21st Conference on Computational Natural Language Learning (CoNLL 2017)

Vancouver, Canada
3 – 4 August 2017

ISBN: 978-1-5108-4564-0

CoNLL 2017

The 21st Conference on
Computational Natural Language Learning

Proceedings of the Conference

August 3 - August 4, 2017
Vancouver, Canada

Introduction

The 2017 Conference on Computational Natural Language Learning (CoNLL) is the 21st in the series of annual meetings organized by SIGNLL, the ACL special interest group on natural language learning. CoNLL 2017 will be held on August 3–4, 2017, and is co-located with the 55th annual meeting of the Association for Computational Linguistics (ACL) in Vancouver, Canada.

As in most previous years, in order to accommodate papers with experimental material and detailed analysis/proofs, CoNLL 2017 invited only long papers, allowing eight pages of content plus unlimited pages of references and supplementary material in initial submission. Final, camera-ready submissions were allowed one additional page, so that all papers in the proceedings have a maximum of nine content pages plus unlimited pages of references and supplementary material.

CoNLL 2017 received a record number of 280 submissions in total, out of which 2 had to be rejected for formal reasons, and 12 were withdrawn by the authors during the review period. Of the remaining 271 papers, 50 papers were chosen to appear in the conference program, with an overall acceptance rate of 18.7%, the lowest ever for the conference. Seven of these were withdrawn after the notification, resulting in 43 papers for the final program: 20 selected for oral presentation, and the remaining 23 for poster presentation plus lightning oral presentation. All 43 papers appear here in the conference proceedings.

CoNLL 2017 features two invited talks, given by Chris Dyer (Google DeepMind) and Naomi Feldman (University of Maryland), and two shared tasks: one on Universal Morphological Reinflection and one on Multilingual Parsing from Raw Text to Universal Dependencies. Papers accepted for the shared tasks are published in companion volumes of the CoNLL 2017 proceedings.

We would like to thank all the authors who submitted their work to CoNLL 2017, and the program committee for helping us select the best papers out of many high-quality submissions. We are grateful to the many program committee members who answered positively to our late requests for reviewing assistance due to the unexpectedly large number of submissions. For this year's CoNLL, we allowed simultaneous submission to other conferences, and in order to ease the burden on the community of reviewers we implemented limited, partial cross-conference review sharing with EMNLP for papers submitted to both conferences. We are grateful to the EMNLP chairs, Rebecca Hwa and Sebastian Riedel, for working together with us, and to the EMNLP program committee members who participated in this process. We are also grateful to our invited speakers and to the SIGNLL board members. In particular, we are immensely thankful to Julia Hockenmaier for her valuable advice and assistance in putting together this year's program and proceedings. We also thank Ben Verhoeven, for maintaining the CoNLL 2017 website. We are grateful to the ACL organization for helping us with the program, proceedings and logistics. Finally, our gratitude goes to our sponsor, Google Inc., for supporting the best paper award at CoNLL 2017.

We hope you enjoy the conference!

Roger Levy and Lucia Specia

CoNLL 2017 conference co-chairs

Conference Chairs:

Lucia Specia, University of Sheffield (UK)
Roger Levy, MIT (USA)

Invited Speakers:

Chris Dyer, CMU (USA) and Google DeepMind (UK)
Naomi Feldman, Department of Linguistics and Institute for Advanced Computer Studies,
University of Maryland (USA)

Program Committee:

Steven Abney
Željko Agić
Roee Aharoni
Héctor Martínez Alonso
Waleed Ammar
Tom Anderson
Ron Artstein
Yoav Artzi
Wilker Aziz
Collin Baker
Omid Bakhshandeh
Timothy Baldwin
Miguel Ballesteros
Roy Bar-Haim
Timo Baumann
Daniel Beck
Barend Beekhuizen
Yonatan Belinkov
Dane Bell
Jonathan Berant
Yevgeni Berzak
Chandra Bhagavatula
Suma Bhat
Pushpak Bhattacharyya
Joachim Bingel
Yonatan Bisk
Johannes Bjerva
Frédéric Blain
Michael Bloodgood
Bernd Bohnet
Francesca Bonin
Chloé Braud
Chris Brockett

Julian Brooke
Kris Cao
Cornelia Caragea
Gracinda Carvalho
Francisco Casacuberta
Baobao Chang
Kai-Wei Chang
Snigdha Chaturvedi
Boxing Chen
Danqi Chen
Wei-Te Chen
David Chiang
Hai Leong Chieu
Eunah Cho
Yejin Choi
Christos Christodoulopoulos
Grzegorz Chrupała
Volkan Cirik
Alexander Clark
Stephen Clark
Arman Cohan
Trevor Cohn
Benoit Crabbé
Walter Daelemans
Andrew Dai
Bhavana Dalvi
Vera Demberg
Steve DeNeefe
Lingjia Deng
Nina Dethlefs
Mark Dras
Rotem Dror
Kevin Duh
Greg Durrett
Chris Dyer
Judith Eckle-Kohler
Jacob Eisenstein
Meng Fang
Geli Fei
Raquel Fernandez
José A. R. Fonollosa
George Foster
Stella Frank
Stefan L. Frank
Lea Frermann
Richard Futrell
Matt Gardner
Michaela Geierhos
Daniel Gildea
Roxana Girju

Dan Goldwasser
Carlos Gómez-Rodríguez
Alvin Grissom II
Cyril Grouin
Sonal Gupta
Masato Hagiwara
Keith Hall
Jey Han Lau
Homa B. Hashemi
Hua He
Julian Hitschler
Julia Hockenmaier
Andrea Horbach
Yufang Hou
Diana Inkpen
Laura Jehl
Charles Jochim
Anders Johannsen
Sariya Karimova
Casey Kennington
Fabio Kepler
Daniel Khashabi
Tracy Holloway King
Sigrid Klerke
Roman Klinger
Philipp Koehn
Mikhail Kozhevnikov
Julia Kreutzer
Jayant Krishnamurthy
Germán Kruszewski
Sandra Kübler
Marco Kuhlmann
Jonathan K. Kummerfeld
Ophélie Lacroix
Chiraag Lala
Carolin Lawrence
Tao Lei
Alessandro Lenci
Omer Levy
Qi Li
Tal Linzen
Ting Liu
Yi Luan
Marco Lui
Franco M. Luque
Pranava Swaroop Madhyastha
Daniel Marcu
Alex Marin
Bruno Martins
Luis Marujo

Yuji Matsumoto
Yevgen Matusevych
David McClosky
Kathy McKeown
Marissa Milne
Ashutosh Modi
Alessandro Moschitti
Nasrin Mostafazadeh
Skatje Myers
Preslav Nakov
Jason Naradowsky
Shashi Narayan
Jan Niehues
Joakim Nivre
Pierre Nugues
Alexis Palmer
Denis Paperno
Viktor Pekar
Nanyun Peng
Xiaochang Peng
Johann Petrak
Luis Nieto Piña
Yuval Pinter
Barbara Plank
David Powers
Nazneen Fatema Rajani
Carlos Ramisch
Roi Reichart
Corentin Ribeyre
Laura Rimell
Alan Ritter
Brian Roark
Kirk Roberts
Salvatore Romeo
Dan Roth
Michael Roth
Alla Rozovskaya
Kenji Sagae
Benoît Sagot
Bahar Salehi
Ryohei Sasano
Carolina Scarton
Shigehiko Schamoni
Marten van Schijndel
Jonathan Schler
William Schuler
Roy Schwartz
Djamé Seddah
Yee Seng Chan
Chaitanya Shivade

Vered Shwartz
Khalil Simaan
Patrick Simianer
Kairit Sirts
Noah A. Smith
Anders Søgaard
Artem Sokolov
Luca Soldaini
Vivek Srikumar
Shashank Srivastava
Gabriel Stanovsky
Ian Stewart
Kevin Stowe
Simon Suster
Swabha Swayamdipta
Partha Talukdar
Chenhao Tan
Sam Thomson
James Thorne
Shubham Toshniwal
Reut Tsarfaty
Oren Tsur
Lifu Tu
Anh Tuan Luu
Marco Turchi
Marc Verhagen
Yannick Versley
Aline Villavicencio
Andreas Vlachos
Svitlana Volkova
Ivan Vulić
Ekaterina Vylomova
Zhiguo Wang
Zeerak Waseem
Taro Watanabe
Ingmar Weber
Ralph Weischedel
Michael Wiegand
John Wieting
Michael Wojatzki
Rui Xia
Berrin Yanikoglu
Marcos Zampieri
Qi Zhang
Xingxing Zhang
Hai Zhao
Muhua Zhu

Table of Contents

Conference Program

Thursday, August 3, 2017

8:45–9:00   *Opening Remarks*

Invited Talk by Chris Dyer

9:00–10:00   *Should Neural Network Architecture Reflect Linguistic Structure?*
Chris Dyer

Session 1

10:00–10:15   *Exploring the Syntactic Abilities of RNNs with Multi-task Learning*
Émile Enguehard, Yoav Goldberg and Tal Linzen

Session 1L: Lightning Talks for Poster Session

10:15–10:17   *The Effect of Different Writing Tasks on Linguistic Style:*
A Case Study of the ROC Story Cloze Task
Roy Schwartz, Maarten Sap, Ioannis Konstas, Leila Zilles,
Yejin Choi and Noah A. Smith

10:17–10:19   *Parsing for Grammatical Relations via Graph Merging*
Weiwei Sun, Yantao Du and Xiaojun Wan

10:19–10:21   *Leveraging Eventive Information for Better Metaphor Detection and Classification*
I-Hsuan Chen, Yunfei Long, Qin Lu and Chu-Ren Huang

10:21–10:23   *Collaborative Partitioning for Coreference Resolution*
Olga Uryupina and Alessandro Moschitti

10:23–10:25   *Named Entity Disambiguation for Noisy Text*
Yotam Eshel, Noam Cohen, Kira Radinsky, Shaul Markovitch,
Ikuya Yamada and Omer Levy

Session 2

4:00–4:15   *Embedding Words and Senses Together via Joint Knowledge-Enhanced Training*
Massimiliano Mancini, Jose Camacho-Collados, Ignacio Iacobacci
and Roberto Navigli

4:15–4:30   *Automatic Selection of Context Configurations for Improved Class-Specific Word Representations*
Ivan Vulić, Roy Schwartz, Ari Rappoport, Roi Reichart and Anna Korhonen

4:30–4:45   *Modeling Context Words as Regions: An Ordinal Regression Approach to Word Embedding*
Shoaib Jameel and Steven Schockaert

4:45–5:00   *An Artificial Language Evaluation of Distributional Semantic Models*
Fatemeh Torabi Asr and Michael Jones

5:00–5:15   *Learning Word Representations with Regularization from Prior Knowledge*
Yan Song, Chia-Jung Lee and Fei Xia

Session 2L: Lightning Talks for Poster Session

5:15–5:17   *Attention-based Recurrent Convolutional Neural Network for Automatic Essay Scoring*
Fei Dong, Yue Zhang and Jie Yang

5:17–5:19   *Feature Selection as Causal Inference: Experiments with Text Classification*
Michael J. Paul

5:19–5:21   *A Joint Model for Semantic Sequences: Frames, Entities, Sentiments*
Haoruo Peng, Snigdha Chaturvedi and Dan Roth

5:21–5:23   *Neural Sequence-to-sequence Learning of Internal Word Structure*
Tatyana Ruzsics and Tanja Samardzic

5:23–5:25   *A Supervised Approach to Extractive Summarisation of Scientific Papers*
Ed Collins, Isabelle Augenstein and Sebastian Riedel

Session 3L: Lightning Talks for Poster Session

10:15–10:17 *Learning Contextual Embeddings for Structural Semantic Similarity using Categorical Information*
Massimo Nicosia and Alessandro Moschitti

10:17–10:19 *Making Neural QA as Simple as Possible but not Simpler*
Dirk Weissenborn, Georg Wiese and Laura Seiffe

10:19–10:21 *Neural Domain Adaptation for Biomedical Question Answering*
Georg Wiese, Dirk Weissenborn and Mariana Neves

10:21–10:23 *A phoneme clustering algorithm based on the obligatory contour principle*
Mans Hulden

10:23–10:25 *Learning Stock Market Sentiment Lexicon and Sentiment-Oriented Word Vector from StockTwits*
Quanzhi Li and Sameena Shah

10:25–10:27 *Learning local and global contexts using a convolutional recurrent network model for relation classification in biomedical text*
Desh Raj, Sunil Sahu and Ashish Anand

10:27–10:29 *Idea density for predicting Alzheimer's disease from transcribed speech*
Kairit Sirts, Olivier Piguet and Mark Johnson

10:29–11:00 *Coffee Break*

11:00–2:00 *Poster Session and Lunch*

Session 5

Invited Talk

Should Neural Network Architecture Reflect Linguistic Structure?

Chris Dyer
DeepMind/CMU

Abstract: I explore the hypothesis that conventional neural network models (e.g., recurrent neural networks) are incorrectly biased for making linguistically sensible generalizations when learning, and that a better class of models is based on architectures that reflect hierarchical structures for which considerable behavioral evidence exists. I focus on the problem of modeling and representing the meanings of sentences. On the generation front, I introduce recurrent neural network grammars (RNNGs), a joint, generative model of phrase-structure trees and sentences. RNNGs operate via a recursive syntactic process reminiscent of probabilistic context-free grammar generation, but decisions are parameterized using RNNs that condition on the entire (top-down, left-to-right) syntactic derivation history, thus relaxing context-free independence assumptions, while retaining a bias toward explaining decisions via "syntactically local" conditioning contexts. Experiments show that RNNGs obtain better results in generating language than models that don't exploit linguistic structure. On the representation front, I explore unsupervised learning of syntactic structures based on distant semantic supervision using a reinforcement-learning algorithm. The learner seeks a syntactic structure that provides a compositional architecture that produces a good representation for a downstream semantic task. Although the inferred structures are quite different from traditional syntactic analyses, the performance on the downstream tasks surpasses that of systems that use sequential RNNs and tree-structured RNNs based on treebank dependencies. This is joint work with Adhi Kuncoro, Dani Yogatama, Miguel Ballesteros, Phil Blunsom, Ed Grefenstette, Wang Ling, and Noah A. Smith.

Bio: Chris Dyer is a research scientist at DeepMind and an assistant professor in the School of Computer Science at Carnegie Mellon University. In 2017, he received the Presidential Early Career Award for Scientists and Engineers (PECASE). His work has occasionally been nominated for best paper awards in prestigious NLP venues and has, much more occasionally, won them. He lives in London and, in his spare time, plays cello.

Proceedings of the 21st Conference on Computational Natural Language Learning (CoNLL 2017), page 1,
Vancouver, Canada, August 3 - August 4, 2017. ©2017 Association for Computational Linguistics

Rational Distortions of
Learners' Linguistic Input

Naomi Feldman
University of Maryland

Abstract: Language acquisition can be modeled as a statistical inference problem: children use sentences and sounds in their input to infer linguistic structure. However, in many cases, children learn from data whose statistical structure is distorted relative to the language they are learning. Such distortions can arise either in the input itself, or as a result of children's immature strategies for encoding their input. This work examines several cases in which the statistical structure of children's input differs from the language being learned. Analyses show that these distortions of the input can be accounted for with a statistical learning framework by carefully considering the inference problems that learners solve during language acquisition

Bio: Naomi Feldman is an associate professor in the Department of Linguistics and the Institute for Advanced Computer Studies at the University of Maryland. She received her PhD in Cognitive Science from Brown University in 2011. Her research lies at the intersection of cognitive science, computer science, and linguistics. She uses methods from machine learning to create formal models of how people learn and represent the structure of their language, and has been developing methods that take advantage of naturalistic speech corpora to study how listeners encode information from their linguistic environment.

Proceedings of the 21st Conference on Computational Natural Language Learning (CoNLL 2017), page 2,
Vancouver, Canada, August 3 - August 4, 2017. ©2017 Association for Computational Linguistics

Exploring the Syntactic Abilities of RNNs with Multi-task Learning

Émile Enguehard[1]   **Yoav Goldberg**[2]   **Tal Linzen**[3,4]

[1]Département d'informatique, ENS, PSL Research University
[2]Computer Science Department, Bar Ilan University
[3]LSCP & IJN, CNRS, EHESS and ENS, PSL Research University
[4]Department of Cognitive Science, Johns Hopkins University

`{emile.enguehard,tal.linzen}@ens.fr`   `yoav.goldberg@gmail.com`

Abstract

Recent work has explored the syntactic abilities of RNNs using the subject-verb agreement task, which diagnoses sensitivity to sentence structure. RNNs performed this task well in common cases, but faltered in complex sentences (Linzen et al., 2016). We test whether these errors are due to inherent limitations of the architecture or to the relatively indirect supervision provided by most agreement dependencies in a corpus. We trained a single RNN to perform both the agreement task and an additional task, either CCG supertagging or language modeling. Multi-task training led to significantly lower error rates, in particular on complex sentences, suggesting that RNNs have the ability to evolve more sophisticated syntactic representations than shown before. We also show that easily available agreement training data can improve performance on other syntactic tasks, in particular when only a limited amount of training data is available for those tasks. The multi-task paradigm can also be leveraged to inject grammatical knowledge into language models.

1 Introduction

Recurrent neural networks (RNNs) have seen rapid adoption in natural language processing applications. Since these models are not equipped with explicit linguistic representations such as dependency parses or logical forms, new methods are needed to characterize the linguistic generalizations that they capture. One such method is drawn from behavioral psychology: the network is tested on cases that are carefully selected to be informative as to the generalizations that the network has acquired.

Linzen et al. (2016) have recently applied this methodology to evaluate how well a trained RNN captures sentence structure, using the **agreement prediction task** (Bock and Miller, 1991; Elman, 1991). The form of an English verb often depends on its subject. Identifying the subject of a given verb of requires sensitivity to sentence structure. Consequently, testing an RNN on its ability to choose the correct form of a verb in context can shed light on the sophistication of its syntactic representations (see Section 2.1 for details).

RNNs trained specifically to perform the agreement task can achieve very good average performance on a corpus, with accuracy close to 99%. However, error rates increase substantially on complex sentences (Linzen et al., 2016, 2017), suggesting that the syntactic knowledge acquired by the RNN is imperfect. Finally, when the RNN is trained as a language model rather than specifically on the agreement task, its sensitivity to subject-verb agreement, measured as the relative probability of the grammatical and ungrammatical forms of the verb, degrades dramatically.

Are the limitations that RNNs showed in previous work inherent to their architecture, or can these limitations be mitigated by stronger supervision? We address this question using multi-task learning, where the same model is encouraged to develop representations that are simultaneously useful for multiple tasks. To provide the RNN with an incentive to develop more sophisticated representations, we trained it to perform one of two tasks: the first is combinatory categorical grammar (CCG) supertagging (Bangalore and Joshi, 1999), a sequence labeling task likely to require robust syntactic representations; the second task is language modeling.

We also investigate the inverse question: can

Proceedings of the 21st Conference on Computational Natural Language Learning (CoNLL 2017), pages 3–14,
Vancouver, Canada, August 3 - August 4, 2017. ©2017 Association for Computational Linguistics

tasks such as supertagging benefit from joint training with the agreement task? This question is of practical interest. Large training sets for the agreement task are much easier to create than training sets for supertagging, which are based on manually parsed sentences. If the training signal from the agreement prediction task proves to be beneficial for supertagging, this could lead to improved supertagging (and therefore parsing) performance in languages in which we only have a small amount of parsed training sentences.

We found that multi-task learning, either with LM or with CCG supertagging, improved the performance of the RNN on the agreement prediction task. The benefits of combined training with supertagging can be quite large: accuracy in challenging relative clause sentences increased from 50.6% to 76.2%. This suggests that RNNs are in principle capable of acquiring much better syntactic representations than those they learned from the corpus in Linzen et al. (2016).

In the other direction, joint training on the agreement prediction task did not improve overall language model perplexity, but made the model more syntax-aware: grammatically appropriate verb forms had higher probability than grammatically inappropriate ones. When a limited amount of CCG training data was available, joint training on agreement prediction led to improved supertagging accuracy. These findings suggest that multi-task training with auxiliary syntactic tasks such as agreement prediction can lead to improved performance on standard NLP tasks.

2 Background and Related Work

2.1 Agreement Prediction

English present-tense third-person verbs agree in number with their subject: singular subjects require singular verbs (*the boy smiles*) and plural subjects require plural verbs (*the boys smile*). Subjects in English are not overtly marked, and complex sentences often have multiple subjects corresponding to different verbs. Identifying the subject of a particular verb can therefore be non-trivial in sentences that have multiple nouns:

(1)   The only championship **banners** that are currently displayed within the building **are** for national or NCAA Championships.

Determining that the subject of the verb in boldface is *banners* rather than the singular nouns *championship* and *building* requires an understanding of the structure of the sentence.

In the agreement task, the learner is given the words leading up to a verb (a "preamble"), and is instructed to predict whether that verb will take the plural or singular form. This task is modeled after a standard psycholinguistic task, which is used to study syntactic representations in humans (Bock and Miller, 1991; Franck et al., 2002; Staub, 2009; Bock and Middleton, 2011).

Any English sentence with a third-person present-tense verb can be used as a training example for this task: all we need is a tagger that can identify such verbs and determine whether they are plural or singular. As such, large amounts of training data for this task can be obtained from a corpus.

The agreement task can often be solved using simple heuristics, such as copying the number of the most recent noun. It can therefore be useful to evaluate the model using sentences in which such a heuristic would fail because one or more nouns of the opposite number from the subject intervene between the subject and the verb; such nouns "attract" the agreement away from the grammatical subject. In general, the more such attractors there are the more difficult the task is for a sequence model that does not represent syntax (we focus on sentences in which **all** of the nouns between the subject and the verb are of the opposite number from the subject):

(2)   The **number** of <u>men</u> **is** not clear. (One attractor)

(3)   The **ratio** of <u>men</u> to <u>women</u> **is** not clear. (Two attractors)

(4)   The **ratio** of <u>men</u> to <u>women</u> and <u>children</u> **is** not clear. (Three attractors)

2.2 CCG Supertagging

Combinatory Categorial Grammar (CCG) is a syntactic formalism that relies on a large inventory of lexical categories (Steedman, 2000). These categories are known as *supertags*, and can be thought of as a fine-grained extension of the usual part-of-speech tags. For example, intransitive verbs (*smile*), transitive verbs (*build*) and raising verbs (*seem*) all have different tags: $S\backslash NP$, $(S\backslash NP)/NP$ and $(S\backslash NP)/(S\backslash NP)$, respectively.

CCG parsers typically rely on a supertagging step where each word in a sentence is associated with an appropriate tag. In fact, supertagging is almost as difficult as finding the full CCG parse of the sentence: once the supertags are determined, only a small number of parses are possible. At the same time, supertagging is simple to set up as a machine learning problem, since at each word it amounts to a straightforward classification problem (Bangalore and Joshi, 1999). RNNs have shown excellent performance on this task, at least in English (Xu et al., 2015; Lewis et al., 2016; Vaswani et al., 2016).

In contrast with the agreement task, training data for supertagging needs to be obtained from parsed sentences which require expert annotation (Hockenmaier and Steedman, 2007); the amount of training data is therefore limited even in English, and much more sparse in other languages.

2.3 Language Modeling

The goal of a language model is to learn the distribution $\hat{p}(w_j|w_1, \ldots, w_{j-1})$ of the j-th word in a sentence given the $j - 1$ words preceding it. We seek to minimize the mean negative log-likelihood of all sentences $s_i = w_{i,1} \ldots w_{i,n_i}$ in our data:

$$L(\hat{p}) = -\frac{1}{Z} \sum_{i=1}^{N} \sum_{j=1}^{n_i} \log \hat{p}(w_{i,j}|w_{i,1:j-1}) \quad (1)$$

where $Z = \sum_{i=1}^{N} n_i$. Language modeling performance is often quantified using the perplexity $2^{L(\hat{p})}$. The effectiveness of RNNs in language modeling, in particular LSTMs, has been demonstrated in numerous studies (Mikolov et al., 2010; Sundermeyer et al., 2012; Jozefowicz et al., 2016).

2.4 Multitask Learning

The benefits of multi-task learning in neural networks are straightforward. Neural networks often require a large amount of training data to achieve good performance on a task. Even with a significant amount of training data, the signal may be too sparse for them to pick it up given their weak inductive biases. By training a network on a simple task for which large quantities of data are available, we can encourage it to evolve representations that would help its performance on the primary task (Caruana, 1998; Bakker and Heskes, 2003). This logic has been applied to various NLP tasks, with generally encouraging results (Collobert and Weston, 2008; Hashimoto et al., 2016; Søgaard

and Goldberg, 2016; Martínez Alonso and Plank, 2017; Bingel and Søgaard, 2017).

3 Methods

3.1 Datasets

We used two training datasets. The first is the corpus of approximately 1.5 million sentences from the English Wikipedia compiled by Linzen et al. (2016). All sentences had at most 50 words and contained at least one third-person present-tense agreement dependency. Following Linzen et al. (2016), we replaced rare words by their part-of-speech tags, using the Penn Treebank tag set (Marcus et al., 1993).[1]

The second data set we used is the CCG-Bank (Hockenmaier and Steedman, 2007), a CCG version of the Penn Treebank. This corpus contained 48934 English sentences, 27299 of which include a present tense third-person verb agreement dependency. A negligible number of sentences longer than 90 words were removed. We applied the traditional split where Sections 2-21 are used for training and Section 23 for testing (41294 and 2407 sentences respectively).[2] Out of the 1363 different supertags that occur in the corpus, we only attempted to predict the 452 supertags that occurred at least ten times; we replaced the rest (0.2% of the tokens) by a dummy value.

3.2 Model

The model in all of our experiments was a standard single-layer LSTM.[3] The first layer was a vector embedding of word tokens into D-dimensional space. The second was a D-dimensional LSTM. The following layers depended on the task. For agreement, the output layers consisted of a linear layer with a one-dimensional output and a sigmoid activation; for language modeling, a linear layer with an N-dimensional output, where N is the size of the lexicon, and a softmax activation; and for supertagging, a linear layer with an S-dimensional

---

[1] In the LM experiments, we restricted ourselves to 10000 words, amounting to 91.2% of the all occurrences. In the CCG supertagging experiments, we used those $12,126$ words that occurred more than 150 times, amounting to 92.2% of the total number of occurrences.

[2] For experiments using this corpus, we use 15784 words occurring at least four times, amounting to 95.9% of occurrences, and replace other words by their POS tags.

[3] Our code and data are available at `https://github.com/emengd/multitask-agreement`.

output, where S is the number of possible tags, followed by a softmax activation.

The language modeling loss is the mean negative log-likelihood of the data given in Equation (1); the loss for agreement is the mean binary cross-entropy of the classifier:

$$L_{\text{agr}} = -\frac{1}{|S|} \sum_{s \in S} \log\left(\hat{q}(\text{num}(s)|s_{:vb})\right)$$

where $\hat{q}$ is the estimated distribution of verb numbers, S the set of sentences, $\text{num}(s)$ the correct verb number in s and $s_{:vb}$ the sentence up to the verb. The loss for CCG supertagging is the mean cross-entropy of the classifiers:

$$L_{\text{ST}} = -\frac{1}{\sum_s |s|} \sum_{s \in S} \sum_{w_j \in s} \log\left(\hat{r}(\text{tag}(w_j)|s_{:w_j})\right)$$

where $\hat{r}$ is the estimated distribution of CCG supertags, $\text{tag}(w_j)$ is the correct tag of word w_j in s, and $s_{:w_j}$ is the sentence s up to and including w_j.

We had at most two tasks in any given experiment. We considered two separate setups for learning from those two tasks: joint training and pre-training.

Joint training: In this setup we had parallel output layers for each task. Both output layers received the shared LSTM representations as their input. We define the global loss L as follows:

$$L = \frac{1}{1+r}L_1 + \frac{r}{1+r}L_2 \qquad (2)$$

where L_1 and L_2 are the losses associated with each task, and r is the weighting ratio of task 2 relative to task 1. This means that r is a hyperparameter that needs to be tuned. Note that sample averaging occurs before formula (2) is applied.

Pre-training: In this setup, we first trained the network on one of the tasks; we then used the weights learned by the network for the embedding layer and the LSTM layer as the initial weights of a new network which we then trained on the second task.

3.3 Training

All neural networks were implemented in Keras (Chollet, 2015) and Theano (Theano Development Team, 2016). We use the AdaGrad optimizer. We use batch training with batch sizes 128 for language modeling experiments and 256 for supertagging experiments on supertagging.

4 Agreement and Supertagging

For the supertagging experiments we used the full CCG corpus as well as 30% of the Wikipedia corpus for the agreement task (20% for training and 10% for testing). We trained the model for 20 epochs. The accuracy figures we report are averaged across three runs. We set the size of the network D to 500 hidden units.[4] We ran a single pre-training experiment in each direction, as well as four joint training experiments, with the weight r of the agreement task set to 0.1, 1, 10 or 100.

We considered two baselines for the agreement task: the last noun baseline predicts the number of the verb based on the number of the most recent noun, and the majority baseline always predicts a singular verb (singular verbs are more common than plural ones in our corpus). Our baseline for supertagging was a majority baseline that predicts for each word its most common supertag.

The agreement task predicts the number of the verb based only on its left context (the preamble). We trained our supertagging model in the same setup. Since our model did not have access to the right context of a word when determining its supertag, we could not expect to compete with state-of-the-art taggers that use right-context lookahead (Xu et al., 2015) or even bidirectional RNNs that read the entire sentence from right to left (Vaswani et al., 2016; Lewis et al., 2016); we therefore did not compare our accuracy to these taggers.

4.1 Overall Results

Figure 1 shows the overall results of the experiment. Multi-task training with supertagging significantly improved overall accuracy on the agreement task (Figure 1a), either with pre-training or joint training: compared to the single-task setup, the agreement error rate decreased by up to 40% in relative terms (from 2.04% to 1.24%). Conversely, multi-task training with agreement did not improve supertagging accuracy, either in the pre-training or in the joint training regime; supertagging accuracy decreased the higher the weight of the agreement task (Figure 1b).

Comparing the two multi-task learning regimes, the pre-training setup performed about as well as the joint training setup with the optimal r. In the following supertagging experiments we dispensed with the joint training setup, which is time con-

---

[4]In initial experiments $D = 50$ yielded supertagging results inferior to a majority choice baseline.

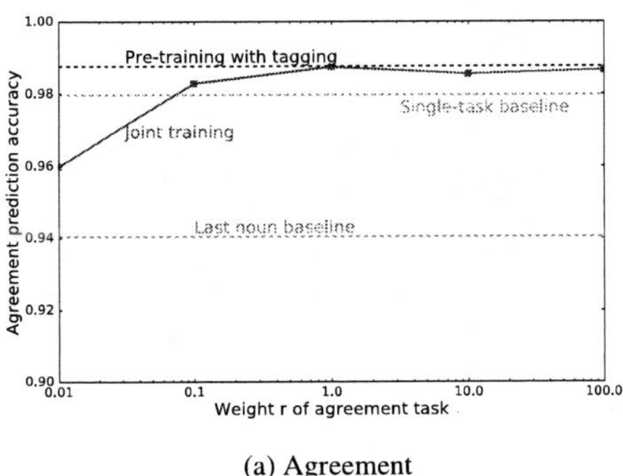

(a) Agreement

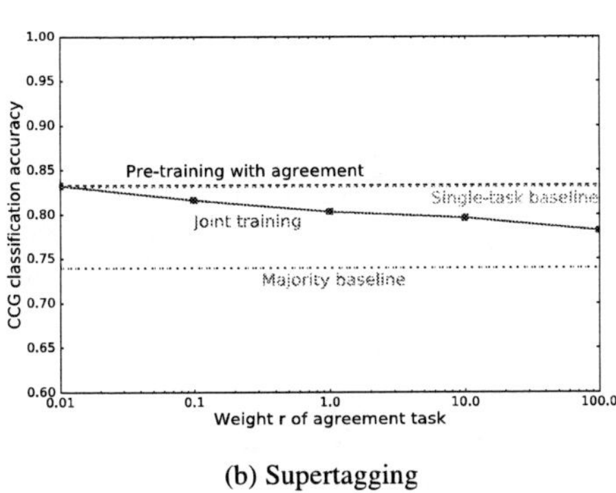

(b) Supertagging

Figure 1: Overall results of supertagging + agreement multi-task training.

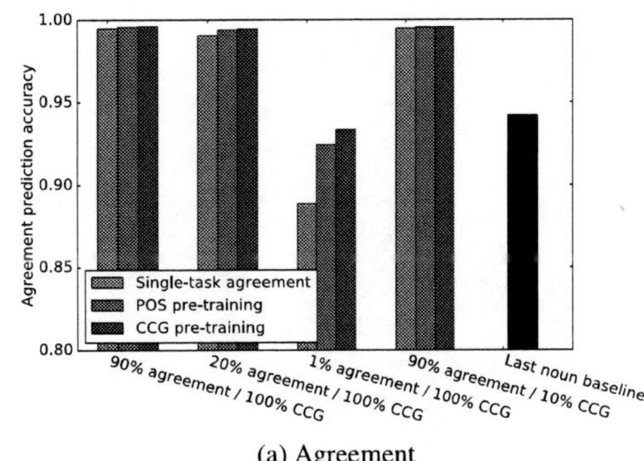

(a) Agreement

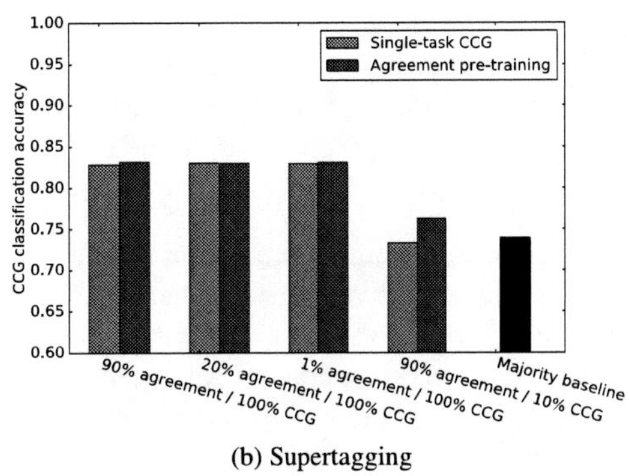

(b) Supertagging

Figure 2: The effect of corpus size on agreement and supertagging accuracy in multi-task settings.

suming since it requires trying multiple values of r, and focused only on the pre-training setup.

4.2 Effect of Corpus Size

To further investigate the relative contribution of the two supervision signals, we conducted a series of follow-up experiments in the pre-training setup, using subsets of varying size of both corpora. We also included POS tagging as an auxiliary task to determine to what extent the full parse of the sentence (approximated by supertags) is crucial to the improvements we have seen in the agreement task. Since POS tags contain less syntactic information than CCG supertags, we expect them to be less helpful as an auxiliary task. Penn Treebank POS tags distinguish singular and plural nouns and verbs, but CCG supertags do not; to put the two tasks on equal footing we removed number information from the POS tags. We trained for 15 epochs and averaged our results over 5 runs.

The results for the agreement task are shown in Figure 2a (baseline values are always calculated over the full corpora). The figure confirms

the beneficial effect of supertagging pre-training (note that the scale starts at 0.8, not 0.9 as in Figure 1a). This effect was amplified when we used less training data for the agreement task. Pre-training on POS tagging yielded a similar though slightly weaker effect. This suggests that much of the improvement in syntactic representations due to pre-training on supertagging can also be gained from pre-training on POS tagging.

Finally, Figure 2b shows that pre-training on the agreement task improved supertagging accuracy when we only used 10% of the CCG corpus (increase in accuracy from 73.4% to 76.3%); however, even with agreement pre-training supertagging accuracy is lower than when the model is trained on the full CCG corpus (where accuracy was 83.1%).

In summary, the data for each task can be used to supplement the data for the other, but there is a large imbalance in the amount of information provided by each task. This is not surprising given that the CCG supertagging data is much richer than the agreement data for any individual sentence. Still, we showed that the syntactic sig-

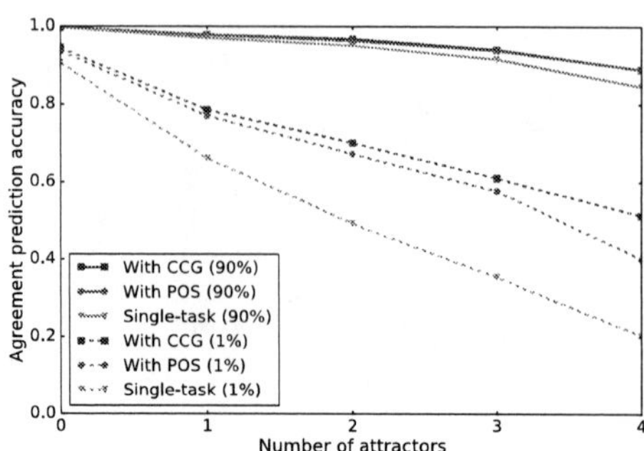

Figure 3: Agreement accuracy as a function of the number of attractors intervening between the subject and the verb, for two different subsets of the agreement corpus (90% and 1% of the corpus).

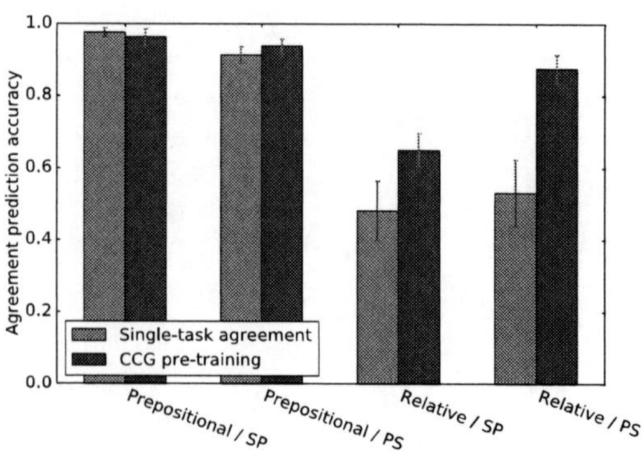

Figure 4: Accuracy on sentences from Bock and Cutting (1992). Error bars indicate standard deviation across runs.

nal from the agreement prediction task can help improve parsing performance when CCG training data is sparse; this weak but widely available source of syntactic supervision may therefore have a practical use in languages with smaller treebanks than English.

4.3 Attraction Errors

Most sentences are syntactically simple and do not pose particular challenges to the models: the accuracy of the last noun baseline in Figure 1a was close to 95%. To investigate the behavior of the model on more difficult sentences, we next break down our test sentences by the number of agreement attractors (see Section 2.1).

Our results, shown in Figure 3, confirm that attractors make the agreement task more difficult, and that pre-training helps overcome this difficulty. This effect is amplified when we only use a small subset of the agreement corpus. In this scenario, the accuracy of the single-task model on sentences with four attractors is only 20.4%. Pre-training makes it possible to overcome this difficulty to a significant extent (though not entirely), increasing the accuracy to 40.1% in the case of POS tagging and 51.2% in the case of supertagging. This suggests that a network that has developed sophisticated syntactic representations can transfer its knowledge to a new syntactic task using only a moderate amount of data.

4.4 Relative Clauses

In Linzen et al. (2016), attraction errors were particularly severe when the attractor was inside a rel-

ative clause. To gain a more precise understanding of the errors and the extent to which pre-training can mitigate them, we turn to two sets of carefully constructed sentences from the psycholinguistic literature (Linzen et al., 2017). Bock and Cutting (1992) compared preambles with prepositional phrase modifiers to closely matched relative clause modifiers:

(5)   PREPOSITIONAL: The demo tape(s) from the popular rock singer(s)...

(6)   RELATIVE: The demo tape(s) that promoted the popular rock singer(s)...

They constructed 24 such sentence pairs. Each of the sentences in each pair has four versions, with all possible combinations of the number of the subject and the attractor. We refer to them as SS for singular-singular (*tape*, *singer*), SP for singular-plural (*tape*, *singers*), and likewise PS and PP. We replaced out-of-vocabulary words with their POS, and further streamlined the materials by always using *that* as the relativizer.

We retrained the single-task and pre-trained models on 90% of the Wikipedia corpus. Like humans, neither model had any issues with SS and PP sentences, which do not have an attractor. The results for SP and PS sentences are shown in Figure 4. The comparison between prepositional and relative modifiers shows that the single-task model was much more likely to make errors when the attractor was in a relative clause (whereas humans are not sensitive to this distinction). This asymmetry was substantially mitigated, though not completely eliminated, by CCG pre-training.

Our second set of sentences was based on the experimental materials of Wagers et al. (2009). We adapted them by deleting the relativizer and creating two preambles from each sentence in the original experiment:

(7) EMBEDDED VERB: The player(s) the coach(es)...

(8) MAIN CLAUSE VERB: The player(s) the coach(es) like the best...

In the first preamble, the verb is expected to agree with the embedded clause subject (*the coach(es)*), whereas in the second one it is expected to agree with the main clause subject (*the player(s)*).

Figure 5 shows that both models made very few errors predicting the embedded clause verb, and more errors predicting the main clause verb. The relative improvement of the pre-trained model compared to the single-task one is more modest in these sentences, possibly because the single-task model does better to begin with on these sentences than on the Bock and Cutting (1992) ones. This in turn may be because the attractor immediately precedes the verb in Bock and Cutting (1992) but not in Wagers et al. (2009), and an immediately adjacent noun may be a stronger attractor. The Appendix contains additional figures tracking the predictions of the network as it processes a sample of sentences with relative clauses; it also illustrates the activation of particular units over the course of such a sentence.

5 Agreement and Language Modeling

We now turn our attention to the language modeling task. The previous experiments confirmed that

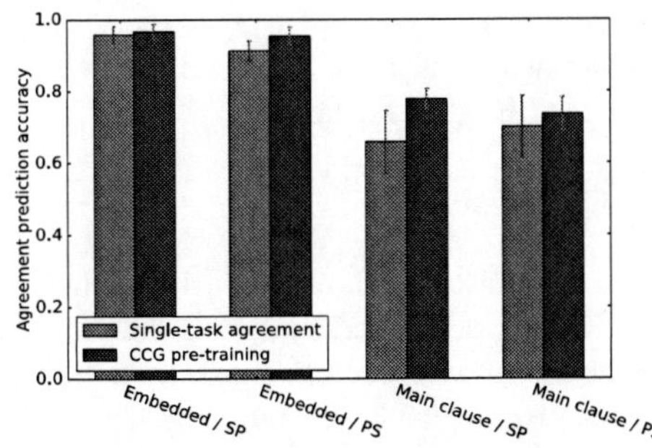

Figure 5: Accuracy on sentences based on Wagers et al. (2009). Error bars indicate standard deviation across runs.

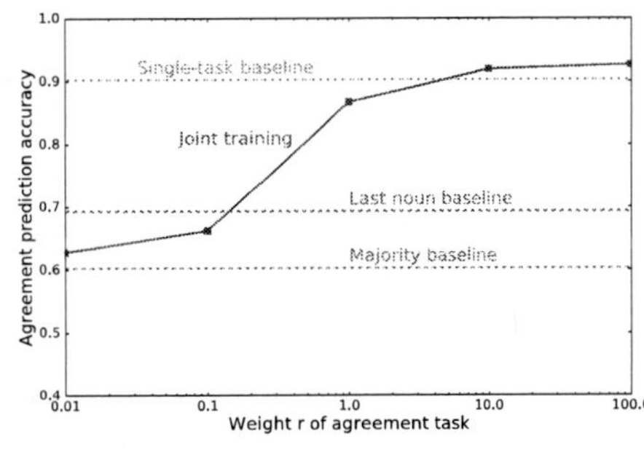

(a) Agreement

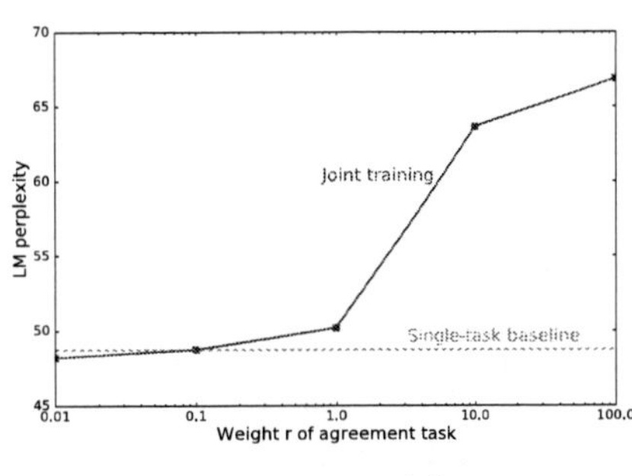

(b) Language modeling

Figure 6: Overall results of language modeling + agreement multi-task training (trained only on sentences with an intervening noun).

agreement in sentences without attractors is easy to predict. We therefore limited ourselves in the language modeling experiments to sentences with potential attractors. Concretely, within the subset of 30% of the Wikipedia corpus, we trained our language model only on sentences with at least one noun (of any number) between the subject and the verb. There were 60680 sentences in the training set. We averaged our results over three runs. Training was stopped after 10 epochs, and the number of hidden units was set to $D = 50$.

5.1 Overall Results

The overall results are shown in Figure 6. Joint training with the LM task improves the performance of the agreement task to a significant extent, bringing accuracy up from 90.2% to 92.6% (a relative reduction of 25% in error rate). This may be due to the higher quality of the word representations that can be learned from the language modeling signal, which in turn help the model make more accurate syntactic predictions.

In the other direction, we do not obtain clear improvements in perplexity from jointly training the LM with agreement. Surprisingly, visual inspection of Figure 6b suggests that the jointly trained LM may achieve somewhat better performance than the single-task baseline for *small* values of r (that is, when the agreement task has a small effect on the overall training loss). To assess the statistical significance of this difference, we repeated the experiment with $r = 0.01$ with 20 random initializations. The standard deviation in LM loss was about 0.018, yielding a standard deviation of 0.011 for three-run averages under Gaussian assumptions. Since the difference of 0.015 between the mean LM losses of the single-task and joint training setups is of comparable magnitude, we conclude that there is no clear evidence that joint training reduces perplexity.

5.2 Grammaticality of LM Predictions

To evaluate the syntactic abilities of an RNN trained as a language model, Linzen et al. (2016) proposed to perform the agreement task by comparing the probability under the learned LM of the correct and incorrect verb forms, under the assumption that all other things being equal a grammatical sequence should have a higher probability than an ungrammatical one (Lau et al., 2016; Le Godais et al., 2017). For instance, if the sentence starts with *the dogs*, we compute:

$$\hat{p}_{\text{correct}} = \frac{\hat{p}(w_2 = \text{are}|w_{0:1} = \text{the dogs})}{\hat{p}(w_2 = \text{are}|\dots) + \hat{p}(w_2 = \text{is}|\dots)} \tag{3}$$

The prediction for the agreement task is derived by thresholding $\hat{p}_{\text{correct}}$ at 0.5.

Is the LM learned in the joint training setup with high r more aware of subject-verb agreement than a single-task LM? Note that this is not a circular question: we are not asking whether the explicit agreement prediction output layer can perform the agreement task — that would be unsurprising — but whether joint training with this task rearranges the probability distributions that the LM defines over the entire vocabulary in a way that is more consistent with English grammar.

As the method outlined in Equation 3 may be sensitive to the idiosyncrasies of the particular verb being predicted, we also explored an unlexicalized way of performing the task. Recall that since we replace uncommon words by their POS

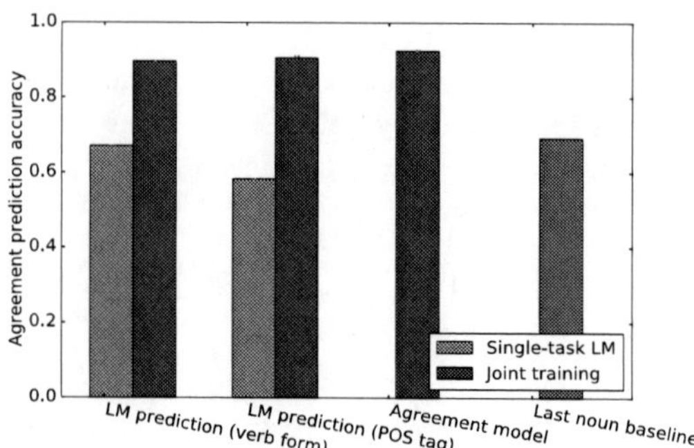

Figure 7: Language model agreement evaluation. Red bars indicate the results obtained on the single-task LM model, blue bars those obtained in a joint training setup with $r = 100$.

tags, POS tags are part of our lexicon. We can use this fact to compare the LM probabilities of the POS tags for the correct and incorrect verb forms: in the example of the preamble *the dogs*, the correct POS would be VBP and the incorrect one VBZ.

The results can be seen in Figure 7. The accuracy of the LM predictions from the jointly trained models is almost as high as that obtained through the agreement model itself. Conversely, the single-task model trained only on language modeling performed only slightly better than chance, and worse than our last noun baseline (recall that the dataset only included sentences with an intervening noun between the subject and the verb, though possibly of the same number as the subject). Predictions based on POS tags are somewhat worse than predictions based on the specific verb. In summary, while joint training with the explicit agreement task does not noticeably reduce language model perplexity, it does help the LM capture syntactic dependencies: the ranking of upcoming words is more consistent with the constraints of English syntax.

6 Conclusions

Previous work has shown that the syntactic representations developed by RNNs that are trained on the agreement prediction task are sufficient for the majority of sentences, but break down in more complex sentences (Linzen et al., 2016, 2017). These deficiencies could be due to fundamental limitations of the architecture, which can only be addressed by switching to more expressive architectures (Socher, 2014; Grefenstette et al., 2015; Dyer et al., 2016). Alternatively, they could be due to insufficient supervision signal in the agreement prediction task, for example because relative clauses with agreement attractors are infrequent in a natural corpus.

We showed that additional supervision from pre-training on syntactic tagging tasks such as CCG supertagging can help the RNN develop more effective syntactic representations which substantially improve its performance on complex sentences, supporting the second hypothesis.

The syntactic representations developed by the RNNs were still not perfect even in the multitask setting, suggesting that stronger inductive biases expressed as richer representational assumptions may lead to further improvements in syntactic performance. The weaker performance on complex sentences in the single-task setting indicates that the inductive bias inherent in RNNs is insufficient for learning adequate syntactic representations from unannotated strings; improvements due to a stronger inductive bias are therefore likely to be particularly pronounced in languages for which parsed corpora are small or unavailable. Finally, the strong syntactic supervision required to promote sophisticated syntactic representations in RNNs may limit their viability as models of language acquisition in children (though children may have sources of supervision that were not available to our models).

We also explored whether multi-task training with the agreement task can improve performance on more standard NLP tasks. We found that it can indeed lead to improved supertagging accuracy when there is a limited amount of training data for that task; this form of weak syntactic supervision can be used to improve parsers for low-resource languages for which only small treebanks are available.

Finally, for language modeling, multi-task training with the agreement task did not reduce perplexity, but did improve the grammaticality of the predictions of the language model (as measured by the relative ranking of grammatical and ungrammatical verb forms); such a language model that favors grammatical sentences may produce more natural-sounding text.

Acknowledgments

We thank Emmanuel Dupoux for discussion. This research was supported by the European Research Council (grant ERC-2011-AdG 295810 BOOT-PHON), the Agence Nationale pour la Recherche (grants ANR-10-IDEX-0001-02 PSL and ANR-10-LABX-0087 IEC) and the Israeli Science Foundation (grant number 1555/15).

References

Bart Bakker and Tom Heskes. 2003. Task clustering and gating for Bayesian multitask learning. *Journal of Machine Learning Research* 4:83–99.

Srinivas Bangalore and Aravind K. Joshi. 1999. Supertagging: An approach to almost parsing. *Computational Linguistics* 25(2):237–265.

Joachim Bingel and Anders Søgaard. 2017. Identifying beneficial task relations for multi-task learning in deep neural networks. In *Proceedings of the 15th Conference of the European Chapter of the Association for Computational Linguistics: Volume 2, Short Papers*. Association for Computational Linguistics, Valencia, Spain, pages 164–169.

Kathryn Bock and J. Cooper Cutting. 1992. Regulating mental energy: Performance units in language production. *Journal of Memory and Language* 31(1):99–127.

Kathryn Bock and Erica L. Middleton. 2011. Reaching agreement. *Natural Language & Linguistic Theory* 29(4):1033–1069.

Kathryn Bock and Carol A. Miller. 1991. Broken agreement. *Cognitive Psychology* 23(1):45–93.

Rich Caruana. 1998. Multitask learning. In Sebastian Thrun and Lorien Pratt, editors, *Learning to learn*, Kluwer Academic Publishers, Boston, pages 95–133.

François Chollet. 2015. Keras. https://github.com/fchollet/keras.

Ronan Collobert and Jason Weston. 2008. A unified architecture for natural language processing: Deep neural networks with multitask learning. In *Proceedings of the 25th International Conference on Machine Learning*. New York, NY, USA, pages 160–167.

Chris Dyer, Adhiguna Kuncoro, Miguel Ballesteros, and A. Noah Smith. 2016. Recurrent neural network grammars. In *Proceedings of the 2016 Conference of the North American Chapter of the Association for Computational Linguistics: Human Language Technologies*. Association for Computational Linguistics, pages 199–209.

Jeffrey L. Elman. 1991. Distributed representations, simple recurrent networks, and grammatical structure. *Machine Learning* 7(2-3):195–225.

Julie Franck, Gabriella Vigliocco, and Janet Nicol. 2002. Subject-verb agreement errors in French and English: The role of syntactic hierarchy. *Language and Cognitive Processes* 17(4):371–404.

Edward Grefenstette, Karl Moritz Hermann, Mustafa Suleyman, and Phil Blunsom. 2015. Learning to transduce with unbounded memory. In *Advances in Neural Information Processing Systems 28*. pages 1828–1836.

Kazuma Hashimoto, Caiming Xiong, Yoshimasa Tsuruoka, and Richard Socher. 2016. A joint many-task model: Growing a neural network for multiple NLP tasks. In *NIPS 2016 Continual Learning and Deep Networks Workshop*.

Julia Hockenmaier and Mark Steedman. 2007. CCGbank: A corpus of CCG derivations and dependency structures extracted from the Penn Treebank. *Computational Linguistics* 33(3):355–396.

Rafal Jozefowicz, Oriol Vinyals, Mike Schuster, Noam Shazeer, and Yonghui Wu. 2016. Exploring the limits of language modeling. *arXiv preprint arXiv:1602.02410* .

Jey Han Lau, Alexander Clark, and Shalom Lappin. 2016. Grammaticality, acceptability, and probability: A probabilistic view of linguistic knowledge. *Cognitive Science* .

Gaël Le Godais, Tal Linzen, and Emmanuel Dupoux. 2017. Comparing character-level neural language models using a lexical decision task. In *Proceedings of the 15th Conference of the European Chapter of the Association for Computational Linguistics: Volume 2, Short Papers*. Association for Computational Linguistics, Valencia, Spain, pages 125–130.

Mike Lewis, Kenton Lee, and Luke Zettlemoyer. 2016. LSTM CCG parsing. In *Proceedings of the 2016 Conference of the North American Chapter of the Association for Computational Linguistics: Human Language Technologies*. pages 221–231.

Tal Linzen, Emmanuel Dupoux, and Yoav Goldberg. 2016. Assessing the ability of LSTMs to learn syntax-sensitive dependencies. *Transactions of the Association for Computational Linguistics* 4:521–535.

Tal Linzen, Yoav Goldberg, and Emmanuel Dupoux. 2017. Agreement attraction errors in neural networks. In *Proceedings of the CUNY Conference on Human Sentence Processing*.

Mitchell P. Marcus, Mary Ann Marcinkiewicz, and Beatrice Santorini. 1993. Building a large annotated corpus of English: The Penn Treebank. *Computational Linguistics* 19(2):313–330.

Héctor Martínez Alonso and Barbara Plank. 2017. When is multitask learning effective? Semantic sequence prediction under varying data conditions. In *Proceedings of the Conference of the European Chapter of the Association for Computationl Linguistics*.

Tomas Mikolov, Martin Karafiát, Lukas Burget, Jan Cernockỳ, and Sanjeev Khudanpur. 2010. Recurrent neural network based language model. In *Proceedings of Interspeech*.

Richard Socher. 2014. *Recursive Deep Learning for Natural Language Processing and Computer Vision*. Ph.D. thesis, Stanford University.

Anders Søgaard and Yoav Goldberg. 2016. Deep multi-task learning with low level tasks supervised at lower layers. In *Proceedings of the 54th Annual Meeting of the Association for Computational Linguistics (Volume 2: Short Papers)*. Association for Computational Linguistics, Berlin, Germany, pages 231–235.

Adrian Staub. 2009. On the interpretation of the number attraction effect: Response time evidence. *Journal of Memory and Language* 60(2):308–327.

Mark Steedman. 2000. *The syntactic process*. MIT Press.

Martin Sundermeyer, Ralf Schlüter, and Hermann Ney. 2012. LSTM neural networks for language modeling. In *Proceedings of the 13th Annual Conference of the International Speech Communication Association (INTERSPEECH)*. pages 194–197.

Theano Development Team. 2016. Theano: A Python framework for fast computation of mathematical expressions. *arXiv e-prints* abs/1605.02688. http://arxiv.org/abs/1605.02688.

Ashish Vaswani, Yonatan Bisk, Kenji Sagae, and Ryan Musa. 2016. Supertagging with LSTMs. In *Proceedings of NAACL-HLT*. pages 232–237.

Matthew W. Wagers, Ellen F. Lau, and Colin Phillips. 2009. Agreement attraction in comprehension: Representations and processes. *Journal of Memory and Language* 61(2):206–237.

Wenduan Xu, Michael Auli, and Stephen Clark. 2015. CCG supertagging with a recurrent neural network. In *Proceedings of the 53rd Annual Meeting of the Association for Computational Linguistics and the 7th International Joint Conference on Natural Language Processing (Volume 2: Short Papers)*. Association for Computational Linguistics, Beijing, China, pages 250–255.

A Appendix

This appendix presents figures based on sentences with relative clause (see Section 4.4). Figure 8 tracks the word-by-word predictions that the single-task model and the pre-trained model make for three sample sentences; the grammatical ground truth is indicated with a dotted black line. Overall, the pre-trained model is closer to the ground truth than the single-task model, even in cases where both models ultimately make the correct prediction (Figure 8b). Figures 8a and 8c show cases in which an attractor in an embedded clause misleads the single-task but not the pre-trained one. Finally, Figure 9 shows a sample of four units that appear to track interpretable aspects of the sentence.

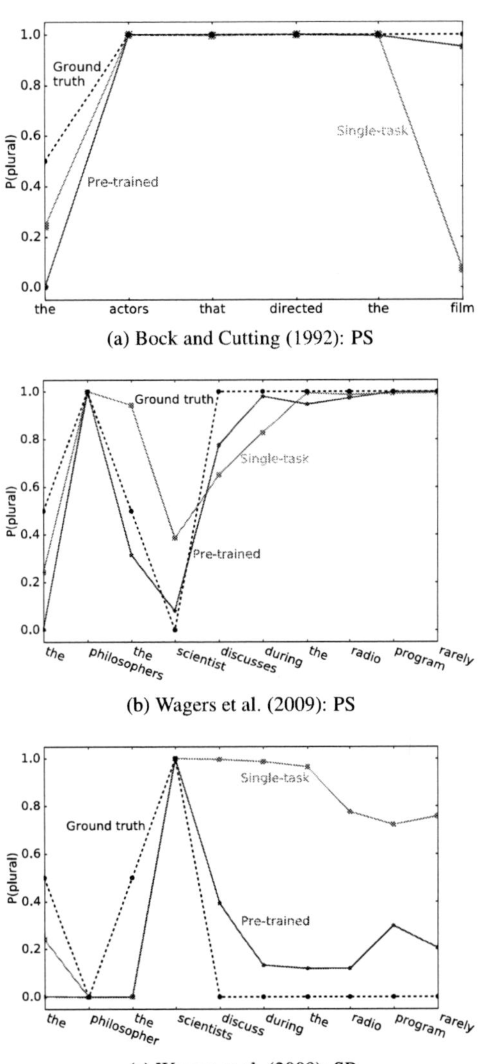

(a) Bock and Cutting (1992): PS

(b) Wagers et al. (2009): PS

(c) Wagers et al. (2009): SP

Figure 8: Probability of a plural prediction after each word in the sentence for three sample sentences. The black dotted line indicates the grammatical ground truth.

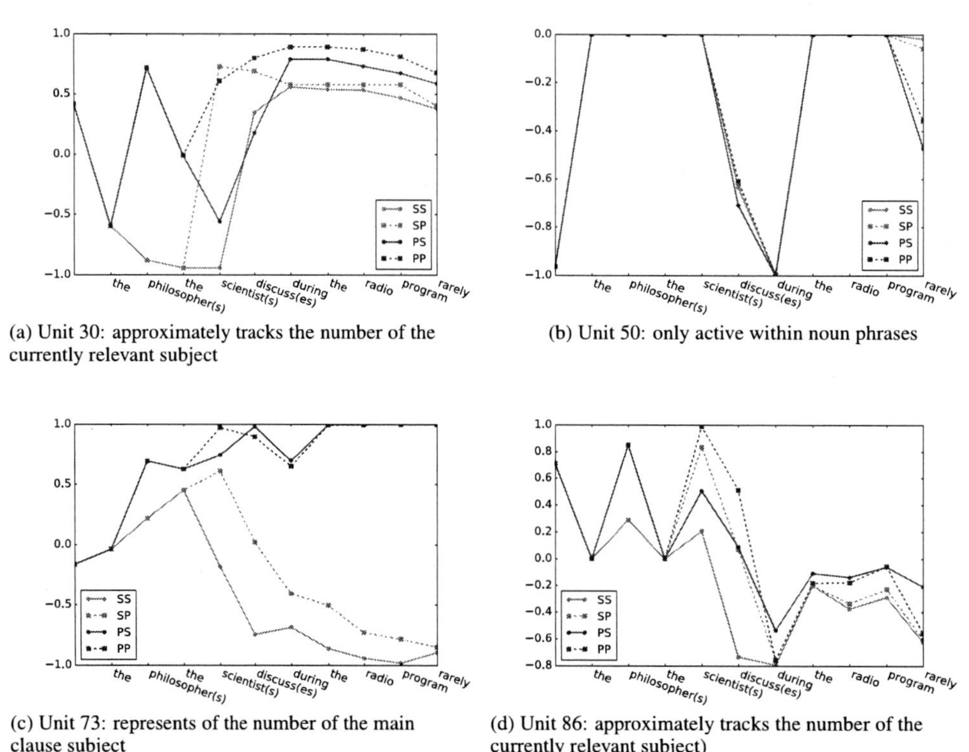

(a) Unit 30: approximately tracks the number of the currently relevant subject

(b) Unit 50: only active within noun phrases

(c) Unit 73: represents of the number of the main clause subject

(d) Unit 86: approximately tracks the number of the currently relevant subject)

Figure 9: Activations of a sample of interpretable units throughout an example sentence from Wagers et al. (2009), for all four number configurations.

The Effect of Different Writing Tasks on Linguistic Style:
A Case Study of the ROC Story Cloze Task

Roy Schwartz[1,2], Maarten Sap[1], Ioannis Konstas[1],
Li Zilles[1], Yejin Choi[1] and Noah A. Smith[1]

[1]Paul G. Allen School of Computer Science & Engineering,
University of Washington, Seattle, WA, USA
[2]Allen Institute for Artificial Intelligence, Seattle, WA, USA
`{roysch,msap,ikonstas,lzilles,yejin,nasmith}@cs.washington.edu`

Abstract

A writer's style depends not just on personal traits but also on her intent and mental state. In this paper, we show how variants of the same writing task can lead to measurable differences in writing style. We present a case study based on the *story cloze task* (Mostafazadeh et al., 2016a), where annotators were assigned similar writing tasks with different constraints: (1) writing an entire story, (2) adding a story ending for a given story context, and (3) adding an incoherent ending to a story. We show that a simple linear classifier informed by stylistic features is able to successfully distinguish among the three cases, without even looking at the story context. In addition, combining our stylistic features with language model predictions reaches state of the art performance on the story cloze challenge. Our results demonstrate that different task framings can dramatically affect the way people write.[1]

1 Introduction

Writing style is expressed through a range of linguistic elements such as words, sentence structure, and rhetorical devices. It is influenced by personal factors such as age and gender (Schler et al., 2006), by personality traits such as agreeableness and openness (Ireland and Mehl, 2014), as well as by mental states such as sentiment (Davidov et al., 2010), sarcasm (Tsur et al., 2010), and deception (Feng et al., 2012). In this paper, we study the extent to which writing style is affected by the nature of the writing task the writer was asked to perform,

Story Prefix	Ending
John liked a girl at his work. He tried to get her attention by acting silly. She told him to grow up. John confesses he was trying to make her like him more.	**She feels flattered and asks John on a date.**
	The girl found this charming, and gave him a second chance.
	John was happy about being rejected.

Table 1: Examples of stories from the story cloze task. The table shows a story prefix with three contrastive endings: The **original** ending, a *coherent* ending and a incoherent one.

since different tasks likely engage different cognitive processes (Campbell and Pennebaker, 2003; Banerjee et al., 2014).[2]

We show that similar writing tasks with different constraints on the author can lead to measurable differences in her writing style. As a case study, we present experiments based on the recently introduced ROC story cloze task (Mostafazadeh et al., 2016a). In this task, authors were asked to write five-sentence self-contained stories, henceforth *original* stories. Then, each original story was given to a different author, who was shown only the first four sentences as a story context, and asked to write two contrasting story endings: a *right* (coherent) ending, and a *wrong* (incoherent) ending. Framed as a story cloze task, the goal of this dataset is to serve as a common-sense challenge for NLP and AI research. Table 1 shows an example of an original story, a coherent story, and an incoherent story.

While the story cloze task was originally de-

---

[1]This paper extends our LSDSem 2017 shared task submission (Schwartz et al., 2017).

[2]For the purposes of this paper, *style* is defined as content-agnostic writing characteristics, such as the number of words in a sentence.

Proceedings of the 21st Conference on Computational Natural Language Learning (CoNLL 2017), pages 15–25,
Vancouver, Canada, August 3 - August 4, 2017. ©2017 Association for Computational Linguistics

signed to be a story understanding challenge, its annotation process introduced three variants of the same writing task: writing an *original*, *right*, or *wrong* ending to a short story. In this paper, we show that a linear classifier informed by stylistic features can distinguish among the different endings to a large degree, even without looking at the story context (64.5–75.6% binary classification results).

Our results allow us to make a few key observations. First, people adopt a different writing style when asked to write coherent vs. incoherent story endings. Second, people change their writing style when writing the entire story on their own compared to writing only the final sentence for a given story context written by someone else.

In order to further validate our method, we also directly tackle the story cloze task. Adapting our classifier to the task, we obtain 72.4% accuracy, only 2.3% below state of the art results. We also show that the style differences captured by our model can be combined with neural language models to make a better use of the story context. Our final model that combines context with stylistic features achieves a new state of the art—75.2%—an additional 2.8% gain.

The contributions of our study are threefold. First, findings from our study can potentially shed light on how different kinds of cognitive load influence the style of written language. Second, combined with recent similar findings of Cai et al. (2017), our results indicate that when designing new NLP tasks, special attention needs to be paid to the instructions given to authors. Third, we establish a new state of the art result on the commonsense story cloze challenge. Our code is available at `https://github.com/roys174/writing_style`.

2 Background: The Story Cloze Task

To understand how different writing tasks affect writing style, we focus on the *story cloze task* (Mostafazadeh et al., 2016a). While this task was developed to facilitate representation and learning of commonsense story understanding, its design included a few key choices which make it ideal for our study. We describe the task below.

ROC stories. The ROC story corpus consists of 49,255 five-sentence stories, collected on Ama-

zon Mechanical Turk (AMT).[3] Workers were instructed to write a coherent self-contained story, which has a clear beginning and end. To collect a broad spectrum of commonsense knowledge, there was no imposed subject for the stories, which resulted in a wide range of different topics.

Story cloze task. After compiling the story corpus, the *story cloze task*—a task based on the corpus—was introduced. A subset of the stories was selected, and only the first four sentences of each story were presented to AMT workers. Workers were asked to write a pair of new story endings for each story context: one *right* and one *wrong*. Both endings were required to complete the story using one of the characters in the story context. Additionally, the endings were required to be "realistic and sensible" (Mostafazadeh et al., 2016a) when read out of context.

The resulting stories, both *right* and *wrong*, were then individually rated for coherence and meaningfulness by additional AMT workers. Only stories rated as simultaneously coherent with a *right* ending and neutral with a *wrong* ending were selected for the task. It is worth noting that workers rated the stories as a whole, not only the endings.

Based on the new stories, Mostafazadeh et al. (2016a) proposed the *story cloze task*. The task is simple: given a pair of stories that differ only in their endings, the system decides which ending is *right* and which is *wrong*. The official training data contains only the original stories (without alternative endings), while development and test data consist of the revised stories with alternative endings (for a different set of original stories that are not included in the training set). The task was suggested as an extensive evaluation framework: as a commonsense story understanding task, as the shared task for the Linking Models of Lexical, Sentential and Discourse-level Semantics workshop (LSDSem 2017, Roth et al., 2017), and as a testbed for vector-space evaluation (Mostafazadeh et al., 2016b).

Interestingly, only very recently, one year after the task was first introduced, the published benchmark on this task surpassed 60%. This comes in contrast to other recent similar machine reading tasks such as CNN/DailyMail (Hermann et al., 2015), SNLI (Bowman et al., 2015), LAMBADA

---

[3]Recently, additional 53K stories were released, which results in roughly 100K stories.

(Paperno et al., 2016) and SQuAD (Rajpurkar et al., 2016), for which results improved dramatically over similar or much shorter periods of time. This suggests that this task is challenging and that high performance is hard to achieve.

In addition, Mostafazadeh et al. (2016a) made substantial efforts to ensure the quality of this dataset. First, each pair of endings was written by the same author, which ensured that style differences between authors could not be used to solve the task. Furthermore, Mostafazadeh et al. implemented nine baselines for the task, using surface level features as well as narrative-informed ones, and showed that each of them reached roughly chance-level. These results suggest that real understanding of text is required in order to solve the task. In this paper, we show that this is not necessarily the case, by demonstrating that a simple linear classifier informed with style features reaches near state of the art results on the task—72.4%.

Different writing tasks in the story cloze task. Several key design decisions make the task an interesting testbed for the purpose of this study. First, the training set for the task (ROC Stories corpus) is not a training set in the usual sense,[4] as it contains only positive (*right*) examples, and not negative (*wrong*) ones.

On top of that, the *original* endings, which serve as positive training examples, were generated differently from the *right* endings, which serve as the positive examples in the development and test sets. While the former are part of a single coherent story written by the same author, the latter were generated by letting an author read four sentences, and then asking her to generate a fifth *right* ending.

Finally, although the *right* and *wrong* sentences were generated by the same author, the tasks for generating them were quite different: in one case, the author was asked to write a *right* ending, which would create a coherent five-sentence story along with the other four sentences. In the other case, the author was asked to write a *wrong* ending, which would result in an incoherent five-sentence story.

3 Surface Analysis of the Story Cloze Task

We begin by computing several characteristics of the three types of endings: *original* endings (from the ROC story corpus training set), *right* endings and *wrong* endings (both from the story cloze task development set). Our analysis reveals several style differences between different groups. First, *original* endings are on average longer (11 words per sentence) than *right* endings (8.75 words), which are in turn slightly longer than *wrong* ones (8.47 words). The latter finding is consistent with previous work, which has shown that sentence length is also indicative of whether a text was deceptive (Qin et al., 2004; Yancheva and Rudzicz, 2013). Although writing *wrong* sentences is not the same as deceiving, it is not entirely surprising to observe similar trends in both tasks.

Second, Figure 1a shows the distribution of five frequent POS tags in all three groups. The figure shows that both *original* and *right* endings use pronouns more frequently than *wrong* endings. Once again, deceptive text is also characterized by fewer pronouns compared to truthful text (Newman et al., 2003).

Finally, Figure 1b presents the distribution of five frequent words across the different groups. The figure shows that *original* endings use coordinations ("and") more than *right* endings, and substantially more than *wrong* ones. Furthermore, *original* and *right* endings seem to prefer enthusiastic language (e.g., "!"), while *wrong* endings tend to use more negative language ("hates"), similar to deceptive text (Newman et al., 2003). Next we show that these style differences are not anecdotal, but can be used to distinguish among the different types of story endings.

4 Model

To what extent do different writing constraints lead authors to adopt different writing styles? In order to answer this question, we first use simple methods that have been shown to be very effective for recognizing style (see Section 8). We describe our model below.

We train a logistic regression classifier to categorize an ending, either as *right* vs. *wrong* or as *original* vs. *new* (*right*). Each feature vector is computed using the words in one ending, without considering earlier parts of the story. We use the following style features.

- **Length:** the number of words in the sentence.

- **Word *n*-grams:** we use sequences of 1–5 words. Following Tsur et al. (2010) and

---

[4]I.e., the training instances are not drawn from a population similar to the one that future testing instances will be drawn from.

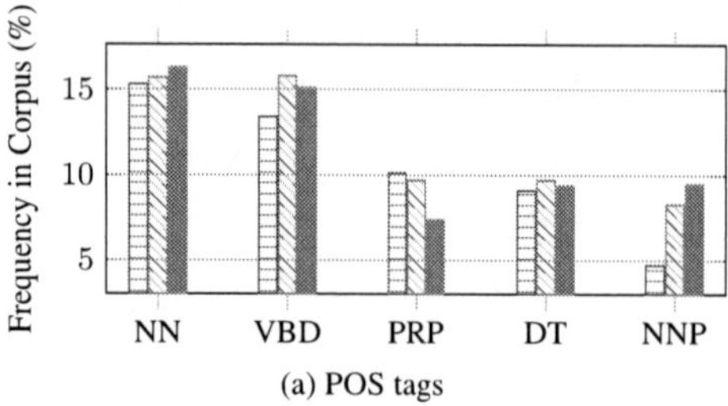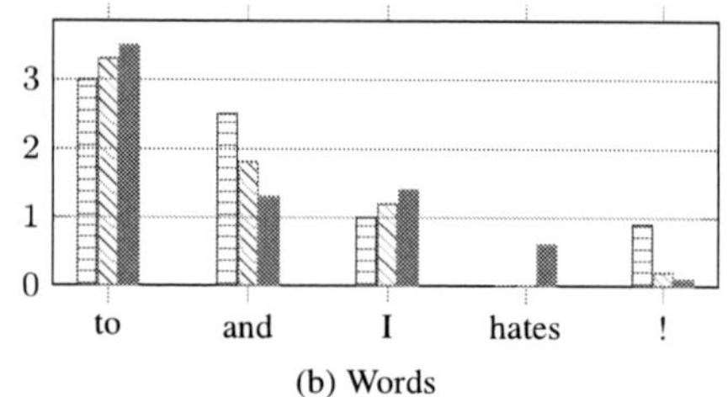

Figure 1: The distribution of five frequent POS tags (1a) and words (1b) across *original* endings (horizontal lines) from the story cloze training set, and *right* (diagonal lines) and *wrong* (solid lines) endings, both from the story cloze task development set.

Schwartz et al. (2013b), we distinguish between high frequency and low frequency words. Specifically, we replace content words (nouns, verbs, adjectives, and adverbs), which are often low frequency, with their part-of-speech tags.

- **Character *n*-grams:** character *n*-grams are one of the most useful features in identifying author style (Stamatatos, 2009). We use character 4-grams.[5]

5 Experiments

We design two experiments to answer our research questions. The first is an attempt to distinguish between *right* and *wrong* endings, the second between *original* endings and *new* (*right*) endings. For completeness, we also run a third experiment, which compares between *original* and *wrong* endings.

Experiment 1: right/wrong endings. The goal of this experiment is to measure the extent to which style features capture differences between the *right* and *wrong* endings. As the story cloze task doesn't have a training corpus for the *right* and *wrong* endings (see Section 2), we use the development set as our training set, holding out 10% for development (3,366 training endings, 374 for development). We keep the story cloze test set as is (3,742 endings).

It is worth noting that our classification task is slightly different from the story cloze task. Instead of classifying pairs of endings, one which is *right* and another which is *wrong*, our classifier decides about each ending individually, whether it

is *right* (positive instance) or *wrong* (negative instance). By ignoring the coupling between *right* and *wrong* pairs, we are able to decrease the impact of author-specific style differences, and focus on the difference between the styles accompanied with *right* and *wrong* writings.

Experiment 2: original/new endings. Here the goal is to measure whether writing the ending as part of a story imposes different style compared to writing a *new* (*right*) ending to an existing story. We use the endings of the ROC stories as our *original* examples and *right* endings from the story cloze task as *new* examples. As there are far more *original* instances than *new* instances, we randomly select five *original* sets, each with the same number of instances as we have *new* instances (3,366 training endings, 374 development endings, and 3,742 test endings). We train five classifiers, one with each of the *original* training sets, and report the average classification result.

Experiment 3: original/wrong endings. For completeness, we measure the extent to which our classifier can discriminate between *original* and *wrong* endings. We replicate Experiment 2, this time replacing *right* endings with *wrong* ones.

Experimental setup. In all experiments, we add a START symbol at the beginning of each sentence.[6] For computing our features, we keep *n*-gram (character or word) features that occur at least five times in the training set. All feature values are normalized to $[0, 1]$. For the POS features, we tag all endings with the Spacy POS tagger.[7] We use Python's sklearn logistic regression imple-

---

[5] Experiments with 5-grams on our development set reached similar performance.

[6] 99% of all sentences end with a period or an exclamation mark, so we do not add a STOP symbol.

[7] http://spacy.io/

Experiment	Accuracy
right vs. wrong	0.645
original vs. right	0.685
original vs. wrong	0.756

Table 2: Results of experiments 1 (*right vs. wrong*), 2 (*original vs. right (new)*) and 3 (*original vs. wrong (new)* endings). In all cases, our setup implies a 50% random baseline.

Model	Acc.
DSSM (Mostafazadeh et al., 2016a)	0.585
ukp (Mihaylov and Frank, 2017)	0.711
tbmihaylov (Mihaylov and Frank, 2017)	0.724
†EndingsOnly (Cai et al., 2017)	0.725
cogcomp	0.744
HIER,ENCPLOTEND,ATT (Cai et al., 2017)	0.747
RNN	0.677
†Ours	0.724
Combined (ours + RNN)	**0.752**
Human judgment	1.000

Table 3: Results on the test set of the story cloze task. The middle block are our results. *cogcomp* results and human judgement scores are taken from Mostafazadeh et al. (2017). Methods marked with (†) do not use the story context in order to make a prediction.

mentation (Pedregosa et al., 2011) with L_2 regularization, performing grid search on the development set to tune a single hyperparameter—the regularization parameter.

5.1 Results

Table 2 shows our results. In all experiments, our model achieves performance well above what would be expected under chance (50% by design). Noting again that our model ignores the story context (the preceding four sentences), our model is unable to capture any notion of coherence. This finding provides strong evidence that the authors' style was affected by the writing task they were given to perform.

5.2 Story Cloze Task

The results of Experiment 1 indicate that *right* and *wrong* endings are characterized by different styles. In order to further estimate the quality of our classification results, we tackle the story cloze task using our classifier. This classification task is more constrained than Experiment 1, as two endings are given and the question is which is *right* and which is *wrong*. We apply the classifier from Experiment 1 as follows: if it assigns different labels to the two given endings, we keep them. Otherwise, the label whose posterior probability is lower is reversed.

Table 3 shows our results on the story cloze test set. Our classifier obtains 72.4% accuracy, only 2.3% lower than state of the art results. Importantly, unlike previous approaches,[8] our classifier does not require the story corpus training data, and in fact doesn't even consider the first four sentences of the story in question. These numbers further support the claim that the styles of *right* and *wrong* endings are indeed very different.

Combination with a neural language model. We investigate whether our model can benefit from state of the art text comprehension models, for which this task was designed. Specifically, we experiment with an LSTM-based (Hochreiter and Schmidhuber, 1997) recurrent neural network language model (RNNLM; Mikolov et al., 2010). Unlike the model in this paper, which only considers the story endings, this language model follows the protocol suggested by the story cloze task designers, and harnesses their ROC Stories training set, which consists of single-ending stories, as well as the story context for each pair of endings. We show that adding our features to this powerful language model gives improvements over our classifier as well as the language model.

We train the RNNLM using a single-layer LSTM of hidden dimension 512. We use the ROC stories for training,[9] setting aside 10% for validation of the language model. We replace all words occurring less than 3 times with an out-of-vocabulary token, yielding a vocabulary size of 21,582. Only during training, we apply a dropout rate of 60% while running the LSTM over all 5 sentences of the stories. Using the Adam optimizer (Kingma and Ba, 2015) and a learning rate of $\eta = 0.001$, we train to minimize cross-entropy.

To apply the language model to the classification problem, we select as *right* the ending with the higher value of

$$\frac{p_\theta(\text{ending} \mid \text{story})}{p_\theta(\text{ending})} \tag{1}$$

---

[8]One exception is the EndingsOnly system (Cai et al., 2017), which was published in concurrence with this work, and obtains roughly the same results.

[9]We use the extended, 100K stories corpus (see Section 2).

Feature Type	Accuracy
Word n-grams	0.612
Character n-grams	0.639
Full model	0.645

Table 4: Results on Experiment 1 with different subsets of features.

The intuition is that a *right* ending should be unsurprising (to the model) given the four preceding sentences of the story (the numerator), controlling for the inherent surprisingness of the words in that ending (the denominator).

On its own, our neural language model performs moderately well on the story cloze test. Selecting endings based on $p_\theta(\text{ending} \mid \text{story})$ (i.e., the numerator of Equation 1), we obtained only 55% accuracy. The ratio in Equation 1 achieves 67.7% (see Table 3).[10]

We combine our linear model with the RNNLM by adding three features to our classifier: the numerator, denominator, and ratio in Equation 1, all in log space. We retrain our linear model with the new feature set, and gain 2.8% absolute, reaching 75.2%, a new state of the art result for the task. These results indicate that context-ignorant style features can be used to obtain high accuracy on the task, adding value even when context and a large training dataset are used.

6 Further Analysis

6.1 Most Discriminative Feature Types

A natural question that follows from this study is which style features are most helpful in detecting the underlying task an author was asked to perform. To answer this question, we re-ran Experiment 1 with different sub-groups of features. Table 4 shows our results. Results show that character n-grams are the most effective style predictors, reaching within 0.6% of the full model, but that word n-grams also capture much of the signal, yielding 61.2%, which is only 3.3% worse than the full model. These findings are in line with previous work that used character n-grams along with other types of features to predict writing style (Schwartz et al., 2013b).

---

[10]Note that taking the logarithm of the expression in Equation 1 gives the pointwise mutual information between the story and the ending, under the language model.

6.2 Most Salient Features

A follow-up question is which individual features contribute most to the classification process, as these could shed light on the stylistic differences imposed by each of the writing tasks.

In order to answer this question, we consider the highest absolute positive and negative coefficients in the logistic regression classifier in Experiments 1 and 2, an approach widely used as a method of extracting the most salient features (Nguyen et al., 2013; Burke et al., 2013; Brooks et al., 2013). It is worth noting that its reliability is not entirely clear, since linear models like logistic regression can assign large coefficients to rare features (Yano et al., 2012). To mitigate this concern, we consider only features appearing in at least 5% of the endings in our training set.

Experiment 1. Table 5a shows the most salient features for *right* (coherent) and *wrong* (incoherent) endings in Experiment 1, along with their corpus frequency. The table shows a few interesting trends. First, authors tend to structure their sentences differently when writing coherent vs. incoherent endings. For instance, incoherent endings are more likely to start with a proper noun and end with a common noun, while coherent endings have a greater tendency to end with a past tense verb.

Second, *right* endings make wider use of coordination structures, as well as adjectives. The latter might indicate that writing coherent stories inspires the authors to write more descriptive text compared to incoherent ones, as is the case in truthful vs. deceptive text (Ott et al., 2011). Finally, we notice a few syntactic differences: *right* endings more often use infinitive verb structure, while *wrong* endings prefer gerunds (VBG).

Experiment 2. Table 5b shows the same analysis for Experiment 2. As noted in Section 2, *original* endings tend to be much longer, which is indeed the most salient feature for them. An interesting observation is that exclamation marks are a strong indication for an *original* ending. This suggests that authors are more likely to show or evoke enthusiasm when writing their own text compared to ending an existing text.

Finally, when comparing the two groups of salient features from both experiments, we find an interesting trend. Several features, such as "START NNP" and "NN .", which indicate *wrong* sentences in Experiment 1, are used to predict

Right	Weight	Freq.	*Wrong*	Weight	Freq.
'ed .'	0.17	6.5%	START NNP	0.21	54.8%
'and '	0.15	13.6%	NN .	0.17	47.5%
JJ	0.14	45.8%	NN NN .	0.15	5.1%
to VB	0.13	20.1%	VBG	0.11	10.1%
'd th'	0.12	10.9%	START NNP VBD	0.11	41.9%

(a) Experiment 1

Right	Weight	Freq.	*Wrong*	Weight	Freq.
length	0.81	100.0%	'.'	0.74	93.0%
'!'	0.46	6.1%	START NNP	0.40	39.2%
NN	0.35	78.9%	START NNP VBD	0.23	29.0%
RB	0.34	44.7%	NN .	0.20	42.3%
','	0.32	12.7%	the NN .	0.20	10.6%

(b) Experiment 2

Table 5: The top 5 most heavily weighted features for predicting *right* vs. *wrong* endings (5a) and *original* vs. *new* (*right*) endings (5b). *length* is the sentence length feature (see Section 4).

new (i.e., *right*) endings in Experiment 2. This indicates that, for instance, incoherent endings have a stronger tendency to begin with a proper noun compared to coherent endings, which in turn are more likely to do so than original endings. This partially explains why distinguishing between *original* and *wrong* endings is an easier task compared to the other pairs (Section 5.1).

7 Discussion

The effect of writing tasks on mental states. In this paper we have shown that different writing tasks affect a writer's writing style in easily detected ways. Our results indicate that when authors are asked to write the last sentence of a five-sentence story, they will use different style to write a *right* ending compared to a *wrong* ending. We have also shown that writing the ending as part of one's own five-sentence story is very different than reading four sentences and then writing the fifth. Our findings hint that the nature of the writing task imposes a different mental state on the author, which is expressed in ways that can be observed using extremely simple automatic tools.

Previous work has shown that a writing task can affect mental state. For instance, writing deceptive text leads to a significant cognitive burden accompanied by a writing style that is different from truthful text (Newman et al., 2003; Banerjee et al., 2014). Writing tasks can even have a long-term effect, as writing emotional texts was observed to benefit both physical and mental health (Lep-ore and Smyth, 2002; Frattaroli, 2006). Campbell and Pennebaker (2003) also showed that the health benefits of writing emotional text are accompanied by changes in writing style, mostly in the use of pronouns.

Another line of work has shown that writing style is affected by mental state. First, an author's personality traits (e.g., depression, neuroticism, narcissism) affect her writing style (Schwartz et al., 2013a; Ireland and Mehl, 2014). Second, temporary changes, such as a romantic relationship (Ireland et al., 2011; Bowen et al., 2016), work collaboration (Tausczik, 2009; Gonzales et al., 2009), or negotiation (Ireland and Henderson, 2014) may also affect writing style. Finally, writing style can also change from one sentence to another, for instance between positive and negative text (Davidov et al., 2010) or when writing sarcastic text (Tsur et al., 2010).

This large body of work indicates a tight connection between writing tasks, mental states, and variation in writing style. This connection hints that the link discovered in this paper, between different writing tasks and resulting variation in writing style, involves differences in mental state. Additional investigation is required in order to further validate this hypothesis.

Design of NLP tasks. Our study also provides important insights for the future design of NLP tasks. The story cloze task was very carefully designed. Many factors, such as topic diversity and temporal and causal relation diversity, were controlled for (Mostafazadeh et al., 2016a). The authors also made sure each pair of endings was written by the same author, partly in order to avoid author-specific style effects. Nonetheless, despite these efforts, several significant style differences can be found between the story cloze training and test set, as well as between the positive and negative labels.

Our findings suggest that careful attention must be paid to instructions given to authors, especially in unnatural tasks such as writing a *wrong* ending. The COPA dataset (Roemmele et al., 2011), which was also designed to test commonsense knowledge, explicitly addressed potential style differences in their instructions. In this task, systems are presented with premises like *I put my plate in the sink*, and then decide between two alternatives, e.g.: (a) *I finished eating.* and (b) *I skipped dinner.* Importantly, when writing the alternatives, annotators were asked to be as brief as possible and avoid proper names, as well as slang.

Applying our story cloze classifier to this dataset yields 53.2% classification accuracy— close to a random baseline. While this could be partially explained by the smaller data size of the COPA dataset (1,000 examples compared to 3,742 in the story cloze task), this indicates that simple instructions may help alleviate the effects of writing style found in this paper. Another way to avoid such effects is to have people rate naturally occurring sentences by parameters such as coherence (or, conversely, the level of surprise), rather than asking them to generate new text.

8   Related Work

Writing style.   Writing style has been an active topic of research for decades. The models used to characterize style are often linear classifiers with style features such as character and word n-grams (Stamatatos, 2009; Koppel et al., 2009). Previous work has shown that different authors can be grouped by their writing style, according to factors such as age (Pennebaker and Stone, 2003; Argamon et al., 2003; Schler et al., 2006; Rosenthal and McKeown, 2011; Nguyen et al., 2011), gender (Argamon et al., 2003; Schler et al., 2006; Bamman et al., 2014), and native language (Koppel et al., 2005; Tsur and Rappoport, 2007; Bergsma et al., 2012). At the extreme case, each individual author adopts a unique writing style (Mosteller

and Wallace, 1963; Pennebaker and King, 1999; Schwartz et al., 2013b).

The line of work that most resembles our work is the detection of deceptive text. Several researchers have used stylometric features to predict deception (Newman et al., 2003; Hancock et al., 2007; Ott et al., 2011; Feng et al., 2012). Some works even showed that gender affects a person's writing style when lying (Pérez-Rosas and Mihalcea, 2014a,b). In this work, we have shown that an even more subtle writing task—writing coherent and incoherent story endings—imposes different styles on the author.

Machine reading.   The story cloze task, which is the focus of this paper, is part of a wide set of machine reading/comprehension challenges published in the last few years. These include datasets like bAbI (Weston et al., 2016), SNLI (Bowman et al., 2015), CNN/DailyMail (Hermann et al., 2015), LAMBADA (Paperno et al., 2016) and SQuAD (Rajpurkar et al., 2016). While these works have presented resources for researchers, it is often the case that these datasets suffer from methodological problems caused by applying noisy automatic tools to generate them (Chen et al., 2016).[11] In this paper, we have pointed to another methodological challenge in designing machine reading tasks: different writing tasks used to generated the data affect writing style, confounding classification problems.

9   Conclusion

Different writing tasks assigned to an author result in different writing styles for that author. We experimented with the story cloze task, which introduces two interesting comparison points: the difference between writing a story on one's own and continuing someone else's story, and the difference between writing a coherent and an incoherent story ending. In both cases, a simple linear model reveals measurable differences in writing styles, which in turn allows our final model to achieve state of the art results on the story cloze task.

The findings presented in this paper have cognitive implications, as they motivate further research

---

[11] Similar problems have been shown in visual question answering datasets, where simple models that rely mostly on the question text perform competitively with state of the art models by exploiting language biases (Zhou et al., 2015; Jabri et al., 2016).

on the effects that a writing prompt has on an author's mental state, and also her concrete response. They also provide valuable lessons for designing new NLP datasets.

10 Acknowledgments

The authors thank Chenhao Tan, Luke Zettlemoyer, Rik Koncel-Kedziorski, Rowan Zellers, Yangfeng Ji and several anonymous reviewers for helpful feedback. This research was supported in part by Darpa CwC program through ARO (W911NF-15-1-0543), Samsung GRO, NSF IIS-1524371, and gifts from Google and Facebook.

References

Shlomo Argamon, Moshe Koppel, Jonathan Fine, and Anat Rachel Shimoni. 2003. Gender, genre, and writing style in formal written texts. *Text* 23(3):321–346.

David Bamman, Jacob Eisenstein, and Tyler Schnoebelen. 2014. Gender identity and lexical variation in social media. *Journal of Sociolinguistics* 18(2):135–160.

Ritwik Banerjee, Song Feng, Jun S. Kang, and Yejin Choi. 2014. Keystroke patterns as prosody in digital writings: A case study with deceptive reviews and essays. In *Proc. of EMNLP*.

Shane Bergsma, Matt Post, and David Yarowsky. 2012. Stylometric analysis of scientific articles. In *Proc. of NAACL*.

Jeffrey D. Bowen, Lauren A. Winczewski, and Nancy L. Collins. 2016. Language style matching in romantic partners? conflict and support interactions. *Journal of Language and Social Psychology* pages 1–24.

Samuel R. Bowman, Gabor Angeli, Christopher Potts, and Christopher D. Manning. 2015. A large annotated corpus for learning natural language inference. In *Proc. of EMNLP*.

Michael Brooks, Katie Kuksenok, Megan K. Torkildson, Daniel Perry, John J. Robinson, Taylor J. Scott, Ona Anicello, Ariana Zukowski, Paul Harris, and Cecilia R. Aragon. 2013. Statistical affect detection in collaborative chat. In *Proc. of CSCW*.

Moira Burke, Lada A. Adamic, and Karyn Marciniak. 2013. Families on facebook. In *Proc. of ICWSM*.

Zheng Cai, Lifu Tu, and Kevin Gimpel. 2017. Pay attention to the ending: Strong neural baselines for the ROC story cloze task. In *Proc. of ACL*.

R. Sherlock Campbell and James W. Pennebaker. 2003. The secret life of pronouns flexibility in writing style and physical health. *Psychological Science* 14(1):60–65.

Danqi Chen, Jason Bolton, and Christopher D. Manning. 2016. A thorough examination of the CNN/Daily Mail reading comprehension task. In *Proc. of ACL*.

Dmitry Davidov, Oren Tsur, and Ari Rappoport. 2010. Enhanced sentiment learning using Twitter hashtags and smileys. In *Proc. of COLING*.

Song Feng, Ritwik Banerjee, and Yejin Choi. 2012. Syntactic stylometry for deception detection. In *Proc. of ACL*.

Joanne Frattaroli. 2006. Experimental disclosure and its moderators: a meta-analysis. *Psychological bulletin* 132(6):823.

Amy L. Gonzales, Jeffrey T. Hancock, and James W. Pennebaker. 2009. Language style matching as a predictor of social dynamics in small groups. *Communication Research* 37(1):3–19.

Jeffrey T. Hancock, Lauren E. Curry, Saurabh Goorha, and Michael Woodworth. 2007. On lying and being lied to: A linguistic analysis of deception in computer-mediated communication. *Discourse Processes* 45(1):1–23.

Karl Moritz Hermann, Tomáš Kočiský, Edward Grefenstette, Lasse Espeholt, Will Kay, Mustafa Suleyman, and Phil Blunsom. 2015. Teaching machines to read and comprehend. In *Proc. of NIPS*.

Sepp Hochreiter and Jürgen Schmidhuber. 1997. Long short-term memory. *Neural Computation* 9(8):1735–1780.

Molly E. Ireland and Marlone D. Henderson. 2014. Language style matching, engagement, and impasse in negotiations. *Negotiation and Conflict Management Research* 7(1):1–16.

Molly E. Ireland and Matthias R. Mehl. 2014. *Natural language use as a marker of personality*, Oxford University Press, USA, pages 201–237. The Oxford Handbook of Language and Social Psychology.

Molly E. Ireland, Richard B. Slatcher, Paul W. Eastwick, Lauren E. Scissors, Eli J. Finkel, and James W. Pennebaker. 2011. Language style matching predicts relationship initiation and stability. *Psychological Science* 22(1):39–44.

Allan Jabri, Armand Joulin, and Laurens van der Maaten. 2016. Revisiting visual question answering baselines. In *Proc. of ECCV*.

Diederik Kingma and Jimmy Ba. 2015. Adam: A method for stochastic optimization. In *Proc. of ICLR*.

Moshe Koppel, Jonathan Schler, and Shlomo Argamon. 2009. Computational methods in authorship attribution. *Journal of the American Society for information Science and Technology* 60(1):9–26.

Moshe Koppel, Jonathan Schler, and Kfir Zigdon. 2005. Determining an author's native language by mining a text for errors. In *Proc. of KDD*.

Stephen J. Lepore and Joshua M. Smyth. 2002. *The Writing Cure: How Expressive Writing Promotes Health and Emotional Well-being*. American Psychological Association.

Todor Mihaylov and Anette Frank. 2017. Simple story ending selection baselines. In *Proc. of LSDSem*.

Tomáš Mikolov, Martin Karafiát, Lukáš Burget, Jan Černocký, and Sanjeev Khudanpur. 2010. Recurrent neural network based language model. In *Proc. of Interspeech*.

Nasrin Mostafazadeh, Nathanael Chambers, Xiaodong He, Devi Parikh, Dhruv Batra, Lucy Vanderwende, Pushmeet Kohli, and James Allen. 2016a. A corpus and cloze evaluation for deeper understanding of commonsense stories. In *Proc. of NAACL*.

Nasrin Mostafazadeh, Michael Roth, Annie Louis, Nathanael Chambers, and James F. Allen. 2017. LSDSem 2017 shared task: The story cloze test. In *Proc. of LSDSem*.

Nasrin Mostafazadeh, Lucy Vanderwende, Wen-tau Yih, Pushmeet Kohli, and James Allen. 2016b. Story cloze evaluator: Vector space representation evaluation by predicting what happens next. In *Proc. of RepEval*.

Frederick Mosteller and David L. Wallace. 1963. Inference in an authorship problem. *Journal of the American Statistical Association* 58(302):275–309.

Matthew L. Newman, James W. Pennebaker, Diane S. Berry, and Jane M. Richards. 2003. Lying words: Predicting deception from linguistic styles. *Personality and Social Psychology Bulletin* 29(5):665–675.

Dong Nguyen, Rilana Gravel, Dolf Trieschnigg, and Theo Meder. 2013. "How old do you think i am?" a study of language and age in Twitter. In *Proc. of ICWSM*.

Dong Nguyen, Noah A. Smith, and Carolyn P. Rosé. 2011. Author age prediction from text using linear regression. In *Proc. of LaTeCH*.

Myle Ott, Yejin Choi, Claire Cardie, and Jeffrey T. Hancock. 2011. Finding deceptive opinion spam by any stretch of the imagination. In *Proc. of ACL*.

Denis Paperno, Germán Kruszewski, Angeliki Lazaridou, Ngoc Quan Pham, Raffaella Bernardi, Sandro Pezzelle, Marco Baroni, Gemma Boleda, and Raquel Fernández. 2016. The LAMBADA dataset: Word prediction requiring a broad discourse context. In *Proc. of ACL*.

Fabian Pedregosa, Gaël Varoquaux, Alexandre Gramfort, Vincent Michel, Bertrand Thirion, Olivier Grisel, Mathieu Blondel, Peter Prettenhofer, Ron Weiss, Vincent Dubourg, Jake Vanderplas, Alexandre Passos, David Cournapeau, Matthieu Brucher, Matthieu Perrot, and Édouard Duchesnay. 2011. Scikit-learn: Machine learning in Python. *JMLR* 12:2825–2830.

James W. Pennebaker and Laura A. King. 1999. Linguistic styles: language use as an individual difference. *Journal of Personality and Social Psychology* 77(6):1296–1312.

James W. Pennebaker and Lori D. Stone. 2003. Words of wisdom: language use over the life span. *Journal of Personality and Social Psychology* 85(2):291–301.

Verónica Pérez-Rosas and Rada Mihalcea. 2014a. Cross-cultural deception detection. In *Proc. of ACL*.

Verónica Pérez-Rosas and Rada Mihalcea. 2014b. Gender differences in deceivers writing style. *Lecture Notes in Computer Science* 8856:163–174.

Tiantian Qin, Judee Burgoon, and Jay F. Nunamaker Jr. 2004. An exploratory study on promising cues in deception detection and application of decision tree. In *Proc. of HICSS*.

Pranav Rajpurkar, Jian Zhang, Konstantin Lopyrev, and Percy Liang. 2016. SQuAD: 100,000+ questions for machine comprehension of text. In *Proc. of EMNLP*.

Melissa Roemmele, Cosmin Adrian Bejan, and Andrew S. Gordon. 2011. Choice of plausible alternatives: An evaluation of commonsense causal reasoning. In *AAAI Spring Symposium: Logical Formalizations of Commonsense Reasoning*.

Sara Rosenthal and Kathleen McKeown. 2011. Age prediction in blogs: A study of style, content, and online behavior in pre- and post-social media generations. In *Proc. of ACL*.

Michael Roth, Nasrin Mostafazadeh, Nathanael Chambers, and Annie Louis, editors. 2017. *Proceedings of the 2nd Workshop on Linking Models of Lexical, Sentential and Discourse-level Semantics*. Association for Computational Linguistics.

Jonathan Schler, Moshe Koppel, Shlomo Argamon, and James Pennebaker. 2006. Effects of age and gender on blogging. In *AAAI Spring Symposium: Computational Approaches to Analyzing Weblogs*.

Andrew H. Schwartz, Johannes C. Eichstaedt, Margaret L. Kern, Lukasz Dziurzynski, Stephanie M. Ramones, Megha Agrawal, Achal Shah, Michal Kosinski, David Stillwell, Martin E.P. Seligman, and Lyle H. Unger. 2013a. Personality, gender, and age in the language of social media: The open-vocabulary approach. *PloS one* 8(9):e73791.

Roy Schwartz, Maarten Sap, Ioannis Konstas, Leila Zilles, Yejin Choi, and Noah A. Smith. 2017. Story cloze task: UW NLP system. In *Proc. of LSDSem*.

Roy Schwartz, Oren Tsur, Ari Rappoport, and Moshe Koppel. 2013b. Authorship attribution of micro-messages. In *Proc. of EMNLP*.

Efstathios Stamatatos. 2009. A survey of modern authorship attribution methods. *Journal of the American Society for information Science and Technology* 60(3):538–556.

Yla Rebecca Tausczik. 2009. *Linguistic analysis of workplace computer-mediated communication.* Master's thesis, University of Texas.

Oren Tsur, Dmitry Davidov, and Ari Rappoport. 2010. ICWSM—a great catchy name: Semi-supervised recognition of sarcastic sentences in online product reviews. In *Proc. of ICWSM*.

Oren Tsur and Ari Rappoport. 2007. Using classifier features for studying the effect of native language on the choice of written second language words. In *Proc. of CACLA*.

Jason Weston, Antoine Bordes, Sumit Chopra, Alexander M Rush, Bart van Merriënboer, Armand Joulin, and Tomas Mikolov. 2016. Towards AI-complete question answering: A set of prerequisite toy tasks. In *Proc. of ICLR*.

Maria Yancheva and Frank Rudzicz. 2013. Automatic detection of deception in child-produced speech using syntactic complexity features. In *Proc. of ACL*.

Tae Yano, Noah A. Smith, and John D. Wilkerson. 2012. Textual predictors of bill survival in congressional committees. In *Proc. of NAACL*.

Bolei Zhou, Yuandong Tian, Sainbayar Sukhbaatar, Arthur Szlam, and Rob Fergus. 2015. Simple baseline for visual question answering. ArXiv:1512.02167.

Parsing for Grammatical Relations via Graph Merging

Weiwei Sun, Yantao Du and **Xiaojun Wan**
Institute of Computer Science and Technology, Peking University
The MOE Key Laboratory of Computational Linguistics, Peking University
`{ws,duyantao,wanxiaojun}@pku.edu.cn`

Abstract

This paper is concerned with building deep grammatical relation (GR) analysis using data-driven approach. To deal with this problem, we propose graph merging, a new perspective, for building flexible dependency graphs: Constructing complex graphs via constructing simple subgraphs. We discuss two key problems in this perspective: (1) how to decompose a complex graph into simple subgraphs, and (2) how to combine subgraphs into a coherent complex graph. Experiments demonstrate the effectiveness of graph merging. Our parser reaches state-of-the-art performance and is significantly better than two transition-based parsers.

1 Introduction

Grammatical relations (GRs) represent functional relationships between language units in a sentence. Marking not only local but also a wide variety of long distance dependencies, GRs encode in-depth information of natural language sentences. Traditionally, GRs are generated as a by-product by grammar-guided parsers, e.g. RASP (Carroll and Briscoe, 2002), C&C (Clark and Curran, 2007b) and Enju (Miyao et al., 2007). Very recently, by representing GR analysis using general directed dependency graphs, Sun et al. (2014) and Zhang et al. (2016) showed that considerably good GR structures can be directly obtained using data-driven, transition-based parsing techniques. We follow their encouraging work and study the data-driven approach for producing GR analyses.

The key challenge of building GR graphs is due to their flexibility. Different from surface syntax, the GR graphs are not constrained to trees, which is a fundamental consideration in design-

ing parsing algorithms. To deal with this problem, we propose graph merging, a new perspective, for building flexible representations. The basic idea is to decompose a GR graph into several subgraphs, each of which captures most but not the complete information. On the one hand, each subgraph is *simple* enough to allow efficient construction. On the other hand, the combination of all subgraphs enables whole target GR structure to be produced.

There are two major problems in the graph merging perspective. First, how to decompose a complex graph into simple subgraphs in a principled way? To deal with this problem, we considered structure-specific properties of the syntactically-motivated GR graphs. One key property is their reachability: In a given GR graph, almost every node is reachable from a same and unique root. If a node is not reachable, it is disconnected from other nodes. This property ensures a GR graph to be successfully decomposed into limited number of forests, which in turn can be accurately and efficiently built via tree parsing. We model the graph decomposition problem as an optimization problem and employ Lagrangian Relaxation for solutions.

Second, how to merge subgraphs into one coherent structure in a principled way? The problem of finding an optimal graph that consistently combines the subgraphs obtained through individual models is non-trivial. We treat this problem as a combinatory optimization problem and also employ Lagrangian Relaxation to solve the problem. In particular, the parsing phase consists of two steps. First, graph-based models are applied to assign scores to individual arcs and various tuples of arcs. Then, a Lagrangian Relaxation-based joint decoder is applied to efficiently produces globally optimal GR graphs according to all graph-based models.

We conduct experiments on Chinese GRBank

Proceedings of the 21st Conference on Computational Natural Language Learning (CoNLL 2017), pages 26–35,
Vancouver, Canada, August 3 - August 4, 2017. ©2017 Association for Computational Linguistics

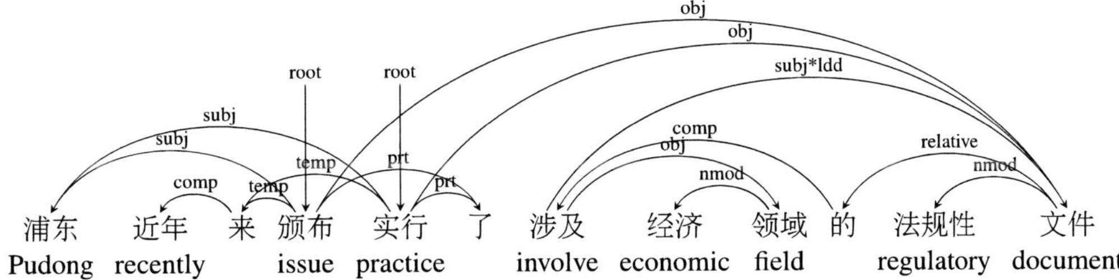

Figure 1: An example: *Pudong recently enacted regulatory documents involving the economic field.*

(Sun et al., 2014). Though our parser does not use any phrase-structure information, it produces high-quality GR analysis with respect to dependency matching. Our parsers obtain a labeled f-score of 84.57 on the test set, resulting in an error reduction of 15.13% over Sun et al. (2014)'s single system. and 10.86% over Zhang et al. (2016)'s system. The remarkable parsing result demonstrates the effectiveness of the graph merging framework. This framework can be adopted to other types of flexible representations, e.g. semantic dependency graphs (Oepen et al., 2014, 2015) and abstract meaning representations (Banarescu et al., 2013).

2 Background

In this paper, we focus on building GR analysis for Mandarin Chinese. Mandarin is an analytic language that lacks inflectional morphology (almost) entirely and utilizes highly configurational ways to convey syntactic and semantic information. This analytic nature allows to represent all GRs as bilexical dependencies. Sun et al. (2014) showed that analysis for a variety of complicated linguistic phenomena, e.g. coordination, raising/control constructions, extraction, topicalization, can be conveniently encoded with directed graphs. Moreover, such deep syntactic dependency graphs can be effectively derived from Chinese TreeBank (Xue et al., 2005) with very high quality. Figure 1 is an example. In this graph, "subj*ldd" between the word "涉及/involve" and the word "文件/documents" represents a long-distance subject-predicate relation. The arguments and adjuncts of the coordinated verbs, namely "颁布/issue" and "实行/practice," are separately yet distributively linked to the two heads.

By encoding GRs as directed graphs over words, Sun et al. (2014) and Zhang et al. (2016) showed that the data-driven, transition-based approach can be applied to build Chinese GR structures with very promising results. This architecture is complementary to the traditional approach to English GR analysis, which leverages grammar-guided parsing under deep formalisms, such as LFG (Kaplan et al., 2004), CCG (Clark and Curran, 2007a) and HPSG (Miyao et al., 2007). We follow Sun et al.'s and Zhang et al.'s encouraging work and study the discriminative, factorization models for obtaining GR analysis.

3 The Idea

The key idea of this work is constructing a complex structure via constructing simple partial structures. Each partial structure is *simple* in the sense that it allows efficient construction. For instance, projective trees, 1-endpoint-corssing trees, non-crossing dependency graphs and 1-endpoint-crossing, pagenumber-2 graphs can be taken as simple structures, given that low-degree polynomial time parsing algorithms exist (Eisner, 1996; Pitler et al., 2013; Kuhlmann and Jonsson, 2015; Cao et al., 2017; Sun et al., 2017). To construct each partial structure, we can employ mature parsing techniques. To get the final target output, we also require the total of all partial structures enables whole target structure to be produced. In this paper, we exemplify the above idea by designing a new parser for obtaining GR graphs. Take the GR graph in Figure 1 for example. It can be decomposed into two tree-like subgraphs, shown in Figure 2. If we can parse the sentence into subgraphs and combine them in a principled way, we get the original GR graph.

Under this perspective, we need to develop a principled method to decompose a complex structure into simple sturctures, which allows us to generate data to train simple solvers. We also need to develop a principled method to integrate partial structures, which allows us to produce coherent

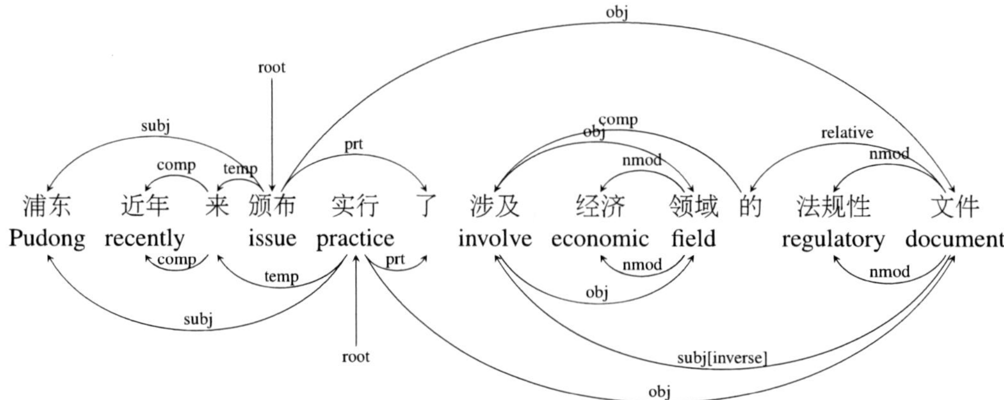

Figure 2: A graph decomposition for the GR graph in Figure 1. The two subgraphs are shown on two sides of the sentence respectively. The subgraph on the upper side of the sentence is exactly a tree, while the one on the lower side is slightly different. The edge from the word "文件/document" to "涉及/involve" is tagged "[inverse]" to indicate that the direction of the edge in the subgraph is in fact opposite to that in the original graph.

structures as outputs. We are going to demonstrate the techniques we use to solve these two problems.

4 Decomposing GR Graphs

4.1 Graph Decomposition as Optimization

Given a sentence $s = \mathbf{w}_1\mathbf{w}_2 \cdots \mathbf{w}_n$ of length n, we use a vector y of length n^2 to denote a graph on it. We use indices i and j to index the elements in the vector, $y(i, j) \in \{0, 1\}$, denoting whether there is an arc from w_i to w_j ($1 \leq i, j \leq n$).

Given a graph y, we hope to find m subgraphs y_1, ..., y_m, each of which belongs to a specific class of graphs $\mathcal{G}_k$ ($k = 1, 2, \cdots, m$). Each class should allow efficient construction. For example, we may need a subgraph to be a tree or a non-crossing dependency graph. The combination of all y_k gives enough information to construct y. Furthermore, the graph decomposition procedure is utilized to generate training data for building sub-models. Therefore, we hope each subgraph y_k is informative enough to train a good disambiguation model. To do so, for each y_k, we define a score function s_k that indicates the "goodness" of y_k. Integrating all ideas, we can formalize graph decomposition as an optimization problem,

$$\begin{aligned} \text{max.} \quad & \sum_k s_k(y_k) \\ \text{s.t.} \quad & y_i \text{ belongs to } \mathcal{G}_i \\ & \sum_k y_k(i, j) \geq y(i, j), \forall i, j \end{aligned}$$

The last condition in this optimization problem en-

sures that all edges in y appear at least in one subgraph.

For a specific graph decomposition task, we should define good score functions s_k and graph classes $\mathcal{G}_k$ according to key properties of the target structure y.

4.2 Decomposing GR Graphs into Tree-like Subgraphs

One key property of GR graphs is their reachability: Every node is either reachable from a unique root or by itself an independent connected component. This property allows a GR graph to be decomposed into limited number of *tree-like* subgraphs. By tree-like we mean if we treat a graph on a sentence as undirected, it is a tree, or it is a subgraph of some tree on the sentence. The advantage of tree-like subgraphs is that they can be effectively built by adapting data-driven tree parsing techniques. Take the sentence in Figure 1 for example. For every word, there is at least one path link the virtual root and this word. Furthermore, we can decompose the graph into two tree-like subgraphs, as shown in Figure 2. In this decomposition, one subgraph is exactly a tree, and the other is very close to a tree.

We restrict the number of subgraphs to 3. The intuition is that we use one tree to capture long distance information and the other two to capture coordination information.[1] In other words, we decompose each given graph y into three tree-like subgraphs g_1, g_2 and g_3. The goal is to let g_1, g_2 and g_3 carry important information of the graph as well as cover all edges in y. The optimization problem can be written as

max. $s_1(g_1) + s_2(g_2) + s_3(g_3)$
s.t. g_1, g_2, g_3 are tree-like
     $g_1(i,j) + g_2(i,j) + g_3(i,j) \geq y(i,j), \forall i,j$

4.2.1 Scoring a Subgraph

We score a subgraph in a first order *arc-factored* way, which first scores the edges separately and then adds up the scores. Formally, the score function is $s_k(g) = \sum \omega_k(i,j)g_k(i,j)$ ($k = 1,2,3$) where $\omega_k(i,j)$ is the score of the edge from i to j. Under this score function, we can use the Maximum Spanning Tree (MST) algorithm (Chu and Liu, 1965; Edmonds, 1967; Eisner, 1996) to decode the tree-like subgraph with the highest score.

After we define the score function, extracting a subgraph from a GR graph works like this: We first assign heuristic weights $\omega_k(i,j)$ ($1 \leq i,j \leq n$) to the potential edges between all the pairs of words, then compute a best projective tree g_k using the Eisner's Algorithm:

$$g_k = \arg\max_g s_k(g) = \arg\max_g \sum \omega_k(i,j)g(i,j).$$

g_k is not exactly a subgraph of y, because there may be some edges in the tree but not in the graph. To guarantee we get a subgraph of the original graph, we add labels to the edges in trees to encode necessary information. We label $g_k(i,j)$ with the original label, if $y(i,j) = 1$; with the original label appended by "$\sim$R" if $y(j,i) = 1$; with "None" else. With this labeling, we can have a function $t2g$ to transform the extracted trees into tree-like graphs. $t2g(g_k)$ is not necessary the same as the original graph y, but must be a subgraph of it.

4.2.2 Three Variations of Scoring

With different weight assignments, we can extract different trees from a graph, obtaining different

subgraphs. We devise three variations of weight assignment: ω_1, ω_2, and ω_3. Each ω_k (k is 1,2 or 3) consists of two parts. One is shared by all, denoted by S, and the other is different from each other, denoted by V. Formally, $\omega_k(i,j) = S(i,j) + V_k(i,j)$ ($k = 1,2,3$ and $1 \leq i,j \leq n$).

Given a graph y, S is defined as $S(i,j) = S_1(i,j) + S_2(i,j) + S_3(i,j) + S_4(i,j)$, where

$$S_1(i,j) = \begin{cases} c_1 & \text{if } y(i,j) = 1 \text{ or } y(j,i) = 1 \\ 0 & \text{else} \end{cases}$$

$$S_2(i,j) = \begin{cases} c_2 & \text{if } y(i,j) = 1 \\ 0 & \text{else} \end{cases}$$

$$S_3(i,j) = c_3(n - |i - j|)$$

$$S_4(i,j) = c_4(n - l_p(i,j))$$

In the definitions above, c_1, c_2, c_3 and c_4 are coefficients, satisfying $c_1 \gg c_2 \gg c_3$, and l_p is a function of i and j. $l_p(i,j)$ is the length of shortest path from i to j that either i is a child of an ancestor of j or j is a child of an ancestor of i. That is to say, the paths are in the form $i \leftarrow n_1 \leftarrow \cdots \leftarrow n_k \rightarrow j$ or $i \leftarrow n_1 \rightarrow \cdots \rightarrow n_k \rightarrow j$. If no such path exits, then $l_p(i,j) = n$. The intuition behind the design is illustrated below.

S_1 indicates whether there is an edge between i and j, and we want it to matter mostly;

S_2 indicates whether the edge is from i to j, and we want the edge with correct direction to be selected more likely;

S_3 indicates the distance between i and j, and we like the edge with short distance because it is easier to predict;

S_4 indicates the length of certain type of path between i and j that reflects c-commanding relationships, and the coefficient remains to be tuned.

We want the score V to capture different information of the GR graph. In GR graphs, we have an additional information (as denoted as "*ldd" in Figure 1) for long distance dependency edges. Moreover, we notice that conjunction is another important structure, and they can be derived from the GR graph. Assume that we tag the edges relating to conjunctions with "*cjt." The three variation scores, i.e. V_1, V_2 and V_3, reflect long distance and the conjunction information in different ways.

---

[1] In this paper, we employ projective parsers. The minimal number of sub-graphs is related to the pagenumber of GR graphs. The pagenumber of 90.96% GR graphs is smaller than or equal to 2, while the pagenumber of 98.18% GR graphs is at most 3. That means 3 projective trees are perhaps good enough to handle Chinese sentences, but 2 projective trees are not. Due to the empirical results in Table 3, using three projective trees can handle 99.55% GR arcs. Therefore, we think three is suitable for our problem.

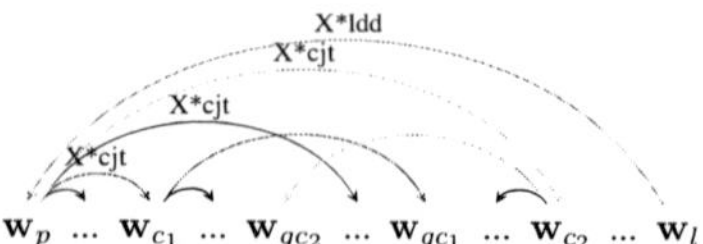

Figure 3: Examples to illustrate the additional weights.

V_1. First for edges $y(i,j)$ whose label is tagged with *ldd, we assign $V_1(i,j) = d$. d is a co-efficient to be tuned on validation data.. Whenever we come across a parent p with a set of conjunction children $cjt_1, cjt_2, \cdots, cjt_n$, we find the rightmost child gc_{1r} of the leftmost child in conjunction cjt_1, and add d to each $V_1(p, cjt_1)$ and $V_1(cjt_1, gc_{1r})$. The edges in conjunction that are added additional d's to are shown in blue in Figure 3.

V_2. Different from V_1, for edges $y(i,j)$ whose label is tagged with *ldd, we assign an $V_2(j,i) = d$. Then for each conjunction structure with a parent p and a set of conjunction children $cjt_1, cjt_2, \cdots, cjt_n$, we find the leftmost child gc_{nl} of the rightmost child in conjunction cjt_n, and add d to each $V_2(p, cjt_n)$ and $V_2(cjt_n, gc_{nl})$. The concerned edges in conjunction are shown in green in Figure 3.

V_3. We do not assign d's to the edges with tag *ldd. For each conjunction with parent p and conjunction children $cjt_1, cjt_2, \cdots, cjt_n$, we add an d to $V_3(p, cjt_1)$, $V_3(p, cjt_2)$, $\cdots$, and $V_3(p, cjt_n)$.

4.3 Lagrangian Relaxation with Approximation

As soon as we get three trees g_1, g_2 and g_3, we get three subgraphs $t2g(g_1)$, $t2g(g_2)$ and $t2g(g_3)$. As is stated above, we want every edge in a graph y to be covered by at least one subgraph, and we want to maximize the sum of the edge weights of all trees. Note that the inequality in the constrained optimization problem above can be replaced by a maximization, written as

$$
\begin{aligned}
\text{max.} \quad & s_1(g_1) + s_2(g_2) + s_3(g_3) \\
\text{s.t.} \quad & g_1, g_2, g_3 \text{ are trees} \\
& \max\{t2g(g_1)(i,j), t2g(g_2)(i,j), \\
& t2g(g_3)(i,j)\} = y(i,j), \forall i,j
\end{aligned}
$$

where $s_k(g_k) = \sum \omega_k(i,j) g_k(i,j)$

Let $g_m = \max\{t2g(g_1), t2g(g_2), t2g(g_3)\}$, and by $\max\{g_1, g_2, g_3\}$ we mean to take the maximum of three vectors pointwisely. The Lagrangian

---

Algorithm 1: The Tree Extraction Algorithm

Initialization: set $u^{(0)}$ to 0
for $k = 0$ **to** K **do**
    $g_1 \leftarrow \arg\max_{g_1} s_1(g_1) + u^{(k)\top} g_1$
    $g_2 \leftarrow \arg\max_{g_2} s_2(g_2) + u^{(k)\top} g_2$
    $g_3 \leftarrow \arg\max_{g_3} s_3(g_3) + u^{(k)\top} g_3$
    if $\max\{g_1, g_2, g_3\} = y$ **then**
        return g_1, g_2, g_3
    $u^{(k+1)} \leftarrow$
        $u_{(k)} - \alpha^{(k)} (\max\{g_1, g_2, g_3\} - y)$
return g_1, g_2, g_3

---

of the problem is

$$
\mathcal{L}(g_1, g_2, g_3; u) = s_1(g_1) + s_2(g_2) + s_3(g_3) \\
+ u^\top (g_m - y)
$$

where u is the Lagrangian multiplier.

Then the dual is

$$
\begin{aligned}
\mathcal{L}(u) &= \max_{g_1, g_2, g_3} \mathcal{L}(g_1, g_2, g_3; u) \\
&= \max_{g_1}(s_1(g_1) + \frac{1}{3} u^\top g_m) \\
&\quad + \max_{g_2}(s_2(g_2) + \frac{1}{3} u^\top g_m) \\
&\quad + \max_{g_3}(s_3(g_3) + \frac{1}{3} u^\top g_m) - u^\top y
\end{aligned}
$$

According to the duality principle, $\max_{g_1, g_2, g_3; u} \min_u \mathcal{L}(g_1, g_2, g_3) = \min_u \mathcal{L}(u)$, so we can find the optimal solution for the problem if we can find $\min_u \mathcal{L}(u)$. However it is very hard to compute $\mathcal{L}(u)$, not to mention $\min_u \mathcal{L}(u)$. The challenge is that g_m in the three maximizations must be consistent.

The idea is to separate the overall maximization into three maximization problems by approximation. We observe that g_1, g_2, and g_3 are very close to g_m, so we can approximate $\mathcal{L}(u)$ by

$$
\begin{aligned}
\mathcal{L}'(u) &= \max_{g_1, g_2, g_3} \mathcal{L}(g_1, g_2, g_3; u) \\
&= \max_{g_1}(s_1(g_1) + \frac{1}{3} u^\top g_1) \\
&\quad + \max_{g_2}(s_2(g_2) + \frac{1}{3} u^\top g_2) \\
&\quad + \max_{g_3}(s_3(g_3) + \frac{1}{3} u^\top g_3) - u^\top y
\end{aligned}
$$

In this case, the three maximization problem can be decoded separately, and we can try to find the optimal u using the subgradient method.

4.4 The Algorithm

Algorithm 1 is our tree decomposition algorithm. In the algorithm, we use subgradient method to find $\min_u \mathcal{L}'(u)$ iteratively. In each iteration, we first compute g_1, g_2, and g_3 to find $\mathcal{L}'(u)$, then update u until the graph is covered by the subgraphs. The coefficient $\frac{1}{3}$'s can be merged into the steps $\alpha^{(k)}$, so we omit them. The three separate problems $g_k \leftarrow \arg\max_{g_k} s_k(g_k) + u^\top g_k$ ($k = 1, 2, 3$) can be solved using Eisner's algorithm, similar to solving $\arg\max_{g_k} s_k(g_k)$. Intuitively, the Lagrangian multiplier u in our Algorithm can be regarded as additional weights for the score function. The update of u is to increase weights to the edges that are not covered by any tree-like subgraph, so that it will be more likely for them to be selected in the next iteration.

5 Graph Merging

The extraction algorithm gives three classes of trees for each graph. We apply the algorithm to the graph training set, and get three training tree sets. After that, we can train three parsing models with the three tree sets. In this work, the parser we use to train models and parse trees is Mate (Bohnet, 2010), a second-order graph-based dependency parser.

Let the scores the three models use be f_1, f_2, f_3 respectively. Then the parsers can find trees with highest scores for a sentence. That is solving the following optimization problems: $\arg\max_{g_1} f_1(g_1)$, $\arg\max_{g_2} f_2(g_2)$ and $\arg\max_{g_2} f_3(g_3)$. We can parse a given sentence with the three models, obtain three trees, and then transform them into subgraphs, and combine them together to obtain the graph parse of the sentence by putting all the edges in the three subgraphs together. That is to say, we obtain the graph $y = \max\{t2g(g_1), t2g(g_2), t2g(g_3)\}$. We call this process **simple merging**.

However, the simple merging process omits some consistency that the three trees extracted from the same graph achieve, thus losing some important information. The information is that when we decompose a graph into three subgraphs, some edges tend to appear in certain classes of subgraphs at the same time. We want to retain the co-occurrence relationship of the edges when doing parsing and merging. To retain the hidden consistency, we must do *joint* decoding instead of decode the three models separately.

5.1 Capturing the Hidden Consistency

In order to capture the hidden consistency, we add consistency tags to the labels of the extracted trees to represent the co-occurrence. The basic idea is to use additional tag to encode the relationship of the edges in the three trees. The tag set is $\mathcal{T} = \{0, 1, 2, 3, 4, 5, 6\}$. Given a tag $t \in \mathcal{T}$, $t\&1$, $t\&2$, $t\&4$ denote whether the edge is contained in g_1, g_2, g_3 respectively, where the operator "&" is the bitwise AND operator. Specially, since we do not need to consider first bit of the tags of edges in g_1, the second bit in g_2, and the third bit in g_3, we always assign 0 to them. For example, if $y(i, j) = 1$, $g_1(i, j) = 1$, $g_2(j, i) = 1$, $g_3(i, j) = 0$ and $t_3(j, i) = 0$, we tag $g_1(i, j)$ as 2 and $g_2(j, i)$ as 1.

When it comes to parsing, we also get labels with consistency information. Our goal is to guarantee the tags in edges of the parse trees for a same sentence are consistent while graph merging. Since the consistency tags emerge, for convenience we index the graph and tree vector representation using three indices. $g(i, j, t)$ denotes whether there is an edge from word $\mathbf{w}_i$ to word $\mathbf{w}_j$ with tag t in graph g.

The joint decoding problem can be written as a constrained optimization problem as

$$
\begin{aligned}
\text{max.} \quad & f_1(g_1) + f_2(g_2) + f_3(g_3) \\
\text{s.t.} \quad & g_1'(i, j, 2) + g_1'(i, j, 6) \leq \sum_t g_2'(i, j, t) \\
& g_1'(i, j, 4) + g_1'(i, j, 6) \leq \sum_t g_3'(i, j, t) \\
& g_2'(i, j, 1) + g_2'(i, j, 5) \leq \sum_t g_1'(i, j, t) \\
& g_2'(i, j, 4) + g_2'(i, j, 5) \leq \sum_t g_3'(i, j, t) \\
& g_3'(i, j, 1) + g_3'(i, j, 3) \leq \sum_t g_1'(i, j, t) \\
& g_3'(i, j, 2) + g_3'(i, j, 3) \leq \sum_t g_2'(i, j, t) \\
& \forall i, j
\end{aligned}
$$

where $g_k' = t2g(g_k)(k = 1, 2, 3)$.

The inequality constraints in the problem are the consistency constraints. Each of them gives the constraint between two classes of trees. For example, the first inequality says that an edge in g_1 with tag $t\&2 \neq 0$ exists only when the same edge in g_2 exist. If all of these constraints are satisfied, the subgraphs achieve the consistency.

5.2 Lagrangian Relaxation with Approximation

To solve the constrained optimization problem above, we do some transformations and then apply the Lagrangian Relaxation to it with approximation.

Let $\boldsymbol{a}_{12}(i,j) = \boldsymbol{g}_1(i,j,2) + \boldsymbol{g}_1(i,j,6)$, then the first constraint can be written as an equity constraint

$$\boldsymbol{g}_1(:,:,2) + \boldsymbol{g}_1(:,:,6) = \boldsymbol{a}_{12}. * \left(\sum_t \boldsymbol{g}_2(:,:,t)\right)$$

where ":" is to take out all the elements in the corresponding dimension, and ".*" is to do multiplication pointwisely. So can the other inequality constraints. If we take $\boldsymbol{a}_{12}, \boldsymbol{a}_{13}, \cdots, \boldsymbol{a}_{32}$ as constants, then all the constraints are linear. The constraints thus can be written as

$$A_1\boldsymbol{g}_1 + A_2\boldsymbol{g}_2 + A_3\boldsymbol{g}_3 = \boldsymbol{0}$$

where A_1, A_2, and A_3 are matrices that can be constructed from $\boldsymbol{a}_{12}, \boldsymbol{a}_{13}, \cdots, \boldsymbol{a}_{32}$.

The Lagrangian of the optimization problem is

$$\mathcal{L}(\boldsymbol{g}_1, \boldsymbol{g}_2, \boldsymbol{g}_3; u) = f_1(\boldsymbol{g}_1) + f_2(\boldsymbol{g}_2) + f_3(\boldsymbol{g}_3) + u^\top(A_1\boldsymbol{g}_1 + A_2\boldsymbol{g}_2 + A_3\boldsymbol{g}_3)$$

where u is the Lagrangian multiplier. Then the dual is

$$\begin{aligned}
\mathcal{L}(u) &= \max_{\boldsymbol{g}_1,\boldsymbol{g}_2,\boldsymbol{g}_3} \mathcal{L}(\boldsymbol{g}_1, \boldsymbol{g}_2, \boldsymbol{g}_3; u) \\
&= \max_{\boldsymbol{g}_1}(f_1(\boldsymbol{g}_1) + u^\top A_1\boldsymbol{g}_1) \\
&\quad + \max_{\boldsymbol{g}_2}(f_2(\boldsymbol{g}_2) + u^\top A_2\boldsymbol{g}_2) \\
&\quad + \max_{\boldsymbol{g}_3}(f_3(\boldsymbol{g}_3) + u^\top A_3\boldsymbol{g}_3)
\end{aligned}$$

Again, we use the subgradient method to minimize $\mathcal{L}(u)$. During the deduction, we take $\boldsymbol{a}_{12}, \boldsymbol{a}_{13}, \cdots, \boldsymbol{a}_{32}$ as constants, but unfortunately they are not. We propose an approximation for the $\boldsymbol{a}$'s in each iteration: Using the $\boldsymbol{a}$'s we got in the previous iteration instead. It is a reasonable approximation given that the u's in two consecutive iterations are similar and so are the $\boldsymbol{a}$'s.

5.3 The Algorithm

The pseudo code of our algorithm is shown in Algorithm 2. We know that the score functions f_1, f_2, and f_3 each consist of first-order scores and higher order scores. So they can be written as

$$f_k(\boldsymbol{g}) = s_k^{1st}(\boldsymbol{g}) + s_k^h(\boldsymbol{g})$$

where $s_k^{1st}(\boldsymbol{g}) = \sum \omega_k(i,j)\boldsymbol{g}(i,j)$ $(k = 1, 2, 3)$. With this property, each individual problem $\boldsymbol{g}_k \leftarrow \arg\max_{\boldsymbol{g}_k} f_k(\boldsymbol{g}_k) + u^\top A_k \boldsymbol{g}_k$ can be decoded easily, with modifications to the first order weights

---

Algorithm 2: The Joint Decoding Algorithm

Initialization: set $u^{(0)}, A_1, A_2, A_3$ to 0,

for $k = 0$ **to** K **do**

  $\boldsymbol{g}_1 \leftarrow \arg\max_{\boldsymbol{g}_1} f_1(\boldsymbol{g}_1) + u^{(k)\top} A_1\boldsymbol{g}_1$

  $\boldsymbol{g}_2 \leftarrow \arg\max_{\boldsymbol{g}_2} f_2(\boldsymbol{g}_2) + u^{(k)\top} A_2\boldsymbol{g}_2$

  $\boldsymbol{g}_3 \leftarrow \arg\max_{\boldsymbol{g}_3} f_3(\boldsymbol{g}_3) + u^{(k)\top} A_3\boldsymbol{g}_3$

  update A_1, A_2, A_3

  if $A_1\boldsymbol{g}_1 + A_2\boldsymbol{g}_2 + A_3\boldsymbol{g}_3 = \boldsymbol{0}$ **then**

     return $\boldsymbol{g}_1, \boldsymbol{g}_2, \boldsymbol{g}_3$

  $u^{(k+1)} \leftarrow$

    $u_{(k)} - \alpha^{(k)}(A_1\boldsymbol{g}_1 + A_2\boldsymbol{g}_2 + A_3\boldsymbol{g}_3)$

return $\boldsymbol{g}_1, \boldsymbol{g}_2, \boldsymbol{g}_3$

---

of the edges in the three models. Specifically, let $\mathbf{w}_k = u^\top A_k$, then we can modify the ω_k in s_k to ω_k', such that $\omega_k'(i,j,t) = \omega_k(i,j,t) + \mathbf{w}_k(i,j,t) + \mathbf{w}_k(j,i,t)$.

The update of $\mathbf{w}_1$, $\mathbf{w}_2$, $\mathbf{w}_3$ can be understood in an intuitive way. When one of the constraints is not satisfied, without loss of generality, say, the first one for edge $\boldsymbol{y}(i,j)$. We know $\boldsymbol{g}_1(i,j)$ is tagged to represent that $\boldsymbol{g}_2(i,j) = 1$, but it is not the case. So we increase the weight of that edge with all kinds of tags in $\boldsymbol{g}_2$, and decrease the weight of the edge with tag representing $\boldsymbol{g}_2(i,j) = 1$ in $\boldsymbol{g}_1$. After the update of the weights, the consistency is more likely to be achieved.

5.4 Labeled Parsing

For sake of formal concision, we illustrate our algorithms omitting the labels. It is straightforward to extend the algorithms to labeled parsing. In the joint decoding algorithm, we just need to extend the weights $\mathbf{w}_1$, $\mathbf{w}_2$, $\mathbf{w}_3$ for every label that appears in the three tree sets, and the algorithm can be deduced similarly.

6 Evaluation and Analysis

6.1 Experimental Setup

We conduct experiments on Chinese GRBank (Sun et al., 2014), an LFG-style GR corpus for Mandarin Chinese. Linguistically speaking, this deep dependency annotation directly encodes information such as coordination, extraction, raising, control as well as many long-range dependencies. The selection for training, development, test data is also according to Sun et al. (2014)'s experiments. Gold standard POS-tags are used for deriving features for disambiguation.

		UP	UR	UF	UCompl	LP	LR	LF	LCompl
SM	subgraph1	88.63	76.19	81.94	18.09	85.94	73.88	79.46	16.11
	subgraph2	88.04	78.20	82.83	17.47	85.31	75.77	80.26	15.43
	subgraph3	88.91	81.12	84.84	20.36	86.57	78.99	82.61	17.30
	Merged	83.23	**88.45**	85.76	22.97	80.59	**85.64**	83.04	19.29
LR	subgraph1	**89.76**	77.48	83.17	18.60	**87.17**	75.25	80.77	16.39
	subgraph2	89.30	79.18	83.93	18.66	86.68	76.85	81.47	16.56
	subgraph3	89.42	81.55	85.31	20.53	87.09	79.43	83.08	17.81
	Merged	88.07	85.14	**86.58**	**26.32**	85.55	82.70	**84.10**	**21.61**

Table 1: Results on development set. *SM* is for Simple Merging, and *LR* for Lagrangian Relaxation.

	UP	UR	UF	UCompl	LP	LR	LF	LCompl
subgraph1	**89.80**	76.74	82.76	18.69	**87.81**	75.04	80.93	17.13
subgraph2	89.34	78.66	83.66	18.46	87.26	76.84	81.72	16.97
subgraph3	89.57	81.23	85.19	20.18	87.78	79.61	83.49	18.22
Merged	88.06	**85.11**	**86.56**	**26.24**	86.03	**83.16**	**84.57**	**22.84**
Sun et al.	-	-	-	-	83.93	79.82	81.82	-
Zhang et al.[Single]	-	-	-	-	82.28	83.11	82.69	-
Zhang et al.[Ensemble]	-	-	-	-	84.92	85.28	85.10	-

Table 2: Lagrangian Relaxation Results on test set.

The measure for comparing two dependency graphs is precision/recall of GR tokens which are defined as $\langle w_h, w_d, l \rangle$ tuples, where w_h is the head, w_d is the dependent and l is the relation. Labeled precision/recall (LP/LR) is the ratio of tuples correctly identified by the automatic generator, while unlabeled precision/recall (UP/UR) is the ratio regardless of l. F-score is a harmonic mean of precision and recall. These measures correspond to attachment scores (LAS/UAS) in dependency tree parsing. To evaluate our GR parsing models that will be introduced later, we also report these metrics.

	Coverage	Edge	Sentence
SD	subgraph1	85.52	28.73
	subgraph2	88.42	28.36
	subgraph3	90.40	34.37
	Merged	96.93	71.66
LR	subgraph1	85.66	29.01
	subgraph2	88.48	28.63
	subgraph3	90.67	34.72
	Merged	**99.55**	**96.90**

Table 3: Results of graph decomposition. *SD* is for Simple Decomposition and *LR* for Lagrangian Relaxation

6.2 Results of Graph Decomposition

Table 3 shows the results of graph decomposition on the training set. If we use simple decomposition, say, directly extracting three trees from a graph, we get three subgraphs. On the training set, each kind of the subgraphs cover around 90% edges and 30% sentences. When we merge them together, they cover nearly 97% edges and over 70% sentences. This indicates that the ability of a single tree is limited and three trees can cover most of the edges.

When we apply Lagrangian Relaxation to the decomposition process, both the edge coverage and the sentence coverage gain great error reduc-tion, indicating that Lagrangian Relaxation is very effective on the task of decomposition.

6.3 Results of Graph Merging

Table 1 shows the results of graph merging on the development set, and Table 2 on test set. The three training sets of trees are from the decomposition with Lagrangian Relaxation and the models are trained from them. In both tables, simple merging (SM) refers to first decode the three trees for a sentence then combine them by putting all the edges together. As is shown, the merged graph achieves higher f-score than other single models. With Lagrangian Relaxation, the performance of not only the merged graph but also the three subgraphs are improved, due to capturing the consistency information.

When we do simple merging, though the recall of each kind of subgraphs is much lower than the precision of them, it is opposite of the merged graph. This is because the consistency between three models is not required and the models tend to give diverse subgraph predictions. When we require the consistency between the three models, the precision and recall become comparable, and higher f-scores are achieved.

The best scores reported by previous work, i.e. (Sun et al., 2014) and (Zhang et al., 2016) are also listed in Table 2. We can see that our subgraphs already achieve competitive scores, and the merged graph with Lagrangian Relaxation improves both unlabeled and labeled f-scores substantially, with an error reduction of 15.13% and 10.86%. We also include Zhang et al.'s parsing result obtained by an ensemble model that integrate six different transition-based models. We can see that parser ensemble is very helpful for deep dependency parsing and the accuracy of our graph merging parser is sightly lower than this ensemble model. Given that the architecture of graph merging is quite different from transition-based parsing, we think system combination of our parser and the transition-based parser is promising.

7 Conclusion

To construct complex linguistic graphs beyond trees, we propose a new perspective, namely graph merging. We take GR parsing as a case study and exemplify the idea. There are two key problems in this perspective, namely graph decomposition and merging. To solve these two problems in a principled way, we treat both problems as optimization problems and employ combinatorial optimization techniques. Experiments demonstrate the effectiveness of the graph merging framework. This framework can be adopted to other types of flexible representations, e.g. semantic dependency graphs (Oepen et al., 2014, 2015) and abstract meaning representations (Banarescu et al., 2013).

Acknowledgments

This work was supported by 863 Program of China (2015AA015403), NSFC (61331011), and Key Laboratory of Science, Technology and Standard in Press Industry (Key Laboratory of Intelligent Press Media Technology). We thank anonymous reviewers for their valuable comments.

References

Laura Banarescu, Claire Bonial, Shu Cai, Madalina Georgescu, Kira Griffitt, Ulf Hermjakob, Kevin Knight, Philipp Koehn, Martha Palmer, and Nathan Schneider. 2013. Abstract meaning representation for sembanking. In *Proceedings of the 7th Linguistic Annotation Workshop and Interoperability with Discourse*. Association for Computational Linguistics, Sofia, Bulgaria, pages 178–186. http://www.aclweb.org/anthology/W13-2322.

Bernd Bohnet. 2010. Top accuracy and fast dependency parsing is not a contradiction. In *Proceedings of the 23rd International Conference on Computational Linguistics (Coling 2010)*. Coling 2010 Organizing Committee, Beijing, China, pages 89–97. http://www.aclweb.org/anthology/C10-1011.

Junjie Cao, Sheng Huang, Weiwei Sun, and Xiaojun Wan. 2017. Parsing to 1-endpoint-crossing, pagenumber-2 graphs. In *Proceedings of the 55th Annual Meeting of the Association for Computational Linguistics*. Association for Computational Linguistics.

John Carroll and Ted Briscoe. 2002. High precision extraction of grammatical relations. In *Proceedings of the 19th International Conference on Computational Linguistics - Volume 1*. Association for Computational Linguistics, Stroudsburg, PA, USA, COLING '02, pages 1–7. https://doi.org/10.3115/1072228.1072241.

Y.J. Chu and T.H. Liu. 1965. On the shortest arborescence of a directed graph. *Science Sinica* pages 14:1396–1400.

Stephen Clark and James Curran. 2007a. Formalism-independent parser evaluation with CCG and DepBank. In *Proceedings of the 45th Annual Meeting of the Association of Computational Linguistics*. Association for Computational Linguistics, Prague, Czech Republic, pages 248–255. http://www.aclweb.org/anthology/P07-1032.

Stephen Clark and James R. Curran. 2007b. Wide-coverage efficient statistical parsing with CCG and log-linear models. *Computational Linguistics* 33(4):493–552. https://doi.org/10.1162/coli.2007.33.4.493.

J. Edmonds. 1967. Optimum branchings. *Journal of Research of the NationalBureau of Standards* pages 71B:233–240.

Jason M. Eisner. 1996. Three new probabilistic models for dependency parsing: an exploration. In *Proceedings of the 16th conference on Computational linguistics - Volume 1*. Association for Computational Linguistics, Stroudsburg, PA, USA, pages 340–345.

Ron Kaplan, Stefan Riezler, Tracy H King, John T Maxwell III, Alex Vasserman, and Richard Crouch. 2004. Speed and accuracy in shallow and deep stochastic parsing. In Daniel Marcu Susan Dumais and Salim Roukos, editors, *HLT-NAACL 2004: Main Proceedings*. Association for Computational Linguistics, Boston, Massachusetts, USA, pages 97–104.

Marco Kuhlmann and Peter Jonsson. 2015. Parsing to noncrossing dependency graphs. *Transactions of the Association for Computational Linguistics* 3:559–570.

Yusuke Miyao, Kenji Sagae, and Jun'ichi Tsujii. 2007. Towards framework-independent evaluation of deep linguistic parsers. In Ann Copestake, editor, *Proceedings of the GEAF 2007 Workshop*. CSLI Publications, CSLI Studies in Computational Linguistics Online, pages 238–258. http://www.cs.cmu.edu/ sagae/docs/geaf07miyaoetal.pdf.

Stephan Oepen, Marco Kuhlmann, Yusuke Miyao, Daniel Zeman, Silvie Cinková, Dan Flickinger, Jan Hajic, and Zdenka Uresová. 2015. Semeval 2015 task 18: Broad-coverage semantic dependency parsing. In *Proceedings of the 9th International Workshop on Semantic Evaluation (SemEval 2015)*.

Stephan Oepen, Marco Kuhlmann, Yusuke Miyao, Daniel Zeman, Dan Flickinger, Jan Hajic, Angelina Ivanova, and Yi Zhang. 2014. Semeval 2014 task 8: Broad-coverage semantic dependency parsing. In *Proceedings of the 8th International Workshop on Semantic Evaluation (SemEval 2014)*. Association for Computational Linguistics and Dublin City University, Dublin, Ireland, pages 63–72. http://www.aclweb.org/anthology/S14-2008.

Emily Pitler, Sampath Kannan, and Mitchell Marcus. 2013. Finding optimal 1-endpoint-crossing trees. *TACL* 1:13–24. http://www.transacl.org/wp-content/uploads/2013/03/paper13.pdf.

Weiwei Sun, Junjie Cao, and Xiaojun Wan. 2017. Semantic dependency parsing via book embedding. In *Proceedings of the 55th Annual Meeting of the Association for Computational Linguistics*. Association for Computational Linguistics.

Weiwei Sun, Yantao Du, Xin Kou, Shuoyang Ding, and Xiaojun Wan. 2014. Grammatical relations in Chinese: GB-ground extraction and data-driven parsing. In *Proceedings of the 52nd Annual Meeting of the Association for Computational Linguistics (Volume 1: Long Papers)*. Association for Computational Linguistics, Baltimore, Maryland, pages 446–456. http://www.aclweb.org/anthology/P14-1042.

Naiwen Xue, Fei Xia, Fu-dong Chiou, and Marta Palmer. 2005. The penn Chinese treebank: Phrase structure annotation of a large corpus. *Natural Language Engineering* 11:207–238. https://doi.org/10.1017/S135132490400364X.

Xun Zhang, Yantao Du, Weiwei Sun, and Xiaojun Wan. 2016. Transition-based parsing for deep dependency structures. *Computational Linguistics* 42(3):353–389. http://aclweb.org/anthology/J16-3001.

Leveraging Eventive Information for
Better Metaphor Detection and Classification

I-Hsuan Chen[1], Yunfei Long[2], Qin Lu[2], Chu-Ren Huang[1]
[1]Department of Chinese & Bilingual Studies, The Hong Kong Polytechnic University
{ihsuan.chen, churen.huang}@polyu.edu.hk
[2]Department of Computing, The Hong Kong Polytechnic University
{csylong, csluqin}@comp.polyu.edu.hk

Abstract

Metaphor detection has been both challenging and rewarding in natural language processing applications. This study offers a new approach based on eventive information in detecting metaphors by leveraging the Chinese writing system, which is a culturally bound ontological system organized according to the basic concepts represented by radicals. As such, the information represented is available in all Chinese text without pre-processing. Since metaphor detection is another culturally based conceptual representation, we hypothesize that sub-textual information can facilitate the identification and classification of the types of metaphoric events denoted in Chinese text. We propose a set of syntactic conditions crucial to event structures to improve the model based on the classification of radical groups. With the proposed syntactic conditions, the model achieves a performance of 0.8859 in terms of F-scores, making 1.7% of improvement than the same classifier with only Bag-of-word features. Results show that eventive information can improve the effectiveness of metaphor detection. Event information is rooted in every language, and thus this approach has a high potential to be applied to metaphor detection in other languages.

1 Introduction

Metaphors are a cross linguistic phenomenon in everyday language as shown in a great amount of corpus linguistic and experimental studies. The Conceptual Metaphor Theory (Lakoff, 1989; Lakoff and Johnson, 1981) shows how linguistic expressions reflect the mapping of two conceptual domains. For example, the expression *I see what you mean* instantiates the conceptual metaphor of KNOWING IS SEEING. The phrase is the result of mapping the source domain SEEING, which is embodied daily experience onto the target domain, KNOWING, as exemplified in the examples of *shed some light* on this, an *illuminating* article, and take a *close look*. Due to the pervasive use of metaphors, there is an enormous amount of studies in the techniques of detecting metaphors. Relevant studies of detecting metaphors primarily rely on contextual information.

This study provides a novel approach to detect and classify metaphors by analyzing eventive information. Concepts can be classified into a wide array of event types according to ontology, the organization of knowledge (Huang et al., 2007). Eventive information thus can be applied to the classification of metaphors, which concern mappings of conceptual structures from a source domain to a target domain.

The classification of metaphoric and literal senses has been approached by different methods such as vector-space models with distributional statistics (Hovy et al., 2013; Tsvetkov et al., 2014) and compositional distributional semantic models (CDSMs) (Kartsaklis and Sadrzadeh, 2013a). Most of the studies regarding metaphoric detection have been done in English, while the task in Chinese is at the incipient stage. The relevant studies such as clustering models and similarity computation in context (Fu et al., 2016; Wang, 2010) mainly focus on the metaphoric sense of each individual noun or adjectival phrase because the analyses are highly dependent on contextual information. However, metaphoric senses of verbs are less touched because it is difficult to define regularities of their contextual information. This study deals with the challenge of the verb category by including eventive information, which is the basis of the classification of metaphors.

Proceedings of the 21st Conference on Computational Natural Language Learning (CoNLL 2017), pages 36–46,
Vancouver, Canada, August 3 - August 4, 2017. ©2017 Association for Computational Linguistics

Chinese is featured by its semantic-based orthography in the writing system. Specifically, Chinese characters are composed of radicals and components, which are ideographic or phonetic symbols. Radicals, which represent core conceptual properties, encode eventive information of the literal senses of characters (Huang 2009, Huang and Hsieh, 2015). For instance, the verb 踢 *ti* 'kick' contains the radical 足 'foot'; the verb 吃 *chi* 'eat' has the radical 口 'mouth'. The radicals clearly identify the body parts executing the actions. Chinese radicals, in particular, evoke the whole event structure such as the initiation, the process, and the termination of a kicking or an eating action. Also, radicals are good indicators of different types of events. For instance, radicals can encode the information of tools in the concept of separation. The radical 刀 *dao* 'knife' of the character 切 *qie* 'cut' implies that the action results in two pieces, while the radical 石 *shi* 'stone' of the character 破 *po* 'break' emphasizing that the action results into pieces. The radicals can thus provide detailed eventive information to identify the source domain in the task of metaphor detection.

Event information characterizes detailed properties such as the volition of the subject and the resulted status of the object. The properties can be accessed by their corresponding syntactic constructions. We propose 17 syntactic conditions which are appropriate to differentiate different event types. First, we implement the algorithm of metaphor detection based on a Support Vector Machine (SVM) classifier. The syntactic conditions serve as additional features using Bag-of-word features as the baseline. Second, we apply the SVM classifier to predict the senses, either literal or metaphoric, of each verb in *Baidu Baike* corpus, which has 1,543,669 million entries and 7.6 billion tokens.[1] We then measure the semantic similarities among different radical groups by the vector representation according to each sense of each character. The similarity of vectors based on word representation and sense representation proves that radicals can predict semantic groups of the literal senses. We delimit the syntactic environments where the literal senses tend to occur. When a sense does not occur in the defined set of syntactic conditions, it is highly possible to be metaphoric.

In this study, NLP technology is applied to two deeply culturally bound phenomena: (i) the Chinese writing system and (ii) the classification of metaphors. The Chinese character orthography is an ontological system organized based on the primitive concepts represented by radicals (Chou and Huang, 2010). Thus, the information represented by radicals is not only cultural specific but also available in all Chinese text without the need for processing. Metaphor detection, as another culturally based conceptual representation, has been proven to be both challenging and extremely valuable in natural language processing. Based on their shared event information, we hypothesize that sub-textual information can leverage the effectiveness to identify and classify different types of metaphoric events hidden in the Chinese text. Our experiments prove the effectiveness of eventive information in detecting metaphors. The approach of leveraging event type information by radicals increases both the precision and the recall in metaphor detection. Although this approach is especially effective for Chinese because of the information embedded in radicals, broader implications include the possibility of leveraging eventive information from different sources in other languages.

2   Related Work

The task of metaphor detection has been handled in a wide variety of approaches including clustering models (Birke and Sarkar, 2006; Shutova et al., 2010; Li and Sporleder, 2010), semantic similarity graphs (Sporleder and Li, 2009), topic modeling (Li et al., 2010; Heintz et al., 2013), and compositional distributional semantic models (CDSMs) (Gutiérrez et al. 2016). Feature-based classification, in particular, attracts most attention since a wide array of contextual information is included (Sporleder and Li, 2009; Dunn., 2013; Hovy et al., 2011; Mohler et al., 2013; Neuman et al., 2013; Tsvetkov et al., 2013; Tsvetkov et al., 2014). Since the studies regarding metaphor identification have primarily focused on English, there are more available datasets in English in both manually-tagged linguistic resources (Gedigian et al., 2006; Krishnakumaran and Zhu, 2007; Broadwell et al., 2013) and corpus-based approach (Birke and Sarker, 2007; Shutova et al., 2013; Neuman et al., 2013; Hovy et al., 2013). Metaphor detection in Chinese is at the incipient stage. Fu et al., (2016) uses hierarchical clustering

---

[1] https://en.wikipedia.org/wiki/Baidu_Baike

for Chinese noun phrases according to their contextual information to recognize metaphoric phrases. Zhou et al. (2011) use the Maximum Entrophy model to detect the metaphoric reading of verb phrases based on collocation with noun phrases, and point out that there is no mature syntactic and semantic tool for metaphor analysis in Chinese. Our study will close the gap by building a model of metaphor detection based on syntactic conditions.

Regarding metaphor detection, most papers emphasize on distinguishing metaphoric senses from literal senses in a polysemy network. Disambiguation of senses has been handled by DSMs based on the availability of contextual information (Baroni et al., 2014; Boleda et al., 2012; Erk and Padó, 2010; Kartsaklis and Sadrzadeh 2013). When more contextual information is incorporated, disambiguation would be more successful. It should be noted that the senses of one form have different degrees of transparency to be traced in semantics. The senses of a form which can be chained together via overlapping semantics, as in the case of polysemy (cut a new *window* in the wall vs. the ball broke a *window*), are more likely to be traced. On the contrary, when the senses of a linguistic form are discrete as in the case of *homonymy* (e.g. piano *keys* vs. *key* point), they may be problematic to DSM (Baroni et al., 2014). Gutiérrez et al. (2016) point out that the challenge arises from the highly context-dependent property of *homonymies* since the relations of senses are not unsystematic. In contrast, the senses of a polysemy form a systematic system, and thus CDSM has a better chance to detect metaphoric senses (Gutiérrez et al. 2016). Nevertheless, how to group a variety of senses including metonymic and metaphoric senses as a polysemy has been a challenge in Chinese (Fu et al., 2016). In this paper, the use of Chinese radicals for grouping senses can avoid the confusion of polysemy and homonym because Chinese radicals stand for semantic classification, reflecting the structure of our ontological knowledge structure (Huang 2009).

Contextual information has been regarded as an important determinant in identifying metaphors. Previous studies thus primarily focus on the adjectives or nouns as in the studies of English metaphors due to the abundant contextual information from these categories. This study, instead, focuses on the verb category and shows the literal and metaphoric senses of a verb can be predicted by their syntactic conditions. The event structure evoked by a verb offers reliable information for metaphor detection.

3 Methodology

Our task is to define the syntactic environments where the metaphoric sense of a verb would be more likely to occur. Each verb corresponds to a type of event structure. Chinese radicals denote the most profiled element in an event structure. For example, the literal sense of 灌 *guan* 'pour', which has a water radical 氵, specifies the material of this action is water. Based on the properties of water, the verb emphasizes dynamic flows. Thus the verb tends to appear in non-passive constructions for expressing the dynamics. The literal meaning of 墊 *dian* 'pad', which has the mud radical 土, profiles mud as a loctum, and therefore it tends to appear with a locative phrase in order to specify the object to be padded. The literal sense of 切 *qie* 'cut', which has a knife radical 刀, specifies the instrument of the separation. The verb occurs mostly in the VO word order, as in 切蛋糕 *qie diangao* 'cut cakes' to emphasize on transitivity. In summary, each verb has its own event structure, which can be observed in the syntactic environments where the verb frequently occurs. Since a metaphoric sense describes a concept different from that of a literal sense, it should have a different event structure from that of a literal sense. According to corpus data, it can be observed that the literal senses of a verb tend to occur under a set of syntactic conditions, while the metaphoric senses of the same verb tend to occur in the environments deviating from the standards. For instance, the metaphoric sense of 灌 *guan* 'pour' frequently appears in passive constructions, while the literal sense generally occurs in non-passive constructions. The metaphoric sense of 墊 *dian* 'pad' is more likely to occur without a locative phrase, whereas the literal senses normally occur with a locative phrase. The metaphoric sense of 切 *qie* 'cut' as in 'cannot cut the relationship' occurs more frequently in the OV word order, while the literal sense tends to occur in the VO word order. The change of event types is expected since the source domain and the target domain refer to different settings although their underlying conceptual structures are organized in a similar way. For instance, both the literal and metaphoric senses of

Radical	Sample Characters	Radical	Sample Characters
火 *huo* 'fire'	熬 *ao* 'simmer' 烤 *kao* 'grill'	糸 *mi* 'thread'	綁 *bang* 'tight' 織 *zhi* 'weave'
水 *shui* 'water'	灌 *guan* 'pour' 沖 *chong* 'flush'	力 *li* 'power'	動 *dong* 'move' 加 *jia* 'add'
土 *tu* 'mud'	墊 *dian* 'pad' 塞 *sai* 'pack'	扌 *shou* 'hand'	抱 *bao* 'hug' 推 *tui* 'push'
金 *jin* 'gold'	釘 *ding* 'pin 鑽 *zuan* 'drill'	口 *kou* 'mouth'	吃 *chi* 'eat' 咬 *yao* 'bite'
石 *shi* 'stone'	砍 *kan* 'chop' 破 *po* 'break' 碰 *peng* 'clash'	辵/辶 *chuo* 'interval walk'	逃 *tiao* 'escape' 追 *zhui* 'chase'
刀 *dao* 'knife'	刷 *shua* 'brush' 切 *qie* 'cut'	足 *zu* 'foot'	跳 *tiao* 'jump' 踢 *ti* 'kick'
斤 *jin* 'ax'	斬 *zan* 'cut' 斷 *duan* 'snap'	走 *zou* 'walk'	走 *zou* 'walk' 趕 *gan* 'chase'

Table 1: Types of radicals and sample characters

切 *qie* 'cut' refer to the concept of separation which results in two entities, but the separation is employed to describe different contexts. The literal one refers to the separation of an entity with a specific instrument, while the metaphoric one refers to the discontinuation of a relationship. It is the change of event types that provides information of predicting which sense is in use.

3.1 Syntactic conditions and Radicals

Radicals: The advantages of radical-based analysis are the transparency and traceability of semantic relations among different senses in a polysemy network. The current experiments include 14 types of radicals as listed in Table 1. Each type of radicals has two to three verbs which have high frequency in *Chinese Gigaword* (Huang 2009) as the representatives.

Syntactic conditions: We hypothesize that the literal senses of a verb tend to appear in a set of syntactic conditions whereas the metaphoric senses tend to deviate from those conditions due to the

change of event types. To test this hypothesis, we propose a variety of syntactic conditions to characterize each sense and its relevant event structure. The conditions are selected based on the frequency of where the literal senses of these verbs occur.

(i) Word order (VO): If a verb can take an object, the verb and its object may occur in either VO or OV word order.

(ii) Compounding (VV): The verb may form a compound with another verb in VV form. The target verb is the second one.

(iii) Transitivity (Vt): The verb may be transitive or intransitive.

(iv) Passivity (Pass): The verb may occur in a passive construction. The indicators are the occurrences of passive markers.

(v) Disposal constructions (Disposal): The verb may occur with the disposal markers to foreground the semantic patient or the direct object.

(vi) Aspectual markers (Asp): The verb may appear with aspectual markers to specify the status of the process.

(vii) Double-object construction (DO): The verb may take both a direct object and an indirect object.

(viii) Relative clauses (RC): The verbs may occur with a relative clause. This feature is indicated by the markers of a relative clause.

(ix) Numeral phrases (Num): Amounts relevant to the event are specified by numeral-classifier phrases.

(x) Locative phrases (Loc): Location of the event is specified. The locative phrase can occur either before or after the verb.

(xi) Negation (Neg): Negative markers appear in the main clause which contains

(xii) Postpositions (Post): The verb may take a postposition phrase.

(xiii) Prepositions (Prep): The verb may occur with a preposition phrase. . The indicators are the occurrences of a variety of prepositions.

(xiv) Instrumental 用 *yong* 'use' (yong): The instruments are profiled.

(xv) 對 *dui* 'to/ toward' (dui): The goal of the verb is profiled by this marker.

(xvi) Beneficiary/ maleficent marker 給 *gei* (gei): The affectiveness of the event relevant to the target verb is specified.

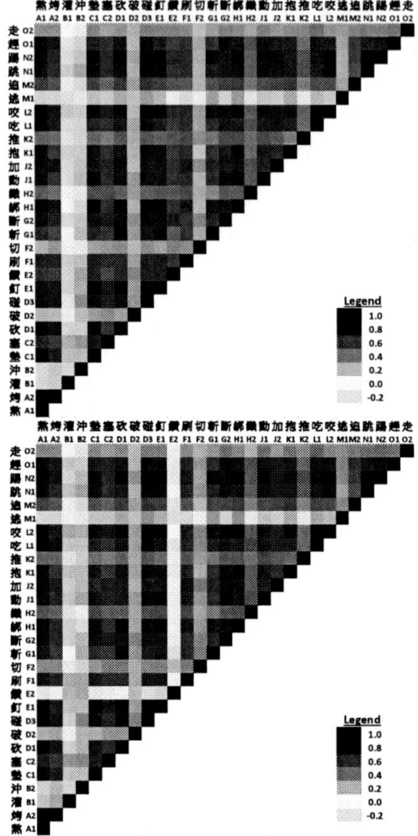

Figure 1: Semantic closeness among different verbs [upper graph: literal sense; lower graph: metaphoric sense]

(xvii) Postverbal adverbs (Vadv): The verb may be followed by an adverb which specifies degrees or durations of time.

3.2 Design of classification model

In order to evaluate the effectiveness of our proposed syntactic conditions, we have to extract the syntactic features which are relevant to the literal and metaphoric senses. The task of detecting the metaphor/literal senses is modeled as a binary class classification. The proposed syntactic conditions are implemented as additional features in this model.

SVM are well performed in higher dimension, particularly when targeted instances only hold a small portion in a dataset. Since our design focuses on the effectiveness of syntactic conditions in metaphor detection rather than on a classifier, we choose SVM with linear kernel as our classifier for its linear binary classification and use LibSVM (Chang and Lin, 2011) as the SVM tool.

3.3 Word embedding for word similarity

Word embedding is known as a special form of word vectors which represents a word through a low dimensional dense vector and has been used in different lexical tasks, such as semantic similarity, word analogy, word synonym detection, and concept categorization (Baroni, 2014), (Levy, 2015). Our goal is to increase the precision of metaphor detection with the aid of the semantic classification of radicals. Thus we conduct word embedding to show how different concepts are categorized in terms of their semantic similarities. Based on the similarity from word embedding, we can infer semantic distance among verbs with different radicals and further quantify the differences between the metaphoric and literal senses of the same verb.

Various models are proposed to learn the dense vector representation of words, which are all based on the distributional hypothesis that words occur in similar context have similar meanings (Harris, 1954). Among those models, the most widely used one is the Skip-Gram model with negative sampling (Mikolov, 2013). In our task, word embedding is trained through the Skip-Gram model with default parameters on the *Baidu Baike* corpus[2] with word segmentation performed by the HIT LTP tool[3].

Since Chinese radicals encode semantic categorizations, verbs which belong to the same radical group are expected to be close semantically. In order to capture the predictive power of radicals in semantics, we use multi-dimensional vector space to show the distribution of verbs when they are used in their literal senses and metaphoric senses respectively (Baroni, 2014, Levy, 2015). First, we use our proposed classifier to predict the senses of 29 selected verbs, and treat metaphor /literal sense of each word as an individual word. And we calculate the cosine similarity between different senses. Figure 1 shows that verbs having the same radical are relatively similar to each other compared to verbs which belong to different radical groups. However, the grouping by radicals does not work well in the metaphoric senses, as shown in the lower graph. The sharp contrast supports the claim that the metaphoric senses of a verb have a

---

[2] http://www.nlpcn.org/resource/7
[3] http://www.ltp-cloud.com/

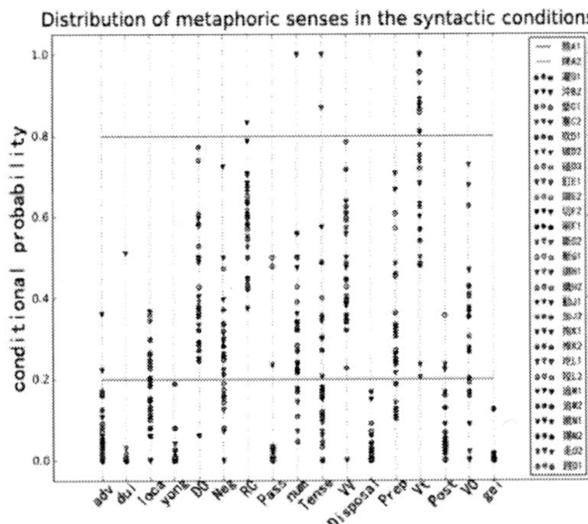

Figure 2: Probability of metaphoric senses in each syntactic condition

Type	Precision	Recall	F score
Basic	0.8824	0.8559	0.8689
All features	0.8952	0.8768	0.8859
Feature group 1	**0.8925**	**0.8821**	**0.8872**
Feature group 2	0.8752	0.8631	0.8691
Feature group 3	0.8705	0.8521	0.8612

Table 2: Performance in different condition groups

- **Base group**: Using Bag-of-word features only
- **Group1**: transitivity (Vt), numeral phrases (Num), relative clauses (RC), compounding (VV), tense, word order (VO), and double-object construction (DO).
- **Group 2:** negation (Neg), prepositions (Prep), locative phrases (Loc), postverbal adverbial (Vadv), passivity (Pass), and aspectual markers (Asp).
- **Group 3:** disposal constructions (Disposal), postpositions (Post), instrumental 用 *yong* 'use' (yong), 對 *dui* 'to/ toward' (dui), and beneficiary/maleficient marker 給 *gei* (gei).

different event structure from that of the literal senses.

4 Experiments

Experiments of feature analysis are conducted to show whether our proposed syntactic conditions can improve the model of metaphor detection.

4.1 Dataset

The dataset is structured based on the 29 verbs from 14 radical groups introduced in Section 3.1. For each verb, a random sample of 200-300 sentences are collected from the *Chinese Gigaword* corpus (Huang, 2009), a comprehensive archive of newswire text data. Two Chinese native speakers manually annotated the metaphoric and literal senses of each token based on *Hantology* (Chou and Huang, 2006), a character-based Chinese language resource in which each character is sense-tagged. In the 6,047 tokens, 1,738 of them are labeled as a metaphoric sense and 4,309 are labeled as a literal sense. Our annotation task has kappa statistics (Banerjee, 1999) over 0.81 indicating strong inter-annotator consistency.

4.2 Model and analysis

We evaluate the 17 syntactic conditions using the SVM classification model in the dataset introduced in Section 4.1. In order to avoid overfitting, we perform 10-fold cross validation. To test the efficiency of our proposed syntactic conditions, the 17 conditions are divided into 3 feature groups.

The three groups are defined based on two principles: (i) the probability of the occurrence of the metaphoric senses in the syntactic condition in question; (ii) the clusters of the verbs. As shown in Figure 2, the metaphoric senses frequently occur in a few syntactic conditions, such as Vt, VO, and relative clauses. Regarding the principle of the clusters, the condition which has less overlapping data points is more effective in distinguishing different senses.

The results of the experiment given in Table 2 show that the proposed syntactic conditions have improved the performance of the model. The incorporation of all the 17 features does improve the classification model by 1.70% in F-score. However, Group 1 has the best performance, outperforming the result when all the 17 features are used. However, when Group 2 and Group 3 are used alone, they do not contribute to improving the model. In fact, Group 3 decreases the effectiveness of the model. The decrease in performance is on both Precision and Recall. However, while the model incorporates Group 1, the precision is improved at the expense of a slight decrease in recall. This increase in precision indicates that the features of Group 2 and Group 3 still provide useful information in metaphor detection.

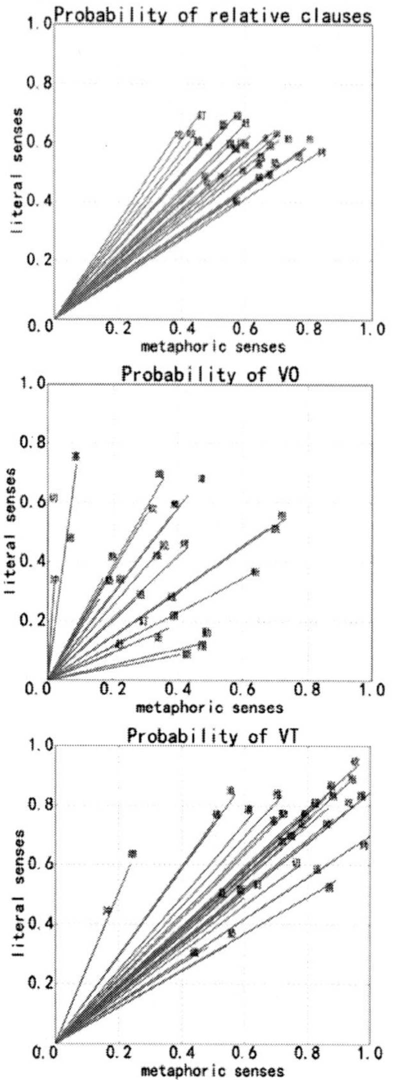

Figure 3: Distribution of example literal-metaphoric pair of verbs under individual syntactic conditions.

5 Discussion

Our experimental result shows that the proposed syntactic conditions can predict where the literal and metaphoric senses of the same verb occur. This is because the two senses tend to be used in different event structure. For example, the literal sense of the verb 灌 *guan* 'pour' as in 灌良田 *guan liang tian* 'irrigating good farms' specifies the location right after the verb, while the metaphoric sense as in 灌水 *guan shui* pour water 'artificially increasing the amount' has water as the

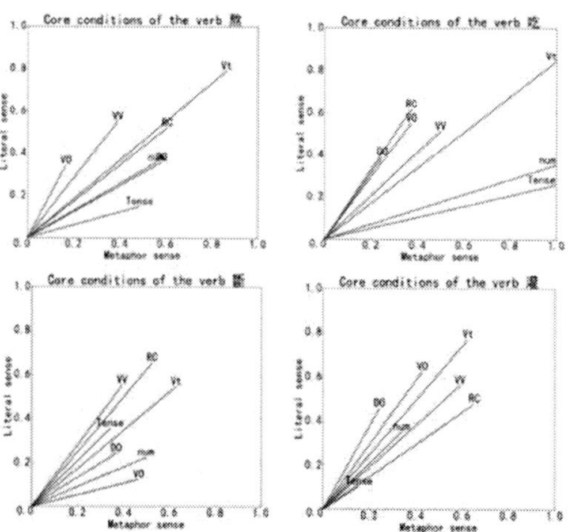

Figure 4: Examples of metaphoric and literal senses of verbs characterized by a core set of syntactic conditions.

material without specifying the location. The literal sense of 走 *zhou* 'walk' appears as an intransitive verb as in 他走了 *ta zhou le* he-walk-ASP 'he left', while the metaphoric sense tends to have a noun phrase following it as in 走好運 *zhou hao yun* walk-luck 'being lucky'. Since the metaphoric sense describes an event different from that of the literal sense, the syntactic properties of the metaphoric sense should differ from those of the literal sense. Among our proposed syntactic conditions, seven of them, transitivity, relative clauses, double objects, compounds, word order, aspectual markers, and numeral phrases, are the most effective conditions in detecting metaphors. Figure 3 shows examples from these syntactic conditions including transitivity, word order, and relative clauses. The horizontal axis shows conditional probabilities in metaphoric sense. The vertical axis shows the conditional probabilities in literal sense. A condition with a stronger predictive power has a bigger difference in the probability between the literal and metaphoric senses. For example, the literal sense and metaphoric sense of the verb 切 *qie* 'cut' have saliently different probabilities in the feature of word order. The literal sense is frequently found in the VO word order, while the metaphoric sense seldom occurs in the VO word order. It is the difference that can serve to predict which sense, literal or metaphoric, is in use.

Each syntactic condition is regarded as a measurement. The syntactic conditions then can be grouped to precisely identify the event types of the literal and metaphoric senses for each verb as

Category	Radicals
Materials	火 *huo* 'fire' 水 *shui* 'water' 土 *tu* 'mud'
Body parts	扌 *shou* 'hand' 口 *kou* 'mouth'
Instruments	走 *zou* 'walk' 辵/辶 *chuo* 'interval walk' 足 *zu* 'foot' 力 *li* 'power'
Movements	石 *shi* 'stone' 刀 *dao* 'knife' 斤 *jin* 'ax' 糸 *mi* 'thread' 金 *jin* 'gold'

Table 3: Higher-level Ontological Categories of Radicals

shown in the examples of Figure 4. The horizontal axis shows conditional probabilities in metaphoric sense. The vertical axis shows the conditional probabilities in literal sense. Each condition has different relevancy to a verb because each verb belongs to a different event type. For example, the condition of word order (labeled as VO) has higher effectiveness in the verb 吃 *chi* 'eat' than in the verb 斷 *duan* 'snap'. In other words, the senses of each verb can be identified by the most relevant syntactic conditions. Therefore, the syntactic environments of where a verb occurs can be used to predict whether it is metaphoric.

Furthermore, grouping verbs by Chinese radicals can offer generalizations of the event types associated with a particular semantic group. A group of relevant radicals denote a higher-level category in the ontological structure, which refers to the organization of knowledge structure and the representation of knowledge system in terms of relations between concepts (Prévot et al., 2010). For example, the radicals discussed in this paper can be classified into four larger semantic categories, which are instruments, body parts, materials, movements, as given in Table 3.

The differences in the distribution of the literal and metaphoric senses of the four semantic groups can be characterized by the rankings of the syntactic conditions. As shown in Figure 5, the group of the material radicals and the group of the movement radicals have different arrangement of the

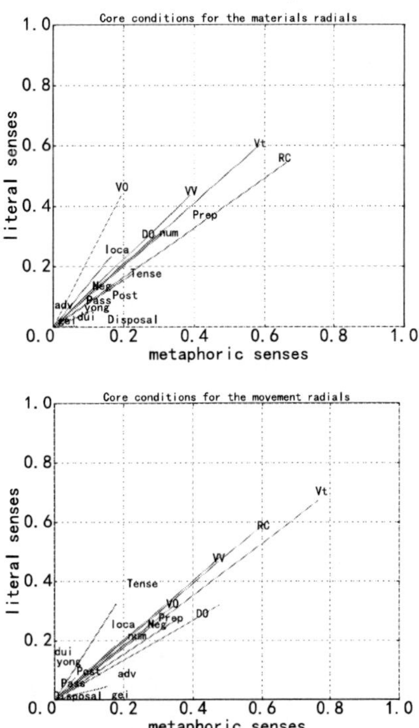

Figure 5: Examples of the syntactic conditions characterizing a higher-level semantic category

conditions. In other words, the literal sense of a larger semantic group can also be identified by its syntactic distribution. When a verb belonging to a larger semantic group does not occur in the set of syntactic conditions where the literal senses generally occur, it is highly possible to be metaphoric. Our design shows that syntactic conditions can offer informative clues in detecting metaphoric senses based on the fact that each sense of a verb has its own preferred syntactic environments.

The syntactic conditions can be further classified based on their effectiveness. As discussed in Section 4.2, the syntactic conditions of Group 1 in our model, transitivity (Vt), numeral phrases (Num), relative clauses (RC), compounding (VV), word order (VO), double-object construction (DO), are proven to be more efficient. The effectiveness of the conditions reflects three generalizations of where metaphoric senses tend to occur. First, a sense tends to be non-metaphoric when a numeral phrase is involved. The involvement of numeral phrases specifies the exact numbers of the object. Since the object has concrete details, the verb is more likely to be a literal. Second, a metaphoric sense is generally used to modify a concept. Due to this modification property, metaphoric senses tend to occur when there is a presence of a relative clause a relative clause, which serves the purpose of modification. Third, due to the changes of event types, the inherent properties of a verb are likely to change. More specifically, the transitivity of a verb changes when the verb is used in its metaphoric sense. For example, when a transitive verb becomes intransitive, the verb is likely not to be in its literal sense. Regarding the occurrence of compounding, the addition of another verb provides additional information and thus creates an event structure which differs from the original one. Similarly, when a verb which does not have two objects in its argument structure appears in the double-object construction, it is a sign of changing event types because the additional object cannot be accommodated in the original event structure. As for word order, it is associated with the information structure, which is a key component of an event structure. The change of word order therefore indicates the change of an event structure. Since each of the syntactic conditions links to a particular aspect of a conceptual event, its change is an informative indicator of which sense, literal or metaphoric, is in use.

On the other hand, the conditions in Group 3 do not contribute much to detecting senses. Although they provide additional information, the information is proven to be peripheral in indicating changes of event types. In brief, our experiments can successfully rank the relevancy of syntactic conditions with event types. The syntactic conditions which are related to the core elements of an event structure can improve the model of detecting metaphors.

6   Conclusion

This study offers an effective and precise way of detecting metaphoric and literal senses by including eventive information encoded in radicals. A set of syntactic conditions core to the event structure of a verb can define where its literal senses tend to occur. When a verb appears in the environments deviating from the defined set, it has a higher chance to be metaphoric. Instead of focusing on individual lexemes, we offer larger generalizations by event types encoded by radicals. Event types correspond to larger conceptual categories. Thus verbs of the same group have similar syntactic distribution. The generalizations can increase the efficiency of the model for metaphor detection.

Our study shows that other eventive information parsed in the existing platforms such as WordNet, FrameNet, and Tongyici Cilin should also have a high potential to be leveraged in the detecting of metaphors. The tools relevant to eventive information such as aspectual markers and word order can be applied to determine event types. This new approach refocuses metaphor detection in the inherent eventive information of metaphors instead of its contextual information, and thus it is more reliable. Our algorithm of modeling eventive information can provide a pathway to incorporate analysis of event types in deep learning as future studies.

In summary, our study show that by leveraging the Chinese writing system, culturally bound eventive information can facilitate processing of metaphor. This method is not only applicable to all Sinitic languages and a small sub-set of languages sharing Chinese orthography as their cultural heritage, such as Japanese and Korean. Huang and Chou (2015) already showed that lexical processing in Japanese and others based on Chinese orthography can be automatically bootstrapped. This study suggests the potential applications for the use of eventive information to conceptual processing such as automatic classification of metaphor. Eventive information in many languages can be automatically or semi-automatically extracted through the OntoLex interface approach (Huang et al. 2010). Eventive information in turn will be a powerful tool in the extraction of event types for studies based on eventive structures such as sarcasm and sentiment detection.

Acknowledgment

The work is partially supported by the following research grants from Hong Kong Polytechnic University: 1-YW1V, 4-ZZFE and RTVU; as well as GRF grants (PolyU 15211/14E and PolyU 152006/16E).

References

Marco Baroni, Raffaela Bernardi, and Roberto Zamparelli. 2014. Frege in space: A program of compositional distributional semantics. *Linguistic Issues in Language Technology*, 9.

Marco Baroni, Georgiana Dinu, and German´ Kruszewski. 2014. Don't count, predict! A systematic comparison of context-counting vs. context-predicting semantic vectors. In *Proceedings of the 52nd Annual Meeting of the Association for Computational Linguistics*. Association for Computational Linguistics, pages 238-247. https:/doi.org/10.3115/v1/P14-1023

George Aaron Broadwell, Umit Boz, Ignacio Cases, Tomek Strzalkowski, Laurie Feldman, Sarah Taylor, Samira Shaikh, Ting Liu, Kit Cho, and Nick Webb. 2013. Using imageability and topic chaining to locate metaphors in linguistic corpora. In *Social Computing, Behavioral-Cultural Modeling and Prediction*. Springer, pages 102-110.

Julia Birke and Anoop Sarkar. 2007. A clustering approach for nearly unsupervised recognition of nonliteral language. In *Proceedings of the 11th Conference of the European Chapter of the Association for Computational Linguistics*, pages 329-336.

Gemma Boleda, Eva Maria Vecchi, Miquel Cornudella, and Louise McNally. 2012. First-order vs. higher order modification in distributional semantics. In *Proceedings of the Joint Conference on Empirical Methods in Natural Language Processing and Computational Natural Language Learning*. Association for Computational Linguistics, pages 1223-1233. http://www.aclweb.org/anthology/D12-1112

Yaming Chou and Chu-ren Huang. 2006. Hantology - A linguistic resource for Chinese language processing and studying. Paper presented at the *5th International Conference on Language Resources and Evaluation*, Genoa, Italy.

Ya-Min Chou and Chu-Ren Huang. 2010. Hantology: conceptual system discovery based on orthographic convention. In *Ontology and the Lexicon: A Natural Language Processing Perspective*. Cambridge University Press, page 122-143.

Jonathan Dunn. 2013. Evaluating the premises and results of four metaphor identification systems. In *Computational Linguistics and Intelligent Text Processing*. Springer, pages 471-486.

Katrin Erk and Sebastian Padó. 2010. Exemplar-based models for word meaning in context. In *Proceedings of the ACL 2010 Conference Short Papers*. Association for Computational Linguistics, pages 92-97.

Jianhui Fu, Shi Wang, Ya Wang, Cungen Cao. 2016. A Practical Method of Identifying Chinese Metaphor Phrases from Corpus. In *International Conference on Knowledge Science, Engineering and Management*. Springer, pages 43-54.

Matt Gedigian, John Bryant, Srini Narayanan, and Branimir Ciric. 2006. Catching metaphors. In *Proceedings of the Third Workshop on Scalable Natural Language Understanding*. Association for Computational Linguistics, pages 41-48.

Gutiérrez Darıo, Ekaterina Shutova, Tyler Marghetis, and Benjamin Bergen. 2016. Literal and metaphorical senses in compositional distributional semantic models. In *Proceedings of the 54th Meeting of the Association for Computational Linguistics*. Association for Computational Linguistics, pages 160-170.

Harris, Zellig, 1954. Distributional structure. *Word*, 10(23):146-162.

Ilana Heintz, Ryan Gabbard, Mahesh Srinivasan, David Barner, Donald S Black, Marjorie Freedman, and Ralph Weischedel. 2013. Automatic extraction of linguistic metaphor with lda topic modeling. In *Proceedings of the First Workshop on Metaphor in NLP*, pages 58-66.

Dirk Hovy, Shashank Srivastava, Sujay Kumar Jauhar, Mrinmaya Sachan, Kartik Goyal, Huiying Li, Whitney Sanders, and Eduard Hovy. 2013. Identifying metaphorical word use with tree kernels. In *Proceedings of the First Workshop on Metaphor in NLP*, pages 5257.

Chu-Ren Huang. 2009. Tagged Chinese Gigaword Version 2.0, LDC2009T14. Linguistic Data Consortium.

Chu-Ren Huang. 2009. Semantics as an Orthography-Relevant Level for Mandarin Chinese. In *The 17th Annual Conference of the International Association of Chinese Linguistics*.

Chu-Ren Huang, Siaw-Fong Chung, and Kathleen Ahrens, 2007. An ontology-based exploration of knowledge systems for metaphor. In *Ontologies* Springer, page 489-517.

Chu-Ren Huang, Nicoletta Calzolari, Aldo Gangemi, Alessandro Lenci, Alessandro Oltramari, and Laurent Prévot. 2010 (Eds.) *Ontology and the lexicon: A natural language processing perspective*. Cambridge: Cambridge University Press,

Chu-Ren Huang and Chou Ya-Min. 2015. Multilingual conceptual access to lexicon based on shared orthography: an ontology-driven study of Chinese and Japanese. In *Language Production, Cognition, and the Lexicon*, ed. Núria Gala, Reinhard Rapp, and Gemma Bel-Enguix. Springer, pages 135-150.

Chu-Ren Huang and Shu-Kai Hsieh. 2015. Chinese lexical semantics: from radicals to event structure. In *The Oxford Handbook of Chinese Linguistics*, ed. William S.-Y. Wang and Chao-Fen Sun. Oxford University Press, pages 290-305.

Dimitri Kartsaklis and Mehrnoosh Sadrzadeh. 2013. Prior disambiguation of word tensors for constructing sentence vectors. In *Proceedings of the 2013 Conference on Empirical Methods in Natural Language Processing*, pages 1590-1601.

Dimitri Kartsaklis, Mehrnoosh Sadrzadeh, and Stephen Pulman. 2013. Separating disambiguation from composition in distributional semantics. In *Proceedings of the 2013 Conference on Computational Natural Language Learning*, pages 114-123.

Saisuresh Krishnakumaran and Xiaojin Zhu. 2007. Hunting elusive metaphors using lexical resources. In *Proceedings of the Workshop on Computational approaches to Figurative Language*. Association for Computational Linguistics, pages 13-20.

George Lakoff and Mark Johnson. 1981. *Metaphors we live by*. University of Chicago Press, Chicago, IL.

George Lakoff. 1989. Some empirical results about the nature of concepts. *Mind & Language*, 4(1-2): 103-109.

Prévot, Laurent, Chu-Ren Huang, Nicoletta Calzolari, Aldo Gangemi, Alessandro Lenci, and Alessandro Oltramari. 2010. Ontology and the lexicon: A multidisciplinary perspective. In *Ontology and the lexicon: A natural language processing perspective*, eds. Chu-Ren Huang, Nicoletta Calzolari, Aldo Gangemi, Alessandro Lenci, Alessandro Oltramari, and Laurent Prévot. Cambridge: Cambridge University Press, pages 3-24.

Omer Levy, Yoav Goldberg, Ido Dagan, and Israel Ramat-Gan. 2015. Improving distributional similarity with lessons learned from word embeddings. *Transactions of the Association for Computational Linguistics*, 3.

Linlin Li, Benjamin Roth, and Caroline Sporleder. 2010. Topic models for word sense disambiguation and token-based idiom detection. In *Proceedings of the 48th Annual Meeting of the Association for Computational Linguistics*. Association for Computational Linguistics, pages 1138-1147.

Linlin Li and Caroline Sporleder. 2010. Using Gaussian mixture models to detect figurative language in context. In *Human Language Technologies: The 2010 Annual Conference of the North American Chapter of the Association for Computational Linguistics*. Association for Computational Linguistics, pages 297-300.

Michael Mohler, David Bracewell, David Hinote, and Marc Tomlinson. 2013. Semantic signatures for example-based linguistic metaphor detection. In *Proceedings of the First Workshop on Metaphor in NLP*, pages 27–35.

Yair Neuman, Dan Assaf, Yohai Cohen, Mark Last, Shlomo Argamon, Newton Howard, and Ophir Frieder. 2013. Metaphor identification in large texts corpora. *PLoS ONE*, 8:e62343.

Tomas Mikolov, Ilya Sutskever, Kai Chen, Greg Corrado, and Jeff Dean. 2013. Distributed representations of words and phrases and their compositionality. In *Proceedings of NIPS*, pages 3111-3119.

Yulia Tsvetkov, Leonid Boytsov, Anatole Gershman, Eric Nyberg, and Chris Dyer. 2014. Metaphor detection with cross-lingual model transfer. In *Proceedings of the 52nd Annual Meeting of the Association for Computational Linguistics*. Association for Computational Linguistics, pages 248-258

Ekaterina Shutova. 2010. Models of metaphor in NLP. In *Proceedings of the 48th Annual Meeting of the Association for Computational Linguistics*. Association for Computational Linguistics, pages 688-697.

Ekaterina Shutova, Lin Sun, and Anna Korhonen. 2010. Metaphor identification using verb and noun clustering. In *Proceedings of the 23rd International Conference on Computational Linguistics*. Association for Computational Linguistics, pages 1002-1010.

Ekaterina Shutova, Simone Teufel, and Anna Korhonen. 2013. Statistical metaphor processing. *Computational Linguistics*, 39(2):301-353.

Caroline Sporleder and Linlin Li. 2009. Unsupervised recognition of literal and non-literal use of idiomatic expressions. In *Proceedings of the 12th Conference of the European Chapter of the Association for Computational Linguistics*, pages 754-762.

Tomek Strzalkowski, George A. Broadwell, Sarah Taylor, Laurie Feldman, Boris Yamrom, Samira Shaikh, Ting Liu, Kit Cho, Umit Boz, Ignacio Cases, and Kyle Elliot. 2013. Robust extraction of metaphors from novel data. In *Proceedings of the First Workshop on Metaphor in NLP*. Association for Computational Linguistics, pages 67-76.

Yulia Tsvetkov, Elena Mukomel, and Anatole Gershman. 2013. Cross-lingual metaphor detection using common semantic features. In *Proceedings of the First Workshop on Metaphor in NLP*. Association for Computational Linguistics, pages 45-51.

Yulia Tsvetkov, Leonid Boytsov, Anatole Gershman, Eric Nyberg, and Chris Dyer. 2014. Metaphor detection with cross-lingual model transfer. In *Proceedings of the 52nd Annual Meeting of the Association for Computational Linguistics*. Association for Computational Linguistics, page 248-258. http://www.aclweb.org/anthology/P14-1024

Zhao Hongyan, Qu Weiguang, Zhang Fen, and Zhou Junsheng. 2011. Chinese verb metaphor recognition based on machine learning and semantic knowledge. *Journal of Nanjing Normal University (Engineering and Technology)* 11(3):59-64.

Collaborative Partitioning for Coreference Resolution

Olga Uryupina[◇] and **Alessandro Moschitti**
◇DISI, University of Trento 38123 Povo (TN), Italy
Qatar Computing Research Institute, HBKU, 34110, Doha, Qatar
`{uryupina,amoschitti}@gmail.com`

Abstract

This paper presents a collaborative partitioning algorithm—a novel ensemble-based approach to coreference resolution. Starting from the all-singleton partition, we search for a solution close to the ensemble's outputs in terms of a task-specific similarity measure. Our approach assumes a loose integration of individual components of the ensemble and can therefore combine arbitrary coreference resolvers, regardless of their models. Our experiments on the CoNLL dataset show that collaborative partitioning yields results superior to those attained by the individual components, for ensembles of both strong and weak systems. Moreover, by applying the collaborative partitioning algorithm on top of three state-of-the-art resolvers, we obtain the second-best coreference performance reported so far in the literature (MELA v08 score of 64.47).

1 Introduction

Coreference resolution has been one of the key areas of NLP for several decades. Major modeling breakthroughs have been achieved, not surprisingly, following three successful shared tasks, such as MUC (Hirschman and Chinchor, 1997), ACE (Doddington et al., 2004) and, most recently, CoNLL (Pradhan et al., 2011; Pradhan et al., 2012). As of today, several high-performing systems are available publicly and, in addition, novel algorithms are being proposed regularly, even if without any code release. Our study aims at making a good use of these resources through a novel ensemble resolution method.

Coreference is a heterogeneous task that requires a combination of accurate and robust processing for relatively easy cases (e.g., name-matching) with very complex modeling of difficult cases (e.g., nominal anaphora or some types of pronouns). The general feeling in the community is that we are currently approaching the upper bound for the easy cases and our next step should involve more complex resolution. If true, this means that most state-of-the-art systems should produce very similar outputs: correctly resolving easy anaphora and failing on less trivial examples. Table 1 scores the outputs of the three best systems from the CoNLL-2012 shared task against each other. As it can be seen, the three systems are rather different, each of them being only slightly closer to each other than to the gold key.[1] This suggests that a meta-algorithm could merge their outputs in an intelligent way, combining the correct decisions of individual systems to arrive at a superior partition.

Although several coreference resolution toolkits exist for over a decade, to our knowledge, there have been no attempts at trying to merge their outputs. The very few ensemble methods reported in the literature focus on combining several resolution strategies within the same system. Following the success of the CoNLL shared task (Pradhan et al., 2011; Pradhan et al., 2012), however, multiple complex approaches have been investigated, with very different underlying models. This means that a re-implementation of all these algorithms within a single system requires a considerable engineering effort. In the present study, we combine the final outputs of the individual systems, without making any assumptions on their specifications. This means that our approach is completely modular, allowing to combine third-party software as black boxes.

The present study aims at finding a partition

---

[1]Across all the systems, the two most different submissions are `zhekova` vs. `li` (34.10 MELA) and the two closest ones are `chunyang` vs. `shou` (95.85 MELA).

Proceedings of the 21st Conference on Computational Natural Language Learning (CoNLL 2017), pages 47–57,
Vancouver, Canada, August 3 - August 4, 2017. ©2017 Association for Computational Linguistics

	key	fernandes	martschat	bjorkelund
fernandes	60.64	100	66.74	67.07
martschat	57.67		100	64.22
bjorkelund	57.41			100

Table 1: Scoring top CoNLL-2012 systems against each other, MELA v08.

combining the outputs of individual coreference resolvers in a collaborative way. To this end, we search the space of possible partitions, starting from the all-singleton solution and incrementally growing coreference entities, with the objective of getting a partition similar to the individual outputs. As a measure of similarity, we rely on task-specific metrics, such as, for example, MUC or MELA scores. To our knowledge, this is the first ensemble-based approach to coreference, operating directly on the partition level. While traditional ensemble techniques, such as boosting or co-training, have been successfully used for coreference resolution before, they are applicable to classification tasks and can only be used on lower levels (e.g., for classifying mention pairs). Combining partitions directly is a non-trivial problem that requires an extra modeling effort.

The rest of the paper is organized as follows. In the next section, we discuss the previous ensemble-based approaches to coreference resolution. Section 3 presents our collaborative partitioning algorithm. In Section 4, we evaluate our approach on the English portion of the OntoNotes dataset. Section 5 summarizes our contributions and highlights directions for future research.

2 Related Work

Only very few studies have so far investigated possibilities of using multiple resolvers for coreference. The first group of approaches aim at parameter optimization for choosing the best overall partition from the components' outputs. This line of research is motivated by the fact that in most approaches to coreference, the underlying classifier does not take into account the task metric, such as, for example, MUC or MELA scores. For instance, in the classical mention-pair model (Soon et al., 2001), the classifier is trained to distinguish between coreferent and non-coreferent pairs. The output of this classifier is then processed heuristically to create coreference partitions. There is therefore no guarantee that the classifier optimized on pairs would lead to the best-scoring partition. One way to overcome this issue involves training a

collection of models and then picking the globally best one on the development data (Munson et al., 2005; Saha et al., 2011). Another possible solution is to learn a ranker that would pick the best model on a per-document basis, using partition-specific features (Ng, 2005). While these approaches can integrate arbitrary systems, they only allow to pick the best output partition, thus, only considering a single solution at a given time. Our algorithm, on the contrary, builds a new partition in a collaborative way, manipulating entities produced by individual components.

The second research line involves training ensembles of classifiers within the same model, using bagging, boosting or co-training (Vemulapalli et al., 2009; Ng and Cardie, 2003b; Ng and Cardie, 2003a; Kouchnir, 2004). Building upon these studies, Rahman and Ng (2011) combine different coreference algorithms in an ensemble-based approach. For each mention in the document, they run several models (mention-pair, mention-ranking, entity-ranking) and heuristically merge their outputs. All these approaches, however, assume a very tight integration of individual components into the ensemble. Thus, they all assume the same set of mentions to be classified.[2] Moreover, most algorithms can only make ensembles of rather similar components, for example, varying feature sets or parameters within the same model of coreference. While Rahman and Ng (2011) allow for a combination of different models, they do it via model-specific rules, assuming the same set of mentions and a left-to-right per-mention resolution strategy—so a completely different novel model cannot be integrated. Finally, most ensembles use some internal information from their individual components, e.g., the confidence scores for mention-pairs. In practice, these considerations mean that all the individual systems should be re-implemented in a single framework before they can be combined in an ensemble. Our study, on the contrary, makes no assumptions about individual components. We combine their outputs at the partition level, without any requirements on their internal structure. Thus, the individual systems can rely on different mention detection approaches. They can have arbitrary models. We do not use any system-internal information, which

---

[2]The CoNLL systems differ considerably with respect to their underlying mentions, thus, the mention detection F-score between two systems varies from 50.11 (`xinxin` vs. `li`) to 99.07 (`chunyang` vs. `shou`).

allows us to use individual components as black boxes. Most importantly, our approach can be run without any modification on top of any resolver, present or future, thus benefiting from other studies on coreference and advancing the state of the art performance.

The machine learning community offers several algorithms combining multiple solutions for tasks going beyond simple classification or regression. The work of Strehl and Ghosh (2003) is of particular relevance for our problem. Thus, Strehl and Ghosh (2003) introduce the task of *ensemble* or *consensus clustering*, where the combiner aims at creating a meta-clustering on top of several individual solutions, without accessing their internal representations, e.g., features. The formulation of Strehl and Ghosh (2003) is identical to ours. However, there are several important differences. Thus, Strehl and Ghosh (2003) focus on the clustering problem, in particular, for large sets of data points. They show that the optimal solution to the consensus clustering problem is not computationally feasible and investigate several very greedy approaches.

Although coreference is formally a partitioning problem, the setting is rather different from a typical clustering scenario. Thus, individual mentions and mention properties are very important for coreference and should carefully be assessed one by one. The resolution clues are very heterogeneous and different elements (mentions) of clusters (entities) can be rather dissimilar in a strict sense. This is why, for example, clustering evaluation measures are not reliable for coreference— and, indeed, task-specific metrics have been put forward. While algorithms of (Strehl and Ghosh, 2003) constitute the state of the art in the ensemble clustering in general, we propose a coreference-specific approach. More specifically, (i) while Strehl and Ghosh (2003) rely on task-agnostic measures of similarity between partitions (mutual information), approximating the search for its maximum with various heuristics, we explicitly integrate coreference metrics, such as MUC and MELA and (ii) since our partitions are much smaller than typical clustering outputs, we can afford a less greedy agglomerative search strategy, again, motivated by the specifics of the final task. In our future work, we plan to evaluate our approach against the general-purpose algorithms proposed in (Strehl and Ghosh, 2003).

Algorithm 1 Collaborative Partitioning

Require: $P = \{p^1..p^n\}$: list of partitions generated by n systems; each partition p^i is a set of entities $p^i = \{e_1^i..e_{k_n}^i\}$, each entity is a set of mentions m
Require: $coreference\_score$: an external metric, e.g. MUC or MELA
1: **begin**
2: create a list of all the mentions $M = \{m_1..m_k\}$
3: init the all-singleton partition $p = \{e_1..e_k\}, e_i = \{m_i\}$
4: **while** $\|p\| > 1$ **do**
5:     $current\_similarity = vote(p, P)$
6:     $max = 0$
7:     **for all** $e_a, e_b \in p$ **do**
8:         $p' = p \cup \{e_a \cup e_b\} \setminus \{e_a\} \setminus \{e_b\}$
9:         $cand\_similarity = vote(p', P)$
10:        **if** $cand\_similarity > max$ **then**
11:           $max = cand\_similarity, maxp = p'$
12:     **if** $max < current\_similarity$ **then**
13:        $break;$
14:     $p = maxp$
15: **end**
16: **function** VOTE(p,P)
17:    $sim = 0$
18:    **for all** $p^i \in P$ **do**
19:       $sim\mathrel{+}= coreference\_score(p, p^i)$
20:    **return** sim

---

3 Collaborative Partitioning

This section first describes our collaborative partitioning algorithms, summarized in Algorithm 1 and then addresses technical details essential for running it in a practical scenario. The main idea behind collaborative partitioning is rather straightforward: we aim at finding a partition that is similar to all the outputs produced by the individual components of the ensemble. To implement this strategy, we have to specify two aspects: (a) the procedure to effectively search the space of possible partitions generating outputs to be tested and (b) the way to measure similarity between a candidate partition and a component's output. In both cases, we propose task-specific solutions.

Thus, we start with the all-singleton partition, where each mention makes its own entity and then try to incrementally grow our entities. At each iteration, we try to merge two clusters, comparing the similarity to the components' outputs before and after the candidate merge. If a candidate merge leads to the highest voting score, we execute this merge and proceed to the next iteration. If no candidate merges improve the similarity score for more than a predefined termination threshold, the algorithm stops. Several things should be noted. First, when trying to build a new partition, we only allow for merging: we never go back and split already constructed entities. This

President Clinton has told a memorial service for the victims of the deadly bomb attack on the USS Cole that justice will prevail . Mr. Clinton promised the gathering at the Norfolk Naval station Wednesday that those who carried out the deadly attack that killed 17 sailors will be found . To those who attacked them , we say you will not find a safe harbor , we will find you and justice will prevail . Meanwhile , in Yemen President Ali Abdul Salay said important evidence had been uncovered in the investigation . President Salay was quoted as saying two people responsible for the blast were killed in a suicide mission and that the attack had been planned for a long time . His comments were not immediately confirmed by US officials who are leading the investigation with Yemen 's help .

fernandes	martschat	bjorkelund	ensemble
[1,2]: President Clinton [25,26] Mr. Clinton	[1,2]: President Clinton [25,26] Mr. Clinton	[1,2]: President Clinton [25,26] Mr. Clinton	[1,2] President Clinton [25,26] Mr. Clinton
[12,15]: the deadly bomb attack [115,116]: the attack	[115,116]: the attack [41,47]: the deadly attack .. sailors	[12,19]: the deadly .. Cole [115,116]: the attack [41,47]: the deadly attack .. sailors	[12,15]: the deadly bomb attack [115,116]: the attack [41,47]: the deadly attack .. sailors
[56,56]: them	[46,47]: 17 sailors [56,56] them	[46,47]: 17 sailors [56,56] them	[46,47]: 17 sailors [56,56] them
[37,47]: those who carried .. sailors [53,56]: those who attacked them [60,60]: you [71,71]: you	[37,47]: those who carried .. sailors [53,56]: those who attacked them	[60,60]: you [71,71]: you	[37,47]: those who carried .. sailors [53,56]: those who attacked them [60,60]: you [71,71]: you
[58,58]: we [68,68]: we	[58,58]: we [68,68]: we	[58,58]: we [68,68]: we	[58,58]: we [68,68]: we
[80,80]: Yemen [140,141]: Yemen 's	[80,80]: Yemen [140,141]: Yemen 's	[80,80]: Yemen [140,141]: Yemen 's	[80,80]: Yemen [140,141]: Yemen 's
[81,84]: President Ali Abdul Salay [95,96]: President Salay [125,125]: His	[81,84]: President Ali Abdul Salay [95,96]: President Salay [125,125]: His	[95,96]: President Salay [125,125]: His	[81,84]: President Ali Abdul Salay [95,96]: President Salay [125,125]: His
[92,93]: the investigation [137,138]: the investigation		[92,93]: the investigation [137,142]: the inv. with Yemen 's help	[92,93]: the investigation [137,138]: the investigation

Table 2: Collaborative partitioning on a sample OntoNotes document: 3 top systems and their ensemble, using MELA similarity. Each row corresponds to a mention, each (multi-row) cell corresponds to an entity created by a specific system. Bracketed numbers indicate word ids.

decision is motivated by the cost of a single operation: while there is only one way to merge two entities, there are exponentially many ways to split an entity in two, making the latter operation much more computationally expensive. Second, unlike most approaches to coreference, we do not process the text in the left-to-right order. Instead, we consider the whole set of mentions from the initial iteration, doing first the merges supported by the majority of the components in the ensemble.

To compute the voting score, we first define the similarity between two partitions, based on coreference metrics, as implemented in the CoNLL scorer (Pradhan et al., 2014): we score our generated partitions against the outputs of the ensemble components. This way we ensure that the final partition is related to the individual outputs in the way that is relevant for the task. There are multiple ways to derive the voting score from existing metrics. The parameters to consider here are: the specific measure to be used (e.g., MUC vs. CEAF vs. MELA), the granularity (e.g., whether to measure the increase/decrease of the specific metric as a continuous or binary value) and the way to combine measures from the different ensemble components in a single score (e.g., weighted vs. unweighted voting). In Section 3.1 below, we discuss several practical considerations for making this choice.

Note that our approach does not make any assumptions about mention detection for individual components: to initialize the run, we simply lump together all the mentions. This, however, leads to performance drops if several individual systems suggest different boundaries for the same mention: the final solution will then keep all the variants merging them into the same entity. To avoid this issue, we implement a post-processing cleanup step: if the final solution contains entities with nested mentions, we keep the most popular variants (or the shorter one for the same popularity). This post-processing helps us avoid any complex merging machinery at the mention level.

Table 2 shows a sample OntoNotes document with outputs of the three top systems and the partition created by the collaborative ensemble. Some entities (e.g. *Yemen*) are easy for all the systems. Some entities (*attack*; *investigation*; *Salay*) are recovered fully only by two systems, probably for the lack of required features. Note that although each system misses some coreference relations, altogether they resolve all the three entities, leading to a considerable improvement in the collaborative partition. Finally, the two entities for *attackers* and *sailors*, central to the document, are represented with pronominal mentions that are hard to resolve. Not surprisingly, the systems make several spurious decisions w.r.t. these entities. The collaborative partitioning algorithm, however, manages to filter out erroneous assignments and produce the correct partition.

3.1 Performance Issues

The collaborative partitioning algorithm starts from the all-singleton solution and tries to incrementally merge entities. Each candidate merge is evaluated with the coreference scorer. This means that, in the worst case, the system requires $O(n^3)$ scorer runs, where n is the total number of mentions: it does n merges and for each merge i, it searches for a pair among $n - i + 1$ entities that maximizes the overall similarity score, requiring $\frac{(n-i+1)*(n-i)}{2}$ scorer runs. This can become prohibitively slow, making the approach not practical. Below we discuss three solutions to speed up the algorithm.

First, the voting function can be simplified. Thus, instead of using continuous similarity values (i.e., how much a candidate merge brings the solution closer to the components' output via increasing or decreasing the specific coreference metric), we can rely on binary indicators: the component up-/down- votes a merge if the metric's value increases/decreases. To compute the final score, we use unweighted voting (or, alternatively, weighted voting with very simple integer weights). This way, the final score can only take a small number of values and, for each merge, we can stop the search once the highest possible score is observed, instead of assessing all the $\frac{(n-i+1)*(n-i)}{2}$ possible pairs. This trick does not affect the worst-case complexity, but can help a lot on the average. Moreover, a simple voting function is necessary for the second speed-up adjustment.

Each merge only involves two entities. Thus, at the merge iteration i, the system observes $n-i$ entities it has already seen before and one new entity generated at the merge iteration $i-1$. To speed up the processing, we can therefore store voting values for merge attempts and reuse them at each iteration. With this adjustments, the algorithm needs only to evaluate candidate merges with the newly constructed entity and therefore each iteration requires a linear number of scoring runs, leading to $O(n^2)$ runs overall. Two considerations should be taken into account. Suppose we evaluate a merge attempt for two entities, e_1 and e_2, at the iteration i and store the value for the voting function. If we then attempt to merge the same two entities at the iteration i', the coreference scoring functions will be different, since they assess the whole partition. This means that this speed-up trick only works if

the ensemble voting function is very simple and is not affected by slight changes in the individual coreference scores. The second consideration is more troublesome. Hashing of voting results only works if the underlying coreference scoring function respects certain monotonicity properties: suppose a (candidate) merge of two entities, e_1 and e_2 at iteration i improves the coreference score with respect to a component's output; the same merge should improve the coreference score also at any later iteration i'. Intuitively speaking, this means that two entities should or shouldn't be merged, according to a specific coreference metric, regardless of the rest of the partition. While link- or mention-based metrics respect this property, the CEAF scores evaluate partitions as a whole and therefore are not monotonic.

Finally, some coreference metrics, such as B^3 and, most importantly, MUC are very fast to compute. The CEAF scores, on the contrary, require a computationally expensive partition alignment procedure. A considerable speed-up can be achieved by opting for a faster scorer. In the experimental section, we evaluate the algorithm's performance with different scoring metrics.

3.2 Algorithm adjustments for the CoNLL/OntoNotes setting

Following the state of the art, we evaluate our approach within the CoNLL framework (Pradhan et al., 2012): we use the OntoNotes dataset (Hovy et al., 2006) and rely on the official release (v8) of the scorer (Pradhan et al., 2014). Several important adjustments should be made to our algorithm to account for peculiarities of this set-up. In particular, (a) the OntoNotes guidelines do not provide annotations for singleton entities and (b) the official shared task score (MELA) relies strongly on B^3 and CEAF metrics. These two properties in combination lead to a number of counter-intuitive effects. We refer the reader to a recent study by Moosavi and Strube (2016) for an extensive discussion of problematic issues with the CoNLL scoring strategy.

The following adjustments have been made to run the algorithm in the CoNLL setting. First, each mention has been duplicated to mitigate the mention identification effect (Moosavi and Strube, 2016): we expand each document by several lines and fill them with dummy mentions. This prevents the system from making spurious merges at the initial iterations as a result of problematic CEAF values.

Second, we employ several clean-up strategies to post-process the final partition. Thus, we remove mentions recognized by a single system only, unless they are considered coreferent with exactly one popular (recognized by multiple systems) mention. This rather inelegant solution could be replaced with a simple requirement that each mention should be recognized by several systems if the singletons were not removed from the evaluation.

4 Experiments

In this section, we evaluate empirically the performance of the collaborative partitioning approach for a variety of ensembles. In particular, we investigate ensembles of different size and composition with respect to the components' quality and assess different coreference scoring metrics as criteria for partition similarity.

4.1 Experimental setup

In our experiments, we rely on the English portion of the CoNLL-2012 dataset (Pradhan et al., 2012). We use the outputs of the CoNLL submissions on the test data, made available publicly by the organizers.

To speed up the system, we use the techniques discussed in Section 3.1 above. In particular, we rely on a very simple unweighted voting scheme: each component contributes equally to the final score. The per-component score for a candidate merge between e_1 and e_2 is computed as follows: if either e_1 or e_2 are not represented in a component's output, it abstains from voting ($score = 0$). Otherwise, the component upvotes candidate merges if the underlying coreference score increases ($score = 2$) and downvotes, if it decreases ($score = -1$). The preference for positive votes (2 vs. 1) is motivated by the fact, that most state-of-the-art models explicitly model coreference, but not non-coreference: if two entities are annotated as non-coreferent by the system, it can be due to several factors, such as the lack of relevant features or algorithm peculiarities that limit the search space. The positive information in the systems' output is therefore more reliable than the negative one. The specific threshold (2 : 1) has been chosen arbitrary without any tuning. Finally, the termination threshold has been set to 0.

4.2 Choosing the scoring metric

In our first experiment, we evaluate different ways of defining similarity between partitions. Recall that each merge is evaluated based on whether it makes the constructed partition closer to the outputs of individual components. The similarity between two partitions is assessed with a task-specific measure. Multiple metrics have been proposed to evaluate coreference resolvers, we refer the reader to (Luo and Pradhan, 2016) for a detailed description and to (Moosavi and Strube, 2016) for a discussion of their problematic properties. In the present experiment, we assess three commonly accepted metrics, MUC, B^3 and CEAFE as well as their average, MELA, used for the official ranking of the CoNLL shared task.

Table 3 summarizes the results achieved by ensembles of the top-3 CoNLL systems. The upper half of the table presents individual components, re-evaluated with the v8 scorer. The lower part presents the performance achieved by four different ensembles, varying the underlying similarity measure used for growing up the partitions. For each performance metric, we highlight the best approach with boldface.

This experiment suggests several findings. First, the collaborative partitioning clearly brings a considerable improvement: depending on the underlying similarity score, the ensemble performs up to 3.5 percentage points better than the best individual components. Moreover, all the four created ensembles yield scores comparable to the very best state-of-the-art systems.

Second, all the four ensembles outperform individual components according to all the evaluation metrics. This means that the overall improvement (MELA) reflects a real quality increase and not just some fortunate re-shuffling of the individual scores to be averaged.

Third, the best overall improvement is achieved with the voting function based on the MELA similarity. The much faster MUC-based method performs 1.5 percentage points worse. This is an ambiguous result: on the one hand, a difference of 1.5% on the CoNLL dataset is non-negligible. On the other hand, even the MUC-based method outperforms each individual component.

4.3 Ensembles of top vs. bottom CoNLL systems

The performance of different systems submitted to CoNLL varies considerably, from 36.11 to 60.64 (MELA score, v08). In this experiment, we try to combine different types of systems. We split all the CoNLL systems into "tiers" of 3 submissions,

components	MUC F	CEAFE F	B^3 F	MELA
CoNLL system outputs				
fernandes	70.51	53.86	57.58	60.64
martschat	66.97	51.46	54.62	57.67
bjorkelund	67.58	50.21	54.47	57.41
Per-tier ensembles (3 systems per ensemble), score>0				
fernandes, martschat,bjorkelund; MUC similarity	**72.45**	55.71	59.87	62.67
fernandes, martschat,bjorkelund; CEAFE similarity	71.73	58.04	61.00	63.58
fernandes, martschat,bjorkelund; B^3 similarity	71.75	58.31	61.08	63.70
fernandes, martschat,bjorkelund; MELA similarity	71.96	**58.95**	**61.35**	**64.08**

Table 3: Collaborative partitioning with the 3 top CoNLL-2012 systems, using different coreference metrics when assessing candidate merges. Boldface indicates the best performing system for each score.

components	MUC F	CEAFE F	B^3 F	MELA
CoNLL system outputs				
tier1: fernandes, martschat,bjorkelund	70.51 66.97 67.58	53.86 51.46 50.21	57.58 54.62 54.47	60.65 57.68 57.42
tier2: chang,chen,chunyang	**66.38** 63.71 63.82	48.94 48.10 47.58	52.99 51.76 51.21	56.10 54.52 54.20
tier3: stamborg,yuan,xu	64.26 62.55 66.18	46.60 45.99 41.25	51.66 50.11 50.30	54.17 52.88 52.57
tier4: shou,uryupina,songyang	62.91 60.89 59.83	46.66 42.93 42.36	49.44 46.24 45.90	53.00 50.02 49.36
tier5: zhekova,xinxin,li	53.52 48.27 50.84	32.16 31.90 25.21	35.66 35.73 32.29	40.44 38.63 36.11
Per-tier ensembles (3 systems per ensemble)				
tier1: fernandes, martschat,bjorkelund	**71.96**	**58.95**	**61.35**	**64.08**
tier2: chang,chen,chunyang	66.35	**53.54**	**56.11**	**58.66**
tier3: stamborg,yuan,xu	**68.60**	**52.98**	**57.89**	**59.22**
tier4: shou,uryupina,songyang	**66.75**	**51.25**	**55.10**	**57.70**
tier5: zhekova,xinxin,li	**56.18**	**34.67**	**41.51**	**44.12**

Table 4: Ensembles of 3 classifiers for different tiers, using MELA for merging. Boldface indicates the best performing system for each tier.

components	tier MUC (R)	tier MUC (P)	tier MUC (F)	tier MELA
CoNLL system outputs				
tier1: fernandes,martschat,bjorkelund	65.83 65.21 65.23	**75.91** 68.83 70.10	70.51 66.97 67.58	60.64 57.67 57.41
tier2: chang,chen,chunyang	64.77 63.47 64.08	**68.06** 63.96 63.57	66.38 63.71 63.82	**56.10** 54.51 54.20
tier3: stamborg,yuan,xu	65.41 62.08 59.11	63.15 63.02 **75.18**	64.26 62.55 66.18	54.17 52.87 52.57
tier4: shou,uryupina,songyang	63.45 61.00 55.29	62.38 60.78 65.19	62.91 60.89 59.83	**53.00** 50.01 49.35
tier5: zhekova,xinxin,li	54.28 55.48 39.12	52.79 42.72 **72.57**	53.52 48.27 50.84	40.44 38.62 36.11
Per-tier ensembles (3 systems per ensemble)				
tier1: fernandes,martschat,bjorkelund	**69.60**	75.55	**72.45**	**62.67**
tier2: chang,chen,chunyang	**69.26**	64.61	**66.85**	54.63
tier3: stamborg,yuan,xu	**67.48**	69.12	**68.29**	**54.26**
tier4: shou,uryupina,songyang	**69.26**	66.07	**67.63**	52.23
tier5: zhekova,xinxin,li	**57.07**	61.77	**59.33**	**40.85**

Table 5: Ensembles of 3 classifiers for different tiers, using MUC for merging. Boldface indicates the best performing system for each tier.

based on their ranking. We do not use the system scores; however, we rely on the ranking computed on the same dataset.[3]

Tables 4 and 5 report the performance figures for ensembles composed of systems from each tier. The former uses MELA as a similarity measure, the latter—MUC. In both tables, the upper half reports performance figures for individual components (each cell in the upper half contains three values for the performance of the three systems of each tier). The lower half reports performance figures for collaborative partitioning with the components from each tier. The best-performing system for each performance metric is shown in boldface: for example, the MUC-based ensemble of the three tier1 systems outperforms its individual components in MUC Recall, MUC F and MELA (Table 5, lower half, first row), with the scores of 69.6%, 72.45% and 62.67% respectively; the best MUC Precision for tier1 (75.91%) is, however, achieved by an individual component, the system fernandes (Table 5, upper half, first row).

As these two tables suggest, collaborative partitioning yields improvement over individual components, for both stronger and weaker tiers. This suggests that collaborative partitioning can be used on top of any systems: unlike many other ensemble techniques, it does not suffer from the error propagation problem when operating on ensembles of weaker components.

The final partition depends on the similarity measure used by the collaborative algorithm. Thus, the MELA measure, being an average of

<hr>

[3]This is a rather unfortunate set-up, but there are no means to roughly evaluate CoNLL systems without using the test data. We assume, however, that an external evaluation, if possible, would be able to differentiate top against bottom submissions.

components	MUC R	MUC P	MUC F	MELA
best individual component (fernandes)				
fernandes	65.83	75.91	70.51	60.65
ensembles, default termination threshold ($= 0$)				
tier1	69.60	75.55	72.45	62.67
tier1+2	74.85	61.73	67.66	52.38
tier1+2+3	75.78	56.43	64.69	43.97
tier1+2+3+4	74.85	53.34	62.29	39.58
tier1+2+3+4+5 (all)	74.08	48.02	58.27	33.10
ensembles, optimal termination threshold				
tier1	69.60	75.55	72.45	62.67
tier1+2	70.53	75.93	73.13	53.60
tier1+2+3	71.54	75.24	73.35	44.41
tier1+2+3+4	68.50	77.12	72.55	49.06
tier1+2+3+4+5 (all)	65.36	80.24	72.04	45.78

Table 6: Ensembles of different sizes, using MUC for merging.

	MUC	CEAFE	B^3	MELA
competitive upper bound, tier1	71.53	56.46	59.74	62.57
competitive upper bound, tier1+2	71.53	56.46	59.74	62.57
competitive upper bound , all	**72.12**	57.55	60.53	63.39
collaborative, tier1	71.96	**58.95**	**61.35**	**64.08**

Table 7: Competitive vs. collaborative partitioning, using MELA for selection (competitive) or merging (collaborative).

MUC, B^3 and CEAF, leads to more balanced final partitions, improving on each individual score. MUC-based ensembles, on the contrary, improve on MUC (through a drastic increase in MUC recall without much precision loss), but do not guarantee any increase in B^3 or CEAF, leading to mixed results on MELA.

4.4 Ensembles of different size

In this experiment, we consider ensembles of different sizes, starting from tier1 and adding less performing components. Table 6 reports the results for ensembles of different size, using MUC for measuring the similarity while growing partitions. The upper half presents the results with the default termination parameter. As it shows, the inclusion of more lower-quality systems leads to better MUC recall values at the cost of the sharp deterioration in precision and the overall scores.

The lower half shows the results obtained with the optimal value of the termination parameter. In a practical scenario, this parameter can be tuned on the development data. Here, the best MUC results ($F = 73.35$) are achieved with the top nine systems. However, this MUC improvement comes at a high cost in B^3 and CEAF, leading to low MELA values even with the optimal parametrization.

4.5 Collaborative vs. Competitive Partitioning

One of the key advantages of the collaborative partitioning algorithm is its loose coupling approach

components	MUC	CEAFE	B^3	MELA
berkeleycoref	69.13	54.30	57.40	60.27
ims-hotcoref	70.25	55.44	58.03	61.23
LSPE	**72.34**	57.40	60.36	63.36
ensemble	71.98	**60.01**	**61.44**	**64.47**

Table 8: Collaborative partitioning for state-of-the-art systems, using MELA for merging. Boldface indicates the best result for each score.

with respect to individual components. This allows for straightforward integration of any coreference resolver at the moment of its release. The only other approach with the same property has been advocated by Ng (2005), where a ranker is learned to select the best partition from the individual outputs. We refer to this algorithm as *competitive partitioning*, since individual components compete with each other for each document instead of collaborating to build a new improved partition.

The competitive partitioning algorithm has a natural upper bound: by using an oracle to always select the best-performing component for each individual document, we can get the highest performance level possibly attainable with this model. Table 7 shows these upper bounds for the first 3, 6 and 15 (all) CoNLL systems. Note that these numbers are obtained with an oracle—the results with a real ranker will, obviously, be lower. The last row of the table shows, for comparison, the tier1 performance for the collaborative partitioning algorithm.

First, it is clear that competitive partitioning on top of CoNLL systems is hardly promising: even in the oracle setting, the performance improves by only 2-3 percentage points. This is due to the fact that CoNLL has a clear winner, the system fernandes, yielding the best solution for more than half of the documents and never losing too much for the remaining half.

Second, collaborative partitioning, on the contrary, seems more beneficial, yielding the results superior to the upper bound of the competitive partitioning algorithm. This is due to the fact that the collaborative approach makes a better use of individual components, combining their entities to arrive at a better new solution.

4.6 Ensembles of post-CoNLL systems

In our last experiment, we depart from the CoNLL outputs to run the collaborative partitioning algorithm on top of the state-of-the-art coreference resolvers. In particular, we combine three very different high-performing systems, `berkeleycoref` (Durrett et al., 2013), `ims-hotcoref` (Björkelund and Kuhn, 2014) and `lspe` (Haponchyk and Moschitti, 2017b; Haponchyk and Moschitti, 2017a). The former relies on an entity-level modeling, whereas the latter two use different structural learning approaches to coreference. All these systems represent state-of-the-art research in the field. Note that we do not include the very latest deep learning based approaches (Wiseman et al., 2016; Clark and Manning, 2016) to allow for a fair comparison: since, as we have seen in the experiments above, the collaborative partitioning algorithm consistently improves over individual ensemble components, integrating the very best systems would be a trivial but not very informative way of advancing the state of the art.

Table 8 shows the performance level of each of these systems on the English portion of the CoNLL-2012 dataset, individually and of the collaborative ensemble. The best performing system according to each metric is shown in bold. The numbers were obtained by running the v08 scorer on the outputs provided by the developers (`berkeleycoref`, `lspe`) or created using the official distribution and the provided pre-trained model (`ims-hotcoref`). No adjustments have been made to the collaborative partitioning algorithm.

Similarly to the experimental findings presented in the previous sections, the collaborative partitioning algorithm outperforms the best individual components. Most importantly, it yields the second-best results reported in the literature, outperforming the system of Wiseman et al. (2016) by 0.26 percentage points.

5 Conclusion

This paper presents collaborative partitioning—a novel ensemble-based approach to coreference resolution. Starting from the all-singleton solution, we search the space of all partitions, aiming at finding the solution close to the components' partitions according to a coreference-specific metric. Our algorithm assumes a loose coupling of individual components within the ensemble, allowing for a straightforward integration of any third party coreference resolution system.

Our evaluation experiments on the CoNLL dataset show that the collaborative partitioning method improves upon individual components, both for high and low performing ensembles. This performance improvement is consistent across all the metrics. Moreover, when combining three state-of-the-art systems, the collaborative ensemble achieves the second-best results reported in the literature so far (MELA score of 64.47).

In the future, we plan to concentrate on improving the voting scheme for the ensemble. Currently, the model relies on a very simplistic unweighted voting strategy. This choice is motivated by practical considerations: a more complex scheme would not make possible the necessary system speed up techniques. The unweighted voting, however, is problematic for ensembles that (a) contain components of very different quality or (b) contain some extremely similar components. This issue has been investigated within the ensemble classification framework, where several approaches have been put forward to construct large ensembles that ensure diversity of their components, e.g., through splitting training data and/or feature sets. In our scenario, however, we can not rely on such techniques, since we build ensembles of few existing high-quality systems, each of them being an outcome of a considerable research and engineering effort. We plan to overcome these issues, investigating different versions of heterogeneous voting.

Another direction of our future work involves an extensive comparison of our approach with ensemble clustering algorithms proposed within the machine learning and data mining community, in particular, by Strehl and Ghosh (2003). Thus, we plan to (i) evaluate our model against these general-purpose techniques in terms of both accuracy and efficiency and (ii) investigate possibilities of adapting the existing ensemble clustering algorithms to explicitly incorporate task-specific metrics.

Finally, we plan to extend our approach to other NLP tasks, investigating collaborative ensembles for other problems with complex outputs, going beyond simple classification-based ensemble techniques.

Acknowledgments

This work has been partially supported by the EC project CogNet, 671625 (H2020-ICT-2014-2, Research and Innovation action).

References

Anders Björkelund and Jonas Kuhn. 2014. Learning structured perceptrons for coreference resolution with latent antecedents and non-local features. In *Proceedings of the 52nd Annual Meeting of the Association for Computational Linguistics (Volume 1: Long Papers)*, pages 47–57, Baltimore, Maryland, June. Association for Computational Linguistics.

Kevin Clark and Christopher D. Manning. 2016. Improving coreference resolution by learning entity-level distributed representations. In *Proceedings of the 54th Annual Meeting of the Association for Computational Linguistics (Volume 1: Long Papers)*, pages 643–653, Berlin, Germany, August. Association for Computational Linguistics.

George Doddington, Alexis Mitchell, Mark Przybocki, Lance Ramshaw, Stephanie Strassell, and Ralph Weischedel. 2004. The automatic content extraction (ACE) program–tasks, data, and evaluation. In *Proceedings of the Language Resources and Evaluation Conference*.

Greg Durrett, David Hall, and Dan Klein. 2013. Decentralized entity-level modeling for coreference resolution. In *Proceedings of the 51st Annual Meeting of the Association for Computational Linguistics (Volume 1: Long Papers)*, pages 114–124, Sofia, Bulgaria, August. Association for Computational Linguistics.

Iryna Haponchyk and Alessandro Moschitti. 2017a. Dont understand a measure? Learn it: Structured prediction for coreference resolution optimizing its measures. In *Proceedings of the 55th Annual Conference of the Association for Computational Linguistics (ACL)*, Vancouver, Canada, July. Association for Computational Linguistics.

Iryna Haponchyk and Alessandro Moschitti. 2017b. A practical perspective on latent structured prediction for coreference resolution. In *Proceedings of the 15th Conference of the European Chapter of the Association for Computational Linguistics: Volume 2, Short Papers*, pages 143–149, Valencia, Spain, April. Association for Computational Linguistics.

Lynette Hirschman and Nancy Chinchor. 1997. MUC-7 coreference task definition. In *Message Understanding Conference Proceedings*.

Eduard Hovy, Mitchell Marcus, Martha Palmer, Lance Ramshaw, and Ralph Weischedel. 2006. Ontonotes: the 90% solution. In *Proceedings of the human language technology conference of the NAACL, Companion Volume: Short Papers*, pages 57–60. Association for Computational Linguistics.

Beata Kouchnir. 2004. A machine learning approach to german pronoun resolution. In *Proceedings of the ACL 2004 Workshop on Student Research*, ACLstudent '04, Stroudsburg, PA, USA. Association for Computational Linguistics.

Xiaoqiang Luo and Sameer Pradhan. 2016. Evaluation metrics. In *Anaphora Resolution*, pages 141–163. Springer Berlin Heidelberg.

Nafise Sadat Moosavi and Michael Strube. 2016. Which coreference evaluation metric do you trust? a proposal for a link-based entity aware metric. In *Proceedings of the 54th Annual Meeting of the Association for Computational Linguistics*, volume 1, pages 632–642.

Art Munson, Claire Cardie, and Rich Caruana. 2005. Optimizing to arbitrary NLP metrics using ensemble selection. In *Proceedings of HLT/EMNLP*, pages 539–546.

Vincent Ng and Claire Cardie. 2003a. Bootstrapping coreference classifiers with multiple machine learning algorithms. In *Proceedings of the 2003 Conference on Empirical Methods in Natural Language Processing*, pages 113–120. Association for Computational Linguistics.

Vincent Ng and Claire Cardie. 2003b. Weakly supervised natural language learning without redundant views. In *Proceedings of the 2003 Conference of the North American Chapter of the Association for Computational Linguistics - Volume 1*, pages 173–180. Association for Computational Linguistics.

Vincent Ng. 2005. Machine learning for coreference resolution: From local classification to global ranking. In *Proceedings of the 43rd Annual Meeting of the ACL*, pages 157–164.

Sameer Pradhan, Lance Ramshaw, Mitchell Marcus, Martha Palmer, Ralph Weischedel, and Nianwen Xue. 2011. Conll-2011 shared task: Modeling unrestricted coreference in ontonotes. In *Proceedings of the Fifteenth Conference on Computational Natural Language Learning (CoNLL 2011)*, Portland, Oregon, June.

Sameer Pradhan, Alessandro Moschitti, Nianwen Xue, Olga Uryupina, and Yuchen Zhang. 2012. CoNLL-2012 shared task: Modeling multilingual unrestricted coreference in OntoNotes. In *Proceedings of the Sixteenth Conference on Computational Natural Language Learning (CoNLL'12)*, Jeju, Korea.

Sameer Pradhan, Xiaoqiang Luo, Marta Recasens, Eduard H Hovy, Vincent Ng, and Michael Strube. 2014. Scoring coreference partitions of predicted mentions: A reference implementation. In *ACL (2)*, pages 30–35.

Altaf Rahman and Vincent Ng. 2011. Ensemble-based coreference resolution. In *Proceedings of the 22nd International Joint Conference on Artificial Intelligence*, pages 1994–1889.

Sriparna Saha, Asif Ekbal, Olga Uryupina, and Massimo Poesio. 2011. Single and multi-objective optimization for feature selection in anaphora resolution. In *Proceedings of the International Joint Conference on Natural Language Processing (IJCNLP'11)*.

Wee Meng Soon, Hwee Tou Ng, and Daniel Chung Yong Lim. 2001. A machine learning approach to coreference resolution of noun phrases. *Computational Linguistic*, 27(4):521–544.

Alexander Strehl and Joydeep Ghosh. 2003. Cluster ensembles — a knowledge reuse framework for combining multiple partitions. *The Journal of Machine Learning Research*, 3:583–617, March.

Smita Vemulapalli, Xiaoqiang Luo, John F. Pitrelli, and Imed Zitouni. 2009. Classifier combination techniques applied to coreference resolution. In *Proceedings of Human Language Technologies: The 2009 Annual Conference of the North American Chapter of the Association for Computational Linguistics, Companion Volume: Student Research Workshop and Doctoral Consortium*, SRWS '09, pages 1–6, Stroudsburg, PA, USA. Association for Computational Linguistics.

Sam Wiseman, Alexander M. Rush, and Stuart M. Shieber. 2016. Learning global features for coreference resolution. In Kevin Knight, Ani Nenkova, and Owen Rambow, editors, *NAACL HLT 2016, The 2016 Conference of the North American Chapter of the Association for Computational Linguistics: Human Language Technologies*, pages 994–1004. The Association for Computational Linguistics.

Named Entity Disambiguation for Noisy Text

Yotam Eshel[1]   Noam Cohen[1]   Kira Radinsky[1,2]
Shaul Markovitch[1]   Ikuda Yamada[3]   Omer Levy[4]

[1]Technion - Israel Institute of Technology, Haifa, Israel
[2]eBay Research, Israel
[3]Studio Ousia, Fujisawa, Kanagawa, Japan
[4]University of Washington, Seattle, WA

Abstract

We address the task of Named Entity Disambiguation (NED) for noisy text. We present WikilinksNED, a large-scale NED dataset of text fragments from the web, which is significantly noisier and more challenging than existing news-based datasets. To capture the limited and noisy local context surrounding each mention, we design a neural model and train it with a novel method for sampling informative negative examples. We also describe a new way of initializing word and entity embeddings that significantly improves performance. Our model significantly outperforms existing state-of-the-art methods on WikilinksNED while achieving comparable performance on a smaller newswire dataset.

1 Introduction

Named Entity Disambiguation (NED) is the task of linking mentions of entities in text to a given knowledge base, such as Freebase or Wikipedia. NED is a key component in Entity Linking (EL) systems, focusing on the disambiguation task itself, independently from the tasks of Named Entity Recognition (detecting mention bounds) and Candidate Generation (retrieving the set of potential candidate entities). NED has been recognized as an important component in NLP tasks such as semantic parsing (Berant and Liang, 2014).

Current research on NED is mostly driven by a number of standard datasets, such as CoNLL-YAGO (Hoffart et al., 2011), TAC KBP (Ji et al., 2010) and ACE (Bentivogli et al., 2010). These datasets are based on news corpora and Wikipedia, which are naturally coherent, well-structured, and rich in context. Global disambiguation models (Guo and Barbosa, 2014; Pershina et al., 2015; Globerson et al., 2016) leverage this coherency by jointly disambiguating all the mentions in a single document. However, domains such as web-page fragments, social media, or search queries, are often short, noisy, and less coherent; such domains lack the necessary contextual information for global methods to pay off, and present a more challenging setting in general.

In this work, we investigate the task of NED in a setting where only *local* and *noisy* context is available. In particular, we create a dataset of 3.2M short text fragments extracted from web pages, each containing a mention of a named entity. Our dataset is far larger than previously collected datasets, and contains 18K unique mentions linking to over 100K unique entities. We have empirically found it to be noisier and more challenging than existing datasets. For example:

> "I had no choice but to experiment with other indoor games. I was born in Atlantic City so the obvious next choice was **Monopoly**. I played until I became a successful Captain of Industry."

This short fragment is considerably less structured and with a more personal tone than a typical news article. It references the entity *Monopoly_(Game)*, however expressions such as "experiment" and "Industry" can distract a naive disambiguation model because they are also related the much more common entity *Monopoly* (economics term). Some sense of local semantics must be considered in order to separate the useful signals (e.g. "indoor games", "played") from the noisy ones.

We therefore propose a new model that leverages local contextual information to disambiguate entities. Our neural approach (based on RNNs with attention) leverages the vast amount of training data in WikilinksNED to learn representations

Proceedings of the 21st Conference on Computational Natural Language Learning (CoNLL 2017), pages 58–68,
Vancouver, Canada, August 3 - August 4, 2017. ©2017 Association for Computational Linguistics

for entity and context, allowing it to extract signals from noisy and unexpected context patterns.

While convolutional neural networks (Sun et al., 2015; Francis-Landau et al., 2016) and probabilistic attention (Lazic et al., 2015) have been applied to the task, this is the first model to use RNNs and a neural attention model for NED. RNNs account for the sequential nature of textual context while the attention model is applied to reduce the impact of noise in the text.

Our experiments show that our model significantly outperforms existing state-of-the-art NED algorithms on WikilinksNED, suggesting that RNNs with attention are able to model short and noisy context better than current approaches. In addition, we evaluate our algorithm on CoNLL-YAGO (Hoffart et al., 2011), a dataset of annotated news articles. We use a simple domain adaptation technique since CoNLL-YAGO lacks a large enough training set for our model, and achieve comparable results to other state-of-the-art methods. These experiments highlight the difference between the two datasets, indicating that our NED benchmark is substantially more challenging.

Code and data used for our experiments can be found at `https://github.com/yotam-happy/NEDforNoisyText`

2 Related Work

Local vs Global NED   Early work on Named Entity Disambiguation, such as Bunescu and Paşca (2006) and Mihalcea and Csomai (2007) focused on local approaches where each mention is disambiguated separately using hand-crafted features. While local approaches provide a hard-to-beat baseline (Ratinov et al., 2011), recent work has largely focused on global approaches. These disambiguate all mentions within a document simultaneously by considering the coherency of entity assignments within a document. For example the local component of the GLOW algorithm (Ratinov et al., 2011) was used as part of the relational inference system suggested by Cheng and Roth (2013). Similarly, Globerson et al. (2016) achieved state-of-the-art results by extending the local-based selective-context model of Lazic et al. (2015) with an attention-like coherence model.

Global models can tap into highly-discriminative semantic signals (e.g. coreference and entity relatedness) that are unavailable to local methods, and have significantly outperformed the local approach on standard datasets (Guo and Barbosa, 2014; Pershina et al., 2015; Globerson et al., 2016). However, global approaches are difficult to apply in domains where only short and noisy text is available, as often occurs in social media, questions and answers, and other short web documents. For example, Huang et al. (2014) collected many tweets from the same author in order to apply a global disambiguation method. Since this work focuses on disambiguating entities within short fragments of text, our algorithmic approach tries to extract as much information from the local context, without resorting to external signals.

Neural Approaches   The first neural approach for NED (He et al., 2013) used stacked auto-encoders to learn a similarity measure between mention-context structures and entity candidates. More recently, convolutional neural networks (CNNs) were employed for learning semantic similarity between context, mention, and candidate inputs (Sun et al., 2015; Francis-Landau et al., 2016). Neural embedding techniques have also inspired a number of works that measure entity-context relatedness using their embeddings (Yamada et al., 2016; Hu et al., 2015). In this paper, we train a recurrent neural network (RNN) model, which unlike CNNs and embeddings, is designed to exploit the sequential nature of text. We also utilize an attention mechanism, inspired by results from Lazic et al. (2015) that successfully used a probabilistic attention-like model for NED.

Noisy Data   Chisholm and Hachey (2015) showed that despite the noisy nature of web data, augmenting Wikipedia-derived data with web-links from the Wikilinks corpus (Singh et al., 2012) can improve performance on standard datasets. In our work, we find noisy web data to be a unique and challenging test case for disambiguation. We therefore use Wikilinks to construct a new stand-alone disambiguation benchmark that focuses on noisy text, rather than use it for training alone. Moreover, we differ from Chisholm at el. by taking a neural approach that implicitly discovers useful signals from contexts, instead of manually crafting features.

Commonly-used benchmarks for NED systems have mostly focused on news-based corpora. CoNLL-YAGO (Hoffart et al., 2011) is a dataset based on Reuters, created by hand-annotating the CoNLL 2003 Named Entity Recognition task dataset with YAGO (Suchanek et al., 2007) entities. It contains $1,393$ documents split into train, development and test sets. TAC KBP 2010 (Ji et al., 2010) and ACE Bentivogli et al. (2010) are also news-based datasets that contain only a limited amount of examples. Ratinov et al. (2011) used a random sample of paragraphs from Wikipedia for evaluation; however, they did not make their sample publicly available.

Our WikilinksNED dataset is substantially different from currently available datasets since they are all based on high-quality content from either news articles or Wikipedia, while WikilinksNED is a benchmark for noisier, less coherent, and more colloquial text. The annotation process is significantly different as well, as our dataset reflects the annotation preferences of real-world website authors. It is also significantly larger in size, being over 100 times larger than CoNLL-YAGO.

Recently, a number of Twitter-based datasets were compiled as well (Meij et al., 2012; Fromreide et al., 2014). These represent a much more extreme case than our dataset in terms of noise, shortness and spelling variations, and are much smaller in size. Due to the unique nature of tweets, proposed algorithms tend to be substantially different from algorithms used for other NED tasks.

3   The WikilinksNED Dataset: Entity Mentions in the Web

We introduce WikilinksNED, a large-scale NED dataset based on text fragments from the web. Our dataset is derived from the Wikilinks corpus (Singh et al., 2012), which was constructed by crawling the web and collecting hyperlinks (mentions) linking to Wikipedia concepts (entities) and their surrounding text (context). Wikilinks contains 40 million mentions covering 3 million entities, collected from over 10 million web pages.

Wikilinks can be seen as a large-scale, naturally-occurring, crowd-sourced dataset where thousands of human annotators provide ground truths for mentions of interest. This means that the dataset contains various kinds of noise, especially due to incoherent contexts. The contextual noise presents an interesting test-case that supplements existing datasets that are sourced from mostly coherent and well-formed text.

To get a sense of textual noise we have set up a small experiment where we measure the similarity between entities mentioned in WikilinksNED and their surrounding context, and compare the results to CoNLL-YAGO. We use state-of-the-art word and entity embeddings obtained from Yamada et al. (2016) and compute cosine similarity between embeddings of the correct entity assignment and the mean of context words. We compare results from all mentions in CoNLL-YAGO to a sample of 50000 web fragments taken from WikilinksNED, using a window of words of size 40 around entity mentions. We find that similarity between context and correct entity is indeed lower for web mentions (0.163) than for CoNLL-YAGO mentions (0.188), and find this result to be statistically significant with very high probability $(p < 10^{-5})$. This result indicates that web fragments in WikilinksNED are indeed noisier compared to CoNLL-YAGO documents.

We prepare our dataset from the local-context version of Wikilinks[1], and resolve ground-truth links using a Wikipedia dump from April 2016[2]. We use the *page* and *redirect* tables for resolution, and keep the database *pageid* column as a unique identifier for Wikipedia entities. We discard mentions where the ground-truth could not be resolved (only 3% of mentions).

We collect all pairs of mention m and entity e appearing in the dataset, and compute the number of times m refers to e ($\#(m, e)$), as well as the conditional probability of e given m: $P(e|m) = \#(m, e) / \sum_{e'} \#(m, e')$. Examining these distributions reveals many mentions belong to two extremes – either they have very little ambiguity, or they appear in the dataset only a handful of times and refer to different entities only a couple of times each. We deem the former to be less interesting for the purpose of NED, and suspect the latter to be noise with high probability. To filter these cases, we keep only mentions for which at least two different entities have 10 mentions each ($\#(m, e) \geq 10$) and consist of at least 10% of occurrences ($P(e|m) \geq 0.1$). This procedure aggressively filters our dataset and we are left with $3.2M$ mentions.

Finally, we randomly split the data into train (80%), validation (10%), and test (10%), according to website domains in order to minimize lexical memorization (Levy et al., 2015).

---

[1]http://www.iesl.cs.umass.edu/data/wiki-links
[2]https://dumps.wikimedia.org/

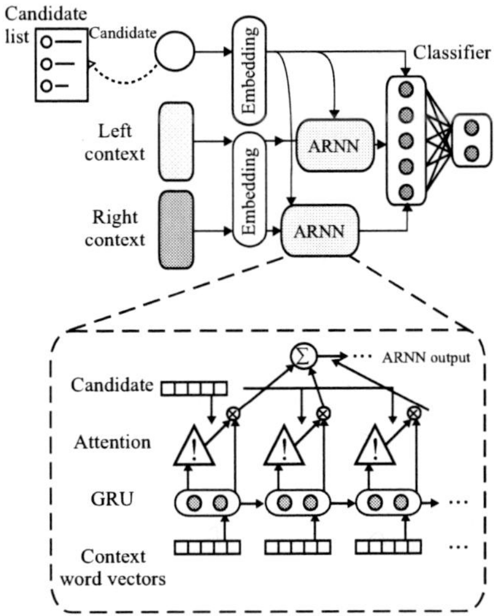

Figure 1: The architecture of our Neural Network model. A close-up of the Attention-RNN component appears in the dashed box.

4　Algorithm

Our DNN model is a discriminative model which takes a pair of local context and candidate entity, and outputs a probability-like score for the candidate entity being correct. Both words and entities are represented using embedding dictionaries and we interpret local context as a window-of-words to the left and right of a mention. The left and right contexts are fed into a duo of Attention-RNN (ARNN) components which process each side and produce a fixed length vector representation. The resulting vectors are concatenated and along with the entity embedding are and then fed into a classifier network with two output units that are trained to emit a probability-like score of the candidate being a correct or corrupt assignment.

4.1　Model Architecture

Figure 1 illustrates the main components of our architecture: an embedding layer, a duo of ARNNs, each processing one side of the context (left and right), and a classifier.

Embedding　The embedding layer first embeds both the entity and the context words as vectors (300 dimensions each).

ARNN　The ARNN unit is composed from an RNN and an attention mechanism. Equation 1 represents the general semantics of an RNN unit. An RNN reads a sequence of vectors $\{v_t\}$ and maintains a hidden state vector $\{h_t\}$. At each step a new hidden state is computed based on the previous hidden state and the next input vector using some function f, and an output is computed using g. This allows the RNN to "remember" important signals while scanning the context and to recognize signals spanning multiple words.

$$h_t = f_{\Theta_1}(h_{t-1}, v_t)$$
$$o_t = g_{\Theta_2}(h_t) \tag{1}$$

Our implementation uses a standard GRU unit (Cho et al., 2014) as an RNN. We fit the RNN unit with an additional attention mechanism, commonly used with state-of-the-art encoder-decoder models (Bahdanau et al., 2014; Xu et al., 2015). Since our model lacks a decoder, we use the entity embedding as a control signal for the attention mechanism.

Equation 2 details the equations governing the attention model.

$$a_t \in \mathbb{R}; a_t = r_{\Theta_3}(o_t, v_{candidate})$$
$$a'_t = \frac{1}{\sum_{i=1}^{t} \exp\{a_i\}} \exp\{a_t\}$$
$$o_{attn} = \sum_t a'_t o_t \tag{2}$$

The function r computes an attention value at each step, using the RNN output o_t and the candidate entity $v_{candidate}$. The final output vector o_{attn} is a fixed-size vector, which is the sum of all the output vectors of the RNN weighted according to the attention values. This allows the attention mechanism to decide on the importance of different context parts when examining a specific candidate. We follow Bahdanau et al. (2014) and parametrize the attention function r as a single layer NN as shown in equation 3.

$$r_{\Theta_3}(o_t, v_{candidate}) = Ao_t + Bv_{candidate} + b \tag{3}$$

Classifier　The classifier network consists of a hidden layer[3] and an output layer with two output units in a softmax. The output units are trained by optimizing a cross-entropy loss function.

---

[3] 300 dimensions with ReLU, and $p = 0.5$ dropout.

4.2 Training

We assume our model is only given training examples for correct entity assignments and therefore use *corrupt-sampling*, where we automatically generate examples of wrong assignments. For each context-entity pair (c, e), where e is the correct assignment for c, we produce k corrupt examples with the same context c but with a different, corrupt entity e'. We considered two alternatives for corrupt sampling and provide an empirical comparison of the two approaches (Section 5):

Near-Misses: Sampling out of the candidate set of each mention. We have found this to be more effective where the training data reliably reflects the test-set distribution.

All-Entity: Sampling from the entire dictionary of entities. Better suited to cases where the training data or candidate generation does not reflect the test-set well. Has an added benefit of allowing us to utilize unambiguous training examples where only a single candidate is found.

We sample corrupt examples uniformly in both alternatives since with uniform sampling the ratio between the number of positive and negative examples of an entity is higher for popular entities, thus biasing the network towards popular entities. In the All-Entity case, this ratio is approximately proportional to the prior probability of the entity.

We note that preliminary experiments revealed that corrupt-sampling according to the distribution of entities in the dataset (as is done by Mikolov at el. (2013)), rather than uniform sampling, did not perform well in our settings due to the lack of biasing toward popular entities.

Model optimization was carried out using standard backpropagation and an AdaGrad optimizer (Duchi et al., 2011). We allowed the error to propagate through all parts of the network and fine tune all trainable parameters, including the word and entity embeddings themselves. We found the performance of our model substantially improves for the first few epochs and then continues to slowly converge with marginal gains, and therefore trained all models for 8 epochs with $k = 5$ for corrupt-sampling.

4.3 Embedding Initialization

Training our model implicitly embeds the vocabulary of words and collection of entities in a common space. However, we found that explicitly initializing these embeddings with vectors pre-trained over a large collection of unlabeled data significantly improved performance (see Section 5.3). To this end, we implemented an approach based on the Skip-Gram with Negative-Sampling (SGNS) algorithm by Mikolov et al. (2013) that simultaneously trains both word and entity vectors.

We used `word2vecf`[4] (Levy and Goldberg, 2014a), which allows one to train word and context embeddings using arbitrary definitions of "word" and "context" by providing a dataset of word-context pairs (w, c), rather than a textual corpus. In our usage, we define a context as an entity e. To compile a dataset of (w, e) pairs, we consider every word w that appeared in the Wikipedia article describing entity e. We limit our vocabularies to words that appeared at least 20 times in the corpus and entities that contain at least 20 words in their articles. We ran the process for 10 epochs and produced vectors of 300 dimensions; other hyperparameters were set to their defaults.

Levy and Goldberg (2014b) showed that SGNS implicitly factorizes the word-context PMI matrix. Our approach is doing the same for the word-entity PMI matrix, which is highly related to the word-entity TFIDF matrix used in Explicit Semantic Analysis (Gabrilovich and Markovitch, 2007).

5 Evaluation

In this section, we describe our experimental setup and compare our model to the state of the art on two datasets: our new WikilinksNED dataset, as well as the commonly-used CoNLL-YAGO dataset (Hoffart et al., 2011). We also examine the effect of different corrupt-sampling schemes, and of initializing our model with pre-trained word and entity embeddings.

In all experiments, our model was trained with fixed-size left and right contexts (20 words in each side). We used a special padding symbol when the actual context was shorter than the window. Further, we filtered stopwords using NLTK's stopword list prior to selecting the window in order to focus on more informative words. Our model was implemented using the Keras (Chollet, 2015) and Tensorflow (Abadi et al., 2015) libraries.

---

[4] `http://bitbucket.org/yoavgo/word2vecf`

Wikilinks Test-Set Evaluation		
Model	**Sampled Test Set (10K)**	**Full Test Set (300K)**
Baseline (MPS)	60	59.6
Cheng (2013)	50.7	-
Yamada (2016)	67.6	66.9
Our Attention-RNN	**73.2**	**73**
Our RNN, w/o Attention	72.1	72.2

Table 1: Evaluation on noisy web data (WikilinksNED)

5.1 WikilinksNED

Training we use Near-Misses corrupt-sampling which was found to perform well due to a large training set that represents the test set well.

Candidate Generation To isolate the effect of candidate generation algorithms, we used the following simple method for all systems: given a mention m, consider all candidate entities e that appeared as the ground-truth entity for m at least once in the training corpus. This simple method yields 97% ground-truth recall on the test set.

Baselines Since we are the first to evaluate NED algorithms on WikilinksNED, we ran a selection of existing local NED systems and compared their performance to our algorithm's.

Yamada et al. (2016) created a state-of-the-art NED system that models entity-context similarity with word and entity embeddings trained using the skip-gram model. We obtained the original embeddings from the authors, and trained the statistical features and ranking model on the WikilinksNED training set. Our configuration of Yamada et al.'s model used only their local features.

Cheng et al. (2013) have made their global NED system publicly available[5]. This algorithm uses GLOW (Ratinov et al., 2011) for local disambiguation. We compare our results to the ranking step of the algorithm, without the global component. Due to the long running time of this system, we only evaluated their method on the smaller test set, which contains 10,000 randomly sampled instances from the full 320,000-example test set.

Finally, we include the **Most Probable Sense (MPS)** baseline, which selects the entity that was seen most with the given mention during training.

Results We used standard micro P@1 accuracy for evaluation. Experimental results comparing our model with the baselines are reported in Table 1. Our RNN model significantly outperforms Yamada at el. on this data by over 5 points, indicating that the more expressive RNNs are indeed beneficial for this task. We find that the attention mechanism further improves our results by a small, yet statistically significant, margin.

5.2 CoNLL-YAGO

Training CoNLL-YAGO has a training set with 18505 non-NIL mentions, which our experiments showed is not sufficient to train our model on. To fit our model to this dataset we first used a simple domain adaptation technique and then incorporated a number of basic statistical and string based features.

Domain Adaptation We used a simple domain adaptation technique where we first trained our model on an available large corpus of label data derived from Wikipedia, and then trained the resulting model on the smaller training set of CoNLL (Mou et al., 2016). The Wikipedia corpus was built by extracting all cross-reference links along with their context, resulting in over 80 million training examples. We trained our model with All-Entity corrupt sampling for 1 epoch on this data. The resulting model was then adapted to CoNLL-YAGO by training 1 epoch on CoNLL-YAGO's training set, where corrupt examples were produced by considering all possible candidates for each mention as corrupt-samples (Near-Misses corrupt sampling).

Additional Features We proceeded to use the model in a similar setting to Yamada et al. (2016) where a Gradient Boosting Regression Tree (GBRT) (Friedman, 2001) model was trained with our model's prediction as a feature along with a number of statistical and string based features defined by Yamada. The statistical features include entity prior probability, conditional proba-

---

[5]`https://cogcomp.cs.illinois.edu/page/software_view/Wikifier`

bility, number of candidates for the given mention and maximum conditional probability of the entity in the document. The string based features include edit distance between mention and entity title and two boolean features indicating whether the entity title starts or ends with the mention and vice versa. The GBRT model parameters where set to the values reported as optimal by Yamada[6].

Candidate Generation   For comparability with existing methods we used two publicly available candidates datasets: (1) PPRforNED - Pershina at el. (2015); (2) YAGO - Hoffart at el. (2011).

Baselines   As a baseline we took the standard Most Probable Sense (MPS) prediction, which selects the entity that was seen most with the given mention during training. We also compare to the following papers - Francis-Landau et al. (2016), Yamada at el. (2016), and Chisholm et al. (2015), as they are all strong local approaches and a good source for comparison.

Results   Table 2 displays the micro and macro P@1 scores on CoNLL-YAGO test-b for the different training steps. We find that when using only the training set of CoNLL-YAGO our model is under-trained and that the domain adaptation significant boosts performance. We find that incorporating extra statistical and string features yields a small extra improvement in performance.

The final micro and macro P@1 scores on CoNLL-YAGO test-b are displayed in table 3. On this dataset our model achieves comparable results, however it does not outperform the state-of-the-art, probably because of the relatively small training set and our reliance on domain adaptation.

5.3   Effects of initialized embeddings and corrupt-sampling schemes

We performed a study of the effects of using pre-initialized embeddings for our model, and of using either All-Entity or Near-Misses corrupt-sampling. The evaluation was done on a 10% sample of the evaluation set of the WikilinksNED corpus and can be seen in Table 4.

We have found that using pre-initialized embeddings results in significant performance gains, due to the better starting point. We have also found that using Near-Misses, our model achieves significantly improved performance. We attribute this

---

[6]Learning rate of 0.02; maximal tree depth of 4; 10, 000 trees.

CoNLL-YAGO test-b - Training Steps Eval		
Model	**Micro P@1**	**Macro P@1**
PPRforNED		
CoNLL training set	82	82
+ domain adaptation	86.6	87.7
+ GBRT	87.3	88.6
Yago		
CoNLL training set	74.8	73.5
+ domain adaptation	83.6	85.1
+ GBRT	83.3	86.3

Table 2:   Evaluation of training steps on CoNLL-YAGO.

CoNLL-YAGO test-b (Local methods)		
Model	**Micro P@1**	**Macro P@1**
PPRforNED		
Our ARNN + GBRT	87.3	88.6
Yamada (2016) local	90.9	92.4
Yamada (2016) global	93.1	92.6
Yago		
Our ARNN + GBRT	83.3	86.3
Yamada (2016) local	87.2	89.6
Francis-Landau (2016)	85.5	-
Chisholm (2015) local	86.1	-
Yamada (2016) global	91.5	90.9
Chisholm (2015) global	88.7	-

Table 3:   Evaluation on CoNLL-YAGO.

difference to the more efficient nature of training with near misses. Both these results were found to be statistically significant.

6   Error Analysis

We randomly sampled and manually analyzed 200 cases of prediction errors made by our model. This set was obtained from WikilinksNED's validation set that was not used for training.

Working with crowd-sourced data, we expected some errors to result from noise in the ground truths themselves. Indeed, we found that 19.5% (39/200) of the errors were not false, out of which 5% (2) where wrong labels, 33% (13) were predictions with an equivalent meaning as the correct entity, and in 61.5% (24) our model suggested a more convincing solution than the original author by using specific hints from the context. In this manner, the mention *'Supreme leader'*, which was

Wikilinks Evaluation-Set	
Model	**Micro accuracy**
Near-misses, with init.	**72.5**
Near-misses, random init.	67.2
All-Entity, with init.	70
All-Entity, random init.	67.1

Table 4: Corrupt-sampling and Initialization

contextually associated to the Iranian leader Ali Khamenei, was linked by our model with *'supreme leader of Iran'* while the "correct" tag was the general *'supreme leader'* entity.

In addition, 15.5% (31/200) were cases where a Wikipedia disambiguation-page was either the correct or predicted entity (2.5% and 14%, respectively). We considered the rest of the 130 errors as true semantic errors, and analyzed them in-depth.

Error type	**Fraction**	
False errors		
Not errors	19.5%	(39/200)
- Annotation error	5%	(2/39)
- Better suggestion	61.5%	(24/39)
- Equivalent entities	33%	(13/39)
Disambiguation page	15.5%	(31/200)
True semantic errors		
Too specific/general	31.5%	(41/130)
'almost correct' errors	26%	(34/130)
insufficient training	21.5%	(28/130)

Table 5: Error distribution in 200 samples. Categories of true errors are not fully distinct.

First, we noticed that in 31.5% of the true errors (41/130) our model selected an entity that can be understood as a specific (6.5%) or general (25%) realization of the correct solution. For example, instead of predicting *'Aroma of wine'* for a text on the scent and flavor of Turkish wine, the model assigned the mention *'Aroma'* with the general *'Odor'* entity. We observed that in 26% (34/130) of the error cases, the predicted entity had a very strong semantic relationship to the correct entity. A closer look discovered two prominent types of 'almost correct' errors occurred repeatedly in the data. The first was a film/book/theater type of error (8.4%), where the actual and the predicted entities were a different display of the same narrative. Even though having different jargon and produc-

ers, those fields share extremely similar content, which may explain why they tend to be frequently confused by the algorithm. A third (4/14) of those cases were tagged as truly ambiguous even for human reader. The second prominent type of 'almost correct' errors where differentiating between adjectives that are used to describe properties of a nation. Particularity, mentions such as *'Germanic'*, *'Chinese'* and *'Dutch'* were falsely assigned to entities that describe language instead of people, and vice versa. We observed this type of mistake in 8.4% of the errors (11/130).

Another interesting type of errors where in cases where the correct entity had insufficient training. We defined insufficient training errors as errors where the correct entity appeared less than 10 times in the training data. We saw that the model followed the MPS in 75% of these cases, showing that our model tends to follow the baseline in such cases. Further, the amount of generalization error in insufficient-training conditions was also significant (35.7%), as our model tended to select more general entities.

7 Conclusions

Our results indicate that the expressibility of attention-RNNs indeed allows us to extract useful features from noisy context, when sufficient amounts of training examples are available. This allows our model to significantly out-perform existing state-of-the-art models. We find that both using pre-initialized embedding vocabularies, and the corrupt-sampling method employed are very important for properly training our model.

However, the gap between results of all systems tested on both CoNLL-YAGO and WikilinksNED indicates that mentions with noisy context are indeed a challenging test. We believe this to be an important real-world scenario, that represents a distinct test-case that fills a gap between existing news-based datasets and the much noisier Twitter data (Ritter et al., 2011) that has received increasing attention. We find recurrent neural models are a promising direction for this task.

Finally, our error analysis shows a number of possible improvements that should be addressed. Since we use the training set for candidate generation, non-nonsensical candidates (i.e. disambiguation pages) cause our model to err and should be removed from the candidate set. In addition, we observe that lack of sufficient training for long-tail entities is still a problem, even when a large training set is available. We believe this, and some subtle semantic cases (book/movie) can be at least partially addressed by considering semantic properties of entities, such as types and categories. We intend to address these issues in future work.

References

Martín Abadi, Ashish Agarwal, Paul Barham, Eugene Brevdo, Zhifeng Chen, Craig Citro, Greg S. Corrado, Andy Davis, Jeffrey Dean, Matthieu Devin, Sanjay Ghemawat, Ian Goodfellow, Andrew Harp, Geoffrey Irving, Michael Isard, Yangqing Jia, Rafal Jozefowicz, Lukasz Kaiser, Manjunath Kudlur, Josh Levenberg, Dan Mané, Rajat Monga, Sherry Moore, Derek Murray, Chris Olah, Mike Schuster, Jonathon Shlens, Benoit Steiner, Ilya Sutskever, Kunal Talwar, Paul Tucker, Vincent Vanhoucke, Vijay Vasudevan, Fernanda Viégas, Oriol Vinyals, Pete Warden, Martin Wattenberg, Martin Wicke, Yuan Yu, and Xiaoqiang Zheng. 2015. TensorFlow: Large-scale machine learning on heterogeneous systems. Software available from tensorflow.org. http://tensorflow.org/.

Dzmitry Bahdanau, Kyunghyun Cho, and Yoshua Bengio. 2014. Neural machine translation by jointly learning to align and translate. *CoRR* abs/1409.0473. http://arxiv.org/abs/1409.0473.

Luisa Bentivogli, Pamela Forner, Claudio Giuliano, Alessandro Marchetti, Emanuele Pianta, and Kateryna Tymoshenko. 2010. *Proceedings of the 2nd Workshop on The People's Web Meets NLP: Collaboratively Constructed Semantic Resources*, Coling 2010 Organizing Committee, chapter Extending English ACE 2005 Corpus Annotation with Ground-truth Links to Wikipedia, pages 19–27. http://aclweb.org/anthology/W10-3503.

Jonathan Berant and Percy Liang. 2014. Semantic parsing via paraphrasing. In *Proceedings of the 52nd Annual Meeting of the Association for Computational Linguistics (Volume 1: Long Papers)*. Association for Computational Linguistics, pages 1415–1425. https://doi.org/10.3115/v1/P14-1133.

Razvan Bunescu and Marius Paşca. 2006. Using encyclopedic knowledge for named entity disambiguation. In *11th Conference of the European Chapter of the Association for Computational Linguistics*. http://aclweb.org/anthology/E06-1002.

Xiao Cheng and Dan Roth. 2013. Relational inference for wikification. In *Proceedings of the 2013 Conference on Empirical Methods in Natural Language Processing*. Association for Computational Linguistics, pages 1787–1796. http://aclweb.org/anthology/D13-1184.

Andrew Chisholm and Ben Hachey. 2015. Entity disambiguation with web links. *Transactions of the Association of Computational Linguistics* 3:145–156. http://aclweb.org/anthology/Q15-1011.

Kyunghyun Cho, Bart van Merrienboer, Caglar Gulcehre, Dzmitry Bahdanau, Fethi Bougares, Holger Schwenk, and Yoshua Bengio. 2014. Learning phrase representations using rnn encoder–decoder for statistical machine translation. In *Proceedings of the 2014 Conference on Empirical Methods in Natural Language Processing (EMNLP)*. Association for Computational Linguistics, pages 1724–1734. https://doi.org/10.3115/v1/D14-1179.

François Chollet. 2015. Keras. https://github.com/fchollet/keras.

John C. Duchi, Elad Hazan, and Yoram Singer. 2011. Adaptive subgradient methods for online learning and stochastic optimization. *Journal of Machine Learning Research* 12:2121–2159. http://dl.acm.org/citation.cfm?id=2021068.

Matthew Francis-Landau, Greg Durrett, and Dan Klein. 2016. Capturing semantic similarity for entity linking with convolutional neural networks. In *Proceedings of the 2016 Conference of the North American Chapter of the Association for Computational Linguistics: Human Language Technologies*. Association for Computational Linguistics, pages 1256–1261. https://doi.org/10.18653/v1/N16-1150.

Jerome H Friedman. 2001. Greedy function approximation: a gradient boosting machine. *Annals of statistics* pages 1189–1232. https://doi.org/10.1214/aos/1013203451.

Hege Fromreide, Dirk Hovy, and Anders Søgaard. 2014. Crowdsourcing and annotating ner for twitter #drift. In *Proceedings of the Ninth International Conference on Language Resources and Evaluation (LREC-2014)*. European Language Resources Association (ELRA). http://www.lrec-conf.org/proceedings/lrec2014/pdf/421_Paper.pdf.

Evgeniy Gabrilovich and Shaul Markovitch. 2007. Computing semantic relatedness using wikipedia-based explicit semantic analysis. In *Proceedings of the 20th International Joint Conference on Artifical Intelligence*. Morgan Kaufmann Publishers Inc., San Francisco, CA, USA, IJCAI'07, pages 1606–1611. http://dl.acm.org/citation.cfm?id=1625275.1625535.

Amir Globerson, Nevena Lazic, Soumen Chakrabarti, Amarnag Subramanya, Michael Ringaard, and Fernando Pereira. 2016. Collective entity resolution with multi-focal attention. In *Proceedings of the 54th Annual Meeting of the Association for Computational Linguistics (Volume 1: Long Papers)*. Association for Computational Linguistics, pages 621–631. https://doi.org/10.18653/v1/P16-1059.

Zhaochen Guo and Denilson Barbosa. 2014. Entity linking with a unified semantic representation. In *Proceedings of the 23rd International Conference on World Wide Web*. ACM, New York, NY,

USA, WWW '14 Companion, pages 1305–1310. https://doi.org/10.1145/2567948.2579705.

Zhengyan He, Shujie Liu, Mu Li, Ming Zhou, Longkai Zhang, and Houfeng Wang. 2013. Learning entity representation for entity disambiguation. In *Proceedings of the 51st Annual Meeting of the Association for Computational Linguistics (Volume 2: Short Papers)*. Association for Computational Linguistics, pages 30–34. http://aclweb.org/anthology/P13-2006.

Johannes Hoffart, Amir Mohamed Yosef, Ilaria Bordino, Hagen Fürstenau, Manfred Pinkal, Marc Spaniol, Bilyana Taneva, Stefan Thater, and Gerhard Weikum. 2011. Robust disambiguation of named entities in text. In *Proceedings of the 2011 Conference on Empirical Methods in Natural Language Processing*. Association for Computational Linguistics, pages 782–792. http://aclweb.org/anthology/D11-1072.

Zhiting Hu, Poyao Huang, Yuntian Deng, Yingkai Gao, and Eric Xing. 2015. Entity hierarchy embedding. In *Proceedings of the 53rd Annual Meeting of the Association for Computational Linguistics and the 7th International Joint Conference on Natural Language Processing (Volume 1: Long Papers)*. Association for Computational Linguistics, pages 1292–1300. https://doi.org/10.3115/v1/P15-1125.

Hongzhao Huang, Yunbo Cao, Xiaojiang Huang, Heng Ji, and Chin-Yew Lin. 2014. Collective tweet wikification based on semi-supervised graph regularization. In *Proceedings of the 52nd Annual Meeting of the Association for Computational Linguistics (Volume 1: Long Papers)*. Association for Computational Linguistics, pages 380–390. https://doi.org/10.3115/v1/P14-1036.

Heng Ji, Ralph Grishman, Hoa Trang Dang, Kira Griffitt, and Joe Ellis. 2010. Overview of the tac 2010 knowledge base population track. In *Third Text Analysis Conference (TAC 2010)*. volume 3, pages 3–3.

Nevena Lazic, Amarnag Subramanya, Michael Ringgaard, and Fernando Pereira. 2015. Plato: A selective context model for entity resolution. *Transactions of the Association of Computational Linguistics* 3:503–515. http://aclweb.org/anthology/Q15-1036.

Omer Levy and Yoav Goldberg. 2014a. Dependency-based word embeddings. In *Proceedings of the 52nd Annual Meeting of the Association for Computational Linguistics (Volume 2: Short Papers)*. Association for Computational Linguistics, pages 302–308. https://doi.org/10.3115/v1/P14-2050.

Omer Levy and Yoav Goldberg. 2014b. Neural word embedding as implicit matrix factorization. In *Advances in Neural Information Processing Systems 27: Annual Conference on Neural Information Processing Systems 2014, December 8-13 2014, Montreal, Quebec, Canada*. pages 2177–2185. http://papers.nips.cc/paper/5477-neural-word-embedding-as-implicit-matrix-factorization.

Omer Levy, Steffen Remus, Chris Biemann, and Ido Dagan. 2015. Do supervised distributional methods really learn lexical inference relations? In *Proceedings of the 2015 Conference of the North American Chapter of the Association for Computational Linguistics: Human Language Technologies*. Association for Computational Linguistics, pages 970–976. https://doi.org/10.3115/v1/N15-1098.

Edgar Meij, Wouter Weerkamp, and Maarten de Rijke. 2012. Adding semantics to microblog posts. In *Proceedings of the Fifth ACM International Conference on Web Search and Data Mining*. ACM, New York, NY, USA, WSDM '12, pages 563–572. https://doi.org/10.1145/2124295.2124364.

Rada Mihalcea and Andras Csomai. 2007. Wikify!: Linking documents to encyclopedic knowledge. In *Proceedings of the Sixteenth ACM Conference on Conference on Information and Knowledge Management*. ACM, New York, NY, USA, CIKM '07, pages 233–242. https://doi.org/10.1145/1321440.1321475.

Tomas Mikolov, Ilya Sutskever, Kai Chen, Gregory S. Corrado, and Jeffrey Dean. 2013. Distributed representations of words and phrases and their compositionality. In *Advances in Neural Information Processing Systems 26: 27th Annual Conference on Neural Information Processing Systems 2013. Proceedings of a meeting held December 5-8, 2013, Lake Tahoe, Nevada, United States.*. pages 3111–3119. http://papers.nips.cc/paper/5021-distributed-representations-of-words-and-phrases-and-their-compositionality.

Lili Mou, Zhao Meng, Rui Yan, Ge Li, Yan Xu, Lu Zhang, and Zhi Jin. 2016. How transferable are neural networks in nlp applications? In *Proceedings of the 2016 Conference on Empirical Methods in Natural Language Processing*. Association for Computational Linguistics, pages 479–489. http://aclweb.org/anthology/D16-1046.

Maria Pershina, Yifan He, and Ralph Grishman. 2015. Personalized page rank for named entity disambiguation. In *Proceedings of the 2015 Conference of the North American Chapter of the Association for Computational Linguistics: Human Language Technologies*. Association for Computational Linguistics, pages 238–243. https://doi.org/10.3115/v1/N15-1026.

Lev Ratinov, Dan Roth, Doug Downey, and Mike Anderson. 2011. Local and global algorithms for disambiguation to wikipedia. In *Proceedings of the 49th Annual Meeting of the Association for Computational Linguistics: Human Language Technologies*. Association for Computational Linguistics, pages 1375–1384. http://aclweb.org/anthology/P11-1138.

Alan Ritter, Sam Clark, Mausam, and Oren Etzioni. 2011. Named entity recognition in
tweets: An experimental study. In *Proceedings of the 2011 Conference on Empirical Methods in Natural Language Processing*. Association
for Computational Linguistics, pages 1524–1534.
http://aclweb.org/anthology/D11-1141.

Sameer Singh, Amarnag Subramanya, Fernando
Pereira, and Andrew McCallum. 2012. Wikilinks:
A large-scale cross-document coreference corpus
labeled via links to wikipedia. *University of
Massachusetts, Amherst, Tech. Rep. UM-CS-2012-
015* https://web.cs.umass.edu/publication/docs
/2012/UM-CS-2012-015.pdf.

Fabian M. Suchanek, Gjergji Kasneci, and Gerhard Weikum. 2007. Yago: A core of semantic knowledge. In *Proceedings of the 16th International Conference on World Wide Web*. ACM,
New York, NY, USA, WWW '07, pages 697–706.
https://doi.org/10.1145/1242572.1242667.

Yaming Sun, Lei Lin, Duyu Tang, Nan Yang, Zhen-
zhou Ji, and Xiaolong Wang. 2015. Modeling
mention, context and entity with neural networks
for entity disambiguation. In *Proceedings of the
Twenty-Fourth International Joint Conference on
Artificial Intelligence, IJCAI 2015, Buenos Aires,
Argentina, July 25-31, 2015*. pages 1333–1339.
http://ijcai.org/Abstract/15/192.

Kelvin Xu, Jimmy Ba, Ryan Kiros, Kyunghyun
Cho, Aaron C. Courville, Ruslan Salakhutdinov, Richard S. Zemel, and Yoshua Bengio.
2015. Show, attend and tell: Neural image
caption generation with visual attention. In
*Proceedings of the 32nd International Confer-
ence on Machine Learning, ICML 2015, Lille,
France, 6-11 July 2015*. pages 2048–2057.
http://jmlr.org/proceedings/papers/v37/xuc15.html.

Ikuya Yamada, Hiroyuki Shindo, Hideaki Takeda,
and Yoshiyasu Takefuji. 2016. Joint learning of the embedding of words and entities
for named entity disambiguation. In *Proceedings of The 20th SIGNLL Conference on Computational Natural Language Learning*. Association for Computational Linguistics, pages 250–259.
https://doi.org/10.18653/v1/K16-1025.

Tell Me Why: Using Question Answering as Distant Supervision for Answer Justification

Rebecca Sharp[*], **Mihai Surdeanu**[*], **Peter Jansen**[*],
Marco A. Valenzuela-Escárcega[*], **Peter Clark**[†] **and Michael Hammond**[*]

[*]University of Arizona
[†]Allen Institute for Artificial Intelligence
[*]{bsharp, msurdeanu, pajansen, marcov, hammond}@email.arizona.edu
[†]peterc@allenai.org

Abstract

For many applications of question answering (QA), being able to explain why a given model chose an answer is critical. However, the lack of labeled data for answer justifications makes learning this difficult and expensive. Here we propose an approach that uses answer ranking as distant supervision for learning how to select informative justifications, where justifications serve as inferential connections between the question and the correct answer while often containing little lexical overlap with either. We propose a neural network architecture for QA that reranks answer justifications as an intermediate (and human-interpretable) step in answer selection. Our approach is informed by a set of features designed to combine both learned representations and explicit features to capture the connection between questions, answers, and answer justifications. We show that with this end-to-end approach we are able to significantly improve upon a strong IR baseline in both justification ranking (+9% rated highly relevant) and answer selection (+6% P@1).

1 Introduction

Developing interpretable machine learning (ML) models, that is, models where a human user can *understand* what the model is learning, is considered by many to be crucial for ensuring usability and accelerating progress (Craven and Shavlik, 1996; Kim et al., 2015; Letham et al., 2015; Ribeiro et al., 2016). For many applications of question answering (QA), i.e., finding short answers to natural language questions, simply providing an answer is not sufficient. A complete

Question:
Which of these is a response to an internal stimulus?
(A) A sunflower turns to face the rising sun.
(B) A cucumber tendril wraps around a wire.
(C) A pine tree knocked sideways in a landslide grows upward in a bend.
(D) Guard cells of a tomato plant leaf close when there is little water in the roots .

Justification: Plants rely on hormones to send signals within the plant in order to respond to internal stimuli such as a lack of water or nutrients.

Table 1: Example of an 8th grade science question with a justification for the correct answer. Note the lack of direct lexical overlap present between the justification and the correct answer, demonstrating the difficulty of the task of finding justifications using traditional distant supervision methods.

approach must be interpretable, i.e., able to *explain* why an answer is correct. For example, in the medical domain, a QA approach that answers treatment questions would not be trusted if the treatment recommendation is not explained in terms that can be understood by the human user.

One approach to interpreting complex models is to make use of human-interpretable information generated by the model to gain insight into what the model is learning. We follow the intuition of Lei et al. (2016), whose two-component network first generates text spans from an input document, and then uses these text spans to make predictions. Lei et al. utilize these intermediate text spans to infer the model's preferences. By learning these human-readable intermediate representations end-to-end with a downstream task, the representations are optimized to correlate with what the model learns is discriminatory for the task, and they can be evaluated against what a human would consider to be important. Here we apply this general framework for model interpretability to QA.

In this work, we focus on answering multiple-choice science exam questions (Clark (2015); see example in Table 1). This domain is challenging as: (a) approximately 70% of science exam ques-

69

Proceedings of the 21st Conference on Computational Natural Language Learning (CoNLL 2017), pages 69–79,
Vancouver, Canada, August 3 - August 4, 2017. ©2017 Association for Computational Linguistics

tion shave been shown to require complex forms of inference to solve (Clark et al., 2013; Jansen et al., 2016), and (b) there are few structured knowledge bases to support this inference. Within this domain, we propose an approach that learns to both select and explain answers, when the only supervision available is for which answer is correct (but not how to explain it). Intuitively, our approach chooses the justifications that provide the most help towards ranking the correct answers higher than incorrect ones. More formally, our neural network approach alternates between using the current model with max-pooling to choose the highest scoring justifications for correct answers, and optimizing the answer ranking model given these justifications. Crucially, these reranked texts serve as our human-readable answer justifications, and by examining them, we gain insight into what the model learned was useful for the QA task.

The specific contributions of this work are:

1. We propose an end-to-end neural method for learning to answer questions and select a high-quality justification for those answers. Our approach re-ranks free-text answer justifications without the need for structured knowledge bases. With supervision only for the correct answers, we learn this re-ranking through a form of distant supervision – i.e., the answer ranking supervises the justification re-ranking.

2. We investigate two distinct categories of features in this "little data" domain: explicit features, and learned representations. We show that, with limited training, explicit features perform far better despite their simplicity.

3. We demonstrate a large (+9%) improvement in generating high-quality justifications over a strong information retrieval (IR) baseline, while maintaining near state-of-the-art performance on the multiple-choice science-exam QA task, demonstrating the success of the end-to-end strategy.

2   Related work

In many ways, deep learning has become the canonical example of the "black box" of machine learning and many of the approaches to explaining it can be loosely categorized into two types: approaches that try to interpret the parameters themselves (e.g., with visualizations and heat maps (Zeiler and Fergus, 2014; Hermann et al., 2015; Li et al., 2016), and approaches that generate human-interpretable information that is ideally correlated with what is being learned inside the model (e.g., Lei et al. (2016)). Our approach falls into the latter type – we use our model's reranking of human-readable justifications to give us insight into what the model considers informative for answering questions. This allows us to see where we do well (Section 6.2), and where we can improve (Section 6.3).

Deep learning has been successfully applied to many recent QA approaches and related tasks (Bordes et al., 2015; Hermann et al., 2015; He and Golub, 2016; Dong et al., 2015; Tan et al., 2016, inter alia). However, large quantities of data are needed to train the millions of parameters often contained in these models. Recently, simpler model architectures have been proposed that greatly reduce the number of parameters while maintaining high performance (e.g., Iyyer et al., 2015; Chen et al., 2016; Parikh et al., 2016). We take inspiration from this trend and propose a simple neural architecture for our task to offset the limited available training data.

Another way to mitigate sparse training data is to include higher-level explicit features. Like Sachan et al. (2016), we make use of explicit features alongside features from distributed representations to capture connections between questions, answers, and supporting text. However, we use a simpler set of features and while they use structured and semi-structured knowledge bases, we use only free-text.

Our approach to learning justification reranking end-to-end with answer selection is similar to the Jansen et al. (2017) latent reranking perceptron, which also operates over free text. However, our approach does not require decomposing the text into an intermediate representation, allowing our technique to more easily extend to larger textual knowledge bases.

The way we have formulated our justification selection (as a re-ranking of knowledge base sentences) is related to, but distinct from the task of answer sentence selection (Wang and Manning, 2010; Severyn and Moschitti, 2012, 2013; Severyn et al., 2013; Severyn and Moschitti, 2015; Wang and Nyberg, 2015, inter alia). Answer sentence selection is typically framed as a fully or semi-supervised task for factoid questions, where

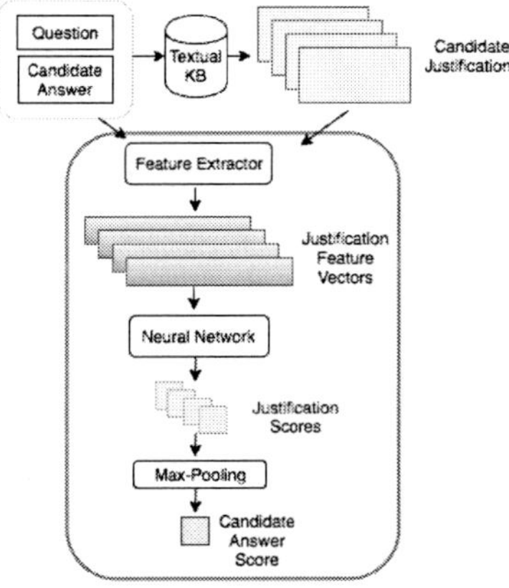

Figure 1: Architecture of our question answering approach. Given a question, candidate answer, and a free-text knowledge base as inputs, we generate a pool of candidate justifications, from which we extract feature vectors. We use a neural network to score each and then use max-pooling to select the current best justification. This serves as the score for the candidate answer itself. The red border indicates the components that are trained online.

a correctly selected sentence fully contains the answer text. Here, we have a variety of questions, many of which are non-factoid. Additionally, we have no direct supervision for our justification selection (i.e., no labels as to which sentences are good justifications for our answers), motivating our distant supervision approach where the performance on our QA task serves as supervision for selecting good justifications. Further, we are not actually looking for sentences that *contain* the answer choice, as with answer sentence selection, but rather sentences which close the "lexical chasm" (Berger et al., 2000) between question and answer. This distinction is demonstrated in the example in Table 1, where the correct answer does not overlap lexically with the question and only minimally with the justification. Instead, the justification serves as a bridge between the question and answer, filling in the missing information for the required inference.

3 Approach

One of the primary difficulties with the explainable QA task addressed here is that, while we have supervision for the correct answer, we do not have annotated answer justifications. Here we tackle this challenge by using the QA task performance as supervision for the justification reranking, allowing us to learn to choose both the correct answer and a compelling, human-readable justification for that answer.

Additionally, similar to the strategy Chen and Manning (2014) applied to parsing, we combine representation-based features with explicit features that capture additional information that is difficult to model through embeddings, especially with limited training data.

The architecture of our approach is summarized in Figure 1. Given a question and a candidate answer, we first query an textual knowledge base (KB) to retrieve a pool of potential justifications for that answer candidate. For each justification, we extract a set of features designed to model the relations between questions, answers, and answer justifications based on word embeddings, lexical overlap with the question and answer candidate, discourse, and information retrieval (IR) (Section 4.2). These features are passed into a simple neural network to generate a score for each justification, given the current state of the model. A final max-pooling layer selects the top-scoring justification for the candidate answer and this max score is used also as the score for the answer candidate. The system is trained using correct-incorrect answer pairs with a pairwise margin ranking loss objective function to enforce that the correct answer be ranked higher than any of the incorrect answers.

With this end-to-end approach, the model learns to select justifications that allow it to correctly answer questions. We hypothesize that this approach enables the model to indirectly learn to choose justifications that provide good explanations as to why the answer is correct. We empirically test this hypothesis in Section 6, where we show that indeed the model learns to correctly answer questions, as well as to select high-quality justifications for those answers.

4 Model and Features

Our approach consists of three main components: (a) the retrieval of a pool of candidate answer justifications (Section 4.1); (b) the extraction of features for each (Section 4.2); and (c) the scoring of the answer candidate itself based on this pool of justifications (Section 4.3). The architecture of this latter scoring component is shown in Figure 2.

4.1 Candidate Justification Retrieval

The first step in our process is to use standard information retrieval (IR) methods to retrieve a set of candidate justifications for each candidate answer to a given question. To do this, we build a bag-of-

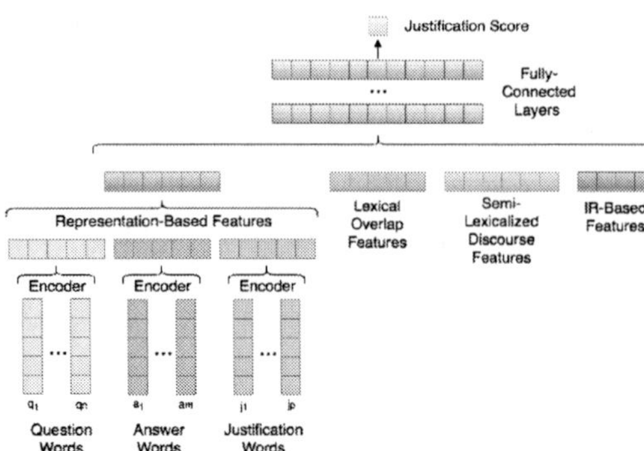

Figure 2: Detailed architecture of the model's scoring component. The question, candidate answer, and justification are encoded (by summing their word embeddings) to create vector representations of each. These representations are combined in several ways to create a set of representation-based similarity features that are concatenated to additional explicit features capturing lexical overlap, discourse and IR information and fed into a feed-forward neural network. The output layer of the network is a single node that represents the score of the justification candidate.

words (BOW) query using the content lemmas for the question and answer candidate, boosting the answer lemmas to have four times more weight[1]. We used Lucene[2] with a *tf-idf* based scoring function to return the top-scoring documents from the KB. Each of these indexed documents consists of a single sentence from our corpora, and serves as one potential justification.

4.2 Feature Extraction

For each retrieved candidate justification, we extract a set of features based on (a) distributed representations of the question, candidate answer, and justification terms; (b) strict lexical overlap; (c) discourse relations present in the justification; and (d) the IR scores for the justification.

Representation-based features (Emb): To model the similarity between the text of each question (Q), candidate answer (A), and candidate justification (J), we include a set of features that utilize distributed representations of the words found in each. First we encode each by summing the vectors for each of their words[3]. We then compute $sim(Q, A)$, $sim(Q, J)$, and $sim(A, J)$ us-

ing cosine similarity. Using another vector representation of only the *unique* words in the justification, i.e., the words that do not occur in either the question or the candidate answer, we also compute $sim(Q, uniqueJ)$ and $sim(A, uniqueJ)$.

To create a feature which captures the relationship between the question, answer, *and* justification, we take inspiration from TransE, a popular relation extraction framework (Bordes et al., 2013). TransE is based on the premise that if two entities, e_1 and e_2 are related by a relation r, then a mapping into k dimensions, $m(x) \in \mathbb{R}^k$ can be learned such that $m(e_1) + m(r) \approx m(e_2)$. Here, we modify this intuition for QA by suggesting that given the vectorized representations of the question, answer candidate, and justification above, $Q + J \approx A$, i.e., a question combined with a strong justification will point towards an answer. Here we model this as an explicit feature, the euclidean distance between $Q + J$ and A, and hypothesize that as a consequence the model will learn to select passages that maximize the quality of the justifications. This makes a total of six features based on distributed representations.

Lexical overlap features (LO): We additionally characterize each justification in terms of a simple set of explicit features designed to capture the size of the justification, as well as the lexical overlap (and difference) between the justification and the question and answer candidate. We include these five features: the proportion of question words, of answer words, and of the combined set of question and answer words that also appear in the justification; the proportion of justification words that do not appear in either the question or the answer; and the length of the justification in words.[4]

Semi-Lexicalized Discourse features (lexDisc): These features use the discourse structure of the justification text, which has been shown to be useful for QA (Jansen et al., 2014; Sharp et al., 2015; Sachan et al., 2016).

We use the discourse parser of Surdeanu et al. (2015) to fragment the text into elementary discourse units (EDUs) and then recursively connect neighboring EDUs with binary discourse relations. For each of the 18 possible relation labels, we create a set of semi-lexicalized discourse features that indicate the presence of a given discourse relation as well as whether or not the head

---

[1]We empirically found this answer term boosting to ensure retrieval of documents which were relevant to the particular answer candidate.

[2]https://lucene.apache.org

[3]While this BOW approach is not ideal in many ways, it performed equivalently to far more complicated approaches such as LSTMs and GRUs, also noted by (Iyyer et al., 2015), likely due to the limited training data in this domain.

[4]We normalized this value by the maximum justification length.

and modifier texts contain words from the question and/or the answer.

For example, for the question *Q: What makes water a good solvent...? A: strong polarity*, with a discourse-parsed justification [*Water is an efficient solvent*]$_{e1}$ [*because of this polarity.*]$_{e2}$, we create the semi-lexicalized feature Q_cause_A, because there is a *Cause* relation between EDUs $e1$ and $e2$, $e1$ overlaps with the question, and $e2$ overlaps with the answer. Since there are 18 possible discourse relation labels, and the prefix and suffix can be any of *Q, A, QA* or *None*, this creates a set of 288 indicator features.

IR-based features (IR^{++}): Finally, we also use a set of four IR-based features which are assigned at the level of the answer candidate (i.e., these features are identical for each of the candidate justifications for that answer choice). Using the same query method as described in Section 4.1, for each question and answer candidate we retrieve a set of indexed documents. Using the *tf-idf* based retrieval scores of these returned documents, $s(d_i)$ for $d_i \in D$, we rank the answer candidates using two methods:

- by the maximum retrieved document score for each candidate, and

- by the weighted sum of all retrieved document scores[5]:

$$\sum_{d_i \in D} \frac{1}{i} s(d_i) \qquad (1)$$

We repeat this process using an unboosted query as well, for a total of four rankings of the answer candidates. We then use these rankings to make a set of four reciprocal rank features, IR$_0^{++}$, ..., IR$_3^{++}$, for each answer candidate (i.e., IR$_0^{++} = 1.0$ for the top-ranked candidate in the first ranking, IR$_0^{++} = 0.5$ for the next candidate, etc.)

4.3 Neural Network

As shown in Figure 2, the extracted features for each candidate justification are concatenated and passed into a fully-connected feed-forward neural network (NN). The output layer is a single node representing the justification score. We then use max-pooling over these scores to select the current best justification for the answer candidate, and use its score as the score for the answer candidate itself. For training, the correct answer for a given

question is paired with each of the incorrect answers, and each are scored as above. We compute the pair-wise margin ranking loss for each training pair:

$$L = \max(0, m - F(a^+) + F(a^-)) \qquad (2)$$

where $F(a^+)$ and $F(a^-)$ are the model scores for a correct and incorrect answer candidate and m is the margin, and backpropagate the gradients. At testing time, we use the trained model to score each answer choice (again using the maximum justification score) and select the highest-scoring.

As we are interested in not only correctly answering questions, but also selecting valid justification for those answers, we keep track of the scores of *all* justifications and use this information to return the top k justifications for each answer choice. These are evaluated along with the answer selection performance in Section 6.

5 Experiments

5.1 Data and Setup

We evaluated our model on the set of 8th grade science questions that was provided by the Allen Institute for Artificial Intelligence (AI2) for a recent Kaggle challenge. The training set contained 2,500 question, each with 4 answer candidates. For our test set, we used the 800 publicly-released questions that were used as the validation set in the actual evaluation.[6] We tuned our model architectures and hyper-parameters on the training data using five-fold cross-validation (training on 4 folds, validating on 1). During testing, we froze the model architecture and all hyperparameters and re-trained on all the training data, setting aside a random 15% of training questions to facilitate early stopping.

5.2 Baselines

In addition to previous work, we compare our model against two strong IR baselines:

- **IR Baseline:** For this baseline, we rank answer candidates by the maximum *tf.idf* document retrieval score using an unboosted query of question and answer terms (see Section 4.1 for retrieval details).

- **IR^{++}:** This baseline uses the same architecture as the full model, as described in Section 4.3, but with only the IR^{++} feature group.

---

[5]Weighted sum was based on the IR scores used in the winning Kaggle system from user Cardal (https://github. com/Cardal/Kaggle_AllenAIscience)

[6]The official testing dataset is not publicly available.

5.3 Corpora

For our pool of candidate justifications (as well as the scores for our IR baselines) we used the corpora that were cited as being most helpful to the top-performing systems of the Kaggle challenge. These consisted of short, flash-card style texts gathered from two online resources: about 700K sentences from StudyStack[7] and 25K sentences from Quizlet[8]. From these corpora, we use the top 50 sentences retrieved by the IR model as our set of candidate justifications. All of our corpora were annotated using using the Stanford CoreNLP toolkit (Manning et al., 2014), the dependency parser of Chen and Manning (2014), and the discourse parser of Surdeanu et al. (2015).

While our model is able to learn a set of embeddings, we found performance was improved when using pre-trained embeddings, and in this low-data domain, fixing these embeddings to not update during training substantially reduced the amount of model over-fitting. In order to pre-train domain-relevant embeddings for our vocabulary, we used the documents from the StudyStack and Quizlet corpora, supplemented by the newly released Aristo MINI corpus (December 2016 release)[9], which contains 1.2M science-related sentences from various web sources. The training was done using the `word2vec` algorithm (Mikolov et al., 2010, 2013) as implemented by Levy and Goldberg (2014), such that the context for each word in a sentence is composed of all the other words in the same sentence. We used embeddings of size 50 as we did not see a performance improvement with higher dimensionality.

5.4 Model Tuning

The neural model was implemented in Keras (Chollet, 2015) using the Theano (Theano Development Team, 2016) backend. For our feed-forward component, we use a shallow neural network that we lightly tuned to have a single fully-connected layer containing 10 nodes, glorot uniform initialization, a $tanh$ activation, and an L2-regularization of 0.1. We trained with the RMSProp optimizer (Tieleman and Hinton, 2012), a learning rate of 0.001, 100 epochs, a batch size of 32, and early stopping with a patience of 5 epochs. Our loss function used a margin of 1.0.

[7] https://www.studystack.com/
[8] https://quizlet.com/
[9] http://allenai.org/

#	Model	P@1 Val	P@1 Test
1	Random	25	25
2	IR Baseline	47.2	47
3	IR^{++}	50.7**	36.35
4	Iyyer et al. (2015)	–	32.52
5	Khot et al. (2017)	–	46.17
6	Our approach w/o IR	50.54*	48.66
7	Our approach	**54.0****††	**53.3****†

Table 2: Performance on the AI2 Kaggle questions, measured by precision-at-one (P@1). *s indicate that the difference between the corresponding model and the IR baseline is statistically significant (* indicates $p < 0.05$ and ** indicates $p < 0.001$) and †s indicate significance compared to IR^{++}, All significance values were determined through a one-tailed bootstrap resampling test with 100,000 iterations.

Ablated Model	P@1 Val
IR^{++} + LO	53.4**††
IR^{++} + LO + lexDisc	53.6**††
Full Model (IR^{++} + LO + lexDisc + Emb)	**54.0****††

Table 3: Ablation of feature groups results, measured by precision-at-one (P@1) on validation data. Significance is indicated as in Table 2.

We experimented with burn-in, i.e., using the best justification chosen by the IR model for the first mini-batches, but found that models without burn-in performed better, indicating that the model benefited from being able to select its own justification.

6 Results

Rather than seeking to outperform all other systems at selecting the correct answer to a question, here we aimed to construct a system system that can produce substantially better justifications for why the answer choice is correct to a human user, without unduly sacrificing accuracy on the answer selection task. Accordingly, we evaluate our system both in terms of it's ability to correctly answer questions (Section 6.1), as well as provide high-quality justifications for those answers (6.2). Additionally, we perform an error analysis (Section 6.3), taking advantage of the insight the reranked justifications provide into what the model is learning.

6.1 QA Performance

We evaluated the accuracy of our system as well as the baselines on the held-out 800 set of test questions. Performance, measured in precision at 1 (P@1)(Manning et al., 2008), is shown in Table 2 for both the validation (i.e., cross validation on training) and test partitions. Because NNs are sensitive to initialization, each experimental result shown is the average performance across five runs, each using different random seeds.

The best performing baseline on the validation data was a model using only IR^{++} features (line 3), but its performance dropped substantially when evaluated on test due to the failure of several random seed initializations to learn. For this reason, we assessed significance of our model combinations with respect to both the IR baseline as well as the IR^{++} (indicated by * and †s, respectively).

Our full model that combines IR^{++}, lexical overlap, discourse, and embeddings-based features, has a P@1 of 53.3% (line 7), an absolute gain of 6.3% over the strong IR baseline despite using the same background knowledge.

Comparison to Previous Work: We compared our performance against another model that achieves state of the art performance on a different set of 8th grade science questions, TUPLE-INF(T+T') (Khot et al., 2017). TUPLEINF(T+T') uses Integer Linear Programming to find support for questions via tuple representations of KB sentences[10]. On our test data, TUPLEINF(T+T') achieves 46.17% P@1 (line 5). As this model is independent of an IR component, we compare its performance against our full system without the IR-based features (line 6), whose performance is 48.66% P@1, an absolute improvement of 2.49% P@1 (5.4% relative) despite our unstructured text inputs and the far smaller size of our knowledge base (three orders of magnitude).

Sachan et al. (2016) also tackle the AI2 Kaggle question set with an approach that learns alignments between questions and structured and semi-structured KB data. They use only the training questions (splitting them into training, validation, and testing partitions), supplemented by questions found in online study guides, and report an accuracy of 47.84%. By way of a loose comparison (since we are evaluating on different data partitions), our model has approximately 5% higher performance despite our simpler set of features and unstructured KB.

We also compare our model to our implementation of the basic Deep-Averaged Network (DAN) Architecture of Iyyer et al. (2015). We used the same 50-dimensional embeddings in both models, so with the reduced embedding dimension, we re-duced the size of each of the DAN dense layer to 50 as well. For simplicity, we also did not implement their word-dropout, a feature that they reported as providing a performance boost. Using this implementation, the performance on the test set was 31.50% P@1. To help with observed overfitting, we tried removing the dense layers and received a small boost to 32.52% P@1 (line 4). The lower performance of their model, which relies exclusively on latent representations of the data, underscores the benefit of including explicit features alongside latent features in a deep-learning approach for this domain[11].

In comparison to other systems that competed in the Kaggle challenge, our system comes in in 7th place out of 170 competitors (top 4%).[12] Compared with the systems which disclosed their methods, we use a subset of their corpora and substantially less hyperparameter tuning, and yet we achieve competitive results.

Feature Ablation: To evaluate the contribution of the individual feature groups, we additionally performed an ablation experiment (see Table 3). Each of our ablated models performed significantly better than the IR baseline on the validation set, including our simplest model, IR^{++}+LO.

6.2 Justification Performance

One of our key claims is that our approach addresses the related, but more challenging problem of performing *explainable* question answering, i.e., providing a high-quality, compelling justification for the chosen answer. To evaluate this claim, we evaluated a random set of 100 test questions that both the IR baseline and our full system answered correctly. For each question, we assessed the quality of each of the top five justifications. For IR, these were the highest-scoring retrieved documents, and for our system, these were

---

[10]Notably, one portion of the tuple KB used was constructed based on a different 8th grade question set than the one we use here.

[11]Another difference between our system and that of the DAN baseline is our usage of a text justification. However, we suspect this difference is not the source of the performance difference: see Jansen et al. (2017), where a variant of the DAN baseline that included an averaged representation of a justification alongside the averaged representations of the question and answer failed to show a performance increase.

[12]Based on the public leaderboard (https://www.kaggle.com/c/the-allen-ai-science-challenge/leaderboard). The best scoring submission had an accuracy of 59.38%. Note that for the systems that participated, this set served as *validation* while for us it was test, and thus it is likely that these scores are slightly overfitted to this dataset, but for us it was blind. As such this is a conservative comparison, and in reality the difference is likely to be smaller.

Question
Q: Scientists use ice cores to help predict the impact of future atmospheric changes on climate. Which property of ice cores do these scientists use?   **A:** The composition of ancient materials trapped in air bubbles

Rating	Example Justification
Good	Ice cores: cylinders of ice that scientist use to study trapped atmospheric gases and particles frozen with in the ice in air bubbles
Half	Ice core: sample from the accumulation of snow and ice over many years that have recrystallized and have trapped air bubbles from previous time periods
Topical	Vesicular texture formation [has] trapped air bubbles.
Off-topic	Physical change: change during which some properties of material change but ...

Table 4: Example justifications from the our model and their associated ratings.

Model	Good@1	Good@5	NDCG@5
IR Baseline	0.52	0.64	0.55
Our Approach	**0.61**	**0.74**	**0.62****

Table 5: Percentage of questions that have at least one *good* justification within the top 1 (Good@1) and the top 5 (Good@5) justifications, as well as the normalized discounted cumulative gain at 5 (NDCG@5) of the ranked justifications. Significance indicated as in Table 2.

the top-scoring justifications as re-ranked by our model. Each of these justifications was composed of a single sentence from our corpus, though a future version could use multi-sentence passages, or aggregate several sentences together, as in Jansen et al. (2017).

Following the methodology of Jansen et al. (2017), each justification received a rating of either *Good* (if the connection between the question and correct answer was fully covered), *Half* (if there was a missing link), *Topical* (if the justification was simply of the right topic), or *Off-Topic* (if the justification was completely unrelated to the question). Examples of each rating are provided in Table 4.

Results of this analysis are shown using three evaluation metrics in Table 5. The first two columns show the percentage of questions which had a *Good* justification at position 1 (Good@1), and within the top 5 (Good@5). Note that 61% of the top-ranked justifications from our system were rated as *Good* as compared to 52% from the IR baseline (a gain of 9%), despite the systems using identical corpora.

We also evaluated the justification ratings using normalized discounted cumulative gain at 5 (NDCG@5) (as formulated in Manning et al.

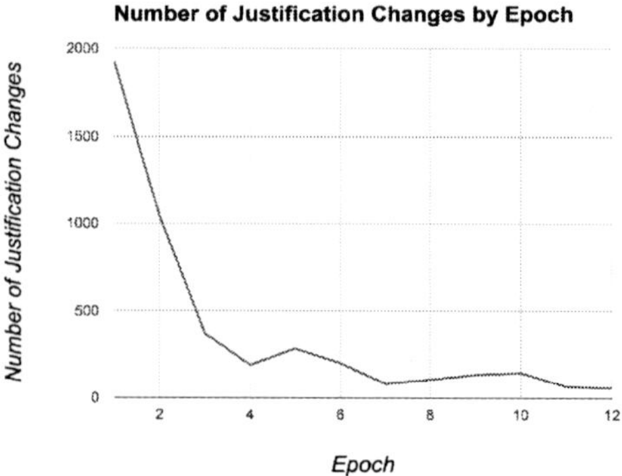

Figure 3: Number of questions for which our complete model chooses a new justification at each epoch during training. While this is for a single random seed, we see essentially identical graphs for each random initialization.

(2008), p.163), where we assigned *Good* justifications a gain of 3.0, *Half* a gain of 2.0, *Topical* a gain of 1.0, and *Off-Topic* a gain of 0.0. With this formulation, our system had a NDCG@5 of 0.62 while the IR baseline had a significantly lower NDCG@5 of 0.55 ($p < 0.001$), shown in the third column of Table 5.

Contribution of Learning to Rerank Justifications: The main assertion of this work is that through learning to rank answers and justifications for those answer candidates in an end-to-end manner, we both answer questions correctly and provide compelling justifications as to why the answer is correct. To confirm that this is the case, we also ran a version of our system that does not re-rank justifications, but uses the top-ranked justification retrieved by IR. This configuration dropped our performance on test to 48.7% P@1, a decrease of 4.6%, and we additionally lose all justification improvements from our system (see Section 6.2), demonstrating that learning this reranking is key to our approach.

Additionally, we tracked the number of times a new justification was chosen by the model as it trained. We found that our system converges to a stable set of justifications during training, shown in Figure 3.

6.3 Error Analysis

To better understand the limitations of our current system, we performed an error analysis of 30 incorrectly answered questions. We examined the top 5 justifications returned for both the correct and chosen answers. Notably, 50% of the questions analyzed had one or more good justifications

Error Type	Percent
Short justification/High lexical overlap	53.3%
Complex inference required	43.3%
Knowledge Base Noise	6.7%
Word order necessary	6.7%
Coverage	6.7%
Negation	3.3%
Other	6.7%

Table 6: Summary of the findings of the 30 question error analysis. Note that a given question may fall into more than one category.

Type:	**Short justification/High lexical overlap**
Question:	The length of time between night and day on Earth varies throughout the year. This time variance is explained primarily by ______.
Correct:	Earth 's angle of tilt *... the days are very short in the winter because the sun's rays hit the earth at an extreme angle ... due to the tilt of the earth's axis.*
Chosen:	Earth 's distance from the Sun *Is light year time or distance? Distance*

Table 7: Example of the system preferring a justification for which all the terms were found in either the question or answer candidate. (Justifications shown in italics)

in the top 5 returned by our system, but for a variety of reasons, summarized in Table 6, the system incorrectly ranked another justification higher.

The table shows that the most common form of error was the system's preference for short justifications with a large degree of lexical overlap with the question and answer choice itself, shown by the example in Table 7. The effect was magnified when the correct answer required more explanation to connect the question to the answer. This suggests that the system has learned that generally many unmatched words are indicative of an incorrect answer. While this may typically be true, extending the system to be able to prefer the *opposite* with certain types of questions would potentially help with these errors.

Type:	**Complex inference required**
Question:	Mr. Harris mows his lawn twice each month. He claims that it is better to leave the clippings on the ground. Which long term effect will this most likely have on his lawn?
Correct:	It will provide the lawn with needed nutrients.

Table 8: Example of a question for which complex inference is required. In order to answer the question, you would need to assemble the event chain: cut grass left on the ground → grass decomposes → decomposed material provides nutrients.

The second largest source of errors came from questions requiring complex inference (causal, process, quantitative, or model-based reasoning) as with the question shown in Table 8. This demonstrates not only the difficulty of the ques-

Type:	**Knowledge base noise**
Question:	If an object traveling to the right is acted upon by an unbalanced force from behind it the object will ______.
Correct:	speed up
Chosen	change direction *Unbalanced force: force that acts on an object that will change its direction*

Table 9: Example of a question for which knowledge base noise (here, in the form of over-generalization) was an issue.

tion set but also the need for systems that can robustly handle a variety of question types and their corresponding information needs.

Aside from these primary sources of error, there were some smaller trends: 7% of the incorrectly chosen answers actually had justifications which "validated" them due to noise in the knowledge base (e.g., the example shown in Table 9), 7% required word-order to answer (e.g., *mass divided by acceleration* vs. *acceleration divided by mass*), another 7% of questions suffered from lack of coverage of the question concept in the knowledge base, and 3% failed to appropriately handle negation (i.e., questions of the format *Which of the following are NOT ...*).

7 Conclusion

Here we propose an end-to-end question answering (QA) model that learns to correctly answer questions as well as provide compelling, human-readable justifications for its answers, despite not having access to labels for justification quality. We do this by using the question answering task as a form of distant supervision for learning justification re-ranking. We show that our accuracy and justification quality are significantly better than a strong IR baseline, while maintaining near state-of-the-art performance for the answer selection task as well.

Acknowledgments

We thank the Allen Institute for Artificial Intelligence for funding this work. Additionally, this work was partially funded by the Defense Advanced Research Projects Agency (DARPA) Big Mechanism program under ARO contract W911NF-14-1-0395. Dr. Mihai Surdeanu discloses a financial interest in Lum.ai. This interest has been disclosed to the University of Arizona Institutional Review Committee and is being managed in accordance with its conflict of interest policies.

References

Adam Berger, Rich Caruana, David Cohn, Dayne Freytag, and Vibhu Mittal. 2000. Bridging the lexical chasm: Statistical approaches to answer finding. In *Proceedings of the 23rd Annual International ACM SIGIR Conference on Research & Development on Information Retrieval*. Athens, Greece.

Antoine Bordes, Nicolas Usunier, Sumit Chopra, and Jason Weston. 2015. Large-scale simple question answering with memory networks. *CoRR* abs/1506.02075.

Antoine Bordes, Nicolas Usunier, Alberto García-Durán, Jason Weston, and Oksana Yakhnenko. 2013. Translating embeddings for modeling multi-relational data. In *NIPS*.

Danqi Chen, Jason Bolton, and Christopher D. Manning. 2016. A thorough examination of the cnn/daily mail reading comprehension task. In *Association for Computational Linguistics (ACL)*.

Danqi Chen and Christopher D Manning. 2014. A fast and accurate dependency parser using neural networks. In *Proceedings of the 2014 Conference on Empirical Methods in Natural Language Processing*. pages 740–750.

F. Chollet. 2015. Keras. https://github.com/fchollet/keras.

Peter Clark. 2015. Elementary school science and math tests as a driver for AI: take the Aristo challenge! In Blai Bonet and Sven Koenig, editors, *Proceedings of the Twenty-Ninth AAAI Conference on Artificial Intelligence, January 25-30, 2015, Austin, Texas, USA.*. AAAI Press, pages 4019–4021.

Peter Clark, Philip Harrison, and Niranjan Balasubramanian. 2013. A study of the knowledge base requirements for passing an elementary science test. In *Proceedings of the 2013 Workshop on Automated Knowledge Base Construction*. AKBC'13, pages 37–42.

Mark W Craven and Jude W Shavlik. 1996. Extracting tree-structured representations of trained networks. *Advances in neural information processing systems* pages 24–30.

Li Dong, Furu Wei, Ming Zhou, and Ke Xu. 2015. Question answering over freebase with multi-column convolutional neural networks. In *Proceedings of Association for Computational Linguistics*. pages 260–269.

Xiaodong He and David Golub. 2016. Character-level question answering with attention. In *Proceedings of the 2016 Conference on Empirical Methods in Natural Language Processing*. Association for Computational Linguistics, pages 1598–1607.

Karl Moritz Hermann, Tomáš Kočiský, Edward Grefenstette, Lasse Espeholt, Will Kay, Mustafa Suleyman, and Phil Blunsom. 2015. Teaching machines to read and comprehend. In *Advances in Neural Information Processing Systems (NIPS)*.

Mohit Iyyer, Varun Manjunatha, Jordan Boyd-Graber, and Hal Daumé III. 2015. Deep unordered composition rivals syntactic methods for text classification. In *Association for Computational Linguistics*.

Peter Jansen, Niranjan Balasubramanian, Mihai Surdeanu, and Peter Clark. 2016. What's in an explanation? characterizing knowledge and inference requirements for elementary science exams. In *Proceedings of COLING 2016, the 26th International Conference on Computational Linguistics: Technical Papers*. The COLING 2016 Organizing Committee, Osaka, Japan, pages 2956–2965.

Peter Jansen, Rebecca Sharp, Mihai Surdeanu, and Peter Clark. 2017. Framing qa as building and ranking intersentence answer justifications. *Computational Linguistics* .

Peter Jansen, Mihai Surdeanu, and Peter Clark. 2014. Discourse complements lexical semantics for non-factoid answer reranking. In *Proceedings of the 52nd Annual Meeting of the Association for Computational Linguistics (ACL)*.

Tushar Khot, Ashish Sabharwal, and Peter Clark. 2017. Answering complex questions using open information extraction. In *Proceedings of Association for Computational Linguistics (ACL)*.

Been Kim, Julie A. Shah, and Finale Doshi-Velez. 2015. Mind the gap: A generative approach to interpretable feature selection and extraction. In *NIPS*.

Tao Lei, Regina Barzilay, and Tommi S. Jaakkola. 2016. Rationalizing neural predictions. In *Proceedings of the 2016 Conference on Empirical Methods in Natural Language Processing*.

Benjamin Letham, Cynthia Rudin, Tyler H McCormick, David Madigan, et al. 2015. Interpretable classifiers using rules and bayesian analysis: Building a better stroke prediction model. *The Annals of Applied Statistics* 9(3):1350–1371.

O. Levy and Y. Goldberg. 2014. Dependency-based word embeddings. In *Proceedings of the 52nd Annual Meeting of the Association for Computational Linguistics (ACL)*. pages 302–308.

Jiwei Li, Xinlei Chen, Eduard Hovy, and Dan Jurafsky. 2016. Visualizing and understanding neural models in nlp. In *Proceedings of the 2016 Conference of the North American Chapter of the Association for Computational Linguistics: Human Language Technologies*. Association for Computational Linguistics, pages 681–691.

Christopher D. Manning, Prabhakar Raghavan, and Hinrich Schütze. 2008. *Introduction to Information Retrieval*. Cambridge University Press.

Christopher D Manning, Mihai Surdeanu, John Bauer, Jenny Finkel, Steven J Bethard, and David McClosky. 2014. The stanford corenlp natural language processing toolkit. In *Proceedings of 52nd Annual Meeting of the Association for Computational Linguistics: System Demonstrations*. pages 55–60.

Tomas Mikolov, Kai Chen, Greg Corrado, and Jeffrey Dean. 2013. Efficient estimation of word representations in vector space. In *Proceedings of the International Conference on Learning Representations (ICLR)*.

Tomas Mikolov, Martin Karafiat, Lukas Burget, Jan Cernocky, and Sanjeev Khudanpur. 2010. Recurrent neural network based language model. In *Proceedings of the 11th Annual Conference of the International Speech Communication Association (INTERSPEECH 2010)*.

Ankur P. Parikh, Oscar Täckström, Dipanjan Das, and Jakob Uszkoreit. 2016. A decomposable attention model for natural language inference. In *Proceedings of the 2016 Conference on Empirical Methods in Natural Language Processing*.

Marco Ribeiro, Sameer Singh, and Carlos Guestrin. 2016. "Why Should I Trust You?": Explaining the predictions of any classifier. In *Proceedings of the 2016 Conference of the North American Chapter of the Association for Computational Linguistics: Demonstrations*. Association for Computational Linguistics, pages 97–101.

Mrinmaya Sachan, Avinava Dubey, and Eric P Xing. 2016. Science question answering using instructional materials. In *The 54th Annual Meeting of the Association for Computational Linguistics*. page 467.

Aliaksei Severyn and Alessandro Moschitti. 2012. Structural relationships for large-scale learning of answer re-ranking. In *Proceedings of the 35th International ACM SIGIR Conference on Research and Development in Information Retrieval*.

Aliaksei Severyn and Alessandro Moschitti. 2013. Automatic feature engineering for answer selection and extraction. In *Proceedings of the Conference on Empirical Methods in Natural Language Processing (EMNLP)*.

Aliaksei Severyn and Alessandro Moschitti. 2015. Learning to rank short text pairs with convolutional deep neural networks. In *Proceedings of the 38th International ACM SIGIR Conference on Research and Development in Information Retrieval*.

Aliaksei Severyn, Massimo Nicosia, and Alessandro Moschitti. 2013. Learning adaptable patterns for passage reranking. In *Proceedings of the Seventeenth Conference on Computational Natural Language Learning (CoNLL)*.

Rebecca Sharp, Peter Jansen, Mihai Surdeanu, and Peter Clark. 2015. Spinning straw into gold: Using free text to train monolingual alignment models for non-factoid question answering. In *Proceedings of the 2015 Conference of the North American Chapter of the Association for Computational Linguistics: Human Language Technologies*. Association for Computational Linguistics, Denver, Colorado, pages 231–237.

Mihai Surdeanu, Thomas Hicks, and Marco A. Valenzuela-Escárcega. 2015. Two practical rhetorical structure theory parsers. In *Proceedings of the North American Chapter of the Association for Computational Linguistics (NAACL): Software Demonstrations*.

Ming Tan, Cicero dos Santos, Bing Xiang, and Bowen Zhou. 2016. Improved representation learning for question answer matching. In *Proceedings of the 54th Annual Meeting of the Association for Computational Linguistics (Volume 1: Long Papers)*. Association for Computational Linguistics, pages 464–473.

Theano Development Team. 2016. Theano: A Python framework for fast computation of mathematical expressions. *arXiv e-prints* abs/1605.02688.

Tijmen Tieleman and Geoffrey Hinton. 2012. Lecture 6.5-rmsprop: Divide the gradient by a running average of its recent magnitude. COURSERA: Neural Networks for Machine Learning.

Di Wang and Eric Nyberg. 2015. A long short-term memory model for answer sentence selection in question answering. In *Proceedings of the 53rd Annual Meeting of the Association for Computational Linguistics and the 7th International Joint Conference on Natural Language Processing (Volume 2: Short Papers)*. Association for Computational Linguistics, pages 707–712.

Mengqiu Wang and Christopher Manning. 2010. Probabilistic tree-edit models with structured latent variables for textual entailment and question answering. In *Proceedings of the 23rd International Conference on Computational Linguistics (Coling 2010)*. Coling 2010 Organizing Committee, pages 1164–1172.

Matthew D. Zeiler and Rob Fergus. 2014. *Visualizing and Understanding Convolutional Networks*, Springer International Publishing, Cham, pages 818–833.

Learning What is Essential in Questions

Daniel Khashabi[†]   **Tushar Khot**   **Ashish Sabharwal**   **Dan Roth**[†]

Univ. of Pennsylvania   Allen Institute for AI   Univ. of Pennsylvania

danielkh@cis.upenn.edu   tushark,ashishs@allenai.org   danroth@cis.upenn.edu

Abstract

Question answering (QA) systems are easily distracted by irrelevant or redundant words in questions, especially when faced with long or multi-sentence questions in difficult domains. This paper introduces and studies the notion of *essential question terms* with the goal of improving such QA solvers. We illustrate the importance of essential question terms by showing that humans' ability to answer questions drops significantly when essential terms are eliminated from questions. We then develop a classifier that reliably (90% mean average precision) identifies and ranks essential terms in questions. Finally, we use the classifier to demonstrate that the notion of question term essentiality allows state-of-the-art QA solvers for elementary-level science questions to make better and more informed decisions, improving performance by up to 5%.

We also introduce a new dataset of over 2,200 crowd-sourced essential terms annotated science questions.

1 Introduction

Understanding what a question is really about is a fundamental challenge for question answering systems that operate with a natural language interface. In domains with multi-sentence questions covering a wide array of subject areas, such as standardized tests for elementary level science, the challenge is even more pronounced (Clark, 2015). Many QA systems in such domains

derive significant leverage from relatively shallow Information Retrieval (IR) and statistical correlation techniques operating on large unstructured corpora (Kwok et al., 2001; Clark et al., 2016). Inference based QA systems operating on (semi-)structured knowledge formalisms have also demonstrated complementary strengths, by using optimization formalisms such as Semantic Parsing (Yih et al., 2014), Integer Linear Program (ILP) (Khashabi et al., 2016), and probabilistic logic formalisms such as Markov Logic Networks (MLNs) (Khot et al., 2015).

These QA systems, however, often struggle with seemingly simple questions because they are unable to reliably identify which question words are redundant, irrelevant, or even intentionally distracting. This reduces the systems' precision and results in questionable "reasoning" even when the correct answer is selected among the given alternatives. The variability of subject domain and question style makes identifying essential question words challenging. Further, essentiality is context dependent—a word like 'animals' can be critical for one question and distracting for another. Consider the following example:

> One way animals usually respond to a sudden drop in temperature is by (A) sweating (B) shivering (C) blinking (D) salivating.

A state-of-the-art optimization based QA system called TableILP (Khashabi et al., 2016), which performs reasoning by aligning the question to semi-structured knowledge, aligns only the word 'animals' when answering this question. Not surprisingly, it chooses an incorrect answer. The issue is that it does not recognize that "drop in temperature" is an essential aspect of the question.

Towards this goal, we propose a system that can assign an essentiality score to each term in the question. For the above example, our system gen-

† Most of the work was done when the first and last authors were affiliated with the University of Illinois, Urbana-Champaign.

Proceedings of the 21st Conference on Computational Natural Language Learning (CoNLL 2017), pages 80–89,
Vancouver, Canada, August 3 - August 4, 2017. ©2017 Association for Computational Linguistics

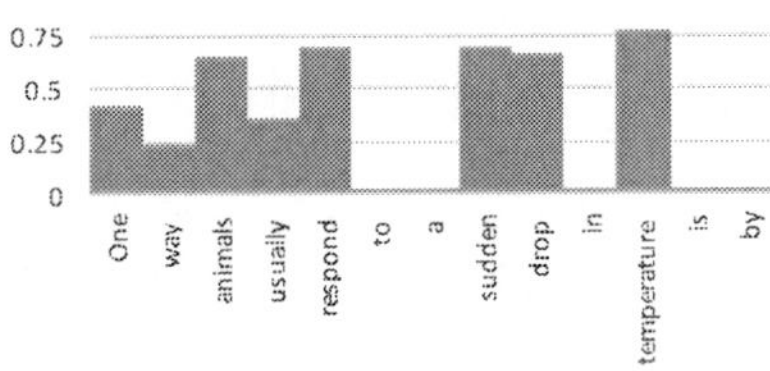

Figure 1: Essentiality scores generated by our system, which assigns high essentiality to "drop" and "temperature".

erates the scores shown in Figure 1, where more weight is put on "temperature" and "sudden drop". A QA system, when armed with such information, is expected to exhibit a more informed behavior.

We make the following contributions:

(A) We introduce the notion of *question term essentiality* and release a new dataset of 2,223 crowd-sourced essential term annotated questions (total 19K annotated terms) that capture this concept.[1] We illustrate the importance of this concept by demonstrating that humans become substantially worse at QA when even a few essential question terms are dropped.

(B) We design a classifier that is effective at predicting question term essentiality. The F1 (0.80) and per-sentence mean average precision (MAP, 0.90) scores of our classifier supercede the closest baselines by 3%-5%. Further, our classifier generalizes substantially better to unseen terms.

(C) We show that this classifier can be used to improve a surprisingly effective IR based QA system (Clark et al., 2016) by 4%-5% on previously used question sets and by 1.2% on a larger question set. We also incorporate the classifier in TableILP (Khashabi et al., 2016), resulting in fewer errors when sufficient knowledge is present for questions to be meaningfully answerable.

1.1 Related Work

Our work can be viewed as the study of an intermediate layer in QA systems. Some systems implicitly model and learn it, often via indirect signals from end-to-end training data. For instance, Neural Networks based models (Wang et al., 2016; Tymoshenko et al., 2016; Yin et al., 2016) implicitly compute some kind of *attention*. While this is intuitively meant to weigh key words in the question more heavily, this aspect hasn't been system-

[1] Annotated dataset and classifier available at `https://github.com/allenai/essential-terms`

atically evaluated, in part due to the lack of ground truth annotations.

There is related work on extracting *question type* information (Li and Roth, 2002; Li et al., 2007) and applying it to the design and analysis of end-to-end QA systems (Moldovan et al., 2003). The concept of term essentiality studied in this work is different, and so is our supervised learning approach compared to the typical rule-based systems for question type identification.

Another line of relevant work is sentence compression (Clarke and Lapata, 2008), where the goal is to minimize the content while maintaining grammatical soundness. These approaches typically build an internal importance assignment component to assign significance scores to various terms, which is often done using language models, co-occurrence statistics, or their variants (Knight and Marcu, 2002; Hori and Sadaoki, 2004). We compare against unsupervised baselines inspired by such importance assignment techniques.

In a similar spirit, Park and Croft (2015) use translation models to extract key terms to prevent semantic drift in query expansion.

One key difference from general text summarization literature is that we operate on questions, which tend to have different essentiality characteristics than, say, paragraphs or news articles. As we discuss in Section 2.1, typical indicators of essentiality such as being a proper noun or a verb (for event extraction) are much less informative for questions. Similarly, while the opening sentence of a Wikipedia article is often a good summary, it is the last sentence (in multi-sentence questions) that contains the most pertinent words.

In parallel to our effort, Jansen et al. (2017) recently introduced a science QA system that uses the notion of *focus words*. Their rule-based system incorporates grammatical structure, answer types, etc. We take a different approach by learning a supervised model using a new annotated dataset.

2 Essential Question Terms

In this section, we introduce the notion of *essential question terms*, present a dataset annotated with these terms, and describe two experimental studies that illustrate the importance of this notion—we show that when dropping terms from questions, humans' performance degrades significantly faster if the dropped terms are essential question terms.

Given a question q, we consider each non-stopword token in q as a candidate for being an essential question term. Precisely defining what is essential and what isn't is not an easy task and involves some level of inherent subjectivity. We specified *three broad criteria*: 1) altering an essential term should change the intended meaning of q, 2) dropping non-essential terms should not change the correct answer for q, and 3) grammatical correctness is not important. We found that given these relatively simple criteria, human annotators had a surprisingly high agreement when annotating elementary-level science questions. Next we discuss the specifics of the crowd-sourcing task and the resulting dataset.

2.1 Crowd-Sourced Essentiality Dataset

We collected 2,223 elementary school science exam questions for the annotation of essential terms. This set includes the questions used by Clark et al. (2016)[2] and additional ones obtained from other public resources such as the Internet or textbooks. For each of these questions, we asked crowd workers[3] to annotate essential question terms based on the above criteria as well as a few examples of essential and non-essential terms. Figure 2 depicts the annotation interface.

The questions were annotated by 5 crowd workers,[4] and resulted in 19,380 annotated terms. The Fleiss' kappa statistic (Fleiss, 1971) for this task was $\kappa = 0.58$, indicating a level of inter-annotator agreement very close to 'substantial'. In particular, all workers agreed on 36.5% of the terms and at least 4 agreed on 69.9% of the terms. We use the proportion of workers that marked a term as essential to be its annotated essentiality score.

On average, less than one-third (29.9%) of the terms in each question were marked as essential (i.e., score > 0.5). This shows the large proportion of distractors in these science tests (as compared to traditional QA datasets), further showing the importance of this task. Next we provide some insights into these terms.

We found that part-of-speech (POS) tags are not a reliable predictor of essentiality, making it difficult to hand-author POS tag based rules. Among

the proper nouns (NNP, NNPS) mentioned in the questions, fewer than half (47.0%) were marked as essential. This is in contrast with domains such as news articles where proper nouns carry perhaps the most important information. Nearly two-thirds (65.3%) of the mentioned comparative adjectives (JJR) were marked as essential, whereas only a quarter of the mentioned superlative adjectives (JJS) were deemed essential. Verbs were marked essential less than a third (32.4%) of the time. This differs from domains such as math word problems where verbs have been found to play a key role (Hosseini et al., 2014).

The best single indicator of essential terms, not surprisingly, was being a scientific term[5] (such as *precipitation* and *gravity*). 76.6% of such terms occurring in questions were marked as essential.

In summary, we have a term essentiality annotated dataset of 2,223 questions. We split this into train/development/test subsets in a 70/9/21 ratio, resulting in 483 test sentences used for per-question evaluation.

We also derive from the above an annotated dataset of 19,380 terms by pooling together all terms across all questions. Each term in this larger dataset is annotated with an essentiality score in the context of the question it appears in. This results in 4,124 test instances (derived from the above 483 test questions). We use this dataset for per-term evaluation.

2.2 The Importance of Essential Terms

Here we report a second crowd-sourcing experiment that validates our hypothesis that the question terms marked above as essential are, in fact, essential for understanding and answering the questions. Specifically, we ask: *Is the question still answerable by a human if a fraction of the essential question terms are eliminated?* For instance, the sample question in the introduction is unanswerable when "drop" and "temperature" are removed from the question: *One way animals usually respond to a sudden * in * is by ___?*

To this end, we consider both the annotated essentiality scores as well as the score produced by our trained classifier (to be presented in Section 3). We first generate candidate sets of terms to eliminate using these essentiality scores based on a threshold $\xi \in \{0, 0.2, \ldots, 1.0\}$: (a) **essential set**: terms with score $\geq \xi$; (b) **non-essential set**: terms

---

[2]These are the only publicly available state-level science exams. http://www.nysedregents.org/Grade4/Science/

[3]We use Amazon Mechanical Turk for crowd-sourcing.

[4]A few invalid annotations resulted in about 1% of the questions receiving fewer annotations. 2,199 questions received at least 5 annotations (79 received 10 annotations due to unintended question repetition), 21 received 4 annotations, and 4 received 3 annotations.

[5]We use 9,144 science terms from Khashabi et al. (2016).

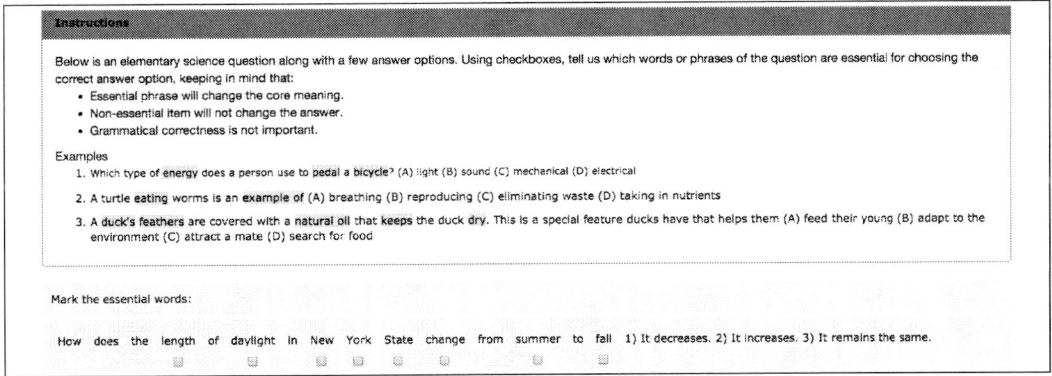

Figure 2: Crowd-sourcing interface for annotating essential terms in a question, including the criteria for essentiality and sample annotations.

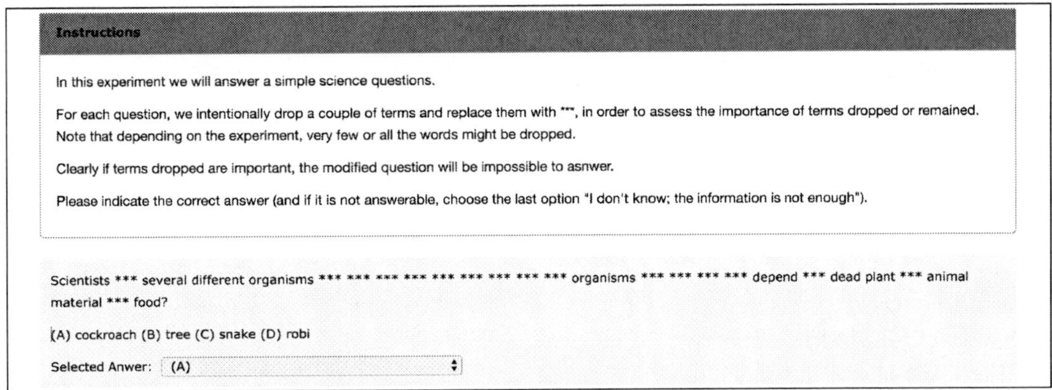

Figure 3: Crowd-sourcing interface for verifying the validity of essentiality annotations generated by the first task. Annotators are asked to answer, if possible, questions with a group of terms dropped.

with score $< \xi$. We then ask crowd workers to try to answer a question after replacing each candidate set of terms with "***". In addition to four original answer options, we now also include "I don't know. The information is not enough" (cf. Figure 3 for the user interface).[6] For each value of ξ, we obtain 5×269 annotations for 269 questions. We measure how often the workers feel there is sufficient information to attempt the question and, when they do attempt, how often do they choose the right answer.

Each value of ξ results in some fraction of terms to be dropped from a question; the exact number depends on the question and on whether we

use annotated scores or our classifier's scores. In Figure 4, we plot the average fraction of terms dropped on the horizontal axis and the corresponding fraction of questions attempted on the vertical axis. Solid lines indicate annotated scores and dashed lines indicate classifier scores. Blue lines (bottom left) illustrate the effect of eliminating essential sets while red lines (top right) reflect eliminating non-essential sets.

We make two observations. First, the solid blue line (bottom-left) demonstrates that dropping even a small fraction of question terms marked as essential dramatically reduces the QA performance of humans. E.g., dropping just 12% of the terms (with high essentiality scores) makes 51% of the questions unanswerable. The solid red line (top-right), on the other hand, shows the opposite trend for terms marked as not-essential: even after drop-

---

[6]It is also possible to directly collect essential term groups using this task. However, collecting such sets of essential terms would be substantially more expensive, as one must iterate over exponentially many subsets rather than the linear number of terms used in our annotation scheme.

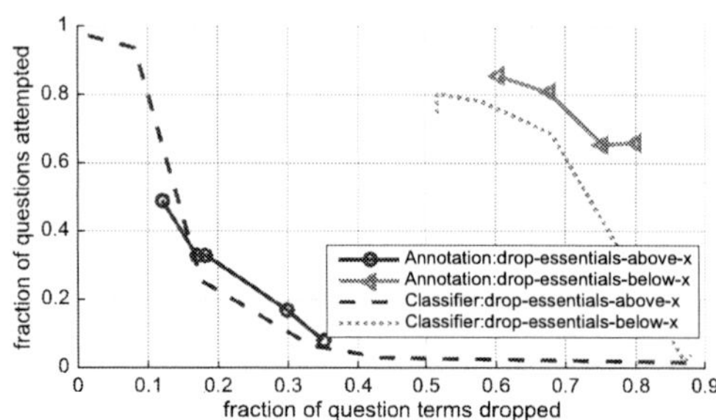

Figure 4: The relationship between the fraction of question words dropped and the fraction of the questions attempted (fraction of the questions workers felt comfortable answering). Dropping most essential terms (blue lines) results in very few questions remaining answerable, while least essential terms (red lines) allows most questions to still be answerable. Solid lines indicate human annotation scores while dashed lines indicate predicted scores.

ping 80% of such terms, 65% of the questions remained answerable.

Second, the dashed lines reflecting the results when using scores from our ET classifier are very close to the solid lines based on human annotation. This indicates that our classifier, to be described next, closely captures human intuition.

3 Essential Terms Classifier

Given the dataset of questions and their terms annotated with essential scores, is it possible to learn the underlying concept? Towards this end, given a question q , answer options a, and a question term q_l, we seek a classifier that predicts whether q_l is essential for answering q. We also extend it to produce an essentiality score $et(q_l, q, a) \in [0, 1]$.[7] We use the annotated dataset from Section 2, where real-valued essentiality scores are binarized to 1 if they are at least 0.5, and to 0 otherwise.

We train a linear SVM classifier (Joachims, 1998), henceforth referred to as **ET classifier**. Given the complex nature of the task, the features of this classifier include syntactic (e.g., dependency parse based) and semantic (e.g., Brown

cluster representation of words (Brown et al., 1992), a list of scientific words) properties of question words, as well as their combinations. In total, we use 120 types of features (cf. Appendix **??** of our Extended edition (Khashabi et al., 2017)).

Baselines. To evaluate our approach, we devise a few simple yet relatively powerful baselines.

First, for our supervised baseline, given (q_l, q, a) as before, we ignore q and compute how often is q_l annotated as essential in the entire dataset. In other words, the score for q_l is the proportion of times it was marked as essential in the annotated dataset. If the instance is never observer in training, we choose an arbitrary label as prediction. We refer to this baseline as *label proportion baseline* and create two variants of it: PROPSURF based on surface string and PROPLEM based on lemmatizing the surface string. For unseen q_l, this baseline makes a random guess with uniform distribution.

Our unsupervised baseline is inspired by work on sentence compression (Clarke and Lapata, 2008) and the PMI solver of Clark et al. (2016), which compute word importance based on co-occurrence statistics in a large corpus. In a corpus $\mathcal{C}$ of 280 GB of plain text (5×10^{10} tokens) extracted from Web pages,[8] we identify unigrams, bigrams, trigrams, and skip-bigrams from q and each answer option a_i. For a pair (x, y) of n-grams, their pointwise mutual information (PMI) (Church and Hanks, 1989) in $\mathcal{C}$ is defined as $\log \frac{p(x,y)}{p(x)p(y)}$ where $p(x, y)$ is the co-occurrence frequency of x and y (within some window) in $\mathcal{C}$. For a given word x, we find all pairs of question n-grams and answer option n-grams. MAXPMI and SUMPMI score the importance of a word x by max-ing or summing, resp., PMI scores $p(x, y)$ across all answer options y for q. A limitation of this baseline is its dependence on the existence of answer options, while our system makes essentiality predictions independent of the answer options.

We note that all of the aforementioned baselines produce real-valued confidence scores (for each term in the question), which can be turned into binary labels (essential and non-essential) by thresholding at a certain confidence value.

---

[7]The essentiality score may alternatively be defined as $et(q_l, q)$, independent of the answer options a. This is more suitable for non-multiple choice questions. Our system uses a only to compute PMI-based statistical association features for the classifier. In our experiments, dropping these features resulted in only a small drop in the classifier's performance.

[8]Collected by Charles Clarke at the University of Waterloo, and used previously by Turney (2013).

3.1 Evaluation

We consider two natural evaluation metrics for essentiality detection, first treating it as a binary prediction task at the level of individual terms and then as a task of ranking terms within each question by the degree of essentiality.

Binary Classification of Terms. We consider all question terms pooled together as described in Section 2.1, resulting in a dataset of 19,380 terms annotated (in the context of the corresponding question) independently as essential or not. The ET classifier is trained on the train subset, and the threshold is tuned using the dev subset.

	AUC	Acc	P	R	F1
MAXPMI [†]	0.74	0.67	0.88	0.65	0.75
SUMPMI [†]	0.74	0.67	0.88	0.65	0.75
PROPSURF	0.79	0.61	0.68	0.64	0.66
PROPLEM	0.80	0.63	0.76	0.64	0.69
ET Classifier	**0.79**	**0.75**	**0.91**	**0.71**	**0.80**

Table 1: Effectiveness of various methods for identifying essential question terms in the test set, including area under the PR curve (AUC), accuracy (Acc), precision (P), recall (R), and F1 score. ET classifier substantially outperforms all supervised and unsupervised (denoted with [†]) baselines.

For each term in the corresponding test set of 4,124 instances, we use various methods to predict whether the term is essential (for the corresponding question) or not. Table 1 summarizes the resulting performance. For the threshold-based scores, each method was tuned to maximize the F1 score based on the dev set. The ET classifier achieves an F1 score of 0.80, which is 5%-14% higher than the baselines. Its accuracy at 0.75 is statistically significantly better than all baselines based on the Binomial[9] exact test (Howell, 2012) at p-value 0.05.

As noted earlier, each of these essentiality identification methods are parameterized by a threshold for balancing precision and recall. This allows them to be tuned for end-to-end performance of the downstream task. We use this feature later when incorporating the ET classifier in QA systems. Figure 5 depicts the PR curves for various methods as the threshold is varied, highlighting that the ET classifier performs reliably at various recall points. Its precision, when tuned to optimize F1, is 0.91, which is very suitable for

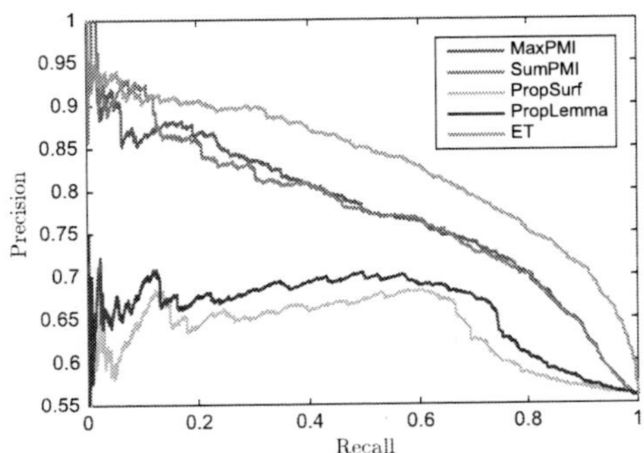

Figure 5: Precision-recall trade-off for various classifiers as the threshold is varied. ET classifier (green) is significantly better throughout.

	AUC	Acc	P	R	F1
MAXPMI [†]	0.75	0.63	0.81	0.65	0.72
SUMPMI [†]	0.75	0.63	0.80	0.66	0.72
PROPSURF	0.57	0.51	0.49	0.61	0.54
PROPLEM	0.58	0.49	0.50	0.59	0.54
ET Classifier	**0.78**	**0.71**	**0.88**	**0.71**	**0.78**

Table 2: Generalization to unseen terms: Effectiveness of various methods, using the same metrics as in Table 1. As expected, supervised methods perform poorly, similar to a random baseline. Unsupervised methods generalize well, but the ET classifier again substantially outperforms them.

high-precision applications. It has a 5% higher AUC (area under the curve) and outperforms baselines by roughly 5% throughout the precision-recall spectrum.

As a second study, we assess how well our classifier **generalizes to unseen terms**. For this, we consider only the 559 test terms that do not appear in the train set.[10] Table 2 provides the resulting performance metrics. We see that the frequency based supervised baselines, having never seen the test terms, stay close to the default precision of 0.5. The unsupervised baselines, by nature, generalize much better but are substantially dominated by our ET classifier, which achieves an F1 score of 78%. This is only 2% below its own F1 across all seen and unseen terms, and 6% higher than the second best baseline.

Ranking Question Terms by Essentiality. Next, we investigate the performance of the ET classifier as a system that ranks all terms within a question in the order of essentiality. Thus,

---

[9]Each test term prediction is assumed to be a binomial.

[10]In all our other experiments, test and train questions are always distinct but may have some terms in common.

System	MAP
MAXPMI [†]	0.87
SUMPMI [†]	0.85
PROPSURF	0.85
PROPLEM	0.86
ET Classifier	**0.90**

Table 3: Effectiveness of various methods for ranking the terms in a question by essentiality. [†] indicates unsupervised method. Mean-Average Precision (MAP) numbers reflect the mean (across all test set questions) of the average precision of the term ranking for each question. ET classifier again substantially outperforms all baselines.

unlike the previous evaluation that pools terms together across questions, we now consider each question as a unit. For the ranked list produced by each classifier for each question, we compute the average precision (AP).[11] We then take the mean of these AP values across questions to obtain the mean average precision (MAP) score for the classifier.

The results for the test set (483 questions) are shown in Table 3. Our ET classifier achieves a MAP of 90.2%, which is 3%-5% higher than the baselines, and demonstrates that one can learn to reliably identify essential question terms.

4 Using ET Classifier in QA Solvers

In order to assess the utility of our ET classifier, we investigate its impact on two end-to-end QA systems. We start with a brief description of the question sets.

Question Sets. We use three question sets of 4-way multiple choice questions.[12] REGENTS and AI2PUBLIC are two publicly available elementary school science question set. REGENTS comes with 127 training and 129 test questions; AI2PUBLIC contains 432 training and 339 test questions that subsume the smaller question sets used previously (Clark et al., 2016; Khashabi et al., 2016). REGTSPERTD set, introduced by Khashabi et al. (2016), has 1,080 questions obtained by automatically perturbing incorrect answer choices for 108 New York Regents 4th grade science questions.

We split this into 700 train and 380 test questions.

For each question, a solver gets a score of 1 if it chooses the correct answer and $1/k$ if it reports a k-way tie that includes the correct answer.

QA Systems. We investigate the impact of adding the ET classifier to two state-of-the-art QA systems for elementary level science questions. Let q be a multiple choice question with answer options $\{a_i\}$. The *IR Solver* from Clark et al. (2016) searches, for each a_i, a large corpus for a sentence that best matches the (q, a_i) pair. It then selects the answer option for which the match score is the highest. The inference based *TableILP Solver* from Khashabi et al. (2016), on the other hand, performs QA by treating it as an optimization problem over a semi-structured knowledge base derived from text. It is designed to answer questions requiring multi-step inference and a combination of multiple facts.

For each multiple-choice question (q, a), we use the ET classifier to obtain essential term scores s_l for each token q_l in q; $s_l = et(q_l, q, a)$. We will be interested in the subset ω of all terms T_q in q with essentiality score above a threshold ξ: $\omega(\xi; q) = \{l \in T_q \mid s_l > \xi\}$. Let $\overline{\omega}(\xi; q) = T_q \setminus \omega(\xi; q)$. For brevity, we will write $\omega(\xi)$ when q is implicit.

4.1 IR solver + ET

To incorporate the ET classifier, we create a parameterized IR system called IR + ET(ξ) where, instead of querying a (q, a_i) pair, we query $(\omega(\xi; q), a_i)$.

While IR solvers are generally easy to implement and are used in popular QA systems with surprisingly good performance, they are often also sensitive to the nature of the questions they receive. Khashabi et al. (2016) demonstrated that a minor perturbation of the questions, as embodied in the REGTSPERTD question set, dramatically reduces the performance of IR solvers. Since the perturbation involved the introduction of distracting incorrect answer options, we hypothesize that a system with better knowledge of what's important in the question will demonstrate increased robustness to such perturbation.

Table 4 validates this hypothesis, showing the result of incorporating ET in IR, as IR + ET($\xi = 0.36$), where ξ was selected by optimizing end-to-end performance on the training set. We observe a 5% boost in the score on REGTSPERTD, showing that incorporating the notion of essentiality makes

---

[11] We rank all terms within a question based on their essentiality scores. For any true positive instance at rank k, the precision at k is defined to be the number of positive instances with rank no more than k, divided by k. The average of all these precision values for the ranked list for the question is the *average precision*.

[12] Available at `http://allenai.org/data.html`

Dataset	Basic IR	IR + ET
REGENTS	59.11	**60.85**
AI2PUBLIC	57.90	**59.10**
REGTSPERTD	61.84	**66.84**

Table 4: Performance of the IR solver without (Basic IR) and with (IR + ET) essential terms. The numbers are solver scores (%) on the test sets of the three datasets.

the system more robust to perturbations.

Adding ET to IR also improves its performance on standard test sets. On the larger AI2PUBLIC question set, we see an improvement of 1.2%. On the smaller REGENTS set, introducing ET improves IRsolver's score by 1.74%, bringing it close to the state-of-the-art solver, TableILP, which achieves a score of 61.5%. This demonstrates that the notion of essential terms can be fruitfully exploited to improve QA systems.

4.2 TableILP solver + ET

Our essentiality guided query filtering helped the IR solver find sentences that are more relevant to the question. However, for TableILP an added focus on essential terms is expected to help only when the requisite knowledge is present in its relatively small knowledge base. To remove confounding factors, we focus on questions that are, in fact, answerable.

To this end, we consider three (implicit) requirements for TableILP to demonstrate reliable behavior: (1) the existence of relevant knowledge, (2) correct alignment between the question and the knowledge, and (3) a valid reasoning chain connecting the facts together. Judging this for a question, however, requires a significant manual effort and can only be done at a small scale.

Question Set. We consider questions for which the TableILP solver does have access to the requisite knowledge and, as judged by a human, a reasoning chain to arrive at the correct answer. To reduce manual effort, we collect such questions by starting with the correct reasoning chains ('support graphs') provided by TableILP. A human annotator is then asked to paraphrase the corresponding questions or add distracting terms, while maintaining the general meaning of the question. Note that this is done independent of essentiality scores. For instance, the modified question below changes two words in the question without affecting its core intent:

> **Original question:** A fox grows thicker fur as a season changes. This adaptation helps the fox to (A) find food(B) keep warmer(C) grow stronger(D) escape from predators
> **Generated question:** An animal grows thicker hair as a season changes. This adaptation helps to (A) find food(B) keep warmer(C) grow stronger(D) escape from predators

While these generated questions should arguably remain correctly answerable by TableILP, we found that this is often not the case. To investigate this, we curate a small dataset Q_R with 12 questions (cf. Appendix C of the extended version (Khashabi et al., 2017)) on each of which, despite having the required knowledge and a plausible reasoning chain, TableILP fails.

Modified Solver. To incorporate question term essentiality in the TableILP solver while maintaining high recall, we employ a *cascade* system that starts with a strong essentiality requirement and progressively weakens it.

Following the notation of Khashabi et al. (2016), let $x(q_l)$ be a binary variable that denotes whether or not the l-th term of the question is used in the final reasoning graph. We enforce that terms with essentiality score above a threshold ξ must be used: $x(q_l) = 1, \forall l \in \omega(\xi)$. Let TableILP+ET($\xi$) denote the resulting system which can now be used in a cascading architecture.

$$\boxed{\text{TableILP+ET}(\xi_1)} \;\rightarrow\; \boxed{\text{TableILP+ET}(\xi_2)} \;\rightarrow\; \cdots$$

where $\xi_1 < \xi_2 < \ldots < \xi_k$ is a sequence of thresholds. Questions unanswered by the first system are delegated to the second, and so on. The cascade has the same recall as TableILP, as long as the last system is the vanilla TableILP. We refer to this configuration as CASCADES($\xi_1, \xi_2, \ldots, \xi_k$).

This can be implemented via repeated calls to TableILP+ET(ξ_j) with j increasing from 1 to k, stopping if a solution is found. Alternatively, one can simulate the cascade via a single extended ILP using k new binary variables z_j with constraints: $|\omega(\xi_j)| * z_j \le \sum_{l \in \omega(\xi_j)} x(q_l)$ for $j \in \{1, \ldots, k\}$, and adding $M * \sum_{j=1}^{k} z_j$ to the objective function, for a sufficiently large constant M.

We evaluate CASCADES(0.4, 0.6, 0.8, 1.0) on our question set, Q_R. By employing essentiality information provided by the ET classifier, CASCADES corrects 41.7% of the mistakes made by vanilla TableILP. This error-reduction illustrates that the extra attention mechanism added to TableILP via the concept of essential question terms helps it cope with distracting terms.

5 Conclusion

We introduced the concept of essential question terms and demonstrated its importance for question answering via two empirical findings: (a) humans becomes substantially worse at QA even when a few essential question terms are dropped, and (b) state-of-the-art QA systems can be improved by incorporating this notion. While text summarization has been studied before, questions have different characteristics, requiring new training data to learn a reliable model of essentiality. We introduced such a dataset and showed that our classifier trained on this dataset substantially outperforms several baselines in identifying and ranking question terms by the degree of essentiality.

Acknowledgments

The authors would like to thank Peter Clark, Oyvind Tafjord, and Peter Turney for valuable discussions and insights.

This work is supported by DARPA under agreement number FA8750-13-2-0008. The U.S. Government is authorized to reproduce and distribute reprints for Governmental purposes notwithstanding any copyright notation thereon. The views and conclusions contained herein are those of the authors and should not be interpreted as necessarily representing the official policies or endorsements, either expressed or implied, of DARPA or the U.S. Government.

References

P. F. Brown, P. V. Desouza, R. L. Mercer, V. J. D. Pietra, and J. C. Lai. 1992. Class-based n-gram models of natural language. *Computational linguistics* 18(4):467–479.

K. W. Church and P. Hanks. 1989. Word association norms, mutual information and lexicography. In *27th Annual Meeting of the Association for Computational Linguistics*. pages 76–83.

P. Clark. 2015. Elementary school science and math tests as a driver for AI: take the Aristo challenge! In *29th AAAI/IAAI*. Austin, TX, pages 4019–4021.

P. Clark, O. Etzioni, T. Khot, A. Sabharwal, O. Tafjord, P. Turney, and D. Khashabi. 2016. Combining retrieval, statistics, and inference to answer elementary science questions. In *30th AAAI*.

J. Clarke and M. Lapata. 2008. Global inference for sentence compression: An integer linear programming approach. *Journal of Artificial Intelligence Research* 31:399–429.

J. L. Fleiss. 1971. Measuring nominal scale agreement among many raters. *Psychological bulletin* 76(5):378.

C. Hori and F. Sadaoki. 2004. Speech summarization: an approach through word extraction and a method for evaluation. *IEICE TRANSACTIONS on Information and Systems* 87(1):15–25.

Mohammad Javad Hosseini, Hannaneh Hajishirzi, Oren Etzioni, and Nate Kushman. 2014. Learning to solve arithmetic word problems with verb categorization. In *2014 EMNLP*. pages 523–533.

D. Howell. 2012. *Statistical methods for psychology*. Cengage Learning.

P. Jansen, R. Sharp, M. Surdeanu, and P. Clark. 2017. Framing qa as building and ranking intersentence answer justifications. *Computational Linguistics* .

T. Joachims. 1998. Text categorization with support vector machines: Learning with many relevant features. *Machine learning: ECML-98* pages 137–142.

D. Khashabi, T. Khot, A. Sabharwal, P. Clark, O. Etzioni, and D. Roth. 2016. Question answering via integer programming over semi-structured knowledge (extended version). In *Proc. 25th Int. Joint Conf. on Artificial Intelligence* (IJCAI).

D. Khashabi, T. Khot, A. Sabharwal, and D. Roth. 2017. Learning what is essential in questions (extended version).

T. Khot, N. Balasubramanian, E. Gribkoff, A. Sabharwal, P. Clark, and O. Etzioni. 2015. Exploring Markov logic networks for question answering. In *2015 EMNLP*. Lisbon, Portugal.

K. Knight and D. Marcu. 2002. Summarization beyond sentence extraction: A probabilistic approach to sentence compression. *Artificial Intelligence* 139(1):91–107.

C. Kwok, O. Etzioni, and D. S. Weld. 2001. Scaling question answering to the web. In *WWW*.

F. Li, X. Zhang, J. Yuan, and X. Zhu. 2007. Classifying what-type questions by head noun tagging. In *Proc. 22nd Int. Conf. on Comput. Ling.* (COLING).

X. Li and D. Roth. 2002. Learning question classifiers. In *Proceedings of the 19th International Conference on Computational Linguistics - Volume 1*. Association for Computational Linguistics, Stroudsburg, PA, USA, COLING '02, pages 1–7.

D. Moldovan, M. Paşca, S. Harabagiu, and M. Surdeanu. 2003. Performance issues and error analysis in an open-domain question answering system. *ACM Transactions on Information Systems (TOIS)* 21(2):133–154.

J. H. Park and W. B. Croft. 2015. Using key concepts in a translation model for retrieval. In *Proceedings of the 38th International ACM SIGIR Conference on Research and Development in Information Retrieval.* ACM, pages 927–930.

P. D. Turney. 2013. Distributional semantics beyond words: Supervised learning of analogy and paraphrase. *TACL* 1:353–366.

Kateryna Tymoshenko, Daniele Bonadiman, and Alessandro Moschitti. 2016. Convolutional neural networks vs. convolution kernels: Feature engineering for answer sentence reranking. In *HLT-NAACL.*

B. Wang, K. Liu, and J. Zhao. 2016. Inner attention based recurrent neural networks for answer selection. In *ACL.*

W.-t. Yih, X. He, and C. Meek. 2014. Semantic parsing for single-relation question answering. In *Proc. 52nd Annual Meeting of the Ass. for Comp. Linguistics* (ACL). pages 643–648.

W. Yin, S. Ebert, and H. Schütze. 2016. Attention-based convolutional neural network for machine comprehension. In *NAACL HCQA Workshop.*

Top-Rank Enhanced Listwise Optimization
for Statistical Machine Translation

Huadong Chen,[†] Shujian Huang,[†*] David Chiang,[‡] Xinyu Dai,[†] Jiajun Chen[†]
[†]State Key Laboratory for Novel Software Technology, Nanjing University
{chenhd, huangsj, daixinyu, chenjj}@nlp.nju.edu.cn
[‡]Department of Computer Science and Engineering, University of Notre Dame
dchiang@nd.edu

Abstract

Pairwise ranking methods are the basis of many widely used discriminative training approaches for structure prediction problems in natural language processing (NLP). Decomposing the problem of ranking hypotheses into pairwise comparisons enables simple and efficient solutions. However, neglecting the global ordering of the hypothesis list may hinder learning. We propose a listwise learning framework for structure prediction problems such as machine translation. Our framework directly models the entire translation list's ordering to learn parameters which may better fit the given listwise samples. Furthermore, we propose *top-rank enhanced* loss functions, which are more sensitive to ranking errors at higher positions. Experiments on a large-scale Chinese-English translation task show that both our listwise learning framework and top-rank enhanced listwise losses lead to significant improvements in translation quality.

1 Introduction

Discriminative training methods for structured prediction in natural language processing (NLP) aim to estimate the parameters of a model that assigns a score to each hypothesis in the (possibly very large) search space. For example, in statistical machine translation (SMT), the model assigns a score to each possible translation, and in syntactic parsing, the function assigns a score to each possible syntactic tree. Ideally, the model should assign scores that rank hypotheses according to their true quality. In this paper, we consider the problem of discriminative training for SMT.

Traditional SMT systems use log-linear models with only about a dozen features, such as translation probabilities and language model probabilities (Yamada and Knight, 2001; Koehn et al., 2003; Chiang, 2005; Liu et al., 2006). These models can be tuned by minimum error rate training (MERT) (Och, 2003), which directly optimizes BLEU using coordinate ascent combined with a global line search.

To enable training of modern SMT systems, which can have thousands of features or more, many research efforts have been made towards scalable discriminative training methods (Chiang et al., 2008; Hopkins and May, 2011; Bazrafshan et al., 2012). Most of these methods either define loss functions that push the model to correctly compare pairs of hypotheses, or use approximate optimization methods that effectively do the same. For practical reasons, only a subset of the pairs are considered; these pairs are selected by either sampling (Hopkins and May, 2011) or heuristic methods (Watanabe et al., 2007; Chiang et al., 2008).

But this pairwise approach neglects the global ordering of the list of hypotheses, which may lead to problems trying to learn good parameter values. Inspired by research in information retrieval (IR) (Cao et al., 2007; Xia et al., 2008), we propose to directly model the ordering of the whole translation list, instead of decomposing it into translation pairs.

Previous research has tried to integrate listwise methods into SMT, but almost all of them focus on the reranking task, which aims to rescore the fixed translation lists generated by a baseline system. They try to either use listwise approaches to training the reranking model (Li et al., 2013; Niehues et al., 2015) or replace the pointwise ranking function, i.e. the log-linear model, with a listwise ranking function by introducing listwise features (Zhang et al., 2016). In this paper, we

---

*Corresponding author.

90

Proceedings of the 21st Conference on Computational Natural Language Learning (CoNLL 2017), pages 90–99,
Vancouver, Canada, August 3 - August 4, 2017. ©2017 Association for Computational Linguistics

focus on listwise approaches that can learn better discriminative models for SMT. We present a listwise learning framework for tuning translation systems that uses two listwise ranking objectives originally developed for IR, ListNet (Cao et al., 2007) and ListMLE (Xia et al., 2008). But unlike standard IR problems, structured prediction problems usually have a huge search space, and at each training iteration, the list of search results can vary. The usual strategy is to form the union of all lists of search results, but this can lead to a "patchy" list that doesn't represent the full search space well. The listwise approaches always based on the permutation probability distribution over the list. Modeling the distribution over a "patchy" list, whose elements were generated by different parameters will affect listwise approaches' performance. To address this issue, we design an *instance-aggregating* method: Instead of treating the data as a fixed-size set of lists that each grow over time as new translations are added at each iteration, we treat the data as a growing set of lists; each time a sentence is translated, the k-best list of translations is added as a new list.

We also extend standard listwise training by considering the importance of different instances in the list. Based on the intuition that instances at the top may be more important for ranking, we propose *top-rank enhanced* loss functions, which incorporate a position-dependent cost that penalizes errors occurring at the top of the list more strongly.

We conduct large-scale Chinese-to-English translation experiments showing that our top-rank enhanced listwise learning methods significantly outperform other tuning methods with high dimensional feature sets. Additionally, even with a small basic feature set, our methods still obtain better results than MERT.

2 Background

2.1 Log-linear models

In this paper, we assume a log-linear model, which defines a scoring function on target translation hypotheses e, given a source sentence **f**:

$$Pr(\mathbf{e} \mid \mathbf{f}) = \frac{\exp s(\mathbf{e}, \mathbf{f})}{\sum_{\mathbf{e'}} \exp s(\mathbf{e'}, \mathbf{f})} \quad (1)$$

$$s(\mathbf{e}, \mathbf{f}) = \mathbf{w} \cdot \mathbf{h}(\mathbf{e} \mid \mathbf{f}) \quad (2)$$

where $\mathbf{h}(\mathbf{e} \mid \mathbf{f})$ is the feature vector and **w** is the feature weight vector.

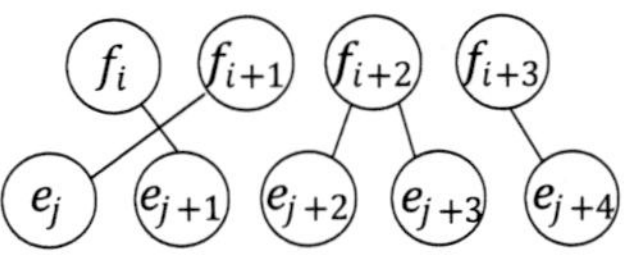

Figure 1: An example of word-phrase features for a phrase translation. The f_i and e_j represent the i-th in the source phrase and j-th word in the target phrase, respectively.

The process of training a SMT system includes both learning the sub-models, which are included in the feature vector **h**, and learning the weight vector **w**.

Then the decoding of SMT systems can be formulated as a search for the translation $\hat{\mathbf{e}}$ with the highest model score:

$$\hat{\mathbf{e}} = \arg\max_{\mathbf{e} \in \mathcal{E}} s(\mathbf{e}, \mathbf{f}) \quad (3)$$

where $\mathcal{E}$ is the set of all reachable hypotheses.

2.2 SMT Features

In this paper, we use a hierarchical phrase based translation system (Chiang, 2005). For convenient comparison, we divide features of SMT into the following three sets.

Basic Features: The basic features are those commonly used in hierarchical phrase based translation systems, including a language model, four translation model features, word, phrase and rule penalties, and penalties for unknown words, the glue rule and null translations.

Extended Features: Inspired by Chen et al. (2013), we manually group the parallel training data into 15 sets, according to their genre and origin. The translation models trained on each set are used as separate features. We also add an indicator feature for each individual training set to mark where the translation rule comes from. The extended features provide additional 60 translation model features and 16 indicator features, which is too many to be tuned with MERT.

Sparse Features: We use word-phrase pair features as our sparse features, which reflect the word-phrase correspondence in a hierarchical phrase (Watanabe et al., 2007). Figure 1 illustrates an example of word-phrase pair features for a phrase translation pair $f_i, ..., f_{i+3}$ and $e_j, ..., e_{j+4}$. Word-phrase pair features (f_i, e_{j+1}), (f_{i+1}, e_j), $(f_{i+2}, e_{j+2}e_{j+3})$, (f_{i+3}, e_{j+4}) will be fired for the translation rule with the given word alignment. In practice, these feature only fire when all the source and target words in the feature are both in the top 100 most frequent words.

2.3 Tuning via Pairwise Ranking

The beam search strategy for SMT decoding process makes it convenient to get a k-best translation list for each source sentence. Given a set of source sentences and their corresponding translation lists, the tuning problem could be regarded as a ranking task. Many recently proposed SMT tuning methods are based on the pairwise ranking framework (Chiang et al., 2008; Hopkins and May, 2011; Bazrafshan et al., 2012).

Pairwise ranking optimization (PRO) (Hopkins and May, 2011) is a commonly used tuning method. The idea of PRO is to sample pairs $(\mathbf{e}, \mathbf{e}')$ from the k-best list, and train a linear binary classifier to predict whether $eval(\mathbf{e}) > eval(\mathbf{e}')$ or $eval(\mathbf{e}) < eval(\mathbf{e}')$, where $eval(\cdot)$ is an extrinsic metric like BLEU. In this paper, we use sentence-level BLEU with add-one smoothing (Lin and Och, 2004).

The method gets a comparable BLEU score to MERT and MIRA (Chiang et al., 2008), and scales well on large feature sets. Other pairwise ranking methods employ similar procedures.

3 Listwise Learning Framework

Although ranking methods have shown their effectiveness in tuning for SMT systems (Hopkins and May, 2011; Watanabe, 2012; Dreyer and Dong, 2015), most proposed ranking approaches view tuning as pairwise ranking. These approaches decompose the ranking of the hypothesis list into pairs, which might limit the training method's ability to learn better parameters. To preserve the ranking information, we first formulate training as an instance of the listwise ranking problem. Then we propose a learning method based on the iterative learning framework of SMT tuning and further investigate the top-rank enhanced losses.

3.1 Training Objectives

3.1.1 The Permutation Probability Model

In order to directly model the translation list, we first introduce a probabilistic model proposed by Guiver and Snelson (2009). A ranking of a list of k translations can be thought of as a function π from $[1, k]$ to translations, where each $\pi(t)$ is the t-th translation candidate in the ranking. A scoring function z (which could be either the model score, s, or the BLEU score, $eval$) induces a probability distribution over rankings:

$$P_z(\pi) = \prod_{j=1}^{k} \frac{\exp z(\pi(j))}{\sum_{t=j}^{k} \exp z(\pi(t))}. \tag{4}$$

3.1.2 Loss Functions

Based on the probabilistic model above, the loss function can be defined as the difference between the distribution over the ranking according to $eval(\cdot)$ and $s(\cdot)$. Thus, we introduce the following two standard listwise losses.

ListNet: The ListNet loss is the cross entropy between the distributions calculated from $eval(\cdot)$ and $s(\cdot)$, respectively, over all permutations.

Due to the exponential number of permutations, Cao et al. (2007) propose a top-one loss instead. Given the function $eval(\cdot)$ and $s(\cdot)$, the top-one loss is defined as:

$$L_{\text{Net-T}} = -\sum_{j=1}^{k} P'_{eval}(\mathbf{e}_j) \, \log P'_s(\mathbf{e}_j)$$

$$P'_z(\mathbf{e}_j) = \frac{\exp z(\mathbf{e}_j)}{\sum_{i=1}^{k} \exp z(\mathbf{e}_i)}$$

where $\mathbf{e}_j$ is the j-th element in the k-best list, and $P'_z(\mathbf{e}_j)$ is the probability that translation $\mathbf{e}_j$ is ranked at the top by the function z.

ListMLE: The ListMLE loss is the negative log-likelihood of the permutation probability of the correct ranking π_{eval}, calculated according to $s(\cdot)$ (Xia et al., 2008):

$$L_{\text{MLE}} = -\log P_s(\pi_{eval})$$

$$= -\sum_{j=1}^{k} \log \frac{\exp s(\pi_{eval}(j))}{\sum_{t=j}^{k} \exp s(\pi_{eval}(t))}. \tag{5}$$

The training objective, which we want to minimize, is simply the total loss over all the lists in the tuning set.

3.2 Training with Instance Aggregating

Because there can be exponentially many possible translations of a sentence, it's only feasible to rank the k best translations rather than all of them; because the feature weights change at each iteration, we have a different k-best list to rank at each iteration. This is different from standard ranking problems in which the training instances stay the same each iteration.

Algorithm 1 MERT-like tuning algorithm

Require: Training sentences $\{\mathbf{f}\}$, maximum number of iterations I, randomly initialized model parameters $\mathbf{w}^0$.

1: **for** $i = 0$ to I **do**
2:    **for** source sentences $\mathbf{f}$ **do**
3:       Decode $\mathbf{f}$: $\mathcal{E}_{\mathbf{f}}^i = \text{KbestDecoder}(\mathbf{f}, \mathbf{w}^i)$
4:       $T \leftarrow T \cup \{\mathcal{E}_{\mathbf{f}}^i\}$
5:    **end for**
6:    Training: $\mathbf{w}^{i+1} = \text{Optimization}(T, \mathbf{w}^i)$
7: **end for**

Many previous tuning methods address this problem by merging the k-best list at the current iteration with the k-best lists at all previous iterations into a single list (Hopkins and May, 2011). We call this *k-best merging*. More formally, if $\mathcal{E}_{\mathbf{f}}^i$ is the k-best list of source sentence $\mathbf{f}$ at iteration i, then at each iteration, the model is trained on the set of lists:

$$\mathcal{E}_{\mathbf{f}} = \bigcup_{j=0}^{i} \mathcal{E}_{\mathbf{f}}^j$$

$$T = \{\mathcal{E}_{\mathbf{f}} \mid \forall \mathbf{f}\}$$

For each source sentence $\mathbf{f}$, T has only one training sample, which is a better and better approximation to the full hypothesis set of $\mathbf{f}$ as more iterations pass.

Unlike previous tuning methods, our tuning method focuses on the distribution over permutation of the whole list. Moreover, unlike with listwise optimization methods used in IR, the k-best list produced for a source sentence at one iteration can differ dramatically from the k-best list produced at the next iteration. Merging k-best lists across iterations, each of which represents only a tiny fraction of the full search space, will lead to a "patchy" list that may hurt the learning performance of the listwise optimization algorithms.

To address this challenge, we propose *instance aggregating*: instead of merging k-best lists across different iterations, we view the translation lists from different iterations as individual training instances:

$$T = \{\mathcal{E}_{\mathbf{f}}^j \mid \forall \mathbf{f}, 0 \leq j \leq i\}.$$

With this method, each source sentence $\mathbf{f}$ has i training instances at the i-th training iteration. In this way, we avoid "patchy" lists and obtain a better set of instances for tuning.

Algorithm 2 Listwise Optimization Algorithm

Require: Training instances T, model parameters $\mathbf{w}$, maximum number of epochs J, batch size b, number of batches B

1: **for** $j = 0$ to J **do**
2:    **for** $i = 0$ to B **do**
3:       Sample a minibatch of b lists from T without replacement
4:       Calculate loss function L
5:       Calculate gradient ∇L
6:       $\mathbf{w}_{t+1} = \text{AdaDelta}(\mathbf{w}_t, L, \Delta \mathbf{w})$
7:    **end for**
8: **end for**
9: $\mathbf{w} = \text{BestBLEU}([\mathcal{E}]_1^m)$

The above instance aggregating method can be used in a MERT-like iterative tuning algorithm as shown in Algorithm 1, which can be easily integrated into current open source systems. The two standard listwise losses can be easily optimized using gradient-based methods (Algorithm 2); both losses are convex, so convergence to a global optimum is guaranteed. The gradients of ListNET and ListMLE with respect to the parameters $\mathbf{w}$ for a single sentence are:

$$\frac{\partial L_{\text{Net-T}}}{\partial \mathbf{w}} = -\sum_{j=1}^{k} P'_{eval}(\mathbf{e}_j)\left(\frac{\partial s(\mathbf{e}_j)}{\partial \mathbf{w}}\right.$$
$$\left. - \sum_{j=1}^{k} \frac{\exp s(\mathbf{e}_j)}{\sum_{j'=1}^{k} \exp s(\mathbf{e}_{j'})} \frac{\partial s(\mathbf{e}_j)}{\partial \mathbf{w}}\right)$$

$$\frac{\partial L_{\text{MLE}}}{\partial \mathbf{w}} = -\sum_{j=1}^{k}\left(\frac{\partial s(\pi_{eval}(j))}{\partial \mathbf{w}}\right.$$
$$\left. - \sum_{t=j}^{k} \frac{\exp s(\pi_{eval}(t))}{\sum_{t'=j}^{k} \exp s(\pi_{eval}(t'))} \frac{\partial s(\pi_{eval}(t))}{\partial \mathbf{w}}\right)$$

For optimization, we use a mini-batch stochastic gradient descent (SGD) algorithm together with AdaDelta (Zeiler, 2012) algorithm to adaptively set the learning rate.

4   Top-Rank Enhanced Losses

In evaluating an SMT system, one naturally cares much more about the top-ranked results than the lower-ranked results. Therefore, we think that getting the ranking right at the top of a list is more relevant for tuning. Therefore, we should pay more attention to the top-ranked translations instead of forcing the model to rank the entire list correctly.

Position-dependent Attention: To do this, we assign a higher cost to ranking errors that occur at the top and a lower cost to errors at the bottom. To make the cost sensitive to position, we define it as:

$$c(j) = \frac{k - j + 1}{\sum_{t=1}^{k} t} \quad (6)$$

where j is the position in the ranking and k is the size of the list.

Based on this cost function, we propose simple top-rank enhanced listwise losses as extensions of both the ListNet loss and the ListMLE loss. The loss functions are defined as follows:

$$L_{\text{MLE-TE}} = -\sum_{j=1}^{k} c(j) \log \frac{\exp s(\pi_{eval}(j))}{\sum_{t=j}^{k} \exp s(\pi_{eval}(t))}$$

$$L_{\text{Net-TE}} = -\sum_{\forall \pi \in \Omega_k} P''_{eval}(\pi) \sum_{j=1}^{k} c(j) \log q_j(\pi)$$

$$q_j(\pi) = \frac{\exp z(\pi(j))}{\sum_{t=j}^{k} \exp z(\pi(t))}.$$

Along similar lines, Xia et al. (2008) also proposed a top-n ranking method, which assumes that only the correct ranking of top-n hypotheses is useful. Compared to our top-rank enhanced losses, it may be too harsh to discard information about the rest of the ordering altogether; our method retains the whole ordering but weights it by position.

5 Experiments and Results

5.1 Data and Preparation

We conduct experiments on a large scale Chinese-English translation task. The parallel data comes from LDC corpora[1], which consists of 8.2 million of sentence pairs. Monolingual data includes Xinhua portion of Gigaword corpus. We use NIST MT03 evaluation test data as the development set, MT02, MT04 and MT05 as the test set.

The Chinese side of the corpora is word segmented using ICTCLAS[2]. Word alignments of the

---

[1]The corpora include LDC2002E18, LDC2003E14, LDC2004E12, LDC2004T08, LDC2005T10 and LDC2007T09

[2]http://ictclas.nlpir.org/

Data	Usage	Sents.
LDC	TM train	8,260,093
Gigaword	LM train	14,684,074
MT03	train	919
MT02	test	878
MT04	test	1,788
MT05	test	1,082

Table 1: Experimental data and statistics.

parallel data are learned by running GIZA++ (Och and Ney, 2003) in both directions and refined under the "grow-diag-final-and" method. We train a 5-gram language model on the monolingual data with Modified Kneser-Ney smoothing(Chen and Goodman, 1999). Throughout the experiments, our translation system is an in-house implementation of the hierarchical phrase-based translation system (Chiang, 2005). The translation quality is evaluated by 4-gram case-insensitive BLEU (Papineni et al., 2002). Statistical significance testing between systems is conducted by bootstrap resampling implemented by Clark et al. (2011).

5.2 Tuning Settings

We build baselines for extended and sparse feature sets with two different tuning methods. First, we tune with PRO (Hopkins and May, 2011). As reported by Cherry and Foster (2012), it's hard to find the setting that performs well in general. We use MegaM version (Daumé III, 2004) with 30 iterations for basic feature set and 100 iterations for extended and sparse feature sets. Second, we run the k-best batch MIRA (KB-MIRA) which shows comparable results with online version of MIRA (Cherry and Foster, 2012; Green et al., 2013). In our experiments, we run KB-MIRA with standard settings in Moses[3]. For the basic feature set, the baseline is tuned with MERT (Och, 2003).

For all our listwise tuning methods, we set batch size to 10. In our experiments, we can't find a epoch size perform well in general, so we set epoch size to 100 for ListMLE with basic features, 200 for ListMLE with extended and sparse features, and 300 for ListNet. These values are set to achieve the best performance on the development set.

We set beam size to 20 throughout our experiments unless otherwise noted. Following Clark et al. (2011), we run the same training procedure 3 times and present the average results for stability. All tuning methods are executed for 40 iter-

---

[3]http://www.statmt.org/moses/

Methods	MT02	MT04	MT05	AVG
Net_m	40.36	38.30	37.93	38.86(+0.00)
ListNet	40.75	38.69	38.31	39.25(+0.39)
MLE_m	39.82	37.88	37.65	38.45(+0.00)
ListMLE	40.40	38.21	38.04	38.88(+0.43)

Table 2: The comparison of instances aggregating and k-best merging on the extended feature set.(Net_m and MLE_m denote ListNet and ListMLE with k-best merging respectively.)

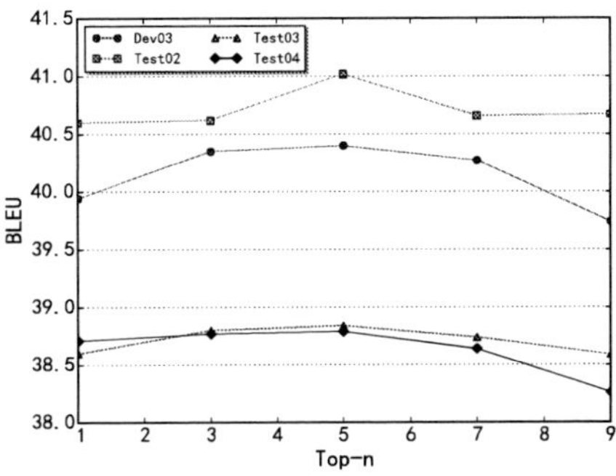

Figure 2: Effect of different n for Top-n ListMLE. We investigate the effect on the extended feature set.

ations of the outer loop and returned the weights that achieve the best development BLEU scores. For all tuning methods on sparse feature set, we use the weight vector tuned by PRO on the extended feature set as initial weights.

5.3 Experiments of Listwise Learning Framework

We first investigate the effectiveness of our instance aggregating training procedure. The results are presented in Table 2. The table compare training with instance aggregating and k-best merging. As the result suggested, with the instance aggregating method, the performance improves on both listwise tuning approaches. For the rest of this paper, we use the instance aggregating as standard setting for listwise tuning approaches.

To verify the performance of our proposed listwise learning framework, we first compare systems with standard listwise losses to the baseline systems. The first four rows in Table 3 show the results. ListNet can outperform PRO by 0.55 BLEU score and 0.26 BLEU score on extended feature set and sparse feature set, respectively. Its main reason is that our listwise methods can obtain structured order information when we take com-

plete translation list as instance.

We also observe that ListMLE can only get a modest performance compare to ListNet. We think the objective function of standard ListMLE which forces the whole list ranking in a correct order is too hard. ListNet mainly benefits from its top one permutation probability which only concerns the permutation with the best object ranked first.

5.4 Effect of Top-rank Enhanced Losses

To verify our assumption that the correct rank in the top portion of a list is more informative, we conduct this set of experiments. Figure 2 shows the results of top-n ListMLE with different n. Compared to ListMLE in Table 2, we find top-n ListMLE can make significant improvements, which means that the top rank is more important. We can observe an improvement in all test sets when we set n from 1 to 5, but when we further increase n, the results dropped. This situation indicates that the correct ranking at the top of the list is more informative and forcing the model to rank the bottom correctly as important as the top will sacrifice the ability to guide better search.

In Table 3, top-5 ListMLE which only aims to rank the top five translations correctly can outperform the baseline and standard ListMLE. With our position-dependent attention, the top-rank enhanced ListMLE can make further improvement over the baseline system(+1.07 and +0.73 on extended and sparse feature sets, respectively.) and achieves the best performance.

The top-n loss might be too loose as an approximation of the measure of BLEU. Compared to top-n ListMLE, our top-rank enhanced ListMLE can further utilize the different portions of the list by different weights. To verify the claim, we further examined the learning processes of the two losses. For simplicity, the experiment is conducted on a translation list generated by random parameters. The results are shown in Figure 3. We can see that our top-rank enhanced loss almost completely inversely correlates with BLEU after iteration 70. In contrast, after iteration 150, although top-5 loss is still decreasing, BLEU starts to drop.

Due to the high computation cost of ListNet, we only perform the top-rank enhanced ListMLE in this paper. Our preliminary experiments indicate that the performance of ListNet can be further improved with a top-2 loss. We think our top-rank

Method	Extended Features				Sparse Features			
	MT02	MT04	MT05	AVG	MT02	MT04	MT05	AVG
PRO	40.30	38.12	37.69	38.70(+0.00)	40.63	38.46	38.24	39.11(+0.00)
KB-MIRA	40.48	37.71	37.37	38.52(-0.18)	40.67	38.48	38.21	39.12(+0.01)
ListNet	**40.75**[*]	**38.69**[+]	**38.31**[*]	**39.25(+0.55)**	**40.91**[*]	**38.77**[*]	**38.42**	**39.37(+0.26)**
ListMLE	40.40	38.21	38.04	38.88(+0.18)	40.63	38.68	38.24	39.18(+0.07)
ListMLE-T5	41.02[*]	38.84[+]	38.79[+]	39.55(+0.85)	41.12[*]	38.91[*]	38.89[*]	39.64(+0.53)
ListMLE-TE	**41.15**[+]	**39.01**[+]	**39.16**[+]	**39.77(+1.07)**	**41.25**[+]	**39.00**[+]	**39.27**[+]	**39.84(+0.73)**

Table 3: BLEU4 in percentage for comparing of baseline systems and systems with listwise losses. [+], [*] marks results that are significant better than the baseline system with $p < 0.01$ and $p < 0.05$. (ListMLE-T5 and ListMLE-TE refer to top-5 LisMLE and our top-rank enhanced ListMLE, respectively.)

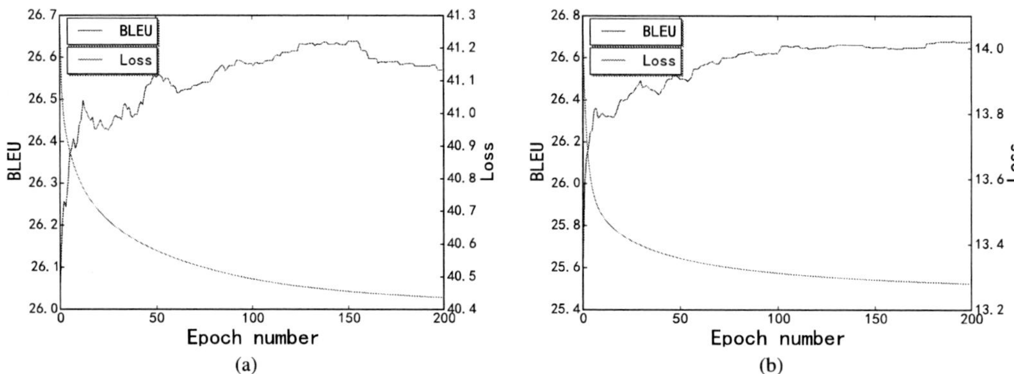

Figure 3: Listwise losses v.s. BLEU in (a) top-5 ListMLE and (b) top-rank enhanced ListMLE

Methods	MT02	MT04	MT05	AVG
PRO	40.90	38.84	38.64	39.64(+0.00)
KB-MIRA	41.09	38.49	38.62	39.40(-0.06)
ListNet	41.49[+]	39.25[*]	39.17[*]	39.97(+0.51)
ListMLE-T5	41.26[*]	39.63[+]	39.32[*]	40.07(+0.61)
ListMLE-TE	**41.85**[+]	**39.96**[+]	**39.88**[+]	**40.56(+1.10)**

Table 4: Comparison of baselines and listwise approaches with a larger k-best list on extended feature set.

enhanced method is also useful for ListNet, but due to its computational demands it needs to be further investigated.

5.5 Impact of the Size of Candidate Lists

Our listwise tuning methods directly model the order of the translation list, it is clear that the choice of the translation list size k has an impact on our methods. A larger candidate list size may result in the availability of more information during tuning. In order to verify our tuning methods' capability of handling the larger translation list, we increase k from 20 to 100. The comparison results are shown in Table 4. With a larger size k, our tuning methods also perform better than baselines. For List-

Net and top-5 ListMLE, we observe that the improvements over baseline is smaller than size 20. This results show that the order information loss caused by directly drop the bottom is aggravated with larger list size. However, our top-rank enhanced method still get a slight better result than size 20 and significant improvement over baseline by 1.1 BLEU score. This indicate that our top-rank enhanced method is more stable and can still effectively exploit the larger size translation list.

5.6 Performance on Basic Feature Set

Since the effectiveness of high dimensional feature set, recent work pays more attention to this scenario. Although previous discriminative tuning methods can effectively handle high dimensional feature set, MERT is still the dominant tuning method for basic features. Here, we investigate our top-rank enhanced tuning methods' capability of handling basic feature set. Table 5 summarizes the comparison results. Firstly, we observe that ListNet and ListMLE can perform comparable with MERT. With our top-ranked enhanced method, we can get a better performance than

Methods	MT02	MT04	MT05	AVG
MERT	37.72	37.13	36.77	37.21(+0.00)
PRO	37.85	37.21	36.68	37.24(+0.03)
KB-MIRA	37.97	37.28	36.58	37.28(+0.07)
ListNet	37.71	37.47*	36.78	37.32(+0.11)
ListMLE	37.54	**37.54**	36.65	37.24(+0.03)
ListMLE-T5	37.90	37.32	36.84	37.35(+0.14)
ListMLE-TE	**38.03**	37.49*	**36.85**	**37.46(+0.25)**

Table 5: Comparison of baseline and liswise approaches on basic feature set.

MERT by 0.25 BLEU score. These results show that our top-ranked enhanced tuning method can learn more informations of translation list even with a basic feature set.

6 Related Work

The ranking problem is well studied in IR community. There are many methods been proposed, including pointwise (Nallapati, 2004), pairwise (Herbrich et al., 1999; Burges et al., 2005) and listwise (Cao et al., 2007; Xia et al., 2008) algorithms. Experiment results show that listwise methods deliver better performance than pointwise and pairwise methods in general (Liu, 2010).

Most NLP researches take ranking as an extra step after searching from its output space (Charniak and Johnson, 2005; Collins and Terry Koo, 2005; Duh, 2008). In SMT research, listwise approaches also have been employed for the reranking tasks. For example, Li et al. (2013) utilized two listwise approaches to rerank the translation outputs and achieved the best segment-level correlation with human judgments. Niehues et al. (2015) employed ListNet to rescore the k-best translations, which significantly outperforms MERT, KB-MIRA and PRO. Zhang et al. (2016) viewed the log-linear model as a pointwise ranking function and shifted it to listwise ranking function by introducing listwise features and outperformed the log-linear model. Compared to these efforts, our method takes a further step by integrating listwise ranking methods into the iterative training.

There are also some researches use ranking methods for tuning to guide better search. In SMT, previous attempts on using ranking as a tuning methods usually perform pairwise comparisons on a subset of translation pairs (Chiang et al., 2008; Hopkins and May, 2011; Watanabe, 2012; Bazrafshan et al., 2012; Guzmán et al., 2015). Dreyer and Dong (2015) even took all translation pairs of the k-best list as training instances, which only ob-

tained a comparable result with PRO and the implementation is more complicate. In this paper, we model the entire list as a whole unit, and propose training objectives that are sensitive to different parts of the list.

7 Conclusion

In this paper, we propose a listwise learning framework for statistical machine translation. In order to adapt listwise approaches, we use an iterative training framework in which instances from different iterations are aggregated into the training set. To emphasize the top order of the list, we further propose top-rank enhanced listwise learning losses. Compared to previous efforts in SMT tuning, our method directly models the order information of the complete translation list. Experiments show our method could lead to significant improvements of translation quality in different feature sets and beam size.

Our current work focuses on the traditional SMT task. For future work, it will be interesting to integrate our methods to modern neural machine translation systems or other structure prediction problems. It may also be interesting to explore more methods on listwise tuning framework, such as investigating different methods to enhance top order of translation list directly w.r.t a given evaluation metric.

Acknowledgments

The authors would like to thank the anonymous reviewers for their valuable comments. This work is supported by the National Science Foundation of China (No. 61672277, 61300158 and 61472183). Part of Huadong Chen's contribution was made while visiting University of Notre Dame. His visit was supported by the joint PhD program of China Scholarship Council.

References

Marzieh Bazrafshan, Tagyoung Chung, and Daniel Gildea. 2012. Tuning as linear regression. In *Proceedings of the 2012 Conference of the North American Chapter of the Association for Computational Linguistics: Human Language Technologies*. Association for Computational Linguistics, pages 543–547. http://aclweb.org/anthology/N12-1062.

Chris Burges, Tal Shaked, Erin Renshaw, Ari Lazier, Matt Deeds, Nicole Hamilton, and Greg Hullender. 2005. Learning to rank using gradient descent. In *Proceedings of the 22Nd International Conference on Machine Learning*. ACM, New York, NY, USA, ICML '05, pages 89–96. https://doi.org/10.1145/1102351.1102363.

Zhe Cao, Tao Qin, Tie-Yan Liu, Ming-Feng Tsai, and Hang Li. 2007. Learning to rank: From pairwise approach to listwise approach. In *Proceedings of the 24th International Conference on Machine Learning*. ACM, New York, NY, USA, ICML '07, pages 129–136. https://doi.org/10.1145/1273496.1273513.

Eugene Charniak and Mark Johnson. 2005. Coarse-to-fine n-best parsing and maxent discriminative reranking. In *Proceedings of the 43rd Annual Meeting of the Association for Computational Linguistics (ACL'05)*. Association for Computational Linguistics, pages 173–180. http://aclweb.org/anthology/P05-1022.

Boxing Chen, Roland Kuhn, and George Foster. 2013. Vector space model for adaptation in statistical machine translation. In *Proceedings of the 51st Annual Meeting of the Association for Computational Linguistics (Volume 1: Long Papers)*. Association for Computational Linguistics, pages 1285–1293. http://aclweb.org/anthology/P13-1126.

Stanley F Chen and Joshua Goodman. 1999. An empirical study of smoothing techniques for language modeling. *Computer Speech & Language* 13(4):359–394.

Colin Cherry and George Foster. 2012. Batch tuning strategies for statistical machine translation. In *Proceedings of the 2012 Conference of the North American Chapter of the Association for Computational Linguistics: Human Language Technologies*. Association for Computational Linguistics, pages 427–436. http://aclweb.org/anthology/N12-1047.

David Chiang. 2005. A hierarchical phrase-based model for statistical machine translation. In *Proceedings of the 43rd Annual Meeting of the Association for Computational Linguistics (ACL'05)*. Association for Computational Linguistics, pages 263–270. http://aclweb.org/anthology/P05-1033.

David Chiang, Yuval Marton, and Philip Resnik. 2008. Online large-margin training of syntactic and structural translation features. In *Proceedings of the 2008 Conference on Empirical Methods in Natural Language Processing*. Association for Computational Linguistics, pages 224–233. http://aclweb.org/anthology/D08-1024.

H. Jonathan Clark, Chris Dyer, Alon Lavie, and A. Noah Smith. 2011. Better hypothesis testing for statistical machine translation: Controlling for optimizer instability. In *Proceedings of the 49th Annual Meeting of the Association for Computational Linguistics: Human Language Technologies*. Association for Computational Linguistics, pages 176–181. http://aclweb.org/anthology/P11-2031.

Collins and Michael Terry Koo. 2005. Discriminative reranking for natural language parsing. *Computational Linguistics, Volume 31, Number 1, March 2005* http://aclweb.org/anthology/J05-1003.

Hal Daumé III. 2004. Notes on CG and LM-BFGS optimization of logistic regression.

Markus Dreyer and Yuanzhe Dong. 2015. Apro: All-pairs ranking optimization for mt tuning. In *Proceedings of the 2015 Conference of the North American Chapter of the Association for Computational Linguistics: Human Language Technologies*. Association for Computational Linguistics, pages 1018–1023. https://doi.org/10.3115/v1/N15-1106.

Kevin Duh. 2008. Ranking vs. regression in machine translation evaluation. In *Proceedings of the Third Workshop on Statistical Machine Translation*. Association for Computational Linguistics, Stroudsburg, PA, USA, StatMT '08, pages 191–194. http://dl.acm.org/citation.cfm?id=1626394.1626425.

Spence Green, Sida Wang, Daniel Cer, and D. Christopher Manning. 2013. Fast and adaptive online training of feature-rich translation models. In *Proceedings of the 51st Annual Meeting of the Association for Computational Linguistics (Volume 1: Long Papers)*. Association for Computational Linguistics, pages 311–321. http://aclweb.org/anthology/P13-1031.

John Guiver and Edward Snelson. 2009. Bayesian inference for plackett-luce ranking models. In *Proceedings of the 26th Annual International Conference on Machine Learning*. ACM, New York, NY, USA, ICML '09, pages 377–384. https://doi.org/10.1145/1553374.1553423.

Francisco Guzmán, Preslav Nakov, and Stephan Vogel. 2015. Analyzing optimization for statistical machine translation: Mert learns verbosity, pro learns length. In *Proceedings of the Nineteenth Conference on Computational Natural Language Learning*. Association for Computational Linguistics, Beijing, China, pages 62–72. http://www.aclweb.org/anthology/K15-1007.

Ralf Herbrich, Thore Graepel, and Klaus Obermayer. 1999. Support vector learning for ordinal regression. In *Artificial Neural Networks, 1999. ICANN 99. Ninth International Conference on (Conf. Publ. No. 470)*. IET, volume 1, pages 97–102.

Mark Hopkins and Jonathan May. 2011. Tuning as ranking. In *Proceedings of the 2011 Conference on Empirical Methods in Natural Language Processing*. Association for Computational Linguistics, pages 1352–1362. http://aclweb.org/anthology/D11-1125.

Philipp Koehn, Franz J. Och, and Daniel Marcu. 2003. Statistical phrase-based translation. In *Proceedings of the 2003 Human Language Technology Conference of the North American Chapter*

of the Association for Computational Linguistics.
http://aclweb.org/anthology/N03-1017.

Maoxi Li, Aiwen Jiang, and Mingwen Wang. 2013.
Listwise approach to learning to rank for automatic
evaluation of machine translation. *Proceedings of
the XIV Machine Translation Summit* .

Chin-Yew Lin and Franz Josef Och. 2004. ORANGE:
A method for evaluating automatic evaluation metrics for machine translation. In *Proceedings of
the 20th International Conference on Computational
Linguistics.*

Tie-Yan Liu. 2010. Learning to rank for information retrieval. In *Proceedings of the 33rd International ACM SIGIR Conference on Research
and Development in Information Retrieval.* ACM,
New York, NY, USA, SIGIR '10, pages 904–904.
https://doi.org/10.1145/1835449.1835676.

Yang Liu, Qun Liu, and Shouxun Lin. 2006. Tree-
to-string alignment template for statistical machine translation. In *Proceedings of the 21st
International Conference on Computational Linguistics and 44th Annual Meeting of the Association for Computational Linguistics.* Association for Computational Linguistics, pages 609–616.
http://aclweb.org/anthology/P06-1077.

Ramesh Nallapati. 2004. Discriminative models for information retrieval. In *Proceedings of the 27th Annual International ACM SIGIR Conference on Research and Development in Information Retrieval.*
ACM, New York, NY, USA, SIGIR '04, pages 64–
71. https://doi.org/10.1145/1008992.1009006.

Jan Niehues, Quoc-Khanh DO, Alexandre Allauzen,
and Alex Waibel. 2015. Listnet-based mt rescoring. In *Proceedings of the Tenth Workshop
on Statistical Machine Translation.* Association
for Computational Linguistics, pages 248–255.
http://aclweb.org/anthology/W15-3030.

Franz Josef Och. 2003. Minimum error rate training in statistical machine translation. In *ACL
'03: Proceedings of the 41st Annual Meeting
on Association for Computational Linguistics.* Association for Computational Linguistics, Morristown, NJ, USA, pages 160–167.
https://doi.org/http://dx.doi.org/10.3115/1075096.1075117.

Franz Josef Och and Hermann Ney. 2003. A
systematic comparison of various statistical
alignment models. *Comput. Linguist.* 29(1):19–51.
https://doi.org/http://dl.acm.org/citation.cfm?id=778824.

Kishore Papineni, Salim Roukos, Todd Ward, and
Wei-Jing Zhu. 2002. Bleu: a method for automatic evaluation of machine translation. In
*Proceedings of the 40th Annual Meeting of
the Association for Computational Linguistics.*
http://aclweb.org/anthology/P02-1040.

Taro Watanabe. 2012. Optimized online rank learning for machine translation. In *Proceedings of
the 2012 Conference of the North American Chapter of the Association for Computational Linguistics: Human Language Technologies.* Association for Computational Linguistics, pages 253–262.
http://aclweb.org/anthology/N12-1026.

Taro Watanabe, Jun Suzuki, Hajime Tsukada, and
Hideki Isozaki. 2007. Online large-margin training for statistical machine translation. In *Proceedings of the 2007 Joint Conference on Empirical
Methods in Natural Language Processing and Computational Natural Language Learning (EMNLP-
CoNLL).* http://aclweb.org/anthology/D07-1080.

Fen Xia, Tie-Yan Liu, Jue Wang, Wensheng
Zhang, and Hang Li. 2008. Listwise approach to learning to rank: Theory and algorithm. In *Proceedings of the 25th International
Conference on Machine Learning.* ACM, New
York, NY, USA, ICML '08, pages 1192–1199.
https://doi.org/10.1145/1390156.1390306.

Kenji Yamada and Kevin Knight. 2001. A
syntax-based statistical translation model. In
*Proceedings of the 39th Annual Meeting of
the Association for Computational Linguistics.*
http://aclweb.org/anthology/P01-1067.

Matthew D Zeiler. 2012. Adadelta: An adaptive learning rate method. *arXiv preprint arXiv:1212.5701* .

M. Zhang, Y. Liu, H. Luan, and M. Sun. 2016. Listwise
ranking functions for statistical machine translation. *IEEE/ACM Transactions on Audio, Speech,
and Language Processing* 24(8):1464–1472.
https://doi.org/10.1109/TASLP.2016.2560527.

Embedding Words and Senses Together
via Joint Knowledge-Enhanced Training

Massimiliano Mancini*, Jose Camacho-Collados*, Ignacio Iacobacci and **Roberto Navigli**
Department of Computer Science
Sapienza University of Rome
`mancini@dis.uniroma1.it`
`{collados,iacobacci,navigli}@di.uniroma1.it`

Abstract

Word embeddings are widely used in Natural Language Processing, mainly due to their success in capturing semantic information from massive corpora. However, their creation process does not allow the different meanings of a word to be automatically separated, as it conflates them into a single vector. We address this issue by proposing a new model which learns word and sense embeddings jointly. Our model exploits large corpora and knowledge from semantic networks in order to produce a unified vector space of word and sense embeddings. We evaluate the main features of our approach both qualitatively and quantitatively in a variety of tasks, highlighting the advantages of the proposed method in comparison to state-of-the-art word- and sense-based models.

1 Introduction

Recently, approaches based on neural networks which embed words into low-dimensional vector spaces from text corpora (i.e. word embeddings) have become increasingly popular (Mikolov et al., 2013; Pennington et al., 2014). Word embeddings have proved to be beneficial in many Natural Language Processing tasks, such as Machine Translation (Zou et al., 2013), syntactic parsing (Weiss et al., 2015), and Question Answering (Bordes et al., 2014), to name a few. Despite their success in capturing semantic properties of words, these representations are generally hampered by an important limitation: the inability to discriminate among different meanings of the same word.

Previous works have addressed this limitation by automatically inducing word senses from monolingual corpora (Schütze, 1998; Reisinger and Mooney, 2010; Huang et al., 2012; Di Marco and Navigli, 2013; Neelakantan et al., 2014; Tian et al., 2014; Li and Jurafsky, 2015; Vu and Parker, 2016; Qiu et al., 2016), or bilingual parallel data (Guo et al., 2014; Ettinger et al., 2016; Šuster et al., 2016). However, these approaches learn solely on the basis of statistics extracted from text corpora and do not exploit knowledge from semantic networks. Additionally, their induced senses are neither readily interpretable (Panchenko et al., 2017) nor easily mappable to lexical resources, which limits their application. Recent approaches have utilized semantic networks to inject knowledge into existing word representations (Yu and Dredze, 2014; Faruqui et al., 2015; Goikoetxea et al., 2015; Speer and Lowry-Duda, 2017; Mrksic et al., 2017), but without solving the meaning conflation issue. In order to obtain a representation for each sense of a word, a number of approaches have leveraged lexical resources to learn sense embeddings as a result of post-processing conventional word embeddings (Chen et al., 2014; Johansson and Pina, 2015; Jauhar et al., 2015; Rothe and Schütze, 2015; Pilehvar and Collier, 2016; Camacho-Collados et al., 2016).

Instead, we propose SW2V (*Senses and Words to Vectors*), a neural model that exploits knowledge from both text corpora and semantic networks in order to simultaneously learn embeddings for both words and senses. Moreover, our model provides three additional key features: (1) both word and sense embeddings are represented in the same vector space, (2) it is flexible, as it can be applied to different predictive models, and (3) it is scalable for very large semantic networks and text corpora.

Authors marked with an asterisk (*) contributed equally.

100

Proceedings of the 21st Conference on Computational Natural Language Learning (CoNLL 2017), pages 100–111,
Vancouver, Canada, August 3 - August 4, 2017. ©2017 Association for Computational Linguistics

2   Related work

Embedding words from large corpora into a low-dimensional vector space has been a popular task since the appearance of the probabilistic feed-forward neural network language model (Bengio et al., 2003) and later developments such as word2vec (Mikolov et al., 2013) and GloVe (Pennington et al., 2014). However, little research has focused on exploiting lexical resources to overcome the inherent ambiguity of word embeddings.

Iacobacci et al. (2015) overcame this limitation by applying an off-the-shelf disambiguation system (i.e. Babelfy (Moro et al., 2014)) to a corpus and then using word2vec to learn sense embeddings over the pre-disambiguated text. However, in their approach words are replaced by their intended senses, consequently producing as output sense representations only. The representation of words and senses in the same vector space proves essential for applying these knowledge-based sense embeddings in downstream applications, particularly for their integration into neural architectures (Pilehvar et al., 2017). In the literature, various different methods have attempted to overcome this limitation. Chen et al. (2014) proposed a model for obtaining both word and sense representations based on a first training step of conventional word embeddings, a second disambiguation step based on sense definitions, and a final training phase which uses the disambiguated text as input. Likewise, Rothe and Schütze (2015) aimed at building a shared space of word and sense embeddings based on two steps: a first training step of only word embeddings and a second training step to produce sense and synset embeddings. These two approaches require multiple steps of training and make use of a relatively small resource like WordNet, which limits their coverage and applicability. Camacho-Collados et al. (2016) increased the coverage of these WordNet-based approaches by exploiting the complementary knowledge of WordNet and Wikipedia along with pre-trained word embeddings. Finally, Wang et al. (2014) and Fang et al. (2016) proposed a model to align vector spaces of words and entities from knowledge bases. However, these approaches are restricted to nominal instances only (i.e. Wikipedia pages or entities).

In contrast, we propose a model which learns both words and sense embeddings from a single joint training phase, producing a common vector

space of words and senses as an emerging feature.

3   Connecting words and senses in context

In order to jointly produce embeddings for words and senses, SW2V needs as input a corpus where words are connected to senses[1] in each given context. One option for obtaining such connections could be to take a sense-annotated corpus as input. However, manually annotating large amounts of data is extremely expensive and therefore impractical in normal settings. Obtaining sense-annotated data from current off-the-shelf disambiguation and entity linking systems is possible, but generally suffers from two major problems. First, supervised systems are hampered by the very same problem of needing large amounts of sense-annotated data. Second, the relatively slow speed of current disambiguation systems, such as graph-based approaches (Hoffart et al., 2012; Agirre et al., 2014; Moro et al., 2014), or word-expert supervised systems (Zhong and Ng, 2010; Iacobacci et al., 2016; Melamud et al., 2016), could become an obstacle when applied to large corpora.

This is the reason why we propose a simple yet effective unsupervised *shallow word-sense connectivity* algorithm, which can be applied to virtually any given semantic network and is linear on the corpus size. The main idea of the algorithm is to exploit the connections of a semantic network by associating words with the senses that are most connected within the sentence, according to the underlying network.

Shallow word-sense connectivity algorithm. Formally, a corpus and a semantic network are taken as input and a set of connected words and senses is produced as output. We define a semantic network as a graph (S, E) where the set S contains synsets (nodes) and E represents a set of semantically connected synset pairs (edges). Algorithm 1 describes how to connect words and senses in a given text (sentence or paragraph) T. First, we gather in a set S_T all candidate synsets of the words (including multiwords up to trigrams) in T (lines 1 to 3). Second, for each candidate synset s we calculate the number of synsets which are connected with s in the semantic network and are included in S_T, excluding connections of synsets which only appear as candidates of the

---

[1]In this paper we focus on senses but other items connected to words may be used (e.g. supersenses or images).

Algorithm 1 Shallow word-sense connectivity

Input: Semantic network (S, E) and text T represented as a bag of words
Output: Set of connected words and senses $T^* \subset T \times S$
1: Set of synsets $S_T \leftarrow \emptyset$
2: **for each** word $w \in T$
3: $\quad$ $S_T \leftarrow S_T \cup S_w$ (S_w: set of candidate synsets of w)
4: Minimum connections threshold $\theta \leftarrow \frac{|S_T|+|T|}{2\,\delta}$
5: Output set of connections $T^* \leftarrow \emptyset$
6: **for each** $w \in T$
7: $\quad$ Relative maximum connections $max = 0$
8: $\quad$ Set of senses associated with w, $C_w \leftarrow \emptyset$
9: $\quad$ **for each** candidate synset $s \in S_w$
10: $\quad\quad$ Number of edges $n = |s' \in S_T : (s, s') \in E$ & $\exists w' \in T : w' \neq w$ & $s' \in S_{w'}|$
11: $\quad\quad$ **if** $n \geq max$ & $n \geq \theta$ **then**
12: $\quad\quad\quad$ **if** $n > max$ **then**
13: $\quad\quad\quad\quad$ $C_w \leftarrow \{(w, s)\}$
14: $\quad\quad\quad\quad$ $max \leftarrow n$
15: $\quad\quad\quad$ **else**
16: $\quad\quad\quad\quad$ $C_w \leftarrow C_w \cup \{(w, s)\}$
17: $\quad$ $T^* \leftarrow T^* \cup C_w$
18: **return** Output set of connected words and senses T^*

---

same word (lines 5 to 10). Finally, each word is associated with its top candidate synset(s) according to its/their number of connections in context, provided that its/their number of connections exceeds a threshold $\theta = \frac{|S_T|+|T|}{2\,\delta}$ (lines 11 to 17).[2] This parameter aims to retain relevant connectivity across senses, as only senses above the threshold will be connected to words in the output corpus. θ is proportional to the reciprocal of a parameter δ,[3] and directly proportional to the average text length and number of candidate synsets within the text.

The complexity of the proposed algorithm is $N + (N \times \alpha)$, where N is the number of words of the training corpus and α is the average polysemy degree of a word in the corpus according to the input semantic network. Considering that non-content words are not taken into account (i.e. polysemy degree 0) and that the average polysemy degree of words in current lexical resources (e.g. WordNet or BabelNet) does not exceed a small constant (3) in any language, we can safely assume that the algorithm is linear in the size of the training corpus. Hence, the training time is not significantly increased in comparison to training words

---

[2]As mentioned above, all unigrams, bigrams and trigrams present in the semantic network are considered. In the case of overlapping instances, the selection of the final instance is performed in this order: mention whose synset is more connected (i.e. n is higher), longer mention and from left to right.

[3]Higher values of δ lead to higher recall, while lower values of δ increase precision but lower the recall. We set the value of δ to 100, as it was shown to produce a fine balance between precision and recall. This parameter may also be tuned on downstream tasks.

only, irrespective of the corpus size. This enables a fast training on large amounts of text corpora, in contrast to current unsupervised disambiguation algorithms. Additionally, as we will show in Section 5.2, this algorithm does not only speed up significantly the training phase, but also leads to more accurate results.

Note that with our algorithm a word is allowed to have more than one sense associated. In fact, current lexical resources like WordNet (Miller, 1995) or BabelNet (Navigli and Ponzetto, 2012) are hampered by the high granularity of their sense inventories (Hovy et al., 2013). In Section 6.2 we show how our sense embeddings are particularly suited to deal with this issue.

4 Joint training of words and senses

The goal of our approach is to obtain a shared vector space of words and senses. To this end, our model extends conventional word embedding models by integrating explicit knowledge into its architecture. While we will focus on the Continuous Bag Of Words (CBOW) architecture of word2vec (Mikolov et al., 2013), our extension can easily be applied similarly to Skip-Gram, or to other predictive approaches based on neural networks. The CBOW architecture is based on the feedforward neural network language model (Bengio et al., 2003) and aims at predicting the current word using its surrounding context. The architecture consists of input, hidden and output layers. The input layer has the size of the word vocabulary and encodes the context as a combination of one-hot vector representations of surrounding words of a given target word. The output layer has the same size as the input layer and contains a one-hot vector of the target word during the training phase.

Our model extends the input and output layers of the neural network with word senses[4] by exploiting the intrinsic relationship between words and senses. The leading principle is that, since a word is the surface form of an underlying sense, updating the embedding of the word should produce a consequent update to the embedding representing that particular sense, and vice-versa. As a consequence of the algorithm described in the previous section, each word in the corpus may be connected with zero, one or more senses. We re-

---

[4]Our model can also produce a space of words and synset embeddings as output: the only difference is that all synonym senses would be considered to be the same item, i.e. a synset.

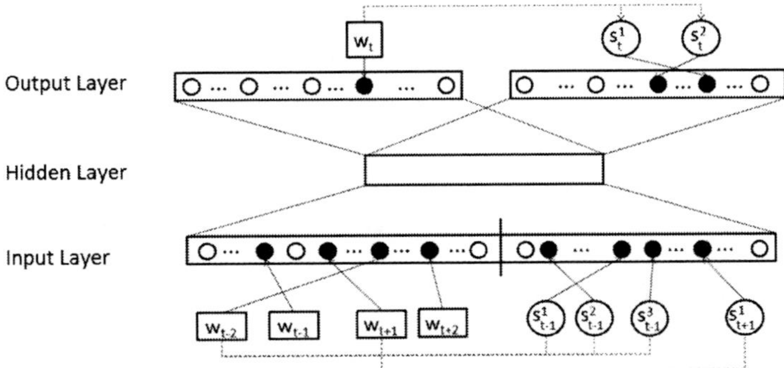

Figure 1: The SW2V architecture on a sample training instance using four context words. Dotted lines represent the virtual link between words and associated senses in context. In this example, the input layer consists of a context of two previous words (w_{t-2}, w_{t-1}) and two subsequent words (w_{t+1}, w_{t+2}) with respect to the target word w_t. Two words (w_{t-1}, w_{t+2}) do not have senses associated in context, while w_{t-2}, w_{t+1} have three senses (s_{t-1}^1, s_{t-1}^2, s_{t-1}^3) and one sense associated (s_{t+1}^1) in context, respectively. The output layer consists of the target word w_t, which has two senses associated (s_t^1, s_t^2) in context.

fer to the set of senses connected to a given word within the specific context as its *associated senses*.

Formally, we define a training instance as a sequence of words $W = w_{t-n}, ..., w_t, ..., w_{t+n}$ (being w_t the target word) and $S = S_{t-n}, ..., S_t, ..., S_{t+n}$, where $S_i = s_i^1, ..., s_i^{k_i}$ is the sequence of all associated senses in context of $w_i \in W$. Note that S_i might be empty if the word w_i does not have any associated sense. In our model each target word takes as context both its surrounding words and all the senses associated with them. In contrast to the original CBOW architecture, where the training criterion is to correctly classify w_t, our approach aims to predict the word w_t and its set S_t of associated senses. This is equivalent to minimizing the following loss function:

$$E = -\log(p(w_t|W^t, S^t)) - \sum_{s \in S_t} \log(p(s|W^t, S^t))$$

where $W^t = w_{t-n}, ..., w_{t-1}, w_{t+1}, ..., w_{t+n}$ and $S^t = S_{t-n}, ..., S_{t-1}, S_{t+1}, ..., S_{t+n}$. Figure 1 shows the organization of the input and the output layers on a sample training instance. In what follows we present a set of variants of the model on the output and the input layers.

4.1 Output layer alternatives

Both words and senses. This is the default case explained above. If a word has one or more associated senses, these senses are also used as target on a separate output layer.

Only words. In this case we exclude senses as target. There is a single output layer with the size of the word vocabulary as in the original CBOW model.

Only senses. In contrast, this alternative excludes words, using only senses as target. In this case, if a word does not have any associated sense, it is not used as target instance.

4.2 Input layer alternatives

Both words and senses. Words and their associated senses are included in the input layer and contribute to the hidden state. Both words and senses are updated as a consequence of the backpropagation algorithm.

Only words. In this alternative only the surrounding words contribute to the hidden state, i.e. the target word/sense (depending on the alternative of the output layer) is predicted only from word features. The update of an input word is propagated to the embeddings of its associated senses, if any. In other words, despite not being included in the input layer, senses still receive the same gradient of the associated input word, through a virtual connection. This configuration, coupled with the only-words output layer configuration, corresponds exactly to the default CBOW architecture of word2vec with the only addition of the update step for senses.

Only senses. Words are excluded from the input layer and the target is predicted only from the senses associated with the surrounding words. The weights of the words are updated through the updates of the associated senses, in contrast to the only-words alternative.

5   Analysis of Model Components

In this section we analyze the different components of SW2V, including the nine model configurations (Section 5.1) and the algorithm which generates the connections between words and senses in context (Section 5.2). In what follows we describe the common analysis setting:

- **Training model and hyperparameters.** For evaluation purposes, we use the CBOW model of word2vec with standard hyperparameters: the dimensionality of the vectors is set to 300 and the window size to 8, and hierarchical softmax is used for normalization. These hyperparameter values are set across all experiments.

- **Corpus and semantic network.** We use a 300M-words corpus from the UMBC project (Han et al., 2013), which contains English paragraphs extracted from the web.[5] As semantic network we use BabelNet 3.0[6], a large multilingual semantic network with over 350 million semantic connections, integrating resources such as Wikipedia and WordNet. We chose BabelNet owing to its wide coverage of named entities and lexicographic knowledge.

- **Benchmark.** Word similarity has been one of the most popular benchmarks for *in-vitro* evaluation of vector space models (Pennington et al., 2014; Levy et al., 2015). For the analysis we use two word similarity datasets: the similarity portion (Agirre et al., 2009, WS-Sim) of the WordSim-353 dataset (Finkelstein et al., 2002) and RG-65 (Rubenstein and Goodenough, 1965). In order to compute the similarity of two words using our sense embeddings, we apply the standard closest senses strategy (Resnik, 1995; Budanitsky and Hirst, 2006; Camacho-Collados

et al., 2015), using cosine similarity (cos) as comparison measure between senses:

$$sim(w_1, w_2) = \max_{s \in S_{w_1}, s' \in S_{w_2}} \cos(\vec{s}_1, \vec{s}_2) \quad (1)$$

where S_{w_i} represents the set of all candidate senses of w_i and $\vec{s}_i$ refers to the sense vector representation of the sense s_i.

5.1   Model configurations

In this section we analyze the different configurations of our model in respect of the input and the output layer on a word similarity experiment. Recall from Section 4 that our model could have words, senses or both in either the input and output layers. Table 1 shows the results of all nine configurations on the WS-Sim and RG-65 datasets.

As shown in Table 1, the best configuration according to both Spearman and Pearson correlation measures is the configuration which has only senses in the input layer and both words and senses in the output layer.[7] In fact, taking only senses as input seems to be consistently the best alternative for the input layer. Our hunch is that the knowledge learned from both the co-occurrence information and the semantic network is more balanced with this input setting. For instance, in the case of including both words and senses in the input layer, the co-occurrence information learned by the network would be duplicated for both words and senses.

5.2   Disambiguation / Shallow word-sense connectivity algorithm

In this section we evaluate the impact of our *shallow word-sense connectivity algorithm* (Section 3) by testing our model directly taking a pre-disambiguated text as input. In this case the network exploits the connections between each word and its disambiguated sense in context. For this comparison we used Babelfy[8] (Moro et al., 2014), a state-of-the-art graph-based disambiguation and entity linking system based on BabelNet. We compare to both the default Babelfy system which

---

[5]http://ebiquity.umbc.edu/blogger/2013/05/01/umbc-webbase-corpus-of-3b-english-words/
[6]http://babelnet.org

[7]In this analysis we used the word similarity task for optimizing the sense embeddings, without caring about the performance of word embeddings or their interconnectivity. Therefore, this configuration may not be optimal for word embeddings and may be further tuned on specific applications. More information about different configurations in the documentation of the source code.

[8]http://babelfy.org

	Output											
	Words				Senses				Both			
	WS-Sim		RG-65		WS-Sim		RG-65		WS-Sim		RG-65	
	r	ρ	r	ρ	r	ρ	r	ρ	r	ρ	r	ρ
Input Words	0.49	0.48	0.65	0.66	0.56	0.56	0.67	0.67	0.54	0.53	0.66	0.65
Senses	0.69	0.69	0.70	0.71	0.69	0.70	0.70	**0.74**	**0.72**	**0.71**	**0.71**	**0.74**
Both	0.60	0.65	0.67	0.70	0.62	0.65	0.66	0.67	0.65	**0.71**	0.68	0.70

Table 1: Pearson (r) and Spearman (ρ) correlation performance of the nine configurations of SW2V

	WS-Sim		RG-65	
	r	ρ	r	ρ
Shallow	**0.72**	**0.71**	**0.71**	**0.74**
Babelfy	0.65	0.63	0.69	0.70
Babelfy*	0.63	0.61	0.65	0.64

Table 2: Pearson (r) and Spearman (ρ) correlation performance of SW2V integrating our *shallow* word-sense connectivity algorithm (default), Babelfy, or Babelfy*.

uses the *Most Common Sense* (MCS) heuristic as a back-off strategy and, following (Iacobacci et al., 2015), we also include a version in which only instances above the Babelfy default confidence threshold are disambiguated (i.e. the MCS back-off strategy is disabled). We will refer to this latter version as Babelfy* and report the best configuration of each strategy according to our analysis.

Table 2 shows the results of our model using the three different strategies on RG-65 and WS-Sim. Our shallow word-sense connectivity algorithm achieves the best overall results. We believe that these results are due to the semantic connectivity ensured by our algorithm and to the possibility of associating words with more than one sense, which seems beneficial for training, making it more robust to possible disambiguation errors and to the sense granularity issue (Erk et al., 2013). The results are especially significant considering that our algorithm took a tenth of the time needed by Babelfy to process the corpus.

6 Evaluation

We perform a qualitative and quantitative evaluation of important features of SW2V in three different tasks. First, in order to compare our model against standard word-based approaches, we evaluate our system in the word similarity task (Section 6.1). Second, we measure the quality of our sense embeddings in a sense-specific application:

sense clustering (Section 6.2). Finally, we evaluate the coherence of our unified vector space by measuring the interconnectivity of word and sense embeddings (Section 6.3).

Experimental setting. Throughout all the experiments we use the same standard hyperparameters mentioned in Section 5 for both the original word2vec implementation and our proposed model SW2V. For SW2V we use the same optimal configuration according to the analysis of the previous section (only senses as input, and both words and senses as output) for all tasks. As training corpus we take the full 3B-words UMBC webbase corpus and the Wikipedia (Wikipedia dump of November 2014), used by three of the comparison systems. We use BabelNet 3.0 (SW2V$_{BN}$) and WordNet 3.0 (SW2V$_{WN}$) as semantic networks.

Comparison systems. We compare with the publicly available pre-trained sense embeddings of four state-of-the-art models: Chen et al. (2014)[9] and AutoExtend[10] (Rothe and Schütze, 2015) based on WordNet, and SensEmbed[11] (Iacobacci et al., 2015) and NASARI[12] (Camacho-Collados et al., 2016) based on BabelNet.

6.1 Word Similarity

In this section we evaluate our sense representations on the standard SimLex-999 (Hill et al., 2015) and MEN (Bruni et al., 2014) word similarity datasets[13]. SimLex and MEN contain 999 and 3000 word pairs, respectively, which constitute, to our knowledge, the two largest similar-

---

[9] http://pan.baidu.com/s/1eQcPK8i
[10] We used the AutoExtend code (http://cistern.cis.lmu.de/~sascha/AutoExtend/) to obtain sense vectors using W2V embeddings trained on UMBC (GoogleNews corpus used in their pre-trained models is not publicly available). We also tried the code to include BabelNet as lexical resource, but it was not easily scalable (BabelNet is two orders of magnitude larger than WordNet).
[11] http://lcl.uniroma1.it/sensembed/
[12] http://lcl.uniroma1.it/nasari/
[13] To enable a fair comparison we did not perform experiments on the small datasets used in Section 5 for validation.

			SimLex-999		MEN	
	System	**Corpus**	r	ρ	r	ρ
Senses	SW2V$_{BN}$	UMBC	**0.49**	**0.47**	0.75	0.75
	SW2V$_{WN}$	UMBC	0.46	0.45	**0.76**	**0.76**
	AutoExtend	UMBC	0.47	0.45	0.74	0.75
	AutoExtend	Google-News	0.46	0.46	0.68	0.70
	SW2V$_{BN}$	Wikipedia	0.47	0.43	0.71	0.73
	SW2V$_{WN}$	Wikipedia	0.47	0.43	0.71	0.72
	SensEmbed	Wikipedia	0.43	0.39	0.65	0.70
	Chen et al. (2014)	Wikipedia	0.46	0.43	0.62	0.62
Words	Word2vec	UMBC	0.39	0.39	0.75	0.75
	Retrofitting$_{BN}$	UMBC	0.47	0.46	0.75	**0.76**
	Retrofitting$_{WN}$	UMBC	0.47	0.46	**0.76**	**0.76**
	Word2vec	Wikipedia	0.39	0.38	0.71	0.72
	Retrofitting$_{BN}$	Wikipedia	0.35	0.32	0.66	0.66
	Retrofitting$_{WN}$	Wikipedia	0.47	0.44	0.73	0.73

Table 3: Pearson (r) and Spearman (ρ) correlation performance on the SimLex-999 and MEN word similarity datasets.

ity datasets comprising a balanced set of noun, verb and adjective instances. As explained in Section 5, we use the closest sense strategy for the word similarity measurement of our model and all sense-based comparison systems. As regards the word embedding models, words are directly compared by using cosine similarity. We also include a *retrofitted* version of the original word2vec word vectors (Faruqui et al., 2015, Retrofitting[14]) using WordNet (Retrofitting$_{WN}$) and BabelNet (Retrofitting$_{BN}$) as lexical resources.

Table 3 shows the results of SW2V and all comparison models in SimLex and MEN. SW2V consistently outperforms all sense-based comparison systems using the same corpus, and clearly performs better than the original word2vec trained on the same corpus. Retrofitting decreases the performance of the original word2vec on the Wikipedia corpus using BabelNet as lexical resource, but significantly improves the original word vectors on the UMBC corpus, obtaining comparable results to our approach. However, while our approach provides a shared space of words and senses, Retrofitting still conflates different meanings of a word into the same vector.

Additionally, we noticed that most of the score divergences between our system and the gold standard scores in SimLex-999 were produced on

antonym pairs, which are over-represented in this dataset: 38 word pairs hold a clear antonymy relation (e.g. *encourage-discourage* or *long-short*), while 41 additional pairs hold some degree of antonymy (e.g. *new-ancient* or *man-woman*).[15] In contrast to the consistently low gold similarity scores given to antonym pairs, our system varies its similarity scores depending on the specific nature of the pair[16]. Recent works have managed to obtain significant improvements by tweaking usual word embedding approaches into providing low similarity scores for antonym pairs (Pham et al., 2015; Schwartz et al., 2015; Nguyen et al., 2016; Mrksic et al., 2017), but this is outside the scope of this paper.

6.2 Sense Clustering

Current lexical resources tend to suffer from the high granularity of their sense inventories (Palmer et al., 2007). In fact, a meaningful clustering of their senses may lead to improvements on downstream tasks (Hovy et al., 2013; Flekova and Gurevych, 2016; Pilehvar et al., 2017). In this section we evaluate our synset representations on the Wikipedia sense clustering task. For a fair comparison with respect to the BabelNet-based com-

---

[14]https://github.com/mfaruqui/retrofitting

[15]Two annotators decided the degree of antonymy between word pairs: *clear antonyms*, *weak antonyms* or *neither*.

[16]For instance, the pairs *sunset-sunrise* and *day-night* are given, respectively, 1.88 and 2.47 gold scores in the 0-10 scale, while our model gives them a higher similarity score. In fact, both pairs appear as coordinate synsets in WordNet.

	Accuracy	F-Measure
SW2V	**87.8**	**63.9**
SensEmbed	82.7	40.3
NASARI	87.0	62.5
Multi-SVM	85.5	-
Mono-SVM	83.5	-
Baseline	17.5	29.8

Table 4: Accuracy and F-Measure percentages of different systems on the SemEval Wikipedia sense clustering dataset.

parison systems that use the Wikipedia corpus for training, in this experiment we report the results of our model trained on the Wikipedia corpus and using BabelNet as lexical resource only. For the evaluation we consider the two Wikipedia sense clustering datasets (500-pair and SemEval) created by Dandala et al. (2013). In these datasets sense clustering is viewed as a binary classification task in which, given a pair of Wikipedia pages, the system has to decide whether to cluster them into a single instance or not. To this end, we use our synset embeddings and cluster Wikipedia pages[17] together if their similarity exceeds a threshold γ. In order to set the optimal value of γ, we follow Dandala et al. (2013) and use the first 500-pairs sense clustering dataset for tuning. We set the threshold γ to 0.35, which is the value leading to the highest F-Measure among all values from 0 to 1 with a 0.05 step size on the 500-pair dataset. Likewise, we set a threshold for NASARI (0.7) and SensEmbed (0.3) comparison systems.

Finally, we evaluate our approach on the SemEval sense clustering test set. This test set consists of 925 pairs which were obtained from a set of highly ambiguous words gathered from past SemEval tasks. For comparison, we also include the supervised approach of Dandala et al. (2013) based on a multi-feature Support Vector Machine classifier trained on an automatically-labeled dataset of the English Wikipedia (Mono-SVM) and Wikipedia in four different languages (Multi-SVM). As naive baseline we include the system which would cluster all given pairs.

Table 4 shows the F-Measure and accuracy results on the SemEval sense clustering dataset. SW2V outperforms all comparison systems according to both measures, including the sense rep-

resentations of NASARI and SensEmbed using the same setup and the same underlying lexical resource. This confirms the capability of our system to accurately capture the semantics of word senses on this sense-specific task.

6.3 Word and sense interconnectivity

In the previous experiments we evaluated the effectiveness of the sense embeddings. In contrast, this experiment aims at testing the interconnectivity between word and sense embeddings in the vector space. As explained in Section 2, there have been previous approaches building a shared space of word and sense embeddings, but to date little research has focused on testing the semantic coherence of the vector space. To this end, we evaluate our model on a Word Sense Disambiguation (WSD) task, using our shared vector space of words and senses to obtain a *Most Common Sense* (MCS) baseline. The insight behind this experiment is that a semantically coherent shared space of words and senses should be able to build a relatively strong baseline for the task, as the MCS of a given word should be closer to the word vector than any other sense. The MCS baseline is generally integrated into the pipeline of state-of-the-art WSD and Entity Linking systems as a back-off strategy (Navigli, 2009; Jin et al., 2009; Zhong and Ng, 2010; Moro et al., 2014; Raganato et al., 2017) and is used in various NLP applications (Bennett et al., 2016). Therefore, a system which automatically identifies the MCS of words from non-annotated text may be quite valuable, especially for resource-poor languages or large knowledge resources for which obtaining sense-annotated corpora is extremely expensive. Moreover, even in a resource like WordNet for which sense-annotated data is available (Miller et al., 1993, SemCor), 61% of its polysemous lemmas have no sense annotations (Bennett et al., 2016).

Given an input word w, we compute the cosine similarity between w and all its candidate senses, picking the sense leading to the highest similarity:

$$MCS(w) = \operatorname*{argmax}_{s \in S_w} \cos(\vec{w}, \vec{s}) \qquad (2)$$

where $\cos(\vec{w}, \vec{s})$ refers to the cosine similarity between the embeddings of w and s. In order to assess the reliability of SW2V against previous models using WordNet as sense inventory, we test our model on the all-words SemEval-2007 (task 17) (Pradhan et al., 2007) and SemEval-2013 (task

---

[17] Since Wikipedia is a resource included in BabelNet, our synset representations are expandable to Wikipedia pages.

	SemEval-07	SemEval-13
SW2V	**39.9**	**54.0**
AutoExtend	17.6	31.0
Baseline	24.8	34.9

Table 5: F-Measure percentage of different MCS strategies on the SemEval-2007 and SemEval-2013 WSD datasets.

12) (Navigli et al., 2013) WSD datasets. Note that our model using BabelNet as semantic network has a far larger coverage than just WordNet and may additionally be used for Wikification (Mihalcea and Csomai, 2007) and Entity Linking tasks. Since the versions of WordNet vary across datasets and comparison systems, we decided to evaluate the systems on the portion of the datasets covered by all comparison systems[18] (less than 10% of instances were removed from each dataset).

Table 5 shows the results of our system and AutoExtend on the SemEval-2007 and SemEval-2013 WSD datasets. SW2V provides the best MCS results in both datasets. In general, AutoExtend does not accurately capture the predominant sense of a word and performs worse than a baseline that selects the intended sense randomly from the set of all possible senses of the target word.

In fact, AutoExtend tends to create clusters which include a word and all its possible senses. As an example, Table 6 shows the closest word and sense[19] embeddings of our SW2V model and AutoExtend to the *military* and *fish* senses of, respectively, *company* and *school*. AutoExtend creates clusters with all the senses of *company* and *school* and their related instances, even if they belong to different domains (e.g., $firm_n^2$ or $business_n^1$ clearly concern the *business* sense of *company*). Instead, SW2V creates a semantic cluster of word and sense embeddings which are semantically close to the corresponding $company_n^2$ and $school_n^7$ senses.

7 Conclusion and Future Work

In this paper we proposed SW2V (*Senses and Words to Vectors*), a neural model which learns vector representations for words and senses in a joint training phase by exploiting both text corpora and knowledge from semantic networks. Data (in-

$company_n^2$ (military unit)		$school_n^7$ (group of fish)	
AutoExtend	**SW2V**	**AutoExtend**	**SW2V**
$company_n^9$	$battalion_n^1$	school	$schools_n^7$
company	battalion	$school_n^4$	$sharks_n^1$
$company_n^8$	$regiment_n^1$	$school_n^6$	sharks
$company_n^6$	$detachment_n^4$	$school_v^1$	$shoals_n^3$
$company_n^7$	$platoon_n^1$	$school_n^3$	$fish_n^1$
$company_v^1$	$brigade_n^1$	elementary	$dolphins_n^1$
firm	regiment	schools	$pods_n^3$
$business_n^1$	$corps_n^1$	$elementary_a^3$	eels
$firm_n^2$	brigade	$school_n^5$	dolphins
$company_n^1$	platoon	$elementary_a^1$	$whales_n^2$

Table 6: Ten closest word and sense embeddings to the senses $company_n^2$ (military unit) and $school_n^7$ (group of fish).

cluding the preprocessed corpora and pre-trained embeddings used in the evaluation) and source code to apply our extension of the word2vec architecture to learn word and sense embeddings from any preprocessed corpus are freely available at `http://lcl.uniroma1.it/sw2v`. Unlike previous sense-based models which require post-processing steps and use WordNet as sense inventory, our model achieves a semantically coherent vector space of both words and senses as an emerging feature of a single training phase and is easily scalable to larger semantic networks like BabelNet. Finally, we showed, both quantitatively and qualitatively, some of the advantages of using our approach as against previous state-of-the-art word- and sense-based models in various tasks, and highlighted interesting semantic properties of the resulting unified vector space of word and sense embeddings.

As future work we plan to integrate a WSD and Entity Linking system for applying our model on downstream NLP applications, along the lines of Pilehvar et al. (2017). We are also planning to apply our model to languages other than English and to study its potential on multilingual and cross-lingual applications.

Acknowledgments

 The authors gratefully acknowledge the support of the ERC Consolidator Grant MOUSSE No. 726487.

Jose Camacho-Collados is supported by a Google Doctoral Fellowship in Natural Language Processing. We would also like to thank Jim McManus for his comments on the manuscript.

---

[18] We were unable to obtain the word embeddings of Chen et al. (2014) for comparison even after contacting the authors.

[19] Following Navigli (2009), $word_n^p$ is the nth sense of *word* with part of speech p (using WordNet 3.0).

References

Eneko Agirre, Enrique Alfonseca, Keith Hall, Jana Kravalova, Marius Paşca, and Aitor Soroa. 2009. A study on similarity and relatedness using distributional and WordNet-based approaches. In *Proceedings of NAACL*. pages 19–27.

Eneko Agirre, Oier Lopez de Lacalle, and Aitor Soroa. 2014. Random walks for knowledge-based word sense disambiguation. *Computational Linguistics* 40(1):57–84.

Yoshua Bengio, Réjean Ducharme, Pascal Vincent, and Christian Janvin. 2003. A Neural Probabilistic Language Model. *The Journal of Machine Learning Research* 3:1137–1155.

Andrew Bennett, Timothy Baldwin, Jey Han Lau, Diana McCarthy, and Francis Bond. 2016. Lexsemtm: A semantic dataset based on all-words unsupervised sense distribution learning. In *Proceedings of ACL*. pages 1513–1524.

Antoine Bordes, Sumit Chopra, and Jason Weston. 2014. Question answering with subgraph embeddings. In *Proceedings of EMNLP*. pages 615–620.

Elia Bruni, Nam-Khanh Tran, and Marco Baroni. 2014. Multimodal distributional semantics. *J. Artif. Intell. Res.(JAIR)* 49(1-47).

Alexander Budanitsky and Graeme Hirst. 2006. Evaluating WordNet-based measures of Lexical Semantic Relatedness. *Computational Linguistics* 32(1):13–47.

José Camacho-Collados, Mohammad Taher Pilehvar, and Roberto Navigli. 2015. A Unified Multilingual Semantic Representation of Concepts. In *Proceedings of ACL*. Beijing, China, pages 741–751.

José Camacho-Collados, Mohammad Taher Pilehvar, and Roberto Navigli. 2016. Nasari: Integrating explicit knowledge and corpus statistics for a multilingual representation of concepts and entities. *Artificial Intelligence* 240:36–64.

Xinxiong Chen, Zhiyuan Liu, and Maosong Sun. 2014. A unified model for word sense representation and disambiguation. In *Proceedings of EMNLP*. Doha, Qatar, pages 1025–1035.

Bharath Dandala, Chris Hokamp, Rada Mihalcea, and Razvan C. Bunescu. 2013. Sense clustering using Wikipedia. In *Proc. of RANLP*. Hissar, Bulgaria, pages 164–171.

Antonio Di Marco and Roberto Navigli. 2013. Clustering and diversifying web search results with graph-based word sense induction. *Computational Linguistics* 39(3):709–754.

Katrin Erk, Diana McCarthy, and Nicholas Gaylord. 2013. Measuring word meaning in context. *Computational Linguistics* 39(3):511–554.

Allyson Ettinger, Philip Resnik, and Marine Carpuat. 2016. Retrofitting Sense-Specific Word Vectors Using Parallel Text. In *Proceedings of NAACL-HLT*. pages 1378–1383.

Wei Fang, Jianwen Zhang, Dilin Wang, Zheng Chen, and Ming Li. 2016. Entity disambiguation by knowledge and text jointly embedding. In *Proceedings of CoNLL*. pages 260–269.

Manaal Faruqui, Jesse Dodge, Sujay K. Jauhar, Chris Dyer, Eduard Hovy, and Noah A. Smith. 2015. Retrofitting word vectors to semantic lexicons. In *Proceedings of NAACL*. pages 1606–1615.

Lev Finkelstein, Gabrilovich Evgeniy, Matias Yossi, Rivlin Ehud, Solan Zach, Wolfman Gadi, and Ruppin Eytan. 2002. Placing search in context: The concept revisited. *ACM Transactions on Information Systems* 20(1):116–131.

Lucie Flekova and Iryna Gurevych. 2016. Supersense embeddings: A unified model for supersense interpretation, prediction, and utilization. In *Proceedings of ACL*. pages 2029–2041.

Josu Goikoetxea, Aitor Soroa, Eneko Agirre, and Basque Country Donostia. 2015. Random walks and neural network language models on knowledge bases. In *Proceedings of NAACL*. pages 1434–1439.

Jiang Guo, Wanxiang Che, Haifeng Wang, and Ting Liu. 2014. Learning sense-specific word embeddings by exploiting bilingual resources. In *Proceedings of COLING*. pages 497–507.

Lushan Han, Abhay Kashyap, Tim Finin, James Mayfield, and Jonathan Weese. 2013. UMBC EBIQUITY-CORE: Semantic textual similarity systems. In *Proceedings of the Second Joint Conference on Lexical and Computational Semantics*. volume 1, pages 44–52.

Felix Hill, Roi Reichart, and Anna Korhonen. 2015. Simlex-999: Evaluating semantic models with (genuine) similarity estimation. *Computational Linguistics* .

Johannes Hoffart, Stephan Seufert, Dat Ba Nguyen, Martin Theobald, and Gerhard Weikum. 2012. Kore: keyphrase overlap relatedness for entity disambiguation. In *Proceedings of CIKM*. pages 545–554.

Eduard H. Hovy, Roberto Navigli, and Simone Paolo Ponzetto. 2013. Collaboratively built semistructured content and Artificial Intelligence: The story so far. *Artificial Intelligence* 194:2–27.

Eric H. Huang, Richard Socher, Christopher D. Manning, and Andrew Y. Ng. 2012. Improving word representations via global context and multiple word prototypes. In *Proc. of ACL*. Jeju Island, Korea, pages 873–882.

Ignacio Iacobacci, Mohammad Taher Pilehvar, and Roberto Navigli. 2015. Sensembed: Learning sense embeddings for word and relational similarity. In *Proceedings of ACL*. Beijing, China, pages 95–105.

Ignacio Iacobacci, Mohammad Taher Pilehvar, and Roberto Navigli. 2016. Embeddings for Word Sense Disambiguation: An Evaluation Study. In *Proceedings of ACL*. pages 897–907.

Sujay Kumar Jauhar, Chris Dyer, and Eduard Hovy. 2015. Ontologically grounded multi-sense representation learning for semantic vector space models. In *Proceedings of NAACL*.

Peng Jin, Diana McCarthy, Rob Koeling, and John Carroll. 2009. Estimating and exploiting the entropy of sense distributions. In *Proceedings of NAACL (2)*. pages 233–236.

Richard Johansson and Luis Nieto Pina. 2015. Embedding a semantic network in a word space. In *Proceedings of NAACL*. pages 1428–1433.

Omer Levy, Yoav Goldberg, and Ido Dagan. 2015. Improving distributional similarity with lessons learned from word embeddings. *TACL* 3:211–225.

Jiwei Li and Dan Jurafsky. 2015. Do multi-sense embeddings improve natural language understanding? In *Proceedings of EMNLP*. Lisbon, Portugal.

Oren Melamud, Jacob Goldberger, and Ido Dagan. 2016. context2vec: Learning Generic Context Embedding with Bidirectional LSTM. In *Proc. of CONLL*. pages 51–61.

Rada Mihalcea and Andras Csomai. 2007. Wikify! Linking documents to encyclopedic knowledge. In *Proceedings of the Sixteenth ACM Conference on Information and Knowledge management*. Lisbon, Portugal, pages 233–242.

Tomas Mikolov, Kai Chen, Greg Corrado, and Jeffrey Dean. 2013. Efficient estimation of word representations in vector space. *CoRR* abs/1301.3781.

George A Miller. 1995. Wordnet: a lexical database for english. *Communications of the ACM* 38(11):39–41.

George A. Miller, Claudia Leacock, Randee Tengi, and Ross Bunker. 1993. A semantic concordance. In *Proceedings of the 3rd DARPA Workshop on Human Language Technology*. Plainsboro, N.J., pages 303–308.

Andrea Moro, Alessandro Raganato, and Roberto Navigli. 2014. Entity Linking meets Word Sense Disambiguation: a Unified Approach. *TACL* 2:231–244.

Nikola Mrksic, Ivan Vulić, Diarmuid Ó Séaghdha, Ira Leviant, Roi Reichart, Milica Gai, Anna Korhonen, and Steve Young. 2017. Semantic Specialisation of Distributional Word Vector Spaces using Monolingual and Cross-Lingual Constraints. *TACL* .

Roberto Navigli. 2009. Word Sense Disambiguation: A survey. *ACM Computing Surveys* 41(2):1–69.

Roberto Navigli, David Jurgens, and Daniele Vannella. 2013. SemEval-2013 Task 12: Multilingual Word Sense Disambiguation. In *Proceedings of SemEval 2013*. pages 222–231.

Roberto Navigli and Simone Paolo Ponzetto. 2012. BabelNet: The automatic construction, evaluation and application of a wide-coverage multilingual semantic network. *AIJ* 193:217–250.

Arvind Neelakantan, Jeevan Shankar, Alexandre Passos, and Andrew McCallum. 2014. Efficient nonparametric estimation of multiple embeddings per word in vector space. In *Proceedings of EMNLP*. Doha, Qatar, pages 1059–1069.

Kim Anh Nguyen, Sabine Schulte im Walde, and Ngoc Thang Vu. 2016. Integrating distributional lexical contrast into word embeddings for antonym-synonym distinction. In *Proceedings of ACL*. pages 454–459.

Martha Palmer, Hoa Dang, and Christiane Fellbaum. 2007. Making fine-grained and coarse-grained sense distinctions, both manually and automatically. *Natural Language Engineering* 13(2):137–163.

Alexander Panchenko, Eugen Ruppert, Stefano Faralli, Simone Paolo Ponzetto, and Chris Biemann. 2017. Unsupervised does not mean uninterpretable: The case for word sense induction and disambiguation. In *Proceedings of EACL*. pages 86–98.

Jeffrey Pennington, Richard Socher, and Christopher D Manning. 2014. GloVe: Global vectors for word representation. In *Proceedings of EMNLP*. pages 1532–1543.

Nghia The Pham, Angeliki Lazaridou, and Marco Baroni. 2015. A multitask objective to inject lexical contrast into distributional semantics. In *Proceedings of ACL*. pages 21–26.

Mohammad Taher Pilehvar, Jose Camacho-Collados, Roberto Navigli, and Nigel Collier. 2017. Towards a Seamless Integration of Word Senses into Downstream NLP Applications. In *Proceedings of ACL*. Vancouver, Canada.

Mohammad Taher Pilehvar and Nigel Collier. 2016. De-conflated semantic representations. In *Proceedings of EMNLP*. Austin, TX.

Sameer Pradhan, Edward Loper, Dmitriy Dligach, and Martha Palmer. 2007. SemEval-2007 task-17: English lexical sample, SRL and all words. In *Proceedings of SemEval*. pages 87–92.

Lin Qiu, Kewei Tu, and Yong Yu. 2016. Context-dependent sense embedding. In *Proceedings of EMNLP*. Austin, Texas, pages 183–191.

Alessandro Raganato, Jose Camacho-Collados, and Roberto Navigli. 2017. Word Sense Disambiguation: A Unified Evaluation Framework and Empirical Comparison. In *Proceedings of EACL*. pages 99–110.

Joseph Reisinger and Raymond J. Mooney. 2010. Multi-prototype vector-space models of word meaning. In *Proceedings of ACL*. pages 109–117.

Philip Resnik. 1995. Using information content to evaluate semantic similarity in a taxonomy. In *Proceedings of IJCAI*. pages 448–453.

Sascha Rothe and Hinrich Schütze. 2015. AutoExtend: Extending Word Embeddings to Embeddings for Synsets and Lexemes. In *Proceedings of ACL*. Beijing, China, pages 1793–1803.

Herbert Rubenstein and John B. Goodenough. 1965. Contextual correlates of synonymy. *Commun. ACM* 8(10):627–633.

Hinrich Schütze. 1998. Automatic word sense discrimination. *Computational linguistics* 24(1):97–123.

Roy Schwartz, Roi Reichart, and Ari Rappoport. 2015. Symmetric pattern based word embeddings for improved word similarity prediction. In *Proceedings of CoNLL*. pages 258–267.

Robert Speer and Joanna Lowry-Duda. 2017. Conceptnet at semeval-2017 task 2: Extending word embeddings with multilingual relational knowledge. In *Proceedings of the 11th International Workshop on Semantic Evaluation (SemEval-2017)*. pages 76–80.

Simon Šuster, Ivan Titov, and Gertjan van Noord. 2016. Bilingual learning of multi-sense embeddings with discrete autoencoders. In *Proceedings of NAACL-HLT*. pages 1346–1356.

Fei Tian, Hanjun Dai, Jiang Bian, Bin Gao, Rui Zhang, Enhong Chen, and Tie-Yan Liu. 2014. A probabilistic model for learning multi-prototype word embeddings. In *Proceedings of COLING*. pages 151–160.

Thuy Vu and D Stott Parker. 2016. K-embeddings: Learning conceptual embeddings for words using context. In *Proceedings of NAACL-HLT*. pages 1262–1267.

Zhen Wang, Jianwen Zhang, Jianlin Feng, and Zheng Chen. 2014. Knowledge graph and text jointly embedding. In *Proceedings of EMNLP*. pages 1591–1601.

David Weiss, Chris Alberti, Michael Collins, and Slav Petrov. 2015. Structured training for neural network transition-based parsing. In *Proceedings of ACL*. Beijing, China, pages 323–333.

Mo Yu and Mark Dredze. 2014. Improving lexical embeddings with semantic knowledge. In *Proceedings of ACL (2)*. pages 545–550.

Zhi Zhong and Hwee Tou Ng. 2010. It Makes Sense: A wide-coverage Word Sense Disambiguation system for free text. In *Proc. of ACL System Demonstrations*. pages 78–83.

Will Y. Zou, Richard Socher, Daniel M Cer, and Christopher D Manning. 2013. Bilingual word embeddings for phrase-based machine translation. In *Proceedings of EMNLP*. pages 1393–1398.

Automatic Selection of Context Configurations for Improved Class-Specific Word Representations

Ivan Vulić[1], Roy Schwartz[2,3], Ari Rappoport[4]
Roi Reichart[5], Anna Korhonen[1]
[1] Language Technology Lab, DTAL, University of Cambridge
[2] CS & Engineering, University of Washington and [3] Allen Institute for AI
[4] Institute of Computer Science, The Hebrew University of Jerusalem
[5] Faculty of Industrial Engineering and Management, Technion, IIT
{iv250,alk23}@cam.ac.uk   roysch@cs.washington.edu
arir@cs.huji.ac.il   roiri@ie.technion.ac.il

Abstract

This paper is concerned with identifying contexts useful for training word representation models for different word classes such as adjectives (A), verbs (V), and nouns (N). We introduce a simple yet effective framework for an automatic selection of *class-specific context configurations*. We construct a context configuration space based on universal dependency relations between words, and efficiently search this space with an adapted beam search algorithm. In word similarity tasks for each word class, we show that our framework is both effective and efficient. Particularly, it improves the Spearman's ρ correlation with human scores on SimLex-999 over the best previously proposed class-specific contexts by 6 (A), 6 (V) and 5 (N) ρ points. With our selected context configurations, we train on only 14% (A), 26.2% (V), and 33.6% (N) of all dependency-based contexts, resulting in a reduced training time. Our results generalise: we show that the configurations our algorithm learns for one English training setup outperform previously proposed context types in another training setup for English. Moreover, basing the configuration space on universal dependencies, it is possible to *transfer* the learned configurations to German and Italian. We also demonstrate improved per-class results over other context types in these two languages.

1 Introduction

Dense real-valued word representations (embeddings) have become ubiquitous in NLP, serving as invaluable features in a broad range of tasks (Turian et al., 2010; Collobert et al., 2011; Chen and Manning, 2014). The omnipresent word2vec skip-gram model with negative sampling (SGNS) (Mikolov et al., 2013) is still considered a robust and effective choice for a word representation model, due to its simplicity, fast training, as well as its solid performance across semantic tasks (Baroni et al., 2014; Levy et al., 2015). The original SGNS implementation learns word representations from local bag-of-words contexts (BOW). However, the underlying model is equally applicable with other context types (Levy and Goldberg, 2014a).

Recent work suggests that "not all contexts are created equal". For example, reaching beyond standard BOW contexts towards contexts based on dependency parses (Bansal et al., 2014; Melamud et al., 2016) or symmetric patterns (Schwartz et al., 2015, 2016) yields significant improvements in learning representations for particular word classes such as *adjectives (A)* and *verbs (V)*. Moreover, Schwartz et al. (2016) demonstrated that a subset of dependency-based contexts which covers only coordination structures is particularly effective for SGNS training, both in terms of the quality of the induced representations and in the reduced training time of the model. Interestingly, they also demonstrated that despite the success with adjectives and verbs, BOW contexts are still the optimal choice when learning representations for *nouns (N)*.

In this work, we propose a simple yet effective framework for selecting *context configurations*, which yields improved representations for verbs, adjectives, *and* nouns. We start with a definition of our context configuration space (Sect. 3.1). Our basic definition of a context refers to a single typed (or labeled) dependency link between words (e.g., the amod link or the dobj link). Our configuration space then naturally consists of all possible subsets of the set of labeled dependency links between words. We employ the universal dependencies (UD) scheme to make our framework applicable across

Proceedings of the 21st Conference on Computational Natural Language Learning (CoNLL 2017), pages 112–122,
Vancouver, Canada, August 3 - August 4, 2017. ©2017 Association for Computational Linguistics

languages. We then describe (Sect. 3.2) our adapted beam search algorithm that aims to select an optimal context configuration for a given word class.

We show that SGNS requires different context configurations to produce improved results for each word class. For instance, our algorithm detects that the combination of `amod` and `conj` contexts is effective for adjective representation. Moreover, some contexts that boost representation learning for one word class (e.g., `amod` contexts for adjectives) may be uninformative when learning representations for another class (e.g., `amod` for verbs). By removing such dispensable contexts, we are able both to speed up the SGNS training and to improve representation quality.

We first experiment with the task of predicting similarity scores for the A/V/N portions of the benchmarking SimLex-999 evaluation set, running our algorithm in a standard SGNS experimental setup (Levy et al., 2015). When training SGNS with our learned context configurations it outperforms SGNS trained with the best previously proposed context type *for each word class*: the improvements in Spearman's ρ rank correlations are 6 (A), 6 (V), and 5 (N) points. We also show that by building context configurations we obtain improvements on the entire SimLex-999 (4 ρ points over the best baseline). Interestingly, this context configuration is not the optimal configuration for any word class.

We then demonstrate that our approach is robust by showing that transferring the optimal configurations learned in the above setup to three other setups yields improved performance. First, the above context configurations, learned with the SGNS training on the English Wikipedia corpus, have an even stronger impact on SimLex999 performance when SGNS is trained on a larger corpus. Second, the transferred configurations also result in competitive performance on the task of solving class-specific TOEFL questions. Finally, we transfer the learned context configurations across languages: these configurations improve the SGNS performance when trained with German or Italian corpora and evaluated on class-specific subsets of the multilingual SimLex-999 (Leviant and Reichart, 2015), without any language-specific tuning.

2 Related Work

Word representation models typically train on (*word, context*) pairs. Traditionally, most models use bag-of-words (BOW) contexts, which represent a word using its neighbouring words, irrespective of the syntactic or semantic relations between them (Collobert et al., 2011; Mikolov et al., 2013; Mnih and Kavukcuoglu, 2013; Pennington et al., 2014, inter alia). Several alternative context types have been proposed, motivated by the limitations of BOW contexts, most notably their focus on topical rather than functional similarity (e.g., *coffee:cup* vs. *coffee:tea*). These include dependency contexts (Padó and Lapata, 2007; Levy and Goldberg, 2014a), pattern contexts (Baroni et al., 2010; Schwartz et al., 2015) and substitute vectors (Yatbaz et al., 2012; Melamud et al., 2015).

Several recent studies examined the effect of context types on word representation learning. Melamud et al. (2016) compared three context types on a set of intrinsic and extrinsic evaluation setups: BOW, dependency links, and substitute vectors. They show that the optimal type largely depends on the task at hand, with dependency-based contexts displaying strong performance on semantic similarity tasks. Vulić and Korhonen (2016) extended the comparison to more languages, reaching similar conclusions. Schwartz et al. (2016), showed that symmetric patterns are useful as contexts for V and A similarity, while BOW still works best for nouns. They also indicated that coordination structures, a particular dependency link, are more useful for verbs and adjectives than the entire set of dependencies. In this work, we generalise their approach: our algorithm systematically and efficiently searches the space of dependency-based context configurations, yielding *class-specific* representations with substantial gains *for all three word classes*.

Previous attempts on specialising word representations for a particular relation (e.g., similarity vs relatedness, antonyms) operate in one of two frameworks: (1) modifying the prior or the regularisation of the original training procedure (Yu and Dredze, 2014; Wieting et al., 2015; Liu et al., 2015; Kiela et al., 2015; Ling et al., 2015b); (2) post-processing procedures which use lexical knowledge to refine previously trained word vectors (Faruqui et al., 2015; Wieting et al., 2015; Mrkšić et al., 2017). Our work suggests that the induced representations can be specialised by directly training the word representation model with carefully selected contexts.

3 Context Selection: Methodology

The goal of our work is to develop a methodology for the identification of optimal context configura-

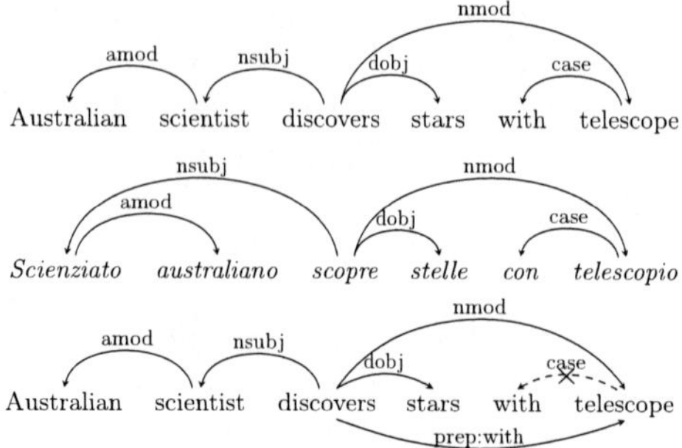

Figure 1: Extracting dependency-based contexts. **Top**: An example English sentence from (Levy and Goldberg, 2014a), now UD-parsed. **Middle**: the same sentence in Italian, UD-parsed. Note the similarity between the two parses which suggests that our context selection framework may be extended to other languages. **Bottom**: prepositional arc collapsing. The uninformative short-range `case` arc is removed, while a "pseudo-arc" specifying the exact link (`prep:with`) between *discovers* and *telescope* is added.

tions for word representation model training. We hope to get improved word representations and, at the same time, cut down the training time of the word representation model. Fundamentally, we are not trying to design a new word representation model, but rather to find valuable configurations for existing algorithms.

The motivation to search for such training context configurations lies in the intuition that the distributional hypothesis (Harris, 1954) should not necessarily be made with respect to BOW contexts. Instead, it may be restated as a series of statements according to particular word relations. For example, the hypothesis can be restated as: "two adjectives are similar if they modify similar nouns", which is captured by the `amod` typed dependency relation. This could also be reversed to reflect noun similarity by saying that "two nouns are similar if they are modified by similar adjectives". In another example, "two verbs are similar if they are used as predicates of similar nominal subjects" (the `nsubj` and `nsubjpass` dependency relations).

First, we have to define an expressive context configuration space that contains potential training configurations and is effectively decomposed so that useful configurations may be sought algorithmically. We can then continue by designing a search algorithm over the configuration space.

3.1 Context Configuration Space

We focus on the configuration space based on dependency-based contexts (DEPS) (Padó and Lapata, 2007; Utt and Padó, 2014). We choose this space due to multiple reasons. First, dependency structures are known to be very useful in capturing functional relations between words, even if these relations are long distance. Second, they have been proven useful in learning word embeddings (Levy and Goldberg, 2014a; Melamud et al., 2016). Finally, owing to the recent development of the Universal Dependencies (UD) annotation scheme (McDonald et al., 2013; Nivre et al., 2016)[1] it is possible to reason over dependency structures in a multilingual manner (e.g., Fig. 1). Consequently, a search algorithm in such DEPS-based configuration space can be developed for multiple languages based on the same design principles. Indeed, in this work we show that the optimal configurations for English translate to improved representations in two additional languages, German and Italian.

And so, given a (UD-)parsed training corpus, for each target word w with modifiers $m_1, \ldots, m_k$ and a head h, the word w is paired with context elements $m_1\_r_1, \ldots, m_k\_r_k, h\_r_h^{-1}$, where r is the type of the dependency relation between the head and the modifier (e.g., `amod`), and r^{-1} denotes an inverse relation. To simplify the presentation, we adopt the assumption that all training data for the word representation model are in the form of such (*word, context*) pairs (Levy and Goldberg, 2014a,c), where *word* is the current target word, and *context* is its observed context (e.g., BOW, positional, dependency-based). A naive version of DEPS extracts contexts from the parsed corpus without any post-processing. Given the example from Fig. 1, the DEPS contexts of *discovers* are: *scientist_nsubj, stars_dobj, telescope_nmod*.

DEPS not only emphasises functional similarity, but also provides a natural implicit grouping of related contexts. For instance, all pairs with the shared relation r and r^{-1} are taken as an r-based *context bag*, e.g., the pairs {*(scientist, Australian_amod), (Australian, scientist_amod^{-1})*} from Fig. 1 are inserted into the `amod` context bag, while {*(discovers, stars_dobj), (stars, discovers_dobj^{-1})*} are labelled with `dobj`.

Assume that we have obtained M distinct dependency relations $r_1, \ldots, r_M$ after parsing and post-processing the corpus. The j-th *individual context*

---

[1] http://universaldependencies.org/ (V1.4 used)

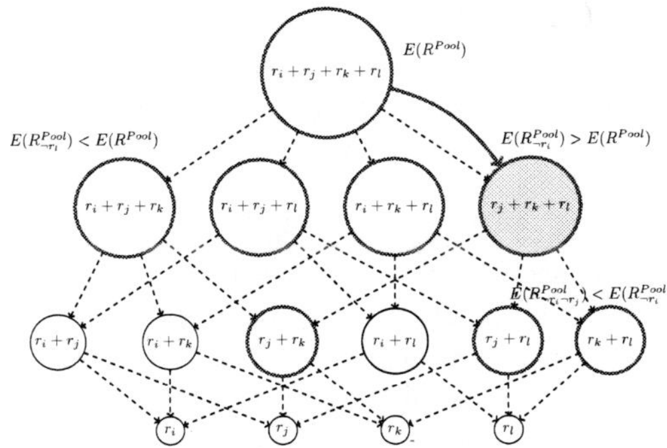

Figure 2: An illustration of Alg. 1. The search space is presented as a DAG with direct links between origin configurations (e.g., $r_i + r_j + r_k$) and all its children configurations obtained by removing exactly one individual bag from the origin (e.g., $r_i + r_j, r_j + r_k$). After automatically constructing the initial pool (line 1), the entry point of the algorithm is the R^{Pool} configuration (line 2). Thicker blue circles denote visited configurations, while the gray circle denotes the best configuration found.

bag, $j = 1, \ldots, M$, labelled r_j, is a bag (or a multiset) of $(word, context)$ pairs where *context* has one of the following forms: v_r_j or $v\_r_j^{-1}$, where v is some vocabulary word. A *context configuration* is then simply a set of individual context bags, e.g., $R = \{r_i, r_j, r_k\}$, also labelled as $R: r_i + r_j + r_k$. We call a configuration consisting of K individual context bags a K-set configuration (e.g., in this example, R is a 3-set configuration).[2]

Although a brute-force exhaustive search over all possible configurations is possible in theory and for small pools (e.g., for adjectives, see Tab. 2), it becomes challenging or practically infeasible for large pools and large training data. For instance, based on the pool from Tab. 2, the search for the optimal configuration would involve trying out $2^{10} - 1 = 1023$ configurations for nouns (i.e., training 1023 different word representation models). Therefore, to reduce the number of visited configurations, we present a simple heuristic search algorithm inspired by beam search (Pearl, 1984).

---

[2] A note on the nomenclature and notation: Each context configuration may be seen as a set of context bags, as it does not allow for repetition of its constituent context bags. For simplicity and clarity of presentation, we use dependency relation types (e.g., r_i = amod, r_j = acl) as labels for context bags. The reader has to be aware that a configuration $R = \{r_i, r_j, r_k\}$ is not by any means a set of relation types/names, but is in fact a multiset of all $(word, context)$ pairs belonging to the corresponding context bags labelled with r_i, r_j, r_k.

Algorithm 1: Best Configuration Search

> **Input** : Set of M individual context bags:
> $$S = \{r'_1, r'_2, \ldots, r'_M\}$$
>
> **1** **build**: *pool* of those $K \leq M$ candidate individual context bags $\{r_1, \ldots, r_K\}$ for which $E(r_i) >= threshold, i \in \{1, \ldots, M\}$, where $E(\cdot)$ is a fitness function.
>
> **2** **build**: K-set configuration $R^{Pool} = \{r_1, \ldots, r_K\}$;
>
> **3** **initialize:** (1) set of candidate configurations $\mathbf{R} = \{R^{Pool}\}$; (2) current level $l = K$; (3) best configuration $R_o = \emptyset$;
>
> **4** **search**:
> **5** **repeat**
> **6** $\quad$ $\mathbf{R_n} \leftarrow \emptyset$;
> **7** $\quad$ $R_o \leftarrow \arg\max\limits_{R \in \mathbf{R} \cup \{R_o\}} E(R)$;
> **8** $\quad$ **foreach** $R \in \mathbf{R}$ **do**
> **9** $\quad\quad$ **foreach** $r_i \in R$ **do**
> **10** $\quad\quad\quad$ **build** new $(l-1)$-set context configuration $R_{\neg r_i} = R - \{r_i\}$;
> **11** $\quad\quad\quad$ **if** $E(R_{\neg r_i}) \geq E(R)$ **then**
> **12** $\quad\quad\quad\quad$ $\mathbf{R_n} \leftarrow \mathbf{R_n} \cup \{R_{\neg r_i}\}$;
> **13** $\quad$ $l \leftarrow l - 1$;
> **14** $\quad$ $\mathbf{R} \leftarrow \mathbf{R_n}$;
> **15** **until** $l == 0$ *or* $\mathbf{R} == \emptyset$;
> **Output** : Best configuration R_o

3.2 Class-Specific Configuration Search

Alg. 1 provides a high-level overview of the algorithm. An example of its flow is given in Fig. 2. Starting from S, the set of all possible M individual context bags, the algorithm automatically detects the subset $S_K \subseteq S, |S_K| = K$, of candidate individual bags that are used as the initial pool (line 1 of Alg. 1). The selection is based on some fitness (goal) function E. In our setup, $E(R)$ is Spearman's ρ correlation with human judgment scores obtained on the development set after training the word representation model with the configuration R. The selection step relies on a simple threshold: we use a threshold of $\rho \geq 0.2$ without any fine-tuning in all experiments with all word classes.

We find this step to facilitate efficiency at a minor cost for accuracy. For example, since amod denotes an adjectival modifier of a noun, an efficient search procedure may safely remove this bag from the pool of candidate bags for verbs.

The search algorithm then starts from the full K-set R^{Pool} configuration (line 3) and tests K $(K - 1)$-set configurations where exactly one individual bag r_i is removed to generate each such configuration (line 10). It then retains only the set of configurations that score higher than the origin K-set configuration (lines 11-12, see Fig. 2). Using this principle, it continues searching only over lower-level $(l - 1)$-set configurations that further improve performance over their l-set origin configuration. It stops if it reaches the lowest level or if it cannot improve the goal function any more (line 15). The best scoring configuration is returned (n.b., not guaranteed to be the global optimum).

In our experiments with this heuristic, the search for the optimal configuration for verbs is performed only over 13 1-set configurations plus 26 other configurations (39 out of 133 possible configurations).[3] For nouns, the advantage of the heuristic is even more dramatic: only 104 out of 1026 possible configurations were considered during the search.[4]

4 Experimental Setup

4.1 Implementation Details

Word Representation Model We experiment with SGNS (Mikolov et al., 2013), the standard and very robust choice in vector space modeling (Levy et al., 2015). In all experiments we use `word2vecf`, a reimplementation of `word2vec` able to learn from arbitrary $(word, context)$ pairs.[5] For details concerning the implementation, we refer the reader to (Goldberg and Levy, 2014; Levy and Goldberg, 2014a).

The SGNS preprocessing scheme was replicated from (Levy and Goldberg, 2014a; Levy et al., 2015). After lowercasing, all words and contexts that appeared less than 100 times were filtered. When considering all dependency types, the vocabulary spans approximately 185K word types.[6] Further, all representations were trained with $d = 300$ (very similar trends are observed with $d = 100, 500$).

The same setup was used in prior work (Schwartz et al., 2016; Vulić and Korhonen, 2016). Keeping the representation model fixed across experiments and varying only the context type allows us to attribute any differences in results to a sole factor: the context type. We plan to experiment with other representation models in future work.

Universal Dependencies as Labels The adopted UD scheme leans on the universal Stanford dependencies (de Marneffe et al., 2014) complemented with the universal POS tagset (Petrov et al., 2012). It is straightforward to "translate" previous annotation schemes to UD (de Marneffe et al., 2014). Providing a consistently annotated inventory of categories for similar syntactic constructions across languages, the UD scheme facilitates representation learning in languages other than English, as shown in (Vulić and Korhonen, 2016; Vulić, 2017).

Individual Context Bags Standard post-parsing steps are performed in order to obtain an initial list of individual context bags for our algorithm: (1) Prepositional arcs are collapsed ((Levy and Goldberg, 2014a; Vulić and Korhonen, 2016), see Fig. 1). Following this procedure, all pairs where the relation r has the form `prep:X` (where X is a preposition) are subsumed to a context bag labelled `prep`; (2) Similar labels are merged into a single label (e.g., direct (`dobj`) and indirect objects (`iobj`) are merged into `obj`); (3) Pairs with infrequent and uninformative labels are removed (e.g., `punct`, `goeswith`, `cc`).

Coordination-based contexts are extracted as in prior work (Schwartz et al., 2016), distinguishing between left and right contexts extracted from the `conj` relation; the label for this bag is `conjlr`. We also utilise the variant that does not make the distinction, labeled `conjll`. If both are used, the label is simply `conj=conjlr+conjll`.[7]

Consequently, the individual context bags we use in all experiments are: `subj`, `obj`, `comp`, `nummod`, `appos`, `nmod`, `acl`, `amod`, `prep`, `adv`, `compound`, `conjlr`, `conjll`.

4.2 Training and Evaluation

We run the algorithm for context configuration selection only once, with the SGNS training setup described below. Our main evaluation setup is presented below, but the learned configurations are tested in additional setups, detailed in Sect. 5.

Training Data Our training corpus is the cleaned and tokenised English Polyglot Wikipedia data (Al-Rfou et al., 2013),[8] consisting of approxi-

---

[3] The total is 133 as we have to include 6 additional 1-set configurations that have to be tested (line 1 of Alg. 1) but are not included in the initial pool for verbs (line 2).

[4] We also experimented with a less conservative variant which does not stop when lower-level configurations do not improve E; it instead follows the path of the best-scoring lower-level configuration even if its score is lower than that of its origin. As we do not observe any significant improvement with this variant, we opt for the faster and simpler one.

[5] https://bitbucket.org/yoavgo/word2vecf

[6] SGNS for all models was trained using stochastic gradient descent and standard settings: 15 negative samples, global learning rate: 0.025, subsampling rate: $1e − 4$, 15 epochs.

[7] Given the coordination structure *boys and girls*, `conjlr` training pairs are *(boys, girls_conj)*, *(girls, boys_conj^{-1})*, while `conjll` pairs are *(boys, girls_conj)*, *(girls, boys_conj)*.

[8] https://sites.google.com/site/rmyeid/projects/polyglot

mately 75M sentences and 1.7B word tokens. The Wikipedia data were POS-tagged with universal POS (UPOS) tags (Petrov et al., 2012) using the state-of-the art TurboTagger (Martins et al., 2013).[9] The parser was trained using default settings (SVM MIRA with 20 iterations, no further parameter tuning) on the TRAIN+DEV portion of the UD treebank annotated with UPOS tags. The data were then parsed with UD using the graph-based Mate parser v3.61 (Bohnet, 2010)[10] with standard settings on TRAIN+DEV of the UD treebank.

Evaluation   We experiment with the verb pair (222 pairs), adjective pair (111 pairs), and noun pair (666 pairs) portions of SimLex-999. We report Spearman's ρ correlation between the ranks derived from the scores of the evaluated models and the human scores. Our evaluation setup is borrowed from Levy et al. (2015): we perform 2-fold cross-validation, where the context configurations are optimised on a development set, separate from the unseen test data. Unless stated otherwise, the reported scores are always the averages of the 2 runs, computed in the standard fashion by applying the cosine similarity to the vectors of words participating in a pair.

4.3   Baselines

Baseline Context Types   We compare the context configurations found by Alg. 1 against baseline contexts from prior work:
- **BOW**: Standard bag-of-words contexts.
- **POSIT**: Positional contexts (Schütze, 1993; Levy and Goldberg, 2014b; Ling et al., 2015a), which enrich BOW with information on the sequential position of each context word. Given the example from Fig. 1, POSIT with the window size 2 extracts the following contexts for *discovers*: *Australian_-2, scientist_-1, stars_+2, with_+1*.
- **DEPS-All**: All dependency links without any context selection, extracted from dependency-parsed data with prepositional arc collapsing.
- **COORD**: Coordination-based contexts are used as fast lightweight contexts for improved representations of adjectives and verbs (Schwartz et al., 2016). This is in fact the `conjlr` context bag, a subset of DEPS-All.
- **SP**: Contexts based on symmetric patterns (SPs, (Davidov and Rappoport, 2006; Schwartz et al., 2015)). For example, if the word X and the word

Context Group	Adj	Verb	Noun
`conjlr` (A+N+V)	0.415	0.281	0.401
`obj` (N+V)	-0.028	0.309	0.390
`prep` (N+V)	0.188	0.344	0.387
`amod` (A+N)	0.479	0.058	0.398
`compound` (N)	-0.124	-0.019	0.416
`adv` (V)	0.197	0.342	0.104
`nummod` (-)	-0.142	-0.065	0.029

Table 1: 2-fold cross-validation results for an illustrative selection of individual context bags. Results are presented for the noun, verb and adjective subsets of SimLex-999. Values in parentheses denote the class-specific initial pools to which each context is selected based on its ρ score (line 1 of Alg. 1).

Adjectives	Verbs	Nouns
`amod,` `conjlr,` `conjll`	`prep,` `acl,` `obj,` `comp,` `adv,` `conjlr,` `conjll`	`amod,` `prep,` `compound,` `subj,` `obj,` `appos,` `acl,` `nmod,` `conjlr,` `conjll`

Table 2: Automatically constructed initial pools of candidate bags for each word class (Sect. 3.2).

Y appear in the lexico-syntactic symmetric pattern "X or Y" in the SGNS training corpus, then Y is an SP context instance for X, and vice versa.

The development set was used to tune the window size for BOW and POSIT (to 2) and the parameters of the SP extraction algorithm.[11]

Baseline Greedy Search Algorithm   We also compare our search algorithm to its greedy variant: at each iteration of lines 8-12 in Alg. 1, R_n now keeps only the best configuration of size $l - 1$ that perform better than the initial configuration of size l, instead of all such configurations.

5   Results and Discussion

5.1   Main Evaluation Setup

Not All Context Bags are Created Equal   First, we test the performance of *individual* context bags across SimLex-999 adjective, verb, and noun subsets. Besides providing insight on the intuition behind context selection, these findings are important for the automatic selection of class-specific pools (line 1 of Alg. 1). The results are shown in Tab. 1.

The experiment supports our intuition (see Sect. 3.2): some context bags are definitely not useful for some classes and may be safely removed

---

[9]http://www.cs.cmu.edu/~ark/TurboParser/
[10]https://code.google.com/archive/p/mate-tools/

[11]The SP extraction algorithm is available online: homes.cs.washington.edu/~roysch/software/dr06/dr06.html

Baselines	(Verbs)
BOW (`win=2`)	0.336
POSIT (`win=2`)	0.345
COORD (`conjlr`)	0.283
SP	0.349
DEPS-All	0.344
Configurations: Verbs	
`POOL-ALL`	0.379
`prep+acl+obj+adv+conj`	0.393
`prep+acl+obj+comp+conj`	0.344
`prep+obj+comp+adv+conj`	*0.391*[†]
`prep+acl+adv+conj` (BEST)	**0.409**
`prep+acl+obj+adv`	0.392
`prep+acl+adv`	0.407
`prep+acl+conj`	0.390
`acl+obj+adv+conj`	0.345
`acl+obj+adv`	0.385

Baselines	(Nouns)
BOW (`win=2`)	0.435
POSIT (`win=2`)	0.437
COORD (`conjlr`)	0.392
SP	0.372
DEPS-All	0.441
Configurations: Nouns	
`POOL-ALL`	0.469
`amod+subj+obj+appos+compound+nmod+conj`	0.478
`amod+subj+obj+appos+compound+conj`	0.487
`amod+subj+obj+appos+compound+conjlr`	*0.476*[†]
`amod+subj+obj+compound+conj` (BEST)	**0.491**
`amod+subj+obj+appos+conj`	0.470
`subj+obj+compound+conj`	0.479
`amod+subj+compound+conj`	0.481
`amod+subj+obj+compound`	0.478
`amod+obj+compound+conj`	0.481

Table 3: Results on the SimLex-999 test data over (a) **verbs** and (b) **nouns** subsets. Only a selection of context configurations optimised for verb and noun similarity are shown. POOL-ALL denotes a configuration where all individual context bags from the verbs/nouns-oriented pools (see Table 2) are used. BEST denotes the best performing configuration found by Alg. 1. Other configurations visited by Alg. 1 that score higher than the best scoring baseline context type for each word class are in gray. Scores obtained using a greedy search algorithm instead of Alg. 1 are in italic, marked with a cross ([†]).

Baselines	(Adjectives)
BOW (`win=2`)	0.489
POSIT (`win=2`)	0.460
COORD (`conjlr`)	0.407
SP	0.395
DEPS-All	0.360
Configurations: Adjectives	
`POOL-ALL: amod+conj` (BEST)	**0.546**[†]
`amod+conjlr`	0.527
`amod+conjll`	0.531
`conj`	0.470

Table 4: Results on the SimLex-999 **adjectives** subset with adjective-specific configurations.

when performing the class-specific SGNS training. For instance, the `amod` bag is indeed important for adjective and noun similarity, and at the same time it does not encode any useful information regarding verb similarity. `compound` is, as expected, useful only for nouns. Tab. 1 also suggests that some context bags (e.g., `nummod`) do not encode any informative contextual evidence regarding similarity, therefore they can be discarded. The initial results with individual context bags help to reduce the pool of candidate bags (line 1 in Alg. 1), see Tab. 2.

Searching for Improved Configurations Next, we test if we can improve class-specific representations by selecting class-specific configurations. Results are summarised in Tables 3 and 4. Indeed, class-specific configurations yield better representations, as is evident from the scores: the improve-

ments with the best class-specific configurations found by Alg. 1 are approximately 6 ρ points for adjectives, 6 points for verbs, and 5 points for nouns over the best baseline for each class.

The improvements are visible even with configurations that simply pool all candidate individual bags (POOL-ALL), without running Alg. 1 beyond line 1. However, further careful context selection, i.e., traversing the configuration space using Alg. 1 leads to additional improvements for V and N (gains of 3 and 2.2 ρ points). Very similar improved scores are achieved with a variety of configurations (see Tab. 3), especially in the neighbourhood of the best configuration found by Alg. 1. This indicates that the method is quite robust: even sub-optimal[12] solutions result in improved class-specific representations. Furthermore, our algorithm is able to find better configurations for verbs and nouns compared to its greedy variant. Finally, our algorithm generalises well: the best scoring configuration on the dev set is always the best one on the test set.

Training: Fast and/or Accurate? Carefully selected configurations are also likely to reduce SGNS training times. Indeed, the configuration-based model trains on only 14% (A), 26.2% (V), and 33.6% (N) of all dependency-based contexts. The training times and statistics for each context type are displayed in Tab. 5. All models

---

[12]The term *optimal* here and later in the text refers to the best configuration returned by our algorithm.

Context Type	Training Time	# Pairs
BOW (win=2)	179mins 27s	5.974G
POSIT (win=2)	190mins 12s	5.974G
COORD (conjlr)	4mins 11s	129.69M
SP	1mins 29s	46.37M
DEPS-All	103mins 35s	3.165G
BEST-ADJ	14mins 5s	447.4M
BEST-VERBS	29mins 48s	828.55M
BEST-NOUNS	41mins 14s	1.063G

Table 5: Training time (wall-clock time reported) in minutes for SGNS ($d = 300$) with different context types. BEST-* denotes the best scoring configuration for each class found by Alg. 1. *#Pairs* shows a total number of pairs used in SGNS training for each context type.

Context Type	Adj	Verbs	Nouns	All
BOW (win=2)	0.604	0.307	0.501	0.464
POSIT (win=2)	0.585	0.400	0.471	0.469
COORD (conjlr)	0.629	0.413	0.428	0.430
SP	0.649	**0.458**	0.414	0.444
DEPS-All	0.574	0.389	0.492	0.464
BEST-ADJ	**0.671**	0.348	0.504	0.449
BEST-VERBS	0.392	0.455	0.478	0.448
BEST-NOUNS	0.581	0.327	**0.535**	0.489
BEST-ALL	0.616	0.402	0.519	**0.506**

Table 6: Results on the A/V/N SimLex-999 subsets, and on the entire set (*All*) in the setup from Schwartz et al. (2016). $d = 500$. BEST-* are again the best class-specific configs returned by Alg. 1.

were trained using parallel training on 10 Intel(R) Xeon(R) E5-2667 2.90GHz processors. The results indicate that class-specific configurations are not as lightweight and fast as SP or COORD contexts (Schwartz et al., 2016). However, they also suggest that such configurations provide a good balance between accuracy and speed: they reach peak performances for each class, outscoring all baseline context types (including SP and COORD), while training is still much faster than with "heavyweight" context types such as BOW, POSIT or DEPS-All.

Now that we verified the decrease in training time our algorithm provides for the final training, it makes sense to ask whether the configurations it finds are valuable *in other setups*. This will make the fast training of practical importance.

5.2 Generalisation: Configuration Transfer

Another Training Setup We first test whether the context configurations learned in Sect. 5.1 are useful when SGNS is trained in another English setup (Schwartz et al., 2016), with more training data and other annotation and parser choices, while evaluation is still performed on SimLex-999.

In this setup the training corpus is the 8B words corpus generated by the `word2vec` script.[13] A preprocessing step now merges common word pairs and triplets to expression tokens (e.g., *Bilbo_Baggins*). The corpus is parsed with labelled Stanford dependencies (de Marneffe and Manning, 2008) using the Stanford POS Tagger (Toutanova et al., 2003) and the stack version of the MALT parser (Goldberg and Nivre, 2012). SGNS preprocessing and parameters are also replicated; we now

train 500-dim embeddings as in prior work.[14]

Results are presented in Tab. 6. The imported class-specific configurations, computed using a much smaller corpus (Sect. 5.1), again outperform competitive baseline context types for adjectives and nouns. The BEST-VERBS configuration is outscored by SP, but the margin is negligible. We also evaluate another configuration found using Alg. 1 in Sect. 5.1, which targets the overall improved performance without any finer-grained division to classes (BEST-ALL). This configuration (`amod+subj+obj+compound+prep+adv+conj`) outperforms all baseline models on the entire benchmark. Interestingly, the non-specific BEST-ALL configuration falls short of A/V/N-specific configurations for each class. This unambiguously implies that the "trade-off" configuration targeting all three classes at the same time differs from specialised class-specific configurations.

Experiments on Other Languages We next test whether the optimal context configurations computed in Sect. 5.1 with English training data are also useful for other languages. For this, we train SGNS models on the Italian (IT) and German (DE) Polyglot Wikipedia corpora with those configurations, and evaluate on the IT and DE multilingual SimLex-999 (Leviant and Reichart, 2015).[15]

Our results demonstrate similar patterns as for English, and indicate that our framework can be easily applied to other languages. For instance, the BEST-ADJ configuration (the same configuration as in Tab. 4 and Tab. 7) yields an improvement of 8

---

[14] The "translation" from labelled Stanford dependencies into UD is performed using the mapping from de Marneffe et al. (2014), e.g., nn is mapped into compound, and rcmod, partmod, infmod are all mapped into one bag: acl.

[15] http://leviants.com/ira.leviant/MultilingualVSMdata.html

[13] code.google.com/p/word2vec/source/browse/trunk/

Context Type	Adj-Q	Verb-Q	Noun-Q
BOW (`win=2`)	31/41	14/19	16/19
POSIT (`win=2`)	**32/41**	13/19	15/19
COORD (`conjlr`)	26/41	11/19	8/19
SP	26/41	11/19	12/19
DEPS-All	31/41	14/19	16/19
BEST-ADJ	**32/41**	12/19	15/19
BEST-VERBS	24/41	**15/19**	16/19
BEST-NOUNS	30/41	14/19	**17/19**

Table 7: Results on the A/V/N TOEFL question subsets. The reported scores are in the following form: *correct_answers/overall_questions*. *Adj-Q* refers to the subset of TOEFL questions targeting adjectives; similar for *Verb-Q* and *Noun-Q*. BEST-* refer to the best class-specific configurations from Tab. 3 and Tab. 4.

ρ points and 4 ρ points over the strongest adjectives baseline in IT and DE, respectively. We get similar improvements for nouns (IT: 3 ρ points, DE: 2 ρ points), and verbs (IT: 2, DE: 4).

TOEFL Evaluation We also verify that the selection of class-specific configurations (Sect. 5.1) is useful beyond the core SimLex evaluation. For this aim, we evaluate on the A, V, and N TOEFL questions (Landauer and Dumais, 1997). The results are summarised in Tab. 7. Despite the limited size of the TOEFL dataset, we observe positive trends in the reported results (e.g., V-specific configurations yield a small gain on verb questions), showcasing the potential of class-specific training in this task.

6 Conclusion and Future Work

We have presented a novel framework for selecting class-specific context configurations which yield improved representations for prominent word classes: adjectives, verbs, and nouns. Its design and dependence on the Universal Dependencies annotation scheme makes it applicable in different languages. We have proposed an algorithm that is able to find a suitable class-specific configuration while making the search over the large space of possible context configurations computationally feasible. Each word class requires a different class-specific configuration to produce improved results on the class-specific subset of SimLex-999 in English, Italian, and German. We also show that the selection of context configurations is robust as once learned configuration may be effectively transferred to other data setups, tasks, and languages without additional retraining or fine-tuning.

In future work, we plan to test the framework with finer-grained contexts, investigating beyond POS-based word classes and dependency links. Exploring more sophisticated algorithms that can efficiently search richer configuration spaces is also an intriguing direction. Another research avenue is application of the context selection idea to other representation models beyond SGNS tested in this work, and experimenting with assigning weights to context subsets. Finally, we plan to test the portability of our approach to more languages.

Acknowledgments

This work is supported by the ERC Consolidator Grant LEXICAL: Lexical Acquisition Across Languages (no 648909). Roy Schwartz was supported by the Intel Collaborative Research Institute for Computational Intelligence (ICRI-CI). The authors are grateful to the anonymous reviewers for their helpful and constructive suggestions.

References

Rami Al-Rfou, Bryan Perozzi, and Steven Skiena. 2013. Polyglot: Distributed word representations for multilingual NLP. In *CoNLL*. pages 183–192. http://www.aclweb.org/anthology/W13-3520.

Mohit Bansal, Kevin Gimpel, and Karen Livescu. 2014. Tailoring continuous word representations for dependency parsing. In *ACL*. pages 809–815. http://www.aclweb.org/anthology/P14-2131.

Marco Baroni, Georgiana Dinu, and Germán Kruszewski. 2014. Don't count, predict! A systematic comparison of context-counting vs. context-predicting semantic vectors. In *ACL*. pages 238–247. http://www.aclweb.org/anthology/P14-1023.

Marco Baroni, Brian Murphy, Eduard Barbu, and Massimo Poesio. 2010. Strudel: A corpus-based semantic model based on properties and types. *Cognitive Science* pages 222–254. https://doi.org/10.1111/j.1551-6709.2009.01068.x.

Bernd Bohnet. 2010. Top accuracy and fast dependency parsing is not a contradiction. In *COLING*. pages 89–97. http://www.aclweb.org/anthology/C10-1011.

Danqi Chen and Christopher D. Manning. 2014. A fast and accurate dependency parser using neural networks. In *EMNLP*. pages 740–750. http://www.aclweb.org/anthology/D14-1082.

Ronan Collobert, Jason Weston, Léon Bottou, Michael Karlen, Koray Kavukcuoglu, and

Pavel P. Kuksa. 2011. Natural language processing (almost) from scratch. *Journal of Machine Learning Research* 12:2493–2537. http://dl.acm.org/citation.cfm?id=1953048.2078186.

Dmitry Davidov and Ari Rappoport. 2006. Efficient unsupervised discovery of word categories using symmetric patterns and high frequency words. In *ACL*. pages 297–304. http://www.aclweb.org/anthology/P06-1038.

Marie-Catherine de Marneffe, Timothy Dozat, Natalia Silveira, Katri Haverinen, Filip Ginter, Joakim Nivre, and Christopher D. Manning. 2014. Universal Stanford dependencies: A cross-linguistic typology. In *LREC*. pages 4585–4592. http://www.lrec-conf.org/proceedings/lrec2014/summaries/1062.html.

Marie-Catherine de Marneffe and Christopher D. Manning. 2008. The Stanford typed dependencies representation. In *Proceedings of the Workshop on Cross-Framework and Cross-Domain Parser Evaluation*. pages 1–8. http://www.aclweb.org/anthology/W08-1301.

Manaal Faruqui, Jesse Dodge, Sujay Kumar Jauhar, Chris Dyer, Eduard Hovy, and Noah A. Smith. 2015. Retrofitting word vectors to semantic lexicons. In *NAACL-HLT*. pages 1606–1615. http://www.aclweb.org/anthology/N15-1184.

Yoav Goldberg and Omer Levy. 2014. Word2vec explained: Deriving Mikolov et al.'s negative-sampling word-embedding method. *CoRR* abs/1402.3722. http://arxiv.org/abs/1402.3722.

Yoav Goldberg and Joakim Nivre. 2012. A dynamic oracle for arc-eager dependency parsing. In *COLING*. pages 959–976. http://www.aclweb.org/anthology/C12-1059.

Zellig S. Harris. 1954. Distributional structure. *Word* 10(23):146–162. https://doi.org/10.1080/00437956.1954.11659520.

Douwe Kiela, Felix Hill, and Stephen Clark. 2015. Specializing word embeddings for similarity or relatedness. In *EMNLP*. pages 2044–2048. http://aclweb.org/anthology/D15-1242.

Thomas K. Landauer and Susan T. Dumais. 1997. Solutions to Plato's problem: The Latent Semantic Analysis theory of acquisition, induction, and representation of knowledge. *Psychological Review* 104(2):211–240. https://doi.org/10.1037/0033-295X.104.2.211.

Ira Leviant and Roi Reichart. 2015. Separated by an un-common language: Towards judgment language informed vector space modeling. *CoRR* abs/1508.00106. http://arxiv.org/abs/1508.00106.

Omer Levy and Yoav Goldberg. 2014a. Dependency-based word embeddings. In *ACL*. pages 302–308. http://www.aclweb.org/anthology/P14-2050.

Omer Levy and Yoav Goldberg. 2014b. Linguistic regularities in sparse and explicit word representations. In *CoNLL*. pages 171–180. http://www.aclweb.org/anthology/W14-1618.

Omer Levy and Yoav Goldberg. 2014c. Neural word embedding as implicit matrix factorization. In *NIPS*. pages 2177–2185. http://papers.nips.cc/paper/5477.pdf.

Omer Levy, Yoav Goldberg, and Ido Dagan. 2015. Improving distributional similarity with lessons learned from word embeddings. *Transactions of the ACL* 3:211–225.

Wang Ling, Chris Dyer, Alan W. Black, and Isabel Trancoso. 2015a. Two/too simple adaptations of Word2Vec for syntax problems. In *NAACL-HLT*. pages 1299–1304. http://www.aclweb.org/anthology/N15-1142.

Wang Ling, Yulia Tsvetkov, Silvio Amir, Ramon Fermandez, Chris Dyer, Alan W Black, Isabel Trancoso, and Chu-Cheng Lin. 2015b. Not all contexts are created equal: Better word representations with variable attention. In *EMNLP*. pages 1367–1372. http://aclweb.org/anthology/D15-1161.

Quan Liu, Hui Jiang, Si Wei, Zhen-Hua Ling, and Yu Hu. 2015. Learning semantic word embeddings based on ordinal knowledge constraints. In *ACL*. pages 1501–1511. http://www.aclweb.org/anthology/P15-1145.

André F. T. Martins, Miguel B. Almeida, and Noah A. Smith. 2013. Turning on the Turbo: Fast third-order non-projective turbo parsers. In *ACL*. pages 617–622. http://www.aclweb.org/anthology/P13-2109.

Ryan T. McDonald, Joakim Nivre, Yvonne Quirmbach-Brundage, Yoav Goldberg, Dipanjan Das, Kuzman Ganchev, Keith B. Hall, Slav Petrov, Hao Zhang, Oscar Täckström, Claudia Bedini, Núria Bertomeu Castelló, and Jungmee Lee. 2013. Universal dependency annotation for multilingual parsing. In *ACL*. pages 92–97. http://www.aclweb.org/anthology/P13-2017.

Oren Melamud, Ido Dagan, and Jacob Goldberger. 2015. Modeling word meaning in context with substitute vectors. In *NAACL-HLT*. pages 472–482. http://www.aclweb.org/anthology/N15-1050.

Oren Melamud, David McClosky, Siddharth Patwardhan, and Mohit Bansal. 2016. The role of context types and dimensionality in learning word embeddings. In *NAACL-HLT*. http://www.aclweb.org/anthology/N16-1118.

Tomas Mikolov, Ilya Sutskever, Kai Chen, Gregory S. Corrado, and Jeffrey Dean. 2013. Distributed representations of words and phrases and their compositionality. In *NIPS*. pages 3111–3119.

Andriy Mnih and Koray Kavukcuoglu. 2013. Learning word embeddings efficiently with noise-contrastive estimation. In *NIPS*. pages 2265–2273.

Nikola Mrkšić, Ivan Vulić, Diarmuid Ó Séaghdha, Ira Leviant, Roi Reichart, Milica Gašić, Anna Korhonen, and Steve Young. 2017. Semantic specialisation of distributional word vector spaces using monolingual and cross-lingual constraints. *Transactions of the ACL* https://arxiv.org/abs/1706.00374.

Joakim Nivre et al. 2016. Universal Dependencies 1.4. LINDAT/CLARIN digital library at Institute of Formal and Applied Linguistics, Charles University in Prague.

Sebastian Padó and Mirella Lapata. 2007. Dependency-based construction of semantic space models. *Computational Linguistics* 33(2):161–199. https://doi.org/10.1162/coli.2007.33.2.161.

Judea Pearl. 1984. Heuristics: Intelligent search strategies for computer problem solving .

Jeffrey Pennington, Richard Socher, and Christopher Manning. 2014. Glove: Global vectors for word representation. In *EMNLP*. pages 1532–1543. http://www.aclweb.org/anthology/D14-1162.

Slav Petrov, Dipanjan Das, and Ryan T. McDonald. 2012. A universal part-of-speech tagset. In *LREC*. pages 2089–2096. http://www.lrecconf.org/proceedings/lrec2012/summaries/274.html.

Hinrich Schütze. 1993. Part-of-speech induction from scratch. In *ACL*. pages 251–258. http://www.aclweb.org/anthology/P93-1034.

Roy Schwartz, Roi Reichart, and Ari Rappoport. 2015. Symmetric pattern based word embeddings for improved word similarity prediction. In *CoNLL*. pages 258–267. http://www.aclweb.org/anthology/K15-1026.

Roy Schwartz, Roi Reichart, and Ari Rappoport. 2016. Symmetric patterns and coordinations: Fast and enhanced representations of verbs and adjectives. In *NAACL-HLT*. pages 499–505. http://www.aclweb.org/anthology/N16-1060.

Kristina Toutanova, Dan Klein, Christopher D. Manning, and Yoram Singer. 2003. Feature-rich part-of-speech tagging with a cyclic dependency network. In *NAACL-HLT*. pages 173–180. http://aclweb.org/anthology/N/N03/.

Joseph P. Turian, Lev-Arie Ratinov, and Yoshua Bengio. 2010. Word representations: A simple and general method for semi-supervised learning. In *ACL*. pages 384–394. http://www.aclweb.org/anthology/P10-1040.

Jason Utt and Sebastian Padó. 2014. Crosslingual and multilingual construction of syntax-based vector space models. *Transactions of the ACL* 2:245–258.

Ivan Vulić. 2017. Cross-lingual syntactically informed distributed word representations. In *EACL*. pages 408–414. http://www.aclweb.org/anthology/E17-2065.

Ivan Vulić and Anna Korhonen. 2016. Is "universal syntax" universally useful for learning distributed word representations? In *ACL*. pages 518–524. http://anthology.aclweb.org/P16-2084.

John Wieting, Mohit Bansal, Kevin Gimpel, and Karen Livescu. 2015. From paraphrase database to compositional paraphrase model and back. *Transactions of the ACL* 3:345–358. http://aclweb.org/anthology/Q15-1025.

Mehmet Ali Yatbaz, Enis Sert, and Deniz Yuret. 2012. Learning syntactic categories using paradigmatic representations of word context. In *EMNLP*. pages 940–951. http://www.aclweb.org/anthology/D12-1086.

Mo Yu and Mark Dredze. 2014. Improving lexical embeddings with semantic knowledge. In *ACL*. pages 545–550. http://www.aclweb.org/anthology/P14-2089.

Modeling Context Words as Regions:
An Ordinal Regression Approach to Word Embedding

Shoaib Jameel and Steven Schockaert
School of Computer Science and Informatics
Cardiff University
{JameelS1, SchockaertS1}@cardiff.ac.uk

Abstract

Vector representations of word meaning have found many applications in the field of natural language processing. Word vectors intuitively represent the average context in which a given word tends to occur, but they cannot explicitly model the diversity of these contexts. Although region representations of word meaning offer a natural alternative to word vectors, only few methods have been proposed that can effectively learn word regions. In this paper, we propose a new word embedding model which is based on SVM regression. We show that the underlying ranking interpretation of word contexts is sufficient to match, and sometimes outperform, the performance of popular methods such as Skip-gram. Furthermore, we show that by using a quadratic kernel, we can effectively learn word regions, which outperform existing unsupervised models for the task of hypernym detection.

1 Introduction

Word embedding models such as Skip-gram (Mikolov et al., 2013b) and GloVe (Pennington et al., 2014) represent words as vectors of typically around 300 dimensions. The relatively low-dimensional nature of these word vectors makes them ideally suited for representing textual input to neural network models (Goldberg, 2016; Nayak, 2015). Moreover, word embeddings have been found to capture many interesting regularities (Mikolov et al., 2013b; Kim and de Marneffe, 2013; Gupta et al., 2015; Rothe and Schütze, 2016), which makes it possible to use them as a source of semantic and linguistic knowledge, and to align word embeddings with visual features (Frome et al., 2013) or across different languages (Zou et al., 2013; Faruqui and Dyer, 2014).

Notwithstanding the practical advantages of representing words as vectors, a few authors have advocated the idea that words may be better represented as regions (Erk, 2009), possibly with gradual boundaries (Vilnis and McCallum, 2015). One important advantage of region representations is that they can distinguish words with a broad meaning from those with a more narrow meaning, and should thus in principle be better suited for tasks such as hypernym detection and taxonomy learning. However, it is currently not well understood how such region based representations can best be learned. One possible approach, suggested in (Vilnis and McCallum, 2015), is to learn a multivariate Gaussian for each word, essentially by requiring that words which frequently occur together are represented by similar Gaussians. However, for large vocabularies, this is computationally only feasible with diagonal covariance matrices.

In this paper, we propose a different approach to learning region representations for words, which is inspired by a geometric view of the Skip-gram model. Essentially, Skip-gram learns two vectors p_w and $\tilde{p_w}$ for each word w, such that the probability that a word c appears in the context of a target word t can be expressed as a function of $p_t \cdot \tilde{p_c}$ (see Section 2). This means that for each threshold $\lambda \in [-1, 1]$ and context word c, there is a hyperplane H_λ^c which (approximately) separates the words t for which $p_t \cdot \tilde{p_c} \geq \lambda$ from the others. Note that this hyperplane is completely determined by the vector $\tilde{p_c}$ and the choice of λ. An illustration of this geometric view is shown in Figure 1(a), where e.g. the word c is strongly related to a (i.e. a has a high probability of occurring in the context of c) but not closely related to b. Note in particular that there is a half-space containing those words which are strongly related to a (w.r.t.

Proceedings of the 21st Conference on Computational Natural Language Learning (CoNLL 2017), pages 123–133,
Vancouver, Canada, August 3 - August 4, 2017. ©2017 Association for Computational Linguistics

a given threshold λ).

Our contribution is twofold. First, we empirically show that effective word embeddings can be learned from purely ordinal information, which stands in contrast to the probabilistic view taken by e.g. Skip-gram and GloVe. Specifically, we propose a new word embedding model which uses (a ranking equivalent of) max-margin constraints to impose the requirement that $p_t \cdot \tilde{p}_c$ should be a monotonic function of the probability $P(c|t)$ of seeing c in the context of t. Geometrically, this means that, like Skip-gram, our model associates with each context word a number of parallel hyperplanes. However, unlike in the Skip-gram model, only the relative position of these hyperplanes is imposed (i.e. if $\lambda_1 < \lambda_2 < \lambda_3$ then $H_c^{\lambda_2}$ should occur between $H_c^{\lambda_1}$ and $H_c^{\lambda_3}$). Second, by using a quadratic kernel for the max-margin constraints, we obtain a model that can represent context words as a set of nested ellipsoids, as illustrated in Figure 1(b). From these nested ellipsoids we can then estimate a Gaussian which acts as a convenient region based word representation.

Note that our model thus jointly learns a vector representation for each word (i.e. the target word representations) as well as a region based representation (i.e. the nested ellipsoids representing the context words). We present experimental results which show that the region based representations are effective for measuring synonymy and hypernymy. Moreover, perhaps surprisingly, the region based modeling of context words also benefits the target word vectors, which match, and in some cases outperform the vectors obtained by standard word embedding models on various benchmark evaluation tasks.

2   Background and Related Work

2.1   Word Embedding

Various methods have already been proposed for learning vector space representations of words, e.g. based on matrix factorization (Turney and Pantel, 2010) or neural networks. Here we briefly review Skip-gram and GloVe, two popular models which share some similarities with our model.

The basic assumption of Skip-gram (Mikolov et al., 2013b) is that the probability $P(c|t)$ of seeing word c in the context of word t is given as:

$$P(c|t) = \frac{p_t \cdot \tilde{p}_c}{\sum_{c'} p_t \cdot \tilde{p}_{c'}}$$

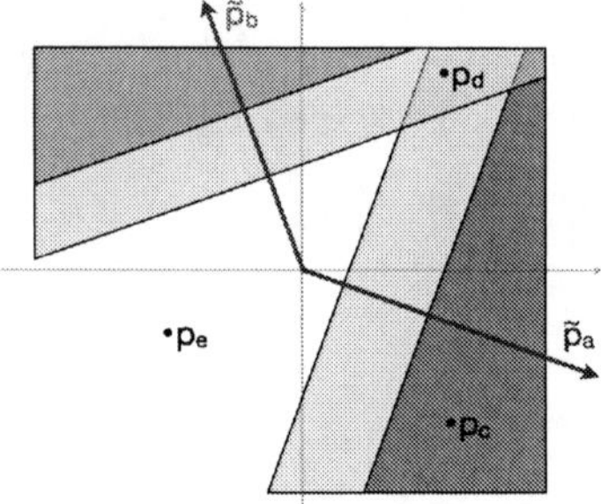

(a) Linear kernel

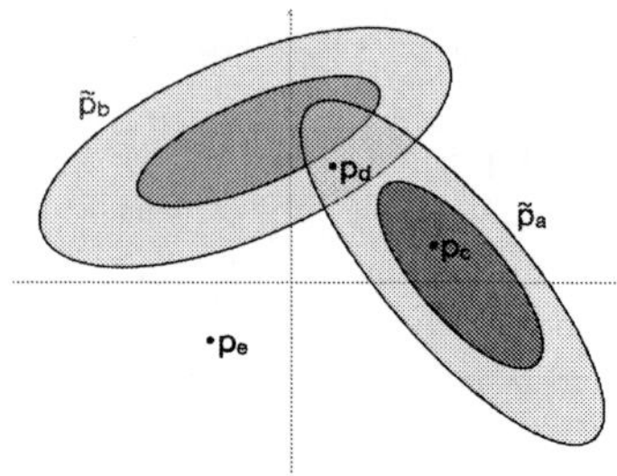

(b) Quadratic kernel

Figure 1: The (dark) green region covers words that are (strongly) related to a. Similarly, the (dark) blue region expresses relatedness to b.

In principle, based on this view, the target vectors p_w and context vectors $\tilde{p}_w$ could be learned by maximizing the likelihood of a given corpus. Since this is computationally not feasible, however, it was proposed in (Mikolov et al., 2013b) to instead optimize the following objective:

$$\sum_{i=1}^{N} \sum_{c' \in C_i} \log(\sigma(p_{w_i} \cdot \tilde{p}_c)) + \sum_{c' \in \overline{C}_i} \log(-\sigma(p_{w_i} \cdot \tilde{p}_{c'}))$$

where the left-most summation is over all N word occurrences in the corpus, w_i is the ith word in the corpus, C_i are the words appearing in the context of w_i and $\overline{C}_i$ consists of $k \cdot |C_i|$ randomly chosen words, called the negative samples for w_i. The context C_i contains the t_i words immediately preceding and succeeding w_i, where t_i is randomly sampled from $\{1, ..., t_{max}\}$ for each i (Goldberg and Levy, 2014). The probability of choosing word w as a negative sample is proportional to $\left(\frac{occ(w)}{N}\right)^{0.75}$, with $occ(w)$ the number of occurrences of word w in the corpus. Finally, to reduce the impact of frequent words, some word occurrences are removed from the corpus before applying the model, with the probability of removing an occurrence of word w being $1 - \sqrt{\frac{\theta}{occ(w)}}$. Default parameter values are $t_{max} = 5$ and $\theta = 10^{-5}$.

GloVe is another popular model for word embedding (Pennington et al., 2014). Rather than explicitly considering all word occurrences, it directly uses a global co-occurrence matrix $X = (x_{ij})$ where x_{ij} is the number of times the word w_j appears in the context of w_i. Like Skip-gram, it learns both a target vector p_w and context vector $\tilde{p}_w$ for each word w, but instead learns these vectors by optimizing the following objective:

$$\sum_i \sum_j f(x_{ij})(p_{w_i} \cdot \tilde{p}_{w_j} + b_{w_i} + \tilde{b}_{w_j} - \log x_{ij})^2$$

where b_{w_i} and $\tilde{b}_{w_j}$ are bias terms, and f is a weighting function to reduce the impact of very rare terms, defined as:

$$f(x_{ij}) = \begin{cases} (\frac{x_{ij}}{x_{max}})^\alpha & \text{if } x_{ij} < x_{max} \\ 1 & \text{otherwise} \end{cases}$$

The default values are $x_{max} = 100$ and $\alpha = 0.75$.

2.2 Region Representations

The idea of representing words as regions was advocated in (Erk, 2009), as a way of modeling the diversity of the contexts in which a word appears. It was argued that such regions could be used to more accurately model the meaning of polysemous words and to model lexical entailment. Rather than learning region representations directly, it was proposed to use a vector space representation of word occurrences. Two alternatives were investigated for estimating a region from these occurrence vectors, respectively inspired by prototype and exemplar based models of categorization. The first approach defines the region as the set of points whose weighted distance to a prototype vector for the word is within a given radius, while the second approach relies on the k-nearest neighbor principle.

In contrast, (Vilnis and McCallum, 2015) proposed a method that directly learns a representation in which each word corresponds to a Gaussian. The model uses an objective function which requires the Gaussians of words that co-occur to be more similar than the Gaussians of words of negative samples (which are obtained as in the Skipgram model). Two similarity measures are considered: the inner product of the Gaussians and the KL-divergence. It is furthermore argued that the asymmetric nature of KL-divergence makes it a natural choice for modeling hypernymy. In particular, it is proposed that the word embeddings could be improved by imposing that words that are in a hypernym relation have a low KL-divergence, allowing for a natural way to combine corpus statistics with available taxonomies.

Finally, another model that represents words using probability distributions was proposed in (Jameel and Schockaert, 2016). However, their model is aimed at capturing the uncertainty about vector representations, rather than at modeling the diversity of words. They show that capturing this uncertainty leads to vectors that outperform those of the GloVe model, on which their model is based. However, the resulting distributions are not suitable for modeling hypernymy. For example, since more information is available for general terms than for narrow terms, the distributions associated with general terms have a smaller variance, whereas approaches that are aimed at modeling the diversity of words have the opposite behavior.

2.3 Ranking Embedding

The model we propose only relies on the rankings induced by each context word, and tries to embed these rankings in a vector space. This problem of "ranking embedding" has already been studied by a few authors. An elegant approach for embedding a given set of rankings, based on the product order, is proposed in (Vendrov et al., 2016). However, this method is specifically aimed at completing partially ordered relations (such as taxonomies), based on observed statistical correlations, and would not be directly suitable as a basis for a word embedding method. The computational complexity of the ranking embedding problem was characterized in (Schockaert and Lee, 2015), where the associated decision problem was shown to be complete for the class $\exists \mathbb{R}$ (which sits between NP and PSPACE).

Note that the problem of ranking embedding is different from the learning-to-rank task (Liu, 2009). In the former case we are interested in learning a vector space representation that is somehow in accordance with a given completely specified set of rankings, whereas in the latter case the focus is on representing incompletely specified rankings in a given vector space representation.

3 Ordinal Regression Word Embedding

3.1 Learning the Embedding

In this section we explain how a form of ordinal regression can be used to learn both word vectors and word regions at the same time. First we introduce some notations.

Recall that the Positive Pointwise Mutual Information (PPMI) between two words w_i and w_j is defined as $PPMI(w_i, w_j) = \max(0, PMI(w_i, w_j))$, with $PMI(w_i, w_j)$ given by:

$$\log \left(\frac{n(w_i, w_j) \cdot (\sum_{w \in W} \sum_{w' \in W} n(w, w'))}{(\sum_{w \in W} n(w_i, w)) \cdot (\sum_{w \in W} n(w, w_j))} \right)$$

where we write $n(w_i, w_j)$ for the number of times word w_j occurs in the context of w_i, and W represents the vocabulary. For each word w_j, we write $W_0^j, ..., W_{n_j}^j$ for the stratification of the words in the vocabulary according to their PPMI value with w_j, i.e. we have that:

1. $PPMI(w, w_j) = 0$ for $w \in W_0^j$;

2. $PPMI(w, w_j) < PPMI(w', w_j)$ for $w \in W_i^j$ and $w' \in W_k^j$ with $i < k$; and

3. $PPMI(w, w_j) = PPMI(w', w_j)$ for $w, w' \in W_i^j$.

As a toy example, suppose $W = \{w_1, w_2, w_3, w_4, w_5\}$ and:

$$PPMI(w_2, w_1) = 3.4 \quad PPMI(w_3, w_1) = 4.1$$
$$PPMI(w_4, w_1) = 0 \quad PPMI(w_5, w_1) = 0$$
$$PPMI(w_1, w_1) = 0$$

Then we would have $W_0^1 = \{w_1, w_4, w_5\}$, $W_1^1 = \{w_2\}$ and $W_2^1 = \{w_3\}$.

To learn the word embedding, we use the following objective function, which requires that for each context word w_j there is a sequence of parallel hyperplanes that separate the representations of the words in W_{i-1}^j from the representations of the words in W_i^j ($i \in \{1, ..., n_j\}$):

$$\sum_j \left(\sum_{i=1}^{n_j} \frac{pos(j, i-1) + neg(j, i)}{|W_{i-1}^j \cup W_i^j|} \right) + \lambda \|\tilde{p}_{w_j}\|^2$$

where

$$pos(j, i-1) = \sum_{w \in W_{i-1}^j} [1 - (\phi(p_w) \cdot \tilde{p}_{w_j} + b_j^i)]_+^2$$

$$neg(j, i) = \sum_{w \in W_i^j} [1 + (\phi(p_w) \cdot \tilde{p}_{w_j} + b_j^i)]_+^2$$

subject to[1] $b_j^1 < ... < b_j^{n_j}$ for each j. Note that we write $[x]_+$ for $\max(0, x)$ and ϕ denotes the feature map of the considered kernel function. In this paper, we will in particular consider linear and quadratic kernels. If a linear kernel is used, then ϕ is simply the identity function. Using a quadratic kernel leads to a quadratic increase in the dimensionality of $\phi(p_w)$ and $\tilde{p}_{w_j}$. In practice, we found our model to be about 3 times slower when a quadratic kernel is used, when the word vectors p_w are chosen to be 300-dimensional. Note that $\tilde{p}_{w_j}$ and b_j^i define a hyperplane, separating the kernel space into a positive and a negative half-space. The constraints of the form $pos(j, i-1)$ essentially encode that the elements from W_{i-1}^j should be represented in the positive half-space, whereas the constraints of the form $neg(j, i)$ encode that the elements from W_i^j should be represented in the negative half-space.

When using a linear kernel, the model is similar in spirit to Skip-gram, in the sense that it associates with each context word a sequence of parallel hyperplanes. In our case, however, only the ordering of these hyperplanes is specified, i.e. the specific offsets b_j^i are learned. In other words, we make the assumption that the higher $PPMI(w, w_j)$ the stronger w is related to w_j, but we do not otherwise assume that the numerical value of $PPMI(w, w_j)$ is relevant. When using a quadratic kernel, each context word is essentially modeled as a sequence of nested ellipsoids. This gives the model a lot more freedom to satisfy the constraints, which may potentially lead to more informative vectors.

The model is similar in spirit to the fixed margin variant for ranking with large-margin constraints proposed in (Shashua and Levin, 2002), but with the crucial difference that we are learning word vectors and hyperplanes at the same time, rather than finding hyperplanes for a given vector space representation. We use stochastic gradient descent to optimize the proposed objective. Note that we use a squared hinge loss, which makes optimizing the objective more straightforward. As usual, the parameter λ controls the trade-off between maintaining a wide margin and minimizing classifica-

---

[1] While it may seem at first glance that this constraint is redundant, this is not actually the case; see (Chu and Keerthi, 2005) for a counterexample in a closely related framework.

tion errors. Throughout the experiments we have kept λ at a default value of 0.5. We have also added L2 regularization for the word vectors w_t with a weight of 0.01, which was found to increase the stability of the model. In practice, W_0^j is typically very large (containing most of the vocabulary), which would make the model too inefficient. To address this issue, we replace it by a small subsample, which is similar in spirit to the idea of negative sampling in the Skip-gram model. In our experiments we use $2k$ randomly sampled words from W, where $k = \sum_{i=1}^{n_j} |W_i^j|$ is the total number of positive samples. We simply use a uniform distribution to obtain the negative samples, as initial experiments showed that using other sampling strategies had almost no effect on the result.

3.2 Using Region Representations

When using a quadratic kernel, the hyperplanes defined by the vector $\tilde{p}_{w_j}$ and offsets b_j^i define a sequence of nested ellipsoids. To represent the word w_j, we estimate a Gaussian from these nested ellipsoids. The use of Gaussian representations is computationally convenient and intuitively acts as a form of smoothing. In Section 3.2.1 we first explain how these Gaussians are estimated, after which we explain how they are used for measuring word similarity in Section 3.2.2

3.2.1 Estimating Gaussians

Rather than estimating the Gaussian representation of a given word w_j from the vector $\tilde{p}_{w_j}$ and offsets b_j^i directly, we will estimate it from the locations of the words that are inside the corresponding ellipsoids. In this way, we can also take into account the distribution of words within each ellipsoid. In particular, for each word w_j, we first determine a set of words w whose vector p_w is inside these ellipsoids. Specifically, for each word w that occurs at least once in the context of w_j, or is among the 10 closest neighbors in the vector space of such a word, we test whether $\phi(p_w) \cdot \tilde{p}_{w_j} < -b_j^1$, i.e. whether w is in the outer ellipsoid for w_j. Let M_{w_j} be the set of all words w for which this is the case. We then represent w_j as the Gaussian $G(.; \mu_{w_j}, C_{w_j})$, where μ_{w_j} and C_{w_j} are estimated as the sample mean and covariance of the set $\{p_w \mid w \in M_{w_j}\}$.

We also consider a variant in which each word w from M_{w_j} is weighted as follows. First, we determine the largest k in $\{1, ..., n_j\}$ for which $\phi(p_w) \cdot \tilde{p}_{w_j} < -b_j^k$; note that since $w \in M_{w_j}$

such a k exists. The weight λ_w of w is defined as the PPMI value that is associated with the set W_j^k. When using this weighted setting, the mean μ_{w_j} and covariance matrix C_{w_j} are estimated as:

$$\mu_{w_j} = \frac{\sum_{w \in M_{w_j}} \lambda_w p_w}{\sum_{w \in M_{w_j}} \lambda_w}$$

$$C_{w_j} = \frac{\sum_{w \in M_{w_j}} \lambda_w (p_w - \mu)(p_w - \mu)^T}{\sum_{w \in M_{w_j}} \lambda_w}$$

Note that the two proposed methods to estimate the Gaussian $G(.; \mu_{w_j}, C_{w_j})$ do not depend on the choice of kernel, hence they could also be applied in combination with a linear kernel. However, given the close relationships between Gaussians and ellipsoids, we can expect quadratic kernels to lead to higher-quality representations. This will be confirmed experimentally in Section 4.

3.2.2 Measuring similarity

To compute the similarity between w and w', based on the associated Gaussians, we consider two alternatives. First, following (Vilnis and McCallum, 2015), we consider the inner product, defined as follows:

$$E(w, w') = \int G(x; \mu_w, C_w) G(x; \mu_{w'}, C_{w'}) dx$$

$$= G(0; \mu_w - \mu_{w'}, C_w + C_{w'})$$

The second alternative is the Jensen-Shannon divergence, given by:

$$JS(w, w') = KL(f_w \| f_{w'}) + KL(f_{w'} \| f_w)$$

with $f_w = G(.; \mu_w, C_w)$, $f_{w'} = G(.; \mu_{w'}, C_{w'})$, and KL the Kullback-Leibler divergence. When computing the KL-divergence we add a small value δ to the diagonal elements of the covariance matrices, following (Vilnis and McCallum, 2015); we used 0.01. This is needed, as for rare words, the covariance matrix may otherwise be singular.

Finally, to measure the degree to which w entails w', we use KL-divergence, again in accordance with (Vilnis and McCallum, 2015).

4 Experiments

In this section we evaluate both the vector and region representations produced by our model. In our experiments, we have used the Wikipedia dump from November 2nd, 2015 consisting of 1,335,766,618 tokens. We used a basic text preprocessing strategy, which involved removing punctuations, removing HTML/XML tags and lowercasing all tokens. We have removed words with less than 10 occurrences in the entire corpus. We used the Apache sentence segmentation tool[2] to detect sentence boundaries. In all our experiments, we have set the number of dimensions as 300, which was found to be a good choice in previous work, e.g. (Pennington et al., 2014). We use a context window of 10 words before and after the target word, but without crossing sentence boundaries. The number of iterations for SGD was set to 20. The results of all baseline models have been obtained using their publicly available implementations. We have used 10 negative samples in the word2vec code, which gave better results than the default value of 5. For the baseline models, we have used the default settings, apart from the D-GloVe model for which no default values were provided by the authors. For D-GloVe, we have therefore tuned the parameters using the ranges discussed in (Jameel and Schockaert, 2016). Specifically we have used the parameters that gave the best results on the Google Analogy Test Set (see below).

As baselines we have used the following standard word embedding models: the Skip-gram (SG) and Continuous Bag-of-Words (CBOW) models[3], proposed in (Mikolov et al., 2013a), the GloVe model[4], proposed in (Pennington et al., 2014), and the D-GloVe model[5] proposed in (Jameel and Schockaert, 2016). We have also compared against the Gaussian word embedding model[6] from (Vilnis and McCallum, 2015), using the means of the Gaussians as vector representations, and the Gaussians themselves as region representations. As in (Vilnis and McCallum, 2015), we consider two variants: one with diagonal covariance matrices (Gauss-D) and one with spherical covariance matrices (Gauss-S). For our model, we will consider the following configurations:

Reg-li-cos word vectors, obtained using linear kernel, compared using cosine similarity;

[2]https://opennlp.apache.org/documentation/1.5.3/manual/opennlp.html#tools.sentdetect
[3]https://code.google.com/archive/p/word2vec/
[4]https://nlp.stanford.edu/projects/glove/
[5]https://github.com/bashthebuilder/pGlove
[6]https://github.com/seomoz/word2gauss

Table 1: Results for the analogy completion task (accuracy). Reg-li-* and Reg-qu-* are our models with a linear and quadratic kernel.

	Gsem	Gsyn	MSR
SG	71.5	64.2	**68.6**
CBOW	74.2	62.3	66.2
GloVe	80.2	58.0	50.3
D-GloVe	**81.4**	59.1	59.6
Gauss-D-cos	61.5	53.6	50.7
Gauss-D-eucl	61.5	53.6	50.7
Gauss-S-cos	61.2	53.2	49.8
Gauss-S-eucl	61.4	53.3	49.8
Reg-li-cos	77.8	62.4	62.6
Reg-li-eucl	77.9	62.6	62.6
Reg-qu-cos	78.6	**65.7**	63.5
Reg-qu-eucl	78.7	**65.7**	63.6

Reg-li-eucl word vectors, obtained using linear kernel, compared using Euclidean distance;

Reg-qu-cos word vectors, obtained using quadratic kernel, compared using cosine similarity;

Reg-qu-eucl word vectors, obtained using quadratic kernel, compared using Euclidean distance;

Reg-li-prod Gaussian word regions, obtained using linear kernel, compared using the inner product E;

Reg-li-wprod Gaussian word regions estimated using the weighted variant, obtained using linear kernel, compared using the inner product E;

Reg-li-JS Gaussian word regions, obtained using linear kernel, compared using the Jensen-Shannon divergence;

Reg-li-wJS Gaussian word regions estimated using the weighted variant, obtained using linear kernel, compared using Jensen-Shannon divergence.

4.1 Analogy Completion

Analogy completion is a standard evaluation task for word embeddings. Given a pair (w_1, w_2) and a word w_3 the goal is to find the word w_4 such that w_3 and w_4 are related in the same way as w_1 and w_2. To solve this task, we predict the word w_4 which is most similar to $w_2 - w_1 + w_3$, either in terms of cosine similarity or Euclidean distance. The evaluation metric is accuracy. We use two popular benchmark data sets: the Google Analogy

Test Set[7] and the Microsoft Research Syntactic Analogies Dataset[8]. The former contains both semantic and syntactic relations, for which we show the results separately, respectively referred to as Gsem and Gsyn; the latter only contains syntactic relations and will be referred to as MSR. The results are shown in Table 1. Recall that the parameters of D-GloVe were tuned on the Google Analogy Test Set, hence the results reported for this model for Gsem and Gsyn might be slightly higher than what would normally be obtained. Note that for our model, we can only use word vectors for this task.

We outperform SG and CBOW for Gsem and Gsyn but not for MSR, and we outperform GloVe and D-GloVe for Gsyn and MSR but not for Gsem. The vectors from the Gaussian embedding model are not competitive for this task. For our model, using Euclidean distance slightly outperforms using cosine. For GloVe, SG and CBOW, we only show results for cosine, as this led to the best results. For D-GloVe, we used the likelihood-based similarity measure proposed in the original paper, which was found to outperform both cosine and Euclidean distance for that model.

For our model, the quadratic kernel leads to better results than the linear kernel, which is somewhat surprising since this task evaluates a kind of linear regularity. This suggests that the additional flexibility that results from the quadratic kernel leads to more faithful context word representations, which in turn improves the quality of the target word vectors.

4.2 Similarity Estimation

To evaluate our model's ability to measure similarity we use 12 standard evaluation sets[9], for which we will use the following abbreviations: S1: MTurk-287, S2:RG-65, S3:MC-30, S4:WS-353-REL, S5:WS-353-ALL, S6:RW-STANFORD, S7: YP-130, S8:SIMLEX-999, S9:VERB-143, S10: WS-353-SIM, S11:MTurk-771, S12:MEN-TR-3K. Each of these datasets contains similarity judgements for a number of word pairs. The task evaluates to what extent the similarity scores produced by a given word embedding model lead to

the same ordering of the word pairs as the provided ground truth judgments. The evaluation metric is the Spearman ρ rank correlation coefficient. For this task, we can either use word vectors or word regions. The results are shown in Table 2.

For our model, the best results are obtained when using word vectors and the Euclidean distance (Reg-qu-eucl), although the differences with the word regions (Reg-qu-wprod) are small. We use *prod* to refer to the configuration where similarity is estimated using the inner product, whereas we write JS for the configurations that use Jensen-Shannon divergence. Moreover, we use *wprod* and wJS to refer to the weighted variant for estimating the Gaussians. We can again observe that using a quadratic kernel leads to better results than using a linear kernel. As the weighted versions for estimating the Gaussians do not lead to a clear improvement, for the remainder of this paper we will only consider the unweighted variant.

With the exception of S9, our model substantially outperforms the Gaussian word embedding model. Of the standard models SG and D-GloVe obtain the strongest performance. Compared to our model, these baseline models achieve similar results for S2, S10, S11 and S12, worse results for S1, S3, S4, S5, S6 and better results for S7, S8 and S9. Two general trends can be observed. First, the data sets where our model performs better tend to be datasets which describe semantic relatedness rather than pure synonymy. Second, the standard models appear to perform better on data sets that contain verbs and adjectives, as opposed to nouns.

4.3 Modeling properties

In (Rubinstein et al., 2015), it was analysed to what extent word embeddings can be used to identify concepts that satisfy a given attribute. While good results were obtained for taxonomic properties, attributive properties such as 'dangerous', 'round', or 'blue' proved to be considerably more problematic. We may expect region-based models to perform well on this task, since each of these attributes then explicitly corresponds to a region in space. To test this hypothesis, Table 3 shows the results for the same 7 taxonomic properties and 13 attributive properties as in (Rubinstein et al., 2015), where the positive and negative examples for all 20 properties are obtained from the McRae feature norms data (McRae et al., 2005). Following (Rubinstein et al., 2015), we use

---

[7] https://nlp.stanford.edu/projects/glove/

[8] http://research.microsoft.com/en-us/um/people/gzweig/Pubs/myz_naacl13_test_set.tgz

[9] https://github.com/mfaruqui/eval-word-vectors

Table 2: Results for similarity estimation (Spearman ρ). Reg-li-* and Reg-qu-* are our models with a linear and quadratic kernel.

	S1	S2	S3	S4	S5	S6	S7	S8	S9	S10	S11	S12
SG	0.656	0.773	0.789	0.648	0.709	0.459	0.500	**0.415**	**0.435**	0.773	0.655	0.731
CBOW	0.644	0.768	0.740	0.532	0.622	0.419	0.341	0.361	0.343	0.707	0.597	0.693
GloVe	0.595	0.755	0.746	0.515	0.577	0.318	0.533	0.382	0.354	0.690	0.652	0.724
D-GloVe	0.659	**0.788**	0.785	0.555	0.651	0.401	**0.535**	0.413	0.388	0.778	**0.656**	**0.746**
Gauss-D-cos	0.591	0.622	0.661	0.403	0.501	0.249	0.388	0.337	0.411	0.640	0.599	0.643
Gauss-D-eucl	0.591	0.623	0.661	0.403	0.501	0.250	0.388	0.338	0.411	0.641	0.599	0.643
Gauss-D-prod	0.588	0.618	0.658	0.399	0.498	0.213	0.356	0.326	0.409	0.631	0.588	0.633
Gauss-D-JS	0.598	0.619	0.665	0.403	0.532	0.288	0.381	0.339	0.410	0.643	0.599	0.644
Gauss-S-cos	0.593	0.632	0.681	0.409	0.506	0.256	0.392	0.337	0.416	0.649	0.601	0.644
Gauss-S-eucl	0.593	0.632	0.681	0.409	0.507	0.356	0.393	0.337	0.416	0.649	0.603	0.644
Gauss-S-prod	0.591	0.619	0.659	0.403	0.505	0.312	0.389	0.328	0.412	0.633	0.591	0.633
Gauss-S-JS	0.598	0.622	0.667	0.405	0.533	0.288	0.385	0.349	0.410	0.643	0.601	0.644
Reg-li-cos	0.666	0.764	0.821	0.652	0.713	0.489	0.469	0.354	0.361	0.734	0.642	0.739
Reg-li-eucl	0.668	0.766	0.821	0.654	0.715	0.489	0.469	0.359	0.361	0.734	0.643	0.739
Reg-li-prod	0.661	0.759	0.818	0.634	0.710	0.481	0.445	0.358	0.360	0.724	0.641	0.729
Reg-li-wprod	0.663	0.761	0.819	0.638	0.711	0.482	0.446	0.359	0.361	0.725	0.642	0.731
Reg-li-JS	0.663	0.758	0.815	0.638	0.709	0.479	0.443	0.359	0.361	0.723	0.641	0.729
Reg-li-wJS	0.665	0.760	0.816	0.638	0.710	0.481	0.445	0.359	0.361	0.725	0.641	0.731
Reg-qu-cos	0.684	0.781	**0.839**	0.662	**0.723**	0.505	0.479	0.367	0.368	0.777	**0.656**	0.744
Reg-qu-eucl	**0.685**	0.781	**0.839**	**0.664**	**0.723**	**0.509**	0.479	0.367	0.368	**0.779**	**0.656**	0.744
Reg-qu-prod	0.681	0.780	0.831	0.658	0.719	0.501	0.478	0.355	0.331	0.778	0.653	0.741
Reg-qu-wprod	0.684	**0.788**	0.831	0.663	0.721	0.501	0.475	0.370	0.365	0.778	0.653	0.739
Reg-qu-JS	0.680	0.781	0.826	0.661	0.715	0.497	0.471	0.328	0.355	0.771	0.649	0.721
Reg-qu-wJS	0.678	0.782	0.824	0.662	0.712	0.498	0.469	0.326	0.351	0.771	0.644	0.720

Table 3: Results for McRae feature norms (F1). Reg-li and Reg-qu are our models with a linear and quadratic kernel.

	Taxonomic		Attributive	
	lin	quad	lin	quad
SG	0.781	0.784	0.365	0.378
CBOW	0.775	0.781	0.361	0.371
GloVe	0.785	0.786	0.364	0.377
D-GloVe	0.743	0.749	0.342	0.364
Gauss-D	0.787	0.789	0.406	0.414
Gauss-S	0.781	0.784	0.401	0.406
Reg-li	0.791	0.796	0.399	0.406
Reg-qu	**0.795**	**0.799**	**0.411**	**0.421**

5-fold cross-validation to train a binary SVM for each property and compute the average F-score due to unbalanced class label distribution. We separately present results for SVMs with a linear and a quadratic kernel. The results indeed support the hypothesis that region-based models are well-suited for this task, as both the Gaussian embedding model and our model outperform the standard word embedding models.

4.4 Hypernym Detection

For hypernym detection, we have used the following 5 benchmark data sets[10]: H1 (Baroni et al., 2012), H2 (Baroni and Lenci, 2011), H3 (Kotler-

man et al., 2010), H4 (Levy et al., 2014) and H5 (Turney and Mohammad, 2015). Each of the data sets contains positive and negative examples, i.e. word pairs that are in a hypernym relation and word pairs that are not. Rather than treating this problem as a classification task, which would require selecting a threshold in addition to producing a score, we treat it as a ranking problem. In other words, we evaluate to what extent the word pairs that are in a valid hypernym relation are the ones that receive the highest scores. We use average precision as our evaluation metric.

Apart from our model, the Gaussian embedding model is the only word embedding model that can by design support unsupervised hyperynym detection. As an additional baseline, however, we also show how Skip-gram performs when using cosine similarity. While such a symmetric measure cannot faithfully model hypernyny, it was nonetheless found to be a strong baseline for hypernymy models (Vulić et al., 2016), due to the inherent difficulty of the task. We also compare with a number of standard bag-of-words based models for detecting hypernyms: WeedsPrec (Kotlerman et al., 2010), ClarkeDE (Clarke, 2009) and invCL (Lenci and Benotto, 2012). These latter models take as input the PPMI weighted co-occurrence counts.

The results are shown in Table 4, where Reg-li-KL and Reg-qu-KL refer to variants of our model

[10]https://github.com/stephenroller/ emnlp2016

Table 4: Results for hypernym detection (AP). Reg-li-* and Reg-qu-* are our models with a linear and quadratic kernel.

Model	H1	H2	H3	H4	H5
WeedsPrec	0.565	0.376	0.611	0.414	0.685
ClarkeDE	0.588	0.397	0.621	0.426	0.699
invCL	0.603	0.416	0.693	0.439	0.756
SG	0.682	0.434	0.712	0.455	0.789
Gauss-D-KL	0.865	0.505	0.806	0.515	0.815
Gauss-S-KL	0.823	0.498	0.801	0.507	0.789
Gauss-D-Cos	0.846	0.499	0.801	0.509	0.811
Gauss-S-Cos	0.813	0.484	0.799	0.501	0.778
Gauss-D-KLC	0.868	0.511	0.809	0.519	0.815
Gauss-S-KLC	0.835	0.501	0.804	0.511	0.795
Reg-li-KL	0.867	0.501	0.805	0.505	0.801
Reg-qu-KL	0.871	0.512	0.811	0.521	0.814
Reg-li-Cos	0.871	0.502	0.807	0.508	0.804
Reg-qu-Cos	0.873	0.513	0.818	0.525	0.819
Reg-li-KLC	0.874	0.509	0.812	0.511	0.806
Reg-qu-KLC	**0.878**	**0.519**	**0.825**	**0.531**	**0.823**

Table 5: Results for HyperLex (Spearman ρ). Reg-li-* and Reg-qu-* are our models with a linear and quadratic kernel.

Model	All	Nouns	Verbs
WeedsPrec	0.166	0.153	0.201
ClarkeDE	0.165	0.151	0.189
invCL	0.168	0.154	0.198
SG	0.158	0.164	**0.297**
Gauss-D-KL	0.185	0.171	0.198
Gauss-S-KL	0.181	0.168	0.184
Gauss-D-Cos	0.179	0.158	0.161
Gauss-S-Cos	0.166	0.151	0.158
Gauss-D-KLC	0.191	0.177	0.199
Gauss-S-KLC	0.189	0.171	0.189
Reg-li-KL	0.181	0.165	0.179
Reg-qu-KL	0.188	0.169	0.191
Reg-li-Cos	0.184	0.168	0.181
Reg-qu-Cos	0.190	0.180	0.196
Reg-li-KLC	0.189	0.171	0.185
Reg-qu-KLC	**0.208**	**0.188**	0.201

in which Kullback-Leibler divergence is used to compare word regions. Surprisingly, both for our model and for the Gaussian embedding model, we find that using cosine similarity between the word vectors outperforms using the word regions with KL-divergence. In general, our model outperforms the Gaussian embedding model and the other baselines. Given the effectiveness of the cosine similarity, we have also experimented with the following metric:

$$hyp(w_1, w_2) = (1 - \cos(w_1, w_2)) \cdot KL(f_{w_1} || f_{w_2})$$

The results are referred to as Reg-li-KLC and Reg-qu-KLC in Table 4. These results suggest that the word regions can indeed be useful for detecting hypernymy, when used in combination with cosine similarity. Intuitively, for w_2 to be a hypernym of w_1, both words need to be similar and w_2 needs to be more general than w_1. While word regions are not needed for measuring similarity, they seem essential for modeling generality (in an unsupervised setting).

The datasets considered so far all treat hypernyms as a binary notion. In (Vulić et al., 2016) a evaluation set was introduced which contains graded hypernym pairs. The underlying intuition is that e.g. cat and dog are more typical/natural hyponyms of animal than dinosaur or amoeba. The results for this data set are shown in Table 5. In this case, we use Spearman ρ as an evaluation metric, measuring how well the rankings induced by different models correlate with the ground truth. Following (Vulić et al., 2016), we separately mention results for nouns and verbs. In the case of

nouns, our findings here are broadly in agreement with those from Table 4 Interesting, for verbs we find that Skip-gram substantially outperforms the region based models, which is in accordance with our findings in the word similarity experiments.

5 Conclusions

We have proposed a new word embedding model, which is based on ordinal regression. The input to our model consists of a number of rankings, capturing how strongly each word is related to each context word in a purely ordinal way. Word vectors are then obtained by embedding these rankings in a low-dimensional vector space. Despite the fact that all quantitative information is disregarded by our model (except for constructing the rankings), it is competitive with standard methods such as Skip-gram, and in fact outperforms them in several tasks. An important advantage of our model is that it can be used to learn region representations for words, by using a quadratic kernel. Our experimental results suggest that these regions can be useful for modeling hypernymy.

Acknowledgments

This work was supported by ERC Starting Grant 637277. This work was performed using the computational facilities of the Advanced Research Computing@Cardiff (ARCCA) Division, Cardiff University. The authors would like to thank the anonymous reviewers for their insightful comments.

References

Marco Baroni, Raffaella Bernardi, Ngoc-Quynh Do, and Chung-chieh Shan. 2012. Entailment above the word level in distributional semantics. In *Proceedings of the 13th Conference of the European Chapter of the Association for Computational Linguistics.* pages 23–32.

Marco Baroni and Alessandro Lenci. 2011. How we blessed distributional semantic evaluation. In *Proceedings of the GEMS 2011 Workshop on GEometrical Models of Natural Language Semantics.* Association for Computational Linguistics, pages 1–10.

Wei Chu and S Sathiya Keerthi. 2005. New approaches to support vector ordinal regression. In *ICML.* pages 145–152.

Daoud Clarke. 2009. Context-theoretic semantics for natural language: an overview. In *Proceedings of the Workshop on Geometrical Models of Natural Language Semantics.* pages 112–119.

Katrin Erk. 2009. Representing words as regions in vector space. In *Proceedings of the Thirteenth Conference on Computational Natural Language Learning.* pages 57–65.

Manaal Faruqui and Chris Dyer. 2014. Improving vector space word representations using multilingual correlation. In *Proceedings of the 14th Conference of the European Chapter of the Association for Computational Linguistics.* pages 462–471.

Andrea Frome, Gregory S. Corrado, Jonathon Shlens, Samy Bengio, Jeffrey Dean, Marc'Aurelio Ranzato, and Tomas Mikolov. 2013. Devise: A deep visual-semantic embedding model. In *Proc. NIPS.* pages 2121–2129.

Yoav Goldberg. 2016. A primer on neural network models for natural language processing. *Journal of Artificial Intelligence Research* 57:345–420.

Yoav Goldberg and Omer Levy. 2014. word2vec explained: Deriving mikolov et al.'s negative-sampling word-embedding method. *arXiv preprint arXiv:1402.3722* .

Abhijeet Gupta, Gemma Boleda, Marco Baroni, and Sebastian Padó. 2015. Distributional vectors encode referential attributes. In *Proc. EMNLP.* pages 12–21.

Shoaib Jameel and Steven Schockaert. 2016. D-glove: A feasible least squares model for estimating word embedding densities. In *Proceedings of the 26th International Conference on Computational Linguistics.* pages 1849–1860.

Joo-Kyung Kim and Marie-Catherine de Marneffe. 2013. Deriving adjectival scales from continuous space word representations. In *Proc. EMNLP.* pages 1625–1630.

Lili Kotlerman, Ido Dagan, Idan Szpektor, and Maayan Zhitomirsky-Geffet. 2010. Directional distributional similarity for lexical inference. *Natural Language Engineering* 16:359–389.

Alessandro Lenci and Giulia Benotto. 2012. Identifying hypernyms in distributional semantic spaces. In *Proceedings of *SEM.* pages 75–79.

Omer Levy, Yoav Goldberg, and Israel Ramat-Gan. 2014. Linguistic regularities in sparse and explicit word representations. In *Proc. CoNLL.* pages 171–180.

Tie-Yan Liu. 2009. Learning to rank for information retrieval. *Foundations and Trends in Information Retrieval* 3:225–331.

Ken McRae, George S Cree, Mark S Seidenberg, and Chris McNorgan. 2005. Semantic feature production norms for a large set of living and nonliving things. *Behavior Research Methods* 37:547–559.

Tomas Mikolov, Kai Chen, Greg Corrado, and Jeffrey Dean. 2013a. Efficient estimation of word representations in vector space. In *International Conference on Learning Representations.*

Tomas Mikolov, Ilya Sutskever, Kai Chen, Gregory S. Corrado, and Jeffrey Dean. 2013b. Distributed representations of words and phrases and their compositionality. In *Proceedings of the 27th Annual Conference on Neural Information Processing Systems.* pages 3111–3119.

Neha Nayak. 2015. In learning hyperonyms over word embeddings. Technical report, Student technical report.

Jeffrey Pennington, Richard Socher, and Christopher D. Manning. 2014. Glove: Global vectors for word representation. In *Proc. EMNLP.* pages 1532–1543.

Sascha Rothe and Hinrich Schütze. 2016. Word embedding calculus in meaningful ultradense subspaces. In *Proceedings of the 54th Annual Meeting of the Association for Computational Linguistics.* pages 512–517.

Dana Rubinstein, Effi Levi, Roy Schwartz, and Ari Rappoport. 2015. How well do distributional models capture different types of semantic knowledge? In *Proceedings of the 53rd Annual Meeting of the Association for Computational Linguistics.* pages 726–730.

Steven Schockaert and Jae Hee Lee. 2015. Qualitative reasoning about directions in semantic spaces. In *Proceedings of the International Joint Conference on Artificial Intelligence.* pages 3207–3213.

Amnon Shashua and Anat Levin. 2002. Ranking with large margin principle: Two approaches. In *NIPS.* pages 937–944.

P. D. Turney and P. Pantel. 2010. From frequency to meaning: Vector space models of semantics. *Journal of Artificial Intelligence Research* 37:141–188.

Peter D Turney and Saif M Mohammad. 2015. Experiments with three approaches to recognizing lexical entailment. *Natural Language Engineering* 21(03):437–476.

Ivan Vendrov, Ryan Kiros, Sanja Fidler, and Raquel Urtasun. 2016. Order-embeddings of images and language. In *International Conference on Learning Representations*.

Luke Vilnis and Andrew McCallum. 2015. Word representations via gaussian embedding. In *Proceedings of the International Conference on Learning Representations*.

Ivan Vulić, Daniela Gerz, Douwe Kiela, Felix Hill, and Anna Korhonen. 2016. Hyperlex: A large-scale evaluation of graded lexical entailment. *arXiv* .

Will Y Zou, Richard Socher, Daniel M Cer, and Christopher D Manning. 2013. Bilingual word embeddings for phrase-based machine translation. In *Proc. EMNLP*. pages 1393–1398.

An Artificial Language Evaluation of Distributional Semantic Models

Fatemeh Torabi Asr
Cognitive Science Program
Indiana University, Bloomington
`fatorabi@indiana.edu`

Michael N. Jones
Psychological and Brain Sciences
Indiana University, Bloomington
`jonesmn@indiana.edu`

Abstract

Recent studies of distributional semantic models have set up a competition between word embeddings obtained from predictive neural networks and word vectors obtained from count-based models. This paper is an attempt to reveal the underlying contribution of additional training data and post-processing steps on each type of model in word similarity and relatedness inference tasks. We do so by designing an artificial language, training a predictive and a count-based model on data sampled from this grammar, and evaluating the resulting word vectors in paradigmatic and syntagmatic tasks defined with respect to the grammar.

1 Introduction

The distributional tradition in linguistics (e.g., Harris, 1954) classically posits that a word's meaning can be estimated by its pattern of co-occurrence with other words. Modern distributional semantic models (DSMs) formalize this process to construct vector representations for word meaning from statistical regularities in large-scale corpora. A typical approach in NLP has been to apply dimensional reduction algorithms borrowed from linear algebra to a word-by-context frequency matrix representation of a text corpus (Deerwester et al. 1990, Landauer & Dumais, 1997). Words that frequently appear in similar contexts will have similar patterns across resulting latent components, even if they never directly co-occur (for reviews, see Jones, Willits, & Dennis, 2015; Turney & Pantel, 2010). These models dominated the literature over direct count methods for over two decades (Bullinaria & Levy, 2007, 2012). Recently, DSMs based on neural networks have rapidly grown in popularity (e.g., Bengio et al., 2003; Collobert et al., 2011; Mikolov et al., 2013). Given a word, the model attempts to predict the context words that it occurs with, or vice-versa. After training on a text corpus, the pattern of elements across the model's hidden layer come to reflect semantic similarities, i.e., will be similar for words that predict similar contexts even if those words do not predict each other. In this sense, neural embedding models come to a distributed vector representation of word meaning that is reminiscent of traditional dimensional reduction DSMs, albeit with a considerably different learning algorithm.

Mikolov et al. (2013a, 2013b) have demonstrated state-of-the-art performance using a neural embedding model with an efficient objective function called `word2vec`. This model rapidly emerged as the leader of the DSM pack, outperforming other models on a broad range of lexical semantic tasks (Baroni et al. 2014). However, since the early surge in excitement for `word2vec`, the literature has now become more focused on trying to understand the conditions under which embedding or traditional DSMs are optimal. Levy and Goldberg (2014) demonstrated analytically that `word2vec` is implicitly factorizing a word-by-context matrix whose cell values are shifted PMI values. In other words, the objective function and the input to `word2vec` are formally equivalent to traditional DSMs; thus the models should behave alike in the limit. The distinction is really one of process and parameterization. With optimum parameterization of traditional DSMs, more recent research is finding insignificant performance differences between `word2vec` and SVD factorizations of a PMI matrix (Sahlgren & Lenci, 2016). Levy et al. (2015) even found a slight advantage for a factorization of the bias shifted log-count matrix and for traditional PPMI over `word2vec` on some tasks when hyperparameters were optimized.

One general distinction between the two types of models is that neural embedding models such as `word2vec` seem to underperform when the training corpus is small, particularly for low-frequency words (Asr et al., 2016; Sahlgren &

Proceedings of the 21st Conference on Computational Natural Language Learning (CoNLL 2017), pages 134–142,
Vancouver, Canada, August 3 - August 4, 2017. ©2017 Association for Computational Linguistics

Lenci, 2016). Levy et al. (2015) note that there is often a benefit in `word2vec` of tuning a larger parameter space over using a larger training corpus. With limited-data mining scenarios becoming more common, a better understanding of how model type and corpus size interact with optimal parameterization is an important topic of inquiry.

Secondly, interest has shifted from trying to determine the best overall model towards a better understanding of what kinds of word relations each model is best at learning, and under what parameterizations. Count-based PMI models are very good at representing first-order statistical patterns that reflect **syntagmatic** relationships in language (aka "relatedness" data). In contrast, the training scheme used by `word2vec` attempts to optimize it for detecting second-order statistical patterns that reflect **paradigmatic** relationships in language (aka "similarity" data). Indeed, this was the pattern demonstrated by Levy et al. (2015): After tuning hyperparameters, `word2vec` performed best on similarity-based tasks while PPMI performed best on relatedness tasks. SVD-based models attempt to represent both statistical patterns. This count-based model outperformed both `word2vec` and PPMI in Levy et al. on both types of relations when standard parameter sets were used; however, the advantage disappeared when hyperparameters were tuned. Standard `word2vec` is optimized for paradigmatic tasks but architectural adaptations exist to make the model better suited for syntagmatic tasks (e.g., Kiela et al., 2015; Ling et al., 2015). Making a model better at one type of task might come at the cost of making it worse at the other if the two types of word relations are orthogonal (Andreas & Klein, 2014; Mitchell & Steedman, 2015). Optimizing for a particular task is also closely tied to the issue of training data size (Melamud et al., 2016).

Finally, both of these issues are intricately tied to post-processing of the embeddings. Levy et al. (2015) inspired by Pennington et al., (2014) pointed out an important parametrization of the `word2vec` model, where co-occurrence information encoded between hidden and output layers (context vectors) are used as well as weighs between the input and hidden layers (word vectors) to construct the final word embeddings (w+c representation). When calculating word similarity based on this composite representation, a mixture between first- and second-order coocurrence information are considered. This is remarkably similar to cognitive models that construct composite memory representations from both paradigmatic and syntagmatic information (Jones & Mewhort, 2007). Recent empirical studies in developmental psychology have found that children learn word relations that have both sources of information before relations with either source alone (Unger et al., 2016). Levy et al. (2015) found a consistent benefit for `word2vec` and PPMI when the $w+c$ post-processing combination was applied. Even though, this is an efficient adaptation in that the scheme does not require retraining, most studies on word similarity and relatedness have only employed the default `word2vec` setting (i.e., only using word vectors) and the usefulness of context vectors has been left underexplored.

It is very plausible to assume that the above three issues (corpus size, relation type, post-processing) interact: Higher-order paradigmatic word relations likely require more training data to discover, and the merging of $w+c$ blends different relation types. The goal of this paper is to elaborate on the effect of corpus size and post-processing on the reflection of syntagmatic and paradigmatic relations between words within the resulting vector space. It has proven impossible in psycholinguistics to select real words that cleanly separate paradigmatic and syntagmatic relations (McNamara, 2005). Hence, we opted to bring the statistical structure of the language under experimental control using an artificial language adapted from Elman (1990). Unlike in natural language corpora, the sources are independent: e.g., *dog* never directly appears with *cat*, and hence any learned relation between them could not be due to first-order information. Thus by defining crisp semantic categories and sentence frames, we investigate how first and second-order co-occurrence information sources are consumed and represented in terms of similarity between words by *count-based* and *predictive* DSMs. Given current uncertainty in the literature on the role of corpus size, relation type, and $w+c$ post-processing regarding the performance of various DSM architectures, this approach affords experimental control to evaluate relative performance as a factorial combination of information sources and parameters while controlling for the many confounding factors that exist in natural language corpora; including the ambiguity of similarity vs. relatedness of two words in evaluation datasets. Section 2 describes our framework in details, and section 3 presents several experiments exploring the capacity of count vs. predict DSMs in modeling relations between words.

2 Experiment Setup

2.1 Creation of Corpus

The artificial language grammar that we use for generating sentences in our test corpora is depicted in Table 1. This grammar was first introduced by Elman (1990) in his exploration of language modeling by Recurrent Neural Networks (RNNs). The language consists of a small vocabulary, a set of explicitly defined semantic categories on top of the vocabulary, and finally, a set of syntactic rules or possible sentence frames, which specifies how words can be put together in a sentence with regard to their semantic categories. The language generation algorithm enumerates all possible sentences in the language and the corpus generator returns a random sample of the language using a uniform distribution across sentence types. The corpus size is a variable in our experiments, and we mention explicitly when we repeat an experiment by re-sampling a corpus to validate the results on the semantic similarity tasks.

2.2 Semantic Similarity Tasks

All experiments in the current paper are centered on the idea that, at least, two types of semantic similarity can be identified for word pairs.

Table 1. Artificial language grammar (Elman 1990)

Sentence Frames	Example
NOUN-HUM VERB-EAT NOUN-FOOD	*man eat cookie*
NOUN-HUM VERB-PERCEPT NOUN-INANIM	*woman see book*
NOUN-HUM VERB-DESTROY NOUN-FRAG	*man smash glass*
NOUN-HUM VERB-INTRAN	*woman sleep*
NOUN-HUM VERB-TRAN NOUN-HUM	*man chase woman*
NOUN-HUM VERB-AGPAT NOUN-INANIM	*woman brake book*
NOUN-HUM VERB-AGPAT	*man move*
NOUN-ANIM VERB-EAT NOUN-FOOD	*cat eat cookie*
NOUN-ANIM VERB-TRAN NOUN-ANIM	*mouse see cat*
NOUN-ANIM VERB-AGPAT NOUN-INANIM	*cat chase mouse*
NOUN-ANIM VERB-AGPAT	*mouse move*
NOUN-INANIM VERB-AGPAT	*rock move*
NOUN-AGRESS VERB-DESTROY NOUN-FRAG	*dragon brake plate*
NOUN-AGRESS VERB-EAT NOUN-HUM	*monster eat man*
NOUN-AGRESS VERB-EAT NOUN-ANIM	*dragon eat cat*
NOUN-AGRESS VERB-EAT NOUN-FOOD	*monster eat cookie*

Semantic Categories
NOUN-HUM: [man, woman]
NOUN-ANIM: [cat, mouse]
NOUN-AGRESS: [dragon, monster]
NOUN-INANIM: [book, rock]
NOUN-FRAG: [glass, plate]
NOUN-FOOD: [cookie, sandwich]
VERB-INTRAN: [think, sleep]
VERB-TRAN: [see, chase]
VERB-PERCEPT: [smell, see]
VERB-AGPAT: [move, break]
VERB-DESTROY: [break, smash]
VERB-EAT: [eat]

Thus, we define two distinct methods to evaluate performance of the DSMs in learning semantic similarity from our artificial language—the syntagmatic task and the paradigmatic task.

Syntagmatic task: the objective of this task is to identify word pairs that can occur in context together (here the scope of a sentence). For example, the word pair *smash* and *cookie* cannot appear in each other's context according to the grammar in Table 1, because no legal sentence frame includes the semantic category of both words. Conversely, the word pair *eat* and *cookie*s are related in the sense that the two words can co-occur within a sentence. Evaluation of the vectors produced by different DSMs in this task is based on the cosine similarity between words occurring in common vs. different context frames and is calculated by the following accuracy measure:

$$Accuracy_{syn} = Avg\ sim(w_i, w_j) - Avg\ sim(w_k, w_l)$$

where (w_i, w_j) is indicative of the word pairs in the vocabulary that appear together in at least one sentence frame, and (w_k, w_l) is indicative of word pairs that do not appear in any common frame given their semantic categories (e.g., *glass* and *chase* belong to *NOUN-FRAG* and *VERB-TRAN*, respectively, which never co-occur within a sentence).

The syntagmatic task is a strict version of finding first-order related, directly co-occurring, or similar topic words in a natural language. Since word pairs are exclusively labeled as co-occurring vs. non-co-occurring based on the grammar of the artificial language, we will have the possibility to look into the performance of the DSM models in drawing syntagmatic similarities without having to deal with other confounds present in natural languages. This type of evaluation is almost impossible in a natural language given the openness of the semantic categories and enormous grammar size. In our modeling framework, if words are distributed in a DSM mostly based on first-order co-occurrence information, accuracy of the syntagmatic task would be high.

Paradigmatic task: two words should be similar if they tend to occur in similar contexts even if they never co-occur in the same sentence. Our paradigmatic task is defined based on this intuition, and the idea of taxonomically similar words in natural languages. According to Table

1, if two words come from the same semantic category (e.g., *man* and *woman*) they appear in similar sentence frames, thus ideally (when all possible sentence formulations exist in the generated sample of the language) they should be found as fully substitutable words. The paradigmatic task evaluates the quality of word vectors generated by a DSM by calculating the cosine similarity of word pairs belonging to same vs. different sematic categories.

$$Accuracy_{par} = Avg\ sim(w_i, w_j) - Avg\ sim(w_k, w_l)$$

where (w_i, w_j) indicates all word pairs coming from same semantic categories, and (w_k, w_l) indicates word pairs belong to different semantic categories. Based on this formulation, the paradigmatic accuracy of a model emphasizing second-order information would be higher than a model favoring first-order information to distribute words in the vector space. The reason is that, in the former model, the cosine similarity between vectors of interchangeable words like *man* and *woman* would converge to 1, or will be at least higher than similarity between other word vectors.[1] Both $Accuracy_{syn}$ and $Accuracy_{par}$ are bounded measures within the range of [-2, 2]; in practice though, they tend to come out within the range of [0, 1].

The above two tasks define the basics of our discriminative approach to investigate which models or parameter settings work best for each type of semantic similarity induction.

2.3 Distributional Methods

In our experiments, we use the implementations of `word2vec` Skip-Gram with Negative Sampling (SGNS) and PMI matrix factorization via Singular Value Decomposition (SVD) by Levy et al. (2015).

The Skip-gram model (SGNS) is one of the two `word2vec` architectures that predicts based on a target word one of its context words at a time. Error of prediction is calculated in the output via softmax and back-propagated to update two

weight matrices: the context matrix (*CM*) between the output and the hidden layer $[]_{vd}$, and the word matrix (*WM*) between the input and the hidden layer $[]_{vd}$, where v is the vocabulary size and d is the size of the hidden layer, thus dimensionality of the final word vectors. In the majority of previous work, the word matrix was used as the final output of the model. When context words are sampled from the same vocabulary as that of target words, the final *CM* will have the same dimensionality as *WM*, thus it can also be used as a semantic representation of the words. Averaging both matrices for a final word representation, rather than just the *WM*, is an optional post-processing method indicated by *w+c*.

Singular Value Decomposition (SVD) is a classic representation learning technique for projecting data into a new, and usually, smaller feature space. Other similar techniques in machine learning include eigenvalue decomposition, the basis of Principle Component Analysis. The SVD model in our study is representative of the count-based distributional semantic models. It begins by calculating a $v*v$ matrix of point-wise mutual information between word-context pairs. The matrix is then factorized and reduced to a $v*d$ matrix, where each row will be a word vector in the new semantic space.

2.4 Implementation and Parameter Balancing

In all our experiments, we try to equate the two models by keeping the common parameters constant and iterating over different values of the method-specific parameters to obtain the best performance for each.

Fixed parameters: parameters that we keep constant throughout all experimental conditions are the context window size (set to 2, in order to cover all words within a sentence in the artificial grammar), subsampling & dynamic context (set to off; no frequency-based smoothing or prioritization is applied to co-occurrence counts), rare word removal (set to off, no minimum cut-off is applied to context words). Therefore, in all experimental conditions that result from manipulating other parameters exactly the same word-context population is extracted from a given corpus and fed as input data to the SGNS and SVD models. We also use one iteration (epoch) in SGNS to keep it equated with SVD, and examine the effect of re-occurrences by manipulating the corpus size instead.

Variable parameters: for comparative experiments on small vs. big data, we generate 5

---

[1] The paradigmatic task can also be defined based on higher-level taxonomic relations. For example, given the grammar in Table 1, we expect models to cluster Verbs and Nouns because each of these higher-level word types share some within-category contextual similarities and between-category differences (e.g., all nouns in the grammar have a verb in context, whereas verbs don't have verbs in their context). In section 3.5 where semantic spaces are visualized we will return to this important point, but for the rest of our experiments model performance is evaluated based on the two basic tasks defined above.

independent corpora of each size (between 1K and 30K sentences) according to the sampling procedure described in Section 2.1. There are three important parameters that strongly affect the performance of the models, but since they are not the focus of our study we chose their values through a performance maximization procedure in all our experiments. One parameter called *dim* is the number of reduced dimensions or the size of final vectors, which is enumerated between 2 and 14 in our experiments. The other parameter *neg* is only applicable to SGNS and indicates the number of negative samples (we try between zero and 6 negative samples). Finally, a parameter in SVD determines the asymmetry of factorization, which was simulated with 0, 0.5 and 1 *eig* (for more details refer to Levy et al., 2015).

3 Results

3.1 Vanilla Comparison

Our first comparison explores the overall performance of the two DSMs with their common post-processing practice. We only use the W matrix to construct the word vectors after training SGNS, and the SVD factorization is also performed in its default manner. As explained in 2.4, we sampled five corpora of each size and measured the maximum likelihood of a model's performance by manipulating the variable parameters.

Table 2 shows that both models had very low overall accuracies in grouping syntagmatically related words. This observation indicates that, by default, both SVD and SGNS consume first-order co-occurrence information but infer second-order information, i.e., paradigmatic similarities between words by generalizing over context types in which two words can be seen. This finding suggests that neither of the models with its default configuration is suitable for performing word relatedness tasks. Reported best performances in the table for SVD were obtained at eig = 0.0, and for SGNS at neg = 1. Optimal dimensionality was variable but always above 5.

Table 2. Vanilla setup accuracy in paradigmatic and syntagmatic tasks with different size training corpuses.

Corpus size	Method	Paradigmatic	Syntagmatic
1K	SVD	**0.828**	**0.253**
	SGNS	0.535	0.113
10K	SVD	**0.832**	**0.258**
	SGNS	0.775	0.092

3.2 Corpus Size

Accuracy scores in Table 2 suggest that, even with small training data SVD can produce good vectors for the paradigmatic task. However, the performance of SGNS increases with more training data. This quick observation is consistent with previous findings regarding the superior performance of count models on word similarity and categorization tasks when models were trained on small corpora and with their default post-processing setting (Asr et al., 2016; Sahlgren & Lenci, 2016). The main reason stated in the literature is that SGNS requires tuning a large number of parameters and seeing more and more data (either through extra epochs or by feeding in a larger corpus of the same distribution of words and sentences) helps the model to converge. In the next sections we will see how otherwise we could enhance this model's performance, possibly in both syntagmatic and paradigmatic tasks.

3.3 Inclusion of Context Vectors

We hypothesized that using a post-processing setup emphasizing first-order information should enhance models' performance in the syntagmatic task. To test this, we repeated experiments on training corpora of size 1K to 30K with the alternative post-processing approaches (inclusion of context vectors, i.e., *w+c* vs. *w,* which was the default setting).

Figure 1 shows that the inclusion of context vectors enhances the accuracy of both models in the syntagmatic task (red lines are on top of the blue lines). This enhancement is more pronounced in the SGNS model: more data increases the accuracy of syntagmatic similarity inference consistently when the *w+c* option is used. SVD also benefits from a *w+c* equivalent setting proposed by Levy & Goldberg (2015) in performing the syntagmatic task, however the enhancement is tightly bounded for this model.

For the paradigmatic task, we expected an inverse pattern: explicit inclusion of first-order co-occurrence information in similarity measurement by considering both word and context vectors should hurt model's performance because only second-order information is important for the paradigmatic task. We can see in Figure 2 that our hypothesis is supported for SVD, where the accuracy declines significantly with the inclusion of the context vectors (compare the red and blue dotted lines). However, the SGNS model does not exhibit a dramatic change of performance in the paradigmatic task with or without the $w+c$ option (compare the solid lines). In fact, the performance in the paradigmatic task was slightly enhanced too. Putting this together with what we saw above regarding SGNS performance in the syntagmatic task brings us to an interesting conclusion about the "optimal parameter setting" for this model: using the $w+c$ option is a good choice adding to the robustness of SGNS, particularly when unsure of which type of similarity inference we would like the model to perform at the end. The SVD model, on the other hand, does not show the capability to learn both tasks at the same time; it gets better in one at the expense of the other. In the next section we try to explain this difference by looking into the way the two models distribute words within the high dimensional vector space.

3.4 Metric Space Expansion/Compression

The above experiments showed a lower ceiling for SVD performance compared to SGNS in both tasks when sufficient data was available to the models and the parameter space was thoroughly explored. In order to explain this observation, we took a closer look at the vectors generated by each model and specifically examined the range of the similarity scores of all word pairs in the vocabulary. We found that SVD generated numerically closer vectors compared to SGNS. This results in a smaller range of similarity scores: totally interchangeable words, such as *man* and *woman* get a cosine similarity score close to 1.0; completely different words (that neither appear in a sentence together, nor share similar contexts) such as *glass* and *chase* get a negative similarity score typically close to 0.0, or around -0.5 in a best case scenario.

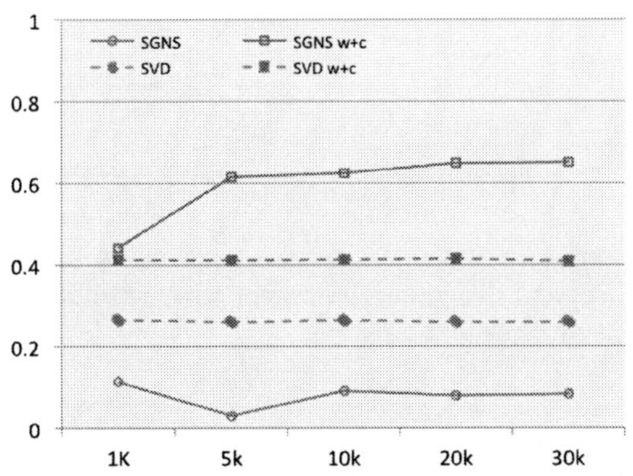

Figure 1. Accuracy of SGNS and SVD with word only vs. word+context vectors trained on corpuses of different sizes (1K to 30K sentences) in the syntagmatic task.

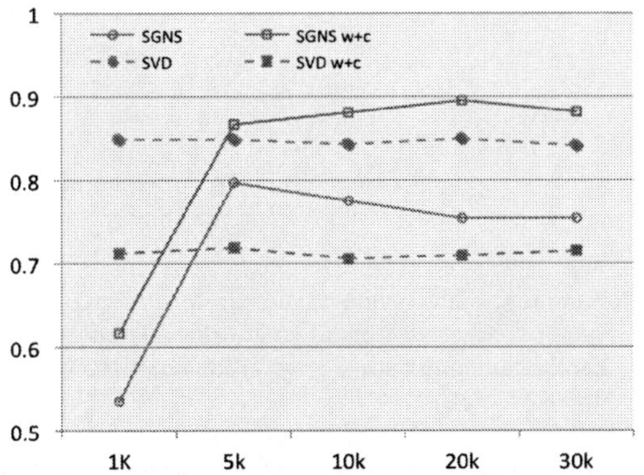

Figure 2. Accuracy of SGNS and SVD with word only vs. word+context vectors trained on corpuses of different sizes (1K to 30K sentences) in the paradigmatic task.

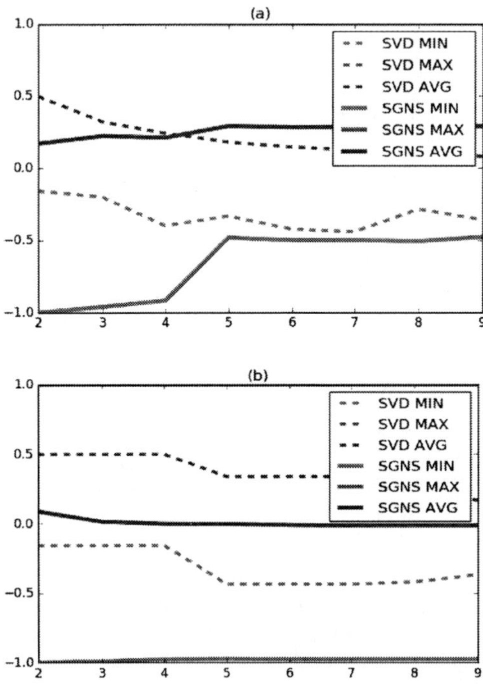

Figure 3. Spectrum of similarity scores between words in SVD and SGNS (10K corpus, neg = 1, eig = 0, dim = 2 to 9 on the x-axis): (a) with w and, (b) with $w+c$ post-processing.

Figure 3 depicts the minimum, maximum and average similarity scores obtained for all word pairs from the vocabulary through repeated experiments on a 10K corpus by manipulating the dimensionality (x-axis). It is almost the same for SGNS and SVD when the word-only post-processing is applied, but as soon as the context vectors are included, the spectrum of similarity scores widens up for SGNS. This investigation may explain why SVD is unable to manifest paradigmatic and syntagmatic relations at the same time.

SVD does not get a huge benefit from more training data or the post-processing step for inclusion of the context vectors. The underlying reason is that SVD always uses a sub-space of the entire similarity spectrum [-0.5, 1.0] so everything is squeezed – we refer to this phenomenon as *space compression*, which we hypothesize is due to the limitations of the dimensionality reduction mechanism. On the other hand, the distribution of words in the vector space obtained from SGNS changes drastically both by training on more data and considering context vectors.

As Figure 3 shows, SGNS has the capacity to use up the entire similarity spectrum [-1.0, 1.0], i.e., *space expansion*. We conjecture that this is due both to the design of the objective function and to the larger number of parameters in the neural model being updated independently, making it a more flexible method to encode fine-grained differences between word groups, while keeping them in meaningful clusters. More data helps the model fine-tune its parameters. Furthermore, averaging the word and context vectors provides an ensemble voting for syntagmatic (relatedness) and paradigmatic (similarity) at the same time.

3.5 Word Clusters in the Semantic Space

The space expansion of the SGNS model by inclusion of the context vectors can be visualized with a 2-dimensional projection of the vectors obtained from w vs. $w+c$ post-processing conditions, depicted in Figures 4 and 5 respectively. A comparison between the two plots shows how the vicinity of paradigmatically similar words (interchangeable words such as *cat* and *mouse*) can be preserved while syntagmatic clusters are emphasized (*cat* and *chase*) by inclusion of context vectors.

It is important, however, to note that higher-level paradigmatic relations are negatively affected as the model tries to bring syntagmatically related words closer to one another. For example, verbs and nouns (clustered in gray ovals in Figures 4), which are paradigmatically different, get mixed up once the syntagmatic clusters start to shape (gray rectangles in Figure 5). On the other hand, nouns referring to animate categories (that have some

level of paradigmatic similarity) fall apart in the $w+c$ space (red dashed cluster in Figures 4, distorted in Figure 5). These observations emphasize the importance of the post-processing choices based on the final inferences we expect from the model. When generalized to a natural language setting, the models depending on the $w+c$ parameterization would demonstrate synonymy, similarity and associative relatedness differently.

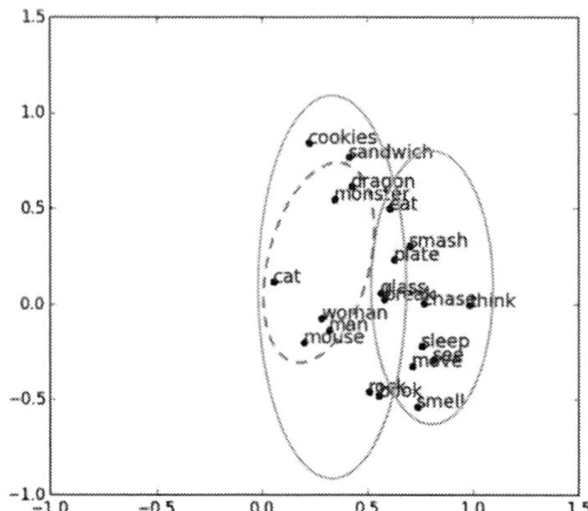

Figure 4. Paradigmatic clusters in SGNS w vector space; Syntagmatic clusters not easily identified (10K corpus, dim = 14, neg = 1)

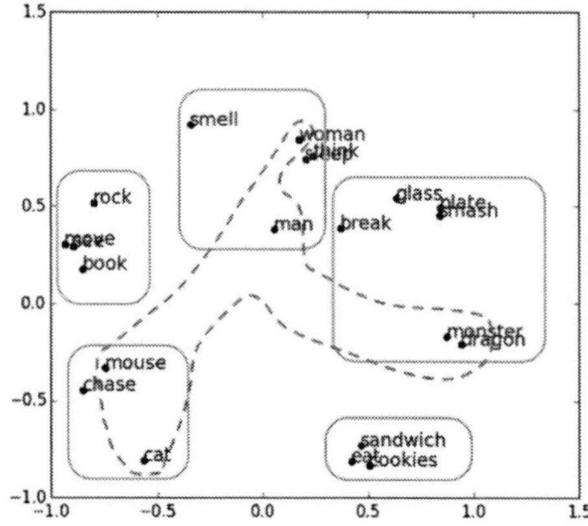

Figure 5. Clear syntagmatic clusters in SGNS $w+c$ vector space; some paradigmatically related words are kept together and some have fallen apart (10K corpus, dim = 14, neg = 1)

One should consider that while dimensionality reduction to two dimensions is possible and helpful for visualization purposes, these images do not reflect the exact distances between words in the high-dimension space. Therefore, these observations should be understood in combination with other results, e.g., similarity spectrums demonstrated in the previous section.

4   Conclusion

We proposed a methodology based on artificial language generation for studying distributional semantic models. This methodology was inspired by the prominent study of Elman (1990) and we mainly selected that to bring confound factors in natural languages under control while assessing the effect of model parameters on produced word vectors.

The experiments in this paper revealed an interaction between the training corpus size and a variety of parameter settings of two opponent DSMs in word similarity/relatedness evaluation. Confirming previous findings with small training data, we showed that SVD could easily organize words based on paradigmatic similarities obtained from second-order co-occurrence information, whereas SGNS needed more data to acquire the same type of knowledge. When it comes to syntagmatic relatedness between words, both models required accurate parameter settings. In particular, the default configuration of both SVD and SGNS aims at optimizing the space in a way that paradigmatically similar words are put together.

The optimal setting of the SGNS for an overall superior performance in both paradigmatic and syntagmatic tasks involved the inclusion of context vectors, which is not the typically tested setting of word2vec in previous studies. Our analysis of similarity scores between vectors generated for all words in the artificial language showed that averaging word and context vectors would result in a more organized SGNS vector space. The equivalent post-processing of the matrices in SVD for explicit inclusion of first-order similarity suggested by Levy et al. (2015) enhanced the performance of this model in the syntagmatic (relatedness) task only in the expense of making it worse for the paradigmatic (similarity) task.

Our observations suggest that SVD has some limitations in populating the distributional space as evenly as SGNS; thus it always comes up with vectors that are on average closer to one another. Further study is needed to explain this finding in a fundamental way perhaps via mathematical derivations. The trade-off between performance in paradigmatic and syntagmatic task, specially for the SVD model, can explain the occasional superiority and inferiority of this model against the neural opponents in previous studies:

similarity and relatedness rankings for words in natural languages manifest a mixture of paradigmatic and syntagmatic relations among words, thus a certain SVD model (with its post-processing optimized for reflecting either type of relation) might outperform SGNS in one task and not in the other.

Our experiments were a first step towards understanding the differences between classic and neural distributional models in a more controlled setting. The proposed methodology can be used in future research, e.g. to assess the effect of vocabulary and grammar size on resulting word vectors by different models, and in turn to select the right distributional approach in specific research context. We hope also that our work will initiate a general methodology for understanding the mechanism of neural networks employed in a variety of natural language processing tasks.

Acknowledgement

We are thankful to our reviewers for their helpful feedback on the initial version of the paper and suggestions for extension of the work. This research was funded by grant R305A140382 from the Institute of Education Sciences.

References

Andreas, J., & Klein, D. (2014). How much do word embeddings encode about syntax? In *Proceedings of ACL* (pp. 822-827).

Asr, F. T., Willits, J. A., & Jones, M. N. (2016). Comparing Predictive and Co-occurrence Based Models of Lexical Semantics Trained on Child-directed Speech. In *Proceedings of the Annual Meeting of Cognitive Science Society*.

Baroni, M., Dinu, G., & Kruszewski, G. (2014). Don't count, predict! A systematic comparison of context-counting vs. context-predicting semantic vectors. In *Proceedings of ACL* (pp. 238-247).

Bengio, Y., Ducharme, R., Vincent, P., & Jauvin, C. (2003). A neural probabilistic language model. *Machine Learning Research*, *3*(Feb), 1137-1155.

Bullinaria, J. A., & Levy, J. P. (2007). Extracting semantic representations from word co-occurrence statistics: A computational study. *Behavior Research Methods*, 39, 510-526.

Collobert, R., Weston, J., Bottou, L., Karlen, M., Kavukcuoglu, K., & Kuksa, P. (2011). Natural language processing (almost) from scratch. *Journal of Machine Learning Research*, *12*(Aug), 2493-2537.

Deerwester, S., Dumais, S. T., Furnas, G. W., Landauer, T. K., & Harshman, R. (1990). Indexing by latent semantic analysis. *Journal of the American society for information science*, *41*(6), 391.

Elman, J.L. (1990). Finding structure in time. *Cognitive Science*, 14, 179-211.

Harris, Z. (1970). Distributional structure. In *Papers in Structural and Transformational Linguistics* (pp. 775–794).

Kiela, D., Hill, F., & Clark, S. (2015). Specializing word embeddings for similarity or relatedness. In *Proceedings of EMNLP*.

Jones, M. N., & Mewhort, D. J. (2007). Representing word meaning and order information in a composite holographic lexicon. *Psychological Review*, 114(1), 1.

Jones, M. N., Willits, J., Dennis, S., & Jones, M. (2015). Models of semantic memory. *Oxford Handbook of Mathematical and Computational Psychology*, 232-254

Landauer, T. K., & Dumais, S. T. (1997). A solution to Plato's problem: The latent semantic analysis theory of acquisition, induction, and representation of knowledge. *Psychological Review*, 104(2), 211.

Levy, O., & Goldberg, Y. (2014). Neural word embedding as implicit matrix factorization. In *Advances in Neural Information Processing Systems* (pp. 2177-2185).

Levy, O., Goldberg, Y., & Dagan, I. (2015). Improving distributional similarity with lessons learned from word embeddings. *Transactions of the Association for Computational Linguistics*, *3*, 211-225.

Li, J., Chen, X., Hovy, E. and Jurafsky, D. (2016). Visualizing and Understanding Neural Models in NLP. In *Proceedings of NAACL*.

Ling, W., Dyer, C., Black, A., & Trancoso, I. (2015). Two/too simple adaptations of word2vec for syntax problems. In *Proceedings of ACL-HLT* (pp. 1299-1304).

McNamara, T. P. (2005). Semantic priming: Perspectives from memory and word recognition. *Psychology Press*.

Melamud, O., McClosky, D., Patwardhan, S., & Bansal, M. (2016). The role of context types and dimensionality in learning word embeddings. *arXiv preprint arXiv:1601.00893*.

Miller, G. A. (1958). Free recall of redundant strings of letters. Journal of Experimental Psychology, 56(6), 485.

Mitchell, J., & Steedman, M. (2015). Orthogonality of syntax and semantics within distributional spaces. In *Proceedings of ACL*.

Mikolov, T., Sutskever, I., Chen, K., Corrado, G.S. and Dean, J. (2013a). Efficient estimation of word representations in vector space. In *ICLR*.

Mikolov, T., Sutskever, I., Chen, K., Corrado, G.S., and Dean., J. (2013b) Distributed Representations of Words and Phrases and their Compositionality. In *Proceedings of NIPS*, 2013.

Pennington, J., Socher, R., & Manning, C. D. (2014). Glove: Global Vectors for Word Representation. In *EMNLP* (Vol. 14, pp. 1532-43).

Sahlgren, M., & Lenci, A. (2016). The Effects of Data Size and Frequency Range on Distributional Semantic Models. *arXiv preprint arXiv:1609.08293*.

Turney, P. D., & Pantel, P. (2010). From frequency to meaning: Vector space models of semantics. *Journal of Artificial Intelligence Research*, 37(1), 141-188.

Unger, L., Fisher, A. V., Nugent, R., Ventura, S. L., & MacLellan, C. J. (2016). Developmental changes in semantic knowledge organization. *Journal of Experimental Child Psychology*, *146*, 202-222.

Learning Word Representations with Regularization from Prior Knowledge

Yan Song
Tencent AI Lab
clksong@tencent.com

Chia-Jung Lee
Microsoft
cjlee@microsoft.com

Fei Xia
University of Washington
fxia@uw.edu

Abstract

Conventional word embeddings are trained with specific criteria (e.g., based on language modeling or co-occurrence) inside a single information source, disregarding the opportunity for further calibration using external knowledge. This paper presents a unified framework that leverages pre-learned or external priors, in the form of a regularizer, for enhancing conventional language model-based embedding learning. We consider two types of regularizers. The first type is derived from topic distribution by running latent Dirichlet allocation on unlabeled data. The second type is based on dictionaries that are created with human annotation efforts. To effectively learn with the regularizers, we propose a novel data structure, trajectory softmax, in this paper. The resulting embeddings are evaluated by word similarity and sentiment classification. Experimental results show that our learning framework with regularization from prior knowledge improves embedding quality across multiple datasets, compared to a diverse collection of baseline methods.

1 Introduction

Distributed representation of words (or word embedding) has been demonstrated to be effective in many natural language processing (NLP) tasks (Bengio et al., 2003; Collobert and Weston, 2008; Turney and Pantel, 2010; Collobert et al., 2011; Mikolov et al., 2013b,d; Weston et al., 2015). Conventional word embeddings are trained with a single objective function (e.g., language modeling (Mikolov et al., 2013c) or word co-occurrence factorization (Pennington et al.,

2014)), which restricts the capability of the learned embeddings from integrating other types of knowledge. Prior work has leveraged relevant sources to obtain embeddings that are best suited for the target tasks, such as Maas et al. (2011) using a sentiment lexicon to enhance embeddings for sentiment classification. However, learning word embeddings with a particular target makes the approach less generic, also implying that customized adaptation has to be made whenever a new knowledge source is considered.

Along the lines of improving embedding quality, semantic resources have been incorporated as guiding knowledge to refine objective functions in a joint learning framework (Bian et al., 2014; Xu et al., 2014; Yu and Dredze, 2014; Nguyen et al., 2016), or used for retrofitting based on word relations defined in the semantic lexicons (Faruqui et al., 2015; Kiela et al., 2015). These approaches, nonetheless, require explicit word relations defined in semantic resources, which is a difficult prerequisite for knowledge preparation.

Given the above challenges, we propose a novel framework that extends typical context learning by integrating external knowledge sources for enhancing embedding learning. Compared to a well known work by Faruqui et al. (2015) that focused on tackling the task using a retrofitting[1] framework on semantic lexicons, our method has an emphasis on joint learning where two objectives are considered for optimization simultaneously. In the meantime, we design a general-purpose infrastructure which can incorporate arbitrary external sources into learning as long as the sources can be encoded into vectors of numerical values (e.g. multi-hot vector according to the topic distributions from a topic model). In prior work by Yu and Dredze (2014) and Kiela et al. (2015), the ex-

---

[1]In their study, joint learning was reported to be less effective than retrofitting.

Proceedings of the 21st Conference on Computational Natural Language Learning (CoNLL 2017), pages 143–152,
Vancouver, Canada, August 3 - August 4, 2017. ©2017 Association for Computational Linguistics

ternal knowledge has to be clustered beforehand according to their semantic relatedness (e.g., *cold, icy, winter, frozen*), and words of similar meanings are added as part of context for learning. This may set a high bar for preparing external knowledge since finding the precise word-word relations is required. Our infrastructure, on the other hand, is more flexible as knowledge that is learned elsewhere, such as from topic modeling or even a sentiment lexicon, can be easily encoded and incorporated into the framework to enrich embeddings.

The way we integrate external knowledge is performed by the notion of a regularizer, which is an independent component that can be connected to the two typical architectures, namely, continuous bag-of-words (CBOW) and skip-gram (SG), or used independently as a retrofitter. We construct the regularizers based on the knowledge learned from both unlabeled data and manually crafted information sources. As an example of the former, a topic model from latent Dirichlet allocation (LDA) (Blei et al., 2003) is first generated from a given corpus, based on which per-word topical distributions are then added as extra signals to aid embedding learning. As an example of the latter, one can encode a dictionary into the regularizer and thus adapt the learning process with the encoded knowledge.

Another contribution of this paper is that we propose a novel data structure, trajectory softmax, to effectively learn prior knowledge in the regularizer. Compared to conventional tree based hierarchical softmax, trajectory softmax can greatly reduce the space complexity when learning over a high-dimension vector. Our experimental results on several different tasks have demonstrated the effectiveness of our approach compared to up-to-date studies.

The rest of the paper is organized as follows. In section 2, we describe in detail our framework and show how we learn the regularizer in section 3. Section 4 presents and analyzes our experimental results and section 5 surveys related work. Finally, conclusions and directions of future work are discussed in section 6.

2 Approach

Conventionally word embeddings are learned from word contexts. In this section, we describe our method of extending embedding learning to incorporate other types of information sources.

Previous work has shown that many different sources can help learn better embeddings, such as semantic lexicons (Yu and Dredze, 2014; Faruqui et al., 2015; Kiela et al., 2015) or topic distributions (Maas et al., 2011; Liu et al., 2015b). To provide a more generic solution, we propose a unified framework that learns word embeddings from context (e.g., CBOW or SG) together with the flexibility of incorporating arbitrary external knowledge using the notion of a regularizer. Details are unfolded in following subsections.

2.1 The Proposed Learning Framework

Preliminaries: The fundamental principle for learning word embeddings is to leverage word context, with a general goal of maximizing the likelihood that a word is predicted by its context. For example, the CBOW model can be formulated as maximizing

$$\mathcal{L} = \frac{1}{|V|} \sum_{i=1}^{|V|} \log p(w_i \mid \sum_{0<|j|\leq c} v_{i+j}), \ \forall \, w_i \in V \tag{1}$$

where v_{i+j} refers to the embedding of a word in w_{i-c}^{i+c}, and c defines the window size of words adjacent to the word w_i. The optimization for $\mathcal{L}$ over the entire corpus is straightforward.

The left part of Figure 1 illustrates the concept of such context learning. It is a typical objective function for language modeling, where w_i is learned by the association with its neighboring words. Since context greatly affects the choice of the current word, this modeling strategy can help finding reasonable semantic relationships among words.

Regularizer: To incorporate additional sources for embedding learning, we introduce the notion of a regularizer, which is designed to encode information from arbitrary knowledge corpora.

Given a knowledge resource Ψ, one can encode the knowledge carried by a word w with $\psi(w)$, where ψ can be any function that maps w to the knowledge it encapsulates. For example, a word has a topic vector $\psi(w) = \overrightarrow{e^{(w_i)}} \Phi_{[1:K,:]}$, resulting $\psi(w) = \overrightarrow{\Phi}_w = (\phi_{1,w}, \phi_{2,w}, ..., \phi_{K,w})$, where $\Phi_{[1:K,:]}$ is the topic distribution matrix for all words with K topics; $\overrightarrow{e^{(w_i)}}$ is the standard basis vector with 1 at the i-th position in the vocabulary V. Therefore, regularization for all w with given

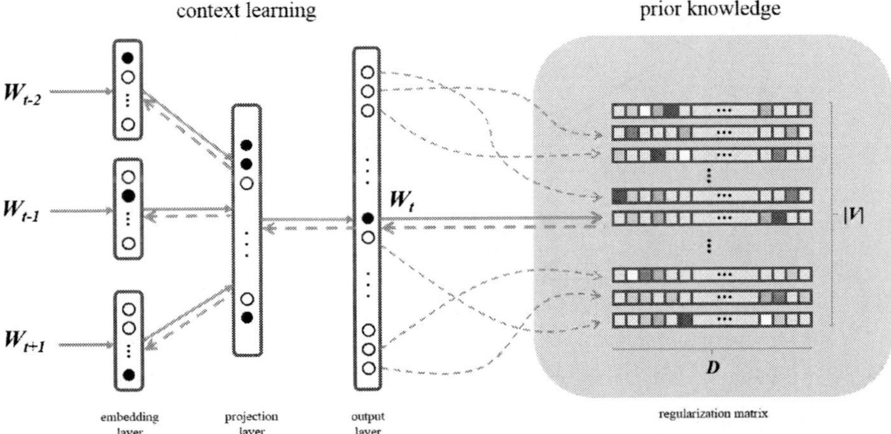

Figure 1: Illustration of joint learning word embeddings with context and regularization from prior knowledge. The green lines refer to the prediction and the red dotted lines refer to the updating process.

a knowledge source can be conceptually used to maximize $\sum_{w \in V} R(v)$, where R is the regularizer, defined as a function of the embedding v of a given word w and formulated as:

$$R(v) = \log p(\psi(w)|v), \ \forall \ w \in V, \Psi \quad (2)$$

The right part of Figure 1 shows an instantiation of a regularizer that encodes prior knowledge of vocabulary size $|V|$, each with D dimensions.

Joint Learning: To extend conventional embedding learning, we combine context learning from an original corpus with external knowledge encoded by a regularizer, where the shared vocabulary set forms a bridge connecting the two spaces. In particular, the objective function for CBOW with integrating the regularizer can be formulated as maximizing

$$\mathcal{L} = \frac{1}{|V|} \sum_{i=1}^{|V|} \log p(w_i, \psi(w_i) \mid \sum_{0<|j|\leq c} v_{i+j}) \quad (3)$$

where not only w_i, but also $R(w_i)$ is predicted by the context words w_{i+j} via their embeddings v_{i+j}.

Figure 1 as a whole illustrates this idea. Recall that each row of the matrix corresponds to a vector of a word in V, representing prior knowledge across D dimensions (e.g., semantic types, classes or topics). When learning/predicting a word within this framework, the model needs to predict not only the correct word as shown in the context learning part in the figure, but also the correct vector in the regularizer. In doing so, the prior knowledge will be carried to word embed-

dings from regularization to context learning by back-propagation through the gradients obtained from the learning process based on the regularization matrix.

Retrofitting: With joint learning as our goal, we should emphasize that the proposed framework supports simultaneous context learning and prior knowledge retrofitting with a unified objective function. This means that the retrofitters can be considered as a stand-alone component at disposal, where the external knowledge vectors are regarded as supervised-learning target and the embeddings are updated through the course of fitting to the target. In §4, we will evaluate the performance of both joint learner and retrofitter in detail.

2.2 Parameter Estimation

As shown in Equation 3, prior knowledge participates in the optimization process for predicting the current word and contributes to embedding updating during training a CBOW model. Using stochastic gradient descent (SGD), embeddings can be easily updated by both objective functions for language modeling and regularization through:

$$v_{i+j}^{\star} = v_{i+j} - \lambda \nabla_v [\log p(w_i| \sum_{0<|j|\leq c} v_{i+j}) + R(v_i^{\star})]$$

$$(4)$$

where R is defined as in Eq.2 for $\psi(w_i)$. For SG model, prior knowledge is introduced in a similar way, with the difference being that context words are predicted instead of the current word.

Therefore, when learned from the context, em-

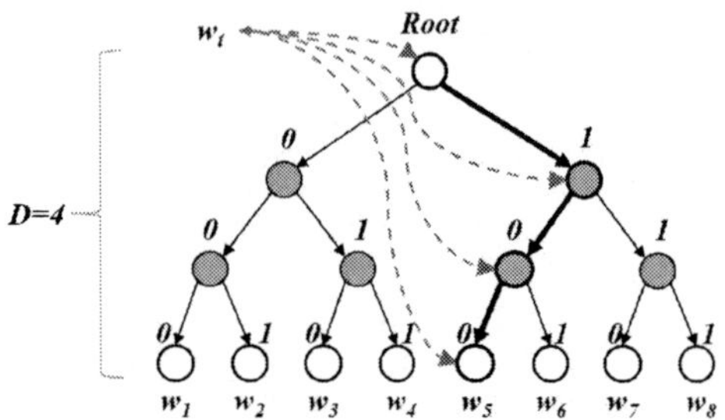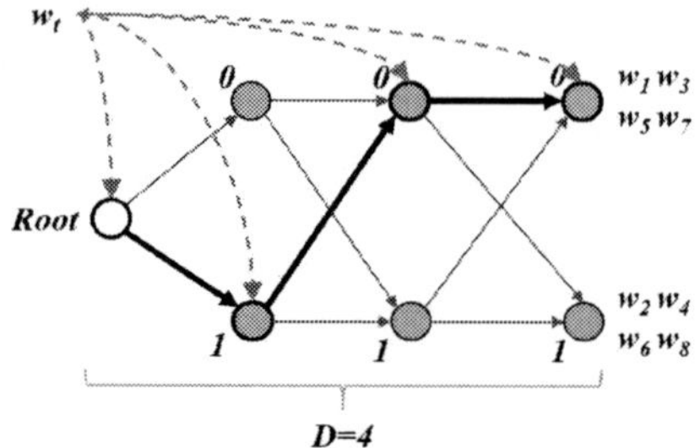

Figure 2: Comparison of hierarchical softmax (left) and trajectory softmax (right) based on an example of eight words in binary coding. The bold arrow lines refer to the path for encoding w_5 in both hierarchical and trajectory softmax.

beddings are updated in the same way as in normal CBOW and SG models. When learned from the regularizer, embeddings are updated via a supervised learning over Ψ, on the condition that Ψ is appropriately encoded by ψ. The details of how it is performed will be illustrated in the next subsection.

2.3 Trajectory Softmax

Hierarchical softmax is a good choice for reducing the computational complexity when training probabilistic neural network language models. Therefore, for context learning on the left part of Figure 1, we continue using hierarchical softmax based on Huffman coding tree (Mikolov et al., 2013a). Typically to encode the entire vocabulary, the depth of the tree falls in a manageable range around 15 to 18.

However, different from learning context words, to encode a regularizer as shown on the right part of Figure 1, using hierarchical softmax is intractable due to exponential space demand. Consider words expressed with D-dimensional vectors in a regularizer, a tree-based hierarchical softmax may require $2^D - 1$ nodes, as illustrated in the left hand side of Figure 2. Since each node contains a d-dimensional "node vector" that is to be updated through training, the total space required is $O(2^D \cdot d)$ for hierarchical softmax to encode the regularizer. When D is very large, such as $D = 50$ meaning that tree depth is 50, the space demand tends to be unrealistic as the number of nodes in the tree grows to 2^{50}.

To avoid the exponential requirement in space, in this work, we propose a trajectory softmax activation to effectively learn over the D-dimensional vectors. Our approach follows a grid hierarchical

structure along a path when conducting learning in the regularizer. From the right hand side of Figure 2, we see that the same regularizer entry is encoded with a path of D nodes, using a grid structure instead of a tree one. Consequently the total space required will be reduced to $O(2 \cdot D \cdot d)$.

As a running example, Figure 2 shows that when $D = 4$, the conventional hierarchical softmax needs at least 15 nodes to perform softmax over the path, while trajectory softmax greatly reduces space to only 7 nodes. Compared to tree-based hierarchical softmax, the paths in trajectory softmax are not branches of a tree, but a fully connected grid of nodes with space complexity of $D \times |C|$ in general. Here $|C|$ refers to the number of choices on the paths for a node to the next node, and thus $|C| = 2$ is the binary case. In Figure 2, we see an activation trajectory for a sequence of "*Root→100*" for encoding word w_5. w_t is then learned and updated through the nodes on the trajectory when w_5 is predicted by w_t. The learning and updating are referred by the dashed arrow lines. Overall, trajectory softmax greatly reduces the space complexity than hierarchical softmax, especially when words sharing similar information, in which case the paths of these words will be greatly overlapped.

More formally, learning with trajectory softmax in the binary case is similar to hierarchical softmax, which is to maximize p over the path for a vector encoded in $\psi(w)$, where p is defined below with an input vector v:

$$p(\psi(w)|v) = \prod_{i=1}^{D-1} \sigma([\![n(i+1)]\!] \cdot v_i^\top v) \quad (5)$$

where v_i is the inner vector in i-th node on the trajectory. $[\![n(i+1)]\!] = 1$ or -1 when $(i+1)$-th node is encoded with 0 or 1, respectively. The final update to word embedding v with the regularizer is conducted by:

$$v^* = v - \gamma(\sigma(v_i^\top v) - t_i) \cdot v_i \qquad (6)$$

which is applied to $i = 1, 2, ..., D - 1$, where $\sigma(x) = \exp(x)/(1 + \exp(x))$; $t_i = [\![n(i + 1)]\!]$; γ is a discount learning rate.

Since the design of trajectory softmax is compatible with the conventional hierarchical softmax, one can easily implement the joint learning by concatenating its *Root* with the terminal node in the hierachical tree. The learning process is thus to traverse all the nodes from the hierarchical tree and the trajectory path.

3 Constructing Regularizers

We consider two categories of information sources for constructing regularizers. The first type of regularizer is built based on resources without annotation. On the contrary, the second type uses text collections with annotation. For brevity, throughout the paper we refer to the former as unannotated regularizer whereas the latter is recognized as annotated regularizer.

3.1 Unannotated Regularizer

The unannotated regularizer constructs its regularization matrix based on an LDA learned topic distribution, which reflects topical salience information of a given word from prior knowledge. Using LDA not only serves our purpose of learning according to word semantics reflected by co-occurrences but can also bring in knowledge inexpensively (i.e., no annotations needed).

To start, a classic LDA is first performed on an arbitrary base corpus for retrieving word topical distribution, resulting in a topic model with K topics. All the units in the corpus are then assigned with a word-topic probability ϕ_i corresponding to topic k, based on which a matrix is formed with all $\overrightarrow{\Phi}_w$, as described in §2.1. Next we convert each $\overrightarrow{\Phi}$ into a 0-1 vector based on the maximum values in $\overrightarrow{\Phi}$. In particular, positions with maximum values are set to 1 and the rest are set to 0 (e.g. $[0.1, 0.1, 0.4, 0.4] \rightarrow [0, 0, 1, 1]$). This converted matrix functions as the final regularization matrix as shown in right hand side of Figure 1. We set $K = 50$ in our experiments.[2] An in-house LDA

implementation[3] is used for training $\Phi_{[1:K,:]}$, with 1,000 iterations.

3.2 Annotated Regularizer

We use three sources for training annotated regularizers in this work. Two of the sources are semantic lexicons, namely, the Paraphrase Database (PPDB)[4] (Ganitkevitch et al., 2013) and synonyms in the WordNet (WN_{syn})[5] (Miller, 1995). They are used in the word similarity task. The third source is a semantic dictionary, SentiWordNet 3.0 (SWN) (Baccianella et al., 2010), which is used in the sentiment classification task. All of the three sources were created with annotation efforts, where either lexical or semantic relations were provided by human experts beforehand.

Before constructing the regularizer, we need encode each word in the sources as a vector according to its relations to other words or predefined information. For PPDB and WN_{syn}, we use them in different ways for joint learning and retrofitting. In order to optimize the efficiency in joint learning, we compress the word relations with topic representations. We use an LDA learner to get topic models for the lexicons[6], with $K = 50$. Therefore, the word relations are transferred into topic distributions that are learned from their co-occurrences defined in the lexicon. The way we construct regularization matrix may be lossy, risking losing information that is explicitly delivered in the lexicon. However, it provides us effective encodings for words, and also yields better learning performance empirically in our experiments. In retrofitting, we directly use words' adjacent matrices extracted from their relations defined in the lexicons, then take the adjacent vector for each word as the regularization vector.

The SWN includes 83K words (147K words and phrases in total). Every word in SWN has two scores for its degree towards positive and negative polarities. For example, the word "pretty" receives 0.625 and 0 for positive and negative respectively, which means it is strongly associated with positive sentiment. The scores range from 0 to 1 with step

---

[2] We experimented with other numbers for K, and their performance didn't vary too much when $K > 40$. We didn't include this comparison due to the similar results.

[3] It is a Markov Chain Monte Carlo (MCMC) based LDA using Gibbs sampling.

[4] We use PPDB-XL in this paper.

[5] We use WN_{syn} because in our experiment only using synonyms perform better than using synonyms, hypernyms and hyponyms.

[6] The lexicons are organized in the similar way as in Faruqui et al. (2015), where synonyms are grouped together and treated as a document for LDA learning.

Embeddings		MEN-3k		SimLex-999		WordSim-353	
		γ	ρ	γ	ρ	γ	ρ
LDA		57.17	58.86	20.39	22.12	55.48	54.81
CBOW		62.93	65.84	28.34	28.31	68.50	66.67
Yu and Dredze (2014)	+PPDB	65.35	65.84	35.56	33.30	72.75	72.43
	+WN$_{syn}$	65.20	65.74	36.15	33.65	**72.79**	**72.58**
This work	+LDA	**67.33**	**69.51**	29.79	29.78	71.19	69.58
	+PPDB	65.25	66.87	**36.43**	33.28	69.45	68.89
	+WN$_{syn}$	64.42	66.98	33.86	**33.69**	66.13	67.11
SG		64.79	66.71	26.97	26.59	68.88	67.80
Kiela et al. (2015)	+PPDB	61.13	60.04	36.47	34.29	70.14	68.76
	+WN$_{syn}$	57.02	59.84	29.02	29.99	63.61	61.22
This work	+LDA	65.02	65.32	25.19	24.04	66.16	69.21
	+PPDB	**70.83**	**71.35**	**37.10**	35.72	**73.94**	**73.11**
	+WN$_{syn}$	66.58	68.14	36.72	**35.91**	68.50	67.90

Table 1: Word similarity results for **joint learning** on three datasets in terms of Pearson's coefficient correlation (γ) and Spearman's rank correlation (ρ) in percentages. Higher score indicates better correlation of the model with respect to the gold standard. Bold indicates the highest score for each embedding type.

of 0.125 for both positive and negative polarities. Therefore there are 9 different degrees for a word to be annotated for the two sentiments. For encoding this dictionary, we design a 18-dimension vector, in which the first 9 dimension represents the positive sentiment while the last 9 for negative sentiment. A word is thus encoded into a binary form where the corresponding dimension is set to 1 with others 0. For the aforementioned word "*pretty*", its encoded vector will be "*000001000 000000000*", in which the score 0.625 of positive activates the 6th dimension in the vector. In doing so, we form a $83K \times 18$ regularization matrix for the SWN dictionary.

4 Experiments

The resulting word embeddings based on joint learning as well as retrofitting are evaluated intrinsically and extrinsically. For intrinsic evaluation, we use word similarity benchmark to directly test the quality of the learned embeddings. For extrinsic evaluation, we use sentiment analysis as a downstream task with different input embeddings. Regularizers based on LDA, PPDB and WN$_{syn}$ are used in word similarity experiment, while SentiWordNet regularization is used in sentiment analysis. The experimental results will be discussed in §4.1 and §4.2.

We experiment with three learning paradigms, namely CBOW, SG and GloVe. GloVe is only tested in retrofitting since our regularizer is not compatible with GloVe learning objective in joint learning. In all of our retrofitting experiments, we only train the regularizer with one iteration, consistent with Kiela et al. (2015).

The base corpus that we used to train initial word embeddings is from the latest articles dumped from Wikipedia and newswire[7], which contains approximately 8 billion words. When training on this corpus, we set the dimension of word embeddings to be 200 and cutoff threshold of word frequency threshold to be 5 times of occurrence. These are common setups shared across the following experiments.

4.1 Word Similarities Evaluation

We use the MEN-3k (Bruni et al., 2012), SimLex-999 (Hill et al., 2015) and WordSim-353 (Finkelstein et al., 2002) datasets to perform quantitative comparisons among different approaches to generating embeddings. The cosine scores are computed between the vectors of each pair of words in the datasets[8]. The measures adopted are Pearson's coefficient of product-moment correlation (γ) and Spearman's rank correlation (ρ), which reflect how

---

[7]This corpus is constructed by the script demo-train-big-model-v1.sh from https://storage.googleapis.com/google-code-archive-source/v2/code.google.com/word2vec/source-archive.zip

[8]For LDA embeddings (topic distributions), we tried Jenson-Shannon divergence, which is much worse than cosine scores in measuring the similarity. Therefore we still use cosine for LDA embeddings.

Embeddings		MEN-3k		SimLex-999		WordSim-353	
		γ	ρ	γ	ρ	γ	ρ
GloVe		66.84	66.97	28.87	27.52	59.78	61.46
Faruqui et al. (2015)	+PPDB	66.98	67.04	29.25	28.25	61.44	63.35
	+WN$_{syn}$	64.29	63.92	27.32	24.39	57.40	58.88
This work	+LDA	59.65	60.23	22.25	22.70	55.65	57.57
	+PPDB	**68.99**	**68.99**	**31.35**	**29.85**	**62.31**	**63.96**
	+WN$_{syn}$	66.72	66.84	29.78	28.47	59.62	61.34
CBOW		62.93	65.84	28.34	28.31	68.50	66.67
Yu and Dredze (2014)	+PPDB	65.08	65.52	36.16	34.01	**72.75**	72.39
	+WN$_{syn}$	**65.34**	65.77	35.68	33.33	72.72	**72.74**
Faruqui et al. (2015)	+PPDB	65.07	67.55	37.07	35.02	71.76	71.18
	+WN$_{syn}$	63.71	66.44	30.15	29.83	71.24	69.39
This work	+LDA	50.07	56.64	21.47	23.01	41.56	47.27
	+PPDB	65.30	**67.68**	**37.34**	**35.74**	72.01	72.05
	+WN$_{syn}$	63.89	66.74	33.96	33.82	68.70	66.91
SG		64.79	66.71	26.97	26.59	68.88	67.80
Kiela et al. (2015)	+PPDB	**67.38**	69.05	32.49	31.84	71.59	69.82
	+WN$_{syn}$	64.58	67.02	29.43	28.12	69.15	68.36
Faruqui et al. (2015)	+PPDB	65.44	67.02	34.12	33.72	71.24	70.31
	+WN$_{syn}$	65.65	66.71	28.25	27.61	70.21	69.47
This work	+LDA	64.02	65.33	24.64	24.28	59.43	60.60
	+PPDB	67.17	**69.09**	**34.93**	**34.57**	**72.63**	**71.15**
	+WN$_{syn}$	65.62	67.38	29.96	29.82	69.70	68.91

Table 2: Word similarity results for **retrofitting** on three datasets in terms of Pearson's coefficient correlation (γ) and Spearman's rank correlation (ρ) in percentages. Higher score indicates better correlation of the model with respect to the gold standard. Bold indicates the highest score for each embedding type.

close the similarity scores to human judgments.

For both joint learning and retrofitting, we test our approach with using PPDB and WN$_{syn}$ as the prior knowledge applied to our regularizer. Considering that LDA can be regarded as soft clustering for words, it is very hard to present words with deterministic relations like in PPDB and WN$_{syn}$, therefore we do not apply retrofitting on LDA results for previous studies.

The evaluation results are shown in Table 1 and Table 2 for joint learning and retrofitting, respectively. Each block in the tables indicates an embedding type and its corresponding enhancement approaches. For comparison, we also include the results from the approaches proposed in previous studies, i.e., Yu and Dredze (2014)[9] for CBOW, Kiela et al. (2015)[10] for SG and Faruqui et al. (2015)[11] for all initial embeddings. Their settings are equal to that used in our approach.

Table 1 shows that directly using LDA topic distributions as embeddings can give reasonable results for word similarities. Because LDA captures word co-occurrences globally so that words share similar contexts are encoded similarly via topic distributions. This is a good indication showing that LDA could be a useful guidance to help our regularize to incorporate global information.

For other joint learning results in Table 1, our approach shows significant gain over the baselines, the same for the approaches from previous studies (Yu and Dredze, 2014; Faruqui et al., 2015). However, using WN$_{syn}$ in Kiela et al. (2015) does not help, this may owe to the fact that using the words defined in WN$_{syn}$ as contexts will affect the real context learning and thus deviate the joint objective function. Interestingly, using LDA in regularizer significantly boosts the performance on MEN-3k, even better than that with using semantic lexicons. The reason might be that LDA enhances word embeddings with the relatedness inherited in topic distributions.

[9]https://github.com/Gorov/JointRCM
[10]We re-implemented their approach in our own code.
[11]https://github.com/mfaruqui/retrofitting

For retrofitting, Table 2 shows that our approach demonstrates its effectiveness for enhancing initial embeddings with prior knowledge. It performs consistently better than all other approaches in a wide range of settings, including three embedding types on three datasets, with few exceptions. Since retrofitting only updates those words in the external sources, e.g., LDA word list or lexicons, it is very sensitive to the quality of the corresponding sources. Consequently, it can be observed from our experiment that unannotated knowledge, i.e., topic distributions, is not an effective source as a good guidance. In contrast, PPDB, which is of high quality of semantic knowledge, outperforms other types of information in most cases.

4.2 Sentiment Classification Evaluation

We perform sentiment classification on the IMDB review data set (Maas et al., 2011), which has 50K labeled samples with equal number of positive and negative reviews. The data set is pre-divided into training and test sets, with each set containing 25K reviews. The classifier is based on a bi-directional LSTM model as described in Dai and Le (2015), with one hidden layer of 1024 units. Embeddings from different approaches are used as inputs for the LSTM classifier. For determining the hyper-parameters (e.g., training epoch and learning rate), we use 15% of the training data as the validation set and we apply early stopping strategy when the error rate on the validation set starts to increase. Note that the final model for testing is trained on the entire training set.

As reported in Table 3, the embeddings trained by our approach work effectively for sentiment classification. Both joint learning and retrofitting with our regularizer outperform other baseline approaches from previous studies, with joint learning being somewhat better than retrofitting. Overall, our joint learning with CBOW achieves the best performance on this task. A ten-partition two-tailed paired t-test at $p < 0.05$ level is performed on comparing each score with the baseline result for each embedding type. Considering that sentiment is not directly related to word meaning, the results indicate that our regularizer is capable of incorporating different type of knowledge for a specific task, even if it is not aligned with the context learning. This task demonstrates the potential of our framework for encoding external knowledge and using it to enrich the representa-

Embeddings		Accuracy
Maas et al. (2011)		88.89
	GloVe	90.66
Faruqui et al. (2015)	+Retro	90.43
This work	+Retro	**90.89**
	CBOW	91.29
Yu and Dredze (2014)	+Joint	91.14
	+Retro	90.71
Faruqui et al. (2015)	+Retro	90.77
This work	+Joint	**92.09**[*]
	+Retro	91.81[*]
	SG	91.30
Faruqui et al. (2015)	+Retro	91.03
Kiela et al. (2015)	+Joint	91.45
	+Retro	91.14
This work	+Joint	**92.07**[*]
	+Retro	91.42

Table 3: Sentiment classification results on IMDB data set (Maas et al., 2011). Bold indicates the highest score for each embedding type. * indicates t-test significance at $p < 0.05$ level when compared with the baseline.

tions of words, without the requirement to build a task-specific, customized model.

5 Related Work

Early research on representing words as distributed continuous vectors dates back to Rumelhart et al. (1986). Recent previous studies (Collobert and Weston, 2008; Collobert et al., 2011) showed that, the quality of embeddings can be improved when training multi-task deep models on task-specific corpora, domain knowledge that is learned over the process. Yet one downside is that huge amounts of labeled data is often required. Another methodology is to update embeddings by learning with external knowledge. Joint learning and retrofitting are two mainstreams of this methodology. Leveraging semantic lexicons (Yu and Dredze, 2014; Bian et al., 2014; Faruqui et al., 2015; Liu et al., 2015a; Kiela et al., 2015; Wieting et al., 2015; Nguyen et al., 2016) or word distributional information (Maas et al., 2011; Liu et al., 2015b) has been proven as effective in enhancing word embeddings, especially for specific down-stream tasks. Bian et al. (2014) proposed to improve embedding learning with different kinds of knowledge, such as morphological, syntactic and semantic information. Wieting et al. (2015) improves embeddings by leveraging paraphrase pairs from the PPDB for learning phrase embeddings in the paraphrasing task. In a similar way, Hill et al. (2016) uses learned word embeddings as supervised knowledge for learning phrase embeddings.

Although our approach is conceptually similar to previous work, it is different in several ways. For leveraging unlabeled data, the regularizer in this work is different from applying topic distributions as word vectors (Maas et al., 2011) or treating topics as conditional contexts (Liu et al., 2015b). For leveraging semantic knowledge, our regularizer does not require explicit word relations as used in previous studies (Yu and Dredze, 2014; Faruqui et al., 2015; Kiela et al., 2015), but takes encoded information of words. Moreover, in order to appropriately learn the encoded information, we use trajectory softmax to perform the regularization. As a result, it provides a versatile data structure to incorporate any vectorized information into embedding learning. The above novelties make our approach versatile so that it can integrate different types of knowledge.

6 Conclusion and Future Work

In this paper we proposed a regularization framework for improving the learning of word embeddings with explicit integration of prior knowledge. Our approach can be used independently as a retrofitter or jointly with CBOW and SG to encode prior knowledge. We proposed trajectory softmax for learning over the regularizer, which can greatly reduce the space complexity compared to hierarchical softmax using the Huffman coding tree, which enables the regularizer to learn over a long vector. Moreover, the regularizer can be constructed from either unlabeled data (e.g., LDA trained from the base corpus) or manually crafted resources such as a lexicon. Experiments on word similarity evaluation and sentiment classification show the benefits of our approach.

For the future work, we plan to evaluate the effectiveness of this framework with other types of prior knowledge and NLP tasks. We also want to explore different ways of encoding external knowledge for regularization.

References

Stefano Baccianella, Andrea Esuli, and Fabrizio Sebastiani. 2010. SentiWordNet 3.0: An Enhanced Lexical Resource for Sentiment Analysis and Opinion Mining. In *Proceedings of the Seventh conference on International Language Resources and Evaluation (LREC'10)*. European Language Resources Association (ELRA), Valletta, Malta.

Yoshua Bengio, Réjean Ducharme, Pascal Vincent, and Christian Janvin. 2003. A neural probabilistic language model. *J. Mach. Learn. Res.* 3:1137–1155.

Jiang Bian, Bin Gao, and Tie-Yan Liu. 2014. Knowledge-Powered Deep Learning for Word Embedding. In *Proceedings of the European Conference on Machine Learning and Knowledge Discovery in Databases - Volume 8724*. New York, NY, USA, ECML PKDD 2014, pages 132–148.

David M. Blei, Andrew Y. Ng, and Michael I. Jordan. 2003. Latent Dirichlet Allocation. *Journal of Machine Learning Research* 3:993–1022.

Elia Bruni, Gemma Boleda, Marco Baroni, and Nam Khanh Tran. 2012. Distributional Semantics in Technicolor. In *Proceedings of the 50th Annual Meeting of the Association for Computational Linguistics (Volume 1: Long Papers)*. Jeju Island, Korea, pages 136–145.

Ronan Collobert and Jason Weston. 2008. A unified architecture for natural language processing: Deep neural networks with multitask learning. In *Proceedings of the 25th International Conference on Machine Learning*. ACM, New York, NY, USA, ICML '08, pages 160–167.

Ronan Collobert, Jason Weston, Léon Bottou, Michael Karlen, Koray Kavukcuoglu, and Pavel Kuksa. 2011. Natural Language Processing (Almost) from Scratch. *Journal of Machine Learning Research* 12:2493–2537.

Andrew M. Dai and Quoc V. Le. 2015. Semi-supervised Sequence Learning. In *Advances in Neural Information Processing Systems 28: Annual Conference on Neural Information Processing Systems 2015, December 7-12, 2015, Montreal, Quebec, Canada*. pages 3079–3087.

Manaal Faruqui, Jesse Dodge, Sujay Kumar Jauhar, Chris Dyer, Eduard Hovy, and Noah A. Smith. 2015. Retrofitting word vectors to semantic lexicons. In *Proceedings of the 2015 Conference of the North American Chapter of the Association for Computational Linguistics: Human Language Technologies*. Denver, Colorado, pages 1606–1615.

Lev Finkelstein, Evgeniy Gabrilovich, Yossi Matias, Ehud Rivlin, Zach Solan, Gadi Wolfman, and Eytan Ruppin. 2002. Placing Search in Context: the Concept Revisited. *ACM Transaction on Information Systems* 20(1):116–131.

Juri Ganitkevitch, Benjamin Van Durme, and Chris Callison-Burch. 2013. PPDB: The Paraphrase Database. In *Proceedings of the 2013 Conference of the North American Chapter of the Association for*

Computational Linguistics: Human Language Technologies. Atlanta, Georgia, pages 758–764.

Felix Hill, KyungHyun Cho, Anna Korhonen, and Yoshua Bengio. 2016. Learning to Understand Phrases by Embedding the Dictionary. *Transactions of the Association for Computational Linguistics* 4:17–30.

Felix Hill, Roi Reichart, and Anna Korhonen. 2015. Simlex-999: Evaluating Semantic Models with Genuine Similarity Estimation. *Computational Linguistics* 41(4):665–695.

Douwe Kiela, Felix Hill, and Stephen Clark. 2015. Specializing word embeddings for similarity or relatedness. In *Proceedings of the 2015 Conference on Empirical Methods in Natural Language Processing*. Lisbon, Portugal, pages 2044–2048.

Quan Liu, Hui Jiang, Si Wei, Zhen-Hua Ling, and Yu Hu. 2015a. Learning semantic word embeddings based on ordinal knowledge constraints. In *Proceedings of the 53rd Annual Meeting of the Association for Computational Linguistics and the 7th International Joint Conference on Natural Language Processing (Volume 1: Long Papers)*. Beijing, China, pages 1501–1511.

Yang Liu, Zhiyuan Liu, Tat-Seng Chua, and Maosong Sun. 2015b. Topical Word Embeddings. In *Proceedings of the Twenty-Ninth AAAI Conference on Artificial Intelligence*. AAAI'15, pages 2418–2424.

Andrew L. Maas, Raymond E. Daly, Peter T. Pham, Dan Huang, Andrew Y. Ng, and Christopher Potts. 2011. Learning Word Vectors for Sentiment Analysis. In *Proceedings of the 49th Annual Meeting of the Association for Computational Linguistics: Human Language Technologies*. Portland, Oregon, USA, pages 142–150.

Tomas Mikolov, Kai Chen, Greg Corrado, and Jeffrey Dean. 2013a. Efficient Estimation of Word Representations in Vector Space. *arXiv preprint* abs/1301.3781.

Tomas Mikolov, Quoc V. Le, and Ilya Sutskever. 2013b. Exploiting Similarities among Languages for Machine Translation. *arXiv preprint* abs/1309.4168.

Tomas Mikolov, Ilya Sutskever, Kai Chen, Greg S Corrado, and Jeff Dean. 2013c. Distributed representations of words and phrases and their compositionality. In C.J.C. Burges, L. Bottou, M. Welling, Z. Ghahramani, and K.Q. Weinberger, editors, *Advances in Neural Information Processing Systems 26*, pages 3111–3119.

Tomas Mikolov, Wen-tau Yih, and Geoffrey Zweig. 2013d. Linguistic Regularities in Continuous Space Word Representations. In *Proceedings of the 2013 Conference of the North American Chapter of the Association for Computational Linguistics: Human Language Technologies*. Association for Computational Linguistics, Atlanta, Georgia, pages 746–751.

George A. Miller. 1995. WordNet: A Lexical Database for English. *Commun. ACM* 38(11):39–41.

Kim Anh Nguyen, Sabine Schulte im Walde, and Ngoc Thang Vu. 2016. Integrating distributional lexical contrast into word embeddings for antonym-synonym distinction. In *Proceedings of the 54th Annual Meeting of the Association for Computational Linguistics (Volume 2: Short Papers)*. Berlin, Germany, pages 454–459.

Jeffrey Pennington, Richard Socher, and Christopher Manning. 2014. Glove: Global Vectors for Word Representation. In *Proceedings of the 2014 Conference on Empirical Methods in Natural Language Processing (EMNLP)*. Doha, Qatar, pages 1532–1543.

David E. Rumelhart, Geoffrey E. Hinton, and Ronald J. Williams. 1986. Learning Representations by Back-propagating Errors. *Nature* pages 533–536.

Peter D. Turney and Patrick Pantel. 2010. From Frequency to Meaning: Vector Space Models of Semantics. *Journal of Artificial Intelligence Research* 37(1):141–188.

Jason Weston, Antoine Bordes, Sumit Chopra, and Tomas Mikolov. 2015. Towards AI-Complete Question Answering: A Set of Prerequisite Toy Tasks. *arXiv preprint* abs/1502.05698.

John Wieting, Mohit Bansal, Kevin Gimpel, and Karen Livescu. 2015. From Paraphrase Database to Compositional Paraphrase Model and Back. *Transactions of the Association for Computational Linguistics* 3:345–358.

Chang Xu, Yalong Bai, Jiang Bian, Bin Gao, Gang Wang, Xiaoguang Liu, and Tie-Yan Liu. 2014. RC-NET: A General Framework for Incorporating Knowledge into Word Representations. In *Proceedings of the 23rd ACM International Conference on Conference on Information and Knowledge Management*. ACM, New York, NY, USA, CIKM '14, pages 1219–1228.

Mo Yu and Mark Dredze. 2014. Improving lexical embeddings with semantic knowledge. In *Proceedings of the 52nd Annual Meeting of the Association for Computational Linguistics (Volume 2: Short Papers)*. Baltimore, Maryland, pages 545–550.

Attention-based Recurrent Convolutional Neural Network for Automatic Essay Scoring

Fei Dong and **Yue Zhang*** and **Jie Yang**
Singapore University of Technology and Design
{fei_dong, jie_yang}@mymail.sutd.edu.sg
yue_zhang@sutd.edu.sg

Abstract

Neural network models have recently been applied to the task of automatic essay scoring, giving promising results. Existing work used recurrent neural networks and convolutional neural networks to model input essays, giving grades based on a single vector representation of the essay. On the other hand, the relative advantages of RNNs and CNNs have not been compared. In addition, different parts of the essay can contribute differently for scoring, which is not captured by existing models. We address these issues by building a hierarchical sentence-document model to represent essays, using the attention mechanism to automatically decide the relative weights of words and sentences. Results show that our model outperforms the previous state-of-the-art methods, demonstrating the effectiveness of the attention mechanism.

1 Introduction

Automatic essay scoring (AES) is the task of automatically assigning grades to student essays. It can be highly challenging, requiring not only knowledge on spelling and grammars, but also on semantics, discourse and pragmatics. Traditional models use sparse features such as bag-of-words, part-of-speech tags, grammar complexity measures, word error rates and essay lengths, which can suffer from the drawbacks of time-consuming feature engineering and data sparsity.

Recently, neural network models have been used for AES (Alikaniotis et al., 2016; Dong and Zhang, 2016; Taghipour and Ng, 2016), giving better results compared to statistical models with handcrafted features. In particular, distributed word representations are used for the input, and

a neural network model is employed to combine word information, resulting in a single dense vector form of the whole essay. A score is given based on a non-linear neural layer on the representation. Without handcrafted features, neural network models have been shown to be more robust than statistical models across different domains (Dong and Zhang, 2016).

Both recurrent neural networks (Williams and Zipser, 1989; Mikolov et al., 2010) and convolutional neural networks (LeCun et al., 1998; Kim, 2014) have been used for modelling input essays. In particular, Alikaniotis et al. (2016) and Taghipour and Ng (2016) use a single-layer LSTM (Hochreiter and Schmidhuber, 1997) over the word sequence to model the essay, and Dong and Zhang (2016) use a two-level hierarchical CNN structure to model sentences and documents separately. It has been commonly understood that CNNs can capture local ngram information effectively, while LSTMs are strong in modelling long history. No previous work has compared the effectiveness of LSTMs and CNNs under the same settings for AES. To better understand the contrast, we adopt the two-layer structure of Dong and Zhang (2016), comparing CNNs and LSTMs for modelling sentences and documents.

Not all sentences contribute equally to the scoring of a given essay, and not all words contribute equally within a sentence. We adopt the neural attention model (Xu et al., 2015; Luong et al., 2015) to automatically calculate weights for convolution features of CNNs and hidden state values of LSTMs, which has been used for obtaining the most pertinent information for machine translation (Luong et al., 2015), sentiment analysis (Shin et al., 2016; Wang et al., 2016; Liu and Zhang, 2017) and other tasks. In our case, the attention mechanism can intuitively select sentences and grams that are more aligned with the props or obviously incorrect. To our knowledge, no prior

---

* Corresponding author.

Proceedings of the 21st Conference on Computational Natural Language Learning (CoNLL 2017), pages 153–162,
Vancouver, Canada, August 3 - August 4, 2017. ©2017 Association for Computational Linguistics

work has investigated the effectiveness of attention models for AES.

Results show that CNN is relatively more effective for modelling sentences, and LSTMs are relatively more effective for modelling documents. This is likely because local ngram information are more relevant to the scoring of sentence structures, and global information is more relevant for scoring document level coherence. In addition, attention gives significantly more accurate results. Our final model achieves the best result reported on the ASAP[1] test set. We release our code at `https://github.com/feidong1991/aes`.

2 Automatic Essay Scoring

2.1 Task

The task of AES is usually treated as a supervised learning problem, typical models of which can be divided into three categories: classification, regression and preference ranking. In the classification scenario, scores are divided into several categories, each score or score range is regarded as one class and the ordinary classification models are employed such as Naive Bayes (NB) and SVMs (Larkey, 1998; Rudner and Liang, 2002). In the regression scenario, each score is treated as continous values for the essay and regression models are considered, like linear regression, Bayesian linear ridge regression (Attali and Burstein, 2004; Phandi et al., 2015). In the preference ranking scenario, AES task is considered as a ranking problem in which pair-wise ranking and list-wise ranking are employed (Yannakoudakis et al., 2011; Chen and He, 2013; Cummins et al., 2016). The former considers the ranking between each pair of essays, while the latter considers the absolute ranking of each essay in the whole set.

Formally, an AES model is trained to minimize the difference between its automatically output scores and human given scores on a set of training data:

$$\min \sum_{i=1}^{N} f(y_i^*, y_i),$$

$$\text{s.t. } y_i = g(t_i), i = 1, 2, ..., N \tag{1}$$

where N is the total number of essays in the training set, y_i^* and y_i are the golden score assigned by human raters and prediction score made by the

AES system of i-th essay in the set respectively, t_i is feature representation of i-th essay, f is the metric function between golden score and prediction score, such as mean square error and mean absolute error, and g is the mapping function from feature t_i to score y_i.

2.2 Evaluation Metric

Many measurement metrics have be adopted to assess the quality of AES systems, including Pearson's correlation, Spearman's ranking correlation, Kendall's Tau and kappa, especially quadratic weighted kappa (QWK). We follow the Automated Student Assessment Prize (ASAP) competition official criteria which takes QWK as evaluation metric, which is also adopted as evaluation metric in (Dong and Zhang, 2016; Taghipour and Ng, 2016; Phandi et al., 2015).

Kappa measures inter-raters agreement on the qualitive items, here inter-raters refer to AES system and human rater. QWK is modified from kappa which takes quadratic weights. The quadratic weight matrix in QWK is defined as:

$$W_{i,j} = \frac{(i-j)^2}{(R-1)^2}, \tag{2}$$

where i and j are the reference rating (assigned by a human rater) and the system rating (assigned by an AES system), respectively, and R is the number of possible ratings.

An observed score matrix O is calculated such that $O_{i,j}$ refers to the number of essays that receive a rating i by the human rater and a rating j by the AES system. An expected score matrix E is calculated as the outer product of histogram vectors of the two (reference and system) ratings. The matrix E needs to be normalized such that the sum of elements in E and the sum of elements in O keep the same. Finally, given the three matrices W, O and E, the QWK value is calculated according to Equation 3:

$$\kappa = 1 - \frac{\sum W_{i,j} O_{i,j}}{\sum W_{i,j} E_{i,j}} \tag{3}$$

We evaluate our model using QWK as the metric, and perform one-tailed t-test to determine the significance of improvements.

3 Model

We employ a hierarchical neural model similar to the sentence-document model of Dong and Zhang

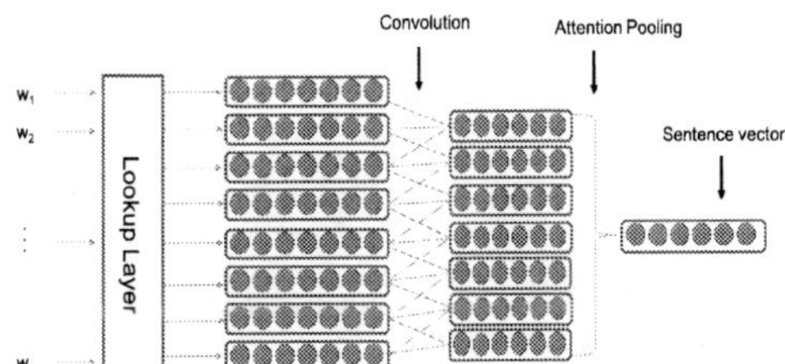

Figure 1: Sentence representation using ConvNet and attention pooling

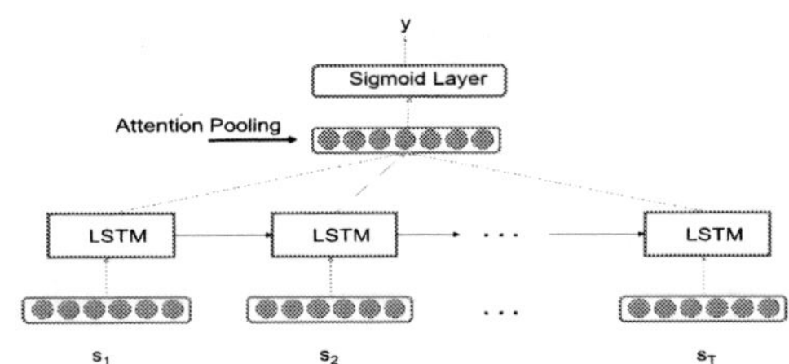

Figure 2: Document (Text) representation using LSTM and attention pooling

(2016) who consider essay script as being composed of sentence sequences rather than word sequences. Different from their model, our neural model learns text representation with LSTMs, which could model the coherence and coreference among sequences of sentences (i.e. capturing more global information compared to CNNs). Besides, attention pooling is both used on words and sentences, which aims to capture more relevant words and sentences that contribute to the final quality of essays.

We investiage two types of word representations, one being character-based embedding, which utilizes a convolutinal layer to learn word representations from raw characters, and the other being word embedding.

Characters For character-based word representation, we employ a convolutional layer over characters in each word, followed by max-pooling and average-pooling layers. The concatenation of max-pooling and average-pooling forms the final word representation for each word.

Let $c_i^1, c_i^2, ..., c_i^m$ be one-hot representation of characters that make up the word w_i, we have the following word representation for w_i using make-up characters:

$$\mathbf{x}_{c_i} = \mathbf{E}_c \mathbf{c}_i \tag{4}$$

$$\mathbf{z}_{c_i}^j = f(\mathbf{W}_c \cdot [\mathbf{x}_{c_i}^j : \mathbf{x}_{c_i}^{j+h-1}] + \mathbf{b}_c) \tag{5}$$

$$\tilde{\mathbf{x}}_i = \max_j \mathbf{z}_{c_i}^j \tag{6}$$

$$\hat{\mathbf{x}}_i = avg_j \, \mathbf{z}_{c_i}^j \tag{7}$$

$$\mathbf{x}_i = \tilde{\mathbf{x}}_i \oplus \hat{\mathbf{x}}_i, \tag{8}$$

where $\mathbf{E}_c$ is the embedding matrix, $\mathbf{x}_{c_i}$ is the embedding vector for $\mathbf{c}_i$, $\mathbf{z}_{c_i}^j$ is the feature map for j-th character in i-th word w_i after convolutional layer, $\mathbf{W}_c$, $\mathbf{b}_c$ are the weights matrix and bias vector respectively, h specifies the window size in the convolutional layer and f is the activation function, here hyperbolic tangent function $tanh$ is used. $\tilde{\mathbf{x}}_i$ and $\hat{\mathbf{x}}_i$ are max-pooling and average-pooling vectors over $\mathbf{z}_{c_i}^j$, and the final word w_i's representation $\mathbf{x}_i$ is the concatenation of $\tilde{\mathbf{x}}_i$ and $\hat{\mathbf{x}}_i$.

Words Given a sentence of words sequence $\mathbf{w}_1, \mathbf{w}_2, ..., \mathbf{w}_n$, an lookup layer map each $\mathbf{w}_i$ into a dense vector $\mathbf{x}_i, i = 1, 2, ..., n$.

$$\mathbf{x}_i = \mathbf{E}\mathbf{w}_i, i = 1, 2, ..., n \tag{9}$$

where $\mathbf{w}_i$ is one-hot representation of the i-th word in the sentence, $\mathbf{E}$ is the embedding matrix, $\mathbf{x}_i$ is the embedding vector of i-th word.

3.1 Sentence Representation

After obtaining the word representations $\mathbf{x}_i, i = 1, 2, ..., n$, we employ a convolutional layer on each sentence:

$$\mathbf{z}_i = f(\mathbf{W}_z \cdot [\mathbf{x}_i^j : \mathbf{x}_i^{j+h_w-1}] + \mathbf{b}_z), \tag{10}$$

where $\mathbf{W}_z$, $\mathbf{b}_z$ are weight matrix and bias vector, respectively, h_w is the window size in the convolutional layer and $\mathbf{z}_i$ is the result feature representation.

Above the convolutional layer, attention pooling is employed to acquire a sentence representation. The structure of a sentence representation is depicted in Figure 1. The details of convolutional and attention pooling layers are defined in the following equations.

$$\mathbf{m}_i = tanh(\mathbf{W}_m \cdot \mathbf{z}_i + \mathbf{b}_m) \tag{11}$$

$$u_i = \frac{e^{\mathbf{w}_u \cdot \mathbf{m}_i}}{\sum e^{\mathbf{w}_u \cdot \mathbf{m}_j}} \tag{12}$$

$$\mathbf{s} = \sum u_i \mathbf{z}_i, \tag{13}$$

where $\mathbf{W}_m$, $\mathbf{w}_u$ are weight matrix and vector, respectively, $\mathbf{b}_m$ is the bias vector, $\mathbf{m}_i$ and u_i are attention vector and attention weight respectively for i-th word. $\mathbf{s}$ is the final sentence representation, which is the weighted sum of all the word vectors.

3.2 Text Representation

A recurrent layer is used to compose a document (text) representation similar to the models of Alikaniotis et al. (2016) and Taghipour and Ng (2016). The main difference is that both earlier work treat the essay script as a sequence of words rathter than a sequence of sentences. Alikaniotis et al. (2016) use score-specific word embeddings as word features and take the last hidden state of LSTM as text representation. Taghipour and Ng (2016) take the average value over all the hidden states of LSTM as text representation. In contrast to the previous LSTM models, we use LSTM to learn from sentence sequences and attention pooling on the hidden states of LSTM to obtain the contribution of each sentence to the final quality of essays. The structure of a text representation using LSTM is depicted in Figure 2.

Long short-term memory units are the modified recurrent units which are proposed to handle the problem of vanishing gradients effectively (Hochreiter and Schmidhuber, 1997; Pascanu et al., 2013). LSTMs use gates to control information flow, preserving or forgetting information for each cell units. In order to control information flow when processing a vector sequence, an input gate, a forget gate and an output gate are employed to decide the passing of information at each time step. Assuming that an essay script consists of T sentences, s_1, s_2, ..., s_T with $\mathbf{s}_t$ being the feature representation of t-th word s_t, we have LSTM cell units addressed in the following equations:

$$
\begin{aligned}
\mathbf{i}_t &= \sigma(\mathbf{W}_i \cdot \mathbf{s}_t + \mathbf{U}_i \cdot \mathbf{h}_{t-1} + \mathbf{b}_i) \\
\mathbf{f}_t &= \sigma(\mathbf{W}_f \cdot \mathbf{s}_t + \mathbf{U}_f \cdot \mathbf{h}_{t-1} + \mathbf{b}_f) \\
\tilde{\mathbf{c}}_t &= tanh(\mathbf{W}_c \cdot \mathbf{s}_t + \mathbf{U}_c \cdot \mathbf{h}_{t-1} + \mathbf{b}_c) \\
\mathbf{c}_t &= \mathbf{i}_t \circ \tilde{\mathbf{c}}_t + \mathbf{f}_t \circ \mathbf{c}_{t-1} \\
\mathbf{o}_t &= \sigma(\mathbf{W}_o \cdot \mathbf{s}_t + \mathbf{U}_o \cdot \mathbf{h}_{t-1} + \mathbf{b}_o) \\
\mathbf{h}_t &= \mathbf{o}_t \circ tanh(\mathbf{c}_t),
\end{aligned}
\tag{14}
$$

where $\mathbf{s}_t$ and $\mathbf{h}_t$ are the input sentence and output sentence vectors at time t, respectively. $\mathbf{W}_i$, $\mathbf{W}_f$,$\mathbf{W}_c$, $\mathbf{W}_o$, $\mathbf{U}_i$, $\mathbf{U}_f$, $\mathbf{U}_c$, and $\mathbf{U}_o$ are weight matrices and $\mathbf{b}_i$, $\mathbf{b}_f$, $\mathbf{b}_c$, and $\mathbf{b}_o$ are bias vectors. The symbol $\circ$ denotes element-wise multiplication and σ represents the sigmoid function.

After obtaining the intermediate hidden states of LSTM $\mathbf{h}_1, \mathbf{h}_2, ..., \mathbf{h}_T$, we use another attention pooling layer over the sentences to learn the final text representation. The attention pooling helps to acuquire the weights of sentences' contribution to final quality of the text. The attention pooling over sentences is addressed as:

$$
\mathbf{a}_i = tanh(\mathbf{W}_a \cdot \mathbf{h}_i + \mathbf{b}_a)
\tag{15}
$$

$$
\alpha_i = \frac{e^{\mathbf{w}_\alpha \cdot \mathbf{a}_i}}{\sum e^{\mathbf{w}_\alpha \cdot \mathbf{a}_j}}
\tag{16}
$$

$$
\mathbf{o} = \sum \alpha_i \mathbf{h}_i,
\tag{17}
$$

where $\mathbf{W}_a$, $\mathbf{w}_\alpha$ are weight matrix and vector respectively, $\mathbf{b}_a$ is the bias vector, $\mathbf{a}_i$ is attention vector for i-th sentence, and α_i is the attention weight of i-th sentence. $\mathbf{o}$ is the final text representation, which is the weighted sum of all the sentence vectors.

Finally, one linear layer with sigmoid function applied on the text representation to get the final score as described in Equation 18.

$$
y = sigmoid(\mathbf{w}_y \mathbf{o} + \mathbf{b}_y)
\tag{18}
$$

where $\mathbf{w}_y$, $\mathbf{b}_y$ are weight vector and bias vector, y is the final score of the essay.

4 Training

Objective We use mean square error (MSE) loss, which is also used in previous models. MSE is widely used in regression tasks, which measures the average value of square error between gold standard scores y_i^* and prediction scores y_i assigned by the AES system among all the essays. Given N essays, we calculate MSE according to Equation 19.

$$
mse(y, y^*) = \frac{1}{N} \sum_{i=1}^{N} (y_i - y_i^*)^2
\tag{19}
$$

The model is trained on a fixed number of epochs and evaluated on the development set at every epoch. We set the batch size to 10 and the best model is selected on the performance of quadratic weighted kappa on the development set. The details of model hyper-parameters are listed in Table 1.

Character Embeddings The character embeddings are initialized with uniform distribution from [-0.05, 0.05]. The dimension of character embeddings is set to 30. During the training process, character embeddings are fine-tuned.

Layer	Parameter Name	Parameter Value
Lookup	char embedding dim	30
	word embedding dim	50
CNN	window size	5
	number of filters	100
LSTM	hidden units	100
Dropout	dropout rate	0.5
	epochs	50
	batch size	10
	initial learning rate η	0.001
	momentum	0.9

Table 1: Hyper-parameters

Set	#Essays	Genre	Avg Len.	Range	Med.
1	1783	ARG	350	2-12	8
2	1800	ARG	350	1-6	3
3	1726	RES	150	0-3	1
4	1772	RES	150	0-3	1
5	1805	RES	150	0-4	2
6	1800	RES	150	0-4	2
7	1569	NAR	250	0-30	16
8	723	NAR	650	0-60	36

Table 2: Statistics of the ASAP dataset; Range refers to score range and Med. refers to median scores. For genre, ARG specifies *argumentative* essays, RES means *response* essays and NAR denotes *narrative* essays.

Word Embeddings We take the Stanford's publicly available GloVe 50-dimensional embeddings[2] as word pretrained embeddings, which are trained on 6 billion words from Wikipedia and web text (Pennington et al., 2014). During the training process, word embeddings are fine-tuned.

Optimization We use RMSprop (Dauphin et al., 2015) as our optimizer to train the whole model. The initial learning rate η is set to 0.001 and momentum is set to 0.9. Dropout regularization is used to avoid overfitting and drop rate is 0.5.

5 Experiments

5.1 Setup

Data The ASAP dataset is used as evaluation data of our AES system. The ASAP dataset consists of 8 different prompts of genres as listed in Table 2.

There are no released labeled test data from the ASAP competition, thus we separate test set and development set from the training set. The partition exactly follows the setting used by Taghipour and Ng (2016), which adopts 5-fold cross-validation, in each fold, 60% of the data is used as our training set, 20% as the development

---

set, and 20% as the test set. The data is tokenized with NLTK[3] tokenizer. All the words are converted to lowercase and the scores are scaled to the range [0, 1]. During evaluation phase, the scaled scores are rescaled to original integer scores, which are used to calculate evaluation metric QWK values. The vocabulary size of the data is set to 4000, by following Taghipour and Ng (2016), selecting the most 4000 frequent words in the training data and treating all other words as unknown words.

Baseline models We take LSTM with Mean-over-Time Pooling (LSTM-MoT) (Taghipour and Ng, 2016) and hierarchical CNN (CNN-CNN-MoT) (Dong and Zhang, 2016) as our baselines. The former takes the essay script as a sequence of words, which is text-level model and the latter regards the script as a sequence of sentences, which is sentence-level model.

LSTM-MoT uses one layer of LSTM over the word sequences, and takes the average pooling over all time-step states as the final text representation, which is called Mean-over-Time (MoT) pooling (Taghipour and Ng, 2016). A linear layer with sigmoid function follows the MoT layer to predict the score of an essay script.

CNN-CNN-MoT uses two layers of CNN, in which one layer operates over each sentence to obtain representation for each sentence and the other CNN is stacked above, followed by mean-over-time pooling to get the final text representation.

LSTM-MoT is the current state-of-the-art neural model on the text-level and CNN-CNN-MoT is a state-of-the-art model on the sentence-level. Besides, LSTM-LSTM-MoT and LSTM-CNN-MoT are adopted as another two baseline models. The former model takes LSTMs to represent both sentences and texts, and the latter uses CNN representing sentences and LSTM representing texts. Both models use MoT pooling and are sentence-level models. We compare our model (LSTM-CNN-attent) with the baseline models to study CNN representing sentences and LSTM representing texts.

5.2 Results

The results are listed in Table 3. Our model LSTM-CNN-attent outperforms the baseline model CNN-CNN-MoT by 3.0%, LSTM-MoT by 2.2% on average quadratic weighted

---

[2]http://nlp.stanford.edu/projects/glove/

[3]http://www.nltk.org

Prompts	LSTM-MoT	CNN-CNN-MoT	LSTM-CNN-att
1	0.818	0.805	0.822
2	0.688	0.613	0.682
3	0.679	0.662	0.672
4	0.805	0.778	0.814
5	0.808	0.800	0.803
6	0.817	0.809	0.811
7	0.797	0.758	0.801
8	0.527	0.644	0.705
Avg.	0.742	0.734	**0.764**

Table 3: Comparison of quadratic weighted kappa between different models on the test data.

LSTM-CNN-attent	Average QWK
char	0.738
word	**0.764**
word + char	0.761

Table 4: Comparison of quadratic weight kappa using different features on the test data.

kappa. The results are statistically significant with $p < 0.05$ by one-tailed t-test. Even compared with the ensemble model used by Taghipour and Ng (2016), which ensembles 10 instances of CNN and LSTM of different initializations, our model still achieves 0.3% improvement on QWK.

5.3 Analysis

We perform several development experiments to verify the effectiveness of sentence-document model and text representation with LSTM and attention pooling.

Characters and Words We explore a convolutional layer to learn word representation from char-based CNN to replace word embeddings. In Table 4, we compare the performance of using character embeddings, word embeddings and concatenation of two embeddings. Empirical results show that with only character embedding features, the performance of our model outperforms CNN-CNN-MoT, and is close to LSTM-MoT. However, there is still a big gap between character embedding and word embedding models, which could come from the fact that we use pretrained word embeddings, which helps improve the performance. When both the word and character embeddings are used, the performance does not improve. One possible explanation is that the ASAP dataset is rather small given the model parameters, which has a potential for overfitting if both words and characters are used.

Model	Model Type	Pooling	Avg QWK
LSTM-MoT	document-level	MoT	0.742
LSTM-attent	document-level	attention	0.731
CNN-CNN-MoT	sentence-level	MoT	0.734
LSTM-LSTM-MoT	sentence-level	MoT	0.758
LSTM-CNN-MoT	sentence-level	MoT	0.759
LSTM-LSTM-attent	sentence-level	attention	0.762
LSTM-CNN-attent	sentence-level	attention	**0.764**

Table 5: Comparison between different model types and pooling methods on the test data (only word embeddings used).

Granularity The previous model LSTM-MoT tackles the AES task by treating each essay script as a sequence of words, which makes an essay an extra long sequence. The word number of one essay usually exceeds several hundreds, which makes it difficult to directly use LSTM to learn text representation if only last hidden state is used. It has been verified by Taghipour and Ng (2016) that LSTM with Mean-over-Time pooling outperforms LSTM with only last state. Though MoT pooling could alleviate this problem by considering all the states information, the model is still built on text-level rather than sentence-level. Both LSTM-CNN-MoT and LSTM-LSTM-MoT are sentence-document models. The former explores CNN for sentence representation and LSTM for text representation, and the latter use both LSTMs for sentence and text representation with MoT pooling. In Table 5, LSTM-CNN-MoT and LSTM-LSTM-MoT obtain large improvements compared to LSTM-MoT, especially for prompt 8 essays, of which the average script length is the biggest. This shows that sentence-document model tends to be more effective for long essays.

Local vs Global In Table 5, we compare LSTM-CNN-MoT with CNN-CNN-MoT to analyze the effectiveness of LSTM for text representation over CNN. Both CNN-CNN-MoT and LSTM-CNN-MoT learn hierarchical sentence-document representations. The former employs two-level CNNs for sentence representation and text representation respectively, and mean-over-time pooling is both used after two-level CNNs. The latter employs a CNN to learn sentence representation at the bottom, stacks one layer of LSTM above to learn text representation, and mean-over-time pooling is also used after CNN and LSTM. Compared with CNN-CNN-MoT in Table 5, LSTM-CNN-MoT gives a big improvement. We believe that on text representation layer, LSTMs can learn more global information, such as sentence coherence, while CNNs learn more local features, such as n-grams and bag-of-words. LSTM-LSTM-MoT outperforms CNN-CNN-MoT and gets slightly worse than LSTM-CNN-MoT, which also shows that LSTM is relatively more effective for modeling the documents.

Mean-over-Time vs Attention pooling We compare the two pooling methods adopted in our model, namely mean-over-time pooling and attention pooling in Table 5. The pooling layers are used after both CNN and LSTM layer to get sentence representation and text representation respectively. We find that by attending over words and sentences, we achieve the best performance, which demonstrates that attention pooling helps find the key words and sentences that contribute to judging quality of essays. In contrast to MoT, each word and sentence will be treated equally, which violates human raters' assessing process. Since our model is based on the sentence-level rather than the text-level, we can exert attention pooling to focus on pertinent words and sentences. Note that attention can be weakened when used for an extra long sequence, such as the scenario in the text-level model. Taghipour and Ng (2016) tried to attend over words on their one-layer LSTM model, but failed to beat the baseline model that employs mean-over-time pooling, because of that text-level model contains a quite long sequence of words, which may weaken the effect of attention. On the contrary, sentence-level model contains relatively short sequences of words, which makes attention more effective.

In Table 6, we briefly show two prompts from the AES data, namely Prompt 4 and Prompt 8. Prompt 4 asks for a response based on the last paragraph of a given story and Prompt 8 requires a true story about laughter. Prompt 4 has few number of sentences compared with Prompt 8. For convenience, we take Prompt 4 essays as our examples to analyze the attention mechanism on sentences, and Prompt 8 essays to analyze the attention mechanism on words n-grams. In Table 7, we list all five sentences in order that make up of one response essay from test set in Prompt 4. Each

	Prompt Contents
Prompt 4	Read the last paragraph of the story. "When they come back, Saeng vowed silently to herself, in the spring, when the snows melt and the geese return and this hibiscus is budding, then I will take that test again." Write a response that explains why the author concludes the story with this paragraph. In your response, include details and examples from the story that support your ideas. [5]
Prompt 8	We all understand the benefits of laughter. For example, someone once said, "Laughter is the shortest distance between two people." Many other people believe that laughter is an important part of any relationship. Tell a true story in which laughter was one element or part.

Table 6: Contents of Prompt 4 and Prompt 8

sentence is associated with its attention weight as shown in the table. The 4-th sentence has the biggest attention weight among the five sentence, then followed by the 5-th sentence. Intuitively, we know the 4-th and 5-th sentence can give strong supporting ideas to illustrate why the author concludes the story with the last paragraph. Therefore, it proves that our attention mechanism on sentences captures the key sentences to represent essays indeed.

In Table 8, we list three example sentences in one essay from the prompt 8 test data. The essay is written by students given the prompt described in the Table 6. The highlighted words are the 5-grams[4] that have the highest attention score. It can be easily seen that the highlighted 5-grams are the most relevant to the prompt, which demonstrates our attention-pooling takes an effect on learning sentence representation.

6 Related Work

The first AES system dates back to 1960s (Page, 1968, 1994) when Project Essay Grade (PEG) was developed. Following that, IntelliMetric 2, Intelligent Essay Assessor (IEA) (Landauer et al., 1998; Foltz et al., 1999) have come out. IEA uses Latent Semantic Analysis (LSA) to calculate the semantic similarity between texts and assigns a score to test text based on the score of the training text which is most similar to the given test text. Other commercial system, like e-rater system (Attali and

---

[4]Since we use a window size of 5 in CNN layer, the attention pooling after CNN layer is attending over 5-grams features.

[5]As Prompt 4 contains a long story in the prompt descriptions, we only pick up the most relevant contents here.

No.	Sentences	Attention weights
1	there was a specific reason as to why the author concluded the story with that quote .	0.17568
2	the author wanted to show how the plant gave saeng a new sense of determination .	0.20358
3	saeng previously was upset and tearing the plant apart .	0.19651
4	but it seemed that she realized how the plant was able to bud to the <unk> and survive .	0.21264
5	so she now was determined to <unk> the <unk> as well and retake the test she failed .	0.21159

Table 7: Attention weights of sentences coming from one student essay in Prompt 4 (The darkness of blue indicates the relative magnitude of attention weights.

Prompt 8	
Example 1	when i was a young boy i used to laugh at anything i could , but as a kid who did n't ?
Example 2	as i got older and grew more , i developed a great sense of humor that to my advantage made me a young people <unk> .
Example 3	i grew more and more <unk> a stronger , more confident sense of humor .

Table 8: Examples of attention pooling over n-grams features in Prompt 8 (The first row specifies the prompt given by the essay designer).

Burstein, 2004), has been deployed in the English language test, such as Test of English as a Foreign Language (TOEFL) and Graduate Record Examination (GRE). Step-wise linear regression is employed in the e-rater systems along with grammatical errors, lexical complexity as handcrafted features.

In the research literature, Larkey (1998) uses Naive Bayes model and takes AES as a classification model. Rudner and Liang (2002) explore multinomial Bernoulli Naive Bayes models to classify texts into several categories of text quality based on content and style features. Chen et al. (2010) formulates the AES task into a weakly supervised framework and employ a voting algorithm.

Other recent work formulate the task as a preference ranking problem (Yannakoudakis et al., 2011; Phandi et al., 2015). Yannakoudakis et al. (2011) formulate AES as a pairwise ranking problem by ranking the order of pair essays based on their quality. Features consist of word n-grams, deep linguistic features, including grammatical complexity, POS n-grams and parsing trees features. Chen and He (2013) formulate AES into a list-wise ranking problem by considering the order relation among the whole essays. Features contain syntactical features, grammar and fluency features as well as content and prompt-specific features. Phandi et al. (2015) use correlated Bayesian Linear Ridge Regression focusing on domain-adaptation tasks. All these previous methods are traditional discrete models using handcrafted discrete features.

Recently, Alikaniotis et al. (2016) employ a long short-term memory model to learn features for essay scoring task automatically without any predefined feature templates. It leverages score-specific word embeddings (SSWEs) for word representations, and takes the last hidden states of a two-layer bidirectional LSTM for essay representations. Taghipour and Ng (2016) also adopt a LSTM model for AES, but use ordinary word embedding and take the average pooling value of all the hidden states of LSTM layer as the essay representations. Dong and Zhang (2016) develop a hierarchical CNN model for regression on AES task by processing texts into sentences and using two layers CNN on both sentence-level and text-level to get the final text representation. Our work contributes to the research literature by systematically investigating CNN and LSTM on sentence-level and text-level modeling, and the effectiveness of attention network on automatically selecting more relevant ngrams and sentences for the task.

Our work is also inline with recent work on building hierarchical sentence-document level representations of documents. Li et al. (2015) build a hierarchical LSTM auto-encoder for documents. Yang et al. (2016) build hierarchical LSTM models with attention for document and Tang et al. (2015) use a hierarchical Gated RNN for sentiment classification. Ren and Zhang (2016) use hierarchical CNN-LSTM model for spam detection. We use a hierarchical CNN-LSTM model for essay scoring, which is a regression task.

7 Conclusion

We investigated a recurrent convolutional neural network to learn text representation and grade essays automatically. Our model treated input essays as sentence-document hierarchies, and employed attention pooling to find the pertinent words and sentences. Empirical results on ASAP essay data show that our model outperforms state-of-art neural models for automatic essay scoring task, giving the best performance. Future work explores the advantage of neural models on cross-domain AES task.

Acknowledgments

We thank the anonymous reviewers for their insightful comments. Yue Zhang is the corresponding author.

References

Dimitrios Alikaniotis, Helen Yannakoudakis, and Marek Rei. 2016. Automatic text scoring using neural networks. *arXiv preprint arXiv:1606.04289* .

Yigal Attali and Jill Burstein. 2004. Automated essay scoring with e-rater® v. 2.0. *ETS Research Report Series* 2004(2):i–21.

Hongbo Chen and Ben He. 2013. Automated essay scoring by maximizing human-machine agreement. In *EMNLP*. pages 1741–1752.

Yen-Yu Chen, Chien-Liang Liu, Chia-Hoang Lee, Tao-Hsing Chang, et al. 2010. An unsupervised automated essay scoring system. *IEEE Intelligent systems* 25(5):61–67.

Ronan Cummins, Meng Zhang, and Ted Briscoe. 2016. Constrained multi-task learning for automated essay scoring. Association for Computational Linguistics.

Yann Dauphin, Harm de Vries, and Yoshua Bengio. 2015. Equilibrated adaptive learning rates for non-convex optimization. In *Advances in Neural Information Processing Systems*. pages 1504–1512.

Fei Dong and Yue Zhang. 2016. Automatic features for essay scoring an empirical study. In *Proceedings of the 2016 Conference on Empirical Methods in Natural Language Processing, pages 968974,*. Association for Computational Linguistics, Austin, Texas, pages 1072–1077. https://www.aclweb.org/anthology/D/D16/D16-1115.pdf.

Peter W Foltz, Darrell Laham, and Thomas K Landauer. 1999. Automated essay scoring: Applications to educational technology. In *proceedings of EdMedia*. volume 99, pages 40–64.

Sepp Hochreiter and Jürgen Schmidhuber. 1997. Long short-term memory. *Neural computation* 9(8):1735–1780.

Yoon Kim. 2014. Convolutional neural networks for sentence classification. *arXiv preprint arXiv:1408.5882* .

Thomas K Landauer, Peter W Foltz, and Darrell Laham. 1998. An introduction to latent semantic analysis. *Discourse processes* 25(2-3):259–284.

Leah S Larkey. 1998. Automatic essay grading using text categorization techniques. In *Proceedings of the 21st annual international ACM SIGIR conference on Research and development in information retrieval*. ACM, pages 90–95.

Yann LeCun, Léon Bottou, Yoshua Bengio, and Patrick Haffner. 1998. Gradient-based learning applied to document recognition. *Proceedings of the IEEE* 86(11):2278–2324.

Jiwei Li, Minh-Thang Luong, and Dan Jurafsky. 2015. A hierarchical neural autoencoder for paragraphs and documents. *arXiv preprint arXiv:1506.01057* .

Jiangming Liu and Yue Zhang. 2017. Attention modeling for targeted sentiment. *EACL 2017* page 572.

Minh-Thang Luong, Hieu Pham, and Christopher D Manning. 2015. Effective approaches to attention-based neural machine translation. *arXiv preprint arXiv:1508.04025* .

Tomas Mikolov, Martin Karafiát, Lukas Burget, Jan Cernocký, and Sanjeev Khudanpur. 2010. Recurrent neural network based language model. In *Interspeech*. volume 2, page 3.

Ellis B Page. 1968. The use of the computer in analyzing student essays. *International review of education* 14(2):210–225.

Ellis Batten Page. 1994. Computer grading of student prose, using modern concepts and software. *The Journal of experimental education* 62(2):127–142.

Razvan Pascanu, Tomas Mikolov, and Yoshua Bengio. 2013. On the difficulty of training recurrent neural networks. *ICML (3)* 28:1310–1318.

Jeffrey Pennington, Richard Socher, and Christopher D Manning. 2014. Glove: Global vectors for word representation. In *EMNLP*. volume 14, pages 1532–1543.

Peter Phandi, Kian Ming A Chai, and Hwee Tou Ng. 2015. Flexible domain adaptation for automated essay scoring using correlated linear regression .

Yafeng Ren and Yue Zhang. 2016. Deceptive opinion spam detection using neural network. In *Proceedings of COLING 2016*. Association for Computational Linguistics, Osaka, Japan, pages 140–150. http://www.aclweb.org/anthology/C/C16/C16-1014.pdf.

Lawrence M Rudner and Tahung Liang. 2002. Automated essay scoring using bayes' theorem. *The Journal of Technology, Learning and Assessment* 1(2).

Bonggun Shin, Timothy Lee, and Jinho D Choi. 2016. Lexicon integrated cnn models with attention for sentiment analysis. *arXiv preprint arXiv:1610.06272* .

Kaveh Taghipour and Hwee Tou Ng. 2016. A neural approach to automated essay scoring. In *Proceedings of the 2016 Conference on Empirical Methods in Natural Language Processing, EMNLP 2016, Austin, Texas, USA, November 1-4, 2016.* pages 1882–1891. http://aclweb.org/anthology/D/D16/D16-1193.pdf.

Duyu Tang, Bing Qin, and Ting Liu. 2015. Document modeling with gated recurrent neural network for sentiment classification. In *EMNLP*. pages 1422–1432.

Yequan Wang, Minlie Huang, Li Zhao, and Xiaoyan Zhu. 2016. Attention-based lstm for aspect-level sentiment classification. In *EMNLP*. pages 606–615.

Ronald J Williams and David Zipser. 1989. A learning algorithm for continually running fully recurrent neural networks. *Neural computation* 1(2):270–280.

Kelvin Xu, Jimmy Ba, Ryan Kiros, Kyunghyun Cho, Aaron C Courville, Ruslan Salakhutdinov, Richard S Zemel, and Yoshua Bengio. 2015. Show, attend and tell: Neural image caption generation with visual attention. In *ICML*. volume 14, pages 77–81.

Zichao Yang, Diyi Yang, Chris Dyer, Xiaodong He, Alex Smola, and Eduard Hovy. 2016. Hierarchical attention networks for document classification. In *Proceedings of NAACL-HLT*. pages 1480–1489.

Helen Yannakoudakis, Ted Briscoe, and Ben Medlock. 2011. A new dataset and method for automatically grading esol texts. In *Proceedings of the 49th Annual Meeting of the Association for Computational Linguistics: Human Language Technologies-Volume 1*. Association for Computational Linguistics, pages 180–189.

Feature Selection as Causal Inference:
Experiments with Text Classification

Michael J. Paul
University of Colorado
Boulder, CO 80309, USA
`mpaul@colorado.edu`

Abstract

This paper proposes a matching technique for learning causal associations between word features and class labels in document classification. The goal is to identify more meaningful and generalizable features than with only correlational approaches. Experiments with sentiment classification show that the proposed method identifies interpretable word associations with sentiment and improves classification performance in a majority of cases. The proposed feature selection method is particularly effective when applied to out-of-domain data.

1 Introduction

A major challenge when building classifiers for high-dimensional data like text is learning to identify features that are not just correlated with the classes in the training data, but associated with classes in a meaningful way that will generalize to new data. Methods for regularization (Hoerl and Kennard, 1970; Chen and Rosenfeld, 2000) and feature selection (Yang and Pedersen, 1997; Forman, 2003) are critical for obtaining good classification performance by removing or minimizing the effects of noisy features. While empirically successful, these techniques can only identify features that are correlated with classes, and these associations can still be caused by factors other than the direct relationship that is assumed.

A more meaningful association is a **causal** one. In the context of document classification using bag-of-words features, we ask the question, which word features "cause" documents to have the class labels that they do? For example, it might be reasonable to claim that adding the word *horrible* to a review would cause its sentiment to become neg-

ative, while this is less plausible for a word like *said*. Yet, in one of our experimental datasets of doctor reviews, *said* has a stronger correlation with negative sentiment than *horrible*.

Inspired by methods for causal inference in other domains, we seek to learn causal associations between word features and document classes. We experiment with propensity score matching (Rosenbaum and Rubin, 1985), a technique attempts to mimic the random assignment of subjects to treatment and control groups in a randomized controlled trial by matching subjects with a similar "propensity" to receive treatment. Translating this idea to document classification, we match documents with similar propensity to contain a word, allowing us to compare the effect a word has on the class distribution after controlling for the context in which the word appears. We propose a statistical test for measuring the importance of word features on the matched training data.

We experiment with binary sentiment classification on three review corpora from different domains (doctors, movies, products) using propensity score matching to test for statistical significance of features. Compared to a chi-squared test, the propensity score matching test for feature selection yields superior performance in a majority of comparisons, especially for domain adaptation and for identifying top word associations. After presenting results and analysis in Sections 4–5, we discuss the implications of our findings and make suggestions for areas of language processing that would benefit from causal learning methods.

2 Causal Inference and Confounding

A challenge in statistics and machine learning is identifying causal relationships between variables. Predictive models like classifiers typically learn only correlational relationships between variables,

Proceedings of the 21st Conference on Computational Natural Language Learning (CoNLL 2017), pages 163–172,
Vancouver, Canada, August 3 - August 4, 2017. ©2017 Association for Computational Linguistics

and if spurious correlations are built into a model, then performance will worsen if the underlying distributions change.

A common cause of spurious correlations is **confounding**. A confounding variable is a variable that explains the association between a dependent variable and independent variables. A commonly used example is the positive correlation of ice cream sales and shark attacks, which are correlated because they both increase in warm weather (when more people are swimming). As far as anyone is aware, ice cream does not cause shark attacks; rather, both variables are explained by a confounding variable, the time of year.

There are experimental methods to reduce confounding bias and identify causal relationships. Randomized controlled trials, in which subjects are randomly assigned to a group that receives treatment versus a control group that does not, are the gold standard for experimentation in many domains. However, this type of experiment is not always possible or feasible. (In text processing, we generally work with documents that have already been written: the idea of assigning features to randomly selected documents to measure their effect does not make sense, so we cannot directly translate this idea.)

A variety of methods exist to attempt to infer causality even when direct experiments, like randomized controlled trials, cannot be conducted (Rosenbaum, 2002). In this work, we propose the use of one such method, propensity score matching (Rosenbaum and Rubin, 1985), for reducing the effects of confounding when identifying important features for classification. We describe this method, and its application to text, in Section 3. First, we discuss why causal methods may be important for document classification, and describe previous work in this space.

2.1 Causality in Document Classification

We now discuss where these ideas are relevant to document classification. Our study performs sentiment classification in online reviews using bag-of-words (unigram) features, so we will use examples that apply to this setting.

There are a number of potentially confounding factors in document classification (Landeiro and Culotta, 2016). Consider a dataset of restaurant reviews, in which fast food restaurants have a much lower average score than other types of restau-rants. Word features that are associated with fast food, like *drive-thru*, will be correlated with negative sentiment due to this association, even if the word itself has neutral sentiment. In this case, the type of restaurant is a confounding variable that causes spurious associations. If we had a method for learning causal associations, we would know that *drive-thru* itself does not affect sentiment.

What does it mean for a word to have a causal relationship with a document class? It is difficult to give a natural explanation for a bag-of-words model that ignores pragmatics and discourse, but here is an attempt. Suppose you are someone who understands bag-of-words representations of documents, and you are given a bag of words corresponding to a restaurant review. Suppose someone adds the word *terrible* to the bag. If you previously recognized the sentiment to be neutral or even positive, it is possible that the addition of this new word would cause the sentiment to change to negative. On the other hand, it is hard to imagine a set of words to which adding the word *drive-thru* would change the sentiment in any direction.

In this example, we would say that the word *terrible* "caused" the sentiment to change, while *drive-thru* did not. While most real documents will not have a clean interpretation of a word "causing" a change in sentiment, this may still serve as a useful conceptual model for identifying features that are meaningfully associated with class labels.

2.2 Previous Work

Recent studies have used text data, especially social media, to make causal claims (Cheng et al., 2015; Reis and Culotta, 2015; Pavalanathan and Eisenstein, 2016). The technique we use in this work, propensity score matching, has recently been applied to user-generated text data (Rehman et al., 2016; De Choudhury and Kiciman, 2017).

For the task of document classification specifically, Landeiro and Culotta (2016) experiment with multiple methods to make classifiers robust to confounding variables such as gender in social media and genre in movie reviews. This work requires confounding variables to be identified and included explicitly, whereas our proposed method requires only the features used for classification.

Causal methods have previously been applied to feature selection (Guyon et al., 2007; Cawley, 2008; Aliferis et al., 2010), but not with the match-

People	Text
Subject	Document
Treatment	Word
Outcome	Class label

Table 1: A mapping of standard terminology of randomized controlled trials (left) to our application of these ideas to text classification (right).

ing methods proposed in this work, and not for document classification.

3 Propensity Score Matching for Document Classification

Propensity score matching (PSM) (Rosenbaum and Rubin, 1985) is a technique that attempts to simulate the random assignment of treatment and control groups by matching treated subjects to untreated subjects that were similarly likely to be in the same group. This is centered around the idea of a **propensity score**, which Rosenbaum and Rubin (1983) define as the probability of being assigned to a treatment group based on observed characteristics of the subject, $P(z_i|x_i)$, typically estimated with a logistic regression model. In other words, what is the "propensity" of a subject to obtain treatment? Subjects that did and did not receive treatment are matched based their propensity to receive treatment, and we can then directly compare the outcomes of the treated and untreated groups.

In the case of document classification, we want to measure the effect of each word feature. Using the terminology above, each word is a "treatment" and each document is a "subject". Each word has a treatment group, the documents that contain the word, and a "control" group, the documents that do not. The "outcome" is the document class label.

Each subject has a propensity score for a treatment. In document classification, this means that each document has a propensity score for each word, which is the probability that the word would appear in the document. For a word w, we define this as the probability of the word appearing given all other words in the document: $P(w|\mathbf{d_i} - \{w\})$, where $\mathbf{d_i}$ is the set of words in the ith document. We estimate these probabilities by training a logistic regression model with word features.

Using our example from the previous section, the probability that a document contains the word *drive-thru* is likely to be higher in reviews that describe fast food that those that do not. Match-

ing reviews based on their likelihood of containing this word should adjust for any bias caused by the type of restaurant (fast food) as a confounding variable. This is done without having explicitly included this as a variable, since it will implicitly be learned when estimating the probability of words associated with fast food, like *drive-thru*.

3.1 Creating Matched Samples

Once propensity scores have been calculated, the next step is to match documents containing a word to documents that do not contain the word but have a similar score. There are a number of strategies for matching, summarized by Austin (2011a). For example, matching could be done one-to-one or one-to-many, sampling either with or without replacement. Another approach is to group similar scoring samples into strata (Cochran, 1968).

In this work, we perform one-to-one matching without replacement using a greedy matching algorithm; Gu and Rosenbaum (1993) found no quality difference using greedy versus optimal matching. We also experiment with thresholding how similar two scores must be to match them.

Implementation Even greedy matching is expensive, so we use a fast approximation. We place documents into 100 bins based on their scores (e.g., scores between .50 and .51). For each "treatment" document, we match it to the approximate closest "control" document by pointing to the treatment document's bin and iterating over bins outward until we find the first non-empty bin, and then select a random control document from that bin. Placing documents into bins is related to stratification approaches (Rosenbaum and Rubin, 1984), except that we use finer bins that typical strata and we still return one-to-one pairs.

3.1.1 Comparing Groups

Since our instances are paired (after one-to-one matching), we can use McNemar's test (McNemar, 1947), which tests if there is a significant change in the distribution of a variable in response to a change in the other. The test statistic is:

$$\chi^2 = \frac{(TN - CP)^2}{TN + CP} \tag{1}$$

where TN is the number of treatment instances with a negative outcome (in our case, the number of documents containing the target word with a negative sentiment label) and CP is the number of control instances with a positive outcome (the

	# documents	# tokens	# word types
Doctors	20,000	432,636	2,422
Movies	50,000	9,420,645	3,124
Products	100,000	7,416,381	2,343

Table 2: Corpus summary.

Training Corpus	Test Corpus					
	Doctors		*Movies*		*Products*	
	PSM	χ^2	PSM	χ^2	PSM	χ^2
Doctors	**.8569**	.8560	**.6796**	.6657	**.6670**	.6367
Movies	**.6510**	.5497	**.8094**	.7421	**.6658**	.4917
Products	.7799	**.7853**	**.8299**	.8245	.8234	**.8277**

Table 3: Area under the feature selection curve (see Figure 1) using F1-score as the evaluation metric. All differences between corresponding PSM and χ^2 results are statistically significant with $p \ll 0.01$ except for (*Doctors*, *Doctors*).

number of documents that do not contain the word with a positive sentiment label).

This test statistic has a chi-squared distribution with 1 degree of freedom. This test is related to a traditional chi-squared test used for feature selection (which we compare to experimentally in Section 4), except that it assumes paired data with a "before" and "after" measurement. In our case, we do not have two outcome measurements for the same subject, but we have two subjects that have been matched in a way that approximates this.

We perform this test for every feature (every word in the vocabulary). The goal of the test is to measure there is a significant difference in the class distribution (positive versus negative, in the case of sentiment) in documents that do and do not contain the word (the "after" and "before" conditions, respectively, when considering words as treatments).

4 Experiments with Feature Selection

To evaluate the ability of propensity score matching to identify meaningful word features, we use it for feature selection (Yang and Pedersen, 1997) in sentiment classification (Pang and Lee, 2004).

4.1 Datasets

We used datasets of reviews from three domains:

- *Doctors:* Doctor reviews from RateMDs.com (Wallace et al., 2014). Doctors are rated on a scale from 1–5 along four different dimensions (knowledgeability, staff, helpfulness, punctuality). We averaged the four ratings for each review and labeled a review positive if the average rating was ≥ 4 and negative if ≤ 2.
- *Movies:* Movie reviews from IMDB (Maas et al., 2011). Movies are rated on a scale from 1–10. Reviews rated ≥ 7 are labeled positive and reviews rated ≤ 4 are labeled negative.
- *Products:* Product reviews from Amazon (Jindal and Liu, 2008). Products are rated on a scale from 1–5, with reviews rated ≥ 4 labeled positive and reviews rated ≤ 2 labeled negative.

All datasets were sampled to have an equal class balance. We used unigram word features. For ef-

ficiency reasons (a limitation that is discussed in Section 7), we pruned the long tail of features, removing words appearing in less than 0.5% of each corpus. The sizes of the processed corpora and their vocabularies are summarized in Table 2.

4.2 Experimental Details

For each corpus, we randomly selected 50% for training, 25% for development, and 25% for testing. The training set is used for training classifiers as well as calculating all feature selection metrics.

We used the development set to measure classification performance for different hyperparameter values. Our propensity score matching method has two hyperparameters. First, when building logistic regression models to estimate the propensity scores, we adjusted the ℓ_2 regularization strength. Second, when matching documents, we required the difference between scores to be less than $\tau \times SD$ to count as a match, where SD is the standard deviation of the propensity scores. We performed a grid search over different values of τ and different regularization strengths, described more in our analysis in Section 5.2, and used the best combination of hyperparameters for each dataset.

We used logistic regression classifiers for sentiment classification. While we experimented with ℓ_2 regularization for constructing propensity scores, we used no regularization for the sentiment classifiers. Since regularization and feature selection are both used to avoid overfitting, we did not want to conflate the effects of the two, so by using unregularized classifiers we can directly assess the efficacy of our feature selection methods on held-out data. All models were implemented with `scikit-learn` (Pedregosa et al., 2011).

Baseline We compare propensity score matching with McNemar's test (**PSM**) to a standard chi-squared test (χ^2) for feature selection, one of the

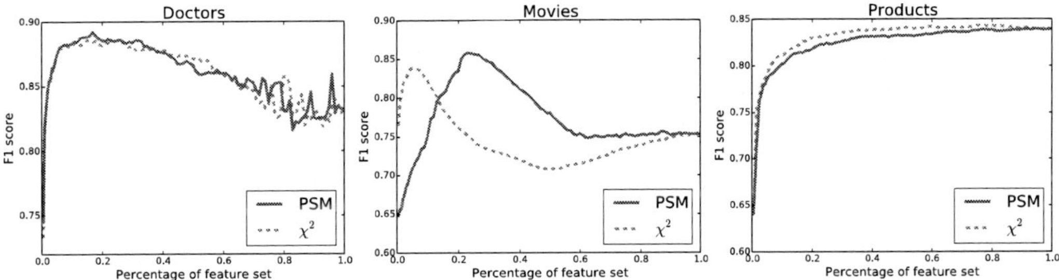

Figure 1: F1 scores when using a varying numbers of features ranked by two feature selection tests.

most common statistical tests for features in document classification (Manning et al., 2008). Since both tests follow a chi-squared distribution, and since McNemar's test is loosely like a chi-squared test for paired data, we believe this baseline offers the most direct comparison.

4.3 Results

We calculated the F1 scores of the sentiment classifiers when using different numbers of features ranked by significance. For example, when training a classifier with 1% of the feature set, this is the most significant 1% (with the lowest p-values). Results for varying feature set sizes on the three test datasets are shown in Figure 1.

To summarize the curves with a concise metric, we calculated the area under these curves (AUC). AUC scores for each dataset can be found along the diagonal of Table 3. We find that PSM gives higher AUC scores than χ^2 in two out of three datasets, though one is not statistically significant based on a paired t-test of the F1 scores.

PSM gives a large improvement over χ^2 on the *Movies* corpus, though the feature selection curve is unusual in that it rises gradually and peaks much later than χ^2. This appears to be because the highest ranking words with PSM have mostly positive sentiment. There is a worse balance of class associations in the top features with PSM than χ^2, so the classifier has a harder time discriminating with few features. However, PSM eventually achieves a higher score than the peak from χ^2 and the performance does not drop as quickly after peaking.

In the next two subsections, we examine additional settings in which PSM offers larger advantages over the χ^2 baseline.

4.3.1 Generalizability

A motivation for learning features with causal associations with document classes is to learn robust

Doctors		Movies		Products	
PSM	χ^2	PSM	χ^2	PSM	χ^2
great	told	great	worst	excellent	waste
caring	great	excellent	bad	wonderful	money
rude	rude	wonderful	and	great	great
best	best	best	great	waste	worst
excellent	said	love	waste	bad	best

Table 4: The highest scoring words from the two feature selection methods.

	$M=5$		$M=10$		$M=20$	
	PSM	χ^2	PSM	χ^2	PSM	χ^2
Doctors	**.5573**	.4806	**.6318**	.5520	**.6999**	.6503
Movies	**.5211**	.4962	.5841	**.6196**	.6171	**.6921**
Products	**.5388**	.3478	**.5514**	.4696	**.6031**	.5622

Table 5: Area under the feature selection curve when using only a small number of features, M.

features that can generalize to changes in the data distribution. To test this, we evaluated each of the three classifiers on the other two datasets (for example, testing the classifier trained on *Doctors* on the *Products* dataset). The AUC scores for all pairs of datasets are shown in Table 3.

On average, PSM improves the AUC over χ^2 by an average of .021 when testing on the same domain as training, while the improvement increases to an average of .053 when testing on out-of-domain data. In thus seems that PSM may be particularly effective at identifying features that can be applied across domains.

4.3.2 Top Features

Having measured performance across the entire feature set, we now focus on only the most highly associated features. The top features are important because these can give insights into the classification task, revealing which features are most associated with the target classes. Having top features that are meaningful and interpretable will lead to more trust in these models (Paul, 2016), and identifying meaningful features can itself be the goal of a study (Eisenstein et al., 2011b).

We experimented with a small number of features $M \in \{5, 10, 20\}$. Under the assumption that optimal hyperparameters may be different when using such a small number of features, we retuned the PSM parameters again for the experiments in this subsection, using $M = 10$.

Table 4 shows the five words with the lowest p-values with both methods. At a glance, the top words from PSM seem to have strong sentiment associations; for example, *excellent* is a top five feature in all three datasets using PSM, and none of the datasets using χ^2. Words without obvious sentiment associations seem to appear more often in the top χ^2 features, like *and*.

To quantify if there is a difference in quality, we again calculated the area under the feature selection F1 curves, where the number of features ranged from 1 to M. Results are shown in Table 5. For M of 10 and 20, PSM does worse on *Movies*, which is not surprising based on our finding above that the top features in this dataset are not balanced across the two labels, so PSM does worse for smaller numbers of features. For the other two datasets, PSM substantially outperforms χ^2. PSM appears to be an effective method for identifying strong feature associations.

5 Empirical Analysis

We now perform additional analyses to gain a deeper understanding of the behavior of propensity score matching applied to feature selection.

5.1 An Example

To better understand what happens during matching, we examined the word *said* on the *Doctors* corpus. This word does not have an obvious sentiment association, but is the fifth-highest scoring word with χ^2. It is still highly ranked when using propensity score matching, but this approach reduces its rank to ten.

Upon closer inspection, we find that reviews tend to use this word when discussing logistical issues, like interactions with office staff. These issues seem to be discussed primarily in a negative context, giving *said* a strong association with negative sentiment. If, however, reviews that discussed these logistical issues were matched, then within these matched reviews, those containing *said* are probably not more negative than those that

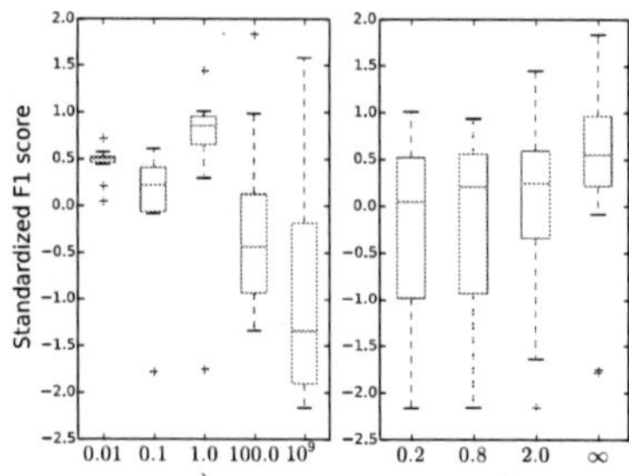

Figure 2: The distribution of the area under the feature selection curve scores when using different hyperparameter settings (propensity inverse regularization strength λ and matching threshold τ).

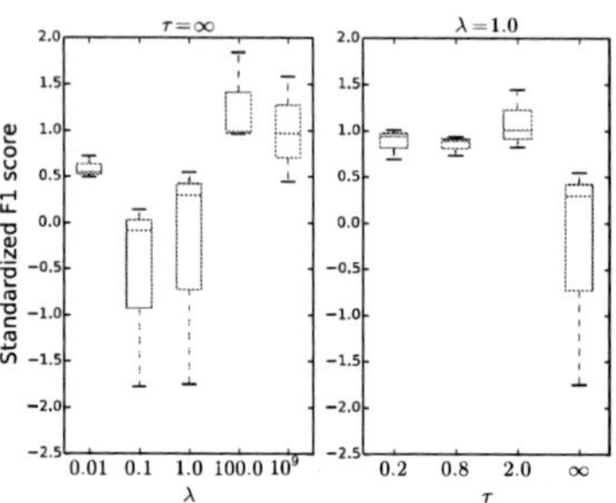

Figure 3: The distribution of scores when using different hyperparameter settings, restricted to the best performing setting for each independent parameter as shown in Figure 2 (varying λ with the optimal τ, and varying τ with the optimal λ).

do not. With propensity score matching, documents are matched based on how likely they are to contain the word *said*, which is meant to control for the negative context that this word has a tendency (or propensity) to appear in.

Table 6 shows example reviews that do (the "treatment" group) and do not (the "control" group) contain *said*. We see that the higher propensity reviews do tend to discuss issues like receptionists and records, and controlling for this context may explain why this method produced a lower ranking for this word.

5.2 Hyperparameter Settings

We investigate the effect of different hyperparameter settings. To do this, we first standardized the results across the three development datasets by converting them to z-scores so that they can be directly compared. The distribution of scores (specifically, the area under the F1 curve scores from Table 3) is summarized in Figure 2.

	"Treatment"		"Control"
	High Propensity		
.8040 −	She repeatedly said, "I don't care how you feel" when my wife told her the medication (birth control) was causing issues. She failed to mention a positive test result, giving a clean bill of health.	.7880 −	After a long, long conversation during which I tried to explain that I did not have records as I was only looked at by a sport trainer, they still would not see me without previous records.
.6320 −	I went for a checkup and he ended up waiting for over 2 hours just to get into the room. Then I waited some more until he eventually came in and dedicated the whole 10 minutes of his time. When I asked what exactly is going to take place, the assistant said, no big deal, just a little scrape.	.5047 +	The receptionist was able to get me in the next day and really worked around my busy schedule. I downloaded my paperwork off the website and had it ready at my appointment. I waited maybe 10 minutes and was in the exam room. The doctor was really nice and took the time to talk to me.
	Low Propensity		
.2012 +	I said he was on time but usually you have to wait because he does procedures in all hospitals in town, has emergencies and runs a little late. No matter how busy he is, he greets you warmly and chats with you.	.1959 −	For over a week I was going to the pharmacy every day after being told by her staff that it had been called in. Finally after a week then told she would not call it in, I had to come in to see her!
.0597 −	This doctor did not do what he said he would, was massively late, unwilling to talk to us about the condition we were facing.	.0598 −	DR.Taylor is usually not around. Staff is rude and antagonistic. They do not care about you as a person or your children.

Table 6: Examples of reviews that were matched based on the word *said*. Reviews on the left contain the word *said* while those on the right do not. Each row corresponds to a pair of matched documents (edited for length). The propensity score and sentiment label (+ or −) is shown for each document.

Regularization When training the logistic regression model to create propensity scores, we experimented with the following values of the inverse regularization parameter: $\lambda \in \{0.01, 0.1, 1.0, 100.0, 10^9\}$, where $\lambda=10^9$ is essentially no regularization other than to keep the optimal parameter values finite. We make two observations. First, high λ values (less regularization) generally result in worse scores. Second, small λ values lead to more consistent results, with less variance in the score distribution. Based on these results, we recommend a value of $\lambda=1.0$ based on its high median score, competitive maximum score, and low variance.

Matching We required that the scores of two documents were within $\tau \times SD$ of each other, and experimented with the following thresholds: $\tau \in \{0.2, 0.8, 2.0, \infty\}$. Austin (2011b) found that $\tau=0.2$ was optimal for continuous features and $\tau=0.8$ was optimal for binary features. Based on these guidelines, 0.8 would be appropriate for our scenario, but we also compared to a larger threshold (2.0) and no threshold (∞). We find that scores consistently increase as τ increases.

Coupling Looking at the two hyperparameters independently does not tell the whole story, due to interactions between the two. In particular, we observe that lower thresholds (lower τ) work better when using heavier regularization (lower λ), and

vice versa. It turns out that it is ill-advised to use $\tau=\infty$, as Figure 2 would suggest, when using our recommendation of $\lambda=1.0$. Figure 3 shows the λ distribution when set to $\tau=\infty$ and the τ distribution when set to $\lambda=1.0$. This shows that when $\lambda=1.0$, scores are much worse when $\tau=\infty$. When $\tau=\infty$, scores are better with higher λ values.

The best combinations of hyperparameters are $(\lambda = 100.0, \tau = \infty)$ and $(\lambda = 1.0, \tau = 2.0)$. Between these, we recommend $(\lambda = 1.0, \tau = 2.0)$ due to its higher median and lower variance.

5.3 P-Values

Lastly, we examine the p-values produced by McNemar's test on propensity score matched data compared to the standard chi-squared test. Figure 4 shows the distribution of the log of the p-values from both methods, using the same hyperparameters as in Section 4.3. We find that χ^2 tends to assign lower p-values, with more extreme values. This suggests that propensity score matching yields more conservative estimates of the statistical significance of features.

6 Related Work

In addition to the prior work already discussed, we wish to draw attention to work in related areas with respect to text classification.

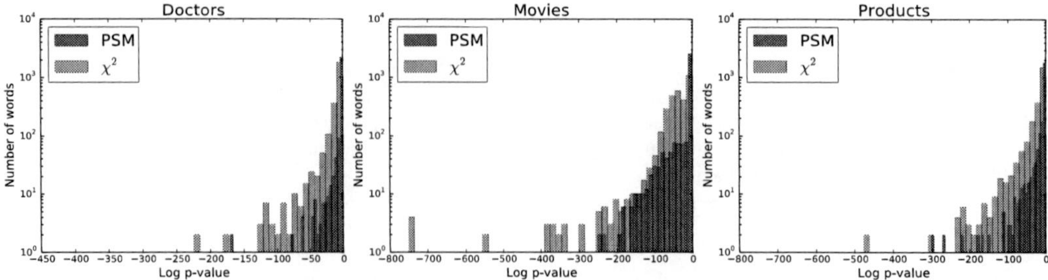

Figure 4: Distribution of p-values of features from the two methods of testing. Counts are on a log scale.

Matching There have been instances of using matching techniques to improve text training data. Tan et al. (2014) built models to estimate the number of retweets of Twitter messages and addressed confounding factors by matching tweets of the same author and topic (based on posting the same link). Zhang et al. (2016) built classifiers to predict media coverage of journal articles used matching sampling to select negative training examples, choosing articles from the same journal issue. While motivated differently, contrastive estimation (Smith and Eisner, 2005) is also related to matching. In contrastive estimation, negative training examples are synthesized by perturbing positive instances. This strategy essentially matches instances that have the same semantics but different syntax.

Annotation Perhaps the work that most closely gets at the concept of causality in document classification is work that asks for annotators to identify which features are important. There are branches of active learning which ask annotators to label not only documents, but to label features for importances or relevance (Raghavan et al., 2006; Druck et al., 2009). Work on annotator rationales (Zaidan et al., 2007; Zaidan and Eisner, 2008) seeks to model **why** annotators labeled a document a certain way—in other words, what "caused" the document to have its label? These ideas could potentially be integrated with causal inference methods for document classification.

7 Future Work

Efficiency is a drawback of the current work. The standard way of defining propensity scores with logistic regression models is not designed to scale to the large number of variables used in text classification. Our proposed method is slow because it requires training a logistic regression model for every word in the vocabulary. Perhaps documents could instead be matched based on another metric, like cosine similarity. This would match documents with similar context, which is what the PSM method appears to be doing based on our analysis.

We emphasize that the results of the PSM statistical analysis could be used in ways other than using it to select features ahead of training, which is less common today than doing feature selection directly through the training process, for example with sparse regularization (Tibshirani, 1994; Eisenstein et al., 2011a; Yogatama and Smith, 2014). One way to integrate PSM with regularization would be to use each feature's test statistic to weight its regularization penalty, discouraging features with high p-values from having large coefficients in a classifier.

In general, we believe this work shows the utility of controlling for the context in which features appear in documents when learning associations between features and classes, which has not been widely considered in text processing. Prior work that used matching and related techniques for text classification was generally motivated by specific factors that needed to be controlled for, but our study found that a general-purpose matching approach can also lead to better feature discovery. We want this work to be seen not necessarily as a specific prescription for one method of feature selection, but as a general framework for improving learning of text categories.

8 Conclusion

We have introduced and experimented with the idea of using propensity score matching for document classification. This method matches documents of similar propensity to contain a word as a way to simulate the random assignment to treatment and control groups, allowing us to more reliably learn if a feature has a significant, causal effect on document classes. While the concept of causality does not apply to document classification as naturally as in other tasks, the methods used for causal inference may still lead to more interpretable and generalizable features. This was evidenced by our experiments with feature selection using corpora from three domains, in which our proposed approach resulted in better performance than a comparable baseline in a majority of cases, particularly when testing on out-of-domain data. In future work, we hope to consider other metrics for matching to improve the efficiency, and to consider other ways of integrating the proposed feature test into training methods for text classifiers.

References

C.F. Aliferis, A. Statnikov, I. Tsamardinos, S. Mani, and X.D. Koutsoukos. 2010. Local causal and markov blanket induction for causal discovery and feature selection for classification. *Journal of Machine Learning Research* 11:171–234.

P.C. Austin. 2011a. An introduction to propensity score methods for reducing the effects of confounding in observational studies. *Multivariate Behav Res* 46(3):399–424.

P.C. Austin. 2011b. Optimal caliper widths for propensity-score matching when estimating differences in means and differences in proportions in observational studies. *Pharm Stat* 10(2):150–161.

G.C. Cawley. 2008. Causal & non-causal feature selection for ridge regression. In *Proceedings of the Workshop on the Causation and Prediction Challenge at WCCI 2008*.

S.F. Chen and R. Rosenfeld. 2000. A survey of smoothing techniques for maximum entropy models. *IEEE Transactions on Speech and Audio Processing* 8(1):37–50.

J. Cheng, C. Danescu-Niculescu-Mizil, and J. Leskovec. 2015. Antisocial behavior in online discussion communities. In *International Conference on Web and Social Media (ICWSM)*.

W.G. Cochran. 1968. The effectiveness of adjustment by subclassification in removing bias in observational studies. *Biometrics* 24:295–313.

M. De Choudhury and E. Kiciman. 2017. The language of social support in social media and its effect on suicidal ideation risk. In *International Conference on Web and Social Media (ICWSM)*.

G. Druck, B. Settles, and A. McCallum. 2009. Active learning by labeling features. In *Conference on Empirical Methods in Natural Language Processing (EMNLP)*.

J. Eisenstein, A. Ahmed, and E.P. Xing. 2011a. Sparse additive generative models of text. In *International Conference on Machine Learning (ICML)*.

J. Eisenstein, N.A. Smith, and E.P. Xing. 2011b. Discovering sociolinguistic associations with structured sparsity. In *Proceedings of the Association for Computational Linguistics (ACL)*.

G. Forman. 2003. An extensive empirical study of feature selection metrics for text classification. *Journal of Machine Learning Research* 3:1289–1305.

X.S. Gu and P.R. Rosenbaum. 1993. Comparison of multivariate matching methods: Structures, distances, and algorithms. *Journal of Computational and Graphical Statistics* 2:405–420.

I. Guyon, C. Aliferis, and A. Elisseeff. 2007. Causal feature selection. In H. Liu and H. Motoda, editors, *Computational Methods of Feature Selection*, Chapman and Hall/CRC Press.

A.E. Hoerl and R.W. Kennard. 1970. Ridge regression: Biased estimation for nonorthogonal problems. *Technometrics* 12:55–67.

N. Jindal and B. Liu. 2008. Opinion spam and analysis. In *International Conference on Web Search and Data Mining (WSDM)*.

V. Landeiro and A. Culotta. 2016. Robust text classification in the presence of confounding bias. In *AAAI*.

A.L. Maas, R.E. Daly, P.T. Pham, D. Huang, A.Y. Ng, and C. Potts. 2011. Learning word vectors for sentiment analysis. In *Annual Meeting of the Association for Computational Linguistics (ACL)*.

C.D. Manning, P. Raghavan, and H. Schütze. 2008. *Introduction to Information Retrieval*. Cambridge University Press.

Q. McNemar. 1947. Note on the sampling error of the difference between correlated proportions or percentages. *Psychometrika* 12(2):153–157.

B. Pang and L. Lee. 2004. A sentimental education: Sentiment analysis using subjectivity summarization based on minimum cuts. In *Proceedings of the 42nd Annual Meeting on Association for Computational Linguistics (ACL)*.

M.J. Paul. 2016. Interpretable machine learning: lessons from topic modeling. In *CHI Workshop on Human-Centered Machine Learning*.

U. Pavalanathan and J. Eisenstein. 2016. Emoticons vs. emojis on Twitter: A causal inference approach. In *AAAI Spring Symposium on Observational Studies through Social Media and Other Human-Generated Content*.

F. Pedregosa, G. Varoquaux, A. Gramfort, V. Michel, B. Thirion, O. Grisel, M. Blondel, P. Prettenhofer, R. Weiss, V. Dubourg, J. Vanderplas, A. Passos, D. Cournapeau, M. Brucher, M. Perrot, and

E. Duchesnay. 2011. Scikit-learn: Machine learning in Python. *Journal of Machine Learning Research* 12:2825–2830.

H. Raghavan, O. Madani, and R. Jones. 2006. Active learning with feedback on features and instances. *J. Mach. Learn. Res.* 7:1655–1686.

N.A. Rehman, J. Liu, and R. Chunara. 2016. Using propensity score matching to understand the relationship between online health information sources and vaccination sentiment. In *AAAI Spring Symposium on Observational Studies through Social Media and Other Human-Generated Content*.

V.L.D. Reis and A. Culotta. 2015. Using matched samples to estimate the effects of exercise on mental health from Twitter. In *AAAI*.

P.R. Rosenbaum. 2002. *Observational Studies*. Springer-Verlag.

P.R. Rosenbaum and D.B. Rubin. 1983. The central role of the propensity score in observational studies for causal effects. *Biometrika* 70:41–55.

P.R. Rosenbaum and D.B. Rubin. 1984. Reducing bias in observational studies using subclassification on the propensity score. *Journal of the American Statistical Association* 79:516–524.

P.R. Rosenbaum and D.B. Rubin. 1985. Constructing a control group using multivariate matched sampling methods that incorporate the propensity score. *The American Statistician* 39:33–38.

N.A. Smith and J. Eisner. 2005. Contrastive estimation: Training log-linear models on unlabeled data. In *Proceedings of the Association for Computational Linguistics (ACL)*.

C. Tan, L. Lee, and B. Pang. 2014. The effect of wording on message propagation: Topic- and author-controlled natural experiments on Twitter. In *Annual Meeting of the Association for Computational Linguistics (ACL)*.

R. Tibshirani. 1994. Regression shrinkage and selection via the lasso. *Journal of the Royal Statistical Society, Series B* 58:267–288.

B.C. Wallace, M.J. Paul, U. Sarkar, T.A. Trikalinos, and M. Dredze. 2014. A large-scale quantitative analysis of latent factors and sentiment in online doctor reviews. *Journal of the American Medical Informatics Association* 21(6):1098–1103.

Y. Yang and J.O. Pedersen. 1997. A comparative study on feature selection in text categorization. In *Proceedings of the Fourteenth International Conference on Machine Learning (ICML)*.

D. Yogatama and N.A. Smith. 2014. Linguistic structured sparsity in text categorization. In *Annual Meeting of the Association for Computational Linguistics (ACL)*.

O.F. Zaidan and J. Eisner. 2008. Modeling annotators: A generative approach to learning from annotator rationales. In *Proceedings of EMNLP 2008*. pages 31–40.

O.F. Zaidan, J. Eisner, and C. Piatko. 2007. Using "annotator rationales" to improve machine learning for text categorization. In *NAACL HLT 2007; Proceedings of the Main Conference*. pages 260–267.

Y. Zhang, E. Willis, M.J. Paul, N. Elhadad, and B.C. Wallace. 2016. Characterizing the (perceived) newsworthiness of health science articles: A data-driven approach. *JMIR Med Inform* 4(3):e27.

A Joint Model for Semantic Sequences: Frames, Entities, Sentiments

Haoruo Peng   Snigdha Chaturvedi   Dan Roth
University of Illinois, Urbana-Champaign
`{hpeng7,snigdha,danr}@illinois.edu`

Abstract

Understanding stories – sequences of events – is a crucial yet challenging natural language understanding task. These events typically carry multiple aspects of semantics including actions, entities and emotions. Not only does each individual aspect contribute to the meaning of the story, so does the interaction among these aspects. Building on this intuition, we propose to jointly model important aspects of semantic knowledge – frames, entities and sentiments – via a semantic language model. We achieve this by first representing these aspects' semantic units at an appropriate level of abstraction and then using the resulting vector representations for each semantic aspect to learn a joint representation via a neural language model. We show that the joint semantic language model is of high quality and can generate better semantic sequences than models that operate on the word level. We further demonstrate that our joint model can be applied to story cloze test and shallow discourse parsing tasks with improved performance and that each semantic aspect contributes to the model.

1 Introduction

Understanding a story requires understanding sequences of events. It is thus vital to model semantic sequences in text. This modeling process necessitates deep semantic knowledge about what can happen next. Since events involve actions, participants and emotions, semantic knowledge about these aspects must be captured and modeled.

Consider the examples in Figure 1. In Ex.1, we observe a sequence of actions (commit, arrest, charge, try), each corresponding to a predicate

---

Ex.1 (Actions - Frames) Steven Avery *committed* murder. He was *arrested, charged* and *tried*.
Opt.1 Steven Avery was <u>convicted</u> of murder.
Opt.2 Steven <u>went</u> to the movies with friends.
Alter. Steven was <u>held in jail</u> during his trial.

Ex.2 (Participants - Entities) It was my first time ever playing *football* and I was so nervous. During the game, I got tackled and it did not hurt at all!
Opt.1 I then felt more confident playing <u>football</u>.
Opt.2 I realized playing <u>baseball</u> was a lot of fun.
Alter. However, I still <u>love baseball more</u>.

Ex.3 (Emotions - Sentiments) Joe wanted to become a professional plumber. So, he applied to a trade school. Fortunately, he was *accepted*.
Opt.1 It made Joe very <u>happy</u>.
Opt.2 It made Joe very <u>sad</u>.
Alter. However, Joe <u>decided not to enroll</u> because he did not have enough money to pay tuition.

Figure 1: **Examples of short stories requiring different aspects of semantic knowledge.** For all stories, Opt.1 is the correct follow-up, while Opt.2 is the contrastive wrong follow-up demonstrating the importance of each aspect. Alter. showcases an alternative correct follow-up, which requires considering different aspects of semantics jointly.

frame. Clearly, "convict" is more likely than "go" to follow such sequence. This semantic knowledge can be learned through modeling frame sequences observed in a large corpus. This phenomena has already been studied in script learning works (Chatman, 1980; Chambers and Jurafsky, 2008b; Ferraro and Van Durme, 2016; Pichotta and Mooney, 2016a; Peng and Roth, 2016). However, modeling actions is not sufficient; participants in actions and their emotions are also important. In Ex. 2, Opt.2 is not a plausible answer because the story is about "football", and it does not make sense to suddenly change the key en-

Proceedings of the 21st Conference on Computational Natural Language Learning (CoNLL 2017), pages 173–183,
Vancouver, Canada, August 3 - August 4, 2017. ©2017 Association for Computational Linguistics

Models	Context Input	Generated Ending
4-gram	Steven Avery committed murder. He was arrested, charged and tried.	With law by the judge <UNK> ...
RNNLM	*same as above*	The information under terrorism ...
Seq2Seq	*same as above*	He decided for a case.
FC-SemLM	commit.01 arrest.01 charge.05 try.01	convict.01
FES-LM	PER[new]-commit.01-ARG[new](NEG) ARG[new]-arrest.01-PER[old](NEU) ARG[new]-charge.05-PER[old](NEU) ARG[new]-try.01-PER[old](NEG)	ARG[new]-convict.01-PER[old](NEG)

Table 1: **Comparison of generative ability for different models.** For each model, we provide Ex.1 as context and compare the generated ending. 4-gram and RNNLM models are trained on NYT news data while Seq2Seq model is trained on the story data (details see Sec. 5). These are models operated on the word level. We compare them with FC-SemLM (Peng and Roth, 2016), which works on frame abstractions, i.e. "predicate.sense". For the proposed FES-LM, we further assign the arguments (subject and object) of a predicate with NER types ("PER, LOC, ORG, MISC") or "ARG" if otherwise. Each argument is also associated with a "[new/old]" label indicating if it is first mentioned in the sequence (decided by entity co-reference). Additionally, the sentiment of a frame is represented as positive (POS), neural (NEU) or negative (NEG). FES-LM can generate better endings in terms of soundness and specificity. The FES-LM ending can be understood as "[Something] convict a person, who has been mentioned before (with an overall negative sentiment)", which can be instantiated as "Steven Avery was convicted." given current context.

tity to "baseball". In Ex.3, one needs understand that "being accepted" typically indicates a positive sentiment and that it applies to "Joe".

As importantly, we believe that modeling these semantic aspects should be done jointly; otherwise, it may not convey the complete intended meaning. Consider the alternative follow-ups in Figure 1: in Ex.1, the entity "jail" gives strong indication that it follows the storyline that mentions "murder"; in Ex.2, even though "football" is not explicitly mentioned, there is a comparison between "baseball" and "football" that makes this continuation coherent; in Ex.3, "decided not to enroll" is a reasonable action after "being accepted", although the general sentiment of the sentence is negative. These examples show that in order to model semantics in a more complete way, we need to consider interactions between frames, entities and sentiments.

In this paper, we propose a joint semantic language model, FES-LM, for semantic sequences, which captures Frames, Entities and Sentiment information. Just as "standard" language models built on top of words, we construct FES-LM by building language models on top of joint semantic representations. This joint semantic representation is a mixture of representations corre-

sponding to different semantic aspects. For each aspect, we capture semantics via abstracting over and disambiguating text surface forms, i.e. semantic frames for predicates, entity types for semantic arguments, and sentiment labels for the overall context. These abstractions provide the basic vocabulary for FES-LM and are essential for capturing the underlying semantics of a story. In Table 1, we provide Ex.1 as context input (although FC-SemLM and FES-LM automatically generate a more abstract representation of this input) and examine the ability of different models to generate an ending. 4-gram, RNNLM and Seq2Seq models operate on the word level, and the generated endings are not satisfactory. FC-SemLM (Peng and Roth, 2016) works on basic frame abstractions and the proposed FES-LM model adds abstracted entity and sentiment information into frames. The results show that FES-LM produces the best ending among all compared models in terms of semantic soundness and specificity.

We build the joint language model from plain text corpus with automatic annotation tools, requiring no human effort. In the empirical study, FES-LM is first built on news documents. We provide perplexity analysis of different variants of FES-LM as well as for the narrative cloze test, where we test the system's ability to recover a randomly dropped frame. We further show that FES-LM improves the performance of sense disambiguation for shallow discourse parsing. We then re-train the model on short commonsense stories (with the model trained on news as initialization). We perform story cloze test (Mostafazadeh et al., 2017), i.e. given a four-sentence story, choose the fifth sentence from two provided options. Our joint model achieves the best known results in the unsupervised setting. In all cases, our ablation study demonstrates that each aspect of FES-LM contributes to the model.

The main contributions of our work are: 1) the design of a joint neural language model for semantic sequences built from frames, entities and sentiments; 2) showing that FES-LM trained on news is of high quality and can help to improve shallow discourse parsing; 3) achieving the state-of-the-art result on story cloze test in an unsupervised setting with the FES-LM tuned on stories.

2 Semantic Aspect Modeling

This section describes how we capture different aspects of the semantic information in a text snippet via semantic frames, entities and sentiments.

2.1 Semantic Frames

Semantic frame is defined by Fillmore (1976): *frames are certain schemata or frameworks of concepts or terms which link together as a system, which impose structure or coherence on some aspect of human experience, and which may contain elements which are simultaneously parts of other such frameworks.* In this work, we simplify it by defining a semantic frame as a composition of a predicate and its corresponding argument participants. The design of PropBank frames (Kingsbury and Palmer, 2002) and FrameNet frames (Baker et al., 1998) perfectly fits our needs. Here we require the predicate to be disambiguated to a specific sense, thus each frame can be uniquely represented by its predicate sense. These frames provide a good level of generalization as each frame can be instantiated into various surface forms in natural texts. For example, in Ex.1, the semantic frame in Opt.1 would be abstracted as "convict.01". We associate each of these frames with an embedding. The arguments of the frames are modeled as entities, as described next.

Additionally, in accordance with the idea pro-

Ex.4 <u>The doctor</u> told <u>Susan</u> that *she* was busy.
<u>The doctor</u> told <u>Susan</u> that *she* had cancer.
<u>Mary</u> told <u>Susan</u> that *she* had cancer.

Figure 2: **Examples of the need for different levels of entity abstraction.** For each sentence, one wants to understand what the pronoun "she" refers to, which requires different abstractions for two underlined entity choices depending on context.

posed by Peng and Roth (2016), we also extend the frame representations to include discourse markers since they model relationships between frames. In this work, we only consider explicit discourse markers between abstracted frames. We use surface forms to represent discourse markers because there is only a limited set. We also assign an embedding with the same dimension as frames to each discourse marker.

To unify the representation, we formally use e_f to represent an embedding of a disambiguated frame/discourse marker. Such embedding would later be learned during language model training.

2.2 Entities

We consider the subject and object of a predicate as the essential entity information for modeling semantics. To achieve a higher level of abstraction, we model entity types instead of entity surface forms. We choose to assign entities with labels produced by Named Entity Recognition (NER), as NER typing is reliable.[1]

In fact, it is difficult to abstract each entity into an appropriate level since the decision is largely affected by context. Consider the examples shown in Figure 2. For the first sentence, to correctly understand what "she" refers to, it is enough to just abstract both entities "the doctor" and "Susan" to the NER type "person", i.e. the semantic knowledge being *person A told person B that person A was busy*. However, when we change the context in the second sentence, the "person" abstraction becomes too broad as it loses key information for this "doctor - patient" situation. The ideal semantic abstraction would be "a doctor told a patient that the patient had a disease". For the third sentence, it is ambiguous without further context from other sentences. Thus, entity abstraction is a delicate balance between specificity and correctness.

---

[1]Though there are a number works on fine-grained entity typing (Yogatama et al., 2015; Ren et al., 2016), their performances are between 65% and 75%, much lower than NER.

Besides type information, Ex.2 in Figure 1 shows the necessity of providing *new entity* information, i.e whether or not an entity is appeared for the first time in the whole semantic sequence. This corresponds well with the definition of *anaphrocity* in co-reference resolution, i.e. whether or not the mention starts a co-reference chain. Thus, we can encode this binary information as an additional dimension in the entity representation.

Thus, we formally define r_e as the entity representation. It is the concatenation of two entity vectors r_{sub} and r_{obj} for subject entity and object entity respectively. Both r_{sub} and r_{obj} are constructed as a one hot vector[2] to represent an entity type, plus an additional dimension indicating whether or not it is a *new entity* (1 if it is new).

2.3 Sentiments

For a piece of text, we can assign a sentiment value to it. It can either be positive, negative, or neutral. In order to decide which one is most appropriate, we first use a look-up table from word lexicons to sentiment, and then count the number of words which corresponds to positive (n_{pos}) and negative (n_{neg}) sentiment respectively. If $n_{pos} > n_{neg}$, we determine the text as positive; and if $n_{pos} < n_{neg}$, we assign the negative label; and if the two numbers equal, we deem the text as neutral. We use one hot vector for three sentiment choices, and define sentiment representation as r_s.

3 FES-LM - Joint Modeling

We present our joint model FES-LM and the neural language model implementation in this section. The joint model considers frames, entities and sentiments together to construct FES representations in order to model semantics more completely. Moreover, we build language models on top of such representations to reflect the sequential nature of semantics.

3.1 FES Representation

We propose FES-LM as a joint model to embed frame, entity and sentiment information together. Thus for each sentence/clause (specific to a frame), we can get individual representations for the frame (i.e. e_f), entity types and new entity information corresponds to subject and object of the frame (i.e. r_e), and sentiment information (i.e. r_s).

Thus, we construct the FES representation as:

$$r_{\text{FES}} = e_f + W_e r_e + W_s r_s.$$

W_e, W_s are two matrices transforming entity and sentiment representations into the frame embedding space, which are added to the corresponding frame embedding. These two parameters are shared across all FES representations. During language model training, we learn frame embeddings e_f as well as W_e and W_s. An overview of the FES representation in a semantic sequence is shown in Figure 3. Note that if the frame embedding represents a discourse marker, we set the corresponding entity and sentiment representations as zero vectors since no entity/sentiment is matched to a discourse marker. It is our design choice to add the entity and sentiment vectors to the frame embeddings, which creates a unified semantic space. During training, the interactions between different semantic aspects are captured by optimizing the loss on the joint FES representations.[3]

3.2 Neural Language Model

To model semantic sequences and train FES representations, we build neural language models. Theoretically, we can utilize any existing neural language model. We choose to implement the log-bilinear language model (LBL) (Mnih and Hinton, 2007) as our main method since previous works have reported best performance using it (Rudinger et al., 2015; Peng and Roth, 2016).

For ease of explanation, we assume that a semantic sequence of FES representations is $[\text{FES}_1, \text{FES}_2, \text{FES}_3, \dots, \text{FES}_k]$, with FES_i being the i_{th} FES representation in the sequence. It assigns each token (i.e. FES representation) with three components: a target vector $v(\text{FES})$, a context vector $v'(\text{FES})$ and a bias $b(\text{FES})$. Thus, we model the conditional probability of a token FES_t given its context $c(\text{FES}_t)$:

$$p(\text{FES}_t | c(\text{FES}_t)) =$$
$$\frac{\exp(v(\text{FES}_t)^\intercal u(c(\text{FES}_t)) + b(\text{FES}_t))}{\sum_{\text{FES} \in \mathcal{V}} \exp(v(\text{FES})^\intercal u(c(\text{FES}_t)) + b(\text{FES}))}.$$

Here, $\mathcal{V}$ denotes the vocabulary (all possible FES representations) and we define

---

[2] Each dimension of the vector indicates an entity type (binary 0/1), and the vector contains exactly one element of 1.

[3] An alternative design choice is to concatenate the vector representations from different semantic aspects together, but we did not get better empirical results compared to our current design.

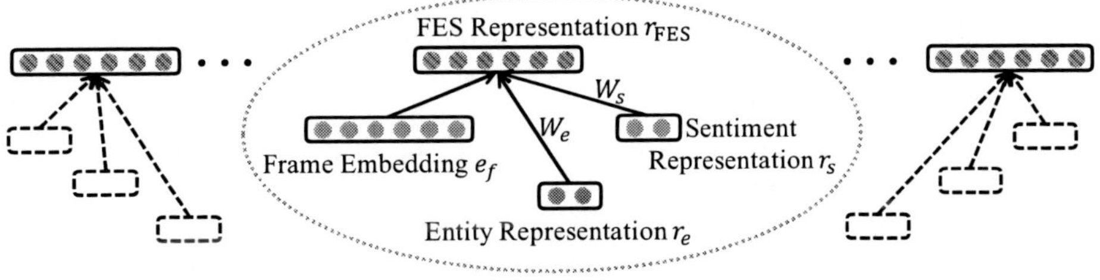

Figure 3: **An overview of the FES representation in a semantic sequence.** Semantic frames are represented by vector r_f. The entity representation r_e is the concatenation of r_{sub} and r_{obj}, both consist of two parts: an one-hot vector for entity type plus an additional dimension to indicate whether or not it is a *new entity*. The sentiment representation r_s is also one-hot.

$$u(c(\text{FES}_t)) = \sum_{c_i \in c(\text{FES}_t)} q_i \odot v'(c_i).$$

Note that $\odot$ represents element-wise multiplication and q_i is a vector that depends only on the position of an FES representation in context, which is also a model parameter. For language model training, we maximize the overall sequence probability $\prod_{t=1}^{k} p(\text{FES}_t | c(\text{FES}_t))$.

4 Building FES-LM

In this section, we explain how we build FES-LM from un-annotated plain text.

4.1 Dataset and Preprocessing

Dataset We first use the New York Times (NYT) Corpus[4] (from year 1987 to 2007) to train FES-LM. It contains over 1.8M documents in total. To fine tune the model on short stories, we re-train FES-LM on the ROCStories dataset (Mostafazadeh et al., 2017) with the model trained on NYT as initialization. We use the train set of ROCStories, which contains around 100K short stories (each consists of five sentences) [5].

Preprocessing We pre-process all documents with Semantic Role Labeling (SRL) (Punyakanok et al., 2004) and Part-of-Speech (POS) tagger (Roth and Zelenko, 1998). We also implement the explicit discourse connective identification module of a shallow discourse parser (Song et al., 2015). Additionally, we utilize within document entity co-reference (Peng et al., 2015a) to produce co-reference chains to get the *new entity*

information. To obtain all annotations, we employ the Illinois NLP tools[6].

4.2 FES Representation Generation

As shown in Sec. 3, each FES representation is built from basic semantic units: frame / entity / sentiment. We describe our implementation details on how we extract these units from text and how we further construct their vector representations respectively.

Frame Abstraction and Enrichment We directly derive semantic frames from semantic role labeling annotations. As the Illinois SRL package is built upon PropBank frames, we map them to FrameNet frames via VerbNet senses to achieve a higher level of abstraction. The mapping is deterministic and partial[7]. For unmapped PropBank frames, we retain their original PropBank forms. We then enrich the frames by augmenting them to verb phrases. We apply three heuristic rules: 1) if a preposition immediately follows a predicate, we append the preposition e.g. *"take over"*; 2) if we encounter the role label AM-PRD which indicates a secondary predicate, we append it to the main predicate e.g. *"be happy"*; 3) if we see the semantic role label AM-NEG which indicates negation, we append "not" e.g. *"not like"*. We further connect compound verbs together as they represent a unified semantic meaning. For this, we apply a rule that if the gap between two predicates is less than two tokens, we treat them as a unified semantic frame defined by the conjunction of the two (augmented) semantic frames, e.g. *"decide to*

---

[4]Available at https://catalog.ldc.upenn.edu/LDC2008T19

[5]Available at http://cs.rochester.edu/nlp/rocstories/

[6]Available at http://cogcomp.org/page/software/

[7]We use the mapping file http://verbs.colorado.edu/verb-index/fn/vn-fn.xml to do it. For example, "place" and "put" with the same VerbNet sense id "9.1-2" are both mapped to the FrameNet frame "Placing".

	Vocabulary Size				Sequence Size	
	FES	F	E	S	#seq	#token
NYT	4M	15K	100	7	1.2M	25.4M
ROCStories	200K	1K	98	7	100K	630K

Table 2: **Statistics on FES-LM vocabularies and sequences.** We compare FES-LM trained on NYT vs. ROCStories; "FES" stands for unique FES representations while "F" for frame embeddings, "E" for entity representations, and "S" for sentiment representations. "#seq" is the number of sequences, and "#token" is the total number of tokens (FES representations) used for training.

buy" being represented by "decide.01-buy.01".

To sum up, we employ the same techniques to deal with frames as discussed in Peng and Roth (2016), which allows us to model more fine-grained semantic frames. As an example of this processing step, *"He didn't want to give up."* is represented as "(not)want.01-give.01[up]". Each semantic frame (here, including discourse markers) is represented by a 200-dimensional vector e_f.

Entity Label Assignment For each entity (here we refer to subject and object of the predicate), we first extract its syntactic head using Collins' Head Rule. To assign entity types, we then check if the head is inside a named entity generated by NER. If so, we directly assign the NER label to this entity. Otherwise, we check if the entity is a pronoun that refers to a person i.e. *I, me, we, you, he, him, she, her, they, them*; in which case, we assign "PER" label to it. For all other cases, we simply assign "ARG" label to indicate the type is unknown.

In order to assign "new entity" labels, we check if the head is inside a mention identified by the co-reference system to start a new co-reference chain. If so, we assign 1; otherwise, we assign 0. On ROCStories dataset, we add an additional rule that all pronouns indicating a person will not be "new entities". This makes the co-reference decisions more robust on short stories.[8]

The entity representation r_e is eventually constructed as a one-hot vector for types of 5 dimensions and an additional dimension for "new entity" information. As we consider both subjects and objects of a frame, r_e is of 12 dimensions in total. If either one of the entities within a frame is missing from SRL annotations, we set its corresponding 6 dimensions as zeros.

Sentiment Representation Generation We first determine the polarity of a word by a look-up table from two pre-trained sentiment lexicons (Liu et al., 2005; Wilson et al., 2005). We then count the number of positive words versus negative words to decide the sentiment of a piece of text as detailed in Sec. 2. This process is done on text corresponding to each frame, i.e. a sentence or a clause. Since we have two different lexicons, we get two separate one-hot sentiment vectors, each with a dimension of 3. Thus, the sentiment representation is the concatenation of the two vectors, a total dimension of 6.

4.3 Neural Language Model Training

For the NYT corpus, we treat each document as a single semantic sequence while on ROCStories, we see each story as a semantic sequence. Additionally, we filter out rare frames which appear less than 20 times in the NYT corpus. Statistics on the eventual FES-LM vocabularies (unique FES representations) and semantic sequences in both datasets are shown in Table 2. Note that the number of unique FES representations reflects the richness of the semantic space that we model. On both datasets, it is about 200 times over what is modeled by only frame representations. At the same time, we do not incur burden on language model training. It is because we do not model unique FES representations directly, and instead we are still operating in the frame embedding space.[9]

We use the OxLM toolkit (Baltescu et al., 2014) with Noise-Constrastive Estimation (Gutmann and Hyvarinen, 2010) to implement the LBL model. We set the context window size to 5 and produce 200-dimension embeddings for FES representations. In addition to learning language model parameters, we also learn frame embeddings e_f along with parameters for W_e (12x200 matrix) and W_s (6x200 matrix).

5 Evaluation

We first show that our proposed FES-LM is of high quality in terms of language modeling ability. We then evaluate FES-LM for shallow discourse parsing on news data as well as application for story cloze test on short common sense stories. In all studies, we verify that each semantic aspect contributes to the joint model.

---

[8]The same rule is not applied on news, since pronouns indicating a person can start a co-reference chain in news.

[9]The FES representation space can be seen as entity and sentiment infused frame embedding space.

	CBOW	SG	LBL
Perplexity			
FES-LM	133.8	135.8	**126.0**
Narrative Cloze Test (Recall@30)			
FES-LM	38.9	37.3	**43.2**
FES-LM - Entity	35.3	33.1	38.4
FES-LM - Sentiment	34.9	32.8	36.3

Table 3: **Quality comparison of neural language models.** We report results for perplexity and narrative cloze test. Both evaluations are done on the gold PropBank data (annotated with gold frames). LBL outperforms CBOW and SG on both tests. We carry out ablation studies for narrative cloze test for FES-LM without entity and sentiment aspects respectively.

5.1 Quality of FES-LM

To evaluate the modeling ability of different neural language models, we train each variant of FES-LM on NYT corpus and report perplexity and narrative cloze test results. Here, we choose the Skip-Gram (SG) model (Mikolov et al., 2013b) and Continuous-Bag-of-Words (CBOW) model (Mikolov et al., 2013a) for comparison with the LBL model. We utilize the word2vec package to implement both SG and CBOW. We set the context window size to be 10 for SG and 5 for CBOW.

We employ the same experimental setting as detailed in Peng and Roth (2016). Results are shown in Table 3. They confirm that LBL model performs the best with the lowest perplexity and highest recall for narrative cloze test.[10] Note that the numbers reported are not directly comparable with those in literature (Rudinger et al., 2015; Peng and Roth, 2016), as we model much richer semantics even though the numbers seem inferior. We further carry out ablation studies for narrative cloze test for FES-LM without entity and sentiment aspects respectively[11]. The results show that sentiment contributes more than entity information.

5.2 Application on News

We choose shallow discourse parsing as the task to show FES-LM's applicability on news. In particular, we evaluate on identifying the correct sense of discourse connectives (both explicit and implicit

ones). We choose Song et al. (2015), which uses a supervised pipeline approach, as our base system. We follow the same experimental setting as described in Peng and Roth (2016), i.e. we add additional conditional probability features generated from FES-LM into the base system. We evaluate on CoNLL16 (Xue et al., 2016) test and blind sets, following the train and development split from the Shared Task, and report F1 using the official shared task scorer.

Table 4 shows the results for shallow discourse parsing with added FES-LM features. We get significant improvement over the base system(*) (based on McNemar's Test) and outperform SemLM, which only utilizes frame information in the semantic sequences. We also rival the top system (Mihaylov and Frank, 2016) in the CoNLL16 Shared Task (connective sense classification subtask). Note that the FES-LM used here is trained on NYT corpus. The ablation study shows that entity aspect contributes less than sentiment aspect in this application.

5.3 Application on Stories

For the story cloze test on the ROCStories dataset. We evaluate in an unsupervised setting, where we disregard the labeled development set and directly test on the test set[12]. We believe this is a better setting to reflect a system's ability to model semantic sequences compared to the supervised setting where we simply treat the task as a binary classification problem with a development set to tune.

We first generate a set of conditional probability features from FES-LM. For each story, we extract semantic aspect information as described in Sec. 2 and construct the joint FES representation according to the learned FES-LM. We then utilize the conditional probability of the fifth sentence s_5 given previous context sentences C as features. Suppose the semantic information in the fifth sentence can be represented by $r_{\text{FES\_k}}$, we can then define the features as $p(s_5|C) = p(r_{\text{FES\_k}}|r_{\text{FES\_(k-1)}}, r_{\text{FES\_(k-2)}}, \cdots, r_{\text{FES\_(k-t)}})$, $t = 1, 2, \cdots, k$. We get multiple features depending on how long we go back in the context in terms of FES representations. Note that one sentence can contain multiple FES representations depending on how many semantic frames it has. For simplicity, we assume a single FES representation $r_{\text{FES\_k}}$

---

[10]We also tried Neural-LSTM (Pichotta and Mooney, 2016a) and context2vec (Melamud et al., 2016) model, but we cannot get better results.

[11]The ablation study is not done for perplexity test because FES-LM with less semantic aspects yields smaller vocabulary, which naturally leads to lower perplexity.

[12]The test set contains $1,871$ four-sentences long stories with two fifth sentence options for each, of which only one is correct; and we report the accuracy.

	CoNLL16 Test			CoNLL16 Blind		
	Explicit	Implicit	Overall	Explicit	Implicit	Overall
Base (Song et al., 2015)*	89.8	35.6	60.4	75.8	31.9	52.3
SemLM (Peng and Roth, 2016)	**91.1**	36.3	61.4	77.3	33.2	53.8
Top (Mihaylov and Frank, 2016)	89.8	**39.2**	**63.3**	78.2	**34.5**	**54.6**
FES-LM (this work)	91.0	37.5	61.8	**78.3**	34.4	54.5
FES-LM - Entity	90.8	37.1	61.6	77.9	34.0	54.1
FES-LM - Sentiment	90.5	36.9	61.3	77.3	33.8	53.9

Table 4: **Shallow discourse parsing results.** With added FES-LM features, we get significant improvement (based on McNemar's Test) over the base system(*) and outperform SemLM, which only models frame information. We also rival the top system (Mihaylov and Frank, 2016) in the CoNLL16 Shared Task (connective sense classification subtask).

Baselines		
Seq2Seq		58.0%
DSSM (Mostafazadeh et al., 2016)		58.5%
Seq2Seq with attention		**59.1%**
Individual Aspect	S.	M.V.
F-LM	57.8%	56.3%
E-LM	52.1%	52.6%
S-LM	54.2%	54.9%
Joint Model	S.	M.V.
FES-LM (this work)	**62.3%**	61.6%
FES-LM - Entity	61.5%	61.7%
FES-LM - Sentiment	61.1%	60.9%

Table 5: **Accuracy results for story cloze text in the unsupervised setting.** "S." represents the inference method with the single most informative feature while "M.V." means majority voting. FES-LM outperforms the strongest baseline (Seq2Seq with attention) by 3 points. The difference is statistically significant based on McNemar's Test. Additional ablation studies show that each semantic aspect contributes to the joint model.

for s_5. In practice, we get at most 12 FES representations as context. We align the features by t, indicating how long we consider the story context. Thus, for each story, we generate at most 12 pairs of conditional probability features. Evey pair of such features can yield a decision on which ending is more probable. Here, we test two different inference methods: a single most informative feature (where we go with the decision made by the pair of features which have the highest ratio) or majority voting based on all feature pairs. Note that we need to re-train FES-LM on the stories (train set of ROCStories, 5-sentence stories, no negative examples provided)[13].

We compare FES-LM with Seq2Seq baselines (Sutskever et al., 2014). We also train the Seq2Seq model on the train set of ROCStories, where we set input as the 4-sentence context and the output as the 5th ending sentence for each story. At test time, we get probability of each option ending from the soft-max layer and choose the higher one as the answer. We use an LSTM encoder (300 hidden units) and decode with an LSTM of the same size. Since it is operated on the word level, we use pre-trained 300-dimensional GloVe embeddings (Pennington et al., 2014) and keep them fixed during training. In addition, we add an attention mechanism (Bahdanau et al., 2014) to make the Seq2Seq baseline stronger. We also report DSSM from Mostafazadeh et al. (2016) as the previously best reported result[14]. To study how each individual aspect affects the performance, we develop neural language models on frames (F-LM), entities (E-LM) and sentiments (S-LM) as additional baseline models separately. We use the same language model training and feature generation techniques as FES-LM. Particularly, for F-LM, it is the same model as FC-SemLM defined in Peng and Roth (2016). Note that individual aspects cannot capture the semantic difference between two given options for all instances. For those instances that the baseline model fails to handle, we set the accuracy as 50% (expectation of random guesses).

The accuracy results are shown in Table 5. The best result we achieve (62.3%) outperforms the strongest baseline (Seq2Seq with attention, 59.1%). It is statistically significant based on McNemar's Test ($\alpha = 0.01$), illustrating the superior

---

[13]It is because of domain difference, e.g. average length of semantic sequence is different (stories are shorter while news are longer, see in Table 2).

[14]DSSM's model parameters are trained on the ROCStories corpus while hyper parameters are determined on the development set.

semantic modeling ability of FES-LM. Results are mixed comparing the two inference methods. The ablation study further confirms that each semantic aspect has its worth in the joint model.

6 Related Work

Our work is built upon the previous work (Peng and Roth, 2016). It generated a probabilistic model on semantic frames while taking into account discourse information, and showed applications to both co-reference resolution and shallow discourse parsing. This line of work is in general inspired by script learning. Early works (Schank and Abelson, 1977; Mooney and DeJong, 1985) tried to learn scripts via construction of knowledge bases from text. More recently, researchers focused on utilizing statistical models to extract high-quality scripts from large amounts of data (Chambers and Jurafsky, 2008a; Bejan, 2008; Jans et al., 2012; Pichotta and Mooney, 2014; Granroth-Wilding et al., 2015; Rudinger et al., 2015; Pichotta and Mooney, 2016b,a). Other works aimed at learning a collection of structured events (Chambers, 2013; Cheung et al., 2013; Balasubramanian et al., 2013; Bamman and Smith, 2014; Nguyen et al., 2015; Inoue et al., 2016). In particular, Ferraro and Van Durme (2016) presented a unified probabilistic model of syntactic and semantic frames while also demonstrating improved coherence. Several works have employed neural embeddings (Modi and Titov, 2014b,a; Frermann et al., 2014; Titov and Khoddam, 2015). Some prior works have used scripts-related ideas to help improve NLP tasks (Irwin et al., 2011; Rahman and Ng, 2011; Peng et al., 2015b). Most recently, Mostafazadeh et al. (2016, 2017) proposed story cloze test as a standard way to test a system's ability to model semantics. They released ROCStories dataset, and organized a shared task for LSDSem'17.

7 Conclusion

This paper proposes FES-LM, a joint neural language model for semantic sequences built upon frames, entities and sentiments. Abstractions on these semantic aspects enable FES-LM to generate better semantic sequences than models working on the word level. Evaluations show that the joint model helps to improve shallow discourse parsing and achieves the best result for story cloze test in the unsupervised setting. In future work, we plan to extend FES-LM to capture more semantic aspects and work towards building a general semantic language model.

Acknowledgments

This work is supported by the US Defense Advanced Research Projects Agency (DARPA) under contract HR0011-15-2-0025, and by the Army Research Laboratory (ARL) under agreement W911NF-09-2-0053, and also by IBM-ILLINOIS Center for Cognitive Computing Systems Research (C3SR) - a research collaboration as part of the IBM Cognitive Horizon Network. The views expressed are those of the authors and do not reflect the official policy or position of the Department of Defense or the U.S. Government.

References

D. Bahdanau, K. Cho, and Y. Bengio. 2014. Neural machine translation by jointly learning to align and translate. *arXiv preprint arXiv:1409.0473* .

C. F. Baker, C. J. Fillmore, and J. B. Lowe. 1998. The berkeley framenet project. In *COLING/ACL*.

N. Balasubramanian, S. Soderland, O. E. Mausam, and O. Etzioni. 2013. Generating coherent event schemas at scale. In *EMNLP*.

P. Baltescu, P. Blunsom, and H. Hoang. 2014. Oxlm: A neural language modelling framework for machine translation. *The Prague Bulletin of Mathematical Linguistics* .

D. Bamman and N. A. Smith. 2014. Unsupervised discovery of biographical structure from text. *TACL* .

C. A. Bejan. 2008. Unsupervised discovery of event scenarios from texts. In *FLAIRS Conference*.

N. Chambers. 2013. Event schema induction with a probabilistic entity-driven model. In *EMNLP*.

N. Chambers and D. Jurafsky. 2008a. Jointly combining implicit constraints improves temporal ordering. In *EMNLP*.

N. Chambers and D. Jurafsky. 2008b. Unsupervised learning of narrative event chains. In *ACL*.

S. B. Chatman. 1980. *Story and discourse: Narrative structure in fiction and film.* Cornell University Press.

J. C. K. Cheung, H. Poon, and L. Vanderwende. 2013. Probabilistic frame induction. *arXiv:1302.4813* .

F. Ferraro and B. Van Durme. 2016. A unified bayesian model of scripts, frames and language. In *AAAI*.

C. J. Fillmore. 1976. Frame semantics and the nature of language. *Annals of the New York Academy of Sciences* .

L. Frermann, I. Titov, and Pinkal. M. 2014. A hierarchical bayesian model for unsupervised induction of script knowledge. In *EACL*.

M. Granroth-Wilding, S. Clark, M. T. Llano, R. Hepworth, S. Colton, J. Gow, J. Charnley, N. Lavrač, M. Žnidaršič, and M. Perovšek. 2015. What happens next? event prediction using a compositional neural network model. In *AAAI*.

M. Gutmann and A. Hyvarinen. 2010. Noise-contrastive estimation: A new estimation principle for unnormalized statistical models. In *AISTATS*.

N. Inoue, Y. Matsubayashi, M. Ono, N. Okazaki, and K. Inui. 2016. Modeling context-sensitive selectional preference with distributed representations. In *COLING*.

J. Irwin, M. Komachi, and Y. Matsumoto. 2011. Narrative schema as world knowledge for coreference resolution. In *CoNLL Shared Task*.

B. Jans, S. Bethard, I. Vulić, and M. F. Moens. 2012. Skip n-grams and ranking functions for predicting script events. In *EACL*.

P. Kingsbury and M. Palmer. 2002. From Treebank to PropBank. In *Proceedings of LREC-2002*.

B. Liu, M. Hu, and J. Cheng. 2005. Opinion observer: Analyzing and comparing opinions on the web. In *WWW*.

O. Melamud, J. Goldberger, and I. Dagan. 2016. context2vec: Learning generic context embedding with bidirectional lstm. In *CoNLL*.

T. Mihaylov and A. Frank. 2016. Discourse relation sense classification using cross-argument semantic similarity based on word embeddings. In *CoNLL Shared Task*.

Tomas Mikolov, Kai Chen, Greg Corrado, and Jeffrey Dean. 2013a. Efficient estimation of word representations in vector space. *arXiv preprint arXiv:1301.3781* .

Tomas Mikolov, Wen-tau Yih, and Geoffrey Zweig. 2013b. Linguistic regularities in continuous space word representations. In *NAACL*.

A. Mnih and G. Hinton. 2007. Three new graphical models for statistical language modelling. In *ICML*.

A. Modi and I. Titov. 2014a. Inducing neural models of script knowledge. In *CoNLL*.

A. Modi and I. Titov. 2014b. Learning semantic script knowledge with event embeddings. In *ICLR Workshop*.

R. Mooney and G. DeJong. 1985. Learning schemata for natural language processing. In *IJCAI*.

N. Mostafazadeh, N. Chambers, X. He, D. Parikh, D. Batra, L. Vanderwende, P. Kohli, and J. Allen. 2016. A corpus and cloze evaluation for deeper understanding of commonsense stories. In *NAACL*.

N. Mostafazadeh, M. Roth, A. Louis, N. Chambers, and J. F. Allen. 2017. Lsdsem 2017 shared task: The story cloze test. In *LSDSEM workshop at EACL*.

K.-H. Nguyen, X. Tannier, O. Ferret, and R. Besançon. 2015. Generative event schema induction with entity disambiguation. In *ACL*.

H. Peng, K. Chang, and D. Roth. 2015a. A joint framework for coreference resolution and mention head detection. In *CoNLL*.

H. Peng, D. Khashabi, and D. Roth. 2015b. Solving hard coreference problems. In *NAACL*.

H. Peng and D. Roth. 2016. Two discourse driven language models for semantics. In *ACL*.

J. Pennington, R. Socher, and C. D. Manning. 2014. Glove: Global vectors for word representation. In *EMNLP*.

K. Pichotta and R. J. Mooney. 2014. Statistical script learning with multi-argument events. In *EACL*.

K. Pichotta and R. J. Mooney. 2016a. Learning statistical scripts with lstm recurrent neural networks. In *AAAI*.

K. Pichotta and R. J. Mooney. 2016b. Using sentence-level lstm language models for script inference. In *ACL*.

V. Punyakanok, D. Roth, W. Yih, and D. Zimak. 2004. Semantic role labeling via integer linear programming inference. In *COLING*.

A. Rahman and V. Ng. 2011. Coreference resolution with world knowledge. In *ACL*.

X. Ren, W. He, M. Qu, L. Huang, H. Ji, and J. Han. 2016. Afet: Automatic fine-grained entity typing by hierarchical partial-label embedding. In *EMNLP*.

D. Roth and D. Zelenko. 1998. Part of speech tagging using a network of linear separators. In *ACL-COLING*.

R. Rudinger, P. Rastogi, F. Ferraro, and B. Van Durme. 2015. Script induction as language modeling. In *EMNLP*.

R. C. Schank and R. P. Abelson. 1977. Scripts, plans, goals, and understanding: An inquiry into human knowledge structures. In *JMZ*.

Y. Song, H. Peng, P. Kordjamshidi, M. Sammons, and D. Roth. 2015. Improving a pipeline architecture for shallow discourse parsing. In *CoNLL Shared Task*.

I. Sutskever, O. Vinyals, and Q. V. Le. 2014. Sequence to sequence learning with neural networks. In *NIPS*.

I. Titov and E. Khoddam. 2015. Unsupervised induction of semantic roles within a reconstruction-error minimization framework. In *NAACL*.

Theresa Wilson, Janyce Wiebe, and Paul Hoffmann. 2005. Recognizing contextual polarity in phrase-level sentiment analysis. In *EMNLP*.

N. Xue, H. T. Ng, A. Rutherford, B. Webber, C. Wang, and H. Wang. 2016. Conll 2016 shared task on multilingual shallow discourse parsing. *CoNLL* .

Dani Yogatama, Daniel Gillick, and Nevena Lazic. 2015. Embedding methods for fine grained entity type classification. In *ACL*.

Neural Sequence-to-sequence Learning of Internal Word Structure

Tatyana Ruzsics   **Tanja Samardžić**
CorpusLab, URPP Language and Space,
University of Zurich, Switzerland
{tatiana.ruzsics, tanja.samardzic}@uzh.ch

Abstract

Learning internal word structure has recently been recognized as an important step in various multilingual processing tasks and in theoretical language comparison. In this paper, we present a neural encoder-decoder model for learning canonical morphological segmentation. Our model combines character-level sequence-to-sequence transformation with a language model over canonical segments. We obtain up to 4% improvement over a strong character-level encoder-decoder baseline for three languages. Our model outperforms the previous state-of-the-art for two languages, while eliminating the need for external resources such as large dictionaries. Finally, by comparing the performance of encoder-decoder and classical statistical machine translation systems trained with and without corpus counts, we show that including corpus counts is beneficial to both approaches.

1 Introduction

One of the most obvious structural differences between languages is the variation in the complexity of internal word structure. In some languages, such as English, words are relatively short and morphologically less complex. In other languages, such as Chintang in Example 1[1], words tend to be long and encapsulate rather rich structure. The Chintang verb *thaptakha* in Example 1 consists of a number of morphemes expressing the imperative mode, aspect and deixis. The information expressed by a single Chintang verb requires several

words in English, as it can be seen in the glosses.[2] and in the translation.

Example 1

a.		cuwa thaptakha			
b.	cuwa	thapt	-a	-khag	-a
c.	water	move	-IMP	-see	-IMP
		across			[2sS]
d.		Bring some water over here!			

The variation in word structure is observed even in common categories such as plural, which is typically part of a word, but expressed using different structures. The items in Example 2[3] show three different structural types associated with expressing plural across languages.

Example 2

Type		Sg.	Pl.
Suffix	Turkish	*ev*	*ev-ler*
		'house'	'houses'
Prefix	Swahili	*m-toto*	*wa-toto*
		'child'	'children'
Redupli-cation	Malay	*anak*	*anak-anak*
		'child'	'children'

With the spread of natural language processing to a wider range of languages, learning internal word structure becomes increasingly important for developing practical applications. Analysis of internal word structure, usually termed morphological segmentation, has been shown helpful in tasks such as machine translation (Dyer et al., 2008; Narasimhan et al., 2014), speech processing (Creutz et al., 2007) and parsing (Seeker and Çetinoglu, 2015). Additionally, there is a growing interest in automatic learning of morphological segmentation for the purpose of theoretical lan-

---

[1]The example is adapted from (Stoll et al., In press)

[2]Cf. Leipzig Glossing Rules at `https://www.eva.mpg.de/lingua/resources/glossing-rules.php`

[3]The examples are adapted from (Eifring and Theil, 2005)

Proceedings of the 21st Conference on Computational Natural Language Learning (CoNLL 2017), pages 184–194,
Vancouver, Canada, August 3 - August 4, 2017. ©2017 Association for Computational Linguistics

guage comparison (Bentz et al., 2017). In this context, it becomes particularly important to be able to process a wide variety of languages, for which the available data sets consist of small, annotated corpora.

In the present work, we cast the task of morphological segmentation as supervised neural sequence-to-sequence learning over characters. Our goal is to define a method for automatic segmentation that can be easily ported across languages, taking advantage of the relatively small, manually analyzed corpora increasingly available in the linguistic community. Our approach therefore needs to rely only on the data available in an annotated corpus.

We follow the line of research based on the soft-attention encoder-decoder paradigm (Bahdanau et al., 2014). This paradigm was recently applied to the task of canonical segmentation by Kann et al. (2016). It was shown to achieve the state-of-the-art performance when combined with a neural re-ranker method that employs additional external dictionary information (Kann et al., 2016). Our approach improves the results achieved by Kann et al. (2016) in case of Indonesian and German languages eliminating at the same time the need for resources outside of annotated corpora.

2 Related Work

The task of the morphological segmentation can be defined in two ways, illustrated with the Chintang verb from Example 1:

  a. Surface segmentation:
     thaptakha → thapt-a-**kh**-a

  b. Canonical segmentation:
     thaptakha → thapt-a-**khag**-a

The term *surface* or *allomorph* segmentation is used by Creutz and Linden (2004) to refer to the analysis where the input word is segmented into substrings without any further string transformation. This definition is most widely applied in computational processing; it is, however, too simplistic for the majority of languages. It does not allow, for instance, to identify *-es* in *bus-es* and *-s* in *car-s* as two variants of the same English plural marker.

More recently, the term *canonical segmentation* was used by Cotterell et al. (2016) to refer to the same definition that was termed *morpheme* segmentation by Creutz and Linden (2004). In this

case, a more abstract internal word structure is learned by transforming the resulting substrings into their canonical forms.

While a great variety of methods has been proposed for surface segmentation, canonical segmentation, which is address in our work, has started being addressed only recently.

The task of surface morphological segmentation is traditionally approached using finite-state technology, such as OpenFst library (Allauzen and Riley, 2012) and OpenGrm Thrax Grammar Compiler library (Roark et al., 2012), with sequence modeling used to disambiguate the finite-state output (Heintz, 2008).

Another line of research has addressed surface segmentation with unsupervised algorithms (MORFESSOR (Creutz and Lagus, 2002), MORFESSOR CAT-MAP (Creutz and Lagus, 2005)), and, more recently, with semi-supervised approaches (Poon et al., 2009; Kohonen et al., 2010)). Narasimhan et al. (2015) include semantic information in the unsupervised learning, staying at the level of surface segmentation. Their approach is extended by Bergmanis and Goldwater (2017), who make a step towards canonical segmentation, proposing a method to generalize over spelling variants of functionally similar morphemes.

Supervised approaches to learning morphological structure are rather rare. Ruokolainen et al. (2013) apply conditional random fields algorithm, used for different sequence classification tasks, to the task of surface segmentation. Their CRF-MORPH system tags each character of a morphologically complex word with one of the tags 'B' for the beginning, 'M' middle, and 'E' end of a segment, and 'S' for a single character segment. The CHIPMUNK model of Cotterell et al. (2015) based on a semi-Markov model extends the CRF-MORPH approach by adding features from stand-alone dictionaries and affix lists.

Canonical segmentation is tackled by Cotterell et al. (2016), who develop a log-linear model on conjunction of a finite-state transduction model for modeling orthographic changes and a semi-Markov segmentation model.

Recently, neural network models achieved state-of-the-art results for both types of segmentation tasks. Wang et al. (2016) applied window LSTM model for surface segmentation. Kann et al. (2016) improved the results by Cotterell et al. (2016) on canonical segmentation by applying the encoder-decoder RNN framework. Kann et al. (2016) achieve the current state-of-the-art for canonical segmentation by re-ranking the output of the encoder-decoder system. The re-ranking component is a multilayer perception run on the morphemes embeddings (Kann et al., 2016). The morphemes embedding used for this re-ranking model are calculated using additional information from the Aspell dictionaries. We follow Kann et al. (2016) in using the encoder-decoder RNN framework, but we do not use any external resources. Instead of that, we extract and exploit more information from the training corpus.

Our approach is in the spirit of the "shallow fusion" approach to machine translation of Gulcehre et al. (2017). Like Gulcehre et al. (2017), we integrate a language model into an encoder-decoder framework. There are, however, several important differences.

First of all, the role of the language model is different. Integrating a language model allows Gulcehre et al. (2017) to augment the parallel training data with additional monolingual corpora on the target side. In this way, they add new information about sequencing, not captured in training on parallel data alone. Both components of their system are trained on the same kind of units — characters. As opposed to this, we use a language model to extract more information from the parallel data. We add new information by training the system at two levels: the basic encoder-decoder component is trained on character sequences and the language model component is trained on the sequences of morphemes. In the case of Gulcehre et al. (2017), the use of a language model is motivated by the fact that external monolingual target-side data is almost always universally available. The situation is reversed for the task of morphological segmentation: morphologically segmented corpora are produced manually by experts in the process of linguistic analysis and they tend to be small and expensive. Our approach is motivated by the need to extract as much information as possible from relatively small target-side data sets.

Second, we add a third component to our model which controls for the difference in characters length between the input word string and the output segmentation string. This helps overcome language model preference for a short output.

Last, while Gulcehre et al. (2017) use a language model implemented with recurrent neural networks, we employ a statistical language model, which is better adapted to our settings with small data sets.

Finally, we note that corpus frequencies are not used in previous supervised approaches, but that systems are trained on word types (training data consist of a list of word types and a segmentation for each type). In the present work, we study token versus types training set up and how this difference affects the performance of statistical models.

3 Model Description

Given an input sequence, such as the Chintang sentence in Example 1 (line a.), we produce a canonical segmentation (line b.), where we recognize that the sequence *kh* in the surface form is an instance of the light verb *khag*.

We follow the notations of Kann et al. (2016) in the formalization of the task of canonical segmentation. First, we define two discrete alphabets, Σ of the surface symbols and Σ_{can} of the canonical symbols. For many languages these two alphabets coincide, for example in the case of English they consist of 26 letters of the Latin alphabet. In the case of Chintang, these alphabets are different: the surface symbols express more specific pronunciation features. Our task is to learn a mapping from a surface word form $w \in \Sigma^*$ (e.g., w='thaptakha'), to its canonical segmentation $c \in \Omega^*$ (e.g., c=thapt|-a|-khag|-a). We define $\Omega = \Sigma_{can} \cup \{|\}$, where the symbol '|' marks segmentation boundaries.[4]

To learn the mappings, we combine the general sequence transformation framework — known as the encoder-decoder RNN — trained on a character level with a language model trained on morphemes. Note that a kind of a language model over characters is implicitly included as a part of the decoder in the character-based encoder-decoder RNN. The language model in our approach is trained over higher level units, providing additional information about the sequences. This, however, poses a challenge for its integration in the general framework. We tackle this problem with our "synchronization" method applied at the decoding stage: the segmentation hypotheses

---

[4]Furthermore, specifically to the Chintang corpus, the canonical symbols additionally use a dash element '-' to distinguish between suffixes, prefixes and roots. We do not exclude this symbol in our experiments.

are expanded and scored using a log-linear combination of (a) scores from a lower-level encoder-decoder model and (b) higher-level scores of the language model. The fusion of the scores is triggered only at the segmentation boundaries.

In this section, we first review the encoder-decoder RNN framework. Then, we present our fusion approach for integrating a language model into the encoder-decoder system.

3.1 Background: Standard Encoder-Decoder Set-up (cED)

The canonical segmentation problem fits the general sequence-to-sequence framework, that is mapping a variable-length sequence to another variable-length sequence. In machine translation, a relatively standard way to perform this task is using encoder-decoder RNN (Cho et al., 2014; Sutskever et al., 2014), extended with a bidirectional encoder and attention mechanism of Bahdanau et al. (2014). For the task of canonical segmentation, the input and the output to the encoder-decoder model is represented as a sequence of characters separated by spaces. Formally, we use the following set up.

The encoder RNN processes the input sequence of vectors, $X = (x^1, \ldots, x^{n_x})$, into a sequence of vectors representing hidden states:

$$h_t = f(h_{t-1}, x_t), \quad t = 1, \ldots, n_x \qquad (1)$$

where f stands for gated recurrent units (Cho et al., 2014). The decoder RNN is conditioned on the information produced by the encoder to generate the output sequence $Y = (y^1, \ldots, y^{n_y})$. Specifically, the decoder RNN models a conditional probability at each step as a function of previous output, current decoder hidden state and current context vector:

$$p(y_t|y_1, \ldots, y_{t-1}, X) = g(y_{t-1}, s_t, c_t), \qquad (2)$$

$$s_t = f(s_{t-1}, y_{t-1}, c_t), \quad t = 1, \ldots, n_y \qquad (3)$$

The context vector c_t is computed at each step as a weighted sum of the hidden states:

$$c_t = \sum_{k=1}^{n_x} \alpha_{tk} h_k, \qquad (4)$$

where the weights are calculated by an alignment model which scores how well the inputs around the position k and the output at the position t match. Intuitively, the decoder produces an output element one at a time, each time focusing (putting attention) on a different part of the input sequence in order to gather the details that are required to produce the next output element.

We use the bidirectional setting of the encoder model (Bahdanau et al., 2014): the hidden state h_t for each time step is obtained by concatenating a forward and backward state $h_t = [\overrightarrow{h_t}; \overleftarrow{h_t}]$. This means that the hidden state contains the summaries of both the preceding elements and the following elements. We refer to this standard framework as cED.

3.2 Integrating a Morpheme Language Model (LM) into cED

Before the integration, we assume that cED system and language model LM have been trained separately. The cED system is trained on character sequences in a parallel corpus where the source side consists of unsegmented words and the target side consist of the aligned canonically segmented words. During the training the cED model learns conditional probability distribution over the character sequences (2). The LM is trained over morpheme sequences on the target side of the corpus and scores how likely a given sequence is in a given language.

We can find the most probable segmentation using a beam search algorithm guided by "synchronized" character-level cED and morpheme-level LM scores. At each time step t, the cED system computes a score for each possible next character y_t in the vocabulary Ω as a continuation of the segmentation hypothesis from the previous step $\{(y_1 y_2 \ldots y_{t-1})^i\}$, $i = 1, \ldots, K$ where K is the beam size (how many best scored segmentation hypothesis we keep from each step). This score is a logarithm of the probability (2). Then, each possible continuation $\{(y_1 y_2 \ldots y_{t-1})^i y_t\}$, $y_t \in \Omega$, $i = 1, \ldots, K$ gets a score which is a sum of cED scores for each character, that is, a sum of the scores for a hypothesis from a previous time step $(y_1 y_2 \ldots y_{t-1})^i$ and a score for the next character y_t. Thus we get a set of $|\Omega| \times K$ new hypothesis of length $|t|$ together with their respective scores. All these new hypotheses at the step t are then sorted according to their respective scores, and the top K ones are selected as candidates for the expansion at the next time step.

In order to guide the described beam decoding with the LM scores we perform a "synchronization". Specifically, we continue the beam search based on the character cED scores till the step $s1$ where all the segmentation hypothesis $\{(y_1 y_2 \ldots y_{s1})^i\}$ $i = 1, \ldots, K$ end with a boundary symbol. The boundary symbol can be either end of word symbol '$< /w >$' or a segmentation boundary symbol '|'. At this step, we re-score the segmentation hypotheses with a weighted sum of the cED score and the LM score:

$$\log p(y_{s1}|y_1, \ldots, y_{s1-1}, X)$$
$$= \log p_{cED}(y_{s1}|y_1, \ldots, y_{s1-1}, X)$$
$$+ \alpha_{LM} \log p_{LM}(y_1, \ldots, y_{s1-1}) \quad (5)$$

At this step, $y_1, \ldots, y_{s1}$ is considered a sequence of $s1$ characters by the cED system and $y_1, \ldots, y_{s1-1}$ (without the last boundary symbol) is considered one morpheme by the LM.

From this synchronization point $s1$ we continue to expand the re-scored hypothesis $\{(y_1 y_2 \ldots y_{s1})^i\}$ $i = 1, \ldots, K$ at the next time step using again only cED scores. We continue this process until we get to the next synchronization point $s2$ where all the hypothesis $\{(y_1 y_2 \ldots y_{s2})^i\}$ $i = 1, \ldots, K$ end with a boundary symbol. After rescoring them with a weighted sum of cED and LM we continue this process again till the next synchronization point. The decoding process ends at a synchronization point where the last symbol of the best scored hypothesis (using the combined cED and LM score) is an end-of-word symbol.

The described decoding process therefore scores the segmentation hypotheses at two levels: normally working at the character level with cED scores and adding the LM scores only when it hits a boundary symbol. In this way, the LM score helps to evaluate how probable the last generated morpheme is based on the morpheme history, that is the sequence of morphemes generated at the previous synchronization time steps.

3.3 The Length Constraint

It is well known that language models give higher preference to shorter sequences. This becomes an issue in the proposed fused model described above: at the synchronization points high LM scores tend to stop further hypothesis expansion. For example, only the first segment can be generated as a model output if it happens to be a fre-quent standalone word. This leads to favoring segmentation predictions where the output is shorter than the input, which is rarely plausible in segmentation. Our early experiments confirmed this intuition, therefore we consider the length constraint component to be an integral part of the language model inclusion and we do not report experiments without this component.

To deal with the length issue, we add a "length constraint" component LC. The LC score is based on the difference in character length between the input word and its segmentation hypothesis. To synchronize the LC score with LM scoring process described before we assign it only at the synchronization time steps and attach it to the boundary symbol. Therefore, the LC score, combined with the LM score, helps to evaluate how probable is the last generated morpheme given the sequence of morphemes generated at the previous steps.

Assume that the input word is $X = x_1 \ldots x_n$ and the produced segmentation hypothesis at the first synchronization step $s1$ is $y_1 \ldots y_{s1}$ where y_{s1} is a boundary symbol. Then the LC score assigned to the morpheme $y_1 \ldots y_{s1-1}$ and attached to the boundary symbol y_{s1} is calculated as the negative value of the absolute difference between the morpheme length and input word length divided by the the input length: $LC(y_1 \ldots y_{s1-1}) = -(|y_1 \ldots y_{s1-1}| - |X|)/|X| = -|s1 - 1 - n|/n$. At the next synchronization point $s2$ the LC score is calculated using the length of the next produced segment: $LC(y_{s1+1} \ldots y_{s2-1}) = -(|y_{s1+1} \ldots y_{s2-1}| - |X|)/|X|$. In a general case, the LC score for the last generated segment σ_i can be expressed as

$$LC(\sigma_i) = -(|\sigma_i| - |X|)/|X| \quad (6)$$

Note that boundary symbols are excluded for the segments length calculation.

The intuition behind the LC score is that it gives a contribution to the total score of a segmentation hypothesis showing how different the length of the so far produced hypothesis is compared to the length of the input word. The characters in the canonical segments tend to be either inserted or deleted compared to their surface form equivalents, therefore we measure LC score using an absolute difference in the length. The higher the absolute value of the difference between the input and the hypothesis, the higher the penalty.

With the inclusion of the LC score for the length

control the total score of our fusion model becomes:

$$\log p(y_{s1}|y_1, \ldots, y_{s1-1}, X)$$
$$= \log p_{cED}(y_{s1}|y_1, \ldots, y_{s1-1}, X)$$
$$+ \alpha_{LM} \log p_{LM}(y_1, \ldots, y_{s1-1})$$
$$+ \alpha_{LC} LC(y_1, \ldots, y_{s1-1}) \quad (7)$$

where the weights α_{LM} and α_{LC} are optimized on a development set.

4 Data and Experiments

In this section, we first give a description of the corpora that we employ for the experiments. Then, we discuss the experimental setup for our model. Finally, we discuss the different configurations of the corpus we employ to explore encoder-decoder model behavior with and without corpus frequencies.

4.1 Corpora

We run our experiments on the datasets for English, German and Indonesian released by Cotterell et al. (2016).[5] The corpus for each language is constructed based on the 10,000 forms selected at random from a uniform distribution over types. This data is further used to sample 5 splits into 8000 training forms, 1000 development forms and 1000 test forms. Following Cotterell et al. (2016) and Kann et al. (2016), we report the results on each of the 5 splits for all three languages.

In addition to these sets, we use a manually segmented and glossed corpus of Chintang (Bickel et al., 2004-2015), a language that features a high degree of synthesis and free prefix ordering (Bickel et al., 2007). The total corpus size of 955,025 word tokens makes the Chintang corpus an exceptional resource for the task of morphological segmentation. As discussed in Section 2, the target segmented data is not easily available and corpora of this size are not likely to be developed for many langauges. We are interested in experimenting with a realistic setup, therefore we use around 150,000 tokens out of the total corpus size. This set is divided into the training set (around 100,000 word tokens) and development and test set (around 25,000 word tokens each).

The data set taken from Cotterell et al. (2016) allows us a comparison of our system with the previous state-of-the-art. The Chintang set allows us to run the segmentation models in different training regimes, with and without corpus frequencies, and therefore to assess the influence of the corpus counts on the performance.

4.2 Tools

We combine the three different components, cED, LM and LC, into a single fused model using the SGNMT (syntactically guided neural machine translation) framework of Stahlberg et al. (2016).[6] This framework provides an elegant solution to decomposing an encoder-decoder system into three components: training, decoding and scoring.

The training module implements the encoder-decoder model with attention mechanism using the Blocks framework built on top of Theano.[7]. We employ this implementation for the cED model.

The scoring component of SGNMT consists of predictor modules, which define scores over the target vocabulary given the current internal predictor state, the history, the source sentence, and external side information. Predictors can be combined with other predictors to form complex decoding tasks. In the case of our model, we use three predictors: cED, LM and LC.

The decoding component is represented by the decoder modules which are search strategies that traverse the space spanned by the predictors. We use a beam search module.

We train the language model LM over morpheme sequences using SRILM toolkit.[8]. The model is trained on the target side of the parallel corpus, i.e. the canonical segmentations.

The weights of the predictors are optimized using MERT (Och, 2003). This is a standard optimization routine in statistical machine translation which searches for the weights of the model components by directly maximizing the performance of the system on a development set. We use the Z-MERT tool[9] in our implementation. The code is available on our GitHub account.[10]

---

[5]ryancotterell.github.io/
canonical-segmentation

[6]http://ucam-smt.github.io/sgnmt
[7]https://github.com/mila-udem/blocks
[8]http://www.speech.sri.com/projects/
srilm/
[9]http://www.cs.jhu.edu/~ozaidan/zmert/
[10]https://github.com/tatyana-ruzsics/
uzh-corpuslab-morphological-segmentation

4.3 Experimental Setup

Baseline and comparison As a baseline, we use the basic component of our model (cED), an ensemble of 5 character-level attention encoder-decoder models with the hyperparameters described below.

We also compare the encoder-decoder model to the character-level statistical machine translation (cSMT). This approach is a natural choice in machine translation with small training sets, but no results have been reported so far for the task of canonical segmentation. We used the Moses toolkit with the following settings: distortion is disallowed and build-in MERT optimization is used to optimize the translation model and language model.

As a reference, we compare our results to the state-of-the-art neural re-ranker model of Kann et al. (2016) Note, however, that the results cannot be directly compared since Kann et al. (2016) use extra training material in the form of external dictionaries.

Evaluation Since our method is intended to be used for processing corpora, the evaluation is performed at the level of word tokens using accuracy of the full segmentation. In addition, we evaluate the performance on subsets of test words. Besides the seen words, we distinguish between two kinds of test words that are not seen in the training corpus: a) new combinations of morphemes already seen during training and b) words that contain unseen morphemes.

Hyperparameters The bidirectional encoder consists of a forward and a backward recurrent RNN each having 100 hidden units. The decoder also has 100 hidden units. The dimensionality of the character embedding is 300. We use a minibatch stochastic gradient descent (SGD) algorithm together with Adadelta to train each model. Each update direction is computed using a minibatch of 20 training examples. At decoding, we use a beam search with a beam size of 12 to find the segmentation that approximately maximizes the conditional probability. All the described hyperparameters are the same as in the work of Kann et al. (2016).

Initialization of all weights (encoder, decoder, embeddings) to the identity matrix and the biases to zero (Le et al., 2015) results in a very fast convergence rate compared to other initializations. We train a single model for 20 epochs with an early stopping based on the development set performance. We also shuffle the training data between the epochs.

Finally, we use an ensemble of five encoder-decoder models with different random initializations. We shuffle the training data for each of the model using different seed value. The ensemble model is based on a combined score from all 5 models and is used to guide the decoding process.

Following earlier experiments, we use morpheme 3-gram language model and apply Kneser-Ney smoothing.

As the objective for the MERT weight optimization we use accuracy on the development set.

Tokens vs Types The Chintang corpus allows us to assess the influence of the corpus counts on the performance of the models used for canonical segmentation. In these experiments, we run only the two baseline models, cSMT and cED (without our language model component), in order to evaluate directly the relevance of such corpus signal to these two training paradigms.[11]

We run each model, cSMT and cED, in two regimes. In the first, type regime, we train the models using a parallel corpus which consists of word types, i.e. unique pairs of surface form and its canonical segmentation. The size of such type corpus is around 21,000 word forms. In the second regime, we train the models using a parallel corpus where each pair of surface form and its canonical segmentation appears as many time as the corresponding word appears in the corpus. The size of the token-based corpus is then 100,000 tokens.

In the type regime, the amount of training examples is substantially smaller than in the token regime. In order to make the comparison between the token regime and the type regime more fair in terms of the amount of training and testing data, we add one more experiment. Specifically, we train the cED model in the type regime using the same number of iterations as in the token regime: 100,000 iterations. In this way, each word type is seen multiple times both in the type and the token regime. The difference is that all the types are equally frequent in the type regime, while we observe their natural text frequency in the token

---

[11]One way to include language model into SMT would be the n-best list reranking which is not exactly the same as our synchronization approach that guides the decoding process. Integrating our fusion approach for a higher-level language model into MOSES is not trivial, and the systems are not comparable without that.

regime.

5 Results and Discussion

The performance of our fused model cED+LM together with the two baseline models is reported for English, German, Indonesian in Table 1.[12] We show the average results over five splits for each language along with the standard deviation (in brackets). Additionally, we present the results on the words not seen in the training which make up for 99% of the test sets in this corpora.

Our fused approach gives an improvement from 1% to 4% over the stronger cED baseline. The bigger improvement for Indonesian could be attributed to the regular patterns of orthographic changes which appear on the segmentation boundaries. In the category of unseen data, the LM component helps to correct errors for the words consisting of new combinations of seen morphemes. In case of Indonesian, around 80% of new words (an average over five splits) belongs to this category, while its share is only around 25% for German and English. The overall lower performance for English and German thus might be due to the less regular patterns and more unseen roots in the training data.

We observe that out of the two baseline models, cED and cSMT, cED performs on average better although their behavior is very similar with a difference of only 1% in accuracy in the case of German and Indonesian.

For reference, we also show the results of the joint model of Cotterell et al. (2016) and the state-of-the-art neural reranker model of Kann et al. (2016) which are available for these data sets. We can see that our approach (cED+LM) gives an improvement of 1% for German and 2% for Indonesian over the state-of-the-art performance while we do not employ extra information from external dictionaries. Note that the languages for which we improve the state of the art are morphologically richer than English.

Table 2 shows the cED and cSMT model on Chintang in two training regimes, word types and word tokens. We also report the results for comparative setting of the type-based regime.

We observe that the corpus-wide training based on word tokens increases the overall performance for both, the cED and cSMT models. The observed improvement can be partially explained by the fact that our evaluation is token based: we count the same result as many times as it appears in the test set. Nevertheless, the score is informative because it shows the coverage over the whole corpus. Additionally, our comparable setting shows that seeing a segmentation for a word type multiple times is not what helps learning. What is beneficial is knowing the actual distribution in the corpus.

It can be seen in Table 2 that cSMT outperforms cED in the token regime. One possible explanation for this outcome is that the inclusion of the word counts helps to learn the character alignments better. This explanation would be in line with the results of Aharoni and Goldberg (2017), who showed that using pretrained character-level statistical alignments to guide the encoder-decoder network in training time can help to improve over the end-to-end soft attention approach for morphological inflection generation task, which also falls into the category of a more general sequence transduction task.

Regarding the different subsets of the test data, the highest improvement on unseen words with new morphemes is achieved by the cED model, while the cSMT model generalizes better in the category of unseen words that consist of new combination of seen morphemes. Both models behave similarly on seen words with the cSMT being slightly better. This leads to an overall best performance of the cSMT model, since the category of seen words has the largest weight among all the word tokens in the test data.

6 Conclusion and Future Work

We presented a neural model based on character level encoder-decoder framework for morphological canonical segmentation in a low-resource setting. The model is fused with a language model over morpheme segments and length control model. Our approach gives higher results than the state-of-the-art approach to canonical segmentation for languages with more morphology, Indonesian and German, while using only the information contained in the training corpus.

Future work may include a development of a single canonical segmentation model where the

---

[12] We obtained significantly better results for cED model than those reported in Kann et al. (2016). We speculate that the difference might be due to the shuffling of the data between the training epochs and early stopping based on the validation set performance.

			Error Rate (%)				
				Types Regime			
		cED+LM	cED Baseline	cSMT Baseline	Joint*	cED+RR*
English	Total	**0.21** (.01)	0.22 (.01)	0.27 (.02)	0.27 (.02)	0.19 (.01)
	New comb.	0.15 (.03)	0.24 (.01)	-	-	-
	New morph.	0.23 (.01)	0.20 (.01)	-	-	-
German	Total	**0.19** (.00)	0.23 (.02)	0.24 (.02)	0.41 (.03)	0.20 (.01)
	New comb.	0.11 (.02)	0.33 (.03)	-	-	-
	New morph.	0.21 (.01)	0.20 (.01)	-	-	-
Indonesian	Total	**0.03** (.02)	0.07 (.01)	0.06 (.01)	0.10 (.01)	0.05 (.01)
	New comb.	0.02 (.03)	0.06 (.01)	-	-	-
	New morph.	0.09 (.03)	0.09 (.03)	-	-	-

Table 1: Performance on the task of canonical segmentation for English, German and Indonesian. Type-based regime. cED+LM - character based encoder-decoder model fused with morpheme based language model. Baseline models: cED - character based encoder-decoder model, cSMT - character based statistical machine translation model. For reference only: Joint* - model of Cotterell et al. (2016), cED+RR* - model of Kann et al. (2016), not directly comparable since based on external dictionary information)

	No. of	Correct predictions (%)				
		Types Regime			Tokens Regime	
		cED	cSMT Baseline	cED Compar.	cED	cSMT Baseline
Total	24,606	0.19	0.18	0.23	0.16	**0.14**
Seen words	19,920	0.13	0.12	0.18	0.08	**0.07**
New comb.	3,959	0.44	**0.41**	0.42	0.47	**0.41**
New morph.	727	0.53	0.57	0.60	**0.48**	0.56

Table 2: Performance on the task of canonical segmentation for Chintang. Type-based vs token-based training regime. cED - character based encoder-decoder model, cSMT - character based statistical machine translation model. Comparative setting for cED: training in types regime for the same number of iterations as in the individual setting of token regime.

optimization of model components is performed using neural approaches.

Another idea relevant to explore in future work is to consider the networks that are designed to be strong at character copying which is the most common operation in string transduction tasks such as morphological segmentation, morphological reinflection and normalization (Gu et al., 2016; See et al., 2017; Makarov et al., 2017).

We also analyzed the effect of incorporating corpus counts for the purpose of training statistical and neural models for canonical segmentation. The results show that incorporating counts as they are seen in the corpora is beneficial for such task for both types of models. Our findings suggest that training sets including real word counts should be further developed for this and similar tasks and would be beneficial for development of future models.

References

Roee Aharoni and Yoav Goldberg. 2017. Morphological inflection generation with hard monotonic attention. In *ACL*.

Cyril Allauzen and Michael Riley. 2012. A pushdown transducer extension for the openfst library. In *Implementation and Application of Automata - 17th International Conference, CIAA 2012, Porto, Portugal, July 17-20, 2012. Proceedings*. pages 66–77.

Dzmitry Bahdanau, Kyunghyun Cho, and Yoshua Bengio. 2014. Neural machine translation by jointly learning to align and translate. *CoRR* abs/1409.0473.

Christian Bentz, Dimitrios Alikaniotis, Tanja Samardi,

and Paula Buttery. 2017. Variation in word frequency distributions: Definitions, measures and implications for a corpus-based language typology. *Journal of Quantitative Linguistics* pages 128–162. https://doi.org/10.1080/09296174.2016.1265792.

Toms Bergmanis and Sharon Goldwater. 2017. From segmentation to analyses: a probabilistic model for unsupervised morphology induction. In *Proceedings of the 15th Conference of the European Chapter of the Association for Computational Linguistics*. Valencia, Spain.

Balthasar Bickel, Goma Banjade, Martin Gaenszle, Elena Lieven, Netra Prasad Paudyal, Ichchha Purna Rai, Manoj Rai, Novel Kishore Rai, and Sabine Stoll. 2007. Free prefix ordering in chintang. *Language* 83(1):43–73. https://muse.jhu.edu/article/214599.

Balthasar Bickel, Sabine Stoll, Martin Gaenszle, Novel Kishor Rai, Elena Lieven, Goma Banjade, Toya Nath Bhatta, Netra Paudyal, Judith Pettigrew, Ichchha P. Rai, and Manoj Rai. 2004-2015. Audiovisual corpus of the chintang language, including a longitudinal corpus of language acquisition by six children. http://www.mpi. nl/DOBES.

Kyunghyun Cho, Bart van Merrienboer, Dzmitry Bahdanau, and Yoshua Bengio. 2014. On the properties of neural machine translation: Encoder-decoder approaches. In *Proceedings of SSST@EMNLP 2014, Eighth Workshop on Syntax, Semantics and Structure in Statistical Translation, Doha, Qatar, 25 October 2014*. pages 103–111.

Ryan Cotterell, Thomas Müller, Alexander Fraser, and Hinrich Schütze. 2015. Labeled morphological segmentation with semi-markov models. In *Proceedings of the Nineteenth Conference on Computational Natural Language Learning*. Association for Computational Linguistics, pages 164–174.

Ryan Cotterell, Tim Vieira, and Hinrich Schütze. 2016. A joint model of orthography and morphological segmentation. In *NAACL HLT 2016, The 2016 Conference of the North American Chapter of the Association for Computational Linguistics: Human Language Technologies, San Diego California, USA, June 12-17, 2016*. pages 664–669.

Mathias Creutz, Teemu Hirsimäki, Mikko Kurimo, Antti Puurula, Janne Pylkkönen, Vesa Siivola, Matti Varjokallio, Ebru Arisoy, Murat Saraçlar, and Andreas Stolcke. 2007. Morph-based speech recognition and modeling of out-of-vocabulary words across languages. *ACM Trans. Speech Lang. Process.* 5(1):3:1–3:29.

Mathias Creutz and Krista Lagus. 2002. Unsupervised discovery of morphemes. In *Proceedings of the ACL-02 Workshop on Morphological and Phonological Learning*. Association for Computational Linguistics, pages 21–30.

Mathias Creutz and Krista Lagus. 2005. Inducing the morphological lexicon of a natural language from unannotated text. In *Proc. International and Interdisciplinary Conference on Adaptive Knowledge Representation and Reasoning (AKRR-05)*. Espoo, Finland, pages 106–113.

Mathias Creutz and Krister Linden. 2004. Morpheme segmentation gold standards for finnish and english.

Christopher Dyer, A Muresan, and Philip Resnik. 2008. Generalizing word lattice translation. In *In ACL-HLT*.

H. Eifring and R. Theil. 2005. *Linguistics for Students of Asian and African Languages*. [available at http://www.uio.no/studier/emner/ hf/ikos/EXFAC03-AAS/h05/larestoff/ linguistics/], Universitetet i Oslo.

Jiatao Gu, Zhengdong Lu, Hang Li, and Victor O. K. Li. 2016. Incorporating copying mechanism in sequence-to-sequence learning. *CoRR* http://arxiv.org/abs/1603.06393.

Caglar Gulcehre, Orhan Firat, Kelvin Xu, Kyunghyun Cho, and Yoshua Bengio. 2017. On integrating a language model into neural machine translation. *Computer Speech and Language* https://doi.org/http://doi.org/10.1016/j.csl.2017.01.014.

Ilana Heintz. 2008. Arabic language modeling with finite state transducers. In *ACL 2008, Proceedings of the 46th Annual Meeting of the Association for Computational Linguistics, June 15-20, 2008, Columbus, Ohio, USA, Student Research Workshop*. pages 37–42.

Katharina Kann, Ryan Cotterell, and Hinrich Schütze. 2016. Neural morphological analysis: Encoding-decoding canonical segments. In *Proceedings of the 2016 Conference on Empirical Methods in Natural Language Processing, EMNLP 2016, Austin, Texas, USA, November 1-4, 2016*. pages 961–967.

Oskar Kohonen, Sami Virpioja, and Krista Lagus. 2010. Semi-supervised learning of concatenative morphology. In *Proceedings of the 11th Meeting of the ACL Special Interest Group on Computational Morphology and Phonology*. Association for Computational Linguistics, pages 78–86.

Quoc V. Le, Navdeep Jaitly, and Geoffrey E. Hinton. 2015. A simple way to initialize recurrent networks of rectified linear units. *CoRR* abs/1504.00941.

Peter Makarov, Tatyana Ruzsics, and Simon Clematide. 2017. Align and copy: Uzh at sigmorphon 2017 shared task for morphological reinflection. In *Proceedings of the CoNLL-SIGMORPHON 2017 Shared Task: Universal Morphological Reinflection*. Vancouver, Canada.

Karthik Narasimhan, Regina Barzilay, and Tommi Jaakkola. 2015. An unsupervised method for uncovering morphological chains. *Transactions of the Association for Computational Linguistics* 3:157–167.

Karthik Narasimhan, Damianos Karakos, Richard Schwartz, Stavros Tsakalidis, and Regina Barzilay. 2014. Morphological segmentation for keyword spotting. *EMNLP* .

Franz Josef Och. 2003. Minimum error rate training in statistical machine translation. In *Proceedings of the 41st Annual Meeting of the Association for Computational Linguistics, 7-12 July 2003, Sapporo Convention Center, Sapporo, Japan.*. pages 160–167.

Hoifung Poon, Colin Cherry, and Kristina Toutanova. 2009. Unsupervised morphological segmentation with log-linear models. In *Proceedings of Human Language Technologies: The 2009 Annual Conference of the North American Chapter of the Association for Computational Linguistics*. Association for Computational Linguistics, pages 209–217.

Brian Roark, Richard Sproat, Cyril Allauzen, Michael Riley, Jeffrey Sorensen, and Terry Tai. 2012. The opengrm open-source finite-state grammar software libraries. In *Proceedings of the ACL 2012 System Demonstrations*. Association for Computational Linguistics, ACL '12, pages 61–66.

Teemu Ruokolainen, Oskar Kohonen, Sami Virpioja, and Mikko Kurimo. 2013. Supervised morphological segmentation in a low-resource learning setting using conditional random fields. In *Proceedings of the Seventeenth Conference on Computational Natural Language Learning*. Association for Computational Linguistics, pages 29–37.

Abigail See, Peter J Liu, and Christopher D Manning. 2017. Get To The Point: Summarization with Pointer-Generator Networks. In *ACL*.

Wolfgang Seeker and Özlem Çetinoglu. 2015. A graph-based lattice dependency parser for joint morphological segmentation and syntactic analysis. *TACL* 3:359–373.

Felix Stahlberg, Eva Hasler, Aurelien Waite, and Bill Byrne. 2016. Syntactically guided neural machine translation. In *Proceedings of the 54th Annual Meeting of the Association for Computational Linguistics, ACL 2016, August 7-12, 2016, Berlin, Germany, Volume 2: Short Papers*.

Sabine Stoll, Jekaterina Mazara, and Balthasar Bickel. In press. The acquisition of polysynthetic verb forms in chintang. In Michael Fortescue, Marianne Mithun, and Nicholas Evans, editors, *Handbook of Polysynthesis*, Oxford University Press, Oxford.

Ilya Sutskever, Oriol Vinyals, and Quoc V. Le. 2014. Sequence to sequence learning with neural networks. In *Advances in Neural Information Processing Systems 27: Annual Conference on Neural Information Processing Systems 2014, December 8-13 2014, Montreal, Quebec, Canada.* pages 3104–3112.

Linlin Wang, Zhu Cao, Yu Xia, and Gerard de Melo. 2016. Morphological segmentation with window LSTM neural networks. In *Proceedings of the Thirtieth AAAI Conference on Artificial Intelligence, February 12-17, 2016, Phoenix, Arizona, USA.*. pages 2842–2848.

A Supervised Approach to Extractive Summarisation of Scientific Papers

Ed Collins and **Isabelle Augenstein** and **Sebastian Riedel**
Department of Computer Science,
University College London (UCL), UK
{edward.collins.13|i.augenstein|s.riedel}@ucl.ac.uk

Abstract

Automatic summarisation is a popular approach to reduce a document to its main arguments. Recent research in the area has focused on neural approaches to summarisation, which can be very data-hungry. However, few large datasets exist and none for the traditionally popular domain of scientific publications, which opens up challenging research avenues centered on encoding large, complex documents. In this paper, we introduce a new dataset for summarisation of computer science publications by exploiting a large resource of author provided summaries and show straightforward ways of extending it further. We develop models on the dataset making use of both neural sentence encoding and traditionally used summarisation features and show that models which encode sentences as well as their local and global context perform best, significantly outperforming well-established baseline methods.

1 Introduction

Automatic summarisation is the task of reducing a document to its main points. There are two streams of summarisation approaches: *extractive summarisation*, which copies parts of a document (often whole sentences) to form a summary, and *abstractive summarisation*, which reads a document and then generates a summary from it, which can contain phrases not appearing in the document. Abstractive summarisation is the more difficult task, but useful for domains where sentences taken out of context are not a good basis for forming a grammatical and coherent summary, like novels.

Here, we are concerned with summarising scientific publications. Since scientific publications are a technical domain with fairly regular and explicit language, we opt for the task of *extractive summarisation*. Although there has been work on summarisation of scientific publications before, existing datasets are very small, consisting of tens of documents (Kupiec et al., 1995; Visser and Wieling, 2009). Such small datasets are not sufficient to learn supervised summarisation models relying on neural methods for sentence and document encoding, usually trained on many thousands of documents (Rush et al., 2015; Cheng and Lapata, 2016; Chopra et al., 2016; See et al., 2017).

In this paper, we introduce a dataset for automatic summarisation of computer science publications which can be used for both abstractive and extractive summarisation. It consists of more than 10k documents and can easily be extended automatically to an additional 26 domains. The dataset is created by exploiting an existing resource, ScienceDirect,[1] where many journals require authors to submit highlight statements along with their manuscripts. Using such highlight statements as gold statements has been proven a good gold standard for news documents (Nallapati et al., 2016a). This new dataset offers many exciting research challenges, such how best to encode very large technical documents, which are largely ignored by current research.

In more detail, our contributions are as follows:

- We introduce a new dataset for summarisation of scientific publications consisting of over 10k documents
- Following the approach of (Hermann et al., 2015) in the news domain, we introduce a method, *HighlightROUGE*, which can be used to automatically extend this dataset and

---

[1] http://www.sciencedirect.com/

Proceedings of the 21st Conference on Computational Natural Language Learning (CoNLL 2017), pages 195–205,
Vancouver, Canada, August 3 - August 4, 2017. ©2017 Association for Computational Linguistics

	#documents	#instances
CSPubSum Train	10148	85490
CSPubSumExt Train	10148	263440
CSPubSum Test	150	N/A
CSPubSumExt Test	10148	131720

Table 2: The CSPubSum and CSPubSumExt datasets as described in Section 2.2. Instances are items of training data.

Paper Title Statistical estimation of the names of HTTPS servers with domain name graphs
Highlights we present the domain name graph (DNG), which is a formal expression that can keep track of cname chains and characterize the dynamic and diverse nature of DNS mechanisms and deployments. We develop a framework called service-flow map (sfmap) that works on top of the DNG.sfmap estimates the hostname of an HTTPS server when given a pair of client and server IP addresses. It can statistically estimate the hostname even when associating DNS queries are unobserved due to caching mechanisms, etc through extensive analysis using real packet traces, we demonstrate that the sfmap framework establishes good estimation accuracies and can outperform the state-of-the art technique called dn-hunter. We also identify the optimized setting of the sfmap framework. The experiment results suggest that the success of the sfmap lies in the fact that it can complement incomplete DNS information by leveraging the graph structure. To cope with large-scale measurement data, we introduce techniques to make the sfmap framework scalable. We validate the effectiveness of the approach using large-scale traffic data collected at a gateway point of internet access links .
Summary Statements Highlighted in Context from Section of Main Text Contributions: in this work, we present a novel methodology that aims to infer the hostnames of HTTPS flows, given the three research challenges shown above. The key contributions of this work are summarized as follows. We present the domain name graph (DNG), which is a formal expression that can keep track of cname chains (challenge 1) and characterize the dynamic and diverse nature of DNS mechanisms and deployments (challenge 3). We develop a framework called service-flow map (sfmap) that works on top of the DNG. sfmap estimates the hostname of an https server when given a pair of client and server IP addresses. It can statistically estimate the hostname even when associating DNS queries are unobserved due to caching mechanisms, etc (challenge 2). Through extensive analysis using real packet traces , we demonstrate that the sfmap framework establishes good estimation accuracies and can outperform the state-of the art technique called dn-hunter, [2]. We also identify the optimized setting of the sfmap framework. The experiment results suggest that the success of the sfmap lies in the fact that it can complement incomplete DNS information by leveraging the graph structure. To cope with large-scale measurement data, we introduce techniques to make the sfmap framework scalable. We validate the effectiveness of the approach using large-scale traffic data collected at a gateway point of internet access links. The remainder of this paper is organized as follows: section2 summarizes the related work. [...]

Table 1: An example of a document with summary statements highlighted in context.

show empirically that this improves summarisation performance

- Taking inspiration from previous work in summarising scientific literature (Kupiec et al., 1995; Saggion et al., 2016), we introduce a metric we use as a feature, *AbstractROUGE*, which can be used to extract summaries by exploiting the abstract of a paper
- We benchmark several neural as well traditional summarisation methods on the dataset and use simple features to model the global context of a summary statement, which contribute most to the overall score
- We compare our best performing system to several well-established baseline methods, some of which use more elaborate methods to model the global context than we do, and show that our best performing model outperforms them on this extractive summarisation task by a considerable margin
- We analyse to what degree different sections in scientific papers contribute to a summary

We expect the research documented in this paper to be relevant beyond the document summarisation community, for other tasks in the space of automatically understand scientific publications, such as keyphrase extraction (Kim et al., 2010; Sterckx et al., 2016; Augenstein et al., 2017; Augenstein and Søgaard, 2017), semantic relation extraction (Gupta and Manning, 2011; Marsi and Öztürk, 2015) or topic classification of scientific articles (Ó Séaghdha and Teufel, 2014).

2 Dataset and Problem Formulation

We release a novel dataset for extractive summarisation comprised of 10148 Computer Science publications.[2] Publications were obtained from ScienceDirect, where publications are grouped into 27 domains, Computer Science being one of them. As such, the dataset could easily be extended to more domains. An example document is shown in Table 1. Each paper in this dataset is guaranteed to have a title, abstract, author written highlight statements and author defined keywords. The highlight statements are sentences that should effectively convey the main takeaway of each paper and are a good gold summary, while the keyphrases are the key topics of the paper. Both abstract and highlights can be thought of as a summary of a paper. Since highlight statements, unlike sentences in the abstract, generally do not have dependencies between them, we opt to use those as gold summary statements for developing our summarisation models, following Hermann et al. (2015); Nallapati et al. (2016b) in their approaches to news summarisation.

---

[2]The dataset along with the code is available here: https://github.com/EdCo95/scientific-paper-summarisation

2.1 Problem Formulation

As shown by Cao et al. (2015), sentences can be good summaries even when taken out of the context of the surrounding sentences. Most of the highlights have this characteristic, not relying on any previous or subsequent sentences to make sense. Consequently, we frame the extractive summarisation task here as a binary sentence classification task, where we assign each sentence in a document a label $y \in 0, 1$. Our training data is therefore a list of sentences, sentence features to encode context and a label all stored in a randomly ordered list.

2.2 Creation of the Training and Testing Data

We used the 10k papers to create two different datasets: *CSPubSum* and *CSPubSumExt* where CSPubSumExt is CSPubSum extended with HighlightROUGE. The number of training items for each is given in Table 2.

CSPubSum This dataset's positive examples are the highlight statements of each paper. There are an equal number of negative examples which are sampled randomly from the bottom 10% of sentences which are the worst summaries for their paper, measured with ROUGE-L (see below), resulting in 85490 training instances. CSPubSum Test is formed of 150 full papers rather than a randomly ordered list of training sentences. These are used to measure the summary quality of each summariser, not the accuracy of the trained models.

CSPubSumExt The CSPubSum dataset has two drawbacks: 1) it is an order of magnitude behind comparable large summarisation datasets (Hermann et al., 2015; Nallapati et al., 2016b); 2) it does not have labels for sentences in the context of the main body of the paper. We generate additional training examples for each paper with *HighlightROUGE* (see next section), which finds sentences that are similar to the highlights. This results in 263k instances for CSPubSumExt Train and 132k instances for CSPubSumExt Test. CSPubSumExt Test is used to test the accuracy of trained models. The trained models are then used in summarisers whose quality is tested on CSPubSum Test with the ROUGE-L metric (see below).

3 ROUGE Metrics

ROUGE metrics are evaluation metrics for summarisation which correspond well to human judgements of good summaries (Lin, 2004). We elect to use ROUGE-L, inline with other research into summarisation of scientific articles (Cohan and Goharian, 2015; Jaidka et al., 2016).

3.1 HighlightROUGE

HighlightROUGE is a method used to generate additional training data for this dataset, using a similar approach to (Hermann et al., 2015). As input it takes a gold summary and body of text and finds the sentences within that text which give the best ROUGE-L score in relation to the highlights, like an oracle summariser would do. These sentences represent the ideal sentences to extract from each paper for an extractive summary.

We select the top 20 sentences which give the highest ROUGE-L score with the highlights for each paper as positive instances and combine these with the highlights to give the positive examples for each paper. An equal number of negative instances are sampled from the lowest scored sentences to match.

When generating data using HighlightROUGE, no sentences from the abstracts of any papers were included as training examples. This is because the abstract is already a summary; our goal is to extract salient sentences from the main paper to supplement the abstract, not from the preexisting summary.

3.2 AbstractROUGE

AbstractROUGE is used as a feature for summarisation. It is a metric presented by this work which exploits the known structure of a paper by making use of the abstract, a preexisting summary. The idea of AbstractROUGE is that sentences which are good summaries of the abstract are also likely to be good summaries of the highlights. The AbstractROUGE score of a sentence is simply the ROUGE-L score of that sentence and the abstract. The intuition of comparing sentences to the abstract is one often used in summarising scientific literature, e.g. (Saggion et al., 2016; Kupiec et al., 1995), however these authors generally encode sentences and abstract as TF-IDF vectors, then compare them, rather than directly comparing them with an evaluation metric. While this may seem somewhat like cheating, all scientific papers are guaranteed to have an abstract so it makes sense to exploit it as much as possible.

4 Method

We encode each sentence in two different ways: as their mean averaged word embeddings and as their Recurrent Neural Network (RNN) encoding.

4.1 Summariser Features

As the sentences in our dataset are randomly ordered, there is no readily available context for each sentence from surrounding sentences (taking this into account is a potential future development). To provide local and global context, a set of 8 features are used for each sentence which are described below. These contextual features contribute to achieving the best performances. Some recent work in summarisation uses as many as 30 features (Dlikman and Last, 2016; Litvak et al., 2016). We choose only a minimal set of features to focus more on learning from raw data than on feature engineering, although this could potentially further improve results.

AbstractROUGE A new metric presented by this work, described in Section 3.2.

Location Authors such as Kavila and Radhika (2015) only chose summary sentences from the Abstract, Introduction or Conclusion, thinking these more salient to summaries; and we show that certain sections within a paper are more relevant to summaries than others (see Section 5.1). Therefore we assign sentences an integer location for 7 different sections: Highlight, Abstract, Introduction, Results / Discussion / Analysis, Method, Conclusion, all else.[3] Location features have been used in other ways in previous work on summarising scientific literature; Visser and Wieling (2009) extract sentence location features based on the headings they occurred beneath while Teufel and Moens (2002) divide the paper into 20 equal parts and assign each sentence a location based on which segment it occurred in - an attempt to capture distinct zones of the paper.

Numeric Count is the number of numbers in a sentence, based on the intuition that sentences containing heavy maths are unlikely to be good summaries when taken out of context.

Title Score In Visser and Wieling (2009) and Teufel and Moens (2002)'s work on summarising

scientific papers, one of the features used is Title Score. Our feature differs slightly from Visser and Wieling (2009) in that we only use the main paper title whereas Visser and Wieling (2009) use all section headings. To calculate this feature, the non-stopwords that each sentence contains which overlap with the title of the paper are counted.

Keyphrase Score Authors such as Spärck Jones (2007) refer to the keyphrase score as a useful summarisation feature. The feature uses author defined keywords and counts how many of these keywords a sentence contains, the idea being that important sentences will contain more keywords.

TF-IDF Term Frequency, Inverse Document Frequency (TF-IDF) is a measure of how relevant a word is to a document (Ramos et al., 2003). It takes into account the frequency of a word in the current document and the frequency of that word in a background corpus of documents; if a word is frequent in a document but infrequent in a corpus it is likely to be important to that document. TF-IDF was calculated for each word in the sentence, and averaged over the sentence to give a TF-IDF score for the sentence. Stopwords were ignored.

Document TF-IDF Document TF-IDF calculates the same metric as TF-IDF, but uses the count of words in a sentence as the term frequency and count of words in the rest of the paper as the background corpus. This gives a representation of how important a word is in a sentence in relation to the rest of the document.

Sentence Length Teufel et al. (2002) created a binary feature for if a sentence was longer than a threshold. We simply include the length of the sentence as a feature; an attempt to capture the intuition that short sentences are very unlikely to be good summaries because they cannot possibly convey as much information as longer sentences.

4.2 Summariser Architectures

Models detailed in this section could take any combination of four possible inputs, and are named accordingly:

- S: The sentence encoded with an RNN.

- A: a vector representation of the abstract of a paper, created by averaging the word vectors of every non-stopword word in the abstract. Since an abstract is already a summary, this

---

[3]based on a small manually created gazetteer of alternative names

gives a good sense of relevance. It is another way of taking the abstract into consideration by using neural methods as opposed to a feature. A future development is to encode this with an RNN.

- F: the 8 features listed in Section 4.1.

- Word2Vec: the sentence represented by taking the average of every non-stopword word vector in the sentence.

Models containing "Net" use a neural network with one or multiple hidden layers. Models ending with "Ens" use an ensemble. All non-linearity functions are Rectified Linear Units (ReLUs), chosen for their faster training time and recent popularity (Krizhevsky et al., 2012).

Single Feature Models The simplest class of summarisers use a single feature from Section 4.1 (Sentence Length, Numeric Count and Section are excluded due to lack of granularity when sorting by these).

Features Only: FNet A single layer neural net to classify each sentence based on all of the 8 features given in Section 4.1. A future development is to try this with other classification algorithms.

Word Vector Models: Word2Vec and Word2VecAF Both single layer networks. Word2Vec takes as input the sentence represented as an averaged word vector of 100 numbers.[4] Word2VecAF takes the sentence average vector, abstract average vector and handcrafted features, giving a 208-dimensional vector for classification.

LSTM-RNN Method: SNet Takes as input the ordered words of the sentence represented as 100-dimensional vectors and feeds them through a bi-directional RNN with Long-Short Term Memory (LSTM, Hochreiter and Schmidhuber (1997)) cells, with 128 hidden units and dropout to prevent overfitting. Dropout probability was set to 0.5 which is thought to be near optimal for many tasks (Srivastava et al., 2014). Output from the forwards and backwards LSTMs is concatenated and projected into two classes.[5]

---

[4]Word embeddings are obtained by training a Word2Vec skip-gram model on the 10000 papers with dimensionality 100, minimum word count 5, a context window of 20 words and downsample setting of 0.001

[5]The model is trained until loss convergence on a small dev set

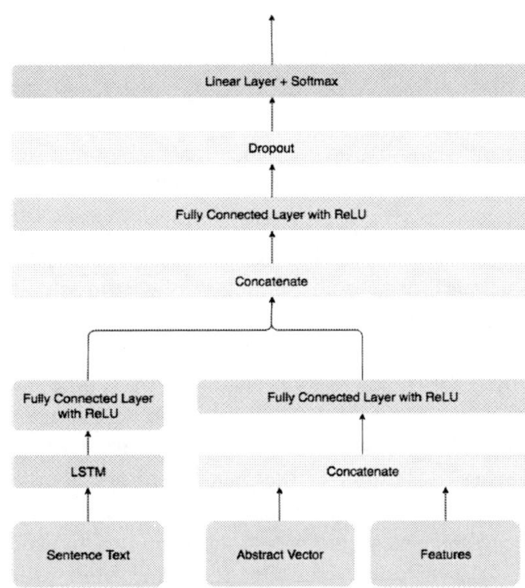

Figure 1: SAFNet Architecture

LSTM and Features: SFNet SFNet processes the sentence with an LSTM as in the previous paragraph and passes the output through a fully connected layer with dropout. The handcrafted features are treated as separate inputs to the network and are passed through a fully connected layer. The outputs of the LSTM and features hidden layer are then concatenated and projected into two classes.

SAFNet SAFNet, shown in Figure 1 is the most involved architecture presented in this paper, which further to SFNet also encodes the abstract.

Ensemble Methods: SAF+F and S+F Ensemblers The two ensemble methods use a weighted average of the output of two different models:

$$p_{\text{summary}} = \frac{S_1(1 - C) + S_2(1 + C)}{2}$$

Where S_1 is the output of the first summariser, S_2 is the output of the second and C is a hyperparameter. SAF+F Ensembler uses SAFNet as as S_1 and FNet as S_2. S+F Ensembler uses SNet as S_1 and FNet as S_2.

5 Results and Analysis

5.1 Most Relevant Sections to a Summary

A straight-forward heuristic way of obtaining a summary automatically would be to identify which sections of a paper generally represent good summaries and take those sections as a summary of the paper. This is precisely what Kavila and Radhika (2015) do, constructing summaries only from the Abstract, Introduction and Conclusion. This approach works from the intuition that certain sections are more relevant to summaries.

To understand how much each section contributes to a gold summary, we compute the ROUGE-L score of each sentence compared to the gold summary and average sentence-level ROUGE-L scores by section. ROUGE-type metrics are not the only metrics which we can use to determine how relevant a sentence is to a summary. Throughout the data, there are approximately 2000 occurrences of authors directly copying sentences from within the main text to use as highlight statements. By recording from which sections of the paper these sentences came, we can determine from which sections authors most frequently copy sentences to the highlights, so may be the most relevant to a summary. This is referred to as the *Copy/Paste Score* in this paper.

Figure 2 shows the average ROUGE score for each section over all papers, and the normalised Copy/Paste score. The title has the highest ROUGE score in relation to the gold summary, which is intuitive as the aim of a title is to convey information about the research in a single line.

A surprising result is that the introduction has the third-lowest ROUGE score in relation to the highlights. Our hypothesis was that the introduction would be ranked highest after the abstract and title because it is designed to give the reader a basic background of the problem. Indeed, the introduction has the second highest Copy/Paste score of all sections. The reason the introduction has a low ROUGE score but high Copy/Paste score is likely due to its length. The introduction tends to be longer (average length of 72.1 sentences) than other sections, but still of a relatively simple level compared to the method (average length of 41.6 sentences), thus has more potential sentences for an author to use in highlights, giving the high Copy/Paste score. However it would also have more sentences which are not good summaries and thus reduce the overall average ROUGE score of the introduction.

Hence, although some sections are slightly more likely to contain good summary sentences, and assuming that we do not take summary sen-

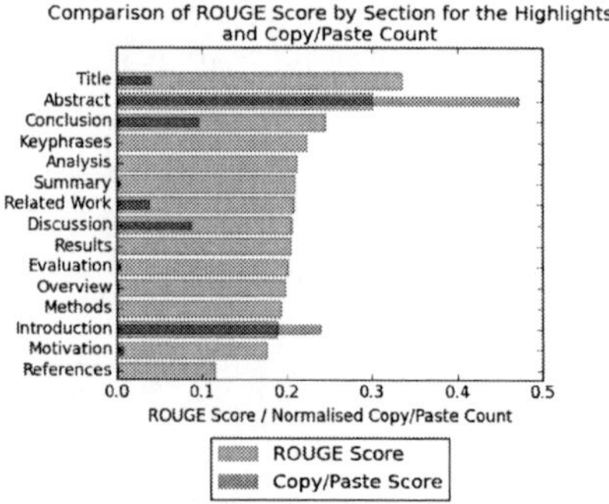

Figure 2: Comparison of the average ROUGE scores for each section and the Normalised Copy-/Paste score for each section, as detailed in Section 5.1. The wider bars in ascending order are the ROUGE scores for each section, and the thinner overlaid bars are the Copy/Paste count.

tences from the abstract which is already a summary, then Figure 2 suggests that there is no definitive section from which summary sentences should be extracted.

5.2 Comparison of Model Performance and Error Analysis

Figure 3 shows comparisons of the best model we developed to well-established external baseline methods. Our model can be seen to significantly outperform these methods, including graph-based methods which take account of global context: LexRank (Radev, 2004) and TextRank (Mihalcea and Tarau, 2004); probabilistic methods in KL-Sum (KL divergence summariser, Haghighi and Vanderwende (2009)); methods based on singular value decomposition with LSA (latent semantic analysis, Steinberger and Ježek (2004)); and simple methods based on counting in SumBasic (Vanderwende et al., 2007). This is an encouraging result showing that our methods that combine neural sentence encoding and simple features for representing the global context and positional information are very effective for modelling an extractive summarisation problem.

Figure 4 shows the performance of all models developed in this work measured in terms of accuracy and ROUGE-L on CSPubSumExt Test and CSPubSum Test, respectively. Architectures which use a combination of sentence encoding and additional features performed best by both mea-

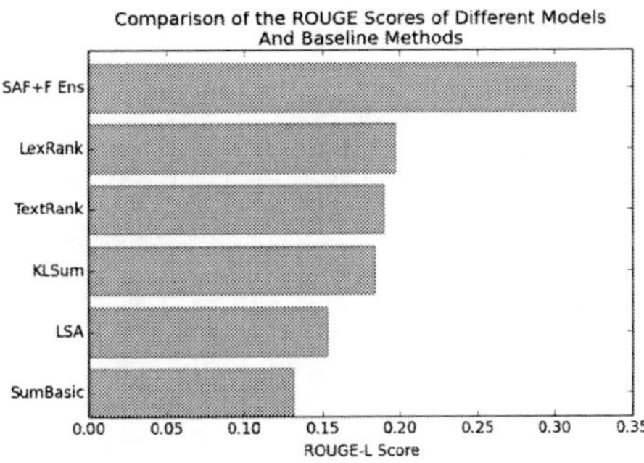

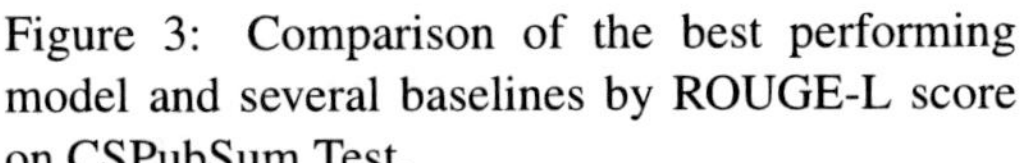

Figure 3: Comparison of the best performing model and several baselines by ROUGE-L score on CSPubSum Test.

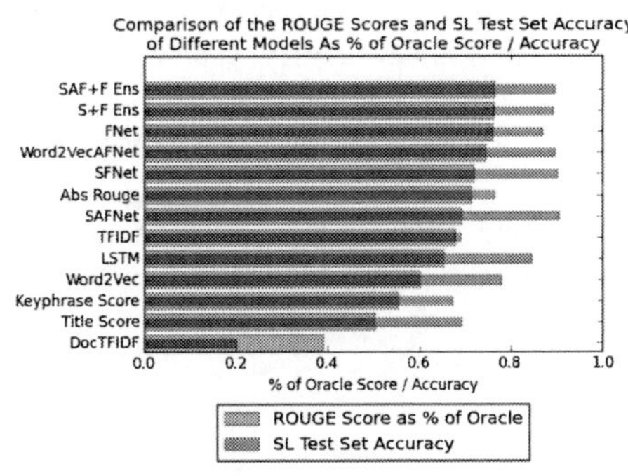

Figure 4: Comparison of the accuracy of each model on CSPubSumExt Test and ROUGE-L score on CSPubSum Test. ROUGE Scores are given as a percentage of the Oracle Summariser score which is the highest score achievable for an extractive summariser on each of the papers. The wider bars in ascending order are the ROUGE scores. There is a statistically significant difference between the performance of the top four summarisers and the 5th highest scoring one (unpaired t-test, p=0.0139).

sures. The LSTM encoding on its own outperforms models based on averaged word embeddings by 6.7% accuracy and 2.1 ROUGE points. This shows that the ordering of words in a sentence clearly makes a difference in deciding if that sentence is a summary sentence. This is a particularly interesting result as it shows that encoding a sentence with an RNN is superior to simple arithmetic, and provides an alternative to the recursive autoencoder proposed by (Socher et al., 2011) which performed worse than vector addition.

Another interesting result is that the highest accuracy on CSPubSumExt Test did not translate into the best ROUGE score on CSPubSum Test, although they are strongly correlated (Pearson correlation, R=0.8738). SAFNet achieved the highest accuracy on CSPubSumExt Test, however was worse than the AbstractROUGE Summariser on CSPubSum Test. This is most likely due to imperfections in the training data. A small fraction of sentences in the training data are mislabelled due to bad examples in the highlights which are exacerbated by the HighlightROUGE method. This leads to confusion for the summarisers capable of learning complex enough representations to classify the mislabelled data correctly.

We manually examined 100 sentences from CSPubSumExt which were incorrectly classified by SAFNet. Out of those, 37 are mislabelled examples. The primary cause of *false positives* was lack of context (16 / 50 sentences) and long range dependency (10 / 50 sentences). Other important causes of false positives were mislabelled data (12 / 50 sentences) and a failure to recog-

nise that mathematically intense sentences are not good summaries (7 / 50 sentences). Lack of context is when sentences require information from the sentences immediately before them to make sense. For example, the sentence "The performance of such systems is commonly evaluated using the data in the matrix" is classified as positive but does not make sense out of context as it is not clear what systems the sentence is referring to. A long-range dependency is when sentences refer to an entity that is described elsewhere in the paper, e.g. sentences referring to figures. These are more likely to be classified as summary statements when using models trained on automatically generated training data with HighlightROUGE, because they have a large overlap with the summary.

The primary cause of *false negatives* was mislabelled data (25 / 50 sentences) and failure to recognise an entailment, observation or conclusion (20 / 50 sentences). Mislabelled data is usually caused by the presence of some sentences in the highlights which are of the form "we set m=10 in this approach", which are not clear without context. Such sentences should only be labelled as positive if they are part of multi-line summaries, which is difficult to determine automatically.

Failure to recognise an entailment, observation or conclusion is where a sentence has the form "entity X seems to have a very small effect on Y" for example, but the summariser has not learnt that this information is useful for a summary, possibly because it was occluded by mislabelled data.

SAFNet and SFNet achieve high accuracy on the automatically generated CSPubSumExt Test dataset, though a lower ROUGE score than other simpler methods such as FNet on CSPubSum Test. This is likely due to overfitting, which our simpler summarisation models are less prone to. One option to solve this would be to manually improve the CSPubSumExt labels, the other to change the form of the training data. Rather than using a randomised list of sentences and trying to learn objectively good summaries (Cao et al., 2015), each training example could be all the sentences in order from a paper, classified as either summary or not summary. The best summary sentences from within the paper would then be chosen using HighlightROUGE and used as training data, and an approach similar to Nallapati et al. (2016a) could be used to read the whole paper sequentially and solve the issue of long-range dependencies and context.

The issue faced by SAFNet does not affect the ensemble methods so much as their predictions are weighted by a hyperparameter tuned with CSPubSum Test rather than CSPubSumExt. Ensemblers ensure good performance on both test sets as the two models are adapted to perform better on different examples.

In summary, our model performances show that: reading a sentence sequentially is superior to averaging its word vectors, simple features that model global context and positional information are very effective and a high accuracy on an automatically generated test set does not guarantee a high ROUGE-L score on a gold test set, although they are correlated. This is most likely caused by models overfitting data that has a small but significant proportion of mislabelled examples as a byproduct of being generated automatically.

5.3 Effect of Using ROUGE-L to Generate More Data

This work used a method similar to Hermann et al. (2015) to generate extra training data (Section 3.1). Figure 5 compares three models trained on CSPubSumExt Train and the same models trained

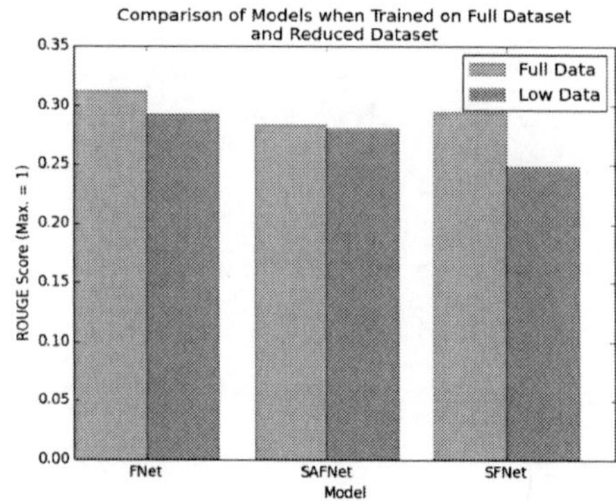

Figure 5: Comparison of the ROUGE scores of FNet, SAFNet and SFNet when trained on CSPubSumExt Train (bars on the left) and CSPubSum Train (bars on the right) and .

on CSPubSum Train (the feature of which section the example appeared in was removed to do this). The FNet summariser and SFNet suffer statistically significant ($p = 0.0147$ and $p < 0.0001$) drops in performance from using the unexpanded dataset, although interestingly SAFNet does not, suggesting it is a more stable model than the other two. These drops in performance however show that using the method we have described to increase the amount of available training data does improves model performance for summarisation.

5.4 Effect of the AbstractROUGE Metric on Summariser Performance

This work suggested use of the AbstractROUGE metric as a feature (Section 3.2). Figure 6 compares the performance of 3 models trained with and without it. This shows two things: the AbstractROUGE metric does improve performance for summarisation techniques based only on feature engineering; and learning a representation of the sentence directly from the raw text as is done in SAFNet and SFNet as well as learning from features results in a far more stable model. This model is still able to make good predictions even if AbstractROUGE is not available for training, meaning the models need not rely on the presence of an abstract.

6 Related Work

Datasets Datasets for extractive summarisation often emerged as part of evaluation campaigns for summarisation of news, organised by the

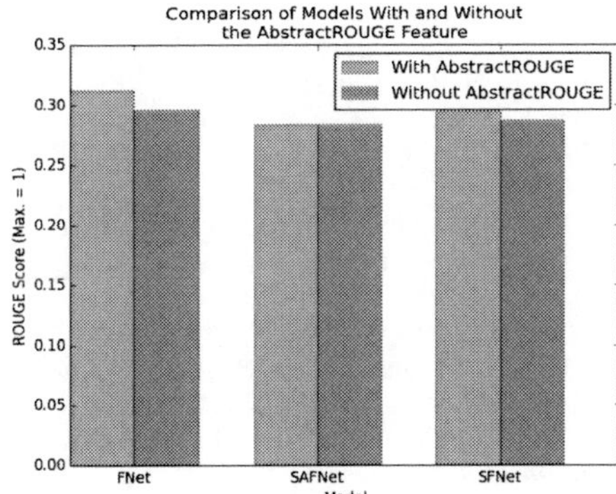

Figure 6: Comparison of ROUGE scores of the Features Only, SAFNet and SFNet models when trained with (bars on the left) and without (bars on the right) AbstractROUGE, evaluated on CSPub-Sum Test. The FNet classifier suffers a statistically significant (p=0.0279) decrease in performance without the AbstractROUGE metric.

Document Understanding Conference (DUC), and the Text Analysis Conference (TAC). DUC proposed single-document summarisation (Harman and Over, 2002), whereas TAC datasets are for multi-document summarisation (Dang and Owczarzak, 2008, 2009). All of the datasets contain roughly 500 documents.

The largest summarisation dataset (1 million documents) to date is the DailyMail/CNN dataset (Hermann et al., 2015), first used for single-document abstractive summarisation by (Nallapati et al., 2016b), enabling research on data-intensive sequence encoding methods.

Existing datasets for summarisation of scientific documents of which we are aware are small. Kupiec et al. (1995) used only 21 publications and CL-SciSumm 2017[6] contains 30 publications. Ronzano and Saggion (2016) used a set of 40 papers, Kupiec et al. (1995) used 21 and Visser and Wieling (2009) used only 9 papers. The largest known scientific paper dataset was used by Teufel and Moens (2002) who used a subset of 80 papers from a larger corpus of 260 articles.

The dataset we introduce in this paper is, to our knowledge, the only large dataset for extractive summarisation of scientific publications. The size of the dataset enables training of data-intensive neural methods and also offers exciting research

challenges centered around how to encode very large documents.

Extractive Summarisation Methods Early work on extractive summarisation focuses exclusively on easy to compute statistics, e.g. word frequency (Luhn, 1958), location in the document (Baxendale, 1958), and TF-IDF (Salton et al., 1996). Supervised learning methods which classify sentences in a document binarily as summary sentences or not soon became popular (Kupiec et al., 1995). Exploration of more cues such as sentence position (Yang et al., 2017), sentence length (Radev et al., 2004), words in the title, presence of proper nouns, word frequency (Nenkova et al., 2006) and event cues (Filatova and Hatzivassiloglou, 2004) followed.

Recent approaches to extractive summarisation have mostly focused on neural approaches, based on bag of word embeddings approaches (Kobayashi et al., 2015; Yogatama et al., 2015) or encoding whole documents with CNNs and/or RNNs (Cheng and Lapata, 2016).

In our setting, since the documents are very large, it is computationally challenging to read a whole publication with a (possibly hierarchical) neural sequence encoder. In this work, we therefore opt to only encode the target sequence with an RNN and the global context with simpler features. We leave fully neural approaches to encoding publications to future work.

7 Conclusion

In this paper, we have introduced a new dataset for summarisation of computer science publications, which is substantially larger than comparable existing datasets, by exploiting an existing resource. We showed the performance of several extractive summarisation models on the dataset that encode sentences, global context and position, which significantly outperform well-established summarisation methods. We introduced a new metric, AbstractROUGE, which we show increases summarisation performance. Finally, we show how the dataset can be extended automatically, which further increases performance. Remaining challenges are to better model the global context of a summary statement and to better capture cross-sentence dependencies.

Acknowledgments

This work was partly supported by Elsevier.

---

[6] http://wing.comp.nus.edu.sg/
cl-scisumm2017/

References

Isabelle Augenstein, Mrinal Kanti Das, Sebastian Riedel, Lakshmi Nair Vikraman, and Andrew McCallum. 2017. SemEval 2017 Task 10: ScienceIE - Extracting Keyphrases and Relations from Scientific Publications. In *Proceedings of SemEval*.

Isabelle Augenstein and Anders Søgaard. 2017. Multi-Task Learning of Keyphrase Boundary Classification. In *Proceedings of ACL*.

Phyllis B Baxendale. 1958. Machine-Made Index for Technical Literature An Experiment. *IBM Journal of Research and Development* 2(4):354–361.

Ziqiang Cao, Furu Wei, Sujian Li, Wenjie Li, Ming Zhou, and Houfeng Wang. 2015. Learning Summary Prior Representation for Extractive Summarization. *Proceedings of ACL* .

Jianpeng Cheng and Mirella Lapata. 2016. Neural Summarization by Extracting Sentences and Words. In *Proceedings of ACL*.

Sumit Chopra, Michael Auli, and Alexander M. Rush. 2016. Abstractive Sentence Summarization with Attentive Recurrent Neural Networks. In *Proceedings NAACL-HLT*.

Arman Cohan and Nazli Goharian. 2015. Scientific Article Summarization Using Citation-Context and Article's Discourse Structure. In *Proceedings of EMNLP*. September, pages 390–400.

Hoa Trang Dang and Karolina Owczarzak. 2008. Overview of the TAC 2008 Update Summarization Task. In *Proceedings of TAC*.

HT Dang and K Owczarzak. 2009. Overview of the TAC 2009 Summarization Track. In *Proceedings of TAC*.

Alexander Dlikman and Mark Last. 2016. Using Machine Learning Methods and Linguistic Features in Single-Document Extractive Summarization. *CEUR Workshop Proceedings* 1646:1–8.

Elena Filatova and Vasileios Hatzivassiloglou. 2004. Event-Based Extractive Summarization. In *Proceedings of ACL Workshop on Summarization*.

Sonal Gupta and Christopher Manning. 2011. Analyzing the Dynamics of Research by Extracting Key Aspects of Scientific Papers. In *Proceedings of IJCNLP*.

Aria Haghighi and Lucy Vanderwende. 2009. Exploring Content Models for Multi-Document Summarization. In *Proceedings of ACL-HLT*. June, pages 362–370.

Donna Harman and Paul Over. 2002. The duc summarization evaluations. In *Proceedings HLT*.

Karl Moritz Hermann, Tomas Kocisky, Edward Grefenstette, Lasse Espeholt, Will Kay, Mustafa Suleyman, and Phil Blunsom. 2015. Teaching Machines to Read and Comprehend. In *Proceedings of NIPS*.

Sepp Hochreiter and Jürgen Schmidhuber. 1997. Long short-term memory. *Neural Computation* 9(8):1735–1780.

Kokil Jaidka, Muthu Kumar Chandrasekaran, Sajal Rustagi, and Min Yen Kan. 2016. Overview of the CL-SciSumm 2016 Shared Task. *CEUR Workshop Proceedings* 1610:93–102.

Selvani Deepthi Kavila and Y Radhika. 2015. Extractive Text Summarization Using Modified Weighing and Sentence Symmetric Feature Methods. *International Journal of Modern Education and Computer Science* 7(10):33.

Su Nam Kim, Olena Medelyan, Min-Yen Kan, and Timothy Baldwin. 2010. SemEval-2010 Task 5 : Automatic Keyphrase Extraction from Scientific Articles. In *Proceedings of the 5th International Workshop on Semantic Evaluation*. Association for Computational Linguistics, Uppsala, Sweden, pages 21–26.

Hayato Kobayashi, Masaki Noguchi, and Taichi Yatsuka. 2015. Summarization Based on Embedding Distributions. In *Proceedings of EMNLP*.

Alex Krizhevsky, Ilya Sutskever, and Geoffrey E Hinton. 2012. ImageNet Classification with Deep Convolutional Neural Networks. In *Proceedings of NIPS*. pages 1–9.

Julian Kupiec, Jan Pedersen, and Francine Chen. 1995. A Trainable Document Summarizer. In *Proceedings of SIGIR*.

C Y Lin. 2004. ROUGE: A Package for Automatic Evaluation of Summaries. In *Proceedings of the ACL Workshop on Text Summarization Branches Out (WAS)*. 1, pages 25–26.

Marina Litvak, Natalia Vanetik, Mark Last, and Elena Churkin. 2016. MUSEEC: A Multilingual Text Summarization Tool. *Proceedings of ACL System Demonstrations* pages 73–78.

Hans Peter Luhn. 1958. The Automatic Creation of Literature Abstracts. *IBM Journal of research and development* 2(2):159–165.

Erwin Marsi and Pinar Öztürk. 2015. Extraction and generalisation of variables from scientific publications. In *Proceedings of EMNLP*.

Rada Mihalcea and Paul Tarau. 2004. TextRank: Bringing order into texts. *Proceedings of EMNLP* 85:404–411.

Ramesh Nallapati, Feifei Zhai, and Bowen Zhou. 2016a. SummaRuNNer: A Recurrent Neural Network based Sequence Model for Extractive Summarization of Documents. *Association for the Advancement of Artificial Intelligence* .

Ramesh Nallapati, Bowen Zhou, Caglar Gulcehre, Bing Xiang, et al. 2016b. Abstractive Text Summarization Using Sequence-to-Sequence RNNs and Beyond. In *Proceedings of CoNLL*.

Ani Nenkova, Lucy Vanderwende, and Kathleen McKeown. 2006. A Compositional Context Sensitive Multi-document Summarizer: Exploring the Factors That Influence Summarization. In *Proceedings of SIGIR*.

Diarmuid Ó Séaghdha and Simone Teufel. 2014. Unsupervised learning of rhetorical structure with untopic models. In *Proceedings of Coling*.

Dragomir R Radev. 2004. LexRank : Graph-based Centrality as Salience in Text Summarization. *Journal of Artificial Intelligence Research* 22(22):457–479.

Dragomir R Radev, Timothy Allison, Sasha Blair-Goldensohn, John Blitzer, Arda Celebi, Stanko Dimitrov, Elliott Drabek, Ali Hakim, Wai Lam, Danyu Liu, et al. 2004. MEAD-A Platform for Multidocument Multilingual Text Summarization. In *Proceedings of LREC*.

Juan Ramos, Juramos Eden, and Rutgers Edu. 2003. Using TF-IDF to Determine Word Relevance in Document Queries. *Processing* .

Francesco Ronzano and Horacio Saggion. 2016. Knowledge Extraction and Modeling from Scientific Publications. In *Proceedings of WWW Workshop on Enhancing Scholarly Data*.

Alexander M. Rush, Sumit Chopra, and Jason Weston. 2015. A Neural Attention Model for Abstractive Sentence Summarization. In *Proceedings of EMNLP*.

Horacio Saggion, Ahmed Abura'ed, and Francesco Ronzano. 2016. Trainable citation-enhanced summarization of scientific articles. *CEUR Workshop Proceedings* 1610:175–186.

Gerard Salton, James Allan, Chris Buckley, and Amit Singhal. 1996. Automatic Analysis, Theme Generation, and Summarization of Machine-Readable Texts. In *Information retrieval and hypertext*, Springer, pages 51–73.

Abigail See, Peter J Liu, and Christopher D Manning. 2017. Get To The Point: Summarization with Pointer-Generator Networks. In *Proceedings of ACL*.

Richard Socher, Jeffrey Pennington, Eric H Huang, Andrew Y Ng, and Christopher D Manning. 2011. Semi-Supervised Recursive Autoencoders for Predicting Sentiment Distributions. In *Proceedings of EMNLP*. pages 151–161.

Karen Spärck Jones. 2007. Automatic summarising: The state of the art. *Information Processing and Management* 43(6):1449–1481.

Nitish Srivastava, Geoffrey Hinton, Alex Krizhevsky, Ilya Sutskever, and Ruslan Salakhutdinov. 2014. Dropout: A Simple Way to Prevent Neural Networks from Overfitting. *Journal of Machine Learning Research* 15:1929–1958.

Josef Steinberger and Karel Ježek. 2004. Using Latent Semantic Analysis in Text Summarization. In *Proceedings of ISIM*. pages 93–100.

Lucas Sterckx, Cornelia Caragea, Thomas Demeester, and Chris Develder. 2016. Supervised Keyphrase Extraction as Positive Unlabeled Learning. In *Proceedings of EMNLP*.

Simone Teufel and Marc Moens. 2002. Summarizing Scientific Articles: Experiments with Relevance and Rhetorical Status. *Computational linguistics* 28(4):409–445.

Lucy Vanderwende, Hisami Suzuki, Chris Brockett, and Ani Nenkova. 2007. Beyond SumBasic: Task-focused summarization with sentence simplification and lexical expansion. *Information Processing and Management* 43(6):1606–1618.

W. T. Visser and M .B. Wieling. 2009. Sentence-based Summarization of Scientific Documents .

Yinfei Yang, Forrest Bao, and Ani Nenkova. 2017. Detecting (Un)Important Content for Single-Document News Summarization. In *Proceedings of EACL (Short Papers)*.

Dani Yogatama, Fei Liu, and Noah A Smith. 2015. Extractive Summarization by Maximizing Semantic Volume. In *Proceedings of EMNLP*. pages 1961–1966.

An Automatic Approach for Document-level Topic Model Evaluation

Shraey Bhatia[1]   **Jey Han Lau**[1,2]   **Timothy Baldwin**[1]

[1] School of Computing and Information Systems,
The University of Melbourne

[2] IBM Research

`shraeybhatia@gmail.com`, `jeyhan.lau@gmail.com`, `tb@ldwin.net`

Abstract

Topic models jointly learn topics and document-level topic distribution. Extrinsic evaluation of topic models tends to focus exclusively on topic-level evaluation, e.g. by assessing the coherence of topics. We demonstrate that there can be large discrepancies between topic- and document-level model quality, and that basing model evaluation on topic-level analysis can be highly misleading. We propose a method for automatically predicting topic model quality based on analysis of document-level topic allocations, and provide empirical evidence for its robustness.

1 Introduction

Topic models such as latent Dirichlet allocation (Blei et al., 2003) jointly learn latent topics (in the form of multinomial distributions over words) and topic allocations to individual documents (in the form of multinomial distributions over topics), and provide a powerful means of document collection navigation and visualisation (Newman et al., 2010a; Chaney and Blei, 2012; Smith et al., 2017). One property of LDA-style topic models that has contributed to their popularity is that they are highly configurable, and can be structured to capture a myriad of statistical dependencies, such as between topics (Blei and Lafferty, 2006), between documents associated with the same individual (Rosen-Zvi et al., 2004), or between documents associated with individuals in different network relations (Wang and Blei, 2011). This has led to a wealth of topic models of different types, and the need for methods to evaluate different styles of topic model over the same document collections. Test data perplexity is the obvious solution, but it has been shown to correlate poorly with direct

human assessment of topic model quality (Chang et al., 2009), motivating the need for automatic topic model evaluation methods which emulate human assessment. Research in this vein has focused primarily on evaluating the quality of individual topics (Newman et al., 2010b; Mimno et al., 2011; Aletras and Stevenson, 2013; Lau et al., 2014; Fang et al., 2016) and largely ignored evaluation of topic allocations to individual documents, and it has become widely accepted that topic-level evaluation is a reliable indicator of the intrinsic quality of the overall topic model (Lau et al., 2014). We challenge this assumption, and demonstrate that topic model evaluation should operate at both the topic and document levels.

Our primary contributions are as follows: (1) we empirically demonstrate that there can be large discrepancies between topic- and document-level topic model evaluation; (2) we demonstrate that previously-proposed document-level evaluation approaches can be misleading, and propose an alternative evaluation method; and (3) we propose an automatic approach to topic model evaluation based on analysis of document-level topic distributions, which we show to correlate strongly with manual annotations.

2 Related Work

Perplexity or held-out likelihood has long been used as an intrinsic metric to evaluate topic models (Wallach et al., 2009). Chang et al. (2009) proposed two human judgement tasks, at the topic and document levels, and showed that there is low correlation between perplexity and direct human evaluations of topic model quality. The two tasks took the form of "intruder" tasks, whereby subjects were tasked with identifying an intruder topic word for a given topic, or an intruder topic for a given document. Specifically, in the word intrusion

Proceedings of the 21st Conference on Computational Natural Language Learning (CoNLL 2017), pages 206–215,
Vancouver, Canada, August 3 - August 4, 2017. ©2017 Association for Computational Linguistics

task, an intruder word was added to the top-5 topic words, and annotators were asked to identify the intruder word. Similarly in the topic intrusion task, a document and 4 topics were presented — the top-3 topics corresponding to the document and a random intruder topic — and subjects were asked to spot the intruder topic. The intuition behind both methods is that the higher the quality of the topic or topic allocation for a given document, the easier it should be to detect the intruder.

Newman et al. (2010b) proposed to measure topic coherence directly in the form of "observed coherence", in which human judges rated topics directly on an ordinal 3-point scale. They experimented with a range of different methods to automate the rating task, and reported the best results by simply aggregating pointwise mutual information (pmi) scores for different pairings of topic words, based on a sliding window over English Wikipedia.

Building on the work of Chang et al. (2009), Lau et al. (2014) proposed an improved method for estimating observed coherence based on normalised pmi (npmi), and further automated the word intruder detection task based on a combination of word association features (pmi, npmi, CP1, and CP2) in a learn-to-rank model (Joachims, 2006). Additionally, the authors showed a strong correlation between word intrusion and observed coherence, and suggested that it is possible to perform topic model evaluation based on aggregation of word intrusion or observed coherence scores across all topics.

3 Datasets and Topic Models

We use two document collections for our experiments: APNEWS and the British National Corpus ("BNC": Burnard (1995)). APNEWS is a collection of Associated Press[1] news articles from 2009 to 2016, while BNC is an amalgamation of extracts from different sources such as books, journals, letters, and pamphlets. We sample 50K and 15K documents from APNEWS and BNC, respectively, to create two datasets for our experiments.

In terms of preprocessing, we use Stanford CoreNLP (Manning et al., 2014) to tokenise words and sentences. We additionally remove stop words,[2] lower-case all word tokens, filter word types which occur less than 10 times, and exclude

the top 0.1% most frequent word types. Statistics for each of the preprocessed datasets are provided in Table 1.

Similarly to Chang et al. (2009), we base our analysis on a representative selection of topic models, each of which we train over APNEWS and BNC to generate 100 topics:

- **lda** (Blei et al., 2003) uses a symmetric Dirichlet prior to model both document-level topic mixtures and topic-level word mixtures. It is one of the most commonly used topic model implementations and serve as a benchmark for comparison. We use Mallet's implementation of lda for our experiments. Note that Mallet implements various enhancements to the basic LDA model, including the use of an asymmetric–symmetric prior.

- **ctm** (Blei and Lafferty, 2006) is an extension of lda that uses a logistic normal prior over topic proportions instead of a Dirichlet prior to model correlations between different topics and reduce overlap in topic content.

- **hca** (Buntine and Mishra, 2014) is an extension to LDA to capture word burstiness (Doyle and Elkan, 2009), based on the observation that there tends to be higher likelihood of generating a word which has already been seen recently. Word generation is modelled by a Pitman–Yor process (Chen et al., 2011).

- **ntm** (Cao et al., 2015) is a neural topic model, where topic–word multinomials are modelled as a look-up layer of words, and topic–document multinomials are modelled as a look-up layer of documents. The output layer of the network is given by the dot product of the two vectors. There are 2 variants of ntm: unsupervised and supervised. We use only the unsupervised variant in our experiments.

- **cluster** is a baseline topic model, specifically designed to produce highly coherent topics but "bland" topic allocations. We represent word types in the documents with pre-trained word2vec vectors (Mikolov et al., 2013a,b), pre-trained on Google News,[3] and create word clusters using k-means clustering ($k = 100$) to generate the topics. We derive the multinomial distribution for each topic based on the cosine distance to the cluster centroid, and

---

[1] https://www.ap.org/en-gb/

[2] We use Mallet's stop word list: https://github.com/mimno/Mallet/tree/master/stoplists

[3] Available from: https://code.google.com/archive/word2vec.

Dataset	#Docs	#Tokens
APNEWS	50K	15M
BNC	15K	18M

Table 1: Statistics for the two document collections used in our experiments

Model	APNEWS	BNC
lda	0.16	0.14
ctm	0.07	0.09
hca	0.14	0.08
ntm	0.10	0.08
cluster	0.18	0.17

Table 2: Topic coherence scores (npmi)

linear normalisation across all words.

To generate the topic allocation for a given document, we first calculate a document representation based on the mean of the `word2vec` vectors of its content words. For each cluster, we represent them by calculating the mean `word2vec` vectors of its top-10 words. Given the document vector and clusters/topics, we calculate the similarity of the document to each cluster based on cosine similarity, and finally (linearly) normalise the similarities to generate a probability distribution.

4 Topic-level Evaluation: Topic Coherence

Pointwise mutual information (and its normalised variant `npmi`) is a common association measure to estimate topic coherence (Newman et al., 2010b; Mimno et al., 2011; Aletras and Stevenson, 2013; Lau et al., 2014; Fang et al., 2016). Although the method is successful in assessing topic quality, it tells us little about the association between documents and topics. As we will see, a topic model can produce topics that are coherent — in terms of `npmi` association — but poor descriptor of the overall concepts in the document collection.

We first compute topic coherence for all 5 topic models over APNEWS and BNC using `npmi` (Lau et al., 2014) and present the results in Table 2.[4] We see that `lda` and `cluster` perform consistently well across both datasets. `hca` performs well over

APNEWS but poorly over BNC. Both `ctm` and `ntm` topics appear to have low coherence over the two datasets.

Based on these results, one would conclude that `cluster` is a good topic model, as it produces very coherent topics. To better understand the nature and quality of the topics, we present a random sample of `lda` and `cluster` topics in Table 3.

Looking at the topics, we see that `cluster` tends to include different inflectional forms of the same word (e.g. *prohibited*, *probihiting*) and near-synonyms/sister words (e.g. *river*, *lake*, *creeks*) in a single topic. This explains the strong `npmi` association of the `cluster` topics. On the other hand, `lda` discovers related words that collectively describe concepts rather than just clustering (near) synonyms. This suggests that the topic coherence metric alone may not completely capture topic model quality, leading us to also investigate the topic distribution associated with documents from our collections.

5 Human Evaluation of Document-level Topic Allocations

In this section, we describe a series of manual evaluations of document-level topic allocations, in order to get a more holistic evaluation of the true quality of the different topic models (in line with the original work of Chang et al. (2009)).

5.1 Topic Intrusion

The goal of the topic intrusion task is to examine whether the document–topic allocations from a given topic model accord with manual judgements. We formulate the task similarly to Chang et al. (2009), in presenting the human judges with a snippet from each document, along with four topics. The four topics comprise the top-3 highest probability topics related to document, and one intruder topic. Each annotator is required to pick the topic that is least representative of the document, with the expectation that the better the topic model, the more readily they should be able to pick the intruder topic. The intruder topic is sampled randomly, subject to the following conditions: (1) it should be a low probability topic for the target document; and (2) it should be a high probability topic for at least one other document. The first constraint is intended to ensure that the intruder topic is unrelated to the target document, while the second constraint is intended to select a topic that is highly

---

[4]We use the following open source toolkit to compute topic coherence: `https://github.com/jhlau/topic_interpretability`.

Model	Topics
lda	oil gas drilling gulf spill natural pipeline wells industry energy computer video screen program text disk windows electronic machine graphics health care hospital services medical staff patients service child authority
cluster	river creek lake rivers dam tributary lakes reservoir tributaries creeks prohibited forbid prohibiting prohibits violated prohibit contravened forbids violate barred terrace courtyard staircase staircases courtyards walls pergola walkway stairways walkways

Table 3: Example `lda` and `cluster` topics.

Topic Model	Mean Model Precision	
	APNEWS	BNC
lda	0.84	0.66
ctm	0.64	0.66
hca	0.60	0.44
ntm	0.26	0.17
cluster	0.39	0.48

Table 4: Mean model precision for human judgements

Topic Model	Mean Topic Log Odds	
	APNEWS	BNC
lda	-0.78	-1.84
ctm	-1.04	-1.60
hca	-2.09	-3.61
ntm	-7.16	-6.32
cluster	-0.12	-0.10

Table 5: Mean topic log odds for human judgements

associated with some documents, and hence likely to be coherent and not a junk topic. Each topic is represented by its top-10 most probable words, and the target document is presented in the form of the first three sentences, with an option to view more of the document if further context is needed.

We used Amazon Mechanical Turk to collect the human judgements, with five document–topic combinations forming a single HIT, one of which acts as a quality control. The control items were sourced from an earlier annotation task where subjects were asked to score the top-5 topics for a target document on a scale of 0–3. The 50 top-scoring documents from this annotation task, with their top-3 topics, were chosen as controls. The intruder topic for the control was generated by randomly selecting 10 words from the corpus vocabulary. In order to pass quality control, each worker had to correctly select the intruder topic for the control document–topic item over 60% of time (across all HITs they completed). Each document–topic pair was rated by 10 annotators initially, and for HITs where less than 3 annotations passed quality control, we reposted them for a second round of annotation.

For our annotation task, we randomly sampled 100 documents from each of our two datasets, for each of which we generate document–topic items based on the five different topic models. In total, therefore, we annotated 1000 (100 documents × 2 collections × 5 topic models) document–topic combinations. After quality control, the final dataset contains an average of 5.4 and 5.5 valid intruder topic annotations for APNEWS and BNC, respectively.

Chang et al. (2009) proposed topic log odds ("TLO") as a means of evaluating the topic intrusion task. The authors defined topic log odds for a document–topic pair as the difference in the log-probability assigned to the intruder and the log-probability assigned to the topic chosen by a given annotator, which they then averaged across annotators to get a TLO score for a single document. Separately, Chang et al. (2009) proposed model precision as a means of evaluating the word intrusion task, whereby they simply calculated the proportion of annotators who correctly selected the intruder word for a given topic. In addition to presenting results based on TLO, we apply the model precision methodology in our evaluation of the topic intrusion task, in calculating the proportion of annotators who correctly selected the intruder topic for a given document, which we then average across documents to derive a model score.

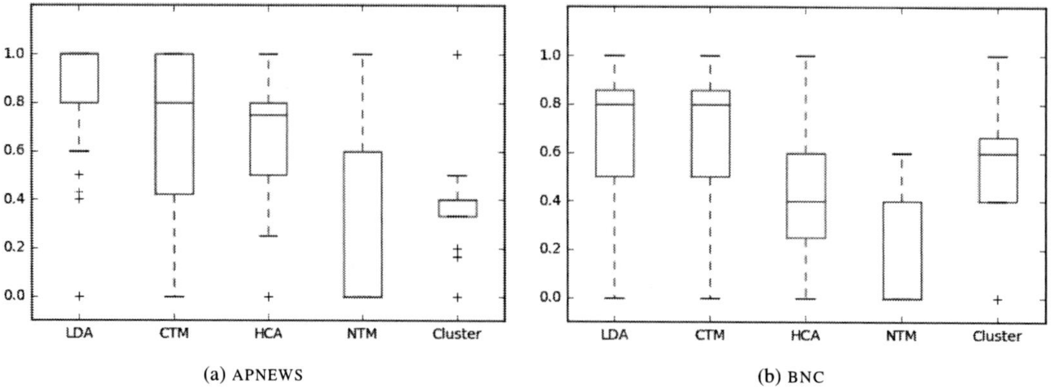

(a) APNEWS   (b) BNC

Figure 1: Boxplots of model precision

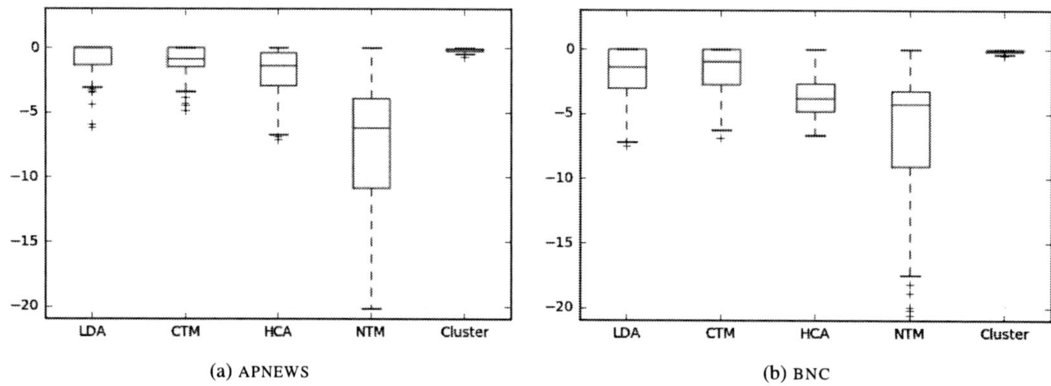

(a) APNEWS   (b) BNC

Figure 2: Boxplots of topic log odds

The results of the human annotation task are summarised in Tables 4 and 5. Looking at model precision for APNEWS first, we see that `lda` outperforms the other topic models. `ctm` and `hca` perform credibly, whereas `ntm` and `cluster` are quite poor. Moving on to BNC, we see a drop in score for `lda`, to a level comparable with `ctm`. `cluster` improves slightly higher than BNC, whereas `hca` drops considerably (despite being designed specifically to deal with word burstiness in the longer documents characteristic of BNC). Figure 1 shows boxplots for topic-level model precision, and reflects a similar trend.

Looking next to TLO in Table 5, we see a totally different picture, with `cluster` being rated as the best topic model by a clear margin. This exposes a flaw in the TLO formulation, in the case of adversarial topic models such as `cluster` which assign near-uniform probabilities across all topics. This results in the difference in probability mass being very close to the upper bound of zero in all cases, meaning that even for random topic selection, TLO is near perfect. We can also see this in Figure 2, where the boxes for `cluster` have nearly zero range. Indeed, if we combined the results for TLO with those for topic coherence, we would (very wrongly!) conclude that `cluster` performs best over both document collections. More encouragingly, for the other four topic models, the results for TLO are much more consistent with those based on model precision.

5.2 Direct Annotation of Topic Assignments

Newman et al. (2010b) proposed a more direct approach to topic coherence, by asking people to rate topics directly based on the top-N words. Taking inspiration from their methodology, we propose to directly annotate each topic assigned to a target document. We present the human annotators with the target document and the top-ranked (high-

Topic Model	Average rating	
	APNEWS	BNC
lda	1.26	1.01
ctm	0.96	1.02
hca	0.95	0.90
ntm	0.36	0.46
cluster	0.41	0.66

Table 6: Top-1 document–topic rating for each topic model

est probability) topic from each of the five topic models, and ask them to rate each topic on an ordinal scale of 0–3. At the model level, we take the mean rating over all document–topic pairings for that topic model (based, once again, on 100 documents per collection).[5] We summarise the findings in Table 6.

We observe that, in the case of APNEWS, lda does considerably better than ctm and hca, whereas for BNC, lda and ctm are quite close, with hca close behind. cluster and ntm do poorly across both datasets. The overall trend for APNEWS of lda > ctm > hca > cluster > ntm is consistent with the model precision results in Table 4. In the case of BNC, the observation of ctm ≈ lda > hca > cluster > ntm is also broadly the same, except that hca does not do as well over the topic intrusion task. Here, we are more interested in the relative performance of topic models than absolute numbers, although the low absolute scores are an indication that it is a difficult annotation task.

Broadly combined across the two evaluation methodologies, lda and ctm are top-performing, hca gets mixed results, and cluster and ntm are the lowest performers. These results generally agree with the model precision findings, demonstrating that model precision is a more robust metric than TLO.

6 Automatic Evaluation

A limitation of the topic intrusion task is that it requires manual annotation, making it ill-suited for large-scale or automatic evaluation. We present the first attempt to automate the prediction of the intruder topic, with the aim of developing an approach to topic model evaluation which comple-

ments topic coherence (as motivated in Sections 4 and 5).

6.1 Methodology

We build a support vector regression (SVR) model (Joachims, 2006) to rank topics given a document to select the intruder topic. We first explain an intuition of the features that are driving the SVR.

To rank topics for a document, we need to first compute the probability of a topic t given document d, i.e. $P(t|d)$. We can invert the condition using Bayes rule:

$$P(t|d) = \frac{P(d|t)P(t)}{P(d)}$$
$$\propto P(d|t)P(t)$$

We can omit $P(d)$ as the probability of document d is constant for the topics that we are ranking.

Next we represent topic t using its top-N highest probability words, giving:

$$P(t|d) \propto P(d|w_1, ..., w_N)P(w_1, ..., w_N)$$
$$\propto \log P(d|w_1, ..., w_N)+$$
$$\log P(w_1, ..., w_N)$$

The first term $\log P(d|w_1, ..., w_N)$ can be interpreted from an information retrieval perspective, where we are computing the relevance of document d given query terms w_1, w_2, ..., w_N. This term constitutes the first feature for the SVR. We use Indri[6] to index the document collection, and compute $\log P(d|w_1, ..., w_N)$ given a set of query words and a document.[7]

We estimate the second term, $\log P(w_1, ..., w_N)$, using the pairwise probability of the topic words:

$$\sum_{0 < i \le m} \sum_{i+1 \le j \le m} \log \frac{\#(w_i, w_j)}{\#(\cdot)}$$

where m denotes the number of topic words used, $\#(w_i, w_j)$ is the number of documents where word w_i and w_j co-occur, and $\#(\cdot)$ is the total number of documents. We explore using two values of m here: 5 and 10.[8] These two values constitute the second and third features of the SVR.

To train the SVR, we sample 1700 random documents and split them into 1600/100 documents for the training and test partitions, respectively.

---

[5]The 100 documents used for this task were different to the ones used in Section 5.1.

[6]http://www.lemurproject.org

[7]$N = 10$.

[8]That is, if $m = 5$, we compute pairwise probabilities using the top-5 topic words.

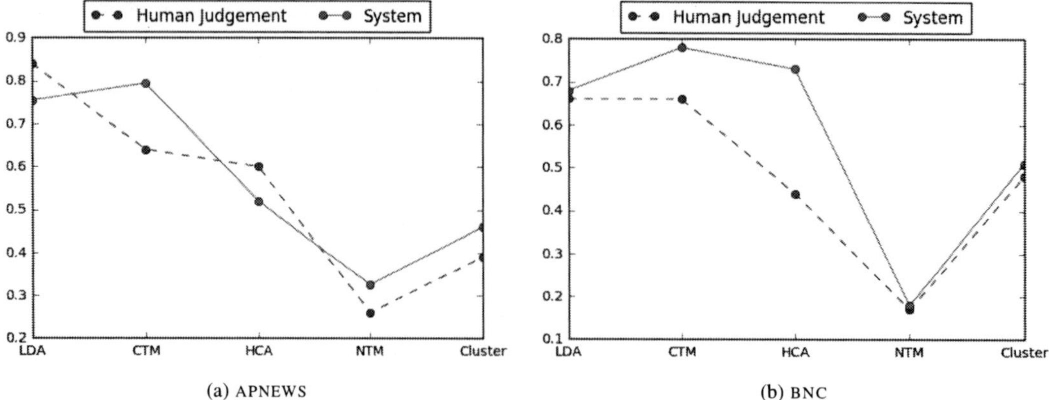

(a) APNEWS   (b) BNC

Figure 3: Mean Model Precision Comparison

The test documents are the same 100 documents that were previously used for intruder topics (Section 5.1). As the intruder topics are artificially generated, we can sample additional documents to create a larger training set for the SVR; the ability to generate arbitrary training data is a strength of our method.

We pool together all 5 topic models when training the SVR, thereby generating 8000 training and 500 development and testing instances for each dataset. For each document, the SVR is trained to rank the topics in terms of their likelihood of being an intruder topic.[9] The top-ranking topic is selected as the system-predicted intruder word, and model precision is computed as before (Section 5.1).[10]

6.2 System results

In Figure 3, we present the human vs. system mean model precision on the test partition for each of the topic models. We see that the trend line for the system model precision very closely tracks that of human model precision. In general, the best systems — `lda` and `ctm` — and the worst systems — `ntm` and `cluster` — are predicted correctly. The correlation between the two is very high, at $r = 0.88$ and 0.87 for APNEWS and BNC, respectively. This suggests that the automated method is a reliable means of evaluating document-level topic model quality.

---

[9]We use the default hyper-parameter values for the SVR ($C = 0.01$), and hence do no require a development set for tuning.

[10]Note that the system model precision for each document–topic combination is a binary value as there is only 1 system — as opposed to multiple annotators — selecting an intruder word.

7 Discussion

To better understand the differences between human- and system-predicted intruder topics, we present a number of documents and their associated topics in Table 7, focusing specifically on: (a) intruder topics that humans struggle to identify but our automatic method reliably detects; and (b) conversely, intruder topics which humans readily identify but our method struggles to detect.

Looking at the topics across the two types of errors, we notice that there are often multiple "bad" topics for these documents: occasionally the annotators are able to single out the worst topic while the system fails (1st and 2nd document), but sometimes the opposite happens (3rd and 4th document). In the first case, the top-ranking topic (*church, gay, ...*) from the topic model is associated with the document because of the service, but actually capturing a very different aspect of religion to what is discussed in the document, which leads our method astray. A similar effect is seen with the second document. In the case of the third and fourth documents, there is actually content further down in the document which is relevant to the topics the human annotators select, but it is not apparent in the document snippet presented to the annotators. That is, the effect is caused by resource limitations for the annotation task, that our automated method does not suffer from.

When we aggregate the top-level model precision values for a topic model, these differences are averaged out (hence the strong correlation in Section 6.2), but these qualitative analyses reveal that there are still slight disparities between human

Error Type: High human MP Low system MP	**Document**	more than 2,000 attendees are expected to attend public funeral services for former nevada gov. kenny guinn . a catholic mass on tuesday morning will be followed by a memorial reception at palace station . the two-term governor who served from 1999 to 2007 died thursday after falling from the roof of his las vegas home while making repairs . he was 73 . guinn 's former chief of staff pete ernaut says attendance to the services will be limited only by the size of the venues . services start at 10 a.m. at st. joseph , husband of mary roman catholic church ...
	Topics	0: church gay marriage religious catholic same-sex couples pastor members bishop 1: died family funeral honor memorial father death wife cemetery son 2: casino las vegas nevada gambling casinos ford vehicles cars car X: students college student campus education tuition universities colleges high degree
	Document	the milwaukee art museum is exhibiting more than 70 works done by 19th century portrait painter thomas sully . it 's the first retrospective of the artist in 30 years and the first to present the artist 's portraits and subject pictures . sully was known for employing drama and theatricality to his works . in some of his full-length portraits , he composed his figures as if they were onstage . some of his subjects even seem to be trying to directly engage the viewer . milwaukee art museum director daniel keegan says the exhibit provides a new look ...
	Topics	0: china art chinese arts artist painting artists cuba world beijing 1: show music film movie won festival tickets game band play 2: online information internet book video media facebook phone computer technology X: kelley family letter leave absence left united jay weeks director
Error Type: Low human MP High system MP	**Document**	(ap) ? the west virginia lottery is celebrating its 28th birthday by doing what it does best : awarding large sums of money . the lottery will mark the milestone on thursday by giving away prizes of $ 1 million , $ 100,000 and $ 10,000 . the three finalists were selected out of thousands of entries from the lottery 's monopoly millionaire instant game . the finalists are josh schoolcraft of given , douglas schafer of wheeling and todd kingrey of charleston . all three are due at lottery headquarters in charleston to collect their winnings ...
	Topics	0: jackpot powerball mega lottery lotto jackpots prizes ticket megaplier tickets 1: mingo earl wheeling virginia ap charleston wvu huntington coalfields rockefeller 2: museum artifacts exhibit paintings artwork historical curator sculpture exhibition exhibits X: abercrombie ridley solace daley enclosures hobbyists hawaiian seventeen secondhand probate
	Document	a 75-year-old driver has died after a collision near o'neill in northern nebraska . the holt county sheriff 's office says the accident occurred wednesday afternoon , less than a mile east of o'neill . the office says thomas schneider halted at a stop sign and then turned east onto nebraska highway 108 . but he apparently turned too wide and went into the oncoming lane . his vehicle struck a westbound vehicle driven by 52-year-old gerald kemp , of niobrara . schneider was pronounced at the scene . the sheriff 's office says kemp suffered no visible injuries ...
	Topics	0: officers shot car shooting officer sheriff woman died killed hospital 1: service weather area storm miles airport snow river bridge emergency 2: prison prosecutors charges guilty trial judge case charged murder pleaded X: toll road rocky carpenter hogan indiana long harvey private director

Table 7: Document and topic examples for two types of errors. "MP" denotes model precision, "X" the intruder topic, and the indices the ranking of the topics. Topics highlighted in pink (yellow) are those incorrectly selected by the system (humans) as intruder topics.

annotators and the automated method in intruder topic selection.

To further understand how the topics relate to the documents in different topic models, we present documents with the corresponding topics for different topic models in Table 8.

In the human annotation task, we use the top-10 most probable words to represent a topic. We use 10 words as it is the standard approach to visualising topics, but this is an important hyper-parameter which needs to be investigated further (Lau and Baldwin, 2016), which we leave to future work.

8 Conclusion

We demonstrate empirically that there can be large discrepancies between topic coherence and document–topic associations. By way of designing an artificial topic model, we showed that a topic model can simultaneously produce topics that are coherent but be largely undescriptive of the document collection. We propose a method to automatically predict document-level topic quality and found encouraging correlation with manual evaluation, suggesting that it can be used as an alternative approach for extrinsic topic model evaluation.

lda	**Document**	more than 2,000 attendees are expected to attend public funeral services for former nevada gov. kenny guinn . a catholic mass on tuesday morning will be followed by a memorial reception at palace station . the two-term governor who served from 1999 to 2007 died thursday after falling from the roof of his las vegas home while making repairs . he was 73 . guinn 's former chief of staff pete ernaut says attendance to the services will be limited only by the size of the venues . services start at 10 a.m. at st. joseph , husband of mary roman catholic church ...
	Topics	0: church gay marriage religious catholic same-sex couples pastor members bishop 1: died family funeral honor memorial father death wife cemetery son
hca	**Document**	usa today founder al neuharth has died in cocoa beach , florida . he was 89 . the news was announced friday by usa today and by the newseum , which he also founded . neuharth changed american newspapers by putting easy-to-read articles and bright graphics in his national daily publication , which he began in 1982 when he ran the gannett co. newspaper group . he wanted to create a bright , breezy , fun newspaper that would catch people 's attention and not take itself too seriously. its annual revenues increased from 200 million to more than 3 billion ...
	Topics	0: honorary commencement philanthropist journalism distinguished honored bachelor pulitzer doctorate harvard 1: shortfall premiums budget reductions cuts shortfalls salaries pensions revenues budgets
ctm	**Document**	a teenage driver who survived a southeastern indiana crash that killed three other youths will spend 90 days in juvenile detention and surrender his driver 's license until age 21 . the 17-year-old driver admitted to charges of reckless homicide and reckless driving during a ripley county juvenile court hearing thursday in versailles , indiana state police sgt. noel houze jr. told the associated press . the teenager choked back sobs throughout the half-hour hearing . the teen will be sent to a juvenile facility in muncie . he also must complete 350 hours of community service ..
	Topics	0: officers shot car shooting officer sheriff woman died killed hospital 1: prison prosecutors charges guilty trial judge case charged murder pleaded
ntm	**Document**	a judge in will county has approved further testing on the coat an oswego man was wearing when his wife and three children were found shot to death in 2007 . christopher vaughn is accused of killing his family inside their suv , which was parked on a frontage road along interstate 55 . authorities found kimberly vaughn shot to death , along with their children , 12-year-old abigayle , 11-year-old cassandra and 8-year-old blake . assistant state 's attorney mike fitzgerald on monday said prosecutors asked for more dna testing on the coat ...
	Topics	0: arraigned burglarizing arrested bigamy detectives motorcyclist arraignment coroner accomplice fondled 1: quarterly pretax dividend profit annualized earnings profits stockholders writedown premarket
cluster	**Document**	a southwest idaho district court judge has been arrested on suspicion of misdemeanor driving under the influence . the idaho press-tribune reports (http://bit.ly/npiita) that 3rd district court judge renae hoff was taken into custody early saturday morning in meridian . meridian deputy police chief tracy basterrechea says an officer pulled the 61-year-old hoff over after she failed to " maintain the lane of travel . "
	Topics	0: suppliers manufacturers companies importers supplier exporters distributors market wholesalers export 1: deported deportation incarcerated prison detention jail parole imprisoned convicts incarceration

Table 8: Example documents and their corresponding topics for different topic models

Acknowledgements

This research was supported in part by the Australian Research Council.

References

Nikos Aletras and Mark Stevenson. 2013. Evaluating topic coherence using distributional semantics. In *Proceedings of the Tenth International Workshop on Computational Semantics (IWCS-10)*. Potsdam, Germany, pages 13–22.

David Blei and John Lafferty. 2006. Correlated topic models. *Advances in Neural Information Processing Systems* 18.

David M Blei, Andrew Y Ng, and Michael I Jordan. 2003. Latent Dirichlet allocation. *Journal of Machine Learning Research* 3:993–1022.

Wray L Buntine and Swapnil Mishra. 2014. Experiments with non-parametric topic models. In *Proceedings of the 20th ACM SIGKDD International Conference on Knowledge Discovery and Data Mining*. pages 881–890.

Lou Burnard. 1995. User guide for the British National Corpus.

Ziqiang Cao, Sujian Li, Yang Liu, Wenjie Li, and Heng

Ji. 2015. A novel neural topic model and its supervised extension. In *Proceedings of AAAI 2015*. pages 2210–2216.

Allison June-Barlow Chaney and David M. Blei. 2012. Visualizing topic models. In *Proceedings of the 6th International Conference on Weblogs and Social Media (ICWSM 2012)*. Dublin, Ireland.

Jonathan Chang, Sean Gerrish, Chong Wang, Jordan L. Boyd-Graber, and David M. Blei. 2009. Reading tea leaves: How humans interpret topic models. In *Advances in Neural Information Processing Systems 21 (NIPS-09)*. Vancouver, Canada, pages 288–296.

Changyou Chen, Lan Du, and Wray Buntine. 2011. Sampling table configurations for the hierarchical poisson-dirichlet process. *Machine Learning and Knowledge Discovery in Databases* pages 296–311.

Gabriel Doyle and Charles Elkan. 2009. Accounting for burstiness in topic models. In *Proceedings of the 26th Annual International Conference on Machine Learning*. pages 281–288.

Anjie Fang, Craig Macdonald, Iadh Ounis, and Philip Habel. 2016. Using word embedding to evaluate the coherence of topics from Twitter data. In *Proceedings of the 39th International ACM SIGIR conference on Research and Development in Information Retrieval*. pages 1057–1060.

Thorsten Joachims. 2006. Training linear SVMs in linear time. In *Proceedings of the 12th ACM SIGKDD International Conference on Knowledge Discovery and Data Mining*. pages 217–226.

Jey Han Lau and Timothy Baldwin. 2016. The sensitivity of topic coherence evaluation to topic cardinality. In *Proceedings of NAACL-HLT*. pages 483–487.

Jey Han Lau, David Newman, and Timothy Baldwin. 2014. Machine reading tea leaves: Automatically evaluating topic coherence and topic model quality. In *Proceedings of EACL 2014*. pages 530–539.

Christopher D. Manning, Mihai Surdeanu, John Bauer, Jenny Finkel, Steven J. Bethard, and David McClosky. 2014. The Stanford CoreNLP natural language processing toolkit. In *Association for Computational Linguistics (ACL) System Demonstrations*. Baltimore, USA, pages 55–60.

Tomas Mikolov, Kai Chen, Greg Corrado, and Jeffrey Dean. 2013a. Efficient estimation of word representations in vector space. In *Proceedings of Workshop at the International Conference on Learning Representations, 2013*. Scottsdale, USA.

Tomas Mikolov, Ilya Sutskever, Kai Chen, Greg S Corrado, and Jeff Dean. 2013b. Distributed representations of words and phrases and their compositionality. In *Advances in Neural Information Processing Systems*. pages 3111–3119.

David Mimno, Hanna Wallach, Edmund Talley, Miriam Leenders, and Andrew McCallum. 2011. Optimizing semantic coherence in topic models. In *Proceedings of the 2011 Conference on Empirical Methods in Natural Language Processing (EMNLP 2011)*. Edinburgh, UK, pages 262–272.

David Newman, Timothy Baldwin, Lawrence Cavedon, Sarvnaz Karimi, David Martinez, and Justin Zobel. 2010a. Visualizing document collections and search results using topic mapping. *Journal of Web Semantics* 8(2–3):169–175.

David Newman, Jey Han Lau, Karl Grieser, and Timothy Baldwin. 2010b. Automatic evaluation of topic coherence. In *Human Language Technologies: The 2010 Annual Conference of the North American Chapter of the Association for Computational Linguistics*. pages 100–108.

Michal Rosen-Zvi, Thomas Griffiths, Mark Steyvers, and Padhraic Smyth. 2004. The author-topic model for authors and documents. In *Proceedings of the 20th Conference on Uncertainty in Artificial Intelligence*. pages 487–494.

Alison Smith, Tak Yeon Lee, Forough Poursabzi-Sangdeh, Jordan Boyd-Graber, Kevin Seppi, Niklas Elmqvist, and Leah Findlater. 2017. Evaluating visual representations for topic understanding and their effects on manually generated labels. *Transactions of the Association for Computational Linguistics* 5:1–15.

Hanna M Wallach, Iain Murray, Ruslan Salakhutdinov, and David Mimno. 2009. Evaluation methods for topic models. In *Proceedings of the 26th International Conference on Machine Learning (ICML 2009)*. Montreal, Canada, pages 1105–1112.

Chong Wang and David M. Blei. 2011. Collaborative topic modeling for recommending scientific articles. In *Proceedings of the 17th ACM SIGKDD International Conference on Knowledge Discovery and Data Mining*. pages 448–456.

Robust Coreference Resolution and Entity Linking on Dialogues:
Character Identification on TV Show Transcripts

Henry Y. Chen, Ethan Zhou, Jinho D. Choi
Math and Computer Science
Emory University
Atlanta, GA 30322, USA
{henry.chen, ethan.zhou, jinho.choi}@emory.edu

Abstract

This paper presents a novel approach to character identification, that is an entity linking task that maps mentions to characters in dialogues from TV show transcripts. We first augment and correct several cases of annotation errors in an existing corpus so the corpus is clearer and cleaner for statistical learning. We also introduce the agglomerative convolutional neural network that takes groups of features and learns mention and mention-pair embeddings for coreference resolution. We then propose another neural model that employs the embeddings learned and creates cluster embeddings for entity linking. Our coreference resolution model shows comparable results to other state-of-the-art systems. Our entity linking model significantly outperforms the previous work, showing the F1 score of 86.76% and the accuracy of 95.30% for character identification.

1 Introduction

Character identification (Chen and Choi, 2016) is a task that identifies each mention as a character in a multiparty dialogue.[1] Let a mention be a nominal referring to a human (e.g., *she*, *mom*, *Judy*), and an entity be a character in the dialogue. The objective is to assign each mention to an entity, who may or may not appear as a speaker in the dialogue. For the example in Table 1, the mention *comedian* is not one of the speakers in the dialogue; nonetheless, it clearly refers to a real person that may appear in some other dialogues. Identifying such mentions as actual characters requires cross-document entity resolution, which makes this task challenging.

Character identification can be viewed as a task of entity linking. Most of the previous work on entity linking focuses on Wikification (Mihalcea and Csomai, 2007a; Ratinov et al., 2011a; Guo et al., 2013). Unlike Wikification, entities in this task have no precompiled information from a knowledge base, which is another challenging aspect. This task is similar to coreference resolution in the sense that it groups mentions into entities, but distinct because it requires the identification of mention groups as real entities. Furthermore, even if it can be tackled as a coreference resolution task, only a few coreference resolution systems are designed to handle dialogues well (Rocha, 1999; Niraula et al., 2014) although several state-of-the-art systems have been proposed for the general domain (Peng et al., 2015; Clark and Manning, 2016; Wiseman et al., 2016).

Due to the nature of multiparty dialogues where speakers take turns to complete a context, character identification becomes a critical step to adapt higher-level NLP tasks (e.g., question answering, summarization) to this domain. This task can also bring another level of sophistication to intelligent personal assistants and intelligent tutoring systems. Perhaps the most challenging aspect comes from colloquial writing that consists of ironies, metaphors, or rhetorical questions. Despite all the challenges, we believe that the output of this task will enhance inference on dialogue contexts by providing finer-grained information about individuals.

In this paper, we augment and correct the existing corpus for character identification, and propose an end-to-end deep-learning system that combines neural models for coreference resolution and entity linking to tackle the task of character identification. The updated corpus and the source code of our models are published and publicly available.[2] This combined system utilizes the strengths from both

---

[1]The dialogues are extracted from TV show transcripts by the previous work (Chen and Choi, 2016).

[2]nlp.mathcs.emory.edu/character-mining/

Proceedings of the 21st Conference on Computational Natural Language Learning (CoNLL 2017), pages 216–225,
Vancouver, Canada, August 3 - August 4, 2017. ©2017 Association for Computational Linguistics

Speaker	Utterance
Joey	Yeah, right! ... You$_1$ serious?
Rachel	Everything you$_2$ need to know is in that first kiss.
Chandler	Yeah. For us$_3$, it's like the stand-up comedian$_4$ you$_5$ have to sit through before the main dude$_6$ starts.
Ross	It's not that we$_7$ don't like the comedian$_8$, it's that ... that's not why we$_9$ bought the ticket.

$\{$You$_1\} \rightarrow$ *Rachel*, $\{$us$_3$, we$_{7,9}\} \rightarrow$ *Collective*, $\{$you$_{2,5}\} \rightarrow$ *General*, $\{$comedian$_{4,8}\} \rightarrow$ *Generic*, $\{$dude$_6\} \rightarrow$ *Other*

Table 1: An example of a multiparty dialogue extracted from the corpus.

models. We introduce a novel approach, agglomerative convolution neural network, for coreference resolution to learn mention, mention-pair, and cluster embeddings, and the results are taken as input to our entity linking model that assigns mentions to their real entities. Entities, including main characters and recurring support characters, are selected from a TV show to mimic a realistic scenario. To the best of our knowledge, this is the first end-to-end model that performs character identification on multiparty dialogues.

2 Related Work

The latest coreference systems employ advanced context features in tandem with deep networks to achieve state-of-the-art performance (Clark and Manning, 2016; Wiseman et al., 2015). Since our task is similar to coreference resolution, we take a similar approach to feature engineering by building mention and cluster embeddings with word embeddings (Clark and Manning, 2016) and include additional mention features described by Wiseman et al. (2015). We are motivated to use convolutional networks through the work of Wu and Ma (2017), but we distinguish our approach by using deep convolution to build embeddings for character identification.

Entity linking has traditionally relied heavily on knowledge databases, most notably, Wikipedia, for entities (Mihalcea and Csomai, 2007b; Ratinov et al., 2011b; Gattani et al., 2013; Francis-Landau et al., 2016).[3] Although we do not make use of knowledge bases, our task is closely aligned to entity linking. Recent advances in entity linking are also applicable to our task since we see Francis-Landau et al. (2016) use convolutional nets to capture semantic similarity between a mention and an entity by comparing context of the mention with the description of the entity. This work validates our usage of deep learning for character identification.

Dialogue tracking has been an expanding task as shown by the Dialogue State Tracking Challenges hosted by Microsoft (Kim et al., 2015). That an ongoing conversation can be dynamically tracked (Henderson et al., 2013) is exciting and applicable to our task because the state of a conversation may yield significant hints for entity linking and coreference resolution. Speaker identification, a task similar to character identification, has already shown some success with partial dialogue tracking by dynamically identifying speakers at each turn in a dialogue using conditional random field models.

3 Corpus

The character identification corpus created by Chen and Choi (2016) includes entity annotation of personal mentions specific to the domain of multiparty dialogues. While the corpus covers a large amount of entities that appear in the first two seasons of the TV show, *Friends*, some of its annotation remains ambiguous, particularly around the label *Unknown*.

An example of *Unknown* mentions in a snippet of a conversation is provided in Table 1. Mentions *comedian*$_{4,8}$ and *dude*$_6$ are originally labeled *Unknown*, but they are two different entities such that their labels should be distinguished. Even though their entities are not immediately identifiable, the *Unknown* label provides no clarity; thus, mentions under this label needs to be subcategorized. We propose to disambiguate these *Unknown* mentions (Section 3.2), comprising 10% of the annotation. Such disambiguation allows finer-grained categories of entity annotations of mentions. We believe the resultant annotations are more realistic and can be used to train more robust model on character identification.

3.1 Corpus Correction

Before disambiguating the corpus, we find some recurring data malformations and errors in mention detection within the corpus. For example:

---

[3]This task is known as 'Wikification'.

Rachel: (To *guy* with a phone) Hello, excuse me.

The underlined action note is accidentally included in the utterance as a part of the dialogue due to a missing parentheses, and the mention *guy* is consequently incorporated into the corpus. These malformations are fixed, and mentions included are removed from the corpus manually before disambiguation. The correction is necessary since the inclusion of action notes is inconsistent throughout the corpus, and they are removed to avoid confusion for our models.

3.2 Corpus Disambiguation

Three labels are introduced to disambiguate *Unknown* mentions: *General*, *Generic*, and *Other*. *Generic* provides abstract groupings for unidentifiable entities, and each group is assigned a unique number for differentiation:

- *General*: Mention used in reference to a general case (e.g., $you_{2,5}$ in Table 1).

- *Generic*: Mention referring to a unidentifiable entity (e.g., $comedian_{4,8}$ in Table 1).

- *Other*: Mention referred to insignificant singleton entity (e.g., $dude_6$ in Table 1).

We perform this disambiguation manually with two main guidelines: only mentions originally labeled *Unknown* are included, and the labels introduced above are provided to annotators in addition to the known entities. We limit the *Generic* mention groups to 5 per iteration of disambiguation for simplicity, and the scenes that requires more than 5 groups are recursively annotated until all unknowns are disambiguated. Unlike the previous work, our annotators are familiar with the TV show, and the task takes about 3 weeks to complete.

	P	S	C	G	N	O	Σ
F1	5,101	2,610	1,259	109	152	184	9,306
F2	5,312	2,432	1,280	42	111	167	9,304
Σ	10,413	5,042	2,388	151	263	351	18,608

Table 2: Counts of disambiguated mentions. P/S: main and secondary character entities. C/G/N/O: *Collective/General/Generic/Other*.

4 Coreference Resolution

The task of character identification needs rich features extracted from mention clusters generated by a coreference resolution system. Thus, the end result of this task largely depends on the quality of the coreference resolution model. Several coreference resolution systems have been proposed and shown state-of-the-art performance (Pradhan et al., 2012); however, they are not necessarily designed for the genre of multiparty dialogue, where each document comprises utterances from multiple speakers.

This section describes a novel approach to coreference resolution using Convolutional Neural Networks (CNN). Our model takes groups of features incorporating several dialogue aspects, feeds them into deep convolution layers, and dynamically generates mention embeddings and mention-pair embeddings, which are used to create the cluster embeddings that significantly improve the performance of our entity linking model (Section 5).

4.1 Agglomerative CNN

Our coreference resolution model, Agglomerative Convolutional Neural Network (ACNN), takes advantage of deep layers in CNN. The model is called *agglomerative* since it aggregates multiple feature groups into several convolution layers for the generation of mention and mention-pair embeddings. Each layer aims to consolidate and learn different combinations of the input features, and additional features are included at each layer. The unique nature of our model allows incremental feature aggregations to create more robust embeddings. Figure 1 illustrates the complete architecture of ACNN.

The first part of the network learns the mention embedding for each of two mentions compared for a coreferent relation. Given two feature maps $\phi_e^k(m)$ and $\phi_d(m)$ where m is a mention, $\phi_e^k(m)$ extracts the embedding features based on word embeddings, and $\phi_d(m)$ extracts the discrete features (Table 3). The first convolution layer CONV_1^k with n-gram filters of size d is applied to each embedding group k, and the result from each filter is max-pooled to generate a feature vector $\in \mathcal{R}^{1 \times d}$. The second convolution layer CONV_2 is then applied to the 3D feature matrix $\in \mathcal{R}^{n \times d \times k}$ from the previous convolution layer on all embedding groups. The result of CONV_2 is max-pooled and concatenated with discrete features extracted by $\phi_d(m)$ to form the mention embedding $\mathbf{r}_s(m)$, defined as follows:

$$\mathbf{r}_s(m) = \text{CONV}_2\left(\begin{bmatrix} \text{CONV}_1^1(\phi_e^1(m)) \\ \vdots \\ \text{CONV}_1^k(\phi_e^k(m)) \end{bmatrix} \right) \| \phi_d(m)$$

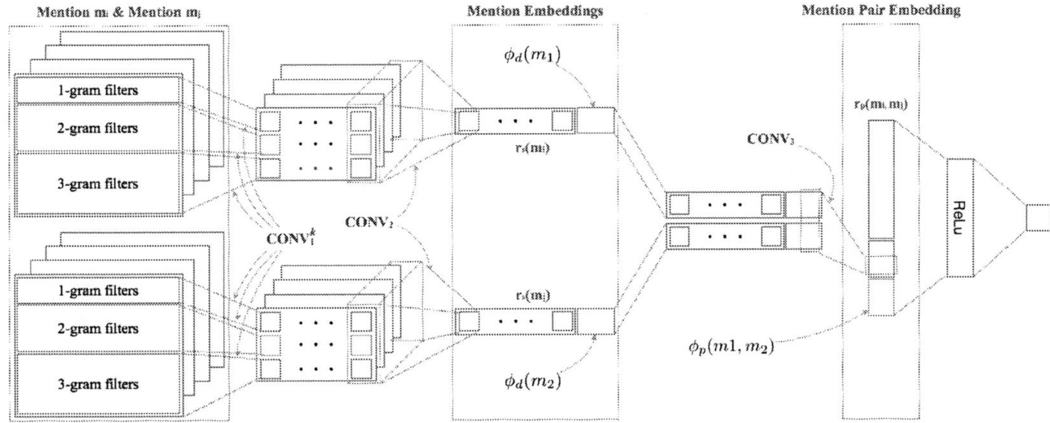

Figure 1: The overview of our agglomerative convolutional neural network.

The second part of the network utilizes the learned mention embedding $\mathbf{r}_s(m)$ to create the mention-pair embedding. Another feature map $\phi_p(m_i, m_j)$ is defined to extract pairwise features between mentions m_i and m_j (Table 3). The third convolution layer CONV_3 is applied to the stacked mention embeddings, $\mathbf{r}_s(m_i)$ and $\mathbf{r}_s(m_j)$. The result is max-pooled and concatenated with the pairwise features extracted by $\phi_p(m_i, m_j)$ to form the mention-pair embedding $\mathbf{r}_p(m_i, m_j)$, defined as follows:

$$\mathbf{r}_p(m_i, m_j) = \text{CONV}_3\left(\begin{bmatrix} \mathbf{r}_s(m_i) \\ \mathbf{r}_s(m_j) \end{bmatrix}\right) \parallel \phi_p(m_i, m_j)$$

The learned mention-pair embedding is put through the hidden layer with the linear rectifier activation function (ReLu) before applying the sigmoid function $\sigma(m_i, m_j)$ to determine the coreferent relation between mentions m_i and m_j, defined as follows:

$$\mathbf{h}(x) = \text{ReLU}(w_h \cdot x + b_h)$$
$$\sigma(m_i, m_j) = \text{sigmoid}(w_s \cdot \mathbf{h}(\mathbf{r}_p(m_i, m_j)) + b_s)$$

The purpose of the sigmoid function $\sigma(m_i, m_j)$ is twofold. For each mention m_i, it performs binary classifications between m_i and m_j where $j \in [1, i)$. If $\max(\sigma(m_i, m_j)) < 0.5$, the model considers no coreferent relation between m_i and any mention prior to it, and create a new cluster containing only m_i s.t. m_i becomes a singleton for the moment. If $\max(\sigma(m_i, m_j)) \geq 0.5$, m_i is put to the existing cluster $\mathcal{C}_{m_k}$ that m_k belongs to, where m_k is $\arg_j \max(\sigma(m_i, m_j))$. This formalism of mention clustering is defined as follows:

- If $\forall_{1 \leq j < i}. \max(\sigma(m_i, m_j)) < 0.5$, then create a new cluster $\mathcal{C}_{m_i}$.

- If $\exists_{1 \leq j < i}. \max(\sigma(m_i, m_j)) \geq 0.5$, then $\mathcal{C}_{m_k} \leftarrow \mathcal{C}_{m_k} \cup \{m_i\}$, where $m_k = \arg_j \max(\sigma(m_i, m_j))$.

Table 3 shows feature templates used for our ACNN model. Sentence and utterance embeddings are the average vectors of all word embeddings in the sentence and utterance, respectively. Speaker embeddings are randomly generated using the Gaussian distribution. Gender and plurality information are from Bergsma and Lin (2006), and word animacy is from Durrett and Klein (2013).

Map	Features
$\phi_e^1(m)$	Embeddings of 1st three words in m
$\phi_e^2(m)$	Embeddings of 3 proceeding words of m
	Embeddings of 3 succeeding words of m
	Average embedding of all words in m
$\phi_e^3(m)$	Embeddings of 3 proceeding sentences
	Embeddings of 1 succeeding sentence
	Embedding of the current sentence
$\phi_e^4(m)$	Embeddings of 3 proceeding utterances
	Embeddings of 1 succeeding utterances
	Embeddings of the current utterance
$\phi_d(m)$	Avg. gender info. of all words in m
	Avg. plurality info. of all words in m
	Avg. word animacy of all words in m
	Embedding of the current speaker
	Embeddings of the previous 2 speakers
$\phi_p(m_i, m_j)$	Exact string match between m_i and m_j
	Relaxed string match between m_i and m_j
	Speaker match between m_i and m_j
	Mention distance between m_i and m_j
	Sentence distance between m_i and m_j

Table 3: Complete feature templates for ACNN. $\phi_e^k(m)$: embedding features, $\phi_d(m)$: discrete features, $\phi_p(m_i, m_j)$: pairwise features.

4.2 Configuration

For our experiments, word embeddings of dimension 50 are trained with FastText (Bojanowski et al., 2016) on the aggregation of New York Times,[4] Wikipedia,[5] and Amazon reviews.[6] The `tanh` activation function and a filter size of 280 is used for all convolution layers. A dropout rate of 0.8 is applied to all max-pooled convoluted results, and ℓ_2 regularization is applied to the sigmoid function. The hidden layer has the same dimension as the filter size. Binary labels of 0 and 1 are assigned to each mention-to-mention pair based on the gold cluster information. The model is trained on a mean squared error loss function with the RMSprop optimizer.

5 Entity Linking

Coreference resolution groups mentions into clusters; however, it does not assign character labels to the clusters, which is required for character identification. This section describes our entity linking model that takes the mention embeddings and the mention-pair embeddings generated ACNN and classifies each mention to one of the character labels (Figure 3). These embeddings are used to create cluster and cluster-mention embeddings through pooling, which give a significant improvement to character identification when included as features in our linker (Section 6).

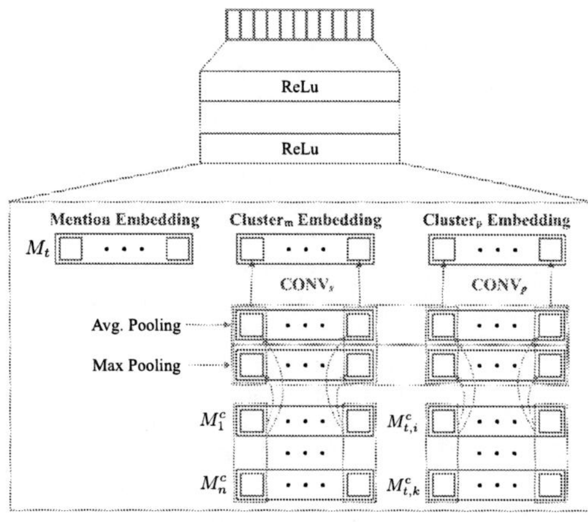

Figure 2: The overview of our entity linking model. Cluster$_m$ and Cluster$_p$ embeddings are derived from mention and mention-pair embeddings, resp.

---

[4] `catalog.ldc.upenn.edu/ldc2008t19`
[5] `dumps.wikimedia.org/enwiki/`
[6] `snap.stanford.edu/data/web-Amazon.html`

Figure 2 illustrates our entity linking model based on a feed-forward neural network with two hidden layers. For each mention m, the model takes the mention embedding $\mathbf{r}_s(m)$ and two cluster embeddings derived from mention embeddings and mention-pair embeddings within the cluster $\mathcal{C}(m)$ (Section 5.2) and classifies m into one of the entity labels using the Softmax regression.

5.1 Cluster Embedding

Two types of cluster embeddings are derived to capture cluster information. Given a mention m and its cluster $\mathcal{C}_m$, cluster embedding $\mathbf{R}_s(\mathcal{C}_m)$ represents the collective mention embedding of all mentions within $\mathcal{C}_m$, and mention-cluster embedding $\mathbf{R}_p(\mathcal{C}_m, m)$ represents the collective mention-pair embedding between m and all the other mentions in $\mathcal{C}_m$ that are compared to m during coreference resolution ($\forall_i.\, m_i \in \mathcal{C}_m$):

$$\mathbf{R}_s(\mathcal{C}_m) = [\mathbf{r}_s(m_1), \mathbf{r}_s(m_2), ..., \mathbf{r}_s(m_{|\mathcal{C}_m|})]$$
$$\mathbf{R}_p(\mathcal{C}_m, m) = [\mathbf{r}_p(m_i, m) \mid m_i \neq m]$$

CONV_s and CONV_p are two separate convolution layers with unigram filters using the `tanh` activation. The results from these layers are max-pooled. The cluster embedding $\mathbf{r}_s(\mathcal{C}_m)$ and the mention-cluster embedding $\mathbf{r}_p(\mathcal{C}_m, m)$ are defined as follows:

$$\mathbf{r}_s(\mathcal{C}_m) = \text{CONV}_s\left(\begin{bmatrix}\texttt{avg\_pool}(\mathbf{R}_s(\mathcal{C}_m)) \\ \texttt{max\_pool}(\mathbf{R}_s(\mathcal{C}_m))\end{bmatrix}\right)$$

$$\mathbf{r}_p(\mathcal{C}_m, m) = \text{CONV}_p\left(\begin{bmatrix}\texttt{avg\_pool}(\mathbf{R}_p(\mathcal{C}_m, m)) \\ \texttt{max\_pool}(\mathbf{R}_p(\mathcal{C}_m, m))\end{bmatrix}\right)$$

The mention embedding, the cluster embedding, and the mention-cluster embedding are concatenated and fed into the network as input, and the scores of all character labels are activated as output.

5.2 Configuration

A dropout layer of rate 0.8 is applied to all inputs. The model is trained as a multi-class classifier with the categorical cross-entropy loss function and the RMSprop optimizer. All hidden layers use the `ReLU` activation function and have the same number of hidden units as the dimension of the mention embeddings. The convolution layers use the same filter sizes as the dimensions of input embeddings.

6 Experiments

Following Chen and Choi (2016), experiments are conducted on two tasks, coreference resolution and

Model	Episode-Level					Scene-Level				
	MUC	B^3	CEAF$_e$	μ	|C|	MUC	B^3	CEAF$_e$	μ	|C|
Clark and Manning (2016)	89.58	69.12	**47.33**	**68.68**	15.19	**90.38**	76.79	56.95	74.70	8.13
Wiseman et al. (2016)	89.80	57.66	45.48	64.31	14.86	89.60	78.08	**65.95**	**77.88**	6.20
This work (ACNN)	**89.92**	**70.33**	44.09	68.11	16.40	88.09	**78.77**	59.72	75.53	7.49

Table 4: Coreference resolution results on the evaluation set (in %).
$\mu = (\text{MUC} + B^3 + \text{CEAF}_e) / 3$. |C|: the average cluster size.

entity linking. Our coreference resolution model shows robust performance compared to other state-of-the-art systems (Section 6.2). Our entity linking model significantly outperforms the heuristic-based approach from the previous work (Section 6.3). All models are evaluated on the gold mentions to focus purely on the analysis of these two tasks.

6.1 Data Split

The corpus is split into the training, development, and evaluation sets (Table 5). For the episode-level, all mentions referring to the same character in each episode are grouped into one cluster (C_{Epi}). For the scene-level, this grouping is done by each scene such that there can be multiple mention clusters that refer to the same character within an episode (C_{Sce}). Ambiguous mention types such as *collective*, *general*, and *other* are excluded from our experiments (Section 3); including those mentions requires developing different resolution models that we shall explore in the future.

	E	S	DC	C_E	C_S	M
TRN	38	362	371	820	2,026	12,842
DEV	3	28	44	58	159	991
TST	5	58	80	113	301	1,885
Total	46	448	444	991	2,486	15,718

Table 5: The training (TRN), development (DEV), and evaluation (TST) sets. E/S/DC/C_E/C_S/M: the numbers of episodes, scenes, distinct characters, episode/scene-level clusters, and mentions.

For entity linking, entity labels are predetermined by collecting characters that appear in all three sets; characters that do not appear in any of the three sets are put together and labeled as *Unknown*. This is reasonable because it is not possible for a statistical model to learn about characters that do not appear in the training set. Likewise, characters that appear in the training set but not in the other sets cannot be developed or evaluated. A total of ten labels are used for entity linking that consist of the top-9

most frequently appeared characters across all sets and *unknown* (Figure 3).

6.2 Coreference Resolution

To benchmark the robustness of our ACNN model (Section 4), two state-of-the-art coreference resolution systems are also experimented. Episode and scene-level models are developed separately for all three systems using the same dataset in Table 5. All system outputs are evaluated with the MUC (Vilain et al., 1995), B^3 (Bagga and Baldwin, 1998), and CEAF$_e$ (Luo, 2005) metrics suggested by the CoNLL'12 shared task (Pradhan et al., 2012). The average score of five trials is reported for each metric to minimize variance because these systems use neural network approaches with random initialization to produce varying results per trial (Table 4).

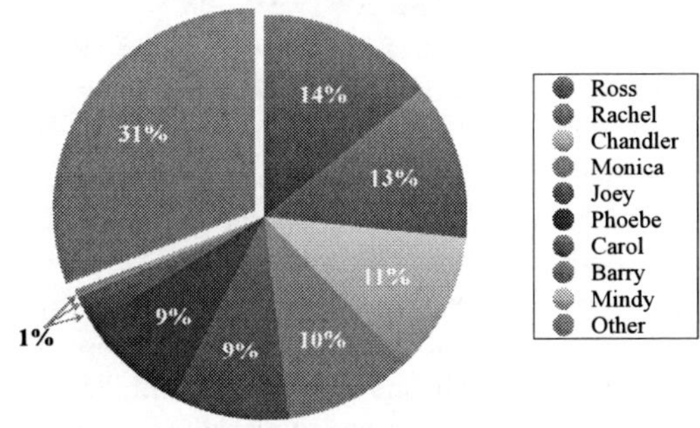

Figure 3: Character labels used for entity linking.

Comparison between the State-of-the-Art

When trained and evaluated on our dataset, both the Stanford (Clark and Manning, 2016) and the Harvard (Wiseman et al., 2016) systems give comparable results to their performance on the CoNLL'12 dataset.[7] The Stanford system using its pre-trained model gives the μ scores of 47.67% and 64.14% for the episode and scene-level respectively, which signifies the importance of the in-domain training data.

---

[7] The Stanford and the Harvard systems reported μ scores of 65.73% and 64.21% on the CoNLL'12 dataset, respectively.

	Model	Ross	Joey	Chandler	Monica	Phoebe	Rachel	Carol	Mindy	Barry	Unk.	Avg	Acc
	B	57.54	80.94	64.91	89.82	87.86	76.47	30.14	0	16.67	70.24	57.46	72.52
E	ME	72.81	80.31	82.43	79.78	82.71	82.94	44.84	20.00	53.05	76.23	67.51	77.80
	CE	93.46	97.90	98.23	95.42	98.24	95.02	100.00	0	95.65	93.71	**86.76**	**95.30**
	B	60.00	69.09	61.05	72.51	57.27	78.77	34.38	0	11.76	67.62	51.24	66.68
S	ME	74.75	81.76	80.71	88.83	84.33	85.43	53.15	20.00	62.90	80.82	71.27	81.07
	CE	91.29	90.64	86.33	94.10	85.41	90.16	65.35	18.71	83.45	85.82	**79.12**	**87.64**

Table 6: Entity linking results on the evaluation set (in %). The F1 score is reported for each character. E/S: episode/scene level. Unk.: *unknown*. Avg: the macro-average F1 score between all characters. Acc: (the number of correctly labeled mentions) / (the total number of mentions).

All systems show higher scores for the scene-level than the episode-level consistently, which confirms the difficulty of this task on larger documents.

Although both systems take advantage of global cluster features, they reveal different strengths on resolving mentions with respect to the cluster size. The Stanford system excels for the episode-level, which is primarily attributed to the cluster-based nature of this system; it is able to find more accurate coreferent chains when the clusters are larger. The Harvard system performs best for the scene-level, indicating that its neural architecture with Long Short-Term Memory cells captures more meaningful cluster features when the clusters are smaller.

Comparison to Agglomerative CNN

In comparison to the other state-of-the-art systems, our ACNN model shows competitive performance; it gives the highest B^3 and comparable μ scores for both episode and scene levels. We measure the average cluster size produced by each system for further analysis ($|C|$ in Table 4). The Harvard system produces smaller clusters than the other two systems. Such a tendency gives more pure clusters, favored by the $CEAF_e$ metric for the scene-level. However, it is prone to breaking up too many links, which leads to poor performance in the B^3 evaluation on the episode-level.

The performance of our model is encouraging although coreference resolution is not the end goal. We design this model to automatically generate mention embeddings and mention-pair embeddings that are used to construct cluster features for entity linking. However, even though this model's success in coreference resolution is not our final objective, its success directly correlates to the success of entity linking because of the similarity between these two tasks. Due to the similar nature of these two tasks, the success of coreference resolution directly correlates to that of entity linking. These embed-dings are the essence of our entity linking model, leading to a huge improvement.

6.3 Entity Linking

The heuristic-based approach proposed by Chen and Choi (2016) is adapted to establish the baseline. Two statistical models are experimented for both the episode and scene levels, one using only mention embeddings and the other using both mention embeddings and cluster embeddings (Section 5). All models are evaluated with the F1 scores of character labels, the macro-average F1 scores between all labels, and the label accuracies. The average scores of five trials are reported in Table 6.

B: Baseline Model

The heuristic-based approach is applied to the mention clusters found by our coreference resolution model. Two rules, [1]proper noun and [2]first-person pronoun matches, are used to assign character labels to all mentions. The label of each cluster is then determined by the majority vote between the mention labels within the cluster. Finally, the cluster label is assigned to all mentions in that cluster. This model performs better when it is applied to the episode-level clusters because larger clusters provide more mention labels, which makes the majority vote more reliable.

ME: Mention Embedding Model

This model takes advantage of the mention embeddings generated by our ACNN model. Compared to the baseline, it gives over a 21% higher average F1 score, and over a 15% higher label accuracy for the episode and the scene levels, respectively. Interestingly, this model shows higher performance for the scene-level, which is not the case for the other two models. This implies that the mention embeddings learned from scene-level documents are more informative than those learned from episode-level ones.

					System						
		Ross	Joey	Chandler	Monica	Phoebe	Rachel	Carol	Mindy	Barry	Unk.	Σ
	Ross	182					7				1	190
	Joey		186								6	192
	Chandler			235								235
	Monica			1	200							201
Gold	Phoebe					141					2	143
	Rachel				2		237					239
	Carol							49				49
	Mindy								0		9	9
	Barry									11		11
	Other	11	1	11	21	4		5		1	562	616
	Σ	193	187	247	223	145	244	54	0	12	580	1,885

Table 7: The confusion matrix between gold and system annotation for all character labels (in #).

This case is also reflected on its coreference resolution performance where the scene-level scores are higher than the episode-level scores (Table 4).

CE: Cluster Embedding Model

While the mention embeddings give a significant improvement over the baseline, further improvement is made when they are coupled with the cluster and mention-cluster embeddings. The episode-level cluster embedding model shows an average F1 score of 86.76% and a label accuracy of 95.30%, which is another 15% improvement, suggesting a practical use of this model in real applications. A couple of important observations are made:

- Cluster and mention-cluster embeddings, although learned during coreference resolution, are crucial for entity linking such that a coreference resolution model specifically designed for multiparty dialogues is necessary to build the state-of-the-art entity linking model for this genre.

- Clusters generated from the episode-level documents provide more information than those from the scene-level do, which aligns with the conclusion made by Chen and Choi (2016).

Error Analysis

An error analysis is performed on the episode-level cluster embedding model. From the confusion matrix in Table 7, two common system errors are detected. First, most of the mispredictions identify *Unknown* as specific characters. Second, the performance on the secondary characters, *Carol, Mindy, and Barry*, is subpar with respect to other entities. This subpar performance likely stems from a paucity of appearances by these secondary characters. For example, *Mindy* constitutes 1% of the dataset (Figure 3) and has only nine occurrences in the evaluation set. Our best model is robust in identifying the primary characters, showing an average F1 score of 96.38% and an accuracy of 98.42% on the evaluation set.

7 Conclusion

In this paper, we explore a relatively new task, character identification on multiparty dialogues, and introduce a novel perspective on approaching the task with coreference resolution and entity linking. We improve and augment finer-grained annotation over the existing corpus that simulates real conversations. We propose a deep convolutional neural network to agglomerate groups of features into mention, mention-pair, cluster, and mention-cluster embeddings that are optimized for entity prediction. Our coreference resolution result shows an improvement on the updated version of the corpus. Our entity linking result reaches to the accuracy that is sufficient for real-world applications.

To the best of our knowledge, our work is the first time that such deep convolution layers have been used for training mention and cluster embeddings. Our results show that the generation of these embeddings is crucial for the success of entity linking on multiparty dialogues. For future work, we will continue to increase the size of the corpus with high-quality and disambiguated annotation. We also wish to improve the embeddings to represent plural and collective mentions, thus we can build upon our entity linking model incorporating many-to-many linkings between entities and mentions.

References

Amit Bagga and Breck Baldwin. 1998. Algorithms for scoring coreference chains. In *The first international conference on language resources and evaluation workshop on linguistics coreference*. Citeseer, volume 1, pages 563–566.

Shane Bergsma and Dekang Lin. 2006. Bootstrapping path-based pronoun resolution. In *Proceedings of the 21st International Conference on Computational Linguistics and 44th Annual Meeting of the Association for Computational Linguistics*. Association for Computational Linguistics, Sydney, Australia, pages 33–40.

Piotr Bojanowski, Edouard Grave, Armand Joulin, and Tomas Mikolov. 2016. Enriching word vectors with subword information. *arXiv preprint arXiv:1607.04606* .

Yu-Hsin Chen and Jinho D. Choi. 2016. Character identification on multiparty conversation: Identifying mentions of characters in tv shows. In *Proceedings of the 17th Annual Meeting of the Special Interest Group on Discourse and Dialogue*. Association for Computational Linguistics, Los Angeles, pages 90–100. http://www.aclweb.org/anthology/W16-3612.

Kevin Clark and Christopher D. Manning. 2016. Deep reinforcement learning for mention-ranking coreference models. In *Proceedings of the 2016 Conference on Empirical Methods in Natural Language Processing*. Association for Computational Linguistics, Austin, Texas, pages 2256–2262. https://aclweb.org/anthology/D16-1245.

Greg Durrett and Dan Klein. 2013. Easy victories and uphill battles in coreference resolution. In *Proceedings of the Conference on Empirical Methods in Natural Language Processing*. Association for Computational Linguistics, Seattle, Washington.

Matthew Francis-Landau, Greg Durrett, and Dan Klein. 2016. Capturing semantic similarity for entity linking with convolutional neural networks. In *Proceedings of the 2016 Conference of the North American Chapter of the Association for Computational Linguistics: Human Language Technologies*. Association for Computational Linguistics, San Diego, California, pages 1256–1261. http://www.aclweb.org/anthology/N16-1150.

Abhishek Gattani, Digvijay S. Lamba, Nikesh Garera, Mitul Tiwari, Xiaoyong Chai, Sanjib Das, Sri Subramaniam, Anand Rajaraman, Venky Harinarayan, and AnHai Doan. 2013. Entity extraction, linking, classification, and tagging for social media: A wikipedia-based approach. *Proc. VLDB Endow.* 6(11):1126–1137. https://doi.org/10.14778/2536222.2536237.

Stephen Guo, Ming-Wei Chang, and Emre Kiciman. 2013. To Link or Not to Link? A Study on End-to-End Tweet Entity Linking. In *Proceedings of the Conference of the North American Chapter of the Association for Computational Linguistics on Human Language Technology*. NAACL, pages 1020–1030.

Matthew Henderson, Blaise Thomson, and Steve Young. 2013. Deep neural network approach for the dialog state tracking challenge. In *Proceedings of the SIGDIAL 2013 Conference*. Association for Computational Linguistics, Metz, France, pages 467–471. http://www.aclweb.org/anthology/W13-4073.

Seokhwan Kim, Luis Fernando DHaro, Rafael E. Banchs, Jason D. Williams, and Matthew Henderson. 2015. The Fourth Dialog State Tracking Challenge. In *Proceedings of the 4th Dialog State Tracking Challenge*. DSTC4.

Xiaoqiang Luo. 2005. On coreference resolution performance metrics. In *Proceedings of the conference on Human Language Technology and Empirical Methods in Natural Language Processing*. Association for Computational Linguistics, pages 25–32.

Rada Mihalcea and Andras Csomai. 2007a. Wikify!: Linking Documents to Encyclopedic Knowledge. In *Proceedings of the Sixteenth ACM Conference on Conference on Information and Knowledge Management*. CIKM'07, pages 233–242.

Rada Mihalcea and Andras Csomai. 2007b. Wikify!: Linking documents to encyclopedic knowledge. In *Proceedings of the Sixteenth ACM Conference on Conference on Information and Knowledge Management*. ACM, New York, NY, USA, CIKM '07, pages 233–242. https://doi.org/10.1145/1321440.1321475.

Nobal B. Niraula, Vasile Rus, Rajendra Banjade, Dan Stefanescu, William Baggett, and Brent Morgan. 2014. The DARE Corpus: A Resource for Anaphora Resolution in Dialogue Based Intelligent Tutoring Systems. In *Proceedings of the Ninth International Conference on Language Resources and Evaluation*. LREC'14, pages 3199–3203.

Haoruo Peng, Kai-Wei Chang, and Dan Roth. 2015. A Joint Framework for Coreference Resolution and Mention Head Detection. In *Proceedings of the 9th Conference on Computational Natural Language Learning*. CoNLL'15, pages 12–21.

Sameer Pradhan, Alessandro Moschitti, Nianwen Xue, Olga Uryupina, and Yuchen Zhang. 2012. CoNLL-2012 Shared Task: Modeling Multilingual Unrestricted Coreference in OntoNotes. In *Proceedings of the Sixteenth Conference on Computational Natural Language Learning: Shared Task*. CoNLL'12, pages 1–40.

Lev Ratinov, Dan Roth, Doug Downey, and Mike Anderson. 2011a. Local and Global Algorithms for Disambiguation to Wikipedia. In *Proceedings of the 49th Annual Meeting of the Association for Computational Linguistics: Human Language Technologies*. ACL'11, pages 1375–1384.

Lev Ratinov, Dan Roth, Doug Downey, and Mike Anderson. 2011b. Local and global algorithms for disambiguation to wikipedia. In *Proceedings of the 49th Annual Meeting of the Association for Computational Linguistics: Human Language Technologies - Volume 1*. Association for Computational Linguistics, Stroudsburg, PA, USA, HLT '11, pages 1375–1384. http://dl.acm.org/citation.cfm?id=2002472.2002642.

Marco Rocha. 1999. Coreference Resolution in Dialogues in English and Portuguese. In *Proceedings of the Workshop on Coreference and Its Applications*. CorefApp'99, pages 53–60.

Marc Vilain, John Burger, John Aberdeen, Dennis Connolly, and Lynette Hirschman. 1995. A model-theoretic coreference scoring scheme. In *Proceedings of the 6th conference on Message understanding*. Association for Computational Linguistics, pages 45–52.

Sam Wiseman, Alexander M. Rush, Stuart Shieber, and Jason Weston. 2015. Learning anaphoricity and antecedent ranking features for coreference resolution. In *Proceedings of the 53rd Annual Meeting of the Association for Computational Linguistics and the 7th International Joint Conference on Natural Language Processing (Volume 1: Long Papers)*. Association for Computational Linguistics, Beijing, China, pages 1416–1426. http://www.aclweb.org/anthology/P15-1137.

Sam Wiseman, Alexander M. Rush, and Stuart M. Shieber. 2016. Learning global features for coreference resolution. In *Proceedings of the 2016 Conference of the North American Chapter of the Association for Computational Linguistics: Human Language Technologies*. Association for Computational Linguistics, San Diego, California, pages 994–1004. http://www.aclweb.org/anthology/N16-1114.

J. L. Wu and W. Y. Ma. 2017. A deep learning framework for coreference resolution based on convolutional neural network. In *2017 IEEE 11th International Conference on Semantic Computing (ICSC)*. pages 61–64. https://doi.org/10.1109/ICSC.2017.57.

Cross-language Learning with Adversarial Neural Networks:
Application to Community Question Answering

Shafiq Joty, Preslav Nakov, Lluís Màrquez and **Israa Jaradat**
ALT Research Group
Qatar Computing Research Institute, HBKU
{sjoty, pnakov, lmarquez, ijaradat}@hbku.edu.qa

Abstract

We address the problem of cross-language adaptation for question-question similarity reranking in community question answering, with the objective to port a system trained on one input language to another input language given labeled training data for the first language and only unlabeled data for the second language. In particular, we propose to use adversarial training of neural networks to learn high-level features that are discriminative for the main learning task, and at the same time are invariant across the input languages. The evaluation results show sizable improvements for our cross-language adversarial neural network (CLANN) model over a strong non-adversarial system.

1 Introduction

Developing natural language processing (NLP) systems that can work indistinctly with different input languages is a challenging task; yet, such a setup is useful for many real-world applications. One expensive solution is to annotate data for each input language and then to train a separate system for each one. Another option, which can be also costly, is to translate the input, e.g., using machine translation (MT), and then to work monolingually in the target language (Hartrumpf et al., 2008; Lin and Kuo, 2010; Ture and Boschee, 2016). However, the machine-translated text can be of low quality, might lose some input signal, e.g., it can alter sentiment (Mohammad et al., 2016), or may not be really needed (Bouma et al., 2008; Pouran Ben Veyseh, 2016). Using a unified cross-language representation of the input is a third, less costly option, which allows any combination of input languages during both training and testing.

In this paper, we take this last approach, i.e., combining languages during both training and testing, and we study the problem of question-question similarity reranking in community Question Answering (cQA), when the input question can be either in English or in Arabic, and the questions it is compared to are always in English. We start with a simple language-independent representation based on cross-language word embeddings, which we input into a feed-forward multilayer neural network to classify pairs of questions, (English, English) or (Arabic, English), regarding their similarity.

Furthermore, we explore the question of whether *adversarial* training can be used to improve the performance of the network when we have some *unlabeled* examples in the target language. In particular, we adapt the Domain Adversarial Neural Network model from (Ganin et al., 2016), which was originally used for domain adaptation, to our cross-language setting. To the best of our knowledge, this is novel for cross-language question-question similarity reranking, as well as for natural language processing (NLP) in general; moreover, we are not aware of any previous work on *cross-language* question reranking for community Question Answering.

In our setup, the basic task-solving network is paired with another network that shares the internal representation of the input and tries to decide whether the input example comes from the source (English) or from the target (Arabic) language. The training of this language discriminator network is *adversarial* with respect to the shared layers by using gradient reversal during backpropagation, which makes the training to *maximize* the loss of the discriminator rather than to minimize it. The main idea is to learn a high-level abstract representation that is discriminative for the main classification task, but is invariant across the input languages.

Proceedings of the 21st Conference on Computational Natural Language Learning (CoNLL 2017), pages 226–237,
Vancouver, Canada, August 3 - August 4, 2017. ©2017 Association for Computational Linguistics

We apply this method to an extension of the SemEval-2016 Task 3, subtask B benchmark dataset for question-question similarity reranking (Nakov et al., 2016b). In particular, we hired professional translators to translate the original English questions to Arabic, and we further collected additional unlabeled questions in English, which we also got translated into Arabic. We show that using the unlabeled data for adversarial training allows us to improve the results by a sizable margin in both directions, i.e., when training on English and adapting the system with the Arabic unlabeled data, and vice versa. Moreover, the resulting performance is comparable to the best monolingual English systems at SemEval. We also compare our unsupervised model to a semi-supervised model, where we have some labeled data for the target language.

The remainder of this paper is organized as follows: Section 2 discusses some related work. Section 3 introduces our model for adversarial training for cross-language problems. Section 4 describes the experimental setup. Section 5 presents the evaluation results. Finally, Section 6 concludes and points to possible directions for future work.

2   Related Work

Below we discuss three relevant research lines: (*a*) adversarial training, (*b*) question-question similarity, and (*c*) cross-language learning.

Adversarial training of neural networks has shown a big impact recently, especially in areas such as computer vision, where generative unsupervised models have proved capable of synthesizing new images (Goodfellow et al., 2014; Radford et al., 2016; Makhzani et al., 2016). One crucial challenge in adversarial training is to find the right balance between the two components: the generator and the adversarial discriminator. Thus, several methods have been proposed recently to stabilize training (Metz et al., 2017; Arjovsky et al., 2017). Adversarial training has also been successful in training predictive models. More relevant to our work is the work of Ganin et al. (2016), who proposed domain adversarial neural networks (DANN) to learn discriminative but at the same time domain-invariant representations, with domain adaptation as a target. Here, we use adversarial training to learn task-specific representations in a *cross-language* setting, which is novel for this task, to the best of our knowledge.

Question-question similarity was part of Task 3 on cQA at SemEval-2016/2017 (Nakov et al., 2016b, 2017); there was also a similar subtask as part of SemEval-2016 Task 1 on Semantic Textual Similarity (Agirre et al., 2016). Question-question similarity is an important problem with application to question recommendation, question duplicate detection, community question answering, and question answering in general. Typically, it has been addressed using a variety of textual similarity measures. Some work has paid attention to modeling the question topic, which can be done explicitly, e.g., using a graph of topic terms (Cao et al., 2008), or implicitly, e.g., using LDA-based topic language model that matches the questions not only at the term level but also at the topic level (Zhang et al., 2014). Another important aspect is syntactic structure, e.g., Wang et al. (2009) proposed a retrieval model for finding similar questions based on the similarity of syntactic trees, and Da San Martino et al. (2016) used syntactic kernels. Yet another emerging approach is to use neural networks, e.g., dos Santos et al. (2015) used convolutional neural networks (CNNs), Romeo et al. (2016) used long short-term memory (LSTMs) networks with neural attention to select the important part when comparing two questions, and Lei et al. (2016) used a combined recurrent–convolutional model to map questions to continuous semantic representations. Finally, translation models have been popular for question-question similarity (Jeon et al., 2005; Zhou et al., 2011). Unlike that work, here we are interested in *cross-language adaptation* for question-question similarity reranking. The problem was studied in (Martino et al., 2017) using cross-language kernels and deep neural networks; however, they used no adversarial training.

Cross-language Question Answering was the topic of several challenges, e.g., at CLEF 2008 (Forner et al., 2008), at NTCIR-8 (Mitamura et al., 2010), and at BOLT (Soboroff et al., 2016). Cross-language QA methods typically use machine translation directly or adapt MT models to the QA setting (Echihabi and Marcu, 2003; Soricut and Brill, 2006; Riezler et al., 2007; Hartrumpf et al., 2008; Lin and Kuo, 2010; Surdeanu et al., 2011; Ture and Boschee, 2016). They can also map terms across languages using Wikipedia links or BabelNet (Bouma et al., 2008; Pouran Ben Veyseh, 2016). However, *adversarial training* has not been tried in that setting.

q: *give tips? did you do with it; if the answer is yes, then what the magnitude of what you avoid it? In our country, we leave a 15-20 percent.*

q_1' Tipping in Qatar. Is Tipping customary in Qatar ? What is considered "reasonable" amount to tip : 1. The guy that pushes the shopping trolley for you 2. The person that washes your car 3. The tea boy that makes coffee for you in the office 4. The waiters at 5-star restaurants 5. The petrol pump attendants etc
Relevant

q_2' Tipping Beauty Salon. What do you think how much i should tip the stuff in a beauty salon for manicure/pedicure; massage or haircut?? Any idea what is required in Qatar?
Relevant

. . .

q_9' Business Meeting? Guys; I'm just enquiring about what one should wear to business meetings in Doha? Are there certain things a man should or shouldn't wear (Serious replys only - not like A man shouldn't wear a dress)!!!! Thanks - Gino
Irrelevant

q_{10}' what to do? I see this man every morning; cleaning the road. I want to give him some money(not any big amount)but I feel odd to offer money to a person who is not asking for it. I am confused; I kept the money handy in the car.... because of the traffic the car moves very slowly in that area; I can give it to him easily..but am not able to do it for the past 4 days; and I feel so bad about it. If I see him tomorrow; What to do?
Irrelevant

Figure 1: An input question and some of the potentially relevant questions retrieved for it.

3 Adversarial Training for Cross-Language Problems

We demonstrate our approach for cross-language representation learning with adversarial training on a cross-lingual extension of the *question–question similarity reranking* subtask of SemEval-2016 Task 3 on community Question Answering.

An example for the monolingual task is shown in Figure 1. We can see an original English input question q and a list of several potentially similar questions q_i' from the Qatar Living[1] forum, retrieved by a search engine. The original question (also referred to as a new question) asks about how to tip in Qatar. Question q_1' is relevant with respect to it as it asks the same thing, and so is q_2', which asks how much one should tip in a specific situation. However, q_9' and q_{10}' are irrelevant: the former asks about what to wear at business meetings, and the latter asks about how to tip a kind of person who does not normally receive tips.

---

[1] http://www.qatarliving.com/forum

In our case, the input question q is in a different language (Arabic) than the language of the retrieved questions (English). The goal is to rerank a set of K retrieved questions $\{q_k'\}_{k=1}^{K}$ written in a source language (e.g., English) according to their similarity with respect to an input user question q that comes in another (target) language, e.g., Arabic. For simplicity, henceforth we will use Arabic as target and English as source. However, in principle, our method generalizes to any source-target language pair.

3.1 Unsupervised Language Adaptation

We approach the problem as a classification task, where given a question pair (q, q'), the goal is to decide whether the retrieved question q' is *similar* (i.e., relevant) to q or not. Let $c \in \{0, 1\}$ denote the class label: 1 for similar, and 0 for not similar. We use the posterior probability $p(c = 1|q, q', \theta)$ as a score for ranking all retrieved questions by similarity, where θ are the model parameters.

More formally, let $\mathcal{R}_n = \{q_{n,k}'\}_{k=1}^{K}$ denote the set of K retrieved questions for a new question q_n. Note that the questions in $\mathcal{R}_n$ are always in English. We consider a training scenario where we have labeled examples $\mathcal{D}_S = \{q_n, q_{n,k}', c_{n,k}\}_{n=1}^{N}$ for English q_n, but we only have unlabeled examples $\mathcal{D}_T = \{q_n, q_{n,k}'\}_{n=N+1}^{M}$ for Arabic q_n, with $c_{n,k}$ denoting the class label for the pair $(q_n, q_{n,k}')$. We want to train a cross-language model that can classify any test example $\{q_n, q_{n,k}'\}$, where q_n is in Arabic. This scenario is of practical importance, e.g., when an Arabic speaker wants to query the system in Arabic, and the database of related information is only in English. Here, we adapt the idea for adversarial training for domain adaptation as proposed by Ganin et al. (2016).

Figure 2 shows the architecture of our cross-language adversarial neural network (CLANN) model. The input to the network is a pair (q, q'), which is first mapped to fixed-length vectors $(\mathbf{z}_q, \mathbf{z}_{q'})$. To generate these word embeddings, one can use existing tools such as *word2vec* (Mikolov et al., 2013) and monolingual data from the respective languages. Alternatively, one can use cross-language word embeddings, e.g., trained using the *bivec* model (Luong et al., 2015). The latter can yield better initialization, which could be potentially crucial when the labeled data is too small to train the input representations with the end-to-end system.

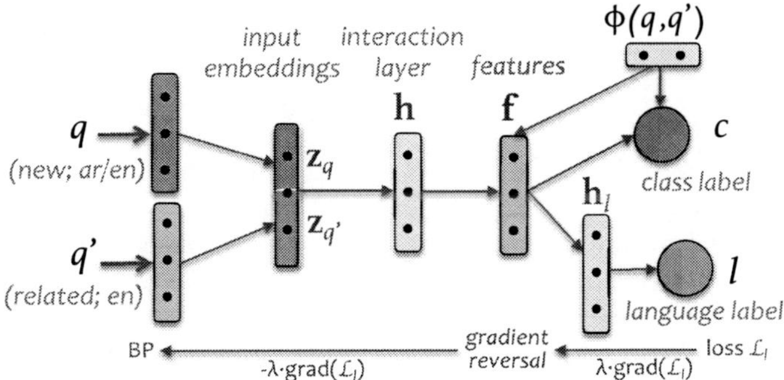

Figure 2: Architecture of CLANN for the question to question similarity problem in cQA.

The network then models the interactions between the input embeddings by passing them through two non-linear hidden layers, **h** and **f**. Additionally, the network considers *pairwise* features $\phi(q, q')$ that go directly to the output layer, and also through the second hidden layer.

The following equations describe the transformations through the hidden layers:

$$\mathbf{h} = g(U[\mathbf{z}_q; \mathbf{z}_{q'}]) \tag{1}$$
$$\mathbf{f} = g(V[\mathbf{h}; \phi(q, q')]) \tag{2}$$

where $[.;.]$ denotes concatenation of two column vectors, U and V are the weight matrices in the first and in the second hidden layer, and g is a nonlinear activation function; we use rectified linear units or ReLU (Nair and Hinton, 2010).

The pairwise features $\phi(q, q')$ encode different types of similarity between q and q', and task-specific properties that we describe later in Section 4. In our earlier work (Martino et al., 2017), we found it beneficial to use them directly to the output layer as well as through a hidden-layer transformation. The non-linear transformation allows us to learn high-level abstract features from the raw similarity measures, while the adversarial training, as we describe below, will make these abstract features language-invariant.

The output layer computes a sigmoid:

$$\hat{c}_\theta = p(c = 1|\mathbf{f}, \mathbf{w}) = \text{sigm}(\mathbf{w}^T[\mathbf{f}; \phi(q, q')]) \tag{3}$$

where **w** are the output layer weights.

We train the network by minimizing the negative log-probability of the gold labels:

$$\mathcal{L}_c(\theta) = -c \log \hat{c}_\theta - (1 - c) \log (1 - \hat{c}_\theta) \tag{4}$$

The network described so far learns the abstract features through multiple hidden layers that are discriminative for the classification task, i.e., *similar* vs. *non-similar*. However, our goal is also to make these features invariant across languages. To this end, we put a language discriminator, another neural network that takes the internal representation of the network **f** (see Equation 2) as input, and tries to discriminate between *English* and *Arabic* inputs — in our case, whether the input comes from $\mathcal{D}_S$ or from $\mathcal{D}_T$.

The language discriminator is again defined by a sigmoid function:

$$\hat{l}_\omega = p(l = 1|\mathbf{f}, \omega) = \text{sigm}(\mathbf{w}_l^T \mathbf{h}_l) \tag{5}$$

where $l \in \{0, 1\}$ denotes the language of q (1 for English, and 0 for Arabic), $\mathbf{w}_l$ are the final layer weights of the discriminator, and $\mathbf{h}_l = g(U_l \mathbf{f})$ defines the hidden layer of the discriminator with U_l being the layer weights and g being the ReLU activations.

We use the negative log-probability as the discrimination loss:

$$\mathcal{L}_l(\omega) = -l \log \hat{l}_\omega - (1 - l) \log \left(1 - \hat{l}_\omega\right) \tag{6}$$

The overall training objective of the composite model can be written as follows:

$$\mathcal{L}(\theta, \omega) = \sum_{n=1}^{N} \mathcal{L}_c^n(\theta) - \lambda\Big[\sum_{n=1}^{N} \mathcal{L}_l^n(\omega) + \sum_{n=N+1}^{M} \mathcal{L}_l^n(\omega)\Big] \tag{7}$$

where $\theta = \{U, V, \mathbf{w}\}$, $\omega = \{U, V, \mathbf{w}, U_l, \mathbf{w}_l\}$, and the hyper-parameter λ controls the relative strength of the two networks.

In training, we look for parameter values that satisfy a min-max optimization criterion as follows:

$$\theta^* = \operatorname*{argmin}_{U,V,\mathbf{w}} \max_{U_l,\mathbf{w}_l} \mathcal{L}(U, V, \mathbf{w}, U_l, \mathbf{w}_l) \qquad (8)$$

which involves a maximization (gradient ascent) with respect to $\{U_l, \mathbf{w}_l\}$ and a minimization (gradient descent) with respect to $\{U, V, \mathbf{w}\}$. Note that maximizing $\mathcal{L}(U, V, \mathbf{w}, U_l, \mathbf{w}_l)$ with respect to $\{U_l, \mathbf{w}_l\}$ is equivalent to minimizing the discriminator loss $\mathcal{L}_l(\omega)$ in Equation (6), which aims to improve the discrimination accuracy. In other words, when put together, the updates of the shared parameters $\{U, V, \mathbf{w}\}$ for the two classifiers work adversarially with respect to each other.

In our gradient descent training, the above min-max optimization is performed by reversing the gradients of the language discrimination loss $\mathcal{L}_l(\omega)$, when they are backpropagated to the shared layers. As shown in Figure 2, the gradient reversal is applied to layer **f** and also to the layers that come before it.

Our optimization setup is related to the training method of Generative Adversarial Networks or GANs (Goodfellow et al., 2014), where the goal is to build deep generative models that can generate realistic images. The discriminator in GANs tries to distinguish real images from model-generated images, and thus the training attempts to minimize the discrepancy between the two image distributions, i.e., *empirical* as in the training data vs. *model-based* as produced by the generator. When backpropagating to the generator network, they consider a slight variation of the reverse gradients with respect to the discriminator loss. In particular, if ρ is the discriminator probability, instead of reversing the gradients of $\log(1 - \rho)$, they use the gradients of $\log \rho$. Reversing the gradient is a different way to achieve the same goal.

Training. Algorithm 1 shows pseudocode for the algorithm we use to train our model, which is based on stochastic gradient descent (SDG). We first initialize the model parameters by using samples from glorot-uniform distribution (Glorot and Bengio, 2010). We then form minibatches of size b by randomly sampling $b/2$ labeled examples from $\mathcal{D}_S$ and $b/2$ unlabeled examples from $\mathcal{D}_T$. For the labeled instances, both $\mathcal{L}_c(\theta)$ and $\mathcal{L}_l(\omega)$ losses are active, while only the $\mathcal{L}_l(\omega)$ loss is active for the unlabeled instances.

Algorithm 1: Model Training with SGD

Input : data $\mathcal{D}_S$, $\mathcal{D}_T$, batch size b
Output : learned model parameters
$\qquad\qquad \{U, V, \mathbf{w}, U_l, \mathbf{w}_l\}$
1. Initialize model parameters;
2. **repeat**
    (*a*) Randomly sample $\frac{b}{2}$ labeled examples
        from $\mathcal{D}_S$
    (*b*) Randomly Sample $\frac{b}{2}$ unlabeled
        examples from $\mathcal{D}_T$
    (*c*) Compute $\mathcal{L}_c(\theta)$ and $\mathcal{L}_l(\omega)$
    (*d*) Take a gradient step for $\frac{2}{b}\nabla_\theta \mathcal{L}_c(\theta)$
    (*e*) Take a gradient step for
        $\frac{2\lambda}{b}\nabla_{U_l,\mathbf{w}_l} \mathcal{L}_l(\omega)$
    `// Gradient reversal`
    (*f*) Take a gradient step for $-\frac{2\lambda}{b}\nabla_\theta \mathcal{L}_l(\omega)$
until *convergence*;

As mentioned above, the main challenge in adversarial training is to balance the two components of the network. If one component becomes smarter, its loss to the shared layer becomes useless, and the training fails to converge (Arjovsky et al., 2017). Equivalently, if one component gets weaker, its loss overwhelms that of the other, causing training to fail. In our experiments, the language discriminator was weaker. This could be due to the use of *cross-language* word embeddings to generate input embedding representations for q and q'. To balance the two components, we would want the error signals from the discriminator to be fairly weak initially, with full power unleashed only as the classification errors start to dominate. We follow the weighting schedule proposed by Ganin et al. (2016, p. 21), who initialize λ to 0, and then change it gradually to 1 as training progresses. I.e., we start training the task classifier first, and we gradually add the discriminator's loss.

3.2 Semi-supervised Extension

Above we considered an unsupervised adaptation scenario, where we did not have any labeled instance for the target language, i.e., when the new question q_n is in Arabic. However, our method can be easily generalized to a semi-supervised setting, where we have access to some labeled instances in the target language, $\mathcal{D}_{T*} = \{q_n, \mathcal{R}_n, c_n\}_{n=M+1}^{L}$. In this case, each minibatch during training is formed by labeled instances from both $\mathcal{D}_S$ and $\mathcal{D}_{T*}$, and unlabeled instances from $\mathcal{D}_T$.

System	Input	Discrim.	Target	Hyperparam. (b, d, $\mathbf{h}$, $\mathbf{f}$, l_2)	MAP	MRR	AvgRec
FNN	en	–	ar	8, 0.2, 10, 100, 0.03	75.28	84.26	89.48
CLANN	en	en vs. ar'	ar	8, 0.2, 15, 100, 0.02	**76.64**	**84.52**	**90.92**
FNN	ar	–	en	8, 0.4, 20, 125, 0.03	75.32	84.17	89.26
CLANN	ar	ar vs. en'	en	8, 0.4, 15, 75, 0.02	**76.70**	**84.52**	**90.61**

Table 1: Performance on the test set for our cross-language systems, with and without adversarial adaptation (CLANN and FNN, respectively), and for both language directions (en-ar and ar-en). The prime notation under the *Discrim.* column represents using a counterpart from the unlabeled data.

4 Experimental Setting

In this section, we describe the datasets we used, the generation of the input embeddings, the nature of the pairwise features, and the general training setup of our model.

4.1 Datasets

SemEval-2016 Task 3 (Nakov et al., 2016b), provides 267 input questions for training, 50 for development, and 70 for testing, and ten times as many potentially related questions retrieved by an IR engine for each input question: 2,670, 500, and 700, respectively. Based on this data, we simulated a *cross-language setup* for question-question similarity reranking. We first got the 387 original train+dev+test questions translated into Arabic by professional translators. Then, we used these Arabic questions as an input with the goal to rerank the ten related English questions. As an example, this is the Arabic translation of the original English question from Figure 1:

هل تعطون الاكراميات؟ ماذا تفعلون بهذا الشأن؛

اذا كانت الاجابة نعم ، ما هو قوة ما تتجنبونه؟

في بلادنا ، نترك من ١٥ إلى ٢٠ بالمئة.

We further collected 221 additional original questions and 1,863 related questions as unlabeled data, and we got the 221 English questions translated to Arabic.[2]

4.2 Cross-language Embeddings

We used the TED (Abdelali et al., 2014) and the OPUS parallel Arabic–English bi-texts (Tiedemann, 2012) to extract a bilingual dictionary, and to learn cross-language embeddings. We chose these bi-texts as they are conversational (TED talks and movie subtitles, respectively), and thus informal, which is close to the style of our community question answering forum.

We trained Arabic-English cross-language word embeddings from the concatenation of these bi-texts using *bivec* (Luong et al., 2015), a bilingual extension of *word2vec*, which has achieved excellent results on semantic tasks close to ours (Upadhyay et al., 2016). In particular, we trained 200-dimensional vectors using the parameters described in (Upadhyay et al., 2016), with a context window of size 5 and iterating for 5 epochs. We then compute the representation for a question by averaging the embedding vectors of the words it contains. Using these cross-language embeddings allows us to compare directly representations of an Arabic or an English input question q to English potentially related questions q'_i.

4.3 Pairwise Features

In addition to the embeddings, we also used some pairwise features that model the similarity or some other relation between the input question and the potentially related questions.[3] These features were proposed in the previous literature for the question–question similarity problem, and they are necessary to obtain state-of-the-art results.

In particular, we calculated the similarity between the two questions using machine translation evaluation metrics, as suggested in (Guzmán et al., 2016). In particular, we used BLEU (Papineni et al., 2002); NIST (Doddington, 2002); TER v0.7.25 (Snover et al., 2006); METEOR v1.4 (Lavie and Denkowski, 2009) with paraphrases; Unigram PRECISION; Unigram RECALL. We also used features that model various components of BLEU, as proposed in (Guzmán et al., 2015): n-gram precisions, n-gram matches, total number of n-grams (n=1,2,3,4), hypothesis and reference length, length ratio, and brevity penalty.

---

[2]Our cross-language dataset and code are available at `https://github.com/qcri/CLANN`

[3]This required translating the Arabic input question to English. For this, we used an in-house Arabic–English phrase-based statistical machine translation system, trained on the TED and on the OPUS bi-texts; for language modeling, it also used the English Gigaword corpus.

We further used as features the cosine similarity between question embeddings. In particular, we used (*i*) 300-dimensional pre-trained Google News embeddings from (Mikolov et al., 2013), (*ii*) 100-dimensional embeddings trained on the entire Qatar Living forum (Mihaylov and Nakov, 2016), and (*iii*) 25-dimensional Stanford neural parser embeddings (Socher et al., 2013). The latter are produced by the parser internally, as a by-product.

Furthermore, we computed various task-specific features, most of them introduced in the 2015 edition of the SemEval task by (Nicosia et al., 2015; Joty et al., 2015). This includes some question-level features: (1) number of URLs/images/emails/phone numbers; (2) number of tokens/sentences; (3) average number of tokens; (4) type/token ratio; (5) number of nouns/verbs/adjectives/adverbs/ pronouns; (6) number of positive/negative smileys; (7) number of single/double/ triple exclamation/interrogation symbols; (8) number of interrogative sentences (based on parsing); (9) number of words that are not in WORD2VEC's Google News vocabulary. Also, some question-question pair features: (10) count ratio in terms of sentences/tokens/nouns/verbs/ adjectives/adverbs/pronouns; (11) count ratio of words that are not in WORD2VEC's Google News vocabulary. Finally, we also have one meta feature: (12) reciprocal rank of the related question in the list of related questions.

4.4 Model settings

We trained our CLANN model by optimizing the objective in Equation (7) using ADAM (Kingma and Ba, 2015) with default parameters. For this, we used up to 200 epochs. In order to avoid overfitting, we used dropout (Srivastava et al., 2014) of hidden units, l_2 regularization on weights, and *early stopping* by observing MAP on the development dataset —if MAP did not increase for 15 consecutive epochs, we exited with the best model recorded so far. We optimized the values of the hyper-parameters using grid search: for minibatch (*b*) size in $\{8, 12, 16\}$, for dropout (*d*) rate in $\{0.2, 0.3, 0.4, 0.5\}$, for **h** layer size in $\{10, 15, 20\}$, for **f** layer size in $\{75, 100, 125\}$, and for l_2 strength in $\{0.01, 0.02, 0.03\}$. The fifth column in Table 1 shows the optimal hyper-parameter setting for the different models. Finally, we used the best model as found on the development dataset for the final evaluation on the test dataset.

System	MAP	MRR	AvgRec
Monolingual (English) from SemEval-2016			
1. IR rank	*74.75*	*83.79*	*88.30*
2. UH-PRHLT (1st)	76.70	83.02	90.31
3. ConvKN (2nd)	76.02	84.64	90.70
Cross-language (Arabic into English)			
4. CLANN	76.70	84.52	90.61

Table 2: Comparison of our cross-language approach (CLANN) to the best results at SemEval-2016 Task 3, subtask B.

5 Evaluation Results

Below we present the experimental results for the unsupervised and semi-supervised language adaptation settings. We compare our cross-language adversarial network (CLANN) to a feed forward neural network (FNN) that has no adversarial part.

5.1 Unsupervised Adaptation Experiments

Table 1 shows the main results for our cross-language adaptation experiments. Rows 1-2 present the results when the target language is Arabic and the system is trained with English input. Rows 3-4 show the reverse case, i.e., adaptation into English when training on Arabic. *FNN* stands for *feed-forward neural network*, and it is the upper layer in Figure 2, excluding the language discriminator. *CLANN* is the full *cross-language adversarial neural network*, training the discriminator with English inputs paired with random Arabic related questions from the unlabeled dataset. We show three ranking-oriented evaluation measures that are standard in the field of Information Retrieval: mean average precision (MAP), mean reciprocal rank (MRR), and average recall (AvgRec). We computed them using the official scorer from SemEval-2016 Task 3.[4] Similarly to that task, we consider Mean Average Precision (MAP) as the main evaluation metric. The table also presents, for reproducibility, the values of the neural network hyper-parameters after tuning (in the fifth column).

We can see that the MAP score for FNN with Arabic target is 75.28. When doing the adversarial adaptation with the unlabeled Arabic examples (CLANN), the MAP score is boosted to 76.64 (+1.36 points). Going in the reverse direction, with English as the target, yields very comparable results: MAP goes from 75.32 to 76.70 (+1.38).

---

[4]`http://alt.qcri.org/semeval2016/task3/`

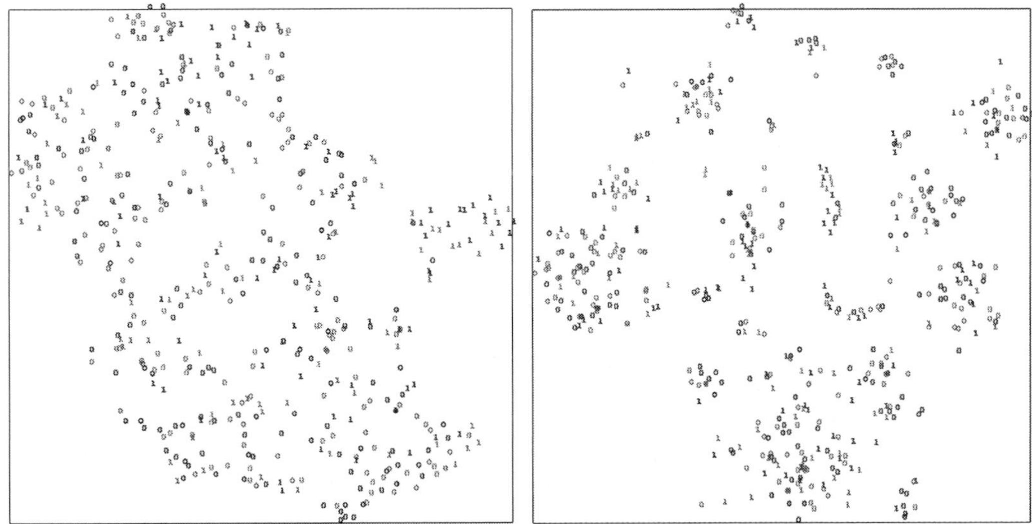

Figure 3: Scatter plots showing Arabic and English test examples, after training the adversarial network. Arabic is shown in blue, and English is in red. 0-1 are the class labels. Left: ar→en, right: en→ar.

To put these results into perspective, Table 2 shows the results for the top-2 best-performing systems from SemEval-2016 Task 3, which used a monolingual English setting. We can see that our FNN approach based on cross-language input embeddings is already not far from the best systems. Yet, when we consider the full adversarial network, in any of the two directions, we get performance that is on par with the best, in all metrics.

We conclude that the adversarial component in the network does the expected job, and improves the performance by focusing the language-independent features in the representation layer. The scatter plots in Figure 3 are computed by projecting the representation layer vectors of the first 500 test examples into two dimensions using t-SNE visualization (van der Maaten and Hinton, 2008). The first 250 are taken with Arabic input (blue), the second 250 are taken with English input (red). 0-1 are the class labels (similar vs. non-similar). The top plot corresponds to CLANN training with English and adapting with Arabic examples, while the second one covers the opposite direction. The plots look as expected. CLANN really mixes the blue and the red examples, as the adversarial part of the network pushes for learning shared abstract features that are language-insensitive. At the same time, the points form clusters with clear majorities of 0s or 1s, as the supervised part of the network learns how to classify them in these classes.

5.2 Semi-supervised Experiments

We now study the semi-supervised scenario when we also have some labeled data from the target language, i.e., where the original question q is in the target language. This can be relevant in practical situations, as sometimes we might be able to annotate some data in the target language. It is also an exploration of training with data in multiple languages all together.

To simulate this scenario, we split the training set in two halves. We train with one half as the source language, and we use the other half with the target language as extra supervised data. At the same time, we also use the unlabeled examples as before. We introduced the semi-supervised model in subsection 3.2, which is a straightforward adaptation of the CLANN model.

Table 3 shows the main results of our cross-language semi-supervised experiments. The table is split into two blocks by source and target language (en-ar or ar-en). We also use the same notation as in Table 1. The suffixes *-unsup* and *-semisup* indicate whether CLANN is trained in unsupervised mode (same as in Table 1) or in semi-supervised mode. The language discriminator in this setting is trained to discriminate between labeled source and labeled target examples, and labeled source and unlabeled target examples. This is indicated in the *Discrim.* column using asterisk and prime symbols, respectively.

233

System	Input	Discrim.	Target	Hyperparam. $(b, d, \mathbf{h}, \mathbf{f}, l_2)$	MAP	MRR	AvgRec
FNN	en	—	ar	8, 0.3, 10, 100, 0.03	74.69	83.79	88.16
CLANN-unsup	en	en vs. ar'	ar	12, 0.3, 15, 75, 0.02	75.93	84.15	89.63
CLANN-semisup	en+ar*	$\left\{\begin{array}{l}\text{en vs. ar}^*\\ \text{en vs. ar'}\end{array}\right.$	ar	8, 0.4, 15, 75, 0.02	76.65	84.52	90.84
FNN	ar	—	en	8, 0.2, 10, 75, 0.03	75.38	84.05	89.12
CLANN-unsup	ar	ar vs. en'	en	12, 0.2, 15, 75, 0.03	75.89	84.29	89.54
CLANN-semisup	ar+en*	$\left\{\begin{array}{l}\text{ar vs. en}^*\\ \text{ar vs. en'}\end{array}\right.$	en	8, 0.2, 10, 75, 0.03	76.63	84.52	90.82

Table 3: Semi-supervised experiments, when training on half of the training dataset, and evaluating on the full testing dataset. Shown is the performance of our cross-language models, with and without adversarial adaptation (i.e., using CLANN and FNN, respectively), using the unsupervised and the semi-supervised settings, and for both language directions: English–Arabic and Arabic–English. The prime notation in the *Discrim.* column represents choosing a counterpart for the discriminator from the unlabeled data. The asterisks stand for choosing an unpaired labeled example from the other half of the training dataset.

There are several interesting observations that we can make about Table 3. First, since here we are training with only 50% of the original training data, both FNN and CLANN-unsup yield lower results compared to before, i.e., compared to Table 1; this is to be expected. However, the unsupervised adaptation, i.e., using the CLANN-unsup model, still yields improvements over the FNN model by a sizable margin, according to all three evaluation measures. When we also train using the additional labeled examples in the target language, i.e., using the CLANN-semisup model, the results are boosted again to a final MAP score that is very similar to what we had obtained before with the full source-language training dataset. In the English into Arabic adaptation, the MAP score jumps from 74.69 to 76.65 (+1.96 points) when going from the FNN to the CLANN-semisup model, the MRR score goes from 83.79 to 84.52 (+0.73), and the AvgRec score is boosted from 88.16 to 90.84 (+2.68). The results in the opposite adaptation direction, i.e., from Arabic into English, follow a very similar pattern.

These results demonstrate the effectiveness and the flexibility of our general adversarial training framework within our CLANN architecture when applied to a cross-language setting for question-question similarity, taking advantage of the unlabeled examples in the target language (i.e., when using unsupervised adaptation) and also taking advantage of any labeled examples in the target language that we may have at our disposal (i.e., when using semi-supervised training with input examples in the two languages simultaneously).

6 Conclusion

We have studied the problem of cross-language adaptation for the task of question-question similarity reranking in community question answering, when the input question can be either in English or in Arabic with the objective to port a system trained on one input language to another input language given labeled data for the source language and only unlabeled data for the target language. We used a discriminative adversarial neural network, which we trained to learn task-specific representations directly. This is novel in a cross-language setting, and we have shown that it works quite well. The evaluation results have shown sizable improvements over a strong neural network model that uses simple projection with cross-language word embeddings.

In future work, we want to extend the present research in several directions. For example, we would like to start with monolingual word embeddings and to try to learn the shared cross-language representation directly as part of the end-to-end training of our neural network. We further plan to try LSTM and CNN for generating the initial representation of the input text (instead of simple averaging of word embeddings). We also want to experiment with more than two languages at a time. Another interesting research direction we want to explore is to try to adapt our general CLANN framework to other tasks, e.g., to answer ranking in community Question Answering (Joty et al., 2016; Nakov et al., 2016a) in a cross-language setting, as well as to cross-language representation learning for words and sentences.

Acknowledgment

This research was performed by the Arabic Language Technologies group at Qatar Computing Research Institute, HBKU, within the Interactive sYstems for Answer Search project (IYAS).

References

Ahmed Abdelali, Francisco Guzmán, Hassan Sajjad, and Stephan Vogel. 2014. The AMARA corpus: Building parallel language resources for the educational domain. In *Proceedings of the 9th International Conference on Language Resources and Evaluation*. Reykjavik, Iceland, LREC '14, pages 1856–1862.

Eneko Agirre, Carmen Banea, Daniel Cer, Mona Diab, Aitor Gonzalez-Agirre, Rada Mihalcea, German Rigau, and Janyce Wiebe. 2016. SemEval-2016 task 1: Semantic textual similarity, monolingual and cross-lingual evaluation. In *Proceedings of the 10th International Workshop on Semantic Evaluation*. San Diego, CA, USA, SemEval '16, pages 497–511.

Martín Arjovsky, Soumith Chintala, and Léon Bottou. 2017. Wasserstein GAN. *CoRR* abs/1701.07875.

Gosse Bouma, Jori Mur, and Gertjan van Noord. 2008. Question answering with Joost at CLEF 2008. In *Proceedings of the 9th Workshop of the Cross-Language Evaluation Forum: Evaluating Systems for Multilingual and Multimodal Information Access*. Aarhus, Denmark, CLEF '08, pages 257–260.

Yunbo Cao, Huizhong Duan, Chin-Yew Lin, Yong Yu, and Hsiao-Wuen Hon. 2008. Recommending questions using the MDL-based tree cut model. In *Proceedings of the 17th International Conference on World Wide Web*. Beijing, China, WWW '08, pages 81–90.

Giovanni Da San Martino, Alberto Barrón-Cedeño, Salvatore Romeo, Antonio Uva, and Alessandro Moschitti. 2016. Learning to re-rank questions in community question answering using advanced features. In *Proceedings of the 25th ACM International Conference on Information and Knowledge Management*. Indianapolis, IN, USA, CIKM '16, pages 1997–2000.

George Doddington. 2002. Automatic evaluation of machine translation quality using n-gram co-occurrence statistics. In *Proceedings of the 2nd International Conference on Human Language Technology Research*. San Diego, CA, USA, HLT '02, pages 138–145.

Cicero dos Santos, Luciano Barbosa, Dasha Bogdanova, and Bianca Zadrozny. 2015. Learning hybrid representations to retrieve semantically equivalent questions. In *Proceedings of the 53rd Annual Meeting of the Association for Computational Linguistics and the 7th International Joint Conference on Natural Language Processing*. Beijing, China, ACL-IJCNLP '15, pages 694–699.

Abdessamad Echihabi and Daniel Marcu. 2003. A noisy-channel approach to question answering. In *Proceedings of the 41st Annual Meeting of the Association for Computational Linguistics*. Sapporo, Japan, ACL '03, pages 16–23.

Pamela Forner, Anselmo Peñas, Eneko Agirre, Iñaki Alegria, Corina Forascu, Nicolas Moreau, Petya Osenova, Prokopis Prokopidis, Paulo Rocha, Bogdan Sacaleanu, Richard F. E. Sutcliffe, and Erik F. Tjong Kim Sang. 2008. Overview of the CLEF 2008 Multilingual Question Answering Track. In *Proceedings of the 9th Workshop of the Cross-Language Evaluation Forum: Evaluating Systems for Multilingual and Multimodal Information Access*. Aarhus, Denmark, CLEF '08, pages 262–295.

Yaroslav Ganin, Evgeniya Ustinova, Hana Ajakan, Pascal Germain, Hugo Larochelle, François Laviolette, Mario Marchand, and Victor Lempitsky. 2016. Domain-adversarial training of neural networks. *Journal of Machine Learning Research* 17(1):2096–2030.

Xavier Glorot and Yoshua Bengio. 2010. Understanding the difficulty of training deep feedforward neural networks. In *JMLR W&CP: Proceedings of the Thirteenth International Conference on Artificial Intelligence and Statistics*. Sardinia, Italy, volume 9 of *AISTATS '10*, pages 249–256.

Ian Goodfellow, Jean Pouget-Abadie, Mehdi Mirza, Bing Xu, David Warde-Farley, Sherjil Ozair, Aaron Courville, and Yoshua Bengio. 2014. Generative adversarial nets. In *Proceedings of Advances in Neural Information Processing Systems Conference 27*. Montréal, Canada, NIPS '14, pages 2672–2680.

Francisco Guzmán, Shafiq Joty, Lluís Màrquez, and Preslav Nakov. 2015. Pairwise neural machine translation evaluation. In *Proceedings of the 53rd Annual Meeting of the Association for Computational Linguistics and the 7th International Joint Conference on Natural Language Processing (Volume 1: Long Papers)*. Beijing, China, ACL-IJCNLP '15, pages 805–814.

Francisco Guzmán, Lluís Màrquez, and Preslav Nakov. 2016. Machine translation evaluation meets community question answering. In *Proceedings of the 54th Annual Meeting of the Association for Computational Linguistics*. Berlin, Germany, ACL '16, pages 460–466.

Sven Hartrumpf, Ingo Glöckner, and Johannes Leveling. 2008. Efficient question answering with question decomposition and multiple answer streams. In *Proceedings of the 9th Workshop of the Cross-Language Evaluation Forum: Evaluating Systems for Multilingual and Multimodal Information Access*. Aarhus,Denmark, CLEF '08, pages 421–428.

Jiwoon Jeon, W. Bruce Croft, and Joon Ho Lee. 2005. Finding similar questions in large question and answer archives. In *Proceedings of the 14th ACM International Conference on Information and Knowledge Management*. Bremen, Germany, CIKM '05, pages 84–90.

Shafiq Joty, Alberto Barrón-Cedeño, Giovanni Da San Martino, Simone Filice, Lluís Màrquez, Alessandro Moschitti, and Preslav Nakov. 2015. Global Thread-level Inference for Comment Classification in Community Question Answering. In *Proc. of the 2015 Conference on Empirical Methods in Natural Language Processing*. ACL, Lisbon, Portugal, pages 573–578.

Shafiq Joty, Lluís Màrquez, and Preslav Nakov. 2016. Joint learning with global inference for comment classification in community question answering. In *Proceedings of the 2016 Conference of the North American Chapter of the Association for Computational Linguistics*. San Diego, CA, USA, NAACL-HLT '16.

Diederik P. Kingma and Jimmy Ba. 2015. Adam: A method for stochastic optimization. In *Proceedings of the 3rd International Conference for Learning Representations*. San Diego, CA, USA, ICLR '15.

Alon Lavie and Michael Denkowski. 2009. The METEOR metric for automatic evaluation of machine translation. *Machine Translation* 23(2–3):105–115.

Tao Lei, Hrishikesh Joshi, Regina Barzilay, Tommi S. Jaakkola, Kateryna Tymoshenko, Alessandro Moschitti, and Lluís Màrquez. 2016. Semi-supervised question retrieval with gated convolutions. In *Proceedings of the 15th Annual Conference of the North American Chapter of the Association for Computational Linguistics*. San Diego, CA, USA, NAACL-HLT '16, pages 1279–1289.

Chuan-Jie Lin and Yu-Min Kuo. 2010. Description of the NTOU complex QA system. In *Proceedings of the 8th NTCIR Workshop Meeting on Evaluation of Information Access Technologies: Information Retrieval, Question Answering, and Cross-Lingual Information Access*. Tokyo, Japan, NTCIR '10, pages 47–54.

Thang Luong, Hieu Pham, and Christopher D. Manning. 2015. Bilingual word representations with monolingual quality in mind. In *Proceedings of the 1st Workshop on Vector Space Modeling for Natural Language Processing*. Denver, CO, USA, pages 151–159.

Alireza Makhzani, Jonathon Shlens, Navdeep Jaitly, and Ian J. Goodfellow. 2016. Adversarial autoencoders. In *Proceedings of the International Conference on Learning Representations 2016*. San Juan, Puerto Rico, ICLR '16.

Giovanni Da San Martino, Salvatore Romeo, Alberto Barrón Cedeño, Shafiq Joty, Lluís Màrquez, Alessandro Moschitti, and Preslav Nakov. 2017. Cross-language question re-ranking. In *Proceedings of the 40th ACM SIGIR Conference on Research and Development in Information Retrieval*. Tokyo, Japan, SIGIR '17.

Luke Metz, Ben Poole, David Pfau, and Jascha Sohl-Dickstein. 2017. Unrolled generative adversarial networks. In *5th International Conference on Learning Representations*. Toulon, France, ICLR '17.

Todor Mihaylov and Preslav Nakov. 2016. SemanticZ at SemEval-2016 Task 3: Ranking relevant answers in community question answering using semantic similarity based on fine-tuned word embeddings. In *Proceedings of the 10th International Workshop on Semantic Evaluation*. San Diego, CA, USA, SemEval '16, pages 879–886.

Tomas Mikolov, Wen-tau Yih, and Geoffrey Zweig. 2013. Linguistic regularities in continuous space word representations. In *Proceedings of the 2013 Conference of the North American Chapter of the Association for Computational Linguistics*. Atlanta, GA, USA, NAACL-HLT '13, pages 746–751.

Teruko Mitamura, Hideki Shima, Tetsuya Sakai, Noriko Kando, Tatsunori Mori, Koichi Takeda, Chin-Yew Song Ruihua Lin, Chuan-Jie Lin, and Cheng-Wei Lee. 2010. Overview of the NTCIR-8 ACLIA tasks: Advanced cross-lingual information access. In *Proceedings of the 8th NTCIR Workshop Meeting on Evaluation of Information Access Technologies: Information Retrieval, Question Answering, and Cross-Lingual Information Access*. Tokyo, Japan, NTCIR '10, pages 15–24.

Saif M. Mohammad, Mohammad Salameh, and Svetlana Kiritchenko. 2016. How translation alters sentiment. *Journal of Artificial Intelligence Research* 55(1):95–130.

Vinod Nair and Geoffrey E. Hinton. 2010. Rectified linear units improve restricted Boltzmann machines. In *Proceedings of the 27th International Conference on Machine Learning*. Haifa, Israel, ICML '10, pages 807–814.

Preslav Nakov, Doris Hoogeveen, Lluís Màrquez, Alessandro Moschitti, Hamdy Mubarak, Timothy Baldwin, and Karin Verspoor. 2017. SemEval-2017 task 3: Community question answering. In *Proceedings of the 11th International Workshop on Semantic Evaluation*. Vancouver, Canada, SemEval '17.

Preslav Nakov, Lluís Màrquez, and Francisco Guzmán. 2016a. It takes three to tango: Triangulation approach to answer ranking in community question answering. In *Proceedings of the 2016 Conference on Empirical Methods in Natural Language Processing*. Austin, TX, USA, EMNLP '16, pages 1586–1597.

Preslav Nakov, Lluís Màrquez, Alessandro Moschitti, Walid Magdy, Hamdy Mubarak, Abed Alhakim Freihat, Jim Glass, and Bilal Randeree. 2016b.

SemEval-2016 task 3: Community question answering. In *Proceedings of the 10th International Workshop on Semantic Evaluation*. San Diego, CA, USA, SemEval '16, pages 525–545.

Massimo Nicosia, Simone Filice, Alberto Barrón-Cedeño, Iman Saleh, Hamdy Mubarak, Wei Gao, Preslav Nakov, Giovanni Da San Martino, Alessandro Moschitti, Kareem Darwish, Lluís Màrquez, Shafiq Joty, and Walid Magdy. 2015. QCRI: Answer selection for community question answering - experiments for Arabic and English. In *Proceedings of the 9th International Workshop on Semantic Evaluation*. Denver, CO,USA, SemEval '15, pages 203–209.

Kishore Papineni, Salim Roukos, Todd Ward, and Wei-Jing Zhu. 2002. BLEU: a method for automatic evaluation of machine translation. In *Proceedings of 40th Annual Meting of the Association for Computational Linguistics*. Philadelphia, PA, USA, ACL '02, pages 311–318.

Amir Pouran Ben Veyseh. 2016. Cross-lingual question answering using common semantic space. In *Proceedings of the 2016 Workshop on Graph-based Methods for Natural Language Processing*. San Diego, CA, USA, TextGraphs '16, pages 15–19.

Alec Radford, Luke Metz, and Soumith Chintala. 2016. Unsupervised representation learning with deep convolutional generative adversarial networks. In *Proceedings of the 4th International Conference on Learning Representations*. San Juan, Puerto Rico, ICLR '16.

Stefan Riezler, Alexander Vasserman, Ioannis Tsochantaridis, Vibhu Mittal, and Yi Liu. 2007. Statistical machine translation for query expansion in answer retrieval. In *Proceedings of the 45th Annual Meeting of the Association of Computational Linguistics*. Prague, Czech Republic, ACL '07, pages 464–471.

Salvatore Romeo, Giovanni Da San Martino, Alberto Barrón-Cedeño, Alessandro Moschitti, Yonatan Belinkov, Wei-Ning Hsu, Yu Zhang, Mitra Mohtarami, and James Glass. 2016. Neural attention for learning to rank questions in community question answering. In *Proceedings of the 26th International Conference on Computational Linguistics*. Osaka, Japan, COLING '16, pages 1734–1745.

Matthew Snover, Bonnie Dorr, Richard Schwartz, Linnea Micciulla, and John Makhoul. 2006. A study of translation edit rate with targeted human annotation. In *Proceedings of the 7th Conference of the Association for Machine Translation in the Americas*. Cambridge, MA, USA, AMTA '06, pages 223–231.

Ian Soboroff, Kira Griffitt, and Stephanie Strassel. 2016. The BOLT IR test collections of multilingual passage retrieval from discussion forums. In *Proceedings of the 39th International Conference on Research and Development in Information Retrieval*. Pisa, Italy, SIGIR '16, pages 713–716.

Richard Socher, John Bauer, Christopher D. Manning, and Ng Andrew Y. 2013. Parsing with compositional vector grammars. In *Proceedings of the 51st Annual Meeting of the Association for Computational Linguistics*. Sofia, Bulgaria, ACL '13, pages 455–465.

Radu Soricut and Eric Brill. 2006. Automatic question answering using the web: Beyond the factoid. *Information Retrieval* 9(2):191–206.

Nitish Srivastava, Geoffrey Hinton, Alex Krizhevsky, Ilya Sutskever, and Ruslan Salakhutdinov. 2014. Dropout: A simple way to prevent neural networks from overfitting. *Journal of Machine Learning Research* 15(1):1929–1958.

Mihai Surdeanu, Massimiliano Ciaramita, and Hugo Zaragoza. 2011. Learning to rank answers to nonfactoid questions from web collections. *Computational Linguistics* 37(2):351–383.

Jörg Tiedemann. 2012. Parallel data, tools and interfaces in OPUS. In *Proceedings of the 8th International Conference on Language Resources and Evaluation*. Istanbul, Turkey, LREC '12, pages 2214–2218.

Ferhan Ture and Elizabeth Boschee. 2016. Learning to translate for multilingual question answering. In *Proceedings of the 2016 Conference on Empirical Methods in Natural Language Processing*. Austin, TX, USA, EMNLP '16, pages 573–584.

Shyam Upadhyay, Manaal Faruqui, Chris Dyer, and Dan Roth. 2016. Cross-lingual models of word embeddings: An empirical comparison. In *Proceedings of the 54th Annual Meeting of the Association for Computational Linguistics*. Berlin, Germany, ACL '16, pages 1661–1670.

Laurens van der Maaten and Geoffrey Hinton. 2008. Visualizing high-dimensional data using t-SNE. *Journal of Machine Learning Research* 9:2579 – 2605.

Kai Wang, Zhaoyan Ming, and Tat-Seng Chua. 2009. A syntactic tree matching approach to finding similar questions in community-based QA services. In *Proceedings of the 32nd international ACM SIGIR conference on Research and development in information retrieval*. Boston, MA, USA, SIGIR '09, pages 187–194.

Kai Zhang, Wei Wu, Haocheng Wu, Zhoujun Li, and Ming Zhou. 2014. Question retrieval with high quality answers in community question answering. In *Proceedings of the 23rd ACM International Conference on Information and Knowledge Management*. Shanghai, China, CIKM '14, pages 371–380.

Guangyou Zhou, Li Cai, Jun Zhao, and Kang Liu. 2011. Phrase-based translation model for question retrieval in community question answer archives. In *Proceedings of the 49th Annual Meeting of the Association for Computational Linguistics*. Portland, OR, USA, ACL '11, pages 653–662.

Knowledge Tracing in Sequential Learning of Inflected Vocabulary

Adithya Renduchintala and **Philipp Koehn** and **Jason Eisner**
Department of Computer Science
Johns Hopkins University
{adi.r,phi,eisner}@jhu.edu

Abstract

We present a feature-rich knowledge tracing method that captures a student's acquisition and retention of knowledge during a foreign language phrase learning task. We model the student's behavior as making predictions under a log-linear model, and adopt a neural gating mechanism to model how the student updates their log-linear parameters in response to feedback. The gating mechanism allows the model to learn complex patterns of retention and acquisition for each feature, while the log-linear parameterization results in an interpretable knowledge state. We collect human data and evaluate several versions of the model.

1 Introduction

Knowledge tracing attempts to reconstruct when a student acquired (or forgot) each of several facts. Yet we often hear that "learning is not just memorizing facts." Facts are not atomic objects to be discretely and independently manipulated. Rather, we suppose, a student who recalls a fact in a given setting is demonstrating a *skill*—by solving a structured prediction problem that is akin to reconstructive memory (Schacter, 1989; Posner, 1989) or pattern completion (Hopfield, 1982; Smolensky, 1986). The attempt at structured prediction may draw on many cooperating feature weights, some of which may be shared with other facts or skills.

In this paper, for the task of foreign-language vocabulary learning, we will adopt a specific structured prediction model and learning algorithm. Different knowledge states correspond to model parameter settings (feature weights). Different learning styles correspond to different hyperparameters that govern the learning algorithm.[1] As we interact with each student through a simple online tutoring system, we would like to track their evolving knowledge state and identify their learning style. That is, we would like to discover parameters and hyperparameters that can explain the evidence so far and predict how the student will react in future. This could help us make good future choices about how to instruct this student, although we leave this reinforcement learning problem to future work. In this paper, we show that we can predict the student's next answer.

In short, we expand the notion of a knowledge tracing model to include representations for a student's (i) current knowledge, (ii) retention of knowledge, and (iii) acquisition of new knowledge. Our reconstruction of the student's knowledge state remains interpretable, since it corresponds to the weights of hand-designed features (sub-skills). Interpretability may help a future teaching system provide useful feedback to students and to human teachers, and help it construct educational stimuli that are targeted at improving particular sub-skills, such as features that select correct verb suffixes.

Our present paper considers a verb conjugation task, where a foreign language learner learns the verb conjugation paradigm by reviewing and interacting with a series of flash cards. This task is a good testbed, as it needs the learner to deploy sub-word features and to generalize to new examples. For example, a student learning Spanish verb conjugation might encounter pairs such as (tú entras, you enter), (yo miro, I watch). Using these examples, the student needs to recognize suffix patterns and apply them to new pairs seen such as (yo entro, I enter).

Vocabulary learning presents a challenging learning environment due to the large number of skills (words) that need to be traced. Learning vocabulary in conjunction with inflection further complicates the challenge due to the number of new sub-skills that are introduced. Huang et al. (2016) suggest that modeling sub-skill interaction is crucial to several knowledge tracing domains. For our domain, a log-linear formulation elegantly allows for arbitrary sub-skills via feature functions.

---

[1] In the present paper, we assume that all students share the same hyperparameters (same learning style), although each student will have their own parameters, which change as they learn.

Proceedings of the 21st Conference on Computational Natural Language Learning (CoNLL 2017), pages 238–247,
Vancouver, Canada, August 3 - August 4, 2017. ©2017 Association for Computational Linguistics

2 Related Work

Bayesian knowledge tracing (Corbett and Anderson, 1994) (BKT) has long been the standard method to infer a student's knowledge from his or her performance on a sequence of task items. In BKT, each skill is modeled by an HMM with two hidden states ("known" or "not-known"), and the probability of success on an item depends on the state of the skill it exercises. Transition and emission probabilities are learned from the performance data using Expectation Maximization (EM). Many extensions of BKT have been investigated, including personalization (e.g., Lee and Brunskill, 2012; Khajah et al., 2014a) and modeling item difficulty (Khajah et al., 2014b).

Our approach could be called **Parametric Knowledge Tracing (PKT)** because we take a student's knowledge to be a vector of prediction parameters (feature weights) rather than a vector of skill bits. Although several BKT variants (Koedinger et al., 2011; Xu and Mostow, 2012; González-Brenes et al., 2014) have modeled the fact that related skills share sub-skills or features, that work does not associate a real-valued weight with each feature at each time. Either skills are still represented with separate HMMs, whose transition and/or emission probabilities are parameterized in terms of shared features with time-invariant weights; or else HMMs are associated with the individual sub-skills, and the performance of a skill depends on which of its subskills are in the "known" state.

Our current version is not Bayesian since it assumes deterministic updates (but see footnote 4). A closely related line of work with deterministic updates is deep knowledge tracing (DKT) (Piech et al., 2015), which applied a classical LSTM model (Hochreiter and Schmidhuber, 1997) to knowledge tracing and showed strong improvements over BKT. Our PKT model differs from DKT in that the student's state at each time step is a more interpretable feature vector, and the state update rule is also interpretable—it is a type of error-correcting learning rule. In addition, the student's state is able to predict the student's actual response and not merely whether the response was correct. We expect that having an interpretable feature vector has better inductive bias (see experiment in section 7.1), and that it may be useful to plan future actions by smart flash card systems. Moreover, in this work we test different plausible state update rules and see how they fit actual student responses, in orer to gain insight about learning.

Most recently, Settles and Meeder (2016)'s half-life regression assumes that a student's retention of a particular skill exponentially decays with time and learns a parameter that models the rate of decay ("half-life regression"). Like González-Brenes et al. (2014) and Settles and Meeder (2016), our model leverages a feature-rich formulation to predict the probability of a learner correctly remembering a skill, but can also capture complex spacing/retention patterns using a neural gating mechanism. Another distinction between our work and half-life regression is that we focus on knowledge tracing within a single session, while half-life regression collapses a session into a single data point and operates on many such data points over longer time spans.

3 Verb Conjugation Task

We devised a flash card training system to teach verb conjugations in a foreign language. In this study, we only asked the student to translate from the foreign language to English, not vice-versa.[2]

3.1 Task Setup

We consider a setting where students go through a series of interactive flash cards during a training session. Figure 1 shows the three types of cards: (i) *Example* (EX) cards simply display a foreign phrase and its English translation (for 7 seconds). (ii) *Multiple-Choice* (MC) cards show a single foreign phrase and require the student to select one of five possible English phrases shown as options. (iii) *Typing* (TP) cards show a foreign phrase and a text input box, requiring the student to type out what they think is the English translation. g Our system can provide feedback for each student response. (i) *Indicative Feedback*: This refers to marking a student's answer as correct or incorrect (Fig. 1c, 1d and 1h). Indicative feedback is always shown for both MC and TP cards. (ii) *Explicit Feedback*: If the student makes an error on a TP card, the system has a 50% chance of showing them the true answer (Fig. 1g). (iii) *Retry*: If the student makes an error on a MC card, the system has a 50% chance of allowing them to try again, up to a maximum of 3 attempts.

3.2 Task Content

In this particular task we used three verb lemmas, each inflected in 13 different ways (Table 1). The inflections included three tenses (simple past,

---

[2] We would regard these as two separate skills that share parameters to some degree, an interesting subject for future study.

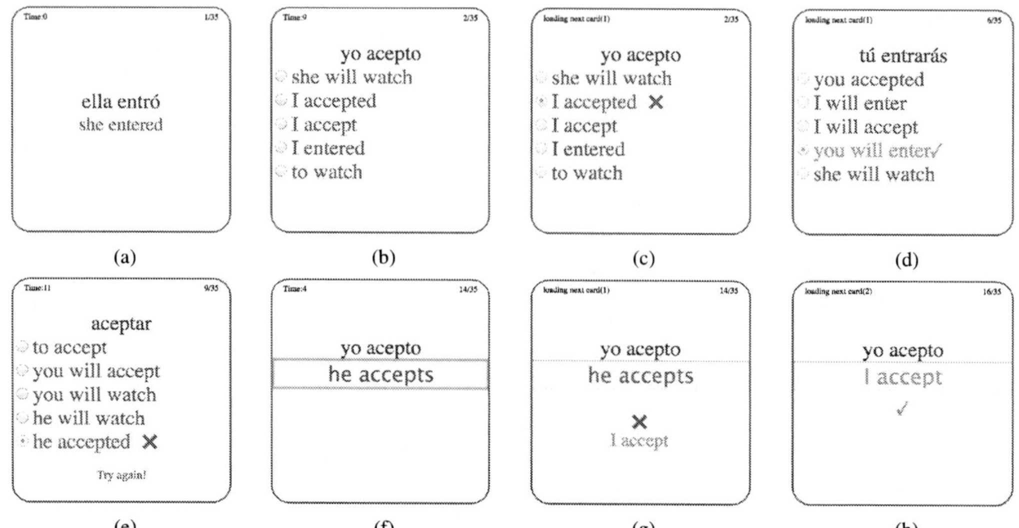

Figure 1: Screen grabs of card modalities during training. These examples show cards for a native English speaker learning Spanish verb conjugation. Fig 1a is an EX card, Fig 1b shows a MC card before the student has made a selection, and Fig 1c and 1d show MC cards after the student has made an incorrect or correct selection respectively, Fig 1e shows a MC card that is giving the student another attempt (the system randomly decides to give the student up to three additional attempts), Fig 1f shows a TP card where a student is completing an answer, Fig 1g shows a TP card that has marked a student answer wrong and then revealed the right answer (the reveal is decided randomly), and finally Fig 1h shows a card that is giving a student feedback for their answer.

Categories	Inf	SPre,1,N	SPre,2,N	SPre,3,M	SPre,3,F	SF,1,N	SF,2,N	SF,3,M	SF,3,F	SP,1,N	SP,2,N	SP,3,M	SP,3,F
	aceptar to accept	yo acepto I accept	tú aceptas you accept	él acepta he accepts	ella acepta she accepts	yo aceptaré I will accept	tú aceptarás you will accept*	él aceptará he will accept	ella aceptará she will accept	yo acepté I accepted*	tú aceptaste you accepted	él aceptó he accepted	ella aceptó she accepted
Lemma	entrar to enter	yo entro I enter	tú entras you enter	él entra he enters	ella entra she enters	yo entraré I will enter	tú entrarás you will enter	él entrará he will enter	ella entrará she will enter	yo entré I entered	tú entraste you entered	él entró he entered	ella entró she entered
	mirar to watch	yo miro I watch*	tú miras you watch*	él mira he watches*	ella mira she watches	yo miraré I will watch	tú mirarás you will watch*	él mirará he will watch	ella mirará she will watch	yo miré I watched	tú miraste you watched	él miró he watched*	ella miró she watched

Table 1: Content used in training sequences. Phrase pairs with * were used for the quiz at the end of the training sequence. This Spanish content was then transformed using the method in section 6.1.

present, and future) in each of four persons (first, second, third masculine, third feminine), as well as the infinitive form. We ensured that each surface realization was unique and regular, resulting in 39 possible phrases.[3] Seven phrases from this set were randomly selected for a quiz, which is shown at the end of the training session, leaving 32 phrases that a student may see in the training session. The student's responses on the quiz do not receive any feedback from the system. We also limited the training session to 35 cards (some of which may require multiple rounds of interaction, owing to retries). All of the methods presented in this paper could be applied to larger content sets as well.

4 Notation

We will use the following conventions in this paper. System actions a_t, student responses y_t, and feedback items a'_t are subscripted by a time $1 \leq t \leq T$. Other subscripts pick out elements of vectors or matrices. Ordinary lowercase letters indicate scalars

---

[3]The inflected surface forms included explicit pronouns.

(α, β, etc.), boldfaced lowercase letters indicate vectors (θ, $\mathbf{y}$, $\mathbf{w}^{zx}$), and boldfaced uppercase letters indicate matrices ($\mathbf{\Phi}$, $\mathbf{W}^{hh}$, etc.). The roman-font superscripts are part of the vector or matrix name.

5 Student Models

5.1 Observable Student Behavior

A flash card is a structured object $a = (x, \mathcal{O})$, where $x \in \mathcal{X}$ is the foreign phrase and $\mathcal{O}$ is a set of allowed responses. For an MC card, $\mathcal{O}$ is the set of 5 multiple-choice options on that card (or fewer on a retry attempt). For a EX or TP card, $\mathcal{O}$ is the set of all 39 English phrases (the TP user interface prevents the student from submitting a guess outside this set).

For non-EX cards, we assume the student samples their response $y \in \mathcal{O}$ from a log-linear distribution parameterized by their knowledge state $\theta \in \mathbb{R}^d$:

$$p(y \mid a; \theta) = p(y \mid x, \mathcal{O}; \theta)$$
$$= \frac{\exp(\theta \cdot \phi(x,y))}{\sum_{y' \in \mathcal{O}} \exp(\theta \cdot \phi(x,y'))} \quad (1)$$

where $\phi(x,y) \in \mathbb{R}^d$ is a feature vector extracted from the (x,y) pair.

5.2 Feature Design

The student's knowledge state is described by the weights θ placed on the features $\phi(x,y)$ in equation (1). We assume the following binary features will suffice to describe the student's behavior.

- *Phrasal* features: We include a unique indicator feature for each possible (x,y) pair, yielding 39^2 features. For example, there exists a feature that fires iff $x = \texttt{yo\_miro} \wedge y = \texttt{I\_enter}$.
- *Word* features: We include indicator features for all (source word, target word) pairs: e.g., $\texttt{yo} \in x \wedge \texttt{enter} \in y$. (These words need not be aligned.)
- *Morpheme* features: We include indicator features for all (w,mc) pairs, where w is a word of the source phrase x, and m is a possible tense, person, or number for the target phrase y (drawn from Table 1). For example, m might be $\texttt{1st}$ (first person) or $\texttt{SPre}$ (simple present).
- *Prefix* and *suffix* features: For each word or morpheme feature that fires, 8 backoff features also fire, where the source word and (if present) the target word are replaced by their first or last i characters, for $i \in \{1,2,3,4\}$.

These templates yield about 4600 features in all, so the knowledge state has $d \approx 4600$ dimensions.

5.3 Learning Models

We now turn to the question of modeling how the student's knowledge state changes during their session. θ_t denotes the state at the start of round t. We take $\theta_1 = 0$ and assume that the student uses a deterministic update rule of the following form:[4]

$$\theta_{t+1} = \beta_t \odot \theta_t + \alpha_t \odot \mathbf{u}_t \qquad (2)$$

where $\mathbf{u}_t$ is an *update vector* that depends on the student's experience (a_t, y_t, a'_t) at round t.

Why this form? First imagine that the student is learning by stochastic gradient descent on some L_2-regularized loss function $C \cdot \| \theta \|^2 + \sum_t \mathcal{L}_t(\theta)$. This algorithm's update rule has the simplified form

$$\theta_{t+1} = \beta_t \cdot \theta_t + \alpha_t \cdot \mathbf{u}_t \qquad (3)$$

where $\mathbf{u}_t = -\nabla \mathcal{L}_t(\theta)$ is the steepest-descent direction on example t, $\alpha_t > 0$ is the learning rate at time t, and $\beta_t = 1 - \alpha_t C$ handles the weight decay due to following the gradient of the regularizer.

Adaptive versions of stochastic gradient descent—such as AdaGrad (Duchi et al., 2011) and AdaDelta (Zeiler, 2012)—are more like our full rule (2) in that they allow different learning rates for different parameters.

In general, we can regard $\alpha_t \in (0,1)^d$ as modeling the rates at which the learner updates the various parameters according to $\mathbf{u}_t$, and $\beta_t \in (0,1)^d$ as modeling the rates at which those parameters are forgotten. These vectors correspond respectively to the *input gates* and *forget gates* in recurrent neural network architectures such as the LSTM (Hochreiter and Schmidhuber, 1997) or GRU (Cho et al., 2014). As in those architectures, we will use neural networks to choose α_t, β_t at each time step t, so that they may be sensitive in nonlinear ways to the context at round t.

5.3.1 Schemes for the Update Vector $\mathbf{u}_t$

We assume that $\mathbf{u}_t$ is the gradient of some log-probability, so that the student learns by trying to increase the log-probability of the correct answer. However, the student does not always *observe* the correct answer y. For example, there is no output label provided when the student only receives feedback that their answer is incorrect. Even in such cases, the student can change their knowledge state.

In this section, we define schemes for defining $\mathbf{u}_t$ from the experience (a_t, y_t, a'_t) at round t. Recall that $a_t = (x_t, \mathcal{O}_t)$. We omit the t subscripts below.

Suppose the student is told that a particular phrase $y \in \mathcal{O}$ is the correct translation of x (via an EX card or via feedback on an answer to an MC or TP card). Then an apt strategy for the student would be to use the following gradient:[5]

$$\boldsymbol{\Delta}^{\checkmark} = \nabla_\theta \log p(y \,|\, x, \mathcal{O}; \theta) \qquad (4)$$
$$= \phi(x,y) - \sum_{y' \in \mathcal{O}} p(y' \,|\, x) \phi(x,y')$$

If the student is told that y is *incorrect*, an apt strategy is to move probability mass collectively to the other available options, increasing their total probability, since one of those options *must* be correct.

---

[4] Since learning is not perfectly predictable, it would be more realistic to compute θ_t by a stochastic update—or equivalently, by a deterministic update that also depends on a random noise vector ϵ_t (which is drawn from, say, a Gaussian). These noise vectors are "nuisance parameters," but rather than integrating over their possible values, a straightforward approximation is to optimize them by gradient descent—along with the other update parameters—so as to locally maximize likelihood.

[5] An objection is that for an EX or TP card, the student may not actually know the exact set of options $\mathcal{O}$ in the denominator. We attempted setting $\mathcal{O}$ to be the set of English phrases the student has seen prior to the current question. Though intuitive, this setting performed worse on all the update and gating schemes.

We call this the *redistribution gradient (RG)*:

$$\Delta^{\boldsymbol{x}} = \nabla_\theta \log p(\mathcal{O} - \{y\} \mid x, \mathcal{O}; \boldsymbol{\theta}) \tag{5}$$

$$= \sum_{y' \in \mathcal{O} - \{y\}} p(y' \mid x, y' \neq y)\phi(x, y') \tag{6}$$

$$- \sum_{y' \in \mathcal{O}} p(y' \mid x)\phi(x, y')$$

where $p(y' \mid x, y' \neq y)$ is a renormalized distribution over just the options $y' \in \mathcal{O} - \{y\}$. Note that if the student selects two wrong answers y_1, y_2 in a row on an MC card, the first update will subtract the average features of $\mathcal{O}$ and add those of $\mathcal{O} - \{y_1\}$; the second update will subtract the average features of $\mathcal{O} - \{y_1\}$ and add those of $\mathcal{O} - \{y_1, y_2\}$. The intermediate addition and subtraction cancel out if the same α vector is used at both rounds, so the net effect is to shift probability mass from the 5 initial options to the 3 remaining ones.[6]

An alternate scheme for incorrect y is to use $-\Delta^{\checkmark}$. We call this *negative gradient (NG)*.

Since the RG and NG update vectors both worked well for handling incorrect y, we also tried linearly interpolating them *(RNG)*, with $\mathbf{u}_t = \boldsymbol{\gamma}_t \odot \Delta^{\boldsymbol{x}} + (1 - \boldsymbol{\gamma}_t) \odot -\Delta^{\checkmark}$. The interpolation vector $\boldsymbol{\gamma}_t$ has elements in $(0, 1)$, and may depend on the context (possibly different for MC and EX cards, for example).

Finally, the *feature vector (FG)* scheme simply adds the features $\phi(x, y)$ when y is correct or subtracts them when y is incorrect. This is appropriate for a student who pays attention only to y, without bothering to note that the alternative options in $\mathcal{O}$ are (respectively) incorrect or correct.

Recall from section 3.1 that the system sometimes gives both indicative and explicit feedback, telling the student that one phrase is incorrect and a different phrase is correct. We treat these as two successive updates with update vectors $\mathbf{u}_t$ and $\mathbf{u}_{t+1}$. Notice that in the FG scheme, adding this pair of update vectors resembles a perceptron update.

Table 2 summarizes our update schemes.

5.3.2 Schemes for the Gates $\alpha_t, \beta_t, \gamma_t$

We characterize each update t by a 7-dimensional context vector $\mathbf{c}_t$, which summarizes what the student has experienced. The first three elements in $\mathbf{c}_t$ are binary indicators of the type of flash card

Update Scheme	Correct	Incorrect
redistribution (RG)	$\mathbf{u}_t = \Delta^{\checkmark}$	$\mathbf{u}_t = \Delta^{\boldsymbol{x}}$
negative grad. (NG)	$\mathbf{u}_t = \Delta^{\checkmark}$	$\mathbf{u}_t = -\Delta^{\checkmark}$
feature vector (FG)	$\mathbf{u}_t = \phi(x, y)$	$\mathbf{u}_t = -\phi(x, y)$

Table 2: Summary of update schemes (other than RNG).

(EX, MC or TP). The next three elements are binary indicators of the type of information that caused the update: correct student answer, incorrect student answer, or revealed answer (via an EX card or explicit feedback). As a reminder, the system can respond with an indication that the answer is correct or incorrect, or it can reveal the answer. Finally, the last element of $\mathbf{c}_t$ is $1/|\mathcal{O}|$, the chance probability of success on this card. From $\mathbf{c}_t$, we define

$$\alpha_t = \sigma(\mathbf{W}^\alpha \mathbf{c}_t + b^\alpha \mathbf{1}) \qquad \in (0,1)^d \tag{7}$$

$$\beta_t = \sigma(\mathbf{W}^\beta \mathbf{c}_{t-1} + b^\beta \mathbf{1}) \qquad \in (0,1)^d \tag{8}$$

$$\gamma_t = \sigma(\mathbf{W}^\gamma \mathbf{c}_t + b^\gamma \mathbf{1}) \qquad \in (0,1)^d \tag{9}$$

where $\mathbf{c}_0 = \mathbf{0}$. Each gate vector is now parameterized by a weight matrix $\mathbf{W} \in \mathbb{R}^{d \times 7}$, where d is the dimensionality of the gradient and knowledge state.

We also tried simpler versions of this model. In the *vector model (VM)*, we define $\alpha_t = \sigma(\mathbf{b}^\alpha)$, and β_t, γ_t similarly. These vectors do not vary with time and simply reflect that some parameters are more labile than others. Finally, the *scalar model (SM)* defines $\alpha_t = \sigma(b^\alpha \mathbf{1})$, so that all parameters are equally labile. One could also imagine tying the gates for features derived from the same template, meaning that some *kinds* of features (in some contexts) are more labile than others, or reducing the number of parameters by learning low-rank $\mathbf{W}$ matrices.

While we also tried augmenting the context vector $\mathbf{c}_t$ with the knowledge state $\boldsymbol{\theta}_t$, this resulted in far too many parameters to train well, and did not help performance in pilot tests.

5.4 Parameter Estimation

We tune the $\mathbf{W}$ and b parameters of the model by maximum likelihood, so as to better predict the students' responses y_t. The likelihood function is

$$p(y_1, \dots y_T \mid a_t, \dots a_T) = \prod_{t=1}^{T} p(y_t \mid a_{1:t}, y_{1:t-1}, a'_{1:t-1})$$

$$= \prod_{t=1}^{T} p(y_t \mid a_t; \boldsymbol{\theta}_t) \tag{10}$$

where we take $p(y_t \mid \cdots) = 1$ at steps where the student makes no response (EX cards and explicit

---

[6]Arguably, a zeroth update should be allowed as well: upon first viewing the MC card, the student should have the chance to subtract the average features of the full set of possibilities and add those of the 5 options in $\mathcal{O}$, since again, the system is implying that one of those 5 options *must* be correct.

feedback). Note that the model assumes that $\boldsymbol{\theta}_t$ is a sufficient statistic of the student's past experiences.

For each (update scheme, gating scheme) combination, we trained the parameters using SGD with RMSProp updates (Tieleman and Hinton, 2012) to maximize the regularized log-likelihood

$$\sum_{t,\tau_t=0} \log p(y_t \mid x_t;\boldsymbol{\theta}_t) - C \cdot \| \mathbf{W} \|^2 \quad (11)$$

summed over all students. Note that $\boldsymbol{\theta}_t$ depends on the parameters through the gated update rule (2).

The development set was used for early stopping and to tune the regularization parameter C.[7]

6 Data Collection

We recruited 153 unique "students" via Amazon Mechanical Turk (MTurk). MTurk participants were compensated \$1 for completing the training and test sessions and a bonus of \$10 was given to the three top scoring students. In our dataset, we retained only the 121 students who answered all questions.

6.1 Language Obfuscation

Fig. 1 shows a few example flash cards for a native English speaker learning Spanish. Fig. 1 shows all our Spanish-English phrase pairs. In our actual task, however, we invented an artificial language for the MTurk students to learn, which allowed us to ignore the problem of students with different initial knowledge levels. We generated our artificial language by enciphering the Spanish orthographic representations. We created a mapping from the true source string alphabet to an alternative, manually defined alphabet, while attempting to preserve pronounceability (by mapping vowels to vowels, etc.). For example, `mirar` was transformed into `melil` and `tú aceptas` became `pi icedpiz`.

6.2 Card Ordering Policy

In the future, we expect to use planning or reinforcement learning to choose the sequence of stimuli for the student. For the present study of student behavior, however, we hand-designed a simple stochastic policy for choosing the stimuli.

The policy must decide what foreign phrase and card modality to use at each training step. Our policy likes to repeat phrases with which participants

had trouble—in hopes that these already-taught phrases are on the verge of being learned. It also likes to pick out new phrases. This was inspired by the popular Leitner (1972) approach, which devised a system of buckets that control how frequently an item is reviewed by a student. Leitner proposed buckets with review frequency rates of every day, every 2 days, every 4 days and so on.

For each foreign phrase $x \in \mathcal{X}$, we maintain a *novelty score* v_x, which is a function of the number of times the phrase is exposed to a student and an *error score* e_x, which is a function of the number of times the student incorrectly responded to the phrase. These scores are initialized to 1 and updated as follows:[8]

$$v_x \leftarrow v_x - 1 \text{ when } x \text{ is viewed}$$

$$e_x \leftarrow \begin{cases} 2e_x & \text{when student gets } x \text{ wrong} \\ 0.5e_x & \text{when student gets } x \text{ right} \end{cases}$$

$$x \sim \frac{g(\mathbf{v}) + g(\mathbf{e})}{2} \quad (12)$$

On each round, we sample a phrase x from either P_v or P_e (equal probability); these distributions are computed by applying a softmax $g(.)$ over the vectors $\mathbf{v}$ and $\mathbf{e}$ respectively (see Eq. 12). Once the phrase x is decided, the modality (EX, MC, TP) is chosen stochastically using probabilities $(0.2, 0.4, 0.4)$, except that probabilities $(1, 0, 0)$ are used for the first example of the session, and $(0.4, 0.6, 0)$ if x is not "TP-qualified." A phrase is TP-qualified if the student has seen both x's pronoun and x's verb lemma on previous cards (even if their correct translation was not revealed). For an MC card, the distractor phrases are sampled uniformly without replacement from the 38 other phrases.

7 Results & Experiments

We partitioned the students into three groups: 80 students for training, 20 for development, and 21 for testing. Most students found the task difficult; the average score on the 7-question quiz—was 2.81 correct, with maximum score of 6. (Recall from section 3.2 that the quiz questions were typing questions, not multiple choice questions.)

After constructing each model, we evaluated it on the held-out data: the 728 responses from the 21 testing students. We measure the log-probability under the model of each actual response ("cross-entropy"), and also the fraction of responses that

---

[7]We searched $C \in \{0.00025, 0.0005, 0.001, ..., 0.01,$ $0.025, 0.05, 0.1\}$ for each gating model and update scheme combination. $C = 0.0025$ gave best results for the CM models, 0.01 for VM and 0.0005 for SM.

[8]Arguably we should have updated e_x instead by adding/subtracting 1, since it will be exponentiated later.

were correctly predicted if our prediction was the model's max-probability response ("accuracy").

Table 3 shows the results of our experiment. All of our models were predictive, doing far better than a uniform baseline that assigned equal probability $1/|\mathcal{O}|$ to all options. Our best models are shown in the final two lines, RNG+VM and RNG+CM.

Which update scheme was best? Interestingly, although the RG update vector is principled from a *machine* learning viewpoint, the NG update vector sometimes achieved better accuracy—though worse perplexity—when predicting the responses of *human* learners.[9] We got our best results on both metrics by interpolating between RG and NG (the RNG scheme). Recall that the NG scheme was motivated by the notion that students who guessed wrong may not study the alternative answers (even though one is correct), either because it is too much trouble to study them or because (for a TP card) those alternatives are not actually shown.

Which gating mechanism was best? In almost all cases, we found that more parameters helped, with CM > VM > SM on accuracy, and a similar pattern on cross-entropy (with VM sometimes winning but only slightly). In short, it helps to use different learning rates for different features, and it probably helps to make them sensitive to the learning context.

Surprisingly, the simple FG scheme outperformed both RG and NG when used in conjunction with a scalar retention and acquisition gate. This, however, did not extend to more complex gates.

Fig. 2 shows a breakdown of the prediction accuracy measures according to whether the card was MC or TP, and according to whether the student's answer was correct (C) or incorrect (IC). Unsurprisingly, all the models have an easier time predicting the student's guess when the student is correct, since the predicted parameters θ_t will often pick the correct answer. However, this is where the vector and context gates far outperform the scalar gates. All the models find predicting the incorrect answers of the students difficult. Moreover, when predicting these incorrect answers, the RG models do slightly better than the NG models.

The models obviously have higher accuracy when predicting student answers for MC cards than for TP cards, as MC cards have fewer options. Again, within both of these modalities, the vector and context gates outperform the scalar gate.

---

[9]Even the FG vector sometimes won (on both metrics!), but this happened only with the worst gating mechanism, SM.

Update Scheme	Gating Mechanism	accuracy	cross-ent.
(Uniform baseline)		0.133	2.459
FG	SM	0.239*	2.362
FG	VM	0.357†	2.130
FG	CM	0.401	2.025
RG	SM	0.135	3.194
RG	VM	0.397†	1.909
RG	CM	0.405	1.938
NG	SM	0.185*	4.674
NG	VM	0.394†	2.320
NG	CM	0.449†*	2.244
RNG (mixed)	SM	0.183	3.502
RNG (mixed)	VM	0.427	1.855
RNG (mixed)	CM	0.449	1.888

Table 3: Table summarizing prediction accuracy and cross-entropy (in nats per prediction) for different models. Larger accuracies and smaller cross-entropies are better. Within an update scheme, the † indicates significant improvement (McNemar's test, $p < 0.05$) over the next-best gating mechanism. Within g a gating mechanism, the * indicates significant improvement over the next-best update scheme. For example, NG+CM is significantly better than NG+VM, so it receives a †; it is also significantly better than RG+CM, and receives a * as well. These comparisons are conducted only among the pure update schemes (above the double line). All other models are significantly better than RG+SM ($p < 0.01$).

Finally, Fig. 3 examines how these models behave when making specific predictions over a training sequence for a single student. At each step we plot the difference in log-probability between our model and a uniform baseline model. Thus, a marker above 0 means that our model assigned the student's answer a probability higher than chance.[10] To contrast the performance difference, we show both the highest-accuracy model (RNG+CM) and the lowest-accuracy model (RG+SM). For a high-scoring student (Fig. 3a), we see RNG+CM has a large margin over RG+SM and a slight upward trend. A higher probability than chance is noticeable even when the student makes mistakes (indicated by hollow markers). In contrast, for an average student (Fig. 3b), the margin between the two models is less perceptible. While the CM+NG model is still above the SM+RG line, there are some answers where CM+NG does very poorly. This is especially true for some of the wrong answers, for example at training steps 25, 29 and 33. Upon closer inspection into the model's error in step 33, we found the prompt received at this training step was `ekki melü` as a MC card, which had been shown to the student on three prior occasions, and the student even answered correctly on one of these occasions. This explains why the model

---

[10]For MC cards, the chance probability is in $\{\frac{1}{5}, \frac{1}{4}, \frac{1}{3}\}$— depending on how many options remain—while for TP cards it is $\frac{1}{39}$.

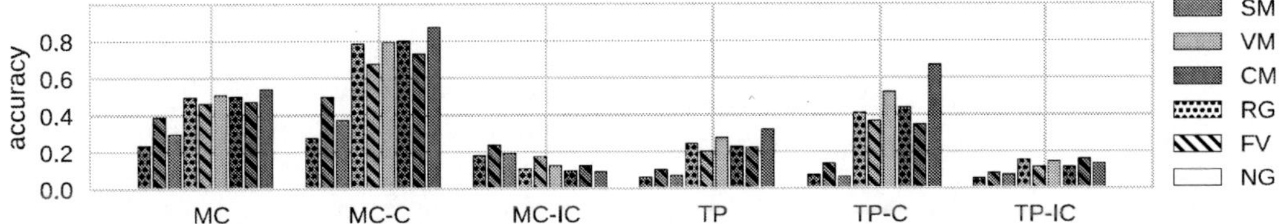

Figure 2: Plot comparing the models on test data under different conditions. Conditions MC and TP indicate Multiple-choice and Typing questions respectively. These are broken down to the cases where the student answers them correctly C and incorrectly IC. SM, VM, and CM represent scalar, vector, and context retention and acquisition gates (shown with different colors), respectively, while RG, NG and FG are redistribution, negative and feature vector update schemes(shown with different hatching patterns).

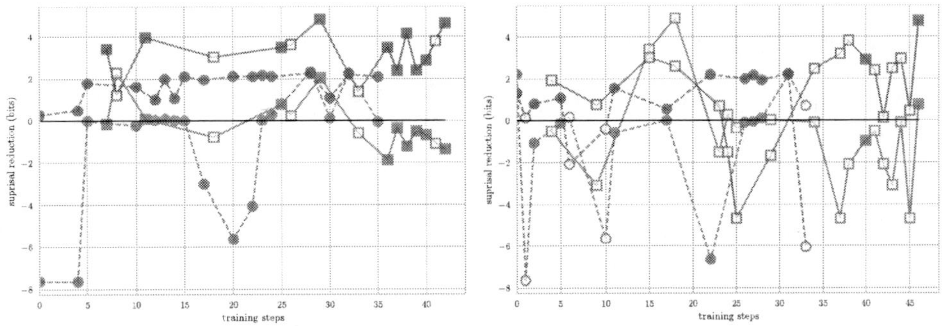

(a) a student with quiz score 6/7   (b) a student with quiz score 2/7

Figure 3: Predicting a specific student's responses. For each response, the plot shows our model's improvement in log-probability over the uniform baseline model. TP cards are the square markers connected by solid lines (the final 7 squares are the quiz), while MC cards—which have a much higher baseline—are the circle markers connected by dashed lines. Hollow and solid markers indicate correct and incorrect answers respectively. The RNG+CM model is shown in blue and the FG+SM model in red.

was surprised to see the student make this error.

7.1 Comparison with Less Restrictive Model

Our parametric knowledge tracing architecture models the student as a typical structured prediction system, which maintains weights for hand-designed features and updates them roughly as an online learning algorithm would. A natural question is whether this restricted architecture sacrifices performance for interpretability, or improves performance via useful inductive bias.

To consider the other end of the spectrum, we implemented a flexible LSTM model in the style of recent deep learning research. This alternative model predicts each response by a student (i.e., on an MC or TP card) given the entire history of previous interactions with that student as summarized by an LSTM. The LSTM architecture is formally capable of capturing update rules exactly like those of PKT, but it is far from limited to such rules.

Much like equation (1), at each time t we predict

$$p(y_t = y \mid a_t) = \frac{\exp(\mathbf{h}_t \cdot \psi(y))}{\sum_{y' \in \mathcal{O}_t} \exp(\mathbf{h}_t \cdot \psi(y))} \quad (13)$$

for each possible response y in the set of options

$\mathcal{O}_t$, where $\psi(y) \in \mathbb{R}^d$ is a learned embedding of response y. Here $\mathbf{h}_t \in \mathbb{R}^d$ denotes the hidden state of the LSTM, which evolves as the student interacts with the system and learns. $\mathbf{h}_t$ depends on the LSTM inputs for all times $< t$, just like the knowledge state θ_t in equations (1)–(2). It also depends on the LSTM input for time t, since that specifies the flash card a_t to which we are predicting the response y_t.

Each flash card $a = (x, \mathcal{O})$ is encoded by a concatenation $\mathbf{a}$ of three vectors: a one-hot 39-dimensional vector specifying the foreign phrase x, a 39-dimensional binary vector $\mathcal{O}$ indicating the possible English options in $\mathcal{O}$, and a one-hot vector indicating whether the card is EX, MC, or TP.

When reading the history of past interactions, the LSTM input at each time step t concatenates the vector representation $\mathbf{a}_t$ of the current flash card with vectors $\mathbf{a}_{t-1}, \mathbf{y}_{t-1}, \mathbf{f}_{t-1}$ that describe the student's experience in round $t - 1$: these respectively encode the previous flash card, the student's response to it (a one-hot 39-dimensional vector), and the resulting feedback (a 39-dimensional binary vector that indicates the remaining options after feedback). Thus, if the student receives no feedback, then $\mathbf{f}_{t-1} = \mathcal{O}_{t-1}$. Indicative feedback sets $\mathbf{f}_{t-1} = \mathbf{y}_{t-1}$

Model	Parameters	Accuracy(test)	Cross-Entropy
RNG+CM	≈ 97K	0.449	1.888
LSTM	≈ 25K	0.429	1.992

Table 4: Comparison of our best-performing PKT model (RNG+CM) to our LSTM model. On our dataset, PKT outperforms the LSTM both in terms of accuracy and cross-entropy.

or $\mathbf{f}_{t-1} = \mathcal{O}_{t-1} - \mathbf{y}_t$, according to whether the student was correct or incorrect. Explicit feedback (including for an EX card) sets $\mathbf{f}_{t-1}$ to a one-hot representation of the correct answer. Thus, $\mathbf{f}_{t-1}$ gives the set of "positive" options that we used in the RG update vector, while $\mathcal{O}_{t-1}$ gives the set of "negative" options, allowing the LSTM to similarly update its hidden state from $\mathbf{h}_{t-1}$ to $\mathbf{h}_t$ to reflect learning.[11]

As in section 5.4, we train the parameters by L_2-regularized maximum likelihood, with early stopping on development data. The weights for the LSTM were initialized uniformly at random $\sim U(-\delta, +\delta)$, where $\delta = 0.01$, and RMSProp was used for gradient descent. We settled on a regularization coefficient of 0.002 after a line search. The number of hidden units d was also tuned using line search. Interestingly, a dimensionality of just $d = 10$ performed best on dev data:[12] at this size, the LSTM has *fewer* parameters than our best model.

The result is shown in Table 4. These results favor our restricted PKT architecture. We acknowledge that the LSTM might perform better when a larger training set was available (which would allow a larger hidden layer), or using a different form of regularization (Srivastava et al., 2014).

Intermediate or hybrid models would of course also be possible. For example, we could predict $p(y \mid a_t)$ via (1), defining θ_t as $\mathbf{h}_t^\top M$, a learned linear function of h_t. This variant would again have access to our hand-designed features $\phi(x, y)$, so that it would know which flash cards were similar. In fact $\theta_t \cdot \phi(x, y)$ in (1) equals $\mathbf{h}_t \cdot (M\phi(x, y))$, so

M can be regarded as projecting $\phi(x, y)$ down to the LSTM's hidden dimension d, learning how to weight and use these features. In this variant, the LSTM would no longer need to take a_t as part of its input at time t: rather, $\mathbf{h}_t$ (just like θ_t in PKT) would be a pure representation of the student's knowledge state at time t, capable of predicting y_t for *any* a_t. This setup more closely resembles PKT—or the DKT LSTM of Piech et al. (2015). Unlike the DKT paper, however, it would still predict the student's specific response, not merely whether they were right or wrong.

8 Conclusion

We have presented a cognitively plausible model that traces a human student's knowledge as he or she interacts with a simple online tutoring system. The student must learn to translate very short inflected phrases from an unfamiliar language into English. Our model assumes that when a student recalls or guesses the translation, he or she is attempting to solve a structured prediction problem of choosing the best translation, based on salient features of the input-output pair. Specifically, we characterize the student's knowledge as a vector of feature weights, which is updated as the student interacts with the system. While the phrasal features memorize the translations of entire input phrases, the other features can pick up on the translations of individual words and sub-words, which are reusable across phrases.

We collected and modeled human-subjects data. We experimented with models using several different update mechanisms, focusing on the student's treatment of negative feedback and the degree to which the student tends to update or forget specific weights in particular contexts. We also found that in comparison to a less constrained LSTM model, we can better fit the human behavior by using weight update schemes that are broadly consistent with schemes used in machine learning.

In the future, we plan to experiment with more variants of the model, including variants that allow noise and personalization. Most important, we mean to use the model for planning which flash cards, feedback, or other stimuli to show next to a given student.

Acknowledgments

This material is based upon work supported by a seed grant from the Science of Learning Institute at Johns Hopkins University.

---

[11]This architecture is formally able to mimic PKT. We would store θ in the LSTM's vector of cell activations, and configure the LSTM's "input" and "forget" gates to update this according to (2) where $\mathbf{u}_t$ is computed from the input. Observe that each feature in section 5.2 has the form $\phi_{ij}(x, y) = \xi_i(x) \cdot \psi_j(y)$. Consider the hidden unit in $\mathbf{h}$ corresponding to this feature, with activation θ_{ij}. By configuring this unit's "output" gate to be $\xi_i(x)$ (where x is the current foreign phrase given in the input), we would arrange for this hidden unit to have output $\xi_i(x) \cdot \theta_{ij}$, which will be multiplied by $\psi_j(y)$ in (13) to recover $\theta_{ij} \cdot \phi_{ij}(x, y)$ just as in (1). (More precisely, the output would be sigmoid$(\xi_i(x) \cdot \theta_{ij})$, but we can evade this nonlinearity if we take the cell activations to be a scaled-down version of θ and scale up the embeddings $\psi(y)$ to compensate.)

[12]We searched $0.001, 0.002, 0.005, 0.01, 0.02, 0.05$ for the regularization coefficient, and $5, 10, 15, 20, 50, 100, 200$ for the number of hidden units.

References

Kyunghyun Cho, Bart van Merrienboer, Caglar Gulcehre, Dzmitry Bahdanau, Fethi Bougares, Holger Schwenk, and Yoshua Bengio. 2014. Learning phrase representations using rnn encoder–decoder for statistical machine translation. In *Proceedings of the 2014 Conference on Empirical Methods in Natural Language Processing (EMNLP)*. Association for Computational Linguistics, Doha, Qatar, pages 1724–1734. http://www.aclweb.org/anthology/D14-1179.

Albert T Corbett and John R Anderson. 1994. Knowledge tracing: Modeling the acquisition of procedural knowledge. *User modeling and user-adapted interaction* 4(4):253–278.

John Duchi, Elad Hazan, and Yoram Singer. 2011. Adaptive subgradient methods for online learning and stochastic optimization. *Journal of Machine Learning Research* 12(Jul):2121–2159.

José González-Brenes, Yun Huang, and Peter Brusilovsky. 2014. General features in knowledge tracing to model multiple subskills, temporal item response theory, and expert knowledge. In *Proceedings of the 7th International Conference on Educational Data Mining*. University of Pittsburgh, pages 84–91.

Sepp Hochreiter and Jürgen Schmidhuber. 1997. Long short-term memory. *Neural computation* 9(8):1735–1780.

J. J. Hopfield. 1982. Neural networks and physical systems with emergent collective computational abilities. In *Proceedings of the National Academy of Sciences of the USA*. volume 79, pages 2554–2558.

Yun Huang, J Guerra, and Peter Brusilovsky. 2016. Modeling skill combination patterns for deeper knowledge tracing. In *Proceedings of the 6th Workshop on Personalization Approaches in Learning Environments (PALE 2016)*. 24th Conference on User Modeling, Adaptation and Personalization, Halifax, Canada.

Mohammad Khajah, Rowan Wing, Robert Lindsey, and Michael Mozer. 2014a. Integrating latent-factor and knowledge-tracing models to predict individual differences in learning. In *Proceedings of the 7th International Conference on Educational Data Mining*.

Mohammad M Khajah, Yun Huang, José P González-Brenes, Michael C Mozer, and Peter Brusilovsky. 2014b. Integrating knowledge tracing and item response theory: A tale of two frameworks. In *Proceedings of Workshop on Personalization Approaches in Learning Environments (PALE 2014) at the 22th International Conference on User Modeling, Adaptation, and Personalization*. University of Pittsburgh, pages 7–12.

K. R. Koedinger, P. I. Pavlick Jr., J. Stamper, T. Nixon, and S. Ritter. 2011. Avoiding problem selection thrashing with conjunctive knowledge tracing. In *Proceedings of the 4th International Conference on Educational Data Mining*. Eindhoven, NL, pages 91–100.

Jung In Lee and Emma Brunskill. 2012. The impact on individualizing student models on necessary practice opportunities. *International Educational Data Mining Society* .

Sebastian Leitner. 1972. *So lernt man lernen: der Weg zum Erfolg*. Herder, Freiburg.

Chris Piech, Jonathan Bassen, Jonathan Huang, Surya Ganguli, Mehran Sahami, Leonidas J Guibas, and Jascha Sohl-Dickstein. 2015. Deep knowledge tracing. In *Advances in Neural Information Processing Systems*. pages 505–513.

Michael I Posner. 1989. *Foundations of cognitive science*. MIT press Cambridge, MA.

D. L. Schacter. 1989. Memory. In M. I. Postner, editor, *Foundations of Cognitive Science*, MIT Press, pages 683–725.

Burr Settles and Brendan Meeder. 2016. A trainable spaced repetition model for language learning. In *Proceedings of the 54th Annual Meeting of the Association for Computational Linguistics (Volume 1: Long Papers)*. Association for Computational Linguistics, Berlin, Germany, pages 1848–1858. http://www.aclweb.org/anthology/P16-1174.

Paul Smolensky. 1986. Information processing in dynamical systems: Foundations of harmony theory. In D. E. Rumelhart, J. L. McClelland, and the PDP Research Group, editors, *Parallel Distributed Processing: Explorations in the Microstructure of Cognition*, MIT Press/Bradford Books, Cambridge, MA, volume 1: Foundations, pages 194–281.

Nitish Srivastava, Geoffrey Hinton, Alex Krizhevsky, Ilya Sutskever, and Ruslan Salakhutdinov. 2014. Dropout: A simple way to prevent neural networks from overfitting. *Journal of Machine Learning Research* 15:1929–1958. http://jmlr.org/papers/v15/srivastava14a.html.

Tijmen Tieleman and Geoffrey Hinton. 2012. Lecture 6.5-rmsprop: Divide the gradient by a running average of its recent magnitude. *COURSERA: Neural networks for machine learning* 4(2).

Yanbo Xu and Jack Mostow. 2012. Comparison of methods to trace multiple subskills: Is LR-DBN best? In *Proceedings of the 5th International Conference on Educational Data Mining*. pages 41–48.

Matthew D Zeiler. 2012. Adadelta: an adaptive learning rate method. *arXiv preprint arXiv:1212.5701* .

A Probabilistic Generative Grammar for Semantic Parsing

Abulhair Saparov
Carnegie Mellon University
Machine Learning Department
Pittsburgh, P.A.
asaparov@cs.cmu.edu

Vijay Saraswat
IBM T.J. Watson
Research Center
Yorktown Heights, N.Y.
vijay@saraswat.org

Tom M. Mitchell
Carnegie Mellon University
Machine Learning Department
Pittsburgh, P.A.
tom.mitchell@cmu.edu

Abstract

We present a generative model of natural language sentences and demonstrate its application to semantic parsing. In the generative process, a logical form sampled from a prior, and conditioned on this logical form, a grammar probabilistically generates the output sentence. Grammar induction using MCMC is applied to learn the grammar given a set of labeled sentences with corresponding logical forms. We develop a semantic parser that finds the logical form with the highest posterior probability exactly. We obtain strong results on the GEOQUERY dataset and achieve state-of-the-art F1 on JOBS.

1 Introduction

Accurate and efficient semantic parsing is a long-standing goal in natural language processing. Existing approaches are quite successful in particular domains (Zettlemoyer and Collins, 2005, 2007; Wong and Mooney, 2007; Liang et al., 2011; Kwiatkowski et al., 2010, 2011, 2013; Li et al., 2013; Zhao and Huang, 2014; Dong and Lapata, 2016). However, they are largely domain-specific, relying on additional supervision such as a lexicon that provides the semantics or the type of each token in a set (Zettlemoyer and Collins, 2005, 2007; Kwiatkowski et al., 2010, 2011; Liang et al., 2011; Zhao and Huang, 2014; Dong and Lapata, 2016), or a set of initial synchronous context-free grammar rules (Wong and Mooney, 2007; Li et al., 2013). To apply the above systems to a new domain, additional supervision is necessary. When beginning to read text from a new domain, humans do not need to re-learn basic English gram-

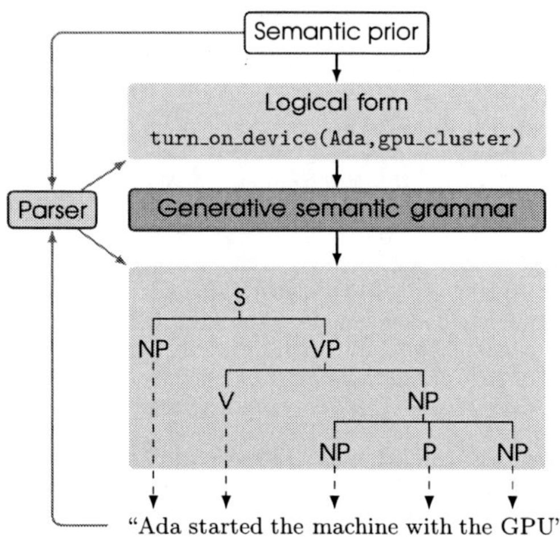

Figure 1: High-level illustration of the setting in which our grammar is applied in this paper. The dark arrows outline the generative process. During parsing, the input is the observed sentence, and we wish to find the most probable logical form and derivation given the training data under the semantic prior.

mar. Rather, they may encounter novel terminology. With this in mind, our approach is akin to that of (Kwiatkowski et al., 2013) where we provide domain-independent supervision to train a semantic parser on a new domain. More specifically, we restrict the rules that may be learned during training to a set that characterizes the general syntax of English. While we do not explicitly present and evaluate an open-domain semantic parser, we hope our work provides *a step* in that direction.

Knowledge plays a critical role in natural language understanding. Even seemingly trivial sentences may have a large number of ambiguous interpretations. Consider the sentence *"Ada started the machine with the GPU,"* for example. Without additional knowledge, such as the fact that "machine" can refer to computing devices that contain GPUs, or that computers generally contain devices such as

Proceedings of the 21st Conference on Computational Natural Language Learning (CoNLL 2017), pages 248–259,
Vancouver, Canada, August 3 - August 4, 2017. ©2017 Association for Computational Linguistics

GPUs, the reader cannot determine whether the GPU is part of the machine or if the GPU is a device that is used to start machines. Context is highly instrumental to quickly and unambiguously understand sentences.

In contrast to most semantic parsers, which are built on discriminative models, our model is fully generative: To generate a sentence, the logical form is first drawn from a prior. A grammar then recursively constructs a derivation tree top-down, probabilistically selecting production rules from distributions that depend on the logical form (see Figure 1 for a high-level schematic diagram). The semantic prior distribution provides a straightforward way to incorporate background knowledge, such as information about the types of entities and predicates, or the context of the utterance. Additionally, our generative model presents a promising direction to *jointly* learn to understand and generate natural language.

This article describes the following contributions:

- In Section 2, we present our grammar formalism in its general form.

- Section 2.2 discusses aspects of the model in its application to the later experiments.

- In Section 3, we present a method to perform grammar induction in this model. Given a set of observed sentences and their corresponding logical forms, we apply Markov chain Monte Carlo (MCMC) to infer the posterior distributions of the production rules in the grammar.

- Given a trained grammar, we also develop a method to perform parsing in Section 4: to find the k-best logical forms for a given sentence, leveraging the semantic prior to guide its search.

- Using the GEOQUERY and JOBS datasets, we demonstrate in Section 6 that this framework can be applied to create natural language interfaces for semantic formalisms as complex as Datalog/lambda calculus, which contain variables, scope ambiguity, and superlatives.

All code and datasets are available at github. com/asaparov/parser.

2 Semantic grammar

A grammar in our formalism operates over a set of nonterminals $\mathcal{N}$ and a set of terminal

$$\text{S} \rightarrow \text{N:select\_arg1} \quad \text{VP:delete\_arg1}$$
$$\text{VP} \rightarrow \text{V:identity} \quad \text{N:select\_arg2}$$
$$\text{VP} \rightarrow \text{V:identity}$$
$$\text{N} \rightarrow \text{``tennis''} \qquad \text{V} \rightarrow \text{``swims''}$$
$$\text{N} \rightarrow \text{``Andre Agassi''} \qquad \text{V} \rightarrow \text{``plays''}$$
$$\text{N} \rightarrow \text{``Chopin''}$$

Figure 2: Example of a grammar in our framework. This grammar operates on logical forms of the form *predicate(first argument, second argument)*. The semantic function `select_arg1` returns the first argument of the logical form. Likewise, the function `select_arg2` returns the second argument. The function `delete_arg1` removes the first argument, and `identity` returns the logical form with no change. In our use of the framework, the interior production rules (the first three listed above) are examples of rules that we specify, whereas the terminal rules and the posterior probabilities of *all* rules are learned via grammar induction. We also use a richer semantic formalism than in this example. Section 2.2 provides more detail.

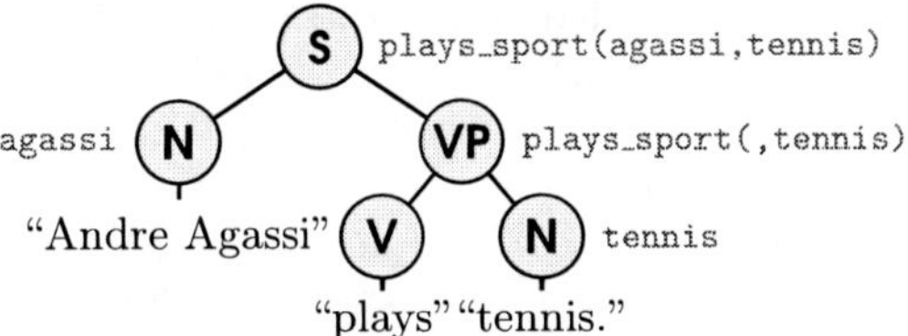

Figure 3: Example of a derivation tree under the grammar given in Figure 2. The logical form corresponding to every node is shown in blue beside the respective node. The logical form for V is `plays_sport(,tennis)` and is omitted above to reduce clutter.

symbols $\mathcal{W}$. It can be understood as an extension of a context-free grammar (CFG) (Chomsky, 1956) where the generative process for the syntax is dependent on a logical form, thereby coupling syntax with semantics. In the top-down generative process of a derivation tree, a logical form guides the selection of production rules. Production rules in our grammar have the form $A \rightarrow B_1{:}f_1 \ldots B_k{:}f_k$ where $A \in \mathcal{N}$ is a nonterminal, $B_i \in \mathcal{N} \cup \mathcal{W}$ are right-hand side symbols, and f_i are *semantic transformation functions*. These functions can encode how to "decompose" this logical form when recursively generating the subtrees rooted at each B_i. Thus, they enable semantic compositionality. An example of a grammar in this framework is shown in Figure 2, and a derivation tree is shown in Figure 3. Let $\mathcal{R}$ be the set of production rules in the grammar and $\mathcal{R}_A$ be the set of production rules with left-hand nonterminal symbol A.

2.1 Generative process

A *parse tree* (or *derivation*) in this formalism is a tree where every interior node is labeled with a nonterminal symbol, every leaf is labeled with a terminal, and the root node is labeled with the root nonterminal S. Moreover, every node in the tree is associated with a logical form: let x^n be the logical form assigned to the tree node n, and $x^0 = x$ for the root node 0.

The generative process to build a parse tree begins with the root nonterminal S and a logical form x. We *expand* S by randomly drawing a production rule from $\mathcal{R}_S$, *conditioned* on the logical form x. This provides the first level of child nodes in the derivation tree. So if, for example, the rule $S \rightarrow B_1{:}f_1 \ldots B_k{:}f_k$ were drawn, the root node would have k child nodes, $n_1, \ldots, n_k$, respectively labeled $B_1, \ldots, B_k$. The logical form associated with each node is determined by the semantic transformation function: $x^{n_i} = f_i(x)$. These functions describe the relationship between the logical form at a child node and that of its parent node. This process repeats recursively with every right-hand side nonterminal symbol, until there are no unexpanded nonterminal nodes. The sentence is obtained by taking the *yield* of the terminals in the tree (a concatenation).

The semantic transformation functions are specific to the semantic formalism and may be defined as appropriate to the application. In our parsing application, we define a domain-independent set of transformation functions (e.g., one function selects the left n conjuncts in a conjunction, another selects the nth argument of a predicate instance, etc).

2.2   Selecting production rules

In the above description, we did not specify the distribution from which rules are selected from $\mathcal{R}_A$. There are many modeling options available when specifying this distribution. In our approach, we choose a hierarchical Dirichlet process (HDP) prior (Teh et al., 2006). Every nonterminal in our grammar $A \in \mathcal{N}$ will be associated with an HDP hierarchy. For each nonterminal, we specify a sequence of *semantic feature functions*, $\{g_1, \ldots, g_m\}$, each of which return a discrete feature (such as an integer) of an input logical form x. We use this sequence of feature functions to define the hierarchy of the HDP: starting with the root node, we add a child node for every possible value of the first feature function g_1. For each of these

child nodes, we add a grandchild node for every possible value of the second feature function g_2, and so forth. The result is a complete tree of depth m. Each node n in this tree is assigned a distribution G^n as follows:

$$G^0 \sim \mathrm{DP}(\alpha^0, H), \qquad (1)$$
$$G^n \sim \mathrm{DP}(\alpha^n, G^{\pi(n)}),$$

where 0 is the root node, $\pi(n)$ is the parent of n, α are a set of concentration parameters, and H is a base distribution over $\mathcal{R}_A$. This base distribution is independent of the logical form x.

To select a rule in the generative process, given the logical form x, we can compute its feature values $(g_1(x), \ldots, g_m(x))$ which specify a unique path in the HDP hierarchy to a leaf node G^x. We then draw the production rule from G^x. The specified set of production rules and semantic features are included with the code package. The specified rules and features do not change across our experiments.

Take, for example, the derivation in Figure 3. In the generative process where the node VP is expanded, the production rule is drawn from the HDP associated with the nonterminal VP. Suppose the HDP was constructed using a sequence of two semantic features: (`predicate`, `arg2`). In the example, the feature functions are evaluated with the logical form `plays_sport(,tennis)` and they return the sequence (`plays_sport`, `tennis`). This sequence uniquely identifies a path in the HDP hierarchy from the root node 0 to a leaf node n. The production rule VP $\rightarrow$ V N is drawn from this leaf node G^n, and the generative process continues recursively.

In our implementation, we divide the set of nonterminals $\mathcal{N}$ into two groups: (1) the set of "interior" nonterminals, and (2) preterminals. The production rules of preterminals are restricted such that the right-hand side contains only terminal symbols. The rules of interior nonterminals are restricted such that only nonterminal symbols appear on the right side.

1. For **preterminals**, we set H to be a distribution over sequences of terminal symbols as follows: we generate each token in the sequence i.i.d. from a uniform distribution over a finite set of terminals and a special *stop* symbol with probability ϕ_A. Once the stop symbol is drawn, we have finished gen-

erating the rule. Note that we do not specify a set of domain-specific terminal symbols in defining this distribution.

2. For **interior nonterminals**, we specify H as a discrete distribution over a domain-independent set of production rules. This requires specifying a set of nonterminal symbols, such as S, NP, VP, etc. Since these production rules contain semantic transformation functions, they are specific to the semantic formalism.

We emphasize that only the prior is specified here, and we will use grammar induction to infer the posterior. In principle, a more relaxed choice of H may enable grammar induction without pre-specified production rules, and therefore without dependence on a particular semantic formalism or natural language, if an efficient inference algorithm can be developed in such cases.

3 Induction

We describe grammar induction independently of the choice of rule distribution. Let θ be the random variables in the grammar: in the case of the HDP prior, θ is the set of all distributions G^n at every node in the hierarchies. Given a set of sentences $y \triangleq \{y_1, \ldots, y_n\}$ and corresponding logical forms $x \triangleq \{x_1, \ldots, x_n\}$, we wish to compute the posterior $p(t, \theta | x, y)$ over the unobserved variables: the grammar θ and the latent derivations/parse trees $t \triangleq \{t_1, \ldots, t_n\}$. This is intractable to compute exactly, and so we resort to Markov chain Monte Carlo (MCMC) (Gelfand and Smith, 1990; Robert and Casella, 2010). To perform blocked Gibbs sampling, we pick initial values for t and θ and repeat the following:

1. For $i = 1, \ldots, n$, sample $t_i | \theta, x_i, y_i$.
2. Sample $\theta | t$.

However, since the sampling of each tree t depends on θ, and we need to resample all n parse trees before sampling θ, this Markov chain can be slow to mix. Thus, we employ collapsed Gibbs sampling by integrating out θ. In this algorithm, we repeatedly sample from $t_i | t_{-i}, x_i, y_i$ where $t_{-i} = t \setminus \{t_i\}$.

$$p(t_i | t_{-i}, x_i, y_i) = \qquad (2)$$

$$\mathbb{1}\{\text{yield}(t_i) = y_i\} \prod_{\substack{A \in \mathcal{N}}} p\left(\bigcap_{\substack{\{n \in t_i : n \\ \text{has label } A\}}} r^n \;\middle|\; t_{-i}, x_i \right),$$

where the intersection is taken over tree nodes $n \in t_i$ labeled with the nonterminal A, r^n is the production rule at node n, and $\mathbb{1}\{\cdot\}$ is 1 if the condition is true and zero otherwise. With θ integrated out, the probability does not necessarily factorize over rules. In the case of the HDP prior, selecting a rule will increase the probability that the same rule is selected again (due to the "rich get richer" effect observed in the Chinese restaurant process). We instead use a Metropolis-Hastings step to sample t_i, where the proposal distribution is given by the fully factorized form:

$$p(t_i^* | t_{-i}, x_i, y_i) = \qquad (3)$$

$$\mathbb{1}\{\text{yield}(t_i^*) = y_i\} \prod_{n \in t_i^*} p\left(r^n \mid t_{-i}, x_i^n\right).$$

After sampling t_i^*, we choose to accept the new sample with probability

$$\frac{\prod_{n \in t_i} p(r^n | x^n, t_{-i})}{p\left(\bigcap_{n \in t_i} r^n | x, t_{-i}\right)} \frac{p\left(\bigcap_{n \in t_i^*} r^n | x, t_{-i}\right)}{\prod_{n \in t_i^*} p(r^n | x^n, t_{-i})},$$

where t_i, here, is the old sample, and t_i^* is the newly proposed sample. In practice, this acceptance probability is very high. This approach is very similar in structure to that in Johnson et al. (2007); Blunsom and Cohn (2010); Cohn et al. (2010).

If an application requires posterior samples of the grammar variables θ, we can obtain them by drawing from $\theta | t$ after the collapsed Gibbs sampler has mixed. Note that this algorithm requries no further supervision beyond the utterances y and logical forms x. However, it is able to exploit additional information such as supervised derivations/parse trees. For example, a lexicon can be provided where each entry is a terminal symbol y_i with a corresponding logical form label x_i. We evaluate our method with and without such a lexicon.

Refer to Saparov and Mitchell (2016) for details on HDP inference and computing $p(r^n | x^n, t_{-i})$.

3.1 Sampling t_i^*

To sample from equation (3), we use inside-outside sampling (Finkel et al., 2006; Johnson et al., 2007), a dynamic programming approach, where the inside step is implemented using an agenda-driven chart parser (Indurkhya and Damerau, 2010). The algorithm fills a chart, which has a cell for every nonterminal A, sentence start position i, end position j, and logical form x. The algorithm aims to compute the *inside probability* of every chart cell: that is, for every cell (A, i, j, x), we compute the probability that t_i^* contains a subtree rooted with the nonterminal A and logical form x, spanning the sentence positions (i, j). Let $I_{(A,i,j,x)}$ be the inside probability at the chart cell (A, i, j, x):

$$I_{(A,i,j,x)} = \sum_{A \to B_1 : f_1 \ldots B_K : f_K}$$
$$\sum_{i=l_1 < \ldots < l_{K+1}=j} \prod_{u=1}^{K} I_{(B_u, l_u, l_{u+1}, f_u(x))}. \quad (4)$$

Each item in the agenda represents a snapshot of the computation of this expression for a single rule $A \to B_1 : f_1 \ldots B_K : f_K$. The agenda item stores the current position in the rule k, the set of sentence spans that correspond to the first k right-hand side symbols $l_1, \ldots, l_{k+1}$, the span of the rule (i, j), the logical form x, and the inside probability of the portion of the rule computed so far. At every iteration, the algorithm pops an item from the agenda and adds it to the chart, and considers the next right-hand side symbol B_k.

- If B_k is a terminal, it will match it against the input sentence. If the terminal does not match the sentence, this agenda item is discarded and the algorithm continues to the next iteration. If the terminal does match, the algorithm *increments* the rule. That is, for each possible value of l_{k+2}, the algorithm constructs a new agenda item containing the same contents as the old agenda item, but with rule position $k + 1$.

- If B_k is a nonterminal, the algorithm will *expand* it (if it was not previously expanded at this cell). The algorithm considers every production rule of the form $B_k \to \beta$, and every possible end position for the next nonterminal $l_{k+2} = l_{k+1} + 1, \ldots, j - 1$, and enqueues a new agenda item with rule $B_k \to \beta$, rule position set to 1, span set to (l_k, l_{k+1}), logical form set to $f_k(x)$, and inside probability initialized to 1. The original agenda item is said to be "waiting" for B_k to be completed later on in the algorithm.

- If the rule is *complete* (there are no subsequent symbols in the rule of this agenda item), we can compute its inner probabil-

ity $p(A \to B_1 : f_1 \ldots B_K : f_K | x, t_{-i})$. First, we record that this rule was used to complete the left-hand nonterminal A at the cell (A, i, j, x). Then, we consider every agenda item in the chart that is currently "waiting" for the left-hand nonterminal A at this sentence span. The search *increments* each "waiting" item, adding a new item to the agenda for each, whose log probability is the sum of the log probability of the old agenda item and the log probability of the completed rule.

We prioritize items in the agenda by $i - j$ (so items with smaller spans are dequeued first). This ensures that whenever the search considers expanding B_k, if B_k was previously expanded at this cell, its inside probability is fully computed. Thus, we can avoid re-expanding B_k and directly increment the agenda item. The algorithm terminates when there are no items in the agenda.

All that remains is the outside step: to sample the tree given the computed inside probabilities. To do so, we begin with the chart cell $(S, 0, |y_i|, x_i)$ where $|y_i|$ is the length of sentence y_i, and we consider all completed rules at this cell (these rules will be of the form $S \to \beta$). Each rule will have a computed inside probability, and we can sample the rule from the categorical distribution according to these inside probabilities. Then, we consider the right-hand side nonterminals in the selected rule, and continue sampling recursively. The end result is a tree sampled from equation (3).

4   Parsing

For a new sentence y_*, we aim to find the logical form x_* and derivation t_* that maximizes

$$p(x_*, t_* | y_*, \boldsymbol{\theta}) \propto p(x_*)p(y_*|t_*)p(t_*|x_*, \boldsymbol{\theta}),$$
$$= \mathbb{1}\{\mathrm{yield}(t_*) = y_*\}p(x_*)\prod_{n \in t_*} p(r^n | x_*^n, \boldsymbol{\theta}). \quad (5)$$

Here, $\boldsymbol{\theta}$ is a point estimate of the grammar, which may be obtained from a single sample, or from a Monte Carlo average over a finite set of samples.

To perform parsing, we first describe an algorithm to compute the derivation t_* that maximizes the above quantity, given the logical form x_* and input sentence y_*. We will later demonstrate how this algorithm can be used to find the optimal logical form and derivation x_*, t_*. To find the optimal t_*, we again use an agenda-driven chart parser to perform the optimization, with a number of important differences. Each agenda item will keep track the derivation tree completed so far.

The algorithm is very similar in structure to the inside algorithm described above. At every iteration of the algorithm, an item is popped from the agenda and added to the chart, applying one of the three operations available to the inside algorithm. The algorithm begins by expanding the root nonterminal S at $(0, |y_*|)$ with the logical form x_*.

4.1 Agenda prioritization

The most important difference from the inside algorithm is the prioritization of agenda items. For a given agenda item with rule $A \rightarrow B_1 : f_1 \ldots B_K : f_K$ with logical form x at sentence position (i, j), we aim to assign as its priority an upper bound on equation (5) for any derivation that contains this rule at this position. To do so, we can split the product in the objective $\prod_{n \in t_*} p(r^n | x_*^n, \boldsymbol{\theta})$ into a product of two components: (1) the *inner probability* is the product of the terms that correspond to the subtree of t_* rooted at the current agenda item, and (2) the *outer probability* is the product of the remaining terms, which correspond to the parts of t_* outside of the subtree rooted at the agenda item. A schematic decomposition of a derivation tree is shown in Figure 4.

We define an upper bound on the log inner probability $I_{(A,i,j)}$ for any subtree rooted at nonterminal A at sentence span (i, j).

$$I_{(A,i,j)} \triangleq \tag{6}$$

$$\max_{A \rightarrow B_1 \ldots B_K} \left(\max_{x'} \log p(A \rightarrow B_1, \ldots, B_K | x', \boldsymbol{\theta}) \right.$$

$$\left. + \max_{l_2 < \ldots < l_K} \sum_{k=1}^{K} I_{(B_k, l_k, l_{k+1})} \right),$$

where $l_1 = i$, $l_{K+1} = j$. Note that the left term is a maximum over all logical forms x', and so this upper bound only considers syntactic information. The right term can be maximized using dynamic programming in $\mathcal{O}(K^2)$. As such, classical syntactic parsing algorithms can be applied to compute I for every chart cell in $\mathcal{O}(n^3)$. For any terminal symbol T, we define $I_{(T,i,j)} = 0$.

We similarly define $O_{(A,i,j,x)}$ representing a bound on the outer probability at every cell.

$$O_{(A,i,j,x)} \triangleq \max_{\{t : \text{yield}(t) = y_*\}} \left(\log p(x) \right. \tag{7}$$

$$\left. + \log p(t_L | x, \boldsymbol{\theta}) + \sum_{(A', i', j') \in r(t_R)} I_{(A', i', j')} \right),$$

where the maximum is taken over t which is a derivation containing a subtree rooted at A at sentence position (i, j). In this expression, t_L is the outer-left portion of the derivation tree t, t_R is the outer-right portion, and $r(t_R)$ is the set of root vertices of the trees in t_R.

Using these two upper bounds, we define the priority of any agenda item with rule $A \rightarrow B_1 : f_1 \ldots B_K : f_K$ at rule position k, with log probability score ρ, and logical form x as:

$$\rho + \max_{l_{k+2} < \ldots < l_{K+1}} \sum_{u=k}^{K} I_{(B_u, l_u, l_{u+1})} + O_{(A,i,j,x)}. \tag{8}$$

Thm 1. *If the priority of agenda items is computed as in equation (8), then at every iteration of the chart parser, the priority of new agenda items will be at most the priority of the current item.*

Proof. See supplementary material A.

Thus, the search is *monotonic*[1]. That is, the maximum priority of items in the agenda never increases.

This property allows us to compute the outer probability bound $O_{(A,i,j,x)}$ for free. Computing it directly is intractable. Consider the expansion step for an agenda item with rule $A \rightarrow B_1 : f_1 \ldots B_K : f_K$ at rule position k, with log probability score ρ, and logical form x. The nonterminal B_k is expanded next at sentence position (l_k, l_{k+1}), and its outer probability is simply

$$O_{(B_k, l_k, l_{k+1}, f_k(x))} = \rho + \tag{9}$$

$$\max_{l_{k+2} < \ldots < l_{K+1}} \sum_{u=k+1}^{K} I_{(B_u, l_u, l_{u+1})} + O_{(A,i,j,x)}.$$

The monotonicity of the search guarantees that any subsequent expansion of B_k at (l_k, l_{k+1}) will not yield a more optimal bound.

Monotonicity also guarantees that when the algorithm completes a derivation for the root nonterminal S, it is optimal (i.e. the Viterbi

---

[1] In the presentation of the algorithm as an A* search, the heuristic is *consistent*.

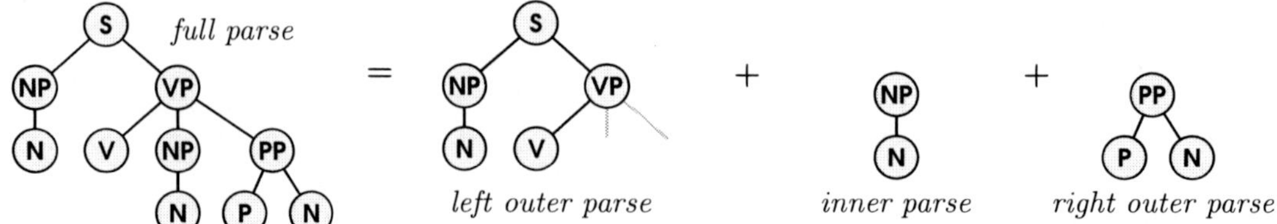

Figure 4: Decomposition of a parse tree into its left outer parse, inner parse, and its right outer parse. This is one example of such a decomposition. For instance, we may similarly produce a decomposition where the prepositional phrase is the inner parse, or where the verb is the inner parse. The terminals are omitted and only the syntactic portion of the parse is displayed here for conciseness.

parse). In this way, we can continue execution to obtain the k-best parses for the given sentence.

4.2 Optimization over logical forms

The above algorithm finds the optimal derivation t_*, given a sentence y_*, logical form x_*, and grammar θ. To jointly optimize over both the derivation and logical form, given θ, imagine running the above algorithm repeatedly for *every* logical form. This approach, implemented naively, is clearly infeasible due to the sheer number of possible logical forms. However, there is a great deal of overlap across the multiple runs, which corresponds to shared substructures across logical forms, which we can exploit to develop an efficient and exact algorithm. At the first step of every run, the root nonterminal is expanded for every logical form. This would create of a new agenda item for every logical form, which are identical in every field except for the logical form (and therefore, its prior probability). Thus, we can represent this set of agenda items as a single agenda item, where instead of an individual logical form x, we store a logical form set X. The outer probability bound is now defined over sets of logical forms: $O_{(A,i,j,X)} \triangleq \max_{x \in X} O_{(A,i,j,x)}$. We can use this quantity in equation (8) to compute the priority of these "aggregated" agenda items. Thus, this algorithm is a kind of branch-and-bound approach to the combinatorial optimization problem. A sparse representation of a set of logical forms is essential for efficient parsing.

Another difference arises after completing the parsing of a rule $A \rightarrow B_1 : f_1 \ldots B_K : f_K$ with a set of logical forms X, where we need to compute $\log p(A \rightarrow B_1 : f_1 \ldots B_K : f_K | x, \theta)$. In the inside algorithm, this was straightforward since there was only a single logical form. But in the parsing setting, X is a set of logical forms, and the aforementioned prob-

ability can vary across instances within this set (for the HDP prior, for example, the set may correspond to multiple distinct paths in the HDP hierarchy). Therefore, we divide X into its equivalence classes. More precisely, consider the set of disjoint subsets of $X = X_1 \bigcup \ldots \bigcup X_m$ where $X_i \bigcap X_j = \varnothing$ for $i \neq j$, such that $p(A \rightarrow B_1 : f_1 \ldots B_K : f_K | x', \theta)$ is the same for every $x' \in X_i$. For each equivalence class X_i, we create a "completed nonterminal" item with the appropriate parse tree, log probability, and logical form set X_i. With these, we continue inspecting the chart for search states "waiting" for the nonterminal A.

The *increment* operation is also slightly different in the parser. When we increment a rule $A \rightarrow B_1 : f_1 \ldots B_K : f_K$ after completing parsing for the symbol B_k with logical form set X, we create a new agenda item with the same contents as the old item, but with the rule position increased by one. The log probability of the new agenda item is the sum of the log probabilities of the old agenda item and the completed subtree. Similarly the logical form set of the new agenda item will be the intersection of $\{f_k^{-1}(x) : x \in X\}$ and the logical forms in the old agenda item.

Our implementation is available for reference at `github.com/asaparov/grammar` and `github.com/asaparov/parser`.

5   Semantic prior

The modular nature of the semantic prior allows us to explore many different models of logical forms. We experiment with a fairly straightforward prior: Predicate instances are generated left-to-right, conditioned only on the last predicate instance that was sampled for each variable. When a predicate instance is sampled, its predicate, arity, and "direction"[2] are simultaneously sampled from a cat-

___
[2]`size(A)`, `size(A,B)`, vs `size(B,A)`, etc.

Method	Additional Supervision	GeoQuery			Jobs		
		P	R	F1	P	R	F1
WASP (Wong and Mooney, 2006)	1,2	87.2	74.8	80.5			
λ-WASP (Wong and Mooney, 2007)	1,2,6	92.0	86.6	89.2			
Extended GHKM (Li et al., 2013)	2,6	93.0	87.6	90.2			
Zettlemoyer and Collins (2005)	3,5,6	**96.3**	79.3	87.0	97.3	79.3	87.4
Zettlemoyer and Collins (2007)	3,5,6	91.6	86.1	88.8			
UBL (Kwiatkowski et al., 2010)	5	94.1	85.0	89.3			
FUBL (Kwiatkowski et al., 2011)	5	88.6	88.6	88.6			
TISP (Zhao and Huang, 2014)	5,6	92.9	**88.9**	**90.9**	85.0	**85.0**	85.0
GSG − lexicon − type-checking	4	86.9	75.7	80.9	89.5	67.1	76.7
GSG + lexicon − type-checking	4,5	88.4	81.8	85.0	91.4	75.7	82.8
GSG − lexicon + type-checking	4,6	89.3	77.9	83.2	93.2	69.3	79.5
GSG + lexicon + type-checking	4,5,6	90.7	83.9	87.2	**97.4**	81.4	**88.7**

Legend for sources of additional supervision are:

1. Training set containing 792 examples,
2. Domain-specific set of initial synchronous CFG rules,
3. Domain-independent set of lexical templates,
4. Domain-independent set of interior production rules,
5. Domain-specific initial lexicon,
6. Type-checking and type specification for entities.

Figure 5: The methods in the top part of the table were evaluated using 10-fold cross validation, whereas those in the bottom part were evaluated with an independent test set.

Logical form:	`answer(A,smallest(A,state(A)))`	`answer(A,largest(B,(state(A),population(A,B))))`
Test sentence:	"Which state is the smallest?"	"Which state has the most population?"
Generated:	"What state is the smallest?"	"What is the state with the largest population?"

Figure 6: Examples of sentences generated from our trained grammar on logical forms in the GeoQuery test set. Generation is performed by computing $\arg\max_{y_*} p(y_* | x_*, \boldsymbol{\theta})$.

egorical distribution. Functions like `largest`, `shortest`, etc, are sampled in the same process. We again use an HDP to model the discrete distribution conditioned on a discrete random variable.

We also follow Wong and Mooney (2007); Li et al. (2013); Zhao and Huang (2014) and experiment with type-checking, where every entity is assigned a type in a type hierarchy, and every predicate is assigned a functional type. We incorporate type-checking into the semantic prior by placing zero probability on type-incorrect logical forms. More precisely, logical forms are distributed according to the original prior, conditioned on the fact that the logical form is type-correct. Type-checking requires the specification of a type hierarchy. Our hierarchy contains 11 types for GeoQuery and 12 for Jobs. We run experiments with and without type-checking for comparison.

6 Results

To evaluate our parser, we use the GeoQuery and Jobs datasets. Following Zettlemoyer and Collins (2007), we use the same 600 GeoQuery sentences for training and an independent test set of 280 sentences. On Jobs, we use the same 500 sentences for training and 140 for testing. We run our parser with two se-

tups: (1) with no domain-specific supervision, and (2) using a small domain-specific lexicon and a set of beliefs (such as the fact that Portland is a city). For each setup, we run the experiments with and without type-checking, for a total of 4 experimental setups. A given output logical form is considered correct if it is semantically equivalent to the true logical form.[3] We measure the precision and recall of our method, where precision is the number of correct parses divided by the number of sentences for which our parser provided output, and recall is the number of correct parses divided by the total number of sentences in each dataset. Our results are shown compared against many other semantic parsers in Figure 5. Our method is labeled GSG for "generative semantic grammar." The numbers for the baselines were copied from their respective papers, and so their specified lexicons/type hierarchies may differ slightly.

Many sentences in the test set contain tokens previously unseen in the training set. In such cases, the maximum possible recall is 88.2 and 82.3 on GeoQuery and Jobs, respectively. Therefore, we also measure the effect of adding a domain-specific lexicon, which

---

[3]The result of execution of the output logical form is identical to that of the true logical form, for any grounding knowledge base/possible world.

maps semantic constants like `maine` to the noun "maine" for example. This lexicon is analogous to the string-matching and argument identification steps previous parsers. We constructed the lexicon manually, with an entry for every city, state, river, and mountain in GEOQUERY (141 entries), and an entry for every city, company, position, and platform in JOBS (180 entries).

Aside from the lexicon and type hierarchy, the only training information is given by the set of sentences y, corresponding logical forms x, and the domain-independent set of interior production rules, as described in section 2.2. In our experiments, we found that the sampler converges rapidly, with only 10 passes over the data. This is largely due to our restriction of the interior production rules to a domain-independent set.

We emphasize that the addition of type-checking and a lexicon are mainly to enable a fair comparison with past approaches. As expected, their addition greatly improves parsing performance. Our method achieves state-of-the-art F1 on the JOBS dataset. However, even without such domain-specific supervision, the parser performs reasonably well.

7   Related work

Our grammar formalism can be related to synchronous CFGs (SCFGs) (Aho and Ullman, 1972) where the semantics and syntax are generated simultaneously. However, instead of modeling the joint probability of the logical form and natural language utterance $p(x, y)$, we model the factorized probability $p(x)p(y|x)$. Modeling each component in isolation provides a cleaner division between syntax and semantics, and one half of the model can be modified without affecting the other (such as the addition of new background knowledge, or changing the language/semantic formalism). We used a CFG in the syntactic portion of our model (although our grammar is not context-free, due to the dependence on the logical form). Richer syntactic formalisms such as combinatory categorial grammar (Steedman, 1996) or head-driven phrase structure grammar (Pollard and Sag, 1994) could replace the syntactic component in our framework and may provide a more uniform analysis across languages. Our model is similar to lexical functional grammar (LFG) (Kaplan and Bresnan, 1995), where f-structures are replaced with logical forms. Nothing in our model precludes incorporating syntactic information like f-structures into the logical form, and as such, LFG is realized in our framework. Our approach can be used to define new generative models of these grammatical formalisms. We implemented our method with a particular semantic formalism, but the grammatical model is agnostic to the choice of semantic formalism or the language. As in some previous parsers, a parallel can be drawn between our parsing problem and the problem of finding shortest paths in hypergraphs using A* search (Klein and Manning, 2001, 2003; Pauls and Klein, 2009; Pauls et al., 2010; Gallo et al., 1993).

8   Discussion

In this article, we presented a generative model of sentences, where each sentence is generated recursively top-down according to a semantic grammar, where each step is conditioned on the logical form. We developed a method to learn the posterior of the grammar using a Metropolis-Hastings sampler. We also derived a Viterbi parsing algorithm that takes into account the prior probability of the logical forms. Through this semantic prior, background knowledge and other information can be easily incorporated to better guide the parser during its search. Our parser provides state-of-the-art results when compared with past approaches.

As a generative model, there are promising applications to interactive learning, caption generation, data augmentation, etc. Richer semantic priors can be applied to perform ontology learning, relation extraction, or context modeling. Applying this work to semi-supervised settings is also interesting. The avenues for future work are numerous.

Acknowledgments

We thank the anonymous reviewers for their helpful feedback, and we also thank Emmanouil A. Platanios for insightful discussion and comments. This research is based upon work supported in part by the Office of the Director of National Intelligence (ODNI), IARPA, and by DARPA under contract number FA8750-13-2-0005. The views and conclusions contained herein are those of the authors and should not be interpreted as necessarily representing the official policies, either expressed or implied of ODNI, IARPA, DARPA, or the US government. The US Government is authorized to reproduce and distribute the reprints for governmental purposed notwithstanding any copyright annotation therein.

References

Albert V. Aho and Jeffery D. Ullman. 1972. *The Theory of Parsing, Translation, and Compiling*, volume 1. Prentice-Hall, Englewood Cliffs, NJ.

Phil Blunsom and Trevor Cohn. 2010. Inducing synchronous grammars with slice sampling. In *HLT-NAACL*. The Association for Computational Linguistics, pages 238–241.

Noam Chomsky. 1956. Three models for the description of language. *IRE Transactions on Information Theory* 2:113–124.

Trevor Cohn, Phil Blunsom, and Sharon Goldwater. 2010. Inducing tree-substitution grammars. *Journal of Machine Learning Research* 11:3053–3096.

Li Dong and Mirella Lapata. 2016. Language to logical form with neural attention. *CoRR* abs/1601.01280.

Jenny Rose Finkel, Christopher D. Manning, and Andrew Y. Ng. 2006. Solving the problem of cascading errors: approximate bayesian inference for linguistic annotation pipelines. In *EMNLP '06: Proceedings of the 2006 Conference on Empirical Methods in Natural Language Processing*. Association for Computational Linguistics, Morristown, NJ, USA, pages 618–626.

Giorgio Gallo, Giustino Longo, and Stefano Pallottino. 1993. Directed hypergraphs and applications. *Discrete Applied Mathematics* 42(2):177–201.

Alan E. Gelfand and Adrian F. M. Smith. 1990. Sampling-based approaches to calculating marginal densities. *Journal of the American Statistical Association* 85(410):398–409.

Nitin Indurkhya and Fred J. Damerau, editors. 2010. *Handbook of Natural Language Processing, Second Edition*. Chapman and Hall/CRC.

M. Johnson, T. L. Griffiths, and S. Goldwater. 2007. Bayesian inference for PCFGs via Markov chain Monte Carlo. In *Proceedings of the North American Conference on Computational Linguistics (NAACL '07)*.

Ronald M. Kaplan and Joan Bresnan. 1995. Lexical-functional grammar: A formal system for grammatical representation.

Dan Klein and Christopher D. Manning. 2001. Parsing and hypergraphs. In *IWPT*. Tsinghua University Press.

Dan Klein and Christopher D. Manning. 2003. A* parsing: Fast exact viterbi parse selection. In *HLT-NAACL*.

Tom Kwiatkowski, Eunsol Choi, Yoav Artzi, and Luke S. Zettlemoyer. 2013. Scaling semantic parsers with on-the-fly ontology matching. In *EMNLP*. ACL, pages 1545–1556.

Tom Kwiatkowski, Luke S. Zettlemoyer, Sharon Goldwater, and Mark Steedman. 2010. Inducing probabilistic ccg grammars from logical form with higher-order unification. In *EMNLP*. ACL, pages 1223–1233.

Tom Kwiatkowski, Luke S. Zettlemoyer, Sharon Goldwater, and Mark Steedman. 2011. Lexical generalization in ccg grammar induction for semantic parsing. In *EMNLP*. ACL, pages 1512–1523.

Peng Li, Yang Liu, and Maosong Sun. 2013. An extended ghkm algorithm for inducing lambda-scfg. In Marie desJardins and Michael L. Littman, editors, *AAAI*. AAAI Press.

Percy Liang, Michael I. Jordan, and Dan Klein. 2011. Learning dependency-based compositional semantics. *CoRR* abs/1109.6841.

Adam Pauls and Dan Klein. 2009. K-best a* parsing. In Keh-Yih Su, Jian Su, and Janyce Wiebe, editors, *ACL/IJCNLP*. The Association for Computer Linguistics, pages 958–966.

Adam Pauls, Dan Klein, and Chris Quirk. 2010. Top-down k-best a* parsing. In *Proceedings of the ACL 2010 Conference Short Papers*. Association for Computational Linguistics, Stroudsburg, PA, USA, ACLShort '10, pages 200–204.

Carl Pollard and Ivan A. Sag. 1994. *Head-driven phrase structure grammar*. University of Chicago Press, Chicago.

C. P. Robert and G. Casella. 2010. *Monte Carlo Statistical Methods*. Springer, New York, NY.

Abulhair Saparov and Tom M. Mitchell. 2016. A probabilistic generative grammar for semantic parsing. In *arXiv:1606.06361*.

Mark Steedman. 1996. *Surface structure and interpretation*. Linguistic inquiry monographs, 30. MIT Press.

Yee Whye Teh, Michael I. Jordan, Matthew J. Beal, and David M. Blei. 2006. Hierarchical dirichlet processes. *Journal of the American Statistical Association* 101(476):1566–1581.

Yuk Wah Wong and Raymond J. Mooney. 2006. Learning for semantic parsing with statistical machine translation. In Robert C. Moore, Jeff A. Bilmes, Jennifer Chu-Carroll, and Mark Sanderson, editors, *HLT-NAACL*. The Association for Computational Linguistics.

Yuk Wah Wong and Raymond J. Mooney. 2007. Learning synchronous grammars for semantic parsing with lambda calculus. In John A. Carroll, Antal van den Bosch, and Annie Zaenen, editors, *ACL*. The Association for Computational Linguistics.

Luke S. Zettlemoyer and Michael Collins. 2005. Learning to map sentences to logical form: Structured classification with probabilistic categorial grammars. In *UAI*. AUAI Press, pages 658–666.

Luke S. Zettlemoyer and Michael Collins. 2007. Online learning of relaxed ccg grammars for parsing to logical form. In Jason Eisner, editor, *EMNLP-CoNLL*. ACL, pages 678–687.

Kai Zhao and Liang Huang. 2014. Type-driven incremental semantic parsing with polymorphism. *CoRR* abs/1411.5379.

A Proof of Thm 1

Induct on the iteration of the algorithm. Let a be the current agenda item, where the production rule of the item is $A \to B_1{:}f_1 \dots B_K{:}f_K$, the rule position is k, the set of sentence spans that correspond to the first k right-hand side symbols is $l_1, \dots, l_{k+1}$, the span of the rule is (i, j), the logical form is x, and the log probability of the first k right-hand side symbols is ρ. For notational brevity, we let $c(a)$ denote the priority of the agenda item a as defined in equation (8). There are three cases:

Case 1 If B_k is a terminal, a new agenda item is created only if the terminal matches the token in the input sentence. Then for each possible value of l_{k+2}, a new agenda item a' is created, where ρ is the same as that in the old agenda item a. Since the logical form is the same, and

$$I_{(B_k,l_k,l_{k+1})} + \max_{l_{k+3}<\dots<l_{K+1}} \sum_{u=k+1}^{K} I_{(B_u,l_u,l_{u+1})}$$

$$\leq \max_{l_{k+2}<\dots<l_{K+1}} \sum_{u=k}^{K} I_{(B_u,l_u,l_{u+1})},$$

the priority of the new agenda item is at most that of the old item $c(a') \leq c(a)$.

Case 2 If B_k is a nonterminal, it proceeds to "expand" it. Suppose to the contrary that we create an agenda item whose priority is greater than that of the current item. This implies that there exists a production rule $B_k \to C_1 \dots C_{K'}$ and a set of sentence spans $l'_2 < \dots < l'_{K'+1}$ such that

$$c(a) =$$

$$\rho + \max_{l_{k+2}<\dots<l_{K+1}} \sum_{u=k}^{K} I_{(B_u,l_u,l_{u+1})} + O_{(A,i,j,x)},$$

$$< \sum_{u=1}^{K'} I_{(C_u,l'_u,l'_{u+1})} + O_{(B_k,l_k,l_{k+1},f_k(x))}$$

$$\leq I_{(B_k,l_k,l_{k+1})} + O_{(B_k,l_k,l_{k+1},f_k(x))},$$

where $l'_1 = l_k$ and $l_{K'+1} = l_{k+1}$. By definition of the bound on the outer probability, the above inequality implies that there exists a derivation t' and logical form x' such that $f_k(x') = f_k(x)$ and

$$c(a) < \log p(x') + \log p(t'_L | x', \boldsymbol{\theta})$$

$$+ I_{(B_k,l_k,l_{k+1})} + \sum_{(A',i',j')\in r(t'_R)} I_{(A',i',j')}. \quad (10)$$

Let $D \to E_1 \dots E_{K''}$ be the production rule in t' that contains the B_k nonterminal at sentence span (l_k, l_{k+1}), and so for some m, $E_m = B_k$. In addition, let s'_i be the sibling derivation tree rooted at E_i for all $i = 1, \dots, m-1$. Therefore, there must exist an agenda item a' with the same production rule, with rule position m, (l_k, l_{k+1}) as the sentence spans of D_m, log probability of the first m right-hand side symbols $\sum_{i=1}^{m-1} \log p(s'_i | x', \boldsymbol{\theta})$, and logical form x'. The priority of this rule state is

$$c(a') = \sum_{i=1}^{m-1} \log p(s'_i | x', \boldsymbol{\theta})$$

$$+ \max_{l_{m+2}<\dots<l_{K''+1}} \sum_{u=m}^{K''} I_{(E_u,l_u,l_{u+1})} + O_{(D,i',j',x')}.$$

By definition of the outer probability bound, we have $O_{(D,i',j',x')} \geq \log p(x') + \log p(t''_L | x', \boldsymbol{\theta}) + \sum_{(A',i',j')\in r(t''_R)} I_{(A',i',j')}$ where t''_L is the outer-left portion of the derivation tree t' not containing the subtree rooted at the nonterminal C, and t''_R is similarly the outer-right portion. Thus, we can lower bound $c(a')$

$$c(a') \geq$$

$$\log p(x') + \log p(t''_L|x',\boldsymbol{\theta}) + \sum_{i=1}^{m-1} \log p(s'_i|x',\boldsymbol{\theta})$$

$$+ \max_{l_{m+2} < \ldots < l_{K''+1}} \sum_{u=m}^{K''} I_{(D_u,l_u,l_{u+1})} + \sum_{(A',i',j') \in r(t''_R)} I_{(A',i',j')},$$

which is at least the quantity in equation (10), since

$$\log p(t'_L|x',\boldsymbol{\theta}) =$$

$$\log p(t''_L|x',\boldsymbol{\theta}) + \sum_{i=1}^{m-1} \log p(s'_i|x',\boldsymbol{\theta}),$$

$$\sum_{(A',i',j') \in r(t'_R)} I_{(A',i',j')} \leq$$

$$\max_{l_{m+2} < \ldots < l_{K''+1}} \sum_{u=m+1}^{K''} I_{(D_u,l_u,l_{u+1})} + \sum_{(A',i',j') \in r(t''_R)} I_{(A',i',j')}.$$

Thus, $c(a') > c(a)$, and so by the inductive hypothesis, a' was processed by the algorithm at an earlier iteration. However, this would mean that the nonterminal B_k is expanded more than once at the sentence location (l_k, l_{k+1}), which is disallowed.

Case 3 If the rule is complete, the algorithm looks for previously-processed agenda items that are "waiting" for a derivation of B_k at positions (l_k, l_{k+1}). The algorithm will combine the completed derivation with the waiting state and create a new agenda item where the rule position is incremented by 1. Suppose to the contrary that the new agenda item a' has priority greater than the current item a. Let the production rule of a' be $D \to E_1 : f_1 \ldots E_{K'} : f_{K'}$ where $E_m = A$ for some m, and so m is the rule position of a'. Additionally, let the sentence spans of the first $m-1$ right-hand symbols be $l'_1, \ldots, l'_{m-1}$, and ρ' is the log probability of the first $m-1$ right-hand symbols, and the logical form is x' where $f_m(x') = x$. Therefore, we can write

$$c(a) = \log p(t'_A|x,\boldsymbol{\theta}) + O_{(A,i,j,x)},$$

$$< \rho' + \log p(t'_A|x,\boldsymbol{\theta}) + O_{(D,i',j',x')}$$

$$+ \max_{l_{m+3} < \ldots < l_{K'}} \sum_{u=m+1}^{K'} I_{(D_u,l'_u,l'_{u+1})} = c(a').$$

This expression implies

$$O_{(A,i,j,x)} < \rho' +$$

$$\max_{l_{m+3} < \ldots < l_{K'}} \sum_{u=m+1}^{K'} I_{(D_u,l'_u,l'_{u+1})} + O_{(C,i',j',x')},$$

but this is not possible by the definition of $O_{(A,i,j,x)}$ in equation (7), as we would have found a derivation with a strictly better objective. ∎

Learning Contextual Embeddings for Structural Semantic Similarity using Categorical Information

Massimo Nicosia◇ and **Alessandro Moschitti**
◇DISI, University of Trento 38123 Povo (TN), Italy
Qatar Computing Research Institute, HBKU, 34110, Doha, Qatar
`{m.nicosia,amoschitti}@gmail.com`

Abstract

Tree kernels (TKs) and neural networks are two effective approaches for automatic feature engineering. In this paper, we combine them by modeling context word similarity in semantic TKs. This way, the latter can operate subtree matching by applying neural-based similarity on tree lexical nodes. We study how to learn representations for the words in context such that TKs can exploit more focused information. We found that neural embeddings produced by current methods do not provide a suitable contextual similarity. Thus, we define a new approach based on a Siamese Network, which produces word representations while learning a binary text similarity. We set the latter considering examples in the same category as similar. The experiments on question and sentiment classification show that our semantic TK highly improves previous results.

1 Introduction

Structural Kernels (Moschitti, 2006) can automatically represent syntactic and semantic structures in terms of substructures, showing high accuracy in several tasks, e.g., relation extraction (Nguyen et al., 2009; Nguyen and Moschitti, 2011; Plank and Moschitti, 2013; Nguyen et al., 2015) and sentiment analysis (Nguyen and Shirai, 2015).

At the same time, deep learning has demonstrated its effectiveness on a plethora of NLP tasks such as Question Answering (QA) (Severyn and Moschitti, 2015a; Rao et al., 2016), and parsing (Andor et al., 2016), to name a few. Deep learning models (DLMs) usually do not include traditional features; they extract relevant signals from distributed representations of words, by applying a sequence of linear and non linear functions to the input. Word representations are learned from large corpora, or directly from the training data of the task at hand.

Clearly, joining the two approaches above would have the advantage of easily integrating structures with kernels, and lexical representations with embeddings into learning algorithms. In this respect, the Smoothed Partial Tree Kernel (SPTK) is a noticeable approach for using lexical similarity in tree structures (Croce et al., 2011). SPTK can match different tree fragments, provided that they only differ in lexical nodes. Although the results were excellent, the used similarity did not consider the fact that words in context assume different meanings or weights for the final task, i.e., it does not consider the context. In contrast, SPTK would benefit to use specific word similarity when matching subtrees corresponding to different constituency. For example, the two questions:

– *What famous model was married to Billy Joel?*

– *What famous model of the Universe was proposed?*

are similar in terms of structures and words but clearly have different meaning and also different categories: the first asks for a human (the answer is Christie Brinkley) whereas the latter asks for an entity (an answer could be *the Expanding Universe*). To determine that such questions are not similar, SPTK would need different embeddings for the word *model* in the two contexts, i.e., those related to *person* and *science*, respectively.

In this paper, we use distributed representations generated by neural approaches for computing the lexical similarity in TKs. We carry out an extensive comparison between different methods, i.e., word2vec, using CBOW and SkipGram, and

Proceedings of the 21st Conference on Computational Natural Language Learning (CoNLL 2017), pages 260–270,
Vancouver, Canada, August 3 - August 4, 2017. ©2017 Association for Computational Linguistics

Glove, in terms of their impact on convolution semantic TKs for question classification (QC). We experimented with composing word vectors and alternative embedding methods for bigger unit of text to obtain context specific vectors.

Unfortunately, the study above showed that standard ways to model context are not effective. Thus, we propose a novel application of Siamese Networks to learn word vectors in context, i.e., a representation of a word conditioned on the other words in the sentence. Since a comprehensive and large enough corpus of disambiguated senses is not available, we approximate them with categorical information: we derive a classification task that consists in deciding if two words extracted from two sentences belong to the same sentence category. We use the obtained contextual word representations in TKs. Our new approach tested on two tasks, question and sentiment classification, shows that modeling the context further improves the semantic kernel accuracy compared to only using standard word embeddings.

2   Related Work

Distributed word representations are an effective and compact way to represent text and are widely used in neural network models for NLP. The research community has also studied them in the context of many other machine learning models, where they are typically used as features.

SPTK is an interesting kernel algorithm that can compute word to word similarity with embeddings (Croce et al., 2011; Filice et al., 2015, 2016). In our work, we go beyond simple word similarity and improve the modeling power of SPTK using contextual information in word representations. Our approach mixes the syntactic and semantic features automatically extracted by the TK, with representations learned with deep learning models (DLMs).

Early attempts to incorporate syntactic information in DLMs use grammatical relations to guide the composition of word embeddings, and recursively compose the resulting substructural embeddings with parametrized functions. In Socher et al. (2012) and Socher et al. (2013), a parse tree is used to guide the composition of word embeddings, focusing on a single parametrized function for composing all words according to different grammatical relations. In Tai et al. (2015), several LSTM architectures that follow an order determined by

syntax are presented. Considering embeddings only, Levy and Goldberg (2014) proposed to learn word representations that incorporate syntax from dependency-based contexts. In contrast, we inject syntactic information by means of TKs, which establish a hard match between tree fragments, while the soft match is enabled by the similarities of distributed representations.

DLMs have been applied to the QC task. Convolutional neural neworks are explored in Kalchbrenner et al. (2014) and Kim (2014). In Ma et al. (2015), convolutions are guided by dependencies linking question words, but it is not clear how the word vectors are initialized. In our case, we only use pre-trained word vectors and the output of a parser, avoiding intensive manual feature engineering, as in Silva et al. (2010). The accuracy of these models are reported in Tab. 1 and can be compared to our QC results (Table 4) on the commonly used test set. In addition, we report our results in a cross-validation setting to better assess the generalization capabilities of the models.

To encode words in context, we employ a Siamese Network, a DLM that has been widely used to model sentence similarity. In a Siamese setting, the same network is used to encode two sentences, and during learning, the distance between the representations of similar sentences is minimized. In Mueller and Thyagarajan (2016), an LSTM is used to encode similar sentences, and their Manhattan distance is minimized. In Neculoiu et al. (2016), a character level bidirectional LSTM is used to determine the similarity between job titles. In Tan et al. (2016), the problem of question/answer matching is treated as a similarity task, and convolutions and pooling on top of LSTM states are used to extract the sentence representations. The paper reports also experiments that include neural attention. Those mechanisms are excluded in our work, since we do not want to break the symmetry of the encoding model.

In Siamese Networks, the similarity is typically computed between pair of sentences. In our work, we compute the similarity of word representations extracted from the states of a recurrent network. Such representations still depend on the entire sentence, and thus encode contextual information.

3   Tree Kernels-based Lexical Similarity

TKs are powerful methods for computing the similarity between tree structures. They can effec-

Model	Features	Accuracy
SVM	Unigram, syntactic information, parser output, WordNet features, hand-coded features	95.0
DCNN	Unsupervised vectors	93.0
CNN_{ns}	CBOW fine-tuned vectors	93.6
DepCNN	Depencency guided filters	95.6
SPTK	SPTK and LSA word vectors	94.8

Table 1: QC accuracy (%) and description of SVM (Silva et al., 2010), DCNN (Kalchbrenner et al., 2014), CNN_{ns} (Kim, 2014), DepCNN, (Ma et al., 2015) and SPTK (Croce et al., 2011) models.

tively encode lexical, syntactic and semantic information in learning algorithms. For this purpose, they count the number of substructures shared by two trees. In most TKs, two tree fragments match if they are identical. In contrast, Croce et al. (2011) proposed the Smoothed Partial Tree Kernel (SPTK), which can also match fragments differing in node labels. For example, consider two constituency tree fragments which differ only for one lexical node. SPTK can establish a soft match between the two fragments by associating the lexicals with vectors and by computing the cosine similarity between the latter. In previous work for QC, vectors were obtained by applying Latent Semantic Analysis (LSA) to a large corpus of textual documents. We use neural word embeddings as in Filice et al. (2015) to encode words. Differently from them, we explore specific embeddings by also deriving a vector representation for the context around each word. Finally, we define a new approach based on the category of the sentence of the target word.

3.1 Smoothed Partial Tree Kernel

SPTK can be defined as follows: let the set $\mathcal{F} = \{f_1, f_2, \ldots, f_{|\mathcal{F}|}\}$ be a tree fragment space and $\chi_i(n)$ be an indicator function, equal to 1 if the target f_i is rooted at node n, and equal to 0 otherwise. A TK function over T_1 and T_2 is:

$$TK(T_1, T_2) = \sum_{n_1 \in N_{T_1}} \sum_{n_2 \in N_{T_2}} \Delta(n_1, n_2),$$

where N_{T_1} and N_{T_2} are the sets of nodes of T_1 and T_2, and $\Delta(n_1, n_2) = \sum_{i=1}^{|\mathcal{F}|} \chi_i(n_1)\chi_i(n_2)$. The latter is equal to the number of common fragments rooted in the n_1 and n_2 nodes. The Δ function for

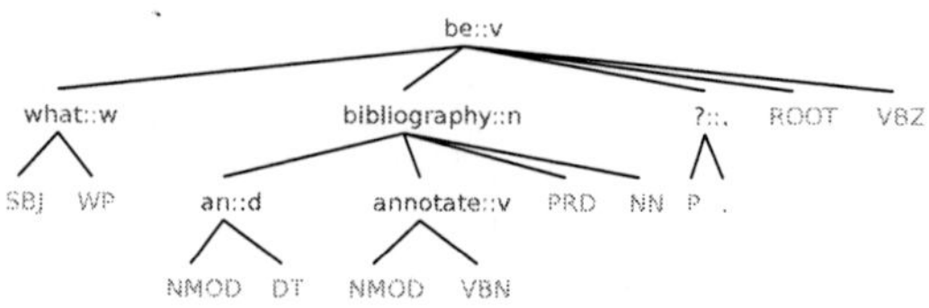

Figure 1: The Lexical Centered Tree (LCT) of the lemmatized sentence: *"What is an annotated bibliography?"*.

SPTK[1] defines a rich kernel space as follows:

1. If n_1 and n_2 are leaves then $\Delta_\sigma(n_1, n_2) = \mu\lambda\sigma(n_1, n_2)$; else

2. $\Delta_\sigma(n_1, n_2) = \mu\sigma(n_1, n_2) \times \left(\lambda^2 + \sum_{\vec{I}_1, \vec{I}_2, l(\vec{I}_1) = l(\vec{I}_2)}\right.$

$$\left.\lambda^{d(\vec{I}_1) + d(\vec{I}_2)} \prod_{j=1}^{l(\vec{I}_1)} \Delta_\sigma(c_{n_1}(\vec{I}_{1j}), c_{n_2}(\vec{I}_{2j}))\right), \quad (1)$$

where σ is any similarity between nodes, e.g., between their lexical labels, $\mu, \lambda \in [0, 1]$ are two decay factors, $\vec{I}_1$ and $\vec{I}_2$ are two sequences of indices, which index subsequences of children u, $\vec{I} = (i_1, \ldots, i_{|u|})$, in sequences of children s, $1 \leq i_1 < \ldots < i_{|u|} \leq |s|$, i.e., such that $u = s_{i_1}..s_{i_{|u|}}$, and $d(\vec{I}) = i_{|u|} - i_1 + 1$ is the distance between the first and last child. c is one of the children of the node n, also indexed by $\vec{I}$. SPTK has been shown to be rather efficient in practice (Croce et al., 2011, 2012).

3.2 Structural representation for text

Syntactic and semantic structures can play an important role in building effective representations for machine learning algorithms. The automatic extraction of features from tree structured representations of text is natural within the TK framework. Therefore, several studies have shown the power of associating rich structural encoding with TKs (Severyn et al., 2013; Tymoshenko and Moschitti, 2015).

In Croce et al. (2011), a wide array of representations derived from the parse tree of a sentence are evaluated. The Lexical Centered Tree (LCT) is shown to be the best performing tree layout for the QC task. An LCT, as shown in Figure 1, contains lexicals at the pre-terminal levels, and their grammatical functions and POS-tags are added as leftmost children. In addition, each lexical node is encoded as a word lemma, and has a suffix which is composed by a special : : symbol and the first

---

[1] For a similarity score between 0 and 1, a normalization in the kernel space, i.e. $\frac{TK(T_1, T_2)}{\sqrt{TK(T_1, T_1) \times TK(T_2, T_2)}}$ is applied.

letter of the POS-tag of the word. These marked lexical nodes are then mapped to their corresponding numerical vectors, which are used in the kernel computation. Only lemmas sharing the same POS-tag are compared in the semantic kernel similarity.

4 Context Word Embeddings for SPTK

We propose to compute the similarity function σ in SPTK as the cosine similarity of word embeddings obtained with neural networks. We experimented with the popular Continuous Bag-Of-Words (CBOW), SkipGram models (Mikolov et al., 2013), and GloVe (Pennington et al., 2014).

4.1 Part-of-speech tags in word embeddings

As in (Croce et al., 2011), we observed that embeddings learned from raw words are not the most effective in the TK computation. Thus, similarly to Trask et al. (2015), we attach a special :: suffix plus the first letter of the part-of-speech (POS) to the word lemmas. This way, we differentiate words by their tags, and learn specific embedding vectors for each of them. This approach increases the performance of our models.

4.2 Modeling the word context

Although a word vector encodes some information about word co-occurrences, the context around a word, as also suggested in Iacobacci et al. (2016), can explicitly contribute to the word similarity, especially when the target words are infrequent. For this reason, we also represent each word as the concatenation of its embedding with a second vector, which is supposed to model the context around the word. We build this vector as (i) a simple average of the embeddings of the other words in the sentence, and (ii) with a method specifically designed to embed longer units of text, namely paragraph2vec (Le and Mikolov, 2014). This is similar to word2vec: a network is trained to predict a word given its context, but it can access to an additional vector specific for the paragraph, where the word and the context are sampled.

5 Recurrent Networks for Encoding Text

As described in Sec. 2, a Siamese Network encodes two inputs into a vectorial representation, reusing the network parameters. In this section, we briefly describe the standard units used in our Siamese Network to encode sentences.

5.1 Recurrent neural network units

Recurrent Neural Networks (RNNs) constitute one of the main architectures used to model sequences, and they have seen a wide adoption in the NLP literature. Vanilla RNNs consume a sequence of vectors one step at the time, and update their internal state as a function of the new input and their previous internal state. For this reason, at any given step, the internal state depends on the entire history of previous states. These networks suffer from the vanishing gradient problem (Bengio et al., 1994), which is mitigated by a popular RNN variant, the Long Short Term Memory (LSTM) network (Hochreiter and Schmidhuber, 1997). An LSTM can control the amount of information from the input that affects its internal state, the amount of information in the internal state that can be forgotten, and how the internal state affects the output of the network.

The Gated Recurrent Unit (GRU) (Chung et al., 2014) is an LSTM variant with similar performance and less parameters, thus faster to train. Since we use this recurrent unit in our model, we briefly review it. Let x_t and s_t be the input vector and state at timestep t, given a sequence of input vectors $(x_1, ..., x_T)$, the GRU computes a sequence of states $(s_1, ..., s_T)$ according to the following equations:

$$z = \sigma(x_t U^z + s_{t-1} W^z)$$
$$r = \sigma(x_t U^r + s_{t-1} W^r)$$
$$h = tanh(x_t U^h + (s_{t-1} \circ r) W^h)$$
$$s_t = (1 - z) \circ h + z \circ s_{t-1}$$

The GRU has an update, z, and reset gate, r, and does not have an internal memory beside the internal state. The U and W matrices are parameters of the model. σ is the logistic function, the $\circ$ operator denotes the elementwise (Hadamard) product, and $tanh$ is the hyperbolic tangent function. All the non-linearities are applied elementwise.

5.2 Bidirectional networks

The aforementioned recurrent units consume the input sequence in one direction, and thus earlier internal states do not have access to future steps. Bidirectional RNNs (Schuster and Paliwal, 1997) solve this issue by keeping a forward and backward internal states that are computed by going through the input sequence in both directions. The state at any given step will be the concatenation of the forward and backward state at that step, and, in our case, will contain useful information from both the left and right context of a word.

6 Contextual Word Similarity Network

The methods to model the context described in Sec. 4.2 augment the target word vector with dimensions derived from the entire sentence. This provides some context that may increase the discriminative power of SPTK. The latter can thus use a similarity between two words dependent on the sentences which they belong to. For example, when SPTK carries out a QC task, the sentences above have higher probability to share similar context if they belong to the same category. Still, this approach is rather shallow as two words of the same sentence would be associated with almost the same context vector. That is, the approach does not really transform the embedding of a given word as a function of its context.

An alternative approach is to train the context embedding using neural networks on a sense annotated corpus, which can remap the word embeddings in a supervised fashion. However, since there are not enough large disambiguated corpora, we need to approximate the word senses with coarse-grained information, e.g., the category of the context. In other words, we can train a network to decide if two target words are sampled from sentences belonging to the same category. This way, the states of the trained network corresponding to each word can be eventually used as word-in-context embeddings.

In the next sections, we present the classification task designed for this purpose, and then the architecture of our Siamese Network for learning contextual word embeddings.

6.1 Defining the derived classification task

The end task that we consider is the categorization of a sentence $s \in D = \{s_1, ..., s_n\}$ into one class $c_i \in C = \{c_1, ..., c_m\}$, where D is our collection of n sentences, and C is the set of m sentence categories. Intuitively, we define the derived task as determining if two words extracted from two different sentences share the same sentence category or not. Our classifier learns word representations while accessing to the entire sentence.

More formally, we sample a pair of labeled sentences $\langle s_i, c_i \rangle$, $\langle s_j, c_j \rangle$ from our training set, where $i \neq j$. Then, we sample a word from each sentence, $w_a \in s_i$ and $w_b \in s_j$, and we assign a label $y \in \{0, 1\}$ to the word pair. We set $y = 0$ if $c_i \neq c_j$, and $y = 1$ if $c_i = c_j$.

Our goal is to learn a mapping f such that:

$$sim(f(s_i, w_a), f(s_j, w_b)) \in [0, 1], \qquad (2)$$

where sim is a similarity function between two vectors that should output values close to 1 when $y = 1$, and values close to 0 when $y = 0$.

6.2 Data construction for the derived task

To generate sentence pairs, we randomly sample sentences from different categories. Pairs labeled as positive are constructed by randomly sampling sentences from the same category, without replacement. Pairs labeled as negative are constructed by randomly sampling the first sentence from one category, and the second sentence from the remaining categories, again without replacement. Note that we oversample low frequency categories, and sample positive and negative examples several times to collect diverse pairs. We remove duplicates, and stop the generation process at approximately 500,000 sentence pairs.

6.3 Bidirectional GRUs for Word Similarity

We model the function f that maps a sentence and one of its words into a fixed size representation as a neural network. We aim at using the f encoder to map different word/sentence pairs into the same embedding space. Since the two input sentences play a symmetric role in our desired similarity and we need to use the same weights for both, we opt for a Siamese architecture (Chopra et al., 2005).

In this setting, the same network is applied to two input instances reusing the weights. Alternatively, the network can be seen as having two branches that share all the parameter weights.

The optimization strategy is what differentiates our Siamese Network from others that compute textual similarity. We do not compute the similarity (and thus the loss) between two sentences. Instead, we compute the similarity between the contextual representations of two random words from the two sentences.

This is clearly depicted in Fig. 2. The input words are mapped to integer ids, which are looked up in an embedding matrix to retrieve the corresponding embedding vectors. The sequence of vectors is then consumed by a 3-layer Bidirectional GRU (BiGRU). We selected a BiGRU for

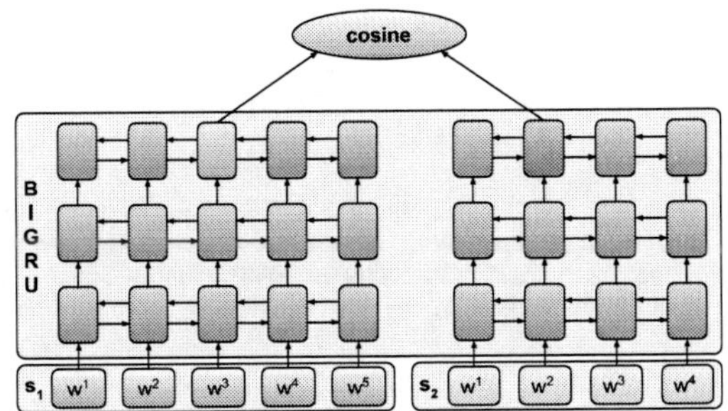

Figure 2: The architecture of the Siamese Network. The network computes $sim(f(s_1, 3), f(s_2, 2))$. The word embeddings of each sentence are consumed by a stack of 3 Bidirectional GRUs. The two branches of the network share the parameter weights.

	CBOW		SkipGram		GloVe
	hs	ns	hs	ns	-
dim					
50	89.8	89.8	91.0	91.6	89.8
100	93.0	93.6	94.2	92.8	91.6
150	94.2	94.0	94.2	93.8	92.4
200	94.6	93.6	93.2	94.2	93.2
250	94.4	94.4	94.2	94.2	93.6
300	94.2	94.0	94.4	94.0	93.8
500	95.2	95.0	94.8	93.8	94.4
750	94.8	94.6	95.0	94.4	94.2
1000	93.4	95.2	95.2	94.6	94.0

Table 2: QC test set accuracies (%) of NSPTK, given embeddings with window size equal to 5, and dimensionality ranging from 50 to 1,000.

our experiments as they are more efficient and accurate than LSTMs for our tasks. We tried other architectures, including convolutional networks, but RNNs gave us better results with less complexity and tuning effort. Note that the weights of the RNNs are shared between the two branches.

Each RNN layer produces a state for each word, which is consumed by the next RNN in the stack. From the top layer, the state corresponding to the word in the similarity pair is selected. This state encodes the word given its sentential context. Thus, the first layer, $BiGRU'$, maps the sequence of input vectors $(x_1, ..., x_T)$, into a sequence of states $(s'_1, ..., s'_T)$, the second, $BiGRU''$, transforms those states into $(s''_1, ..., s''_T)$, and the third, $BiGRU'''$, produces the final representations of the words in context $(s'''_1, ..., s'''_T)$.

Eventually, the network computes the similarity of a pair of encoded words, selected from the two sentences. We optimize the cosine similarity to match the similarity function used in SPTK. We rescale the output similarity in the $[0, 1]$ range and train the network to minimize the log loss between predictions and true labels.

7 Experiments

We compare SPTK models with our tree kernel model using neural word embeddings (NSPTK) on question classification (QC), a central task for question answering, and on sentiment classfication (SC).

7.1 Experimental setup

Data. The QC dataset (Li and Roth, 2006) contains a set of questions labelled according to a two-layered taxonomy, which describes their expected answer type. The coarse layer maps each question into one of 6 classes: Abbreviation, Description, Entity, Human, Location and Number. Our experimental setting mirrors the setting of the original study: we train on 5,452 questions and test on 500.

The SC dataset is the one of SemEval Twitter'13 for message-level polarity classification (Nakov et al., 2013). The dataset is organized in a training, development and test sets containing respectively 9,728, 1,654 and 3,813 tweets. Each tweet is labeled as positive, neutral or negative. The only preprocessing step we perform on tweets is to replace user mentions and url with a <USER> and <URL> token, respectively.

In the cross-validation experiments, we use the training data to produce the training and test folds, whereas we use the original test set as our validation set for tuning the parameters of the network.

Word embeddings. Learning high quality word embeddings requires large textual corpora. We train all the vectors for QC on the ukWaC corpus (Ferraresi et al., 2008), also used in Croce et al. (2011) to obtain LSA vectors. The corpus includes an annotation layer produced with Tree-Tagger [2]. We process the documents by attaching the POS-tag marker to each lemma. We trained paragraph2vec vectors using the Gensim[3] toolkit. Word embeddings for the SC task are learned on a corpus of 50M English tweets collected from the Twitter API over two months, using word2vec and setting the dimension to 100.

Neural model. We use GloVe word embeddings (300 dimensions), and we fix them during training. Embeddings for words that are not present in

---

[2] http://www.cis.uni-muenchen.de/ schmid/tools/TreeTagger/
[3] https://radimrehurek.com/gensim/

	CBOW	SkipGram	GloVe	LSA
	hs	hs	-	-
dim				
100	84.47	84.63	82.92	-
250	85.75	85.85	85.04	85.39
500	86.48	86.32	85.73	-

Table 3: QC cross-validation accuracies (%) of NSPTK given embeddings with the selected dimensionalities.

word	context	QC test accuracy	QC CV accuracy
w2v	-	95.2	86.48
w2v	w2v	95.4	$86.08^{\dagger}$
w2v	p2v	95.0	86.46
p2v	-	92.8	$82.65^{\dagger}$
p2v	p2v	93.6	$83.47^{\dagger}$

Table 4: QC accuracies for the word embeddings (CBOW vectors with 500 dimensions, trained using hierarchical softmax) and paragraph2vec.

the embedding model are randomly initalized by sampling a vector of the same dimension from the uniform distribution $U[-0.25, 0.25]$.

The size of the forward and backward states of the BiGRUs is set to 100, so the resulting concatenated state has 200 dimensions. The number of stacked bidirectional networks is three and it was tuned on a development set. This allows the network to have high capacity, fit the data, and have the best generalization ability. The final layer learns higher order representations of the words in context. We did not use dropout as a regularization mechanism since it did not show a significant difference on the performance of the network. The network parameters are trained using the Adam optimizer (Kingma and Ba, 2014), with a learning rate of 0.001.

The training examples are fed to the network in mini-batches. The latter are balanced between positive and negative examples by picking 32 pairs of sentences sharing the same category, and 32 pairs of sentences from different categories. Batches of 64 sentences are fed to the network. The number of words sampled from each sentence is fixed to 4, and for this reason the final loss is computed over 256 pairs of words in context, for each mini-batch. The network is then trained for 5 epochs, storing the parameters corresponding to the best registered accuracy on the validation set. Those weights are later loaded and used to encode the words in a sentence by taking their corresponding output states from the last BiGRU unit.

Structural models. We trained the tree kernel

word	context	QC CV accuracy	Std. dev
w2v	-	86.48	.005
BiGRUs	-	$84.61^{\dagger}$	.027
w2v	BiGRUs	$\mathbf{88.32}^{\dagger}$	.009

Table 5: QC accuracies for NSPTK, using the word-in-context vector produced by the stacked BiGRU encoder trained with the Siamese Network. Word vectors are trained with CBOW (hs) and have 500 dimensions.

word	context	SC F_1^{PN}
w2v	-	48.65
w2v	w2v	51.59
w2v	BiGRUs	**60.96**

SemEval system	SC F_1^{PN}
Castellucci et al. (2013)	58.27
Dong et al. (2015)	72.8

Table 6: SC results for NSPTK with word embeddings and the word-in-context embeddings. Runs of selected systems are also reported.

models using SVM-Light-TK (Moschitti, 2004), an SVM-Light extension (Joachims, 1999) with tree kernel support. We modified the software to lookup specific vectors for each word in a sentence. We preprocessed each sentence with the LTH parser[4] and used its output to construct the LCT. We used the parameters for the QC classifiers from Croce et al. (2011), while we selected them on the Twitter'13 dev. set for the SC task.

7.2 Context Embedding Results

Table 2 shows the QC accuracy of NSPTK with CBOW, SkipGram and GloVe. The results are reported for vector dimensions (dim) ranging from 50 to 1000, with a fixed window size of 5.

The performance for the CBOW hierarchical softmax (hs) and negative sampling (ns), and for the SkipGram hs settings are similar. For the SkipGram ns settings, the accuracy is slightly lower for smaller dimension sizes. GloVe embeddings yield a lower accuracy, which steadily increases with the size of the embeddings. In general, a higher dimension size produces higher accuracy, but also makes the training more expensive. 500 dimensions seem a good trade-off between performance and computational cost.

To better validate the performance of NSPTK, and since the usual test set may have reached a saturation point, we cross-validate some models.

---

[4]http://nlp.cs.lth.se

Question	Wrong w2v	Correct BiGRU
1) What is the occupation of Nicholas Cage ?	enty	hum
2) What level of government (...) is responsible for dealing with racism?	num	hum
3) What is the Motto for the State of Maryland?	loc	desc
4) What is a virtual IP address?	loc	desc
5) What function does a community's water tower serve?	loc	desc

Table 7: Sample of sentences where NSPTK with word vectors fails, and the BiGRU model produces correct classifications.

We use the training set to perform a 5-fold stratified cross-validation (CV), such that the distribution of labels in each fold is similar. Table 3 shows the cross-validated results for a subset of word embedding models. Neural embeddings seem to give a slightly higher accuracy than LSA. A more substantial performance edge may come from modeling the context, thus we experimented with word embeddings concatenated to context embeddings.

Table 4 shows the results of NSPTK using different word encodings. The *word* and *context* columns refer to the model used for encoding the word and the context, respectively. These models are word2vec (*w2v*) and paragraph2vec (*p2v*). The word2vec vector for the context is produced by averaging the embedding vectors of the other words in the sentence, i.e., excluding the target word. The paragraph2vec model has its own procedure to embed the words in the context. CV results marked with † are significant with a p-value < 0.005. The cross-validation results reveal that word2vec embeddings without context are a tough baseline to beat, suggesting that standard ways to model the context are not effective.

7.3 Results of our Bidirectional GRU for Word Similarity

Table 5 shows the results of encoding the words in context using a more sophisticated approach: mapping the word to a representation learned with the Siamese Network that we optimize on the derived classification task presented in Section 6.1. The NSPTK operating on word vectors (best vectors from Table 3) concatenated with the word-in-context vectors produced by the stacked Bi-GRU encoder, registers a significant improvement over word vectors alone. In this case, the results marked with † are significant with a p-value < 0.002. This indicates that the strong similarity contribution coming from word vectors is successfully affected by the word-in-context vectors from the network. The original similarities are thus modulated to be more effective for the final clas-

sification task. Another possible advantage of the model is that unknown words, which do not participate in the context average of simpler model, have a potentially more useful representation in the internal states of the network.

7.4 Sentiment Classification

Table 6 reports the results on the SC task. This experiment shows that incorporating the context in the similarity computation slightly improves the performance of the NSPTK. The real improvement, 12.31 absolute percent points over using word vectors alone, comes from modeling the words in context with the BiGRU encoder, confirming it as an effective strategy to improve the modeling capabilities of NSPTK.

Interestingly, our model with a single kernel function and without complex text normalization techniques outperforms a multikernel system (Castellucci et al., 2013), when the word-in-context embeddings are incorporated. The multikernel system is applied on preprocessed text and includes a Bag-Of-Words Kernel, a Lexical Semantic Kernel, and a Smoothed Partial Tree Kernel. State-of-the-art systems (Dong et al., 2015; Severyn and Moschitti, 2015b) include many lexical and clustering features, sentiment lexicons, and distant supervision techniques. Our approach does not include any of the former.

7.5 Wins of the BiGRU model

An error analysis on the QC task reveals the *What* questions as the most ambiguous. Table 7 contains some of the successes of the BiGRU model with respect to the model using only word vectors. Those wins can be explained by the effect of the contextual word vectors on the kernel similarity. In Question 1, the meaning of *occupation* is affected by the presence of a person name. In Question 2, the word *level* loses its prevalent association with quantities. In questions 3 to 5, the underlined words are a strong indicator of locations/places, and the kernel similarity may be dominated by their corresponding word vectors. BiGRU vectors are instead able to effectively re-modulate the kernel similarity and induce a correct classification.

8 Conclusions

In this paper, we applied neural network models for learning representations with semantic convolution tree kernels. We evaluated the main distributional representation methods for computing semantic similarity inside the kernel. In addition, we augmented the vectorial representations of words with information coming from the sentential content. Word vectors alone revealed to be difficult to improve upon. To better model the context, we proposed word-in-context representations extracted from the states of a recurrent neural network. Such network learns to decide if two words are sampled from sentences which share the same category label. The resulting embeddings are able to improve on the selected tasks when used in conjunction with the original word embeddings, by injecting more contextual information for the modulation of the kernel similarity. We show that our approach can improve the accuracy of the convolution semantic tree kernel.

Acknowledgments. This work has been supported by the EC project CogNet, 671625 (H2020-ICT-2014-2, Research and Innovation action). The first author was supported by the Google Europe Doctoral Fellowship Award 2015. Many thanks to the anonymous reviewers for their valuable suggestions.

References

Daniel Andor, Chris Alberti, David Weiss, Aliaksei Severyn, Alessandro Presta, Kuzman Ganchev, Slav Petrov, and Michael Collins. 2016. Globally Normalized Transition-Based Neural Networks. In *Proceedings of the 54th Annual Meeting of the Association for Computational Linguistics (Volume 1: Long Papers)*. Association for Computational Linguistics, Berlin, Germany, pages 2442–2452. http://www.aclweb.org/anthology/P16-1231.

Y. Bengio, P. Simard, and P. Frasconi. 1994. Learning Long-term Dependencies with Gradient Descent is Difficult. *Trans. Neur. Netw.* 5(2):157–166. https://doi.org/10.1109/72.279181.

Giuseppe Castellucci, Simone Filice, Danilo Croce, and Roberto Basili. 2013. UNITOR: Combining Syntactic and Semantic Kernels for Twitter Sentiment Analysis. In *Second Joint Conference on Lexical and Computational Semantics (*SEM), Volume 2: Proceedings of the Seventh International Workshop on Semantic Evaluation (SemEval 2013)*. Association for Computational Linguistics, Atlanta, Georgia, USA, pages 369–374. http://www.aclweb.org/anthology/S13-2060.

Sumit Chopra, Raia Hadsell, and Yann LeCun. 2005. Learning a similarity metric discriminatively, with application to face verification. In *Computer Vision and Pattern Recognition, 2005. CVPR 2005. IEEE Computer Society Conference on*. IEEE, volume 1, pages 539–546.

Junyoung Chung, Caglar Gulcehre, KyungHyun Cho, and Yoshua Bengio. 2014. Empirical evaluation of gated recurrent neural networks on sequence modeling. *arXiv preprint arXiv:1412.3555* .

Danilo Croce, Alessandro Moschitti, and Roberto Basili. 2011. Structured Lexical Similarity via Convolution Kernels on Dependency Trees. In *In EMNLP*. Edinburgh, Scotland, UK. http://www.aclweb.org/anthology/D11-1096.

Danilo Croce, Alessandro Moschitti, Roberto Basili, and Martha Palmer. 2012. Verb Classification using Distributional Similarity in Syntactic and Semantic Structures. In *ACL (1)*. The Association for Computer Linguistics, pages 263–272.

Li Dong, Furu Wei, Yichun Yin, Ming Zhou, and Ke Xu. 2015. Splusplus: A Feature-Rich Two-stage Classifier for Sentiment Analysis of Tweets. In *Proceedings of the 9th International Workshop on Semantic Evaluation (SemEval 2015)*. Association for Computational Linguistics, Denver, Colorado, pages 515–519. http://www.aclweb.org/anthology/S15-2086.

Adriano Ferraresi, Eros Zanchetta, Marco Baroni, and Silvia Bernardini. 2008. Introducing and evaluating ukWaC, a very large web-derived corpus of English. In *Proceedings of the 4th Web as Corpus Workshop (WAC-4) Can we beat Google?*. page 47.

Simone Filice, Danilo Croce, Alessandro Moschitti, and Roberto Basili. 2016. KeLP at SemEval-2016 Task 3: Learning Semantic Relations between Questions and Answers. In *Proceedings of the 10th International Workshop on Semantic Evaluation (SemEval-2016)*. Association for Computational Linguistics, San Diego, California, pages 1116–1123. http://www.aclweb.org/anthology/S16-1172.

Simone Filice, Giovanni Da San Martino, and Alessandro Moschitti. 2015. Structural Representations for Learning Relations between Pairs of Texts. In *Proceedings of the 53rd Annual Meeting of the Association for Computational Linguistics and the 7th International Joint Conference on Natural Language Processing (Volume*

1: Long Papers). Association for Computational Linguistics, Beijing, China, pages 1003–1013. http://www.aclweb.org/anthology/P15-1097.

Sepp Hochreiter and Jürgen Schmidhuber. 1997. Long short-term memory. *Neural computation* 9(8):1735–1780.

Ignacio Iacobacci, Mohammad Taher Pilehvar, and Roberto Navigli. 2016. Embeddings for Word Sense Disambiguation: An Evaluation Study. In *Proceedings of the 54th Annual Meeting of the Association for Computational Linguistics (Volume 1: Long Papers)*. Association for Computational Linguistics, Berlin, Germany, pages 897–907. http://www.aclweb.org/anthology/P16-1085.

Thorsten Joachims. 1999. Making Large-scale Support Vector Machine Learning Practical. In Bernhard Schölkopf, Christopher J. C. Burges, and Alexander J. Smola, editors, *Advances in Kernel Methods*, MIT Press, Cambridge, MA, USA, pages 169–184. http://dl.acm.org/citation.cfm?id=299094.299104.

Nal Kalchbrenner, Edward Grefenstette, and Phil Blunsom. 2014. A Convolutional Neural Network for Modelling Sentences. In *Proceedings of the 52nd Annual Meeting of the Association for Computational Linguistics (Volume 1: Long Papers)*. Baltimore, Maryland, pages 655–665. http://www.aclweb.org/anthology/P14-1062.

Yoon Kim. 2014. Convolutional Neural Networks for Sentence Classification. In *Proceedings of the 2014 Conference on Empirical Methods in Natural Language Processing (EMNLP)*. Association for Computational Linguistics, Doha, Qatar, pages 1746–1751. http://www.aclweb.org/anthology/D14-1181.

Diederik P. Kingma and Jimmy Ba. 2014. Adam: A Method for Stochastic Optimization. In *Proceedings of the 3rd International Conference on Learning Representations (ICLR)*.

Quoc V. Le and Tomas Mikolov. 2014. Distributed Representations of Sentences and Documents. *CoRR* abs/1405.4053. http://arxiv.org/abs/1405.4053.

Omer Levy and Yoav Goldberg. 2014. Dependency-Based Word Embeddings. In *Proceedings of the 52nd Annual Meeting of the Association for Computational Linguistics (Volume 2: Short Papers)*. Association for Computational Linguistics, Baltimore, Maryland, pages 302–308. http://www.aclweb.org/anthology/P14-2050.

Xin Li and Dan Roth. 2006. Learning question classifiers: the role of semantic information. *Natural Language Engineering* 12(3):229–249.

Mingbo Ma, Liang Huang, Bowen Zhou, and Bing Xiang. 2015. Dependency-based Convolutional Neural Networks for Sentence Embedding. In *Proceedings of the 53rd Annual Meeting of the Association*

for Computational Linguistics and the 7th International Joint Conference on Natural Language Processing (Volume 2: Short Papers). Association for Computational Linguistics, Beijing, China, pages 174–179. http://www.aclweb.org/anthology/P15-2029.

Tomas Mikolov, Kai Chen, Greg Corrado, and Jeffrey Dean. 2013. Efficient estimation of word representations in vector space. *ICLR Workshop* .

Alessandro Moschitti. 2004. A Study on Convolution Kernels for Shallow Semantic Parsing. In *Proceedings of the 42nd Annual Meeting on Association for Computational Linguistics*. Association for Computational Linguistics, Stroudsburg, PA, USA, ACL '04.

Alessandro Moschitti. 2006. Efficient Convolution Kernels for Dependency and Constituent Syntactic Trees. In *Proceedings of the 17th European Conference on Machine Learning*. Springer-Verlag, Berlin, Heidelberg, ECML'06, pages 318–329. https://doi.org/10.1007/11871842_32.

Jonas Mueller and Aditya Thyagarajan. 2016. Siamese Recurrent Architectures for Learning Sentence Similarity. In *Proceedings of the Thirtieth AAAI Conference on Artificial Intelligence*. AAAI Press, AAAI'16, pages 2786–2792. http://dl.acm.org/citation.cfm?id=3016100.3016291.

Preslav Nakov, Sara Rosenthal, Zornitsa Kozareva, Veselin Stoyanov, Alan Ritter, and Theresa Wilson. 2013. SemEval-2013 Task 2: Sentiment Analysis in Twitter. In *Second Joint Conference on Lexical and Computational Semantics (*SEM), Volume 2: Proceedings of the Seventh International Workshop on Semantic Evaluation (SemEval 2013)*. Association for Computational Linguistics, Atlanta, Georgia, USA, pages 312–320. http://www.aclweb.org/anthology/S13-2052.

Paul Neculoiu, Maarten Versteegh, and Mihai Rotaru. 2016. Learning Text Similarity with Siamese Recurrent Networks. In *Proceedings of the 1st Workshop on Representation Learning for NLP*. Association for Computational Linguistics, Berlin, Germany, pages 148–157. http://anthology.aclweb.org/W16-1617.

Thien Hai Nguyen and Kiyoaki Shirai. 2015. Aspect-Based Sentiment Analysis Using Tree Kernel Based Relation Extraction. In Alexander Gelbukh, editor, *Computational Linguistics and Intelligent Text Processing: 16th International Conference, CICLing 2015*. Springer International Publishing, Cairo, Egypt, pages 114–125.

Thien Huu Nguyen, Barbara Plank, and Ralph Grishman. 2015. Semantic Representations for Domain Adaptation: A Case Study on the Tree Kernel-based Method for Relation Extraction. In *Proceedings of the 53rd Annual Meeting of the Association for Computational Linguistics and the 7th International*

Joint Conference on Natural Language Processing (Volume 1: Long Papers). Association for Computational Linguistics, Beijing, China, pages 635–644. http://www.aclweb.org/anthology/P15-1062.

Truc Vien T. Nguyen and Alessandro Moschitti. 2011. End-to-End Relation Extraction Using Distant Supervision from External Semantic Repositories. In *Proceedings of the 49th Annual Meeting of the Association for Computational Linguistics: Human Language Technologies*. Association for Computational Linguistics, Portland, Oregon, USA, pages 277–282. http://www.aclweb.org/anthology/P11-2048.

Truc-Vien T. Nguyen, Alessandro Moschitti, and Giuseppe Riccardi. 2009. Convolution Kernels on Constituent, Dependency and Sequential Structures for Relation Extraction. In *Proceedings of the 2009 Conference on Empirical Methods in Natural Language Processing*. Association for Computational Linguistics, Singapore, pages 1378–1387. http://www.aclweb.org/anthology/D/D09/D09-1143.

Jeffrey Pennington, Richard Socher, and Christopher D. Manning. 2014. GloVe: Global Vectors for Word Representation. In *Empirical Methods in Natural Language Processing*. pages 1532–1543. http://www.aclweb.org/anthology/D14-1162.

Barbara Plank and Alessandro Moschitti. 2013. Embedding Semantic Similarity in Tree Kernels for Domain Adaptation of Relation Extraction. In *Proceedings of the 51st Annual Meeting of the Association for Computational Linguistics (Volume 1: Long Papers)*. Association for Computational Linguistics, Sofia, Bulgaria, pages 1498–1507. http://www.aclweb.org/anthology/P13-1147.

Jinfeng Rao, Hua He, and Jimmy Lin. 2016. Noise-Contrastive Estimation for Answer Selection with Deep Neural Networks. In *Proceedings of the 25th ACM International on Conference on Information and Knowledge Management*. ACM, New York, NY, USA, CIKM '16, pages 1913–1916.

Mike Schuster and Kuldip K Paliwal. 1997. Bidirectional recurrent neural networks. *IEEE Transactions on Signal Processing* 45(11):2673–2681.

Aliaksei Severyn and Alessandro Moschitti. 2015a. Learning to rank short text pairs with convolutional deep neural networks. In *Proceedings of the 38th International ACM SIGIR Conference on Research and Development in Information Retrieval*. ACM, pages 373–382.

Aliaksei Severyn and Alessandro Moschitti. 2015b. UNITN: Training Deep Convolutional Neural Network for Twitter Sentiment Classification. In *Proceedings of the 9th International Workshop on Semantic Evaluation (SemEval 2015)*. Association for Computational Linguistics, Denver, Colorado, pages 464–469. http://www.aclweb.org/anthology/S15-2079.

Aliaksei Severyn, Massimo Nicosia, and Alessandro Moschitti. 2013. Learning Semantic Textual Similarity with Structural Representations. In *Proceedings of the 51st Annual Meeting of the ACL (Volume 2: Short Papers)*. ACL, pages 714–718. http://aclweb.org/anthology/P13-2125.

João Silva, Luísa Coheur, Ana Cristina Mendes, and Andreas Wichert. 2010. From symbolic to sub-symbolic information in question classification. *Artificial Intelligence Review* 35(2):137–154.

Richard Socher, Brody Huval, Christopher D. Manning, and Andrew Y. Ng. 2012. Semantic Compositionality through Recursive Matrix-Vector Spaces. In *Proceedings of the 2012 Joint Conference on Empirical Methods in Natural Language Processing and Computational Natural Language Learning*. Association for Computational Linguistics, Jeju Island, Korea, pages 1201–1211. http://www.aclweb.org/anthology/D12-1110.

Richard Socher, Alex Perelygin, Jean Wu, Jason Chuang, Christopher D. Manning, Andrew Ng, and Christopher Potts. 2013. Recursive Deep Models for Semantic Compositionality Over a Sentiment Treebank. In *Proceedings of the 2013 Conference on Empirical Methods in Natural Language Processing*. Association for Computational Linguistics, Seattle, Washington, USA, pages 1631–1642. http://www.aclweb.org/anthology/D13-1170.

Kai Sheng Tai, Richard Socher, and Christopher D. Manning. 2015. Improved Semantic Representations From Tree-Structured Long Short-Term Memory Networks. In *Proceedings of the 53rd Annual Meeting of the Association for Computational Linguistics and the 7th International Joint Conference on Natural Language Processing (Volume 1: Long Papers)*. Association for Computational Linguistics, Beijing, China, pages 1556–1566. http://www.aclweb.org/anthology/P15-1150.

Ming Tan, Cicero dos Santos, Bing Xiang, and Bowen Zhou. 2016. Improved Representation Learning for Question Answer Matching. In *Proceedings of the 54th Annual Meeting of the Association for Computational Linguistics (Volume 1: Long Papers)*. Association for Computational Linguistics, Berlin, Germany, pages 464–473. http://www.aclweb.org/anthology/P16-1044.

Andrew Trask, Phil Michalak, and John Liu. 2015. sense2vec - A Fast and Accurate Method for Word Sense Disambiguation In Neural Word Embeddings. *CoRR* abs/1511.06388. http://arxiv.org/abs/1511.06388.

Kateryna Tymoshenko and Alessandro Moschitti. 2015. Assessing the Impact of Syntactic and Semantic Structures for Answer Passages Reranking. In *Proceedings of the 24th ACM International on Conference on Information and Knowledge Management, CIKM 2015, Melbourne, VIC, Australia, October 19 - 23, 2015*. pages 1451–1460.

Making Neural QA as Simple as Possible but not Simpler

Dirk Weissenborn **Georg Wiese** **Laura Seiffe**

Language Technology Lab, DFKI
Alt-Moabit 91c
Berlin, Germany

{dirk.weissenborn, georg.wiese, laura.seiffe}@dfki.de

Abstract

Recent development of large-scale question answering (QA) datasets triggered a substantial amount of research into end-to-end neural architectures for QA. Increasingly complex systems have been conceived without comparison to simpler neural baseline systems that would justify their complexity. In this work, we propose a simple heuristic that guides the development of neural baseline systems for the extractive QA task. We find that there are two ingredients necessary for building a high-performing neural QA system: first, the awareness of question words while processing the context and second, a composition function that goes beyond simple bag-of-words modeling, such as recurrent neural networks. Our results show that FastQA, a system that meets these two requirements, can achieve very competitive performance compared with existing models. We argue that this surprising finding puts results of previous systems and the complexity of recent QA datasets into perspective.

1 Introduction

Question answering is an important end-user task at the intersection of natural language processing (NLP) and information retrieval (IR). QA systems can bridge the gap between IR-based search engines and sophisticated intelligent assistants that enable a more directed information retrieval process. Such systems aim at finding precisely the piece of information sought by the user instead of documents or snippets containing the answer. A special form of QA, namely extractive QA, deals with the extraction of a direct *answer* to a *question* from a given textual *context*.

The creation of large-scale, extractive QA datasets (Rajpurkar et al., 2016; Trischler et al., 2017; Nguyen et al., 2016) sparked research interest into the development of end-to-end neural QA systems. A typical neural architecture consists of an embedding-, encoding-, interaction- and answer layer (Wang and Jiang, 2017; Yu et al., 2017; Xiong et al., 2017; Seo et al., 2017; Yang et al., 2017; Wang et al., 2017). Most such systems describe several innovations for the different layers of the architecture with a special focus on developing powerful *interaction layer* that aims at modeling word-by-word interaction between question and context.

Although a variety of extractive QA systems have been proposed, there is no competitive neural baseline. Most systems were built in what we call a *top-down* process that proposes a complex architecture and validates design decisions by an ablation study. Most ablation studies, however, remove only a single part of an overall complex architecture and therefore lack comparison to a reasonable neural baseline. This gap raises the question whether the complexity of current systems is justified solely by their empirical results.

Another important observation is the fact that seemingly complex questions might be answerable by simple heuristics. Let's consider the following example:

When *did building activity occur on St. Kazimierz Church?*

Building activity occurred in numerous noble palaces and churches [...]. One of the best examples [..] are Krasinski Palace (<u>1677-1683</u>), Wilanow Palace (<u>1677-1696</u>) and St. Kazimierz Church (**<u>1688-1692</u>**)

Although it seems that evidence synthesis of multiple sentences is necessary to fully understand the

Proceedings of the 21st Conference on Computational Natural Language Learning (CoNLL 2017), pages 271–280,
Vancouver, Canada, August 3 - August 4, 2017. ©2017 Association for Computational Linguistics

relation between the answer and the question, answering this question is easily possible by applying a simple *context/type matching heuristic*. The heuristic aims at selecting answer spans that a) match the expected answer type (a time as indicated by "When") and b) are close to important question words ("St. Kazimierz Church"). The actual answer "1688-1692" would easily be extracted by such a heuristic.

In this work, we propose to use the aforementioned *context/type matching heuristic* as a guideline to derive simple neural baseline architectures for the extractive QA task. In particular, we develop a simple neural, bag-of-words (BoW)- and a recurrent neural network (RNN) baseline, namely *FastQA*. Crucially, both models do not make use of a complex interaction layer but model interaction between question and context only through computable features on the word level. FastQA's strong performance questions the necessity of additional complexity, especially in the interaction layer, which is exhibited by recently developed models. We address this question by evaluating the impact of extending FastQA with an additional interaction layer (FastQAExt) and find that it doesn't lead to systematic improvements. Finally, our contributions are the following: **i)** definition and evaluation of a BoW- and RNN-based neural QA baselines guided by a simple heuristic; **ii)** bottom-up evaluation of our FastQA system with increasing architectural complexity, revealing that the awareness of question words and the application of a RNN are enough to reach state-of-the-art results; **iii)** a complexity comparison between FastQA and more complex architectures as well as an in-depth discussion of usefulness of an interaction layer; **iv)** a qualitative analysis indicating that FastQA mostly follows our heuristic which thus constitutes a strong baseline for extractive QA.

2 A Bag-of-Words Neural QA System

We begin by motivating our architectures by defining our proposed context/type matching heuristic: a) the type of the answer span should correspond to the expected answer type given by the question, and b) the correct answer should further be surrounded by a context that fits the question, or, more precisely, it should be surrounded by many question words. Similar heuristics were frequently implemented explicitly in traditional QA systems,

e.g., in the answer extraction step of Moldovan et al. (1999), however, in this work our heuristic is merely used as a guideline for the construction of neural QA systems. In the following, we denote the hidden dimensionality of the model by n, the question tokens by $Q = (q_1, ..., q_{L_Q})$, and the context tokens by $X = (x_1, ..., x_{L_X})$.

2.1 Embedding

The embedding layer is responsible for mapping tokens x to their corresponding n-dimensional representation $\boldsymbol{x}$. Typically this is done by mapping each word x to its corresponding word embedding $\boldsymbol{x}^w$ (*lookup-embedding*) using an embedding matrix E, s.t. $\boldsymbol{x}^w = Ex$. Another approach is to embed each word by encoding their corresponding character sequence $x^c = (c_1, ..., c_{L_X})$ with C, s.t. $\boldsymbol{x}^c = C(x_c)$ (*char-embedding*). In this work, we use a convolutional neural network for C of filter width 5 with max-pooling over time as explored by Seo et al. (2017), to which we refer the reader for additional details. Both approaches are combined via concatenation, s.t. the final embedding becomes $\boldsymbol{x} = [\boldsymbol{x}^w; \boldsymbol{x}^c] \in \mathbb{R}^d$.

2.2 Type Matching

For the BoW baseline, we extract the span in the question that refers to the expected, lexical answer type (LAT) by extracting either the question word(s) (e.g., *who, when, why, how, how many*, etc.) or the first noun phrase of the question after the question words "what" or "which" (e.g., "what *year* did...").[1] This leads to a correct LAT for most questions. We encode the LAT by concatenating the embedding of the first- and last word together with the average embedding of all words within the LAT. The concatenated representations are further transformed by a fully-connected layer followed by a tanh non-linearity into $\tilde{\boldsymbol{z}} \in \mathbb{R}^n$. Note that we refer to a fully-connected layer in the following by FC, s.t. $FC(\boldsymbol{u}) = W\boldsymbol{u} + \boldsymbol{b}$, $W \in \mathbb{R}^{n \times m}, \boldsymbol{b} \in \mathbb{R}^n, \boldsymbol{u} \in \mathbb{R}^m$.

We similarly encode each potential answer span (s, e) in the context, i.e., all spans with a specified, maximum number of words (10 in this work), by concatenating the embedding of the first- and last word together with the average embedding of all words within the span. Because the surrounding context of a potential answer span can give important clues towards the type of an answer span,

---

[1] More complex heuristics can be employed here but for the sake of simplicity we chose a very simple approach.

for instance, through nominal modifiers left of the span (e.g., "... president <u>obama</u> ...") or through an apposition right of the span (e.g., "... <u>obama</u>, president of..."), we additionally concatenate the average embeddings of the 5 words to the left and to the right of a span, respectively. The concatenated span representation, which comprises in total five different embeddings, is further transformed by a fully-connected layer with a tanh non-linearity into $\tilde{x}_{s,e} \in \mathbb{R}^n$.

Finally, the concatenation of the LAT representation, the span representation and their element-wise product, i.e., $[\tilde{z}; \tilde{x}_{s,e}; \tilde{z} \odot \tilde{x}_{s,e}]$, serve as input to a feed-forward neural network with one hidden layer which computes the type score $g_{type}(s, e)$ for each span (s, e).

2.3 Context Matching

In order to account for the number of surrounding words of an answer span as a measure for question to answer span match (context match), we introduce two word-in-question features. They are computed for each context word x_j and explained in the following

binary The binary word-in-question (wiq^b) feature is 1 for tokens that are part of the question and else 0. The following equation formally defines this feature where $\mathbb{I}$ denotes the indicator function:

$$\text{wiq}_j^b = \mathbb{I}(\exists i : x_j = q_i) \qquad (1)$$

weighted The wiq$_j^w$ feature for context word x_j is defined in Eq. 3, where Eq. 2 defines a basic similarity score between q_i and x_j based on their word-embeddings. It is motivated on the one hand by the intuition that question tokens which rarely appear in the context are more likely to be important for answering the question, and on the other hand by the fact that question words might occur as morphological variants, synonyms or related words in the context. The latter can be captured (softly) by using word embeddings instead of the words themselves whereas the former is captured by the application of the softmax operation in Eq. 3 which ensures that infrequent occurrences of words are weighted more heavily.

$$sim_{i,j} = \boldsymbol{v}_{wiq}(\boldsymbol{x}_j \odot \boldsymbol{q}_i) \quad , \boldsymbol{v}_{wiq} \in \mathbb{R}^n \qquad (2)$$

$$\text{wiq}_j^w = \sum_i \text{softmax}(sim_{i,\cdot})_j \qquad (3)$$

A derivation that connects wiq^w with the term-frequencies (a prominent information retrieval measure) of a word in the question and the context, respectively, is provided in Appendix A.

Finally, for each answer span (s, e) we compute the average wiq^b and wiq^w scores of the 5, 10 and 20 token-windows to the left and to the right of the respective (s, e)-span. This results in a total of 2 (kinds of features)$\times$3 (windows)$\times$2 (left/right) $=$ 12 scores which are weighted by trainable scalar parameters and summed to compute the context-matching score $g_{ctxt}(s, e)$.

2.4 Answer Span Scoring

The final score g for each span (s, e) is the sum of the type- and the context matching score: $g(s, e) = g_{type}(s, e) + g_{ctxt}(s, e)$. The model is trained to minimize the softmax-cross-entropy loss given the scores for all spans.

3 FastQA

Although our BoW baseline closely models our intended heuristic, it has several shortcomings. First of all, it cannot capture the compositionality of language making the detection of sensible answer spans harder. Furthermore, the semantics of a question is dramatically reduced to a BoW representation of its expected answer-type and the scalar word-in-question features. Finally, answer spans are restricted to a certain length.

To account for these shortcomings we introduce another baseline which relies on the application of a single bi-directional recurrent neural networks (BiRNN) followed by a answer layer that separates the prediction of the start and end of the answer span. Lample et al. (2016) demonstrated that BiRNNs are powerful at recognizing named entities which makes them sensible choice for context encoding to allow for improved type matching. Context matching can similarly be achieved with a BiRNN by informing it of the locations of question tokens appearing in the context through our wiq-features. It is important to recognize that our model should implicitly learn to capture the heuristic, but is not limited by it.

On an abstract level, our RNN-based model, called FastQA, consists of three basic layers, namely the embedding-, encoding- and answer layer. Embeddings are computed as explained in §2.1. The other two layers are described in detail in the following. An illustration of the basic archi-

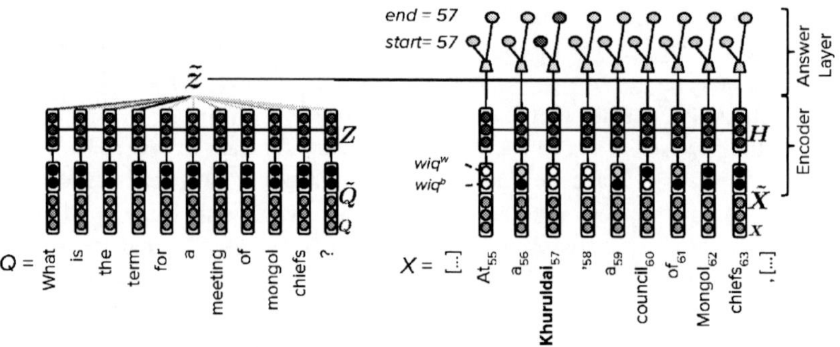

Figure 1: Illustration of FastQA system on example question from SQuAD. The two word-in-question features (wiq^b, wiq^w) are presented with varying degrees of activation.

tecture is provided in Figure 1.

3.1 Encoding

In the following, we describe the encoding of the context which is analogous to that of the question.

To allow for interaction between the two embeddings described in §2.1, they are first projected jointly to a n-dimensional representation (Eq. 4)) and further transformed by a single highway layer (Eq. 5) similar to Seo et al. (2017).

$$x' = Px \quad , P \in \mathbb{R}^{n \times d} \tag{4}$$
$$g_e = \sigma(\mathrm{FC}(x')), \ x'' = \tanh\left(\mathrm{FC}\left(x'\right)\right)$$
$$\tilde{x} = g_e x' + (1 - g_e)x'' \tag{5}$$

Because we want the encoder to be aware of the question words we feed the binary- and the weighted *word-in-question* feature of §2.3 in addition to the embedded context words as input. The complete input $\tilde{X} \in \mathbb{R}^{n+2 \times L_X}$ to the encoder is therefore defined as follows:

$$\tilde{X} = ([\tilde{x}_1; \mathrm{wiq}_1^b; \mathrm{wiq}_1^w], ..., [\tilde{x}_{L_X}; \mathrm{wiq}_{L_X}^b; \mathrm{wiq}_{L_X}^w])$$

$\tilde{X}$ is fed to a bidirectional RNN and its output is again projected to allow for interaction between the features accumulated in the forward and backward RNN (Eq. 6). In preliminary experiments we found LSTMs (Hochreiter and Schmidhuber, 1997) to perform best.

$$H' = \mathrm{Bi\text{-}LSTM}(\tilde{X}) \quad , H' \in \mathbb{R}^{2n \times L_X}$$
$$H = \tanh(BH'^{\top}) \quad , B \in \mathbb{R}^{n \times 2n} \tag{6}$$

We initialize the projection matrix B with $[I_n; I_n]$, where I_n denotes the n-dimensional identity matrix. It follows that H is the sum of the outputs from the forward- and backward-LSTM at the beginning of training.

As mentioned before, we utilize the same encoder parameters for both question and context, except the projection matrix B which is not shared. However, they are initialized the same way, s.t. the context and question encoding is identical at the beginning of training. Finally, to be able to use the same encoder for both question and context we fix the two wiq features to 1 for the question.

3.2 Answer Layer

After encoding context X to $H = [h_1, ..., h_{L_X}]$ and the question Q to $Z = [z_1, ..., z_{L_Q}]$, we first compute a weighted, n-dimensional question representation $\tilde{z}$ of Q (Eq. 7). Note that this representation is context-independent and as such only computed once, i.e., there is no additional word-by-word interaction between context and question.

$$\alpha = \mathrm{softmax}(v_q Z) \quad , v_q \in \mathbb{R}^n$$
$$\tilde{z} = \sum_i \alpha_i z_i \tag{7}$$

The probability distribution p_s for the start location of the answer is computed by a 2-layer feed-forward neural network with a rectified-linear (ReLU) activated, hidden layer s_j as follows:

$$s_j = \mathrm{ReLU}\left(\mathrm{FC}\left([h_j; \tilde{z}; h_j \odot \tilde{z}]\right)\right)$$
$$p_s(j) \propto \exp(v_s s_j) \quad , v_s \in \mathbb{R}^n \tag{8}$$

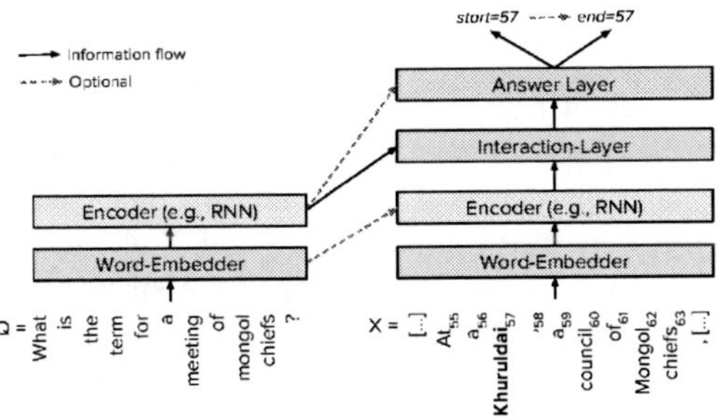

Figure 2: Illustration of the basic architecture which underlies most existing neural QA systems.

The conditional probability distribution p_e for the end location conditioned on the start location s is computed similarly by a feed-forward neural network with hidden layer e_j as follows:

$$e_j = \mathrm{ReLU}\left(\mathrm{FC}\left([h_j; h_s; \tilde{z}; h_j \odot \tilde{z}; h_j \odot h_s]\right)\right)$$
$$p_e(j|s) \propto \exp(v_e e_j) \quad , v_e \in \mathbb{R}^n \tag{9}$$

The overall probability p of predicting an answer span (s, e) is $p(s, e) = p_s(s) \cdot p_e(e|s)$. The model is trained to minimize the cross-entropy loss of the predicted span probability $p(s, e)$.

Beam-search During prediction time, we compute the answer span with the highest probability by employing beam-search using a beam-size of k. This means that ends for the top-k starts are predicted and the span with the highest overall probability is predicted as final answer.

4 Comparison to Prior Architectures

Many neural architectures for extractive QA have been conceived very recently. Most of these systems can be broken down into four basic layers for which individual innovations were proposed. A high-level illustration of these systems is show in Figure 2. In the following, we compare our system in more detail with existing models.

Embedder The embedder is responsible for embedding a sequence of tokens into a sequence of n-dimensional states. Our proposed embedder (§2.1) is very similar to existing ones used for example in Seo et al. (2017); Yang et al. (2017).

Encoder Embedded tokens are further encoded by some form of composition function. A prominent type of encoder is the (bi-directional) recurrent neural network (RNN) which is also used in this work. Feeding additional word-level features similar to ours is rarely done with the exception of Wang et al. (2017); Li et al. (2016).

Interaction Layer Most research focused on the interaction layer which is responsible for word-by-word interaction between context and question. Different ideas were explored such as attention (Wang and Jiang, 2017; Yu et al., 2017), co-attention (Xiong et al., 2017), bi-directional attention flow (Seo et al., 2017), multi-perspective context matching (Wang et al., 2017) or fine-grained gating (Yang et al., 2017). All of these ideas aim at enriching the encoded context with weighted states from the question and in some cases also from the context. These are gathered individually for each context state, concatenated with it and serve as input to an additional RNN. Note that this layer is omitted completely in FastQA and therefore constitutes the main simplification over previous work.

Answer Layer Finally, most systems divide the prediction the start and the end by another network. Their complexity ranges from using a single fully-connected layer (Seo et al., 2017; Wang et al., 2017) to employing convolutional neural networks (Trischler et al., 2017) or recurrent, deep Highway-Maxout-Networks(Xiong et al., 2017). We further introduce *beam-search* to extract the most likely answer span with a simple 2-layer feed-forward network.

5 FastQA Extended

To explore the necessity of the interaction layer and to be architecturally comparable to existing models we extend FastQA with an additional interaction layer (FastQAExt). In particular, we introduce *representation fusion* to enable the exchange of information in between passages of the context (*intra-fusion*), and between the question and the context (*inter-fusion*). Representation fusion is defined as the weighted addition between a state, i.e., its n-dimensional representation, and its respective co-representation. For each context state its corresponding co-representation is retrieved via attention from the rest of the context (intra) or the question (inter), respectively, and "fused" into its own representation. For the sake of brevity we describe technical details of this layer in Appendix B, because this extension is not the focus of this work but merely serves as a representative of the more complex architectures described in §4.

6 Experimental Setup

We conduct experiments on the following datasets.

SQuAD The Stanford Question Answering Dataset (Rajpurkar et al., 2016)[2] comprises over $100k$ questions about paragraphs of 536 Wikipedia articles.

NewsQA The NewsQA dataset (Trischler et al., 2017)[3] contains $100k$ answerable questions from a total of $120k$ questions. The dataset is built from CNN news stories that were originally collected by Hermann et al. (2015).

Performance on the SQuAD and NewsQA datasets is measured in terms of *exact match* (accuracy) and a mean, per answer token-based *F1* measure which was originally proposed by Rajpurkar et al. (2016) to also account for partial matches.

6.1 Implementation Details

BoW Model The BoW model is trained on spans up to length 10 to keep the computation tractable. This leads to an upper bound of about 95% accuracy on SQuAD and 87% on NewsQA. As pre-processing steps we lowercase all inputs and tokenize it using spacy[4]. The binary word in question feature is computed on lemmas provided by spacy and restricted to alphanumeric words that are not stopwords. Throughout all experiments we use a hidden dimensionality of $n = 150$, dropout at the input embeddings with the same mask for all words (Gal and Ghahramani, 2015) and a rate of 0.2 and 300-dimensional fixed word-embeddings from Glove (Pennington et al., 2014). We employed ADAM (Kingma and Ba, 2015) for optimization with an initial learning-rate of 10^{-3} which was halved whenever the $F1$ measure on the development set dropped between epochs. We used mini-batches of size 32.

FastQA The pre-processing of FastQA is slightly simpler than that of the BoW model. We

tokenize the input on whitespaces (exclusive) and non-alphanumeric characters (inclusive). The binary word in question feature is computed on the words as they appear in context. Throughout all experiments we use a hidden dimensionality of $n = 300$, variational dropout at the input embeddings with the same mask for all words (Gal and Ghahramani, 2015) and a rate of 0.5 and 300-dimensional fixed word-embeddings from Glove (Pennington et al., 2014). We employed ADAM (Kingma and Ba, 2015) for optimization with an initial learning-rate of 10^{-3} which was halved whenever the $F1$ measure on the development set dropped between checkpoints. Checkpoints occurred after every 1000 mini-batches each containing 64 examples.

Cutting Context Length Because NewsQA contains examples with very large contexts (up to more than 1500 tokens) we cut contexts larger than 400 tokens in order to efficiently train our models. We ensure that at least one, but at best all answers are still present in the remaining 400 tokens. Note that this restriction is only employed during training.

7 Results

7.1 Model Component Analysis

Model	Dev	
	F1	Exact
Logistic Regression[1]	51.0	40.0
Neural BoW Baseline	56.2	43.8
BiLSTM	58.2	48.7
BiLSTM + wiq^b	71.8	62.3
BiLSTM + wiq^w	73.8	64.3
BiLSTM + wiq^{b+w} (FastQA*)	74.9	65.5
FastQA* + intrafusion	76.2	67.2
FastQA* + intra + inter (FastQAExt*)	77.5	68.4
FastQA* + char-emb. (FastQA)	76.3	67.6
FastQAExt* + char-emb. (FastQAExt)	78.3	69.9
FastQA w/ beam-size 5	76.3	67.8
FastQAExt w/ beam-size 5	**78.5**	**70.3**

Table 1: SQuAD results on development set for increasingly complex architectures. [1]Rajpurkar et al. (2016)

Table 1 shows the individual contributions of each model component that was incrementally added to a plain BiLSTM model without features, character embeddings and beam-search. We see that the most crucial performance boost stems

---

from the introduction of either one of our features
($\approx 15\%$ F1). However, all other extensions also
achieve notable improvements typically between
1 and 2% F1. Beam-search slightly improves results which shows that the most probable start is
not necessarily the start of the best answer span.

In general, these results are interesting in many
ways. For instance, it is surprising that a simple
binary feature like wiq^b can have such a dramatic
effect on the overall performance. We believe that
the reason for this is the fact that an encoder without any knowledge of the actual question has to
account for every possible question that might be
asked, i.e., it has to keep track of the entire context around each token in its recurrent state. An
informed encoder, on the other hand, can selectively keep track of question related information.
It can further abstract over concrete entities to their
respective types because it is rarely the case that
many entities of the same type occur in the question. For example, if a person is mentioned in the
question the context encoder only needs to remember that the "question-person" was mentioned but
not the concrete name of the person.

Another interesting finding is the fact that additional character based embeddings have a notable effect on the overall performance which was
already observed by Seo et al. (2017); Yu et al.
(2017). We see further improvements when employing representation fusion to allow for more interaction. This shows that a more sophisticated interaction layer can help. However, the differences
are not substantial, indicating that this extension
does not offer any systematic advantage.

7.2 Comparing to State-of-the-Art

Our neural BoW baseline achieves good results
on both datasets (Tables 3 and 1)[5]. For instance,
it outperforms a feature rich logistic-regression
baseline on the SQuAD development set (Table 1)
and nearly reaches the BiLSTM baseline system (i.e., FastQA without character embeddings
and features). It shows that more than half or
more than a third of all questions in SQuAD or
NewsQA, respectively, are (partially) answerable
by a very simple neural BoW baseline. However, the gap to state-of-the-art systems is quite
large ($\approx 20\%$F1) which indicates that employing

---

[5]We did not evaluate the BoW baseline on the SQuAD
test set because it requires submitting the model to Rajpurkar
et al. (2016) and we find that comparisons on NewsQA and
the SQuAD development set give us enough insights.

Model	Test	
	F1	Exact
Logistic Regression[1]	51.0	40.4
Match-LSTM[2]	73.7	64.7
Dynamic Chunk Reader[3]	71.0	62.5
Fine-grained Gating[4]	73.3	62.5
Multi-Perspective Matching[5]	75.1	65.5
Dynamic Coattention Networks[6]	75.9	66.2
Bidirectional Attention Flow[7]	77.3	68.0
r-net[8]	77.9	69.5
FastQA w/ beam-size $k = 5$	77.1	68.4
FastQAExt $k = 5$	**78.9**	**70.8**

Table 2: Official SQuAD leaderboard of single-
model systems on test set from 2016/12/29, the
date of submitting our model. [1]Rajpurkar et al.
(2016), [2]Wang and Jiang (2017), [3]Yu et al. (2017),
[4]Yang et al. (2017), [5]Wang et al. (2017), [6]Xiong
et al. (2017), [7]Seo et al. (2017), [8] not published.
Note that systems are regularly uploaded and improved on SQuAD.

Model	Dev		Test	
	F1	Exact	F1	Exact
Match-LSTM[1]	48.9	35.2	48.0	33.4
BARB[2]	49.6	36.1	48.3	34.1
Neural BoW Baseline	37.6	25.8	36.6	24.1
FastQA $k = 5$	**56.4**	**43.7**	55.7	41.9
FastQAExt $k = 5$	56.1	**43.7**	**56.1**	**42.8**

Table 3: Results on the NewsQA dataset.
[1]Wang and Jiang (2017) was re-implemented by
[2]Trischler et al. (2017).

more complex composition functions than averaging, such as RNNs in FastQA, are indeed necessary to achieve good performance.

Results presented in Tables 2 and 3 clearly
demonstrate the strength of the FastQA system. It
is very competitive to previously established state-
of-the-art results on the two datasets and even improves those for NewsQA. This is quite surprising when considering the simplicity of FastQA
putting existing systems and the complexity of
the datasets, especially SQuAD, into perspective.
Our extended version FastQAExt achieves even
slightly better results outperforming all reported
results prior to submitting our model on the very
competitive SQuAD benchmark.

In parallel to this work Chen et al. (2017) introduced a very similar model to FastQA, which
relies on a few more hand-crafted features and a
3-layer encoder instead of a single layer in this

work. These changes result in slightly better performance which is in line with the observations in this work.

7.3 Do we need additional interaction?

In order to answer this question we compare FastQA, a system without a complex word-by-word interaction layer, to representative models that have an interaction layer, namely FastQAExt and the Dynamic Coattention Network (DCN, Xiong et al. (2017)). We measured both time- and space-complexity of FastQAExt and a reimplementation of the DCN in relation to FastQA and found that FastQA is about twice as fast as the other two systems and requires $2 - 4\times$ less memory compared to FastQAExt and DCN, respectively[6].

In addition, we looked for systematic advantages of FastQAExt over FastQA by comparing SQuAD examples from the development set that were answered correctly by FastQAExt and incorrectly by FastQA (589 FastQAExt wins) against FastQA wins (415). We studied the average question- and answer length as well as the question types for these two sets but could not find any systematic difference. The same observation was made when manually comparing the kind of reasoning that is needed to answer a certain question. This finding aligns with the marginal empirical improvements, especially for NewsQA, between the two systems indicating that FastQAExt seems to generalize slightly better but does not offer a particular, systematic advantage. Therefore, we argue that the additional complexity introduced by the interaction layer is not necessarily justified by the incremental performance improvements presented in §7.2, especially when memory or run-time constraints exist.

7.4 Qualitative Analysis

Besides our empirical evaluations this section provides a qualitative error inspection of predictions for the SQuAD development dataset. We analyse 55 errors made by the FastQA system in detail and highlight basic abilities that are missing to reach human level performance.

We found that most errors are based on a lack of either syntactic understanding or a fine-grained semantic distinction between lexemes with similar

---

[6]We implemented all models in TensorFlow (Abadi et al., 2015).

meanings. Other error types are mostly related to annotation preferences, e.g., answer is good but there is a better, more specific one, or ambiguities within the question or context.

> Example FastQA errors. Predicted answers are underlined while correct answers are presented in boldface.
>
> Ex. 1: *What religion did the Yuan discourage, to support Buddhism?*
>
> Buddhism (especially Tibetan Buddhism) flourished, although **Taoism** endured ... persecutions... from the Yuan government
>
> Ex. 2: *Kurt Debus was appointed what position for the Launch Operations Center?*
>
> Launch Operations Center (LOC) ... Kurt Debus, a member of Dr. Wernher von Braun's ... team. Debus was named the LOC's first **Director** .
>
> Ex. 3: *On what date was the record low temperature in Fresno?*
>
> high temperature for Fresno ... set on July 8, 1905, while the official record low ... set on **January 6, 1913**

A prominent type of mistake is a lack of fine-grained understanding of certain answer types (Ex. 1). Another error is the lack of co-reference resolution and context sensitive binding of abbreviations (Ex. 2). We also find that the model sometimes struggles to capture basic syntactic structure, especially with respect to nested sentences where important separators like punctuation and conjunctions are being ignored (Ex. 3).

A manual examination of errors reveals that about 35 out of 55 mistakes (64%) can directly be attributed to the plain application of our heuristic. A similar analysis reveals that about 44 out of 50 (88%) analyzed positive cases are covered by our heuristic as well. We therefore believe that our model and, wrt. empirical results, other models as well mostly learn a simple context/type matching heuristic.

This finding is important because it reveals that an extractive QA system does not have to solve the complex reasoning types of Chen et al. (2016) that were used to classify SQuAD instances (Rajpurkar et al., 2016), in order to achieve current state-of-the-art results.

8 Related Work

The creation of large scale cloze datasets such the DailyMail/CNN dataset (Hermann et al., 2015) or the Children's Book Corpus (Hill et al., 2016) paved the way for the construction of end-to-end neural architectures for reading comprehension. A thorough analysis by Chen et al. (2016), however, revealed that the DailyMail/CNN was too easy and still quite noisy. New datasets were constructed to eliminate these problems including SQuAD (Rajpurkar et al., 2016), NewsQA (Trischler et al., 2017) and MsMARCO (Nguyen et al., 2016).

Previous question answering datasets such as MCTest (Richardson et al., 2013) and TREC-QA (Dang et al., 2007) were too small to successfully train end-to-end neural architectures such as the models discussed in §4 and required different approaches. Traditional statistical QA systems (e.g., Ferrucci (2012)) relied on linguistic pre-processing pipelines and extensive exploitation of external resources, such as knowledge bases for feature-engineering. Other paradigms include template matching or passage retrieval (Andrenucci and Sneiders, 2005).

9   Conclusion

In this work, we introduced a simple, context/type matching heuristic for extractive question answering which serves as guideline for the development of two neural baseline system. Especially FastQA, our RNN-based system turns out to be an efficient neural baseline architecture for extractive question answering. It combines two simple ingredients necessary for building a currently competitive QA system: a) the awareness of question words while processing the context and b) a composition function that goes beyond simple bag-of-words modeling. We argue that this important finding puts results of previous, more complex architectures as well as the complexity of recent QA datasets into perspective. In the future we want to extend the FastQA model to address linguistically motivated error types of §7.4.

Acknowledgments

We thank Sebastian Riedel, Philippe Thomas, Leonhard Hennig and Omer Levy for comments on an early draft of this work as well as the anonymous reviewers for their insightful comments. This research was supported by the German Federal Ministry of Education and Research (BMBF) through the projects ALL SIDES (01IW14002), BBDC (01IS14013E), and Software Campus (01IS12050, sub-project GeNIE).

References

Martin Abadi, Ashish Agarwal, Paul Barham, Eugene Brevdo, Zhifeng Chen, Craig Citro, Greg Corrado, Andy Davis, Jeffrey Dean, Matthieu Devin, Sanjay Ghemawat, Ian Goodfellow, Andrew Harp, Geoffrey Irving, Michael Isard, Yangqing Jia, Lukasz Kaiser, Manjunath Kudlur, Josh Levenberg, Dan Man, Rajat Monga, Sherry Moore, Derek Murray, Jonathon Shlens, Benoit Steiner, Ilya Sutskever, Paul Tucker, Vincent Vanhoucke, Vijay Vasudevan, Oriol Vinyals, Pete Warden, Martin Wicke, Yuan Yu, and Xiaoqiang Zheng. 2015. TensorFlow: Large-Scale Machine Learning on Heterogeneous Distributed Systems .

Andrea Andrenucci and Eriks Sneiders. 2005. Automated question answering: Review of the main approaches. In *ICITA*.

Danqi Chen, Jason Bolton, and Christopher D Manning. 2016. A Thorough Examination of the CNN / Daily Mail Reading Comprehension Task. *ACL* .

Danqi Chen, Adam Fisch, Jason Weston, and Antoine Bordes. 2017. Reading Wikipedia to Answer Open-Domain Questions. *ACL* .

Hoa Trang Dang, Diane Kelly, and Jimmy J Lin. 2007. Overview of the TREC 2007 Question Answering Track. *TREC* .

D. A. Ferrucci. 2012. Introduction to "This is Watson". *IBM Journal of Research and Development* .

Yarin Gal and Zoubin Ghahramani. 2015. Dropout as a Bayesian Approximation : Representing Model Uncertainty in Deep Learning. *ICML* .

Karl Moritz Hermann, Tomáš Kočiský, Edward Grefenstette, Lasse Espeholt, Will Kay, Mustafa Suleyman, and Phil Blunsom. 2015. Teaching Machines to Read and Comprehend. *NIPS* .

Felix Hill, Antoine Bordes, Sumit Chopra, and Jason Weston. 2016. The Goldilocks Principle: Reading Children's Books with Explicit Memory Representations. *ICLR* .

Sepp Hochreiter and Jürgen Schmidhuber. 1997. LONG SHORT-TERM MEMORY. *Neural Computation* .

Diederik Kingma and Jimmy Ba. 2015. Adam: A Method for Stochastic Optimization. *ICLR* .

Guillaume Lample, Miguel Ballesteros, Sandeep Subramanian, Kazuya Kawakami, and Chris Dyer. 2016. Neural Architectures for Named Entity Recognition. *NAACL* .

Peng Li, Wei Li, Zhengyan He, Xuguang Wang, Ying Cao, Jie Zhou, and Wei Xu. 2016. Dataset and Neural Recurrent Sequence Labeling Model for Open-Domain Factoid Question Answering. *arXiv:1607.06275v1 [cs.CL]* .

Dan I. Moldovan, Sanda M. Harabagiu, Marius Pasca, Rada Mihalcea, Richard Goodrum, Roxana Girju, and Vasile Rus. 1999. Lasso: A tool for surfing the answer net. In *TREC*.

Tri Nguyen, Mir Rosenberg, Xia Song, Jianfeng Gao, Saurabh Tiwary, Rangan Majumder, and Li Deng. 2016. Ms Marco: a Human Generated Machine Reading Comprehension Dataset. *NIPS* .

Jeffrey Pennington, Richard Socher, and Christopher D Manning. 2014. GloVe: Global Vectors for Word Representation. *EMNLP* .

Pranav Rajpurkar, Jian Zhang, Konstantin Lopyrev, and Percy Liang. 2016. SQuAD: 100,000+ Questions for Machine Comprehension of Text. *EMNLP* .

Matthew Richardson, Christopher J C Burges, and Erin Renshaw. 2013. MCTest: A Challenge Dataset for the Open-Domain Machine Comprehension of Text. *EMNLP* .

Minjoon Seo, Aniruddha Kembhavi, Ali Farhadi, and Hananneh Hajishirzi. 2017. Bi-Directional Attention Flow for Machine Comprehension. In *ICLR*.

Yelong Shen, Po-Sen Huang, Jianfeng Gao, and Weizhu Chen. 2016. ReasoNet: Learning to Stop Reading in Machine Comprehension. *arXiv:1609.05284* .

Adam Trischler, Tong Wang, Xingdi Yuan, Justin Harris, Alessandro Sordoni, Philip Bachman, and Kaheer Suleman. 2017. NewsQA: A Machine Comprehension Dataset. *arXiv:1611.09830* .

Shuohang Wang and Jing Jiang. 2017. Machine Comprehension Using Match-LSTM and Answer Pointer. In *ICLR*.

Zhiguo Wang, Haitao Mi, Wael Hamza, and Radu Florian. 2017. Multi-Perspective Context Matching for Machine Comprehension. *arXiv:1612.04211* .

Caiming Xiong, Victor Zhong, and Richard Socher. 2017. Dynamic Coattention Networks for Question Answering. *ICLR* .

Zhilin Yang, Bhuwan Dhingra, Ye Yuan, Junjie Hu, William W Cohen, and Ruslan Salakhutdinov. 2017. Words or Characters? Fine-grained Gating for Reading Comprehension. *ICLR* .

Yang Yu, Wei Zhang, Kazi Hasan, Mo Yu, Bing Xiang, and Bowen Zhou. 2017. End-to-End Reading Comprehension with Dynamic Answer Chunk Ranking. In *ArXiv*.

Neural Domain Adaptation for Biomedical Question Answering

Georg Wiese[1,2], Dirk Weissenborn[2] and Mariana Neves[1]

[1] Hasso Plattner Institute, August Bebel Strasse 88, Potsdam 14482 Germany
[2] Language Technology Lab, DFKI, Alt-Moabit 91c, Berlin, Germany
`georg.wiese@student.hpi.de,`
`dewe01@dfki.de, mariana.neves@hpi.de`

Abstract

Factoid question answering (QA) has recently benefited from the development of deep learning (DL) systems. Neural network models outperform traditional approaches in domains where large datasets exist, such as SQuAD ($\approx 100,000$ questions) for Wikipedia articles. However, these systems have not yet been applied to QA in more specific domains, such as biomedicine, because datasets are generally too small to train a DL system from scratch. For example, the BioASQ dataset for biomedical QA comprises less then 900 factoid (single answer) and list (multiple answers) QA instances. In this work, we adapt a neural QA system trained on a large open-domain dataset (SQuAD, *source*) to a biomedical dataset (BioASQ, *target*) by employing various transfer learning techniques. Our network architecture is based on a state-of-the-art QA system, extended with biomedical word embeddings and a novel mechanism to answer list questions. In contrast to existing biomedical QA systems, our system does not rely on domain-specific ontologies, parsers or entity taggers, which are expensive to create. Despite this fact, our systems achieve state-of-the-art results on factoid questions and competitive results on list questions.

1 Introduction

Question answering (QA) is the task of retrieving *answers* to a *question* given one or more *contexts*. It has been explored both in the open-domain setting (Voorhees et al., 1999) as well as domain-specific settings, such as BioASQ for the biomedical domain (Tsatsaronis et al., 2015). The BioASQ challenge provides ≈ 900 *factoid* and *list* questions, i.e., questions with one and several answers, respectively. This work focuses on answering these questions, for example: *Which drugs are included in the FEC-75 regimen? $\rightarrow$ fluorouracil, epirubicin, and cyclophosphamide.*

We further restrict our focus to *extractive* QA, i.e., QA instances where the correct answers can be represented as spans in the contexts. Contexts are relevant documents which are provided by an information retrieval (IR) system.

Traditionally, a QA pipeline consists of named-entity recognition, question classification, and answer processing steps (Jurafsky, 2000). These methods have been applied to biomedical datasets, with moderate success (Zi et al., 2016). The creation of large-scale, open-domain datasets such as SQuAD (Rajpurkar et al., 2016) have recently enabled the development of neural QA systems, e.g., Wang and Jiang (2016), Xiong et al. (2016), Seo et al. (2016), Weissenborn et al. (2017), leading to impressive performance gains over more traditional systems.

However, creating large-scale QA datasets for more specific domains, such as the biomedical, would be very expensive because of the need for domain experts, and therefore not desirable. The recent success of deep learning based methods on open-domain QA datasets raises the question whether the capabilities of trained models are transferable to another domain via *domain adaptation* techniques. Although domain adaptation has been studied for traditional QA systems (Blitzer et al., 2007) and deep learning systems (Chen et al., 2012; Ganin et al., 2016; Bousmalis et al., 2016; Riemer et al., 2017; Kirkpatrick et al., 2017), it has to our knowledge not yet been applied for end-to-end neural QA systems.

To bridge this gap we employ various do-

Proceedings of the 21st Conference on Computational Natural Language Learning (CoNLL 2017), pages 281–289,
Vancouver, Canada, August 3 - August 4, 2017. ©2017 Association for Computational Linguistics

main adaptation techniques to transfer knowledge from a trained, state-of-the-art neural QA system (FastQA, Weissenborn et al. (2017)) to the biomedical domain using the much smaller BioASQ dataset. In order to answer *list questions* in addition to factoid questions, we extend FastQA with a novel answering mechanism. We evaluate various transfer learning techniques comprehensively. For factoid questions, we show that mere fine-tuning reaches state-of-the-art results, which can further be improved by a forgetting cost regularization (Riemer et al., 2017). On list questions, the results are competitive to existing systems. Our manual analysis of a subset of the factoid questions suggests that the results are even better than the automatic evaluation states, revealing that many of the "incorrect" answers are in fact synonyms to the gold-standard answer.

2   Related Work

Traditional Question Answering Traditional factoid and list question answering pipelines can be subdivided into named-entity recognition, question classification, and answer processing components (Jurafsky, 2000). Such systems have also been applied to biomedical QA such as the OAQA system by Zi et al. (2016). Besides a number of domain-independent features, they incorporate a rich amount of biomedical resources, including a domain-specific parser, entity tagger and thesaurus to retrieve concepts and synonyms. A logistic regression classifier is used both for question classification and candidate answer scoring. For candidate answer generation, OAQA employs different strategies for general factoid/list questions, choice questions and quantity questions.

Neural Question Answering Neural QA systems differ from traditional approaches in that the algorithm is not subdivided into discrete steps. Instead, a single model is trained end-to-end to compute an answer directly for a given question and context. The typical architecture of such systems (Wang and Jiang, 2016; Xiong et al., 2016; Seo et al., 2016) can be summarized as follows:

1. **Embedding Layer:** Question and context tokens are mapped to a high-dimensional vector space, for example via GloVe embeddings (Pennington et al., 2014) and (optionally) character embeddings (Seo et al., 2016).

2. **Encoding Layer:** The token vectors are processed independently for question and context, usually by a recurrent neural network (RNN).

3. **Interaction Layer:** This layer allows for interaction between question and context representations. Examples are Match-LSTM (Wang and Jiang, 2016) and Coattention (Xiong et al., 2016).

4. **Answer Layer:** This layer assigns start and end scores to all of the context tokens, which can be done either statically (Wang and Jiang, 2016; Seo et al., 2016) or by a dynamic decoding process (Xiong et al., 2016).

FastQA *FastQA* fits into this schema, but reduces the complexity of the architecture by removing the interaction layer, while maintaining state-of-the-art performance (Weissenborn et al., 2017). Instead of one or several interaction layers of RNNs, FastQA computes two simple word-in-question features for each token, which are appended to the embedding vectors before the encoding layer. We chose to base our work on this architecture because of its state-of-the-art performance, faster training time and reduced number of parameters.

Unsupervised Domain Adaptation Unsupervised domain adaptation describes the task of learning a predictor in a *target domain* while labeled training data only exists in a different *source domain*. In the context of deep learning, a common method is to first train an autoencoder on a large unlabeled corpus from both domains and then use the learned input representations as input features to a network trained on the actual task using the labeled source domain dataset (Glorot et al., 2011; Chen et al., 2012). Another approach is to learn the hidden representations directly on the target task. For example, domain-adversarial training optimizes the network such that it computes hidden representations that both help predictions on the source domain dataset and are indistinguishable from hidden representations of the unlabeled target domain dataset (Ganin et al., 2016). These techniques cannot be straightforwardly applied to the question answering task, because they require a large corpus of biomedical question-context pairs (albeit no answers are required).

Supervised Domain Adaptation In contrast to the unsupervised case, supervised domain adaptation assumes access to a small amount of labeled training data in the target domain. The simplest approach to supervised domain adaptation for neural models is to pre-train the network on data from the source domain and then fine-tune its parameters on data from the target domain. The main drawback of this approach is *catastrophic forgetting*, which describes the phenomenon that neural networks tend to "forget" knowledge, i.e., its performance in the source domain drops significantly when they are trained on the new dataset. Even though we do not directly aim for good performance in the source domain, measures against catastrophic forgetting can serve as a useful regularizer to prevent over-fitting.

Progressive neural networks combat this issue by keeping the original parameters fixed and adding new units that can access previously learned features (Rusu et al., 2016). Because this method adds a significant amount of new parameters which have to be trained from scratch, it is not well-suited if the target domain dataset is small. Riemer et al. (2017) use fine-tuning, but add an additional *forgetting cost* term that punishes deviations from predictions with the original parameters. Another approach is to add an L2 loss which punishes deviation from the original parameters. Kirkpatrick et al. (2017) apply this loss selectively on parameters which are important in the source domain.

3 Model

Our network architecture is based on FastQA (Weissenborn et al., 2017), a state-of-the-art neural QA system. Because the network architecture itself is exchangeable, we treat it as a black box, with subtle changes at the input and output layer as well as to the decoding and training procedure. These changes are described in the following. See Figure 3 for an overview of the system.

3.1 Input Layer

In a first step, words are embedded into a high-dimensional vector space. We use three sources of embeddings, which are concatenated to form a single embedding vector:

- **GloVe embeddings:** 300-dimensional GloVe vectors (Pennington et al., 2014). These are

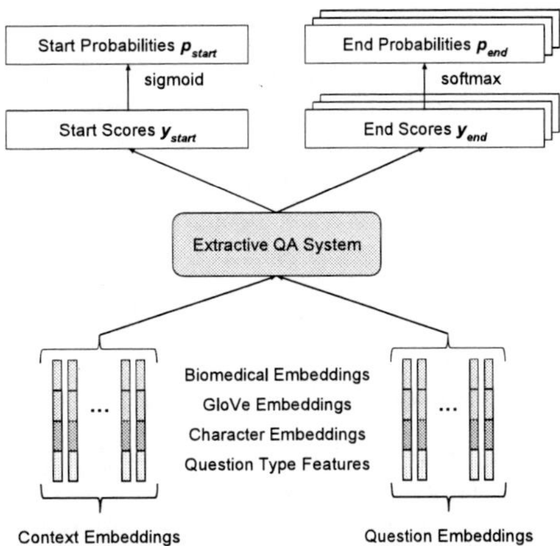

Figure 1: Network architecture of our system for biomedical question answering. At its core, it uses an extractive neural QA system as a black box (we use FastQA (Weissenborn et al., 2017)). The embedding layer is modified in order to include biomedical word embeddings and question type features. The output layer is adjusted to add the ability to answer list questions in addition to factoid questions.

open-domain word vectors trained on 840 billion tokens from web documents. The vectors are not updated during training.

- **Character embeddings:** As used in FastQA (Weissenborn et al., 2017) and proposed originally by Seo et al. (2016), we employ a 1-dimensional convolutional neural network which computes word embeddings from the characters of the word.

- **Biomedical Word2Vec embeddings:** 200-dimensional vectors trained using Word2Vec (Mikolov et al., 2013) on about 10 million PubMed abstracts (Pavlopoulos et al., 2014). These vectors are specific to the biomedical domain and we expect them to help on biomedical QA.

As an optional step, we add entity tag features to the token embeddings via concatenation. Entity tags are provided by a dictionary-based entity tagger based on the UMLS Metathesaurus. The entity tag feature vector is a 127-dimensional bit vector that for each of the UMLS semantic types states whether the current token is part of an entity of that type. This step is only applied if explicitly noted.

Finally, a one-hot encoding of the question type (*factoid* or *list*) is appended to all the input vectors. With these embedding vectors as input, we invoke FastQA to produce start and end scores for each of the n context tokens. We denote start scores by y_{start}^i and end scores conditioned on a predicted start at position i by $y_{end}^{i,j}$, with start index $i \in [1, n]$ and end index $j \in [i, n]$.

3.2 Output Layer

In our adapted output layer, we convert the start and end scores to span probabilities. The computation of these probabilities is independent of the question type. The interpretation, however, depends on the question type: While for factoid questions, the list of answer spans is interpreted as a ranked list of answer candidates, for list questions, answers above a certain probability threshold are interpreted as the set of answers to the question.

Given the start scores $y_{start}^1, ..., y_{start}^n$ and end scores $y_{end}^{i,1}, ..., y_{end}^{i,n}$, we compute the start and end probabilities as follows:

$$p_{start}^i = \sigma(y_{start}^i) \tag{1}$$

$$p_{end}^{i,\cdot} = \text{softmax}(y_{end}^{i,\cdot}) \tag{2}$$

where $\sigma(x)$ is the sigmoid function. As a consequence, multiple tokens can be chosen as likely start tokens, but the network is expected to select a single end token for a given start token, hence the softmax function. Finally, the probability that a given span (i, j) answers the question is $p_{span}^{i,j} = p_{start}^i \cdot p_{end}^{i,j}$. This extension generalizes the FastQA output layer such that multiple answer spans with different start positions can have a high probability, allowing us to retrieve multiple answers for list questions.

3.3 Decoding

Given a trained model, start probabilities can be obtained by running a forward pass and computing the start probability as in Equation 1. For the top 20 starts, we compute the end probabilities as given by Eq. 2. From the start and end probabilities, we extract the top 20 answer spans ranked by $p_{span}^{i,j}$. As a simple post-processing step, we remove duplicate strings and retain only those with the highest probability.

For factoid questions, we output the 5 most likely answer spans as our ranked list of answers. For list questions, we learn a *probability cutoff threshold* t that defines the set of list answers $A = \{(i, j) | p_{span}^{i,j} \geq t\}$. We choose t to be the threshold that optimizes the list F1 score on the respective development set.

3.4 Domain Adaptation

Fine-tuning Our training procedure consists of two phases: In the *pre-training phase*, we train the model on SQuAD, using a token F1 score as the training objective as by Weissenborn et al. (2017). We will refer to the resulting parameters as the *base model*. In the *fine-tuning phase*, we initialize the model parameters with the base model and then continue our optimization on the BioASQ dataset with a smaller learning rate.

Forgetting Cost Regularization To avoid *catastrophic forgetting* during fine-tuning as a means to regularize our model, we optionally add an additional forgetting cost term L_{fc}, as proposed by Riemer et al. (2017). It is defined as the cross-entropy loss between the current predictions and the base model's predictions.

L2 Weight Regularization We also add an L2 loss term L_{l2} which penalizes deviations from the base model's parameters. Note that a more advanced approach would be to apply this loss selectively on weights which are particularly important in the source domain (Kirkpatrick et al., 2017). The final loss is computed as $L_{final} = L_{original} + C_{fc} \cdot L_{fc} + C_{l2} \cdot L_{l2}$ where C_{fc} and C_{l2} are hyperparameters which are set to 0 unless otherwise noted.

4 Experimental Setup

4.1 Datasets

SQuAD *SQuAD* (Rajpurkar et al., 2016) is a dataset of $\approx 100,000$ questions with relevant contexts and answers that sparked research interest into the development of neural QA systems recently. The contexts are excerpts of Wikipedia articles for which crowd-source workers generated questions-answer pairs. Because of the large amount of training examples in SQuAD, it lends itself perfectly as our source dataset.

BioASQ The BioASQ challenge provides a biomedical QA dataset (Tsatsaronis et al., 2015) consisting of questions, relevant contexts (called *snippets*) from PubMed abstracts and possible answers to the question. It was carefully created with the help of biomedical experts.

In this work, we focus on Task B, Phase B of the BioASQ challenge, in which systems must answer questions from gold-standard snippets. These questions can be either yes/no questions, summary questions, factoid questions, or list questions. Because we employ an extractive QA system, we restrict this study to answering factoid and list questions by extracting answer spans from the provided contexts.

The 2017 BioASQ training dataset contains $1,799$ questions, of which 413 are factoid and 486 are list questions. The questions have ≈ 20 snippets on average, each of which are on average ≈ 34 tokens long. We found that around 65% of the factoid questions and around 92% of the list questions have at least one extractable answer. For questions with extractable answers, answers spans are computed via a simple substring search in the provided snippets. All other questions are ignored during training and treated as answered incorrectly during evaluation.

4.2 Training

We minimize the cross-entropy loss for the gold standard answer spans. However, for multiple answer spans that refer to the same answer (e.g. synonyms), we only minimize the loss for the span of the lowest loss. We use the ADAM (Kingma and Ba, 2014) for optimization on SQuAD with a learning rate starting at 10^{-3} which is halved whenever performance drops between checkpoints. During the fine-tuning phase, we continue optimization on the BioASQ dataset with a smaller learning rate starting at 10^{-4}. During both phases, the model is regularized by variational dropout of rate 0.5 (Gal and Ghahramani, 2015).

4.3 Evaluation

The official evaluation measures from BioASQ are mean reciprocal rank (MRR) for factoid questions and F1 score for list questions [1]. For factoid questions, the list of ranked answers can be at most five entries long. The F1 score is measured on the gold standard list elements. For both measures,

case-insensitive string matches are used to check the correctness of a given answer. A list of synonyms is provided for all gold-standard answers. If the system's response matches one of them, the answer counts as correct.

For evaluation, we use two different fine-tuning datasets, depending on the experiment: *BioASQ3B*, which contains all questions of the first three BioASQ challenges, and *BioASQ4B* which additionally contains the test questions of the fourth challenge. *BioASQ4B* is used as the training dataset for the fifth BioASQ challenge whereas *BioASQ3B* was used for training during the fourth challenge.

Because the datasets are small, we perform 5-fold cross-validation and report the average performance across the five folds. We use the larger *BioASQ4B* dataset except when evaluating the ensemble and when comparing to participating systems of previous BioASQ challenges.

All models were implemented using Tensor-Flow (Abadi et al., 2016) with a hidden size of 100. Because the context in BioASQ usually comprises multiple snippets, they are processed independently in parallel for each question. Answers from all snippets belonging to a question are merged and ranked according to their individual probabilities.

5 Results

5.1 Domain Adaptation

In this section, we evaluate various domain adaptation techniques. The results of the experiments are summarized in Table 1.

Baseline As a baseline without transfer learning, Experiment 1 trains the model on BioASQ only. Because the BioASQ dataset by itself is very small, a dropout rate of 0.7 was used, because it worked best in preliminary experiments. We observe a rather low performance, which is expected when applying deep learning to such a small dataset.

Fine-tuning Experiments 2 and 3 evaluate the pure fine-tuning approach: Our *base model* is a system trained on SQuAD only and tested on BioASQ (Experiment 2). For Experiment 3, we fine-tuned the base model on the *BioASQ4B* training set. We observe that performance increases significantly, especially on list questions. This increase is expected, because the network is trained

---

[1] The details can be found at `http://participants-area.bioasq.org/Tasks/b/eval_meas/`

Experiment	Factoid MRR	List F1
(1) Training on BioASQ only	17.9%	19.1%
(2) Training on SQuAD only	20.0%	8.1%
(3) Fine-tuning on BioASQ	24.6%	23.6%
(4) Fine-tuning on BioASQ w/o biomedical embeddings	21.3%	22.4%
(5) Fine-tuning on BioASQ w/ entity features	23.3%	23.8%
(6) Fine-tuning on BioASQ + SQuAD	23.9%	23.8%
(7) Fine-tuning on BioASQ w/ forgetting cost ($C_{fc} = 100.0$)	26.2%	21.1%
(8) Fine-tuning on BioASQ w/ L2 loss on original parameters ($C_{l2} = 0.3$)	22.6%	20.4%

Table 1: Comparison of various transfer learning techniques. In Experiment 1, the model was trained on BioASQ only. In Experiment 2, the model was trained on SQuAD and tested on BioASQ. We refer to it as the *base model*. In Experiment 3, the base model parameters were fine-tuned on the BioASQ training set. Experiments 4-5 evaluate the utility of domain dependent word vectors and features. Experiments 6-8 address the problem of catastrophic forgetting. All experiments have been conducted with the *BioASQ4B* dataset and 5-fold cross-validation.

on biomedical- and list questions, which are not part of the SQuAD dataset, for the first time. Overall, the performance of the fine-tuned model on both question types is much higher than the baseline system without transfer learning.

Features In order to evaluate the impact of using biomedical word embeddings, we repeat Experiment 3 without them (Experiment 4). We see a factoid and list performance drop of 3.3 and 1.2 percentage points, respectively, showing that biomedical word embeddings help increase performance.

In Experiment 5, we append entity features to the word vector, as described in Section 3.1. Even though these features provide the network with domain-specific knowledge, we found that it actually harms performance on factoid questions. Because most of the entity features are only active during fine-tuning with the small dataset, we conjecture that the performance decrease is due to over-fitting.

Catastrophic Forgetting We continue our study with techniques to combat catastrophic forgetting as a means to regularize training during fine-tuning. In Experiment 6 of Table 1 we fine-tune the base model on a half-half mixture of BioASQ and SQuAD questions (BioASQ questions have been upsampled accordingly). This form of joint training yielded no significant performance gains. Experiment 7 regularizes the model via an additional forgetting cost term, as

proposed by Riemer et al. (2017) and explained in Section 3.4. We generally found that this technique only increases performance for factoid questions where the performance boost was largest for $C_{fc} = 100.0$. The fact that the forgetting loss decreases performance on list questions is not surprising, as predictions are pushed more towards the predictions of the base model, which has very poor performance on list questions.

Experiment 8 adds an L2 loss which penalizes deviations from the base model's parameters. We found that performance decreases as we increase the value of C_{l2} which shows that this technique does not help at all. For the sake of completeness we report results for $C_{l2} = 0.3$, the lowest value that yielded a significant drop in performance.

5.2 Ensemble

Model ensembles are a common method to tweak the performance of a machine learning system. Ensembles combine multiple model predictions, for example by averaging, in order to improve generalization and prevent over-fitting. We evaluate the utility of an ensemble by training five models on the *BioASQ3B* dataset using 5-fold cross-validation. Each of the models is evaluated on the 4B test data, i.e., data which is not included in *BioASQ3B*.

During application, we run an ensemble by averaging the start and end scores of individual models before they are passed to the sigmoid / softmax functions as defined in Eq. 1 and 2. In Table 2 we summarize the average performance of

Experiment	Factoid MRR	List F1
Average	23.4%	24.0%
Best	24.3%	27.7%
Ensemble	27.3%	28.6%

Table 2: Performance of a model ensemble. Five models have been trained on the *BioASQ3B* dataset and tested on the 4B test questions. We report the average and best single model performances, as well as the ensemble performance.

the five models, the best performance across the five models, and the performance of the ensemble. We observe performance gains of 3 percentage points on factoid questions and a less than 1 percentage point on list questions, relative to the best single model. This demonstrates a small performance gain that is consistent with the literature.

5.3 Comparison to competing BioASQ systems

Because the final results of the fifth BioASQ challenge are not available at the time of writing, we compare our system to the best systems in last year's challenge [2]. For comparison, we use the best single model and the model ensemble trained on *BioASQ3B* (see Section 5.2). We then evaluate the model on the 5 batches of last year's challenge using the official BioASQ evaluation tool. Each batch contains 100 questions of which only some are factoid and list questions. Note that the results underestimate our system's performance, because our competing system's responses have been manually evaluated by humans while our system's responses are evaluated automatically using string matching against a potentially incomplete list of synonyms. In fact, our qualitative analysis in Section 5.4 shows that many answers are counted as incorrect, but are synonyms of the gold-standard answer. The results are summarized in Table 3 and compared to the best systems in the challenge in each of the batches and question type categories.

With our system winning four out of five batches on factoid questions, we consider it state-of-the-art in biomedical factoid question answering, especially when considering that our results might be higher on manual evaluation. The results on list questions are slightly worse, but still very

[2]Last year's results are available at `http://participants-area.bioasq.org/results/4b/phaseB/`

competitive. This is surprising, given that the network never saw a list question prior to the fine-tuning phase. Due to small test set sizes, the sampling error in each batch is large, causing the single model to outperform the model ensemble on some batches.

5.4 Qualitative Analysis

In order to get a better insight into the quality of the predictions, we manually validated the predictions for the factoid questions of batch 5 of the fourth BioASQ challenge as given by the best single model (see Table 3). There are in total 33 factoid questions, of which 23 have as the gold standard answer a span in one of the contexts. According to the official BioASQ evaluation, only 4 questions are predicted correctly (i.e., the gold standard answer is ranked highest). However, we identified 10 rank-1 answers which are not counted as correct but are synonyms to the gold standard answer. Examples include "CMT4D disease" instead of "Charcot-Marie-Tooth (CMT) 4D disease", "tafazzin" instead of "Tafazzin (TAZ) gene", and "β-glucocerebrosidase" instead of "Beta glucocerebrosidase". In total, we labeled 14 questions as correct and 24 questions as having their correct answer in the top 5 predictions.

In the following, we give examples of mistakes made by the system. Questions are presented in italics. In the context, we underline predicted answers and present correct answers in boldface.

We identified eight questions for which the semantic type of the top answer differs from the question answer type. Some of these cases are completely wrong predictions. However, this category also includes subtle mistakes like the following:

In which yeast chromosome does the rDNA cluster reside?

The rDNA cluster in Saccharomyces cerevisiae is located 450 kb from the left end and 610 kb from the right end of **chromosome XII**...

Here, it predicted a yeast species the rDNA cluster is located in, but ignored that the question is asking for a chromosome.

Another type of mistakes is that the top answer is somewhat correct, but is missing essential information. We labeled four predictions with this category, like the following example:

	Factoid MRR			List F1		
Batch	**Best Participant**	**Single**	**Ensemble**	**Best Participant**	**Single**	**Ensemble**
1	12.2% (fa1)	25.2%	**29.2%**	16.8% (fa1)	**29.1%**	27.9%
2	22.6% (LabZhu-FDU)	16.4%	**24.2%**	15.5% (LabZhu-FDU)	**25.8%**	20.8%
3	24.4% (oaqa-3b-3)	**24.7%**	20.6%	**48.3%** (oaqa-3b-3)	31.8%	33.3%
4	32.5% (oaqa-3b-4)	34.0%	**40.3%**	**31.2%** (oaqa-3b-4)	29.0%	24.1%
5	**28.5%** (oaqa-3b-5)	23.7%	23.2%	**29.0%** (oaqa-3b-5)	23.5%	26.1%
Avg.	24.0%	24.8%	**27.5%**	**28.1%**	27.8%	26.5%

Table 3: Comparison to systems on last year's (fourth) BioASQ challenge for factoid and list questions. For each batch and question type, we list the performance of the best competing system, our single model and ensemble. Note that our qualitative analysis (Section 5.4) suggests that our factoid performance on batch 5 would be about twice as high if all synonyms were contained in the gold standard answers.

How early during pregnancy does non-invasive cffDNA testing allow sex determination of the fetus?
Gold Standard Answer: "6th to 10th week of gestation" or "first trimester of pregnancy"
Given Top Answer: "6th-10th"

In summary, to our judgment, 14 of 33 questions (42.4%) are answered correctly, and 24 of 33 questions (72.7%) are answered correctly in one of the top 5 answers. These are surprisingly high numbers considering low MRR score of 23.7% of the automatic evaluation (Table 3).

6 Discussion and future work

The most significant result of this work is that state-of-the-art results in biomedical question answering can be achieved even in the absence of domain-specific feature engineering. Most competing systems require structured domain-specific resources, such as biomedical ontologies, parsers, and entity taggers. While these resources are available in the biomedical domain, they are not available in most domains.

Our system, on the other hand, requires a large open-domain QA dataset, biomedical word embeddings (which are trained in an unsupervised fashion), and a small biomedical QA dataset. This suggests that our methodology is easily transferable to other domains as well.

Furthermore, we explored several supervised domain adaptation techniques. In particular, we demonstrated the usefulness of forgetting cost for factoid questions. The decreased performance on list questions is not surprising, because the model's performance on those questions is very poor prior to fine-tuning which is due to the lack of list questions in SQuAD. We believe that large scale open-domain corpora for list questions would enhance performance further.

Unsupervised domain adaptation could be an interesting direction for future work, because the biomedical domain offers large amounts of textual data, some of which might even contain questions and their corresponding answers. We believe that leveraging these resources holds potential to further improve biomedical QA.

7 Conclusion

In this paper, we described a deep learning approach to address the task of biomedical question answering by using domain adaptation techniques. Our experiments reveal that mere fine-tuning in combination with biomedical word embeddings yield state-of-the-art performance on biomedical QA, despite the small amount of in-domain training data and the lack of domain-dependent feature engineering. Techniques to overcome catastrophic forgetting, such as a forgetting cost, can further boost performance for factoid questions. Overall, we show that employing domain adaptation on neural QA systems trained on large-scale, open-domain datasets can yield good performance in domains where large datasets are not available.

Acknowledgments

This research was supported by the German Federal Ministry of Education and Research (BMBF) through Software Campus project GeNIE (01IS12050).

References

Martín Abadi, Ashish Agarwal, Paul Barham, Eugene Brevdo, Zhifeng Chen, Craig Citro, Greg S Corrado, Andy Davis, Jeffrey Dean, Matthieu Devin, et al. 2016. Tensorflow: Large-scale machine learning on heterogeneous distributed systems. *arXiv preprint arXiv:1603.04467* .

John Blitzer, Mark Dredze, Fernando Pereira, et al. 2007. Biographies, bollywood, boom-boxes and blenders: Domain adaptation for sentiment classification. In *ACL*. volume 7, pages 440–447.

Konstantinos Bousmalis, George Trigeorgis, Nathan Silberman, Dilip Krishnan, and Dumitru Erhan. 2016. Domain separation networks. In *Advances in Neural Information Processing Systems*. pages 343–351.

Minmin Chen, Zhixiang Xu, Kilian Weinberger, and Fei Sha. 2012. Marginalized denoising autoencoders for domain adaptation. *arXiv preprint arXiv:1206.4683* .

Yarin Gal and Zoubin Ghahramani. 2015. Dropout as a bayesian approximation: Representing model uncertainty in deep learning. *arXiv preprint arXiv:1506.02142* 2.

Yaroslav Ganin, Evgeniya Ustinova, Hana Ajakan, Pascal Germain, Hugo Larochelle, François Laviolette, Mario Marchand, and Victor Lempitsky. 2016. Domain-adversarial training of neural networks. *Journal of Machine Learning Research* 17(59):1–35.

Xavier Glorot, Antoine Bordes, and Yoshua Bengio. 2011. Domain adaptation for large-scale sentiment classification: A deep learning approach. In *Proceedings of the 28th international conference on machine learning (ICML-11)*. pages 513–520.

Dan Jurafsky. 2000. *Speech & language processing*. Pearson Education India.

Diederik Kingma and Jimmy Ba. 2014. Adam: A method for stochastic optimization. *arXiv preprint arXiv:1412.6980* .

James Kirkpatrick, Razvan Pascanu, Neil Rabinowitz, Joel Veness, Guillaume Desjardins, Andrei A Rusu, Kieran Milan, John Quan, Tiago Ramalho, Agnieszka Grabska-Barwinska, et al. 2017. Overcoming catastrophic forgetting in neural networks. *Proceedings of the National Academy of Sciences* page 201611835.

Tomas Mikolov, Ilya Sutskever, Kai Chen, Greg S Corrado, and Jeff Dean. 2013. Distributed representations of words and phrases and their compositionality. In *Advances in neural information processing systems*. pages 3111–3119.

Ioannis Pavlopoulos, Aris Kosmopoulos, and Ion Androutsopoulos. 2014. Continuous space word vectors obtained by applying word2vec to abstracts of biomedical articles http://bioasq.lip6.fr/info/BioASQword2vec/.

Jeffrey Pennington, Richard Socher, and Christopher D. Manning. 2014. Glove: Global vectors for word representation. In *Empirical Methods in Natural Language Processing (EMNLP)*. pages 1532–1543. http://www.aclweb.org/anthology/D14-1162.

Pranav Rajpurkar, Jian Zhang, Konstantin Lopyrev, and Percy Liang. 2016. Squad: 100,000+ questions for machine comprehension of text. *arXiv preprint arXiv:1606.05250* .

Matthew Riemer, Elham Khabiri, and Richard Goodwin. 2017. Representation stability as a regularizer for improved text analytics transfer learning https://openreview.net/pdf?id=HyenWc5gx.

Andrei A Rusu, Neil C Rabinowitz, Guillaume Desjardins, Hubert Soyer, James Kirkpatrick, Koray Kavukcuoglu, Razvan Pascanu, and Raia Hadsell. 2016. Progressive neural networks. *arXiv preprint arXiv:1606.04671* .

Minjoon Seo, Aniruddha Kembhavi, Ali Farhadi, and Hannaneh Hajishirzi. 2016. Bidirectional attention flow for machine comprehension. *arXiv preprint arXiv:1611.01603* .

George Tsatsaronis, Georgios Balikas, Prodromos Malakasiotis, Ioannis Partalas, Matthias Zschunke, Michael R Alvers, Dirk Weissenborn, Anastasia Krithara, Sergios Petridis, Dimitris Polychronopoulos, et al. 2015. An overview of the bioasq large-scale biomedical semantic indexing and question answering competition. *BMC bioinformatics* 16(1):1.

Ellen M Voorhees et al. 1999. The trec-8 question answering track report. In *Trec*. volume 99, pages 77–82.

Shuohang Wang and Jing Jiang. 2016. Machine comprehension using match-lstm and answer pointer. *arXiv preprint arXiv:1608.07905* .

Dirk Weissenborn, Georg Wiese, and Laura Seiffe. 2017. Making neural qa as simple as possible but not simpler. *arXiv preprint arXiv:1703.04816* .

Caiming Xiong, Victor Zhong, and Richard Socher. 2016. Dynamic coattention networks for question answering. *arXiv preprint arXiv:1611.01604* .

Yang Zi, Zhou Yue, and Eric Nyberg. 2016. Learning to answer biomedical questions: Oaqa at bioasq 4b. *ACL 2016* page 23.

A phoneme clustering algorithm based on the obligatory contour principle

Mans Hulden
Department of Linguistics
University of Colorado
`mans.hulden@colorado.edu`

Abstract

This paper explores a divisive hierarchical clustering algorithm based on the well-known Obligatory Contour Principle in phonology. The purpose is twofold: to see if such an algorithm could be used for unsupervised classification of phonemes or graphemes in corpora, and to investigate whether this purported universal constraint really holds for several classes of phonological distinctive features. The algorithm achieves very high accuracies in an unsupervised setting of inferring a consonant-vowel distinction, and also has a strong tendency to detect coronal phonemes in an unsupervised fashion. Remaining classes, however, do not correspond as neatly to phonological distinctive feature splits. While the results offer only mixed support for a universal Obligatory Contour Principle, the algorithm can be very useful for many NLP tasks due to the high accuracy in revealing consonant/vowel/coronal distinctions.

1 Introduction[1]

It has long been noted in phonology that there seems to be a universal cross-linguistic tendency to avoid redundancy or repetition of similar speech features within a word or morpheme, especially if the phonemes are adjacent to one another. Many different names are given to variants of this general phenomenon in the linguistic literature: "identity avoidance" (Yip, 1998), "similar place avoidance" (Pozdniakov and Segerer, 2007), "obligatory contour principle" (OCP) (Leben, 1973), and "dissimilation" (Hempl, 1893). Some special

cases such as haplology (avoidance of adjacent identical syllables) also fall in this general category of avoiding repetition along some dimension.

The general phenomenon itself is supported by robust, although inconsistent, evidence across a number of languages. An early example is the observation of Spitta-Bey (1880),[2] that the Arabic language tends to favor combination of consonant segments (phonemes) in morphemes that have different places of articulation; this was also later pointed out by Greenberg (1950) and those Semitic root outliers that deviate from this pattern were analyzed in depth in Frajzyngier (1979). In Proto-Indo-European (PIE) roots, which are mostly structured CVC, stop-V-stop combinations have been found to be statistically underrepresented (Iverson and Salmons, 1992). That is, PIE seems to obey a cross-linguistic constraint that disfavors two similar consonants in a root. Another specific example comes from Japanese, where the phenomenon called Lyman's law—which effectively says that a morpheme may consist of maximally one voiced obstruent—can also be interpreted as avoidance (Itô and Mester, 1986).

In light of such evidence, proposals have been put forth to define the concept of phoneme by distributional properties alone as opposed to the prevalent distinctive feature systems which are largely based on articulatory features (Fischer-Jørgensen, 1952). Elsewhere, after finding a statistical tendency to avoid similar place of articulation in word-initial and word-medial consonants, Pozdniakov and Segerer (2007) offer the argument

---

[1]All code data sets used are available at `https://github.com/cvocp/cvocp`

[2]Nun hat, wie schon längst bemerkt ist, die arabische Sprache die Neigung, solche Buchstaben in einem Worte zu vereinigen, deren Organe weit von einander entfernt liegen, wie Kehllaute und Dentale. Translation: Now, the Arabic language, as has long been noted, has the tendency to combine such letters in a word where the place of articulation is distant, such as gutturals and dentals (Spitta-Bey, 1880, p. 15).

Proceedings of the 21st Conference on Computational Natural Language Learning (CoNLL 2017), pages 290–300,
Vancouver, Canada, August 3 - August 4, 2017. ©2017 Association for Computational Linguistics

that this phenomenon of "Similar Place Avoidance" is a statistical universal.

This phenomenon is often filed under the generic heading "obligatory contour principle" (Leben, 1973; McCarthy, 1986; Yip, 1988; Odden, 1988; Meyers, 1997; Pierrehumbert, 1993; Rose, 2000; Frisch, 2004). Originally, the OCP was applied as a theoretical constraint only to tone languages, with the argument that adjacent identical tones in *underlying forms* were rare, and this reflected an obligatory contour principle. The usage has since spread, and is assumed to account for segmental features other than tone.

It is unclear why the phenomenon is so widespread and why it manifests itself in the diverse ways it does. Accounts range from information compression to a diachronically visible hypercorrection by listeners who misperceive the signal and make the assumption that repetition is unlikely (Ohala, 1981).

This paper explores the simplest incarnation of the idea of similarity avoidance; namely, that two adjacent segments are preferably different in some way and that this difference reveals itself globally. That is, it is not assumed that the constraint is absolute; rather, an algorithm is developed that induces grouping of unknown phoneme symbols so as to maximize potential alternation of clusters in a sequence of symbols, i.e. a corpus. If the OCP holds for phonological or phonetic features—primarily places of articulation—such a clustering algorithm could group phonemes along the lines of distinctive features. While, as we shall see, the observations do not support the presence of a strong universal OCP effect, the top-level clusters discovered by the algorithm correspond nearly 100% to the distinction of consonants and vowels—or syllabic and non-syllabic elements if expressed in terms of features. Furthermore, a tier-based variant of the algorithm additionally groups consonants somewhat reliably into coronal/non-coronal places of articulation, and also often distinguishes front vowels from back vowels. This is true even if the algorithm is run on alphabetic representations. An evaluation of the ability to detect C/V distinction against a data set of 503 Bible translations (Kim and Snyder, 2013) is included, improving upon earlier work that attempts to distinguish between consonants and vowels in an unsupervised fashion (Kim and Snyder, 2013; Goldsmith and Xanthos, 2009; Moler and Morri-

son, 1983; Sukhotin, 1962). The algorithm is also more robust than earlier algorithms that perform consonant-vowel separation and works with less data, something that is also briefly evaluated.

This paper is structured as follows: an overview of previous work is given in section 2, mostly related to the simpler task of grouping consonants and vowels without labeled data, rather than identifying distinctive features. Following that, the general algorithm is developed in section 3, after which the experiments on both phonemic and graphemic representations in section 4 are reported. Four experiments are evaluated. The first uses phonemic data from 9 languages for clustering and evaluates clustering along distinctive feature lines. The second is a graphemic experiment that uses a data set of Bible translations in 503 languages where the task is to distinguish the vowels from the consonants; here, results are compared to Kim and Snyder (2013) on the same data set. That data is slightly noisy, motivating the third experiment, which is also graphemic and evaluates consonant-vowel distinctions on vetted word lists from data taken from the ACL SIG-MORPHON shared task on morphological reinflection (Cotterell et al., 2016). The ability of a tier-based variant of the algorithm to separate coronals from non-coronals is evaluated in a fourth experiment where Universal Dependencies corpora (Nivre et al., 2017) are used.

The main results are presented in section 5. Given the high accuracy of the algorithm in C/V distinction with very little data and its consequent potential applicability to decipherment tasks, a small practical example application is evaluated which analyzes a fragment of text, a manuscript of only 54 characters.

2 Related Work

The statistical experiments of Andrey Markov (1913) on Alexander Pushkin's poem *Eugene Onegin* constitute what is probably one of the earliest discoveries of the fact that significant latent structure can be found by examining immediate co-occurrence of graphemes in text. Examining a 20,000-letter sample of the poem, Markov found a strong statistical bias that favored alternation of consonants and vowels. A number of computational approaches have since been investigated that attempt to reveal phonological structure in corpora. Often, orthography is used as a proxy for phonology since textual data is easier to come by. A spectral method was introduced by Moler and Morrison (1983) with the explicit purpose of distinguishing consonants from vowels by a dimensionality reduction on a segment co-occurrence matrix through singular value decomposition (SVD). An almost identical SVD-based approach was later applied to phonological data by Goldsmith and Xanthos (2009). Hidden Markov Models coupled with the EM algorithm have also been used to learn consonant-vowel distinctions (Knight et al., 2006) as well as other latent structure, such as vowel harmony (Goldsmith and Xanthos, 2009). Kim and Snyder (2013) use Bayesian inference supported by simultaneous language clustering to infer C/V-distinctions in a large number of scripts simultaneously. We compare our results against a data set published in conjunction with that work. More directly related to the current work are Mayer et al. (2010) and Mayer and Rohrdantz (2013) who work with models for visualizing consonant co-occurrence in a corpus.

2.1 Sukhotin's algorithm

Sukhotin's algorithm (Sukhotin, 1962, 1973) is a well-known algorithm for separating consonants from vowels in orthographic data; good descriptions of the algorithm are given in Guy (1991) and Sassoon (1992). The idea is to start with the assumption that all segments in a corpus are consonants, then repeatedly and greedily find the segment that co-occurs most with other segments, and declare that a vowel. This is performed until a stopping condition is reached. The algorithm is known to perform surprisingly well (Foster, 1992; Goldsmith and Xanthos, 2009), although it is limited to the task it was designed to do—inferring a C/V-distinction (with applications to decipherment) without attempting to reveal any further structure in the segments. All the syllabic/nonsyllabic distinction results in the current work are compared with the performance of Sukhotin's algorithm.

3 General OCP-based algorithm

At the core of the new clustering algorithm is the OCP-observation alluded to above, already empirically established in (Markov, 1913, 2006), that there is a systematic bias toward alternating adjacent segments along some dimension. To reveal this alternation, one can assume that there is a natural grouping of all segments into two initial sets, called **0** and **1**, in such a way that the total number of **0-1** or **1-0** alternations between adjacent segments in a corpus is maximized. For example, consider a corpus of a single string **abc**. This can be split into two nonempty subsets in six different ways: $\mathbf{0} = \{ab\}$ and $\mathbf{1} = \{c\}$; $\mathbf{0} = \{a\}$ and $\mathbf{1} = \{bc\}$; $\mathbf{0} = \{ac\}$ and $\mathbf{1} = \{b\}$, and their symmetric variants which are produced by swapping **0** and **1**. Out of these, the best assignment is $\mathbf{0} = \{ac\}$ and $\mathbf{1} = \{b\}$, since if reflects an alternation of sets where $\mathbf{abc} \mapsto \mathbf{010}$. The 'score' of this assignment is based on the number of adjacent alternations, in this case 2 (**01** and **10**).

Outside of such small examples which split perfectly into alternating sets, once this optimal division of all segments into **0** and **1** is found, there may remain some residue of adjacent segments in the same class (**0-0** and **1-1**). The sets **0** and **1** can then be partitioned anew into subsets **00**, **01** (from **0**) and **10** and **11** (from **1**). Again, there may be some residue, and the partitioning procedure can be applied recursively until no further splitting is possible, i.e. until all of the adjacent segments fall into different clusters in the hierarchy.

More formally, given a corpus of words $w_1, \ldots, w_n$ and where each word is a sequence of symbols $s_1, \ldots, s_m$, this top-level objective function that we want to maximize can be expressed as

$$\sum_w \sum_i \mathbb{1}(\mathbf{Group}(s_i) \neq \mathbf{Group}(s_{i+1})) \qquad (1)$$

where **Group(s)** is the set that segment s is in.

Given a suggested split of all the segments in a corpus into, say, the top-level disjoint sets **0** and **1**, we obviously do not need to examine the whole corpus to establish the score but can do so by simply examining bigram counts of the corpus.

Still, finding just the top-level split of segments into **0** and **1** is computationally expensive if done by brute force by trying all the possible assignments of segments into **0** and **1** and evaluating the score for each assignment. Since there are 2^n ways of partitioning a set of segments into two subsets (ignoring the symmetry of **0** and **1**), such an approach is feasible in reasonable time only for small alphabets (< 25, roughly).

To address the computational search space problem, the algorithm is implemented by a type of simulated annealing (Kirkpatrick et al., 1983; Černý, 1985) to quickly find the optimum. The algorithm for the top-level split proceeds as follows:

(1) Randomly divide the set S into S' and S''

(2) Draw an integer p from $Uniform(1 \ldots K)$, where K depends on the cooling schedule

(3) Swap p random segments between S' and S''

(4) If score is higher after swap, keep swap else discard swap. Go to (2).

The idea is to begin with an arbitrary partition of S into S' and S'', then randomly trying successively smaller and smaller random swaps of segments between the two sets according to a cooling schedule, always keeping the swap if the score improves. The cooling schedule was tested against corpora that use smaller alphabets where the answer is known beforehand by a brute-force calculation. The cooling was made slow enough to give the correct answer in 100/100 tries on such development corpora. In practice, this yields an annealing schedule where early swaps (the size of K) are sometimes as large as $|S|$, ending in K equaling 1 for several iterations before termination. This splitting is repeated recursively to produce new sub-splits until no splitting is possible, i.e. the score cannot improve by splitting a set into two subsets.

3.1 A tier-based variant

Many identity avoidance effects have been documented that seem to operate not by strict adjacency, but over intervening material, such as consonants and vowels, as discussed in the introduction. For example, Rose (2000) argues that OCP effects apply to adjacent consonants across intervening vowels in Semitic languages. This motivates a tier-based variant of the algorithm. In this modification, instead of repeatedly splitting sets based on a residue of adjacent segments that belong to the same set, we instead modify the corpus, removing segments after each split. Each time we split a set S into S' and S'' based on a corpus C, we also create new corpora C' and C'' where segments in S'' are removed from C' and segments in S' are removed from C''. Splitting then resumes recursively for S' and S'', where S' uses the corpus C' and S'' the corpus C''. Figure 1 shows an example of this. Here, the initial

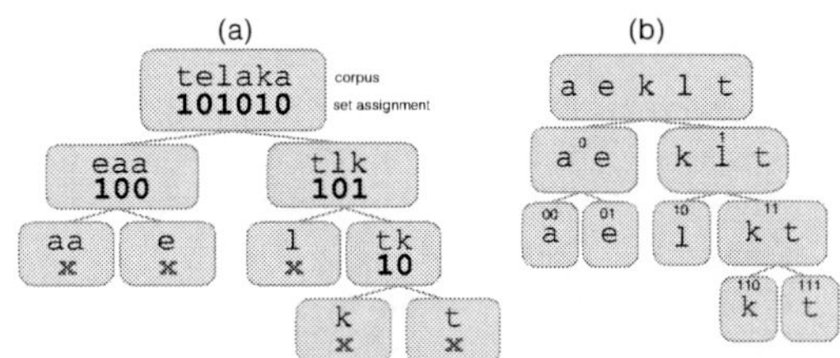

Figure 1: Illustration of the tier-based variant of the clustering algorithm. The left-hand side (a) shows the original corpus (the single word **telaka**), where each character is assigned a top-level grouping, after which the corpus is modified to remove characters in the respective sets **0** and **1**. The algorithm is then applied recursively to the modified corpora. The resulting clustering is shown in (b).

corpus $C =$ **telaka**, and the initial segment set $S = \{a, e, k, l, t\}$ is split into $S' = \{a, e\}$ and $S'' = \{k, l, t\}$ on a first iteration. Likewise, the corpus is now modified by removing the S' and S'' segments from C'' and C' respectively, yielding new corpora $C' =$ **eaa** and $C'' =$ **tlk**, and splitting proceeds on these subcorpora. This way, if, say, consonants and vowels operate on different tiers and get split first into top-level sets, the remaining consonants will become adjacent to each other on the next iteration, as will the vowels.

4 Experiments

Four experiments are evaluated; the first experiment performs a full hierarchical clustering on phonemic data in 9 typologically divergent languages. The clusters are evaluated according to the following simple criterion: counting the number of splits in the tree that correspond to a split that could be expressed through a single phonological $\pm$ feature. For example, if the top level split in the tree produced corresponds to exactly the consonants and vowels, it is counted as a 1, since this corresponds to the partitioning that would be produced by the phonological feature [$\pm$syllabic]. If there is no way to express the split through a single distinctive feature, it is counted as a 0. A standard phonological feature set like that given in sources such as Hayes (2011) or PHOIBLE (Moran et al., 2014) is assumed. As mentioned above, the hypothesis under examination is that if the OCP is a strong universal principle, some non-significant number of subclusters coinciding with single phonological distinctive features should be

293

Language	Source	Sample
Arapaho	(Cowell and Moss Sr, 2008)	towohei hiiθeti? tohnooke? toothei?eihoo …
Basque	Wikipedia + g2p	meʃikoko iriburuko espetʃe batean sartu zuten eta meʃiko …
English	(Brent and Cartwright, 1996)	ju want tu si ðə bʊk lʊk ðɛrz ə bɔi wɪð hɪz hæt …
Finnish	(Aho, 1884) + g2p	vai oli eilen kolmekymmentæ kotoapæinkø se matti ajelee …
Hawaiian	Wikipedia + g2p	?o ka ?õlelo hawai?i ka ?õlelo makuahine a ka po?e maoli …
Hungarian	(Gervain and Erra, 2012)	idʒ nintʃ jɒj dɛ tʃɛtʃɛ hol ɒ montʃikɒ hol vɒn ɒ montʃi itt ɒ …
Italian	Wikipedia + g2p	tʃitta eterna kon abitanti e il komune piu popoloso ditalia …
Polish	(Boruta and Jastrzebska, 2012)	gdʑie jest bartuɕ gdʑie jest ɲe ma xoɖ tu a kuku tso xovaʃ …
Spanish	(Taulé et al., 2008) + g2p	un akuerdo entre la patronal i los sindikatos franθeses sobre …

Table 1: The data used for the phonemic clustering experiment, with sources indicated and a sample.

found. Both the non-tier algorithm and the tier-based algorithm is evaluated.

In the second experiment, the capacity of the algorithm to distinguish between consonants and vowels is evaluated, this time with graphemic data. To separate consonants from vowels—the most significant dimension of alternation between adjacent segments—the algorithm is run only for the top-level split, and it is assumed that the top two subsets will represent the consonants and vowels. Here, the results are compared with those of Kim and Snyder (2013), who train a hierarchical Bayesian model to perform this distinction over all the 503 languages at the same time. Sukhotin's algorithm is also used as another baseline.

In the third experiment, the capacity to distinguish consonants and vowels in graphemic data in the form of word lists—i.e. where no frequency data is known—is evaluated compared against Sukhotin's algorithm.

4.1 Phonemic splitting

Nine languages from a diverse set of sources were used for this experiment (see Table 1). Some of the language data were already represented as phonemes (English, Hungarian, and Polish), while for the others, which have close-to-phonemic writing systems, a number of grapheme-to-phoneme (g2p) rules were created manually to convert the data into an International Phonetic Alphabet (IPA) representation. The conversion was on the level of the phoneme—actual allophones (such as /n/ being velarized to [ŋ] before /k/ in most languages or /d/ being pronounced [ð] intervocalically in Spanish) were not modeled. Table 1 summarizes the data and gives a sample of each corpus.

For this data, the clustering algorithm was run as described above and each split was annotated

Figure 2: Resulting Finnish clusters with manual annotation of the distinctive feature splits.

with information about whether the split *could* be defined in terms of a single distinctive feature. Figure 2 shows the output of such a tree produced by the algorithm, with manual feature annotations.

The percentage of correctly identified top-level splits (which are syllabic/non-syllabic segments) is also given, together with the corresponding results from Sukhotin's C/V-inference algorithm, and Moler & Morrison's SVD-based algorithm.

4.2 C/V distinction in Bible translations

This experiment relies on word lists and frequency counts from Bible translations covering 503 distinct languages. Of these, 476 use a Latin alphabet, 26 a Cyrillic alphabet, and one uses Greek. The data covers a large number of language groups, and has been used before by Kim and Snyder (2013) to evaluate accuracy in unsupervised C/V-distinction.

The algorithms were evaluated in two different ways: one, on a task where each C and V set is inferred separately for each language, and two, in a task where all languages' consonants and vowels are learned at once, as if the corpus were one language, for clearer comparison with earlier work. Both token-level accuracy and type-level accuracy are given, again, for comparability reasons. For this data set, Sukhotin's C/V-algorithm and Moler & Morrison's algorithm were used as baselines in addition to the results of Kim and Snyder (2013).

4.3 C/V-distinction with word lists

An additional experiment evaluates the algorithm's capacity to perform C/V-distinction against Sukhotin's algorithm on a data set of 10 morphologically complex languages where lists of inflected forms were taken from the ACL SIGMOR-PHON shared task data (Cotterell et al., 2016). In this case, we have no knowledge of the frequency of the forms given, but need to rely only on type information. The Arabic data was transliterated into a latinate alphabet (by DIN 31635), with vowels marked. For the other languages, the native alphabet was used. Per-type accuracy is reported.

5 Results

On the first task, which uses phonemic data, consonant/vowel distinction accuracy is 100% throughout (see Table 2). Sukhotin's algorithm also performs very well in all except two languages. English, in particular, is a surprising outlier, with Sukhotin's algorithm only classifying 21.62% correctly. This is probably due to there existing a proportionately large number of syllabic phonemes in English (13/37). Moler & Morrison's algorithm has less than perfect accuracy in three languages. There is great variation in the OCP algorithm's capacity to produce splits that coincide with phonological features in both the tier-based and non-tier variants. Roughly speaking, the larger the phoneme inventory, the less likely it is for the splits to align themselves in accordance with phonological features. Also, since the tier-based variant naturally leads to more splits, the figures appear higher since splits in lower levels of the tree, which contain few phonemes, can almost always be done along distinctive feature lines. The depth of the induced tree also correlates with the variety of syllable types permitted in the language. An extreme example of this is Hawaiian (Figure 3), which only permits **V** and **CV** syllables, yielding a very shallow tree where no consonants are split beyond the first level. English and Polish lie

Figure 3: Hawaiian clusters reveal a predominantly CV/V syllable type since the non-syllabic branch of the tree is shallow.

at the other extreme, with 37 splits each. This circumstance may perhaps be further leveraged to infer syllable types from unknown scripts.

On the C/V inference task for 503 languages, the OCP algorithm outperforms Sukhotin's algorithm and Kim and Snyder (2013) (K&S) when each language is inspected individually (see Figure 3). However, for the case where we learn all distinctions at once, the OCP algorithm produces an identical result with Sukhotin. Here the token level accuracy also exceeds K&S with 99.89 vs. 98.55.

The already high accuracy rate of the OCP algorithm on the Bible translation data is probably in reality even higher, especially when all languages are inspected at the same time. Out of the 343 grapheme types, OCP and Sukhotin only misclassify 7, and upon closer manual inspection, it is found that only two of these are bona fide errors. Five are errors in the gold standard—all in the Cyrillic-based data (see Table 5 for an overview of the errors in the gold standard or the classifications). The first actual error, Cyrillic s, only occurs in five word types in the entire corpus, and is always surrounded by other consonants. The other error, ŏ, is more difficult to interpret—it occurs in three typologically different languages: Akoose (bss), Northern Grebo (gbo), and Peñoles Mixtec (mil).

On the third task, where only word lists are available from grapheme classification into C/V, the OCP algorithm performs equally to Sukhotin's algorithm, except for one language (Navajo),

Language	Splits OCP		Splits OCP(tier)		C/V (OCP)	C/V (Sukh.)	C/V (M&M)	Inventory size
Arapaho	9/14	(62.29)	11/15	(73.34)	100.0	100.0	100.0	16
Basque	8/14	(57.14)	16/20	(80.00)	100.0	100.0	100.0	21
English	3/12	(25.00)	15/25	(60.00)	**100.0**	21.62	94.59	37
Finnish	14/16	(87.50)	17/19	(89.47)	100.0	100.0	100.0	20
Hawaiian	4/5	(80.00)	8/12	(66.67)	**100.0**	**100.0**	92.30	13
Hungarian	10/20	(50.00)	21/31	(67.74)	**100.0**	96.97	**100.0**	33
Italian	7/11	(63.64)	15/20	(75.00)	100.0	100.0	100.0	22
Polish	10/21	(47.61)	23/33	(69.70)	**100.0**	**100.0**	97.30	37
Spanish	10/15	(66.67)	16/21	(76.19)	100.0	100.0	100.0	22

Table 2: Phonemic data: fraction of cluster splits that go exactly along single distinctive features (Splits with OCP/OCP (tier)), together with percentage. Also given are C/V-distinction accuracy (per type) for the OCP algorithm (OCP), Sukhotin's algorithm (Sukh.), Moler and Morrison's algorithm (M&M).

		OCP	Sukhotin	M&M	K&S
Individual	Type	**95.10**	92.50	94.15	—
	Token	**96.55**	93.65	95.59	95.99
All	Type	**96.43**	**96.43**	89.79	—
	Token	**99.89**	**99.89**	99.79	98.55

Table 3: Results on the 503-language Bible translations on consonant-vowel distinction. Both type and token accuracy are included. The *Individual* column shows the macro-averaged results on running all languages individually, and the *All* column shows the results of running all data at once. Here, 'OCP' is the current algorithm; 'Sukhotin' is Sukhotin's algorithm, 'M&M' is the SVD-method in Moler & Morrison (1983), and 'K&S' is the method given in Kim & Snyder (2013).

where the OCP algorithm misclassifies one symbol less (see Figure 4).

6 Application to text fragments: the arrow of the gods

Given that the algorithm performs very well on consonant-vowel distinctions and groups segments along distinctive features better with small alphabets, an additional experiment was performed on a small manuscript to get a glimpse of potential application to cryptography and the decipherment of substitution ciphers. In this experiment, the writing system is known to be alphabetic (in fact Cyrillic), and the purpose is to examine the clustering induced by so little available data.

Language	OCP	Sukhotin	M&M
Arabic	1/40 (97.50)	1/40 (97.50)	1/40 (97.50)
Finnish	0/31 (100.0)	0/31 (100.0)	0/31 (100.0)
Georgian	1/33 (96.97)	1/33 (96.97)	**0/33 (100.0)**
German	**1/30 (96.67)**	**1/30 (96.67)**	2/30 (93.33)
Hungarian	1/33 (96.97)	1/33 (96.97)	1/33 (96.97)
Maltese	2/30 (93.33)	2/30 (93.33)	**0/30 (100.0)**
Navajo	2/30 (93.33)	3/30 (90.00)	**1/30 (96.67)**
Russian	**0/34 (100.0)**	**0/34 (100.0)**	2/34 (94.12)
Spanish	**0/33 (100.0)**	**0/33 (100.0)**	2/33 (93.94)
Turkish	0/34 (100.0)	0/34 (100.0)	0/34 (100.0)
Average	**97.48**	97.14	97.25

Table 4: Per type accuracy on C/V-distinction on word lists. Listed are the number of misclassifications, and the accuracy per type.

The birch bark letter number 292 found in 1957 in excavations in Novgorod, Russia, is the oldest known document in a Finnic language (Karelian), stemming most likely from the early 13th century (Haavio, 1964). The document consists of only 54 symbols, written in Cyrillic.[3] The clustering method (see Figure 4) identifies the vowels and consonants, except for the grapheme **y** (/u/). This is probably because the short manuscript renders the word **nuoli** (Latinized form) 'arrow' inconsistently in three different ways, with Cyrillic **y** = /u/ occurring in different places, making the segment difficult for the algorithm. The high vowels /i/ and

---

[3]The exact translation of the contents is a matter of dispute; the first translation given by Yuri Yeliseyev in 1959 reads as follows (Haavio, 1964): God's arrow ten [is] your name // This arrow is God's own // [The] God directs judgment.

Symbol	Class	Comments
s	V	Macedonian, only occurs four times.
ь	V	Cyrillic soft sign (neither vowel not consonant).
ө	V	Cyrillic; error, should be CYRILLIC SMALL LETTER BARRED O, a vowel.
ı	V	Halh Mongolian, incorrect words in corpus.
й	C	Cyrillic, corresponds to the palatal approximant /j/, incorrect in gold.
ї	C	Ukrainian iotated vowel sounds /ji/, unclear if vowel or consonant.
ŏ	C	Bantu languages: high tone/long vowel in Bantu languages.

Table 5: The only misclassified segments in the 503-Bible test. The column *Class* gives this 'incorrect' classification of the OCP algorithm. Most of these are errors in the data/gold standard. Only the Cyrillic **s** which occurs four times in the data (always adjacent to other consonants) and the ŏ-symbol are actually incorrect.

/u/ (left) are also separated from the non-high vowels (right) /a/, /o/, and /e/ (the Cyrillic soft sign also falls in this group). Sukhotin's algorithm, which only infers the consonants and vowels, makes one more mistake than the current algorithm.

7 Identifying coronal segments with the tier-based variant

Although the only really robust pattern reliably discovered by the algorithm is the distinction between consonants and vowels, there are strong patterns within some of the clusters that appear to be cross-linguistically constant, specifically with the tier-based variant. The first is that, whenever a five-vowel system is present (such as in Basque, Spanish, and Italian), after the topmost split which divides up the vowels and the consonants, the first split within the vowel group is almost always $\{a, o, u\}$ and $\{e, i\}$. A second pattern concerns coronal segments. The first split within the consonant group tends to divide the segments into coronal/non-coronal segments. This is not an absolute trend, but happens far above chance. This is also true when running the algorithm on graphemic data, where coronals can be identified. Table 6 gives an overview of how cross-linguistically coherent the resulting first consonant splits are. The data set is a selection of 14 languages from the Universal Dependencies 2.0 data (Nivre et al., 2017).

8 Conclusion & future work

This paper has reported on a simple algorithm that rests on the assumption that languages tend to exhibit hierarchical alternation in adjacent phonemes. While such alternation does not always occur for any individual adjacent segment pair, on

Language	Second Consonant Group	#C
Basque	(c)　　l n (ñ) r s　　x　　z	21
Catalan	l n　　r s　　x　　z	22
Irish	d　　l n　　r s	13
Dutch	h l n　　r　　x　　z	19
Estonian	h l n　　r s	16
Finnish	h l n　　r s (š) (x)　　(z)	21
German	j　　l n　　r s　　x　　z	21
Indonesian	l n　　r s　　z	20
Italian	h l n　　r s　　(y)	21
Latin	d h l n　　r s	16
Latvian	č　j　ķ l ļ n ņ r s　　z ž	24
Lithuanian	j　　l n　　r s š　　z ž	19
Portuguese	ç　j　l n (ñ) r s　　x	24
Slovak	c ď j　l ĺ n ň r s š　　z ž	26

Table 6: The second consonant grouping found using the tier-based OCP algorithm. This is the split below the top-level consonant/vowel split. The characters in this set largely correspond to coronal sounds. The data comes from 14 languages in the Universal Dependencies 2.0 data set. Shown in parentheses are symbols outside the native orthography of the language (most likely from named entities and borrowings found in the corpora). The rightmost column shows the total number of identified consonants in the language. In particular, **l**, **n**, and **r** are always in this set, while **s** is nearly always present.

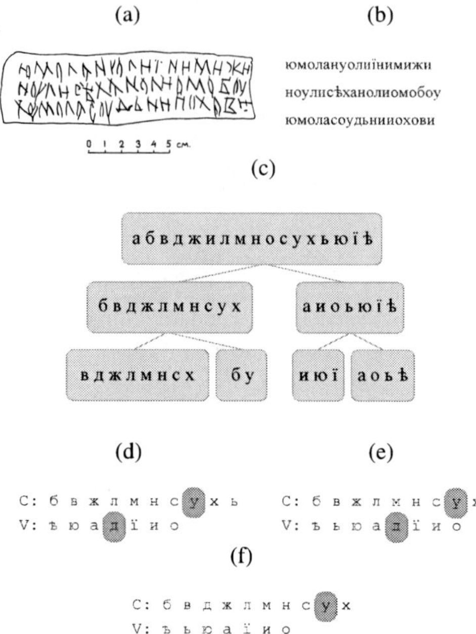

Figure 4: Clustering the graphemes in the 54-symbol *birch bark letter 292* manuscript (a), with transcription given in (b), and the results of OCP clustering (c). Also given are the C/V classifications produced by the Moler and Morrison (1983) algorithm (d), Sukhotin's algorithm (e), and the OCP algorithm (f), with errors marked with red boxes.

the corpus level this alternation largely holds and serves to reveal interesting structure in phonological organization. The top cluster discovered by the algorithm is also a highly reliable indicator of syllabic vs. non-syllabic segments, i.e. consonants and vowels, and improves upon the state-of-the-art in this unsupervised task. Interestingly, Sukhotin's C/V algorithm, which has similar performance (Sukhotin, 1962), can be interpreted as a greedy approximation of the first iteration in the current algorithm. A tier-based variant of the algorithm tends to detect front/back vowel contrasts and coronal/non-coronal contrasts as well, although this is more of a robust trend rather than an absolute.

Lower levels in the clustering approach are less reliable indicators of classical feature alternation, but can serve effectively to reveal aspects of syllable structure. For example, it is obvious from the Hawaiian clustering that the predominant syllable in the language is CV. One is led to conclude that the obligatory contour principle may be manifest in larger classes of segments (such as [±syllabic]), but not necessarily in on the fine-grained level. Some resulting cluster splits such as for example {m,p} vs. {b,f,t} (example from Basque) are often not only inseparable by a single feature split, but are not separable by any combination of features. This lack of evidence for a strong OCP may be in line with the vigorous debate in the phonological literature on the universal role of the OCP (see e.g. McCarthy (1986); Odden (1988)). Some languages (such as Finnish and Hawaiian) yield splits that almost always coincide with a single phonological feature, whereas other languages do not. Smaller inventories typically yield more robust results, although this may be partly due to chance factors—there are more ways to split a small set according to distinctive features than large sets.

Of interest is the utility of the extracted clusters in various supervised and semi-supervised NLP applications. For example, in algorithms that learn to inflect words from annotated examples (Ahlberg et al., 2015; Cotterell et al., 2016), it is often useful to have a subdivision of the segments that alternate, since this allows one to generalize behavior of classes of segments or graphemes, similar to the way e.g. Brown clusters (Brown et al., 1992) generalize over classes of words. Labeling segments with the position in a clustering tree and using that as a feature, for instance, is a cheap and straightforward way to inject this kind of knowledge into supervised systems designed to operate over many languages.

Acknowledgements

Thanks to Andy Cowell for help with the Arapaho and Hawaiian datasets, Mike Hammond and Miikka Silfverberg for comments on an earlier version of this paper, and Francis Tyers for sharing his knowledge of Cyrillic writing systems and comments regarding the error analysis. Thanks also to Zygmunt Frajzyngier and Sharon Rose for general OCP-related discussion and comments. Several anonymous reviewers raised helpful points. This work has been partly sponsored by DARPA I20 in the program Low Resource Languages for Emergent Incidents (LORELEI) issued by DARPA/I20 under Contract No. HR0011-15-C-0113.

References

Malin Ahlberg, Markus Forsberg, and Mans Hulden. 2015. Paradigm classification in supervised learning of morphology. In *Proceedings of NAACL-HLT*. Association for Computational Linguistics, Denver, Colorado, pages 1024–1029. http://www.aclweb.org/anthology/N15-1107.

Juhani Aho. 1884. *Rautatie [The Railroad]*. Werner-Söderström, Porvoo, Finland.

Luc Boruta and Justyna Jastrzebska. 2012. A phonemic corpus of Polish child-directed speech. In *Proceedings of the eighth international conference on Language Resources and Evaluation (LREC)*.

Michael R. Brent and Timothy A. Cartwright. 1996. Distributional regularity and phonotactic constraints are useful for segmentation. *Cognition* 61(1):93–125.

Peter F. Brown, Peter V. deSouza, Robert L. Mercer, Vincent J. Della Pietra, and Jenifer C. Lai. 1992. Class-based n-gram models of natural language. *Computational Linguistics* 18(4):467–479.

Vladimír Černý. 1985. Thermodynamical approach to the traveling salesman problem: An efficient simulation algorithm. *Journal of Optimization Theory and Applications* 45(1):41–51.

Ryan Cotterell, Christo Kirov, John Sylak-Glassman, David Yarowsky, Jason Eisner, and Mans Hulden. 2016. The SIGMORPHON 2016 shared task—morphological reinflection. In *Proceedings of the 2016 Meeting of SIGMORPHON*. Association for Computational Linguistics, Berlin, Germany.

Andrew Cowell and Alonzo Moss Sr. 2008. *The Arapaho Language*. University Press of Colorado.

Eli Fischer-Jørgensen. 1952. On the definition of phoneme categories on a distributional basis. *Acta linguistica* 7(1-2):8–39.

Caxton C. Foster. 1992. A comparison of vowel identification methods. *Cryptologia* 16(3):282–286.

Zygmunt Frajzyngier. 1979. Notes on the $R_1R_2R_2$ stems in Semitic. *Journal of Semitic Studies* 24(1):1–12.

Stefan A. Frisch. 2004. Language processing and segmental OCP effects. In Bruce Hayes, Robert Martin Kirchner, and Donca Steriade, editors, *Phonetically Based Phonology*, Cambridge University Press, pages 346–371.

Judit Gervain and Ramón Guevara Erra. 2012. The statistical signature of morphosyntax: A study of Hungarian and Italian infant-directed speech. *Cognition* 125(2):263–287.

John Goldsmith and Aris Xanthos. 2009. Learning phonological categories. *Language* 85(1):4–38.

Joseph H. Greenberg. 1950. The patterning of root morphemes in Semitic. *Word* 6(2):162–181.

Jacques B. M. Guy. 1991. Vowel identification: an old (but good) algorithm. *Cryptologia* 15(3):258–262.

Martti Haavio. 1964. The oldest source of Finnish mythology: Birchbark letter no. 292. *Journal of the Folklore Institute* 1(1/2):45–66.

Bruce Hayes. 2011. *Introductory Phonology*. John Wiley & Sons.

George Hempl. 1893. Loss of r in English through dissimilation. *Dialect Notes* (1):279–281.

Junko Itô and Ralf-Armin Mester. 1986. The phonology of voicing in Japanese: Theoretical consequences for morphological accessibility. *Linguistic Inquiry* pages 49–73.

Gregory K. Iverson and Joseph C. Salmons. 1992. The phonology of the Proto-Indo-European root structure constraints. *Lingua* 87(4):293–320.

Young-Bum Kim and Benjamin Snyder. 2013. Unsupervised consonant-vowel prediction over hundreds of languages. In *Proceedings of the 51st Annual Meeting of the Association for Computational Linguistics (Volume 1: Long Papers)*. Association for Computational Linguistics, Sofia, Bulgaria, pages 1527–1536.

S. Kirkpatrick, Jr. C. D. Gelatt, and M. P. Vecchi. 1983. Optimization by simulated annealing. *Science* 220(4598):671–680.

Kevin Knight, Anish Nair, Nishit Rathod, and Kenji Yamada. 2006. Unsupervised analysis for decipherment problems. In *Proceedings of the COLING/ACL*. Association for Computational Linguistics, pages 499–506.

William Ronald Leben. 1973. *Suprasegmental Phonology*. Ph.D. thesis, Massachusetts Institute of Technology.

A. A. Markov. 1913. Primer statisticheskogo issledovaniya nad tekstom "Evgeniya Onegina", illyustriruyuschij svyaz ispytanij v cep. *Izvestiya Akademii Nauk* Ser. 6(3):153–162.

A. A. Markov. 2006. An example of statistical investigation of the text "Eugene Onegin" concerning the connection of samples in chains. *Science in Context* 19(4):591–600.

Thomas Mayer and Christian Rohrdantz. 2013. PhonMatrix: Visualizing co-occurrence constraints of sounds. In *Proceedings of the 51st Annual Meeting of the Association for Computational Linguistics: System Demonstrations*. Association for Computational Linguistics, Sofia, Bulgaria, pages 73–78.

Thomas Mayer, Christian Rohrdantz, Frans Plank, Peter Bak, Miriam Butt, and Daniel A Keim. 2010. Consonant co-occurrence in stems across languages: Automatic analysis and visualization of a phonotactic constraint. In *Proceedings of the 2010 Workshop on NLP and Linguistics: Finding the Common Ground*. Association for Computational Linguistics, pages 70–78.

John J. McCarthy. 1986. OCP effects: Gemination and antigemination. *Linguistic Inquiry* 17(2):207–263.

Scott Meyers. 1997. OCP effects in optimality theory. *Natural Language & Linguistic Theory* 15(4):847–892.

Cleve Moler and Donald Morrison. 1983. Singular value analysis of cryptograms. *American Mathematical Monthly* pages 78–87.

Steven Moran, Daniel McCloy, and Richard Wright, editors. 2014. *PHOIBLE Online*. Max Planck Institute for Evolutionary Anthropology, Leipzig. http://phoible.org/.

Joakim Nivre, Željko Agić, Lars Ahrenberg, Maria Jesus Aranzabe, Masayuki Asahara, Aitziber Atutxa, et al. 2017. Universal dependencies 2.0. LINDAT/CLARIN digital library at the Institute of Formal and Applied Linguistics, Charles University in Prague.

David Odden. 1988. Anti antigemination and the OCP. *Linguistic Inquiry* 19(3):451–475.

John Ohala. 1981. The listener as a source of sound change. In Carrie S. Masek, Roberta A. Hendrick, and Mary Frances Miller, editors, *Papers from the Parasession on Language and Behavior*, Chicago Linguistic Society, pages 178–203.

Janet Pierrehumbert. 1993. Dissimilarity in the Arabic verbal roots. In *Proceedings of NELS*. volume 23, pages 367–381.

Konstantin Pozdniakov and Guillaume Segerer. 2007. Similar place avoidance: A statistical universal. *Linguistic Typology* 11(2):307–348.

Sharon Rose. 2000. Rethinking geminates, long-distance geminates, and the OCP. *Linguistic Inquiry* 31(1):85–122.

George T. Sassoon. 1992. The application of Sukhotin's algorithm to certain non-English languages. *Cryptologia* 16(2):165–173.

Wilhelm Spitta-Bey. 1880. *Grammatik des arabischen Vulgärdialectes von Aegypten*. Hinrichs, Leipzig.

Boris V. Sukhotin. 1962. Eksperimental'noe vydelenie klassov bukv s pomoshch'ju EVM. *Problemy strukturnoj lingvistiki* pages 198–206.

Boris V. Sukhotin. 1973. Méthode de déchiffrage, outil de recherche en linguistique. *T. A. Informations* pages 1–43.

Mariona Taulé, Maria Antònia Martí, and Marta Recasens. 2008. AnCora: Multilevel annotated corpora for Catalan and Spanish. In *Proceedings of the sixth international conference on Language Resources and Evaluation (LREC)*.

Moira Yip. 1988. The obligatory contour principle and phonological rules: A loss of identity. *Linguistic Inquiry* 19(1):65–100.

Moira Yip. 1998. Identity avoidance in phonology and morphology. In Steven Lapointe, Diane Brentari, and Patrick Farrell, editors, *Morphology and its Relation to Phonology and Syntax*, CSLI, Stanford, pages 216–246.

Learning Stock Market Sentiment Lexicon and Sentiment-Oriented Word Vector from StockTwits

Quanzhi Li, Sameena Shah
Research and Development
Thomson Reuters
3 Times Square, New York, NY 10036
{quanzhi.li, sameena.shah@thomsonreuters.com}

Abstract

Previous studies have shown that investor sentiment indicators can predict stock market change. A domain-specific sentiment lexicon and sentiment-oriented word embedding model would help the sentiment analysis in financial domain and stock market. In this paper, we present a new approach to learning stock market lexicon from StockTwits, a popular financial social network for investors to share ideas. It learns word polarity by predicting message sentiment, using a neural network. The sentiment-oriented word embeddings are learned from tens of millions of StockTwits posts, and this is the first study presenting sentiment-oriented word embeddings for stock market. The experiments of predicting investor sentiment show that our lexicon outperformed other lexicons built by the state-of-the-art methods, and the sentiment-oriented word vector was much better than the general word embeddings.

1 Introduction

Social media has provided a rich opinion content that is valuable for diverse decision-making processes (Montoyo et al., 2012; Oliveira 2016), and sentiment analysis is being increasingly used to predict stock market variables (Antweiler and Frank 2014; Yu eta l., 2013; Schumaker et al., 2012). In particular, social media messages are a useful source for supporting stock market decisions (Bollen et al., 2011; Oliveira et al., 2013). Users of social media, such as StockTwits and Twitter, post very frequently, and this makes the real-time assessment possible, which can be exploited during the trading day. The two important sentiment data that can help sentiment

analysis greatly are sentiment lexicons and word embeddings learned from large amount of data. Word embedding (word vector) has been used in many NLP tasks and noticeably improved their performance (Socher et al., 2013; Tang et al., 2014b; Vo and Zhang, 2015; Li et al., 2017). However, there has been little effort in constructing sentiment lexicon for financial domain and stock market, and in using social media as the data source. Many terms in financial market have different meanings, especially sentiment polarity, from that in other domains or sources, such as the general news articles and Twitter. For example, terms *long, short, put* and *call* have special meanings in stock market. Another example is the term *underestimate,* which is a negative term in general, but it can suggest an opportunity to buy equities when is used in stock market messages. Domain independent lexicons or general word embedding model may not perform well in financial domain. Therefore, it is necessary and important to built sentiment lexicons and word embeddings specifically for stock market.

The automatic lexicon creation approaches in previous studies are mainly based on statistic measures. There are few studies exploiting machine learning models (Tang et al, 2014a; Vo and Zhang 2016). In this study, we propose a new approach that is based on neural network, and our experiment shows that it outperforms the state-of-the-art methods. Most word embedding models only consider the syntactic and semantic information of a word, and the sentiment information is not coded in the embeddings. In this study, we extend the word vector model from (Collobert et al., 2011) by incorporating the sentiment information into the neural network to learn the embeddings; it captures the sentiment information of sentences as well as the syntactic contexts of words.

Proceedings of the 21st Conference on Computational Natural Language Learning (CoNLL 2017), pages 301–310,
Vancouver, Canada, August 3 - August 4, 2017. ©2017 Association for Computational Linguistics

The main contributions of this study are: first, we proposed a new approach based on neural network for constructing a large scale sentiment lexicon for stock market. Second, we built a sentiment-oriented word embedding (SOWE) model specifically for stock market. To our knowledge, this is the first word embedding model for stock market. The experiment shows that it outperforms the general embedding models. The lexicons and embeddings are available at https://github.com/quanzhili/stocklexicon.

2   Related Studies

There are three approaches to generating a sentiment lexicon (Liu, 2012; Al-Twairesh et al., 2016): the manual approach, dictionary-based approach, and corpus-based approach. The manual approach is usually used in conjunction with automated approaches to check the correction of the resulting lexicons.

The dictionary based method exploits the synonyms and antonyms of a word in dictionary. It usually starts with a small set of seed sentiment words, and they are looked up in the dictionary for their synonyms and antonyms, which are then added to the seed set and a new iteration process starts. Most studies adapting this approach use WordNet with different ways expanding the seed list, such as graph-based methods (Rao and Ravichandran, 2009) and distance-based measures (Kamps, 2004; Williams and Anand, 2009). The SentiWordNet lexicon created by (Esuli and Sebastiani, 2005) is the first important work based on WordNet. SentiWordNet was further expanded by (Esuli and Sebastiani, 2006; Baccianella et al., 2010) later. Bing Liu's lexicon (Hu and Liu, 2004) is also built using a dictionary based method, in which WordNet is used.

In the corpus-based approaches, the lexicon words are extracted from the corpus. Usually they also start with a set of seed sentiment words, and then expand it by discovering words with opposite or similar sentiment. For example, Turney and Littman (2002) used search engines to find a word's sentiment. They first compute the association strength between the word and a set of positive words, and then the association strength between the word and a set of negative ones. The strength with positive words minus the strength with negative ones is this word's sentiment score, which is negative if the result is negative and positive if the result is positive.

Point-wise Mutual Information (PMI) is used to measure the association strength, and it is also used as one baseline method in our study. More details on PMI will be given later. Another example is the MPQA subjectivity lexicon (Wilson et al., 2005), which was built manually by annotating the subjective expressions in the MPQA corpus. As social media became popular, several studies have focused on developing sentiment lexicons from social media data, especially Twitter (Tang et al., 2014; Kiritchenko et al., 2014, Vo and Zhang, 2016; Al-Twairesh et al., 2016).

There are very few lexicons built for stock market or financial domain. A financial lexicon was manually built by (Loughran and McDonald, 2011), using documents extracted from the U.S. Securities and Exchange Commission portal from 1994 to 2008. Mao et al. (2014) proposed a procedure to automatically create a financial lexicon in Chinese, by exploiting a large news corpus, whose documents are classified as positive or negative according to the contemporaneous stock returns. Oliveira et al. (2014; 2016) used statistic measures, such as Information Gain (IG), TF.IDF and PMI, to build sentiment lexicons from StockTwits messages for stock market. The TF.IDF and PMI methods are used as two baseline methods in our study. Tang et al. (2014a) use a neural network to learn word embeddings from tweets, and then expand a set of seed sentiment words by measuring the word vector distance between seed words and other words. Vo and Zhang's approach (2016) is based on a simple neural network, to learn polarity values of a term by optimizing the prediction accuracy of message sentiment using lexicons. Our proposed approach is compared to this method. Both (Tang et al., 2014a) and (Vo and Zhang, 2016) worked on Twitter data, not stock market data.

Embeddings of a word capture both the syntactic structure and semantics of the word. The C&W model and the word2vec model are the two popular word embedding models (Collobert et al., 2011; Mikolov et al., 2013). Word embeddings have been used in many NLP tasks (Socher et al., 2014; Mass, 2012; Matt, 2015; Tang et al., 2014b; Li et al., 2016; Li et al., 2017; Vo and Zhang, 2015). Although there are quite a few studies on word embedding for Twitter data, there is no previous study on word embeddings for stock market.

Year	Number of StockTwits Messages	Number of Messages with Sentiment Label (Bullish or Bearish)	% of Messages with Sentiment Label	Number of Bullish Messages	Number of Bearish Messages	Ratio of Bullish / Bearish
2010	517,435	20,307	3.92%	17,310	2,997	5.78
2011	1,182,172	62,186	5.26%	46,823	15,363	3.05
2012	2,823,990	128,832	4.56%	95,610	33,222	2.88
2013	6,039,500	784,067	12.98%	609,709	174,358	3.50
2014	10,833,688	2,168,000	20.01%	1,774,647	393,353	4.51
2015	15,390,934	3,253,027	21.14%	2,596,182	656,845	3.95
Total	36,787,719	6,416,419	17.44%	5,140,281	1,276,138	4.03

Table 1: Statistics of StockTwits data set. Sentiment labels (bullish or bearish) are provided by message authors.

3 Learning Sentiment Lexicon and Sentiment Oriented Word Embeddings (SOWE)

In this section, we first describe how we collected the data set from StockTwits and the necessary preprocessing steps. The data set was used for both the sentiment lexicon construction and the SOWE model creation. Section 3.2 presents the proposed approach for constructing the lexicon, and Section 3.3 explains the algorithm used for building the SOWE model.

3.1 Data Collection and Preprocessing Steps

In this subsection, we describe the StockTwits data set, the basic data preprocessing steps, and how we identify phrases from StockTwits messages.

StockTwits Data Set: StockTwits is a financial social network for sharing ideas among traders. Anyone on StockTwits can contribute content – short messages limited to 140 characters that cover ideas on specific investments. Most messages have a *cashtag*, which is a stock symbol, such as $aapl, to specify the entity (stock) this message is about. We received the permission from StockTwits to access their historical message archive from year 2010 to 2015. We used this data set to build sentiment lexicons and SOWE for stock market and general financial applications.

Similar to Twitter's tweet, each StockTwits message includes a userId, number of followers, message text, timestamp, and other metadata.

About 17.44% of the StockTwits messages are labeled as "bullish" or "bearish" by their authors, to show their sentiment toward the mentioned stocks. The rest of them do not have this bullish/bearish metadata. Table 1 presents the basic statistics of this data set. This table shows that the total number of messages increased greatly year by year. And we also see that the number of messages labeled as *Bullish* is much higher than that labeled as *Bearish,* with an overall ratio of 4.03. In this study, we extracted 6.4 million messages with the *Bullish* or *Bearish* sentiment label, and used them as the training data for our lexicon construction and SOWE model creation. Overall, we have about 5.1 million *Bullish* messages and 1.3 million *Bearish* messages. Below are some examples of StockTwits messages:

- *Love this company long time. $PYPL*
- *Most bullish stocks during this dip, $GOLD*
- *Another Sell Rating, Sell Rating for $AXP*
- *My favorite stock pick #in2010: $GMCR.*
- *Supermarket Stocks Rally as Tesco Plans to Axe Non-core UK Assets. $MRW*
- *Long $AMZN Oct $240 Calls*
- *for the 2009, $AXP was the $DJIA's best-performing component, having garnered a 118% gain:*
- *$f ford has not seen $10 since 9/05, but it's still a bull, be careful.*

Preprocessing Steps: Some preprocessing steps are performed to clean the messages:

- Messages that contain only cashtags, URLs, or mentions are discarded, since they do not have meaningful terms.
- Message text is converted to lower case.

- All URLs are removed. Most URLs are short URLs and located at the end of a message.
- All mentions are converted to a special symbol, for privacy reason. This includes the mentions appearing in a regular message and the user handles at the beginning of a retweet, e.g. ``RT: @bullguy''.
- All cashtags are replaced by a special symbol, to avoid cashtags to gain a polarity value related to a particular time period.
- Numbers following +, – or white space, but not followed by % (e.g. +23.3, +33, -5.52), are converted to a set of special symbols. These symbols reflect the value range of these numbers, and the range of the number determines which symbol it will be converted to. For example, +12.45 => #increase1, +20.22=> #increase2, -21.45=> #decrease2. These numbers are usually about stock price change, and so they bear sentiment information of the message. Different symbols reflect different degrees of price change.
- Similar to the above step, numbers following +, – or white space, and also followed by % (e.g. +23.34%, -5.8%), are also converted to a set of special symbols. These numbers are usually about price or volume changes. But they are based on percentage, which is different from the numbers discussed in previous step. They also convey important sentiment information.

After passing through the above preprocessing steps, the tweets are used to learn the sentiment lexicon and word embedding model.

Phrase Identification: Phrases usually convey more specific meaning than single-term words, and many phrases have a meaning that is not a simple composition of the meanings of its individual words. To identify phrases, we use the approach described in (Mikolov et al. 2013). We first find words that appear frequently together, and infrequently in other contexts. For example, "short sell" is identified as a phrase; while a bigram "they have" is not. By using this approach, we can form many reasonable phrases without greatly increasing the vocabulary size. To identify phrases, a simple data-driven approach is used, where phrases are formed based on the unigram and bigram counts, using this scoring function:

$$Score(w_i, w_j) = \frac{C(w_i, w_j) - \mu}{C(w_i) * C(w_j)} \qquad (1)$$

Where $C(w_i, w_j)$ is the frequency of word w_i and w_j appearing together. μ is a discounting coefficient to prevent too many phrases consisting of infrequent words to be generated. The bigrams with score above the chosen threshold are then used as phrases. Then the process is repeated a few passes over the training data with decreasing threshold value, so we can identify longer phrases having several words. For the StockTwits data set, we empirically set the maximum length of a phrase to 4 words in this study. Other parameters are set as the default values used in (Mikolov et al. 2013).

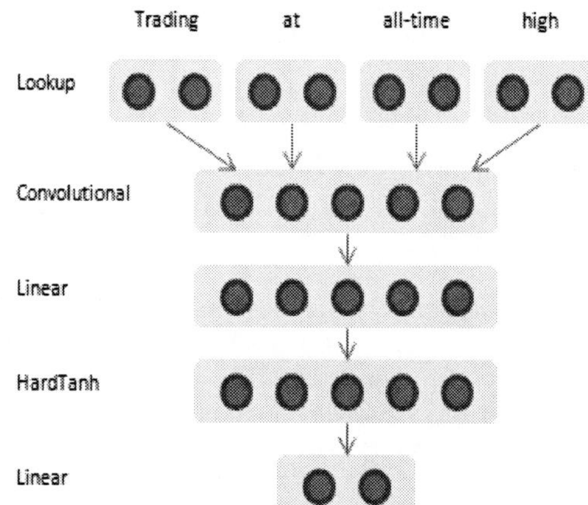

Figure 1: The neural network model for building sentiment lexicon for stock market.

3.2 Sentiment Lexicon Construction

The Proposed Approach: Most corpus-based lexicon construction approaches mainly utilize statistical measures, such as TF-IDF, GI and PMI methods. Our approach is based on a neural network model, inspired by the general network structure for processing NLP tasks (Collobert at al., 2011). Figure 1 shows the neural network we employed for learning the polarity values of a term, by predicting the sentiment value of a StockTwits message. Following (Esuli and Sebastiani, 2006; Vo and Zhang, 2016), we also use two attributes to define the sentiment of a term (word or phrase): positivity and negativity. This means each term has the form of $t = (p, n)$, where p is the positivity value and n is the negativity value. The value range is from 0 to 1 for both p and n. If the value of p is greater than n, we can say that this term has a positive sentiment, and vise versa. If p and n are close to each other, we can say that the term is neutral, bearing little sentiment information.

There are five layers in Figure 1, and from top to bottom, they are: lookup, convolutional, linear, HardTanh and linear. Using the message in this figure as an example, the words of this post are the input of this feed-forward neural network. In this example message, we assume there is no phrase identified, so there are four input terms. If there is a phrase, let's say *all-time high* is detected as a phrase, then these two words will be treated as one input term. The top layer is the lookup table for term polarity values. Because the training input is message, which varies in length, we use a convolutional layer to extract features that can be fed to standard affine layers. There are different ways to generate the representation of text segments with different lengths. In this study, we use the concatenation convolutional layer, which concatenates the layers of max, min and average of the two polarity values of all terms in the input message. This layer gives the best performance, based on our pilot experiments. The concatenation layer is expressed as follow:

$$Z(m) = [Z_p(m), Z_n(m)] \qquad (2)$$

$$Z_p(m) = [Z_{p,max}(m), Z_{p,min}(m), Z_{p,ave}(m)] \qquad (3)$$

$$Z_n(m) = [Z_{n,max}(m), Z_{n,min}(m), Z_{n,ave}(m)] \qquad (4)$$

Where $Z(m)$ is the representation of message m, $Z_p(m)$ is for the positivity values of all the terms in this message, and $Z_n(m)$ is for negativity values of the terms. Given the convolutional layer, we can get the output of the first linear layer:

$$f^1(t) = w_1 Z(m) + b_1 \qquad (5)$$

The HardTanh layer:

$$\alpha = HardTanh(f^1(t)) \qquad (6)$$

And the second linear layer, whose output, $f^2(t)$, is the sentiment score for input message m:

$$f^2(t) = w_2 \alpha + b_2 \qquad (7)$$

Where w_1, w_2, b_1, b_2 are the parameters of the linear layers. The non-linear HardTanh layer is to extract highly non-linear features. Without the HardTanh layer, the network would be a simple linear model. Because the hard version of the hyperbolic tangent is slightly cheaper to compute

and still keep the generalization performance unchanged, it is chosen as the non-linear layer.

The *HardTanh(x)* function is defined as:

$$HardTanh(x) = \begin{cases} -1, & \text{if } x <= -1 \\ x, & \text{if } -1 <= x <= 1 \\ 1, & \text{if } x > 1 \end{cases} \qquad (8)$$

Since we have just two labels for the output, negative and positive, the dimension of the second linear layer is 2. If the polarity of a StockTwits message is positive, the predicted positive score is expected to be larger than the predicted negative score, and vise versa.

The hinge loss of this model is defined as:

$$loss(m) = max(0, 1 - g(m) f_p(m) + g(m) f_n(m)) \qquad (9)$$

Where $g(m)$ is the gold value of message m (positive or negative), $f_p(m)$ is the predicted positive score, and $f_n(m)$ is the predicted negative score.

Model Training: The data set used for training this model is already described in previous section. To train this model, we take the derivative of the loss by back-propagation with respect to the whole set of parameters, and use AdaGrad to update the parameters (Collobert et al., 2011; Duchi et al., 2011). Each term is first initialized by randomly choosing a negative and positive value less than 0.2. The same neural network and parameters setting are used to learn the sentiment polarity for both words and phrases. A validation data set was used to tune the model hyper-parameters.

Baseline Methods for Performance Comparison: We compare our method to three other methods: TF.IDF, PMI and Vo & Zhang from (Vo and Zhang, 2016), which is based on a simple neural network. PMI and TF.IDF are the two most successful approaches building lexicons based on statistic measures. The Vo & Zhang method is the state-of-the-art approach utilizing machine learning technology. We described them briefly below.

TF.IDF is usually used for calculating the weight of a term in text analysis tasks, and it has been used in previous studies for lexicon construction (Oliveira et al. 2014; Oliveira et al., 2016; Al-Twairesh et al., 2016). To use it for computing a term's sentiment score, we first created two documents composed by all the messages of each class (bullish document and bearish document). Then, for each term, we compute its TF.IDF value for the bullish and bearish classes, respectively. And finally we can compute the sentiment score for term t, using the two TF.IDF values:

$$S_{TF.IDF}(t) = \frac{TF.IDF(t,p) - TF.IDF(t,n)}{TF.IDF(t,p) + TF.IDF(t,n)} \qquad (10)$$

The final sentiment class depends on the value of $S_{TF.IDF}(t)$. It is bullish if the value is positive and bearish if it is negative.

PMI is a popular statistic measure used in many previous studies to develop lexicons (Mohammad et al., 2013; Oliveira et al., 2014; Oliveira et al., 2016; Al-Twairesh et al., 2016; Vo and Zhang, 2016). It is defined as:

$$PMI(x,y) = log_2 \frac{p(x,y)}{p(x)p(y)} \qquad (11)$$

Where x and y are two objects, $p(x)$ and $p(y)$ are the probabilities of occurring x and y in the corpus, respectively, $p(x, y)$ is the probability that they co-occur together. If x and y are strongly associated, PMI will be largely positive. It is highly negative if they are complementary. And if there is no significant relationship between them, it is near zero. To compute a term's sentiment score, we use both positive and negative PMI values of a term. The S_{PMI} score for term t is defined as follow:

$$S_{PMI}(t) = PMI(t, bullish) - PMI(t, bearish) \qquad (12)$$

Where *bullish* and *bearish* refer to the sentiment label provided by the message author.

Vo & Zhang approach is a machine learning method that also optimizes the prediction accuracy of message sentiment using lexicons (Vo and Zhang, 2016). To leverage large amount of data, they use a simple neural network to train the lexicon. In this method, each term also has two polarity values: positive and negative. It uses one layer to compute the predicted sentiment probability, by adding the positive and negative values of all the terms in the input message together. Then a softmax function is used to get the predicted sentiment label for the input message. The cross-entropy error is employed as the loss function. Vo and Zhang tested their method on Twitter, using the emotions in a tweet as the indication of its polarity type. They didn't use it in the stock market domain.

3.3 Sentiment-Oriented Word Embedding

Word embedding is a dense, low-dimensional and real-valued vector for a word. The embeddings of a word capture both the syntactic structure and semantics of the word. Traditional bag-of-words and bag-of-n-grams hardly capture the semantics of words (Collobert et al., 2011; Mikolov et al. 2013).

The C&W (Collobert et al., 2011) model is a popular word embedding model. It learns word embeddings based on the syntactic contexts of words. It replaces the center word with a random word and derives a corrupted n-gram. The training objective is that the original n-gram is expected to obtain a higher language model score than the corrupted n-gram. The original and corrupted n-grams are treated as inputs of a feed-forward neural network, respectively. SOWE extends the C&W model by incorporating the sentiment information into the neural network to learn the embeddings (Collobert et al., 2011; Tang et al., 2014b); it captures the sentiment information of messages as well as the syntactic contexts of words. Given an original (or corrupted) n-gram and the polarity of a message as input, it predicts a two-dimensional vector (f_0, f_1), for each input n-gram, where (f_0, f_1) are the language model score and sentiment score of the input n-gram, respectively. There two training objectives: the original n-gram should get a higher language model score than the corrupted n-gram, and the polarity score of the original n-gram should be more aligned to the polarity label of the message than the corrupted one. The loss function is the linear combination of two losses: $loss_0\ (t,\ t')$ - the syntactic loss and $loss_1\ (t,\ t')$ - the sentiment loss:

$$loss\ (t,\ t') = \alpha * loss_0\ (t,\ t') + (1-\alpha) * loss_1\ (t,\ t') \qquad (13)$$

The SOWE model used in this study was trained from the same 6.4 million StockTwits messages used for building sentiment lexicons; this includes 5.1 million bullish and 1.3 million bearish messages. The metadata of the SOWE model will be presented in the Experiments section

4 Experiments and Results

4.1 Evaluation of Sentiment Lexicons

In this experiment, we evaluated the lexicons built by these approaches: TF.IDF, PMI, Vo & Zhang, and our proposed approach. The same data set, which consists of 6.4 million labeled StockTwits messages, is used by these four methods. The messages are preprocessed accordingly for each method. If the difference between a term's learned positive and negative values is very small, then this term has a neutral sentiment. If we use 0.10 as the threshold to differentiate neutral terms from positive and negative terms (i.e. terms with |positive-negative| < 0.10 are neutral), our approach generated 42K sentiment words and phrases. The other three methods have slightly lower amount of sentiment terms.

Sentiment Classification: The lexicons built from these methods can be used in both unsupervised and supervised sentiment classifiers. The former is implemented by summing the sentiment scores of all tokens contained in a given message (Taboada et al., 2011; Kiritchenko et al., 2014; Vo and Zhang, 2016). If the total sentiment score is larger than 0, then the message is classified as positive. Here only one positivity attribute is required to represent a lexicon, so for lexicons with both positive and negative values for a term, the value of (*positive − negative)* is used as the score.

In this experiment, we used a supervised method for performance evaluation. There are different ways to generate features for a message using a lexicon. In this study, we follow the method used in previous studies (Zhu et al., 2014; Vo and Zhang 2016). If a lexicon has both positive and negative values for a term, then a unified score is first computed (i.e. positive − negative), and it is used to generate features described below. Given a message *m*, the features are:
- The number of sentiment tokens in *m*, where sentiment tokens are words or phrases whose sentiment scores are not zero in a lexicon.
- The total scores of negative and positive terms.
- The maximal score of all the terms in this message.
- The total sentiment score of the message.
- The sentiment score of the last term in *m*.

Data Set: we selected 30K messages that were already labeled as bullish or bearish from StockTwits's 2016 data set. They were not included in the data set used for constructing the lexicons. The amounts of bullish and bearish messages in the data set are roughly about 70% vs. 30%. We split this data set into three parts: 70% as training data, 10% as validation data and 20% for testing.

Classifier and Performance Metrics: we tried several classifiers, such as LibLiner, logistic regression and SMO. SMO gave the best results for most cases, and so we used it to compare the four lexicons. SMO is a sequential minimal optimization algorithm for training a support vector

classifier. The F1 measure and accuracy are used as the performance metrics, which have been used by many previous studies.

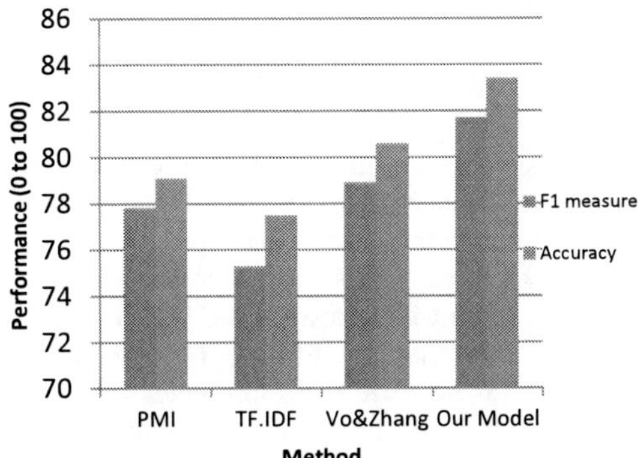

Figure 2: Sentiment classification result, based on lexicons generated by different approaches.

Result: Figure 2 presents the results. It shows that the two methods based on neural network performed better than the two statistic measures. PMI outperformed TF.IDF, which is also demonstrated by other studies (Oliveira et al. 2016). For the two models using neural networks, our proposed model outperformed the Vo & Zhang model, and the result was statistically significant at *p=0.01* using *t-test*. This result also shows that learning lexicon by predicting the accuracy of message is better than the approaches using statistic measures.

Metadata	Model		
	SOWE	StockTwitsWE	TwitterWE
Number of messages	6.4 million	37 million	200 million
Number of words in training data	87 million	505 million	2.9 billion
Number of unique words in the embedding model	165K	616K	3.5 million
Vector dimension size	300	300	300
Term frequency threshold	5	5	5
Learning context windows size	8	8	8

Table 2: Metadata of word embedding models

4.2 Evaluation of the SOWE Model

In this experiment, we evaluated the SOWE embeddings, which encode both the syntactic and sentiment information and are generated specifically for stock market. We also use sentiment classification task to do the evaluation. We compare SOWE to only embedding models, not lexicons. The reason is that they are the same type of data, and so we can use the same feature setting for them, and the experiment setting would not affect the performance comparison result. We didn't compare the SOWE to the lexicons, because they are different types of data and we need to use different approaches to generate features for them, and this will inevitably affect their performance, and make an unfair comparison. We leave this type of comparison for future research.

Word Embedding Models for Comparison: The SOWE model is compared to two types of embeddings:

StockTwitsWE: this is a general word embedding model built from StockTwits data set. This model does not have sentiment information encoded. But because the general embeddings capture both the syntactic structure and semantics of the word, it may know that the term *long* and *buy* have similar meaning in the stock market.

TwitterWE: this is a general word embedding model built from Twitter data set. This model is purely based on Twitter tweets. Although there are some tweets talking about stocks, most of the tweets are about other topics, such as sports and celebrities. We wanted to see how SOWE performs, compared to the embedding model learned from messages of a different social media platform.

These two models are built using word2vec (Mikolov et al., 2013). For StockTwitsWE, we collected 37 million StockTwits messages, which include both the labeled (bullish or bearish) and unlabeled messages. They are preprocessed using the same steps as the data set for creating sentiment lexicon. About 200 million tweets were collected from Twitter for building the TwitterWE model. The tweets date from October 2014 to October 2016. They were acquired through Twitter's public streaming API and the Decahose data (10% of Twitter's streaming data). The basic information of the three models is presented in Table 2. The embedding dimension size, word frequency threshold and window size are set based on our pilot experiments.

Experiment Settings: In this experiment, we used the same data set used in last evaluation, which consists of 30K messages. The performance metrics used are also F1 measure and accuracy. The classifier used is still SMO, which gave the best performance among several classifiers we tried.

Message Representation from Term Embeddings: In this experiment, to derive the message representation from embeddings of its terms, we use the concatenation convolutional layer, which concatenates the layers of max, min and average of message terms. This layer gave the best performance based on our pilot experiments. . The concatenation layer is expressed as follow:

$$Z(t) = [Z_{max}(t), Z_{min}(t), Z_{ave}(t)] \qquad (14)$$

where $Z(t)$ is the representation of tweet t.

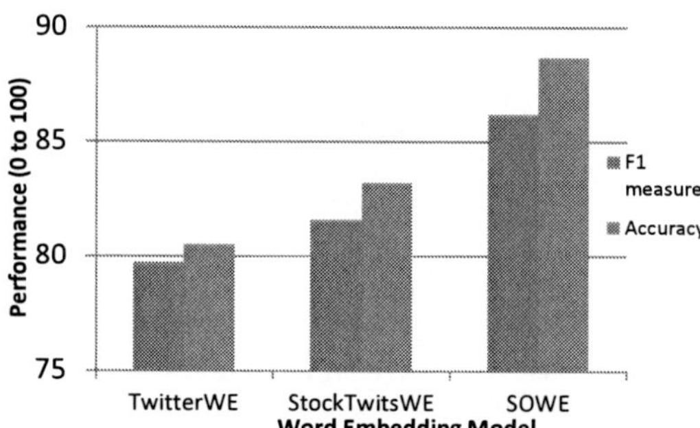

Figure 3: Comparison of the three word embedding models

Result: Figure 3 shows the comparison result of the three models. As we expected, the SOWE models performed the best, and the difference was statistically significant *at p =0.01* using *t-test*. This proves that by integrating the sentiment information into word embeddings, we can greatly improve the sentiment classification performance, although its training data set is much smaller compared to the other two models. The result also shows that the general embedding model trained on StockTwits messages performed better than the model trained on Twitter data set. One reason is that some terms in StockTwits have different sentiment meanings from the same terms in Twitter, such as *put* and *call*.

5 Conclusion

In this paper, we described a new approach based on neural network for building a large scale sentiment lexicon for stock market. We also presented a sentiment-oriented word embedding model, learned from millions of labeled messages on stock market. The experiment of measuring investor sentiment shows that our lexicon construction approach outperformed the state-of-the-art methods, and the sentiment-oriented word embedding model performed well on predicting a message's bullish/bearish polarity. The lexicons and word embedding presented in this study are available to researchers and others interested in sentiment analysis and stock market move prediction. One of our future studies is to apply our lexicon and SOWE on predicting stock market.

References

Alfred. V. Aho and Jeffrey D. Ullman. 1972. *The Theory of Parsing, Translation and Compiling, volume 1*. Prentice-Hall, Englewood Cliffs, NJ.

Nora Al-Twairesh, Hend Al-Khalifa, AbdulMalik Al-Salman, AraSenTi: Large-Scale Twitter-Specific Arabic Sentiment Lexicons, *ACL 2016*

W. Antweiler, M. Z. Frank, Is all that talk just noise? the information content of internet stock message boards, *The Journal of Finance* 59 (3) (2004)

Stefano Baccianella, Andrea Esuli, and Fabrizio Sebastiani. 2010. SentiWordNet 3.0: An Enhanced Lexical Resource for Sentiment Analysis and Opinion Mining. *In LREC*, volume 10

J. Bollen, H. Mao, X. Zeng, Twitter mood predicts the stock market, *Journal of Computational Science* 2 (1), 2011

Collobert, Ronan, Jason Weston, Leon Bottou, Michael Karlen, Koray Kavukcuoglu, and Pavel Kuksa. Natural language processing (almost) from scratch. *The Journal of Machine Learning Research*, 2011

John Duchi, Elad Hazan, and Yoram Singer. 2011. Adaptive subgradient methods for online learning and stochastic optimization. *The Journal of Machine Learning Research*

Andrea Esuli and Fabrizio Sebastiani. 2005. Determining the semantic orientation of terms through gloss classification. *CIKM 2005*.

Andrea Esuli and Fabrizio Sebastiani. 2006. Sentiwordnet: A publicly available lexical resource for opinion mining. *LREC'06*, volume 6

Minqing Hu and Bing Liu. 2004. Mining and summarizing customer reviews. *KDD 2004*

Jaap Kamps. 2004. Using Wordnet to measure semantic orientations of adjectives. *LREC 2004*

Svetlana Kiritchenko, Xiaodan Zhu, and Saif M. Mohammad. 2014. Sentiment analysis of short informal texts. *Journal. of Artificial Intelligence. Research*, 50:723–762.

Quanzhi Li, Sameena Shah, Xiaomo Liu, Armineh Nourbakhsh, Word Embeddings Learned from Tweets and General Data, *The 11th International AAAI Conference on Web and Social Media (ICWSM-17)*. May, 2017.

Quanzhi Li, S. Shah, X. Liu, A. Nourbakhsh & R. Fang, TweetSift: Tweet Topic Classification Based on Entity Knowledge Base and Topic Enhanced Word Embedding, *CIKM* 2016

Bing Liu. 2012. Sentiment analysis and opinion mining. *Synthesis Lectures on Human Language Technologies*, 5(1)

T. Loughran, B. McDonald, When is a liability not a liability? Textual analysis, dictionaries, and 10-Ks., *Journal of Finance, 66* (1) (2011)

Maas, A.; Daly, R.; Pham, P.; Huang, D.; Ng, A. and Potts, C., Learning word vectors for sentiment analysis, *ACL 2012*

H. Mao, P. Gao, Y. Wang, J. Bollen, Automatic construction of financial semantic orientation lexicon from large-scale Chinese news corpus, *Financial Risks International Forum*, 2014.

Matt, T., Document Classification by Inversion of Distributed Language Representations, 2015. *ACL 2015*

Tomas Mikolov, Ilya Sutskever, Kai Chen, Greg Corrado, and Jeffrey Dean. Distributed Representations of Words and Phrases and their Compositionality. *NIPS*, 2013.

Saif M. Mohammad, Svetlana Kiritchenko, and Xiaodan Zhu. 2013. Nrc-canada: Building the state-of-the-art in sentiment analysis of tweets. *SemEval-2013*

Montoyo, P. Martnez-Barco, A. Balahur, Subjectivity and sentiment analysis: An overview of the current state of the area and envisaged developments, *Decision Support Systems* 53 (4) (2012)

N. Oliveira, P. Cortez, N. Areal, On the predictability of stock market behavior using StockTwits sentiment and posting volume, *Progress in Artificial Intelligence, 2013*

N. Oliveira, P. Cortez, N. Areal, Automatic Creation of Stock Market Lexicons for Sentiment Analysis Using StockTwits Data, *IDES 2014*.

N. Oliveira, P. Cortez, N. Areal, stock market sentiment lexicon acquisition using microblogging data and statistical measures, *Decision Support Systems*, 2012.

Delip Rao and Deepak Ravichandran. 2009. Semi-supervised polarity lexicon induction. European Chapter of the Association for Computational Linguistics, 2009.

R. P. Schumaker, Y. Zhang, C.-N. Huang, H. Chen, Evaluating sentiment in financial news articles, Decision Support Systems 53 (3) (2012)

Socher, R.; Perelygin, A.; Wu, J.; Chuang, J.; Manning, C.; Ng, A. and Potts, C., Recursive Deep Models for Semantic Compositionality Over a Sentiment Treebank, EMNLP 2014.

Maite Taboada, Julian Brooke, Milan Tofiloski, Kimberly Voll, and Manfred Stede. 2011. Lexicon-based methods for sentiment analysis. Computational linguistics, 2011

Duyu Tang, Furu Wei, Bing Qin, Ming Zhou, and Ting Liu. 2014a. Building large-scale twitter-specific sentiment lexicon: A representation learning approach. COLING 2014

Duyu Tang, Furu Wei, Nan Yang, Ming Zhou, Ting Liu, and Bing Qin. 2014b. Learning sentiment specific word embedding for Twitter sentiment classification. ACL 2014

Peter Turney and Michael L Littman. 2002. Unsupervised learning of semantic orientation from a hundred-billion-word corpus. Technical report, NRC Institute for Information Technology; National Research Council Canada.

D. Vo and Y. Zhang, Target-dependant twitter sentiment classification with rich automatic features, IJCAI 2015.

D. Vo and Y. Zhang, Don't Count, Predict! An Automatic Approach to Learning Sentiment, ACL2016.

Gbolahan K Williams and Sarabjot Singh Anand. 2009. Predicting the Polarity Strength of Adjectives Using WordNet. ICWSM 2009

Theresa Wilson, Janyce Wiebe, and Paul Hoffmann. 2005. Recognizing contextual polarity in phrase-level sentiment analysis. EMNLP 2005

Xiaodan Zhu, Svetlana Kiritchenko, and Saif Mohammad. 2014. Nrc-canada-2014: Recent improvements in the sentiment analysis of tweets. In Proceedings of SemEval-2014

Learning local and global contexts using a convolutional recurrent network model for relation classification in biomedical text

Desh Raj and **Sunil Kumar Sahu** and **Ashish Anand**
Department of Computer Science and Engineering
Indian Institute of Technology Guwahati
Guwahati, India

Abstract

The task of relation classification in the biomedical domain is complex due to the presence of samples obtained from heterogeneous sources such as research articles, discharge summaries, or electronic health records. It is also a constraint for classifiers which employ manual feature engineering. In this paper, we propose a convolutional recurrent neural network (CRNN) architecture that combines RNNs and CNNs in sequence to solve this problem. The rationale behind our approach is that CNNs can effectively identify coarse-grained local features in a sentence, while RNNs are more suited for long-term dependencies. We compare our CRNN model with several baselines on two biomedical datasets, namely the i2b2-2010 clinical relation extraction challenge dataset, and the SemEval-2013 DDI extraction dataset. We also evaluate an attentive pooling technique and report its performance in comparison with the conventional max pooling method. Our results indicate that the proposed model achieves state-of-the-art performance on both datasets.[1]

1 Introduction

Relation classification is the task of identifying the semantic relation present between a given pair of entities in a piece of text. Since most search queries are some forms of binary factoids (Agichtein et al., 2005), modern question-answering systems rely heavily upon relation classification as a preprocessing step (Fleischman

[1]The code for the can be found at: `https://github.com/desh2608/crnn-relation-classification`.

et al., 2003; Lee et al., 2007). Accurate relation classification also facilitates discourse processing and precise sentence interpretations. Hence, this task has witnessed a great deal of attention over the last decade (Mintz et al., 2009; Surdeanu et al., 2012).

In the biomedical domain, in particular, extracting such tuples from data may be essential for identifying protein and drug interactions, symptoms and causes of diseases, among others. Further, since clinical data tends to be obtained from multiple (and diverse) information sources such as journal articles, discharge summaries, and electronic patient records, relation classification becomes a more challenging task.

To identify relations between entities, a variety of lexical, syntactic, or pragmatic cues may be exploited, which results in a challenging variability in the type of features used for classification purpose. Due to this variability, a number of approaches have been suggested, some of which rely on features extracted from POS tagging, morphological analysis, dependency parsing, and world knowledge (Kambhatla, 2004; Santos et al., 2015; Suchanek et al., 2006; Mooney and Bunescu, 2005; Bunescu and Mooney, 2005). Deep learning architectures have recently gathered much interest because of their ability to conveniently extract relevant features without the need of explicit feature engineering. For this reason, a number of convolutional and recurrent neural network models (Zeng et al., 2014; Xu et al., 2015b) have been used for this task.

In this paper, we propose a model that uses recurrent neural networks (RNNs) and convolutional neural networks (CNNs) in sequence to learn global and local context, respectively. We refer to this as CRNN, following the naming convention used in (Huynh et al., 2016). We argue that in order for any classification task to be effective, the

311

Proceedings of the 21st Conference on Computational Natural Language Learning (CoNLL 2017), pages 311–321,
Vancouver, Canada, August 3 - August 4, 2017. ©2017 Association for Computational Linguistics

regression layer must see a complete representation of the sentence, i.e., both short and long-term dependencies must be appropriately represented in the sentence embedding. This argument forms the basis of our approach. In a deep learning framework, since the complete information available to the classifier at the top-level is obtained through manipulation of the sentence embedding itself, the task of relation classification essentially emulates other popular objectives such as text classification and sentiment analysis if the representation for the entity types are integrated in the sentence. Although our proposed model uses RNNs and CNNs in sequence, it is only two layers deep, as opposed to the very deep architectures proposed earlier (Conneau et al., 2016). This simplicity allows for intuitive understanding of each level of the model, while still learning a sufficiently complex representation of the input sentence.

In addition to local and global contexts, we also experiment with attention for relation classification. Although attention as a concept is relatively well-known, especially in computational neuroscience (Itti et al., 1998; Desimone and Duncan, 1995), it became popular only recently with applications to image captioning and machine translation (Xu et al., 2015a; Vinyals et al., 2015; Bahdanau et al., 2014). Attention has also been employed to some success in relation classification tasks (Wang et al., 2016a; Zhou et al., 2016a). In our experiments, we use an attention-based pooling strategy and compare the results with those obtained using conventional pooling methods. Our model variants are accordingly named **CRNN-Max** and **CRNN-Att**, depending upong the pooling scheme used.

Our model is distinctive in that it does not rely upon any linguistic feature for relation classification. In domains such as biomedicine, texts may not always be written in syntactically/grammatically correct form. Furthermore, lack of necessary training data may not provide good feature extractors such as those in generic domains. Hence, we explored only models without any extra features. Of course, adding other features such as part-of-speech taggers or dependency parsers, if they are available easily, may improve the performance further. Our key contributions in this paper are as follows:

- We propose and validate a two-layer architecture comprising RNNs and CNNs in se-

quence for relation classification in biomedical text. Our model's performance is comparable to the state-of-the-art on two benchmark datasets, namely the i2b2-2010 clinical relation extraction challenge, and the SemEval-2013 DDI extraction dataset, without any need for handcrafted features.

- We analyze and discuss why such a model effectively captures short and long-term dependencies in a sentence, and demonstrate why this representation facilitates classification.

- We evaluate an attention-based pooling technique and compare its performance with conventional pooling strategies.

- We provide evidence to further the argument in favor of using RNNs to obtain regional embeddings in a sentence.

2 Related Research

CNNs have been effectively employed in NLP tasks such as text classification (Kim, 2014), sentiment analysis (Dos Santos and Gatti, 2014), relation classification (Zeng et al., 2014; Nguyen and Grishman, 2015b), and so on. Similarly, RNN models have also been used for similar tasks (Johnson and Zhang, 2016). The improved performance of these models is due to several reasons:

1. Pretrained word vectors are used as inputs for most of these models. These embeddings capture the semantic similarity between words in a global context better than one-hot representations.

2. CNNs are capable of learning local features such as short phrases or recurring n-grams, similar to the way they provide translational, rotational and scale invariance in vision.

3. RNNs utilize the word order in the sentence, and are also able to learn the long-term dependencies.

These observations amply motivate a model which captures both short-term and long-term dependencies using a combination of CNNs and RNNs to form a robust representation of the sentence. Earlier, researchers have proposed RCNN models that compute "regional embeddings" using a CNN at the first level, and these embeddings

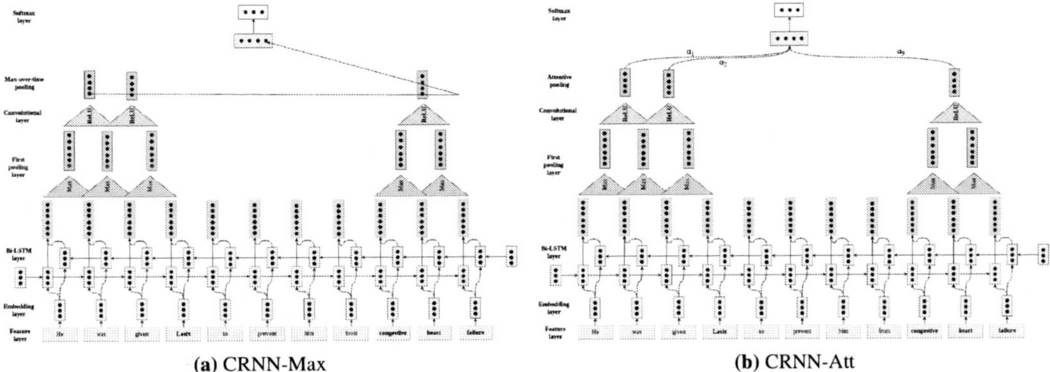

(a) CRNN-Max   (b) CRNN-Att

Figure 1: Architecture of the proposed models. For representation purpose, the following configuration has been used: $d = n_O = 3$, $f_1 = f_2 = 2$, $n_c = 4$, and $|C| = 3$.

are then fed into an RNN layer which uses sequence information to generate the sentence representation (Huynh et al., 2016; Wang et al., 2016b; Chen et al., 2017; Nguyen and Grishman, 2015a). These models are similar to ones that have also been employed to some success for visual recognition (Donahue et al., 2015). However, such models are still limited because the RNN may "forget" features that occurred in the past if the sequence is very long.

We solve this problem by obtaining the output of the RNN at each time step (or word), and then pooling small phrases. This method of using a "recurrent+pooling" module for regional embedding is inspired from (Johnson and Zhang, 2016), who showed that for text categorization, embeddings of text regions, which can convey higher-level concepts than single words in isolation, are more useful than word embeddings. We also experiment with attention-pooling to integrate weighted features from discontinuous regions in the sentence.

3 Proposed Method

Given a sentence S with marked entities e_1 and e_2, belonging to entity types t_1 and t_2, respectively, and a set of relation classes $C = \{c_1, \dots, c_m\}$ we formulate the task of identifying the semantic relation as a supervised classification problem, i.e., we learn a function $f : (\mathbf{S}, E, T) \rightarrow C$, where $\mathbf{S}$ is the set of all sentences, E is the set of entity pairs, and T denotes the set of entity types. Our training objective is to learn a joint representation of the sentence and the entity types, such that a softmax regression layer predicts the correct label. To learn such an embedding, we propose a two-layer neural network architecture consisting of a "recurrent+pooling" layer and a "convolutional+pooling" layer in sequence. This architecture is diagrammatically described in Fig. 1, and the remainder of this section explains each of the layers in detail.

3.1 Embedding layer

The only features we use from S are the words themselves. The vector representation of these words is obtained using the GloVe method (Pennington et al., 2014).

Pre-trained word vectors are used for the word embeddings and the words not present in the embeddings list are initialized randomly. All the word vectors are updated during training.

3.2 Recurrent layer

RNN is a class of artificial neural networks which utilizes sequential information and maintains history through its intermediate layers (Graves et al., 2009). We use long short-term memory (LSTM) based model (Hochreiter and Schmidhuber, 1997), which uses memory and gated mechanism to compute the hidden state. In particular we use a bidirectional LSTM model (Bi-LSTM) similar to the ones used in (Graves, 2013; Huang et al., 2015).

Let $h_l^{(t)}$ and $h_r^{(t)}$ be the outputs obtained from the forward and backward direction of the LSTM at time t. Then the combined output is given as

$$z^{(t)} = h_l^{(t)} : h_r^{(t)}, \quad z^{(t)} \in \mathbb{R}^{n_O}. \quad (1)$$

where : denotes the concatenation operation. We obtain the output at each word and pass it to the first pooling layer.

3.3 First pooling layer

The recurrent layer generates word-level embeddings that incorporate information from the past and future context. Sometimes the word itself may not be important for the sentence representation, and in such cases, it may be better to extract the most important features from short phrases using a pooling technique. If f_1 denotes the length of the filter used for pooling, and $(z_1, \ldots, z_m)$ is the sequence of vectors obtained from the previous layer, then

$$p = (p_1, p_2, \ldots, p_{m-f_1+1}), \qquad (2)$$

where $p_i \in \mathbb{R}^{n_O}$ is given as

$$p_i = \max_{1 \leq j \leq f_1} [z_{i+j}], \qquad (3)$$

i.e. the maximum among all vectors z_{i+1} to z_{i+f_1}.

3.4 Convolutional layer

We apply convolution on p to get local features from each part of the sentence (Collobert and Weston, 2008). Consider a convolutional filter parametrized by weight vector $w_c \in \mathbb{R}^{n_O * f_2}$, where f_2 is the length of filter. Then the output sequence of convolution layer would be

$$h_c^i = f(w_c \cdot p^{i:i+f_2-1} + b_c), \qquad (4)$$

where $i = 1, 2, \ldots, m - f_1 - f_2 + 2$, $\cdot$ is dot product, f is the rectifier linear unit (ReLU) function ($f(x) = \max\{0, x\}$), and $b_c \in \mathbb{R}$ is the bias term. The parameters w_c and b_c are shared across all convolutions $i = 1, 2, \ldots, m - f_1 - f_2 + 2$. On applying n_c such filters, we obtain an output matrix $H_c \in \mathbb{R}^{n_c \times (m-f_1-f_2+2)}$.

3.5 Second pooling layer

The output of the convolutional layer is of variable length ($m - f_1 - f_2 + 2$), since it depends on the length m of the input sentence. To obtain fixed length global features for the entire sentence, we apply pooling over the entire sequence. For this, we experiment with two different pooling schemes based on which our model has two variations, namely CRNN-Max and CRNN-Att.

3.5.1 Max pooling over time

Max pooling over time (Collobert and Weston, 2008) takes the maximum over the entire sentence, with the assumption that all the relevant information is accumulated in that position. Since the input to this layer are the local convolved vectors, this strategy essentially extracts the most important features from several short phrases. The output is then given as

$$z_{pool} = \max_{1 \leq i \leq (m-f_1-f_2+2)} [h_c^i], \qquad (5)$$

where $z_{pool} \in \mathbb{R}^{n_c}$ is the dimension-wise maximum over all h_c^i's.

3.5.2 Attention-based pooling

A max pooling scheme may fail when important cues are distributed across different clauses in the sentence. We solve this problem by using an attention-based pooling scheme, which obtains an optimal feature dimension-wise by taking weighted linear combinations of the vectors. These weights are trained using an attention mechanism such that more important features are weighed higher (Bahdanau et al., 2014; Yang et al., 2016; Zhou et al., 2016b). The attention mechanism produces a vector α of size $m - f_1 - f_2 + 2$, and the values in this vector are the weights for each phrase obtained from the convolutional layer feature vectors.

$$\begin{aligned}
H_{att} &= \tanh(W_1^\alpha H_c) \\
\alpha &= Softmax(W_2^{\alpha T} H_{att}) \\
z_{att} &= \alpha H_c^T
\end{aligned} \qquad (6)$$

Here, H_c is the matrix of CNN output vectors, $W_1^\alpha, W_2^\alpha \in \mathbb{R}^{n_c \times n_c}$ is the parameter matrix, $\alpha \in \mathbb{R}^{m-f_1-f_2+2}$ are the attention weights, and $z_{att} \in \mathbb{R}^{n_c}$ is the output of the pooling layer. The attention weights are a function of the input sentence, and hence α is different for every sentence.

3.6 Fully connected and softmax

To obtain a classifier over the extracted global features, we use a fully connected layer consisting of $|C|$ nodes, where C is the set of all possible relation classes, followed by a softmax layer to generate a probability distribution over the set of all possible labels. The final output is given as

$$p(c_i|x) = Softmax(W_i^o z + b_i^o), \qquad (7)$$

where W^o and b^o are the weight and bias parameters, and z may be either z_{pool} or z_{att}, depending on the second pooling layer scheme. The predicted output y' is obtained as

$$y' = \arg\max_{c_i \in C} p(c_i|x). \qquad (8)$$

Class	Train size	Test size
TrCP	436	108
TrAP	2131	532
TrWP	109	26
TrIP	165	41
TrNAP	140	34
TeRP	2457	614
TeCP	409	101
PIP	1776	443
None	44588	11146
Total	**52211**	**13045**

Table 1: Number of training and testing instances for each relation type in the i2b2 dataset.

Class	Train		Test	
	Before	After	Before	After
Mechanism	1318	1264	302	302
Effect	1685	1620	360	360
Advice	826	820	221	221
Int	189	140	96	96
None	23756	12651	4737	3046
Total	**4018**	**3844**	**979**	**979**

Table 2: Number of training and testing instances for each relation type in the DDI extraction dataset.

4 Experiments

4.1 Datasets

We have used 2 datasets for experimentation, namely the i2b2-2010 clinical relation extraction challenge dataset (Sun et al., 2013), and the SemEval-2013 DDI extraction dataset (Segura Bedmar et al., 2013).

i2b2-2010 relation extraction

This dataset contains sentences from discharge summaries collected from three different hospitals and have 8 relation types: *treatment caused medical problems* (**TrCP**), *treatment administered medical problem* (**TrAP**), *treatment worsen medical problem* (**TrWP**), *treatment improve or cure medical problem* (**TrIP**), *treatment was not administered because of medical problem* (**TrNAP**), *test reveal medical problem* (**TeRP**), *test conducted to investigate medical problem* (**TeCP**), and *medical problem indicates medical problem* (**PIP**). If a sentence has more than two entities, we make an instance for each pair. Since only 170 of the 394 original training documents and 256 of the 477 testing documents were available for download, we combined all the training and testing instances, and then split it in a 80:20 ratio for training and test sets respectively. The statistics of the dataset are described in Table 1.

SemEval 2013 DDI extraction

This dataset contains annotated sentences from two sources, Medline abstracts (biomedical research articles) and DrugBank database (documents written by medical practitioners). The dataset is annotated with following four kinds of interactions: *advice* (opinion or consultation related to the simultaneous use of the two drugs), *effect* (effect of the DDI together with pharmacodynamic effect or mechanism of interaction), *mechanism* (pharmacokinetic mechanism), and *int* (drug interaction without any other information). Dataset provides the training and test instances by sentences. Similar to i2b2 relation extraction dataset if a sentence has more than two drug names, all possible pairs of drugs in the sentence have been separately annotated, such that a single sentence having multiple drug names leads to separate instances of drug pairs and corresponding interaction. Statistics of the dataset (along with negative instance filtering, discussed in Section 4.1.1) is shown in Table 2.

4.1.1 Preprocessing

As a preprocessing step, we replace the entities in the i2b2 dataset with the corresponding entity types. For instance, the sentence: "He was given *Lasix* to prevent him from *congestive heart failure.*" was converted to: "He was given *TREATMENT_A* to prevent him from *PROBLEM_B.*" Similarly, for the DDI extraction dataset, the two targeted drug names are replaced with DRUG-A and DRUG-B respectively, and other drug names in the same sentence are replaced with DRUG-N. Further, all numbers were replaced with the keyword *NUM*. Similar to the earlier studies (Sahu and Anand, 2017; Liu et al., 2016; Rastegar-Mojarad et al., 2013), negative instances were filtered from training sets.

4.2 Implementation details

Pretrained 100-dimensional word vectors in the embedding layer are obtained using the GloVe method (Pennington et al., 2014) trained on a corpus of PubMed open source articles (Muneeb et al., 2015), and are updated during the training process. We use both l_2 regularization and dropout (Srivastava et al., 2014) techniques for regularization. Dropout is applied only on the output of the second pooling layer, and it prevents co-adaptation of hidden units by randomly dropping few nodes. After tuning the hyperparameters on a validation set (20% of training set), the values of 0.01 (0.001) and 0.7 (0.5) were found optimal for the regularization parameter and dropout for the i2b2 (DDI extraction) dataset, respectively. We use Adam technique (Kingma and Ba, 2014) to optimize our loss function, with a learning rate of 0.01. For all the models, n_O and n_C were tuned on the validation set, and values of 200 and 100 were found to be optimal. Hyperparameters of baseline methods were taken from the values suggested in the respective papers. Entire neural network parameters and feature vectors are updated while training. We have implemented the proposed model in Python language using the Tensorflow package (Abadi et al., 2016). We experiment with different filter sizes for f_1 and f_2 and discuss the results in Section 5.1.

4.3 Baseline methods

We compare our models with 5 methods that have earlier been used for relation classification to satisfactory results. These baselines were selected for one of the following three purposes.

Feature-based methods

We selected a feature-based SVM classifier (Rink et al., 2011) that uses several handcrafted features such as distance of word from entities, POS tags, chunk tags, etc., to compare whether our models were able to outperform classifiers with rigorous feature engineering. It is to be noted that we use our own implementation of the SVM classifier (using the scikit-learn (Pedregosa et al., 2011) library), using features as described in (Sahu et al., 2016).

Single-layer neural networks

We selected a multiple-filter CNN with max-pooling (Sahu et al., 2016) and an LSTM model with max and attentive pooling (Sahu and Anand, 2017). In Section 5.5, we compare our models with these single layer models to justify using a combination of RNN and CNN to learn long-term and short-term dependencies, respectively. To observe the effect of the network model independent of the feature set, we use only the word embeddings as features for each of these models. Further, we used the same hyperparameters as mentioned in the respective papers.

Recurrent convolutional neural network

This model, inspired from (Wang et al., 2016b), obtains regional embeddings using a convolutional

$f_1\backslash f_2$	2	3	4	5	6
1	59.97	58.96	59.30	59.18	60.03
2	59.84	56.69	60.89	**62.45**	61.03
3	60.46	61.77	58.85	57.34	59.81

Table 3: Average F1 scores on varying filter sizes f_1 and f_2 in the CRNN-Att model for i2b2 dataset.

layer. These are then fed into a recurrent layer and a single output is obtained after traversing the entire sequence. We compare our models with this RCNN model to observe the effect of obtaining outputs at every word, as opposed to at the end of the sequence.

5 Results and Discussion

5.1 Effect of filter sizes f_1 and f_2

We experiment with various combinations of filter sizes f_1 and f_2 on the i2b2 dataset using our CRNN-Att model. Since f_1 denotes the size of the first pooling filter, it essentially represents the amount of information present in a regional embedding that is fed into the convolutional layer. If f_1 is too small ($f_1 = 1$, i.e., no pooling), embeddings from seemingly unimportant words may get through, and if it is large ($f_1 \geq 3$), individual embeddings may get pooled such that a few words dominate the majority of regions. For the filter size f_2 in the convolutional layer, a midrange value (4 to 6) was found to work well. This may be because this layer learns to identify short phrases which are usually of this length. These observations were common for both datasets. The F1 scores for various combinations of filter sizes on the i2b2 data are shown in Table 3. In the remaining experiments, we choose $(f_1, f_2) = (2,5)$ for both our model variants.

5.2 Initialization and tuning of word embeddings

The only feature used in our models is the word vectors for every word in the sentence. We perform several experiments on the i2b2 data to observe the effect of word vector initialization and update on the model performance. The results are summarized in Table 5.

Interestingly, the best performing model uses randomly initialized word embeddings that are not updated during training. This is in contrast to earlier studies (Sahu and Anand, 2017; Collobert and Weston, 2008) where pretrained embeddings

Model	i2b2-2010			DDI extraction		
	Precision	Recall	F1 score	Precision	Recall	F1 score
SVM (Rink et al., 2011)	**67.44**	57.85	59.31	65.39	40.13	49.74
CNN-Max (Sahu et al., 2016)	55.73	50.08	49.42	68.15	46.58	54.05
LSTM-Max (Sahu and Anand, 2017)	57.54	55.40	55.60	**73.98**	59.96	65.41
LSTM-Att (Sahu and Anand, 2017)	65.23	56.77	60.04	53.43	**64.86**	58.27
RCNN (Wang et al., 2016b)	50.07	45.34	46.47	–	–	–
CRNN-Max	67.91	61.98	**64.38**	72.91	60.88	**65.89**
CRNN-Att	64.62	**62.14**	62.45	69.03	59.04	63.24

Table 4: Comparison of our proposed models CRNN-Max and CRNN-Att, with baselines, on the i2b2-2010 and DDI extraction datasets.

Initialization	update	CRNN-Max	CRNN-Att
Random	Trainable	62.78	61.19
Random	Non-trainable	**64.38**	61.51
PubMed	Trainable	60.60	**62.45**
PubMed	Non-trainable	58.49	59.35

Table 5: Effect of initialization and update of word embeddings in our proposed models, in terms of F1 score, using the i2b2-2010 datset.

Class	Size	SVM	CNN	LSTM-Max	RCNN	CRNN-Max	CRNN-Att
TrCP	108	34.90	34.01	35.48	18.30	43.18	**47.66**
TrAP	532	63.48	46.69	58.74	45.15	**67.39**	63.94
TrWP	26	7.41	10.26	0.00	0.00	**16.67**	9.52
TrIP	41	9.09	21.74	0.00	0.00	25.71	**34.48**
TrNAP	34	5.13	15.87	0.00	0.00	**36.36**	18.60
TeRP	614	**80.44**	63.52	73.50	67.01	80.32	76.31
TeCP	101	30.30	27.63	25.20	11.48	39.46	**39.76**
PIP	443	49.44	49.30	51.54	45.05	**58.04**	55.53

Table 6: Classwise performance (in terms of F1 score) of various models on the i2b2 dataset.

usually improved model performances by 3-4%. However, this result aligns with the observations made in (Johnson and Zhang, 2015) and supports the argument for one-hot LSTMs. It may be enlightening to discuss why such a result is obtained.

First, we note that in the formulas for LSTM, e.g., $\mathbf{u}_t = \tanh(\mathbf{W}^{(u)}\mathbf{x}_t + \mathbf{U}^{(u)}\mathbf{h}_{t-1} + \mathbf{b}^{(u)})$, if $\mathbf{x}_t$ is the one-hot representation of a word, the term $\mathbf{W}^{(u)}\mathbf{x}_t$ serves as a word embedding. Thus, a one-hot LSTM inherently includes a word embedding in its computation. Further, a word vector lookup is a linear operation, and hence it may be merged into the LSTM layer itself by multiplying the LSTM weights by the word embedding matrix. This means that the expressive power of an LSTM which uses pretrained vectors is the same as that of one which uses randomly initialized word embeddings. It has also been shown in earlier studies that pretrained embeddings do not improve the performance of networks as the number of layers increases.

Johnson et al. (2015) even argued that the embedding layer can be replaced with a one-hot representation without compromising on the performance. Empirically, inclusion of an embedding layer makes training from scratch more difficult, even with the help of adaptive learning rates. Similar observations have been made regarding CNNs (Kim, 2014; Johnson and Zhang, 2014).

5.3 Comparison with baseline methods

Table 4 shows the results obtained on the i2b2 and DDI extraction datasets using our proposed models, as compared to the baseline methods. Our models outperform the baselines even without the need for explicit feature engineering. It is interesting to note that our CRNN-Max performs better than the CRNN-Att, and a similar result has also been observed earlier in (Sahu and Anand, 2017).

Class-wise performance analysis

We compare class-wise performance of our models on the i2b2 dataset with some of the baselines, and this is summarized in Table 6. It is evident that performances improve with training size, and from the confusion matrices (not shown here), we found that samples of a lower frequency class were misclassified into a higher frequency class comprising the same entity types. For instance, samples belonging to TrWP (Treatment Worsen medical Problem) were often classified as TrAP (Treatment Administered medical Problem).

5.4 Effect of attention-based pooling

Our CRNN-Att model uses an attention-based technique in the final pooling layer, i.e. it obtains a weighted linear combination of different phrases depending upon their relative importance in the sentence embedding. To confirm this, we visualize attention weights in a CRNN-Att model with $(f_1, f_2) = (1, 3)$, for 5 samples in the i2b2 dataset through a heat map as shown in Figure 2. Since weights are assigned to phrases rather than words, to obtain attention for each word we take the mean

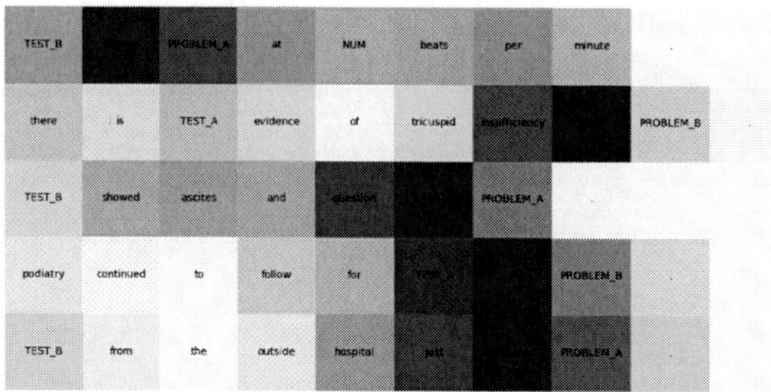

Figure 2: Attention heatmap for 5 sentences selected from the i2b2-2010 dataset. A darker background corresponds to a larger attention weight.

of weights of all phrases that the word is present in. The figure shows that the attentive pooling scheme is able to select important phrases depending upon the classification label. It is evident that the model assigns a higher weight to semantically relevant words such as "showed," "question," and "revealed".

5.5 Long and short term dependencies

We conjecture that our proposed CRNN models perform better than single layer CNNs or RNNs because they capture both local and global contexts efficiently. To confirm our hypothesis, we determine the average sentence lengths and entity separations for several sets of sentences belonging to classes where our models performed well, and for classes where either the CNN model or the LSTM-Max model performed relatively well, for the i2b2-2010 dataset. These results are visualized in the box plots shown in Fig. 3.

From the figure, we note that our models CRNN-Max and CRNN-Att perform significantly better than a CNN model in classifying long sentences with large entity separation, while CNN models work well with shorter sentences where the entities are less separated. This is evident by observing the median and range of lower to upper quartile values in the figure. This confirms our conjecture that our models learn long-term dependencies better than a simple CNN model. Similarly, our proposed models perform better on a larger range of sentence lengths than LSTMs, which may be due to more effective modeling of local contexts.

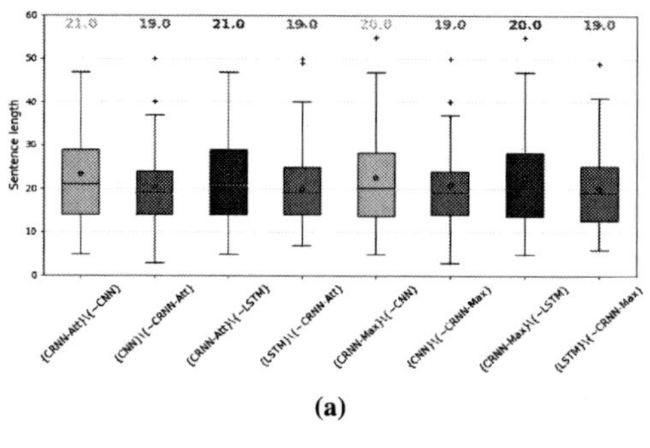

(a)

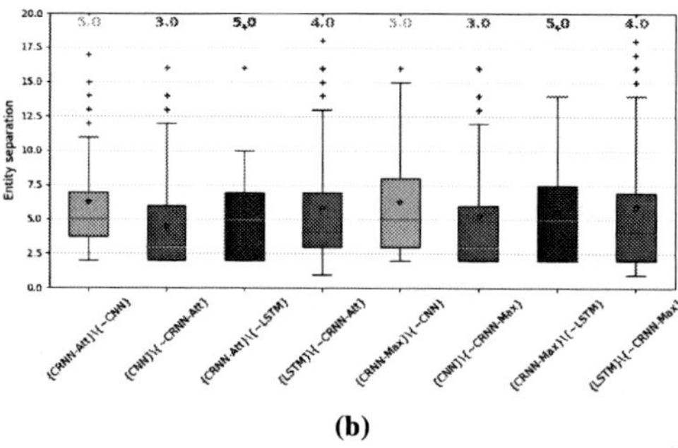

(b)

Figure 3: Box plots for distribution of (a) sentence lengths and (b) entity separation for sentence sets. A representation of the form $\{X\}\backslash\{\tilde{Y}\}$ denotes the set of sentences correctly classified by model X but wrongly classified by model Y. The numbers at the top are the median values for each box.

5.6 Effect of linguistic features

The SVM baseline model described earlier consists of the following features obtained for each word in the sentence: word embedding, part-of-speech (POS) tag, chunk tag, distance from first entity, distance from second entity, and entity type. Of these, the entity type feature is already used in our CRNN model in the preprocessing step

Class	Size	SVM	CRNN-Max	#1	#2
TrCP	108	34.90	36.91	11	30
TrAP	532	63.48	68.85	83	93
TrWP	26	7.41	0.00	1	0
TrIP	41	9.09	0.00	2	0
TrNAP	34	5.13	0.00	1	0
TeRP	614	80.44	81.29	69	83
TeCP	101	30.30	36.90	5	14
PIP	443	49.44	60.66	45	110
Total	1899	59.31	63.78	217	330

Table 7: Classwise performance comparison between SVM and CRNN-Max using linguistic features. #1 denotes number of sentences of a class classified correctly by SVM but incorrectly by CRNN-Max; #2 denotes vice-versa.

by replacing the entities with their corresponding types. Furthermore, we have also described experiments with initialization and update of word embeddings.

In this section, we add the four other linguistic features in our proposed model to observe its performance in comparison with the SVM model. Table 7 summarizes this comparison.

Although the F1 scores for the models are relatively close, the precision (P) and recall (R) vary significantly: P is 67.44 and 61.00, while R is 57.85 and 67.54, for the SVM and CRNN-Max models, respectively. Our CRNN-Max model, therefore, is more sensitive while the SVM classifier has a higher specificity. Furthermore, it is evident that SVM outperforms our model only on classes with a disproportionately low instance count. We may argue that due to the presence of more features and less number of records, our model gets over-trained only on the larger classes. This problem may then be avoided with better regularization, to achieve even higher performance.

6 Conclusion

In this work, we proposed and evaluated a two-layer architecture comprising recurrent and convolutional layers in sequence to learn global and local contexts in a sentence, which was then used for relation classification. To the best of our knowledge, this is the first attempt at combining CNNs and RNNs in sequence for a relation classification task in biomedical domain. Two variants of the model, namely CRNN-Max and CRNN-Att, were evaluated on the i2b2-2010 dataset and the SemEval 2013 DDI extraction dataset, and max-pooling was found to perform better than attentive pooling. Even though our method employed only word embeddings as input feature, it was able to conveniently outperform state-of-the-art techniques that use extensive feature engineering. Finally, our results indicated that a "recurrent+pooling" layer effectively generates regional embedding without the need for pretrained word vectors. It would be interesting to see whether one-hot word vectors perform better than randomly initialized embeddings. We may also benefit from probing whether tree-based or non-continuous convolutions work as well as our CRNN models for learning long and short term dependencies for relation classification.

References

Martın Abadi, Ashish Agarwal, Paul Barham, Eugene Brevdo, Zhifeng Chen, Craig Citro, Greg S Corrado, Andy Davis, Jeffrey Dean, Matthieu Devin, et al. 2016. Tensorflow: Large-scale machine learning on heterogeneous distributed systems. *arXiv preprint arXiv:1603.04467* .

Eugene Agichtein, Silviu Cucerzan, and Eric Brill. 2005. Analysis of factoid questions for effective relation extraction. In *Proceedings of the 28th annual international ACM SIGIR conference on Research and development in information retrieval*. ACM, pages 567–568.

Dzmitry Bahdanau, Kyunghyun Cho, and Yoshua Bengio. 2014. Neural machine translation by jointly learning to align and translate. *arXiv preprint arXiv:1409.0473* .

Razvan C Bunescu and Raymond J Mooney. 2005. A shortest path dependency kernel for relation extraction. In *Proceedings of the conference on human language technology and empirical methods in natural language processing*. Association for Computational Linguistics, pages 724–731.

Guibin Chen, Deheng Ye, Erik Cambria, Jieshan Chen, and Zhenchang Xing. 2017. Ensemble application of convolutional and recurrent neural networks for multi-label text categorization. IJCNN.

Ronan Collobert and Jason Weston. 2008. A unified architecture for natural language processing: Deep neural networks with multitask learning. In *Proceedings of the 25th international conference on Machine learning*. ACM, pages 160–167.

Alexis Conneau, Holger Schwenk, Loïc Barrault, and Yann Lecun. 2016. Very deep convolutional networks for natural language processing. *arXiv preprint arXiv:1606.01781* .

Robert Desimone and John Duncan. 1995. Neural mechanisms of selective visual attention. *Annual review of neuroscience* 18(1):193–222.

Jeffrey Donahue, Lisa Anne Hendricks, Sergio Guadarrama, Marcus Rohrbach, Subhashini Venugopalan, Kate Saenko, and Trevor Darrell. 2015. Long-term recurrent convolutional networks for visual recognition and description. In *Proceedings of the IEEE conference on computer vision and pattern recognition*. pages 2625–2634.

Cícero Nogueira Dos Santos and Maira Gatti. 2014. Deep convolutional neural networks for sentiment analysis of short texts. In *COLING*. pages 69–78.

Michael Fleischman, Eduard Hovy, and Abdessamad Echihabi. 2003. Offline strategies for online question answering: Answering questions before they are asked. In *Proceedings of the 41st Annual Meeting on Association for Computational Linguistics-Volume 1*. Association for Computational Linguistics, pages 1–7.

Alex Graves. 2013. Generating sequences with recurrent neural networks. *arXiv preprint arXiv:1308.0850* .

Alex Graves, Marcus Liwicki, Santiago Fernández, Roman Bertolami, Horst Bunke, and Jürgen Schmidhuber. 2009. A novel connectionist system for unconstrained handwriting recognition. *IEEE transactions on pattern analysis and machine intelligence* 31(5):855–868.

Sepp Hochreiter and Jürgen Schmidhuber. 1997. Long short-term memory. *Neural computation* 9(8):1735–1780.

Zhiheng Huang, Wei Xu, and Kai Yu. 2015. Bidirectional lstm-crf models for sequence tagging. *arXiv preprint arXiv:1508.01991* .

Trung Huynh, Yulan He, Allistair Willis, and Stefan Rüger. 2016. Adverse drug reaction classification with deep neural networks .

Laurent Itti, Christof Koch, Ernst Niebur, et al. 1998. A model of saliency-based visual attention for rapid scene analysis. *IEEE Transactions on pattern analysis and machine intelligence* 20(11):1254–1259.

Rie Johnson and Tong Zhang. 2014. Effective use of word order for text categorization with convolutional neural networks. *arXiv preprint arXiv:1412.1058* .

Rie Johnson and Tong Zhang. 2015. Semi-supervised convolutional neural networks for text categorization via region embedding. In *Advances in neural information processing systems*. pages 919–927.

Rie Johnson and Tong Zhang. 2016. Supervised and semi-supervised text categorization using lstm for region embeddings. *arXiv preprint arXiv:1602.02373* .

Nanda Kambhatla. 2004. Combining lexical, syntactic, and semantic features with maximum entropy models for extracting relations. In *Proceedings of the ACL 2004 on Interactive poster and demonstration sessions*. Association for Computational Linguistics, page 22.

Yoon Kim. 2014. Convolutional neural networks for sentence classification. *arXiv preprint arXiv:1408.5882* .

Diederik Kingma and Jimmy Ba. 2014. Adam: A method for stochastic optimization. *arXiv preprint arXiv:1412.6980* .

Changki Lee, Yi-Gyu Hwang, and Myung-Gil Jang. 2007. Fine-grained named entity recognition and relation extraction for question answering. In *Proceedings of the 30th annual international ACM SIGIR conference on Research and development in information retrieval*. ACM, pages 799–800.

Shengyu Liu, Buzhou Tang, Qingcai Chen, and Xiaolong Wang. 2016. Drug-drug interaction extraction via convolutional neural networks. *Computational and mathematical methods in medicine* 2016.

Mike Mintz, Steven Bills, Rion Snow, and Dan Jurafsky. 2009. Distant supervision for relation extraction without labeled data. In *Proceedings of the Joint Conference of the 47th Annual Meeting of the ACL and the 4th International Joint Conference on Natural Language Processing of the AFNLP: Volume 2-Volume 2*. Association for Computational Linguistics, pages 1003–1011.

Raymond J Mooney and Razvan C Bunescu. 2005. Subsequence kernels for relation extraction. In *Advances in neural information processing systems*. pages 171–178.

TH Muneeb, Sunil Kumar Sahu, and Ashish Anand. 2015. Evaluating distributed word representations for capturing semantics of biomedical concepts. *Proceedings of ACL-IJCNLP* page 158.

Thien Huu Nguyen and Ralph Grishman. 2015a. Combining neural networks and log-linear models to improve relation extraction. *arXiv preprint arXiv:1511.05926* .

Thien Huu Nguyen and Ralph Grishman. 2015b. Relation extraction: Perspective from convolutional neural networks. In *Proceedings of NAACL-HLT*. pages 39–48.

F. Pedregosa, G. Varoquaux, A. Gramfort, V. Michel, B. Thirion, O. Grisel, M. Blondel, P. Prettenhofer, R. Weiss, V. Dubourg, J. Vanderplas, A. Passos, D. Cournapeau, M. Brucher, M. Perrot, and E. Duchesnay. 2011. Scikit-learn: Machine learning in Python. *Journal of Machine Learning Research* 12:2825–2830.

Jeffrey Pennington, Richard Socher, and Christopher D Manning. 2014. Glove: Global vectors for word representation. In *EMNLP*. volume 14, pages 1532–1543.

Majid Rastegar-Mojarad, Richard D Boyce, and Rashmi Prasad. 2013. UWM-TRIADS: classifying drug-drug interactions with two-stage SVM and post-processing. In *Proceedings of the 7th International Workshop on Semantic Evaluation*. pages 667–674.

Bryan Rink, Sanda Harabagiu, and Kirk Roberts. 2011. Automatic extraction of relations between medical concepts in clinical texts. *Journal of the American Medical Informatics Association* 18(5):594–600.

Sunil Kumar Sahu and Ashish Anand. 2017. Drug-drug interaction extraction from biomedical text using long short term memory network. *arXiv preprint arXiv:1701.08303* .

Sunil Kumar Sahu, Ashish Anand, Krishnadev Oruganty, and Mahanandeeshwar Gattu. 2016. Relation extraction from clinical texts using domain invariant convolutional neural network. *arXiv preprint arXiv:1606.09370* .

Cicero Nogueira dos Santos, Bing Xiang, and Bowen Zhou. 2015. Classifying relations by ranking with convolutional neural networks. *arXiv preprint arXiv:1504.06580* .

Isabel Segura Bedmar, Paloma Martínez, and María Herrero Zazo. 2013. Semeval-2013 task 9: Extraction of drug-drug interactions from biomedical texts (ddiextraction 2013). Association for Computational Linguistics.

Nitish Srivastava, Geoffrey E Hinton, Alex Krizhevsky, Ilya Sutskever, and Ruslan Salakhutdinov. 2014. Dropout: a simple way to prevent neural networks from overfitting. *Journal of Machine Learning Research* 15(1):1929–1958.

Fabian M Suchanek, Georgiana Ifrim, and Gerhard Weikum. 2006. Combining linguistic and statistical analysis to extract relations from web documents. In *Proceedings of the 12th ACM SIGKDD international conference on Knowledge discovery and data mining*. ACM, pages 712–717.

Weiyi Sun, Anna Rumshisky, and Ozlem Uzuner. 2013. Evaluating temporal relations in clinical text: 2012 i2b2 challenge. *Journal of the American Medical Informatics Association* 20(5):806–813.

Mihai Surdeanu, Julie Tibshirani, Ramesh Nallapati, and Christopher D Manning. 2012. Multi-instance multi-label learning for relation extraction. In *Proceedings of the 2012 Joint Conference on Empirical*

Methods in Natural Language Processing and Computational Natural Language Learning. Association for Computational Linguistics, pages 455–465.

Oriol Vinyals, Alexander Toshev, Samy Bengio, and Dumitru Erhan. 2015. Show and tell: A neural image caption generator. In *Proceedings of the IEEE Conference on Computer Vision and Pattern Recognition*. pages 3156–3164.

Linlin Wang, Zhu Cao, Gerard de Melo, and Zhiyuan Liu. 2016a. Relation classification via multi-level attention cnns. In *ACL*.

Xingyou Wang, Weijie Jiang, and Zhiyong Luo. 2016b. Combination of convolutional and recurrent neural network for sentiment analysis of short texts. In *Proceedings of the 26th International Conference on Computational Linguistics*. pages 2428–2437.

Kelvin Xu, Jimmy Ba, Ryan Kiros, Kyunghyun Cho, Aaron Courville, Ruslan Salakhutdinov, Richard S Zemel, and Yoshua Bengio. 2015a. Show, attend and tell: Neural image caption generation with visual attention. *arXiv preprint arXiv:1502.03044* 2(3):5.

Kun Xu, Yansong Feng, Songfang Huang, and Dongyan Zhao. 2015b. Semantic relation classification via convolutional neural networks with simple negative sampling. *arXiv preprint arXiv:1506.07650* .

Zichao Yang, Diyi Yang, Chris Dyer, Xiaodong He, Alex Smola, and Eduard Hovy. 2016. Hierarchical attention networks for document classification. In *Proceedings of NAACL-HLT*. pages 1480–1489.

Daojian Zeng, Kang Liu, Siwei Lai, Guangyou Zhou, Jun Zhao, et al. 2014. Relation classification via convolutional deep neural network. In *COLING*. pages 2335–2344.

Peng Zhou, Wei Shi, Jun Tian, Zhenyu Qi, Bingchen Li, Hongwei Hao, and Bo Xu. 2016a. Attention-based bidirectional long short-term memory networks for relation classification. In *ACL*.

Peng Zhou, Wei Shi, Jun Tian, Zhenyu Qi, Bingchen Li, Hongwei Hao, and Bo Xu. 2016b. Attention-based bidirectional long short-term memory networks for relation classification. In *The 54th Annual Meeting of the Association for Computational Linguistics*. page 207.

Idea density for predicting Alzheimer's disease from transcribed speech

Kairit Sirts[1], Olivier Piguet[2,3] and Mark Johnson[4]

[1]Institute of Computer Science, University of Tartu
[2]School of Psychology and Brain & Mind Centre, The University of Sydney
[3]Neuroscience Research Australia, The University of New South Wales
[4]Department of Computing, Macquarie University
`kairit.sirts@ut.ee`, `olivier.piguet@sydney.edu.au`
`mark.johnson@mq.edu.au`

Abstract

Idea Density (ID) measures the rate at which ideas or elementary predications are expressed in an utterance or in a text. Lower ID is found to be associated with an increased risk of developing Alzheimer's disease (AD) (Snowdon et al., 1996; Engelman et al., 2010). ID has been used in two different versions: propositional idea density (PID) counts the expressed ideas and can be applied to any text while semantic idea density (SID) counts pre-defined information content units and is naturally more applicable to normative domains, such as picture description tasks. In this paper, we develop DEPID, a novel dependency-based method for computing PID, and its version DEPID-R that enables to exclude repeating ideas—a feature characteristic to AD speech. We conduct the first comparison of automatically extracted PID and SID in the diagnostic classification task on two different AD datasets covering both closed-topic and free-recall domains. While SID performs better on the normative dataset, adding PID leads to a small but significant improvement (+1.7 F-score). On the free-topic dataset, PID performs better than SID as expected (77.6 vs 72.3 in F-score) but adding the features derived from the word embedding clustering underlying the automatic SID increases the results considerably, leading to an F-score of 84.8.

1 Introduction

Idea density (ID) measures the rate of propositions or ideas expressed per word in a text and it is connected to some very interesting results from neuroscience related to Alzheimer's disease (AD). In

The old gray [MARE] has a very large [NOSE].

Dependencies	Propositions
det(The, mare)	
amod(old, mare)	(OLD, MARE)
amod(gray, mare)	(GRAY, MARE)
nsubj(mare, has)	(HAS, MARE, NOSE)
det(a, nose)	
advmod(very, large)	(VERY, (LARGE, NOSE))
amod(large, nose)	(LARGE, NOSE)
dobj(nose, has)	(HAS, MARE, NOSE)
punct(., has)	

Table 1: The alignment of the dependency and propositional structures. The example sentence is due to Brown et al. (2008). The predicative proposition (HAS, MARE, NOSE) is represented by two dependency arcs.

particular, two longitudinal studies—the Nun Study (Snowdon et al., 1996) and the Precursors Study (Engelman et al., 2010)—suggest that lower ID, as measured from the essays written in young age, is associated with the higher probability of developing AD in later life.

Two alternative definitions of idea density have been used in relation to AD. **Propositional idea density** (PID) counts the number of *any* ideas expressed in the text, setting no restriction to the topic (Turner and Greene, 1977; Chand et al., 2010). An example sentence with its ideas or propositions is given in Table 1. Based on each proposition a question can be formulated with a yes or no answer. Removing a proposition from a sentence changes the semantic meaning of that sentence. For instance, removing the proposition (GRAY, MARE) from the example makes the overall meaning of the sentence more general. The PID is then computed by normalising the proposition count with the token count and thus the PID of the example given in Table 1 is $6/9 \approx 0.667$.

The existing tool for automatic PID computation,

322

Proceedings of the 21st Conference on Computational Natural Language Learning (CoNLL 2017), pages 322–332,
Vancouver, Canada, August 3 - August 4, 2017. ©2017 Association for Computational Linguistics

CPIDR (Brown et al., 2008), is based on counting POS tags. However, we noticed that the propositional structure of a sentence is very similar to its dependency structure, see the first column in Table 1. This motivated us to come up with DEPID, a method for computing PID from dependency structures. In addition, DEPID more easily enables to consider idea repetition which has been shown to be a characteristic feature in Alzheimer's speech (Bayles et al., 1985; Tomoeda et al., 1996; Bayles et al., 2004), resulting in a modified PID version DEPID-R which excludes the repeated ideas.

Semantic idea density (SID) (Ahmed et al., 2013a,b) relies on a set of pre-defined information content units (ICU). ICU is an object or action that can be seen on the picture or is told in the story and is expected to be mentioned in the narrative. For instance, assuming that the words in capital letters and square brackets in the example sentence shown in Table 1 belong to the set of pre-defined ICUs the SID is computed by normalising the ICU count with the token count: $2/9 \approx 0.222$. Recently, Yancheva and Rudzicz (2016), proposed a method for computing SID based on word embedding clusters. We use their method for computing SID as it does not rely on any pre-defined ICU inventory and thus is applicable also on free-topic datasets.

PID and SID are complementary definitions of idea density with SID being naturally applicable in standardised picture description or story re-telling tasks while PID is more suitable on datasets of spontaneous speech on free topics.

In this paper we study the predictiveness of both PID and SID features in the diagnostic classification task for predicting AD. To that end, we conduct experiments on two very different datasets: DementiaBank, which consists of transcriptions of a normative picture description task, and AMI, which contains autobiographical memory interviews describing life events freely chosen by the subjects.

We show that on the DementiaBank data the POS-based PID scores are actually higher for AD patients than they are for normal controls, contrary to the expectations from the AD literature (Engelman et al., 2010; Chand et al., 2012; Kemper et al., 2001). By studying the characteristics of the DementiaBank we are able to adapt DEPID such that its PID values become significantly different between the patient and control groups in the expected direction. Thus, we believe that our proposed DEPID is a better tool for measuring PID as

described by neurolinguists on spontaneous speech transcripts than the POS-based CPIDR.

Secondly, we show that the SID performs better than PID on the constrained-domain DementiaBank corpus but adding the PID feature leads to a small but significant improvement.

Thirdly, we show that on the free-topic AMI dataset the PID performs better than the automatically extracted SID, but adding the features derived from the word embedding clustering underlying the SID, modeling the broad discussion topics, increases the results considerably—an effect which is less visible on the constrained topic DementiaBank.

The contributions of this paper are the following:

1. Development of DEPID, the new dependency-based method for automatically computing PID and its version DEPID-R which enables to detect and exclude idea repetitions;
2. Analysis of the characteristic features of the DementiaBank dataset and the proposal for modifying DEPID to make it applicable to this and other similar closed-topic datasets.
3. Results of extensive diagnostic classification experiments using PID, SID and several related baselines on two very different AD datasets.

2 Idea density and Alzheimer's disease

ID was first associated with AD in the Nun Study (Snowdon et al., 1996), based on a cohort of elderly nuns participating in a longitudinal study of aging and Alzheimer's disease. In this work, they studied the autobiographical essays the nuns had written decades ago in their youth. The nuns were divided into three groups based on their ID score computed from the essays, so that each group covered 33.3% percentile of the whole range of ID values. The lowest group was labeled as having low ID and the medium and highest group as having high ID. These groups were established from a sample of 93 nuns. The association between AD and ID was studied on a sample of 25 nuns who had died by the time of the study, for 10 of whom the cause of death had been marked as AD. The study found that most subjects with AD belonged to the low ID group while most of those, who did not develop AD, belonged to the group with high ID, thus suggesting that the low ID in youth might be associated with the development of the AD in later life.

Similar work was conducted on a group of medical students for whom essays from the time of their admission to the medical school several decades earlier were available (Engelman et al., 2010). The results of this study also showed a significantly lower ID on the AD group as compared to the healthy controls, suggesting that ID could be an important discriminative feature for predicting AD.

2.1 Propositional and semantic idea density

Two different versions of ID have been developed over time, both derived from the propositional base structure developed by Kintsch and Keenan (1973) to describe the semantic complexity of texts in reading experiments.

Propositional idea density (PID), which was used both in the Nun Study and the medical students study, is based on counting the semantic propositions as defined by Turner and Greene (1977) and later refined by Chand et al. (2012). Three main types of propositions where described: 1) predications that are based on verb frames; 2) modifications that include all sorts of modifiers, e.g. adjectival, adverbial, quantifying, qualifying etc.; and 3) connections that join simple propositions into complex ones. For each proposition, a question can be formed with a yes or no answer. For instance, based on the example in Table 1, we could form the following questions:

1. Is the mare old?
2. Is the mare gray?
3. Has the mare a nose?
4. Is the nose large?
5. Is the nose very large?

Each of those questions inquires about a different aspect of the whole sentence and is a basis of an idea or proposition.

Semantic idea density (SID) has retained its relation to the propositional base of some text. It relies on a set of information content units (ICUs) that have been pre-defined for a closed-topic task, such as picture description or story re-telling. For instance, different inventories of 7-25 ICUs have been described for the Cookie Theft picture task (Goodglass and Kaplan, 1983), listing objects visible on the picture such as *"boy"*, *"girl"*, *"cookie"* or *"kitchen"* or actions performed on the scene such as *"boy stealing cookies"* or *"woman drying dishes"*. SID is computed by counting the number of ICUs mentioned in the text and then normalising by the total number of word tokens.

2.2 Related work on AD using ID

PID, computed with CPIDR, has been used in few previous works for predicting AD. Jarrold et al. (2010) used PID as one among many features and reported it as significant. They obtained a classification accuracy of 73% on their dataset, which contained short structured clinical interviews, with their best model and feature set that also included the PID feature. PID was also used by Roark et al. (2011) to detect mild cognitive impairment on a story re-telling dataset. However, they found no significant difference between groups in terms of PID and thus, their feature selection procedure most probably filtered it out.

In terms of SID, most previous work has relied on manually defined ICUs (Ahmed et al., 2013b,a). Fraser et al. (2015) extracted binary and frequency-based ICU features. They searched for words related to the ICU objects and looked at the *nsubj-*relations in the dependency parses to detect the ICUs referring to actions. The binary feature was set when any word related to an ICU was mentioned in the text, while frequency-based features counted the total number of times any word referring to an ICU was mentioned.

Recently, Yancheva and Rudzicz (2016) proposed a method for automatically extracting ICUs and computing SID without relying on a manually defined ICU inventory. This work will be reviewed in more detail in section 4. They found that the automatically extracted ICUs and SID performed as well in a diagnostic AD classification task as the human-defined ICUs.

3 Computation of PID

Automating the computation of PID is difficult because it is essentially a semantic measure. The instructions given by Turner and Greene (1977) for counting the propositions assume the comprehension of the semantic meaning of the text, while the raw text lacks the necessary semantic annotations. However, it has been noticed that the propositions roughly correspond to certain POS tags. In particular, Snowdon et al. (1996) mention that elementary propositions are expressed using verbs, adjectives, adverbs and prepositions. This observation is the basis of the CPIDR program (Brown et al., 2008), a tool for automatically computing PID scores from text. CPIDR first processes the text with a POS-tagger, then counts all verbs, adjectives, adverbs, prepositions and coordinating

Dep rel	Proposition type
advcl	Causal connection
advmod	Qualifying modification
amod	Qualifying modification
appos	Referential predication
cc	Conjunctive connective
csubj	Predication with a clausal subject
csubjpass	Predication with a passive clausal subject
det[a]	Quantifying modification
neg	Negative modification
npadvmod	Qualifying modification
nsubj[b]	Predication subject
nsubjpass	Predication with passive subject
nummod	Quantifying modification
poss	Possessive modification
predet	Qualifying modification
preconj	Conjunctive or disjunctive connection
prep	Proposition denoting purpose, location, intention, etc.
quantmod	Quantifying modification
tmod	Qualifying modification
vmod	Qualifying modification

Table 2: Dependency relations encoding propositions.

[a]except *a*, *an* and *the*
[b]except *it* and *this*

conjunctions as propositions, and then applies a set of 37 rules to adjust the final proposition count.

3.1 DEPID—dependency-based PID

We propose that the dependency structure is better suited for PID computation than the POS tag counting approach adopted by the existing CPIDR program (Brown et al., 2008) because the dependency structure resembles more closely the semantic propositional structure, see Table 1. We treat each dependency type as a separate feature and manually set the feature weights to either one or zero depending on whether this dependency relation encodes a proposition or not. We make these decisions based on the dependency type descriptions in the Stanford dependency manual (de Marneffe and Manning, 2008). The dependency types with non-zero weights are listed in Table 2. The PID is then computed by summing the counts of those dependency relations and normalising by the number of word tokens. We call our dependency-based PID computation method DEPID.

We computed the Spearman correlations between CPIDR, DEPID and manual proposition counts on the 69 example sentences given in chapter 2 in (Turner and Greene, 1977)[1] and the 177

	Spearman r
CPIDR vs Manual	0.795
DEPID vs Manual	0.839
DEPID vs CPIDR	0.864

Table 3: Spearman correlations between CPIDR, DEPID and manual proposition counts on the examples given in Turner and Greene (1977) and Chand et al. (2010).

example sentences given in (Chand et al., 2010), making up the total of 276 sentences. These correlations are given in Table 3. We observe that by just counting the dependency relations given in Table 2, we obtain proposition counts that correlate better with the manual counts than the POS-based CPIDR counts.

3.2 DEPID-R

It is known that the Alzheimer's language is generally fluent and grammatical but in order to maintain the fluency the deficiencies in semantic or episodic memory are compensated with empty speech (Nicholas et al., 1985), such as repetitions, both on the word level but also on the idea, sentence or narrative level. DEPID easily enables to track repeated ideas in the narrative. We consider a proposition as repetition of a previous idea when the *deprel*(DEPENDENT LEMMA, HEAD LEMMA) tuples of the two propositions match. For instance, a sentence *"I had a happy life."* contains three propositions: *nsubj*(I, HAVE), *dobj*(LIFE, HAVE) and *amod*(HAPPY, LIFE). Another sentence *"I've had a very happy life."* later in the same narrative only adds a single proposition to the total count—*advmod*(VERY, HAPPY)—as this is the only new piece of information that was added.

We modify DEPID to exclude the repetitive ideas of a narrative by only counting the proposition *types* expressed with the lexicalised *deprel*(DEPENDENT LEMMA, HEAD LEMMA) dependency arcs. We call this modified version of dependency-based PID computation method DEPID-R. The relation between DEPID-R and DEPID is that DEPID counts the *tokens* of the same propositions.

4 Computation of SID

Recently, Yancheva and Rudzicz (2016) proposed a method for automatically computing SID without

---

[1]Similar to Brown et al. (2008), we exclude the example 17, but for examples 18, 54, 55, 56, we include all paraphrases.

	DB		AMI	
	AD	**Ctrl**	**AD**	**Ctrl**
Subjects	169	98	20	20
Samples	257	241	36	20
Mean samples	1.52	2.46	1.80	1.00
Mean words	104	114	1674	1509
Std words	58	59	778	688

Table 4: Statistics of the DementiaBank (DB) and AMI datasets. *Mean samples* is the average number of samples per subject. *Mean* and *std words* are the mean number of words per sample and the respective standard deviation.

the use of manually defined ICUs. Their method relies on clustering word embeddings of the nouns and verbs found in the transcriptions, assuming that the embeddings of the words related to the same semantic unit are clustered together.

They first perform K-means clustering on the word embeddings. Then, for each cluster they compute the mean distance μ_{cl} and its standard deviation σ_{cl}. The mean distance is the average Euclidean distance of all vectors assigned to a cluster from the centroid of that cluster. Finally, for each word they compute the scaled distance as a z-score of the Euclidean distance d_E between the word embedding and its closest cluster centroid:

$$d_{scaled} = \frac{d_E - \mu_{cl}}{\sigma_{cl}}$$

The words with $d_{scaled} < 3$ are counted as automatic ICUs. SID is then computed by dividing the number of ICUs with the total number of word tokens in the transcription.

In addition to SID, Yancheva and Rudzicz (2016) experiment with distance-based features also derived from the same clustering. The distance feature for each cluster is computed as the average of the scaled distances of the words (nouns or verbs) in the transcript assigned to that cluster. These cluster features are not directly related to the concept of SID but they could be viewed as an automatic approximation of features derived from the human annotated ICUs.

5 Experiments

5.1 Data

We conduct experiments on two very different AD datasets. The first dataset is derived from the DementiaBank (Becker et al., 1994), which is part of a publicly available Talkbank corpus.[2] It contains descriptions of the Cookie Theft picture (Goodglass and Kaplan, 1983) produced by subjects diagnosed with dementia as well as of healthy control cases. The data is manually transcribed and annotated in the CHAT format (MacWhinney, 2000), containing a range of annotations denoting various speech events. This is the same dataset used by Yancheva and Rudzicz (2016) and similar to them, we use the interviews of all control subjects and subjects whose diagnose is either AD or probable AD.

The second dataset, collected at NeuRA[3], contains autobiographical memory interviews (AMI) of both AD patients and healthy control subjects. Each interview consists of four stories, each story describing events from a particular period of the subject's life: teenage years, early adulthood, middle adulthood and last year. Each story has three logical parts: free recall, general probe and specific probe. In the free recall part the subject is asked to talk freely about events he remembers from the given life period. In the general recall part the interviewer helps to narrow down to a particular specific event. In the specific probe part the interviewer asks a number of predefined questions about this specific event. We use all four stories of an interview as a single sample but extract only the free recall part of each story as this is the most spontaneous part of the interview.

We preprocess both data sets similarly, following the procedure described in (Fraser et al., 2015) as closely as possible. We first extract only the patient's dialogue turns. Then we remove any tokens that are not words (e.g. laughs). In DementiaBank corpus, such tokens can be detected by various CHAT annotations. We also remove filled pauses such as *um, uh, er, ah*. The statistics of both datasets are given in Table 4.

5.2 Analysis of the idea density

First, we perform a statistical analysis of the different ID measures in Table 5 on both datasets using the indepedent samples Wilcoxon rank-sum test to test the difference between group means.

The DEPID computed PID values are systematically lower than the CPIDR values on both datasets, suggesting that either CPIDR overestimates or the DEPID underestimates the number of propositions. In order to check that we manually annotated the

---

[2]https://talkbank.org/DementiaBank/
[3]Neuroscience Research Australia

Data	Method	AD mean (sd)	Ctrl mean (sd)
DB	CPIDR*	0.518 (0.069)	0.491 (0.057)
DB	DEPID*	0.371 (0.052)	0.356 (0.046)
DB	DEPID-R	0.339 (0.049)	0.334 (0.042)
DB	DEPID-R-ADD*	0.168 (0.064)	0.194 (0.059)
DB	SID*	0.380 (0.051)	0.427 (0.045)
AMI	CPIDR	0.524 (0.023)	0.532 (0.017)
AMI	DEPID	0.468 (0.022)	0.473 (0.017)
AMI	DEPID-R*	0.334 (0.027)	0.366 (0.027)
AMI	DEPID-R-ADD+*	0.291 (0.032)	0.337 (0.032)
AMI	SID*	0.346 (0.034)	0.385 (0.024)

Table 5: The statistics of the ID values for AD and control groups. DEPID-R ignores the repeated ideas. DEPID-R-ADD for DementiaBank additionally excludes conjunctions, sentences with *I* and *you* subjects and sentences with vague meaning. DEPID-R-ADD+ for AMI only ignores sentences with vague meaning. SID is computed based on the clustering of the whole dataset. Star (*) after the method name indicates that the difference in group means is statistically significant ($p < 0.001$).

propositions of 20 interviews from DementiaBank according to the guidelines given by Chand et al. (2012). We found that both CPIDR and DEPID overestimate the PID values although CPIDR does it to much greater extent. CPIDR both overestimates the number of propositions and underestimates the number of tokens in certain cases leading to higher PID scores. For example, CPIDR does not count contracted forms, such as *"'s"* in *"it's"* or *"n't"* in *"don't"* as distinct tokens. Because there are many such forms in DementiaBank transcriptions, this behaviour considerably lowers CPIDR token counts. Also, CPIDR counts each auxiliary verb in present participle constructions as a separate proposition although these auxiliaries only mark syntax, thus leading to an artificially high proposition count. For instance, the clauses *"she is reaching"* and *"he is taking"* both contain two propositions according to CPIDR, whereas they both really contain only one semantic idea.

Both CPIDR and DEPID PID values differ significantly between AD and control groups on DementiaBank but the mean values are opposite to what was expected—AD patients have significantly higher PID than controls. When the repeated ideas are not counted (DEPID-R), the difference between groups becomes non-significant. However, we were curious about why the association between the lower PID values and the AD diagnosis cannot be observed on DementiaBank. Thus, we investigated this issue and found that the DementiaBank interviews have certain additional characteristics that contribute to the automatic proposition count being too high.

Conjunctive propositions First, we noticed that most *and-conjunctions* are used as lexical fillers in DementiaBank, whereas both CPIDR and DEPID count all conjunctions as propositions. In order to address this problem we excluded the *cc* dependency type from the set of propositions.

Sentences with pronominal subjects Secondly, we noticed that the sentences with subject either *I* or *you* most probably do not say anything about the picture but rather belong to the meta conversation. Two examples of such sentences are for instance *"what else can I tell you about the picture?"* or *"I'd say that's about all."*. To solve this problem we did not count propositions from sentences, where the subject was either *I* or *you*.

Vague sentences Finally, we observed that the AD patients seem to utter more *vague sentences* that do not contain any concrete ideas, such as for instance *"the upper one is there"* or *"they're doing more things on the outside."*. Both CPIDR and DEPID extract propositions from syntactic structures and thus they count pseudo-ideas from those sentences as well. To detect such vague sentences we evaluated the specificity of all sentences using SpeciTeller (Li and Nenkova, 2015). SpeciTeller predicts a specificity score between 0 and 1 for each sentence using features extracted from the sentence surface-level, specific dictionaries and distributional word embeddings. We did not count propositions from sentences whose specificity score was lower than 0.01.

After incorporating all those three measures to DEPID we finally obtain PID values on DementiaBank that are significantly different for patients and controls in the expected direction—the AD patients have significantly lower PID values than control subjects. Note that those measures only affect the proposition count and not the number of tokens. Also note that although these measures were motivated by the observations made on one particular (DementiaBank) dataset, they can be expected to be applicable to other similar closed-topic datasets, containing picture descriptions or story re-tellings.[4]

---

[4]Unfortunately, aside from DementiaBank there are no other publicly available AD datasets and thus we could not test whether our expectations hold true.

On AMI data, the difference between group means is non-significant for both CPIDR and DE-PID values. However, when the repeated ideas are excluded (DEPID-R), the mean PID for AD patients is significantly lower than for controls, as expected. It should be noted that the first two problems observed on DementiaBank—conjunctions and pronominal subjects—are not actual on the free-recall AMI data. In autobiographical memory interviews many sentences are expected to have *I* as subject. Also, the *and*-conjunctions are more likely to convey real ideas there rather than carry the role of lexical fillers. However, AD patients can utter more sentences with very vague meaning in AMI data as well and thus, in the last row of the Table 5 we show the DEPID PID values with vague sentences excluded for AMI dataset as well. We see that the PID values decrease for both patients and controls and the difference between groups remains statistically significant.

SID values differ significantly between the AD and control groups on both datasets with AD patients having significantly lower SID values as expected. The clustering underlying the automatically computed SID is trained on the whole dataset for both DementiaBank and AMI data.

5.3 Classification setup

We test both PID and SID in the diagnostic binary classification task on both DementiaBank and AMI datasets. When computing PID, the repeated ideas are excluded (DEPID-R). In addition, for DementiaBank, we also use the additional measures described in Section 5.2 (DEPID-R-ADD) as, according to Table 5, just DEPID-R cannot be expected to be predictive on that type of dataset. We compute the SID as described in Section 4. In following (Yancheva and Rudzicz, 2016), we cluster the 50-dimensional Glove embeddings[5] of all nouns and verbs found in the transcripts with k-means. Similar to them, we set the number of clusters to 10 on both datasets.

For single feature models (SID or PID) we use a simple logistic regression classifier. For models with multiple features we use the elastic net logistic regression with an elastic net hyperparameter $\alpha = 0.5$. We train and test with 10-fold cross-validation on subjects and repeat each experiment 100 times. We report the mean and stan-

Data	Features	Precision	Recall	F-score
DB	CPIDR	59.8 (0.7)	59.1 (0.5)	58.8 (0.5)
DB	PID	61.1 (0.7)	60.3 (0.6)	60.0 (0.5)
DB	SID	71.4 (0.6)	70.7 (0.5)	70.5 (0.5)
DB	SID+PID	**73.7** (0.9)	**72.1** (0.6)	**72.2** (0.6)
AMI	CPIDR	45.1 (3.2)	63.4 (1.8)	51.9 (2.3)
AMI	PID	79.2 (1.9)	**80.0** (0.5)	77.6 (0.9)
AMI	SID	73.7 (3.0)	75.3 (1.5)	72.3 (2.1)
AMI	SID+PID	**82.9** (3.8)	78.0 (1.8)	**77.7** (1.8)

Table 6: Classification results of various ID measures. The PID is DEPID-R-ADD for DementiaBank and DEPID-R for AMI.

dard deviation of the 100 macro-averaged cross-validated runs. For each experiment we report class-weighted precision, recall and F-score.[6]

5.4 Classification results

The classification results using various ID measures are shown in Table 6. On both datasets, PID and SID are better from the CPIDR baseline although the difference is considerably larger on the free-recall AMI dataset. On DementiaBank, SID performs better than PID and combining SID and PID also gives a small consistent cumulative effect, improving the F-score by 1.7%. On AMI data, the SID performs surprisingly well, considering that the automatic ICUs were extracted from only 10 clusters and the number of clusters was not tuned to that dataset at all. However, PID performs ca 5% better than SID in terms of all measures. Combining PID and SID gives some improvements in precision at the cost the decrease in recall and gives no cumulative gains in F-score. These results are fully in line with our expectations that the syntax-based DEPID performs better on the free-topic dataset, while the SID is better on closed-domain dataset.

For better comparison with Yancheva and Rudzicz (2016) we also experimented with the distance-based cluster features, which are derived from the clusters underlying the automatic SID (see section 4). We also show additional semantic baselines using LIWC features (Tausczik and Pennebaker, 2010) and bag-of-word (BOW) features extracting the counts of nouns and verbs normalised by the number of tokens. These results are shown in Table 7. On DementiaBank dataset, cluster features alone do not perform too well and using cluster features together with PID and SID gives only minor improvements. On the other hand, both the

---

[5]http://nlp.stanford.edu/projects/ glove/

[6]Classification accuracy is omitted because it is equivalent to the class-weighted recall.

Data	Features	Precision	Recall	F-score
DB	Clusters	62.3 (1.6)	62.2 (1.7)	62.2 (1.7)
DB	C+PID	67.4 (1.7)	64.9 (1.5)	65.1 (1.5)
DB	C+SID	73.4 (1.4)	71.5 (1.3)	71.6 (1.3)
DB	C+SID+PID	74.4 (1.5)	72.5 (1.2)	72.7 (1.2)
DB	LIWC	80.0 (0.9)	78.4 (0.7)	78.5 (0.7)
DB	BOW	**80.6** (1.1)	**79.1** (1.0)	**79.3** (1.0)
AMI	Clusters	76.9 (7.7)	71.2 (5.2)	70.5 (5.8)
AMI	C+PID	81.2 (5.0)	75.7 (3.8)	75.3 (3.8)
AMI	C+SID	83.5 (5.0)	77.9 (4.1)	77.7 (4.4)
AMI	C+SID+PID	**84.6** (4.4)	**78.1** (3.8)	**78.4** (4.0)
AMI	LIWC	74.2 (4.7)	67.8 (3.5)	66.8 (3.3)
AMI	BOW	65.1 (7.2)	65.3 (4.1)	61.6 (4.7)

Table 7: Classification results on DementiaBank (DB) and AMI using cluster features (C) combined with PID and SID, and LIWC and BOW baselines. The PID is DEPID-R-ADD for DementiaBank and DEPID-R for AMI.

Data	Features	Precision	Recall	F-score
DB	Clusters	68.0 (1.2)	65.5 (0.9)	65.7 (0.8)
DB	C+PID	69.6 (1.1)	67.1 (0.7)	67.4 (0.7)
DB	C+SID	75.3 (1.0)	73.3 (0.7)	73.5 (0.7)
DB	C+SID+PID	**76.6** (1.1)	**74.8** (0.8)	**75.0** (0.7)
AMI	Clusters	86.0 (3.6)	80.4 (2.2)	80.5 (2.1)
AMI	C+PID	88.4 (3.9)	83.0 (2.7)	83.2 (2.8)
AMI	C+SID	**88.6** (3.0)	**84.8** (1.7)	**84.8** (1.7)
AMI	C+SID+PID	87.3 (3.8)	82.4 (2.6)	82.7 (2.7)

Table 8: Classification results on DementiaBank (DB) and AMI using cluster features (C) combined with PID and SID. The clusters are pre-trained on the whole dataset. The PID is DEPID-R-ADD for DementiaBank and DEPID-R for AMI.

LIWC and BOW baselines perform very well on DementiaBank with BOW features giving the total highest precision of 80.6%, recall of 79.1% and F-score of 79.3%. In fact, these results are very close to the state-of-the-art on this dataset: a recall of 81.9% (Fraser et al., 2015) and an F-score of 80.0% (Yancheva and Rudzicz, 2016). Note however that the BOW features are conceptually much simpler than the acoustic and lexicosyntactic features extracted by Yancheva and Rudzicz (2016) and Fraser et al. (2015).

On the free-recall AMI data, the cluster features perform surprisingly well while the results of the LIWC and BOW baselines are lower. Adding cluster features to ID behaves inconsistently—in case of SID the F-score improves while adding cluster features to PID lowers the F-score. It is also worth noticing that results on AMI data including cluster features vary quite a bit, in some cases having standard deviation even as high as 7.7%.

Finally, we experimented with a scenario where the word embedding clusters are pre-trained on the whole dataset, in which case the clustering and thus also the SID feature reflect the structure of both training and test folds. This scenario assumes retraining the clustering and the classification model for each new test item/set. Although the classification model is then informed by the test set, we do not see it as test set leakage as the clustering is unsupervised. These results, given in Table 8, show that all results on both datasets improve, whereas the improvements are considerably larger on AMI dataset, which is expected because the model trained on the free-topic AMI data is likely to gain more on knowing the topics discussed in the test item/set. This scenario gives the highest F-score of 84.8% on this dataset when adding cluster features to SID.

Note, that the cluster features F-score trained on the full dataset is slightly lower than the 68% reported by Yancheva and Rudzicz (2016). This difference is probably due to the differences in hyperparameters and experimental setup: we use an elastic-net regularised logistic regression classifier while they used a random forest, we perform 10-fold cross-validation while they divided the DementiaBank into 60-20-20 train-dev-test partitions. However, the classification performance of cluster features together with SID are in the same range as their reported 74%.

6 Discussion

This is the first work we are aware of that compares the same methods for predicting AD on two different datasets. Moreover, most previous work has been conducted either on constrained-topic datasets, containing picture descriptions (Orimaye et al., 2014; Fraser et al., 2015; Yancheva and Rudzicz, 2016; Rentoumi et al., 2014), or semi-constrained structured interviews about some particular topic (Thomas et al., 2005; Jarrold et al., 2010, 2014), while our AMI dataset contains free recall samples and thus is probably more spontaneous than the previously used datasets.

We expected PID to perform well on the free-recall AMI dataset, which proved to be the case. However, we were surprised that the small number of automatically extracted clusters perform so well on that dataset too. This raises the natural question what topics those clusters represent. To shed light on this question, we studied the clustering trained on the whole AMI dataset. There were three clusters for which values differed significantly[7] between AD and control subjects: C0 ($p < 0.001$), C6 ($p < 0.001$) and C9 ($p = 0.0044$). C0, which could be denoted as a cluster describing experiences, contained a diverse mix of words, which close to the cluster center denoted specific aspects of something or connoted emotions such as *"rudeness"*, *"flirting"* and *"usher"*, while the farther words contained a range of aspects relevant to people's lives such as *"billiards"*, *"bronchitis"* and *"depression"*. C6 contained close to the cluster center simple work-related words, e.g. *"working"*, *"employed"* and *"student"*, while farther from the center there were more words referring to family members and even further away became the words referring to specific professions such as *"psychologists"*, *"barrister"* and *"chemist"*. The values of C6 feature for AD patients were significantly lower than for controls. Finally, the cluster C9 contained simple business-related words close to the cluster center, such as *"manage"*, *"product"* and *"account"*, while the words got more specific farther away from the centroid, e.g. *"licensed"*, *"reorganisation"* and *"textile"*.

Also, we checked how many words were considered as ICUs (words with $d_{scaled} < 3.0$ to their closest cluster center) on AMI data and found that most words were counted. This suggests that the automatically computed SID is in fact very close to the simple proportion of nouns and verbs in the transcripts. In order to check this, we extracted the normalised counts of nouns and verbs from all transcripts in both datasets and used it to train single feature logistic regression classifiers. We obtained the precision 67.6, recall 66.8 and F-score 66.6 on DementiaBank and precision 77.1, recall 76.0 and F-score 74.3 on AMI dataset. Also, we found that on DementiaBank the simple bag-of-words baseline obtained the results very close to the current state-of-the-art that uses much more complex feature sets, including both acoustic and lexicosyntactic features (Fraser et al., 2015). These two observations suggest that there is still room for studying simple feature sets for predicting AD.

7   Conclusion

We experimented with two different definitions of idea density—propositional idea density and semantic idea density—in the classification task for predicting Alzheimer's disease. In the AD and psycholinguistic literature, PID has been automatically

---

calculated using CPIDR (Engelman et al., 2010; Ferguson et al., 2014; Bryant et al., 2013; Moe et al., 2016). We show that CPIDR has a number of flaws when applied to AD speech, and we propose a new PID computation method DEPID which is more highly correlated with manual estimates of PID. We recommend that AD researchers use our automatic measure, DEPID-R, which also excludes repeating ideas from the total idea count, in place of CPIDR.

This is the first comparison between PID and SID and also the first computational study that evaluates the predictive models for Alzheimer's disease on two very different datasets. While on the closed-topic picture description dataset SID performs better, including PID also adds a small improvement to the classification results. On the open-domain dataset we found that the PID was more predictive than SID as expected. However, the small number of automatically extracted cluster features underlying the SID, modeling the broad discussion topics, led to even better results.

In future we plan to study the usefulness and applicability of both PID and SID also in other clinical tasks, such as in clinical diagnostic tasks for depression or schizophrenia. Another possible avenue for future work would include combining dependency-base PID and embedding-based SID into a unified idea density measure that would take into account both the propositional structure as well as the semantic content of words.

Acknowledgements

This research was supported by a Google award through the Natural Language Understanding Focused Program, and under the Australian Research Council's Discovery Projects funding scheme (project number DP160102156), and in part by funding to ForeFront, a collaborative research group dedicated to the study of frontotemporal dementia and motor neuron disease, from the National Health and Medical Research Council (NHMRC) (APP1037746), and the Australian Research Council (ARC) Centre of Excellence in Cognition and its Disorders Memory Program (CE11000102). OP is supported by an NHMRC Senior Research Fellowship (APP1103258).

References

Samrah Ahmed, Celeste A. de Jager, Anne-Marie Haigh, and Peter Garrard. 2013a. Semantic process-

---

---

[7]We used the Wilcoxon signed rank test.

ing in connected speech at a uniformly early stage of autopsy-confirmed Alzheimer's disease. *Neuropsychology* 27(1):79–85.

Samrah Ahmed, Anne-Marie F. Haigh, Celeste A. de Jager, and Peter Garrard. 2013b. Connected speech as a marker of disease progression in autopsy-proven Alzheimer's disease. *Brain* 136(12):3727–3737.

Kathryn A. Bayles, Cheryl K. Tomoeda, Alfred W. Kaszniak, Lawrence Z. Stern, and Karen K. Eagans. 1985. Verbal perseveration of dementia patients. *Brain and Language* 25(1):102–116.

Kathryn A. Bayles, Cheryl K. Tomoeda, Patrick E. McKnight, Nancy Helm-Estabrooks, and Josh N. Hawley. 2004. Verbal perseveration in individuals with Alzheimer's disease. *Seminars in Speech and Language* 25(4):335–347.

James T. Becker, Francois Boller, Oscar L. Lopez, Judith Saxton, and Karen L. McGonigle. 1994. The natural history of Alzheimer's disease. Description of study cohort and accuracy of diagnosis. *Archives of Neurology* 51(6):585–594.

Cati Brown, Tony Snodgrass, Susan J. Kemper, Ruth Herman, and Michael A. Covington. 2008. Automatic measurement of propositional idea density from part-of-speech tagging. *Behavior research methods* 40(2):540–545.

Lucy Bryant, Elizabeth Spencer, Alison Ferguson, Hugh Craig, Kim Colyvas, and Linda Worrall. 2013. Propositional Idea Density in aphasic discourse. *Aphasiology* 27(8):992–1009.

Vineeta Chand, Kathleen Baynes, Lisa M. Bonnici, and Sarah Tomaszewski Farias. 2010. Analysis of Idea Density (AID): A Manual. Technical report, University of California at Davis.

Vineeta Chand, Kathleen Baynes, Lisa M. Bonnici, and Sarah Tomaszewski Farias. 2012. A rubric for extracting idea density from oral language samples. *Current Protocols in Neuroscience* 1.

Marie-Catherine de Marneffe and Christopher D. Manning. 2008. Stanford Dependencies manual. Technical report, Stanford University.

Michal Engelman, Emily M. Agree, Lucy A. Meoni, and Michael J. Klag. 2010. Propositional density and cognitive function in later life: findings from the Precursors Study. *Journals of Gerontology - Series B Psychological Sciences and Social Sciences* 65(6):706–711.

Alison Ferguson, Elizabeth Spencer, Hugh Craig, and Kim Colyvas. 2014. Propositional idea density in women's written language over the lifespan: computerized analysis. *Cortex* 55:107–121.

Kathleen C. Fraser, Jed A. Meltzer, and Frank Rudzicz. 2015. Linguistic Features Identify Alzheimer's Disease in Narrative Speech. *Journal of Alzheimer's disease* 49(2):407–422.

Harold Goodglass and Edith Kaplan. 1983. *The Assessment of Aphasia and Related Disorders*. Lea & Febiger.

William Jarrold, Bart Peintner, David Wilkins, Dimitra Vergryi, Colleen Richey, Maria Luisa Gorno-Tempini, and Jennifer Ogar. 2014. Aided diagnosis of dementia type through computer-based analysis of spontaneous speech. In *Proceedings of the Workshop on Computational Linguistics and Clinical Psychology: From Linguistic Signal to Clinical Reality*. pages 27–37.

William L. Jarrold, Bart Peintner, Eric Yeh, Ruth Krasnow, Harold S. Javitz, and Gary E. Swan. 2010. Language analytics for assessing brain health: Cognitive impairment, depression and pre-symptomatic alzheimer's disease. In *Proceedings of the 2010 International Conference on Brain Informatics*. pages 299–307.

Susan Kemper, Janet Marquis, and Marilyn Thompson. 2001. Longitudinal change in language production: effects of aging and dementia on grammatical complexity and propositional content. *Psychology and Aging* 16(4):600–614.

Walter Kintsch and Janice Keenan. 1973. Reading rate and retention as a function of the number of propositions in the base structure of sentences. *Cognitive Psychology* 5(3):257–274.

Junyi Jessy Li and Ani Nenkova. 2015. Fast and accurate prediction of sentence specificity. In *Proceedings of the Twenty-Ninth AAAI Conference on Artificial Intelligence*. pages 2281–2287.

Brian MacWhinney. 2000. *The CHILDES Project: Tools for analyzing talk, 3rd edition.*. Lawrence Erlbaum Associates.

Aubrey M. Moe, Nicholas J. K. Breitborde, Mohammed K. Shakeel, Colin J. Gallagher, and Nancy M. Docherty. 2016. Idea density in the life-stories of people with schizophrenia: Associations with narrative qualities and psychiatric symptoms. *Schizophrenia Research* 172(1):201–205.

Marjorie Nicholas, Loraine K. Obler, Martin L. Albert, and Nancy Helm-Estabrooks. 1985. Empty Speech in Alzheimer's Disease and Fluent Aphasia. *Journal of Speech and Hearing Research* 28(3):405–410.

Sylvester O. Orimaye, Jojo Sze-Meng Wong, and Karen J. Golden. 2014. Learning Predictive Linguistic Features for Alzheimer's Disease and related Dementias using Verbal Utterances. In *Proceedings of the Workshop on Computational Linguistics and Clinical Psychology: From Linguistic Signal to Clinical Reality*. pages 78–87.

Vassiliki Rentoumi, Ladan Raoufian, Samrah Ahmed, Celeste A. de Jager, and Peter Garrard. 2014. Features and machine learning classification of connected speech samples from patients with autopsy proven Alzheimer's disease with and without additional vascular pathology. *Journal of Alzheimer's disease* 42(S3):3–17.

Brian Roark, Margaret Mitchell, John-Paul Hosom, Kristy Hollingshead, and Jeffrey Kaye. 2011. Spoken Language Derived Measures for Detecting Mild Cognitive Impairment. *IEEE transactions on audio, speech, and language processing* 19(7):2081–2090.

David A. Snowdon, Susan J. Kemper, James A. Mortimer, Lydia H. Greiner, David R. Wekstein, and William R. Markesbery. 1996. Linguistic ability in early life and cognitive function and Alzheimer's disease in late life. Findings from the Nun Study. *JAMA* 275(7):528–532.

Yla R. Tausczik and James W. Pennebaker. 2010. The Psychological Meaning of Words: LIWC and Computerized Text Analysis Methods. *Journal of Language and Social Psychology* 29(1):24–54.

Calvin Thomas, Vlado Keselj, Nick Cercone, Kenneth Rockwood, and Elissa Asp. 2005. Automatic detection and rating of dementia of Alzheimer type through lexical analysis of spontaneous speech. In *IEEE International Conference Mechatronics and Automation, 2005*. pages 1569–1574.

Cheryl K. Tomoeda, Kathryn A. Bayles, Michael W. Trosset, Tamiko Azuma, and Anna McGeagh. 1996. Cross-sectional analysis of Alzheimer disease effects on oral discourse in a picture description task. *Alzheimer Disease and Associated Disorders* 10(4):204–215.

Althea Turner and Edith Greene. 1977. The construction and use of a propositional text base. Technical report, University of Colorado.

Maria Yancheva and Frank Rudzicz. 2016. Vectorspace topic models for detecting Alzheimer's disease. In *Proceedings of the 54th Annual Meeting of the Association for Computational Linguistics*. pages 2337–2346.

Zero-Shot Relation Extraction via Reading Comprehension

Omer Levy[1]   Minjoon Seo[1]   Eunsol Choi[1]   Luke Zettlemoyer[1,2]

[1]Paul G. Allen School of Computer Science and Engineering
University of Washington, Seattle WA
{omerlevy,minjoon,eunsol,lsz}@cs.washington.edu

[2]Allen Institute for Artificial Intelligence, Seattle, WA

Abstract

We show that relation extraction can be reduced to answering simple reading comprehension questions, by associating one or more natural-language questions with each relation slot. This reduction has several advantages: we can (1) learn relation-extraction models by extending recent neural reading-comprehension techniques, (2) build very large training sets for those models by combining relation-specific crowd-sourced questions with distant supervision, and even (3) do zero-shot learning by extracting new relation types that are only specified at test-time, for which we have no labeled training examples. Experiments on a Wikipedia slot-filling task demonstrate that the approach can generalize to new questions for known relation types with high accuracy, and that zero-shot generalization to unseen relation types is possible, at lower accuracy levels, setting the bar for future work on this task.

1 Introduction

Relation extraction systems populate knowledge bases with facts from an unstructured text corpus. When the type of facts (relations) are predefined, one can use crowdsourcing (Liu et al., 2016) or distant supervision (Hoffmann et al., 2011) to collect examples and train an extraction model for each relation type. However, these approaches are incapable of extracting relations that were *not* specified in advance and observed during training. In this paper, we propose an alternative approach for relation extraction, which can potentially extract facts of new types that were neither specified nor observed a priori.

Relation	Question Template
$educated\_at(x, y)$	Where did x graduate from?
	In which university did x study?
	What is x's alma mater?
$occupation(x, y)$	What did x do for a living?
	What is x's job?
	What is the profession of x?
$spouse(x, y)$	Who is x's spouse?
	Who did x marry?
	Who is x married to?

Figure 1: Common knowledge-base relations defined by natural-language question templates.

We show that it is possible to reduce relation extraction to the problem of answering simple reading comprehension questions. We map each relation type $R(x, y)$ to at least one parametrized natural-language question q_x whose answer is y. For example, the relation $educated\_at(x, y)$ can be mapped to "Where did x study?" and "Which university did x graduate from?". Given a particular entity x ("Turing") and a text that mentions x ("Turing obtained his PhD from Princeton"), a non-null answer to any of these questions ("Princeton") asserts the fact and also fills the slot y. Figure 1 illustrates a few more examples.

This reduction enables new ways of framing the learning problem. In particular, it allows us to perform *zero-shot learning*: define new relations "on the fly", *after* the model has already been trained. More specifically, the zero-shot scenario assumes access to labeled data for N relation types. This data is used to train a reading comprehension model through our reduction. However, at test time, we are asked about a previously unseen relation type R_{N+1}. Rather than providing labeled data for the new relation, we simply list questions that define the relation's slot values. Assuming we learned a good reading comprehension model, the correct values should be extracted.

Our zero-shot setup includes innovations both

Proceedings of the 21st Conference on Computational Natural Language Learning (CoNLL 2017), pages 333–342,
Vancouver, Canada, August 3 - August 4, 2017. ©2017 Association for Computational Linguistics

in data and models. We use distant supervision for a relatively large number of relations (120) from Wikidata (Vrandečić, 2012), which are easily gathered in practice via the WikiReading dataset (Hewlett et al., 2016). We introduce a crowd-sourcing approach for gathering and verifying the questions for each relation. This process produced about 10 questions per relation on average, yielding a dataset of over 30,000,000 question-sentence-answer examples in total. Because questions are paired with relation types, not instances, this overall procedure has very modest costs.

The key modeling challenge is that most existing reading-comprehension problem formulations assume the answer to the question is always present in the given text. However, for relation extraction, this premise does not hold, and the model needs to reliably determine when a question is not answerable. We show that a recent state-of-the-art neural approach for reading comprehension (Seo et al., 2016) can be directly extended to model answerability and trained on our new dataset. This modeling approach is another advantage of our reduction: as machine reading models improve with time, so should our ability to extract relations.

Experiments demonstrate that our approach generalizes to new paraphrases of questions from the training set, while incurring only a minor loss in performance (4% relative F1 reduction). Furthermore, translating relation extraction to the realm of reading comprehension allows us to extract a significant portion of previously unseen relations, from virtually zero to an F1 of 41%. Our analysis suggests that our model is able to generalize to these cases by learning typing information that occurs across many relations (e.g. the answer to "Where" is a location), as well as detecting relation paraphrases to a certain extent. We also find that there are many feasible cases that our model does not quite master, providing an interesting challenge for future work.

2   Related Work

We are interested in a particularly harsh zero-shot learning scenario: given labeled examples for N relation types during training, extract relations of a new type R_{N+1} at test time. The only information we have about R_{N+1} are parametrized questions.

This setting differs from prior art in relation extraction. Bronstein et al. (2015) explore a similar zero-shot setting for event-trigger identification, in which R_{N+1} is specified by a set of trigger words at test time. They generalize by measuring the similarity between potential triggers and the given seed set using unsupervised methods. We focus instead on slot filling, where questions are more suitable descriptions than trigger words.

Open information extraction (open IE) (Banko et al., 2007) is a schemaless approach for extracting facts from text. While open IE systems need no relation-specific training data, they often treat different phrasings as different relations. In this work, we hope to extract a canonical slot value independent of how the original text is phrased.

Universal schema (Riedel et al., 2013) represents open IE extractions and knowledge-base facts in a single matrix, whose rows are entity pairs and columns are relations. The redundant schema (each knowledge-base relation may overlap with multiple natural-language relations) enables knowledge-base population via matrix completion techniques. Verga et al. (2017) predict facts for entity pairs that were not observed in the original matrix; this is equivalent to extracting seen relation types with unseen entities (see Section 6.1). Rocktäschel et al. (2015) and Demeester et al. (2016) use inference rules to predict hidden knowledge-base relations from observed natural-language relations. This setting is akin to generalizing across different manifestations of the same relation (see Section 6.2) since a natural-language description of each target relation appears in the training data. Moreover, the information about the unseen relations is a set of explicit inference rules, as opposed to implicit natural-language questions.

Our zero-shot scenario, in which no manifestation of the test relation is observed during training, is substantially more challenging (see Section 6.3). In universal-schema terminology, we add a new empty column (the target knowledge-base relation), plus a few new columns with a single entry each (reflecting the textual relations in the sentence). These columns share no entities with existing columns, making the rest of the matrix irrelevant. To fill the empty column from the others, we match their descriptions. Toutanova et al. (2015) proposed a similar approach that decomposes natural-language relations and computes their similarity in a universal schema setting; however, they did not extend their method to knowledge-base relations, nor did they attempt to recover out-of-schema relations as we do.

3   Approach

We consider the slot-filling challenge in relation extraction, in which we are given a knowledge-base relation R, an entity e, and a sentence s. For example, consider the relation *occupation*, the entity "Steve Jobs", and the sentence "Steve Jobs was an American businessman, inventor, and industrial designer". Our goal is to find a set of text spans A in s for which $R(e, a)$ holds for each $a \in A$. In our example, $A = \{businessman, inventor, industrial\ designer\}$. The empty set is also a valid answer ($A = \emptyset$) when s does not contain any phrase that satisfies $R(e, ?)$. We observe that given a natural-language question q that expresses $R(e, ?)$ (e.g. "What did Steve Jobs do for a living?"), solving the reading comprehension problem of answering q from s is equivalent to solving the slot-filling challenge.

The challenge now becomes one of *querification*: translating $R(e, ?)$ into q. Rather than querify $R(e, ?)$ for every entity e, we propose a method of querifying the relation R. We treat e as a variable x, querify the parametrized query $R(x, ?)$ (e.g. $occupation(x, ?)$) as a question template q_x ("What did x do for a living?"), and then instantiate this template with the relevant entities, creating a tailored natural-language question for each entity e ("What did *Steve Jobs* do for a living?"). This process, *schema querification*, is by an order of magnitude more efficient than querifying individual instances because annotating a relation type automatically annotates all of its instances.

Applying schema querification to N relations from a pre-existing relation-extraction dataset converts it into a reading-comprehension dataset. We then use this dataset to train a reading-comprehension model, which given a sentence s and a question q returns a set of text spans A within s that answer q (to the best of its ability).

In the zero-shot scenario, we are given a new relation $R_{N+1}(x, y)$ at test-time, which was neither specified nor observed beforehand. For example, the $deciphered(x, y)$ relation, as in "Turing and colleagues came up with a method for efficiently deciphering the Enigma", is too domain-specific to exist in common knowledge-bases. We then querify $R_{N+1}(x, y)$ into q_x ("Which code did x break?") or q_y ("Who cracked y?"), and run our reading-comprehension model for each sentence in the document(s) of interest, while instantiating the question template with different entities that might participate in this relation.[1] Each time the model returns a non-null answer a for a given question q_e, it extracts the relation $R_{N+1}(e, a)$.

Ultimately, all we need to do for a new relation is define our information need in the form of a question.[2] Our approach provides a natural-language API for application developers who are interested in incorporating a relation-extraction component in their programs; no linguistic knowledge or pre-defined schema is needed. To implement our approach, we require two components: training data and a reading-comprehension model. In Section 4, we construct a large relation-extraction dataset and querify it using an efficient crowdsourcing procedure. We then adapt an existing state-of-the-art reading-comprehension model to suit our problem formulation (Section 5).

4   Dataset

To collect reading-comprehension examples as in Figure 2, we first gather labeled examples for the task of relation-slot filling. Slot-filling examples are similar to reading-comprehension examples, but contain a knowledge-base query $R(e, ?)$ instead of a natural-language question; e.g. *spouse*(Angela Merkel, ?) instead of "Who is Angela Merkel married to?". We collect many slot-filling examples via distant supervision, and then convert their queries into natural language.

Slot-Filling Data   We use the WikiReading dataset (Hewlett et al., 2016) to collect labeled slot-filling examples. WikiReading was collected by aligning each Wikidata (Vrandečić, 2012) relation $R(e, a)$ with the corresponding Wikipedia article D for the entity e, under the reasonable assumption that the relation can be derived from the article's text. Each instance in this dataset contains a relation R, an entity e, a document D, and an answer a. We used distant supervision to select the specific sentences in which each $R(e, a)$ manifests. Specifically, we took the first sentence s in D to contain both e and a. We then grouped instances by R, e, and s to merge all the answers for $R(e, ?)$ given s into one answer set A.

---

[1] This can be implemented efficiently by constraining potential entities with existing facts in the knowledge base. For example, any entity x that satisfies $occupation(x, cryptographer)$ or any entity y for which $subclass\_of(y, cipher)$ holds. We leave the exact implementation details of such a system for future work.

[2] While we use questions, one can also use sentences with slots (clozes) to capture an almost identical notion.

Relation	Question	Sentence & Answers
educated_at	What is **Albert Einstein**'s alma mater?	**Albert Einstein** was awarded a PhD by the <u>University of Zürich</u>, with his dissertation titled...
occupation	What did **Steve Jobs** do for a living?	**Steve Jobs** was an American <u>**businessman**</u>, <u>**inventor**</u>, and <u>**industrial designer**</u>.
spouse	Who is **Angela Merkel** married to?	**Angela Merkel**'s second and current husband is quantum chemist and professor <u>**Joachim Sauer**</u>, who has largely...

Figure 2: Examples from our reading-comprehension dataset. Each instance contains a relation R, a question q, a sentence s, and an answer set A. The question explicitly mentions an entity e, which also appears in s. For brevity, answers are underlined instead of being displayed in a separate column.

> (1) The wine is produced in the **X** region of <u>**France**</u>.
> (2) **X**, the capital of <u>**Mexico**</u>, is the most populous city in North America.
> (3) **X** is an unincorporated and organized territory of <u>**the United States**</u>.
> (4) The **X** mountain range stretches across <u>**the United States**</u> and <u>**Canada**</u>.

Figure 3: An example of the annotator's input when querifying the $country(x, ?)$ relation. The annotator is required to ask a question about x whose answer is, for each sentence, the underlined spans.

Schema Querification Crowdsourcing querification at the schema level is not straightforward, because the task has to encourage workers to (a) figure out the relation's semantics (b) be lexically-creative when asking questions. We therefore apply a combination of crowdsourcing tactics over two Mechanical Turk annotation phases: collection and verification.

For each relation R, we present the annotator with 4 example sentences, where the entity e in each sentence s is masked by the variable x. In addition, we underline the extractable answers $a \in A$ that appear in s (see Figure 3). The annotator must then come up with a question about x whose answer, given each sentence s, is the underlined span within that sentence. For example, "In which country is x?" captures the exact set of answers for each sentence in Figure 3. Asking a more general question, such as "Where is x?" might return false positives ("North America" in sentence 2).

Each worker produced 3 different question templates for each example set. For each relation, we sampled 3 different example sets, and hired 3 different annotators for each set. We ran one instance of this annotation phase where the workers were also given, in addition to the example set, the name of the relation (e.g. *country*), and another instance where it was hidden. Out of a potential 54 question templates, 40 were unique on average.

In the verification phase, we measure the question templates' quality by sampling additional sentences and instantiating each question template with the example entity e. Annotators are then asked to answer the question from the sentence s, or mark it as unanswerable; if the annotators' an-swers match A, the question template is valid. We discarded the templates that were not answered correctly in the majority of the examples (6/10).[3]

Overall, we applied schema querification to 178 relations that had at least 100 examples each (accounting for 99.77% of the data), costing roughly \$1,250. After the verification phase, we were left with 1,192 high-quality question templates spanning 120 relations.[4] We then join these templates with our slot-filling dataset along relations, instantiating each template q_x with its matching entities. This process yields a reading-comprehension dataset of over 30,000,000 examples, where each instance contains the original relation R (unobserved by the machine), a question q, a sentence s, and the set of answers A (see Figure 2).

Negative Examples To support relation extraction, our dataset deviates from recent reading comprehension formulations (Hermann et al., 2015; Rajpurkar et al., 2016), and introduces negative examples – question-sentence pairs that have no answers ($A = \emptyset$). Following the methodology of InfoboxQA (Morales et al., 2016), we generate negative examples by matching (for the same entity e) a question q that pertains to one relation with a sentence s that expresses another relation. We also assert that the sentence does not contain the answer to q. For instance, we match "Who

---

[3]We used this relatively lenient measure because many annotators selected the correct answer, but with a slightly incorrect span; e.g. "American businessman" instead of "businessman". We therefore used token-overlap F1 as a secondary filter, requiring an average score of at least 0.75.

[4]58 relations had zero questions after verification due to noisy distant supervision and little annotator quality control.

is Angela Merkel married to?" with a sentence about her occupation: "Angela Merkel is a German politician who is currently the Chancellor of Germany". This process generated over 2 million negative examples. While this is a relatively naive method of generating negative examples, our analysis shows that about a third of negative examples contain good distractors (see Section 7).

Discussion Some recent QA datasets were collected by expressing knowledge-base assertions in natural language. The Simple QA dataset (Bordes et al., 2015) was created by annotating questions about individual Freebase facts (e.g. $educated\_at(Turing, Princeton)$), collecting roughly 100,000 natural-language questions to support QA against a knowledge graph. Morales et al. (2016) used a similar process to collect questions from Wikipedia infoboxes, yielding the 15,000-example InfoboxQA dataset. For the task of identifying predicate-argument structures, QA-SRL (He et al., 2015) was proposed as an open schema for semantic roles, in which the relation between an argument and a predicate is expressed as a natural-language question containing the predicate ("Where was someone educated?") whose answer is the argument ("Princeton"). The authors collected about 19,000 question-answer pairs from 3,200 sentences.

In these efforts, the costs scale linearly in the number of instances, requiring significant investments for large datasets. In contrast, schema querification can generate an enormous amount of data for a fraction of the cost by labeling at the relation level; as evidence, we were able to generate a dataset 300 times larger than Simple QA. To the best of our knowledge, this is the first robust method for collecting a question-answering dataset by crowd-annotating at the schema level.

5   Model

Given a sentence s and a question q, our algorithm either returns an answer span[5] a within s, or indicates that there is no answer.

The task of obtaining answer spans to natural-language questions has been recently studied on the SQuAD dataset (Rajpurkar et al., 2016; Xiong et al., 2016; Lee et al., 2016; Wang et al., 2016). In SQuAD, every question is answerable from the

---

[5]While our problem definition allows for multiple answer spans per question, our algorithm assumes a single span; in practice, less than 5% of our data has multiple answers.

text, which is why these models assume that there exists a correct answer span. Therefore, we modify an existing model in a way that allows it to decide whether an answer exists. We first give a high-level description of the original model, and then describe our modification.

We start from the BiDAF model (Seo et al., 2016), whose input is two sequences of words: a sentence s and a question q. The model predicts the start and end positions $\mathbf{y}^{start}, \mathbf{y}^{end}$ of the answer span in s. BiDAF uses recurrent neural networks to encode contextual information within s and q alongside an attention mechanism to align parts of q with s and vice-versa.

The outputs of the BiDAF model are the confidence scores of $\mathbf{y}^{start}$ and $\mathbf{y}^{end}$, for each potential start and end. We denote these scores as $\mathbf{z}^{start}, \mathbf{z}^{end} \in \mathbb{R}^N$, where N is the number of words in the sentence s. In other words, $\mathbf{z}_i^{start}$ indicates how likely the answer is to start at position i of the sentence (the higher the more likely); similarly, $\mathbf{z}_i^{end}$ indicates how likely the answer is to end at that index. Assuming the answer exists, we can transform these confidence scores into pseudo-probability distributions $\mathbf{p}^{start}, \mathbf{p}^{end}$ via softmax. The probability of each i-to-j-span of the context can therefore be defined by:

$$P(a = s_{i...j}) = \mathbf{p}_i^{start}\mathbf{p}_j^{end} \qquad (1)$$

where $\mathbf{p}_i$ indicates the i-th element of the vector $\mathbf{p}_i$, i.e. the probability of the answer starting at i. Seo et al. (2016) obtain the span with the highest probability during post-processing.

To allow the model to signal that there is no answer, we concatenate a trainable bias b to the end of both confidences score vectors $\mathbf{z}^{start}, \mathbf{z}^{end}$. The new score vectors $\tilde{\mathbf{z}}^{start}, \tilde{\mathbf{z}}^{end} \in \mathbb{R}^{N+1}$ are defined as $\tilde{\mathbf{z}}^{start} = [\mathbf{z}^{start}; b]$ and similarly for $\tilde{\mathbf{z}}^{end}$, where $[;]$ indicates row-wise concatenation. Hence, the last elements of $\tilde{\mathbf{z}}^{start}$ and $\tilde{\mathbf{z}}^{end}$ indicate the model's confidence that the answer has no start or end, respectively. We apply softmax to these augmented vectors to obtain pseudo-probability distributions, $\tilde{\mathbf{p}}^{start}, \tilde{\mathbf{p}}^{end}$. This means that the probability the model assigns to a null answer is:

$$P(a = \emptyset) = \tilde{\mathbf{p}}_{N+1}^{start}\tilde{\mathbf{p}}_{N+1}^{end}. \qquad (2)$$

If $P(a = \emptyset)$ is higher than the probability of the best span, $\arg\max_{i,j \leq N} P(a = s_{i...j})$, then the model deems that the question cannot be answered from the sentence. Conceptually, adding the bias enables the model to be sensitive to the absolute values of the raw confidence scores $\mathbf{z}^{start}, \mathbf{z}^{end}$. We are essentially setting and learning a threshold b that decides whether the model is sufficiently confident of the best candidate answer span.

While this threshold provides us with a dynamic per-example decision of whether the instance is answerable, we can also set a global confidence threshold p_{min}; if the best answer's confidence is below that threshold, we infer that there is no answer. In Section 6.3 we use this global threshold to get a broader picture of the model's performance.

6 Experiments

To understand how well our method can generalize to unseen data, we design experiments for unseen entities (Section 6.1), unseen question templates (Section 6.2), and unseen relations (Section 6.3).

Evaluation Metrics   Each instance is evaluated by comparing the tokens in the labeled answer set with those of the predicted span.[6] Precision is the true positive count divided by the number of times the system returned a non-null answer. Recall is the true positive count divided by the number of instances that have an answer.

Hyperparameters   In our experiments, we initialized word embeddings with GloVe (Pennington et al., 2014), and did not fine-tune them. The typical training set was an order of 1 million examples, for which 3 epochs were enough for convergence. All training sets had a ratio of 1:1 positive and negative examples, which was chosen to match the test sets' ratio.

Comparison Systems   We experiment with several variants of our model. In *KB Relation*, we feed our model a relation indicator (e.g. R_{17}) instead of a question. We expect this variant to generalize reasonably well to unseen entities, but fail on unseen relations. The second variant (*NL Relation*) uses the relation's name (as a natural-language expression) instead of a question (e.g. *educated_at* as "educated at"). We also consider a weakened version of our querification approach (*Single Template*) where, during training, only one question template per relation is observed. The full variant of our model, *Multiple Templates*, is

trained on a more diverse set of questions. We expect this variant to have significantly better paraphrasing abilities than *Single Template*.

We also evaluate how asking about the same relation in multiple ways improves performance (*Question Ensemble*). We create an ensemble by sampling 3 questions per test instance and predicting the answer for each. We then choose the answer with the highest sum of confidence scores.

In addition to our model, we compare three other systems. The first is a random baseline that chooses a named entity in the sentence that does not appear in the question (*Random NE*). We also reimplement the *RNN Labeler* that was shown to have good results on the extractive portion of WikiReading (Hewlett et al., 2016). Lastly, we retrain an off-the-shelf relation extraction system (Miwa and Bansal, 2016), which has shown promising results on a number of benchmarks. This system (and many like it) represents relations as indicators, and cannot extract unseen relations.

6.1   Unseen Entities

We show that our reading-comprehension approach works well in a typical relation-extraction setting by testing it on unseen entities and texts.

Setup   We partitioned our dataset along entities in the question, and randomly clustered each entity into one of three groups: train, dev, or test. For instance, Alan Turing examples appear only in training, while Steve Jobs examples are exclusive to test. We then sampled 1,000,000 examples for train, 1,000 for dev, and 10,000 for test. This partition also ensures that the sentences at test time are different from those in train, since the sentences are gathered from each entity's Wikipedia article.

Results   Table 1 shows that our model generalizes well to new entities and texts, with little variance in performance between *KB Relation*, *NL Relation*, *Multiple Templates*, and *Question Ensemble*. *Single Template* performs significantly worse than these variants; we conjecture that simpler relation descriptions (*KB Relation* & *NL Relation*) allow for easier parameter tying across different examples, whereas learning from multiple questions allows the model to acquire important paraphrases. All variants of our model outperform off-the-shelf relation extraction systems (*RNN Labeler* and *Miwa & Bansal*) in this setting, demonstrating that reducing relation extraction to reading

---

[6]We ignore word order, case, punctuation, and articles ("a", "an", "the"). We also ignore "and", which often appears when a single span captures multiple correct answers (e.g. "United States and Canada").

	Precision	Recall	F1
Random NE	11.17%	22.14%	14.85%
RNN Labeler	62.55%	62.25%	62.40%
Miwa & Bansal	96.07%	58.70%	72.87%
KB Relation	89.08%	91.54%	90.29%
NL Relation	88.23%	91.02%	89.60%
Single Template	77.92%	73.88%	75.84%
Multiple Templates	87.66%	91.32%	89.44%
Question Ensemble	88.08%	91.60%	89.80%

Table 1: Performance on unseen entities.

	Precision	Recall	F1
Seen	86.73%	86.54%	86.63%
Unseen	84.37%	81.88%	83.10%

Table 2: Performance on seen/unseen questions.

comprehension is indeed a viable approach for our Wikipedia slot-filling task.

An analysis of 50 examples that *Multiple Templates* mispredicted shows that 36% of errors can be attributed to annotation errors (chiefly missing entries in Wikidata), and an additional 42% result from inaccurate span selection (e.g. "8 February 1985" instead of "1985"), for which our model is fully penalized. In total, only 18% of our sample were pure system errors, suggesting that our model is very close to the performance ceiling of this setting (slightly above 90% F1).

6.2 Unseen Question Templates

We test our method's ability to generalize to new descriptions of the same relation, by holding out a question template for each relation during training.

Setup We created 10 folds of train/dev/test samples of the data, in which one question template for each relation was held out for the test set, and another for the development set. For instance, "What did x do for a living?" may appear only in the training set, while "What is x's job?" is exclusive to the test set. Each split was stratified by sampling N examples per question template ($N = 1000, 10, 50$ for train, dev, test, respectively). This process created 10 training sets of 966,000 examples with matching development and test sets of 940 and 4,700 examples each.

We trained and tested *Multiple Templates* on each one of the folds, yielding performance on unseen templates. We then replicated the existing test sets and replaced the unseen question templates with templates from the training set, yielding performance on seen templates. Revisiting our example, we convert test-set occurrences of "What is x's job?" to "What did x do for a living?".

	Precision	Recall	F1
Random NE	9.25%	18.06%	12.23%
RNN Labeler	13.28%	5.69%	7.97%
Miwa & Bansal	100.00%	0.00%	0.00%
KB Relation	19.32%	2.54%	4.32%
NL Relation	40.50%	28.56%	33.40%
Single Template	37.18%	31.24%	33.90%
Multiple Templates	43.61%	36.45%	39.61%
Question Ensemble	45.85%	37.44%	41.11%

Table 3: Performance on unseen relations.

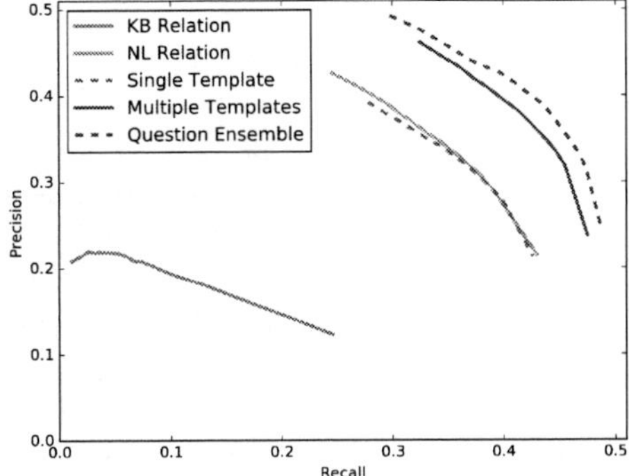

Figure 4: Precision/Recall for unseen relations.

Results Table 2 shows that our approach is able to generalize to unseen question templates. Our system's performance on unseen questions is nearly as strong as for previously observed templates (losing roughly 3.5 points in F1).

6.3 Unseen Relations

We examine a pure zero-shot setting, where test-time relations are unobserved during training.

Setup We created 10 folds of train/dev/test samples, partitioned along relations: 84 relations for train, 12 dev, and 24 test. For example, when *educated_at* is allocated to test, no *educated_at* examples appear in train. Using stratified sampling of relations, we created 10 training sets of 840,000 examples each with matching dev and test sets of 600 and 12,000 examples per fold.

Results Table 3 shows each system's performance; Figure 4 extends these results for variants of our model by applying a global threshold on the answers' confidence scores to generate precision/recall curves (see Section 5). As expected, representing knowledge-base relations as indicators (*KB Relation* and *Miwa & Bansal*) is insufficient in a zero-shot setting; they must be interpreted as natural-language expressions to allow for

Verbatim	Relation	András Dombai **plays for** what team? András Dombai... ...currently **plays** as a goalkeeper **for** *FC Tatabánya*.
	Type	Which **airport** is most closely associated with Royal Jordanian? Royal Jordanian Airlines... ...from its main base at *Queen Alia International **Airport**...*
Global	Relation	Who was responsible for **directing** Les petites fugues? Les petites fugues is a 1979 Swiss comedy film **directed by** *Yves Yersin*.
	Type	**When** was The Snow Hawk released? The Snow Hawk is a *1925* film...
Specific	Relation	Who **started** Fürstenberg China? The Fürstenberg China Factory **was founded**... ...**by** *Johann Georg von Langen*...
	Type	What **voice type** does Étienne Lainez have? Étienne Lainez... ...was a French operatic ***tenor***...

Figure 5: The different types of discriminating cues we observed among positive examples.

some generalization. The difference between using a single question template (*Single Template*) and the relation's name (*NL Relation*) appears to be minor. However, training on a variety of question templates (*Multiple Templates*) substantially increases performance. We conjecture that multiple phrasings of the same relation allows our model to learn answer-type paraphrases that occur across many relations (see Section 7). There is also some advantage to having multiple questions at test time (*Question Ensemble*).

7 Analysis

To understand how our method extracts unseen relations, we analyzed 100 random examples, of which 60 had answers in the sentence and 40 did not (negative examples).

For negative examples, we checked whether a distractor – an incorrect answer of the correct answer type – appears in the sentence. For example, the question "Who is John McCain married to?" does not have an answer in "John McCain chose Sarah Palin as his running mate", but "Sarah Palin" is of the correct answer type. We noticed that 14 negative examples (35%) contain distractors. When pairing these examples with the results from the unseen relations experiment in Section 6.3, we found that our method answered 2/14 of the distractor examples incorrectly, compared to only 1/26 of the easier examples. It appears that while most of the negative examples are easy, a significant portion of them are not trivial.

For positive examples, we observed that some instances can be solved by matching the relation in the sentence to that in the question, while others rely more on the answer's type. Moreover, we notice that each cue can be further categorized according to the type of information needed to detect it: (1) when part of the question appears verba-

	Relation	Type
Verbatim	12%	5%
Global	8%	25%
Specific	22%	28%

Table 4: The distribution of cues by type, based on a sample of 60.

	Relation	Type
Verbatim	*43%*	*33%*
Global	*60%*	*73%*
Specific	*46%*	*18%*

Table 5: Our method's accuracy on subsets of examples pertaining to different cue types. Results in *italics* are based on a sample of less than 10.

tim in the text, (2) when the phrasing in the text deviates from the question in a way that is typical of other relations as well (e.g. syntactic variability), (3) when the phrasing in the text deviates from the question in a way that is unique to this relation (e.g. lexical variability). We name these categories *verbatim*, *global*, and *specific*, respectively. Figure 5 illustrates all the different types of cues we discuss in our analysis.

We selected the most important cue for solving each instance. If there were two important cues, each one was counted as half. Table 4 shows their distribution. Type cues appear to be somewhat more dominant than relation cues (58% vs. 42%). Half of the cues are relation-specific, whereas global cues account for one third of the cases and verbatim cues for one sixth. This is an encouraging result, because we can potentially learn to accurately recognize verbatim and global cues from other relations. However, our method was only able to exploit these cues partially.

We paired these examples with the results from the unseen relations experiment in Section 6.3 to see how well our method performs in each category. Table 5 shows the results for the *Multiple*

Templates setting. On one hand, the model appears agnostic to whether the relation cue is verbatim, global, or specific, and is able to correctly answer these instances with similar accuracy (there is no clear trend due to the small sample size). For examples that rely on typing information, the trend is much clearer; our model is much better at detecting global type cues than specific ones.

Based on these observations, we think that the primary sources of our model's ability to generalize to new relations are: *global type detection*, which is acquired from training on many different relations, and *relation paraphrase detection* (of all types), which probably relies on its pre-trained word embeddings.

8 Conclusion

We showed that relation extraction can be reduced to a reading comprehension problem, allowing us to generalize to unseen relations that are defined on-the-fly in natural language. However, the problem of zero-shot relation extraction is far from solved, and poses an interesting challenge to both the information extraction and machine reading communities. As research into machine reading progresses, we may find that more tasks can benefit from a similar approach. To support future work in this avenue, we make our code and data publicly available.[7]

Acknowledgements

The research was supported in part by DARPA under the DEFT program (FA8750-13-2-0019), the ARO (W911NF-16-1-0121), the NSF (IIS-1252835, IIS-1562364), gifts from Google, Tencent, and Nvidia, and an Allen Distinguished Investigator Award. We also thank Mandar Joshi, Victoria Lin, and the UW NLP group for helpful conversations and comments on the work.

References

Michele Banko, Michael J. Cafarella, Stephen Soderland, Matt Broadhead, and Oren Etzioni. 2007. Open information extraction from the web. In *Proceedings of the 20th International Joint Conference on Artifical Intelligence*. Morgan Kaufmann Publishers Inc., San Francisco, CA, USA, IJCAI'07, pages 2670–2676. http://dl.acm.org/citation.cfm?id=1625275.1625705.

Antoine Bordes, Nicolas Usunier, Sumit Chopra, and Jason Weston. 2015. Large-scale simple question answering with memory networks. *arXiv preprint arXiv:1506.02075* .

Ofer Bronstein, Ido Dagan, Qi Li, Heng Ji, and Anette Frank. 2015. Seed-based event trigger labeling: How far can event descriptions get us? In *Proceedings of the 53rd Annual Meeting of the Association for Computational Linguistics and the 7th International Joint Conference on Natural Language Processing (Volume 2: Short Papers)*. Association for Computational Linguistics, Beijing, China, pages 372–376. http://www.aclweb.org/anthology/P15-2061.

Thomas Demeester, Tim Rocktäschel, and Sebastian Riedel. 2016. Lifted rule injection for relation embeddings. In *Proceedings of the 2016 Conference on Empirical Methods in Natural Language Processing*. Association for Computational Linguistics, Austin, Texas, pages 1389–1399. https://aclweb.org/anthology/D16-1146.

Luheng He, Mike Lewis, and Luke Zettlemoyer. 2015. Question-answer driven semantic role labeling: Using natural language to annotate natural language. In *Proceedings of the 2015 Conference on Empirical Methods in Natural Language Processing*. Association for Computational Linguistics, Lisbon, Portugal, pages 643–653. http://aclweb.org/anthology/D15-1076.

Karl Moritz Hermann, Tomáš Kočiský, Edward Grefenstette, Lasse Espeholt, Will Kay, Mustafa Suleyman, and Phil Blunsom. 2015. Teaching machines to read and comprehend. In *Advances in Neural Information Processing Systems*. http://arxiv.org/abs/1506.03340.

Daniel Hewlett, Alexandre Lacoste, Llion Jones, Illia Polosukhin, Andrew Fandrianto, Jay Han, Matthew Kelcey, and David Berthelot. 2016. Wikireading: A novel large-scale language understanding task over wikipedia. In *Proceedings of the Conference of the Association for Computational Linguistics*.

Raphael Hoffmann, Congle Zhang, Xiao Ling, Luke Zettlemoyer, and Daniel S Weld. 2011. Knowledge-based weak supervision for information extraction of overlapping relations. In *Proceedings of the 49th Annual Meeting of the Association for Computational Linguistics: Human Language Technologies-Volume 1*. Association for Computational Linguistics, pages 541–550.

Kenton Lee, Tom Kwiatkowski, Ankur Parikh, and Dipanjan Das. 2016. Learning recurrent span representations for extractive question answering. *arXiv preprint arXiv:1611.01436* .

Angli Liu, Stephen Soderland, Jonathan Bragg, Christopher H. Lin, Xiao Ling, and Daniel S. Weld. 2016. Effective crowd annotation for relation extraction. In *Proceedings of the 2016 Conference*

---

[7] http://nlp.cs.washington.edu/zeroshot

of the North American Chapter of the Association for Computational Linguistics: Human Language Technologies. Association for Computational Linguistics, San Diego, California, pages 897–906. http://www.aclweb.org/anthology/N16-1104.

Makoto Miwa and Mohit Bansal. 2016. End-to-end relation extraction using lstms on sequences and tree structures. In *Proceedings of the 54th Annual Meeting of the Association for Computational Linguistics (Volume 1: Long Papers)*. Association for Computational Linguistics, Berlin, Germany, pages 1105–1116. http://www.aclweb.org/anthology/P16-1105.

Alvaro Morales, Varot Premtoon, Cordelia Avery, Sue Felshin, and Boris Katz. 2016. Learning to answer questions from wikipedia infoboxes. In *Proceedings of the 2016 Conference on Empirical Methods in Natural Language Processing*. Association for Computational Linguistics, Austin, Texas, pages 1930–1935. https://aclweb.org/anthology/D16-1199.

Jeffrey Pennington, Richard Socher, and Christopher Manning. 2014. Glove: Global vectors for word representation. In *Proceedings of the 2014 Conference on Empirical Methods in Natural Language Processing (EMNLP)*. Association for Computational Linguistics, Doha, Qatar, pages 1532–1543. http://www.aclweb.org/anthology/D14-1162.

P. Rajpurkar, J. Zhang, K. Lopyrev, and P. Liang. 2016. Squad: 100,000+ questions for machine comprehension of text. In *Proceedings of the Conference of the Empirical Methods in Natural Language Processing*.

Sebastian Riedel, Limin Yao, Andrew McCallum, and Benjamin M. Marlin. 2013. Relation extraction with matrix factorization and universal schemas. In *Proceedings of the 2013 Conference of the North American Chapter of the Association for Computational Linguistics: Human Language Technologies*. Association for Computational Linguistics, Atlanta, Georgia, pages 74–84. http://www.aclweb.org/anthology/N13-1008.

Tim Rocktäschel, Sameer Singh, and Sebastian Riedel. 2015. Injecting logical background knowledge into embeddings for relation extraction. In *Proceedings of the 2015 Conference of the North American Chapter of the Association for Computational Linguistics: Human Language Technologies*. Association for Computational Linguistics, Denver, Colorado, pages 1119–1129. http://www.aclweb.org/anthology/N15-1118.

Minjoon Seo, Aniruddha Kembhavi, Ali Farhadi, and Hannaneh Hajishirzi. 2016. Bidirectional attention flow for machine comprehension. *arXiv preprint arXiv:1611.01603* .

Kristina Toutanova, Danqi Chen, Patrick Pantel, Hoifung Poon, Pallavi Choudhury, and Michael Gamon. 2015. Representing text for joint embedding of text and knowledge bases. In *Proceedings of the 2015 Conference on Empirical Methods in Natural Language Processing*. Association for Computational Linguistics, Lisbon, Portugal, pages 1499–1509. http://aclweb.org/anthology/D15-1174.

Patrick Verga, Arvind Neelakantan, and Andrew McCallum. 2017. Generalizing to unseen entities and entity pairs with row-less universal schema. In *Proceedings of the 15th Conference of the European Chapter of the Association for Computational Linguistics: Volume 1, Long Papers*. Association for Computational Linguistics, Valencia, Spain, pages 613–622. http://www.aclweb.org/anthology/E17-1058.

Denny Vrandečić. 2012. Wikidata: A new platform for collaborative data collection. In *Proceedings of the 21st international conference companion on World Wide Web*. ACM, pages 1063–1064.

Zhiguo Wang, Haitao Mi, Wael Hamza, and Radu Florian. 2016. Multi-perspective context matching for machine comprehension. *arXiv preprint arXiv:1612.04211* .

Caiming Xiong, Victor Zhong, and Richard Socher. 2016. Dynamic coattention networks for question answering. *arXiv preprint arXiv:1611.01604* .

The Covert Helps Parse the Overt

Xun Zhang, Weiwei Sun and **Xiaojun Wan**
Institute of Computer Science and Technology, Peking University
The MOE Key Laboratory of Computational Linguistics, Peking University
`{zhangxunah,ws,wanxiaojun}@pku.edu.cn`

Abstract

This paper is concerned with whether deep syntactic information can help surface parsing, with a particular focus on empty categories. We design new algorithms to produce dependency trees in which empty elements are allowed, and evaluate the impact of information about empty category on parsing overt elements. Such information is helpful to reduce the approximation error in a structured parsing model, but increases the search space for inference and accordingly the estimation error. To deal with structure-based overfitting, we propose to integrate disambiguation models with and without empty elements, and perform structure regularization via joint decoding. Experiments on English and Chinese TreeBanks with different parsing models indicate that incorporating empty elements consistently improves surface parsing.

1 Introduction

In the last two decades, there was an increasing interest in producing rich syntactic annotations that are not limited to surface analysis. See, among others, (Callmeier, 2000; Kaplan et al., 2004; Clark and Curran, 2007; Miyao and Tsujii, 2008; Zhang et al., 2016). Such analysis, e.g. deep dependency structures (King et al., 2003), is usually coupled with grammars under deep formalisms, e.g. Combinatory Categorial Grammar (CCG; Steedman, 2000), Head-driven Phrase-Structure Grammar (HPSG; Pollard and Sag, 1994) and Lexical-Functional Grammar (LFG; Bresnan and Kaplan, 1982). Although deep grammar formalisms allow information beyond local construction to be constructed, it is still not clear whether such additional information is helpful for surface syntactic analysis. This is partly because analysis grounded on different grammar formalisms, e.g. HPSG and CFG, are not directly comparable.

In the Government and Binding (GB; Chomsky, 1981) theory, empty category is a key concept bridging S-Structure and D-Structure, due to its possible contribution to trace *movements*. Following the linguistic insights underlying GB, a traditional dependency analysis can be augmented with empty elements, viz. covert elements (Xue and Yang, 2013). See Figure 1 for an example. The new representation provides a considerable amount of deep syntactic information, while keeping intact all dependencies of overt words. Integrating both overt and covert elements in one unified representation provides an effective yet lightweight way to achieve deeper language understanding beyond surface syntax[1]. Even more important, this modest way to modify tree analysis makes possible fair evaluation of the influence of deep syntactic elements on surface parsing.

We study graph-based parsing models for this new representation with a particular focus on the impact of information about the covert on parsing the overt. The major advantage of the graph-based approach to dependency parsing is that its constrained factorization enables the design of polynomial time algorithms for decoding, especially for projective structures. Following GB, an empty element can be only a dependent. Furthermore, the number and distribution of empty elements in one sentence is highly constrained. These properties makes polynomial time decoding for joint empty element detection and dependency parsing still plausible. To exemplify our idea, we design novel second- and third-order algorithms for the

---

[1] In this paper, we arguably call dependencies among overt words only surface analysis.

Proceedings of the 21st Conference on Computational Natural Language Learning (CoNLL 2017), pages 343–353,
Vancouver, Canada, August 3 - August 4, 2017. ©2017 Association for Computational Linguistics

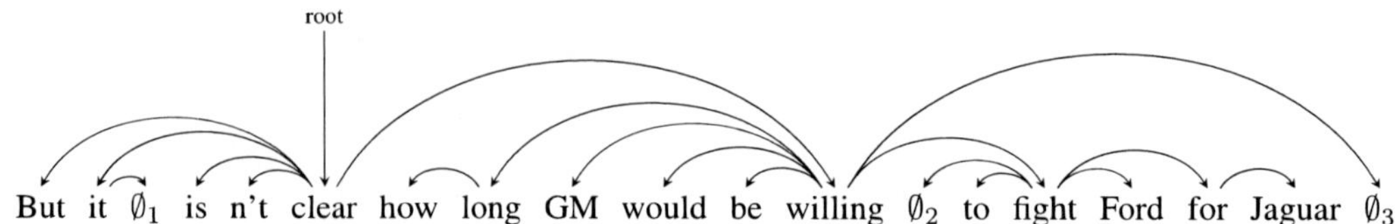

Figure 1: An example from PTB. The dependency structure is according to Stanford Dependency (de Marneffe et al., 2006). "$\emptyset$" denotes an empty element. "$\emptyset_1$" indicates an expletive construction; "$\emptyset_2$" indicates that the subject for *fight*, i.e. *GM*, is located in another place; "$\emptyset_3$" indicates a *wh*-movement.

new problem.

The influence of incorporating empty elements is twofold. On the one hand, the extra information enriches the structural information of the outputs, which is important to reduce the approximation error in a structured prediction problem. On the other hand, predicting empty elements increases the search space for decoding, and thus increases the difficulty of parameter estimation for disambiguation. Our experiments on English Penn TreeBank (PTB; Marcus et al., 1993) and Chinese TreeBank (CTB; Xue et al., 2005) shows that the second effect is prominent. The accuracy of predicting dependencies among overt words sometimes declines slightly.

To ensure that predicting the empty elements helps parse the overt, we need to reduce the new estimation error. To this end, we propose to integrate scores from parsing models with and without empty elements and perform *joint* decoding. The intuition is to leverage parameters estimated without empty elements as a backoff, which exhibit better generalization ability. We evaluate two joint decoders: One is based on chart merging and the other is based on dual decomposition. Experiments demonstrate that information about the covert improves surface analysis in this way. Accuracy evaluated using parsing models with different factorizations and on data sets from different languages is consistently improved. Especially, for those sentences in which there is no empty element, accuracy is improved too. This highlights the fact that empty category can help reduce the approximation error for surface analysis.

The remaining part of the paper is organized as follows. Section 2 is a brief introduction to the problem. Section 3 describes existing algorithms for parsing for overt words only, while Section 4 gives the details of our new algorithms for parsing with empty elements. Section 5 describes the details of the joint models as well as the decoding algorithms. Section 6 presents experimental results and empirical analyses. Section 7 concludes the paper.

2 Syntactic Analysis with Empty Category

In GB, empty categories are an important piece of machinery in representing the syntactic structure of a sentence. An empty category is a covert nominal element that is unpronounced, such as dropped pronouns and traces of dislocated elements. In treebanks, empty categories have been used to indicate long-distance dependencies, discontinuous constituents, and certain dropped elements (Marcus et al., 1993; Xue et al., 2005). Together with labeled brackets and function tags, they make up the full syntactic representation of a sentence.

Empty category is one key concept bridging S-Structure and D-Structure, given that they contain essential information to trace *movements*, i.e. the transformation procedure to convert a D-Structure to an S-Structure. When representing empty categories in dependency trees, we can use a null symbol to depict the idea that there is a mental category at the level being represented. See Figure 1 for an example.

Detecting empty elements is important to the interpretation of the syntactic structure of a sentence. For example, Chung and Gildea (2010) reported preliminary work that has shown a positive impact of automatic empty element detection on statistical machine translation. There are three strategies to find empty categories. Dienes and Dubey (2003) introduced a model that utilizes clues from word forms and POS tags to predict the existence of empty categories. In their method, syntactic parsing was treated as a next-step task and therefore had no influence on finding empty elements. Johnson (2002) and Xue and Yang

(2013) proposed to identify empty categories after syntactic parsing. Different from the above pre-processing strategy, their post-processing models can not use information about empty category to improve parsing. Cai et al. (2011) introduced an integrated model, where empty category detection and phrase-structure parsing are combined in a single model. They, however, did not report any improvement for parsing.[2]

Seeker et al. (2012) evaluted all above strategies to include empty nodes in dependency parsing for German and Hungarian. To predict both empty nodes and dependency relations, they enriched the information encoded in dependency labels. They showed that both pre-processing and integrated strategies failed to leverage empty categories to improve parsing. Especially, their pre-processing method significantly descreased parsing accuracy.

Although empty categories are very important in theory, it is still unclear that they can help parsing in practice.

3 The Existing Parsing Algorithms

Data-driven dependency parsing has received an increasing amount of attention in the past decade. Such approaches, e.g. transition-based (Yamada and Matsumoto, 2003; Nivre, 2008; Andor et al., 2016) and graph-based (McDonald, 2006; Torres Martins et al., 2009; Lei et al., 2014) models have attracted the most attention of dependency parsing in recent years. A graph-based system explicitly parameterizes models over substructures of a dependency tree, and formulates parsing as a Maximum Spanning Tree problem (McDonald et al., 2005). A number of dynamic programming (DP) algorithms have been designed. Here we summarize the design of two widely used algorithms for second- and third-order factorization, since it is the basis of our new algorithms.

3.1 Algorithm 1: Sibling Factorization

Eisner (1996) introduced a widely-used DP algorithm for first-order parsing. Their algorithm includes two interrelated types of DP structures: (1) complete spans, which consist of a head-word and its descendents on one side, and (2) incomplete spans, which consist of a dependency and the region between the head and modifier. To include

---

[2] Comparing their numeric results with other papers', we find that their model does not result in improved parsing.

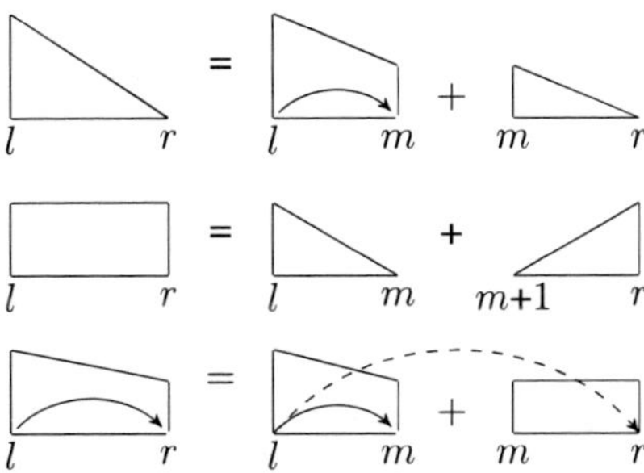

Figure 2: The DP structures and derivations of the standard sibling algorithm. Complete spans are depicted as triangles, incomplete spans as trapezoids, and sibling spans as rectangles. A new dependency is created by applying the last rule. Especially, the score associated with the last rule is determined by a sibling part. For brevity, we elide the right-headed versions.

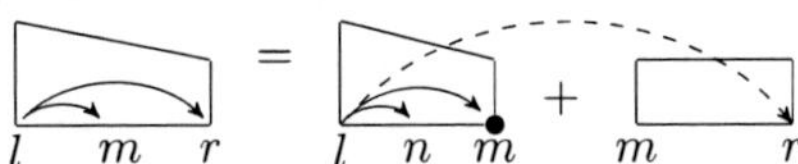

Figure 3: The modified construction rule for the tri-sibling algorithm.

second-order sibling parts, McDonald and Pereira (2006) extended Eisner's algorithm with a third structure, viz. (3) sibling spans, which represent the region between successive modifiers of same head. The second-order algorithm visits all the spans from bottom to top, finding the best combination of smaller structures to form a new one. Each type of span is created by recursively combining two smaller, adjacent spans. The DP structures and their constructions are specified graphically in Figure 2.

3.2 Algorithm 2: Tri-sibling Factorization

It is easy to extend the second-order sibling factorization to parts containing multiple siblings. For example, Koo and Collins (2010) introduced tri-sibling factorization in which a triple of three successive edges on the same side. Here, we consider parsing for tri-sibling factorization only. To this end, we augment the incomplete span structure with an internal index. The modified construction rule is specified graphically in Figure 3. Note that the presentation is slightly different from Koo and Collins's.

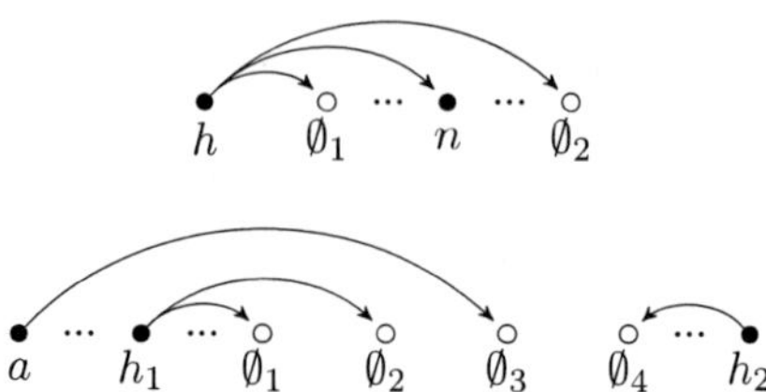

Figure 4: Prototypes of structures related to empty categories.

4 The New Algorithms

We propose three novel algorithms for the new parsing problem. We only consider projective structures. For sake of concision, we call an edge with an empty child empty edge, and call other edges normal ones. Not only normal edges but also empty edges do not cross with each other. We illustrate several properties of empty elements that are fundamental requirements of our algorithms, and then give details of our new algorithms.

4.1 Properties of empty elements

Two theoretical and empirical properties of empty elements results in the design of exact parsing algorithms for simultaneously predicting dependencies as well detecting empty elements.

1. According to GB, an empty element cannot be regarded as a head word.

2. There are very limited number of successive empty elements in between two successive overt words. Therefore, we can treat all successive empty elements governed by same head as one word. We can use the label associated to the corresponding empty edge to distinguish how many empty nodes are there.

According to the first property, we have two prototype structures of empty nodes and their associated edges. If there are two empty elements that are governed by the same head, the overt words in between them must be their siblings or dominated by their siblings. We graphically show this case as the upper figure in Figure 4. If there is a sequence of successive empty elements in between two overt words, the prototype structure is shown as the bottom figure in Figure 4.

Now we consider the emprical coverage of the second property on PTB and CTB. The coverage is evaluated using sentences in the training sets (as defined in Section 6). We show the statistics in Table 1. The length indicates the number of successive empty elements that are governed by the same overt word. At most three empty elements are next to each other.

Length	English	Chinese
1	54800	13115
2	2534	385
3	8	18
Total	57342	13518

Table 1: Coverage relative to the number of successive empty elements that have the same head.

4.2 Algorithm 3: Partial Sibling Model

4.2.1 DP Structures

Now we consider parsing with empty category detection by extending Algorithm 1. We consider six DP structures when we construct a tree with empty elements on a given span $[i, k]$ of vertices. See Figure 5 for graphical visualization. The first two are adapted in concord with Algorithm 1, and we introduce four new DP structures, transformed from incomplete constituent, which can manipulate the empty nodes. These new DP structures are explained below. Without loss of generality, we only illustrate the left-headed versions.

Overt-outside Incomplete Span. The rightmost word must be an overt word.

Overt-both Incomplete Span. Both the rightmost mode and the inner sibling of incomplete spans are overt words. An incomplete span structure is associated with an edge that crosses the whole span. We also care about its left sibling, and thus record it using an extra index. We call this sibling the inner sibling.

Covert-inside Incomplete Span. The rightmost word must be an overt word, while the inner sibling of incomplete span is a covert word.

Covert-ouside Incomplete Span. The rightmost word must be a covert word, while the inner sibling of incomplete span is an overt word.

Note that we already combine all successive empty nodes as one, so there is no *covert-both incomplete span*.

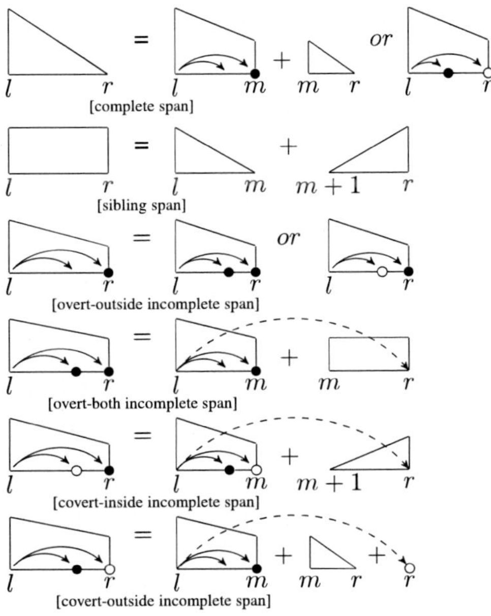

Figure 5: Graphic representations of new DP structures and their derivations of Algorithm 3. For brevity, we elide the right-headed versions.

4.2.2 Construction Rules

Figure 5 provides a graphical specification of the construction of all six DP structures. The following is the explaination for each construction rule.

1. The rightmost child of the head in a complete span may be an empty node. If so, the empty node must located at the boundary, because no empty node can be a head. Therefore a complete span itself is a covert-outside incomplete span. Otherwise, the rightmost child separates the complete span into an overt-outside incomplete span and another smaller complete span.

2. A sibling span is decomposed in the same way to Algorithm 1.

3. An overt-outside incomplete span is the extension of the incomplete span from the old algorithm. We consider two cases according to the type of the inner sibling. So it is either an overt-both or a covert-inside incomplete span.

4. Like a standard incomplete span in Algorithm 1, an overt-both incomplete span is made of an overt-outside incomplete span and a sibling span. A normal edge is created during the construction.

5. A covert-inside incomplete span is built from a covert-outside incomplete span and a complete span in the opposite direction rather than a sibling span. This is because the empty node does not have any child. A normal edge is also created here.

6. A covert-outside incomplete span is made up of an overt-outside incomplete span, an adjacent complete span and a new covert word. In this step, we add a new empty element as well as an empty edge.

4.2.3 Complexity

The set of complete or sibling spans has $O(n^2)$ elements, while the set of each type of incomplete spans has $O(n^2)$ elements. Therefore, the space requirement is of $O(n^2)$. To build a new DP structure in any type, we either change the type of an existing DP structure or search for the best position to separate the whole structure into two parts. The second case is worse and needs time of $O(n^3)$. As a result, Algorithm 3 runs in time of $O(n^3)$.

4.3 Algorithm 4: Full Sibling Model

Now consider the difference between Algorithm 1 and 3. It is easy to figure out that not all sibling factors summed by Algorithm 1 are included by Algorithm 3. Specifically, if two normal edges that are adjacent to each other (say e_1 and e_2) are inserted with an empty edge, e_1 and e_2 are taken as a sibling part by Algorithm 1 but not 3. Now we are going to modify Algorithm 3 to include all such sibling parts. To this end, we modify the covert-inside span structure as well as its the construction rule. In particular, we explictly utilize the index of the inner child provided by a covert-inside span. Figure 6 gives a specification.

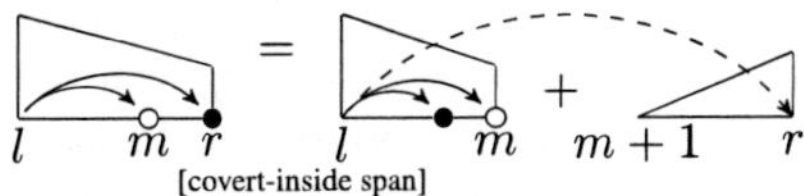

Figure 6: The modified construction rule for overt-both incomplete span in Algorithm 4. For brevity, we elide the right-headed versions.

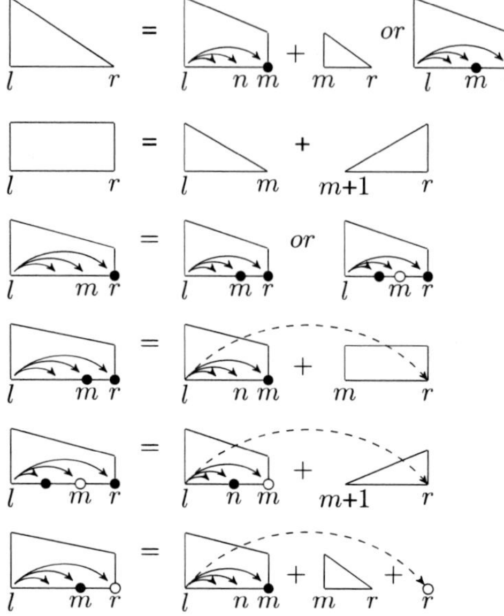

Figure 7: Graphic representations of new DP structures and their derivations of Algorithm 5. For brevity, we elide the right-headed versions.

The modification of the construction rule for the covert-inside incomplete span increases the complexity. The time and space requirements of Algorithm 4 are $O(n^4)$ and $O(n^3)$ respectively, because we must consider the position of the inner sibling, viz. m, in Figure 6.

4.4 Algorithm 5: Partial Tri-sibling Model

Previous work shows that it is relatively easy to extend the second-order sibling factorization to parts containing multiple siblings for standard parsing. It is similar when empty elements are taken into account. Adding the index of one more inner modifier to all incomplete span structures allows tri-sibling features to be calculated. We sketch the idea in Figure 7.

We add one more index to all the four incomplete DP structures in Algorithm 3. The time and space complexity are increased by a factor of $O(n)$. The analysis of the complexity of Algorithm 5 is similar to Algorithm 3. In short, Algorithm 5 runs in time $O(n^4)$ with a space requirement of $O(n^3)$. We can also extend Algorithm 5 to a full version, like what we have done for sibling models. The time complexity will go up to $O(n^5)$, which makes the algorithm somehow impractical.

5 Structure Regularization via Joint Decoding

We can see from the definition of the extended algorithms that the search space for decoding is significantly increased. This results in a side effect for practical parsing. Given the limit of available annotations for training, searching for more complicated structures in a larger space is harmful to the generalization ability in structured prediction (Sun, 2014). Incorporating empty elements significantly increases the difficulty for parameter estimation, and therefore it is harder to find a good disambiguation model. To control structure-based overfitting, we propose a new way to perform structure regularization: combining the two score functions learned from models with and without empty elements.

We formalize the idea as follows. Consider a sentence $s = w_1 w_2 \cdots w_n$. We denote the *index set* of all possible dependencies as $\mathcal{I} = \{(i, j) | i, j \in \{1, \cdots, n\}, i \neq j\}$. A dependency parse then can be represented as a vector

$$\boldsymbol{y} = \{y(i, j) : (i, j) \in \mathcal{I}\}$$

where $y(i, j) = 1$ if there is an arc $i \rightarrow j$ in the graph, 0 otherwise. Let $\mathcal{Y}$ denote the set of all possible $\boldsymbol{y}$. We use another index set $\mathcal{I}' = \{(i, j) | i, j \in \{1, \cdots, n + 1^2\}\}$, where $i > n$ indicates an empty node. Then a dependency parse with empty nodes can be represented as a vector similar to $\boldsymbol{y}$:

$$\boldsymbol{z} = \{z(i, j) : (i, j) \in \mathcal{I}'\}.$$

Let $\mathcal{Z}$ denote the set of all possible $\boldsymbol{z}$. Assume that $f : \mathcal{Y} \rightarrow \mathbb{R}$ and $g : \mathcal{Z} \rightarrow \mathbb{R}$ assign scores to parse trees without and with empty elements. A reasonable model to integrate f and g is to find the optimal parse by solving the following optimization problem:

$$
\begin{aligned}
\text{max.} \quad & \lambda f(\boldsymbol{y}) + (1 - \lambda) g(\boldsymbol{z}) \\
\text{s.t.} \quad & \boldsymbol{y} \in \mathcal{Y}, \boldsymbol{z} \in \mathcal{Z} \\
& y(i, j) = z(i, j), \ \forall (i, j) \in \mathcal{I}
\end{aligned}
\tag{1}
$$

λ is a weight for combining scores. We use the validation data to get an appropriate value for λ[3].

---

[3] Given the similarity of the parsing models with and without empty elements, $\lambda = 0.5$ usually achieves optimal performance.

```
1   $\mathbf{u}^{(0)} \leftarrow 0$
2   for $k \leftarrow 0..T$ do
3       $\mathbf{y} \leftarrow \arg\max_{\mathbf{y} \in \mathcal{Y}}(f(\mathbf{y}) + \sum_{i,j} u(i,j)y(i,j))$
4       $\mathbf{z} \leftarrow \arg\max_{\mathbf{z} \in \mathcal{Z}}(g(\mathbf{z}) - \sum_{i,j} u(i,j)z(i,j))$
5       if $\forall(i,j) \in \mathcal{I}, y(i,j) = z(i,j)$ then
6           return $\mathbf{z}$
7       else
8           $\mathbf{u}^{(k+1)} \leftarrow \mathbf{u}_{(k)} - \alpha^{(k)}(\mathbf{y} - \mathbf{z})$
9   return $\mathbf{z}$
```

Figure 8: Joint decoding based on dual decomposition.

5.1 Chart Merging

The optimization problem (1) can be solved using Algorithm 3 to 5. For example, if we try to combine models coupled with Algorithm 1 and 3, or Algorithm 1 and 4, we can merge the local scores of all sibling parts and then apply Algorithm 4 for solutions. Note that Algorithm 3 here cannot produce the exact solution. If we try to combine models coupled with Algorithm 2 and 5, we can use an algorithm of which the time complexity is $O(n^5)$. We have mentioned such an algorithm at the end of Section 4.4. Similar to sibling factorization, Algorithm 5 can only produce approximate solutions.

5.2 Dual Decomposition

The chart merging method can be applied to algorithms that have highly coherent DP structures. Dual decomposition is an alternative yet more flexible method for solving the optimization problem (1). Heterogeneous models can be combined, and for the majority of input sentences exact solutions can be found in a few iterations. We sketch the solution as follows.

The Lagrangian of (1), i.e. $\mathcal{L}(\mathbf{y}, \mathbf{z}; \mathbf{u})$, is

$$f(\mathbf{y}) + g(\mathbf{z}) + \sum_{(i,j) \in \mathcal{I}} u(i,j)(y(i,j) - z(i,j))$$

where $\mathbf{u}$ is the Lagrangian multiplier. Then the dual is

$$\begin{aligned}
\mathcal{L}(\mathbf{u}) &= \max_{\mathbf{y} \in \mathcal{Y}, \mathbf{z} \in \mathcal{Z}} \mathcal{L}(\mathbf{y}, \mathbf{z}; \mathbf{u}) \\
&= \max_{\mathbf{y} \in \mathcal{Y}}(f(\mathbf{y}) + \sum_{(i,j) \in \mathcal{I}} u(i,j)y(i,j)) \\
&\quad + \max_{\mathbf{z} \in \mathcal{Z}}(g(\mathbf{z}) - \sum_{(i,j) \in \mathcal{I}} u(i,j)z(i,j))
\end{aligned}$$

We instead try to find the solution for $\min_{\mathbf{u}} \mathcal{L}(\mathbf{u})$. By using a subgradient method for this optimiza-

		#{Sent}	#{Overt}	#{Covert}
En	train	38667	909114	57342
	test	2336	54242	3447
Ch	train	8605	193417	13518
	test	941	21797	1520

Table 2: Numbers of sentences, overt and covert elements in training and test sets.

tion problem, we have another joint decoding algorithm, as shown in Figure 8.

6 Experiments

6.1 Data Sets

We conduct experiments on both English and Chinese treebanks. In particular, PTB and CTB are used. Because PTB and CTB are phrase-structure treebanks, we need to convert them into dependency annotations. To do so, we use the tool provided by Stanford CoreNLP to process PTB, and the tool provided by Xue and Yang (2013) to process CTB 5.0. We use gold-standard POS to derive features for disambiguation.

To simpify our experiments, we preprocess the obtained dependency tree in the following way.

1. We combine successive empty elements with identical head into one new empty node which is still linked to the common head word.

2. Because the high-order algorithm spends is very expensive, we only use relatively short sentence. Here we only keep sentences less than 64 tokens.

3. We focus on unlabeled parsing.

The statistics of the data after cleaning is shown in Table 2

We use standard training, validation, and test splits to facilitate comparisons. Accuracy is measured with unlabeled attachment score for all overt words (UAS_o): the percentage of overt words with the correct head. We are also concerned with the prediction accuracy for empty elements. To evaluate performance on empty nodes, we consider the correctness of empty edges. We report the percentage of empty words in right slot with correct head. The i-th slot in the sentence means that the position immediately after the i-th concrete word. So if we have a sentence with length n, we get $n+1$ slots.

$f_{\mathrm{uni}}(X)$:

$X.w$, $Y.p$, $X.w \circ X.p$

$f_{\mathrm{bi}}(X, Y)$:

$X.wp \circ Y.w$, $X.wp \circ Y.p$, $X.w \circ Y.wp$, $X.p \circ Y.wp$, $X.wp \circ Y.wp$

$f_{\mathrm{context}}(X, Y)$:

$X.p \circ Y.p \circ X_1.p \circ Y_{-1}.p$, $X.p \circ Y.p \circ X_{-1}.p \circ Y_{-1}.p$, $X.p \circ Y.p \circ X_1.p \circ Y_1.p$, $X.p \circ Y.p \circ X_{-1}.p \circ Y_1.p$

$X.p \circ Y.p \circ Z.p$, Z is token between X and Y

$f_{\mathrm{sib}}(X, Y)$:

$X.w \circ Y.w$, $X.w \circ Y.p$, $X.p \circ Y.w$, $X.p \circ Y.p$

$f_{\mathrm{sib}}(X, Y, Z)$:

$X.p \circ Y.p \circ Z.p$

$f_{\mathrm{tsib}}(X, Y, Z, W)$:

$X.w \circ Y.w \circ Z.p \circ W.p$, $X.w \circ Y.p \circ Z.w \circ W.p$, $X.w \circ Y.p \circ Z.p \circ W.w$, $X.p \circ Y.w \circ Z.w \circ W.p$, $X.p \circ Y.w \circ Z.p \circ W.w$, $X.p \circ Y.p \circ Z.w \circ W.w$, $X.w \circ Y.p \circ Z.p \circ W.p$, $X.p \circ Y.w \circ Z.p \circ W.p$, $X.p \circ Y.p \circ Z.w \circ W.p$, $X.p \circ Y.p \circ Z.p \circ W.w$

Table 3: Feature template functions.

6.2 Statistical Disambiguation

In the context of data-driven parsing, we still need an extra disambiguation model for building a practical parser. As with many other parsers, we employ a global linear model. To estimate parameters, we utilize the averaged perceptron algorithm (Collins, 2002). Developing features has been shown crucial to advancing the state-of-the-art in dependency parsing. We adopt features from previous work.

We refer to the head/child of the arc as h/c, the k-th inner split point as m_k, and the grand point as g. We list features selected by different algorithm as follows, and all following features should be concatenated with direction and distance of the arc.

- arc features: $f_{\mathrm{uni}}(h)$, $f_{\mathrm{uni}}(c)$, $f_{\mathrm{bi}}(h, c)$, $f_{\mathrm{context}}(h, c)$.

- sibling features: $f_{\mathrm{sib}}(c, m_0)$, $f_{\mathrm{sib}}(h, c, m_k)$.

- tri-sibling features: $f_{\mathrm{sib}}(h, c, m_1)$, $f_{\mathrm{tsib}}(h, c, m, m_1)$.

6.3 Results of Individual Models

Table 4 lists the accuracy of individual models coupled with different decoding algorithms on the test sets. We focus on the prediction for overt

Algo	English	Chinese
1	91.73	89.16
3	91.70 (-0.03)	89.20 ($+0.04$)
4	91.72 (-0.01)	89.28 ($+0.12$)
2	92.23	90.00
5	92.41 ($+0.18$)	89.82 (-0.18)

Table 4: UAS_o of different individual models on test data. The upper and bottom blocks present results obtained by sibling and tri-sibling models respectively.

	Algo	English	Chinese
CM	1+3	91.94 ($+0.21$)	89.53 ($+0.37$)
	1+4	91.88 ($+0.15$)	89.44 ($+0.28$)
DD	1+3	91.96 ($+0.23$)	89.53 ($+0.37$)
	1+4	91.94 ($+0.21$)	89.53 ($+0.37$)
CM	2+5	92.60 ($+0.37$)	90.35 ($+0.35$)
DD	2+5	92.71 ($+0.48$)	90.38 ($+0.38$)

Table 5: UAS_o of different joint decoding models on test data. "CM" and "DD" are short for joint decoders based on chart merging and dual decomposition respectively. The upper and bottom blocks present results obtained by sibling and tri-sibling models respectively. All improvements are statistically significant.

words only. Models coupled with Algorithm 1, 3 and 4 are second-order models, while with 2 and 5 third-order ones. When we take into account empty categories, more information is available. The empirical results suggest that deep linguistic information does not necessarily help surface analysis.

6.4 Results of Joint Decoding

Table 5 lists the accuracy of different joint decoding models on the test sets. We can see that the joint decoding framework is effective to deal with structure-based overfitting. This time, the accuracy of analysis for overt words is consistently improved across a wide range of conditions. Especially, the third-order model is improved more. We use the Hypothesis Tests method (Berg-Kirkpatrick et al., 2012) to evaluate the improvements. When the *p-value* is set to 0.05, all improvements in Figure 5 is statistically significant.

We separate all sentences in test data set into two subsets: One contains sentences that have no

	English		Chinese	
Algo	−EC	+EC	−EC	+EC
3	92.50	91.53	90.92	88.60
1+3	92.83	91.77	91.12	88.97
4	92.82	91.48	91.29	88.58
1+4	92.84	91.74	91.10	88.98
5	93.68	92.13	92.00	89.06
2+5	93.99	92.43	92.10	89.77

Table 6: UAS_o evaluated using different types of sentences. Dual decomposition is used for joint decoding.

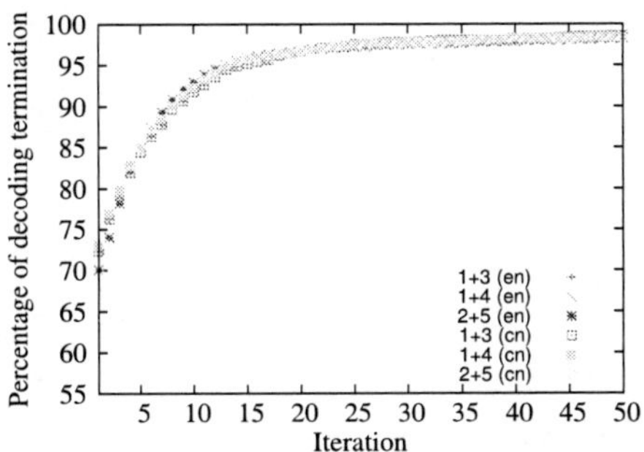

Figure 9: The exact decoding rate on development data.

empty elements and the other contains other sentences. The accuracy evaluated on the two sets are summarized in Table 6. For those sentences in which there is no empty element, accuracy is improved as well. This indicates that empty category can help reduce the approximation error for surface analysis.

6.5 Efficiency of Joint Decoding

One thing worth noting is that the chart merging method with an approximate decoder is comparable to other more complex solutions that produce exact or nearly exact results. Chart merging with approximate decoders only modifies scores assigned to secord- or third-order parts, while keeping intact the decoding procedure. As a result, the efficiency of approximate chart merging is comparable to individual models.

Dual decomposition-based joint decoder iteratively calls individual decoders. Due to the similarity of models with and without empty elements, this iteration procedure usually terminates very fast. We calculate the percentage of finding exact decoding below k iterations, and the result is show in Figure 9. For most sentences, dual decomposition practically gives the exact solutions in a few iterations. One advantage relevant is that such a decoder can integrate parsing models that are somehow heterogeneous. Refer to (Koo et al., 2010) for example.

7 Discussion and Conclusion

Can deep syntactic information help surface parsing, which is the mainstream focus of NLP research. In this paper, we investigate this topic under the umbrella of Transformational Grammar, GB in particular. We focused on empty category augmented dependency analysis. We demonstrate that on the one hand deep information helps reduce the approximation error for traditional (surface) parsing, while on the other hand traditional parsing helps reduce the estimation error for deep parsing. Coupling surface and deep information in an appropriate way is able to produce better syntactic analysis. A natural avenue for further research would be the integrating parsing models under deep and shallow grammar formalisms.

In addition to empty category detection, empty categories should be linked to an overt element if possible. Take the second empty element in Figure 1 for example. The information about its existance is valuable, but knowing it acturally refers to *GM* is more helpful. However, adding such coreference information makes the syntactic representation no long trees and thus brings along new challenges for designing algorithms. How to deal with empty category detection and resolution in one unified model? It would be an interesting topic for future investigation.

Acknowledgments

This work was supported by 863 Program of China (2015AA015403), NSFC (61331011), and Key Laboratory of Science, Technology and Standard in Press Industry (Key Laboratory of Intelligent Press Media Technology). Weiwei Sun is the corresponding author.

References

Daniel Andor, Chris Alberti, David Weiss, Aliaksei Severyn, Alessandro Presta, Kuzman Ganchev, Slav Petrov, and Michael Collins. 2016. Globally normalized transition-based neural networks. In *Proceedings of the 54th Annual Meeting of the Association for Computational Linguistics (Volume 1: Long Papers)*. Association for Computational

Linguistics, Berlin, Germany, pages 2442–2452. http://www.aclweb.org/anthology/P16-1231.

Taylor Berg-Kirkpatrick, David Burkett, and Dan Klein. 2012. An empirical investigation of statistical significance in nlp. In *Proceedings of the 2012 Joint Conference on Empirical Methods in Natural Language Processing and Computational Natural Language Learning*. Association for Computational Linguistics, Jeju Island, Korea, pages 995–1005. http://www.aclweb.org/anthology/D12-1091.

J. Bresnan and R. M. Kaplan. 1982. Introduction: Grammars as mental representations of language. In J. Bresnan, editor, *The Mental Representation of Grammatical Relations*, MIT Press, Cambridge, MA, pages xvii–lii.

Shu Cai, David Chiang, and Yoav Goldberg. 2011. Language-independent parsing with empty elements. In *Proceedings of the 49th Annual Meeting of the Association for Computational Linguistics: Human Language Technologies*. Association for Computational Linguistics, Portland, Oregon, USA, pages 212–216. http://www.aclweb.org/anthology/P11-2037.

Ulrich Callmeier. 2000. Pet. a platform for experimentation with efficient hpsg processing techniques. *Journal of Natural Language Engineering* 6(1):99–108.

Noam Chomsky. 1981. *Lectures on Government and Binding*. Foris Publications, Dordecht.

Tagyoung Chung and Daniel Gildea. 2010. Effects of empty categories on machine translation. In *Proceedings of the 2010 Conference on Empirical Methods in Natural Language Processing*. Association for Computational Linguistics, Cambridge, MA, pages 636–645. http://www.aclweb.org/anthology/D10-1062.

Stephen Clark and James R. Curran. 2007. Wide-coverage efficient statistical parsing with CCG and log-linear models. *Computational Linguistics* 33(4):493–552. https://doi.org/10.1162/coli.2007.33.4.493.

Michael Collins. 2002. Discriminative training methods for hidden markov models: Theory and experiments with perceptron algorithms. In *Proceedings of the 2002 Conference on Empirical Methods in Natural Language Processing*. Association for Computational Linguistics, pages 1–8. https://doi.org/10.3115/1118693.1118694.

Marie-Catherine de Marneffe, Bill MacCartney, and Christopher D. Manning. 2006. Generating typed dependency parses from phrase structure parses. In *IN PROC. INT' L CONF. ON LANGUAGE RESOURCES AND EVALUATION (LREC*. pages 449–454.

Pétr Dienes and Amit Dubey. 2003. Deep syntactic processing by combining shallow methods. In *Proceedings of the 41st Annual Meeting of the Association for Computational Linguistics*. Association for Computational Linguistics, Sapporo, Japan, pages 431–438. https://doi.org/10.3115/1075096.1075151.

Jason M. Eisner. 1996. Three new probabilistic models for dependency parsing: an exploration. In *Proceedings of the 16th conference on Computational linguistics - Volume 1*. Association for Computational Linguistics, Stroudsburg, PA, USA, pages 340–345.

Mark Johnson. 2002. A simple pattern-matching algorithm for recovering empty nodes and their antecedents. In *Proceedings of 40th Annual Meeting of the Association for Computational Linguistics*. Association for Computational Linguistics, Philadelphia, Pennsylvania, USA, pages 136–143. https://doi.org/10.3115/1073083.1073107.

Ron Kaplan, Stefan Riezler, Tracy H King, John T Maxwell III, Alex Vasserman, and Richard Crouch. 2004. Speed and accuracy in shallow and deep stochastic parsing. In Daniel Marcu Susan Dumais and Salim Roukos, editors, *HLT-NAACL 2004: Main Proceedings*. Association for Computational Linguistics, Boston, Massachusetts, USA, pages 97–104.

Tracy Holloway King, Richard Crouch, Stefan Riezler, Mary Dalrymple, and Ronald M. Kaplan. 2003. The PARC 700 dependency bank. In *In Proceedings of the 4th International Workshop on Linguistically Interpreted Corpora (LINC-03)*. pages 1–8.

Terry Koo and Michael Collins. 2010. Efficient third-order dependency parsers. In *Proceedings of the 48th Annual Meeting of the Association for Computational Linguistics*. Association for Computational Linguistics, Uppsala, Sweden, pages 1–11. http://www.aclweb.org/anthology/P10-1001.

Terry Koo, Alexander M. Rush, Michael Collins, Tommi Jaakkola, and David Sontag. 2010. Dual decomposition for parsing with non-projective head automata. In *Proceedings of the 2010 Conference on Empirical Methods in Natural Language Processing*. Association for Computational Linguistics, Cambridge, MA, pages 1288–1298. http://www.aclweb.org/anthology/D10-1125.

Tao Lei, Yu Xin, Yuan Zhang, Regina Barzilay, and Tommi Jaakkola. 2014. Low-rank tensors for scoring dependency structures. In *Proceedings of the 52nd Annual Meeting of the Association for Computational Linguistics (Volume 1: Long Papers)*. Association for Computational Linguistics, Baltimore, Maryland, pages 1381–1391. http://www.aclweb.org/anthology/P14-1130.

Mitchell P. Marcus, Mary Ann Marcinkiewicz, and Beatrice Santorini. 1993. Building a large annotated corpus of english: the penn treebank. *Computational Linguistics* 19(2):313–330. http://dl.acm.org/citation.cfm?id=972470.972475.

Ryan McDonald. 2006. *Discriminative learning and spanning tree algorithms for dependency parsing*. Ph.D. thesis, University of Pennsylvania, Philadelphia, PA, USA.

Ryan McDonald and Fernando Pereira. 2006. Online learning of approximate dependency parsing algorithms. In *Proceedings of 11th Conference of the European Chapter of the Association for Computational Linguistics (EACL-2006)).* volume 6, pages 81–88.

Ryan McDonald, Fernando Pereira, Kiril Ribarov, and Jan Hajic. 2005. Non-projective dependency parsing using spanning tree algorithms. In *Proceedings of Human Language Technology Conference and Conference on Empirical Methods in Natural Language Processing*. Association for Computational Linguistics, Vancouver, British Columbia, Canada, pages 523–530.

Yusuke Miyao and Jun'ichi Tsujii. 2008. Feature forest models for probabilistic hpsg parsing. *Computational Linguistics* 34(1):35–80. https://doi.org/10.1162/coli.2008.34.1.35.

Joakim Nivre. 2008. Algorithms for deterministic incremental dependency parsing. *Computational Linguistics* 34:513–553. https://doi.org/http://dx.doi.org/10.1162/coli.07-056-R1-07-027.

Carl Pollard and Ivan A. Sag. 1994. *Head-Driven Phrase Structure Grammar*. The University of Chicago Press, Chicago.

Wolfgang Seeker, Richárd Farkas, Bernd Bohnet, Helmut Schmid, and Jonas Kuhn. 2012. Data-driven dependency parsing with empty heads. In *Proceedings of COLING 2012: Posters*. The COLING 2012 Organizing Committee, Mumbai, India, pages 1081–1090. http://www.aclweb.org/anthology/C12-2105.

Mark Steedman. 2000. *The syntactic process*. MIT Press, Cambridge, MA, USA.

Xu Sun. 2014. Structure regularization for structured prediction. In Z. Ghahramani, M. Welling, C. Cortes, N. D. Lawrence, and K. Q. Weinberger, editors, *Advances in Neural Information Processing Systems 27*, Curran Associates, Inc., pages 2402–2410. http://papers.nips.cc/paper/5563-structure-regularization-for-structured-prediction.pdf.

Andre Torres Martins, Noah Smith, and Eric Xing. 2009. Concise integer linear programming formulations for dependency parsing. In *Proceedings of the Joint Conference of the 47th Annual Meeting of the ACL and the 4th International Joint Conference on Natural Language Processing of the AFNLP*. Association for Computational Linguistics, Suntec, Singapore, pages 342–350. http://www.aclweb.org/anthology/P/P09/P09-1039.

Naiwen Xue, Fei Xia, Fu-dong Chiou, and Marta Palmer. 2005. The penn Chinese treebank: Phrase structure annotation of a large corpus. *Natural Language Engineering* 11:207–238. https://doi.org/10.1017/S135132490400364X.

Nianwen Xue and Yaqin Yang. 2013. Dependency-based empty category detection via phrase structure trees. In *Proceedings of the 2013 Conference of the North American Chapter of the Association for Computational Linguistics: Human Language Technologies*. Association for Computational Linguistics, Atlanta, Georgia, pages 1051–1060. http://www.aclweb.org/anthology/N13-1125.

Hiroyasu Yamada and Yuji Matsumoto. 2003. Statistical dependency analysis with support vector machines. In *The 8th International Workshop of Parsing Technologies (IWPT2003)*. pages 195–206.

Xun Zhang, Yantao Du, Weiwei Sun, and Xiaojun Wan. 2016. Transition-based parsing for deep dependency structures. *Computational Linguistics* 42(3):353–389. http://aclweb.org/anthology/J16-3001.

German in Flux:
Detecting Metaphoric Change via Word Entropy

Dominik Schlechtweg[*†]**, Stefanie Eckmann**[‡]**, Enrico Santus**[◇]**,**
Sabine Schulte im Walde[*]**, Daniel Hole**[†]

[*]Inst. for Natural Language Processing, University of Stuttgart, Germany
[†]Dept. of Linguistics/German Studies, University of Stuttgart, Germany
[‡]Historical and Indo-European Linguistics, LMU Munich, Germany
[◇]Singapore University of Technology and Design, Singapore
`dominik.schlechtweg@gmx.de, stefanie.eckmann@campus.lmu.de,`
`esantus@mit.edu, schulte@ims.uni-stuttgart.de, holedan@gmail.com`

Abstract

This paper explores the information-theoretic measure entropy to detect metaphoric change, transferring ideas from hypernym detection to research on language change. We also build the first diachronic test set for German as a standard for metaphoric change annotation. Our model shows high performance, is unsupervised, language-independent and generalizable to other processes of semantic change.

1 Introduction

Recently, computational linguistics has shown an increasing interest in language change. This interest is focused on making semantic change measurable. However, even though different types of semantic change are well-known in historical linguistics, little effort has been made to distinguish between them. A very basic distinction in historical linguistics is the one between *innovative meaning change* (also polysemization)— e.g., German *brüten* 'breed' > 'breed, brood over sth.'—and *reductive meaning change*—e.g., German *schinden* 'to skin, torture' > 'to torture' (cf. Koch, 2016, p. 24–27). Metaphoric meaning change is an important sub-process of innovative meaning change. Hence, a computational model of semantic change should be able to distinguish metaphoric change from other—typically less strong—types of change. Such a model, particularly if applicable to different languages, would be beneficial for a number of areas: (i), historical linguists may test their theoretical claims about semantic change on a large-scale empirical basis going beyond the traditional corpus-based approaches; (ii), linguists and psychologists working on metaphor in language or cognition may

benefit by gaining new insights into the diachronic aspects of metaphor which are not yet as central in these fields as the synchronic aspects; and, finally, (iii), the Natural Language Processing research community may benefit by applying the model presented here to a wide range of tasks in which polysemy and non-literalness are involved.

Our aim is to build an unsupervised and language-independent computational model which is able to distinguish metaphoric change from semantic stability. We apply *entropy* (a measure of uncertainty inherited from information theory) to a *Distributional Semantic Model* (DSM). In particular, we exploit the idea of *semantic generality* applied in hypernym detection, to detect metaphoric change as a special process of meaning innovation. German will serve as a sample language, since there is a rich historical corpus available covering a large time period. Nevertheless, our model is presumably applicable to other languages requiring only minor adjustments. With the model, we introduce the first resource for evaluation of models of metaphoric change and propose a structured annotation process that is generalizable to the creation of gold standards for other types of semantic change.[1]

In the next section, we give an overview of related work on semantic change and automatic detection of metaphor. In Section 3, the basic linguistic notions we focus on are introduced and connected to their distributional properties, followed by a description of the corpus used to obtain vector representations of words in Section 4. In Section 5, the information-theoretic measures we apply to word vectors are described. Section 6 presents the annotation study conducted to create a

---

[1]The test set is provided together with the annotation data and the model code (which is based on Shwartz et al. (2016)'s code): `https://github.com/Garrafao/MetaphoricChange`

354

metaphoric change test set for German. Section 7 illustrates how the measures' predictions shall be evaluated. The results are presented and discussed in Section 8. Section 9 will then conclude and give a short outlook to further research objectives.

2 Related Work

There is a number of recent approaches to trace semantic change via distributional methods. This includes mainly (i), semantic *similarity models* assuming one sense for each word and then measuring its spatial displacement by a similarity metric (such as cosine) in a semantic vector space (Gulordava and Baroni, 2011; Kim et al., 2014; Xu and Kemp, 2015; Eger and Mehler, 2016; Hellrich and Hahn, 2016; Hamilton et al., 2016a,b) and (ii), *word sense induction models* (WSI) inferring for each word a probability distribution over different word senses (or topics) in turn modeled as a distribution over words (Wang and Mccallum, 2006; Bamman and Crane, 2011; Wijaya and Yeniterzi, 2011; Lau et al., 2012; Mihalcea and Nastase, 2012; Frermann and Lapata, 2016).

Most of the similarity models seem to be limited to quantify the degree of overall change rather than being able to qualify different types of semantic change.[2] Similarity metrics, in particular, were shown not to distinguish well between words on different levels of the semantic hierarchy (Shwartz et al., 2016). Thus, we cannot expect diachronic similarity models to reflect changes in the semantic generality of a word over time, which was described to be a central effect of semantic change (cf. Bybee, 2015, p. 197). Additionally, they often pose the problem of vector space alignment (especially when relying on word embeddings), occurring when word vectors from different time periods have to be mapped to a common coordinate axis (cf. Hamilton et al., 2016b, p. 1492).

Diachronic WSI models, on the contrary, are able to detect at least innovative (and reductive) meaning change, as they are designed to induce newly arising senses of words. However, they do not measure how these senses relate to each other in terms of semantic generality. Hence, ad hoc, they may not be able to distinguish different subtypes of innovative meaning change such as metaphoric vs. metonymic change. They may fail

to detect meaning changes where no new senses can be induced as, e.g., in grammaticalization. Moreover, some models require elaborate training (e.g., Frermann and Lapata, 2016).

Apart from similarity and WSI models, Sagi et al. (2009) measure semantic broadening and narrowing of words (shifting upwards and downwards in the semantic taxonomy respectively) via *semantic density* calculated as the average cosine of its context word vectors. Just as word entropy, semantic density is based on the measurement of linguistic context dispersion (see Section 3.1). However, this method is only applied in a case study with very limited scope in terms of the number of phenomena covered and there is no verification of the test items via annotation. Hence, it remains to be shown that the method can generally distinguish broadening and narrowing or other types of meaning innovation.

Two previous approaches to language change exploit the notion of entropy. Juola (2003) describes language change on a very general level by computing the relative entropy (or KL-divergence) of language stages, i.e. intuitively speaking, measuring how well later stages of English encode a prior stage. Kisselew et al. (2016) are interested in the diachronic properties of conversion using— among other measures—a word entropy measure.

Finally, research on synchronic metaphor identification has applied a wide range of approaches, including binary classification relying on standard distributional similarity (Birke and Sarkar, 2006), text cohesion measures (Li and Sporleder, 2009), classification relying on abstractness cues (Turney et al., 2011; Köper and Schulte im Walde, 2016) or cross-lingual information (Tsvetkov et al., 2014), and soft clustering (Shutova et al., 2013), among others. As to our knowledge, no previous work has explicitly exploited the idea of generalization (via hypernymy models) in metaphor detection yet.

3 Metaphoric Change

Metaphoric change plays a fundamental role in semantic change (cf. e.g. Ferraresi, 2014, p. 15). Within the framework of Conceptual Metaphor Theory (Lakoff and Johnson, 1980) the metaphorical effect can be described as a mapping from a source domain to a target domain. Following the terminology from Koch (2016, p. 24) *innovative meaning change*, as opposed to *reductive meaning change*, is where the existing meaning M_A (the

---

[2]With the exception of Hamilton et al. (2016a, p. 1) making the rather coarse-grained distinction between cultural shift and "regular processes of linguistic drift".

source concept) of a word acquires a new meaning M_B (the target concept). *Metaphoric Change* is, then, a subcategory of innovative meaning change where M_B is related to M_A by similarity or a reduced comparison (cf. Koch, 2016, p. 47, and also Steen, 2010, p. 10). While language is often used ad hoc in a non-literal meaning in discourse, not every of these uses constitutes an instance of metaphoric change. Only when a metaphoric innovation is conventionalized within the language, we can speak of metaphoric meaning change (cf. Koch, 2016, p. 27). Consider German *umwälzen* as an example. In Early New High German the word was only used in the sense 'to turn around something or someone physically' (M_A) as in (1).[3] In Contemporary New High German, though, the word is also frequently used in the sense 'to change something (possibly abstract) radically' (M_B) as in (2).

(1) *...muß ich mich **vmbweltzen** / vnd kan keinen schlaff in meine augen bringen* [4]

'...I have to turn around and cannot bring sleep into my eyes.'

(2) *Kinadon wollte den Staat **umwälzen**...* [5]

'Kinadon wanted to revolutionize the state...'

3.1 Distributional Properties

As Bybee (2015) notes, and is also commonly agreed-upon, "metaphorical meaning changes create *polysemy*" (p. 199, her italics). Campbell (1998, p. 258) describes this effect as "extensions in the meaning of a word" occurring through metaphoric change. It is only logical to assume that such extensions in meaning range imply an extension in the range of linguistic contexts a word occurs in. This extension, then, distinguishes words undergoing such a change from semantically stable words, but also from words undergoing different types of meaning change such as reductive meaning change where we expect an oppositional effect: a reduction of the range of contexts a word occurs in. Polysemization (and thus context extension) is, yet, not only a typical property of metaphoric change but of all types of innovative meaning change such as *metonymic change*, *generalization*, *specialization*, and *grammaticalization* (cf. Heine and Kuteva, 2007, p. 35). However,

recall that metaphor involves a mapping between two different domains (as introduced in Lakoff and Johnson 1980) in contrast to other types of meaning change, which is why we would expect a relatively strong effect on the contextual distribution here.

Moreover, not only the range of a word's meanings influences the range of contexts it occurs in, but also the particular nature of the individual meanings has an influence. As research in hypernymy detection shows, words at different levels of semantic generality have different distributional properties (Rimell, 2014; Santus et al., 2014; Shwartz et al., 2016). According to the *distributional informativeness hypothesis*, semantically more general words are less informative than special words as they occur in more general contexts (Rimell, 2014; Santus et al., 2014). Hence, differences in *semantic generality* of source and target concept should be reflected by their contextual distribution.[6] Such differences occur particularly with taxonomic meaning changes like generalization and specialization, but also with metaphoric change, as it often results in the emergence of more abstract meanings of a word. Consider, e.g., the development of German *glänzend* with 'luminous' as source and 'very good' as target concept. The source concept only applies to a rather limited range of entities, i.e., physical ones. The target concept, on the contrary, given its abstractness, applies to nearly every entity. Interpreting such changes of words as a change in their semantic generality, we now aim to examine how well it is measurable with distributional methods.

4 Corpus

For our investigation, we use the corpus of *Deutsches Textarchiv (erweitert)* (DTA), which is accessible online and downloadable for free.[7] The DTA provides more than 2447 lemmatized and POS-tagged texts (with more than 140M tokens), covering a time period from the late 15th to the early 20th century. Thus, it covers the developments of German from (late) Early New High German to Contemporary New High German. The corpus is POS-tagged using the STTS tagset (Schiller et al., 1999). The texts used by DTA include literary and scientific texts as well as

---

[3]Early New High German: ca. 1350-1650; Contemporary New High German: 1650-today (cf. Fleischer, 2011, p. 24)

[4]Neomenius, J.: Christliche Leichpredigt. Brieg, 1616.

[5]Müller, K. O.: Die Dorier. Vier Bücher. Bd. 2, 1824.

[6]Related ideas are also indicated, e.g., by Fortson (2003, p. 650) and Bybee (2015, p. 202).

[7]`http://www.deutschestextarchiv.de/`

functional writings, e.g., cookbooks. DTA aims at providing a corpus with a roughly equivalent number of texts from each of the aforementioned genres. The corpus is preprocessed in standard ways. (Find details in Appendix A.) For the creation of the co-occurrence matrices, from which we calculate word entropy and the other measures, a standard model of distributional semantics with a symmetric window of size 2 is used.

5 Entropy

In hypernym detection a number of well-established measures compare the semantic generality of words on the basis of their distributional generality (Weeds and Weir, 2003; Clarke, 2009; Kotlerman et al., 2009). A promising candidate measure seems to be *word entropy*, which is introduced in Santus (2013) and Santus et al. (2014). Amongst other advantages, word entropy is independently measurable over time, which avoids the problem of vector space alignment.

5.1 Entropy in Information Theory

The term 'Entropy' was first introduced by Shannon (1948) who laid the foundations of information theory. Intuitively, it measures the unpredictability of a system. The entropy H of a discrete random variable X with possible values $\{x_1, ..., x_n\}$ and probability mass function $P(X)$ (a probability distribution) is

$$H(X) = -\sum_{i=1}^{n} P(x_i) \log_b P(x_i) \quad (3)$$

where b is typically equal to 2 or 10 (Shannon, 1948, cf. p. 11).

Word Entropy. Examining language statistically, a word w may be represented by its distribution in a corpus. This distribution is determined by the contexts of w, i.e., the words it co-occurs with, and how often it co-occurs with them. The distribution of w is usually recorded in a matrix, intuitively a table where rows correspond to target word distributions and columns to context word distributions. Rows are typically referred to as *vectors* and the whole matrix spans a *vector space*. We can interpret w's (normalized) vector then as a probability distribution where word co-occurrences of w with any other corpus word w' correspond to events in the probability distribution. More specifically, assuming that C and T are

discrete random variables of occurrences of context and target words respectively, we say that w's vector estimates the conditional probability distribution of context words given target word w with discrete random variable C and a probability mass function defined by $P(C \mid T = w)$. For every $c \in C$, $P(c \mid w)$ (the probability that the context word c will occur given the occurrence of w as target word) is estimated by $\frac{Freq(w,c)}{Freq(w)}$.[8] Now, we can apply any notion from probability theory to this distribution. Hence, the entropy of w's probability distribution is given by

$$H(C) = -\sum_{i=1}^{n} P(c_i \mid w) \log_2 P(c_i \mid w) \quad (4)$$

The entropy of w's estimated probability distribution—for the sake of convenience we will just write $H(w)$—measures the unpredictability of w's co-occurrences, i.e., how hard it is to predict with which word w will co-occur if we look at a random occurrence of w. In hypernym detection, word entropy is assumed to reflect semantic generality. While here it is mostly used to compare pairs of different words for their semantic relations, e.g., whether one is the hypernym of the other, we will compare the word entropy of one and the same word w in different time periods assuming this to reflect w's semantic development with respect to its generality.

Normalization

Depending on corpus size and other factors, the frequency of each target word will vary strongly. On top of that, the number of types in the corpus increases with the progression of time. These factors influence word entropy (and also other measures) without being tied to semantic change. Hence, we need a way to normalize for them. We test essentially two ways of normalizing word entropy for word frequency:

Matching Occurrence Number (MON). The first strategy assumes that, for the most part, the influence of word frequency on word entropy comes from the increasing number of context types with increasing number of contexts n used to construct a word vector (where n is dependent on word frequency). Hence, we can suppress the influence of word frequency by comparing only word vectors

---

[8]For convenience, here, we do not distinguish between a word and the mathematical structure corresponding to the event of the occurrence of the word.

constructed from an equal number of contexts (cf. Kisselew et al., 2016). In order to make the vectors of all target words from all time periods comparable, we choose a common number of contexts n for all target words. Additionally, in order to diminish the influence of chance (because we do not use all contexts, we have to pick a random subset), we average over the entropies computed for a number of k vectors, each constructed from a different n-sized set of contexts. (Find information on the setting of hyperparameters in Appendix A.)

Ordinary Least Squares Regression (OLS). Another way of normalizing entropy for frequency relies on the observation that there is a correlation between word entropy and word frequency. We try to approximate this relationship by fitting an OLS model to the observations from the corpus, where each observed word type is a data point. This approximation can then serve as a prediction for the expected change of a word's entropy given a certain change in the word's frequency. Deviations from this expectation can further be interpreted as the change in entropy solely related to semantic generality. In order to get a good approximation for each target word we only fit the model to the local n data points next to the target word in the independent variable (frequency). In Figure 1 we see the result of fitting the model described by Equation 5 to the 1000 data points (from a specific time period) next to the data point for the adjective *locker*, 'loose', in the independent variable. As we can see, the data point for *locker* slightly deviates from the regression curve, more precisely, by $\Delta = 0.136$. Taking this as a starting point for the semantic development of *locker* (reference time) we can now calculate *locker*'s Δ in a later time period (focus time). We assume that Δ stays approximately equal if only *locker*'s frequency changes. If Δ, however, increases, we assume that the word underwent meaning innovation. We apply an analogous procedure to all target words.

$$entropy \sim \alpha + \beta \ln(frequency) \qquad (5)$$

5.2 Other Measures

Word Frequency. Concerning frequency, a similar argument can be brought forward as in Section 3.1: When a word acquires a new meaning and can be applied to a wider range of entities, then we would expect the word to be used more often. Furthermore, it is well known that certain types

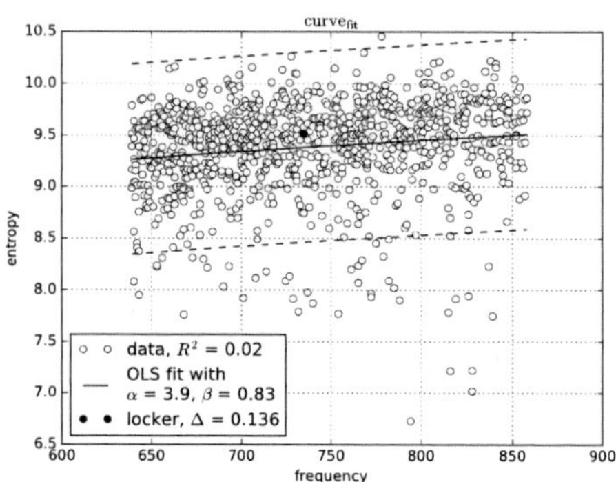

Figure 1: Example of OLS for *locker*

of semantic change correlate with frequency. For instance, *desemanticization* comes with a strong increase in frequency (cf. Bybee, 2015, p. 133). For this, we use the frequency of a word w as a baseline to word entropy (parallel to the practice in hypernym detection). In order to diminish the influence of corpus size we normalize word frequency $Freq(w)$ by the number of tokens N in the relevant slice of the corpus:

$$Freq_n(w) = \frac{Freq(w)}{N} \qquad (6)$$

Second-Order Word Entropy. A variant of word entropy used in hypernym detection is second-order word entropy where entropy is not calculated directly for the word w, but rather for its most-associated context words. Then the median of these is w's second-order word entropy (cf. Santus et al., 2014, p. 40). This measure relies on the hypothesis that the more semantically general a word is, the more it co-occurs with general context words. Presumably, this measure is more immune to the influence of word frequency, because not w's own frequency plays a role, but rather the frequency of its most-associated context words. This may be helpful where we have rather accidental differences in the frequency of a word in different time periods, e.g., due to corpus size or text sort. In such a setting we reckon regular (first-order) word entropy to be more prone to these accidental factors than second-order word entropy.

6 Diachronic Metaphor Annotation

Humans often have different intuitions about what is a metaphor and what is not. According to

Steen (2010, p. 2) "the identification of metaphoric language has become a matter of controversy". Therefore, we did not want to rely solely on our own intuitions, but identify metaphoric change of words via annotation. A number of structured annotation guidelines for synchronic metaphor identification have been proposed (Pragglejaz Group, 2007; Steen, 2010; Shutova, 2015). Steen (cf. 2010, p. 8) distinguishes between linguistic and conceptual metaphor annotation. We adopted the former approach, since we were less interested in the exact mapping underlying a metaphoric use of a word. The crucial difference to synchronic metaphor identification is that we did not want annotators to judge individual uses but pairs of uses of lexical units.[9] The metaphoric relation between the source and the target concept involved in the metaphoric change of a word w should be reflected in w's individual uses which is a common methodological assumption in historical linguistics. Individual uses bearing the meaning of source or target concept allow humans to infer these meanings which can then be judged as being (non-)metaphorical to each other. We operationalize this observation as annotation procedure.

Target Selection. We preselected the target items for annotation so that they were likely to have undergone metaphoric change. For this, we scanned the literature on metaphoric change in German such as Fritz (2006) and Keller and Kirschbaum (2003). The richest list we found in Paul (2002) (ca. 140 items). However, this could not be taken directly as a gold standard. We first checked for every item whether we could attest metaphoric change in the corpus. If so, we determined a rough date of change according to when we found the metaphoric meaning clearly established in the corpus. We then checked whether the item had an occurrence frequency above a threshold of 40 around the date of change. Only then the item was added to the test set for annotation.[10]

For every metaphoric target word m in the test set we added a semantically stable word s with the same POS-tag from the same frequency area. For this, we checked the words in the immediate vicinity to m in the total frequency rank (of the first half of the century in which m's change oc-

curred) in DWDS, a rich online etymological dictionary of German.[11] If there was no meaning change indicated and we could not attest a clear meaning change in the corpus, we added the word to the test set. Thereby, we balanced metaphoric and stable words with respect to frequency. Stable words comprise concrete words, e.g. *Palast* 'palace', as well as more abstract words, e.g. *freundlich* 'friendly'. The test set contains nouns, verbs and adjectives. (Find it in Appendix C.)

Next, parallel to the corpus slicing (see Section 7), we selected 20 contexts from two time periods. These periods were set in such a way that one was located before and one after the pre-identified date of change. Supposing that a word occurs in n contexts in a certain time period, we ordered them according to publication date and picked every $(n/20)^{\text{th}}$ context guaranteeing that contexts are well-distributed over authors and the time period. Contexts with less than 10 words and obvious parsing errors were excluded in order to provide enough information for the annotators and to avoid contexts excluded by them.

Finally, contexts from the earlier period were combined randomly with contexts from the later period yielding 20 context pairs for every target. The order of every second pair was switched, minimizing the possibility that annotators infer the chronology of contexts. The pairs of all 28 target words were randomly sampled such that individual judgments were less influenced by earlier judgments of the same target, resulting in 560 context pairs presented to the annotators.

Annotation Procedure. Three annotators were asked to judge for each of the 560 context pairs whether one of the contexts admitted inference of a meaning of the target word which is related metaphorically to the meaning in the other context. (Find an example in Appendix B.) The annotators were linguists, two of them were marginally acquainted with historical linguistics. The annotation guidelines are a combination and modification of the processes described by Pragglejaz Group (2007), Steen (2010) and Shutova (2015). Whether a meaning of a target word in context 2 (M2) is metaphorically related to the meaning in context 1 (M1) should be identified in 3 steps:

1. For each word its meaning in context is established;

---

[9] A similar procedure is used in Erk et al. (2009, 2013) for annotation of usage similarity.

[10] We provide both: the full list of items and the one filtered for frequency.

[11] https://dwds.de/

2. It is decided whether M1 can be seen as a more basic meaning than M2. This is the case when M2 is related to M1 in one or more of the following ways: (i), M2 is less concrete than M1; (ii), M2 is less human-oriented than M1; (iii), M2 is not related to bodily action in contrast to M1; (iv), M2 is less precise than M1.

3. If this is the case, then it is decided whether M2 contrasts with M1 but can be understood in comparison with it. If yes, M2 is judged as being metaphorically related to M1, otherwise as not being metaphorically related to M1.

Step 2 is intended to exclude cases of non-metaphorical polysemy, for which a more basic meaning should not be identifiable (cf. Pragglejaz Group, 2007, p. 30). It is a rather liberal variation of the existing guidelines in that already the fact that one of the criteria holds is sufficient to consider M1 to be more basic than M2. This is because of cases like *Feder*, 'feather, springclip', *Blatt*, 'leaf, sheet, newspaper', and *Haube*, 'cap, cover, marriage, crest', whose meaning change would else not be captured, although we reckon it metaphoric: The change of *Feder* 'feather' > 'feather, springclip' does not fall under all criteria in step 2, e.g., there is no mapping from concrete to abstract. The existing guidelines seem to implicitly exclude such cases of metaphors, which we want to overcome. Future studies may opt for different decisions here.

Step 3 guarantees that the two meanings identified are sufficiently distinct and that there can be a mapping established between them. We cannot guarantee that annotators judge the context pairs in exactly the way we prescribe in the guidelines. (Find the full guidelines in Appendix B.)

Annotation Results. Annotators reported that they found the task hard, which is not surprising given that some contexts dated back 400 years making it sometimes difficult to interpret them. Accordingly, we expected this to be reflected in the inter-annotator agreement. Annotator 1 and Annotator 2 had a moderate agreement of $\kappa = .40$ (Fleiss' Kappa) for earlier and .46 for later contexts, while Annotator 3 had poor agreement with both, Annotator 1 (.26, .26) and Annotator 2 (.32, .29). Given this deviation, we excluded Annotator 3 from the evaluation. (Further evaluation is performed for the judgments of Annotator 1 and Annotator 2.) The agreement we found is only slightly lower than in comparable synchronic studies. Pragglejaz Group (2007, p. 21), e.g., report a κ between 0.56 and 0.72 for different tasks. We can attribute the difference in agreement to the higher level of difficulty of the task the annotators were faced with.

The annotation results are summarized in Table 1. Target words are ordered decreasingly according to the increase in metaphorically tagged contexts over time (last column). In addition to κ we also give the share of items with perfect agreement ($\%A$), since κ underestimates agreement on rare effects (Feinstein and Cicchetti, 1990). As you can see, the annotators overall confirmed our judgments of the targets, as most metaphoric targets are at the top of the list. Target words differ strongly in the strength of metaphoric change assigned to them: between 82% (*Donnerwetter*) and -14% (*Haube*). Yet, most targets exhibit positive judgment, which we would expect from a test set containing metaphoric and stable targets. Striking is the position of *Feder* and *Haube* at the bottom, which are tagged even negatively metaphoric. This means that the share of metaphorically tagged contexts was higher for the earlier contexts. We conjecture that the reason for this is that both words were already used in other metaphoric meanings in earlier contexts. The high position of *freundlich* and *fett* presumably results from the fact that they are abstract adjectives. Metaphor identification for adjectives is more difficult than for nouns and verbs, because their meanings tend to be less concrete and precise (cf. Pragglejaz Group, 2007, p. 28). They are typically applicable to a wider range of entities, increasing the probability to encounter a context pair in our study with two uses differing in abstractness and preciseness. We will pay particular attention to the targets rated differently by us and the annotators in the analysis of the measures' predictions.

7 Evaluation

As with Gulordava and Baroni (2011) or Hamilton et al. (2016b), we assess the measures' performance by comparing their predictions in a corpus against a gold standard. Our gold standard is the rank of target words in Table 1 obtained by annotation. We obtain the measures' predictions for the target words by first calculating their values in a

lexeme	type	earlier contexts				later contexts				$\Delta\%+$
		time	%+	%A	κ	time	%+	%A	κ	
Donnerwetter	met	1700-1800	.00	1.00	-	1850-1926	.82	.85	.57	.82
peinlich	met	1600-1700	.00	.80	-.11	1800-1900	.67	.60	.17	.67
glänzend	met	1600-1700	.06	.85	.31	1800-1900	.63	.95	.89	.57
erhaben	met	1600-1700	.12	.85	.49	1800-1900	.55	.55	.14	.43
geharnischt	met	1700-1800	.00	.95	-.03	1850-1926	.42	.95	.90	.42
freundlich	sta	1600-1700	.07	.70	.10	1800-1900	.38	.65	.35	.31
fett	sta	1600-1700	.08	.65	.06	1800-1900	.27	.55	.17	.20
flott	met	1700-1800	.00	.85	.72	1850-1926	.20	.75	.59	.20
Blatt	met	1500-1600	.00	.75	-.10	1700-1800	.17	.60	.16	.17
Rausch	met	1600-1700	.00	.85	.50	1800-1900	.15	.65	.36	.15
locker	met	1700-1800	.11	.90	.70	1850-1926	.23	.65	.30	.12
ausstechen	met	1600-1700	.10	1.00	1.00	1800-1900	.21	.95	.86	.11
eitel	met	1600-1700	.00	.35	-.27	1800-1900	.11	.45	-.07	.11
ahnen	sta	1600-1700	.00	.70	.20	1800-1900	.09	.55	.11	.09
brüten	met	1600-1700	.11	.90	.66	1800-1900	.19	.80	.48	.08
erdenklich	sta	1700-1800	.00	.60	-.25	1850-1926	.06	.80	.22	.06
aufwecken	sta	1600-1700	.24	.85	.62	1800-1900	.27	.75	.43	.03
stillschweigend	sta	1700-1800	.07	.75	.13	1850-1926	.08	.60	-.07	.02
bewachsen	sta	1700-1800	.00	.85	-.08	1850-1926	.00	1.00	-	.00
Palast	sta	1700-1800	.00	.80	-.11	1850-1926	.00	.80	-.11	.00
Fenchel	sta	1600-1700	.00	.95	-.03	1800-1900	.00	1.00	-	.00
Wohngebäude	sta	1700-1800	.00	.95	-.03	1850-1926	.00	1.00	-	.00
adelig	sta	1600-1700	.08	.65	.11	1800-1900	.07	.70	.10	-.01
Evangelium	sta	1500-1600	.05	.95	.64	1700-1800	.00	.90	-.05	-.05
Unhöflichkeit	sta	1600-1700	.05	.95	.64	1800-1900	.00	.65	-.21	-.05
heil	sta	1600-1700	.13	.40	-.01	1800-1900	.00	.50	.03	-.13
Feder	met	1700-1800	.28	.90	.76	1850-1926	.13	.75	.28	-.14
Haube	met	1600-1700	.20	.75	.37	1800-1900	.06	.90	.44	-.14
all	-	-	.06	.80	.40	-	.20	.74	.46	.14

Table 1: Annotation results divided into judgments for earlier and later contexts. %+ contains the share of metaphorically tagged items in all items for the respective target word on which there was perfect agreement. %A gives the share of items with perfect agreement and κ the Fleiss' Kappa score for all annotators. The last column, $\Delta\%+$, contains the relative increase or decrease in metaphorically tagged items over time calculated by $(\%+_{later}) - (\%+_{earlier})$. Rows are ordered decreasingly according to the values in $\Delta\%+$.

time period 1 before the starting point of change and in a time period 2 after that. We then compute the difference d in values between period 1 and 2 for each target word and further rank the target words according to d. Next, we compute the rank correlation between each of these predicted ranks and the gold rank as a performance measure.

Time period 1 is usually the century before and period 2 the century after the century of change, e.g., *ausstechen* (1739) will be compared in 1600-1700 and 1800-1900. (Only for targets from 1800-1900 time period 2 is different, i.e., 1850-1926, since the corpus version we use only contains texts until 1926.) Stable words are compared in the same time periods as their metaphoric counterparts (see Section 6). With this procedure we have the possibility to evaluate the measures (i), only on targets from the same century, fixing influential side factors such as corpus size, and (ii), on all targets, which is a much harder task. (Find a list of time periods with corpus sizes in Appendix A.)

8   Results

Table 2 shows Spearman's ρ quantifying the correlation between the measures' predicted ranks and the gold standard rank. We can directly see that word entropy (H) correlates significantly with the gold rank in different conditions. Moreover, the ranking it predicts for targets from 1700-1800 correlates much stronger (.64) with the gold rank than the other measures' predictions. Note that the correlation is highly significant despite the relatively small sample size. In the harder condition, where we look at the ranks across different time periods, H still correlates significantly and stronger than all other measures with the gold rank. However, apart from H, the conclusions we can draw about the other measures can only be preliminary, as there is no significance for their predicted ranks.

At first glance, the normalized versions of entropy do not perform as expected: H_{MON} never outperforms frequency and shows even negative correlation in one time period. Since we reckoned that the reason for this is the low setting of the hyperparameter $n = 29$ (which we adopted with the intention to construct all vectors from a common number of contexts), we also tested the measure on target words from 1700-1800 with a setting of n such that the maximum number of contexts is used to construct the word vector and the number of vectors to average over $k = 10$. In this setting H_{MON}'s prediction has a highly significant correlation with the gold rank which is comparable in strength to H.

Notably, H_{OLS} has the best performance for targets from 1800-1900. We tried out different hyperparameter settings and found that our initial choice of the data window size $n = 1000$ may also not have been optimal, as higher n yield better, yet non-significant, results: $n = 500/10000/20000/50000$ yields $\rho = 0.19/0.32/0.31/0.21$ respectively, for targets from 1700-1800. Another factor possibly biasing H_{OLS} are different variances in different corpora or frequency areas which may also connect to our observation that the measure correlates negatively with absolute changes in frequency, i.e., decrease in frequency often leads to increase in H_{OLS} and vice versa.

H^2 consistently performs poorly. Moreover, testing of different values for N yields a wide range of ρ values between -0.29 and 0.42 for targets from 1700-1800, not allowing conclusions on the performance of the measure because the correlation is not significant.

Analyzing the predicted ranks reveals interesting insights. H and its normalized siblings rank *Donnerwetter*, which is at the top of the gold rank, at the very bottom. This is, presumably, because in its later metaphoric sense 'blowup' the word can be used as an interjection in very short sentences as in (7).

(7) *Potz Donnerwetter!* [12]

    'Man alive!'

This narrows down *Donnerwetter*'s contextual distribution due to our model only considering words within a sentence as context. H^2 and frequency are not sensitive to this and rank the word much higher. This shows that, (i), different factors play a role in determining the contextual distribution of a word suggesting that a model of semantic change should incorporate different types of information and, (ii), that H^2 and frequency may still be helpful in detecting metaphoric change in certain settings. The dominance of H may also be a hint to this direction: Word entropy combines frequency and contextual distribution as it is influenced by both.

Feder and *Haube* from the very bottom of the gold rank are not beyond the bottom-items of any measure's prediction. In H's prediction, which is the best-performing measure, they rank near the middle (12, 18). This indicates that their position at the bottom of the gold rank may not accurately reflect the semantic change they underwent. Similarly for the adjectives *freundlich* and *fett* ranking in all predictions near middle or lower (for H: 18, 10). We still have to assess how these words behave in future studies.

	1600-1700	1700-1800	1800-1900	all
H	1.00	.64***	.10	**.39***
H_{MON}	1.00	.19	-.10	.06
H_{OLS}	1.00	.20	.29	.26
H^2	1.00	.06	.02	.13
$Freq_n$	1.00	.29	-.07	.26

Table 2: Summary of the predictions of word entropy (H), H normalized via MON (H_{MON}), H normalized via OLS (H_{OLS}), second-order word entropy (H^2) and normalized frequency ($Freq_n$) for the respective subset of target words from our test set for each time period. Values in cells refer to Spearman's rank correlation coefficient ρ between the individual measure's predicted rank and the relevant subrank from the annotated gold standard (Table 1).

9 Conclusion

Semantic generality is an important indicator of semantic change. As Bybee (cf. 2015, p. 197) puts it, generalization and specialization are two basic principles of meaning change. We proposed a

---

[12]Hauptmann, Gerhart: Der Biberpelz. Berlin, 1893.

way to detect metaphoric change based on semantic generality and built a test set for the evaluation of computational models of metaphoric change in German. We proposed an annotation procedure strictly derived from comparable synchronic work and showed that annotators can show reasonable agreement. Different distributional measures based on the information-theoretic concept of entropy were compared against the annotators judgments and it was found that raw word entropy correlates strongly and significantly with the gold rank in different settings in contrast to most other entropy measures and frequency. We found evidence that H_{MON} predicts well with certain parameter settings.

Both, the annotation procedure and the computational model, are generalizable to different types of semantic change. Moreover, our model is unsupervised and language-independent as it relies, in principle, on minimal linguistic input, since entropy can be computed already from a raw token co-occurrence matrix. Yet, the model profits from richer input as indicated in Shwartz et al. (2016).

Future studies should test how well word entropy distinguishes metaphoric change from other types of meaning innovation and how well it detects innovative and reductive meaning change in general. The latter may be tested straightforwardly on the English data of Gulordava and Baroni (2011) and Hamilton et al. (2016b). In doing so, it will be interesting to see how our model performs in comparison to diachronic similarity and WSI models.

Acknowledgments

We thank Prof. Dr. Sebastian Padó (Institute for Natural Language Processing, University of Stuttgart) for pointing out his idea to normalize word entropy via OLS. We are very grateful to Prof. Dr. Olav Hackstein (Historical and Indo-European Linguistics, LMU Munich) and his research colloquium for valuable discussions and comments and to Sascha Schlechtweg for statistical advice. We would like to thank Andrew Wigman for careful proof-reading as well as Jörg Förstner, Michael Frotscher, Altina Mujkic, Edona Neziri, Cornelia van Scherpenberg, Christian Soetebier and Veronika Vasileva for help related to the annotation process. Last but not least, we thank the reviewers for constructive criticism helping us to improve the paper substantially.

References

D. Bamman and G. Crane. 2011. Measuring Historical Word Sense Variation. In *Proceedings of the 11th Annual International ACM/IEEE Joint Conference on Digital Libraries*. ACM, New York, NY, USA, JCDL '11, pages 1 – 10.

Julia Birke and Anoop Sarkar. 2006. A Clustering Approach for the Nearly Unsupervised Recognition of Nonliteral Language. In *Proceedings of the 11th Conference of the European Chapter of the ACL*. Trento, Italy, pages 329–336.

Joan L. Bybee. 2015. *Language change*. Cambridge University Press, Cambridge, United Kingdom.

L. Campbell. 1998. *Historical Linguistics: An Introduction*. Edinburgh University Press.

Daoud Clarke. 2009. Context-theoretic semantics for natural language: an overview. In *Proceedings of the Workshop on Geometrical Models of Natural Language Semantics*. Association for Computational Linguistics, Athens, Greece, pages 112–119.

Steffen Eger and Alexander Mehler. 2016. On the linearity of semantic change: Investigating meaning variation via dynamic graph models. In *Proceedings of the 54th Annual Meeting of the Association for Computational Linguistics, ACL 2016, August 7-12, 2016, Berlin, Germany, Volume 2: Short Papers*.

Katrin Erk, Diana McCarthy, and Nicholas Gaylord. 2009. Investigations on word senses and word usages. In *In Proceedings of ACL-09*.

Katrin Erk, Diana McCarthy, and Nicholas Gaylord. 2013. Measuring word meaning in context. *Computational Linguistics* 39(3):511–554.

A. R. Feinstein and D. V. Cicchetti. 1990. High agreement but low Kappa: I. The problems of two paradoxes. *Journal of Clinical Epidemiology* 43(6):543 – 549.

Gisella Ferraresi. 2014. *Grammatikalisierung*. Kurze Einführungen in die germanistische Linguistik. Winter, Heidelberg.

J. Fleischer. 2011. *Historische Syntax des Deutschen*. Narr, Tübingen.

Benjamin Fortson. 2003. *The Handbook of Historical Linguistic*, Blackwell, Oxford, chapter An Approach to Semantic Change, pages 648–666. The Handbook of Historical Linguistics.

Lea Frermann and Mirella Lapata. 2016. A bayesian model of diachronic meaning change. *TACL* 4:31–45.

Gerd Fritz. 2006. *Historische Semantik*. Metzler, Stuttgart/Weimar.

K. Gulordava and M. Baroni. 2011. A distributional similarity approach to the detection of semantic change in the Google Books Ngram corpus. In *Proceedings of GEMS*.

W. L. Hamilton, J. Leskovec, and D. Jurafsky. 2016a. Cultural Shift or Linguistic Drift? Comparing Two Computational Measures of Semantic Change. In *Emnlp*.

W. L. Hamilton, J. Leskovec, and D. Jurafsky. 2016b. Diachronic Word Embeddings Reveal Statistical Laws of Semantic Change. *CoRR* abs - 1605 - 09096.

Bernd Heine and Tania Kuteva. 2007. *The Genesis of Grammar: A Reconstruction*. Oxford University Press.

J. Hellrich and U. Hahn. 2016. Bad Company—Neighborhoods in Neural Embedding Spaces Considered Harmful. *Proceedings of COLING 2016* pages 2785 – 2796.

Patrick Juola. 2003. The Time Course of Language Change. *Computers and the Humanities* 37(1):77–96.

R. Keller and I. Kirschbaum. 2003. *Bedeutungswandel: eine Einführung*. De Gruyter Studienbuch. De Gruyter.

Y. Kim, Y.-I. Chiu, K. Hanaki, D. Hegde, and S. Petrov. 2014. Temporal Analysis of Language through Neural Language Models. *ArXiv e-prints* .

Max Kisselew, Laura Rimell, Alexis Palmer, and Sebastian Pado. 2016. Predicting the direction of derivation in english conversion. In *Proceedings of the 14th SIGMORPHON Workshop on Computational Research in Phonetics, Phonology, and Morphology*. Berlin, Germany.

Peter Koch. 2016. Meaning change and semantic shifts. In Maria Koptjevskaja-Tamm Pänivi Juvonen, editor, *The Lexical Typology of Semantic Shifts*, De Gruyter Mouton.

Maximilian Köper and Sabine Schulte im Walde. 2016. Distinguishing Literal and Non-Literal Usage of German Particle Verbs. In *Proceedings of the Conference of the North American Chapter of the Association for Computational Linguistics: Human Language Technolog ies*. San Diego, California, USA, pages 353–362.

Lili Kotlerman, Ido Dagan, Idan Szpektor, and Maayan Zhitomirsky-Geffet. 2009. Directional distributional similarity for lexical expansion. In *Proceedings of the ACL-IJCNLP 2009 Conference Short Papers*. Association for Computational Linguistics, Stroudsburg, PA, USA, ACLShort '09, pages 69–72.

G. Lakoff and M. Johnson. 1980. *Metaphors We Live By*. Phoenix books. University of Chicago Press.

J. H. Lau, P. Cook, D. McCarthy, D. Newman, and T. Baldwin. 2012. Word Sense Induction for Novel Sense Detection. In *Proceedings of the 13th Conference of the European Chapter of the Association for Computational Linguistics*. Association for Computational Linguistics, Stroudsburg, PA, USA, EACL '12, pages 591 – 601.

Linlin Li and Caroline Sporleder. 2009. Classifier Combination for Contextual Idiom Detection Without Labelled Data. In *Proceedings of the Conference on Empirical Methods in Natural Language Processing*. Singapore, pages 315–323.

R. Mihalcea and V. Nastase. 2012. Word Epoch Disambiguation: Finding How Words Change Over Time. In *Proceedings of the 50th Annual Meeting of ACL.*

H. Paul. 2002. *Deutsches Wörterbuch: Bedeutungsgeschichte und Aufbau unseres Wortschatzes.* Niemeyer, Tübingen, 10 edition.

Pragglejaz Group. 2007. MIP: A method for identifying metaphorically used words in discourse. *Metaphor and Symbol* 22:1–39.

Laura Rimell. 2014. Distributional lexical entailment by topic coherence. In *Proceedings of the 14th Conference of the European Chapter of the Association for Computational Linguistics, EACL 2014, April 26-30, 2014, Gothenburg, Sweden.* pages 511–519.

E. Sagi, S. Kaufmann, and B. Clark. 2009. Semantic Density Analysis: Comparing Word Meaning Across Time and Phonetic Space. In *Proceedings of the Workshop on Geometrical Models of Natural Language Semantics*. Association for Computational Linguistics, Stroudsburg, PA, USA, GEMS '09, pages 104 – 111.

Enrico Santus. 2013. SLQS: An entropy measure. Unpublished Master Thesis, University of Pisa.

Enrico Santus, Alessandro Lenci, Qin Lu, and Sabine Schulte Im Walde. 2014. Chasing hypernyms in vector spaces with entropy. In *Proceedings of the 14th Conference of the European Chapter of the Association for Computational Linguistics, volume 2: Short Papers*. pages 38–42.

Anne Schiller, Simone Teufel, Christine Stöckert, and Christine Thielen. 1999. Guidelines für das Tagging deutscher Textcorpora mit STTS. Technical report, Institut für maschinelle Sprachverarbeitung, Stuttgart.

Claude E. Shannon. 1948. *A Mathematical Theory of Communication*. CSLI Publications.

E. Shutova. 2015. *Annotation of Linguistic and Conceptual Metaphor*, Springer.

Ekaterina Shutova, Simone Teufel, and Anna Korhonen. 2013. Statistical Metaphor Processing. *Computational Linguistics* 39(2):301–353.

V. Shwartz, E. Santus, and D. Schlechtweg. 2016. Hypernyms under Siege: Linguistically-motivated Artillery for Hypernymy Detection. *CoRR* abs - 1612 - 04460.

G. Steen. 2010. *A Method for Linguistic Metaphor Identification: From MIP to MIPVU.* Converging evidence in language and communication research. John Benjamins Publishing Company.

Yulia Tsvetkov, Leonid Boytsov, Anatole Gershman, Eric Nyberg, and Chris Dyer. 2014. Metaphor Detection with Cross-Lingual Model Transfer. In *Proceedings of the 52nd Annual Meeting of the Association for Computational Linguistics*. Baltimore, Maryland, pages 248–258.

Peter Turney, Yair Neuman, Dan Assaf, and Yohai Cohen. 2011. Literal and Metaphorical Sense Identification through Concrete and Abstract Context. In *Proceedings of the Conference on Empirical Methods in Natural Language Processing*. Edinburgh, UK, pages 680–690.

X. Wang and A. Mccallum. 2006. Topics over time: A non-Markov continuous-time model of topical trends. In *In SIGKDD*.

Julie Weeds and David Weir. 2003. A general framework for distributional similarity. In *EMNLP*. pages 81–88.

D. T. Wijaya and R. Yeniterzi. 2011. Understanding Semantic Change of Words over Centuries. In *Proceedings of the 2011 International Workshop on DEtecting and Exploiting Cultural diversiTy on the Social Web*. ACM, New York, NY, USA, DETECT '11, pages 35–40.

Y. Xu and C. Kemp. 2015. A Computational Evaluation of Two Laws of Semantic Change. In *Proceedings of the 37th Annual Meeting of the Cognitive Science Society, CogSci 2015, Pasadena, California, USA, July 22-25, 2015.*

A Hyperparameters and Corpus Preprocessing Details

A.1 Hyperparameters

Second-order word entropy has 3 hyperparameters: (i), the number of positively associated contexts N to compute the average/median from; (ii), whether to use median or average entropy among the top N contexts;[13] and (iii), the association metric used to sort the contexts by relevance (i.e., PPMI or PLMI). We choose the following combination of hyperparameters: $\langle 100, \text{median}, \text{PLMI} \rangle$,

---

[13]Note that for any test pair, N is the *maximal* number of associated contexts, which is reduced to M if a test target has only M ($< N$) positively associated contexts in one of the two matrices to compare.

which is suggested by the work of Shwartz et al. (2016).

For MON entropy normalization we choose $n = 29$, because that is the lowest context number of a word in one of its two relevant time periods, and $k = 10000$. For OLS normalization we choose $n = 1000$.

A.2 Corpus Preprocessing

Words that occur less than 5 times in the whole corpus, functional words and punctuation are deleted. As functional words we regard those which are not tagged with a POS-tag starting with either 'N', 'V' or 'AD'. Every token is then replaced by its lemma form combined with the starting of its POS-tag, e.g., *geht* is replaced by *gehen:V*. Note that both diachronic lemmatization and POS-tagging are provided by DTA.

time period	1500-1600	1600-1700	1700-1800	1800-1900	1850-1926
corpus size	0.2M	13M	23M	34M	23M

Table 3: Time periods for evaluation and their respective corpus sizes after preprocessing.

B Annotation Guidelines

B.1 Introduction

Following the terminology from Koch (cf. 2016, p. 24) *innovative meaning change*, as opposed to *reductive meaning change*, is where the existing meaning M_A of a word acquires a new meaning M_B, where this normally happens over a long period of time.

Metaphoric Change is, then, a subcategory of innovative meaning change (besides metonymic change, generalization...) where M_B is related to M_A by similarity or a reduced comparison Koch (cf. 2016, p. 47). (cf. also Steen, 2010, p. 10)

Note that the annotation process described below is a combination and modification of the processes described by Pragglejaz Group (2007), Steen (2010) and Shutova (2015).

B.2 Annotation Process

You will be given an OpenOffice table document with approximately 560 lines. In every line you will see in columns 2 and 3 two uses of a word (the target word contained in column 1) with its surrounding contexts. The relevant word is marked in bold font in both contexts.

1. For each such use of a word establish its meaning in context, that is, how it applies to an entity, relation, or attribute in the situation evoked by the text (contextual meaning). Take into account what comes before and after the word. Note that the word might be used differently from what you are familiar with. Don't let yourself be confused by alternative spelling.

2. Try to find an interpretation where the meaning in the second context (M2) is related to the meaning in the first context (M1) in one or more of the following ways:

   - M2 is less concrete than M1 (what it evokes is harder to imagine, see, hear, feel, smell, and taste);
   - M2 is less human-oriented than M1;
   - M2 is not related to bodily action in contrast to M1;
   - M2 is less precise than M1 (precise as opposed to vague).

3. If M2 is indeed related to M1 in one or more of these ways, decide whether M2 contrasts with M1 but can be understood in comparison with it. (See below for an example.)

4. (i) If yes, <u>fill in 1</u> into the column headed by 'M2 is metaphorically related to M1', judging M2 as <u>being metaphorically related to M1</u>.

   (ii) If no, <u>fill in 0</u> into the column headed by 'M2 is is metaphorically related to M1', judging M2 as <u>not being metaphorically related to M1</u>.

   (iii) If you cannot decide, e.g., because the word marked in bold font doesn't match the word shown in column 1 in meaning or part of speech, you don't understand either of the contexts, one is too unspecific or other reasons, don't perform evaluation, <u>fill in a 1 into the comments column</u> and go on to the next test item.

5. Compare the two meanings in the other direction, i.e., decide whether M1 is metaphorically related to M2 by going through steps 2 to 4 and fill your judgment into the column headed by 'M1 is metaphoric compared to M2'.

Please make sure that you don't change anything in the file apart from column width, your
judgments and comments. Finally, return the annotated document to the above-mentioned email
address. If you have any further questions on the
task, don't hesitate to ask.

B.3 Annotation Example

The following example illustrates how the procedure operates in practice. Consider Table 4 as an
example table similar to the one you will receive
for annotation.

In line 1 you need to compare two uses of the
word *umwälzen*. In context 1 *umwälzen* is used in
the sense 'to turn around something or someone
physically' (M1). This contrasts with its use in
context 2 where it is used in the sense 'to change
something radically' (M2). M2 is clearly less concrete than M1 and not necessarily related to bodily action. Moreover, M2 is less precise, since
we may have greater disagreement about the question whether something 'changed radically' than
we may have on the question whether someone or
something (was) turned around. (You may have a
different intuition here, which should then be reflected in your judgment accordingly.)

Now, as we saw, M2 contrasts with M1. However, it can be understood in comparison with it:
We can understand abstract change in terms of
physical or local change. Consequently, we fill in
1 in the column headed by 'M2 is metaphorically
related to M1', judging M2 to be metaphorically
related to M1. And, for the same reasons as mentioned above, we fill in a 0 in the column headed
by 'M1 is metaphorically related to M2'.

In line 2 both meanings of *umwälzen*, M1 and
M2, are similarly concrete, human-oriented, related to bodily action and precise. They don't
contrast with each other. (You may want to say
that they are equal.) Hence, neither meaning has
a metaphoric relation to the other. Consequently,
we fill in 0 into both columns.

target word	Context 1	Context 2	M1 is metaphorically related to M2	M2 is metaphorically related to M1	comments
umwälzen	Ein Knecht vnd Tagelöhner hat doch auff den abendt sein Brodt / lohn vnd ruhe / Ein Kriegsman seinen Monat soldt / ich aber mus der elenden nächte viel haben / da mich mein außwendiger schmertz vnd inwendige hertzen angst nit schlaffen lest / ja ich bin der elendeste Mensch auff Erden / wann andere Leute / auch das tumme Vieh in jhrem Stalle jhre leibliche bequeme nachtruhe haben / muß ich mich **vmbweltzen**/ vnd kan keinen schlaff in meine augen bringen	Kinadon wollte den Staat **umwälzen**, weil er nicht, obgleich von starkem und thäigem Geiste, zu den Gleichen gehörte.	0	1	
umwälzen	Bey diesen und ähnlichen Handlungen ist das Auge entweder offen, oder verschlossen, aber in beyden Fällen der Augapfel krampfhaft **umgewälzt**, so dass nur der Rand der Iris unter dem obern Augenliede hervorscheint, die Pupille erweitert, und die Netzhaut unempfindlich selbst gegen die heftigsten Reitzmittel.	Und was sagestu? habe ich deinen so hochgerühmten Ritter dann auch vom Pferde gezaubert / da er sich im Sande **umweltzete**?	0	0	
...					

Table 4: Example Annotation Table

C Metaphoric Change Test Set

lexeme	POS	type	old meaning > new meaning	date	freq.
eitel	AD	met	'empty' > 'arrogant'	1764	1320
freundlich	AD	sta	'cordial, benevolent'	1516	1351
erhaben	AD	met	'pronounced, prominent' > 'distinguished, great'	1725	1003
fett	AD	sta	'obese, greasy, fatty (food)'	1557	951
glänzend	AD	met	'sparkling, luminous' > 'sparkling, luminous, very good'	1753	496
adelig	AD	sta	'aristocratic, noble, virtuous'	1585	481
peinlich	AD	met	'painful' > 'painful, diligent, embarrassing'	1788	440
heil	AD	sta	'safe, sound'	1494	423
locker	AD	met	'not tense/tight' > 'frivolous, loose'	1800	407
stillschweigend	AD	sta	'silent'	1603	498
geharnischt	AD	met	'armoured' > 'sharply-worded, strong'	1825	50
bewachsen	AD	sta	'overgrown'	1603	52
flott	AD	met	'afloat' > 'lively, quick, dressy'	1800	42
erdenklich	AD	sta	'imaginable'	1647	44
Feder	N	met	'feather' > 'feather, springclip'	1852	1121
Palast	N	sta	'palace, chateau'	1500	1111
Blatt	N	met	'leaf' > 'leaf, sheet, newspaper'	1638	410
Evangelium	N	sta	'the Gospel'	1521	405
Haube	N	met	'cap' > 'cap, cover, marriage, crest'	1712	138
Fenchel	N	sta	'fennel'	1531	138
Rausch	N	met	'intoxication (due to use of mind-altering substances)' > 'inebriation'	1756	65
Unhöflichkeit	N	sta	'discourtesy'	1605	65
Donnerwetter	N	met	'thunderstorm' > 'thunderstorm, blowup'	1805	49
Wohngebäude	N	sta	'residential building'	1737	49
brüten	V	met	'breed' > 'breed, brood over sth.'	1754	184
aufwecken	V	sta	'wake up (so.)'	1585	183
ausstechen	V	met	'excise' > 'excise, outrival'	1739	53
ahnen	V	sta	'suspect'	1500	53

Table 5: Historical data: sta (stable), met (metaphoric). The date column indicates the year of the occurrence of the change for metaphoric items, but the year of the first occurrence for stable items. The last column (freq.) lists the frequency of the lexeme in the first half of the century in which the corresponding metaphoric change occurs.

Encoding of phonology in a recurrent neural model of grounded speech

Afra Alishahi
Tilburg University
a.alishahi@uvt.nl

Marie Barking
Tilburg University
m.barking@uvt.nl

Grzegorz Chrupała
Tilburg University
g.chrupala@uvt.nl

Abstract

We study the representation and encoding of phonemes in a recurrent neural network model of grounded speech. We use a model which processes images and their spoken descriptions, and projects the visual and auditory representations into the same semantic space. We perform a number of analyses on how information about individual phonemes is encoded in the MFCC features extracted from the speech signal, and the activations of the layers of the model. Via experiments with phoneme decoding and phoneme discrimination we show that phoneme representations are most salient in the lower layers of the model, where low-level signals are processed at a fine-grained level, although a large amount of phonological information is retain at the top recurrent layer. We further find out that the attention mechanism following the top recurrent layer significantly attenuates encoding of phonology and makes the utterance embeddings much more invariant to synonymy. Moreover, a hierarchical clustering of phoneme representations learned by the network shows an organizational structure of phonemes similar to those proposed in linguistics.

1 Introduction

Spoken language is a universal human means of communication. As such, its acquisition and representation in the brain is an essential topic in the study of the cognition of our species. In the field of neuroscience there has been a long-standing interest in the understanding of neural representations of linguistic input in human brains, most commonly via the analysis of neuro-imaging data of participants exposed to simplified, highly controlled inputs. More recently, naturalistic data has been used and patterns in the brain have been correlated with patterns in the input (e.g. Wehbe et al., 2014; Khalighinejad et al., 2017).

This type of approach is relevant also when the goal is the understanding of the dynamics in complex neural network models of speech understanding. Firstly because similar techniques are often applicable, but more importantly because the knowledge of how the workings of artificial and biological neural networks are similar or different is valuable for the general enterprise of cognitive science.

Recent studies have implemented models which learn to understand speech in a weakly and indirectly supervised fashion from correlated audio and visual signal: Harwath et al. (2016); Harwath and Glass (2017); Chrupała et al. (2017a). This is a departure from typical Automatic Speech Recognition (ASR) systems which rely on large amounts of transcribed speech, and these recent models come closer to the way humans acquire language in a grounded setting. It is thus especially interesting to investigate to what extent the traditional levels of linguistic analysis such as phonology, morphology, syntax and semantics are encoded in the activations of the hidden layers of these models. There are a small number of studies which focus on the syntax and/or semantics in the context of neural models of written language (e.g. Elman, 1991; Frank et al., 2013; Kádár et al., 2016; Li et al., 2016a; Adi et al., 2016; Li et al., 2016b; Linzen et al., 2016). Taking it a step further, Gelderloos and Chrupała (2016) and Chrupała et al. (2017a) investigate the levels of representations in models which learn language from phonetic transcriptions and from the speech signal, respectively. Neither of these tackles the

Proceedings of the 21st Conference on Computational Natural Language Learning (CoNLL 2017), pages 368–378,
Vancouver, Canada, August 3 - August 4, 2017. ©2017 Association for Computational Linguistics

representation of phonology in any great depth. Instead they work with relatively coarse-grained distinctions between form and meaning.

In the current work we use controlled synthetic stimuli, as well as alignment between the audio signal and phonetic transcription of spoken utterances to extract phoneme representation vectors based on the activations on the hidden layers of a model of grounded speech perception. We use these representations to carry out analyses of the representation of phonemes at a fine-grained level. In a series of experiments, we show that the lower layers of the model encode accurate representations of the phonemes which can be used in phoneme identification and classification with high accuracy. We further investigate how the phoneme inventory is organised in the activation space of the model. Finally, we tackle the general issue of the representation of phonological form versus meaning with a controlled task of synonym discrimination.

Our results show that the bottom layers in the multi-layer recurrent neural network learn invariances which enable it to encode phonemes independently of co-articulatory context, and that they represent phonemic categories closely matching usual classifications from linguistics. Phonological form becomes harder to detect in higher layers of the network, which increasingly focus on representing meaning over form, but encoding of phonology persists to a significant degree up to the top recurrent layer.

We make the data and open-source code to reproduce our results publicly available at github.com/gchrupala/encoding-of-phonology.

2   Related Work

Research on encoding of phonology has been carried out from a psycholinguistics as well as computational modeling perspectives. Below we review both types of work.

2.1   Phoneme perception

Co-articulation and interspeaker variability make it impossible to define unique acoustic patterns for each phoneme. In an early experiment, Liberman et al. (1967) analyzed the acoustic properties of the /d/ sound in the two syllables /di/ and /du/. They found that while humans easily noticed differences between the two instances when /d/ was played in isolation, they perceived the /d/ as be-

ing the same when listening to the complete syllables. This phenomenon is often referred to as categorical perception: acoustically different stimuli are perceived as the same. In another experiment Lisker and Abramson (1967) used the two syllables /ba/ and /pa/ which only differ in their *voice onset time* (VOT), and created a continuum moving from syllables with short VOT to syllables with increasingly longer VOT. Participants identified all consonants with VOT below 25 msec as being /b/ and all consonant with VOT above 25 msec as being /p/. There was no grey area in which both interpretations of the sound were equally likely, which suggests that the phonemes were perceived categorically. Supporting findings also come from discrimination experiments: when one consonant has a VOT below 25 msec and the other above, people perceive the two syllables as being different (/ba/ and /pa/ respectively), but they do not notice any differences in the acoustic signal when both syllables have a VOT below or above 25 msec (even when these sounds are physically further away from each other than two sounds that cross the 25 msec dividing line).

Evidence from infant speech perception studies suggests that infants also perceive phonemes categorically (Eimas et al., 1971): one- and four-month old infants were presented with multiple syllables from the continuum of /ba/ to /pa/ sounds described above. As long as the syllables all came from above or below the 25 msec line, the infants showed no change in behavior (measured by their amount of sucking), but when presented with a syllable crossing that line, the infants reacted differently. This suggests that infants, just like adults, perceive speech sounds as belonging to discrete categories. Dehaene-Lambertz and Gliga (2004) also showed that the same neural systems are activated for both infants and adults when performing this task.

Importantly, languages differ in their phoneme inventories; for example English distinguishes /r/ from /l/ while Japanese does not, and children have to learn which categories to use. Experimental evidence suggests that infants can discriminate both native and nonnative speech sound differences up to 8 months of age, but have difficulty discriminating acoustically similar nonnative contrasts by 10-12 months of age (Werker and Hensch, 2015). These findings suggest that by their first birthday, they have learned to focus only on those contrasts that are relevant for their native language and to neglect those which are not. Psycholinguistic theories assume that children learn the categories of their native language by keeping track of the frequency distribution of acoustic sounds in their input. The forms around peaks in this distribution are then perceived as being a distinct category. Recent computational models showed that infant-directed speech contains sufficiently clear peaks for such a distributional learning mechanism to succeed and also that top-down processes like semantic knowledge and visual information play a role in phonetic category learning (ter Schure et al., 2016).

From the machine learning perspective categorical perception corresponds to the notion of learning invariances to certain properties of the input. With the experiments in Section 4 we attempt to gain some insight into this issue.

2.2 Computational models

There is a sizeable body of work on using recurrent neural (and other) networks to detect phonemes or phonetic features as a subcomponent of an ASR system. King and Taylor (2000) train recurrent neural networks to extract phonological features from framewise cepstral representation of speech in the TIMIT speaker-independent database. Frankel et al. (2007) introduce a dynamic Bayesian network for articulatory (phonetic) feature recognition as a component of an ASR system. Siniscalchi et al. (2013) show that a multilayer perceptron can successfully classify phonological features and contribute to the accuracy of a downstream ASR system.

Mohamed et al. (2012) use a Deep Belief Network (DBN) for acoustic modeling and phone recognition on human speech. They analyze the impact of the number of layers on phone recognition error rate, and visualize the MFCC vectors as well as the learned activation vectors of the hidden layers of the model. They show that the representations learned by the model are more speaker-invariant than the MFCC features.

These works directly supervise the networks to recognize phonological information. Another supervised but multimodal approach is taken by Sun (2016), which uses grounded speech for improving a supervised model of transcribing utterances from spoken description of images. We on the other hand are more interested in understanding how the phonological level of representation emerges from weak supervision via correlated signal from the visual modality.

There are some existing models which learn language representations from sensory input in such a weakly supervised fashion. For example Roy and Pentland (2002) use spoken utterances paired with images of objects, and search for segments of speech that reliably co-occur with visual shapes. Yu and Ballard (2004) use a similar approach but also include non-verbal cues such as gaze and gesture into the input for unsupervised learning of words and their visual meaning. These language learning models use rich input signals, but are very limited in scale and variation.

A separate line of research has used neural networks for modeling phonology from a (neuro)-cognitive perspective. Burgess and Hitch (1999) implement a connectionist model of the so-called phonological loop, i.e. the posited working memory which makes phonological forms available for recall (Baddeley and Hitch, 1974). Gasser and Lee (1989) show that Simple Recurrent Networks are capable of acquiring phonological constraints such as vowel harmony or phonological alterations at morpheme boundaries. Touretzky and Wheeler (1989) present a connectionist architecture which performs multiple simultaneous insertion, deletion, and mutation operations on sequences of phonemes. In this body of work the input to the network is at the level of phonemes or phonetic features, not acoustic features, and it is thus more concerned with the rules governing phonology and does not address how representations of phonemes arise from exposure to speech in the first place. Moreover, the early connectionist work deals with constrained, toy datasets. Current neural network architectures and hardware enable us to use much more realistic inputs with the potential to lead to qualitatively different results.

3 Model

As our model of language acquisition from grounded speech signal we adopt the Recurrent Highway Network-based model of Chrupała et al. (2017a). This model has two desirable properties: firstly, thanks to the analyses carried in that work, we understand roughly how the hidden layers differ in terms of the level of linguistic representation they encode. Secondly, the model is trained on clean synthetic speech which makes it appropriate to use for the controlled experiments in Section 5.2. We refer the reader to Chrupała et al. (2017a) for a detailed description of the model architecture. Here we give a brief overview.

The model exploits correlations between two modalities, i.e. speech and vision, as a source of weak supervision for learning to understand speech; in other words it implements language acquisition from the speech signal grounded in visual perception. The architecture is a bi-modal network whose learning objective is to project spoken utterances and images to a joint semantic space, such that corresponding pairs (u, i) (i.e. an utterance and the image it describes) are close in this space, while unrelated pairs are far away, by a margin α:

$$\sum_{u,i} \left(\sum_{u'} \max[0, \alpha + d(u, i) - d(u', i)] \right. \tag{1}$$
$$\left. + \sum_{i'} \max[0, \alpha + d(u, i) - d(u, i')] \right)$$

where $d(u, i)$ is the cosine distance between the encoded utterance u and encoded image i.

The image encoder part of the model uses image vectors from a pretrained object classification model, VGG-16 (Simonyan and Zisserman, 2014), and uses a linear transform to directly project these to the joint space. The utterance encoder takes Mel-frequency Cepstral Coefficients (MFCC) as input, and transforms it successively according to:

$$\text{enc}_u(\mathbf{u}) = \text{unit}(\text{Attn}(\text{RHN}_{k,L}(\text{Conv}_{s,d,z}(\mathbf{u})))) \tag{2}$$

The first layer $\text{Conv}_{s,d,z}$ is a one-dimensional convolution of size s which subsamples the input with stride z, and projects it to d dimensions. It is followed by $\text{RHN}_{k,L}$ which consists of k residualized recurrent layers. Specifically these are Recurrent Highway Network layers (Zilly et al., 2016), which are closely related to GRU networks, with the crucial difference that they increase the depth of the transform between timesteps; this is the recurrence depth L. The output of the final recurrent layer is passed through an attention-like lookback operator Attn which takes a weighted average of the activations across time steps. Finally, both utterance and image projections are L2-normalized. See Section 4.1 for details of the model configuration.

Vowels	i ɪ ʊ u
	e ɛ ə ɚ ɔɪ ɔ o
	aɪ æ ʌ ɑ aʊ
Approximants	j ɹ l w
Nasals	m n ŋ
Plosives	p b t d k g
Fricatives	f v θ ð s z ʃ ʒ h
Affricates	tʃ dʒ

Table 1: Phonemes of General American English.

4 Experimental data and setup

The phoneme representations in each layer are calculated as the activations averaged over the duration of the phoneme occurrence in the input. The average input vectors are similarly calculated as the MFCC vectors averaged over the time course of the articulation of the phoneme occurrence. When we need to represent a phoneme type we do so by averaging the vectors of all its occurrences in the validation set. Table 1 shows the phoneme inventory we work with; this is also the inventory used by Gentle/Kaldi (see Section 4.3).

4.1 Model settings

We use the pre-trained version of the COCO Speech model, implemented in Theano (Bastien et al., 2012), provided by Chrupała et al. (2017a).[1] The details of the model configuration are as follows: convolutional layer with length 6, size 64, stride 3, 5 Recurrent Highway Network layers with 512 dimensions and 2 microsteps, attention Multi-Layer Perceptron with 512 hidden units, Adam optimizer, initial learning rate 0.0002. The 4096-dimensional image feature vectors come from the final fully connect layer of VGG-16 (Simonyan and Zisserman, 2014) pretrained on Imagenet (Russakovsky et al., 2014), and are averages of feature vectors for ten crops of each image. The total number of learnable parameters is 9,784,193. Table 2 sketches the architecture of the utterance encoder part of the model.

4.2 Synthetically Spoken COCO

The Speech COCO model was trained on the Synthetically Spoken COCO dataset (Chrupała et al., 2017b), which is a version of the MS COCO

---

[1] Code, data and pretrained models available from https://github.com/gchrupala/visually-grounded-speech.

Attention: size 512
Recurrent 5: size 512
Recurrent 4: size 512
Recurrent 3: size 512
Recurrent 2: size 512
Recurrent 1: size 512
Convolutional: size 64, length 6, stride 3
Input MFCC: size 13

Table 2: COCO Speech utterance encoder architecture.

dataset (Lin et al., 2014) where speech was synthesized for the original image descriptions, using high-quality speech synthesis provided by gTTS.[2]

4.3 Forced alignment

We aligned the speech signal to the corresponding phonemic transcription with the Gentle toolkit,[3] which in turn is based on Kaldi (Povey et al., 2011). It uses a speech recognition model for English to transcribe the input audio signal, and then finds the optimal alignment of the transcription to the signal. This fails for a small number of utterances, which we remove from the data. In the next step we extract MFCC features from the audio signal and pass them through the COCO Speech utterance encoder, and record the activations for the convolutional layer as well as all the recurrent layers. For each utterance the representations (i.e. MFCC features and activations) are stored in a $t_r \times D_r$ matrix, where t_r and D_r are the number of times steps and the dimensionality, respectively, for each representation r. Given the alignment of each phoneme token to the underlying audio, we then infer the slice of the representation matrix corresponding to it.

5 Experiments

In this section we report on four experiments which we designed to elucidate to what extent information about phonology is represented in the activations of the layers of the COCO Speech model. In Section 5.1 we quantify how easy it is to decode phoneme identity from activations. In Section 5.2 we determine phoneme discriminability in a controlled task with minimal pair stimuli. Section 5.3 shows how the phoneme inventory is

[2]Available at https://github.com/pndurette/gTTS.
[3]Available at https://github.com/lowerquality/gentle.

organized in the activation space of the model. Finally, in Section 5.4 we tackle the general issue of the representation of phonological form versus meaning with the controlled task of synonym discrimination.

5.1 Phoneme decoding

In this section we quantify to what extent phoneme identity can be decoded from the input MFCC features as compared to the representations extracted from the COCO speech. As explained in Section 4.3, we use phonemic transcriptions aligned to the corresponding audio in order to segment the signal into chunks corresponding to individual phonemes.

We take a sample of 5000 utterances from the validation set of Synthetically Spoken COCO, and extract the force-aligned representations from the Speech COCO model. We split this data into $\frac{2}{3}$ training and $\frac{1}{3}$ heldout portions, and use supervised classification in order to quantify the recoverability of phoneme identities from the representations. Each phoneme slice is averaged over time, so that it becomes a D_r-dimensional vector. For each representation we then train $L2$-penalized logistic regression (with the fixed penalty weight 1.0) on the training data and measure classification error rate on the heldout portion.

Figure 1 shows the results. As can be seen from this plot, phoneme recoverability is poor for the representations based on MFCC and the convolutional layer activations, but improves markedly for the recurrent layers. Phonemes are easiest recovered from the activations at recurrent layers 1 and 2, and the accuracy decreases thereafter. This suggests that the bottom recurrent layers of the model specialize in recognizing this type of low-level phonological information. It is notable however that even the last recurrent layer encodes phoneme identity to a substantial degree.

The MFCC features do much better than majority baseline (89% error rate) but poorly reltive to the the recurrent layers. Averaging across phoneme durations may be hurting performance, but interestingly, the network can overcome this and form more robust phoneme representations in the activation patterns.

5.2 Phoneme discrimination

Schatz et al. (2013) propose a framework for evaluating speech features learned in an unsupervised setup that does not depend on phonetically labeled

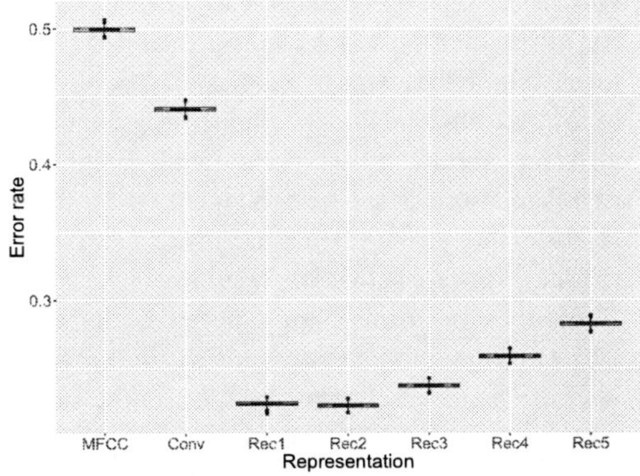

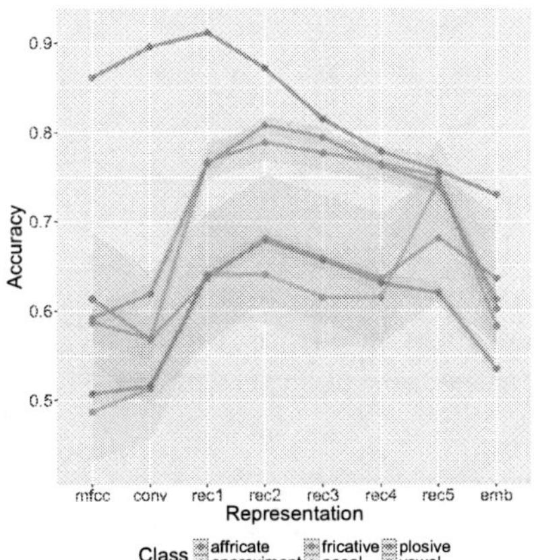

Figure 1: Accuracy of phoneme decoding with input MFCC features and COCO Speech model activations. The boxplot shows error rates bootstrapped with 1000 resamples.

Figure 2: Accuracies for the ABX CV task for the cases where the target and the distractor belong to the same phoneme class. Shaded area extends ± 1 standard error from the mean.

data. They propose a set of tasks called Minimal-Pair ABX tasks that allow to make linguistically precise comparisons between syllable pairs that only differ by one phoneme. They use variants of this task to study phoneme discrimination across talkers and phonetic contexts as well as talker discrimination across phonemes.

Here we evaluate the COCO Speech model on the *Phoneme across Context* (PaC) task of Schatz et al. (2013). This task consists of presenting a series of equal-length tuples (A, B, X) to the model, where A and B differ by one phoneme (either a vowel or a consonant), as do B and X, but A and X are not minimal pairs. For example, in the tuple (*be* /bi/, *me* /mi/, *my* /maɪ/), the task is to identify which of the two syllables /bi/ or /mi/ is closer to /maɪ/. The goal is to measure context invariance in phoneme discrimination by evaluating how often the model recognizes X as the syllable closer to B than to A.

We used a list of all attested consonant-vowel (CV) syllables of American English according to the syllabification method described in Gorman (2013). We excluded the ones which could not be unambiguously represented using English spelling for input to the TTS system (e.g. /baʊ/). We then compiled a list of all possible (A, B, X) tuples from this list where (A, B) and (B, X) are minimal pairs, but (A, X) are not. This resulted in 34,288 tuples in total. For each tuple, we measure $\text{sign}(\text{dist}(A, X) - \text{dist}(B, X))$, where $\text{dist}(i, j)$ is the euclidean distance between the vector rep-

resentations of syllables i and j. These representations are either the audio feature vectors or the layer activation vectors. A positive value for a tuple means that the model has correctly discriminated the phonemes that are shared or different across the syllables.

Table 3 shows the discrimination accuracy in this task using various representations. The pattern is similar to what we observed in the phoneme identification task: best accuracy is achieved using representation vectors from recurrent layers 1 and 2, and it drops as we move further up in the model. The accuracy is lowest when final embedding features are used for this task.

However, the PaC task is most meaningful and

Table 3: Accuracy of choosing the correct target in an ABX task using different representations.

Representation	Accuracy
MFCC	0.72
Convolutional	0.73
Recurrent 1	0.83
Recurrent 2	0.84
Recurrent 3	0.80
Recurrent 4	0.77
Recurrent 5	0.75
Embeddings	0.67

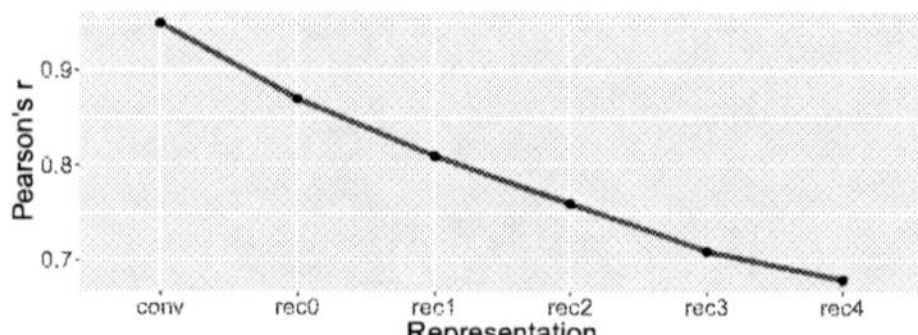

Figure 3: Pearson's correlation coefficients r between the distance matrix of MFCCs and distance matrices on activation vectors.

challenging where the target and the distractor phonemes belong to the same phoneme class. Figure 2 shows the accuracies for this subset of cases, broken down by class. As can be seen, the model can discriminate between phonemes with high accuracy across all the layers, and the layer activations are more informative for this task than the MFCC features. Again, most phoneme classes seem to be represented more accurately in the lower layers (1–3), and the performance of the model in this task drops as we move towards higher hidden layers. There are also clear differences in the pattern of discriminability for the phoneme classes. The vowels are especially easy to tell apart, but accuracy on vowels drops most acutely in the higher layers. Meanwhile the accuracy on fricatives and approximants starts low, but improves rapidly and peaks around recurrent layer 2. The somewhat erratic pattern for nasals and affricates is most likely due to small sample size for these classes, as evident from the wide standard error.

5.3 Organization of phonemes

In this section we take a closer look at the underlying organization of phonemes in the model. Our experiment is inspired by Khalighinejad et al. (2017) who study how the speech signal is represented in the brain at different stages of the auditory pathway by collecting and analyzing electroencephalography responses from participants listening to continuous speech, and show that brain responses to different phoneme categories turn out to be organized by phonetic features.

We carry out an analogous experiment by analyzing the hidden layer activations of our model in response to each phoneme in the input. First, we generated a distance matrix for every pair of phonemes by calculating the Euclidean distance between the phoneme pair's activation vectors for

each layer separately, as well as a distance matrix for all phoneme pairs based on their MFCC features. Similar to what Khalighinejad et al. (2017) report, we observe that the phoneme activations on all layers significantly correlate with the phoneme representations in the speech signal, and these correlations are strongest for the lower layers of the model. Figure 3 shows the results.

We then performed agglomerative hierarchical clustering on phoneme type MFCC and activation vectors, using Euclidean distance as the distance metric and the Ward linkage criterion (Ward Jr, 1963). Figure 5 shows the clustering results for the activation vectors on the first hidden layer. The leaf nodes are color-coded according to phoneme classes as specified in Table 1. There is substantial degree of matching between the classes and the structure of the hierarchy, but also some mixing between rounded back vowels and voiced plosives /b/ and /g/, which share articulatory features such as lip movement or tongue position.

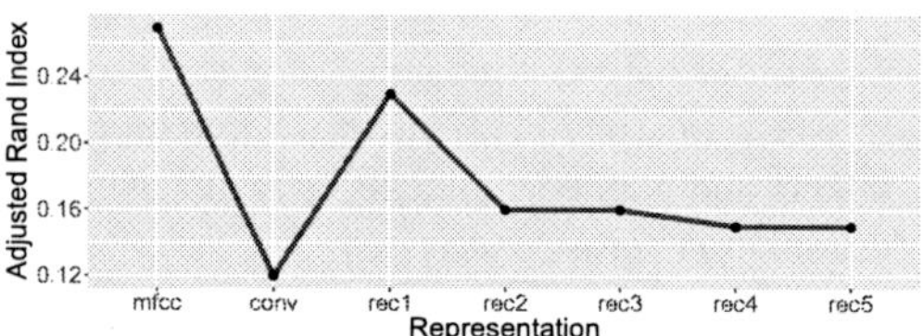

Figure 4: Adjusted Rand Index for the comparison of the phoneme type hierarchy induced from representations against phoneme classes.

We measured the adjusted Rand Index for the match between the hierarchy induced from each representation against phoneme classes, which were obtained by cutting the tree to divide the cluster into the same number of classes as there are phoneme classes. There is a notable drop between the match from MFCC to the activation of the convolutional layer. We suspect this may be explained by the loss of information caused by averaging over phoneme instances combined with the lower temporal resolution of the activations compared to MFCC. The match improves markedly at recurrent layer 1.

5.4 Synonym discrimination

Next we simulate the task of distinguishing between pairs of synonyms, i.e. words with different acoustic forms but the same meaning. With a representation encoding phonological form, our

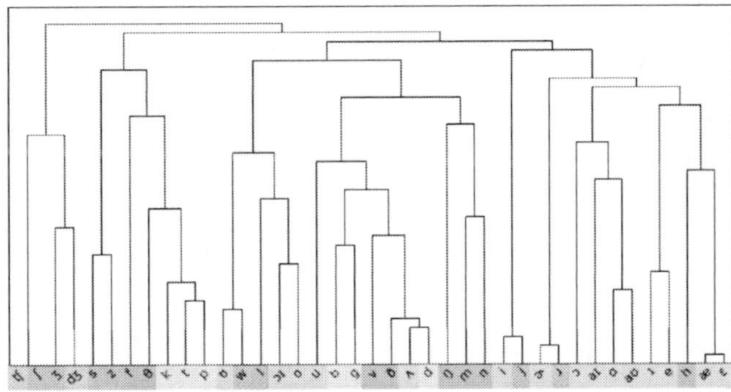

Figure 5: Hierarchical clustering of phoneme activation vectors on the first hidden layer.

expectation is that the task would be easy; in contrast, with a representation which is invariant to phonological form in order to encode meaning, the task would be hard.

We generate a list of synonyms for each noun, verb and adjective in the validation data using Wordnet (Miller, 1995) synset membership as a criterion. Out of these generated word pairs, we select synonyms for the experiment based on the following criteria:

- both forms clearly are synonyms in the sense that one word can be replaced by the other without changing the meaning of a sentence,
- both forms appear more than 20 times in the validation data,
- the words differ clearly in form (i.e. they are not simply variant spellings like *donut/doughnut, grey/gray*),
- the more frequent form constitutes less than 95% of the occurrences.

This gives us 2 verb, 2 adjective and 21 noun pairs.

For each synonym pair, we select the sentences in the validation set in which one of the two forms appears. We use the POS-tagging feature of NLTK (Bird, 2006) to ensure that only those sentences are selected in which the word appears in the correct word category (e.g. *play* and *show* are synonyms when used as nouns, but not when used as verbs). We then generate spoken utterances in which the original word is replaced by its synonym, resulting in the same amount of utterances for both words of each synonym pair.

For each pair we generate a binary classification task using the MFCC features, the average activations in the convolutional layer, the average unit

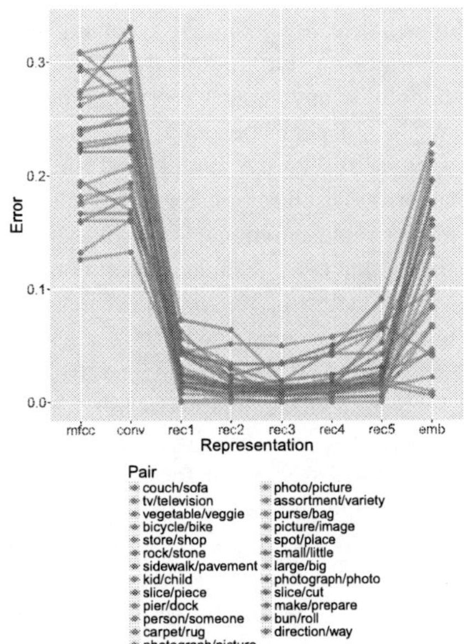

Figure 6: Synonym discrimination error rates, per representation and synonym pair.

activations per recurrent layer, and the sentence embeddings as input features. For every type of input, we run 10-fold cross validation using Logistic Regression to predict which of the two words the utterance contains. We used an average of 672 (minimum 96; maximum 2282) utterances for training the classifiers.

Figure 6 shows the error rate in this classification task for each layer and each synonym pair. Recurrent layer activations are more informative for this task than MFCC features or activations of the convolutional layer. Across all the recurrent layers the error rate is small, showing that some form of phonological information is present throughout this part of the model. However, sentence embeddings give relatively high error rates suggesting that the attention layer acts to focus on semantic information and to filter out much of phonological form.

6 Discussion

Understanding distributed representations learned by neural networks is important but has the reputation of being hard or even impossible. In this work we focus on making progress on this problem for a particular domain: representations of phonology in a multilayer recurrent neural network trained on grounded speech signal. We believe it is important to carry out multiple analyses using diverse methodology: any single experiment may be misleading as it depends on analytical choices such as the type of supervised model used for decoding, the algorithm used for clustering, or the similarity metric for representational similarity analysis. To the extent that more than one experiment points to the same conclusion our confidence in the reliability of the insights gained will be increased.

Earlier work (Chrupała et al., 2017a) shows that encoding of semantics in our RNN model of grounded speech becomes stronger in higher layers, while encoding of form becomes weaker. The main high-level results of our study confirm this pattern by showing that the representation of phonological knowledge is most accurate in the lower layers of the model. This general pattern is to be expected as the objective of the utterance encoder is to transform the input acoustic features in such a way that it can be matched to its counterpart in a completely separate modality. Many of the details of how this happens, however, are far from obvious: perhaps most surprisingly we found that a large amount of phonological information is still available up to the top recurrent layer. Evidence for this pattern emerges from the phoneme decoding task, the ABX task and the synonym discrimination task. The last one also shows that the attention layer filters out and significantly attenuates encoding of phonology and makes the utterance embeddings much more invariant to synonymy.

Our model is trained on synthetic speech, which is easier to process than natural human-generated speech. While small-scale databases of natural speech and image are available (e.g. the Flickr8k Audio Caption Corpus, Harwath and Glass, 2015), they are not large enough to reliably train models such as ours. In future we would like to collect more data and apply our methodology to grounded human speech and investigate whether context and speaker-invariant phoneme representations can be learned from natural, noisy input. We would also like to make comparisons to the results that emerge from similar analyses applied to neuroimaging data.

References

Yossi Adi, Einat Kermany, Yonatan Belinkov, Ofer Lavi, and Yoav Goldberg. 2016. Fine-grained analysis of sentence embeddings using auxiliary prediction tasks. *arXiv preprint arXiv:1608.04207* .

Alan D Baddeley and Graham Hitch. 1974. Working memory. *Psychology of learning and motivation* 8:47–89.

Frédéric Bastien, Pascal Lamblin, Razvan Pascanu, James Bergstra, Ian J. Goodfellow, Arnaud Bergeron, Nicolas Bouchard, and Yoshua Bengio. 2012. Theano: new features and speed improvements. Deep Learning and Unsupervised Feature Learning NIPS 2012 Workshop.

Steven Bird. 2006. NLTK: the natural language toolkit. In *Proceedings of the COLING/ACL on Interactive presentation sessions*. Association for Computational Linguistics, pages 69–72.

Neil Burgess and Graham J Hitch. 1999. Memory for serial order: a network model of the phonological loop and its timing. *Psychological Review* 106(3):551.

Grzegorz Chrupała, Lieke Gelderloos, and Afra Alishahi. 2017a. Representations of language in a model of visually grounded speech signal. In *Proceedings of the 55th Annual Meeting of the Association for Computational Linguistics*.

Grzegorz Chrupała, Lieke Gelderloos, and Afra Alishahi. 2017b. Synthetically spoken COCO. https://doi.org/10.5281/zenodo.400926.

Ghislaine Dehaene-Lambertz and Teodora Gliga. 2004. Common neural basis for phoneme processing in infants and adults. *Journal of Cognitive Neuroscience* 16(8):1375–1387.

Peter D Eimas, Einar R Siqueland, Peter Juscyk, and James Vigorito. 1971. Speech perception in infants. *Science* 171(3968):303–306.

Jeffrey L Elman. 1991. Distributed representations, simple recurrent networks, and grammatical structure. *Machine learning* 7(2-3):195–225.

Robert Frank, Donald Mathis, and William Badecker. 2013. The acquisition of anaphora by simple recurrent networks. *Language Acquisition* 20(3):181–227.

Joe Frankel, Mirjam Wester, and Simon King. 2007. Articulatory feature recognition using dynamic Bayesian networks. *Computer Speech & Language* 21(4):620–640.

Michael Gasser and Ch Lee. 1989. Networks that learn phonology. Technical report, Computer Science Department, Indiana University.

Lieke Gelderloos and Grzegorz Chrupała. 2016. From phonemes to images: levels of representation in a recurrent neural model of visually-grounded language learning. In *Proceedings of COLING 2016, the 26th International Conference on Computational Linguistics: Technical Papers*.

Kyle Gorman. 2013. *Generative phonotactics*. Ph.D. thesis, University of Pennsylvania.

David Harwath and James Glass. 2015. Deep multimodal semantic embeddings for speech and images. In *IEEE Automatic Speech Recognition and Understanding Workshop*.

David Harwath and James R Glass. 2017. Learning word-like units from joint audio-visual analysis. *arXiv preprint arXiv:1701.07481* .

David Harwath, Antonio Torralba, and James Glass. 2016. Unsupervised learning of spoken language with visual context. In *Advances in Neural Information Processing Systems*. pages 1858–1866.

Ákos Kádár, Grzegorz Chrupała, and Afra Alishahi. 2016. Representation of linguistic form and function in recurrent neural networks. *CoRR* abs/1602.08952.

Bahar Khalighinejad, Guilherme Cruzatto da Silva, and Nima Mesgarani. 2017. Dynamic encoding of acoustic features in neural responses to continuous speech. *Journal of Neuroscience* 37(8):2176–2185.

Simon King and Paul Taylor. 2000. Detection of phonological features in continuous speech using neural networks. *Computer Speech & Language* 14(4):333 – 353.

Jiwei Li, Xinlei Chen, Eduard Hovy, and Dan Jurafsky. 2016a. Visualizing and understanding neural models in NLP. In *Proceedings of NAACL-HLT*. pages 681–691.

Jiwei Li, Will Monroe, and Dan Jurafsky. 2016b. Understanding neural networks through representation erasure. *CoRR* abs/1612.08220.

Alvin M Liberman, Franklin S Cooper, Donald P Shankweiler, and Michael Studdert-Kennedy. 1967. Perception of the speech code. *Psychological review* 74(6):431.

Tsung-Yi Lin, Michael Maire, Serge Belongie, James Hays, Pietro Perona, Deva Ramanan, Piotr Dollár, and C Lawrence Zitnick. 2014. Microsoft COCO: Common objects in context. In *Computer Vision–ECCV 2014*, Springer, pages 740–755.

Tal Linzen, Emmanuel Dupoux, and Yoav Goldberg. 2016. Assessing the ability of LSTMs to learn syntax-sensitive dependencies. *Transactions of the Association for Computational Linguistics* 4:521–535.

L. Lisker and A.S. Abramson. 1967. The voicing dimension: some experiments in comparative phonetics. In *Proceedings of the 6th International Congress of Phonetic Sciences*.

George A Miller. 1995. WordNet: a lexical database for english. *Communications of the ACM* 38(11):39–41.

Abdel-rahman Mohamed, Geoffrey Hinton, and Gerald Penn. 2012. Understanding how deep belief networks perform acoustic modelling. In *Acoustics, Speech and Signal Processing (ICASSP), 2012 IEEE International Conference on*. IEEE, pages 4273–4276.

Daniel Povey, Arnab Ghoshal, Gilles Boulianne, Lukas Burget, Ondrej Glembek, Nagendra Goel, Mirko Hannemann, Petr Motlicek, Yanmin Qian, Petr Schwarz, Jan Silovsky, Georg Stemmer, and Karel Vesely. 2011. The Kaldi speech recognition toolkit. In *IEEE 2011 Workshop on Automatic Speech Recognition and Understanding*. IEEE Signal Processing Society. IEEE Catalog No.: CFP11SRW-USB.

Deb K Roy and Alex P Pentland. 2002. Learning words from sights and sounds: a computational model. *Cognitive Science* 26(1):113 – 146. https://doi.org/http://dx.doi.org/10.1016/S0364-0213(01)00061-1.

Olga Russakovsky, Jia Deng, Hao Su, Jonathan Krause, Sanjeev Satheesh, Sean Ma, Zhiheng Huang, Andrej Karpathy, Aditya Khosla, Michael Bernstein, Alexander C. Berg, and Li Fei-Fei. 2014. ImageNet large scale visual recognition challenge.

Thomas Schatz, Vijayaditya Peddinti, Francis Bach, Aren Jansen, Hynek Hermansky, and Emmanuel Dupoux. 2013. Evaluating speech features with the minimal-pair ABX task: Analysis of the classical MFC/PLP pipeline. In *INTERSPEECH 2013: 14th Annual Conference of the International Speech Communication Association*. pages 1–5.

Karen Simonyan and Andrew Zisserman. 2014. Very deep convolutional networks for large-scale image recognition. *CoRR* abs/1409.1556.

Sabato Marco Siniscalchi, Dong Yu, Li Deng, and Chin-Hui Lee. 2013. Exploiting deep neural networks for detection-based speech recognition. *Neurocomputing* 106:148 – 157.

Felix Sun. 2016. *Speech representation models for speech synthesis and multimodal speech recognition*. Ph.D. thesis, Massachusetts Institute of Technology.

SMM ter Schure, CMM Junge, and PPG Boersma. 2016. Semantics guide infants' vowel learning: computational and experimental evidence. *Infant Behavior and Development* 43:44–57.

David S Touretzky and Deirdre W Wheeler. 1989. A computational basis for phonology. In *NIPS*. pages 372–379.

Joe H Ward Jr. 1963. Hierarchical grouping to optimize an objective function. *Journal of the American statistical association* 58(301):236–244.

Leila Wehbe, Brian Murphy, Partha Talukdar, Alona Fyshe, Aaditya Ramdas, and Tom Mitchell. 2014. Simultaneously uncovering the patterns of brain regions involved in different story reading subprocesses. *PloS one* 9(11):e112575.

Janet F Werker and Takao K Hensch. 2015. Critical periods in speech perception: new directions. *Annual review of psychology* 66:173–196.

Chen Yu and Dana H Ballard. 2004. A multimodal learning interface for grounding spoken language in sensory perceptions. *ACM Transactions on Applied Perception (TAP)* 1(1):57–80.

Julian Georg Zilly, Rupesh Kumar Srivastava, Jan Koutník, and Jürgen Schmidhuber. 2016. Recurrent highway networks. *arXiv preprint arXiv:1607.03474* .

Multilingual Semantic Parsing and Code-switching

Long Duong, Hadi Afshar, Dominique Estival, Glen Pink, Philip Cohen, Mark Johnson
Voicebox Technologies
`{longd,hadia,dominiquee,glenp,philipc,markj}@voicebox.com`

Abstract

Extending semantic parsing systems to new domains and languages is a highly expensive, time-consuming process, so making effective use of existing resources is critical. In this paper, we describe a transfer learning method using crosslingual word embeddings in a sequence-to-sequence model. On the NLmaps corpus, our approach achieves state-of-the-art accuracy of 85.7% for English. Most importantly, we observed a consistent improvement for German compared with several baseline domain adaptation techniques. As a by-product of this approach, our models that are trained on a combination of English and German utterances perform reasonably well on code-switching utterances which contain a mixture of English and German, even though the training data does not contain any code-switching. As far as we know, this is the first study of code-switching in semantic parsing. We manually constructed the set of *code-switching test utterances* for the NLmaps corpus and achieve 78.3% accuracy on this dataset.

1 Introduction

Semantic parsing is the task of mapping a natural language query to a logical form (LF) such as Prolog or lambda calculus, which can be executed directly through database query (Zettlemoyer and Collins, 2005, 2007; Haas and Riezler, 2016; Kwiatkowksi et al., 2010).

Semantic parsing needs application or domain specific training data, so the most straightforward approach is to manufacture training data for each combination of language and application domain.

However, acquiring such data is an expensive, lengthy process.

This paper investigates ways of leveraging application domain specific training data in one language to improve performance and reduce the training data needs for the same application domain in another language. This is an increasingly common commercially important scenario, where a single application must be developed for multiple languages simultaneously. In this paper, we investigate the question of transferring a semantic parser from a source language (e.g. English) to a target language (e.g. German). In particular, we examine the situation where there is a large amount of training data for the source language but much less training data for the target language. It is important to note that, despite surface language differences, it has long been suggested that logical forms are the same across languages (Fodor, 1975), motivating transfer learning for this paper.

We conceptualize our work as a form of domain adaptation, where we transfer knowledge about a specific application domain (e.g. navigation queries) from one language to another. Much work has investigated feature-based domain adaptation (Daume III, 2007; Ben-David et al., 2007). However, it is a non-trivial research question to apply these methods to deep learning.

We experiment with several deep learning methods for supervised crosslingual domain adaptation and make two key findings. The first is that we can use a bilingual dictionary to build crosslingual word embeddings, serving as a bridge between source and target language. The second is that machine-translated training data can also be used to effectively improve performance when there is little application domain specific training data in the target language. Interestingly, even when training on the full dataset of the target language, we show that it is still useful to lever-

Proceedings of the 21st Conference on Computational Natural Language Learning (CoNLL 2017), pages 379–389,
Vancouver, Canada, August 3 - August 4, 2017. ©2017 Association for Computational Linguistics

age information from the source language through crosslingual word embeddings. We set new state-of-the-art results on the NLmaps corpus.

Another benefit of joint training of the model is that a single model has the capacity to understand both languages. We show this gives the model the ability to parse code-switching utterances, where the natural language query contains a mixture of two languages. Being able to handle code-switching is valuable in real-world applications that expect spoken natural language input in a variety of settings and from a variety of speakers. Many people around the world are bilingual or multilingual, and even monolingual speakers are liable to use foreign expressions or phrases. Real systems must be able to handle that kind of input, and the method we propose is a simple and efficient way to extend the capabilities of an existing system.

As far as we know, this is the first study of code-switching in semantic parsing. We constructed a new set of *code-switching test utterances* for the NLmaps corpus. Our jointly trained model obtains a logical form exact match accuracy of 78.3% on this test set.

Our contributions are:

- We achieve new state-of-the-art results on the English and German versions of the NLmaps corpus (85.7% and 83.0% respectively).

- We propose a method to incorporate bilingual word embeddings into a sequence-to-sequence model, and apply it to semantic parsing. To the best of our knowledge, we are the first to apply crosslingual word embedding in a sequence-to-sequence model.

- Our joint model allows us to also process input with code-switching. We develop a new dataset for evaluating semantic parsing on code-switching input which we make publicly available.[1]

2 Related work

Deep learning and the sequence-to-sequence approach in particular have achieved wide success in many applications, reaching state-of-the-art performance for semantic parsing (Jia and Liang, 2016; Dong and Lapata, 2016), machine translation (Luong et al., 2015b), image caption generation (Xu et al., 2015), and speech recognition (Chorowski et al., 2014, 2015). Nevertheless, transferring information in a deep learning model about a source language to a target language is still an open research question, and is the focus of this paper.

Our work falls under crosslingual transfer learning category: we want to transfer a semantic parser from one language to another language. The assumption is that there is sufficient application domain specific training data in a source language to train a semantic parser, but only a small amount of application domain specific training data in the target language. We would like to leverage the source language training data to improve semantic parsing in the target language. It is common to exploit the shared structures between languages for POS tagging and Noun Phrase bracketing (Yarowsky and Ngai, 2001), dependency parsing (Täckström et al., 2012; McDonald et al., 2013), named entity recognition (Tsai et al., 2016; Nothman et al., 2013) and machine translation (Zoph et al., 2016). However, as far as we know, there is no prior work on crosslingual transfer learning for semantic parsing, which is the topic of this paper.

There are several common techniques for transfer learning across domains. The simplest approach is *Fine Tune*, where the model is first trained on the source domain and then fine-tuned on the target domain (Watanabe et al., 2016). Using some form of regularization (e.g. L_2) to encourage the target model to remain similar to the source model is another common approach (Duong et al., 2015a). In this approach, the model is trained in the *cascade* style, where the source model is trained first and then used as in a prior when training the target model. It is often beneficial to *jointly* train the source and target models under a single objective function (Collobert et al., 2011; Firat et al., 2016; Zoph and Knight, 2016). Combining source and target data together into a single dataset is a simple way to jointly train for both domains. However, this approach might not work well in the crosslingual case, i.e. transfer from one language to another, because there may not be many shared features between the two languages. We show how to use crosslingual word embeddings (§3.3.1) as the bridge to better share information between languages.

Instead of combining data, a more sophisticated

---

[1]github.com/vbtagitlab/code-switching

	GeoQuery	ATIS
Number of utterances	880	5410
Jia and Liang (2016)	89.3	83.3
Zettlemoyer and Collins (2007)	86.1	84.6
Kočiský et al. (2016)	87.3	-
Dong and Lapata (2016)	87.1	84.6
Liang et al. (2011)	**91.1**	-
Kwiatkowksi et al. (2010)	88.6	82.8
Zhao and Huang (2015)	88.9	84.2
`TGT Only`	86.1	**86.1**

Table 1: Performance of the baseline attentional model (`TGT Only`) on GeoQuery (Zettlemoyer and Collins, 2005) and ATIS (Zettlemoyer and Collins, 2007) dataset compared with prior work. The best performance is shown in bold.

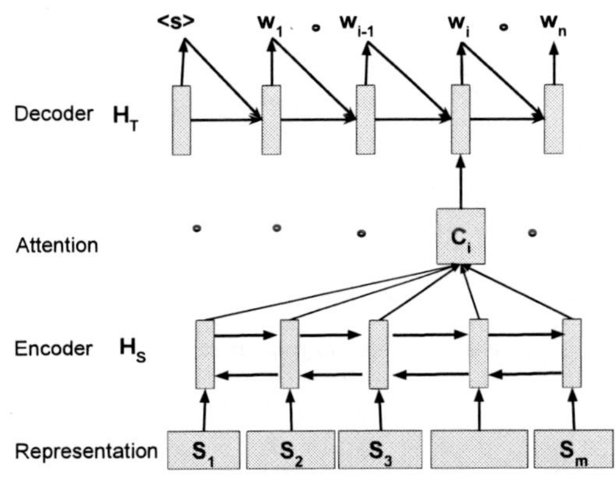

Figure 1: The baseline attentional model as applied to our tasks. The input is the natural language utterance and the output is the logical form.

approach for joint training is to modify the model to adapt for both domains (or languages). Watanabe et al. (2016) propose a dual output model where each output is used for one domain. Kim et al. (2016) extend the feature augmentation approach of Daume III (2007) for deep learning by augmenting different models for each domain. In this paper we experiment with multiple encoders for the sequence-to-sequence attentional model, as described in §3.2. While some of the methods we investigate in this paper have been explored in the domain of syntactic parsing - Tiedemann (2014) used machine translation for cross-lingual transfer, and Ammar et al. (2016) show that a single parser can produce syntactic analyses in multiple languages - our work applies them to semantic parsing.

3 Model

We base our approach on the bidirectional sequence-to-sequence (seq2seq) model with attention of Bahdanau et al. (2014). This attentional model encodes a source as a sequence of vectors, and generates output by decoding these sequences. At each decoding time step, it "attends" to different parts of the encoded sequence.

On a large dataset, it is difficult to improve on a properly tuned seq2seq model with attention. As Table 1 shows, our baseline attentional seq2seq model (described below), which we call `TGT Only` in the figures and tables, achieves competitive results on standard semantic parsing

datasets. We begin by describing the basic attentional model and then present our methods for transfer learning to different languages.

3.1 Baseline attentional model

The baseline attentional seq2seq model (`TGT Only`) is shown in Figure 1. The source utterance is represented as a sequence of vectors $S_1, S_2, \ldots, S_m$. Each S_i is the output of an embeddings lookup. The model has two main components: an encoder and a decoder. For the encoder, we use a bidirectional recurrent neural network (RNN) with Gated Recurrent Units (GRU) (Pezeshki, 2015). The source utterance is encoded as a sequence of vectors $H_S = (H_S^1, H_S^2, \ldots, H_S^m)$ where each vector H_S^j ($1 \leq j \leq m$) is the concatenation of the hidden states of the forward and backward GRU at time j.

The attention mechanism is added to the model through an alignment matrix $\alpha \in \mathbb{R}^{n \times m}$, where n is the number of target tokens in the logical form. We add `<s>` and `</s>` to mark the start and end of the target sentence. The "glimpse" vector c_i of the source when generating w_i is $c_i = \sum_j \alpha_{ij} H_S^j$. The decoder is another RNN with GRU unit. At each time step, the decoder RNN receives c_i in addition to the previously-output word. Thus, the hidden state[2] at time i of the decoder is defined as $H_T^i = \mathrm{GRU}(H_T^{i-1}, c_i, w_{i-1})$, which is used to

---

[2]The GRU also carries a memory cell, along with the hidden state; we exclude this from the presentation for clarity of notation.

Train	
Utt-original:	What is the homepage of the cinema Cinéma Chaplin in Paris?
LF-original:	query(area(keyval('name','Paris'),keyval('is_in:country','France')),nwr(keyval('name', 'Cinéma_Chaplin')), qtype(findkey('website')))
Utt-converted:	What is the homepage of the cinema UNK UNK in Paris?
LF-converted:	query(area(keyval('name','Paris'),keyval('is_in:country','France')),nwr(keyval('name','UNK_UNK')), qtype(findkey('website')))
Test	
Utt-original:	Would you tell me the phone number of Guru Balti in Edinburgh?
Utt-converted:	Would you tell me the phone number of UNK UNK in Edinburgh?
LF-predicted:	query(area(keyval(name,City_of_Edinburgh)),nwr(keyval(name,UNK_UNK)),qtype(findkey(phone)))
LF-lexicalised:	query(area(keyval(name,City_of_Edinburgh)),nwr(keyval(name,'Guru_Balti')), qtype(findkey(phone)))

Figure 2: Handling of unknown word at train and test times. Training examples containing capitalised low-frequency words are duplicated: in one copy, the capitalised low-frequency words are kept in both the utterance (Utt-original) and the LF (LF-original), while in the other copy they are replaced with the symbol UNK in both the utterance (Utt-converted) and the LF (LF-converted). At test time, unknown words in the input utterance are replaced with UNK symbols (in Utt-converted); the UNK symbols in the predicted LF (LF-predicted) are then replaced with the unknown words (LF-lexicalised).

predict word w_i:

$$p(w_i \mid w_1 \cdots w_{i-1}, H_S) = \text{softmax}(g(H_T^i)) \quad (1)$$

where g is a linear transformation.

We use 70 dimensions for both the hidden states and memory cells in the source GRUs and 60 dimensions for target GRUs. We train this model using RMSprop (Tieleman and Hinton, 2012) to minimize the negative log-likelihood using a mini-batch of 256 and early stopping on development data. The initial learning rate is 0.002 and is decayed with decay rate 0.1 if we did not observe any improvement after 1000 iterations. The gradients are rescaled if their L_2 norm is greater than 10. We implemented dropout for both source and target GRU units (Srivastava et al., 2014) with input and output dropout rates of 40% and 25% respectively. The initial state of the source GRU is trainable, and the initial state of target GRU is initialized with the final states of the source GRUs. The non-embeddings weights are initialized using Xavier initialization (Glorot and Bengio, 2010). We also tried stacking several layers of GRUs but did not observe any significant improvement. Choice of hyper-parameters will be discussed in more detail in §4.2.

We initialize the word embeddings in the model with pre-trained monolingual word embeddings trained on a Wikipedia dump using word2vec (Mikolov et al., 2013). We use monolingual word embeddings for all models except for the jointly trained model, where we instead use crosslingual word embeddings (§3.3.1).

In order to handle unknown words, during training, all words that are low frequency and capitalized are replaced with the special symbol UNK in both utterance and logical form. Effectively, we target low-frequency named entities in the dataset. This is a simple but effective version of delexicalization, which does not require a named entity recognizer.[3] However, unlike previous work (Jia and Liang, 2016; Gulcehre et al., 2016; Gu et al., 2016), we also retain the original sentence in the training data, which results in a substantial performance improvement. The intuition is that the model is capable of learning a useful signal even for very rare words. During test time, we replace (from left to right) the UNK in the logical form with the corresponding word in the source utterance. Figure 2 shows examples of handling unknown words during training and testing. At train time, the two words *Cinéma* and *Chaplin* are replaced with UNK in both utterance and logical form. At test time, the first and second UNK in the logical form are replaced with the unknown words *Guru* and *Balti* from the test utterance. We implement this attentional model as our baseline. We now detail our methods for transferring learning to other languages.

---

[3]Using named entity recognition would be another solution but we did not want to rely on additional resources.

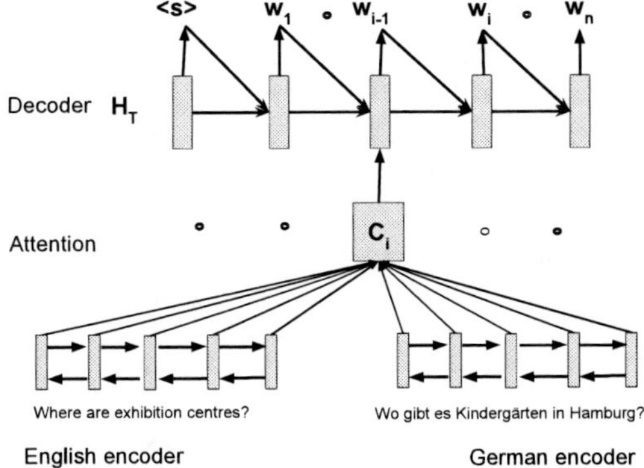

Figure 3: Dual encoder model where each language has a separate encoder but both share the same decoder. Each training mini-batch only has monolingual input, so only one encoder is used for each mini-batch.

3.2 Dual encoder model

Multi-task learning is a common approach for neural domain adaptation (Watanabe et al., 2016; Duong et al., 2015b; Collobert et al., 2011; Luong et al., 2015a). In this approach, the source and target domains are jointly trained under a single objective function. The idea is that many parameters can be shared between the source and target domains, and the errors in the source domain can inform the target domain and vice versa. Following this idea, we extend the baseline attentional model (§3.1) to dual encoders, one for the source language and another for the target language. In this work, we perform the evaluation with English and German as both source and target languages, i.e. in both directions (depending on the model). The decoder is shared across languages as shown in Figure 3. We refer to this as our Dual model. The glimpse vector c_i will be calculated using either the source or target RNN encoder, motivated by the fact that both source and target languages use the same target logical form. The model is trained on the combined data of both the source and target languages. For each mini-batch, we only use the source or target language data, and make use of the corresponding RNN encoder.

3.3 All model

Another straightforward domain adaptation technique is to combine the source and target language data. We create a new training data set $D_{all} = D_s \cup D_t$ where D_s and D_t are the training data for source and target language. We refer to this as our All model. The All model is a Dual model, but both source and target RNNs are shared and only the embedding matrices are different between source and target languages.

3.3.1 Crosslingual word embeddings

Overcoming lexical differences is a key challenge in crosslingual domain adaptation. Prior work on domain adaptation found features that are common across languages, such as high-level linguistic features extracted from the World Atlas of Language Structures (Dryer and Haspelmath, 2013), crosslingual word clusters (Täckström et al., 2012) and crosslingual word embeddings (Ammar et al., 2016). Here, we extend crosslingual word embeddings as the crosslingual features for semantic parsing.

We train crosslingual word embeddings across source and target languages following the approach of Duong et al. (2016), who achieve high performance on several monolingual and crosslingual evaluation metrics. Their work is essentially a multilingual extension of word2vec, where they use a context in one language to predict a target word in another language. The target words in the other language are obtained by looking up that word in a bilingual dictionary. Thus, the input to their model is monolingual data in both languages and a bilingual dictionary. We use monolingual data from pre-processed Wikipedia dump (Al-Rfou et al., 2013) with bilingual dictionary from Panlex (Kamholz et al., 2014).

We initialize the seq2seq source embeddings of both languages with the crosslingual word embeddings. However, we *do not update* these embeddings. We apply crosslingual word embeddings (+XlingEmb) to the All model (§3.3) and the Dual encoder model (§3.2) and jointly train for the source and target language. For other models described in this paper, we initialize with monolingual word embeddings.

3.4 Trans model

The above crosslingual word embeddings need a bilingual dictionary to connect between the source and target language. In addition, we can also leverage a machine translation system as the connection between languages. For this case, we define a Trans model, which applies the baseline attentional model with training data $D_{trans} =$

English utterance (from NLmaps)	How many universities are there in Paris?
German utterance (from NLmaps)	Wie viele Universitäten hat Paris?
Code-switching (constructed)	Wie viele Universitäten are there in Paris?
Logical form	query(area(keyval('name','Paris'),keyval('is_in:country','France')), nwr(keyval('amenity','university')),qtype(count))

Table 2: Example of data from the NLmaps corpus. The English and German utterances are translations of each other and they share the same logical form. We constructed code-switching utterances for all the logical forms in the NLmaps test corpus.

$\texttt{translate}(D_s) \cup D_t$, where $\texttt{translate}$ is the function to translate the data from the source language to the target language. For the experiments reported in this paper, we use Google Translate (Wu et al., 2016).

4 Experiments

In this section, we evaluate the methods proposed in §3 for transfer learning for semantic parsing. The aim is to build a parser for a target language with minimum supervision given application domain specific training data for a source language. The question we want to answer is whether it is possible to share information across languages to improve the performance of semantic parsing.

4.1 Dataset

We use the NLmaps corpus (Haas and Riezler, 2016), a semantic parsing corpus for English and German. We evaluated our approach on this corpus because it is the only dataset which provides data in both English and German. Table 2 presents typical examples from this dataset, together with a constructed code-switching utterance. Utterances from different languages are assigned the same logical forms, thus motivating the approach taken in this paper. We tokenize in way similar to Kočiský et al. (2016).[4] For each language, the corpus contains 1500 pairs of natural language queries and corresponding logical forms for training and 880 pairs for testing. We use 10% of the training set as development data for early stopping and hyper-parameter tuning. For evaluation, we use exact match accuracy for the logical form (Kočiský et al., 2016).

4.2 Hyper-parameter tuning

Hyper-parameter tuning is important for good performance. We tune the baseline attentional model

(§3.1) on the development data by generating 100 configurations which are permutations of different optimizers, source and target RNN sizes, RNN cell type[5], dropout rates and mini-batch sizes. We then use the same configuration for all other models.

4.3 Learning curves

We experimented with transfer learning from $English \rightarrow German$ and $German \rightarrow English$. We use all the data in the NLmaps corpus for the source language and vary the amount of data for the target language. Figure 4 shows the learning curve for transfer learning in both directions.

The first observation is that the baseline attentional model trained on the target only (TGT Only) is very robust when trained on large datasets but performs poorly on small datasets. The Dual model performs similarly to the baseline attentional model for English and slightly worse for German. The simple method of combining the data (All model) performs surprisingly well, especially on small datasets where this model is $\approx 20\%$ better than the baseline attentional model for both languages. Incorporating crosslingual word embeddings (+XlingEmb) consistently improves the performance for all data sizes. The improvement is more marked for the $English \rightarrow German$ direction. Finally, if we have a machine translation system, we can further improve the performance on a target language by augmenting the data with translations from the source language. This simple method substantially improves performance on a target language, especially in the small dataset scenario. More surprisingly, if we don't use any target language data and train on $D_{trans} = \texttt{translate}(D_s)$ we achieve 61.3% and 48.2% accuracy for English and German respectively (Figure 4). This corresponds to a distant supervision baseline where the

---

[4]We remove quotes, add spaces around parenthesis and separate the question mark at the end of the utterance.

[5]We tried with LSTM, GRU and Highway networks.

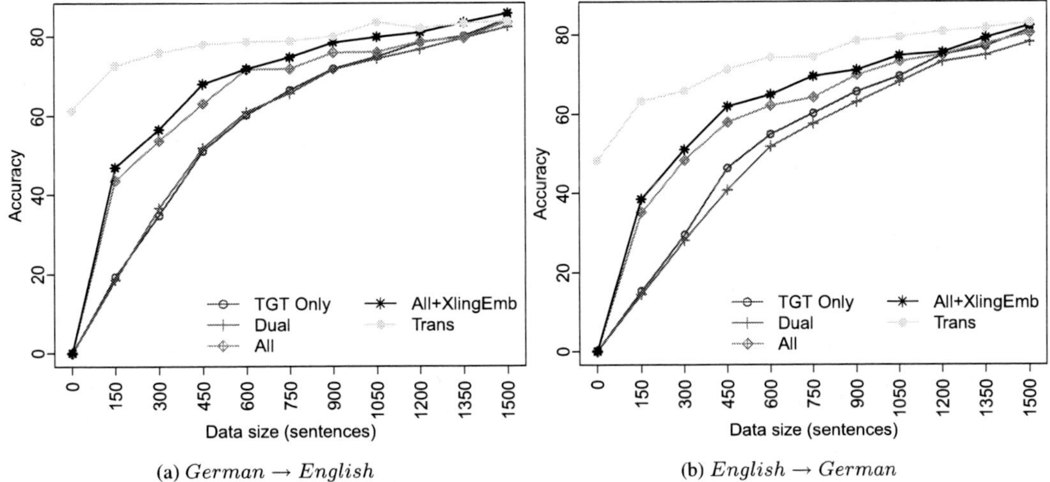

(a) *German → English* (b) *English → German*

Figure 4: Learning curves for English and German with various models. `TGT Only` applies the baseline attentional mode (§3.1) to the target language data alone. `Dual` uses the dual encoders from §3.2. `All` is similar with `TGT Only` but trained on the combined data of both languages. `All+XlingEmb`, instead of monolingual word embeddings, uses crosslingual word embeddings (§3.3.1). `Trans` model uses a machine translation system (§3.4). At 1500 sentences, since we do not have development data for early stopping, we train the model for exactly 10k iterations.

training data is "silver standard" given by a machine translation system. This baseline is equivalent to supervised learning on 600 and 450 gold sentences on English and German respectively.

We also tried several other models such as *Fine Tune*, where the model is trained on the source language first and then fine tuned on the target language but the performance is similar to the `TGT Only` model. The other baseline we implemented is L_2, where we use the source language model as the prior to the target language objective function through an L_2 regularization. However, we did not observe any performance gain, as was also noticed by Watanabe et al. (2016).

4.4 Discussion

Figure 4 shows the learning curves at various data points. Table 3 presents the results for models trained on all target language data (1500 sentences). The `Dual` encoder performs the worst. The baseline supervised learning on target data only (`TGT Only`) performs surprisingly well, probably because it is highly tuned. When training on combined English and German data (`All` model), we observe a slight decrease in performance for both English and German. Even when training on the full target language dataset, using crosslingual word embeddings improves the per-

	English	German
Haas and Riezler (2016)	68.3	-
Kočiský et al. (2016)	78.0	-
`Dual`	82.3	78.1
`TGT Only`	84.2	81.3
`All`	83.6	80.3
`All+XlingEmb`	**85.7**	82.3
`Trans`	83.8	**83.0**

Table 3: Results on the full datasets. The best result is shown in bold.

formance by about 2% in both English and German which highlights the effectiveness of crosslingual word embeddings. As shown in Figure 4, adding a machine translation system helps immensely for small datasets. On a full dataset, however, we only observe a small improvement for German but degradation in performance for English using `Trans` model. This might be because machine translations are hardly perfect. With a high level of confidence when training on full dataset, added translations do not contribute much to the model. Importantly, however, these results are substantially better than the previous state-of-the-art result reported in Kočiský et al. (2016).

Model	Accuracy
German `TGT Only`	14.5
English `TGT Only`	16.3
`All`	76.8
`All+XlingEmb`	**78.3**

Table 4: Accuracy of seq2seq models on the code-switching test utterances. The monolingual English and German seq2seq models (`TGT Only`) are trained only on English and German utterances respectively, while the `All` and `All+XlingEmb` models are trained on both sets of utterances. The best result is shown in bold.

5 Code-switching

An interesting result is that by jointly training the model on both English and German, we can now also handle *code-switching* data, where a natural language utterance is a mixture of English and German. We evaluate our jointly trained model's ability to parse utterances consisting of both English and German on our manually constructed code-switching testset.[6] An example of constructed code-switching utterance is shown in Table 2. Note that our models are only trained on "pure" English and German utterances; there are no code-switching training examples in the input.

Code-switching is a complex linguistic phenomenon and there are different accounts of the socio-linguistic conventions governing its use (Poplack, 2004; Isurin et al., 2009; MacSwan, 2017), as well as of the structural properties of utterances with code-switching (Joshi, 1982). Here we focus on the simple kind of code-switching where a single phrase is produced in a different language than the rest of the utterance. Our dataset was created by a fluent bilingual speaker who generated code-switching utterances for each of the 880 examples in the NLmaps test set. Approximately half of the utterances are "Denglish" (i.e., a German phrase embedded in an English matrix sentence) and half are "Gamerican" (an English phrase embedded in a German matrix sentence). NLmaps includes English and German utterances for each test example, and where possible our code-switching utterance was a combination of these (some of our code-switching examples diverge from the corresponding English and German

---

6github.com/vbtagitlab/code-switching

utterances if this improves fluency).

Table 4 presents the results of our models on this new test set. This makes clear that the `All+XlingEmb` model performs noticeably better than the baseline monolingual models on the code-switching test examples, even though there were no such examples in the training set.

6 Conclusion

In this paper, we investigate ways to transfer information from one (source) language to another (target) language in a single semantic parsing application domain. This paper compared various transfer learning models with a strong sequence-to-sequence baseline. We found that a simple method of combining source and target language data works surprisingly well, much better than more complicated methods such as a `Dual` model or L_2 regularization. If bilingual dictionaries are available, crosslingual word embeddings can be constructed and used to further improve the performance. We observed $\approx 20\%$ improvement for small datasets compared to the strong baseline attentional model. Moreover, this improvement can almost be doubled if we leverage some machine translation system. Even on the full dataset, our jointly trained model with crosslingual word embeddings gives state-of-the-art results for semantic parsing of the English and German versions of NLmaps corpus.

This paper also investigated the performance of semantic parsers on *code-switching utterances* that combine English and German. We created a new code-switching test set, and showed that our simple jointly trained model with crosslingual word embeddings achieves 78.3% exact match accuracy on this set, which is more than 60% better than a corresponding monolingual sequence-to-sequence model.

For future work, we would like to try delexicalization as part of training and experiment with better ways of handling unknown word such as a copy mechanism (Jia and Liang, 2016; Gu et al., 2016; Gulcehre et al., 2016). Investigating a more sophisticated network architecture that can perform multilingual semantic parsing more accurately, or with less training data is another fruitful research direction. This work has only scratched the surface in terms of code switching. We would like to exploit the pragmatic and socio-linguistic context to better handle code-switching.

Acknowledgments

We thank the anonymous reviewers for their insightful comments.

References

Rami Al-Rfou, Bryan Perozzi, and Steven Skiena. 2013. Polyglot: Distributed word representations for multilingual NLP. In *Proceedings of the Seventeenth Conference on Computational Natural Language Learning*. pages 183–192.

Waleed Ammar, George Mulcaire, Miguel Ballesteros, Chris Dyer, and Noah Smith. 2016. Many languages, one parser. *Transactions of the Association for Computational Linguistics* 4:431–444.

Dzmitry Bahdanau, Kyunghyun Cho, and Yoshua Bengio. 2014. Neural machine translation by jointly learning to align and translate. *CoRR* abs/1409.0473.

Shai Ben-David, John Blitzer, Koby Crammer, and Fernando Pereira. 2007. Analysis of representations for domain adaptation. In P. B. Schölkopf, J. C. Platt, and T. Hoffman, editors, *Advances in Neural Information Processing Systems 19*, MIT Press, pages 137–144.

Jan Chorowski, Dzmitry Bahdanau, Kyunghyun Cho, and Yoshua Bengio. 2014. End-to-end continuous speech recognition using attention-based recurrent NN: first results. *CoRR* abs/1412.1602.

Jan Chorowski, Dzmitry Bahdanau, Dmitriy Serdyuk, KyungHyun Cho, and Yoshua Bengio. 2015. Attention-based models for speech recognition. *CoRR* abs/1506.07503.

Ronan Collobert, Jason Weston, Léon Bottou, Michael Karlen, Koray Kavukcuoglu, and Pavel Kuksa. 2011. Natural language processing (almost) from scratch. *J. Mach. Learn. Res.* 12:2493–2537.

Hal Daume III. 2007. Frustratingly easy domain adaptation. In *Proceedings of the 45th Annual Meeting of the Association of Computational Linguistics*. Association for Computational Linguistics, pages 256–263.

Li Dong and Mirella Lapata. 2016. Language to logical form with neural attention. In *Proceedings of the 54th Annual Meeting of the Association for Computational Linguistics (Volume 1: Long Papers)*. Association for Computational Linguistics, pages 33–43.

Matthew S. Dryer and Martin Haspelmath, editors. 2013. *WALS Online – walls.info*. Max Planck Institute for Evolutionary Anthropology.

Long Duong, Trevor Cohn, Steven Bird, and Paul Cook. 2015a. Low resource dependency parsing: Cross-lingual parameter sharing in a neural network parser. In *Proceedings of the 53rd Annual Meeting of the Association for Computational Linguistics and the 7th International Joint Conference on Natural Language Processing*. pages 845–850.

Long Duong, Trevor Cohn, Steven Bird, and Paul Cook. 2015b. A neural network model for low-resource universal dependency parsing. In *Proceedings of the 2015 Conference on Empirical Methods in Natural Language Processing*. Association for Computational Linguistics, pages 339–348.

Long Duong, Hiroshi Kanayama, Tengfei Ma, Steven Bird, and Trevor Cohn. 2016. Learning crosslingual word embeddings without bilingual corpora. In *Proceedings of the 2016 Conference on Empirical Methods in Natural Language Processing*. Association for Computational Linguistics, pages 1285–1295.

Orhan Firat, Kyunghyun Cho, and Yoshua Bengio. 2016. Multi-way, multilingual neural machine translation with a shared attention mechanism. In *Proceedings of the 2016 Conference of the North American Chapter of the Association for Computational Linguistics: Human Language Technologies*. pages 866–875.

Jerry A. Fodor. 1975. *The Language of Thought*. Harvard University Press.

Xavier Glorot and Yoshua Bengio. 2010. Understanding the difficulty of training deep feedforward neural networks. In Yee Whye Teh and Mike Titterington, editors, *Proceedings of the Thirteenth International Conference on Artificial Intelligence and Statistics*. PMLR, volume 9 of *Proceedings of Machine Learning Research*, pages 249–256.

Jiatao Gu, Zhengdong Lu, Hang Li, and Victor O.K. Li. 2016. Incorporating copying mechanism in sequence-to-sequence learning. In *Proceedings of the 54th Annual Meeting of the Association for Computational Linguistics (Volume 1: Long Papers)*. pages 1631–1640.

Caglar Gulcehre, Sungjin Ahn, Ramesh Nallapati, Bowen Zhou, and Yoshua Bengio. 2016. Pointing the unknown words. In *Proceedings of the 54th Annual Meeting of the Association for Computational Linguistics (Volume 1: Long Papers)*. Association for Computational Linguistics, pages 140–149.

Carolin Haas and Stefan Riezler. 2016. A corpus and semantic parser for multilingual natural language querying of openstreetmap. In *Proceedings of the 2016 Conference of the North American Chapter of the Association for Computational Linguistics: Human Language Technologies*. Association for Computational Linguistics, pages 740–750.

Ludmila Isurin, Donald Winford, and Kees De Bot. 2009. *Multidisciplinary Approaches to Code Switching*. John Benjamins Publishing.

Robin Jia and Percy Liang. 2016. Data recombination for neural semantic parsing. In *Proceedings of the 54th Annual Meeting of the Association for Computational Linguistics (Volume 1: Long Papers)*. Association for Computational Linguistics, pages 12–22.

Aravind K Joshi. 1982. Processing of sentences with intra-sentential code-switching. In *Proceedings of the 9th conference on Computational linguistics-Volume 1*. Academia Praha, pages 145–150.

David Kamholz, Jonathan Pool, and Susan Colowick. 2014. PanLex: Building a resource for panlingual lexical translation. In *Proceedings of the Ninth International Conference on Language Resources and Evaluation (LREC'14)*. European Language Resources Association, pages 3145–50.

Young-Bum Kim, Karl Stratos, and Ruhi Sarikaya. 2016. Frustratingly easy neural domain adaptation. In *Proceedings of COLING 2016, the 26th International Conference on Computational Linguistics: Technical Papers*. pages 387–396.

Tomáš Kočiský, Gábor Melis, Edward Grefenstette, Chris Dyer, Wang Ling, Phil Blunsom, and Karl Moritz Hermann. 2016. Semantic parsing with semi-supervised sequential autoencoders. In *Proceedings of the 2016 Conference on Empirical Methods in Natural Language Processing*. Association for Computational Linguistics, pages 1078–1087.

Tom Kwiatkowksi, Luke Zettlemoyer, Sharon Goldwater, and Mark Steedman. 2010. Inducing probabilistic CCG grammars from logical form with higher-order unification. In *Proceedings of the 2010 Conference on Empirical Methods in Natural Language Processing*. Association for Computational Linguistics, pages 1223–1233.

Percy Liang, Michael Jordan, and Dan Klein. 2011. Learning dependency-based compositional semantics. In *Proceedings of the 49th Annual Meeting of the Association for Computational Linguistics: Human Language Technologies*. Association for Computational Linguistics, pages 590–599.

Minh-Thang Luong, Quoc V. Le, Ilya Sutskever, Oriol Vinyals, and Lukasz Kaiser. 2015a. Multi-task sequence to sequence learning. *CoRR* abs/1511.06114.

Thang Luong, Hieu Pham, and Christopher D. Manning. 2015b. Effective approaches to attention-based neural machine translation. In *Proc. Empirical Method in Natural Language Processing (EMNLP)*. pages 1412–1421.

Jeff MacSwan. 2017. A multilingual perspective on translanguaging. *American Educational Research Journal* 54(1):167–201.

Ryan McDonald, Joakim Nivre, Yvonne Quirmbach-Brundage, Yoav Goldberg, Dipanjan Das, Kuzman Ganchev, Keith Hall, Slav Petrov, Hao Zhang, Oscar Täckström, Claudia Bedini, Núria Bertomeu Castelló, and Jungmee Lee. 2013. Universal dependency annotation for multilingual parsing. In *Proceedings of the 51st Annual Meeting of the Association for Computational Linguistics*. pages 92–97.

Tomas Mikolov, Wen-tau Yih, and Geoffrey Zweig. 2013. Linguistic regularities in continuous space word representations. In *Proceedings of the 2013 Conference of the North American Chapter of the Association for Computational Linguistics: Human Language Technologies*. pages 746–751.

Joel Nothman, Nicky Ringland, Will Radford, Tara Murphy, and James R. Curran. 2013. Learning multilingual named entity recognition from Wikipedia. *Artificial Intelligent* 194:151–175.

Mohammad Pezeshki. 2015. Sequence modeling using gated recurrent neural networks. *CoRR* abs/1501.00299.

Shana Poplack. 2004. Code-switching. In *Soziolinguistik: an international handbook of the science of language (2nd edition)*, Walter de Gruyter, pages 589–596.

Nitish Srivastava, Geoffrey Hinton, Alex Krizhevsky, Ilya Sutskever, and Ruslan Salakhutdinov. 2014. Dropout: A simple way to prevent neural networks from overfitting. *Journal of Machine Learning Research* 15:1929–1958.

Oscar Täckström, Ryan McDonald, and Jakob Uszkoreit. 2012. Cross-lingual word clusters for direct transfer of linguistic structure. In *Proceedings of the 2012 Conference of the North American Chapter of the Association for Computational Linguistics: Human Language Technologies*. Association for Computational Linguistics, pages 477–487.

Jörg Tiedemann. 2014. Rediscovering annotation projection for cross-lingual parser induction. In *Proceedings of COLING 2014, the 25th International Conference on Computational Linguistics: Technical Papers*. Dublin City University and Association for Computational Linguistics, Dublin, Ireland, pages 1854–1864. http://www.aclweb.org/anthology/C14-1175.

T. Tieleman and G. Hinton. 2012. Lecture 6.5—RmsProp: Divide the gradient by a running average of its recent magnitude. COURSERA: Neural Networks for Machine Learning.

Chen-Tse Tsai, Stephen Mayhew, and Dan Roth. 2016. Cross-lingual named entity recognition via Wikification. In *The SIGNLL Conference on Computational Natural Language Learning*.

Yusuke Watanabe, Kazuma Hashimoto, and Yoshimasa Tsuruoka. 2016. Domain adaptation for neural networks by parameter augmentation. In *Proceedings of the 1st Workshop on Representation Learning for NLP*. Association for Computational Linguistics, pages 249–257.

Yonghui Wu, Mike Schuster, Zhifeng Chen, Quoc V. Le, Mohammad Norouzi, Wolfgang Macherey, Maxim Krikun, Yuan Cao, Qin Gao, Klaus Macherey, Jeff Klingner, Apurva Shah, Melvin Johnson, Xiaobing Liu, Lukasz Kaiser, Stephan Gouws, Yoshikiyo Kato, Taku Kudo, Hideto Kazawa, Keith Stevens, George Kurian, Nishant Patil, Wei Wang, Cliff Young, Jason Smith, Jason Riesa, Alex Rudnick, Oriol Vinyals, Greg Corrado, Macduff Hughes, and Jeffrey Dean. 2016. Google's neural machine translation system: Bridging the gap between human and machine translation. *CoRR* abs/1609.08144.

Kelvin Xu, Jimmy Ba, Ryan Kiros, Kyunghyun Cho, Aaron C. Courville, Ruslan Salakhutdinov, Richard S. Zemel, and Yoshua Bengio. 2015. Show, attend and tell: Neural image caption generation with visual attention. In *Proceedings of the 32nd International Conference on Machine Learning, ICML 2015, Lille, France, 6-11 July 2015*. pages 2048–2057.

David Yarowsky and Grace Ngai. 2001. Inducing multilingual POS taggers and NP bracketers via robust projection across aligned corpora. In *Proceedings of the Second Meeting of the North American Chapter of the Association for Computational Linguistics on Language technologies*. pages 1–8.

Luke Zettlemoyer and Michael Collins. 2007. Online learning of relaxed CCG grammars for parsing to logical form. In *Proceedings of the 2007 Joint Conference on Empirical Methods in Natural Language Processing and Computational Natural Language Learning (EMNLP-CoNLL)*. pages 678–687.

Luke S. Zettlemoyer and Michael Collins. 2005. Learning to map sentences to logical form: Structured /classification with probabilistic categorial grammars. In *UAI '05, Proceedings of the 21st Conference in Uncertainty in Artificial Intelligence, Edinburgh, Scotland, July 26-29, 2005*. pages 658–666.

Kai Zhao and Liang Huang. 2015. Type-driven incremental semantic parsing with polymorphism. In *Proceedings of the 2015 Conference of the North American Chapter of the Association for Computational Linguistics: Human Language Technologies*. Association for Computational Linguistics, pages 1416–1421.

Barret Zoph and Kevin Knight. 2016. Multi-source neural translation. In *Proceedings of the 2016 Conference of the North American Chapter of the Association for Computational Linguistics: Human Language Technologies*. pages 30–34.

Barret Zoph, Deniz Yuret, Jonathan May, and Kevin Knight. 2016. Transfer learning for low-resource neural machine translation. In *Proceedings of the 2016 Conference on Empirical Methods in Natural Language Processing*. pages 1568–1575.

Optimizing Differentiable Relaxations of Coreference Evaluation Metrics

Phong Le[1]   **Ivan Titov**[1,2]
[1]ILLC, University of Amsterdam
[2]ILCC, School of Informatics, University of Edinburgh
`p.le@uva.nl`   `ititov@inf.ed.ac.uk`

Abstract

Coreference evaluation metrics are hard to optimize directly as they are non-differentiable functions, not easily decomposable into elementary decisions. Consequently, most approaches optimize objectives only indirectly related to the end goal, resulting in suboptimal performance. Instead, we propose a differentiable relaxation that lends itself to gradient-based optimisation, thus bypassing the need for reinforcement learning or heuristic modification of cross-entropy. We show that by modifying the training objective of a competitive neural coreference system, we obtain a substantial gain in performance. This suggests that our approach can be regarded as a viable alternative to using reinforcement learning or more computationally expensive imitation learning.

1 Introduction

Coreference resolution is the task of identifying all mentions which refer to the same entity in a document. It has been shown beneficial in many natural language processing (NLP) applications, including question answering (Hermann et al., 2015) and information extraction (Kehler, 1997), and often regarded as a prerequisite to any text understanding task.

Coreference resolution can be regarded as a clustering problem: each cluster corresponds to a single entity and consists of all its mentions in a given text. Consequently, it is natural to evaluate predicted clusters by comparing them with the ones annotated by human experts, and this is exactly what the standard metrics (e.g., MUC, B^3, CEAF) do. In contrast, most state-of-the-art systems are optimized to make individual co-

reference decisions, and such losses are only indirectly related to the metrics.

One way to deal with this challenge is to optimize directly the non-differentiable metrics using reinforcement learning (RL), for example, relying on the REINFORCE policy gradient algorithm (Williams, 1992). However, this approach has not been very successful, which, as suggested by Clark and Manning (2016a), is possibly due to the discrepancy between sampling decisions at training time and choosing the highest ranking ones at test time. A more successful alternative is using a 'roll-out' stage to associate cost with possible decisions, as in Clark and Manning (2016a), but it is computationally expensive. Imitation learning (Ma et al., 2014b; Clark and Manning, 2015), though also exploiting metrics, requires access to an expert policy, with exact policies not directly computable for the metrics of interest.

In this work, we aim at combining the best of both worlds by proposing a simple method that can turn popular coreference evaluation metrics into differentiable functions of model parameters. As we show, this function can be computed recursively using scores of individual local decisions, resulting in a simple and efficient estimation procedure. The key idea is to replace non-differentiable indicator functions (e.g. the member function $\mathbb{I}(m \in S)$) with the corresponding posterior probabilities ($p(m \in S)$) computed by the model. Consequently, non-differentiable functions used within the metrics (e.g. the set size function $|S| = \sum_m \mathbb{I}(m \in S)$) become differentiable ($|S|_c = \sum_m p(m \in S)$). Though we assume that the scores of the underlying statistical model can be used to define a probability model, we show that this is not a serious limitation. Specifically, as a baseline we use a probabilistic version of the neural mention-ranking

390

Proceedings of the 21st Conference on Computational Natural Language Learning (CoNLL 2017), pages 390–399,
Vancouver, Canada, August 3 - August 4, 2017. ©2017 Association for Computational Linguistics

model of Wiseman et al. (2015b), which on its own outperforms the original one and achieves similar performance to its global version (Wiseman et al., 2016). Importantly when we use the introduced differentiable relaxations in training, we observe a substantial gain in performance over our probabilistic baseline. Interestingly, the absolute improvement (+0.52) is higher than the one reported in Clark and Manning (2016a) using RL (+0.05) and the one using reward rescaling[1] (+0.37). This suggests that our method provides a viable alternative to using RL and reward rescaling.

The outline of our paper is as follows: we introduce our neural resolver baseline and the B^3 and LEA metrics in Section 2. Our method to turn a mention ranking resolver into an entity-centric resolver is presented in Section 3, and the proposed differentiable relaxations in Section 4. Section 5 shows our experimental results.

2 Background

2.1 Neural mention ranking

In this section we introduce neural mention ranking, the framework which underpins current state-of-the-art models (Clark and Manning, 2016a). Specifically, we consider a probabilistic version of the method proposed by Wiseman et al. (2015b). In experiments we will use it as our baseline.

Let $(m_1, m_2, .., m_n)$ be the list of mentions in a document. For each mention m_i, let $a_i \in \{1, ..., i\}$ be the index of the mention that m_i is coreferent with (if $a_i = i$, m_i is the first mention of some entity appearing in the document). As standard in coreference resolution literature, we will refer to m_{a_i} as an antecedent of m_i.[2] Then, in mention ranking the goal is to score antecedents of a mention higher than any other mentions, i.e., if s is the scoring function, we require $s(a_i = j) > s(a_i = k)$ for all j, k such that m_i and m_j are coreferent but m_i and m_k are not.

Let $\phi_a(m_i) \in \mathbb{R}^{d_a}$ and $\phi_p(m_i, m_j) \in \mathbb{R}^{d_p}$ be respectively features of m_i and features of pair

(m_i, m_j). The scoring function is defined by:

$$s(a_i = j) = \begin{cases} \mathbf{u}^T \begin{bmatrix} \mathbf{h}_a(m_i) \\ \mathbf{h}_p(m_i, m_j) \end{bmatrix} + u_0 & \text{if } j < i \\ \mathbf{v}^T \mathbf{h}_a(m_i) + v_0 & \text{if } j = i \end{cases}$$

where

$$\mathbf{h}_a(m_i) = \tanh(\mathbf{W}_a \phi_a(m_i) + \mathbf{b}_a)$$
$$\mathbf{h}_p(m_i, m_j) = \tanh(\mathbf{W}_p \phi_p(m_i, m_j) + \mathbf{b}_p)$$

and $\mathbf{u}, \mathbf{v}, \mathbf{W}_a, \mathbf{W}_p, \mathbf{b}_a, \mathbf{b}_p$ are real vectors and matrices with proper dimensions, u_0, v_0 are real scalars.

Unlike Wiseman et al. (2015b), where the max-margin loss is used, we define a probabilistic model. The probability[3] that m_i and m_j are coreferent is given by

$$p(a_i = j) = \frac{\exp\{s(a_i = j)\}}{\sum_{j'=1}^{i} \exp\{s(a_i = j')\}} \quad (1)$$

Following Durrett and Klein (2013) we use the following softmax-margin (Gimpel and Smith, 2010) loss function:

$$L(\Theta) = -\sum_{i=1}^{n} \log \Big(\sum_{j \in C(m_i)} p'(a_i = j) \Big) + \lambda ||\Theta||_1,$$

where Θ are model parameters, $C(m_i)$ is the set of the indices of correct antecedents of m_i, and $p'(a_i = j) \propto p(a_i = j)e^{\Delta(j, C(m_i))}$. Δ is a cost function used to manipulate the contribution of different error types to the loss function:

$$\Delta(j, C(m_i)) = \begin{cases} \alpha_1 & \text{if } j \neq i \wedge i \in C(m_i) \\ \alpha_2 & \text{if } j = i \wedge i \notin C(m_i) \\ \alpha_3 & \text{if } j \neq i \wedge j \notin C(m_i) \\ 0 & \text{otherwise} \end{cases}$$

The error types are "false anaphor", "false new", "wrong link", and "no mistake", respectively. In our experiments, we borrow their values from Durrett and Klein (2013): $(\alpha_1, \alpha_2, \alpha_3) = (0.1, 3, 1)$. In the subsequent discussion, we refer to the loss as *mention-ranking heuristic cross entropy.*

---

[1] Reward rescaling is a technique that computes error values for a heuristic loss function based on the reward difference between the best decision according to the current model and the decision leading to the highest metric score.

[2] This slightly deviates from the definition of antecedents in linguistics (Crystal, 1997).

[3] For the sake of readability, we do not explicitly mark in our notation that all the probabilities are conditioned on the document (e.g., the mentions) and dependent on model parameters.

2.2 Evaluation Metrics

We use five most popular metrics[4],

- MUC (Vilain et al., 1995),

- B^3 (Bagga and Baldwin, 1998),

- CEAF_m, CEAF_e (Luo, 2005),

- BLANC (Luo et al., 2014),

- LEA (Moosavi and Strube, 2016).

for evaluation. However, because MUC is the least discriminative metric (Moosavi and Strube, 2016), whereas CEAF is slow to compute, out of the five most popular metrics we incorporate into our loss only B^3. In addition, we integrate LEA, as it has been shown to provide a good balance between discriminativity and interpretability.

Let $G = \{G_1, G_2, ..., G_N\}$ and $S = \{S_1, S_2, ..., S_M\}$ be the gold-standard entity set and an entity set given by a resolver. Recall that an entity is a set of mentions. The recall and precision of the B^3 metric is computed by:

$$R_{B^3} = \frac{\sum_{v=1}^{N} \sum_{u=1}^{M} \frac{|G_v \cap S_u|^2}{|G_v|}}{\sum_{v=1}^{N} |G_v|}$$

$$P_{B^3} = \frac{\sum_{u=1}^{M} \sum_{v=1}^{N} \frac{|G_v \cap S_u|^2}{|S_u|}}{\sum_{u=1}^{M} |S_u|}$$

The LEA metric is computed as:

$$R_{LEA} = \frac{\sum_{v=1}^{N} \left(|G_v| \times \sum_{u=1}^{M} \frac{link(G_v \cap S_u)}{link(G_v)} \right)}{\sum_{v=1}^{N} |G_v|}$$

$$P_{LEA} = \frac{\sum_{u=1}^{M} \left(|S_u| \times \sum_{v=1}^{N} \frac{link(G_v \cap S_u)}{link(S_u)} \right)}{\sum_{u=1}^{M} |S_u|}$$

where $link(E) = |E| \times (|E| - 1)/2$ is the number of coreference links in entity E. F_β, for both metrics, is defined by:

$$F_\beta = (1 + \beta^2) \frac{P \times R}{\beta^2 P + R}$$

$\beta = 1$ is used in the standard evaluation.

------

[4]All are implemented in Pradhan et al. (2014), https://github.com/conll/ reference-coreference-scorers.

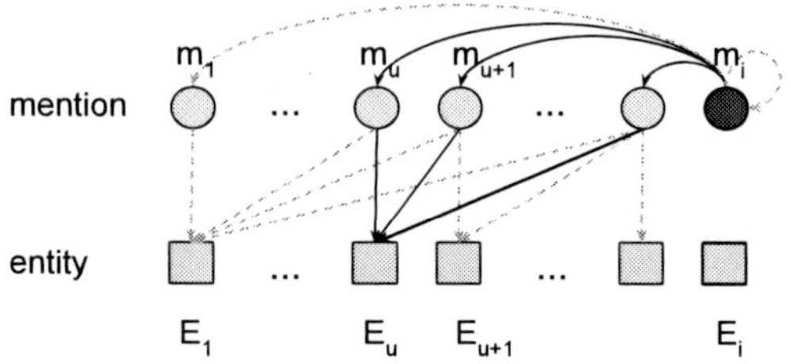

Figure 1: For each mention m_u there is a potential entity E_u so that m_u is the first mention in the chain. Computing $p(m_i \in E_u), u < i$ takes into the account all directed paths from m_i to E_u (black arrows). Noting that there is no directed path from any $m_k, k < u$ to E_u because $p(m_k \in E_u) = 0$. (See text for more details.)

3 From mention ranking to entity centricity

Mention-ranking resolvers do not explicitly provide information about entities/clusters which is required by B^3 and LEA. We therefore propose a simple solution that can turn a mention-ranking resolver into an entity-centric one.

First note that in a document containing n mentions, there are n potential entities $E_1, E_2, ..., E_n$ where E_i has m_i as the first mention. Let $p(m_i \in E_u)$ be the probability that mention m_i corresponds to entity E_u. We now show that it can be computed recursively based on $p(a_i = j)$ as follows:

$$p(m_i \in E_u) =$$
$$\begin{cases} \sum_{j=u}^{i-1} p(a_i = j) \times p(m_j \in E_u) & \text{if } u < i \\ p(a_i = i) & \text{if } u = i \\ 0 & \text{if } u > i \end{cases}$$

In other words, if $u < i$, we consider all possible m_j with which m_i can be coreferent, and which can correspond to entity E_u. If $u = i$, the link to be considered is the m_i's self-link. And, if $u > i$, the probability is zero, as it is impossible for m_i to be assigned to an entity introduced only later. See Figure 1 for extra information.

We now turn to two crucial questions about this formula:

- *Is $p(m_i \in \bullet)$ a valid probability distribution?*

- *Is it possible for a mention m_u to be mostly anaphoric (i.e. $p(m_u \in E_u)$ is low) but for the corresponding cluster E_u to be highly* *probable (i.e. $p(m_i \in E_u)$ is high for some i)?*

The first question is answered in Proposition 1. The second question is important because, intuitively, when a mention m_u is anaphoric, the potential entity E_u does not exist. We will show that the answer is "No" by proving in Proposition 2 that the probability that m_u is anaphoric is always higher than any probability that m_i, $i > u$ refers to E_u.

Proposition 1. $p(m_i \in \bullet)$ *is a valid probability distribution, i.e.,* $\sum_{u=1}^{n} p(m_i \in E_u) = 1$, *for all* $i = 1, ..., n$.

Proof. We prove this proposition by induction.

Basis: it is obvious that $\sum_{u=1}^{n} p(m_1 \in E_u) = p(a_1 = 1) = 1$.

Assume that $\sum_{u=1}^{n} p(m_j \in E_u) = 1$ for all $j < i$. Then,

$$\sum_{u=1}^{i-1} p(m_i \in E_u)$$

$$= \sum_{u=1}^{i-1} \sum_{j=u}^{i-1} p(a_i = j) \times p(m_j \in E_u)$$

Because $p(m_j \in E_u) = 0$ for all $j < u$, this expression is equal to

$$\sum_{u=1}^{i-1} \sum_{j=1}^{i-1} p(a_i = j) \times p(m_j \in E_u)$$

$$= \sum_{j=1}^{i-1} p(a_i = j) \times \sum_{u=1}^{i-1} p(m_j \in E_u)$$

$$= \sum_{j=1}^{i-1} p(a_i = j)$$

Therefore,

$$\sum_{u=1}^{n} p(m_i \in E_u) = \sum_{j=1}^{i-1} p(a_i = j) + p(a_i = i) = 1$$

(according to Equation 1). $\qquad\square$

Proposition 2. $p(m_i \in E_u) \leq p(m_u \in E_u)$ *for all $i > u$.*

Proof. We prove this proposition by induction.

Basis: for $i = u + 1$,

$$p(m_{u+1} \in E_u) = p(a_{u+1} = u) \times p(m_u \in E_u)$$
$$\leq p(m_u \in E_u)$$

Assume that $p(m_j \in E_u) \leq p(m_u \in E_u)$ for all $j \geq u$ and $j < i$. Then

$$p(m_i \in E_u) = \sum_{j=u}^{i-1} p(a_i = j) \times p(m_j \in E_u)$$

$$\leq \sum_{j=u}^{i-1} p(a_i = j) \times p(m_u \in E_u)$$

$$\leq p(m_u \in E_u) \times \sum_{j=1}^{i} p(a_i = j)$$

$$= p(m_u \in E_u)$$

$\qquad\square$

3.1 Entity-centric heuristic cross entropy loss

Having $p(m_i \in E_u)$ computed, we can consider coreference resolution as a multiclass prediction problem. An entity-centric heuristic cross entropy loss is thus given below:

$$L_{ec}(\Theta) = -\sum_{i=1}^{n} \log p'(m_i \in E_{e(m_i)}) + \lambda ||\Theta||_1$$

where $E_{e(m_i)}$ is the correct entity that m_i belongs to, $p'(m_i \in E_u) \propto p(m_i \in E_u)e^{\Gamma(u,e(m_i))}$. Similar to Δ in the mention-ranking heuristic loss in Section 2.1, Γ is a cost function used to manipulate the contribution of the four different error types ("false anaphor", "false new", "wrong link", and "no mistake"):

$$\Gamma(u, e(m_i)) =$$
$$\begin{cases} \gamma_1 & \text{if } u \neq i \wedge e(m_i) = i \\ \gamma_2 & \text{if } u = i \wedge e(m_i) \neq i \\ \gamma_3 & \text{if } u \neq e(m_i) \wedge u \neq i \wedge e(m_i) \neq i \\ 0 & \text{otherwise} \end{cases}$$

4 From non-differentiable metrics to differentiable losses

There are two functions used in computing B^3 and LEA: the set size function $|.|$ and the link function $link(.)$. Because both of them are non-differentiable, the two metrics are non-differentiable. We thus need to make these two functions differentiable.

There are two remarks. Firstly, both functions can be computed using the indicator function

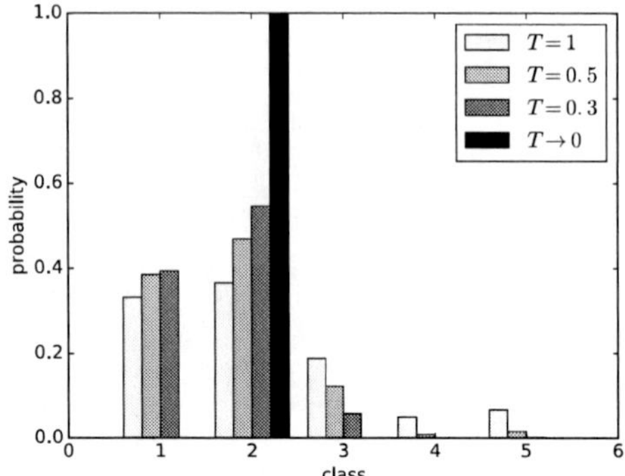

Figure 2: Softmax $\frac{\exp\{\pi_i/T\}}{\sum_j \exp\{\pi_j/T\}}$ with different values of T. The softmax becomes more peaky when the value of T gets smaller. As $T \to 0$ the softmax converges to the indicator function that chooses $\arg\max_i \pi_i$.

$\mathbb{I}(m_i \in S_u)$:

$$|S_u| = \sum_{i=1}^{n} \mathbb{I}(m_i \in S_u)$$

$$link(S_u) = \sum_{j<i} \mathbb{I}(m_i \in S_u) \times \mathbb{I}(m_j \in S_u)$$

Secondly, given $\pi_{i,u} = \log p(m_i \in S_u)$, the indicator function $\mathbb{I}(m_i \in S_{u^*})$, $u^* = \arg\max_u p(m_i \in S_u)$ is the converging point of the following softmax as $T \to 0$ (see Figure 2):

$$p(m_i \in S_u; T) = \frac{\exp\{\pi_{i,u}/T\}}{\sum_v \exp\{\pi_{i,v}/T\}}$$

where T is called *temperature* (Kirkpatrick et al., 1983).

Therefore, we propose to represent each S_u as a *soft*-cluster:

$$S_u = \{p(m_1 \in E_u; T), ..., p(m_n \in E_u; T)\}$$

where, as defined in Section 3, E_u is the potential entity that has m_u as the first mention. Replacing the indicator function $\mathbb{I}(m_i \in S_u)$ by the probability distribution $p(m_i \in E_u; T)$, we then have a *differentiable* version for the set size function and the link function:

$$|S_u|_d = \sum_{i=1}^{n} p(m_i \in E_u; T)$$

$$link_d(S_u) = \sum_{j<i} p(m_i \in E_u; T) \times p(m_j \in E_u; T)$$

$|G_v \cap S_u|_d$ and $link_d(G_v \cap S_u)$ are computed similarly with the constraint that only mentions in G_v are taken into account. Plugging these functions into precision and recall of B^3 and LEA in Section 2.2, we obtain differentiable $\hat{F}_{\beta,B^3}$ and $\hat{F}_{\beta,LEA}$, which are then used in two loss functions:

$$L_{\beta,B^3}(\Theta; T) = -\hat{F}_{\beta,B^3}(\Theta; T) + \lambda||\Theta||_1$$

$$L_{\beta,LEA}(\Theta; T) = -\hat{F}_{\beta,LEA}(\Theta; T) + \lambda||\Theta||_1$$

where λ is the hyper-parameter of the L_1 regularization terms.

It is worth noting that, as $T \to 0$, $\hat{F}_{\beta,B^3} \to F_{\beta,B^3}$ and $\hat{F}_{\beta,LEA} \to F_{\beta,LEA}$.[5] Therefore, when training a model with the proposed losses, we can start at a high temperature (e.g., $T = 1$) and anneal to a small but non-zero temperature. However, in our experiments we fix $T = 1$. Annealing is left for future work.

5   Experiments

We now demonstrate how to use the proposed differentiable B^3 and LEA to train a coreference resolver. The source code and trained models are available at `https://github.com/lephong/diffmetric_coref`.

Setup

We run experiments on the English portion of CoNLL 2012 data (Pradhan et al., 2012) which consists of 3,492 documents in various domains and formats. The split provided in the CoNLL 2012 shared task is used. In all our resolvers, we use not the original features of Wiseman et al. (2015b) but their slight modification described in Wiseman et al. (2016) (section 6.1).[6]

Resolvers

We build following baseline and three resolvers:

- baseline: the resolver presented in Section 2.1. We use the identical configuration as in Wiseman et al. (2016): $\mathbf{W}_a \in \mathbb{R}^{200 \times d_a}$, $\mathbf{W}_p \in \mathbb{R}^{700 \times d_p}$, $\lambda = 10^{-6}$ (where d_a, d_p are respectively the numbers of mention features and pair-wise features). We also employ their pretraining methodology.

---

[5] We can easily prove this using the algebraic limit theorem.

[6] `https://github.com/swiseman/nn_coref/`

- L_{ec}: the resolver using the entity-centric cross entropy loss introduced in Section 3.1. We set $(\gamma_1, \gamma_2, \gamma_3) = (\alpha_1, \alpha_2, \alpha_3) = (0.1, 3, 1)$.

- L_{β,B^3} and $L_{\beta,LEA}$: the resolvers using the losses proposed in Section 4. β is tuned on the development set by trying each value in $\{\sqrt{0.8}, 1, \sqrt{1.2}, \sqrt{1.4}, \sqrt{1.6}, \sqrt{1.8}, 1.5, 2\}$.

To train these resolvers we use AdaGrad (Duchi et al., 2011) to minimize their loss functions with the learning rate tuned on the development set and with one-document mini-batches. Note that we use the baseline as the initialization point to train the other three resolvers.

5.1 Results

We firstly compare our resolvers against Wiseman et al. (2015b) and Wiseman et al. (2016). Results are shown in the first half of Table 1. Our baseline surpasses Wiseman et al. (2015b). It is likely due to using features from Wiseman et al. (2016). Using the entity-centric heuristic cross entropy loss and the relaxations are clearly beneficial: L_{ec} is slightly better than our baseline and on par with the global model of Wiseman et al. (2016). $L_{\beta=1,B^3}, L_{\beta=1,LEA}$ outperform the baseline, the global model of Wiseman et al. (2016), and L_{ec}. However, the best values of β are $\sqrt{1.4}$, $\sqrt{1.8}$ respectively for L_{β,B^3}, and $L_{\beta,LEA}$. Among these resolvers, $L_{\beta=\sqrt{1.8},LEA}$ achieves the highest F_1 scores across all the metrics except BLANC.

When comparing to Clark and Manning (2016a) (the second half of Table 1), we can see that the absolute improvement over the baselines (i.e. 'heuristic loss' for them and the heuristic cross entropy loss for us) is higher than that of reward rescaling but with much shorter training time: +0.37 (7 days[7]) and +0.52 (15 hours) on the CoNLL metric for Clark and Manning (2016a) and ours, respectively. It is worth noting that our absolute scores are weaker than these of Clark and Manning (2016a), as they build on top of a similar but stronger mention-ranking baseline, which employs deeper neural networks and requires a much larger number of epochs to train (300 epochs, including pretraining). For the purpose of illustrating the proposed losses, we started with a simpler model by Wiseman et al. (2015b) which requires

---

[7]As reported in `https://github.com/clarkkev/deep-coref`

(a) [...] that $_{13}$[the virus] could mutate [...] /. In fact some health experts say $_{17}$[it]$^{13*}_{17,17}$'s just a matter of time [...]
(b) Walk a mile in $_{157}$[our] shoes that 's all I have to say because anybody who works in a nursing home will very quickly learn that these are very fragile patients /. $_{165}$[We]$^{157}_{165*,157}$ did the very best $_{167}$[we]$^{165}_{165,165}$ could in these situations [...]

Figure 3: Example predictions: the subscript before a mention is its index. The superscript / subscript after a mention indicates the antecedent predicted by the baseline / $L_{\beta=1,B^3}$, $L_{\beta=\sqrt{1.4},B^3}$. Mentions with the same color are true coreferents. "*"s mark *incorrect* decisions.

a much smaller number of epochs, thus faster, to train (20 epochs, including pretraining).

5.2 Analysis

Table 2 shows the breakdown of errors made by the baseline and our resolvers on the development set. The proposed resolvers make fewer "false anaphor" and "wrong link" errors but more "false new" errors compared to the baseline. This suggests that loss optimization prevents over-clustering, driving the precision up: when antecedents are difficult to detect, the self-link (i.e., $a_i = i$) is chosen. When β increases, they make more "false anaphor" and "wrong link" errors but less "false new" errors.

In Figure 3(a) the baseline, but not $L_{\beta=1,B^3}$ nor $L_{\beta=\sqrt{1.4},B^3}$, mistakenly links $_{17}$[it] with $_{13}$[the virus]. Under-clustering, on the other hand, is a problem for our resolvers with $\beta = 1$: in example (b), $L_{\beta=1,B^3}$ missed $_{165}$[We]. This behaviour results in a reduced recall but the recall is not damaged severely, as we still obtain a better F_1 score. We conjecture that this behaviour is a consequence of using the F_1 score in the objective, and, if undesirable, F_β with $\beta > 1$ can be used instead. For instance, also in Figure 3, $L_{\beta=\sqrt{1.4},B^3}$ correctly detects $_{17}$[it] as non-anaphoric and links $_{165}$[We] with $_{157}$[our].

Figure 4 shows recall, precision, F_1 (average of MUC, B^3, CEAF$_e$), on the development set when training with L_{β,B^3} and $L_{\beta,LEA}$. As expected, higher values of β yield lower precisions but higher recalls. In contrast, F_1 increases until

	MUC	B^3	$CEAF_m$	$CEAF_e$	BLANC	LEA	CoNLL
Wiseman et al. (2015b)	72.60	60.52	-	57.05	-	-	63.39
Wiseman et al. (2016)	73.42	61.50	-	57.70	-	-	64.21
Our proposals							
baseline (heuristic loss)	73.22	61.44	65.12	57.74	62.16	57.52	64.13
L_{ec}	73.2	61.75	65.77	57.8	**63.3**	57.89	64.25
$L_{\beta=1,B^3}$	73.37	61.94	65.79	58.22	63.19	58.06	64.51
$L_{\beta=\sqrt{1.4},B^3}$	73.48	61.99	65.9	58.36	63.1	58.13	64.61
$L_{\beta=1,LEA}$	73.3	61.88	65.69	57.99	63.27	58.03	64.39
$L_{\beta=\sqrt{1.8},LEA}$	**73.53**	**62.04**	**65.95**	**58.41**	63.09	**58.18**	**64.66**
Clark and Manning (2016a)							
baseline (heuristic loss)	74.65	63.03	-	58.40	-	-	65.36
REINFORCE	74.48	63.09	-	58.67	-	-	65.41
Reward Rescaling	74.56	63.40	-	59.23	-	-	65.73

Table 1: Results (F_1) on CoNLL 2012 test set. CoNLL is the average of MUC, B^3, and $CEAF_e$.

	Non-Anaphoric (FA)			Anaphoric (FN + WL)		
	Proper	Nominal	Pronom.	Proper	Nominal	Pronom.
baseline	630	714	1051	374 + 190	821 + 238	347 + 779
L_{ec}	529	609	904	438 + 182	924 + 220	476 + 740
$L_{\beta=1,B^3}$	545	559	883	433 + 172	951 + 192	457 + 761
$L_{\beta=\sqrt{1.4},B^3}$	557	564	926	426 + 178	941 + 194	431 + 766
$L_{\beta=1,LEA}$	513	547	843	456 + 170	960 + 191	513 + 740
$L_{\beta=\sqrt{1.8},LEA}$	577	591	1001	416 + 176	919 + 198	358 + 790

Table 2: Number of: "false anaphor" (FA, a non-anaphoric mention marked as anaphoric), "false new" (FN, an anaphoric mention marked as non-anaphoric), and "wrong link" (WL, an anaphoric mention is linked to a wrong antecedent) errors on the development set.

reaching the highest point when $\beta = \sqrt{1.4} \approx 1.18$ for L_{β,B^3} ($\beta = \sqrt{1.8} \approx 1.34$ for $L_{\beta,LEA}$), it then decreases gradually.

5.3 Discussion

Because the resolvers are evaluated on F_1 score metrics, it should be that L_{β,B^3} and $L_{\beta,LEA}$ perform the best with $\beta = 1$. Figure 4 and Table 1 however do not confirm that: β should be set with values a little bit larger than 1. There are two hypotheses. First, the statistical difference between the training set and the development set leads to the case that the optimal β on one set can be suboptimal on the other set. Second, in our experiments we fix $T = 1$, meaning that the relaxations might not be close to the true evaluation metrics enough. Our future work, to confirm/reject this, is to use annealing, i.e., gradually decreasing T down to (but larger than) 0.

Table 1 shows that the difference between L_{β,B^3} and $L_{\beta,LEA}$ in terms of accuracy is not substan-

tial (although the latter is slightly better than the former). However, one should expect that L_{β,B^3} would outperform $L_{\beta,LEA}$ on B^3 metric while it would be the other way around on LEA metric. It turns out that, B^3 and LEA behave quite similarly in non-extreme cases. We can see that in Figure 2, 4, 5, 6, 7 in Moosavi and Strube (2016).

6 Related work

Mention ranking and entity centricity are two main streams in the coreference resolution literature. Mention ranking (Denis and Baldridge, 2007; Durrett and Klein, 2013; Martschat and Strube, 2015; Wiseman et al., 2015a) considers local and independent decisions when choosing a correct antecedent for a mention. This approach is computationally efficient and currently dominant with state-of-the-art performance (Wiseman et al., 2016; Clark and Manning, 2016a). Wiseman et al. (2015b) propose to use simple neural

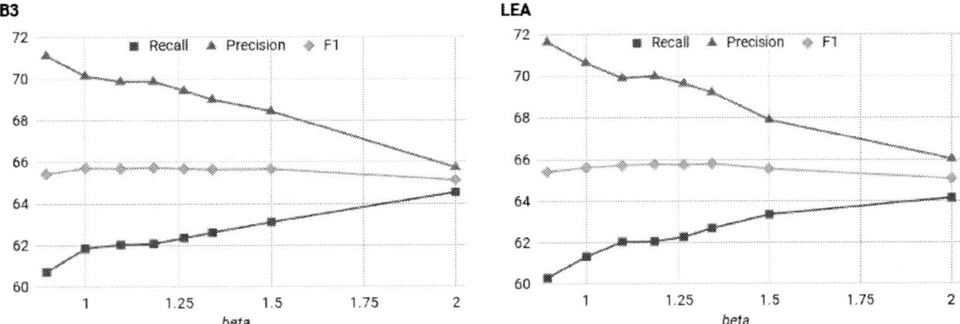

Figure 4: Recall, precision, F_1 (average of MUC, B^3, $CEAF_e$), on the development set when training with L_{β,B^3} (left) and $L_{\beta,LEA}$ (right). Higher values of β yield lower precisions but higher recalls.

networks to compute mention ranking scores and to use a heuristic loss to train the model. Wiseman et al. (2016) extend this by employing LSTMs to compute mention-chain representations which are then used to compute ranking scores. They call these representations *global features*. Clark and Manning (2016a) build a similar resolver as in Wiseman et al. (2015b) but much stronger thanks to deeper neural networks and "better mention detection, more effective, hyperparameters, and more epochs of training". Furthermore, using reward rescaling they achieve the best performance in the literature on the English and Chinese portions of the CoNLL 2012 dataset. Our work is built upon mention ranking by turning a mention-ranking model into an entity-centric one. It is worth noting that although we use the model proposed by Wiseman et al. (2015b), any mention-ranking models can be employed.

Entity centricity (Wellner and McCallum, 2003; Poon and Domingos, 2008; Haghighi and Klein, 2010; Ma et al., 2014a; Clark and Manning, 2016b), on the other hand, incorporates entity-level information to solve the problem. The approach can be top-down as in Haghighi and Klein (2010) where they propose a generative model. It can also be bottom-up by merging smaller clusters into bigger ones as in Clark and Manning (2016b). The method proposed by Ma et al. (2014a) greedily and incrementally adds mentions to previously built clusters using a prune-and-score technique. Importantly, employing imitation learning these two methods can optimize the resolvers directly on evaluation metrics. Our work is similar to Ma et al. (2014a) in the sense that our resolvers incrementally add mentions to previously built clusters.

However, different from both Ma et al. (2014a); Clark and Manning (2016b), our resolvers do not use any discrete decisions (e.g., merge operations). Instead, they seamlessly compute the probability that a mention refers to an entity from mention-ranking probabilities, and are optimized on differentiable relaxations of evaluation metrics.

Using differentiable relaxations of evaluation metrics as in our work is related to a line of research in reinforcement learning where a non-differentiable action-value function is replaced by a differentiable critic (Sutton et al., 1999; Silver et al., 2014). The critic is trained so that it is as close to the true action-value function as possible. This technique is applied to machine translation (Gu et al., 2017) where evaluation metrics (e.g., BLUE) are non-differentiable. A disadvantage of using critics is that there is no guarantee that the critic converges to the true evaluation metric given finite training data. In contrast, our differentiable relaxations do not need to train, and the convergence is guaranteed as $T \rightarrow 0$.

7 Conclusions

We have proposed

- a method for turning any mention-ranking resolver into an entity-centric one by using a recursive formula to combine scores of individual local decisions, and

- differentiable relaxations for two coreference evaluation metrics, B^3 and LEA.

Experimental results show that our approach outperforms the resolver by Wiseman et al. (2016), and gains a higher improvement over the baseline than that of Clark and Manning (2016a) but with much shorter training time.

Acknowledgments

We would like to thank Raquel Fernández, Wilker Aziz, Nafise Sadat Moosavi, and anonymous reviewers for their suggestions and comments. The project was supported by the European Research Council (ERC StG BroadSem 678254), the Dutch National Science Foundation (NWO VIDI 639.022.518) and an Amazon Web Services (AWS) grant.

References

Amit Bagga and Breck Baldwin. 1998. Algorithms for scoring coreference chains. In *The first international conference on language resources and evaluation workshop on linguistics coreference*. volume 1, pages 563–566.

Kevin Clark and Christopher D. Manning. 2016a. Deep reinforcement learning for mention-ranking coreference models. In *Proceedings of the 2016 Conference on Empirical Methods in Natural Language Processing*. Association for Computational Linguistics, Austin, Texas, pages 2256–2262. https://aclweb.org/anthology/D16-1245.

Kevin Clark and Christopher D. Manning. 2016b. Improving coreference resolution by learning entity-level distributed representations. In *Proceedings of the 54th Annual Meeting of the Association for Computational Linguistics (Volume 1: Long Papers)*. Association for Computational Linguistics, Berlin, Germany, pages 643–653. http://www.aclweb.org/anthology/P16-1061.

Kevin Clark and D. Christopher Manning. 2015. Entity-centric coreference resolution with model stacking. In *Proceedings of the 53rd Annual Meeting of the Association for Computational Linguistics and the 7th International Joint Conference on Natural Language Processing (Volume 1: Long Papers)*. Association for Computational Linguistics, pages 1405–1415. https://doi.org/10.3115/v1/P15-1136.

David Crystal. 1997. *Dictionary of Linguistics and Phonetics*. Blackwell Publishers, Cambrindge, MA.

Pascal Denis and Jason Baldridge. 2007. A ranking approach to pronoun resolution. In *IJCAI*. volume 158821593.

John Duchi, Elad Hazan, and Yoram Singer. 2011. Adaptive subgradient methods for online learning and stochastic optimization. *Journal of Machine Learning Research* 12(Jul):2121–2159.

Greg Durrett and Dan Klein. 2013. Easy victories and uphill battles in coreference resolution. In *Proceedings of the 2013 Conference on Empirical Methods in Natural Language Processing*. Association for Computational Linguistics, pages 1971–1982. http://aclweb.org/anthology/D13-1203.

Kevin Gimpel and Noah A. Smith. 2010. Softmax-margin crfs: Training log-linear models with cost functions. In *Human Language Technologies: The 2010 Annual Conference of the North American Chapter of the Association for Computational Linguistics*. Association for Computational Linguistics, Los Angeles, California, pages 733–736. http://www.aclweb.org/anthology/N10-1112.

Jiatao Gu, Kyunghyun Cho, and Victor OK Li. 2017. Trainable greedy decoding for neural machine translation. *arXiv preprint arXiv:1702.02429*.

Aria Haghighi and Dan Klein. 2010. Coreference resolution in a modular, entity-centered model. In *Human Language Technologies: The 2010 Annual Conference of the North American Chapter of the Association for Computational Linguistics*. Association for Computational Linguistics, pages 385–393.

Karl Moritz Hermann, Tomáš Kočiský, Edward Grefenstette, Lasse Espeholt, Will Kay, Mustafa Suleyman, and Phil Blunsom. 2015. Teaching machines to read and comprehend. In *Advances in Neural Information Processing Systems (NIPS)*. http://arxiv.org/abs/1506.03340.

Andrew Kehler. 1997. *Second Conference on Empirical Methods in Natural Language Processing*, chapter Probabilistic Coreference in Information Extraction. http://aclweb.org/anthology/W97-0319.

Scott Kirkpatrick, C Daniel Gelatt, Mario P Vecchi, et al. 1983. Optimization by simulated annealing. *science* 220(4598):671–680.

Xiaoqiang Luo. 2005. On coreference resolution performance metrics. In *Proceedings of Human Language Technology Conference and Conference on Empirical Methods in Natural Language Processing*. http://aclweb.org/anthology/H05-1004.

Xiaoqiang Luo, Sameer Pradhan, Marta Recasens, and Eduard Hovy. 2014. An extension of blanc to system mentions. In *Proceedings of the 52nd Annual Meeting of the Association for Computational Linguistics (Volume 2: Short Papers)*. Association for Computational Linguistics, pages 24–29. https://doi.org/10.3115/v1/P14-2005.

Chao Ma, Janardhan Rao Doppa, J. Walker Orr, Prashanth Mannem, Xiaoli Fern, Tom Dietterich, and Prasad Tadepalli. 2014a. Prune-and-score: Learning for greedy coreference resolution. In *Proceedings of the 2014 Conference on Empirical Methods in Natural Language Processing (EMNLP)*. Association for Computational Linguistics, Doha, Qatar, pages 2115–2126. http://www.aclweb.org/anthology/D14-1225.

Chao Ma, Rao Janardhan Doppa, Walker J. Orr, Prashanth Mannem, Xiaoli Fern, Tom Dietterich, and Prasad Tadepalli. 2014b. Prune-and-score: Learning for greedy coreference resolution. In *Proceedings of the 2014 Conference on Empirical Methods in Natural Language Processing (EMNLP)*. Association for Computational Linguistics, pages 2115–2126. https://doi.org/10.3115/v1/D14-1225.

Sebastian Martschat and Michael Strube. 2015. Latent structures for coreference resolution. *Transactions of the Association for Computational Linguistics* 3:405–418.

Nafise Sadat Moosavi and Michael Strube. 2016. Which coreference evaluation metric do you trust? a proposal for a link-based entity aware metric. In *Proceedings of the 54th Annual Meeting of the Association for Computational Linguistics (Volume 1: Long Papers)*. Association for Computational Linguistics, Berlin, Germany, pages 632–642. http://www.aclweb.org/anthology/P16-1060.

Hoifung Poon and Pedro Domingos. 2008. Joint unsupervised coreference resolution with markov logic. In *Proceedings of the conference on empirical methods in natural language processing*. Association for Computational Linguistics, pages 650–659.

Sameer Pradhan, Xiaoqiang Luo, Marta Recasens, Eduard Hovy, Vincent Ng, and Michael Strube. 2014. Scoring coreference partitions of predicted mentions: A reference implementation. In *Proceedings of the 52nd Annual Meeting of the Association for Computational Linguistics (Volume 2: Short Papers)*. Association for Computational Linguistics, Baltimore, Maryland, pages 30–35. http://www.aclweb.org/anthology/P14-2006.

Sameer Pradhan, Alessandro Moschitti, Nianwen Xue, Olga Uryupina, and Yuchen Zhang. 2012. *Joint Conference on EMNLP and CoNLL - Shared Task*, Association for Computational Linguistics, chapter CoNLL-2012 Shared Task: Modeling Multilingual Unrestricted Coreference in OntoNotes, pages 1–40. http://aclweb.org/anthology/W12-4501.

David Silver, Guy Lever, Nicolas Heess, Thomas Degris, Daan Wierstra, and Martin A. Riedmiller. 2014. Deterministic policy gradient algorithms. In *Proceedings of the 31th International Conference on Machine Learning, ICML 2014, Beijing, China, 21-26 June 2014*. pages 387–395. http://jmlr.org/proceedings/papers/v32/silver14.html.

Richard S Sutton, David A McAllester, Satinder P Singh, Yishay Mansour, et al. 1999. Policy gradient methods for reinforcement learning with function approximation. In *NIPS*. volume 99, pages 1057–1063.

Marc Vilain, John Burger, John Aberdeen, Dennis Connolly, and Lynette Hirschman. 1995. A model-theoretic coreference scoring scheme. In *Sixth Message Understanding Conference (MUC-6): Proceedings of a Conference Held in Columbia, Maryland, November 6-8, 1995*. http://aclweb.org/anthology/M95-1005.

B Wellner and A McCallum. 2003. Towards conditional models of identity uncertainty with application to proper noun coreference. In *IJCAI Workshop on Information Integration and the Web*.

Ronald J Williams. 1992. Simple statistical gradient-following algorithms for connectionist reinforcement learning. *Machine learning* 8(3-4):229–256.

Sam Wiseman, Alexander M Rush, Stuart M Shieber, and Jason Weston. 2015a. Learning anaphoricity and antecedent ranking features for coreference resolution. In *Proceedings of the 53rd Annual Meeting of the Association for Computational Linguistics*. Association for Computational Linguistics, volume 1, pages 92–100.

Sam Wiseman, M. Alexander Rush, and M. Stuart Shieber. 2016. Learning global features for coreference resolution. In *Proceedings of the 2016 Conference of the North American Chapter of the Association for Computational Linguistics: Human Language Technologies*. Association for Computational Linguistics, pages 994–1004. https://doi.org/10.18653/v1/N16-1114.

Sam Wiseman, M. Alexander Rush, Stuart Shieber, and Jason Weston. 2015b. Learning anaphoricity and antecedent ranking features for coreference resolution. In *Proceedings of the 53rd Annual Meeting of the Association for Computational Linguistics and the 7th International Joint Conference on Natural Language Processing (Volume 1: Long Papers)*. Association for Computational Linguistics, pages 1416–1426. https://doi.org/10.3115/v1/P15-1137.

Neural Structural Correspondence Learning for Domain Adaptation

Yftah Ziser and **Roi Reichart**
Faculty of Industrial Engineering and Management, Technion, IIT
syftah@campus.technion.ac.il, roiri@ie.technion.ac.il

Abstract

We introduce a neural network model that marries together ideas from two prominent strands of research on domain adaptation through representation learning: structural correspondence learning (*SCL*, (Blitzer et al., 2006)) and autoencoder neural networks (NNs). Our model is a three-layer NN that learns to encode the non-pivot features of an input example into a low-dimensional representation, so that the existence of pivot features (features that are prominent in both domains and convey useful information for the NLP task) in the example can be decoded from that representation. The low-dimensional representation is then employed in a learning algorithm for the task. Moreover, we show how to inject pre-trained word embeddings into our model in order to improve generalization across examples with similar pivot features. We experiment with the task of cross-domain sentiment classification on 16 domain pairs and show substantial improvements over strong baselines.[1]

1 Introduction

Many state-of-the-art algorithms for Natural Language Processing (NLP) tasks require labeled data. Unfortunately, annotating sufficient amounts of such data is often costly and labor intensive. Consequently, for many NLP applications even resource-rich languages like English have labeled data in only a handful of domains.

Domain adaptation (Daumé III, 2007; Ben-David et al., 2010), training an algorithm on labeled data taken from one domain so that it can perform properly on data from other domains, is therefore recognized as a fundamental challenge in NLP. Indeed, over the last decade domain adaptation methods have been proposed for tasks such as sentiment classification (Bollegala et al., 2011b), POS tagging (Schnabel and Schütze, 2013), syntactic parsing (Reichart and Rappoport, 2007; McClosky et al., 2010; Rush et al., 2012) and relation extraction (Jiang and Zhai, 2007; Bollegala et al., 2011a), if to name just a handful of applications and works.

Leading recent approaches to domain adaptation in NLP are based on Neural Networks (NNs), and particularly on autoencoders (Glorot et al., 2011; Chen et al., 2012). These models are believed to extract features that are robust to cross-domain variations. However, while excelling on benchmark domain adaptation tasks such as cross-domain product sentiment classification (Blitzer et al., 2007), the reasons to this success are not entirely understood.

In the pre-NN era, a prominent approach to domain adaptation in NLP, and particularly in sentiment classification, has been structural correspondence learning (*SCL*) (Blitzer et al., 2006, 2007). Following the auxiliary problems approach to semi-supervised learning (Ando and Zhang, 2005), this method identifies correspondences among features from different domains by modeling their correlations with *pivot* features: features that are frequent in both domains and are important for the NLP task. Non-pivot features from different domains which are correlated with many of the same pivot features are assumed to correspond, providing a bridge between the domains. Elegant and well motivated as it may be, SCL does not form the state-of-the-art since the neural approaches took over.

In this paper we marry these approaches, proposing NN models inspired by ideas from both.

---

[1] Our code is at: https://github.com/yftah89/Neural-SCL-Domain-Adaptation.

Proceedings of the 21st Conference on Computational Natural Language Learning (CoNLL 2017), pages 400–410,
Vancouver, Canada, August 3 - August 4, 2017. ©2017 Association for Computational Linguistics

Particularly, our basic model receives the non-pivot features of an input example, encodes them into a hidden layer and then, instead of decoding the input layer as an autoencoder would do, it aims to decode the pivot features. Our more advanced model is identical to the basic one except that the decoding matrix is not learned but is rather replaced with a fixed matrix consisting of pre-trained embeddings of the pivot features. Under this model the probability of the i-th pivot feature to appear in an example is a (non-linear) function of the dot product of the feature's embedding vector and the network's hidden layer vector. As explained in Section 3, this approach encourages the model to learn similar hidden layers for documents that have different pivot features as long as these features have similar meaning. In sentiment classification, for example, although one positive review may use the unigram pivot feature *excellent* while another positive review uses the pivot *great*, as long as the embeddings of pivot features with similar meaning are similar (as expected from high quality embeddings) the hidden layers learned for both documents are biased to be similar.

We experiment with the task of cross-domain product sentiment classification of (Blitzer et al., 2007), consisting of 4 domains (12 domain pairs) and further add an additional target domain, consisting of sentences extracted from social media blogs (total of 16 domain pairs). For pivot feature embedding in our advanced model, we employ the word2vec algorithm (Mikolov et al., 2013). Our models substantially outperform strong baselines: the SCL algorithm, the marginalized stacked denoising autoencoder (MSDA) model (Chen et al., 2012) and the MSDA-DAN model (Ganin et al., 2016) that combines the power of MSDA with a domain adversarial network (DAN).

2 Background and Contribution

Domain adaptation is a fundamental, long standing problem in NLP (e.g. (Roark and Bacchiani, 2003; Chelba and Acero, 2004; Daume III and Marcu, 2006)). The challenge stems from the fact that data in the source and the target domains are often distributed differently, making it hard for a model trained in the source domain to make valuable predictions in the target domain.

Domain adaptation has various setups, differing with respect to the amounts of labeled and unlabeled data available in the source and target domains. The setup we address, commonly referred to as unsupervised domain adaptation is where both domains have ample unlabeled data, but only the source domain has labeled training data.

There are several approaches to domain adaptation in the machine learning literature, including instance reweighting (Huang et al., 2007; Mansour et al., 2009), sub-sampling from both domains (Chen et al., 2011) and learning joint target and source feature representations (Blitzer et al., 2006; Daumé III, 2007; Xue et al., 2008; Glorot et al., 2011; Chen et al., 2012).

Here, we discuss works that, like us, take the representation learning path. Most works under this approach follow a two steps protocol: First, the representation learning method (be it SCL, an autoencoder network, our proposed network model or any other model) is trained on unlabeled data from both the source and the target domains; Then, a classifier for the supervised task (e.g. sentiment classification) is trained in the source domain and this trained classifier is applied to test examples from the target domain. Each input example of the task classifier, at both training and test, is first run through the representation model of the first step and the induced representation is fed to the classifier. Recently, end-to-end models that jointly learn to represent the data and to perform the classification task have also been proposed. We compare our models to one such method (MSDA-DAN, (Ganin et al., 2016)).

Below, we first discuss two prominent ideas in feature representation learning: pivot features and autoencoder neural networks. We then summarize our contribution in light of these approaches.

Pivot and Non-Pivot Features The definitions of this approach are given in Blitzer et al. (2006, 2007), where SCL is presented in the context of POS tagging and sentiment classification, respectively. Fundamentally, the method divides the shared feature space of both the source and the target domains to the set of pivot features that are frequent in both domains and are prominent in the NLP task, and a complementary set of non-pivot features. In this section we abstract away from the actual feature space and its division to pivot and non-pivot subsets. In Section 4 we discuss this issue in the context of sentiment classification.

For representation learning, SCL employs the pivot features in order to learn mappings from the original feature space of both domains to a shared, low-dimensional, real-valued feature space. This is done by training classifiers whose input consists of the non-pivot features of an input example and their binary classification task (the auxiliary task) is predicting, every classifier for one pivot feature, whether the pivot associated with the classifier appears in the input example or not. These classifiers are trained on unlabeled data from both the target and the source domains: the training supervision naturally occurs in the data, no human annotation is required. The matrix consisting of the weight vectors of these classifiers is then post-processed with singular value decomposition (SVD), to facilitate final compact representations. The SVD derived matrix serves as a transformation matrix which maps feature vectors in the original space into a low-dimensional real-valued feature space.

Numerous works have employed the SCL method in particular and the concept of pivot features for domain adaptation in general. A prominent method is spectral feature alignment (SFA, (Pan et al., 2010)). This method aims to align domain-specific (non-pivot) features from different domains into unified clusters, with the help of domain-independent (pivot) features as a bridge.

Recently, Gouws et al. (2012) and Bollegala et al. (2015) implemented ideas related to those described here within an NN for cross-domain sentiment classification. For example, the latter work trained a word embedding model so that for every document, regardless of its domain, pivots are good predictors of non-pivots, and the pivots' embeddings are similar across domains. Yu and Jiang (2016) presented a convolutional NN that learns sentence embeddings using two auxiliary tasks (whether the sentence contains a positive or a negative domain independent sentiment word), purposely avoiding prediction with respect to a large set of pivot features. In contrast to these works our model can learn useful cross-domain representations for any type of input example and in our cross-domain sentiment classification experiments it learns document level embeddings. That is, unlike Bollegala et al. (2015) we do not learn word embeddings and unlike Yu and Jiang (2016) we are not restricted to input sentences.

Autoencoder NNs An autoencoder is comprised of an encoder function h and a decoder function g, typically with the dimension of h smaller than that of its argument. The reconstruction of an input x is given by $r(x) = g(h(x))$. Autoencoders are typically trained to minimize a reconstruction error $loss(x, r(x))$. Example loss functions are the squared error, the Kullback-Leibler (KL) divergence and the cross entropy of elements of x and elements of $r(x)$. The last two loss functions are appropriate options when the elements of x or $r(x)$ can be interpreted as probabilities of a discrete event. In Section 3 we get back to this point when defining the cross-entropy loss function of our model. Once an autoencoder has been trained, one can stack another autoencoder on top of it, by training a second model which sees the output of the first as its training data (Bengio et al., 2007). The parameters of the stack of autoencoders describe multiple representation levels for x and can feed a classifier, to facilitate domain adaptation.

Recent prominent models for domain adaptation for sentiment classification are based on a variant of the autoencoder called Stacked Denoising Autoencoders (SDA, (Vincent et al., 2008)). In a denoising autoencoder (DEA) the input vector x is stochastically corrupted into a vector $\tilde{x}$, and the model is trained to minimize a denoising reconstruction error $loss(x, r(\tilde{x}))$. SDA for cross-domain sentiment classification was implemented by Glorot et al. (2011). Later, Chen et al. (2012) proposed the marginalized SDA (MSDA) model that is more computationally efficient and scalable to high-dimensional feature spaces than SDA.

Marginalization of denoising autoencoders has gained interest since MSDA was presented. Yang and Eisenstein (2014) showed how to improve efficiency further by exploiting noising functions designed for structured feature spaces, which are common in NLP. More recently, Clinchant et al. (2016) proposed an unsupervised regularization method for MSDA based on the work of Ganin and Lempitsky (2015) and Ganin et al. (2016).

There is a recent interest in models based on variational autoencoders (Kingma and Welling, 2014; Rezende et al., 2014), for example the variational fair autoencoder model (Louizos et al., 2016), for domain adaptation. However, these models are still not competitive with MSDA on the tasks we consider here.

Our Contribution We propose an approach that marries the above lines of work. Our model is similar in structure to an autoencoder. However, instead of reconstructing the input x from the hidden layer $h(x)$, its reconstruction function r receives a low dimensional representation of the non-pivot features of the input ($h(x^{np})$, where x^{np} is the non-pivot representation of x (Section 3)) and predicts whether each of the pivot features appears in this example or not. As far as we know, we are the first to exploit the mutual strengths of pivot-based methods and autoencoders for domain adaptation.

3 Neural SCL Models

We propose two models: the basic *Autoencoder SCL (AE-SCL, 3.2))*, that directly integrates ideas from autoencoders and SCL, and the elaborated *Autoencoder SCL with Similarity Regularization (AE-SCL-SR, 3.3)*, where pre-trained word embeddings are integrated into the basic model.

3.1 Definitions

We denote the feature set in our problem with f, the subset of pivot features with $f_p \subseteq \{1, \ldots, |f|\}$ and the subset of non-pivot features with $f_{np} \subseteq \{1, \ldots, |f|\}$ such that $f_p \cup f_{np} = \{1, \ldots, |f|\}$ and $f_p \cap f_{np} = \emptyset$. We further denote the feature representation of an input example X with x. Following this notation, the vector of pivot features of X is denoted with x^p while the vector of non-pivot features is denoted with x^{np}.

In order to learn a robust and compact feature representation for X we will aim to learn a non-linear prediction function from x^{np} to x^p. As discussed in Section 4 the task we experiment with is cross-domain sentiment classification. Following previous work (e.g. (Blitzer et al., 2006, 2007; Chen et al., 2012) our feature representation consists of binary indicators for the occurrence of word unigrams and bigrams in the represented document. In what follows we hence assume that the feature representation x of an example X is a binary vector, and hence so are x^p and x^{np}.

3.2 Autoencoder SCL (AE-SCL)

In order to solve the prediction problem, we present an NN architecture inspired by autoencoders (Figure 1). Given an input example X with a feature representation x, our fundamental idea is to start from a non-pivot feature representation, x^{np}, encode x^{np} into an intermediate representation $h_{w^h}(x^{np})$, and, finally, predict with a function $r_{w^r}(h_{w^h}(x^{np}))$ the occurrences of pivot features, x^p, in the example.

As is standard in NN modeling, we introduce non-linearity to the model through a non-linear activation function denoted with σ (the sigmoid

function in our models). Consequently we get: $h_{w^h}(x^{np}) = \sigma(w^h x^{np})$ and $r_{w^r}(h_{w^h}(x^{np})) = \sigma(w^r h_{w^h}(x^{np}))$. In what follows we denote the output of the model with $o = r_{w^r}(h_{w^h}(x^{np}))$.

Since the sigmoid function outputs values in the $[0, 1]$ interval, o can be interpreted as a vector of probabilities with the i-th coordinate reflecting the probability of the i-th pivot feature to appear in the input example. Cross-entropy is hence a natural loss function to jointly reason about all pivots:

$$L(o, x^p) = \frac{1}{|f_p|} \sum_{i=1}^{|f_p|} x^p{}_i \cdot log(o_i) + (1-x^p{}_i) \cdot log(1-o_i)$$

As x^p is a binary vector, for each pivot feature, $x^p{}_i$, only one of the two members of the sum that take this feature into account gets a non-zero value. The higher the probability of the correct event is (whether or not $x^p{}_i$ appears in the input example), the lower is the loss.

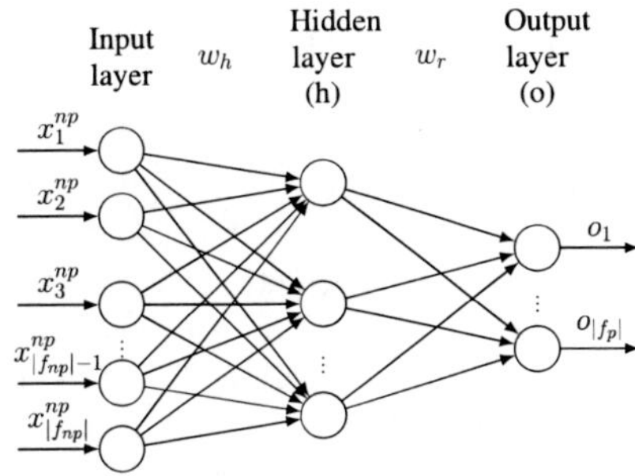

Figure 1: A Sketch of the AE-SCL and AE-SCL-SR models. While in AE-SCL both the encoding matrix w^h and the reconstruction matrix w^r are optimized, in AE-SCL-SR w^r is pre-trained by a word embedding model. See full details in text.

3.3 Autoencoder SCL with Similarity Regularization (AE-SCL-SR)

An important observation of Blitzer et al. (2007), is that some pivot features are similar to each other to the level that they indicate the same information with respect to the classification task. For example, in sentiment classification with word unigram features, the words (unigrams) *great* and *excellent* are likely to serve as pivot features, as the meaning of each of them is preserved across domains. At the same time, both features convey very similar (positive) sentiment information to the level that a sentiment classifier should treat them as equals.

The AE-SCL-SR model is based on two crucial observations. First, in many NLP tasks the pivot features can be pre-embedded into a vector space where pivots with similar meaning have similar vectors. Second, the set $f_p{}^{X_i}$ of pivot features that appear in an example X_i is typically much smaller than the set $\hat{f_p}{}^{X_i}$ of pivot features that do not appear in it. Hence, if the pivot features of X_1 and X_2 convey the same information about the NLP task (e.g. that the sentiment of both X_1 and X_2 is positive), then even if $f_p{}^{X_1}$ and $f_p{}^{X_2}$ are not identical, the intersection between the larger sets $\hat{f_p}{}^{X_1}$ and $\hat{f_p}{}^{X_2}$ is typically much larger than the symmetric difference between $f_p{}^{X_1}$ and $f_p{}^{X_2}$.

For instance, consider two examples, X_1 with the single pivot feature $f_1 = great$, and X_2, with the single pivot feature $f_2 = excellent$. Crucially, even though X_1 and X_2 differ with respect to the existence of f_1 and f_2, due to the similar meaning of these pivot features, we expect both X_1 and X_2 not to contain many other pivot features, such as *terrible, awful* and *mediocre*, whose meanings conflict with that of f_1 and f_2.

To exploit these observations, in AE-SCL-SR the reconstruction matrix w^r is pre-trained with a word embedding model and is kept fixed during the training and prediction phases of the neural network. Particularly, the i-th row of w^r is set to be the vector representation of the i-th pivot feature as learned by the word embedding model. Except from this change, the AE-SCL-SR model is identical to the AE-SCL model described above.

Now, denoting the encoding layer for X_1 with h_1 and the encoding layer for X_2 with h_2, we expect both $\sigma(w^r_{k_i} \cdot h_1)$ and $\sigma(w^r_{k_i} \cdot h_2)$ to get low values (i.e. values close to 0), for those k_i *conflicting pivot features*: pivots whose meanings conflict with that of $f_p{}^{X_1}$ and $f_p{}^{X_2}$. By fixing the representations of similar conflicting features to similar vectors, AE-SCL-SR provides a strong bias for h_1 and h_2 to be similar, as its only way to bias the predictions with respect to these features to be low is by pushing h_1 and h_2 to be similar. Consequently, under AE-SCL-SR the vectors that encode the non-pivot features of documents with similar pivot features are biased to be similar to each other. As mentioned in Section 4 the vector $\tilde{h} = \sigma^{-1}(h)$ forms the feature representation that is fed to the sentiment classifier to facilitate domain adaptation. By definition, when h_1 and h_2 are similar so are their $\tilde{h}_1$ and $\tilde{h}_2$ counterparts.

4 Experiments

In this section we describe our experiments. To facilitate clarity, some details are not given here and instead are provided in the appendices.

Cross-domain Sentiment Classification To demonstrate the power of our models for domain adaptation we experiment with the task of cross-domain sentiment classification (Blitzer et al., 2007). The data for this task consist of Amazon product reviews from four product domains: Books (B), DVDs (D), Electronic items (E) and Kitchen appliances (K). For each domain 2000 labeled reviews are provided: 1000 are classified as positive and 1000 as negative, and these are augmented with unlabeled reviews: 6000 (B), 34741 (D), 13153 (E) and 16785 (K).

We also consider an additional target domain, denoted with *Blog*: the University of Michigan sentence level sentiment dataset, consisting of sentences taken from social media blogs.[2] The dataset for the original task consists of a labeled training set (3995 positive and 3091 negative) and a 33052 sentences test set for which sentiment labels are not provided. We hence used the original test set as our target domain unlabeled set and the original training set as our target domain test set.

Baselines Cross-domain sentiment classification has been studied in a large number of papers. However, the difference in preprocessing methods, dataset splits to train/dev/test subsets and the different sentiment classifiers make it hard to directly compare between the numbers reported in past.

We hence compare our models to three strong baselines, running all models under the same conditions. We aim to select baselines that represent the state-of-the-art in cross-domain sentiment classification in general, and in the two lines of work we focus at: pivot based and autoencoder based representation learning, in particular.

The first baseline is SCL with pivot features selected using the mutual information criterion (SCL-MI, (Blitzer et al., 2007)). This is the SCL method where pivot features are frequent in the unlabeled data of both the source and the target domains, and among those features are the ones with the highest mutual information with the task (sentiment) label in the source domain labeled data. We implemented this method. In our implementation unigrams and bigrams should appear at least

---

[2] https://inclass.kaggle.com/c/si650winter11

10 times in both domains to be considered frequent. For non-pivot features we consider unigrams and bigrams that appear at least 10 times in their domain. The same pivot and non-pivot selection criteria are employed for our AE-SCL and AE-SCL-SR models.

Among autoencoder models, SDA has shown by Glorot et al. (2011) to outperform SFA and SCL on cross-domain sentiment classification and later on Chen et al. (2012) demonstrated superior performance for MSDA over SDA and SCL on the same task. Our second baseline is hence the MSDA method (Chen et al., 2012), with code taken from the authors' web page.[3]

To consider a regularization scheme on top of MSDA representations we also experiment with the MSDA-DAN model (Ganin et al., 2016) which employs a domain adversarial network (DAN) with the MSDA vectors as input. In Ganin et al. (2016) MSDA-DAN has shown to substantially outperform the DAN model when DAN is randomly initialized. The DAN code is taken from the authors' repository. [4]

For reference we compare to the No-DA case where the sentiment classifier is trained in the source domain and applied to the target domain without adaptation. The sentiment classifier we employ, in this case as well as with our methods and with the SCL-MI and MSDA baselines, is a standard logistic regression classifier.[5] [6]

Experimental Protocol Following the unsupervised domain adaptation setup (Section 2), we have access to unlabeled data from both the source and the target domains, which we use to train the representation learning models. However, only the source domain has labeled training data for sentiment classification. The original feature set we start from consists of word unigrams and bigrams.

All methods (baselines and ours), except from MSDA-DAN, follow a two-step protocol at both training and test time. In the first step, the input example is run through the representation model which generates a new feature vector for this example. Then, in the second step, this vector is concatenated with the original feature vector of the example and the resulting vector is fed into the sentiment classifier (this concatenation is a standard convention in the baseline methods).

For MSDA-DAN all the above holds, except from one exception. MSDA-DAN gets an input representation that consists of a concatenation of the original and the MSDA-induced feature sets. As this is an end-to-end model that predicts the sentiment class jointly with the new feature representation, we do not employ any additional sentiment classifier. As in the other models, MSDA-DAN utilizes source domain labeled data as well as unlabeled data from both the source and the target domains at training time.

We experiment with a 5-fold cross-validation on the source domain (Blitzer et al., 2007): 1600 reviews for training and 400 reviews for development. The test set for each target domain of Blitzer et al. (2007) consists of all 2000 labeled reviews of that domain, and for the Blog domain it consists of the 7086 labeled sentences provided with the task dataset. In all five folds half of the training examples and half of the development examples are randomly selected from the positive reviews and the other halves from the negative reviews. We report average results across these five folds, employing the same folds for all models.

Hyper-parameter Tuning The details of the hyper-parameter tuning process for all models (including data splits to training, development and test sets) are described in the appendices. Here we provide a summary.

AE-SCL and AE-SCL-SR: For the stochastic gradient descent (SGD) training algorithm we set the learning rate to 0.1, momentum to 0.9 and weight-decay regularization to 10^{-5}. The number of pivots was chosen among $\{100, 200, \ldots, 500\}$ and the dimensionality of h among $\{100, 300, 500\}$. For the features induced by these models we take their $w^h x^{np}$ vector. For AE-SCL-SR, embeddings for the unigram and bigram features were learned with word2vec (Mikolov et al., 2013). Details about the software and the way we learn bigram representations are in the appendices.

Baselines: For SCL-MI, following (Blitzer et al., 2007) we tuned the number of pivot features between 500 and 1000 and the SVD dimensions among 50,100 and 150. For MSDA we tuned the number of reconstructed features among $\{500, 1000, 2000, 5000, 10000\}$, the number of model layers among $\{1, 3, 5\}$ and the corrup-

---

[3] http://www.cse.wustl.edu/~mchen
[4] https://github.com/GRAAL-Research/domain_adversarial_neural_network
[5] http://scikit-learn.org/stable/
[6] We tried to compare to (Bollegala et al., 2015) but failed to replicate their results despite personal communication with the authors.

Model|Source→Target	D→B	E→B	K→B	B→D	E→D	K→D
AE-SCL-SR	**0.773**[*+◇]	0.7115	0.730[*+]	**0.811**[+◇]	**0.745**[*+◇]	**0.763**[*+◇]
AE-SCL	0.758[◉]	0.701	**0.742**[‡◉]	0.794	0.732[‡]	0.743[‡◉]
MSDA	0.761	**0.719**	0.7	0.783	0.71	0.714
MSDA-DAN	0.75	0.71	0.712	0.797	0.731	0.738
SCL-MI	0.732	0.685	0.693	0.788	0.704	0.722
No-DA	0.736	0.679	0.677	0.76	0.692	0.702

Mod.|So.→Tar.	B→E	D→E	K→E	B→K	D→K	E→K	Test-All
AE-SCL-SR	**0.768**[*+◇]	**0.781**[*+◇]	**0.84**[*+◇]	**0.801**[*+◇]	**0.803**[+◇]	0.846	**0.781**[*+◇]
AE-SCL	0.744	0.763[‡◉]	0.828[◉]	0.795[‡◉]	0.8[‡◉]	0.848	0.770[‡]
MSDA	0.746	0.75	0.824	0.788	0.774	0.845	0.759
MSDA-DAN	0.747	0.745	0.821	0.754	0.776	**0.85**	0.761
SCL-MI	0.719	0.715	0.822	0.772	0.74	0.829	0.743
No-DA	0.7	0.709	0.816	0.74	0.732	0.824	0.731

Mod.|So.→Tar.	B→Blog	D→Blog	E→Blog	K→Blog	Test-All
AE-SCL-SR	**0.705**[*+]	**0.793**[+◇]	0.703[*+◇]	**0.841**[*+◇]	**0.769**[*+◇]
AE-SCL	0.691	0.787[‡◉]	0.645[◉]	0.747[◉]	0.718
MSDA	0.698	0.775	0.646	0.75	0.717
MSDA-DAN	0.694	0.737	**0.764**	0.672	0.716
SCL-MI	0.687	0.767	0.662	0.704	0.705
NO-DA	0.627	0.747	0.620	0.616	0.652

Table 1: Sentiment classification accuracy for the Blitzer et al. (2007) task (top tables), and for adaptation from the Blitzer's product review domains to the Blog domain (bottom table). Test-All presents average results across setups. Statistical significance (with the McNemar paired test for labeling disagreements (Gillick and Cox, 1989; Blitzer et al., 2006), $p < 0.05$) is denoted with: * (AE-SCL-SR vs. AE-SCL), + (AE-SCL-SR vs. MSDA), ◇ (AE-SCL-SR vs. MSDA-DAN), ‡ (AE-SCL vs. MSDA) and ◉ (AE-SCL vs. MSDA-DAN). All the differences between any model and No-DA are statistically significant.

tion probability among $\{0.1, 0.2, \ldots, 0.5\}$. For MSDA-DAN, we followed Ganin et al. (2016): the λ adaptation parameter is chosen among 9 values between 10^{-2} and 1 on a logarithmic scale, the hidden layer size l is chosen among $\{50, 100, 200\}$ and the learning rate μ is 10^{-3}.

5 Results

Table 1 presents our results. In the Blitzer et al. (2007) task (top tables), AE-SCL-SR is the best performing model in 9 of 12 setups and on a unified test set consisting of the test sets of all 12 setups (the Test-All column). AE-SCL, MSDA and MSDA-DAN perform best in one setup each. On the unified test set, AE-SCL-SR improves over SCL-MI by 3.8% (error reduction (ER) of 14.8%) and over MSDA-DAN by 2% (ER of 8.4%), while AE-SCL improves over SCL-MI and MSDA-DAN by 2.7% (ER of 10.5%) and 0.9% (ER of 3.8%), respectively. MSDA-DAN and MSDA perform very similarly on the unified test set (0.761 and 0.759, respectively) with generally minor differences in the individual setups.

When adapting from the product review domains to the Blog domain (bottom table), AE-

SCL-SR performs best in 3 of 4 setups, providing particularly large improvements when training is in the Kitchen (K) domain. The average improvement of AE-SCL-SR over MSDA is 5.2% and over a non-adapted classifier is 11.7%. As before, MSDA-DAN performs similarly to MSDA on the unified test set, although the differences in the individual setups are much higher. The differences between AE-SCL-SR and the other models are statistically significant in most cases.[7]

Class Based Analysis Table 3 presents a class-based comparison between model pairs. Results are presented for the unified test set of the Blitzer et al. (2007) task. The table reveals that the strength of AE-SCL-SR comes from its improved accuracy on positive examples: in 3.97% of the cases over AE-SCL (compared to 2.19% of the positive examples where AE-SCL is better) and in 6.40% of the cases over MSDA (compared to 2.80%). While on negative examples the pattern is reversed and AE-SCL and MSDA outperform AE-

---

[7]The difference between two models in a given setup is considered to be statistically significant if and only if it is significant in all five folds of that setup.

Setup	Gold	Pivots (First doc.)	Pivots (Second doc.)	AE-SCL (Fir.,Sec.)	Rank Diff
E→B	1	very good, good	great	(1,0)	58058 (2.90%)
E→D	1	fantastic	wonderful	(1,0)	44982 (2.25%)
K→E	1	excellent, works fine	well, works well	(1,0)	75222 (3.76%)
K→D	1	the best,best	perfect	(1,0)	98554 (4.93%)
D→B	0	boring, waste of	dull, can't recommend	(1,0)	78999 (3.95%)
B→D	0	very disappointing, disappointing	disappointed	(1,0)	139851 (6.99%)
D→K	0	sadly	unfortunately	(1,0)	63567 (3.17%)
B→K	0	unhappy	disappointed	(1,0)	110544 (5.52%)

Table 2: Document pair examples from eight setups (1st column) with the same gold sentiment class. In all cases, AE-SCL-SR correctly classifies both documents, while AE-SCL misclassifies one (5th column). The 6th column presents the difference in the ranking of the cosine scores between the representation vectors $\tilde{h}$ of the documents according to both models (the rank of AE-SCL minus the rank of AE-SCL-SR), both in absolute values and as a percentage of the 1,999,000 document pairs $(2000 \cdot 1999/2)$ in the test set of each setup. As $\tilde{h}$ is feeded to the sentiment classifer we expect documents that belong to the same class to have more similar $\tilde{h}$ vectors. The differences are indeed positive in all 8 cases.

	Positive	Negative
AE-SCL-SR	954 (3.97 %)	576 (2.40 %)
AE-SCL	527 (2.19 %)	754 (3.14 %)

	Positive	Negative
AE-SCL-SR	1538 (6.40 %)	765 (3.18 %)
MSDA	673 (2.80 %)	1109 (4.60 %)

Table 3: Class based analysis for the unified test set of the Blitzer et al. (2007) task. A *(model,class)* presents the number of test examples from the *class*, for which the *model* is correct while the other model in the table is wrong.

SCL-SR, this is a weaker effect which only moderates the overall superiority of AE-SCL-SR.[8]

The unlabeled documents from all four domains are strongly biased to convey positive opinions (Section 4). This is indicated, for example, by the average score given to these reviews by their authors: 4.29 (B), 4.33 (D), 3.96 (E) and 4.16 (K), on a scale of 1 to 5. This analysis suggests that AE-SCL-SR better learns from of its unlabeled data.

Similar Pivots Recall that AE-SCL-SR aims to learn more similar representations for documents with similar pivot features. Table 2 demonstrates this effect through pairs of test documents from 8 product review setups.[9] The documents contain pivot features with very similar meaning and indeed they belong to the same sentiment class. Yet, in all cases AE-SCL-SR correctly classifies both

documents, while AE-SCL misclassifies one.

The rightmost column of the table presents the difference in the ranking of the cosine similarity between the representation vectors $\tilde{h}$ of the documents in the pair, according to each of the models. Results (in numerical values and percentage) are given with respect to all cosine similarity values between the $\tilde{h}$ vectors of any document pair in the test set. As the documents with the highest similarity are ranked 1, the positive difference between the ranks of AE-SCL and those of AE-SCL-SR indicate that AE-SCL's rank is lower. That is, AE-SCL-SR learns more similar representations for documents with similar pivot features.

6 Conclusions and Future Work

We presented a new model for domain adaptation which combines ideas from pivot based and autoencoder based representation learning. We have demonstrated how to encode information from pre-trained word embeddings to improve the generalization of our model across examples with semantically similar pivot features. We demonstrated strong performance on cross-domain sentiment classification tasks with 16 domain pairs and provided initial qualitative analysis that supports the intuition behind our model. Our approach is general and applicable for a large number of NLP tasks (for AE-SCL-SR this holds as long as the pivot features can be embedded in a vector space).

In future we would like to adapt our model to more general domain adaptation setups such as where adaptation is performed between sets of source and target domains and where some labeled data from the target domain(s) is available.

---

[8]The reported numbers are averaged over the 5 folds and rounded to the closest integer, if necessary. The comparison between AE-SCL-SR and MSDA-DAN yields a very similar pattern and is hence excluded from space considerations.

[9]We consider for each setup one example pair from one of the five folds such that the dimensionality of the hidden layers in both models is identical.

A Hyperparameter Tuning

This appendix describes the hyper-parameter tuning process for the models compared in our paper. Some of these details appear in the full paper, but here we provide a detailed description.

AE-SCL and AE-SCL-SR We tuned the parameters of both our models in two steps. First, we randomly split the unlabeled data from both the source and the target domains in a 80/20 manner and combine the large subsets together and the small subsets together so that to generate unlabeled training and validation sets. On these training/validation sets we tune the hyperparameters of the stochastic gradient descent (SGD) algorithm we employ to train our networks: learning rate (0.1), momentum (0.9) and weight-decay regularization (10^{-5}). Note that these values are tuned on the fully unsupervised task of predicting pivot features occurrence from non-pivot input representation, and are then employed in all the source-traget domain combinations, across all folds. [10]

After tuning the SGD parameters, in the second step we tuned the model's hyper-parameters for each fold of each source-target setup. The hyperparameters are the number of pivots (100 to 500 in steps 100) and the dimensionality of h (100 to 500 in steps of 200). We select the values that yield the best performing model when training on the training set and evaluating on the training domain development set of each fold.[11]

We further explored the quality of the various intermediate representations generated by the models as sources of features for the sentiment classifier. The vectors we considered are: $w^h x^{np}$, $h = \sigma(w^h x^{np})$, $w^r h$ and $r = \sigma(w^r h)$. We chose the $w^h x^{np}$ vector, denoted in the paper in the paper with $\tilde{h}$.

For AE-SCL-SR, embeddings for the unigram and bigram features were learned with word2vec (Mikolov et al., 2013). [12] To learn bigram representations, in cases where a bigram pivot *(w1,w2)* is included in a sentence we generate the triplet

w1,w1-w2, w2. For example, the sentence *It was a very good book* with the bigram pivot *very good* is re-written as: *It was a very very-good good book*. The revised corpus is then fed into word2vec. The dimension of the hidden layer h of AE-SCL-SR is the dimension of the induced embeddings.

In both parameter tuning steps we use the unlabeled validation data for early stopping: the SGD algorithm stops at the first iteration where the validation data error increases rather then when the training error or the loss function are minimized.

SCL-MI Following (Blitzer et al., 2007) we used 1000 pivot features .[13] The number of SVD dimensions was tuned on the labeled development data to the best value among 50,100 and 150.

MSDA Using the labeled dev. data we tuned the number of reconstructed features (among 500, 1000, 2000, 5000 and 10000) the number of model layers (among $\{1,3,5\}$) and the corruption probability (among $\{0.1, 0.2, \ldots, 0.5\}$). For details on these hyper-parameters see (Chen et al., 2012).

MSDA-DAN Following Ganin et al. (2016) we tuned the hyperparameters on the labeled development data as follows. The λ adaptation parameter is chosen among 9 values between 10^{-2} and 1 on a logarithmic scale. The hidden layer size l is chosen among $\{50, 100, 200\}$ and the learning rate μ is fixed to 10^{-3}.

B Experimental Choices

Variants of the Product Review Data There are two releases of the datasets of the Blitzer et al. (2007) cross-domain product review task. We use the one from `http://www.cs.jhu.edu/~mdredze/ datasets/sentiment/index2.html` where the data is imbalanced, consisting of more positive than negative reviews. We believe that our setup is more realistic as when collecting unlabeled data, it is hard to get a balanced set. Note that Blitzer et al. (2007) used the other release where the unlabeled data consists of the same number of positive and negative reviews.

Test Set Size While Blitzer et al. (2007) used only 400 target domain reviews for test, we use the entire set of 2000 reviews. We believe that this decision yields more robust and statistically significant results.

---

[10]Both AE-SCL and AE-SCL-SR converged to the same values. This is probably because for each parameter we consider only a handful of values: learning rate (0.01,0.1,1), momentum (0.1,0.,5,0.9) and weight-decay regularization (10^{-4},10^{-5},10^{-6}).

[11]When tuning the SGD parameters we experimented with 100 and 500 pivots and dimensionality of 100 and 500 for h.

[12]We employed the Gensim package and trained the model on the unlabeled data from both the source and the target domains of each adaptation setup (`https:// radimrehurek.com/gensim/`).

[13]Results with 500 pivots were very similar.

References

Rie Kubota Ando and Tong Zhang. 2005. A framework for learning predictive structures from multiple tasks and unlabeled data. *Journal of Machine Learning Research* 6(Nov):1817–1853. http://www.jmlr.org/papers/v6/ando05a.html.

Shai Ben-David, John Blitzer, Koby Crammer, Alex Kulesza, Fernando Pereira, and Jennifer Wortman Vaughan. 2010. A theory of learning from different domains. *Machine learning* 79(1-2):151–175. https://doi.org/10.1007/s10994-009-5152-4.

Yoshua Bengio, Pascal Lamblin, Dan Popovici, and Hugo Larochelle. 2007. Greedy layer-wise training of deep networks. In *Proc. of NIPS*. http://papers.nips.cc/paper/3048-greedy-layer-wise-training-of-deep-networks.

John Blitzer, Mark Dredze, Fernando Pereira, et al. 2007. Biographies, bollywood, boom-boxes and blenders: Domain adaptation for sentiment classification. In *Proc. of ACL*. http://aclweb.org/anthology/P07-1056.

John Blitzer, Ryan McDonald, and Fernando Pereira. 2006. Domain adaptation with structural correspondence learning. In *Proc. of EMNLP*. http://aclweb.org/anthology/W06-1615.

Danushka Bollegala, Takanori Maehara, and Ken-ichi Kawarabayashi. 2015. Unsupervised cross-domain word representation learning. In *Proc. of ACL*. https://doi.org/10.3115/v1/P15-1071.

Danushka Bollegala, Yutaka Matsuo, and Mitsuru Ishizuka. 2011a. Relation adaptation: learning to extract novel relations with minimum supervision. In *Proc. of IJCAI*. https://doi.org/10.1109/TKDE.2011.250.

Danushka Bollegala, David Weir, and John Carroll. 2011b. Using multiple sources to construct a sentiment sensitive thesaurus for cross-domain sentiment classification. In *Proc. of ACL*. http://aclweb.org/anthology/P11-1014.

Ciprian Chelba and Alex Acero. 2004. Adaptation of maximum entropy capitalizer: Little data can help a lot. In *Proc. of EMNLP*. http://aclweb.org/anthology/W04-3237.

Minmin Chen, Yixin Chen, and Kilian Q Weinberger. 2011. Automatic feature decomposition for single view co-training. In *Proc. of ICML*. http://dblp.uni-trier.de/rec/bib/conf/icml/ChenWC11.

Minmin Chen, Zhixiang Xu, Kilian Weinberger, and Fei Sha. 2012. Marginalized denoising autoencoders for domain adaptation. In *Proc. of ICML*. http://icml.cc/2012/papers/416.pdf.

Stéphane Clinchant, Gabriela Csurka, and Boris Chidlovskii. 2016. A domain adaptation regularization for denoising autoencoders. In *Proc. of ACL* (short papers). https://doi.org/10.18653/v1/P16-2005.

Hal Daumé III. 2007. Frustratingly easy domain adaptation. In *Proc. of ACL*. http://aclweb.org/anthology/P07-1009.

Hal Daume III and Daniel Marcu. 2006. Domain adaptation for statistical classifiers. *Journal of Artificial Intelligence Research* 26:101–126. http://dl.acm.org/citation.cfm?id=1622559.1622562.

Yaroslav Ganin and Victor Lempitsky. 2015. Unsupervised domain adaptation by backpropagation. In *Proc. of ICML*. http://dblp.uni-trier.de/rec/bib/conf/icml/GaninL15.

Yaroslav Ganin, Evgeniya Ustinova, Hana Ajakan, Pascal Germain, Hugo Larochelle, François Laviolette, Mario Marchand, and Victor Lempitsky. 2016. Domain-adversarial training of neural networks. *Journal of Machine Learning Research* 17(59):1–35. http://jmlr.org/papers/v17/15-239.html.

Laurence Gillick and Stephen J Cox. 1989. Some statistical issues in the comparison of speech recognition algorithms. In *Proc. of ICASSP*. IEEE. https://doi.org/10.1109/ICASSP.1989.266481.

Xavier Glorot, Antoine Bordes, and Yoshua Bengio. 2011. Domain adaptation for large-scale sentiment classification: A deep learning approach. In *In proc. of ICML*. pages 513–520. http://dblp.uni-trier.de/rec/bib/conf/icml/GlorotBB11.

Stephan Gouws, GJ Van Rooyen, MIH Medialab, and Yoshua Bengio. 2012. Learning structural correspondences across different linguistic domains with synchronous neural language models. In *Proc. of the xLite Workshop on Cross-Lingual Technologies, NIPS*.

Jiayuan Huang, Arthur Gretton, Karsten M Borgwardt, Bernhard Schölkopf, and Alex J Smola. 2007. Correcting sample selection bias by unlabeled data. In *Proc. of NIPS*. http://papers.nips.cc/paper/3075-correcting-sample-selection-bias-by-unlabeled-data.

Jing Jiang and ChengXiang Zhai. 2007. Instance weighting for domain adaptation in nlp. In *Proc. of ACL*. http://aclweb.org/anthology/P07-1034.

Diederik P Kingma and Max Welling. 2014. Auto-encoding variational bayes. In *Proc. of ICLR*. http://dblp.uni-trier.de/rec/bib/journals/corr/KingmaW13.

Christos Louizos, Kevin Swersky, Yujia Li, Max Welling, and Richard Zemel. 2016. The variational fair autoencoder http://dblp.uni-trier.de/rec/bib/journals/corr/LouizosSLWZ15.

Yishay Mansour, Mehryar Mohri, and Afshin Rostamizadeh. 2009. Domain adaptation with multiple sources. In *Proc. of*

NIPS. http://papers.nips.cc/paper/3550-domain-adaptation-with-multiple-sources.

David McClosky, Eugene Charniak, and Mark Johnson. 2010. Automatic domain adaptation for parsing. In *Proc. of NAACL*. http://aclweb.org/anthology/N10-1004.

Tomas Mikolov, Ilya Sutskever, Kai Chen, Greg Corrado, and Jeffrey Dean. 2013. Distributed representations of words and phrases and their compositionality. In *Proc. of NIPS*. http://papers.nips.cc/paper/5021-distributed-representations-of-words-and-phrases-and-their-compositionality.

Sinno Jialin Pan, Xiaochuan Ni, Jian-Tao Sun, Qiang Yang, and Zheng Chen. 2010. Cross-domain sentiment classification via spectral feature alignment. In *Proceedings of the 19th international conference on World wide web*. ACM, pages 751–760. https://doi.org/10.1145/1772690.1772767.

Roi Reichart and Ari Rappoport. 2007. Self-training for enhancement and domain adaptation of statistical parsers trained on small datasets. In *Proc. of ACL*. http://aclweb.org/anthology/P07-1078.

Danilo Jimenez Rezende, Shakir Mohamed, and Daan Wierstra. 2014. Stochastic backpropagation and approximate inference in deep generative models. In *Proc. of ICML*. http://dblp.uni-trier.de/rec/bib/conf/icml/RezendeMW14.

Brian Roark and Michiel Bacchiani. 2003. Supervised and unsupervised pcfg adaptation to novel domains. In *Proc. of HLT-NAACL*. http://aclweb.org/anthology/N03-1027.

Alexander M Rush, Roi Reichart, Michael Collins, and Amir Globerson. 2012. Improved parsing and pos tagging using inter-sentence consistency constraints. In *Proc. of EMNLP-CoNLL*. http://aclweb.org/anthology/D12-1131.

Tobias Schnabel and Hinrich Schütze. 2013. Towards robust cross-domain domain adaptation for part-of-speech tagging. In *Proc. of IJCNLP*. http://aclweb.org/anthology/I13-1023.

Pascal Vincent, Hugo Larochelle, Yoshua Bengio, and Pierre-Antoine Manzagol. 2008. Extracting and composing robust features with denoising autoencoders. In *Proc. of ICML*. https://doi.org/10.1145/1390156.1390294.

Gui-Rong Xue, Wenyuan Dai, Qiang Yang, and Yong Yu. 2008. Topic-bridged plsa for cross-domain text classification. In *Proc. of SIGIR*. https://doi.org/10.1145/1390334.1390441.

Yi Yang and Jacob Eisenstein. 2014. Fast easy unsupervised domain adaptation with marginalized structured dropout. In *Proc. of ACL (short papers)*. https://doi.org/10.3115/v1/P14-2088.

Jianfei Yu and Jing Jiang. 2016. Learning sentence embeddings with auxiliary tasks for cross-domain sentiment classification. In *Proc. of EMNLP*. http://aclweb.org/anthology/D16-1023.

A Simple and Accurate Syntax-Agnostic Neural Model for Dependency-based Semantic Role Labeling

Diego Marcheggiani[1], Anton Frolov[2], Ivan Titov[1,3]
[1]ILLC, University of Amsterdam
[2]Machine Intelligence Department, Yandex
[3]ILCC, School of Informatics, University of Edinburgh
`marcheggiani@uva.nl`
`anton-fr@yandex-team.ru`
`ititov@inf.ed.ac.uk`

Abstract

We introduce a simple and accurate neural model for dependency-based semantic role labeling. Our model predicts predicate-argument dependencies relying on states of a bidirectional LSTM encoder. The semantic role labeler achieves competitive performance on English, even without any kind of syntactic information and only using local inference. However, when automatically predicted part-of-speech tags are provided as input, it substantially outperforms all previous local models and approaches the best reported results on the English CoNLL-2009 dataset. We also consider Chinese, Czech and Spanish where our approach also achieves competitive results. Syntactic parsers are unreliable on out-of-domain data, so standard (i.e., syntactically-informed) SRL models are hindered when tested in this setting. Our syntax-agnostic model appears more robust, resulting in the best reported results on standard out-of-domain test sets.

1 Introduction

The task of semantic role labeling (SRL), pioneered by Gildea and Jurafsky (2002), involves the prediction of predicate argument structure, i.e., both identification of arguments as well as their assignment to an underlying *semantic role*. These representations have been shown to be beneficial in many NLP applications, including question answering (Shen and Lapata, 2007) and information extraction (Christensen et al., 2011). Semantic banks (e.g., PropBank (Palmer et al., 2005)) often represent arguments as syntactic constituents or, more generally, text spans (Baker

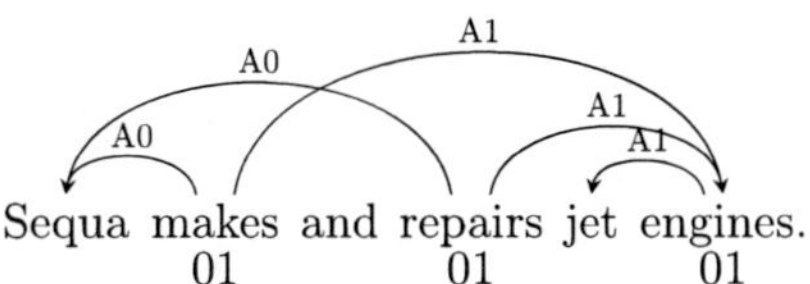

Figure 1: A semantic dependency graph.

et al., 1998). In contrast, CoNLL-2008 and 2009 shared tasks (Surdeanu et al., 2008; Hajic et al., 2009) popularized *dependency-based semantic role labeling* where the goal is to identify syntactic heads of arguments rather than entire constituents. Figure 1 shows an example of such a dependency-based representation: node labels are senses of predicates (e.g., "01" indicates that the first sense from the PropBank sense repository is used for predicate *makes* in this sentence) and edge labels are semantic roles (e.g., A0 is a proto-agent, 'doer').

Until recently, state-of-the-art SRL systems relied on complex sets of lexico-syntactic features (Pradhan et al., 2005) as well as declarative constraints (Punyakanok et al., 2008; Roth and Yih, 2005). Neural SRL models instead exploited feature induction capabilities of neural networks, largely eliminating the need for complex hand-crafted features. Initially achieving state-of-the-art results only in the multilingual setting, where careful feature engineering is not practical (Gesmundo et al., 2009; Titov et al., 2009), neural SRL models now also outperform their traditional counterparts on standard benchmarks for English (FitzGerald et al., 2015; Roth and Lapata, 2016; Swayamdipta et al., 2016; Foland and Martin, 2015).

Recently, it has been shown that an accurate span-based SRL model can be constructed without relying on syntactic features (Zhou and Xu, 2015).

411

Nevertheless, the situation with dependency-based SRL has not changed: even recent state-of-the-art methods for this task heavily rely on syntactic features (Roth and Lapata, 2016; FitzGerald et al., 2015; Lei et al., 2015; Roth and Woodsend, 2014; Swayamdipta et al., 2016). In particular, Roth and Lapata (2016) argue that syntactic features are necessary for the dependency-based SRL and show that performance of their model degrades dramatically if syntactic paths between arguments and predicates are not provided as an input. In this work, we are the first to show that it is possible to construct a very accurate dependency-based semantic role labeler which either does not use any kind of syntactic information or uses very little (automatically predicted part-of-speech tags). This suggests that our LSTM model can largely implicitly capture syntactic information, and this information can, to a large extent, substitute treebank syntax.

Similarly to the span-based model of Zhou and Xu (2015) we use bidirectional LSTMs to encode sentences and rely on their states when predicting arguments of each predicate.[1] We predict semantic dependency edges between predicates and arguments relying on LSTM states corresponding to the predicate and the argument positions (i.e. both edge endpoints). As semantic roles are often specific to predicates or even predicate senses (e.g., in PropBank (Palmer et al., 2005)), instead of predicting the role label (e.g., A0 for *Sequa* in our example), we predict predicate-specific roles (e.g., *make*-A0) using a compositional model. Both these aspects (predicting edges and compositional embeddings of roles) contrast our approach with that of Zhou and Xu (2015) who essentially treat the SRL task as a generic sequence labeling task. We empirically show that using these two ideas is crucial for achieving competitive performance on dependency SRL (+1.0% semantic F_1 in our ablation studies on English). Also, unlike the span-based version, we observe that using automatically predicted POS tags is also important (+0.7% F_1).

The resulting SRL model is very simple. Not only we do not rely on syntax, our model is also local, i.e., we do not globally score or constrain sets of arguments. On the standard English in-domain CoNLL-2009 benchmark we achieve 87.7 F_1 which compares favorable to the best local model (86.7% F_1 for PathLSTM (Roth and Lapata, 2016)) and approaches the best results overall (87.9% for an ensemble of 3 PathLSTM models with a reranker on top). When we experiment with Chinese, Czech and Spanish portions of the CoNLL-2009 dataset, we also achieve competitive results, even without any extra hyper-parameter tuning.

Moreover, as syntactic parsers are not reliable when used out-of-domain, standard (i.e., syntactically-informed) dependency SRL models are crippled when applied to such data. In contrast, our syntax-agnostic model appears to be considerably more robust: we achieve the best result so far on the English and Czech out-of-domain test set (77.7% and 87.2% F_1, respectively). For English, this constitutes a 2.4% absolute improvement over the comparable previous model (75.3% for the local PathLSTM) and substantially outperforms any previous method (76.5% for the ensemble of 3 PathLSTMs). We believe that out-of-domain performance may in fact be more important than in-domain one: in practice linguistic tools are rarely, if ever, used in-domain.

The key contributions can be summarized as follows:

- we propose the first effective syntax-agnostic model for dependency-based SRL;

- it achieves the best results among local models on the English, Chinese and Czech in-domain test sets;

- it substantially outperforms all previous methods on the out-of-domain test set on both English and Czech.

Despite the effectiveness of our syntax-agnostic version, we believe that both integration of treebank syntax and global inference are promising directions and leave them for future work. In fact, the proposed SRL model, given its simplicity and efficiency, may be used as a natural building block for future global and syntactically-informed SRL models.[2]

2   Our Model

The focus of this paper is on argument identification and labeling, as these are the steps which have

---

[1]In the CoNLL-2009 benchmark, predicates do not need to be identified: their positions are provided as input at test time. Consequently, as standard for dependency SRL, we ignore this subtask in further discussion.

[2]The code is available at `https://github.com/ diegma/neural-dep-srl`.

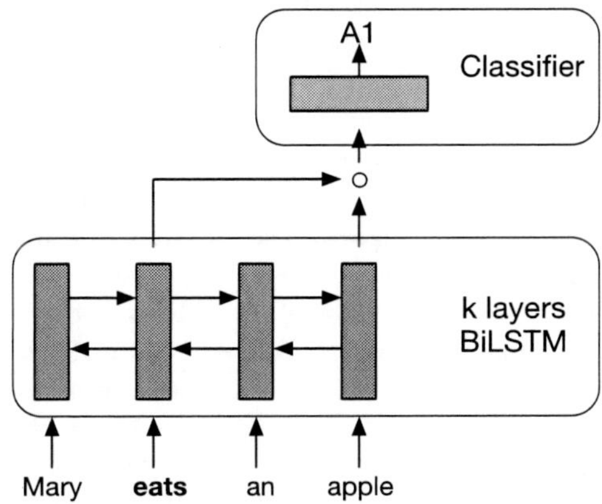

Figure 2: Predicting an argument and its label with an LSTM encoder.

been previously believed to require syntactic information. For the predicate disambiguation subtask we use models from previous work.

In order to identify and classify arguments, we propose a model composed of three components:

- a word representation component that from a word w_i in a sentence **w** build a word representation x_i;

- a Bidirectional LSTM (BiLSTM) encoder which takes as input the word representation x_i and provide a dynamic representation of the word and its context in a sentence;

- a classifier which takes as an input the BiLSTM representation of the candidate argument and the BiLSTM representation of the predicate to predict the role associated to the candidate argument.

2.1 Word representation

We represent each word w as the concatenation of four vectors: a randomly initialized word embedding $x^{re} \in \mathbb{R}^{d_w}$, a pre-trained word embedding $x^{pe} \in \mathbb{R}^{d_w}$, a randomly initialized part-of-speech tag embedding $x^{pos} \in \mathbb{R}^{d_p}$ and a randomly initialized lemma embedding $x^{le} \in \mathbb{R}^{d_l}$ that is only active if the word is one of the predicates. The randomly initialized embeddings x^{re}, x^{pos}, and x^{le} are fine-tuned during training, while the pre-trained ones are kept fixed, as in Dyer et al. (2015). The final word representation is given by

$x = x^{re} \circ x^{pe} \circ x^{pos} \circ x^{le}$, where $\circ$ represents the concatenation operator.

2.2 Bidirectional LSTM encoder

One of the most effective ways to model sequences are recurrent neural networks (RNN) (Elman, 1990), more precisely their gated versions, for example, Long Short-Term Memory (LSTM) networks (Hochreiter and Schmidhuber, 1997).

Formally, we can define an LSTM as a function $LSTM_\theta(x_{1:i})$ that takes as input the sequence $x_{1:i}$ and returns a hidden state $h_i \in \mathbb{R}^{d_h}$. This state can be regarded as a representation of the sentence from the start to the position i, or, in other words, it encodes the word at position i along with its left context. Bidirectional LSTMs make use of two LSTMs: one for the forward pass, and another for the backward pass, $LSTM_F$ and $LSTM_B$, respectively. In this way the concatenation of forward and backward LSTM states encodes both left and right contexts of a word, $BiLSTM(x_{1:n}, i) = LSTM_F(x_{1:i}) \circ LSTM_B(x_{n:i})$. In this work we stack k layers of bidirectional LSTMs, each layer takes the lower layer as its input.

2.3 Predicate-specific encoding

As we will show in the ablation studies in Section 3, encoding a sentence with a bidirectional LSTM in one shot and using it to predict the entire semantic dependency graph does not result in competitive SRL performance. Instead, similarly to Zhou and Xu (2015), we produce predicate-specific encodings of a sentence and use them to predict arguments of the corresponding predicate. This contrasts with most other applications of LSTM encoders (for example, in syntactic parsing (Kiperwasser and Goldberg, 2016; Cross and Huang, 2016) or machine translation (Sutskever et al., 2014)), where sentences are typically encoded once and then used to predict the entire structured output (e.g., a syntactic tree or a target sentence). Specifically, when identifying arguments of a given predicate, we add a predicate-specific feature to the representation of each word in the sentence by concatenating a binary flag to the word representation of Section 2.1. The flag is set to 1 for the word corresponding to the currently considered predicate, it is set to 0 otherwise. In this way, sentences with more than one predicate will be re-encoded by bidirectional LSTMs multiple times.

2.4 Role classifier

Our goal is to predict and label arguments for a given predicate. This can be accomplished by labeling each word in a sentence with a role, including the special 'NULL' role to indicate that it is not an argument of the predicate. We start with explaining the basic role classifier and then discuss two extensions, which we will later show to be crucial for achieving competitive performance.

2.4.1 Basic role classifier

The basic role classifier takes the hidden state of the top-layer bidirectional LSTM corresponding to the considered word at position i and uses it to estimate the probability of the role r. Though we experimented with multilayer perceptrons, we obtained the best results with a simple log-linear model:

$$p(r|v_i, p) \propto \exp(W_r v_i), \qquad (1)$$

where v_i is the hidden state calculated by $BiLSTM(x_{1:n}, i)$, p refers to the predicate and the symbol $\propto$ signifies proportionality. This is essentially equivalent to the approach used in Zhou and Xu (2015) for span-based SRL.[3]

2.4.2 Incorporating predicate state

Since the context of a predicate in the sentence is highly informative for deciding if a word is its argument and for choosing its semantic role, we provide the predicate's hidden state (v_p) as another input to the classifier (as in Figure 2):

$$p(r|v_i, v_p) \propto \exp(W_r(v_i \circ v_p)), \qquad (2)$$

where, as before, $\circ$ denotes concatenation. Note that we are effectively predicting an edge between words i and p in the sentence, so it is quite natural to exploit hidden states corresponding to both endpoints.[4]

Since we use predicate information within the classifier, it may seem that predicate-specific sentence encoding (Section 2.3) is not needed anymore. Moreover, predicting dependency edges relying on LSTM states of endpoints was shown effective in the context of syntactic dependency

parsing without any form of re-encoding (Kiperwasser and Goldberg, 2016). Nevertheless, in our ablation studies we observed that foregoing predicate-specific encoding results in large performance degradation (-6.2% F_1 on English). Though this dramatic drop in performance seems indeed surprising, the nature of the semantic dependencies, especially for nominal predicates, is different from general syntactic dependencies, with many arguments being far away from the predicates. Relations of these arguments to the predicate may be hard to encode with this simpler mechanism.

The two ways of encoding predicate information, using predicate-specific encoding and incorporating the predicate state in the classifier, turn out to be complementary.

2.4.3 Compositional modeling of roles

Instead of using a matrix W_r we found it beneficial to jointly embed the role r and predicate lemma l using a non-linear transformation:

$$p(r|v_i, v_p, l) \propto \exp(W_{l,r}(v_i \circ v_p)), \qquad (3)$$

$$W_{l,r} = ReLU(U(u_l \circ v_r)), \qquad (4)$$

where $ReLU$ is the rectilinear activation function, U is a parameter matrix, whereas $u_l \in \mathbb{R}^{d'_l}$ and $v_r \in \mathbb{R}^{d_r}$ are randomly initialized embeddings of predicate lemmas and roles. In this way each role prediction is predicate-specific, and at the same time we expect to learn a good representation for roles associated to infrequent predicates. This form of compositional embedding is similar to the one used in FitzGerald et al. (2015).

3 Experiments

We applied our model to the English, Chinese, Czech and Spanish CoNLL-2009 datasets with the standard split into training, test and development sets. For English, we used external embeddings of Dyer et al. (2015) learned using the structured skip n-gram approach of Ling et al. (2015), for Chinese, we used external embeddings produced with the neural language model of Bengio et al. (2003). For Czech and Spanish, we used embeddings created with the model proposed by Bojanowski et al. (2016).

Similarly to Kiperwasser and Goldberg (2016) we used word dropout (Iyyer et al., 2015); we replaced a word with the *UNK* token with probability $\frac{\alpha}{fr(w)+\alpha}$, where α is an hyper-parameter and

---

[3]Since they considered span-based SRL, they used BIO encoding (Ramshaw and Marcus, 1995) and ensured the consistency of B, I and O labels with a 1-order Markov CRF. For dependency SRL both BIO encoding and the 1-order Markov CRF would be useless.

[4]We abuse the notation and refer as p both to the predicate word and to its position in the sentence.

$fr(w)$ is the frequency of the word w. The predicted POS tags were provided by the CoNLL-2009 shared-task organizers. We used the same predicate disambiguator as in Roth and Lapata (2016) for English, the one used in Zhao et al. (2009) for Czech and Spanish, and the one used in Björkelund et al. (2009) for Chinese. The training objective was the categorical cross-entropy, and we optimized it with Adam (Kingma and Ba, 2015). The hyperparameter tuning and all model selection was performed on the English development set; the chosen values are shown in Table 1.

Semantic role labeler	
d_w (English word embeddings)	100
d_w (Chinese word embeddings)	128
d_w (Czech word embeddings)	300
d_w (Spanish word embeddings)	300
d_{pos} (POS embeddings)	16
d_l (lemma embeddings)	100
d_h (LSTM hidden states)	512
d_r (role representation)	128
d_l' (output lemma representation)	128
k (BiLSTM depth)	4
α (word dropout)	.25
learning rate	.01

Table 1: Hyperparameter values.

3.1 Results

We compared our full model (with POS tags and the classifier defined in Section 2.4.3) against state-of-the-art models for dependency-based SRL on English, Chinese, Czech and Spanish. For English, our model significantly outperformed all the local counter-parts (i.e., models which do not perform global inference) on the in-domain tests (see Table 2) with 87.6% F_1 for our model vs. 86.7% for PathLSTM (Roth and Lapata, 2016). When compared with global models, our model performed on-par with the state-of-the-art global version of PathLSTM.

Though we had not done any parameter selection for other languages (i.e., used the same parameters as for English), our model performed competitively across all languages we considered.

For Chinese (Table 4), the proposed model outperformed the best previous model (PathLSTM) with an improvement of 1.8% F_1.

For Czech (Table 5), our model, even though unlike previous work it does not use any kind

System	P	R	F_1
Lei et al. (2015) (local)	-	-	86.6
FitzGerald et al. (2015) (local)	-	-	86.7
Roth and Lapata (2016) (local)	88.1	85.3	86.7
Ours (local)	**88.7**	**86.8**	**87.7**
Björkelund et al. (2010) (global)	88.6	85.2	86.9
FitzGerald et al. (2015) (global)	-	-	87.3
Foland and Martin (2015) (global)	-	-	86.0
Swayamdipta et al. (2016) (global)	-	-	85.0
Roth and Lapata (2016) (global)	90.0	85.5	87.7
FitzGerald et al. (2015) (ensemble)	-	-	87.7
Roth and Lapata (2016) (ensemble)	90.3	85.7	87.9

Table 2: Results on the English in-domain test set.

System	P	R	F_1
Lei et al. (2015) (local)	-	-	75.6
FitzGerald et al. (2015) (local)	-	-	75.2
Roth and Lapata (2016) (local)	76.9	73.8	75.3
Ours (local)	**79.4**	**76.2**	**77.7**
Björkelund et al. (2010) (global)	77.9	73.6	75.7
FitzGerald et al. (2015) (global)	-	-	75.2
Foland and Martin (2015) (global)	-	-	75.9
Roth and Lapata (2016) (global)	78.6	73.8	76.1
FitzGerald et al. (2015) (ensemble)	-	-	75.5
Roth and Lapata (2016) (ensemble)	79.7	73.6	76.5

Table 3: Results on the English out-of-domain test set.

of morphological features explicitly,[5] was able to outperform the system that achieved the best score in the CoNLL-2009 shared task. The improvement is 0.8% F_1.

Finally, for Spanish (Table 6), our system, though again achieved competitive results, did not outperform the best CoNLL-2009 model and yielded results very similar to those of PathLSTM. One possible reason for this slightly weaker performance is the relatively small size of the Spanish training set (less then half of the English one). This suggests that our model, tuned on English, is likely over-parametrized or under-regularized for Spanish.

The results are especially strong on out-of-domain data. As shown in Table 3, our approach outperformed even ensemble models on the out-of-domain English data (77.7% vs. 76.5% for

---

[5]However, character level information is encoded in the external embeddings, see (Bojanowski et al., 2016).

System	P	R	F_1
Björkelund et al. (2009)	82.4	75.1	78.6
Zhao et al. (2009)	80.4	75.2	77.7
Roth and Lapata (2016)	83.2	75.9	79.4
Ours	**83.4**	**79.1**	**81.2**

Table 4: Results on the Chinese test set.

In-domain	P	R	F_1
Björkelund et al. (2009)	88.1	82.9	85.4
Zhao et al. (2009)	88.2	82.4	85.2
Ours	**86.6**	**85.4**	**86.0**

Out-of-domain	P	R	F_1
Björkelund et al. (2009)	86.1	81.9	83.9
Zhao et al. (2009)	88.6	82.5	85.4
Ours	**88.0**	**86.5**	**87.2**

Table 5: Results on the Czech test sets.

System	P	R	F_1
Björkelund et al. (2009)	78.9	74.3	76.5
Zhao et al. (2009)	83.1	78.0	80.5
Roth and Lapata (2016)	83.2	77.4	80.2
Ours	**81.4**	**79.3**	**80.3**

Table 6: Results on the Spanish test set.

System	P	R	F_1
Ours (local)	87.7	85.5	86.6
w/o POS tags	87.3	84.5	85.9
w/o predicate-specific encoding	80.9	79.8	80.4
with basic classifier	86.7	84.5	85.6

Table 7: Ablation study on the English development set.

the ensemble of PathLSTMs). Similarly, it performed very well on the out-of-domain Czech dataset scoring 87.2% F_1, with a 1.8% F_1 improvement over the best CoNLL-2009 participant (see Table 5, bottom). The favorable results on out-of-domain test sets are not surprising, as syntactic parsers, even the most accurate ones, usually struggle on domains different from the ones they have been trained on. This means that the syntactic trees they produce are unreliable and compromise the accuracy of SRL systems which rely on them. The error propagation can in principle be mitigated by exploiting a distribution over parse trees (e.g., encoded in a parse forest) rather than using a single ('Viterbi') parse. However, this is rarely feasible in practice. Since our model does not use predicted parse trees and instead relies on the ability of LSTMs to capture long distance dependencies and syntactic phenomena (Linzen et al., 2016), it is less brittle in this setting.

3.2 Ablation studies and analysis

In order to show the contribution of the modeling choices we made, we performed an ablation study on the English development set (Table 7). In these experiments we made individual changes to the model (one by one) and measured their influence on the model performance.

First, we observed that POS tag information is highly beneficial for obtaining competitive performance.

Not using predicate-specific encoding (Section 2.3), or, in other words, doing one-pass encoding with no predicate flags, hurts the performance even more badly (6% drop in F_1 on the development set). This is somewhat surprising given that one-pass LSTM encoders performed competitively for syntactic dependencies (Kiperwasser and Goldberg, 2016; Cross and Huang, 2016) and suggests that major differences between the two problems require the use of different modeling approaches.

We also observed a 1.0% drop in F_1 when we follow Zhou and Xu (2015) and use the basic role classifier (Section 2.4.1). These results show that both predicate-specific encoding (Section 2.3) and exploiting predicate information in the classifier (Sections 2.4.2-2.4.3) are complementary.

We also studied how performance varies depending on the distance between a predicate and an argument (Figure 3). We compared our approach to the global PathLSTM model: PathLSTM is a natural reference point as it is the most accurate previous model, exploits similar modeling and representation techniques (e.g., word embeddings, LSTMs) but, unlike our approach, relies on predicted syntax. Contrary to our expectations, syntactically-driven and global PathLSTM was weaker for longer distances. We may speculate that syntactic paths for arguments further away from the predicate become unreliable. Though LSTMs are likely to be affected by a similar trend, their states may be able to capture the uncertainty about the structure and thus let the

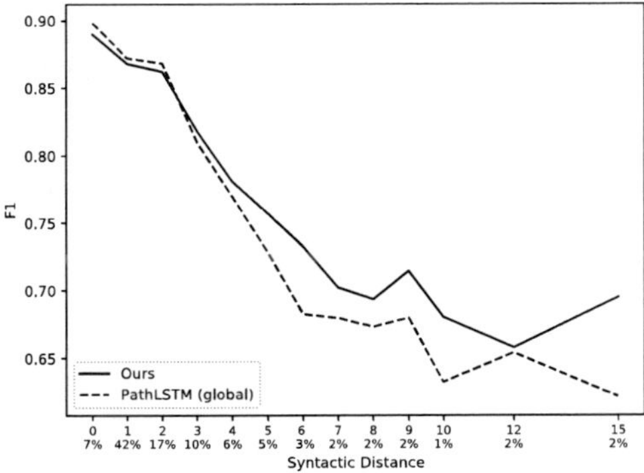

Figure 3: F_1 as function of word distance. Percentages indicate the amount of arguments at a specific distance from a predicate.

		Ours	PathLSTM	Freq. (%)
Verbal	A0	90.5	90.4	15%
	A1	92.0	91.8	21%
	A2	80.3	80.2	5%
	AM-*	77.9	77.0	16%
	All	*86.4*	*86.1*	*61%*
		Ours	PathLSTM	Freq. (%)
Nominal	A0	81.8	81.5	10%
	A1	85.1	85.5	16%
	A2	78.5	79.8	7%
	AM-*	72.5	73.2	5%
	All	*81.1*	*81.8*	*39%*

Table 8: F_1 results on the English test set broken down into verbal and nominal predicates.

role classifier account for this uncertainty without the need to explicitly sum over potential syntactic analysis. In contrast, PathLSTM will have access only to the single (top scoring) parse tree and, thus, may be more brittle.

In Table 8, we break down F_1 results on the English test set into verbal and nominal predicates, and again compare our results with PathLSTM. First, as expected, we observe that both models are less accurate in predicting semantic roles of nominal predicates. For verbal predicates, our model slightly outperformed PathLSTM in core roles (A0-2) and performed much better (0.9% F_1) in predicting modifiers (AM-*). This is very surprising as some information about modifiers is actually explicitly encoded in syntactic dependen-

System	P	R	F_1
Verbal PathLSTM	93.4	87.8	90.5
Ours	**92.7**	**89.8**	**91.2**

System	P	R	F_1
Nom. PathLSTM	92.0	83.9	87.8
Ours	**89.4**	**86.6**	**88.0**

Table 9: Argument recognition results broken down into verbal and nominal predicates.

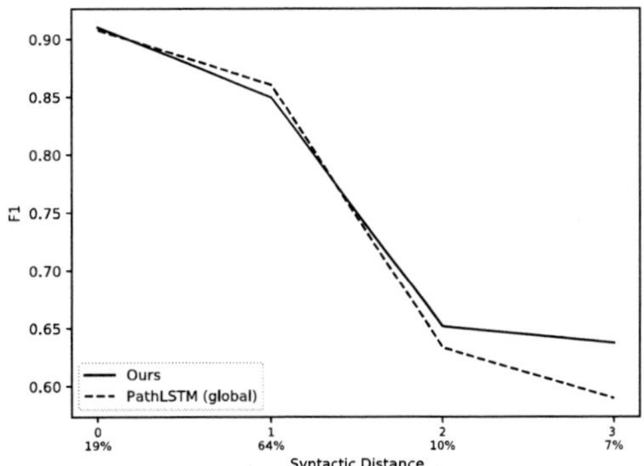

Figure 4: F_1 as function of syntactic distance for nominal predicates. Percentages indicate the amount of arguments at a specific distance from a nominal predicate.

cies exploited by PathLSTM (e.g., the syntactic dependency TMP is predictive of the modifier role AM-TMP). Note though that the syntactic parser was trained on the same sentences (both data originates from WSJ sections 02-22 of Penn Treebank), and this can explain why these syntactic dependencies (e.g., TMP) may convey little beneficial information to the semantic role labeler. For nominal predicates, PathLSTM was more accurate than our model for all roles excluding A0. To get a better idea for what is happening, we plotted the F_1 scores as a function of the length of the shortest path between nominal predicates and their arguments. On one hand, Figure 4 shows that PathLSTM is more accurate on roles one syntactic arc away from the nominal predicate. Note that these are the majority (78%) of arguments. On the other hand, our model appears to be more accurate for arguments syntactically far from nominal predicates. This again suggests that PathLSTM struggles with harder cases.

System	Example
Manual	Most of the stock [A2]selling[\A2] **pressure** came [A0]from[\A0] Wall Street professionals.
PathLSTM	Most of the stock [A2]selling[\A2] **pressure** came from Wall Street professionals.
Ours	Most of the stock [A0]selling[\A0] **pressure** came [A0]from[\A0] Wall Street professionals.

Table 10: Example of errors for the nominal predicate *pressure*: A0 is *a presser* (proto-agent) and A2 is *a goal* .

Unlike verbal predicates, syntactic structure is less predictive of semantic roles for nominals (e.g., many arguments are noun modifiers). Consequently, we hypothesized that our model should be weaker than PathLSTM in recognizing arguments but should be on par with PathLSTM in assigning their roles. To test this, we looked into argument identification performance (i.e., ignored labels). Table 9 shows the accuracy of both models in recognizing arguments of nominal and verbal predicates. Our model appears more accurate in recognizing arguments of both nominal (88.0% vs 87.8% F_1) and verbal predicates (91.2% vs. 90.5% F_1). This, when taken together with weaker labeled F_1 of our model for nominal predicates (Table 8), implies that, contrary to our expectations, it is the role labeling performance for nominals which is problematic for our model. Examples of this behavior can be seen in Table 10: all arguments of the predicate *pressure* are correctly recognized by our model but the role for the argument *selling* is not predicted correctly. In contrast, PathLSTM does not make any mistake with the labeling of the argument *selling* but fails to recognize *from* as an argument.

4   Related Work

Earlier approaches to SRL heavily relied on complex sets of lexico-syntactic features (Gildea and Jurafsky, 2002). Pradhan et al. (2005) used a support vector machine classifier and relied on two syntactic views (obtained with two different parsers), for feature extraction. In addition to hand-crafted features, Roth and Yih (2005) enriched CRFs with an integer linear programming inference procedure in order to encode non-local constraints in SRL; Toutanova et al. (2008) employed a global reranker for dealing with structural constraint; while Surdeanu et al. (2007) studied several combination strategies of local and global features obtained from several independent SRL models.

In the last years there has been a flurry of work that employed neural network approaches for SRL. FitzGerald et al. (2015) used hand-crafted features within an MLP for calculating potentials of a CRF model; Roth and Lapata (2016) extended the features of a non-neural SRL model with LSTM representations of syntactic paths between arguments and predicates; Lei et al. (2015) relied on low-rank tensor factorization that captured interactions between arguments, predicate, their syntactic path and semantic roles; while Collobert et al. (2011) and Foland and Martin (2015) used convolutional networks as sentence encoder and a CRF as a role classifier, both approaches employed a rich set of features as input of the convolutional encoder. Finally, Swayamdipta et al. (2016) jointly modeled syntactic and semantic structures; they extended one of the earliest neural approaches for SRL (Henderson et al., 2008; Titov et al., 2009; Gesmundo et al., 2009), with more sophisticated modeling techniques, for example, using LSTMs instead of vanilla RNNs.

Another related line of work (Naradowsky et al., 2012; Gormley et al., 2014), instead of relying on treebank syntax, integrated grammar induction as a sub-component into their statistical model. In this way, similarly to us, they do not use treebank syntax but rather rely on the ability of their joint model to induce syntax appropriate for SRL. Their focus was primarily on the low resource setting (where syntactic annotation is not available), whereas in standard set-ups their performance was not as strong. It would be interesting to see if explicit modeling of latent syntax is also beneficial when used in conjunction with LSTMs.

5   Conclusions

We proposed a neural syntax-agnostic method for dependency-based SRL. Our model is simple and fast, and surpasses comparable approaches (no system combination, local inference) on the standard in-domain CoNLL-2009 benchmark for English, Chinese, Czech and Spanish. Moreover, it outperforms all previous methods (including ensembles) in the arguably more realistic out-of-domain setting in both English and Czech. In the future, we will consider integration of syntactic information and joint inference.

Acknowledgments

The project was supported by the European Research Council (ERC StG BroadSem 678254), the Dutch National Science Foundation (NWO VIDI 639.022.518) and an Amazon Web Services (AWS) grant. The authors would like to thank Michael Roth for his helpful suggestions.

References

Collin F. Baker, Charles J. Fillmore, and John B. Lowe. 1998. The Berkeley FrameNet project. In *Proceedings of COLING-ACL*.

Yoshua Bengio, Réjean Ducharme, Pascal Vincent, and Christian Janvin. 2003. A neural probabilistic language model. *Journal of Machine Learning Research* 3:1137–1155.

Anders Björkelund, Bernd Bohnet, Love Hafdell, and Pierre Nugues. 2010. A high-performance syntactic and semantic dependency parser. In *Proceedings of COLING*.

Anders Björkelund, Love Hafdell, and Pierre Nugues. 2009. Multilingual semantic role labeling. In *Proceedings of CoNLL*.

Piotr Bojanowski, Edouard Grave, Armand Joulin, and Tomas Mikolov. 2016. Enriching word vectors with subword information. *arXiv preprint arXiv:1607.04606* .

Janara Christensen, Mausam, Stephen Soderland, and Oren Etzioni. 2011. An analysis of open information extraction based on semantic role labeling. In *Proceedings of the 6th International Conference on Knowledge Capture (K-CAP) 2011*.

Ronan Collobert, Jason Weston, Léon Bottou, Michael Karlen, Koray Kavukcuoglu, and Pavel Kuksa. 2011. Natural language processing (almost) from scratch. *JMLR* 12:2493–2537.

James Cross and Liang Huang. 2016. Incremental parsing with minimal features using bi-directional LSTM. In *Proceedings of ACL*.

Chris Dyer, Miguel Ballesteros, Wang Ling, Austin Matthews, and Noah A. Smith. 2015. Transition-based dependency parsing with stack long short-term memory. In *Proceedings of ACL*.

Jeffrey L. Elman. 1990. Finding structure in time. *Cognitive Science* 14(2):179–211.

Nicholas FitzGerald, Oscar Täckström, Kuzman Ganchev, and Dipanjan Das. 2015. Semantic role labeling with neural network factors. In *Proceedings of EMNLP*.

William Foland and James Martin. 2015. Dependency-based semantic role labeling using convolutional neural networks. In *Joint Conference on Lexical and Computational Semantics*.

Andrea Gesmundo, James Henderson, Paola Merlo, and Ivan Titov. 2009. Latent variable model of synchronous syntactic-semantic parsing for multiple languages. In *Proceedings of CoNLL*.

Daniel Gildea and Daniel Jurafsky. 2002. Automatic labeling of semantic roles. *Computational linguistics* 28(3):245–288.

Matthew R. Gormley, Margaret Mitchell, Benjamin Van Durme, and Mark Dredze. 2014. Low-resource semantic role labeling. In *Proceedings of ACL*.

Jan Hajic, Massimiliano Ciaramita, Richard Johansson, Daisuke Kawahara, Maria Antònia Martí, Lluís Màrquez, Adam Meyers, Joakim Nivre, Sebastian Padó, Jan Stepánek, Pavel Stranák, Mihai Surdeanu, Nianwen Xue, and Yi Zhang. 2009. The CoNLL-2009 shared task: Syntactic and semantic dependencies in multiple languages. In *Proceedings of CoNLL*.

James Henderson, Paola Merlo, Gabriele Musillo, and Ivan Titov. 2008. A latent variable model of synchronous parsing for syntactic and semantic dependencies. In *Proceedings of CoNLL*.

Sepp Hochreiter and Jürgen Schmidhuber. 1997. Long short-term memory. *Neural Computation* 9(8):1735–1780.

Mohit Iyyer, Varun Manjunatha, Jordan Boyd-Graber, and Hal Daumé III. 2015. Deep unordered composition rivals syntactic methods for text classification. In *Proceedings of ACL*.

Diederik Kingma and Jimmy Ba. 2015. Adam: A method for stochastic optimization. In *Proceedings of ICLR*.

Eliyahu Kiperwasser and Yoav Goldberg. 2016. Simple and accurate dependency parsing using bidirectional LSTM feature representations. *TACL* .

Tao Lei, Yuan Zhang, Lluís Màrquez, Alessandro Moschitti, and Regina Barzilay. 2015. High-order low-rank tensors for semantic role labeling. In *Proceedings of NAACL*.

Wang Ling, Chris Dyer, Alan W Black, and Isabel Trancoso. 2015. Two/too simple adaptations of word2vec for syntax problems. In *Proceedings of NAACL*.

Tal Linzen, Emmanuel Dupoux, and Yoav Goldberg. 2016. Assessing the ability of LSTMs to learn syntax-sensitive dependencies. *TACL* 4:521–535.

Jason Naradowsky, Sebastian Riedel, and David A Smith. 2012. Improving nlp through marginalization of hidden syntactic structure. In *Proceedings of EMNLP*.

Martha Palmer, Paul Kingsbury, and Daniel Gildea. 2005. The proposition bank: An annotated corpus of semantic roles. *Computational Linguistics* 31(1):71–106.

Sameer Pradhan, Kadri Hacioglu, Wayne H. Ward, James H. Martin, and Daniel Jurafsky. 2005. Semantic role chunking combining complementary syntactic views. In *Proceedings of CoNLL*.

Vasin Punyakanok, Dan Roth, and Wen-tau Yih. 2008. The importance of syntactic parsing and inference in semantic role labeling. *Computational Linguistics* 34(2):257–287.

Lance A. Ramshaw and Mitchell P. Marcus. 1995. Text chunking using transformation-based learning. In *Proceedings of the Third ACL Workshop on Very Large Corpora*.

Dan Roth and Wen-tau Yih. 2005. Integer linear programming inference for conditional random fields. In *Proceedings of ICML*.

Michael Roth and Mirella Lapata. 2016. Neural semantic role labeling with dependency path embeddings. In *Proceedings of ACL*.

Michael Roth and Kristian Woodsend. 2014. Composition of word representations improves semantic role labelling. In *Proceedings of EMNLP*.

Dan Shen and Mirella Lapata. 2007. Using semantic roles to improve question answering. In *Proceedings of EMNLP-CoNLL*.

Mihai Surdeanu, Richard Johansson, Adam Meyers, Lluís Màrquez, and Joakim Nivre. 2008. The CoNLL 2008 shared task on joint parsing of syntactic and semantic dependencies. In *Proceedings of CoNLL*.

Mihai Surdeanu, Lluís Màrquez, Xavier Carreras, and Pere Comas. 2007. Combination strategies for semantic role labeling. *Journal of Artificial Intelligence Research* 29:105–151.

Ilya Sutskever, Oriol Vinyals, and Quoc V. Le. 2014. Sequence to sequence learning with neural networks. In *Proceedings of NIPS*.

Swabha Swayamdipta, Miguel Ballesteros, Chris Dyer, and Noah A. Smith. 2016. Greedy, joint syntactic-semantic parsing with stack LSTMs. In *Proceedings of CoNLL*.

Ivan Titov, James Henderson, Paola Merlo, and Gabriele Musillo. 2009. Online projectivisation for synchronous parsing of semantic and syntactic dependencies. In *Proceedings of IJCAI*.

Kristina Toutanova, Aria Haghighi, and Christopher D. Manning. 2008. A global joint model for semantic role labeling. *Computational Linguistics* 34(2):161–191.

Hai Zhao, Wenliang Chen, Jun'ichi Kazama, Kiyotaka Uchimoto, and Kentaro Torisawa. 2009. Multilingual dependency learning: Exploiting rich features for tagging syntactic and semantic dependencies. In *Proceedings of CoNLL*.

Jie Zhou and Wei Xu. 2015. End-to-end learning of semantic role labeling using recurrent neural networks. In *Proceedings of ACL*.

Joint Prediction of Morphosyntactic Categories for Fine-Grained Arabic Part-of-Speech Tagging Exploiting Tag Dictionary Information

Go Inoue, Hiroyuki Shindo and Yuji Matsumoto
Graduate School of Information and Science
Nara Institute of Science and Technology
8916-5 Takayama, Ikoma, Nara, 630-0192, Japan
`{inoue.go.ib4, shindo, matsu}@is.naist.jp`

Abstract

Part-of-speech (POS) tagging for morphologically rich languages such as Arabic is a challenging problem because of their enormous tag sets. One reason for this is that in the tagging scheme for such languages, a complete POS tag is formed by combining tags from multiple tag sets defined for each morphosyntactic category. Previous approaches in Arabic POS tagging applied one model for each morphosyntactic tagging task, without utilizing shared information between the tasks. In this paper, we propose an approach that utilizes this information by jointly modeling multiple morphosyntactic tagging tasks with a multi-task learning framework. We also propose a method of incorporating tag dictionary information into our neural models by combining word representations with representations of the sets of possible tags. Our experiments showed that the joint model with tag dictionary information results in an accuracy of 91.38% on the Penn Arabic Treebank data set, with an absolute improvement of 2.11% over the current state-of-the-art tagger. [1]

1 Introduction

Part-of-speech (POS) tagging is a fundamental task in natural language processing. The granularity of the POS tag set that reflects language-specific information varies from language to language. In morphologically simple languages such as English, the size of the tag set is typically less than a hundred. On the other hand, in morphologically rich languages such as Arabic, the number of theoretically possible tags can be up to 333,000, of which only 2,200 tags might appear in an actual corpus (Habash and Rambow, 2005). One reason for this is that in the tagging scheme for such languages, a complete POS tag is formed by combining tags from multiple tag sets defined for each morphosyntactic category. For example, a complete POS tag for the word *Hb* ("love")[2] can be defined as the combination of a noun from the coarse POS category, a nominative (n) from the case category, "not applicable" (na) from the mood category, and so on. The enormous number of resulting tags causes fine-grained POS tagging for Arabic to be more challenging.

In order to perform this task, it is beneficial to utilize information from other morphosyntactic categories when predicting a label for one category. For example, if a word is a noun, it should take one of three tags from the case category: nominative (n), accusative (a), or genitive (g), while it should take "not applicable" (na) from the mood category since mood is not defined for nominals. However, most of the previous approaches in Arabic did not utilize this information, applying one model for each task (Habash and Rambow, 2005; Pasha et al., 2014; Shahrour et al., 2015). To make use of this information, we propose an approach that jointly models multiple morphosyntactic prediction tasks using a multi-task learning scheme. Specifically, we adopt parameter sharing in our bi-directional LSTM model in the hope that the shared parameters will store information beneficial to multiple tasks. To further boost the performance, we propose a method of incorporating tag dictionary information into our neural models by combining word representations with representations of the sets of possible tags.

Our experiments showed that the joint model

---

[1] Our code is available at `https://github.com/go-inoue/FineGrainedArabicPOSTagger`

[2] We use the Buckwalter transliteration scheme (Buckwalter, 2002) to represent Arabic characters.

Proceedings of the 21st Conference on Computational Natural Language Learning (CoNLL 2017), pages 421–431,
Vancouver, Canada, August 3 - August 4, 2017. ©2017 Association for Computational Linguistics

Category	Possible values
pos ($n = 35$)	noun, noun_num, noun_quant, noun_prop, adj, adj_comp, adj_num, adv, adv_interrog, adv_rel, pron, pron_dem, pron_exclam, pron_interrog, pron_rel, verb, verb_pseudo, part, part_dem, part_det, part_focus, part_fut, part_interrog, part_neg, part_restrict, part_verb, part_voc, prep, abbrev, punc, conj, conj_sub, interj, digit, latin
gen ($n = 3$)	m (masculine), f (feminine), na (not applicable)
num ($n = 5$)	s (singular), d (dual), p (plural), u (undefined), na
cas ($n = 5$)	n (nominative), a (accusative), g (genitive), u, na
mod ($n = 5$)	i (indicative), j (jussive), s (subjunctive), u, na
asp ($n = 4$)	i (imperfective), p (perfective), c (command), na
per ($n = 4$)	1, 2, 3, na
vox ($n = 4$)	a (active), p (passive), u, na
stt ($n = 5$)	i (indefinite), d (definite), c (constructive/poss/idafa), u, na
prc0 ($n = 10$)	0, na, Aa_prondem, AlmA_detneg, lA_neg, mA_neg, mA_part, mA_rel
prc1 ($n = 27$)	0, na,<i$_interrog, bi_part, bi_prep, bi_prog, Ea_prep, EalaY_prep, fiy_prep, hA_dem, Ha_fut, ka_prep, la_emph, la_prep, la_rc, libi_prep laHa_emphfut, laHa_rcfut, li_jus, li_prep, min_prep, sa_fut, ta_prep, wa_part, wa_prep, wA_voc, yA_voc
prc2 ($n = 9$)	0, na, fa_conj, fa_conn, fa_rc, fa_sub, wa_conj, wa_part, wa_sub
prc3 ($n = 3$)	0, na, >a_ques
enc ($n = 54$)	0, na, 1p_dobj, 1p_poss, 1p_pron, 1s_dobj, 1s_poss, 1s_pron, 2d_dobj, 2d_poss, 2d_pron, 2p_dobj, 2p_poss, 2p_pron, 2fp_dobj, 2fp_poss, 2fp_pron, 2fs_dobj, 2fs_poss, 2fs_pron, 2mp_dobj, 2mp_poss, 2mp_pron, 2ms_dobj, 2ms_poss, 2ms_pron, 3d_dobj, 3d_poss, 3d_pron, 3p_dobj, 3p_poss, 3p_pron, 3fp_dobj, 3fp_poss, 3fp_pron, 3fs_dobj, 3fs_poss, 3fs_pron, 3mp_dobj, 3mp_poss, 3mp_pron, 3ms_dobj, 3ms_poss, 3ms_pron, Ah_voc, lA_neg, ma_interrog, mA_interrog, man_interrog, man_rel, ma_rel, mA_rel, ma_sub, mA_sub

Table 1: The 14 morphosyntactic categories and their possible values used in Pasha et al. (2014). n indicates the size of the tag set.

with tag dictionary information yields the best accuracy on the Penn Arabic Treebank data set with 91.38%, an absolute improvement of 2.11% over the current state-of-the-art.

2 Fined-Grained Arabic POS Tagging

POS tagging takes a sequence of n words $x_{1:n}$ as input and outputs a corresponding sequence of labels $y_{1:n}$, where x_t is the t-th word in a sentence and $y_t \in T$ is the tag of x_t. In English, a POS tag is typically taken from a single tag set T. By contrast, in morphologically rich languages such as Arabic, a complete POS tag is formed by combining tags from multiple tag sets defined for each morphosyntactic category.

For example, a complete POS tag for the word *Hb* ("love") can be defined as the combination of a noun from the coarse POS category, a nominative (*n*) from the case category, "not applicable" (*na*) from the mood category, and so on. Formally, the fine-grained POS tag y_t^{fine} for a word x_t is defined as the conjunction of the tags $y_t^{(1)} \wedge y_t^{(2)} \wedge ... \wedge y_t^{(k)}$ from k tag sets $T^{(1)}, T^{(2)}, ..., T^{(k)}$. Our purpose is then to predict all morphosyntactic categories for each word — in other words, this can be seen as a multi-class and multi-label sequential labeling problem.

In this paper, we use the 14 morphosyntactic categories[3] used in Pasha et al. (2014), a

framework widely used in modern Arabic NLP tools (Pasha et al., 2014; Shahrour et al., 2015; Khalifa et al., 2016). The 14 categories and their possible values are shown in Table 1.

3 Model

In this section, we first briefly describe bi-directional LSTMs. We then present our models which use bi-LSTMs for fine-grained Arabic POS tagging[4]. We also propose a method of incorporating tag dictionary information into our neural models by combining word representations with representations of the sets of possible tags.

3.1 Bi-directional LSTMs

Recurrent neural networks (RNN) (Elman, 1990) are a class of neural networks that are capable of handling sequences of any length. An RNN can be seen as a function that reads the input vector x_t at time step t and calculates a hidden state $\mathbf{h}_t$ using x_t and the previous hidden state $\mathbf{h}_{t-1}$. In classification tasks, the vector $\mathbf{h}_t$ is then fed into the output layer and produces a probability distribution over the possible classes. One of the drawbacks of basic RNNs is their difficulty to train due to the so-called vanishing gradient problem. Long short term memory (LSTM) networks (Hochreiter and Schmidhuber, 1997) address this issue by in-

---

[3]The categories are: coarse POS (pos), gender (gen), number (num), case (cas), mood (mod), aspect (asp), person (per), voice (vox), state (stt), four proclitics (prc0, prc1, prc2, prc3), and one enclitic (enc).

[4]We do not consider a model that directly predicts full complex tags, since complex tags only found in the test set cannot be predicted by such a model.

troducing memory cells and gate units that capture long-term dependencies.

A bi-directional LSTM network (Graves and Schmidhuber, 2005) is an extension of an LSTM network that allows modeling of past and future dependencies in arbitrary-length input sequences. The output vector $\mathbf{h}_t$ of a bi-LSTM is calculated by concatenating the output vector of the forward directional LSTM that reads the sequence from beginning to end with the output vector of the backward directional LSTM that reads the sequence in the reverse direction.

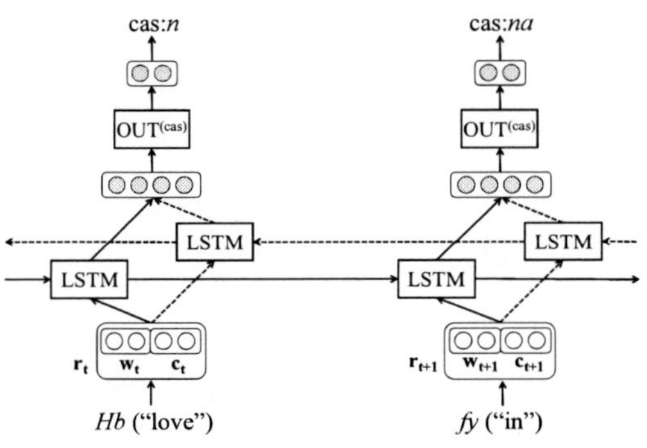

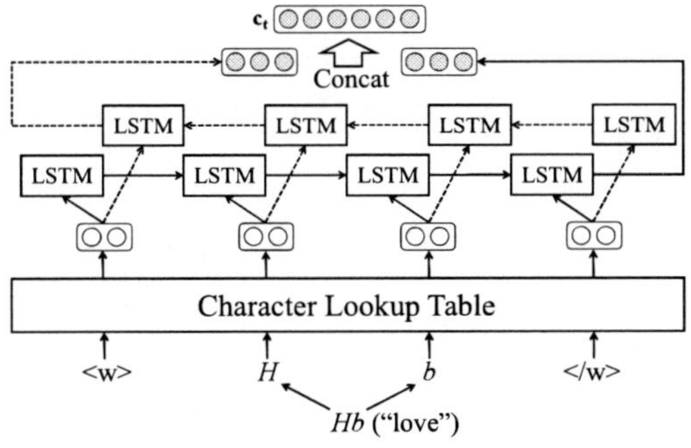

Figure 1: Top: Our baseline model for the category "cas". We have one model for each category, resulting in 14 models in total. Bottom: How to create character-level embeddings. <w> and </w> indicates the beginning and the end of a word.

3.2 Independent Prediction Model

For our baseline method, we use a model that independently predicts each morphosyntactic category using bi-LSTMs. Our baseline is similar to the basic model in Plank et al. (2016). The top part of Figure 1 illustrates an overview of our baseline model. Given a sequence of n words $x_{1:n}$, we encode each word x_t into a vector represen-

tation $\mathbf{r}_t = [\mathbf{w}_t; \mathbf{c}_t]$, which is the concatenation of the word embedding $\mathbf{w}_t$ and the character-level embedding $\mathbf{c}_t$. The character-level embedding is computed by concatenating hidden states of the character-level forward LSTM and those of the backward LSTM as depicted in the bottom part of Figure 1.

The vector representation $\mathbf{r}_t$ is then fed into our bi-LSTM model, giving the forward hidden state $\overrightarrow{\mathbf{h}}_t$ and the backward hidden state $\overleftarrow{\mathbf{h}}_t$. Both hidden states are concatenated into single vector $\mathbf{v}_t = [\overrightarrow{\mathbf{h}}_t; \overleftarrow{\mathbf{h}}_t]$ and fed into the output layer. Finally, we obtain the output label y_t by performing a softmax over the tag set vocabulary. We train models separately for each morphosyntactic category, resulting in 14 models in total.

3.3 Joint Prediction Model

Our baseline model does not share any information between morphosyntactic prediction tasks, as it is trained separately. However, it is beneficial to utilize information from other morphosyntactic categories when predicting a label for one category. In order to do this, we adopt a multi-task learning approach (Collobert et al., 2011; Yang et al., 2016; Søgaard and Goldberg, 2016; Bingel and Søgaard, 2017; Martínez Alonso and Plank, 2017). Specifically, we use parameter sharing in the hidden layers of our bi-LSTM model so that we can generate a unified model that can carry information beneficial to each task.

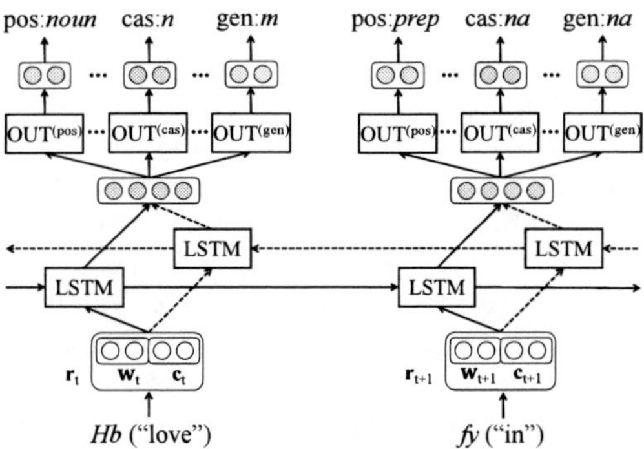

Figure 2: Multi-task bi-directional LSTM model for fine-grained Arabic POS tagging.

Figure 2 shows an overview of our joint model. The output vectors of the bi-LSTMs are fed into multiple output layers, each performing a corresponding morphosyntactic prediction task. Our model trains to minimize the cross-entropy loss averaged across all the tasks. The loss function for each input word is defined as follows:

$$L(\hat{y}^{fine}, y^{fine}) = \frac{1}{|M|} \sum_{m \in M} L(\hat{y}_m, y_m)$$

where $M = \{pos, cas, gen, ...\}$ is the set of morphosyntactic prediction tasks and $L(\hat{y}_m, y_m)$ is the cross-entropy loss for the category m.

3.4 Encoding Tag Dictionary Information

One of our contributions is to incorporate tag dictionary information into our neural models by combining word representations with representations of the sets of possible tags. Unlike previous approaches that use tag dictionary information provided by a morphological analyzer as a hard constraint (Habash and Rambow, 2005; Pasha et al., 2014; Shahrour et al., 2015), we use it as a soft constraint, as well as an additional feature for our model.

The drawback of using a morphological analyzer in a pipeline fashion is that the model cannot find the correct tag in the disambiguation step if the analyzer does not return any tag candidates. Habash et al. (2016) report in their error analysis that 31.3% of their tagging errors were due to this problem. To cope with this issue, we propose a method of encoding tag dictionary information into our neural models instead of using a morphological analyzer in a pipeline fashion. As such, the output of our tagger is not restricted by the output candidates that are generated by the analyzer, and our method can be applied to POS tagging with an arbitrary tag set.

The bottom part of Figure 3 illustrates how to encode tag dictionary information for the word *Hb* ("love"). First, the input word is given to a tag dictionary that generates sets of possible tags for each morphosyntactic category. The outputs from the dictionary are then fed into the corresponding lookup tables, giving vector representations for possible tags. For each category, we sum over the outputs from the lookup table and then concatenate all the summed vectors into a single vector.

Formally, the encoded vector representation $\mathbf{d}_t$ for the input word x_t is computed by concatenating all the sub-vectors defined for each morphosyntactic category m:

$$\mathbf{d}_t = [\mathbf{d}_t^{(pos)}; ... ; \mathbf{d}_t^{(cas)}; ... ; \mathbf{d}_t^{(gen)}]$$

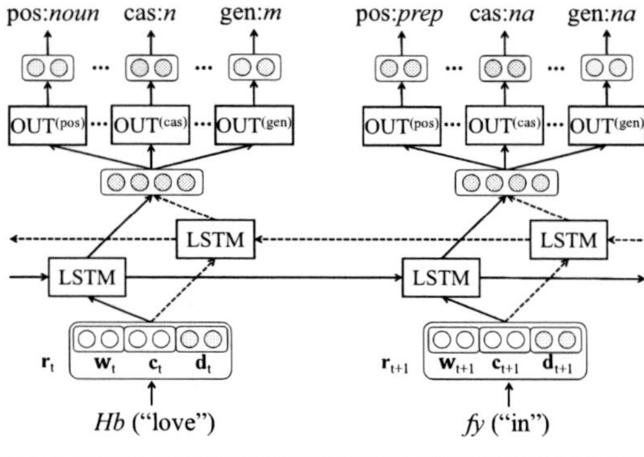

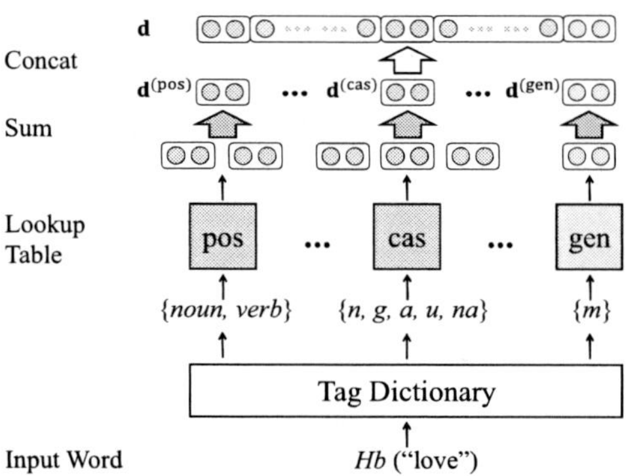

Figure 3: Top: An overview of our proposed model with tag dictionary embeddings. Bottom: Example of how tag dictionary information is encoded.

The sub-vector $\mathbf{d}_t^{(m)}$ is computed with the following equation:

$$\mathbf{d}_t^{(m)} = \sum_{d \in D_t^{(m)}} \mathbf{W}^{(m)} \mathbf{e}_d^{(m)}$$

where $D_t^{(m)}$ is the set of possible tags for the category m given the word x_t, $\mathbf{W}^{(m)}$ is the embedding matrix for the category m, and $\mathbf{e}_d^{(m)}$ is a one-hot vector representing the tag d for the category m. Finally, the resulting vector $\mathbf{d}_t$ is concatenated with the word embedding $\mathbf{w}_t$ and the character-level embedding $\mathbf{c}_t$, forming the input word representation $\mathbf{r}_t = [\mathbf{w}_t; \mathbf{c}_t; \mathbf{d}_t]$ for our model. The top part of Figure 3 illustrates the overall architecture of our proposed model.

4 Experiments

In this section, we present our experimental setup and results. We report tagging accuracy on two data sets: the Penn Arabic Treebank (PATB) data set and the Arabic Universal Dependencies Treebank (UD Arabic) data set. We also report the effects of tag dictionary information in both data sets.

4.1 Experimental Setup

4.1.1 Implementation Details

We implement all bi-LSTM models using the DyNet library (Neubig et al., 2017). We use the same hyperparameters throughout the independent and joint models, i.e., Adam with cross entropy loss, mini-batch size of a single sentence, 100 dimensions for word embeddings, 50 for character-level embeddings, 10 for each morphosyntactic dictionary embedding, 500 hidden states, 100 dimensions for output layers, random initialization for the embeddings, and no dropout regularization. We do not use external resources for the word embeddings in order to emulate the data availability of earlier work as much as possible. The number of epochs is optimized based on evaluation over the development set, to a maximum of 10 epochs. We use ALMOR (Habash, 2007), which is part of the MADAMIRA distribution (Pasha et al., 2014), alongside the SAMA database (Maamouri et al., 2010c) to create the tag dictionary.

4.1.2 Data Sets

The PATB Data Set

In order to compare our models with the current state-of-the-art tagger, we use the Penn Arabic Treebank (PATB, parts 1, 2 and 3) (Maamouri et al., 2010a, 2011, 2010b) with the same partitioning as Diab et al. (2013). The statistics of the data set are shown in Table 2. The data sets are pre-processed as in Pasha et al. (2014) to correct annotation inconsistencies and to obtain the morphosyntactic feature representation for each word. All the Arabic characters are transliterated according to the Buckwalter transliteration scheme (Buckwalter, 2002) and each numerical digit is substituted with 0.

	Train	Dev	Test
# Sentences	15789	1986	1963
# Words	502991	63136	63168
# Tags	2028	1034	1069

Table 2: Number of sentences, space-delimited words, and fine-grained POS tags in the Penn Arabic Treebank data set.

The UD Arabic Data Set

In order to evaluate the performance of our models on different data in a different tagging scheme, we use the Arabic portion of Universal Dependencies Version 1.4 (Nivre et al., 2016) with the provided gold tokenization. We assume gold tokenization for the sake of simplicity. The statistics of the data set are shown in Table 3.

	Train	Dev	Test
# Sentences	6174	786	704
# Tokens	225853	28263	28268
# Tags	327	214	213

Table 3: Number of sentences, tokens, and fine-grained POS tags in the UD Arabic data set.

For the fine-grained POS tag set, we use the universal POS tags and 16 of the morphological features defined in the UD Arabic data set. The annotations in the UD Arabic data set are automatically converted from the Prague Arabic Dependency Treebank (Smrž et al., 2008). Table 4 shows the lists of possible values for each morphosyntactic category. The annotations in UD Arabic are different from those in PATB with regard to the choice of categories and their granularity, although there are some overlaps in categories such as gender and person. For pre-processing, each numerical digit is substituted with 0.

POS ($n = 17$)	ADJ, ADP, ADV, AUX, CONJ, DET, INTEJ, NOUN, NUM, PART, PRON, PROPN, PUNCT, SCONJ, SYM, VERB, X
Gender ($n = 3$)	Fem, Masc, EMPTY
Number ($n = 4$)	Dual, Plur, Sing, EMPTY
Case ($n = 4$)	Acc, Gen, Nom, EMPTY
Mood ($n = 5$)	Imp, Ind, Jus, Sub, EMPTY
Aspect ($n = 3$)	Imp, Perf, EMPTY
Person ($n = 4$)	1, 2, 3, EMPTY
Voice ($n = 3$)	Act, Pass, EMPTY
Definite ($n = 5$)	Com, Cons, Def, Ind, EMPTY
Abbr ($n = 2$)	Yes, EMPTY
AdpType ($n = 2$)	Prep, EMPTY
Foreign ($n = 2$)	Yes, EMPTY
Negative ($n = 2$)	Negative, EMPTY
NumForm ($n = 3$)	Digit, Word, EMPTY
NumValue ($n = 4$)	1, 2, 3, EMPTY
PronType ($n = 4$)	Dem, Prs, Rel, EMPTY
VerbForm ($n = 2$)	Fin, EMPTY

Table 4: The 17 morphosyntactic categories in the UD scheme (i.e., the universal POS tags and 16 morphological features) and their possible values. n indicates the size of the tag set.

4.1.3 Evaluation

Tagging Accuracy on the PATB data set

We report tagging accuracy over the 14 morphosyntactic categories and their combination,

	pos	gen	num	cas	mod	asp	per	vox	stt	prc0	prc1	prc2	prc3	enc	All
CamelParser	96.78	99.41	99.43	92.68	99.13	99.27	99.23	99.08	97.54	99.67	99.63	99.59	99.90	99.61	89.27
Independent	96.31	99.05	99.26	93.17	99.07	99.08	99.10	98.80	97.23	99.62	99.64	99.73	**99.97**	99.44	87.74
+*Dict*	97.07	99.33	99.51	94.70	99.31	99.34	99.35	99.18	98.11	99.48	99.78	**99.78**	**99.97**	99.68	90.17
Joint	96.24	99.27	99.16	93.48	99.18	99.19	99.20	98.91	97.70	99.66	99.64	99.68	**99.97**	99.58	89.49
+*Dict*	**97.21**	**99.50**	**99.59**	**94.76**	**99.41**	**99.44**	**99.47**	**99.25**	**98.24**	**99.71**	**99.81**	99.73	99.96	**99.71**	**91.38**

Table 5: Tagging accuracies on the PATB data set. **All** is the percentage where all categories were correct (i.e., the fine-grained POS tag). +*Dict* indicates the use of the tag dictionary embeddings. Best results are in boldface.

	pos	gen	num	cas	mod	asp	per	vox	stt	prc0	prc1	prc2	prc3	enc	All
Joint	96.24	99.27	99.16	93.48	99.18	99.19	99.20	98.91	97.70	99.66	99.64	99.68	99.97	99.58	89.49
+*pos*	**+0.96**	**+0.25**	+0.27	**+1.00**	**+0.25**	+0.21	+0.23	**+0.38**	+0.46	+0.04	+0.09	+0.09	0.00	+0.08	**+1.48**
+*gen*	+0.35	+0.10	+0.18	+0.34	+0.12	+0.12	+0.09	+0.21	+0.19	0.00	-0.06	0.00	-0.01	+0.02	+0.33
+*num*	+0.36	+0.10	**+0.43**	+0.45	+0.06	+0.07	+0.08	+0.17	+0.13	+0.03	-0.02	+0.02	-0.01	+0.01	+0.63
+*cas*	+0.51	+0.13	+0.25	+0.82	**+0.25**	+0.22	+0.23	+0.32	+0.41	-0.01	+0.08	+0.04	0.00	+0.06	+0.99
+*mod*	+0.38	+0.10	+0.14	+0.77	+0.23	+0.23	+0.21	+0.31	+0.39	-0.01	+0.04	+0.05	-0.01	+0.06	+0.82
+*asp*	+0.47	+0.12	+0.22	+0.48	+0.22	+0.22	+0.24	+0.33	+0.33	+0.02	+0.06	+0.03	0.00	+0.03	+0.68
+*per*	+0.26	+0.16	+0.18	+0.72	+0.24	**+0.28**	**+0.29**	+0.36	+0.32	+0.01	+0.08	+0.06	0.00	+0.07	+0.78
+*vox*	+0.27	+0.13	+0.15	+0.65	+0.21	+0.21	+0.19	+0.31	+0.29	+0.01	-0.07	-0.01	-0.01	+0.04	+0.60
+*stt*	+0.60	+0.12	+0.20	+0.87	+0.23	+0.23	+0.22	+0.35	**+0.47**	+0.03	+0.07	+0.05	-0.01	+0.05	+0.99
+*prc0*	+0.31	+0.10	+0.16	+0.56	+0.06	+0.08	+0.08	+0.16	+0.16	**+0.06**	+0.06	+0.05	0.00	0.00	+0.56
+*prc1*	+0.40	+0.09	+0.21	+0.50	+0.06	-0.02	+0.06	+0.14	+0.11	+0.02	**+0.15**	+0.02	0.00	0.00	+0.69
+*prc2*	+0.23	+0.04	+0.16	+0.23	0.00	-0.01	+0.04	+0.12	+0.05	+0.04	-0.09	**+0.10**	-0.01	-0.02	+0.35
+*prc3*	+0.14	+0.05	+0.16	+0.33	+0.07	+0.04	+0.04	+0.15	+0.09	+0.01	-0.05	+0.05	-0.01	+0.01	+0.28
+*enc*	+0.26	+0.02	+0.12	+0.53	+0.09	+0.07	+0.07	+0.21	+0.22	+0.02	0.00	+0.04	-0.01	**+0.12**	+0.63
+*all*	+0.97	+0.23	+0.43	+1.28	+0.23	+0.25	+0.27	+0.34	+0.54	+0.05	+0.17	+0.05	-0.01	+0.13	+1.89

Table 6: Performance comparison of the different models, each of which uses a single morphosyntactic category in its tag dictionary embeddings, on the PATB data set. +*m* in the leftmost column indicates the use of the category *m* to form the tag dictionary embeddings. +*all* indicates the use of all categories to form the tag dictionary embeddings. Boldfaced numbers represent the largest improvement in the category to predict (minimum of 0.05% absolute).

i.e., the fine-grained POS tag (**All**). For comparison, we use CamelParser (Shahrour et al., 2015), the current state-of-the-art tagger. CamelParser is an improved version of the previous state-of-the-art tagger MADAMIRA (Pasha et al., 2014), which ranks the possible analyses provided by a morphological analyzer using SVMs. Camel-Parser adjusts the outputs of MADAMIRA by utilizing case-state classifiers that incorporate additional syntactic information provided by a dependency parser and hand-written rules. The tag set used in CamelParser is compatible with the 14 morphosyntactic categories we use.

Tagging Accuracy on the UD Arabic data set
For the UD Arabic data set, we report tagging accuracy over the 17 morphosyntactic categories (i.e., the universal POS tags and 16 morphological features) and their combination (**All**). We use independent models with and without tag dictionary information and joint models with and without tag dictionary information for this data set.

Most Influential Categories
For both data sets, we conduct additional experiments to investigate which morphosyntactic category in the tag dictionary embeddings contributes most to the performance. Specifically, instead of using all morphosyntactic categories to create the tag dictionary embeddings, we use only one at a time. In other words, we skip the last step of concatenating all the sub-vectors defined for each morphosyntactic category, and use only one of the sub-vectors for the tag dictionary embeddings.

4.2 Results

4.2.1 The PATB Data Set

Our Models vs CamelParser

Table 5 illustrates our experimental results on the PATB data set. The best performing model was the joint model with tag dictionary embeddings (+*Dict*), achieving an accuracy of 91.38% on the strictest metric "**All**" (i.e., the fine-grained POS tag) with an absolute improvement of 2.11% over CamelParser, the current state-of-the-art tagger. This model outperforms CamelParser in every morphosyntactic category. Among these categories, the most notable improvement is the case category (cas) with an absolute improvement of 2.08% over the current state-of-the-art system. Leaving out the dictionary embeddings (+*Dict*) reduces the performance by 1.89% absolute, but still outperforms CamelParser without using any addi-

	POS	Gender	Number	Case	Mood	Aspect	Person	Voice	Definite
Independent	95.15	97.28	96.38	93.76	99.56	99.35	99.37	99.14	96.40
+Dict	96.08	98.06	97.23	94.86	99.68	99.51	99.47	99.16	97.09
Joint	95.92	97.96	96.69	94.60	99.67	99.50	99.45	99.21	96.67
+Dict	**96.64**	**98.32**	**97.47**	**95.43**	**99.69**	**99.58**	**99.59**	**99.32**	**97.35**

	Abbr	AdpType	Foreign	Negative	NumForm	NumValue	PronType	VerbForm	All
Independent	99.88	99.75	99.16	99.99	99.88	99.80	99.76	99.69	86.45
+Dict	**100.00**	99.84	99.58	99.99	**99.90**	99.80	99.79	99.73	89.17
Joint	99.99	99.85	99.47	99.99	**99.90**	**99.98**	99.81	99.78	90.36
+Dict	99.99	**99.86**	**99.66**	99.99	99.89	**99.98**	**99.84**	**99.84**	**91.68**

Table 7: Tagging accuracies on the UD Arabic data set. **All** is the percentage where all categories were correct (i.e., the fine-grained POS tag). *+Dict* indicates the use of the tag dictionary embeddings.

tional resources such as a morphological analyzer or a dependency parser, indicating the effectiveness of joint modeling of morphosyntactic categories. On the other hand, the independent model gives an accuracy of 87.74%, which is 1.53% absolute worse than CamelParser. However, adding dictionary embeddings (*+Dict*) enhances the performance with an absolute improvement of 2.43% and yields the second-best accuracy, showing the impact of the additional dictionary feature.

Most Influential Categories

Which morphosyntactic category in the tag dictionary embeddings contributes most to the performance? Table 6 compares the performance of the different models, each of which uses a single morphosyntactic category in its tag dictionary embeddings. The category that contributes most in the tag dictionary embeddings is the coarse POS category (*+pos*) with an absolute improvement of 1.48% on the metric "**All**". It is worth mentioning that case and state categories are tied for the second most contributing category, which supports CamelParser's idea that improving the prediction of case and state categories will provide further performance gains.

Looking at the effects on each category to predict, the embeddings for coarse POS (*+pos*) give the best improvement in 5 categories: coarse POS (pos), gender (gen), case (cas), mood (mod), and voice (vox). We can see that the information carried by the coarse POS category plays a central role for predicting other morphosyntactic categories, especially for the case category. On the other hand, in 8 categories, the best improvement was achieved when the category used for the tag dictionary embeddings was the same as the category to predict. The 8 categories were: coarse POS (pos), number (num), person (per), state (stt), three of the proclitics (prc0, prc1, prc2), and en-

clitic (enc). This result suggests that the tag dictionary embeddings of a given category behave as a soft constraint when predicting the same category, which makes intuitive sense.

4.2.2 The UD Arabic Data Set

Results of Our Models

Table 7 illustrates our experimental results on the UD Arabic data set. The independent model gives an accuracy of 86.34% on the metric "**All**" (i.e., the fine-grained POS tag). Adding the tag dictionary embeddings (*+Dict*) improves the accuracy with an absolute improvement of 2.72%. Unlike the PATB data set, the joint model outperformed both independent models regardless of the use of the tag dictionary embeddings. The best performing model was the joint model with the tag dictionary embeddings (*+Dict*), achieving an accuracy of 91.68%. We can observe that the overall results show similar tendencies to the results on the PATB data set in spite of the different annotation schemes.

Most Influential Categories

Table 8 compares the performance of the different models, each of which uses a single morphosyntactic category in its tag dictionary embeddings, on the UD Arabic data set. As in the results on the PATB data set, the coarse POS category (*+pos*) is the category that contributes the most in the tag dictionary embeddings, giving an absolute improvement of 0.92% on the metric "**All**". It also gives the best improvement in 8 categories: POS, Aspect, Case, Definite, Foreign, Gender, Number, Person, and Voice. This result confirmed that the possible tag information from the POS category is more effective than information from the other categories.

On the other hand, unlike in the PATB data set, we do not observe a relationship between the cat-

	POS	Gender	Number	Case	Mood	Aspect	Person	Voice	Definite
Joint	95.92	97.96	96.69	94.60	99.67	99.50	99.45	99.21	96.67
+*pos*	**+0.55**	**+0.30**	**+0.49**	**+0.58**	+0.04	+0.07	**+0.14**	**+0.15**	**+0.56**
+*gen*	-0.20	+0.01	-0.07	+0.05	**+0.06**	**+0.09**	+0.09	+0.13	-0.01
+*num*	+0.12	+0.06	+0.44	+0.32	+0.04	+0.01	+0.13	+0.04	+0.25
+*cas*	+0.19	+0.01	+0.33	+0.33	+0.02	+0.02	+0.08	+0.04	+0.37
+*mod*	+0.15	-0.09	+0.24	+0.26	+0.02	+0.07	+0.13	+0.14	+0.19
+*asp*	+0.19	0.00	+0.23	+0.33	-0.02	+0.06	+0.11	+0.09	+0.29
+*per*	+0.20	+0.03	+0.26	+0.38	+0.01	+0.07	+0.12	+0.07	+0.28
+*vox*	+0.08	+0.01	+0.17	+0.13	-0.01	+0.05	+0.09	+0.14	+0.21
+*stt*	+0.08	-0.06	+0.25	+0.48	-0.04	+0.04	+0.08	+0.07	+0.41
+*prc0*	-0.03	-0.06	+0.27	+0.10	+0.04	+0.02	+0.08	-0.02	+0.31
+*prc1*	-0.01	-0.01	+0.18	+0.20	+0.03	+0.02	+0.06	+0.07	+0.14
+*prc2*	-0.17	-0.12	+0.21	+0.15	+0.03	0.00	+0.01	-0.03	+0.22
+*prc3*	+0.07	-0.14	+0.29	+0.21	-0.02	+0.02	+0.08	+0.06	+0.25
+*enc*	-0.01	-0.22	+0.40	+0.10	-0.02	-0.04	-0.03	-0.05	+0.28
+*all*	+0.72	+0.36	+0.78	+0.83	+0.02	+0.08	+0.14	+0.11	+0.68

	Abbr	AdpType	Foreign	Negative	NumForm	NumValue	PronType	VerbForm	**All**
Joint	99.99	99.85	99.47	99.99	99.90	99.98	99.81	99.78	90.36
+*pos*	+0.01	-0.01	**+0.16**	0.00	+0.01	-0.02	+0.03	+0.03	**+0.92**
+*gen*	+0.01	0.00	+0.03	0.00	0.00	0.00	+0.01	+0.04	+0.08
+*num*	0.00	-0.02	+0.06	0.00	+0.02	0.00	+0.01	+0.03	+0.34
+*cas*	+0.01	0.00	+0.08	0.00	+0.02	0.00	0.00	+0.03	+0.30
+*mod*	0.00	-0.04	+0.03	0.00	0.00	-0.01	+0.01	+0.04	+0.33
+*asp*	+0.01	-0.01	+0.07	0.00	-0.01	0.00	+0.01	+0.02	+0.48
+*per*	0.00	-0.01	+0.16	0.00	+0.02	0.00	0.00	+0.02	+0.50
+*vox*	+0.01	-0.03	+0.09	0.00	-0.01	0.00	+0.01	+0.01	+0.06
+*stt*	+0.01	-0.03	+0.06	0.00	-0.01	-0.01	+0.01	+0.01	+0.28
+*prc0*	+0.01	-0.01	+0.09	0.00	0.00	-0.01	+0.01	+0.03	+0.13
+*prc1*	+0.01	-0.01	+0.12	+0.01	-0.03	-0.01	+0.01	0.00	+0.30
+*prc2*	+0.01	-0.02	+0.11	0.00	-0.02	-0.01	0.00	0.00	-0.02
+*prc3*	+0.01	-0.03	-0.02	0.00	0.00	-0.03	0.00	-0.02	-0.01
+*enc*	+0.01	-0.04	+0.03	-0.01	0.00	0.00	0.00	+0.01	-0.02
+*all*	0.00	+0.01	+0.19	0.00	-0.01	0.00	+0.03	+0.06	+1.32

Table 8: Performance comparison of the different models, each of which uses a single morphosyntactic category in its tag dictionary embeddings, on the UD Arabic data set. +*m* in the leftmost column indicates the use of the category *m* to form the tag dictionary embeddings. +*all* indicates the use of all categories to form the tag dictionary embeddings. Boldfaced numbers represent the largest improvement in the category to predict (minimum of 0.05% absolute).

egory used for the tag dictionary embeddings and the category to predict, presumably because of the difference in the annotation schemes.

5 Related Work

Diab et al. (2004) proposed a segmentation-based approach, in which they tag each clitic-segmented token using SVMs. Mohamed and Kübler (2010) proposed a word-based approach which takes space-delimited words as inputs and uses memory-based learning. Their experiment showed that the word-based approach performed better than the segmentation-based approach, avoiding segmentation error propagation. Zhang et al. (2015) proposed joint modeling of segmentation, POS tagging, and dependency parsing using a randomized greedy algorithm. The aforementioned studies were focused on tagging

with reduced POS tag sets whose sizes ranged from 12 to 993. However, we use one of the most fine-grained POS tag sets, with about 2,000 tags appearing in our training set.

In the context of fine-grained POS tagging, Mueller et al. (2013) presented an approximated higher-order CRF for morphosyntactic tagging across six languages, assuming gold clitic segmentation. Pasha et al. (2014) used an analyze-and-disambiguate approach, in which they ranked the possible analyses provided by a morphological analyzer for each space-delimited word. The state-of-the-art tagger (Shahrour et al., 2015) extended their model by adjusting the outputs of Pasha et al.'s tagger by utilizing case-state classifiers that incorporate additional syntactic information provided by a dependency parser and hand-written rules.

Compared to their approaches, our model is simple but powerful: It does not assume gold clitic segmentation, since segmentation is also modeled as part of the morphosyntactic categories, nor does it require the additional pipeline process of syntactic parsing. Nonetheless, it is more accurate than the current state-of-the-art.

Another related line of work tackles sequential labeling problems using multi-task learning with deep neural networks and investigates situations where multi-task learning leads to improvements in performance (Søgaard and Goldberg, 2016; Bingel and Søgaard, 2017; Martínez Alonso and Plank, 2017). Although our main focus is not on investigating the most effective task combination, it can be worth experimenting with various configurations in our settings.

With regard to the use of outputs from a morphological analyzer as additional features, our work is closely related to Bohnet et al. (2013) and Shen et al. (2016). Bohnet et al. (2013) presented a joint approach for morphological and syntactic analysis for morphologically rich languages, integrating additional features that encode whether a tag is in the dictionary or not. Shen et al. (2016) proposed an approach in which they encode a sequence of possible morphosyntactic tags provided by a morphological analyzer using bi-directional LSTMs. In contrast, we provide an alternative way of encoding this information, as well as an analysis on the most influential categories in the encoded tag embeddings.

6 Conclusions

We presented an approach for fine-grained Arabic POS tagging that jointly models each morphosyntactic tagging task using a multi-task learning framework. We also proposed a method of incorporating tag dictionary information into our neural models by combining word representations with representations of the sets of possible tags. The joint model with tag dictionary information results in the best accuracy of 91.38% with an absolute improvement of 2.11% over the current state-of-the-art tagger. In addition, our experiments showed that the proposed method of encoding tag dictionary information improves the tagging accuracy even on a data set with different annotations.

One potential future direction to explore is domain adaptation to Arabic dialects, since our approach is easily applicable as it does not require construction of a morphological analyzer for each dialect. Another direction is to make use of publicly available dictionaries such as Wiktionary to construct a tag dictionary.

Acknowledgments

We would like to thank the anonymous reviewers, Hiroki Ouchi, Yuichiro Sawai, Taishi Ikeda, Hitoshi Manabe, and Michael Wentao Li for their valuable comments and suggestions. We also appreciate Nizar Habash and Salam Khalifa for providing the pre-processed data and running the CamelParser experiment.

References

Joachim Bingel and Anders Søgaard. 2017. Identifying beneficial task relations for multi-task learning in deep neural networks. In *Proceedings of the 15th Conference of the European Chapter of the Association for Computational Linguistics: Volume 2, Short Papers*. Association for Computational Linguistics, Valencia, Spain, pages 164–169. http://www.aclweb.org/anthology/E17-2026.

Bernd Bohnet, Joakim Nivre, Igor Boguslavsky, Richárd Farkas, Filip Ginter, and Jan Hajič. 2013. Joint Morphological and Syntactic Analysis for Richly Inflected Languages. *Transactions of the Association for Computational Linguistics* 1:415–428.

Tim Buckwalter. 2002. Buckwalter Arabic Morphological Analyzer Version 1.0 LDC2002L49. Linguistic Data Consortium (LDC, Philadelphia US).

Ronan Collobert, Jason Weston, Léon Bottou, Michael Karlen, Koray Kavukcuoglu, and Pavel Kuksa. 2011. Natural Language Processing (Almost) from Scratch. *Journal of Machine Learning Research* 12(Aug):2493–2537.

Mona Diab, Nizar Habash, Owen Rambow, and Ryan Roth. 2013. LDC Arabic Treebanks and Associated Corpora: Data Divisions Manual. In *arXiv preprint arXiv:1309.5652*.

Mona Diab, Kadri Hacioglu, and Daniel Jurafsky. 2004. Automatic Tagging of Arabic Text: From Raw Text to Base Phrase Chunks. In *Proceedings of the 2004 Conference of the North American Chapter of the Association for Computational Linguistics: Human Language Technologies: Short Papers*. Association for Computational Linguistics, Boston, Massachusetts, USA, pages 149–152. http://anthology.aclweb.org/N/N04/N04-4038.pdf.

Jeffrey L Elman. 1990. Finding structure in time. *Cognitive Science* 14(2):179–211.

Alex Graves and Jürgen Schmidhuber. 2005. Frame-wise Phoneme Classification with Bidirectional LSTM and Other Neural Network Architectures. *Neural Networks* 18(5):602–610.

Nizar Habash. 2007. Arabic Morphological Representations for Machine Translation. *Arabic Computational Morphology: Knowledge-based and Empirical Methods* pages 263–285.

Nizar Habash and Owen Rambow. 2005. Arabic Tokenization, Part-of-Speech Tagging and Morphological Disambiguation in One Fell Swoop. In *Proceedings of the 43rd Annual Meeting of the Association for Computational Linguistics (ACL'05)*. Association for Computational Linguistics, Ann Arbor, Michigan, USA, pages 573–580. https://doi.org/10.3115/1219840.1219911.

Nizar Habash, Anas Shahrour, and Muhamed Al-Khalil. 2016. Exploiting Arabic Diacritization for High Quality Automatic Annotation. In *Proceedings of the Tenth International Conference on Language Resources and Evaluation (LREC'16)*. pages 4298–4303. http://www.lrec-conf.org/proceedings/lrec2016/pdf/878_Paper.pdf.

Sepp Hochreiter and Jürgen Schmidhuber. 1997. Long Short-Term Memory. *Neural Computation* 9(8):1735–1780.

Salam Khalifa, Nasser Zalmout, and Nizar Habash. 2016. YAMAMA: Yet Another Multi-Dialect Arabic Morphological Analyzer. In *Proceedings of COLING 2016, the 26th International Conference on Computational Linguistics: System Demonstrations*. The COLING 2016 Organizing Committee, Osaka, Japan, pages 223–227. http://aclweb.org/anthology/C16-2047.

Mohamed Maamouri, Ann Bies, Seth Kulick, Fatma Gaddeche, Wigdan Mekki, Sondos Krouna, Basma Bouziri, and Wadji Zaghouani. 2010a. Arabic Treebank: Part 1 v 4.1. Linguistic Data Consortium (LDC, Philadelphia US).

Mohamed Maamouri, Ann Bies, Seth Kulick, Fatma Gaddeche, Wigdan Mekki, Sondos Krouna, Basma Bouziri, and Wadji Zaghouani. 2011. Arabic Treebank: Part 2 v 3.1. Linguistic Data Consortium (LDC, Philadelphia US).

Mohamed Maamouri, Ann Bies, Seth Kulick, Sondos Krouna, Fatma Gaddeche, and Wadji Zaghouani. 2010b. Arabic Treebank: Part 3 v 3.2. Linguistic Data Consortium (LDC, Philadelphia US).

Mohamed Maamouri, David Graff, Basma Bouziri, Sondos Krouna, Ann Bies, and Seth Kulick. 2010c. LDC Standard Arabic Morphological Analyzer (SAMA) Version 3.1 LDC2010L01. Linguistic Data Consortium (LDC, Philadelphia US).

Héctor Martínez Alonso and Barbara Plank. 2017. When is multitask learning effective? semantic sequence prediction under varying data conditions. In *Proceedings of the 15th Conference of the European Chapter of the Association for Computational Linguistics: Volume 1, Long Papers*. Association for Computational Linguistics, Valencia, Spain, pages 44–53. http://www.aclweb.org/anthology/E17-1005.

Emad Mohamed and Sandra Kübler. 2010. Is Arabic Part of Speech Tagging Feasible Without Word Segmentation? In *Proceedings of Human Language Technologies: The 2010 Annual Conference of the North American Chapter of the Association for Computational Linguistics*. Association for Computational Linguistics, Los Angeles, California, USA, pages 705–708. http://www.aclweb.org/anthology/N10-1105.

Thomas Mueller, Helmut Schmid, and Hinrich Schütze. 2013. Efficient Higher-Order CRFs for Morphological Tagging. In *Proceedings of the 2013 Conference on Empirical Methods in Natural Language Processing*. Association for Computational Linguistics, Seattle, Washington, USA, pages 322–332. http://www.aclweb.org/anthology/D13-1032.

Graham Neubig, Chris Dyer, Yoav Goldberg, Austin Matthews, Waleed Ammar, Antonios Anastasopoulos, Miguel Ballesteros, David Chiang, Daniel Clothiaux, Trevor Cohn, Kevin Duh, Manaal Faruqui, Cynthia Gan, Dan Garrette, Yangfeng Ji, Lingpeng Kong, Adhiguna Kuncoro, Gaurav Kumar, Chaitanya Malaviya, Paul Michel, Yusuke Oda, Matthew Richardson, Naomi Saphra, Swabha Swayamdipta, and Pengcheng Yin. 2017. Dynet: The Dynamic Neural Network Toolkit. *arXiv preprint arXiv:1701.03980* .

Joakim Nivre, Željko Agić, Lars Ahrenberg, Maria Jesus Aranzabe, Masayuki Asahara, Aitziber Atutxa, Miguel Ballesteros, John Bauer, Kepa Bengoetxea, Yevgeni Berzak, Riyaz Ahmad Bhat, Eckhard Bick, Carl Börstell, Cristina Bosco, Gosse Bouma, Sam Bowman, Gülşen Cebirolu Eryiit, Giuseppe G. A. Celano, Fabricio Chalub, Çar Çöltekin, Miriam Connor, Elizabeth Davidson, Marie-Catherine de Marneffe, Arantza Diaz de Ilarraza, Kaja Dobrovoljc, Timothy Dozat, Kira Droganova, Puneet Dwivedi, Marhaba Eli, Tomaž Erjavec, Richárd Farkas, Jennifer Foster, Claudia Freitas, Katarína Gajdošová, Daniel Galbraith, Marcos Garcia, Moa Gärdenfors, Sebastian Garza, Filip Ginter, Iakes Goenaga, Koldo Gojenola, Memduh Gökrmak, Yoav Goldberg, Xavier Gómez Guinovart, Berta Gonzáles Saavedra, Matias Grioni, Normunds Grūzītis, Bruno Guillaume, Jan Hajič, Linh Hà M, Dag Haug, Barbora Hladká, Radu Ion, Elena Irimia, Anders Johannsen, Fredrik Jørgensen, Hüner Kaşkara, Hiroshi Kanayama, Jenna Kanerva, Boris Katz, Jessica Kenney, Natalia Kotsyba, Simon Krek, Veronika Laippala, Lucia Lam, Phng Lê Hng, Alessandro Lenci, Nikola Ljubešić, Olga

Lyashevskaya, Teresa Lynn, Aibek Makazhanov, Christopher Manning, Cătălina Mărănduc, David Mareček, Héctor Martínez Alonso, André Martins, Jan Mašek, Yuji Matsumoto, Ryan McDonald, Anna Missilä, Verginica Mititelu, Yusuke Miyao, Simonetta Montemagni, Keiko Sophie Mori, Shunsuke Mori, Bohdan Moskalevskyi, Kadri Muischnek, Nina Mustafina, Kaili Müürisep, Lng Nguyn Th, Huyn Nguyn Th Minh, Vitaly Nikolaev, Hanna Nurmi, Petya Osenova, Robert Östling, Lilja Øvrelid, Valeria Paiva, Elena Pascual, Marco Passarotti, Cenel-Augusto Perez, Slav Petrov, Jussi Piitulainen, Barbara Plank, Martin Popel, Lauma Pretkalnia, Prokopis Prokopidis, Tiina Puolakainen, Sampo Pyysalo, Alexandre Rademaker, Loganathan Ramasamy, Livy Real, Laura Rituma, Rudolf Rosa, Shadi Saleh, Baiba Saulīte, Sebastian Schuster, Wolfgang Seeker, Mojgan Seraji, Lena Shakurova, Mo Shen, Natalia Silveira, Maria Simi, Radu Simionescu, Katalin Simkó, Mária Šimková, Kiril Simov, Aaron Smith, Carolyn Spadine, Alane Suhr, Umut Sulubacak, Zsolt Szántó, Takaaki Tanaka, Reut Tsarfaty, Francis Tyers, Sumire Uematsu, Larraitz Uria, Gertjan van Noord, Viktor Varga, Veronika Vincze, Lars Wallin, Jing Xian Wang, Jonathan North Washington, Mats Wirén, Zdeněk Žabokrtský, Amir Zeldes, Daniel Zeman, and Hanzhi Zhu. 2016. Universal Dependencies 1.4. LINDAT/CLARIN digital library at the Institute of Formal and Applied Linguistics, Charles University. http://hdl.handle.net/11234/1-1827.

Arfath Pasha, Mohamed Al-Badrashiny, Mona T Diab, Ahmed El Kholy, Ramy Eskander, Nizar Habash, Manoj Pooleery, Owen Rambow, and Ryan Roth. 2014. MADAMIRA: A Fast, Comprehensive Tool for Morphological Analysis and Disambiguation of Arabic. In *Proceedings of the Ninth International Conference on Language Resources and Evaluation (LREC'14)*. Reykjavik, Iceland, volume 14, pages 1094–1101. http://www.lrec-conf.org/proceedings/lrec2014/pdf/593_Paper.pdf.

Barbara Plank, Anders Søgaard, and Yoav Goldberg. 2016. Multilingual Part-of-Speech Tagging with Bidirectional Long Short-Term Memory Models and Auxiliary Loss. In *Proceedings of the 54th Annual Meeting of the Association for Computational Linguistics (Volume 2: Short Papers)*. Association for Computational Linguistics, Berlin, Germany, pages 412–418. http://anthology.aclweb.org/P16-2067.

Anas Shahrour, Salam Khalifa, and Nizar Habash. 2015. Improving Arabic Diacritization through Syntactic Analysis. In *Proceedings of the 2015 Conference on Empirical Methods in Natural Language Processing*. Association for Computational Linguistics, Lisbon, Portugal, pages 1309–1315. http://aclweb.org/anthology/D15-1152.

Qinlan Shen, Daniel Clothiaux, Emily Tagtow, Patrick Littell, and Chris Dyer. 2016. The Role of Context in Neural Morphological Disambiguation.

In *Proceedings of COLING 2016, the 26th International Conference on Computational Linguistics: Technical Papers*. The COLING 2016 Organizing Committee, Osaka, Japan, pages 181–191. http://aclweb.org/anthology/C16-1018.

Otakar Smrž, Viktor Bielicky, and Jan Hajic. 2008. Prague Arabic Dependency Treebank: A Word on the Million Words. In *Proceedings of the Workshop on Arabic and Local Languages (LREC 2008)*. pages 16–23.

Anders Søgaard and Yoav Goldberg. 2016. Deep multi-task learning with low level tasks supervised at lower layers. In *Proceedings of the 54th Annual Meeting of the Association for Computational Linguistics (Volume 2: Short Papers)*. Association for Computational Linguistics, Berlin, Germany, pages 231–235. http://anthology.aclweb.org/P16-2038.

Zhilin Yang, Ruslan Salakhutdinov, and William Cohen. 2016. Multi-Task Cross-Lingual Sequence Tagging from Scratch. *arXiv preprint arXiv:1603.06270* .

Yuan Zhang, Chengtao Li, Regina Barzilay, and Kareem Darwish. 2015. Randomized Greedy Inference for Joint Segmentation, POS Tagging and Dependency Parsing. In *Proceedings of the 2015 Conference of the North American Chapter of the Association for Computational Linguistics: Human Language Technologies*. Association for Computational Linguistics, Denver, Colorado, USA, pages 42–52. http://www.aclweb.org/anthology/N15-1005.

Learning from Relatives: Unified Dialectal Arabic Segmentation

**Younes Samih[1], Mohamed Eldesouki[3], Mohammed Attia[2], Kareem Darwish[3],
Ahmed Abdelali[3], Hamdy Mubarak[3], and Laura Kallmeyer[1]**

[1]Dept. of Computational Linguistics,University of Düsseldorf, Düsseldorf, Germany
[2]Google Inc., New York City, USA
[3]Qatar Computing Research Institute, HBKU, Doha, Qatar
[1]{samih,kallmeyer}@phil.hhu.de
[2]attia@google.com
[3]{mohamohamed,hmubarak,aabdelali,kdarwish}@hbku.edu.qa

Abstract

Arabic dialects do not just share a common koiné, but there are shared pan-dialectal linguistic phenomena that allow computational models for dialects to learn from each other. In this paper we build a unified segmentation model where the training data for different dialects are combined and a single model is trained. The model yields higher accuracies than dialect-specific models, eliminating the need for dialect identification before segmentation. We also measure the degree of relatedness between four major Arabic dialects by testing how a segmentation model trained on one dialect performs on the other dialects. We found that linguistic relatedness is contingent with geographical proximity. In our experiments we use SVM-based ranking and bi-LSTM-CRF sequence labeling.

1 Introduction

Segmenting Arabic words into their constituent parts is important for a variety of applications such as machine translation, parsing and information retrieval. Though much work has focused on segmenting Modern Standard Arabic (MSA), recent work began to examine dialectal segmentation in some Arabic dialects. Dialectal segmentation is becoming increasingly important due to the ubiquity of social media, where users typically write in their own dialects as opposed to MSA. Dialectal text poses interesting challenges such as lack of spelling standards, pervasiveness of word merging, letter substitution or deletion, and foreign word borrowing. Existing work on dialectal segmentation focused on building resources and tools for each dialect separately (Habash et al., 2013;

Pasha et al., 2014; Samih et al., 2017). The rational for the separation is that different dialects have different affixes, make different lexical choices, and are influenced by different foreign languages. However, performing reliable dialect identification to properly route text to the appropriate segmenter may be problematic, because conventional dialectal identification may lead to results that are lower than 90% (Darwish et al., 2014). Thus, building a segmenter that performs reliably across multiple dialects without the need for dialect identification is desirable.

In this paper we examine the effectiveness of using a segmenter built for one dialect in segmenting other dialects. Next, we explore combining training data for different dialects in building a joint segmentation model for all dialects. We show that the joint segmentation model matches or outperforms dialect-specific segmentation models. For this work, we use training data in four different dialects, namely Egyptian (EGY), Levantine (LEV), Gulf (GLF), and Maghrebi (MGR). We utilize two methods for segmentation. The first poses segmentation as a ranking problem, where we use an SVM ranker. The second poses the problem as a sequence labeling problem, where we use a bidirectional Long Short-Term Memory (bi-LSTM) Recurrent Neural Network (RNN) that is coupled with Conditional Random Fields (CRF) sequence labeler.

2 Background

Work on dialectal Arabic is fairly recent compared to MSA. A number of research projects were devoted to dialect identification (Biadsy et al., 2009; Zbib et al., 2012; Zaidan and Callison-Burch, 2014; Eldesouki et al., 2016). There are five major dialects including Egyptian, Gulf, Iraqi, Levantine and Maghrebi. Few resources for these dialects

432

Proceedings of the 21st Conference on Computational Natural Language Learning (CoNLL 2017), pages 432–441,
Vancouver, Canada, August 3 - August 4, 2017. ©2017 Association for Computational Linguistics

are available such as the CALLHOME Egyptian Arabic Transcripts (LDC97T19), which was made available for research as early as 1997. Newly developed resources include the corpus developed by Bouamor et al. (2014), which contains 2,000 parallel sentences in multiple dialects and MSA as well as English translation. These sentences were translated by native speakers into the target dialects from an original dialect, the Egyptian.

For segmentation, Mohamed et al. (2012) built a segmenter based on memory-based learning. The segmenter has been trained on a small corpus of Egyptian Arabic comprising 320 comments containing 20,022 words from `www.masrawy.com` that were segmented and annotated by two native speakers. They reported a 91.90% accuracy on the segmentation task. MADA-ARZ (Habash et al., 2013) is an Egyptian Arabic extension of the Morphological Analysis and Disambiguation of Arabic (MADA) tool. They trained and evaluated their system on both Penn Arabic Treebank (PATB) (parts 1-3) and the Egyptian Arabic Treebank (parts 1-5) (Maamouri et al., 2014) and they achieved 97.5% accuracy. MADAMIRA[1] (Pasha et al., 2014) is a new version of MADA that includes the functionality for analyzing dialectal Egyptian. Monroe et al. (2014) used a single dialect-independent model for segmenting Egyptian dialect in addition to MSA. They argue that their segmenter is better than other segmenters that use sophisticated linguistic analysis. They evaluated their model on three corpora, namely parts 1-3 of Penn Arabic Treebank (PATB), Broadcast News Arabic Treebank (BN), and parts 1-8 of the BOLT Phase 1 Egyptian Arabic Treebank (ARZ) reporting an F1 score of 92.1%.

3 Segmentation Datasets

We used datasets for four dialects, namely Egyptian (EGY), Levantine (LEV), Gulf (GLF), and Maghrebi (MGR) which are available at `http://alt.qcri.org/resources/da_resources/`. Each dataset consists of a sets of 350 manually segmented tweets. Briefly, we obtained a large Arabic collection composed of 175 million Arabic tweets by querying the Twitter API using the query "lang:ar" during March 2014. Then, we identified tweets whose authors identified their location in countries where the dialects of interest are spoken (e.g. Morocco,

---

[1]MADAMIRA release 20160516 2.1

Algeria, Tunisia, and Libya for MGR) using a large location gazetteer (Mubarak and Darwish, 2014) which maps each region/city to its country. Then we filtered the tweets using a list containing 10 strong dialectal words per dialect, such as the MGR word كيما "kymA" (like/as in) and the LEV word هيك "hyk" (like this). Given the filtered tweets, we randomly selected 2,000 unique tweets for each dialect, and we asked a native speaker of each dialect to manually select 350 tweets that are heavily dialectal, i.e. contain more dialectal than MSA words. Table 1 lists the number of tweets that we obtained for each dialect and the number of words they contain.

Dialect	No of Tweets	No of Tokens
Egyptian	350	6,721
Levantine	350	6,648
Gulf	350	6,844
Maghrebi	350	5,495

Table 1: Dataset size for the different dialects

We manually segmented each word in the corpus while preserving the original characters. This decision was made to allow processing real dialectal words in their original form. Table 2 shows segmented examples from the different dialects.

3.1 Segmentation Convention

In some research projects, segmentation of DA is done on a CODA'fied version of the text, where CODA is a standardized writing convention for DA (Habash et al., 2012). CODA guidelines provide directions on to how to normalize words, correct spelling and unify writing. Nonetheless, these guidelines are not available for all dialects. In the absence of such guidelines as well as the dynamic nature of the language, we choose to operate directly on the raw text. As in contrast to MSA, where guidelines for spelling are common and standardized, written DA seems to exhibit a lot of diversity, and hence, segmentation systems need to be robust enough to handle all the variants that might be encountered in such texts.

Our segmentation convention is closer to stemming rather than tokenization in that we separate all prefixes (with the exception of imperfective prefixes with verbs) and suffixes from the stems. The following is a summary to these instructions that were given to the native speakers to segment the data:

Word	Glossary	Segmentation	Dialect
بيقولك "byqwlk"	Is telling you	بـ+يقول+ك "b+yqwl+k"	EGY
ويجي "wyjy"	And he comes	و+يج+ي "w+yj+y"	GLF
برد "brd"	I'll return	بـ+رد "b+rd"	LEV
مغتنفاعهم "mgtnfAEhm"	It will not benefit them	مـ+غ+تنفاع+هم "m+g+tnfAE+hm"	MGR

Table 2: Dialect annotation example

- Separate all prefixes for verbs, nouns, and adjectives, e.g. the conjunction و "w" (and), preposition ل "l" (to), definite article ال "Al" (the), etc.

- Separate all suffixes for verbs, nouns, and adjectives, e.g. the feminine marker ة "p", number marker ون "wn", object or genitive pronouns ه "h" (him), etc.

- Emoticons, user names, and hash-tags are treated as single units.

- Merged words are separated, e.g. عبد+ال+عزيز "Ebd+Al+Ezyz" (Abd Al-Aziz).

- When there is an elongation of a short vowel "a, u ,i" with a preposition, the elongated vowel is segmented with the preposition, e.g. ليهم "lyhm" (for them) ⇒ ليـ+هم "ly+hm".

Complete list of guidelines is found at: `http://alt.qcri.org/resources/da_resources/seg-guidelines.pdf`.

4 Arabic Dialects

4.1 Similarities

There are some interesting observations which show similar behavior of different Arabic dialects (particularly those in our dataset) when they diverge from MSA. These observations show that Arabic dialects do not just share commonalities with MSA, but they also share commonalities among themselves. It seems that dialects share some built-in functionalities to generate words, some of which may have been inherited from classical Arabic, where some of these functionalities are lost or severely diminished in MSA. Some of these commonalities include:

- Dialects have eliminated case endings.

- Dialects introduce a progressive particle, e.g. بـ+يقول "b+yqwl" (EGY), عم+يقول "Em+yqwl"

(LEV), كـ+يقول "k+yqwl" (MGR), and د+يقول "d+yqwl" (Iraqi) for "he says". This does not exist in MSA.

- Some dialects use a post-negation particle, e.g. مـ+يحب+ش "m+yHb+$" (does not like) (EGY, LEV and MGR). This does not also exist in MSA as well as GLF.

- Dialects have future particles that are different from MSA, such as ح "H" (LEV), هـ "h" (EGY), and غ "g" (MGR). Similar to the MSA future particle س "s" that may have resulted from shortening the particle سوف "swf" and then using the shortened version as a prefix, dialectal future particles may have arisen using a similar process, where the Levantine future particle "H" is a shortened version of the word راح "rAH" (he will) (Persson, 2008; Jarad, 2014).

- Dialects routinely employ word merging, particularly when two identical letters appear consecutively. In MSA, this is mostly restricted to the case of the preposition ل "l" (to) when followed by the determiner ال "Al" (the), where the "A" in the determiner is silent. This is far more common in dialects as in يعمل لك "yEml lk" (he does for you) ⇒ يعملك "yEmlk".

- Dialects often change short vowels to long vowels or vice verse (vowel elongation and reduction). This phenomenon infrequently appears in poetry, particularly classical Arabic poetry, but is quite common in dialects such as converting له "lh" (to him) to ليه "lyh".

- Dialects have mostly eliminated dual forms except with nouns, e.g. عيني "Eyny" (my two eyes) and قرشين "qr$yn" (two piasters). Consequently dual agreement markers on adjectives, relative pronouns, demonstrative adjectives, and verbs have largely disappeared. Likewise, masculine nominative plural noun and verb suffix ون "wn" has been largely replaced with the accusative/genitive forms ين "yn" and وا "wA" respectively.

Phenomena that appear in multiple dialects, but may not necessarily appear in MSA, may provide an indication that segmented training data for one dialect may be useful in segmenting other dialects.

4.2 Differences

In this section, we show some differences between dialects that cover surface lexical and morphological features in light of our datasets. Deep lexical and morphological analysis can be applied after POS-tagging of these datasets. Differences can explain why some dialects are more difficult than others, which dialects are closer to each other, and the possible effect of cross-dialect training. The differences may also aid future work on dialect identification.

We start by comparing dialects with MSA to show how close a dialect to MSA is. We randomly selected 300 words from each dialect and we analyzed them using the Buckwalter MSA morphological analyzer (BAMA) (Buckwalter, 2004). Table 3 lists the percentage of words that were analyzed, analysis precision, and analysis recall, which is the percentage of actual MSA words that BAMA was able to analyze. Results show that BAMA was most successful, in terms of coverage and precision, in analyzing GLF, while it faired the worst on MGR, in terms of coverage, and the worst on LEV, in terms of precision. Some dialectal words are incorrectly recognized as MSA by BAMA, such as كده "kdh" (like this), where BAMA analyzed it as "kd+h" (his toil). It seems that GLF is the closest to MSA and MGR is the furthest away.

Dialect	Percent Analyzed	Analysis Precision	Analysis Recall
EGY	83	81	94
LEV	83	76	91
GLF	**86**	**88**	94
MGR	78	78	95

Table 3: Buckwalter analysis

Table 4 shows the overlap between unique words and all words for the different dialect pairs

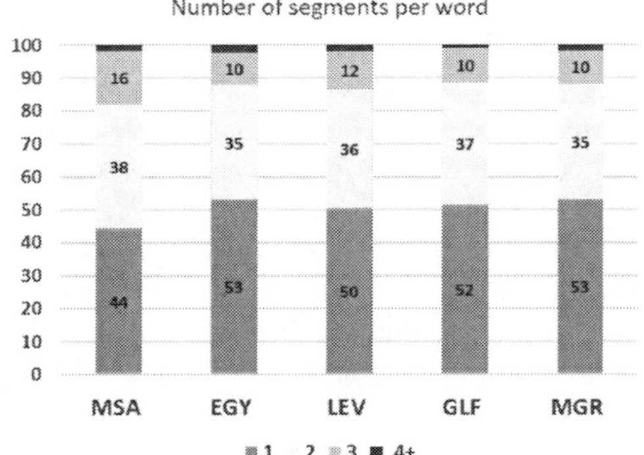

Figure 1: Distribution of segment count per word (percentages are overlaid on the graph)

in our datasets. As the table shows, EGY, LEV, and GLF are closer together and MGR is further away from all of them. Also, LEV is closer to both EGY and GLF than the last two to each other. We also looked at the common words between dialects to see if they had different segmentations. Aside from two words, namely ليه "lyh" (to him, why) and بيه "byh" (with it, gentleman), that both appear in EGY and LEV, all other common words have identical segmentations. This is welcome news for the lookup scheme that we employ in which we use segmentations that are seen in training directly during testing.

Dialect pairs	Unique Overlap	All Overlap
EGY-GLF	16.1%	41.6%
EGY-LEV	18.1%	43.3%
EGY-MGR	14.3%	36.7%
GLF-LEV	17.0%	41.4%
GLF-MGR	15.9%	37.8%
LEV-MGR	16.2%	38.5%

Table 4: Common words across dialects

Figure 1 shows the distribution of segment counts per word for words in our datasets. We obtained the MSA segment counts from the Arabic Penn Treebank (parts 1-3) (Maamouri et al., 2014). The figure shows that dialectal words tend to have a similar distribution of word segment counts and they generally have fewer segments than MSA. This may indicate that dialects may have simpler segmentations than MSA, and cases where words have 4 or more segments, such as

مـ+قلتـ+بها +لـ+و+ش "m+qlt+hA+l+w+$" (I did not say it to him), are infrequent.

Tables 5 and 6 respectively show the number of prefixes or suffixes, the top 5 prefixes and suffixes (listed in descending order), and the unique prefixes and suffixes for each dialect in comparison to MSA. As the tables show, MGR has the most number of prefixes, while GLF has the most number of suffixes. Further, there are certain prefixes and suffixes that are unique to dialects. While the prefix "Al" (the) leads the list of prefixes for all dialects, the prefix ب "b" in LEV and EGY, where it is either a progressive particle or a preposition, is used more frequently than in MSA, where it is used strictly as a preposition. Similarly, the suffix كن "kn" (your) is more frequent in LEV than any other dialect. The Negation suffix ش "$" (not) and feminine suffix marker كي "ky" (your) are used in EGY, LEV, and MGR, but not in GLF or MSA. The appearance of some affixes in some dialects and their absence in others may seem to complicate cross dialect training, and the varying frequencies of affixes across dialects may seem to complicate joint training.

Dialect	No.	Top 5	Unique
MSA	8	Al,w,l,b,f	>, s
EGY	11	Al,b,w,m,h	hA, fA
LEV	11	Al,b,w,l,E	Em
GLF	14	Al,w,b,l,mA	mw,mb,$
MGR	**19**	Al,w,l,b,mA	kA,t,tA,g

Table 5: Prefixes statistics

Dialect	No.	Top 5	Unique
MSA	23	p,At,A,h,hA	hmA
EGY	24	h,p,k,$,hA	Y,kwA,nY,kY
LEV	27	p,k,y,h,w	-
GLF	**30**	h,k,y,p,t	j
MGR	24	p,w,y,k,hA	Aw

Table 6: Suffixes statistics

5 Learning Algorithms

We present here two different systems for word segmentation. The first uses SVM-based ranking (SVM^{Rank})[2] to rank different possible seg-

mentations for a word using a variety of features. The second uses bi-LSTM-CRF, which performs character-based sequence-to-sequence mapping to predict word segmentation.

5.1 SVM^{Rank} Approach

We used the SVM-based ranking approach proposed by Abdelali et al. (2016), in which they used SVM based ranking to ascertain the best segmentation for Modern Standard Arabic (MSA), which they show to be fast and of high accuracy. The approach involves generating all possible segmentations of a word and then ranking them. The possible segmentations are generated based on possible prefixes and suffixes that are observed during training. For example, if hypothetically we only had the prefixes و "w" (and) and ل "l" (to) and the suffix ه "h" (his), the possible segmentations of وليده "wlydh" (his new born) would be {wlydh, w+lydh, w+l+ydh, w+l+yd+h, w+lyd+h, wlyd+h} with "wlyd+h" being the correct segmentation. SVM^{Rank} would attempt to rank the correct segmentation higher than all others. To train SVM^{Rank}, we use the following features:

- Conditional probability that a leading character sequence is a prefix.
- Conditional probability that a trailing character sequence is a suffix.
- probability of the prefix given the suffix.
- probability of the suffix given the prefix.
- unigram probability of the stem.
- unigram probability of the stem with first suffix.
- whether a valid stem template can be obtained from the stem, where we used Farasa (Abdelali et al., 2016) to guess the stem template.
- whether the stem that has no trailing suffixes and appears in a gazetteer of person and location names (Abdelali et al., 2016).
- whether the stem is a function word, such as على "ElY" (on) and من "mn" (from).
- whether the stem appears in the AraComLex[3] Arabic lexicon (Attia et al., 2011) or in the Buckwalter lexicon (Buckwalter, 2004). This is sensible considering the large overlap between MSA and DA.
- length difference from the average stem length.

The segmentations with their corresponding features are then passed to the SVM ranker (Joachims, 2006) for training. Our SVM^{Rank} uses a linear kernel and a trade-off parameter between training error and margin of 100. All segmentations are ranked out of context. Though some words may have multiple valid segmentations in different contexts, previous work on MSA has shown that it holds for 99% of the cases (Abdelali et al., 2016). This assumption allows us to improve segmentation results by looking up segmentations that were observed in the dialectal training sets (DA) or segmentations from the training sets with a back off to segmentation in a large segmented MSA corpus, namely parts 1, 2, and 3 of the Arabic Penn Treebank Maamouri et al. (2014) (DA+MSA).

5.2 Bi-LSTM-CRF Approach

In this subsection we describe the different components of our Arabic segmentation bi-LSTM-CRF based model, shown in Figure 2. It is a slight variant of the bi-LSTM-CRF architecture first proposed by Huang et al. (2015), Lample et al. (2016), and Ma and Hovy (2016)

5.2.1 Recurrent Neural Networks

A recurrent neural network (RNN) together with its variants, i.e. LSTM, bi-LSTM, GRU, belong to a family of powerful neural networks that are well suited for modeling sequential data. Over the last several years, they have achieved many ground-breaking results in many NLP tasks. Theoretically, RNNs can learn long distance dependencies, but in practice they fail due to vanishing/exploding gradients (Bengio et al., 1994).

LSTMs LSTMs (Hochreiter and Schmidhuber, 1997) are variants of the RNNs that can efficiently overcome difficulties with training and efficiently cope with long distance dependencies. Formally, the output of the LSTM hidden layer h_t given input x_t is computed via the following intermediate calculations: (Graves, 2013):

$$i_t = \sigma(W_{xi}x_t + W_{hi}h_{t-1} + W_{ci}c_{t-1} + b_i)$$
$$f_t = \sigma(W_{xf}x_t + W_{hf}h_{t-1} + W_{cf}c_{t-1} + b_f)$$
$$c_t = f_t c_{t-1} + i_t \tanh(W_{xc}x_t + W_{hc}h_{t-1} + b_c)$$
$$o_t = \sigma(W_{xo}x_t + W_{ho}h_{t-1} + W_{co}c_t + b_o)$$
$$h_t = o_t \tanh(c_t)$$

where σ is the logistic sigmoid function, and i, f,

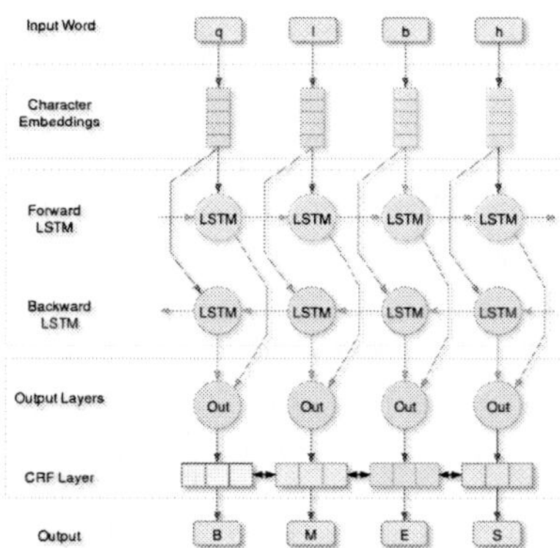

Figure 2: Architecture of our proposed neural network Arabic segmentation model applied to the word قلبه "qlbh" and output "qlb+h".

o and c are respectively the input gate, forget gate, output gate and cell activation vectors. More interpretation about this architecture can be found in (Graves and Schmidhuber, 2005) and(Lipton et al., 2015).

Bi-LSTMs Another extension to the single LSTM networks are the bi-LSTMs (Schuster and Paliwal, 1997). They are also capable of learning long-term dependencies and maintain contextual features from both past and future states. As shown in Figure 2, they are comprised of two separate hidden layers that feed forwards to the same output layer.

CRF In many sequence labeling tasks bi-LSTMs achieve very competitive results against traditional models, still when they are used for some specific sequence classification tasks, such as segmentation and named entity detection, where there is a strict dependence between the output labels, they fail to generalize perfectly. During the training phase of the bi-LSTM networks, the resulting probability distribution of each time step is independent from each other. To overcome this independence assumptions imposed by the bi-LSTM and to exploit this kind of labeling constraints in our Arabic segmentation system, we model label sequence logic jointly using Conditional Random Fields (CRF) (Lafferty et al., 2001)

5.2.2 DA segmentation Model

The concept we followed in bi-LSTM-CRF sequence labeling is that segmentation is a one-to-

437

one mapping at the character level where each character is annotated as either beginning a segment (B), continues a previous segment (M), ends a segment (E), or is a segment by itself (S). After the labeling is complete we merge the characters and labels together. For example, بيقولوا "byqwlwA" (they say) is labeled as "SBM-MEBE", which means that the word is segmented as b+yqwl+wA. The architecture of our segmentation model, shown in Figure 2, is straightforward. At the input layer a look-up table is initialized with randomly uniform sampled embeddings mapping each character in the input to a d-dimensional vector. At the hidden layer, the output from the character embeddings is used as the input to the bi-LSTM layer to obtain fixed-dimensional representations of characters. At the output layer, a CRF is applied on the top of bi-LSTM to jointly decode labels for the whole input characters. Training is performed using stochastic gradient (SGD) descent with momentum 0.9 and batch size 50, optimizing the cross entropy objective function.

Optimization To mitigate overfitting, given the small size of the training data, we employ dropout (Hinton et al., 2012), which prevents co-adaptation of hidden units by randomly setting to zero a proportion of the hidden units during training. We also employ early stopping (Caruana et al., 2000; Graves et al., 2013) by monitoring the models performance on a development set.

6 Experimental Setup and Results

Using the approaches described earlier, we perform several experiments, serving two main objectives. First we want to see how closely related the dialects are and whether we can use one dialect for the augmentation of training data in another dialect. The second objective is to find out whether we can build a one-fits-all model that does not need to know which specific dialect it is dealing with.

In the first set of experiments shown in Table 7, we build segmentation models for each dialect and tested them on all the other dialects. We compare these cross dialect training and testing to training and testing on the same dialect, where we use 5 fold cross validation with 70/10/20 train/dev/test splits. We also use the Farasa MSA segmenter as a baseline. We conduct the experiments at three levels: pure system output (without lookup), with DA lookup, and with DA+MSA lookup. We mean

by "lookup" a post-processing add-on step where we feed segmentation solutions in the test files directly from the training data when a match is found. This is based on the assumption that segmentation is a context-free problem and therefore the utilization of observed data can be maximized.

Using both algorithms (SVM and LSTM) the results show a general trend where EGY segmentation yields better results from the LEV model than from the GLF's. The GLF data benefits more from the LEV model than from the EGY one. For the LEV data both GLF and EGY models are equally good. MGR seems relatively distant in that it does not contribute to or benefit from other dialects independently. This shows a trend where dialects favor geographical proximity. In the case with no lookup, LSTM fairs better than SVM when training and testing is done on the same dialect. However, the opposite is true when training on one dialect and testing on another. This may indicate that the SVM-ranker has better cross-dialect generalization than the bi-LSTM-CRF sequence labeler. When lookup is used, SVM yields better results across the board except in three cases, namely when training and testing on Egyptian with DA+MSA lookup, when training with Egyptian and testing on MGR, and when training with GLF and testing on MGR with DA+MSA lookup. Lastly, the best SVM cross-dialect results with lookup consistently beat the Farasa MSA baseline often by several percentage points for every dialect. The same is true for LSTM when training with relatively related dialects (EGY, LEV, and GLF), but the performance decreases when training or testing using MGR.

In the second set of experiments, we wanted to see whether we can train a unified segmenter that would segment all the dialects in our datasets. For the results shown in Table 8, we also used 5-fold cross validation (with the same splits generated earlier) where we trained on the combined training splits from all dialects and tested on all the test splits with no lookup, DA lookup, and MSA+DA lookup. We refer to these models as "joint" models. Using SVM, the combined model drops by 0.3% to 1.3% compared to exclusively using matching dialectal training data. We also conducted another SVM experiment in which we use the joint model in conjunction with a dialect identification oracle to restrict possible affixes only to those that are possible for that dialect (last two row

	Test Set							
Farasa	85.7		82.6		82.9		82.6	
Training	EGY		LEV		GLF		MGR	
	SVM	LSTM	SVM	LSTM	SVM	LSTM	SVM	LSTM
with no lookup								
EGY	91.0	93.8	87.7	87.1	86.5	85.8	81.3	82.5
LEV	85.2	85.5	87.8	91.0	85.5	85.7	83.42	80.0
GLF	85.7	85.0	86.4	86.9	87.7	89.4	82.6	81.6
MGR	85.0	78.6	85.7	78.8	84.5	78.4	84.7	87.1
with DA lookup								
EGY	94.5	94.2	89.2	87.6	87.5	86.5	81.5	82.8
LEV	89.7	85.9	92.9	91.8	89.6	86.3	83.5	80.4
GLF	89.7	85.5	89.2	87.5	92.8	90.8	83.0	82.4
MGR	88.6	78.9	86.9	78.8	87.3	79.0	90.5	88.5
with DA+MSA lookup								
EGY	94.6	**95.0**	90.5	89.2	88.8	88.3	83.5	89.2
LEV	90.1	87.5	**93.3**	93.0	89.7	87.8	84.3	82.4
GLF	90.3	87.3	89.6	88.6	**93.1**	91.9	84.1	84.8
MGR	88.6	81.2	88.1	80.3	88.1	80.7	**91.2**	90.1

Table 7: Cross dialect results.

	Test Set							
Lookup	EGY		LEV		GLF		MGR	
	SVM	LSTM	SVM	LSTM	SVM	LSTM	SVM	LSTM
No lookup	91.4	94.1	89.8	92.4	88.8	91.7	83.82	89.1
DA	94.1	94.8	92.8	93.3	91.8	92.6	89.6	90.7
DA+MSA	94.3	**95.3**	93.0	**93.9**	92.2	**93.1**	90.0	**91.4**
Joint with restricted affixes								
DA	94.5	-	92.8	-	91.9	-	89.7	-
DA+MSA	94.8	-	93.0	-	92.4	-	90.3	-

Table 8: Joint model results.

in Table 8). The results show improvements for all dialects, but aside for EGY, the improvements do not lead to better results than those for single dialect models. Conversely, the bi-LSTM-CRF joint model with DA+MSA lookup beats every other experimental setup that we tested, leading to the best segmentation results for all dialects, without doing dialect identification. This may indicate that bi-LSTM-CRF benefited from cross-dialect data in improving segmentation for individual dialects.

7 Conclusion

This paper presents (to the best of our knowledge) the first comparative study between closely related languages with regards to their segmentation. Arabic dialects diverged from a single origin, yet they maintained pan-dialectal common features which allow them to cross-fertilize.

Our results show that a single joint segmentation model, based on bi-LSTM-CRF, can be developed for a group of dialects and this model yields results that are comparable to, or even superior to, the performance of single dialect-specific models. Our results also show that there is a degree of closeness between dialects that is contingent with the geographical proximity. For example, we statistically show that Gulf is closer to Levantine than to Egyptian, and similarly Levantine is closer to Egyptian than to Gulf. Cross dialect segmentation experiments also show that Maghrebi is equally distant from the other three regional dialects. This sheds some light on the degree of mutual intelligibility between the speakers of Arabic dialects, assuming that the level of success in inter-dialectal segmentation can be an indicator of how well speakers of the respective dialects can understand each others.

References

Ahmed Abdelali, Kareem Darwish, Nadir Durrani, and Hamdy Mubarak. 2016. Farasa: A fast and furious segmenter for arabic. In *Proceedings of the 2016 Conference of the North American Chapter of the Association for Computational Linguistics: Demonstrations*. Association for Computational Linguistics, San Diego, California, pages 11–16.

Mohammed Attia, Pavel Pecina, Antonio Toral, Lamia Tounsi, and Josef van Genabith. 2011. An open-source finite state morphological transducer for modern standard arabic. In *Proceedings of the 9th International Workshop on Finite State Methods and Natural Language Processing*. Association for Computational Linguistics, pages 125–133.

Yoshua Bengio, Patrice Simard, and Paolo Frasconi. 1994. Learning long-term dependencies with gradient descent is difficult. *IEEE transactions on neural networks* 5(2):157–166.

Fadi Biadsy, Julia Hirschberg, and Nizar Habash. 2009. Spoken arabic dialect identification using phonotactic modeling. In *Proceedings of the EACL 2009 Workshop on Computational Approaches to Semitic Languages*. Association for Computational Linguistics, Stroudsburg, PA, USA, Semitic '09, pages 53–61.

Houda Bouamor, Nizar Habash, and Kemal Oflazer. 2014. A multidialectal parallel corpus of arabic. In Nicoletta Calzolari (Conference Chair), Khalid Choukri, Thierry Declerck, Hrafn Loftsson, Bente Maegaard, Joseph Mariani, Asuncion Moreno, Jan Odijk, and Stelios Piperidis, editors, *Proceedings of the Ninth International Conference on Language Resources and Evaluation (LREC'14)*. European Language Resources Association (ELRA), Reykjavik, Iceland.

Tim Buckwalter. 2004. Buckwalter arabic morphological analyzer version 2.0 .

Rich Caruana, Steve Lawrence, and Lee Giles. 2000. Overfitting in neural nets: Backpropagation, conjugate gradient, and early stopping. In *NIPS*. pages 402–408.

Kareem Darwish, Hassan Sajjad, and Hamdy Mubarak. 2014. Verifiably effective arabic dialect identification. In *EMNLP*. pages 1465–1468.

Mohamed Eldesouki, Fahim Dalvi, Hassan Sajjad, and Kareem Darwish. 2016. Qcri@ dsl 2016: Spoken arabic dialect identification using textual features. *VarDial 3* page 221.

Alex Graves. 2013. Generating sequences with recurrent neural networks. *arXiv preprint arXiv:1308.0850* .

Alex Graves, Abdel-rahman Mohamed, and Geoffrey Hinton. 2013. Speech recognition with deep recurrent neural networks. In *Acoustics, speech and signal processing (icassp), 2013 ieee international conference on*. IEEE, pages 6645–6649.

Alex Graves and Jürgen Schmidhuber. 2005. Framewise phoneme classification with bidirectional lstm and other neural network architectures. *Neural Networks* 18(5):602–610.

Nizar Habash, Mona T Diab, and Owen Rambow. 2012. Conventional orthography for dialectal arabic. In *LREC*. pages 711–718.

Nizar Habash, Ryan Roth, Owen Rambow, Ramy Eskander, and Nadi Tomeh. 2013. Morphological analysis and disambiguation for dialectal arabic. In *Hlt-Naacl*. pages 426–432.

Geoffrey E Hinton, Nitish Srivastava, Alex Krizhevsky, Ilya Sutskever, and Ruslan R Salakhutdinov. 2012. Improving neural networks by preventing co-adaptation of feature detectors. *arXiv preprint arXiv:1207.0580* .

Sepp Hochreiter and Jürgen Schmidhuber. 1997. Long short-term memory. *Neural computation* 9(8):1735–1780.

Zhiheng Huang, Wei Xu, and Kai Yu. 2015. Bidirectional LSTM-CRF models for sequence tagging. *CoRR* abs/1508.01991.

Najib Ismail Jarad. 2014. The grammaticalization of the motion verb "ra" as a prospective aspect marker in syrian arabic. *Al-'Arabiyya* 47:101–118.

Thorsten Joachims. 2006. Training linear svms in linear time. In *Proceedings of the 12th ACM SIGKDD international conference on Knowledge discovery and data mining*. ACM, pages 217–226.

John D. Lafferty, Andrew McCallum, and Fernando C. N. Pereira. 2001. Conditional random fields: Probabilistic models for segmenting and labeling sequence data. In *Proc. ICML*.

Guillaume Lample, Miguel Ballesteros, Sandeep Subramanian, Kazuya Kawakami, and Chris Dyer. 2016. Neural architectures for named entity recognition. *arXiv preprint arXiv:1603.01360* .

Zachary C Lipton, David C Kale, Charles Elkan, and Randall Wetzell. 2015. A critical review of recurrent neural networks for sequence learning. *CoRR* abs/1506.00019.

Xuezhe Ma and Eduard Hovy. 2016. End-to-end sequence labeling via bi-directional lstm-cnns-crf. In *Proceedings of the 54th Annual Meeting of the Association for Computational Linguistics (Volume*

1: Long Papers). Association for Computational Linguistics, Berlin, Germany, pages 1064–1074. http://www.aclweb.org/anthology/P16-1101.

Mohamed Maamouri, Ann Bies, Seth Kulick, Michael Ciul, Nizar Habash, and Ramy Eskander. 2014. Developing an egyptian arabic treebank: Impact of dialectal morphology on annotation and tool development. In *LREC*. pages 2348–2354.

Emad Mohamed, Behrang Mohit, and Kemal Oflazer. 2012. Annotating and learning morphological segmentation of egyptian colloquial arabic. In *LREC*. pages 873–877.

Will Monroe, Spence Green, and Christopher D Manning. 2014. Word segmentation of informal arabic with domain adaptation. In *ACL (2)*. pages 206–211.

Hamdy Mubarak and Kareem Darwish. 2014. Using twitter to collect a multi-dialectal corpus of arabic. In *Proceedings of the EMNLP 2014 Workshop on Arabic Natural Language Processing (ANLP)*. pages 1–7.

Arfath Pasha, Mohamed Al-Badrashiny, Mona Diab, Ahmed El Kholy, Ramy Eskander, Nizar Habash, Manoj Pooleery, Owen Rambow, and Ryan M Roth. 2014. Madamira: A fast, comprehensive tool for morphological analysis and disambiguation of Arabic. *Proc. LREC* .

Maria Persson. 2008. The role of the b-prefix in gulf arabic dialects as a marker of future, intent and/or irrealis 8:26–52.

Younes Samih, Mohammed Attia, Mohamed Eldesouki, Hamdy Mubarak, Ahmed Abdelali, Laura Kallmeyer, and Kareem Darwish. 2017. A neural architecture for dialectal arabic segmentation. *WANLP 2017 (co-located with EACL 2017)* page 46.

Mike Schuster and Kuldip K Paliwal. 1997. Bidirectional recurrent neural networks. *IEEE Transactions on Signal Processing* 45(11):2673–2681.

Omar F Zaidan and Chris Callison-Burch. 2014. Arabic dialect identification. *Computational Linguistics* 40(1):171–202.

Rabih Zbib, Erika Malchiodi, Jacob Devlin, David Stallard, Spyros Matsoukas, Richard Schwartz, John Makhoul, Omar F. Zaidan, and Chris Callison-Burch. 2012. Machine translation of arabic dialects. In *Proceedings of the 2012 Conference of the North American Chapter of the Association for Computational Linguistics: Human Language Technologies*. Association for Computational Linguistics, Stroudsburg, PA, USA, NAACL HLT '12, pages 49–59.

Natural Language Generation for Spoken Dialogue System using RNN Encoder-Decoder Networks

Van-Khanh Tran[1,2] and Le-Minh Nguyen[1]

[1]Japan Advanced Institute of Science and Technology, JAIST
1-1 Asahidai, Nomi, Ishikawa, 923-1292, Japan
{tvkhanh, nguyenml}@jaist.ac.jp
[2]University of Information and Communication Technology, ICTU
Thai Nguyen University, Vietnam
tvkhanh@ictu.edu.vn

Abstract

Natural language generation (NLG) is a critical component in a spoken dialogue system. This paper presents a Recurrent Neural Network based Encoder-Decoder architecture, in which an LSTM-based decoder is introduced to select, aggregate semantic elements produced by an attention mechanism over the input elements, and to produce the required utterances. The proposed generator can be jointly trained both sentence planning and surface realization to produce natural language sentences. The proposed model was extensively evaluated on four different NLG datasets. The experimental results showed that the proposed generators not only consistently outperform the previous methods across all the NLG domains but also show an ability to generalize from a new, unseen domain and learn from multi-domain datasets.

1 Introduction

Natural Language Generation (NLG) plays a critical role in Spoken Dialogue Systems (SDS) with task is to convert a meaning representation produced by the Dialogue Manager into natural language utterances. Conventional approaches still rely on comprehensive hand-tuning templates and rules requiring expert knowledge of linguistic representation, including rule-based (Mirkovic et al., 2011), corpus-based n-gram models (Oh and Rudnicky, 2000), and a trainable generator (Stent et al., 2004).

Recently, Recurrent Neural Networks (RNNs) based approaches have shown promising performance in tackling the NLG problems. The RNN-based models have been applied for NLG as a joint training model (Wen et al., 2015a,b) and an end-to-end training model (Wen et al., 2016c). A recurring problem in such systems is requiring annotated datasets for particular dialogue acts[1] (DAs). To ensure that the generated utterance representing the intended meaning of the given DA, the previous RNN-based models were further conditioned on a 1-hot vector representation of the DA. Wen et al. (2015a) introduced a heuristic gate to ensure that all the slot-value pair was accurately captured during generation. Wen et al. (2015b) subsequently proposed a Semantically Conditioned Long Short-term Memory generator (SC-LSTM) which jointly learned the DA gating signal and language model.

More recently, Encoder-Decoder networks (Vinyals and Le, 2015; Li et al., 2015), especially the attentional based models (Wen et al., 2016b; Mei et al., 2015) have been explored to solve the NLG tasks. The Attentional RNN Encoder-Decoder (Bahdanau et al., 2014) (ARED) based approaches have also shown improved performance on a variety of tasks, e.g., image captioning (Xu et al., 2015; Yang et al., 2016), text summarization (Rush et al., 2015; Nallapati et al., 2016).

While the RNN-based generators with DA gating-vector can prevent the undesirable semantic repetitions, the ARED-based generators show signs of better adapting to a new domain. However, none of the models show significant advantage from out-of-domain data. To better analyze model generalization to an unseen, new domain as well as model leveraging the out-of-domain sources, we propose a new architecture which is an extension of the ARED model. In order to better select, aggregate and control the semantic information, a Refinement Adjustment LSTM-based component (*RALSTM*) is introduced to the

---

[1]A combination of an action type and a set of slot-value pairs. e.g. *inform(name='Bar crudo'; food='raw food')*

442

Proceedings of the 21st Conference on Computational Natural Language Learning (CoNLL 2017), pages 442–451,
Vancouver, Canada, August 3 - August 4, 2017. ©2017 Association for Computational Linguistics

decoder side. The proposed model can learn from unaligned data by jointly training the sentence planning and surface realization to produce natural language sentences. We conducted experiments on four different NLG domains and found that the proposed methods significantly outperformed the state-of-the-art methods regarding BLEU (Papineni et al., 2002) and slot error rate ERR scores (Wen et al., 2015b). The results also showed that our generators could scale to new domains by leveraging the out-of-domain data. To sum up, we make three key contributions in this paper:

- We present an LSTM-based component called *RALSTM* cell applied on the decoder side of an ARED model, resulting in an end-to-end generator that empirically shows significant improved performances in comparison with the previous approaches.

- We extensively conduct the experiments to evaluate the models training from scratch on each in-domain dataset.

- We empirically assess the models' ability to: learn from multi-domain datasets by pooling all available training datasets; and adapt to a new, unseen domain by limited feeding amount of in-domain data.

We review related works in Section 2. Following a detail of proposed model in Section 3, Section 4 describes datasets, experimental setups, and evaluation metrics. The resulting analysis is presented in Section 5. We conclude with a brief summary and future work in Section 6.

2 Related Work

Recently, RNNs-based models have shown promising performance in tackling the NLG problems. Zhang and Lapata (2014) proposed a generator using RNNs to create Chinese poetry. Xu et al. (2015); Karpathy and Fei-Fei (2015); Vinyals et al. (2015) also used RNNs in a multi-modal setting to solve image captioning tasks. The RNN-based Sequence to Sequence models have applied to solve variety of tasks: conversational modeling (Vinyals and Le, 2015; Li et al., 2015, 2016), machine translation (Luong et al., 2015; Li and Jurafsky, 2016)

For task-oriented dialogue systems, Wen et al. (2015a) combined a forward RNN generator, a CNN reranker, and a backward RNN reranker to generate utterances. Wen et al. (2015b) proposed SC-LSTM generator which introduced a control sigmoid gate to the LSTM cell to jointly learn the gating mechanism and language model. A recurring problem in such systems is the lack of sufficient domain-specific annotated data. Wen et al. (2016a) proposed an out-of-domain model which was trained on counterfeited data by using semantically similar slots from the target domain instead of the slots belonging to the out-of-domain dataset. The results showed that the model can achieve a satisfactory performance with a small amount of in-domain data by fine tuning the target domain on the out-of-domain trained model.

More recently, RNN encoder-decoder based models with attention mechanism (Bahdanau et al., 2014) have shown improved performances in various tasks. Yang et al. (2016) proposed a review network to the image captioning, which reviews all the information encoded by the encoder and produces a compact thought vector. Mei et al. (2015) proposed RNN encoder-decoder-based model by using two attention layers to jointly train content selection and surface realization. More close to our work, Wen et al. (2016b) proposed an attentive encoder-decoder based generator which computed the attention mechanism over the slot-value pairs. The model showed a domain scalability when a very limited amount of data is available.

Moving from a limited domain dialogue system to an open domain dialogue system raises some issues. Therefore, it is important to build an open domain dialogue system that can make as much use of existing abilities of functioning from other domains. There have been several works to tackle this problem, such as (Mrkšić et al., 2015) using RNN-based networks for multi-domain dialogue state tracking, (Wen et al., 2016a) using a procedure to train multi-domain via multiple adaptation steps, or (Gašić et al., 2015; Williams, 2013) adapting of SDS components to new domains.

3 Recurrent Neural Language Generator

The recurrent language generator proposed in this paper is based on a neural language generator (Wen et al., 2016b), which consists of three main components: (i) an Encoder that incorporates the target meaning representation (MR) as the model inputs, (ii) an Aligner that aligns and controls the semantic elements, and (iii) an RNN Decoder that

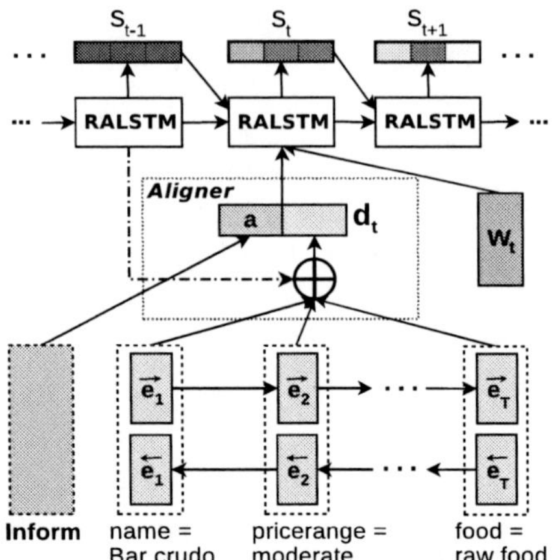

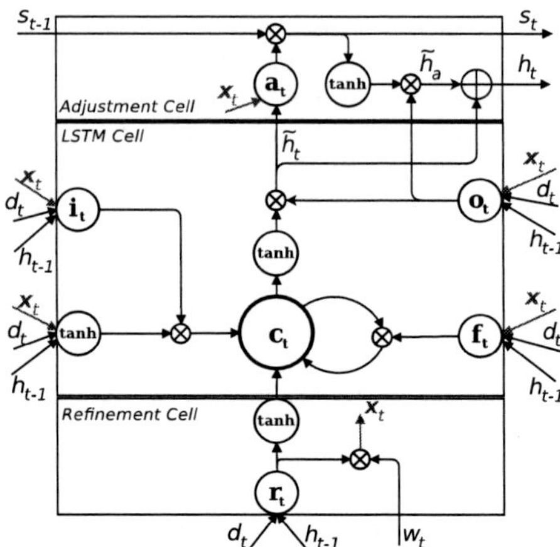

Figure 1: Unrolled presentation of the RNNs-based neural language generator. The Encoder part is a BiLSTM, the Aligner is an attention mechanism over the encoded inputs, and the Decoder is the proposed RALSTM model conditioned on a 1-hot representation vector **s**. The fading color of the vector **s** indicates retaining information for future computational time steps.

Figure 2: The RALSTM cell proposed in this paper, which consists of three components: an Refinement Cell, a traditional LSTM Cell, and an Adjustment Cell. At time step t, while the Refinement cell computes new input tokens $\mathbf{x}_t$ based on the original input tokens and the attentional DA representation $\mathbf{d}_t$, the Adjustment Cell calculates how much information of the slot-value pairs can be generated by the LSTM Cell.

generates output sentences. The generator architecture is shown in Figure 1. The Encoder first encodes the MR into input semantic elements which are then aggregated and selected by utilizing an attention-based mechanism by the Aligner. The input to the RNN Decoder at each time step is a 1-hot encoding of a token[2] $\mathbf{w}_t$ and an attentive DA representation $\mathbf{d}_t$. At each time step t, RNN Decoder also computes how much the feature value vector $\mathbf{s}_{t-1}$ retained for the next computational steps, and adds this information to the RNN output which represents the probability distribution of the next token $\mathbf{w}_{t+1}$. At generation time, we can sample from this conditional distribution to obtain the next token in a generated sentence, and feed it as the next input to the RNN Decoder. This process finishes when an end sign is generated (Karpathy and Fei-Fei, 2015), or some constraints are reached (Zhang and Lapata, 2014). The model can produce a sequence of tokens which can finally be lexicalized[3] to form the required utterance.

3.1 Encoder

The slots and values are separated parameters used in the encoder side. This embeds the source information into a vector representation $\mathbf{z}_i$ which is a concatenation of embedding vector representation of each slot-value pair, and is computed by:

$$\mathbf{z}_i = \mathbf{u}_i \oplus \mathbf{v}_i \qquad (1)$$

where $\mathbf{u}_i$, $\mathbf{v}_i$ are the i-th slot and value embedding vectors, respectively, and $\oplus$ is vector concatenation. The i index runs over the L given slot-value pairs. In this work, we use a 1-layer, Bidirectional LSTM (Bi-LSTM) to encode the sequence of slot-value pairs[4] embedding. The Bi-LSTM consists of forward and backward LSTMs which read the sequence of slot-value pairs from left-to-right and right-to-left to produce forward and backward sequence of hidden states $(\overrightarrow{\mathbf{e}_1}, .., \overrightarrow{\mathbf{e}_L})$, and $(\overleftarrow{\mathbf{e}_1}, .., \overleftarrow{\mathbf{e}_L})$, respectively. We then obtain the sequence of encoded hidden states $\mathbf{E} = (\mathbf{e}_1, \mathbf{e}_2, .., \mathbf{e}_L)$ where $\mathbf{e}_i$

---

[2]Input texts are delexicalized where slot values are replaced by its corresponding slot tokens.

[3]The process in which slot token is replaced by its value.

[4]We treated the set of slot-value pairs as a sequence and use the order specified by slot's name (e.g., slot *address* comes first, *food* follows *address*). We have tried treating slot-value pairs as a set with natural order as in the given DAs. However, this yielded even worse results.

is a sum of the forward hidden state $\overrightarrow{\mathbf{e}_i}$ and the backward one $\overleftarrow{\mathbf{e}_i}$ as follows:

$$\mathbf{e}_i = \overrightarrow{\mathbf{e}_i} + \overleftarrow{\mathbf{e}_i} \qquad (2)$$

3.2 Aligner

The Aligner utilizes attention mechanism to calculate the DA representation as follows:

$$\beta_{t,i} = \frac{\exp e_{t,i}}{\sum_j \exp e_{t,j}} \qquad (3)$$

where

$$e_{t,i} = a(\mathbf{e}_i, \mathbf{h}_{t-1}) \qquad (4)$$

and $\beta_{t,i}$ is the weight of i-th slot-value pair calculated by the attention mechanism. The alignment model a is computed by:

$$a(\mathbf{e}_i, \mathbf{h}_{t-1}) = \mathbf{v}_a^\top \tanh(\mathbf{W}_a \mathbf{e}_i + \mathbf{U}_a \mathbf{h}_{t-1}) \qquad (5)$$

where $\mathbf{v}_a, \mathbf{W}_a, \mathbf{U}_a$ are the weight matrices to learn. Finally, the Aligner calculates dialogue act embedding $\mathbf{d}_t$ as follows:

$$\mathbf{d}_t = \mathbf{a} \oplus \sum_i \beta_{t,i} \mathbf{e}_i \qquad (6)$$

where $\mathbf{a}$ is vector embedding of the action type.

3.3 RALSTM Decoder

The proposed semantic RALSTM cell applied for Decoder side consists of three components: a Refinement cell, a traditional LSTM cell, and an Adjustment cell:

Firstly, instead of feeding the original input token $\mathbf{w}_t$ into the RNN cell, the input is recomputed by using a semantic gate as follows:

$$\begin{aligned} \mathbf{r}_t &= \sigma(\mathbf{W}_{rd}\mathbf{d}_t + \mathbf{W}_{rh}\mathbf{h}_{t-1}) \\ \mathbf{x}_t &= \mathbf{r}_t \odot \mathbf{w}_t \end{aligned} \qquad (7)$$

where $\mathbf{W}_{rd}$ and $\mathbf{W}_{rh}$ are weight matrices. Element-wise multiplication $\odot$ plays a part in word-level matching which not only learns the vector similarity, but also preserves information about the two vectors. $\mathbf{W}_{rh}$ acts like a key phrase detector that learns to capture the pattern of generation tokens or the relationship between multiple tokens. In other words, the new input $\mathbf{x}_t$ consists of information of the original input token $\mathbf{w}_t$, the DA representation $\mathbf{d}_t$, and the hidden context $\mathbf{h}_{t-1}$. $\mathbf{r}_t$ is called a *Refinement* gate because the input tokens are refined by a combination gating information of the attentive DA representation $\mathbf{d}_t$ and the

previous hidden state $\mathbf{h}_{t-1}$. By this way, we can represent the whole sentence based on the refined inputs.

Secondly, the traditional LSTM network proposed by Hochreiter and Schmidhuber (2014) in which the input gate $\mathbf{i}_i$, forget gate $\mathbf{f}_t$ and output gates $\mathbf{o}_t$ are introduced to control information flow and computed as follows:

$$\begin{pmatrix} \mathbf{i}_t \\ \mathbf{f}_t \\ \mathbf{o}_t \\ \hat{\mathbf{c}}_t \end{pmatrix} = \begin{pmatrix} \sigma \\ \sigma \\ \sigma \\ \tanh \end{pmatrix} \mathbf{W}_{4n,4n} \begin{pmatrix} \mathbf{x}_t \\ \mathbf{d}_t \\ \mathbf{h}_{t-1} \end{pmatrix} \qquad (8)$$

where n is hidden layer size, $\mathbf{W}_{4n,4n}$ is model parameters. The cell memory value $\mathbf{c}_t$ is modified to depend on the DA representation as:

$$\begin{aligned} \mathbf{c}_t &= \mathbf{f}_t \odot \mathbf{c}_{t-1} + \mathbf{i}_t \odot \hat{\mathbf{c}}_t + \tanh(\mathbf{W}_{cr}\mathbf{r}_t) \\ \tilde{\mathbf{h}}_t &= \mathbf{o}_t \odot \tanh(\mathbf{c}_t) \end{aligned} \qquad (9)$$

where $\tilde{\mathbf{h}}_t$ is the output.

Thirdly, inspired by work of Wen et al. (2015b) in which the generator was further conditioned on a 1-hot representation vector $\mathbf{s}$ of given dialogue act, and work of Lu et al. (2016) that proposed a visual sentinel gate to make a decision on whether the model should attend to the image or to the sentinel gate, an additional gating cell is introduced on top of the traditional LSTM to gate another controlling vector $\mathbf{s}$. Figure 6 shows how RALSTM controls the DA vector $\mathbf{s}$. First, starting from the 1-hot vector of the DA $\mathbf{s}_0$, at each time step t the proposed cell computes how much the LSTM output $\tilde{\mathbf{h}}_t$ affects the DA vector, which is computed as follows:

$$\begin{aligned} \mathbf{a}_t &= \sigma(\mathbf{W}_{ax}\mathbf{x}_t + \mathbf{W}_{ah}\tilde{\mathbf{h}}_t) \\ \mathbf{s}_t &= \mathbf{s}_{t-1} \odot \mathbf{a}_t \end{aligned} \qquad (10)$$

where $\mathbf{W}_{ax}$, $\mathbf{W}_{ah}$ are weight matrices to be learned. $\mathbf{a}_t$ is called an *Adjustment* gate since its task is to control what information of the given DA have been generated and what information should be retained for future time steps. Second, we consider how much the information preserved in the DA $\mathbf{s}_t$ can be contributed to the output, in which an additional output is computed by applying the output gate $\mathbf{o}_t$ on the remaining information in $\mathbf{s}_t$ as follows:

$$\begin{aligned} \mathbf{c}_a &= \mathbf{W}_{os}\mathbf{s}_t \\ \tilde{\mathbf{h}}_a &= \mathbf{o}_t \odot \tanh(\mathbf{c}_a) \end{aligned} \qquad (11)$$

where $\mathbf{W}_{os}$ is a weight matrix to project the DA presentation into the output space, $\tilde{\mathbf{h}}_a$ is the Adjustment cell output. Final RALSTM output is a combination of both outputs of the traditional LSTM cell and the Adjustment cell, and computed as follows:

$$\mathbf{h}_t = \tilde{\mathbf{h}}_t + \tilde{\mathbf{h}}_a \tag{12}$$

Finally, the output distribution is computed by applying a softmax function g, and the distribution can be sampled to obtain the next token,

$$P(w_{t+1} \mid w_t, ...w_0, \mathbf{DA}) = g(\mathbf{W}_{ho}\mathbf{h}_t)$$
$$w_{t+1} \sim P(w_{t+1} \mid w_t, w_{t-1}, ...w_0, \mathbf{DA}) \tag{13}$$

where $\mathbf{DA} = (\mathbf{s}, \mathbf{z})$.

3.4 Training

The objective function was the negative log-likelihood and computed by:

$$\mathbf{F}(\theta) = -\sum_{t=1}^{T} \mathbf{y}_t^\top \log \mathbf{p}_t \tag{14}$$

where: $\mathbf{y}_t$ is the ground truth token distribution, $\mathbf{p}_t$ is the predicted token distribution, T is length of the input sentence. The proposed generators were trained by treating each sentence as a mini-batch with l_2 regularization added to the objective function for every 5 training examples. The models were initialized with a pretrained Glove word embedding vectors (Pennington et al., 2014) and optimized by using stochastic gradient descent and back propagation through time (Werbos, 1990). Early stopping mechanism was implemented to prevent over-fitting by using a validation set as suggested in (Mikolov, 2010).

3.5 Decoding

The decoding consists of two phases: (i) over-generation, and (ii) reranking. In the over-generation, the generator conditioned on both representations of the given DA use a beam search to generate a set of candidate responses. In the reranking phase, cost of the generator is computed to form the reranking score $\mathbf{R}$ as follows:

$$\mathbf{R} = \mathbf{F}(\theta) + \lambda \mathbf{ERR} \tag{15}$$

where λ is a trade off constant and is set to a large value in order to severely penalize nonsensical outputs. The slot error rate $\mathbf{ERR}$, which is the number of slots generated that is either missing or redundant, and is computed by:

$$\mathbf{ERR} = \frac{\mathbf{p} + \mathbf{q}}{\mathbf{N}} \tag{16}$$

where $\mathbf{N}$ is the total number of slots in DA, and $\mathbf{p}$, $\mathbf{q}$ is the number of missing and redundant slots, respectively.

4 Experiments

We extensively conducted a set of experiments to assess the effectiveness of the proposed models by using several metrics, datasets, and model architectures, in order to compare to prior methods.

4.1 Datasets

We assessed the proposed models on four different NLG domains: finding a restaurant, finding a hotel, buying a laptop, and buying a television. The Restaurant and Hotel were collected in (Wen et al., 2015b), while the Laptop and TV datasets have been released by (Wen et al., 2016a) with a much larger input space but only one training example for each DA so that the system must learn partial realization of concepts and be able to recombine and apply them to unseen DAs. This makes the NLG tasks for the Laptop and TV domains become much harder. The dataset statistics are shown in Table 1.

Table 1: Dataset statistics.

	Restaurant	Hotel	Laptop	TV
# train	3,114	3,223	7,944	4,221
# validation	1,039	1,075	2,649	1,407
# test	1,039	1,075	2,649	1,407
# distinct DAs	248	164	13,242	7,035
# DA types	8	8	14	14
# slots	12	12	19	15

4.2 Experimental Setups

The generators were implemented using the TensorFlow library (Abadi et al., 2016) and trained with training, validation and testing ratio as 3:1:1. The hidden layer size, beam size were set to be 80 and 10, respectively, and the generators were trained with a 70% of dropout rate. We performed 5 runs with different random initialization of the network and the training is terminated by using early stopping. We then chose a model that yields the highest BLEU score on the validation set as shown in Table 2. Since the trained models can

Table 2: Performance comparison on four datasets in terms of the BLEU and the error rate ERR(%) scores. The results were produced by training each network on 5 random initialization and selected model with the highest validation BLEU score. $\sharp$ denotes the Attention-based Encoder-Decoder model. The best and second best models highlighted in **bold** and *italic* face, respectively.

Model	Restaurant		Hotel		Laptop		TV	
	BLEU	ERR	BLEU	ERR	BLEU	ERR	BLEU	ERR
HLSTM	0.7466	0.74%	0.8504	2.67%	0.5134	1.10%	0.5250	2.50%
SCLSTM	0.7525	0.38%	0.8482	3.07%	0.5116	0.79%	0.5265	2.31%
Enc-Dec$^\sharp$	0.7398	2.78%	0.8549	4.69%	0.5108	4.04%	0.5182	3.18%
w/o A$^\sharp$	0.7651	0.99%	0.8940	1.82%	0.5219	1.64%	0.5296	2.40%
w/o R$^\sharp$	*0.7748*	*0.22%*	*0.8944*	*0.48%*	*0.5235*	*0.57%*	*0.5350*	*0.72%*
RALSTM$^\sharp$	**0.7789**	**0.16%**	**0.8981**	**0.43%**	**0.5252**	**0.42%**	**0.5406**	**0.63%**

Table 3: Performance comparison of the proposed models on four datasets in terms of the BLEU and the error rate ERR(%) scores. The results were averaged over 5 randomly initialized networks. **bold** denotes the best model.

Model	Restaurant		Hotel		Laptop		TV	
	BLEU	ERR	BLEU	ERR	BLEU	ERR	BLEU	ERR
w/o A	0.7619	2.26%	0.8913	1.85%	0.5180	1.81%	0.5270	2.10%
w/o R	0.7733	0.23%	0.8901	0.59%	0.5208	0.60%	0.5321	0.50%
RALSTM	**0.7779**	**0.20%**	**0.8965**	**0.58%**	**0.5231**	**0.50%**	**0.5373**	**0.49%**

differ depending on the initialization, we also report the results which were averaged over 5 randomly initialized networks. Note that, except the results reported in Table 2, all the results shown were averaged over 5 randomly initialized networks. We set λ to 1000 to severely discourage the reranker from selecting utterances which contain either redundant or missing slots. For each DA, we over-generated 20 candidate sentences and selected the top 5 realizations after reranking. Moreover, in order to better understand the effectiveness of our proposed methods, we: (i) performed an ablation experiments to demonstrate the contribution of each proposed cells (Tables 2, 3), (ii) trained the models on the Laptop domain with varied proportion of training data, starting from 10% to 100% (Figure 3), (iii) trained general models by merging all the data from four domains together and tested them in each individual domain (Figure 4), and (iv) trained adaptation models on merging data from restaurant and hotel domains, then fine tuned the model on laptop domain with varied amount of adaptation data (Figure 5).

4.3 Evaluation Metrics and Baselines

The generator performance was assessed on the two evaluation metrics: the BLEU and the slot error rate ERR by adopting code from an open source benchmark toolkit for Natural Language Generation[5]. We compared the proposed models against three strong baselines which have been recently published as state-of-the-art NLG benchmarks[5].

- HLSTM proposed by Wen et al. (2015a) which used a heuristic gate to ensure that all of the slot-value information was accurately captured when generating.

- SCLSTM proposed by Wen et al. (2015b) which can jointly learn the gating signal and language model.

- Enc-Dec proposed by Wen et al. (2016b) which applied the attention-based encoder-decoder architecture.

5 Results and Analysis

5.1 Results

We conducted extensive experiments on our models and compared against the previous methods. Overall, the proposed models consistently achieve the better performance regarding both evaluation metrics across all domains in all test cases.

Model Comparison in an Unseen Domain

The ablation studies (Tables 2, 3) demonstrate the contribution of different model components

---

[5]https://github.com/shawnwun/RNNLG

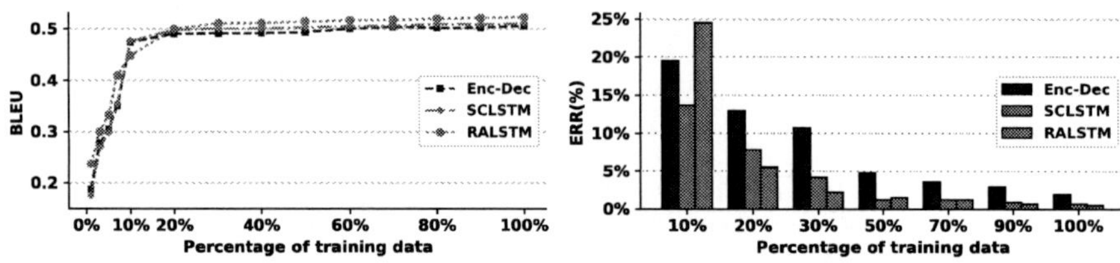

Figure 3: Performance comparison of the models trained on Laptop domain.

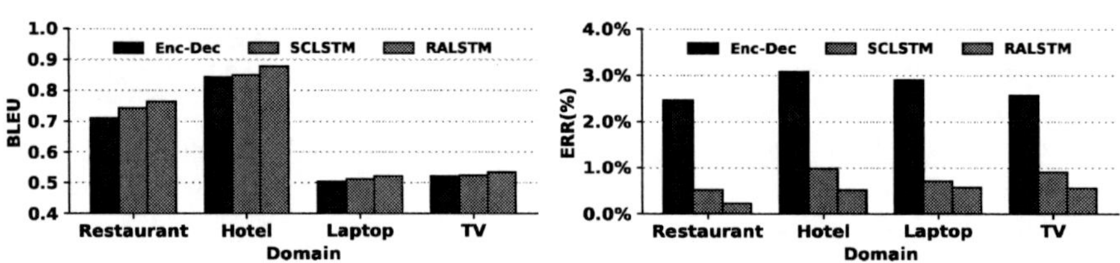

Figure 4: Performance comparison of the general models on four different domains.

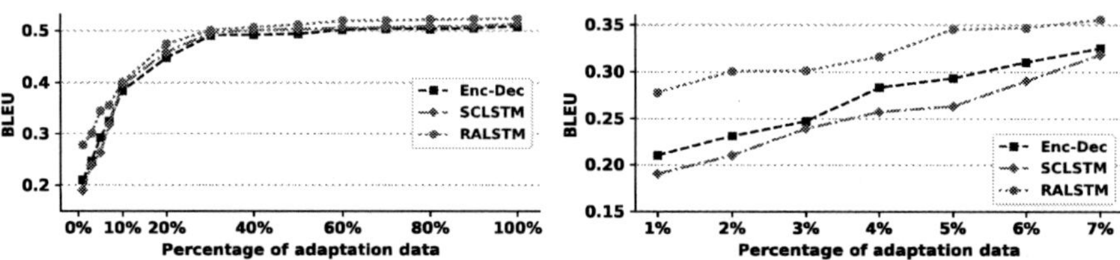

Figure 5: Performance on Laptop domain with varied amount of the adaptation training data when adapting models trained on Restaurant+Hotel dataset.

in which the models were assessed without Adjustment cell (*w/o A*), or without Refinement cell (*w/o R*). It clearly sees that the Adjustment cell contributes to reducing the slot error rate ERR score since it can effectively prevent the undesirable slot-value pair repetitions by gating the DA vector **s**. A comparison between the ARED-based models (denoted by ♯ in Table 2) shows that the proposed models not only have better performance with higher the BLEU score but also significantly reduce the slot error rate ERR score by a large margin about 2% to 4% in every datasets. Moreover, a comparison between the models with gating the DA vector also indicates that the proposed models (*w/o R*, *RALSTM*) have significant improved performance on both the evaluation metrics across the four domains compared to the *SCLSTM* model. The *RALSTM* cell without the Refinement cell is similar as the *SCLSTM* cell. However, it obtained the results much better than the

SCLSTM baselines. This stipulates the necessary of the LSTM encoder and the Aligner in effectively partial learning the correlated order between slot-value representation in the DAs, especially for the unseen domain where there is only one training example for each DA. Table 3 further demonstrates the stable strength of our models since the results' pattern stays unchanged compared to those in Table 2.

Figure 3 shows a comparison of three models (*Enc-Dec*, *SCLSTM*, and *RALSTM*) which were trained from scratch on the unseen laptop domain in varied proportion of training data, from 1% to 100%. It clearly shows that the *RALSTM* outperforms the previous models in all cases, while the *Enc-Dec* has a much greater ERR score comparing to the two models.

A comparison of top responses generated for some input DAs between different models are shown in Table 4. While the previous models still

Table 4: Comparison of top responses generated for some input dialogue acts between different models. Errors are marked in color (missing, misplaced information). *All2** are general models.

#	Model	Generated Responses from Laptop Domain
1	***Input DA***	?compare(name="satellite notus 19", pricerange="budget", drive="500 gb", name="portege thanatos 98", pricerange="expensive", drive="128 gb")
	Reference	the satellite notus 19 has a 500 gb drive and is in the budget price range . on the other hand the portege thanatos 98 has a 128 gb drive and is in the expensive price range . which would you prefer
	HLSTM	the satellite notus 19 is a budget priced laptop with a 500 gb drive and a 128 gb drive . which one do you prefer [portege thanatos 98, expensive]
	Enc-Dec	the satellite notus 19 is in the budget price range . the portege thanatos 98 has a 500 gb drive and is in the expensive price range . which one do you prefer [128 gb]
	SCLSTM	the satellite notus 19 is in the budget price range and has a 500 gb drive and the portege thanatos 98 has a 128 gb drive . which one do you prefer [expensive]
	RALSTM	the satellite notus 19 is in the budget price range with a 500 gb drive , while the portege thanatos 98 is in the expensive price range and has a 128 gb drive . which one do you prefer
	All2Laptop	the satellite notus 19 is a budget price range with a 500 gb drive and the portege thanatos 98 has a 128 gb drive and is in the expensive price range . which one do you prefer

#	Model	Generated Responses from TV Domain
2	***Input DA***	inform_count(count="73", type="television", hasusbport="dontcare", hdmiport="2", screensizerange="dontcare")
	Reference	there are 73 televisions if you do not care about whether it has usb port or not, with 2 hdmi ports and if you do not care about the screen size
	HLSTM	there are 73 televisions with 2 hdmi ports and if you do not care about the number of usb ports [screensizerange]
	Enc-Dec	there are 73 televisions with 2 hdmi ports if you do not care about usb ports [screensizerange]
	SCLSTM	there are 73 televisions with 2 hdmi ports if you do not care about the screen size and if you do not care about the number of usb ports
	RALSTM	there are 73 televisions with 2 hdmi ports if you do not care about screen size or usb ports
	All2Tv	there are 73 televisions with 2 hdmi ports if you do not care about screen size or usb ports

produce some errors (missing and misplaced information), the proposed models (RALSTM and the models *All2** trained by pooling all datasets together) can generate appropriate sentences. We also found that the proposed models tend to generate more complete and concise sentences than the other models.

All these prove the importance of the proposed components: the Refinement cell in aggregating and selecting the attentive information, and the Adjustment cell in controlling the feature vector (see Examples in Figure 6).

General Models

Figure 4 shows a comparison performance of general models as described in Section 4.2. The results are consistent with the Figure 3, in which the *RALSTM* has better performance than the *Enc-Dec* and *SCLSTM* on all domains in terms of the BLEU and the ERR scores, while the *Enc-Dec* has difficulties in reducing the ERR score. This indicates the relevant contribution of the proposed component Refinement and Adjustment cells to the original ARED architecture, in which the Refinement with attentional gating can effectively select and aggregate the information before putting them into the traditional LSTM cell, while the Adjustment with gating DA vector can effectively control the

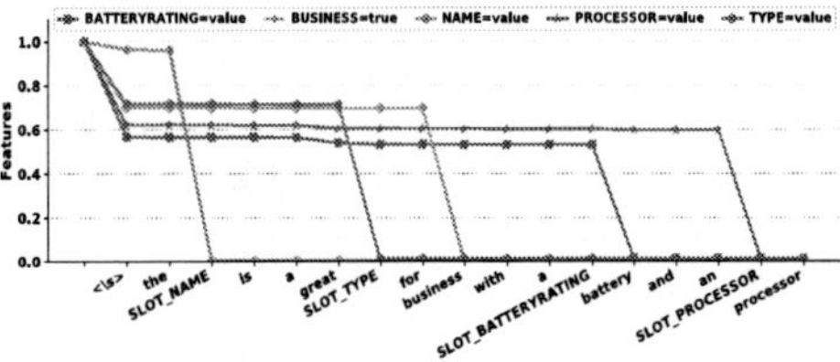

(a) An example from the Laptop domain.

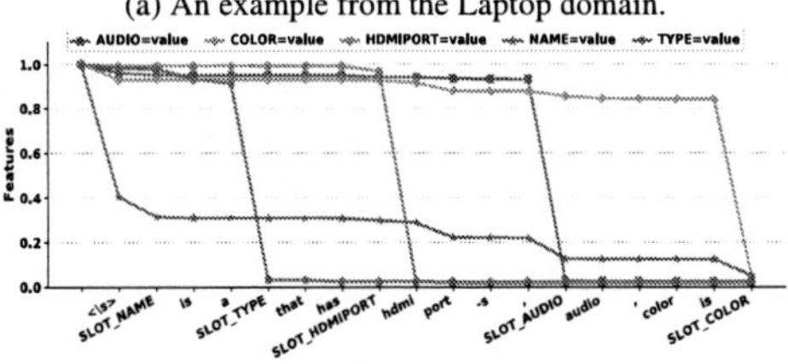

(b) An example from the TV domain.

Figure 6: Example showing how RALSTM drives down the DA feature value vector **s** step-by-step, in which the model generally shows its ability to detect words and phases describing a corresponding slot-value pair.

information flow during generation.

Adaptation Models

Figure 5 shows domain scalability of the three models in which the models were first trained on the merging out-of-domain Restaurant and Hotel datasets, then fine tuned the parameters with varied amount of in-domain training data (laptop domain). The *RALSTM* model outperforms the previous model in both cases where the sufficient in-domain data is used (as in Figure 5-*left*) and the limited in-domain data is used (Figure 5-*right*). The Figure 5-*right* also indicates that the *RALSTM* model can adapt to a new, unseen domain faster than the previous models.

6 Conclusion and Future Work

We present an extension of ARED model, in which an RALSTM component is introduced to select and aggregate semantic elements produced by the Encoder, and to generate the required sentence. We assessed the proposed models on four NLG domains and compared to the state-of-the-art generators. The proposed models empirically show consistent improvement over the previous methods in both the BLEU and ERR evaluation metrics. The proposed models also show an ability to extend to a new, unseen domain no matter how much the in-domain training data was fed. In the future, it would be interesting to apply the proposed model to other tasks that can be modeled based on the encoder-decoder architecture, i.e., image captioning, reading comprehension, and machine translation.

Acknowledgements

This work was supported by JSPS Kakenhi Grant Number JP15K16048 and JST CREST JP-MJCR1513. The first author would like to thank the Vietnamese Government Scholarship (911 project).

References

Martın Abadi, Ashish Agarwal, Paul Barham, Eugene Brevdo, Zhifeng Chen, Craig Citro, Greg S Corrado, Andy Davis, Jeffrey Dean, Matthieu Devin, et al. 2016. Tensorflow: Large-scale machine learning on heterogeneous distributed systems. *arXiv preprint arXiv:1603.04467* .

Dzmitry Bahdanau, Kyunghyun Cho, and Yoshua Bengio. 2014. Neural machine translation by jointly learning to align and translate. *arXiv preprint arXiv:1409.0473* .

Milica Gašić, Dongho Kim, Pirros Tsiakoulis, and Steve Young. 2015. Distributed dialogue policies for multi-domain statistical dialogue management. In *Acoustics, Speech and Signal Processing (ICASSP), 2015 IEEE International Conference on.* IEEE, pages 5371–5375.

Sepp Hochreiter and Jürgen Schmidhuber. 1997. Long short-term memory. *Neural computation* .

Andrej Karpathy and Li Fei-Fei. 2015. Deep visual-semantic alignments for generating image descriptions. In *Proceedings of the IEEE Conference CVPR.* pages 3128–3137.

Jiwei Li, Michel Galley, Chris Brockett, Jianfeng Gao, and Bill Dolan. 2015. A diversity-promoting objective function for neural conversation models. *arXiv preprint arXiv:1510.03055* .

Jiwei Li, Michel Galley, Chris Brockett, Georgios P Spithourakis, Jianfeng Gao, and Bill Dolan. 2016. A persona-based neural conversation model. *arXiv preprint arXiv:1603.06155* .

Jiwei Li and Dan Jurafsky. 2016. Mutual information and diverse decoding improve neural machine translation. *arXiv preprint arXiv:1601.00372* .

Jiasen Lu, Caiming Xiong, Devi Parikh, and Richard Socher. 2016. Knowing when to look: Adaptive attention via a visual sentinel for image captioning. *arXiv preprint arXiv:1612.01887* .

Minh-Thang Luong, Quoc V Le, Ilya Sutskever, Oriol Vinyals, and Lukasz Kaiser. 2015. Multi-task sequence to sequence learning. *arXiv preprint arXiv:1511.06114* .

Hongyuan Mei, Mohit Bansal, and Matthew R Walter. 2015. What to talk about and how? selective generation using lstms with coarse-to-fine alignment. *arXiv preprint arXiv:1509.00838* .

Tomas Mikolov. 2010. Recurrent neural network based language model.

Danilo Mirkovic, Lawrence Cavedon, Matthew Purver, Florin Ratiu, Tobias Scheideck, Fuliang Weng, Qi Zhang, and Kui Xu. 2011. Dialogue management using scripts and combined confidence scores. US Patent 7,904,297.

Nikola Mrkšić, Diarmuid O Séaghdha, Blaise Thomson, Milica Gašić, Pei-Hao Su, David Vandyke, Tsung-Hsien Wen, and Steve Young. 2015. Multi-domain dialog state tracking using recurrent neural networks. *arXiv preprint arXiv:1506.07190* .

Ramesh Nallapati, Bowen Zhou, Caglar Gulcehre, Bing Xiang, et al. 2016. Abstractive text summarization using sequence-to-sequence rnns and beyond. *arXiv preprint arXiv:1602.06023* .

Alice H Oh and Alexander I Rudnicky. 2000. Stochastic language generation for spoken dialogue systems. In *Proceedings of the 2000 ANLP/NAACL Workshop on Conversational systems-Volume 3.* Association for Computational Linguistics, pages 27–32.

Kishore Papineni, Salim Roukos, Todd Ward, and Wei-Jing Zhu. 2002. Bleu: a method for automatic evaluation of machine translation. In *Proceedings of the 40th ACL*. Association for Computational Linguistics, pages 311–318.

Jeffrey Pennington, Richard Socher, and Christopher D Manning. 2014. Glove: Global vectors for word representation. In *EMNLP*. volume 14, pages 1532–43.

Alexander M Rush, Sumit Chopra, and Jason Weston. 2015. A neural attention model for abstractive sentence summarization. *arXiv preprint arXiv:1509.00685*.

Amanda Stent, Rashmi Prasad, and Marilyn Walker. 2004. Trainable sentence planning for complex information presentation in spoken dialog systems. In *Proceedings of the 42nd ACL*. Association for Computational Linguistics, page 79.

Oriol Vinyals and Quoc Le. 2015. A neural conversational model. *arXiv preprint arXiv:1506.05869*.

Oriol Vinyals, Alexander Toshev, Samy Bengio, and Dumitru Erhan. 2015. Show and tell: A neural image caption generator. In *Proceedings of the IEEE Conference on Computer Vision and Pattern Recognition*. pages 3156–3164.

Tsung-Hsien Wen, Milica Gašić, Dongho Kim, Nikola Mrkšić, Pei-Hao Su, David Vandyke, and Steve Young. 2015a. Stochastic Language Generation in Dialogue using Recurrent Neural Networks with Convolutional Sentence Reranking. In *Proceedings SIGDIAL*. Association for Computational Linguistics.

Tsung-Hsien Wen, Milica Gasic, Nikola Mrksic, Lina M Rojas-Barahona, Pei-Hao Su, David Vandyke, and Steve Young. 2016a. Multi-domain neural network language generation for spoken dialogue systems. *arXiv preprint arXiv:1603.01232*.

Tsung-Hsien Wen, Milica Gašic, Nikola Mrkšic, Lina M Rojas-Barahona, Pei-Hao Su, David Vandyke, and Steve Young. 2016b. Toward multi-domain language generation using recurrent neural networks.

Tsung-Hsien Wen, Milica Gašić, Nikola Mrkšić, Pei-Hao Su, David Vandyke, and Steve Young. 2015b. Semantically conditioned lstm-based natural language generation for spoken dialogue systems. In *Proceedings of EMNLP*. Association for Computational Linguistics.

Tsung-Hsien Wen, David Vandyke, Nikola Mrksic, Milica Gasic, Lina M Rojas-Barahona, Pei-Hao Su, Stefan Ultes, and Steve Young. 2016c. A network-based end-to-end trainable task-oriented dialogue system. *arXiv preprint arXiv:1604.04562*.

Paul J Werbos. 1990. Backpropagation through time: what it does and how to do it. *Proceedings of the IEEE* 78(10):1550–1560.

Jason Williams. 2013. Multi-domain learning and generalization in dialog state tracking. In *Proceedings of SIGDIAL*. Citeseer, volume 62.

Kelvin Xu, Jimmy Ba, Ryan Kiros, Kyunghyun Cho, Aaron Courville, Ruslan Salakhudinov, Rich Zemel, and Yoshua Bengio. 2015. Show, attend and tell: Neural image caption generation with visual attention. In *International Conference on Machine Learning*. pages 2048–2057.

Zhilin Yang, Ye Yuan, Yuexin Wu, William W Cohen, and Ruslan R Salakhutdinov. 2016. Review networks for caption generation. In *Advances in Neural Information Processing Systems*. pages 2361–2369.

Xingxing Zhang and Mirella Lapata. 2014. Chinese poetry generation with recurrent neural networks. In *EMNLP*. pages 670–680.

Graph-based Neural Multi-Document Summarization

Michihiro Yasunaga[1]   Rui Zhang[1]   Kshitijh Meelu[1]
Ayush Pareek[2]   Krishnan Srinivasan[1]   Dragomir Radev[1]
[1]Department of Computer Science, Yale University
[2]The LNM Institute of Information Technology
{michihiro.yasunaga,r.zhang,kshitijh.meelu}@yale.edu
{ayush.original}@gmail.com
{krishnan.srinivasan,dragomir.radev}@yale.edu

Abstract

We propose a neural multi-document summarization (MDS) system that incorporates sentence relation graphs. We employ a Graph Convolutional Network (GCN) on the relation graphs, with sentence embeddings obtained from Recurrent Neural Networks as input node features. Through multiple layer-wise propagation, the GCN generates high-level hidden sentence features for salience estimation. We then use a greedy heuristic to extract salient sentences while avoiding redundancy. In our experiments on DUC 2004, we consider three types of sentence relation graphs and demonstrate the advantage of combining sentence relations in graphs with the representation power of deep neural networks. Our model improves upon traditional graph-based extractive approaches and the vanilla GRU sequence model with no graph, and it achieves competitive results against other state-of-the-art multi-document summarization systems.

1   Introduction

Document summarization aims to produce fluent and coherent summaries covering salient information in the documents. Many previous summarization systems employ an extractive approach by identifying and concatenating the most salient text units (often whole sentences) in the document.

Traditional extractive summarizers produce the summary in two steps: sentence ranking and sentence selection. First, they utilize human-engineered features such as sentence position and length (Radev et al., 2004a), word frequency and importance (Nenkova et al., 2006; Hong and Nenkova, 2014), among others, to rank sentence

salience. Then, they select summary-worthy sentences using a range of algorithms, such as graph centrality (Erkan and Radev, 2004), constraint optimization via Integer Linear Programming (McDonald, 2007; Gillick and Favre, 2009; Li et al., 2013), or Support Vector Regression (Li et al., 2007) algorithms. Optionally, sentence reordering (Lapata, 2003; Barzilay et al., 2001) can follow to improve coherence of the summary.

Recently, thanks to their strong representation power, neural approaches have become popular in text summarization, especially in sentence compression (Rush et al., 2015) and single-document summarization (Cheng and Lapata, 2016). Despite their popularity, neural networks still have issues when dealing with multi-document summarization (MDS). In previous neural multi-document summarizers (Cao et al., 2015, 2017), all the sentences in the same document cluster are processed independently. Hence, the relationships between sentences and thus the relationships between different documents are ignored. However, Christensen et al. (2013) demonstrates the importance of considering discourse relations among sentences in multi-document summarization.

This work proposes a multi-document summarization system that exploits the representational power of deep neural networks and the sentence relation information encoded in graph representations of document clusters. Specifically, we apply Graph Convolutional Networks (Kipf and Welling, 2017) on sentence relation graphs. First, we discuss three different techniques to produce sentence relation graphs, where nodes represent sentences in a cluster and edges capture the connections between sentences. Given a relation graph, our summarization model apples a Graph Convolutional Network (GCN), which takes in sentence embeddings from Recurrent Neural Networks as input node features. Through multiple layer-wise prop-

Proceedings of the 21st Conference on Computational Natural Language Learning (CoNLL 2017), pages 452–462,
Vancouver, Canada, August 3 - August 4, 2017. ©2017 Association for Computational Linguistics

agation, the GCN generates high-level hidden features for the sentences. We then obtain sentence salience estimations through a regression on top, and extract salient sentences in a greedy manner while avoiding redundancy.

We evaluate our model on the DUC 2004 multi-document summarization (MDS) task. Our model shows a clear advantage over traditional graph-based extractive summarizers, as well as a baseline GRU model that does not use any graph, and achieves competitive results with other state-of-the-art MDS systems. This work provides a new gateway to incorporating graph-based techniques into neural summarization.

2 Related Work

2.1 Graph-based MDS

Graph-based MDS models have traditionally employed surface level (Erkan and Radev, 2004; Mihalcea and Tarau, 2005; Wan and Yang, 2006) or deep level (Pardo et al., 2006; Antiqueira et al., 2009) approaches based on topological features and the number of nodes (Albert and Barabási, 2002). Efforts have been made to improve decision making of these systems by using discourse relationships between sentences (Radev, 2000; Radev et al., 2001). Erkan and Radev (2004) introduce LexRank to compute sentence importance based on the eigenvector centrality in the connectivity graph of inter-sentence cosine similarity. Mei et al. (2010) propose DivRank to balance the prestige and diversity of the top ranked vertices in information networks and achieve improved results on MDS. Christensen et al. (2013) build multi-document graphs to identify pairwise ordering constraints over the sentences by accounting for discourse relationships between sentences (Mann and Thompson, 1988). In our work, we build on the Approximate Discourse Graph (ADG) model (Christensen et al., 2013) and account for macro level features in sentences to improve sentence salience prediction.

2.2 Summarization Using Neural Networks

Neural networks have recently been popular for text summarization (Kågebäck et al., 2014; Rush et al., 2015; Yin and Pei, 2015; Cao et al., 2016; Wang and Ling, 2016; Cheng and Lapata, 2016; Nallapati et al., 2016, 2017; See et al., 2017). For example, Rush et al. (2015) introduce a neural attention feed-forward network-based model for sentence compression. Wang and Ling (2016)

employ encoder-decoder RNNs to effectively produce short abstractive summaries for opinions. Cao et al. (2016) develop a query-focused summarization system called AttSum which deals with saliency ranking and relevance ranking using query-attention-weighted CNNs.

Very recently, thanks to the large scale news article datasets (Hermann et al., 2015), Cheng and Lapata (2016) train an extractive summarization system with attention-based encoder-decoder RNNs to sequentially label summary-worth sentences in single documents. See et al. (2017), adopting an abstractive approach, augment the standard attention-based encoder-decoder RNNs with the ability to copy words from the source text via pointing and to keep track of what has been summarized. These models (Cheng and Lapata, 2016; See et al., 2017) achieve state-of-the-art performance on the DUC 2002 single-document summarization task. However, scaling up these RNN sequence-to-sequence approaches to the multi-document summarization task has not been successful, 1) due to the lack of large multi-document summarization datasets needed to train the computationally expensive sequence-to-sequence model, and 2) because of the inadequacy of RNNs to capture the complex discourse relations across multiple documents. Our multi-document summarization model resolves these issues 1) by breaking down the summarization task into salience estimation and sentence selection that do not require an expensive decoder architecture, and 2) by utilizing sentence relation graphs.

3 Method

Given a document cluster, our method extracts sentences as a summary in two steps: sentence salience estimation and sentence selection. Figure 1 illustrates our architecture for sentence salience estimation. Given a document cluster, we first build a sentence relation graph, where interacting sentence nodes are connected by edges. For each sentence, we apply an RNN with Gated Recurrent Units (GRU^{sent}) (Cho et al., 2014; Chung et al., 2014) and extract the last hidden state as the sentence embedding. We then apply Graph Convolutional Networks (Kipf and Welling, 2017) on the sentence relation graph with the sentence embeddings as the input node features, to produce final sentence embeddings that reflect the graph representation. Thereafter, a second level GRU (GRU^{doc}) produces the entire cluster embedding

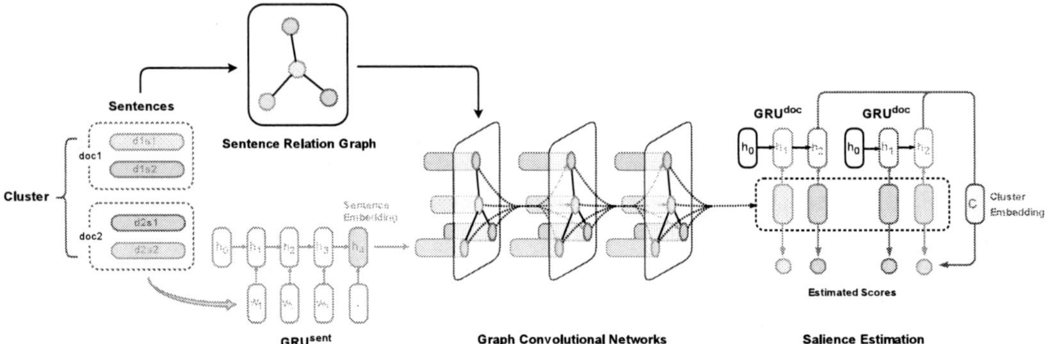

Figure 1: Illustration of our architecture for sentence salience estimation. In this example, there are two documents in the cluster and each document has two sentences. Sentences are processed by the GRU^{sent} to get input sentence embeddings. The GCN takes the input sentence embeddings and the sentence relation graph, and outputs high-level hidden features for individual sentences. GRU^{doc} produces the cluster embedding from the output sentence embeddings. The salience is estimated from the output sentence embeddings and the cluster embedding. w_i: the word embedding for i-th word. h_i: the hidden state of GRU at i-th step.

by sequentially connecting the final sentence embeddings. We estimate the salience of each sentence from the final sentence embeddings and the cluster embedding. Finally, based on the estimated salience scores, we select sentences in a greedy way until reaching the length limit.

3.1 Graph Representation of Clusters

To best evaluate the architecture, we consider three graph representation methods to model sentence relationships within clusters. First, as prior methods in representing document clusters often adhere to the standard of cosine similarity (Erkan and Radev, 2004), our initial baseline approach naturally used this representation. Specifically, we add an edge between two sentences if the tf-idf cosine similarity measure between them, using the bag-of-words model, is above a threshold of 0.2.

Secondly, the G-Flow system (Christensen et al., 2013) utilizes discourse relationships between sentences to create its graph representations, known as Approximate Discourse Graph (ADG). The ADG constructs edges between sentences by counting discourse relation indicators such as deverbal noun references, event and entity continuations, discourse markers, and co-referent mentions. These features allow characterization of sentence relationships, rather than simply their similarity.

While G-Flow's ADG provides many improvements from baseline graph representations, it suffers several disadvantages that diminish its ability

Personalization Features
• Position in Document
• From 1st 3 Sentences?
• No. of Proper Nouns
• > 20 Tokens in Sentence?
• Sentence Length
• No. of Co-referent Verb Mentions
• No. of Co-referent Common Noun Mentions
• No. of Co-referent Proper Noun Mentions

Table 1: List of features that were input to the regression function in obtaining sentence personalization scores.

to aid salience prediction when given to the neural network. Specifically, the ADG lacks much diversity in its assigned edge weights. Because the weights are discretely incremented, they are multiples of 0.5; many edge weights are 1.0. While the presence of an edge provides a remarkable amount of underlying knowledge on the discourse relationships, edge weights can further include information about the strength — and, similarly, importance — of these relationships. We hope to improve the edge weights by making them more diverse, while infusing more information in the weights themselves. In doing so, we contribute our Personalized Discourse Graph (PDG). To advance the ADG's performance in providing predictors for sentence salience, we apply a multiplicative effect to the ADG's edge weights via sentence personalization.

A baseline sentence personalization score $s(v)$, which can be viewed as weighting of sentences, is calculated for every sentence v to account for surface features in each sentence. These features, listed in Table 1, are used as input for linear regression, as per Christensen et al. (2013). The regression is applied to each sentence to obtain the personalization score, $s(v)$. Each edge weight in the original ADG is then transformed by this sentence personalization score and normalized over the total outgoing scores. That is, for directed edge $(u, v) \in E$, the weight is

$$w_{PDG}(u, v) = \frac{w_{ADG}(u, v)s(v)}{\sum_{u' \in V} w_{ADG}(u', v)s(u')} \quad (1)$$

The inclusion of the sentence personalization scores allows the PDG to account for macro-level features in each sentence, augmenting information for salience estimation. To provide more clarity, we include a figure of the PDG in later sections.

Although it may be possible to incorporate the sentence personalization features later into the salience estimation network, we chose to encode them in the PDG to improve the edge weight distribution of sentence relation graphs and to make our salience estimation architecture methodically consistent. Additionally, in order to maintain consistency between graph representations, following two modifications are made to the discourse graphs. First, the directed edges of both the ADG and PDG are made undirected by averaging the edges weights in both directions. Second, edge weights are rescaled to a maximum edge weight of 1 prior to being fed to the GCN.

3.2 Graph Convolutional Networks

We apply Graph Convolutional Networks (GCN) from Kipf and Welling (2017) on top of the sentence relation graph. In this subsection, we explain in detail the formulation of GCN, and how GCN produces the final sentence embeddings.

The goal of GCN is to learn a function $f(X, A)$ that takes as input:

- $A \in \mathbb{R}^{N \times N}$, the adjacency matrix of graph $\mathcal{G}$, where N is the number of nodes in $\mathcal{G}$.
- $X \in \mathbb{R}^{N \times D}$, the input node feature matrix, where D is the dimension of input node feature vectors.

and outputs high-level hidden features for each node, $Z \in \mathbb{R}^{N \times F}$, that encapsulate the graph structure. F is the dimension of output feature vectors. The function $f(X, A)$ takes a form of layer-wise propagation based on neural networks. We compute the activation matrix in the $(l + 1)^{th}$ layer as $H^{(l+1)}$, starting from $H^0 = X$. The output of L-layer GCN is $Z = f(X, A) = H^{(L)}$.

To introduce the formulation, consider a simple form of layer-wise propagation:

$$H^{(l+1)} = \sigma \left(A H^{(l)} W^{(l)} \right) \quad (2)$$

where σ is an activation function such as ReLU($\cdot$) $= \max(0, \cdot)$. $W^{(l)}$ is the parameter to learn in the lth layer. Eq 2 has two limitations. First, multiplying by A means that for each node, we sum up the feature vectors of all neighboring nodes but not the node itself. We fix this by adding self-loops in the graph. Second, since A is not normalized, multiplying by A will change the scale of feature vectors. To overcome this, we apply a symmetric normalization by using $D^{-\frac{1}{2}} A D^{-\frac{1}{2}}$ where D is the node degree matrix. These two renormalization tricks result in the following propagation rule:

$$H^{(l+1)} = \sigma \left(\tilde{D}^{-\frac{1}{2}} \tilde{A} \tilde{D}^{-\frac{1}{2}} H^{(l)} W^{(l)} \right) \quad (3)$$

where $\tilde{A} = A + I_N$ is the adjacency matrix of the graph $\mathcal{G}$ with added self-loops (I_N is the identity matrix). $\tilde{D}$ is the degree matrix with $\tilde{D}_{ii} = \sum_j \tilde{A}_{ij}$. Kipf and Welling (2017) also provide a theoretical justification of Eq 3 as a first-order approximation of spectral graph convolution (Hammond et al., 2011; Defferrard et al., 2016).

As an example, if we have a two-layer GCN, we first calculate $\hat{A} = \tilde{D}^{-\frac{1}{2}} \tilde{A} \tilde{D}^{-\frac{1}{2}}$ in a preprocessing step, and then produce

$$Z = f(X, A) = \sigma \left(\hat{A} \, \sigma \left(\hat{A} X W^{(0)} \right) W^{(1)} \right)$$

3.3 Sentence Embeddings

As the input node features X of GCN, we use sentence embeddings calculated by GRU^{sent}.

Given a document cluster C with N sentences $(s_1, s_2, ..., s_N)$ in total, for each sentence s_i of L words $(w_1, w_2, ..., w_L)$, GRU^{sent} recurrently updates hidden states at each time step t:

$$\mathbf{h}_t^{sent} = \text{GRU}^{sent}(\mathbf{h}_{t-1}^{sent}, \mathbf{w}_t) \quad (4)$$

where $\mathbf{w}_t$ is the word embedding for w_t, $\mathbf{h}_t^{sent}$ is the hidden state of GRU^{sent}. $\mathbf{h}_0$ is initialized as a zero vector, and the input sentence embedding $\mathbf{x}_i$ is the last hidden state:

$$\mathbf{x}_i = \mathbf{h}_L^{sent} \quad (5)$$

All sentence embeddings from the given document cluster are grouped as the node feature matrix X:

$$X = \begin{bmatrix} - & \mathbf{x}_1^T & - \\ - & \mathbf{x}_2^T & - \\ & \vdots & \\ - & \mathbf{x}_N^T & - \end{bmatrix} \quad (6)$$

X is fed into GCN subsequently to obtain the final sentence embeddings $\mathbf{s}_i$ that incorporate the graph representation of sentence relationships:

$$Z = f(X, A) = \begin{bmatrix} - & \mathbf{s}_1^T & - \\ - & \mathbf{s}_2^T & - \\ & \vdots & \\ - & \mathbf{s}_N^T & - \end{bmatrix} \quad (7)$$

3.4 Cluster Embedding

Additionally, in order to have a global view of the entire document cluster, we apply a second-level RNN, GRU^{doc}, to encode the entire document cluster. Given a document cluster C with M documents $(d_1, d_2, ..., d_M)$, for document d_i with $|d_i|$ sentences, GRU^{doc} first builds the document embedding $\mathbf{d}_i$ on top of sentence embeddings:

$$\mathbf{h}_t^{doc} = \text{GRU}^{doc}(\mathbf{h}_{t-1}^{doc}, \mathbf{s}_t) \quad (8)$$

$$\mathbf{d}_i = \mathbf{h}_{|d_i|}^{doc} \quad (9)$$

where $\mathbf{s}_t$ is the sentence embedding in the document d_i. In Eq 9, we extract the last hidden state as the document embedding for d_i. In Eq 10, we average over document embeddings to produce the cluster embedding $\mathbf{C}$:

$$\mathbf{C} = \frac{1}{M} \sum_{i=1}^{M} \mathbf{d}_i \quad (10)$$

All the GRUs we used are forward. We also experimented with backward GRUs and bi-directional GRUs, but neither of them meaningfully improved upon forward GRUs.

3.5 Salience Estimation

For the sentence s_i in the cluster C, we calculate the salience of s_i as the following, similarly to the attention mechanism in neural machine translation (Bahdanau et al., 2015):

$$f(s_i) = \mathbf{v}^T \tanh(\mathbf{W}_1 \mathbf{C} + \mathbf{W}_2 \mathbf{s}_i) \quad (11)$$

$$\text{salience}(s_i) = \frac{f(s_i)}{\sum_{s_j \in C} f(s_j)} \quad (12)$$

where $\mathbf{v}, \mathbf{W}_1, \mathbf{W}_2$ are learnable parameters. In Eq 11, we first calculate the score $f(s_i)$ by considering the sentence embedding itself, $\mathbf{s}_i$, and the cluster embedding $\mathbf{C}$ for the global context of the multi-document. The score is then normalized as $\text{salience}(s_i)$ via softmax in Eq 12.

3.6 Training

The model parameters include the parameters in GRU^{sent} and GRU^{doc}, the weights in GCN layers, and the parameters for salience estimation $(\mathbf{v}, \mathbf{W}_1, \mathbf{W}_2)$. Parameters in GRU^{sent} and GRU^{doc} are not shared. The model is trained end-to-end to minimize the following cross-entropy loss between the salience prediction and the normalized ROUGE score of each sentence:

$$\mathcal{L} = -\sum_{C} \sum_{s_i \in C} R(s_i) \log(\text{salience}(s_i)) \quad (13)$$

$R(s_i)$ is calculated by $R(s_i) = \text{softmax}(\alpha\, r(s_i))$, where $r(s_i)$ is the average of ROUGE-1 and ROUGE-2 Recall scores of sentence s_i by measuring with the ground-truth human-written summaries. α is a constant rescaling factor to make the distribution sharper. The value of α is determined from the validation data set. $\alpha r(s_i)$ is then normalized across the cluster via softmax, similarly to Eq 12.

3.7 Sentence Selection

Given the salience score estimation, we apply a simple greedy procedure to select sentences. Sentences with higher salience scores have higher priorities. First, we sort sentences in descending order of the salience scores. Then, we select one sentence from the top of the list and append to the summary if the sentence is of reasonable length (8-55 words, as in (Erkan and Radev, 2004)) and is not redundant. The sentence is redundant if the tf-idf cosine similarity between the sentence and the current summary is above 0.5 (Hong and Nenkova, 2014). We select sentences this way until we reach the length limit.

4 Experiments

In this section, we evaluate our model on benchmark MDS data sets, and compare with other state-of-the-art systems. We aim to show that our model, by combining sentence relations in graphs with the representation power of deep neural networks, can improve upon other traditional graph-based extractive approaches and the vanilla GRU model which does not use any graph. In addition,

	DUC'01	DUC'02	DUC'03	DUC'04
# of Clusters	30	59	30	50
# of Documents	309	567	298	500
# of Sentences	24498	16090	7721	13270
Vocabulary Size	28188	22174	13248	18036
Summary Length	100 words	100 words	100 words	665 Bytes

Table 2: Statistics for DUC Multi-Document Summarization Data Sets.

we further study the effect of graph and different graph representations on the summarization performance and investigate the correlation of graph structure and sentence salience estimation.

4.1 Data Set and Evaluation

We use the benchmark data sets from the Document Understanding Conferences (DUC) containing clusters of English news articles and human reference summaries. Table 2 shows the statistics of the data sets. We use DUC 2001, 2002, 2003 and 2004 containing 30, 59, 30 and 50 clusters of nearly 10 documents each respectively. Our model is trained on DUC 2001 and 2002, validated on 2003, and tested on 2004. For evaluation, we use the ROUGE-1,2 metric, with stemming and stop words not removed as suggested by Owczarzak et al. (2012).

4.2 Experimental Setup

We conduct four experiments on our model: three using each of the three types of graphs discussed earlier, and one without using any graph. In the experiments with graphs, for each document cluster, we tokenize all the documents into sentences and generate a graph representation of their relations by the three methods: Cosine Similarity Graph, Approximate Discourse Graph (ADG) from G-Flow, and our Personalized Discourse Graph (PDG). Note that for the Cosine Similarity Graph, we compute the tf-idf cosine similarity for every pair of sentences using the bag-of-word model and add an edge for similarity above 0.2. The weight of the edge is the value of similarity. We apply GCNs with the graphs in the final step of sentence encoding. For the experiment without any graph, we omit the GCN part and simply use the GRU sentence and cluster encoders.

We use 300-dimensional pre-trained word2vec embeddings (Mikolov et al., 2013) as input to GRU^{sent} in Eq 4. The word embeddings are fine-tuned during training. We use three GCN hidden

	R-1	R-2
SVR (Li et al., 2007)	36.18	9.34
CLASSY11 (Conroy et al., 2011)	37.22	9.20
CLASSY04 (Conroy et al., 2004)	37.62	8.96
GreedyKL (Haghighi and Vanderwende, 2009)	37.98	8.53
TsSum (Conroy et al., 2006)	35.88	8.15
G-Flow (Christensen et al., 2013)	35.30	8.27
FreqSum (Nenkova et al., 2006)	35.30	8.11
Centroid (Radev et al., 2004b)	36.41	7.97
Cont. LexRank (Erkan and Radev, 2004)	35.95	7.47
RegSum (Hong and Nenkova, 2014)	**38.57**	**9.75**
GRU	$36.64_{\pm 0.11}$	8.47
GRU+GCN: Cosine Similarity Graph	$37.33_{\pm 0.23}$	8.78
GRU+GCN: ADG from G-Flow	$37.41_{\pm 0.32}$	8.97
GRU+GCN: Personalized Discourse Graph	$\mathbf{38.23_{\pm 0.22}}$	**9.48**

Table 3: ROUGE Recalls on DUC 2004. We show mean (and standard deviation for R-1) over 10 repeated trials for each of our experiments.

layers ($L = 3$). The hidden states in GRU^{sent}, GCN hidden layers, and GRU^{doc} are all 300-dimensional vectors ($D = F = 300$).

The rescaling factor α in the objective function (Eq 13) is chosen as 40 from {10, 20, 30, 40, 50, 100} based on the validation performance. The objective function is optimized using Adam (Kingma and Ba, 2015) stochastic gradient descent with a learning rate of 0.001 and a batch size of 1. We use gradient clipping with a maximum gradient norm of 1.0. The model is validated every 10 iterations, and the training is stopped early if the validation performance does not improve for 10 consecutive steps. We trained using a single Tesla K80 GPU. For all the experiments, the training took approximately 30 minutes until a stop.

4.3 Results

Table 3 summarizes our results. First we take our simple GRU model as the baseline of the RNN-based regression approach. As seen from the table, the addition of Cosine Similarity Graph on top of the GRU clearly boosts the performance. Furthermore, the addition of ADG from G-Flow gives a slighly better performance. Our Personalized Discourse Graph (PDG) enhances the R-1 score by more than 1.50. The improvement indicates that the combination of graphs and GCNs processes sentence relations across documents better than the vanilla RNN sequence models.

To gain a global view of our performance, we also compare our result with other baseline multi-document summarizers and the state-of-the-

	PDG	ADG	Cosine Similarity	No Graph
Num of Iterations	200	280	310	250
Train Cost	4.286	5.460	5.458	5.310
Validation Cost	4.559	5.077	5.099	5.214

Table 4: Training statistics for the four experiments. The first row shows the number of iterations the model took to reach the best validation result before an early stop. The train cost and validation cost at that time step are shown in the second row and third row, respectively. All the values are the average over 10 repeated trials.

art systems related to our regression method. We compute ROUGE scores from the actual output summary of each system. We run the G-Flow code released by Christensen et al. (2013) to get the output summary of the G-Flow system. The output summary of other systems are compiled in Hong et al. (2014). To ensure fair comparison, we use ROUGE-1.5.5 with the same parameters as in Hong et al. (2014) across all methods: -n 2 -m -l 100 -x -c 95 -r 1000 -f A -p 0.5 -t 0.

From Table 3, we observe that our GCN system significantly outperforms the commonly used baselines and traditional graph approaches such as Centroid, LexRank, and G-Flow. This indicates the advantage of the representation power of neural networks used in our model. Our system also exceeds CLASSY04, the best peer system in DUC 2004, and Support Vector Regression (SVR), a widely used regression-based summarizer. We remain at a comparable level to RegSum, the state-of-the-art multi-document summarizer using regression. The major difference is that RegSum performs regression on word level and estimates the salience of each word through a rich set of word features, such as frequency, grammar, context, and hand-crafted dictionaries. RegSum then computes sentence salience based on the word scores. On the other hand, our model simply works on sentence level, spotlighting sentence relations encoded as a graph. Incorporating more word-level features into our discourse graphs may be an interesting future direction to explore.

4.4 Discussion

As shown in Table 3, our graph-based models outperform the vanilla GRU model, which has no graph. Additionally, for the three graphs we consider, PDG improves R-1 score by 0.82 over ADG, and ADG outperforms the Cosine Similar-

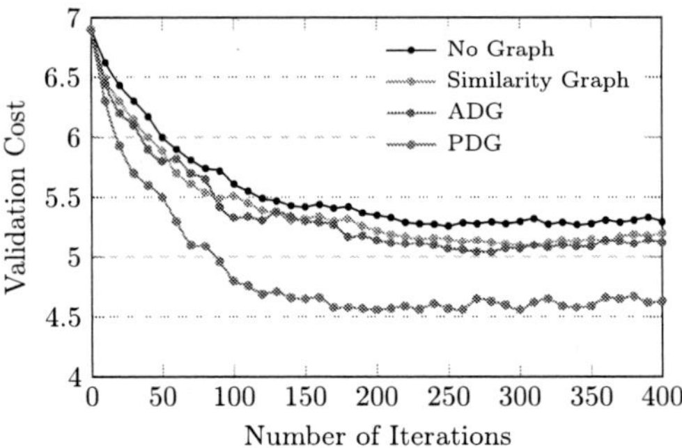

Figure 2: Visualization of the learning curves for the four experiments. The vertical axis displays the validation costs in the interval 4.0 - 7.0.

	PDG	ADG	Cosine Similarity
Number of nodes	265	265	265
Number of edges	1023	1050	884
Average edge weight	0.075	0.295	0.359
Average node degree	0.171	5.136	2.260
ρ of degree and salience	0.136	0.113	0.093

Table 5: Characteristics of the three graph representations, averaged over the clusters (i.e. graphs) in DUC 2004. Note that max edge weight in all three representations is 1.0 due to rescaling for consistency. The degree of each node is calculated as the sum of edge weights.

ity Graph by 0.08 on the R-1 score. While the Cosine Similarity Graph encodes general word-level connections between sentences, discourse graphs, especially our personalized version, specialize in representing the narrative and logical relations between sentences. Therefore, we hypothesize that the PDG provides a more informative guide to estimating the importance of each sentence. In an attempt to better understand the results and validate the effect of sentence relation graphs (especially of the PDG), we have conducted the analysis that follows.

Training Statistics. We compare the learning curves of the four different settings: GRU without any graph, GRU+GCN with the Cosine Similarity Graph, GRU+GCN with ADG, and GRU+GCN with PDG (see Table 4 & Figure 2). Without a graph, the model converges faster and achieves lower training cost than the Cosine Similarity Graph and ADG. This is most likely due to the simplicity of the architecture, but it is also less generalizable, yielding a higher validation cost

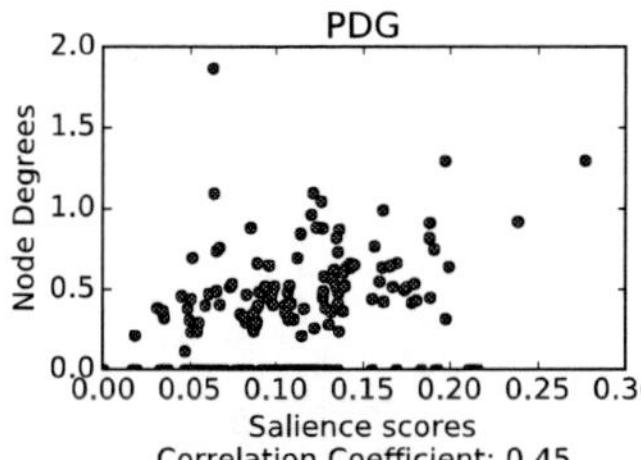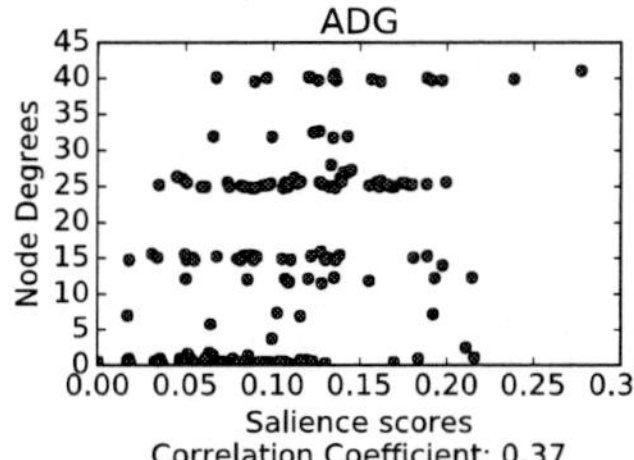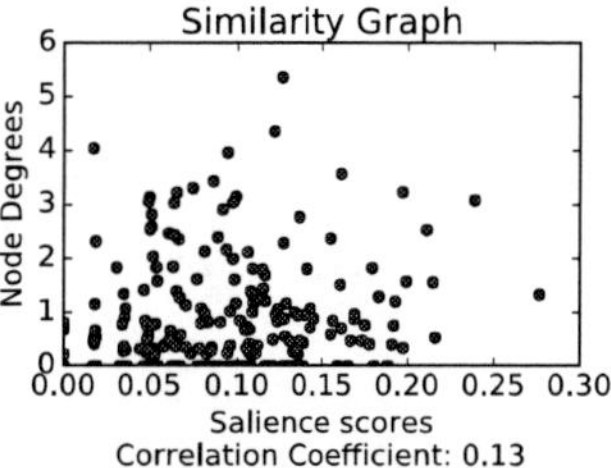

Figure 3: Visualization of the relationship between salience score and node degree for the three graph representation methods. Cluster d30011t from DUC 2004 is chosen as an example.

than the models with graphs. For the three graph methods, ADG converges faster and has better validation performance than the Cosine Similarity Graph. PDG converges even faster than "No Graph" and achieves the lowest training cost and validation cost amongst all methods. This shows that the PDG has particularly strong representation power and generalizability.

Graph Statistics. We also analyze the characteristics of the three graph representation methods on DUC 2004 document clusters. Table 5 summarizes the following basic statistics: the number of nodes (i.e. sentences), the number of edges, average edge weight, and average node degree per graph. We include the correlation between node degree and salience, as well.

As seen from the table, PDG and ADG have approximately the same number of edges. This is expected since the PDG is built by transforming the edge weights in ADG. The Cosine Similarity Graph has slightly fewer edges, simply due to the implemented threshold.

Moreover, note that the ADG has significantly higher average edge weight and node degree as compared to the PDG. These values reflect the discrete nature of the ADG's edge assignment — further evidence of this can be seen in Figure 3. Because the ADG's raw edge weight assignment is done by increments of 0.5, the average node degree tends to be significantly large. This motivated the construction of our PDG, which corrects for this by coercing the average edge weight and node degree to be more diverse and, consequently, smaller (after rescaling). The process of including sentence personalization scores in edge weight assignments of the PDG leads to a select number of edges gaining markedly large distinction. This aids the GCN in identifying the most important edge connections along with the affili-

ated sentences.

Node Degree and Salience. In Table 5, we also calculate the correlation coefficient ρ, per graph, between the degree of each sentence node and its salience score. We observe that all the graph representations show positive correlation between the node degree and the salience score. Moreover, the order of correlation strength is PDG > ADG > Cosine Similarity Graph. Though node degree is a simple measure of these graphs, this observation supports our hypothesis on the efficacy of sentence relation graphs, particularly of PDGs, to provide a guide to salience estimation. [1]

As a case study to illustrate our observation, we chose one cluster (d30011t) from DUC 2004. Figure 3 shows the scatter plots of the node degree and salience score of each sentence.

Visualization of the PDG. Finally, to demonstrate the functionality of the PDG and complement our discussion from Section 3.1, we visualize the PDG on cluster d30011t with the salience score on each node in Figure 4 (also see Figure 5 for the actual sentences).

From the visualization, it can be observed that the nodes representing salient sentences (such as (d_6, s_8), (d_6, s_7), and (d_2, s_4)) tend to have higher degrees in the PDG. We can also observe that the PDG represents edges which connect nodes of sentences from different documents, in contrast with the traditional sequence model.

From Figure 5, we note that the most salient sentence (d_6, s_8) actually describes much of the reference summary. As an example of discourse relation, (d_6, s_7) and (d_2, s_4), the two nodes connected to (d_6, s_8), provide the background for

---

[1] However, we shall add that simply selecting sentences of highest node degrees in PDGs did not itself produce good summaries, compared to our GCN model. Hence, we utilize the graph representations specifically as inputs to the GCN.

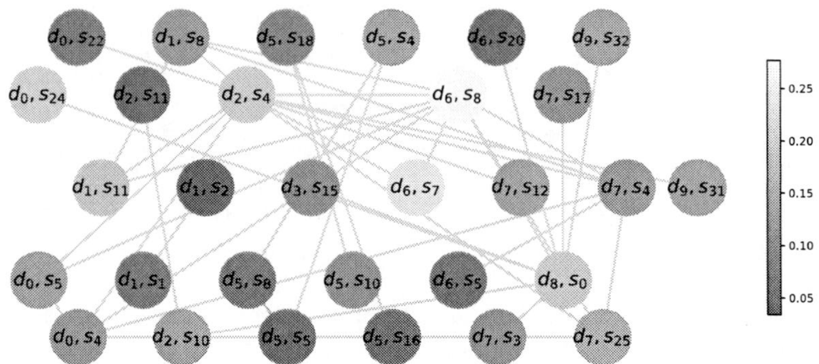

Figure 4: Visualization of the PDG on cluster d30011t. Each node is a sentence, with label (DocumentID, SentenceID). The node color represents the salience score (see the color bar). For simplicity, we only display edges of weight above 0.03. Best viewed in color.

Reference Summary (truncated): Malaysian Prime Minister Mahathir Mohamad ruled adroitly for 17 years until September 1998 when he suddenly reversed his economic policy and fired his popular deputy and heir apparent, Anwar Ibrahim. Anwar organized a political opposition, leading Mahathir to arrest him. (...) Anwar remained in custody as lawyers appealed. (...)

Sent-label (6,8): Anwar was ... after two weeks of nationwide rallies at which he called for government reform and Mahathir's resignation, he was arrested ....

Sent-label (6,7): The two had differed over economic policy and Anwar has said Mahathir feared he was a threat to his 17-year rule.

Sent-label (2,4): Mahathir and Anwar had differed over economic policy and Anwar says Mahathir feared him as an alternative leader.

Sent-label (0,22): Before his arrest, Anwar designated his wife, Azizah Ismail, as the leader of his new ``reform" movement.

Figure 5: Reference summary and illustrative sentences from cluster d30011t.

(d_6, s_8), even though they do not share many words in common with it. On the other hand, (d_0, s_{22}), which is only connected with (d_2, s_4), is not salient as it does not provide a central message for the summary.

5 Conclusion

In this paper, we presented a novel multi-document summarization system that exploits the representational power of neural networks and graph representations of sentence relationships. On top of a simple GRU model as an RNN-based regression baseline, we build a Graph Convolutional Network (GCN) architecture applied on a Personalized Discourse Graph. Our model, unlike traditional RNN models, can capture sentence relations across documents and demonstrates improved salience prediction and summarization, achieving competitive performance with current state-of-the-art systems. Furthermore, through multiple analyses, we have validated the efficacy of sentence relation graphs, particularly of PDG, to help to learn the salience of sentences. This work shows the promise of the GCN models and of discourse graphs applied to processing multi-document inputs.

Acknowledgements

We would like to thank the members of the Sapphire Project (University of Michigan and IBM), as well as all the anonymous reviewers for their helpful suggestions on this work. This material is based in part upon work supported by IBM under contract 4915012629. Any opinions, findings, conclusions, or recommendations expressed herein are those of the authors and do not necessarily reflect the views of IBM.

References

Réka Albert and Albert-László Barabási. 2002. Statistical mechanics of complex networks. *Reviews of modern physics* 74(1):47.

Lucas Antiqueira, Osvaldo N Oliveira, Luciano da Fontoura Costa, and Maria das Graças Volpe Nunes. 2009. A complex network approach to text summarization. *Information Sciences* 179(5):584–599.

Dzmitry Bahdanau, Kyunghyun Cho, and Yoshua Bengio. 2015. Neural machine translation by jointly learning to align and translate. In *ICLR*.

Regina Barzilay, Noemie Elhadad, and Kathleen R McKeown. 2001. Sentence ordering in multidocument summarization. In *Proceedings of the first international conference on Human language technology research*.

Ziqiang Cao, Wenjie Li, Sujian Li, and Furu Wei. 2017. Improving multi-document summarization via text classification. In *AAAI*.

Ziqiang Cao, Wenjie Li, Sujian Li, Furu Wei, and Yanran Li. 2016. Attsum: Joint learning of focusing and summarization with neural attention. In *COLING*.

Ziqiang Cao, Furu Wei, Li Dong, Sujian Li, and Ming Zhou. 2015. Ranking with recursive neural networks and its application to multi-document summarization. In *AAAI*.

Jianpeng Cheng and Mirella Lapata. 2016. Neural summarization by extracting sentences and words. In *ACL*.

Kyunghyun Cho, Bart van Merrienboer, Caglar Gulcehre, Dzmitry Bahdanau, Fethi Bougares, Holger Schwenk, and Yoshua Bengio. 2014. Learning phrase representations using rnn encoder–decoder for statistical machine translation. In *EMNLP*.

Janara Christensen, Mausam, Stephen Soderland, and Oren Etzioni. 2013. Towards coherent multi-document summarization. In *NAACL*.

Junyoung Chung, Caglar Gulcehre, KyungHyun Cho, and Yoshua Bengio. 2014. Empirical evaluation of gated recurrent neural networks on sequence modeling. *NIPS 2014 Deep Learning and Representation Learning Workshop* .

John M Conroy, Judith D Schlesinger, Jade Goldstein, and Dianne P Oleary. 2004. Left-brain/right-brain multi-document summarization. In *Proceedings of the Document Understanding Conference (DUC 2004)*.

John M Conroy, Judith D Schlesinger, Jeff Kubina, Peter A Rankel, and Dianne P O'Leary. 2011. Classy 2011 at tac: Guided and multi-lingual summaries and evaluation metrics. *TAC* 11:1–8.

John M Conroy, Judith D Schlesinger, and Dianne P O'Leary. 2006. Topic-focused multi-document summarization using an approximate oracle score. In *COLING/ACL*.

Michaël Defferrard, Xavier Bresson, and Pierre Vandergheynst. 2016. Convolutional neural networks on graphs with fast localized spectral filtering. In *NIPS*.

Günes Erkan and Dragomir R Radev. 2004. Lexrank: Graph-based lexical centrality as salience in text summarization. *Journal of Artificial Intelligence Research* 22:457–479.

Dan Gillick and Benoit Favre. 2009. A scalable global model for summarization. In *Proceedings of the Workshop on Integer Linear Programming for Natural Langauge Processing*. Association for Computational Linguistics, pages 10–18.

Aria Haghighi and Lucy Vanderwende. 2009. Exploring content models for multi-document summarization. In *NAACL*.

David K Hammond, Pierre Vandergheynst, and Rémi Gribonval. 2011. Wavelets on graphs via spectral graph theory. *Applied and Computational Harmonic Analysis* 30(2):129–150.

Karl Moritz Hermann, Tomas Kocisky, Edward Grefenstette, Lasse Espeholt, Will Kay, Mustafa Suleyman, and Phil Blunsom. 2015. Teaching machines to read and comprehend. In *NIPS*.

Kai Hong, John M Conroy, Benoit Favre, Alex Kulesza, Hui Lin, and Ani Nenkova. 2014. A repository of state of the art and competitive baseline summaries for generic news summarization. In *LREC*.

Kai Hong and Ani Nenkova. 2014. Improving the estimation of word importance for news multi-document summarization. In *EACL*.

Mikael Kågebäck, Olof Mogren, Nina Tahmasebi, and Devdatt Dubhashi. 2014. Extractive summarization using continuous vector space models. In *Proceedings of the 2nd Workshop on Continuous Vector Space Models and their Compositionality (CVSC)@ EACL*. Citeseer, pages 31–39.

Diederik Kingma and Jimmy Ba. 2015. Adam: A method for stochastic optimization. In *ICLR*.

Thomas N Kipf and Max Welling. 2017. Semi-supervised classification with graph convolutional networks. In *ICLR*.

Mirella Lapata. 2003. Probabilistic text structuring: Experiments with sentence ordering. In *ACL*.

Chen Li, Xian Qian, and Yang Liu. 2013. Using supervised bigram-based ilp for extractive summarization. In *ACL*.

Sujian Li, You Ouyang, Wei Wang, and Bin Sun. 2007. Multi-document summarization using support vector regression. In *Proceedings of DUC*. Citeseer.

William C Mann and Sandra A Thompson. 1988. Rhetorical structure theory: Toward a functional theory of text organization. *Text-Interdisciplinary Journal for the Study of Discourse* 8(3):243–281.

Ryan McDonald. 2007. A study of global inference algorithms in multi-document summarization. In *European Conference on Information Retrieval*.

Qiaozhu Mei, Jian Guo, and Dragomir Radev. 2010. Divrank: the interplay of prestige and diversity in information networks. In *SIGKDD*.

Rada Mihalcea and Paul Tarau. 2005. A language independent algorithm for single and multiple document summarization. In *IJCNLP*.

Tomas Mikolov, Ilya Sutskever, Kai Chen, Greg S Corrado, and Jeff Dean. 2013. Distributed representations of words and phrases and their compositionality. In *NIPS*.

Ramesh Nallapati, Feifei Zhai, and Bowen Zhou. 2017. Summarunner: A recurrent neural network based sequence model for extractive summarization of documents. *AAAI* .

Ramesh Nallapati, Bowen Zhou, Caglar Gulcehre, Bing Xiang, et al. 2016. Abstractive text summarization using sequence-to-sequence rnns and beyond. In *CoNLL*.

Ani Nenkova, Lucy Vanderwende, and Kathleen McKeown. 2006. A compositional context sensitive multi-document summarizer: exploring the factors that influence summarization. In *SIGIR*.

Karolina Owczarzak, John M Conroy, Hoa Trang Dang, and Ani Nenkova. 2012. An assessment of the accuracy of automatic evaluation in summarization. In *Proceedings of Workshop on Evaluation Metrics and System Comparison for Automatic Summarization*. Association for Computational Linguistics, pages 1–9.

Thiago Pardo, Lucas Antiqueira, Maria Nunes, Osvaldo Oliveira, and Luciano da Fontoura Costa. 2006. Modeling and evaluating summaries using complex networks. *Computational Processing of the Portuguese Language* pages 1–10.

Dragomir R Radev. 2000. A common theory of information fusion from multiple text sources step one: cross-document structure. In *Proceedings of the 1st SIGdial workshop on Discourse and dialogue-Volume 10*. Association for Computational Linguistics, pages 74–83.

Dragomir R Radev, Timothy Allison, Sasha Blair-Goldensohn, John Blitzer, Arda Celebi, Stanko Dimitrov, Elliott Drabek, Ali Hakim, Wai Lam, Danyu Liu, et al. 2004a. Mead-a platform for multidocument multilingual text summarization. In *LREC*.

Dragomir R Radev, Sasha Blair-Goldensohn, Zhu Zhang, and Revathi Sundara Raghavan. 2001. Newsinessence: A system for domain-independent, real-time news clustering and multi-document summarization. In *Proceedings of the first international conference on Human language technology research*. Association for Computational Linguistics, pages 1–4.

Dragomir R Radev, Hongyan Jing, Małgorzata Styś, and Daniel Tam. 2004b. Centroid-based summarization of multiple documents. *Information Processing & Management* 40(6):919–938.

Alexander M Rush, Sumit Chopra, and Jason Weston. 2015. A neural attention model for abstractive sentence summarization. In *EMNLP*.

Abigail See, Peter J. Liu, and Christopher D. Manning. 2017. Get to the point: Summarization with pointer-generator networks. In *ACL*.

Xiaojun Wan and Jianwu Yang. 2006. Improved affinity graph based multi-document summarization. In *NAACL*.

Lu Wang and Wang Ling. 2016. Neural network-based abstract generation for opinions and arguments. In *NAACL*.

Wenpeng Yin and Yulong Pei. 2015. Optimizing sentence modeling and selection for document summarization. In *IJCAI*.

Author Index

Association for Computational Linguistics
209 N. Eighth Street
Stroudsburg, Pennsylvania 18360

ISBN 978-1-5108-4564-0